INTERNATIONAL LAW OF HUMAN RIGHTS

INTERNATIONAL LAW OF HUMAN RIGHTS

ANTÔNIO AUGUSTO CANÇADO TRINDADE
AND
DAMIÁN A. GONZÁLEZ-SALZBERG

Great Clarendon Street, Oxford, OX2 6DP,
United Kingdom

Oxford University Press is a department of the University of Oxford.
It furthers the University's objective of excellence in research, scholarship,
and education by publishing worldwide. Oxford is a registered trade mark of
Oxford University Press in the UK and in certain other countries

© Oxford University Press 2024

The moral rights of the authors have been asserted

All rights reserved. No part of this publication may be reproduced, stored in
a retrieval system, or transmitted, in any form or by any means, without the
prior permission in writing of Oxford University Press, or as expressly permitted
by law, by licence or under terms agreed with the appropriate reprographics
rights organization. Enquiries concerning reproduction outside the scope of the
above should be sent to the Rights Department, Oxford University Press, at the
address above

You must not circulate this work in any other form
and you must impose this same condition on any acquirer

Public sector information reproduced under Open Government Licence v3.0
(http://www.nationalarchives.gov.uk/doc/open-government-licence/open-government-licence.htm)

Published in the United States of America by Oxford University Press
198 Madison Avenue, New York, NY 10016, United States of America

British Library Cataloguing in Publication Data

Data available

Library of Congress Control Number: 2023944887

ISBN 978-0-19-289349-9

Printed in the UK by
Bell & Bain Ltd., Glasgow

Links to third party websites are provided by Oxford in good faith and
for information only. Oxford disclaims any responsibility for the materials
contained in any third party website referenced in this work.

PRAISE FOR *INTERNATIONAL LAW OF HUMAN RIGHTS*

'A major contribution from Latin America to the core issues of international human rights law by two talented international legal scholars of different generations which provides important insights into the doctrines as well as legal analysis of the normative framework.' **Professor Mónica Pinto, Professor Emerita of International Law and Human Rights Law, University of Buenos Aires**

'This is an invaluable contribution to the study of international human rights law. The authors bring both sense and sensibility to bear on an array of important topics and what emerges is a highly distinctive and potentially transformative resource.' **Professor Natasa Mavronicola, Professor of Human Rights Law, University of Birmingham**

'A succinct and very insightful account of international human rights law, and an excellent example of a collaborative approach between human rights theory and practice.' **Professor Kanstantsin Dzehtsiarou, Professor in Human Rights Law and Director of the International Law and Human Rights Unit, University of Liverpool**

'A very useful textbook with accessible and clear structure. I love its modern approach to the classification of rights—this is a textbook that belongs to our era.' **Aikaterini Tsampi, Assistant Professor of Public International Law, University of Groningen**

'A very comprehensive discussion of the major, foundational themes in international human rights law, with a critical, yet constructive approach and with an eye for cultural, political and regional differences.' **Marjolein van den Brink, Senior Lecturer in Law, Utrecht University**

'Excellent. The coverage and ability to convey a lot of technical detail in such an interesting and accessible way is most impressive. It ensures that the impact of Judge Trindade's work will continue into the next generation.' **Elizabeth Craig, Senior Lecturer in Law, University of Sussex**

'A contemporary, broad but in-depth review of international human rights law, showing a clear mastery of associated scholarship—a great, well-written textbook.' **Dr Nicolas Kang-Riou, Senior Lecturer in Law, University of Lincoln**

ACKNOWLEDGEMENTS

From the Authors

The authors would like to thank the following members of the legal and academic community for their help at different stages of the production of this manuscript.

Dr Justine Bendel, University of Leeds
Dr Pieter Cannoot, Ghent University
Dr Pablo Castillo-Ortiz, University of Sheffield
Prof Kanstantsin Dzehtsiarou, University of Liverpool
Dr Yin Harn Lee, University of Bristol
Prof Paul Lemmens, KU Leuven
Judge Georgios Serghides, European Court of Human Rights
Dr Jens Theilen, Helmut Schmidt University

For the Editorial Advisory Panel

The authors and Oxford University Press would also like to thank the many members of the academic community whose generous and insightful feedback helped to shape this text, including those who wished to remain anonymous.

Dr Marjolein van den Brink, Utrecht University
Dr Koldo Casla, University of Essex
Dr Elizabeth Craig, University of Sussex
Dr Viljam Engström, Åbo Akademi University
Professor Rosa Freedman, University of Reading
Dr Nicolas Kang-Riou, University of Lincoln
Andreea Manea, The Hague University of Applied Sciences
Professor Natasa Mavronicola, University of Birmingham
Professor Ricardo D. Rabinovich-Berkman, University of Buenos Aires
Dr Aikaterini Tsampi, University of Groningen
Dr Vassilis Tzevelekos, University of Liverpool
Dr Stuart Wallace, University of Leeds

From the Publisher

Every effort has been made to trace and contact copyright holders prior to publication. Where this has not proved possible, if notified, the publisher will undertake to rectify any errors or omissions at the earliest opportunity.

OUTLINE CONTENTS

Preface	xiii
Foreword	xv
List of Abbreviations	xix
Table of Cases	xxiii
Table of Treaties	xliii
Epigraph	lxiii

PART I FOUNDATIONS, HISTORY, AND LEGAL FRAMEWORK

1	HUMAN RIGHTS	3
2	THE DEVELOPMENT OF THE INTERNATIONAL LAW OF HUMAN RIGHTS	58
3	THE NORMATIVE FRAMEWORK OF HUMAN RIGHTS UNDER INTERNATIONAL LAW	113

PART II THE UNIVERSAL SYSTEM

4	UNITED NATIONS CHARTER-BASED BODIES	177
5	UNITED NATIONS TREATY (MONITORING) BODIES	231

PART III REGIONAL SYSTEMS

6	THE INTER-AMERICAN HUMAN RIGHTS SYSTEM	299
7	THE EUROPEAN HUMAN RIGHTS SYSTEM	360
8	THE AFRICAN HUMAN RIGHTS SYSTEM	418

PART IV SUBSTANTIVE RIGHTS

9	THE INTERNATIONAL PROTECTION OF SUBSTANTIVE RIGHTS (I)	477
10	THE INTERNATIONAL PROTECTION OF SUBSTANTIVE RIGHTS (II)	543

Index	609

CONTENTS

Preface	xiii
Foreword	xv
List of Abbreviations	xix
Table of Cases	xxiii
Table of Treaties	xliii
Epigraph	lxiii

PART I FOUNDATIONS, HISTORY, AND LEGAL FRAMEWORK

1 HUMAN RIGHTS 3

   1.1 The Meaning of Human Rights 3
   1.2 The Histories of Human Rights 19
   1.3 Human Rights Critiques 38
   1.4 Conclusion 56

2 THE DEVELOPMENT OF THE INTERNATIONAL LAW OF HUMAN RIGHTS 58

   2.1 The International Law of Human Rights 58
   2.2 The International Law of Human Rights: Legislative Stage 60
   2.3 Civil and Political Rights and Economic, Social, and Cultural Rights 74
   2.4 The International Law of Human Rights: Implementation Stage 87
   2.5 The International Protection of the Human Person Through the Evolving Convergence of Legal Regimes 99
   2.6 Further Reflections: Time and the International Law of Human Rights 107
   2.7 Conclusion 111

3 THE NORMATIVE FRAMEWORK OF HUMAN RIGHTS UNDER INTERNATIONAL LAW 113

   3.1 Sources 113
   3.2 The Nature and Scope of International Human Rights Obligations 138
   3.3 The Protected Subjects of Human Rights 164
   3.4 The Interaction of International and Domestic Law in the Protection of Human Rights 170
   3.5 Conclusion 171

PART II THE UNIVERSAL SYSTEM

4 UNITED NATIONS CHARTER-BASED BODIES — 177

4.1 Human Rights under the United Nations Charter — 177
4.2 The United Nations Commission on Human Rights — 179
4.3 The Human Rights Council (HRC) — 185
4.4 The High Commissioner for Human Rights — 211
4.5 The International Court of Justice and the International Protection of Human Rights: a Tribute to Judge Antônio Augusto Cançado Trindade — 218
4.6 Conclusion — 227

5 UNITED NATIONS TREATY (MONITORING) BODIES — 231

5.1 The UN Core Human Rights Treaties — 231
5.2 Treaty (Monitoring) Bodies — 233
5.3 The Committees' Main Functions — 234
5.4 The Committee on the Elimination of Racial Discrimination (CERD) — 245
5.5 The Human Rights Committee (CCPR) — 250
5.6 The Committee on Economic, Social and Cultural Rights (CESCR) — 254
5.7 The Committee on the Elimination of Discrimination Against Women (CEDAW Committee) — 260
5.8 The Committee Against Torture (CAT) — 265
5.9 The Committee on the Rights of the Child (CRC) — 269
5.10 The Committee on the Protection of the Rights of all Migrant Workers and Members of their Families (CMW) — 274
5.11 Committee on the Rights of Persons with Disabilities (CRPD) — 279
5.12 Committee on Enforced Disappearances (CED) — 283
5.13 Further Reflections: Improving the Treaty Body System — 288
5.14 Conclusion — 293

PART III REGIONAL SYSTEMS

6 THE INTER-AMERICAN HUMAN RIGHTS SYSTEM — 299

6.1 The Creation and Development of the Inter-American System — 299
6.2 The Inter-American Commission on Human Rights: Composition and Structure — 313
6.3 The Inter-American Court of Human Rights: Composition and Structure — 317
6.4 The Individual and the Inter-American Human Rights System — 323
6.5 Critical Debates: Backlashes and Lack of Financial Support — 348
6.6 Inter-State Cases — 351
6.7 Further Reflections: the 'Margin of Appreciation' and the 'Conventionality Control' Doctrines — 352

    6.8 Testimonial: Reflections from a Former Judge and President of the Court (Judge Antônio Augusto Cançado Trindade)   355

    6.9 Conclusion   358

7 THE EUROPEAN HUMAN RIGHTS SYSTEM   360

    7.1 The Creation of the European Human Rights System   360

    7.2 The European Court of Human Rights: Composition and Structure   373

    7.3 The Individual and the European Court of Human Rights   375

    7.4 Inter-State Cases   399

    7.5 Compliance with the Court's Judgments   401

    7.6 The Court's Advisory Jurisdiction   404

    7.7 Further Reflections: the 'Margin of Appreciation' Doctrine   408

    7.8 Conclusion   416

8 THE AFRICAN HUMAN RIGHTS SYSTEM   418

    8.1 Origins and Development of the African Human Rights System   418

    8.2 The African Commission on Human and Peoples' Rights   437

    8.3 The African Court on Human and Peoples' Rights   441

    8.4 The Individual and the African Human Rights System   447

    8.5 Advisory Opinions   466

    8.6 Inter-State Communications   468

    8.7 Critical Debates: Towards a New African Court   469

    8.8 Conclusion   472

PART IV SUBSTANTIVE RIGHTS

9 THE INTERNATIONAL PROTECTION OF SUBSTANTIVE RIGHTS (I)   477

    9.1 The Right to Life   477

    9.2 The Right to Personal Integrity   494

    9.3 Freedom of Thought, Conscience, and Religion   509

    9.4 Freedom of Opinion and Expression   523

10 THE INTERNATIONAL PROTECTION OF SUBSTANTIVE RIGHTS (II)   543

    10.1 The Prohibition of Discrimination   543

    10.2 Women's Rights   562

    10.3 Children's Rights   576

    10.4 Group Rights   589

Index   609

PREFACE

I met Antônio in Washington D.C. in 2013. An article I wrote during my PhD studies won the 2013 Human Rights Essay Award and American University gave me a generous scholarship to attend its summer programme, where I took Prof Cançado Trindade's course. Only a few months later, I met him again in Strasbourg. He was teaching another course and I had mastered the courage to sit the week-long examinations for the Diploma in International and Comparative Human Rights Law at the 'René Cassin' Institute. When Antônio found out I had been the candidate awarded the prestigious *diplôme* that year, he sent me a heart-warming message with an invitation to visit him at the International Court of Justice. Over the years, I would visit him at the Court many times; our academic conversations ending with abundant laughter in the same restaurant in The Hague, in the unwavering company of Carmela.

During one of these visits, in May 2017, we came up with the idea to write this book together. Having been teaching international human rights law for a number of years, I found the literature for students to have a very distinctive provenance and approach, and thought that two critical scholars from America's Southern Cone could offer a different perspective. We embarked on this academic adventure in January 2018, soon after his re-election as Judge of the International Court of Justice. Sadly, Antônio died in May 2022. After many years of one of the most enjoyable co-productive endeavours of my academic career, we had completed about 80 per cent of our project. While truthful to our discussions, ideas, and sketches, I take full responsibility for any opinions expressed in Chapter 1 and Chapter 4 of this book, written after Antônio had left us.

Completing this book has been one of the most rewarding, challenging, joyful, yet sad experiences of my career. To co-author a book with one of the most important figures in the development of the international law of human rights was an opportunity that I will forever treasure. The numerous separate opinions of Judge Cançado Trindade, President of the Inter-American Court, were one of the biggest inspirations during my law degree at the Universidad de Buenos Aires; his work at the Court truly helped re-shape the legal landscape of America (the continent). Working with Judge Cançado Trindade, of the International Court of Justice, revealed that the person behind the pen was as inspiring as his judgments, with a real conviction that law can have a significant impact in improving the world. Sharing time with my friend Antônio, always joyful and seemingly untiring, was simply a gift I will never forget.

Judge Antônio Augusto Cançado Trindade died on 29 May 2022. His contribution, not only to academia, but to the progress of human rights in America and the world, will live forever.

FOREWORD

Two critical scholars from the Global South wrote this book, offering a global perspective on the international law of human rights that not only discusses the current state of the discipline, but also engages with multiple challenges that we believe underpin this particular branch of international law. Despite our own personal positionalities, the critiques throughout the book do not originate in one specific school of thought, reflecting an awareness that there is more than one way to approach the field of human rights. In writing this book, we have made use of a plurality of sources, produced at different times, in different geographic locations, and in different languages. Nonetheless, as you will easily grasp, our own Global South background transpires in the heightened attention paid to certain topics and the recurrent emergence of specific concerns, such as the legal legacies of colonialism, or law's over-reliance on Western epistemes. Having said that, we also acknowledge having prioritized the use of more recent sources and those produced in English. We hope these resources will be more accessible for you, our reader, when embarking on your own journey to advance the study of the discipline beyond this book. At the same time, we have consciously endeavoured to provide an even degree of attention to the legal knowledge produced by the multiple international monitoring bodies charged with developing, on a daily basis, the interpretation and scope of the international law of human rights.

The book offers particular features that will support your learning. These include 'case boxes', which provide brief summaries of some of the most relevant judgments and decisions that are mentioned throughout the main discussion, to facilitate the understanding of the overall topic. Similarly, acknowledging that the book might be used by readers at different stages of their studies and from different disciplines, we have marked some discussions as 'further reflections', indicating that the level of detail contained therein might be beyond what is expected in a traditional textbook. We have also selected certain issues for discussion as 'critical debates', emphasizing that— despite our personal stance on them—opinions on the specific topics might differ, and inviting you to form your own views. At the end of each chapter, we suggest a short list of books (including collective works) that have been referred to throughout the chapter and which would be worth considering for delving further into the topics discussed. Lastly, in **Section 6.8** you can find a unique testimonial from Judge Cançado Trindade's experience as Judge and President of the Inter-American Court of Human Rights.

The book is divided into four Parts, each comprising two or three chapters. **Part One** provides an essential introduction to the international law of human rights, encompassing discussions about the meaning and the histories of the idea of human rights, as well as of the development of the protection of human rights under international law. Given that not every reader of this book will have an advanced knowledge of public international law, **Chapter 3** offers an introduction to the sources, obligations, and subjects of international law, as applicable to the international law of human rights. The second and third parts of the book focus on existent international human rights regimes. Across two chapters, **Part Two** explores the human rights framework developed under the United Nations, while **Part Three** engages with the three main regional systems created for the protection of human rights, in chapters dedicated to the Inter-American, European, and African human rights systems. It is worth highlighting that no discussion of European Union law can be found in that part of the book, as further explained in the introduction to **Part Three**. The final part of the book comprises two chapters, which critically discuss selected human rights. Another important remark is that no traditional section on 'economic, social, and cultural rights' will be found in **Part Four**. We placed this discussion within the historical development of the discipline, in **Section 2.3**, due to our strong belief that the classification and compartmentalization of human rights is an undesired consequence of a particular historical, economic, and political context, which acts as an ongoing obstacle for conceiving individuals' rights as fully indivisible and interdependent.

To Susana Salzberg and in memory of Antônio Augusto Cançado Trindade, for their immense inspiration in pursuing an academic career.

With everlasting thanks to Chris for incommensurable support during the many years of writing this book.

LIST OF ABBREVIATIONS

ACERWC	African Committee of Experts on the Rights and Welfare of the Child
ACHPR	African Commission on Human and Peoples' Rights
ACHR	American Convention on Human Rights
ACtHPR	African Court on Human and Peoples' Rights
ADRDM	American Declaration of Rights and Duties of Man
African Charter	African Charter of Human and Peoples' Rights
African Children's Charter	African Charter on the Rights and Welfare of the Child
African Court Protocol	Protocol on the Establishment of an African Court on Human and Peoples' Rights
Arab Charter	Arab Charter of Human Rights
ASEAN	Association of Southeast Asian Nations
AU	African Union
CARICOM	Caribbean Community
CAT	Committee against Torture
CCPR	Human Rights Committee
CED	Committee on Enforced Disappearances
CEDAW	Convention on the Elimination of All Forms of Discrimination against Women
CEDAW Committee	Committee on the Elimination of Discrimination against Women
CERD	Committee on the Elimination of Racial Discrimination
CESCR	Committee on Economic, Social and Cultural Rights
CHR	United Nations Commission on Human Rights
CJEU	Court of Justice of the European Union
Convention of Belém do Pará	Inter-American Convention on the Prevention, Punishment and Eradication of Violence against Women
CRC	Committee on the Rights of the Child
CRPD	Committee on the Rights of Persons with Disabilities
CSW	Commission on the Status of Women
ECHR	European Convention on Human Rights
ECOSOC	Economic and Social Council
ECOWAS	Economic Community of West African States
ECtHR	European Court of Human Rights
EU	European Union
HRC	Human Rights Council
IACHR	Inter-American Commission on Human Rights
IACtHR	Inter-American Court of Human Rights
ICC	International Criminal Court
ICCPR	International Covenant on Civil and Political Rights

ICCPR-OP1	First Optional Protocol to the International Covenant on Civil and Political Rights
ICCPR-OP2	Second Optional Protocol to the International Covenant on Civil and Political Rights, aiming at the abolition of the death penalty
ICERD	International Convention on the Elimination of All Forms of Racial Discrimination
ICESCR	International Covenant on Economic, Social and Cultural Rights
ICJ	International Court of Justice
ICPD	International Conference on Population and Development
ICPPED	International Convention for the Protection of All Persons from Enforced Disappearance
ICRC	International Committee of the Red Cross
ICRMW	International Convention on the Protection of the Rights of All Migrant Workers and Members of Their Families
ICTR	International Criminal Tribunal for Rwanda
ICTY	International Criminal Tribunal for the Former Yugoslavia
ILC	International Law Commission
ILO	International Labour Organization
Malabo Protocol	Protocol on Amendments to the Protocol on the Statute of the African Court of Justice and Human Rights
Maputo Protocol	Protocol on the Rights of Women in Africa
MERCOSUR	Southern Common Market
OAS	Organization of American States
OAU	Organisation of African Unity
OECD	Organisation for Economic Co-operation and Development
OHCHR	Office of the High Commissioner of Human Rights
OP1-CRC	Optional Protocol to the Convention on the Rights of the Child on the sale of children, child prostitution and child pornography
OP2-CRC	Optional Protocol to the Convention on the Rights of the Child on the involvement of children in armed conflict
OP3-CRC	Optional Protocol to the Convention on the Rights of the Child on a communications procedure
OPCAT	Optional Protocol to the Convention against Torture and Other Cruel, Inhuman or Degrading Treatment or Punishment
OP-CEDAW	Optional Protocol to the Convention on the Elimination of All Forms of Discrimination against Women
OPCRPD	Optional Protocol to the Convention on the Rights of Persons with Disabilities
OP-ICESCR	Optional Protocol to the International Covenant on Economic, Social and Cultural Rights
PACE	Parliamentary Assembly of the Council of Europe
PCIJ	Permanent Court of International Justice
Protocol of San Salvador	Additional Protocol to the American Convention on Human Rights in the Area of Economic, Social, and Cultural Rights
SADC	Southern African Development Community

SPT	Subcommittee on Prevention of Torture and Other Cruel, Inhuman or Degrading Treatment or Punishment
UDHR	Universal Declaration of Human Rights
UN	United Nations
UN Women	United Nations Entity for Gender Equality and the Empowerment of Women
UNAIDS	Joint United Nations Programme on HIV and AIDS
UNCAT	Convention against Torture and Other Cruel, Inhuman or Degrading Treatment or Punishment
UNCRC	United Nations Convention on the Rights of the Child
UNCRPD	United Nations Convention on the Rights of Persons with Disabilities
UNDP	United Nations Development Programme
UNECA	United Nations Economic Commission for Africa
UNESCO	United Nations Educational, Scientific and Cultural Organization
UNFPA	United Nations Population Fund
UNGA	United Nations General Assembly
UNHCR	United Nations High Commissioner for Refugees
UNICEF	United Nations Children's Fund (formerly United Nations International Children's Emergency Fund)
UNIFEM	United Nations Development Fund for Women
VCLT	Vienna Convention on the Law of Treaties
WHO	World Health Organization

TABLE OF CASES

COURT OF JUSTICE OF THE EUROPEAN UNION (CJEU)

C-308/06, Intertanko [2008] ECR I-4057 . . . 149

EUROPEAN COMMISSION OF HUMAN RIGHTS (ECHR)

Arrowsmith v. United Kingdom, App. no. 7050/75, 12 October 1978 . . . 511
Bulut v. Turkey, App. no. 18783/91, 3 May 1993 . . . 518
Darby v. Sweden, App. no. 11581/85, 9 May 1989 . . . 511
Greece v the United Kingdom ('The Cyprus Case'), App. no. 176/56 (1958) . . . 18, 409, 410, 412
Karaduman v. Turkey, App. no. 7050/75, 3 May 1993 . . . 518
Lawless v. Ireland, App. no. 332/57, 19 December 1959 . . . 409, 410, 411, 412
The Greek case (1969), App. no. 3321/67 (c), App. no. 3322/67 (Norway v. Greece), App. no. 3323/67 (Sweden v. Greece), App. no. 3344/67 (Netherlands v. Greece) . . . 370, 399, 497, 501, 502
W. v. United Kingdom (dec.), App. no. 18187/91, 10 February 1993 . . . 511

EUROPEAN COURT OF HUMAN RIGHTS (ECtHR)

A, B and C v. Ireland [GC], App. no. 25579/05, ECHR 2010 . . . 414, 415, 479
A. v. the United Kingdom, 23 September 1998, Reports of Judgments and Decisions 1998-VI . . . 505
A.P., Garcon and Nicot v. France, App. nos. 79885/12 and two others, 6 April 2017 . . . 559
Abdulaziz, Cabales and Balkandali v. the United Kingdom, 28 May 1985, Series A App. no. 94 . . . 545
Advisory opinion concerning the recognition in domestic law of a legal parent-child relationship between a child born through a gestational surrogacy arrangement abroad and the intended mother [GC], request no. P16-2018-001, French Court of Cassation, 10 April 2019 . . . 406, 407
Advisory opinion concerning the use of the 'blanket reference' or 'legislation by reference' technique in the definition of an offence and the standards of comparison between the criminal law in force at the time of the commission of the offence and the amended criminal law [GC], request no. P16-2019-001, Armenian Constitutional Court, 29 May 2020 . . . 406, 407
Advisory opinion on certain legal questions concerning the lists of candidates submitted with a view to the election of judges to the European Court of Human Rights [GC], 12 February 2008 . . . 405, 406
Advisory opinion on certain legal questions concerning the lists of candidates submitted with a view to the election of judges to the European Court of Human Rights (No. 2) [GC], 22 January 2010 . . . 405
Advisory opinion on the applicability of statutes of limitation to prosecution, conviction and punishment in respect of an offence constituting, in substance, an act of torture [GC], Request no. P16-2021-001, Armenian Court of Cassation, 26 April 2022 . . . 406
Advisory opinion on the assessment, under Article 3 of Protocol No. 1 to the Convention, of the proportionality of a general prohibition on standing for election after removal from office in impeachment proceedings [GC], Request no. P16-2020-002, Lithuanian Supreme Administrative Court, 8 April 2022 . . . 406
Advisory opinion on the difference in treatment between landowners' associations 'having a recognised existence on the date of the creation of an approved municipal hunters' association' and landowners' associations set up after that date [GC], Request no. P16-2021-002, French Conseil d'Etat, 13 July 2022 . . . 406
Ahmet Arslan and Others v. Turkey, App. no. 41135/98, 23 February 2010 . . . 518, 522
Airey v. Ireland, 9 October 1979, Series A no. 32 . . . 80, 109
Akdivar and Others v. Turkey, 16 September 1996, Reports of Judgments and Decisions 1996-IV . . . 384

Akman v. Turkey (striking out), App. no. 37453/97, ECHR 2001-VI . . . 378
Al-Adsani v. the United Kingdom [GC], App. no. 35763/97, ECHR 2001-XI . . . 135, 495
Alekseyev v. Russia, App. nos. 4916/07 and two others, 21 October 2010 . . . 414, 558
Ali and Ayşe Duran v. Turkey, App. no. 42942/02, 8 April 2008 . . . 489, 505
Al-Jedda v. the United Kingdom [GC], App. no. 27021/08, ECHR 2011 . . . 149, 158
Al-Nashif v. Bulgaria, App. no. 50963/99, 20 June 2002 . . . 388
Al-Saadoon and Mufdhi v. the United Kingdom, App. no. 61498/08, ECHR 2010 . . . 131, 485
Al-Skeini and Others v. the United Kingdom [GC], App. no. 55721/07, ECHR 2011 . . . 157, 158, 163, 164
Animal Defenders International v. the United Kingdom [GC], App. no. 48876/08, ECHR 2013 . . . 413
Artico v. Italy, 13 May 1980, Series A no. 37 . . . 116
Asatruarfelagid v. Iceland (dec.), App. no. 22897/08, 18 September 2012 . . . 511
Assanidze v. Georgia [GC], App. no. 71503/01, ECHR 2004-II . . . 390, 392
Assenov and Others v. Bulgaria, 28 October 1998, Reports of Judgments and Decisions 1998-VIII . . . 504, 505
Association SOS Attentats and De Boery v. France (dec.) [GC], App. no. 76642/01 . . . 378
Axel Springer AG v. Germany [GC], App. no. 39954/08, 7 February 2012 . . . 535
Aydın Tatlav v. Turkey, App. no. 50692/99, 2 May 2006 . . . 538
Aydın v. Turkey, 25 September 1997, Reports of Judgments and Decisions 1997-VI . . . 502
B.S. v. Spain, App. no. 47159/08, 24 July 2012 . . . 553, 561
Bader and Kanbor v. Sweden, No. 13284/04, 8 November 2005 . . . 103
Bah v. the United Kingdom, App. no. 56328/07, ECHR 2011 . . . 544, 555
Baka v. Hungary [GC], App. no. 20261/12, 23 June 2016 . . . 130
Banković and Others v. Belgium and Others (dec.) [GC], App. no. 52207/99, ECHR 2001-XII . . . 157, 162
Bayatyan v. Armenia [GC], App. no. 23459/03, ECHR 2011 . . . 415, 513, 517
Bayev and Others v. Russia, App. nos. 67667/09 and two others, 20 June 2017 . . . 533
Bede Djokaba Lambi Longa v. The Netherlands (dec.), App. no. 33917/12, 9 October 2012 . . . 150

Behrami and Behrami v. France and Saramati v. France, Germany and Norway (dec.) [GC], App. no. 71412/01 and 78166/01, 2 May 2007 . . . 150
Belilos v. Switzerland, 29 April 1988, Series A no. 132 . . . 122, 123
Biblical Centre of the Chuvash Republic v. Russia, App. no. 33203/08, 12 June 2014 . . . 517
Bladet Tromso and Stensaas v. Norway [GC], App. no. 21980/93, ECHR 1999-III . . . 527
Bouton v. France (dec.), App. no. 22636/19, 13 October 2022 . . . 538
Bouyid v. Belgium [GC], App. no. 23380/09, ECHR 2015 . . . 503
Broniowski v. Poland (friendly settlement) [GC], App. no. 31443/96, ECHR 2005-IX . . . 395
Broniowski v. Poland [GC], App. no. 31443/96, ECHR 2004-V . . . 394, 395
Budayeva and Others v. Russia, nos. 15339/02 and four others, ECHR 2008 . . . 412, 487
Buscarini and Others v. San Marino [GC], App. no. 24645/94, ECHR 1999-I . . . 511
Cali and Others v. Italy (striking out), App. no. 52332/99, 19 May 2005 . . . 378
Campbell and Cosans v. the United Kingdom, 25 February 1982, Series A no. 48 . . . 511
Carson and Others v. the United Kingdom, App. no. 42184/05, 4 November 2008 . . . 554
Case 'relating to certain aspects of the laws on the use of languages in education in Belgium' (merits), 23 July 1968, p. 31, Series A no. 6 . . . 18, 410, 412, 553, 554
Castells v. Spain, 23 April 1992, Series A no. 236 . . . 526, 536
Catan and Others v. the Republic of Moldova and Russia [GC], App. nos. 43370/04 and 2 others, ECHR 2012 . . . 158, 163, 164
Chabauty v. France [GC], App. no. 57412/08, 4 October 2012 . . . 561
Chassagnou and Others v. France [GC], App. nos. 25088/94, 28331/95, 28443/95, ECHR 1999 III . . . 555, 561
Christine Goodwin v. the United Kingdom [GC], App. no. 28957/95, ECHR 2002-VI . . . 559
Cossey v. the United Kingdom, 27 September 1990, Series A no. 184 . . . 559
Courten v. the United Kingdom (dec.), App. 4479/06, 4 November 2008 . . . 388
Cyprus v. Turkey [GC], App. no. 25781/94, ECHR 2001-IV . . . 158, 399
D.H. and Others v. the Czech Republic [GC], App. no. 57325/00, ECHR 2007-IV . . . 545, 546, 554, 555, 556
Dahlab v. Switzerland (dec.), App. no. 42393/98, 15 February 2001 . . . 518, 519

De Wilde, Ooms and Versyp v. Belgium, 18 June 1971, Series A App. no. 12 . . . 412
Decision on the Competence of the Court to Give an Advisory Opinion (2 June 2004) . . . 405
Delfi AS v. Estonia (GC), App. no. 64569/09, ECHR 2015 . . . 528
Denmark v. Turkey, App. no. 34382/97, ECHR 2000-IV . . . 399
Dogru v. France, App. no. 27058/05, 4 December 2008 . . . 516, 533
Drozd and Janousek v. France and Spain, 26 June 1992, Series A no. 240 . . . 157
Dudgeon v. the United Kingdom, 22 October 1981, Series A no. 45 . . . 108, 413, 414, 556
E.B. v. France [GC], App. no. 43546/02, 22 January 2008 . . . 544, 554, 555
E.S. v. Austria, App. no. 38450/12, 25 October 2018 . . . 539
Egeland and Hanseid v. Norway, App. no. 34438/04, 16 April 2009 . . . 416
El Majjaoui and Stichting Touba Moskee v. the Netherlands (striking out) [GC], App. no. 25525/03, 20 December 2007 . . . 378
Evans v. the United Kingdom [GC], App. no. 6339/05, ECHR 2007-I . . . 413, 479
Eweida and Others v. the United Kingdom, App. nos. 48420/10 and three others, ECHR 2013 . . . 413, 514, 518, 522
F.H. v. Sweden, App. no. 32621/06, 20 January 2009 . . . 109
Fabian v. Hungary, App. no. 78117/3, 5 September 2017 . . . 545
Federation Hellenique des Syndicats des Employes du Secteur Bancaire v. Greece (dec.), App. no. 72808/10, 6 December 2011 . . . 387
Fedotov v. Russia, App. no. 5140/02, 25 October 2005 . . . 503
Fedotova and Others v. Russia [GC], App. nos. 40792/10 and two others, 17 January 2023 . . . 558
Feldbrugge v. The Netherlands, App 8562/79, 29 May 1986 . . . 18
Finger v. Bulgaria, App. no. 37346/05, 10 May 2011 . . . 389
Folgero and Others v. Norway (dec.), App. no. 15472/02, 14 February 2006 . . . 386, 387
Folgero and Others v. Norway [GC], App. no. 15472/02, ECHR 2007-III . . . 512
Frette v. France, no. 36515/97, ECHR 2002-I . . . 415, 555
Gafgen v. Germany [GC], App. no. 22978/05, ECHR 2010 . . . 507, 508
Gagliano Giorgi v. Italy, App. no. 23563/07, ECHR 2012 . . . 389

Garaudy v. France (dec.), App. no. 65831/01, 24 June 2003 . . . 530, 531
Garib v. the Netherlands, no. 43494/09, 23 February 2016 . . . 560
Genderdoc-M v. Moldova, App. no. 9106/06, 12 June 2012 . . . 557
Georgia v. Russia (I) [GC], App. no. 13255/07, ECHR 2014 . . . 399, 400
Georgia v. Russia (II) [GC], App. no. 38263/08 (21 January 2021) . . . 399
Georgia v. Russia (III) (striking out), App. no. 61186/09, 16 March 2010 . . . 399
Giniewski v. France, App. no. 64016/00, ECHR 2006-I . . . 538
Giusti v. Italy, App. no. 13175/03, 18 October 2011 . . . 389
Gładkowski v. Poland (striking out), App. no. 29697/96, 14 March 2000 . . . 378
Glor v. Switzerland, App. no. 13444/04, ECHR 2009 . . . 544, 555
Golder v. the United Kingdom, 21 February 1975, Series A no. 18 . . . 119, 130
Gongadze v. Ukraine, App. no. 34056/02, ECHR 2005-XI . . . 503
Grimmark v. Sweden (dec.), App. no. 43726/16, 11 February 2020 . . . 514
Guerra v. Italy, Reports of Judgments and Decisions 1998-I (1998) . . . 18
Gurdeniz v. Turkey (dec.), App. no. 59715/10, 18 March 2014 . . . 386, 387
H.L.R. v. France, 29 April 1997, Reports of Judgments and Decisions 1997-III . . . 497, 504
Hadrabova and Others v. the Czech Republic (dec.), App. nos. 42165/02, 466/03, 25 September 2007 . . . 388
Hamalainen v. Finland [GC], App. no. 37359/09, ECHR 2014 . . . 413
Hamidović v. Bosnia and Herzegovina, App. no. 57792/15, 5 December 2017 . . . 522
Handyside v. the United Kingdom, 7 December 1976, Series A no. 24 . . . 18, 410, 412, 525, 526, 533, 534
Hans Jorg Schimanek v. Austria (dec.), App. no. 32307/96, 1 February 2000 . . . 530
Haran v. Turkey, App. no. 25754/94, 26 March 2002 . . . 378
Harkins v. the United Kingdom (dec.) [GC], App. no. 71537/14, 15 June 2017 . . . 386
Hilal Mammadov v. Azerbaijan, App. no. 81553/12, 4 February 2016 . . . 387
Hirsi Jamaa and Others v. Italy, No. 27765/09, 23 February 2012 . . . 103, 158
Hun v. Turkey (striking out), App. no. 5142/04, 10 November 2005 . . . 378

İ.A. v. Turkey, App. no. 42571/98, ECHR 2005-VIII . . . 538
Identoba and Others v. Georgia, App. no. 73235/12, 12 May 2015 . . . 544, 555, 556, 559
Ilaşcu and Others v. Moldova and Russia [GC], App. no. 48787/99, ECHR 2004-VII . . . 157, 162, 381, 390, 392
Ilgar Mammadov v. Azerbaijan, no. 15172/13, 22 May 2014 . . . 403, 404
Ireland v. the United Kingdom, 18 January 1978, Series A no. 25 . . . 92, 115, 399, 400, 497, 500, 502, 503
Issa and Others v. Turkey, App. no. 31821/96, 16 November 2004 . . . 158, 162, 163
Ivanova v. Bulgaria, App. no. 52435/99, 12 April 2007 . . . 509
Jacubowski v. Germany, 23 June 1994, Series A App. no. 291-A . . . 413
Jaggi v. Switzerland, App. no. 58757/00, ECHR 2006-X . . . 412, 413
Jaloud v. the Netherlands [GC], App. no. 47708/08, ECHR 2014 . . . 149
Jerusalem v. Austria, App. no. 26958/95, ECHR 2001-II . . . 536
Jian v. Romania (dec.), no. 46640/99, 30 March 2004 . . . 388
Kafkaris v. Cyprus (dec.), App. no. 9644/09, 21 June 2011 . . . 386
Kalac v. Turkey, 1 July 1997, Reports of Judgments and Decisions 1997-IV . . . 510
Karner v. Austria, App. no. 40016/98, ECHR 2003-IX . . . 378, 379, 544, 554, 555
Karoussiotis v. Portugal, App. no. 23205/08, ECHR 2011 . . . 386
Karsai v. Hungary, App. no. 5380/07, 1 December 2009 . . . 536
Kavala v. Turkey, no. 28749/18, 10 December 2019 . . . 392
Kezer and Others v. Turkey (dec.), App. no. 58058/00, 5 October 2004 . . . 386
Khamtokhu and Aksenchik v. Russia [GC], App. nos. 60367/08 and 961/11, ECHR 2017 . . . 545
Kjeldsen, Busk Madsen and Pedersen v. Denmark, 7 December 1976, Series A App. no. 23 . . . 512
Klein v. Slovakia, App. no. 72208/01, 31 October 2006 . . . 538
Kokkinakis v. Greece, 25 May 1993, Series A no. 260-A . . . 510, 517
Kolk and Kislyiy v. Estonia (dec.), App. nos. 23052/04 and 24018/04, 17 January 2006 . . . 130
Konig v. Germany, 28 June 1978, Series A no. 27 . . . 117
Konstantin Markin v. Russia [GC], App. no. 30078/06, ECHR 2012 . . . 412, 544, 554

Korolev v. Russia (dec.), App. no. 25551/05, 1 July 2010 . . . 389
Kurtulmuş v. Turkey (dec.), App. no. 65500/01, 24 January 2006 . . . 511
L.C.B. v. the United Kingdom, 9 June 1998, Reports of Judgments and Decisions 1998-III . . . 487
La Rosa and Alba v. Italy (striking out), App. no. 58274/00, 28 June 2005 . . . 378
Lachiri v. Belgium, App. no. 3413/09, 18 September 2018 . . . 522
Ladygin v. Russia (dec.), App. no. 35365/05, 3 August 2011 . . . 389
Lambert and Others v. France [GC], App. no. 46043/14, ECHR 2015 . . . 412
Latvia v. Denmark, App. no. 9717/20, 16 June 2020 . . . 399
Lautsi and Others v. Italy [GC], App. no. 30814/06, ECHR 2011 . . . 512, 513
Leander v. Sweden, 26 March 1987, Series A App. no. 116 . . . 413
Leyla Şahin v. Turkey [GC], App. no. 44774/98, ECHR 2005-XI . . . 517, 518, 519
lgar Mammadov v. Azerbaijan (infringement proceedings) [GC], App. no. 15172/13, 29 May 2019 . . . 401, 403, 404
Loizidou v. Turkey (merits), 18 December 1996, Reports of Judgments and Decisions 1996-VI . . . 158, 159
Loizidou v. Turkey (preliminary objections), 23 March 1995, Series A no. 310 . . . 157, 158, 159
Luberti v. Italy, 23 February 1984, Series A App. no. 75 . . . 412
Lustig-Prean and Beckett v. United Kingdom, App. nos. 31417/96 and 32377/96, September 1999 . . . 557
López-Ostra v. Spain (ser. A) 303-C (1994) . . . 18
M.C. v. Bulgaria, App. no. 39272/98, ECHR 2003-XII . . . 412
M.K. v. Greece, App. no. 51312/16, 1 February 2018 . . . 586
Mahmut Kaya v. Turkey, App. no. 22535/93, ECHR 2000-III . . . 147, 505
Makaratzis v. Greece [GC], App. no. 50385/99, ECHR 2004-XI . . . 487
Malcolm Ross v. Canada, Communication No. 736/1997 (18 October 2000) . . . 530
Malsagova and Others v. Russia (dec.), App. no. 27244/03, 6 March 2008 . . . 387
Mamatkulov and Askarov v. Turkey [GC], App. nos. 46827/99, 46951/99, ECHR 2005-I . . . 381, 382
Manenc v. France (dec.), App. no. 66686/09, 21 September 2010 . . . 388

Maravić Markeš v. Croatia, App. no. 70923/11, 9 January 2014 . . . 389
Marckx v. Belgium, 13 June 1979, Series A no. 31 . . . 109, 140, 554
markt intern Verlag GmbH and Klaus Beermann v. Germany, 20 November 1989, Series A no. 165 . . . 413, 526
Marlow v. the United Kingdom (dec.), App. no. 42015/98, 5 December 2000 . . . 414
McCann and Others v. the United Kingdom, 27 September 1995, Series A no. 324 . . . 480
Medvedyev and Others v. France [GC], App. no. 3394/03, ECHR 2010 . . . 158
Menson v. the United Kingdom (dec.), App. no. 47916/99, ECHR 2003-V . . . 488
Meriakri v. Moldova (striking out), App. no. 53487/99, 1 March 2005 . . . 378
Metropolitan Church of Bessarabia and Others v. Moldova, App. no. 45701/99, ECHR 2001-XII . . . 169, 511
Mikolenko, v. Estonia (dec.), App. no. 16944/03, 5 January 2006 . . . 387
Miroļubovs and Others v. Latvia, App. no. 798/05, 15 September 2009 . . . 388
Mouvement raelien suisse v. Switzerland [GC], App. no. 16354/06 . . . 526
Mozer v. the Republic of Moldova and Russia [GC], App. no. 11138/10, 23 February 2016 . . . 163
Muller and Others v. Switzerland, 24 May 1988, Series A no. 133 . . . 526
Murruvet Kucuk v. Turkey (striking out), App. no. 21784/04, 10 November 2005 . . . 378
Nada v. Switzerland [GC], App. no. 10593/08, ECHR 2012 . . . 150
Nagmetov v. Russia [GC], App. no. 35589/08, 30 March 2017 . . . 390
Neulinger and Shuruk v. Switzerland [GC], App. no. 41615/07, ECHR 2010 . . . 579
Nolan and K. v. Russia, App. no. 2512/04, 12 February 2009 . . . 516
OAO Neftyanaya Kompaniya Yukos v. Russia, App. no. 14902/04, 20 September 2011 . . . 386
Observer and Guardian v. the United Kingdom, 26 November 1991, Series A App. no. 216 . . . 169, 413, 526
Ocalan v. Turkey [GC], App. no. 46221/99, ECHR 2005-IV . . . 158
Odievre v. France [GC],App. no. 42326/98, ECHR 2003-III . . . 413
Oğur v. Turkey [GC], App. no. 21594/93, ECHR 1999-III . . . 488
Oleksandr Volkov v. Ukraine, App. no. 21722/11, ECHR 2013 . . . 393
Oneryıldız v. Turkey [GC], App. no. 48939/99, ECHR 2004-XII . . . 487

Open Door and Dublin Well Woman v. Ireland, 29 October 1992, Series A no. 246-A . . . 169
Opuz v. Turkey, App. no. 33401/02, ECHR 2009 . . . 573
Osman v. the United Kingdom [GC], 28 October 1998, Reports of Judgments and Decisions 1998-VIII . . . 487
Otto v. Germany (dec.), App. no. 21425/06, 10 November 2009 . . . 385
P.B. and J.S. v. Austria, App. no. 18984/02, 22 July 2010 . . . 18
P.V. v. Spain, App. no. 35159/09, 30 November 2010 . . . 559
Pad and Others v. Turkey (dec.), App. no. 60167/00, 28 June 2007 . . . 163
Paladi v. Moldova [GC], App. no. 39806/05, 10 March 2009 . . . 381
Palomo Sanchez and Others v. Spain [GC], App. nos. 28955/06 and three others, ECHR 2011 . . . 414
Papamichalopoulos and Others v. Greece (Article 50), 31 October 1995 . . . 390
Paul and Audrey Edwards v. the United Kingdom, App. no. 46477/99, ECHR 2002-II . . . 488
Pedersen and Baadsgaard v. Denmark [GC], App. no. 49017/99, ECHR 2004-XI . . . 536
Pentikainen v. Finland [GC], App. no. 11882/10, ECHR 2015 . . . 527
Peraldi v. France (dec.), App. no. 2096/05, 7 April 2009 . . . 387
Perincek v. Switzerland [GC], App. no. 27510/08, ECHR 2015 . . . 530
Petkoski and Others v. the former Yugoslav Republic of Macedonia, no. 27736/03, 8 January 2009 . . . 412
Predescu v. Romania, App. no. 21447/03, 2 December 2008 . . . 388
Professional Trades Union for Prison, Correctional and Secure Psychiatric Workers and Others (POA and Others) v. the United Kingdom (dec.), App. no. 59253/11, 21 May 2013 . . . 386, 387
Quark Fishing Ltd v. the United Kingdom (dec.), App. no. 15305/06, 19 September 2006 . . . 154, 155
Rabczewska v. Poland, App. no. 8257/13, 15 September 2022 . . . 538
Rees v. the United Kingdom, 17 October 1986, Series A no. 106 . . . 559
Refah Partisi (the Welfare Party) and Others v. Turkey [GC], App. nos. 41340/98 and 3 others, ECHR 2003-II . . . 169
Řehak v. the Czech Republic (dec.), App. no. 67208/01, 18 May 2004 . . . 388

Religionsgemeinschaft der Zeugen Jehovas and Others v. Austria, App. no. 40825/98, 31 July 2008 . . . 511

Ringeisen v. Austria (Art. 50), 22 June 1972, Series A no. 15 . . . 487

S. and Marper v. the United Kingdom [GC], App. nos. 30562/04, 30566/04, ECHR 2008 . . . 412, 413

S.A.S. v. France [GC], App. no. 43835/11, ECHR 2014 . . . 388, 518, 522, 523

S.H. and Others v. Austria [GC], App. no. 57813/00, ECHR 2011 . . . 415

S.L. v. Austria (dec.), App. no. 45330/99, 22 November 2001 . . . 413

Sabri Guneş v. Turkey [GC], App. no. 27396/06, 29 June 2012 . . . 385

Salgueiro da Silva Mouta v. Portugal, App. no 33290/96, ECHR 1999-IX . . . 556, 557, 558

Savda v. Turkey, App. no. 42730/05, 12 June 2012 . . . 386

Schalk and Kopf v. Austria, App. no. 30141/04, ECHR 2010 . . . 415, 558

Schwizgebel v. Switzerland, App. no. 25762/07, ECHR 2010 . . . 544, 555

Scozzari and Giunta v. Italy [GC], App. nos. 39221/98, 41963/98, ECHR 2000-VIII . . . 390

Sejdovic v. Italy [GC], App. no. 56581/00, ECHR 2006-II . . . 384

Selmouni v. France [GC], App. no. 25803/94, ECHR 1999-V . . . 135, 495, 500, 502, 503

Sevgi Erdoğan v. Turkey (striking out), App. no. 28492/95, 29 April 2003 . . . 378

Shamayev and Others v. Georgia and Russia (dec.), App. no. 36378/02, 16 September 2003 . . . 385

Shamayev and Others v. Georgia and Russia, App. no. 36378/02, ECHR 2005-III . . . 385

Sheffield and Horsham v. the United Kingdom, 30 July 1998, Reports of Judgments and Decisions 1998-V . . . 559

Sinan Işık v. Turkey, App. no. 21924/05, ECHR 2010 . . . 393, 394

Sitaropoulos and Giakoumopoulos v. Greece [GC], App. no. 42202/07, ECHR 2012 . . . 415

Slovenia v. Croatia [GC], App. no. 54155/16, 18 November 2020 . . . 399

Smirnova and Smirnova v. Russia (dec.), App. nos. 46133/99, 48183/99, 3 October 2002 . . . 386, 387

Smith and Grady v. United Kingdom, App. nos. 33985/96, 33986/96, ECHR 1999-VI . . . 557

Soering v. United Kingdom, No. 14038/88, 7 July 1989, Series A no. 161 . . . 103, 116, 414, 486

Standard Verlags GmbH v. Austria (no. 2), App. no. 21277/05, 4 June 2009 . . . 536

Stec and Others v. the United Kingdom (dec.) [GC], nos. 65731/01 and 65900/01, ECHR 2005-X . . . 413

Stec and Others v. the United Kingdom [GC], App. nos. 65731/01, 65900/01, ECHR 2006-VI . . . 414

Steen v. Sweden (dec.), App. no. 62309/17, 11 February 2020 . . . 514

Stoll v. Switzerland [GC], App. no. 69698/01, ECHR 2007-V . . . 536

Streletz, Kessler and Krenz v. Germany [GC], App. nos. 34044/96 and two others, ECHR 2001-II . . . 477

Surek v. Turkey (no. 1) [GC], App. no. 26682/95, ECHR 1999-IV . . . 413

Svyato-Mykhaylivska Parafiya v. Ukraine, App. no. 77703/01, 14 June 2007 . . . 516, 517

Taddeucci and McCall v. Italy, App. no. 51362/09, 30 June 2016 . . . 544, 554

Tagiyev and Huseynov v. Azerbaijan, App. no. 13274/08, 5 December 2019 . . . 538

Tahsin Acar v. Turkey (preliminary issue) [GC], App. no. 26307/95, ECHR 2003-VI . . . 377, 378

Tahsin Acar v. Turkey [GC], App. no. 26307/95, ECHR 2004-III . . . 488

Tammer v. Estonia, App. no. 41205/98, ECHR 2001-I . . . 535

The Church of Jesus Christ of Latter-Day Saints v. the United Kingdom, App. no. 7552/09, 4 March 2014 . . . 511

The Sunday Times v. the United Kingdom (No. 1), 26 April 1979, Series A no. 30 . . . 169, 414, 516, 533

Thlimmenos v. Greece [GC], App. no. 34369/97, ECHR 2000-IV . . . 513, 544

Timishev v. Russia, App. nos. 55762/00 and 55974/00, ECHR 2005-XII . . . 555

Tyrer v. the United Kingdom, 25 April 1978, Series A no. 26 . . . 109, 117, 118

Ukraine v. Russia (III) (striking out), App. no. 49537/14, 1 September 2015 . . . 399

Valiulienė v. Lithuania, App. no. 33234/07, 26 March 2013 . . . 412

Valsamis v. Greece, 18 December 1996, Reports of Judgments and Decisions 1996-VI . . . 512

Van der Heijden v. the Netherlands [GC], App. no. 42857/05 . . . 415

Van Houten v. the Netherlands (striking out), App. no. 25149/03, ECHR 2005-IX . . . 378

Varbanov v. Bulgaria, App. no. 31365/96, ECHR 2000-X . . . 388

Varnava and Others v. Turkey [GC], App. nos. 16064/90 and eight others, ECHR 2009 . . . 386

Vavřička and Others v. the Czech Republic [GC], App. nos. 47621/13 and five others, 8 April 2021 . . . 579
Verein gegen Tierfabriken Schweiz (VgT) v. Switzerland (no. 2) [GC], no. 32772/02, ECHR 2009 . . . 386
Vieira & Filhos LDA and Ferreira da Costa LDA v. Portugal (dec.), App. nos. 980/12, 28385/12, 13 November 2012 . . . 388
Vo v. France [GC], App. no. 53924/00, ECHR 2004-VIII . . . 412, 479
Vojnović and Vojnović v. Croatia (dec.), App. no. 4819/10, 26 June 2012 . . . 386
Von Hannover v. Germany (no. 2) [GC], App. nos. 40660/08, 60641/08, ECHR 2012 . . . 414
Weber v. Switzerland, 22 May 1990, Series A no. 177 . . . 122
Wingrove v. the United Kingdom, 25 November 1996, Reports of Judgments and Decisions 1996-V . . . 413, 526, 538
Witzsch v. Germany (dec.), No. 7485/03, 13 December 2005 . . . 530
X and Others v. Austria [GC], App. no. 19010/07, ECHR 2013 . . . 412, 415, 557, 558
X and Y v. Romania, App. nos. 2145/16, 20607/16, 19 January 2021 . . . 559
X and Y v. the Netherlands, 26 March 1985, Series A no. 91 . . . 144, 145
X, Y and Z v. the United Kingdom, 22 April 1997, Reports of Judgments and Decisions 1997-II . . . 415
Yaremenko v. Ukraine (No. 2), App. no. 66338/09, 30 April 2015 . . . 507
Yonghong v. Portugal (dec.), App. no. 50887/99, ECHR 1999-IX . . . 154
Young, James and Webster v. the United Kingdom, 13 August 1981, Series A no. 44 . . . 144, 516
Z and Others v. the United Kingdom [GC], App. no. 29392/95, ECHR 2001-V . . . 505
Z v. Finland, 25 February 1997, Reports of Judgments and Decisions 1997-I . . . 413, 415
Zana v. Turkey, 25 November 1997, Reports of Judgments and Decisions 1997-VII . . . 534
Živić v. Serbia, App. no. 37204/08, 13 September 2011 . . . 389

AFRICAN COMMITTEE OF EXPERTS ON THE RIGHTS AND WELFARE OF THE CHILD (ACERWC)

Legal and Human Rights Centre and Centre for Reproductive Rights (on behalf of Tanzanian girls) v. Tanzania. Communication No. 0012/Com/001/2019, Decision No. 002/2022 . . . 87, 434
Minority Rights Group International and SOS-Esclaves (on behalf of Said Ould Salem and Yarg Ould Salem) v. Mauritania. Communication No. 007/Com/003/2015, Decision 003/2017 (15 December 2017) . . . 87
The Centre for Human Rights (University of Pretoria) and La Rencontre Africaine pour la Defense des Droits de l'Homme (Senegal) v. Senegal. Decision 003/Com/001/2012 (15 April 2014) . . . 87, 587

AFRICAN COMMISSION ON HUMAN AND PEOPLES' RIGHTS (ACHPR)

African Freedom of Expression Exchange & 15 Others (Represented by FOI Attorneys) v. Algeria & 27 Others, Communication 742/20 . . . 447
Amnesty International and Others v. Sudan, Communications 48/90, 50/91, 52/91, 89/93 (1999) . . . 511
Article 19 v. The State of Eritrea, Communication 275/2003 (2007) . . . 428, 465
Centre for Minority Rights Development (Kenya) and Minority Rights Group (on behalf of Endorois Welfare Council) v. Kenya, no. 276/03 (2009) . . . 516, 603, 604
Commission Nationale Des Droits De l'Homme Et Des Liberté v. Chad, Communication 74/92 (1995) . . . 428
Constitutional Rights Project v. Nigeria, Communication 60/91 (1995) . . . 464
Constitutional Rights Project v. Nigeria, Communication 87/93 (1995) . . . 464
Democratic Republic of Congo v. Burundi, Rwanda and Uganda, Communication 227/99 (2003) . . . 92, 468
Free Legal Assistance Group, Lawyers' Committee for Human Rights, Union Interafricaine des Droits de l'Homme, Les Temoins de Jehovah v. Zaire (Democratic Republic of Congo), Communications 25/89-47/90-56/91-100/93 (1995) . . . 86, 423, 464, 493
Garreth Anver Prince v. South Africa, Communication 255/02 (7 December 2004) . . . 510
Huri-Laws v. Nigeria, Communication No. 225/98 (6 November 2000) . . . 503
Ilesanmi v. Nigeria, Communication 268/2003 (2005) . . . 464
Institute for Human Rights and Development in Africa and Others v. Democratic Republic of Congo, Communication 393/10 (2016) . . . 449

Interights (on behalf of Pan African Movement and Citizens for Peace in Eritrea) v. Ethiopia, Communication 233/99 (2003) . . . 463

Interights et al. (on behalf of Mariette Sonjaleen Bosch) v. Botswana, Communication 240/01 (2003) . . . 458

International Pen and Others v. Nigeria, Communications 137/94, 139/94, 154/96, 161/97 (1998) . . . 458

J.E. Zitha & P.J.L .Zitha (represented by Prof. Dr Liesbeth Zegveld) v. Mozambique, Communication 361/08 (2011) . . . 461

Jean-Marie Atangana Mebara v. Cameroon, Communication 416/12 (2015) . . . 449

Katangese Peoples' Congress v. Zaire, Comm. No. 75/92 (1995) . . . 596

Ligue Camerounaise des Droits de l'Homme v. Cameroon, Communication 65/92 (1997) . . . 464

Luke Munyandu Tembani and Benjamin John Freeth (represented by Norman Tjombe) v. Angola and Thirteen Others, Communication 409/12 (2013) . . . 461

Malawi African Association and others v. Mauritania, Communications 54/91, 61/91, 98/93, 164–196/97, 210/98 (2002) . . . 461

Media Rights Agenda and Others v. Nigeria, Communications 105/93, 128/94, 130/94, 152/96 (1998) . . . 427, 428, 464, 525

Media Rights Agenda v. Nigeria, Communications 224/98 (2000) . . . 461

Mekongo v. Cameroon, Communication 59/91 (2000) . . . 449

Mgwanga Gunme v. Cameroon, Communication 266/2003 (2009) . . . 461

Mohammad Abdullah Saleh Al-Asad v. Djibouti, Communication 383/10 (14 October 2014) . . . 164, 461

Movement Burkinabé des Droits de l'Homme et des Peuples v. Burkina Faso, Communication 204/97 (2001) . . . 449

Organisation Mondiale Contre La Torture v. Rwanda, Communications 27/89, 46/91, 49/91, 99/93 (1996) . . . 464

Purohit and Moore v. The Gambia, Communication 241/2001 (2003) . . . 423, 464

Scanlen and Holderness v. Zimbabwe, Communication 297/2005 (2009) . . . 427, 449

Sir Dawda K Jawara v. The Gambia, Communications 147/95 and 149/96 (11 May 2000) . . . 463, 465

Social and Economic Rights Action Center (SERAC) and Center for Economic and Social Rights (CESR) v. Nigeria, Communication 155/96, ACHPR/COMM/A044/1 (27 May 2002) . . . 85, 86, 139, 423, 447, 493, 602

Umuhoza v. Rwanda (merits) (2017) 2 AfCLR 165 . . . 517, 530, 532, 534, 535

Zimbabwe Lawyers for Human Rights & Associated Newspapers of Zimbabwe v. Zimbabwe, Communication 284/03 (2009) . . . 169, 461

AFRICAN COURT ON HUMAN AND PEOPLES' RIGHTS (ACtHPR)

Actions pour la Protection des Droits de l'Homme (APDH) v. Côte d'Ivoire (2016) 1 AfCLR 668 . . . 462

African Commission on Human and Peoples' Rights v. Kenya (merits) (2017) 2 AfCLR 9 . . . 86, 423, 424, 603

African Commission on Human and Peoples' Rights v. Libya (provisional measures) (2013) 1 AfCLR 145 . . . 459

African Commission on Human and Peoples' Rights v. Libya (provisional measures 2) (2015) 1 AfCLR 150 . . . 459

Ajavon v. Benin (merits) (2019) 3 AfCLR 130 . . . 465

Ajavon v. Benin Judgment (2020) 4 AfCLR 133 . . . 463

Alex Thomas v. Tanzania (merits) (2015) 1 AfCLR 465 . . . 442, 462, 464

Ally Rajabu and others v. Tanzania, App. 7/2015, Judgment (28 November 2019) . . . 454, 455, 456, 457, 485

Association pour le Progrès et la Défense des Droits des Femmes Maliennes and the Institute for Human Rights and Development in Africa v. Mali (merits) (2018) 2 AfCLR 380 . . . 443, 462, 568

Atabong Denis Atemnkeng v. African Union (jurisdiction) (2013) 1 AfCLR 182 . . . 444, 445, 461

Beneficiaries of Late Norbert Zongo Abdoulaye Nikiema, Ernest Zongo and Blise Ilboudo & the Burkinabe Movement on Human and Peoples' Rights v. Burkina Faso (preliminary objections) (2013) 1 AfCLR 197 . . . 462, 463

Beneficiaries of Late Norbert Zongo Abdoulaye Nikiema, Ernest Zongo and Blise Ilboudo & the Burkinabe Movement on Human and Peoples' Rights v. Burkina Faso (merits) (2014) 1 AfCLR 219 . . . 463

Beneficiaries of late Norbert Zongo, Abdoulaye Nikiema alias Ablasse, Ernest Zongo, Blaise Ilboudo and Mouvement Burkinabe des Droits de l'Homme et des Peuples v. Burkina Faso (reparations) (2015) 1 AfCLR 258 . . . 169, 455, 461, 487

Bernard Anbataayela Mornah v. Benin, Burkina Faso, Cote d'Ivoire, Ghana, Mali, Malawi, Tanzania, and Tunisia. Judgment, App. no. 028/2018 (22 September 2022) ... 136, 461, 593, 594, 595

Emil Touray and Others v. Gambia (ruling), 24 March 2022 ... 463

Evarist v. Tanzania (merits) (2018) 2 AfCLR 402 ... 464

Femi Falana v. African Commission on Human and Peoples' Rights (jurisdiction) (2015) 1 AfCLR 499 ... 451, 461

Femi Falana v. African Union (jurisdiction) (2012) 1 AfCLR 118 ... 444, 461

Gombert v. Cote d'Ivoire (jurisdiction and admissibility) (2018) 2 AfCLR 270 ... 169, 461, 463

Harold Mbalanda Munthali v. Malawi (merits) 23 June 2022 ... 464

Ingabire Victoire Umuhoza v. Rwanda (jurisdiction) (2016) 1 AfCLR 562 ... 423, 444, 445, 446

Jebra Kambole v. Tanzania, App. 18/2018, Judgment (15 July 2020) 4 AfCLR 460 ... 455, 456, 555

Johnson v. Ghana (jurisdiction and admissibility) (2019) 3 AfCLR 99 ... 449, 463

Kambole v. Tanzania (judgment) (2020) 4 AfCLR 460 ... 555

Kouadio Kobena Fory v. République of Côte d'Ivoire (judgment) (2 December 2021) ... 462

Laurent Munyandilikirwa v. Rwanda, App. no. 23/2015 (2 December 2021) ... 465

Lohe Issa Konaté v. Burkina Faso (merits) (2014) 1 AfCLR 314; (reparations) (2016) 1 AfCLR 346 ... 442, 454, 456, 457, 462, 463, 516, 533

Mango v. Tanzania (merits) (2018) 2 AfCLR 314 ... 464

Mohamed Abubakari v. Tanzania (merits) (2016) 1 AfCLR 599 ... 442, 464

Noudehouenou v. Benin, App. 003/2020, Order (provisional measures) (5 May 2020) ... 459

Request for Advisory Opinion by the African Committee of Experts on the Rights and Welfare of the Child on the Standing of the African Commission of Experts on the Rights and Welfare of the Child before the African Court on Human and Peoples' Rights, Request 2/2013 (4 December 2014) ... 466

Request for Advisory Opinion by the Pan African Lawyers Union (PALU), Advisory Opinion No. 1/2018 (4 December 2020) ... 467

Request for Advisory Opinion by the Pan African Lawyers Union (PALU) on the right to participate in the government of one's country in the context of an election held during a public health emergency or a pandemic, such as the Covid-19 crisis. Advisory Opinion No. 1/2020 (16 July 2021) ... 428, 467

Robert John Penessis v. Tanzania, App. 13/2015, Judgment (28 November 2019) ... 442, 454, 456, 457, 462

Sissoko & 74 Others v. Mali (judgment) (2020) 4 AfCLR 641 ... 465

Tanganyika Law Society, Legal and Human Rights Centre and Reverend Christopher R. Mtikila v. Tanzania (merits) (2013) 1 AfCLR 34 ... 427, 455

Tike Mwambipile and Equality Now v. Tanzania (ruling), 1 December 2022 ... 463

Urban Mkandawire v. Malawi (admissibility) (2013) 1 AfCLR 283 ... 462

Woyome v. Ghana (provisional measures) (2017) 2 AfCLR 213 ... 459

COMMITTEE AGAINST TORTURE (CAT)

G.R.B. v. Sweden, Communication No. 83/1997, CAT/C/20/D/83/1997 (15 May 1998) ... 504

Kepa Urra Guridi v. Spain, Communication No. 212/2002, CAT/C/34/D/212/2002 (17 May 2005) ... 505

Kirsanov v. Russia, Communication No. 478/2011, CAT/C/52/D/478/2011 (14 May 2014) ... 507

Mutombo vs. Switzerland case, Communication No. 13/1993, UN Doc. A/49/44 (1994) ... 103

Suleymane Guengueng et al. v. Senegal, Communication No. 181/2001, CAT/C/36/D/181/2001 (19 May 2006) ... 269

COMMITTEE ON ECONOMIC, SOCIAL AND CULTURAL RIGHTS (CESCR)

Ben Djazia and Bellili v. Spain, Communication 5/2015, E/C.12/61/D/5/2015 (2017) ... 243, 258, 493

Gomez-Limon Pardo v. Spain, Communication 85/2018, E/C.12/67/D/52/2018 (2020) ... 493

I.D.G. v. Spain, Communication 2/2014, E/C.12/55/D/2/2014 (2015) ... 493

Lopez Alban v. Spain, Communication 37/2018 (2019) ... 493

S.C. and G.P. v. Italy, Communication No. 22/2017 (7 March 2019) ... 258

Trujillo Calero v. Ecuador, E/C.12/63/D/10/2015 (2018) ... 561

COMMITTEE ON ENFORCED DISAPPEARANCES (CED)

E.L.A. v. France, CED/C/19/D/3/2019 (25 September 2020) . . . 286
Yrusta v. Argentina, CED/C/10/D/1/2013 (11 March 2016) . . . 286, 287

COMMITTEE ON THE ELIMINATION OF RACIAL DISCRIMINATION (CERD)

Decision of the ad hoc Conciliation Commission on the request for suspension submitted by Qatar concerning the interstate communication Qatar v. the Kingdom of Saudi Arabia (15 March 2021) . . . 247
Documentation and Advisory Centre on Racial Discrimination (DACRD) v. Denmark, Decision on Admissibility, Communication No. 28/2003, UN Doc. CERD/C/63/D/28/2003 (19 August 2003) . . . 169
Jewish community of Oslo; the Jewish community of Trondheim; Rolf Kirchner; Julius Paltiel; the Norwegian Antiracist Centre; and Nadeem Butt v. Norway, Communication No. 30/2003, UN Doc. CERD/C/67/D/30/2003 (15 August 2005) . . . 169, 249
Palestine v. Israel, CERD/C/100/5 (12 December 2019) . . . 245
State of Qatar v. Kingdom of Saudi Arabia, ICERD-ISC 2018/1 (14 December 2018) . . . 92

COMMITTEE ON THE RIGHTS OF THE CHILD (CRC)

S.E.M.A v. France, CRC/C/92/D/130/2020 (25 January 2023) . . . 588
Y.B. and N.S. v. Belgium, CRC/C/79/D/12/2017 (5 November 2018) . . . 243, 584

COMMITTEE ON THE RIGHTS OF PERSONS WITH DISABILITIES (CRPD)

H.M. v. Sweden, CRPD/C/7/D/3/2011 (19 April 2012) . . . 283

CONVENTION ON THE ELIMINATION OF ALL FORMS OF DISCRIMINATION AGAINST WOMEN (CEDAW)

A.T. v. Hungary, Communication No. 2/2003, CEDAW/C/36/D/2/2003 (26 January 2005) . . . 146, 573
Fatma Yildirim (deceased) v. Austria, Communication No. 6/2005, CEDAW/C/39/D/2005 (1 October 2007) . . . 243

HUMAN RIGHTS COMMITTEE (CCPR)

A.S., D.I., O.I. and G.D. v. Italy, Communication No. 3042/2017, CCPR/C/130/D/3042/2017 (27 January 2021) . . . 164
Adam v. The Czech Republic, Communication No. 586/1994, U.N. Doc. CCPR/C/57/D/586/1994 (1996) . . . 561
Bleier v. Uruguay, Communication No. 7/30 (1980), CCPR/C/15/D/30/1978 . . . 488
Brok v. The Czech Republic, Communication No. 774/1997, CCPR/C/73/D/774/1997 (2001) . . . 561
Charles Chitat Ng v. Canada, Communication No. 469/1991, CCPR/C/49/D/469/1991 (7 January 1994) . . . 486
Chief Bernard Ominayak and the Lubicon Lake Band v. Canada, Communication No. 167/1984, U.N. Doc. Supp. No. 40 (A/45/40) (26 March 1990) . . . 602
Damian Thomas v. Jamaica, Communication No. 800/1998, UN Doc. CCPR/C/65/D/800/1998 (26 May 1999) . . . 253
Eversley Thompson v. St. Vincent and the Grenadines, Communication No. 806/1998, CCPR/C/70/D/806/1998 (2000) . . . 485
F.A. v. France, Communication No. 2662/2015, CCPR/C/123/D/2662/2015 (16 July 2018) . . . 520
Giri et al. v. Nepal, Communication No. 1761/2008, CCPR/C/101/D/1761/2008 (24 March 2011) . . . 502
Haraldsson and Sveinsson v. Iceland, Communication No. 1306/2004, CCPR/C/91/D/1306/2004 (2007) . . . 561
Hudoyberganova v. Uzbekistan, Communication No. 931/2000, CCPR/C/82/D/931/2000 (5 November 2004) . . . 518, 520
Ilmari Lansman et al. v. Finland, Communication No. 511/1992, UN Doc. CCPR/C/52/D/511/1992 (26 October 1994) . . . 517
Kaba v. Canada, 21 May 2010, CCPR/C/98/D/1465/2006 . . . 103
Karnel Singh Bhinder v. Canada, Communication No. 208/1986, UN Doc. CCPR/C/37/D/208/1986 (9 November 1989) . . . 518, 545
L.T.K. v. Finland, Communication No. 185/1984, UN Doc. CCPR/C/25/D/185/1984 (9 July 1985) . . . 513

Leirvag v. Norway, Communication No. 1155/2003 (3 November 2004) . . . 512

Lilian Celiberti de Casariego v. Uruguay, Communication No. R.13/56, UN Doc. Supp. No. 40 (A/36/40) . . . 156

Lubuto v. Zambia, Communication No. 390/1990, CCPR/C/55/D/390/1990/Rev. 1 (1995) . . . 484

Maille v. France, Communication No. 689/1996, UN Doc. CCPR/C/69/D/689/1996 (10 July 2000) . . . 513

Mellet v. Ireland, Communication No. 2324/2013, CCPR/C/116/D/2324/2013 (2016) . . . 561

Miriana Hebbadj v. France, Communication No. 2807, CCPR/C/123/D/2807/2016 (17 July 2018) . . . 520

Mr. Edward Young v. Australia, Communication No. 941/2000, UN Doc. CCPR/C/78/D/941/2000 (2003) . . . 143

Mumtaz Karakurt v. Austria, Communication No. 965/2000, CCPR/C/74/D/965/2000 (4 April 2002) . . . 544, 555

Paul Arenz, Thomas Roder and Dagmar Roder v. Germany, Communication No. 1138/2002, CCPR/C/80/D/1138/2002 (24 March 2004) . . . 146

Quinteros v. Uruguay, Communication No. 107/1981 (21 July 1983) . . . 142, 481

Rawle Kennedy v. Trinidad and Tobago, 2 November 1999, Communication No. 845/1999, UN Doc. CCPR/C/67/D/845/1999 . . . 126

Robert Faurisson v. France, Communication No. 550/1993, UN Doc. CCPR/C/58/D/550/1993(1996) . . . 530, 531

Rupert Althammer et al. v. Austria, Communication No. 998/2001, CCPR/C/78/D/998/2001 (8 August 2003) . . . 545

Sayadi and Vinck v. Belgium, Communication No. 1472/2006, UN Doc. CCPR/C/94/D/1472/2006 (22 October 2008) . . . 150

Sergio Euben Lopez Burgos v. Uruguay, Communication No. R.12/52, UN Doc. Supp. No. 40 (A/36/40) . . . 156

Seyma Turkan v. Turkey, Communication No. 2274/2013, CCPR/C/123/D/2274/2013/Rev.1 (17 July 2018) . . . 520

Sonia Yaker, Communication No. 2747/2016, CCPR/C/123/D/2747/2016 (17 July 2018) . . . 520, 521

Sprenger v. The Netherlands, Communication No. 395/1990, CCPR/C/44/D/395/1990 (31 March 1992) . . . 544, 554

Suarez de Guerrero v. Colombia, Communication No. 11/45 (1982) . . . 487

Toonen v. Australia, Communication No. 488/1992, CCPR/C/50/D/488/1992 (31 March 1994) . . . 556, 557

X v. Colombia, Communication No. 1361/2005, CCPR/C/89/D/1361/2005 (2007) . . . 143

Young v. Australia, Communication No. 941/2000, CCPR/C/78/D/941/2000 (18 September 2003) . . . 544, 554, 557

INTER-AMERICAN COMMISSION ON HUMAN RIGHTS (IACHR)

ABC Color v. Paraguay, Report No. 6/84 (17 May 1984) . . . 169

Almir Muniz Da Silva v. Brazil, Petition 1170-09, Report 78/16 (Admissibility) (30 December 2016) . . . 343

Aylwin Azócar, Report No. 137/99, OEA/Ser.L/V/II.106, doc. 6 Rev. (1999) . . . 352

Benito Tide Mendez et al. v. Dominican Republic, Case 12.271, Report No. 64/12 (29 March 2012) . . . 555

Brazil, Case 7615, Report No. 12/85, OEA/Ser.L/V/ II.66, doc. 10 rev.1 (1985) . . . 82

Chirinos Salamanca and others v. Venezuela, Case No. 14.143 (16 February 2022) . . . 308

Cuba, Case 4402, Report No. 45/81, OEA/Ser.L/V/II.54, doc. 9 rev.1 (1980–1981) . . . 82

Danny Honorio Bastidas Meneses and others v. Ecuador, Petition 189-03, Report 153/11 (Admissibility) (2 November 2011) . . . 339

Edgar Tamayo Arias v. United States, Petition 15–12, Report 73/12 (Admissibility) (17 July 2012) . . . 342

Franklin Guillermo Aisalla Molina and family, Inter-State Case 12.779 (Ecuador—Colombia), Report No. 96/13, Decision to Archive, 4 November 2013 . . . 351

Franklin Guillermo Aisalla Molina and family, Inter-State Petition IP-02 (Ecuador—Colombia) Report 112/10 (Admissibility), OEA/Ser.L/V/II.140, doc. 10 (21 October 2012) . . . 339, 351

Hildegard María Feldman v. Colombia, Case 11.010, Report 15/95, OEA/Ser.L/V/II.91, doc. 7 (28 February 1996) . . . 326

Jehovah's Witnesses v. Argentina, Case 2.137 (18 November 1978) . . . 169

Johan Alexis Ortiz Hernández v. Venezuela Petition 12.270, Report 22/05 (Admissibility) (25 February 2005) . . . 343

Jorge Marcial Tzompaxtle Tecpile and others v. Mexico, Petition 211-07, Report No. 67/15 (Admissibility) (27 October 2015) . . . 343

Jose Isabel Salas Galindo and others v. United States, Case 10.573, Report No. 121/18, OEA/Ser.L/V/ II.169 Doc. 138 (5 October 2018) . . . 164

José Tomás Tenorio Morales and others v. Nicaragua, Petition 142-04, Report 41/16 (Admissibility) (11 September 2016) . . . 342

Khaled El-Masri v. United States, Petition 419-08, Report 21/16 (Admissibility) (15 April 2016) . . . 339

Lares Rángel and others v. Venezuela, Case No. 14.170 (6 July 2022) . . . 308

Luis Lizardo Cabrera v. Dominican Republic, Case 10.832, Report Nº 35/96, OEA/Ser.L/V/II.95 Doc. 7 rev. at 821 (1997) . . . 502

Marino Lopez et al v. Colombia, Case 12.573, Report No. 64/11 (31 March 2011) . . . 553

Members of the Trade Union of Workers of the National Federation of Coffee Growers of Colombia v. Colombia, Petition 374-05, Report 15/15 (Admissibility) (24 March 2015) . . . 342

Michael Domingues v. United States, Report No. 62/02 (22 October 2002) . . . 135

Nicaragua v. Costa Rica, Inter-State Case 01/06, Report 11/07 (8 March 2007) . . . 92, 159, 351

Norberto Javier Restrepo v. Colombia, Case 11.726, Report 96/19, OEA/Ser.L/V/II, doc. 105 (14 June 2019) . . . 326

Radio Nanduti v. Paraguay, Report No. 14/87 (28 March 1987) . . . 169

Ríos Montt v. Guatemala, Case 10.804, Report No. 30/93, OEA/Ser.L/V/II.85, doc. 9 Rev. at 206 (1994) . . . 352

Rosendo Radilla Pacheco v. Mexico, Petition 777-01, Report 65/05 (Admissibility), OEA/Ser.L/V/II.124, doc. 5 (27 February 2006) . . . 339

Statehood Solidarity Comm. v. U.S., Case 11.204, Report No. 98/03, OEA/Ser.L/V/II.118, doc. 5 Rev. 2 (2003) . . . 325

Tamara Mariana Adrián Hernández v. Venezuela, Petition 824-12, Report 66/16 (Admissibility), OEA/Ser.L/V/II.159, doc. 75 (6 December 2016) . . . 339

U'wa People v. Colombia, Petition 11.754, Report 33/15 (Admissibility) (22 July 2015) . . . 343

Wallace de Almeida v. Brazil, Case 12.440, Report No. 26/09, (20 March 2009) . . . 547

Yaqui People v. Mexico), Petition 79-06, Report 48/15 (Admissibility), OEA/Ser.L/V/II.155, doc. 28 (28 July 2015) . . . 339

INTER-AMERICAN COURT OF HUMAN RIGHTS (IACtHR)

19 Merchants v. Colombia. Merits, Reparations and Costs. Judgment of July 5, 2004. Series C No. 109 . . . 331

Almonacid Arellano et al. v. Chile. Preliminary Objections, Merits, Reparations and Costs. Judgment of September 26, 2006. Series C No. 154 . . . 130, 135, 137, 352, 353

Aloeboetoe v. Suriname (Reparations and Costs), Serie C 15 (1993) . . . 135

Álvarez Ramos v. Venezuela. Preliminary Objection, Merits, Reparations and Costs. Judgment of August 30, 2019. Series C No. 380 . . . 308

Anzualdo Castro v. Peru. Preliminary Objection, Merits, Reparations and costs. Judgment of September 22, 2009. Series C No. 202 . . . 481

Apitz Barbera et al. ('First Court of Administrative Disputes') v. Venezuela. Preliminary Objection, Merits, Reparations and Costs. Judgment of August 5, 2008. Series C No. 182 . . . 331

Armando Alejandre Jr, Carlos Costa, Mario De La Pena, and Pablo Morales v. Cuba, Report No 86/99 (29 September 1999) . . . 157

Artavia Murillo et al. (In Vitro Fertilization) v. Costa Rica. Preliminary Objections, Merits, Reparations and Costs. Judgment of November 28, 2012. Series C No. 257 . . . 478, 479

'Article 55 of the American Convention on Human Rights'. Advisory Opinion OC-20/09 of September 29, 2009. Series A no. 20 . . . 318

Atala Riffo and daughters v. Chile. Merits, Reparations and Costs. Judgment of February 24, 2012. Series C No. 239 . . . 352, 544, 545, 555, 557, 558

Baena Ricardo et al. v. Panama. Competence. Judgment of November 28, 2003. Series C No. 104 . . . 334, 335, 336

Baena Ricardo et al. v. Panama. Preliminary Objections. Judgment of November 18, 1999. Series C No. 61 . . . 94, 342

Bámaca Velásquez v. Guatemala. Merits. Judgment of November 25, 2000. Series C No. 70 . . . 340, 481

Bámaca Velásquez v. Guatemala. Reparations and Costs. Judgment of February 22, 2002. Series C No. 91 . . . 331, 481

Barreto Leiva v. Venezuela. Merits, Reparations and Costs. Judgment of November 17, 2009. Series C No. 206 . . . 352

Barrios Altos v. Peru. Merits. Judgment March 14, 2001. Series C No. 75 . . . 489, 505

Barrios Altos v. Peru. Reparations and Costs. Judgment of November 30, 2001. Series C No. 87 . . . 330

Blake v. Guatemala. Merits. Judgment of January 24, 1998. Series C No. 36 . . . 107, 108, 115

Blake v. Guatemala. Reparations and Costs. Judgment of January 22, 1999. Series C No. 48 . . . 58, 116

Boyce et al. v. Barbados. Preliminary Objection, Merits, Reparations and Costs. Judgment of November 20, 2007. Series C No. 169 . . . 122, 332, 333, 339

Bueno Alves v. Argentina. Merits, Reparations and Costs. Judgment of May 11, 2007. Series C No. 164 . . . 340, 497

Bulacio v. Argentina. Merits, Reparations and Costs. Judgment of September 18, 2003. Series C No. 100 . . . 330, 332, 488

Caballero Delgado and Santana v. Colombia. Preliminary Objections. Judgment of January 21, 1994. Series C No. 17 . . . 324

Cabrera Garcia and Montiel Flores v. Mexico. Preliminary Objection, Merits, Reparations, and Costs. Judgment of November 26, 2010 Series C No. 220 . . . 507, 508, 509

Caesar v. Trinidad and Tobago. Merits, Reparations and Costs. Judgment of March 11, 2005. Series C No. 123 . . . 115, 116, 119, 120, 121, 122, 124, 135, 495

Cantoral Benavides v. Peru. Merits. Judgment of August 18, 2000. Series C No. 69 . . . 135, 502

Cantoral Benavides v. Peru. Reparations and Costs. Judgment of December 3, 2001. Series C No. 88 . . . 331

Cantoral Huamaní and García Santa Cruz v. Peru. Preliminary Objection, Merits, Reparations and Costs. Judgment of July 10, 2007. Series C No. 167 . . . 330, 331

Caracazo v. Venezuela. Reparations and Costs. Judgment of August 29, 2002. Series C No. 95 . . . 331

Case of Kichwa Indigenous People of Sarayaku v. Ecuador. Merits and Reparations. Judgment of June 27, 2012. Series C No. 245 . . . 604

Cases of Fernández Ortega et al. and Rosendo Cantú and other v. México. Monitoring Compliance with Judgment. Order of the Inter-American Court of Human Rights of November 21, 2014 . . . 335

Cases of the Río Negro Massacres and Gudiel Álvarez et al. v. Guatemala. Monitoring Compliance with Judgment. Order of the Inter-American Court of Human Rights of August 21, 2014 . . . 335

Cases of the Yakye Axa, Sawhoyamaxa and Xákmok Kásek Indigenous Communities v. Paraguay. Monitoring Compliance with Judgment. Order of the President of the Inter-American Court of Human Rights of September 1, 2016 . . . 335

Castañeda Gutman v. Mexico. Preliminary Objections, Merits, Reparations and Costs. Judgment of August 6, 2008. Series C No. 184 . . . 352

Castillo Petruzzi et al. v. Peru. Merits, Reparations and Costs. Judgment of May 30, 1999. Series C No. 52 . . . 130, 331

Castillo Petruzzi et al. v. Peru. Preliminary Objections. Judgment of September 4, 1998. Series C No. 41 . . . 167, 329

Cayara v. Peru. Preliminary Objections. Judgment of February 3, 1993. Series C No. 14 . . . 325, 344

Cepeda Vargas v. Colombia. Preliminary Objections, Merits, Reparations, and Costs. Judgment of May 26, 2010. Series C No. 213 . . . 94

Certain Attributes of the Inter-American Commission on Human Rights. Advisory Opinion OC-13/93, of July 16, 1993. Series A no. 13 . . . 321, 325

Cesti Hurtado v. Peru. Reparations and Costs. Judgment of May 31, 2001. Series C No. 78 . . . 331

Claude Reyes et al. v. Chile. Merits, Reparations and Costs. Judgment of September 19, 2006. Series C No. 151 . . . 528

Coard et al. v. United States, Report No 109/99 (29 September 1999) . . . 157

Compatibility of Draft Legislation with Article 8(2)(h) of the American Convention on Human Rights. Advisory Opinion OC-12/91 of December 6, 1991. Series A no.12 . . . 321

Compulsory Membership in an Association Prescribed by Law for the Practice of Journalism. Advisory Opinion OC-5/85 of November 13, 1985. Series A no. 5 . . . 118

Constitutional Court v. Peru. Provisional Measures. Order of the President of the Inter-American Court of Human Rights of April 7, 2000 . . . 344, 347

Control of due process in the exercise of the powers of the Inter-American Commission on Human Rights. Advisory Opinion OC-19/05 of November 28, 2005. Series A no. 19 . . . 321, 343

Denunciation of the American Convention on Human Rights and the Charter of the Organization of American States and the consequences for State human rights obligations.

Advisory Opinion OC-26/20 of November 9, 2020. Series A no. 26 . . . 321

Díaz Loreto et al. v. Venezuela. Preliminary Objections, Merits, Reparations and Costs. Judgment of November 19, 2019. Series C No. 392 . . . 308

Dismissed Congressional Employees (Aguado Alfaro et al.) v. Peru. Preliminary Objections, Merits, Reparations and Costs. Judgment of November 24, 2006. Series C No. 158 . . . 352, 353, 354

Duque v. Colombia. Preliminary Objections, Merits, Reparations and Costs. Judgment of February 26, 2016. Series C No. 310 . . . 143, 352

Durand and Ugarte v. Peru. Preliminary Objections. Judgment of May 28, 1999. Series C No. 50 . . . 341

Durand and Ugarte v. Peru. Reparations and Costs. Judgment of December 3, 2001. Series C No. 89 . . . 331

El Amparo v. Venezuela. Reparations and Costs. Judgment of September 14, 1996. Series C No. 28 . . . 142, 332, 333, 336, 356, 488

Employees of the Fireworks Factory of Santo Antonio de Jesus and their families v. Brazil. Preliminary Objections, Merits, Reparations and Costs. Judgment of July 15, 2020. Series C No. 407 . . . 553

Enforceability of the Right to Reply or Correction. Advisory Opinion OC-7/85 of August 29, 1986. Series A no. 7 . . . 118

Entitlement of legal entities to hold rights under the Inter-American Human Rights System. Advisory Opinion OC-22/16 of February 26, 2016. Series A no. 22 . . . 169, 323

Escher et al v. Brazil. Monitoring Compliance with Judgment. Order of the Inter-American Court of Human Rights of June 19, 2012 . . . 337

Escué Zapata v. Colombia. Merits, Reparations and Costs. Judgment of July 4, 2007. Series C No. 165 . . . 331

Expelled Dominicans and Haitians v. Dominican Republic. Preliminary Objections, Merits, Reparations and Costs. Judgment of August 28, 2014. Series C No. 282 . . . 350

Fermin Ramirez v. Guatemala. Merits, Reparations and Costs. Judgment of June 20, 2005. Series C No. 126 . . . 135, 495

Five Pensioners v. Peru. Merits, Reparations and Costs. Judgment of February 28, 2003. Series C No. 98 . . . 164

Fontevecchia and D`Amico v. Argentina. Merits, Reparations and Costs. Judgment of November 29, 2011. Series C No. 238 . . . 535, 536

Furlan and family v. Argentina. Preliminary Objections, Merits, Reparations and Costs. Judgment of August 31, 2012. Series C No. 246 . . . 352, 353

Gangaram Panday v. Suriname. Preliminary Objections. Judgment of December 4, 1991. Series C No. 12 . . . 343

Garrido and Baigorria v. Argentina. Reparations and Costs. Judgment of August 27, 1998. Series C No. 39 . . . 155

Gender identity, and equality and non-discrimination with regard to same-sex couples. Advisory Opinion OC-24/17 of November 24, 2017. Series A no. 24 . . . 118, 321, 352, 556, 557, 559

Genie Lacayo v. Nicaragua. Application for Judicial Review of the Judgment of Merits, Reparations and Costs. Order of the Court of September 13, 1997. Series C No. 45 . . . 338

Girls Yean and Bosico v. Dominican Republic. Preliminary Objections, Merits, Reparations and Costs. Judgment of September 8, 2005. Series C No. 130 . . . 143, 544

Godínez Cruz v. Honduras. Preliminary Objections. Judgment of June 26, 1987. Series C No. 3 . . . 324

Goiburu et al. v. Paraguay. Merits, Reparations and Costs. Judgment of September 22, 2006. Series C No. 153 . . . 135, 136

Gómez Murillo et al. v. Costa Rica. Judgment of November 29, 2016. Series C No. 326 . . . 325, 352

Gómez Palomino v. Peru. Merits, Reparations and Costs. Judgment of November 22, 2005. Series C No. 136 . . . 340

Gomez Paquiyauri Brothers v. Peru. Merits, Reparations and Costs. Judgment of July 8, 2004. Series C No. 110 . . . 135, 137, 142, 331, 332, 354, 489

Gonzales Lluy et al. v. Ecuador. Preliminary Objections, Merits, Reparations and Costs. Judgment of September 1, 2015. Series C No. 298 . . . 561

González et al. ('Cotton Field') v. Mexico. Preliminary Objection, Merits, Reparations and Costs. Judgment of November 16, 2009. Series C No. 205 . . . 340, 497, 574

González et al. v. Venezuela. Merits and Reparations. Judgment of September 20, 2021. Series C No. 436 . . . 308

Grande v. Argentina. Preliminary Objections and Merits. Judgment of August 31, 2011. Series C No. 231 . . . 343

Guerrero, Molina et al. v. Venezuela. Merits, Reparations and Costs. Judgment of June 3, 2021. Series C No. 424 . . . 308

Gutiérrez Soler v. Colombia. Provisional Measures. Order of the Inter-American Court of Human Rights of March 11, 2005 . . . 346

Heliodoro Portugal v. Panama. Preliminary Objections, Merits, Reparations and Costs. Judgment of August 12, 2008. Series C No. 186 . . . 340

Herrera Ulloa v. Costa Rica. Preliminary Objections, Merits, Reparations and Costs. Judgment of July 2, 2004. Series C No. 107 . . . 352, 535

Hilaire v. Trinidad and Tobago. Preliminary Objections. Judgment of September 1, 2001. Series C No. 80 . . . 122

Hilaire, Constantine and Benjamin et al. v. Trinidad and Tobago. Merits, Reparations and Costs. Judgment of June 21, 2002. Series C No. 94 . . . 130, 485

Hugh Jordan v. the United Kingdom, App. no. 24746/94, 4 May 2001 . . . 488

Huilca Tecse v. Peru. Merits, Reparations and Costs. Judgment of March 3, 2005. Series C No. 121 . . . 142, 332

In the matter of Viviana Gallardo et al. Series A no. 101 . . . 326

Interpretation of the American Declaration of the Rights and Duties of Man within the Framework of Article 64 of the American Convention on Human Rights. Advisory Opinion OC-10/89 of July 14,1989. Series A no.10 . . . 117, 304, 320, 340

Ivcher Bronstein v. Peru. Competence. Judgment of September 24, 1999. Series C No. 54 . . . 446

Ivcher Bronstein v. Peru. Merits, Reparations and Costs. Judgment of February 6, 2001. Series C No. 74 . . . 526

Ivcher Bronstein v. Peru. Provisional Measures. Order of the Inter-American Court of Human Rights of November 23, 2000 . . . 346

Jebra Kambole v. Tanzania, App. 18/2018, Judgment (28 November 2019) . . . 140, 171

Joint Monitoring Compliance of 11 cases v. Guatemala. Monitoring Compliance with Judgment of the Inter-American Court of Human Rights of August 21, 2014 . . . 335

Juan Humberto Sánchez v. Honduras. Preliminary Objection, Merits, Reparations and Costs. Judgment of June 7, 2003. Series C No. 99 . . . 332

Judicial Guarantees in States of Emergency (Arts. 27(2), 25 and (8) American Convention on Human Rights). Advisory Opinion OC-9/87 of October 6, 1987. Series A no. 9 . . . 141

Judicial Guarantees in States of Emergency. Advisory Opinion OC-9/87 of October 6, 1987. Series A no. 9 . . . 119

Juridical Condition and Human Rights of the Child. Advisory Opinion OC-17/02 of August 28, 2002. Series A no.17 . . . 59, 321, 580

Juridical Condition and Rights of the Undocumented Migrants. Advisory Opinion OC-18/03 of September 17, 2003. Series A no.18 . . . 103, 129, 133, 136, 137, 142, 143, 145, 320, 321, 543, 544, 547

Kawas Fernández v. Honduras. Merits, Reparations and Costs. Judgment of April 3, 2009. Series C No. 196 . . . 332

Kawas Fernandez v. Honduras. Provisional Measures. Order of the Inter-American Court of Human Rights of July 5, 2011 . . . 347

Kichwa Indigenous People of Sarayaku v. Ecuador. Merits and Reparations. Judgment of June 27, 2012. Series C No. 245 . . . 602, 603

Kimel v. Argentina. Merits, Reparations and Costs. Judgment of May 2, 2008 Series C No. 177 . . . 529, 536, 537

Lagos del Campo v. Peru. Preliminary Objections, Merits, Reparations, and Costs. Judgment of August 31, 2017. Series C No. 340 . . . 82, 84

Las Dos Erres Massacre v. Guatemala. Preliminary Objection, Merits, Reparations and Costs. Judgment of November 24, 2009. Series C No. 211 . . . 332

Las Palmeras v. Colombia. Preliminary Objections. Judgment of February 4, 2000. Series C No. 67 . . . 340

Lingens v. Austria, 8 July 1986, Series A no. 103 . . . 535, 536

Loayza Tamayo v. Peru. Interpretation of the Judgment of Merits. Order of the Court of March 8, 1998. Series C No. 47 . . . 337

Loayza Tamayo v. Peru. Merits. Judgment of September 17, 1997. Series C No. 33 . . . 501

Loayza Tamayo v. Peru. Preliminary Objections. Judgment of January 31, 1996. Series C No. 25 . . . 343

Loayza Tamayo v. Peru. Reparations and Costs. Judgment of November 27, 1998. Series C No. 42 . . . 140, 171, 331, 332

López Álvarez v. Honduras. Merits, Reparations and Costs. Judgment of February 1, 2006. Series C No. 141 . . . 353, 526

Lori Berenson Mejía v. Peru. Merits, Reparations and Costs. Judgment of November 25, 2004. Series C No. 119 . . . 326, 332

Mapiripán Massacre v. Colombia. Merits, Reparations and Costs. Judgment of September 15, 2005. Series C No. 134 . . . 331

Mapiripán Massacre v. Colombia. Monitoring compliance with Judgment. Order of the

Inter-American Court of Human Rights of November 23, 2012 . . . 337

Maqueda v. Argentina. Preliminary Objections. Order of January 17, 1995. Series C No. 18 . . . 325

Maritza Urrutia v. Guatemala. Merits, Reparations and Costs. Judgment of November 27, 2003. Series C No. 103 . . . 135, 495, 498, 504, 505

Mariya Alekhina and Others v. Russia, App. no. 38004/12, 17 July 2018 . . . 529

Matter of 'Globovisión' Television Station regarding Venezuela. Provisional Measures. Order of the Inter-American Court of Human Rights of September 4, 2004 . . . 346

Matter of Haitians and Dominicans of Haitian-origin in the Dominican Republic regarding Dominican Republic. Provisional Measures. Order of the Inter-American Court of Human Rights of August 18, 2000 . . . 103, 346

Matter of Haitians and Dominicans of Haitian-origin in the Dominican Republic. Provisional Measures. Order of the Inter-American Court of Human Rights of May 26, 2001 . . . 346

Matter of James et al. regarding Trinidad and Tobago. Provisional Measures. Order of the Inter-American Court of Human Rights of May 25, 1999 . . . 109

Matter of James et al. regarding Trinidad and Tobago. Provisional Measures. Order of the Inter-American Court of Human Rights of August 29, 1998 . . . 347

Matter of James et al. regarding Trinidad and Tobago. Provisional Measures. Order of the Inter-American Court of Human Rights of November 26, 2001 . . . 344

Matter of Kichwa Indigenous People of Sarayaku regarding Ecuador. Provisional Measures. Order of the Inter-American Court of Human Rights of July 6, 2004 . . . 346

Matter of L.M. regarding Paraguay. Provisional Measures. Order of the Inter-American Court of Human Rights of July 1, 2011 . . . 346

Matter of the Mendoza Prisons regarding Argentina. Provisional Measures. Order of the Inter-American Court of Human Rights of November 22, 2004 . . . 344

Matter of the Peace Community of San José de Apartadó regarding Colombia. Provisional Measures. Order of the Inter-American Court of Human Rights of November 24, 2000 . . . 344, 346

Mayagna (Sumo) Awas Tingni Community v. Nicaragua. Merits, Reparations, and Costs. Judgment of August 31, 2001. Series C No. 79 . . . 82, 83, 84, 602

Mayagna (Sumo) Awas Tingni Community v. Nicaragua. Provisional Measures. Order of the Inter-American Court of Human Rights of September 6, 2002 . . . 346

Miguel Castro Castro Prison v. Peru. Interpretation of the Judgment on Merits, Reparations and Costs. Judgment of August 2, 2008 Series C No. 181 . . . 337

Miguel Castro-Castro Prison v. Peru. Merits, Reparations and Costs. Judgment of November 25, 2006. Series C No. 160 . . . 502, 503

Moiwana Community v. Suriname. Preliminary Objections, Merits, Reparations and Costs. Judgment of June 15, 2005. Series C No. 124 . . . 142, 332, 340, 341

Molina Theissen v. Guatemala. Reparations and Costs. Judgment of July 3, 2004. Series C No. 108 . . . 331

Mota Abarullo et al. v. Venezuela. Merits, Reparations and Costs. Judgment of November 18, 2020. Series C No. 417 . . . 308

Myrna Mack Chang v. Guatemala. Merits, Reparations and Costs. Judgment of November 25, 2003. Series C No. 101 . . . 138, 330, 331, 332, 353

Neira Alegría et al. Case. Requests of Review and Interpretation of the Judgment on Preliminary Objections of December 11, 1991. Order of July 3, 1992 . . . 337

Neira Alegria et al. v. Peru. Preliminary Objections. Judgment of December 11, 1991. Series C No. 13 . . . 130, 131, 325, 342

Olivares Muñoz et al. v. Venezuela. Merits, Reparations and Costs. Judgment of November 10, 2020. Series C No. 415 . . . 308

'Other treaties' subject to the consultative jurisdiction of the Court (Art. 64 American Convention on Human Rights). Advisory Opinion OC-1/82 of September 24, 1982. Series A no. 1 . . . 115, 317, 319, 322

Otto-Preminger-Institut v. Austria, 20 September 1994, Series A no. 295-A . . . 538, 539

Ozturk v. Turkey [GC], App. no. 22479/93, ECHR 1999-VI . . . 529

Paniagua Morales et al. Case. Order of September 11, 1995 . . . 318

Perozo et al. v. Venezuela. Preliminary Objections, Merits, Reparations, and Costs. Judgment of January 28, 2009. Series C No. 195 . . . 138

Plan de Sánchez Massacre v. Guatemala. Reparations. Judgment of November 19, 2004. Series C No. 116 . . . 331

Proposed Amendments of the Naturalization Provisions of the Constitution of Costa Rica. Advisory Opinion OC-4/84 of January 19, 1984. Series A no. 4 . . . 142, 321, 322, 352, 554

Pueblo Bello Massacre v. Colombia. Merits, Reparations and Costs. Judgment of January 31, 2006. Series C No. 140 . . . 147, 332, 487

Quispialaya Vilcapoma v. Peru. Preliminary Objections, Merits, Reparations and Costs. Judgment of November 23, 2015. Series C No. 308 . . . 505

Radilla Pacheco v. Mexico. Preliminary Objections, Merits, Reparations and Costs. Judgment of November 23, 2009. Series C No. 209 . . . 340, 353

Raxcacó Reyes v. Guatemala. Merits, Reparations and Costs. Judgment of September 15, 2005. Series C No. 133 . . . 340, 484

Rejection to the Request of an Advisory Opinion submitted by Costa Rica. Order of the IACtHR of May 10, 2005 . . . 321

Rejection to the Request of an Advisory Opinion submitted by the Secretary General of the Organization of American States. Order of the IACtHR of June 23, 2016 . . . 321

Reports of the Inter-American Commission on Human Rights. Advisory Opinion OC-15/97 of November 14, 1997. Series A no. 15 . . . 321, 322

Restrictions to the Death Penalty. Advisory Opinion OC-3/83 of September 8, 1983. Series A no. 3 . . . 121, 309, 319, 322, 483

Ricardo Canese v. Paraguay. Merits, Reparations and Costs. Judgment of August 31, 2004. Series C No. 111 . . . 331

Rights and guarantees of children in the context of migration and/or in need of international protection. Advisory Opinion OC-21/14 of August 19, 2014 . . . 321, 580

Saldano v. Argentina, Report N° 38/99 (11 March 1999) . . . 157

Santo Domingo Massacre v. Colombia. Preliminary Objections, Merits and Reparations. Judgment of November 30, 2012. Series No. 259 . . . 340

Saramaka People v. Suriname. Preliminary Objections, Merits, Reparations, and Costs. Judgment of November 28, 2007 Series C No. 172 . . . 94, 342, 343, 603

Satakunnan Markkinaporssi Oy and Satamedia Oy v. Finland [GC], App. no. 931/13, 27 June 2017 . . . 535

Sawhoyamaxa Indigenous Community v. Paraguay. Merits, Reparations, and Costs. Judgment of March 29, 2006. Series C No. 146 . . . 83, 111, 117, 487, 602, 603

Serrano Cruz Sisters v. El Salvador. Preliminary Objections. Judgment of November 23, 2004. Series C No. 118 . . . 99

Shanaghan v. the United Kingdom, App. no. 37715/97, 4 May 2001 . . . 545

'Street Children' (Villagrán Morales et al.) v. Guatemala. Merits. Judgment of November 19, 1999. Series C No. 63 . . . 82, 310, 340, 503

'Street Children' (Villagrán Morales et al.) v. Guatemala. Reparations and Costs. Judgment of May 26, 2001. Series C No. 77 . . . 330, 331

Suarez Rosero v. Ecuador. Merits. Judgment of November 12, 1997. Series C No. 35 . . . 108

The Effect of Reservations on the Entry into Force of the American Convention on Human Rights. Advisory Opinion OC-2/82 of September 24, 1982. Series A no. 2 . . . 121, 319, 320, 321, 339

The institution of asylum, and its recognition as a human right under the Inter-American System of Protection. Advisory Opinion OC-25/18 of May 30, 2018. Series A no. 25 . . . 321

'The Last Temptation of Christ' (Olmedo Bustos et al.) v. Chile. Merits, Reparations and Costs. Judgment of February 5, 2001. Series C No. 73 . . . 140, 332, 354, 540

The Right to Information on Consular Assistance in the Framework of the Guarantees of the due Process of Law. Advisory Opinion OC-16/99 of October 1, 1999. Series A No.16 . . . 109, 111, 221, 320, 340

The Word 'Laws' in Article 30 of the American Convention on Human Rights. Advisory Opinion OC-6/86 of May 9, 1986. Series A no. 6 . . . 117

Tibi v. Ecuador. Preliminary Objections, Merits, Reparations and Costs. Judgment of September 7, 2004. Series C No. 114 . . . 336, 353

Valencia Hinojosa et al. v. Ecuador. Preliminary Objections, Merits, Reparations and Costs. Judgment of November 29, 2016. Series C No. 327 . . . 488

Valle Jaramillo et al. v. Colombia. Merits, Reparations and Costs. Judgment of November 27, 2008. Series C No. 192 . . . 331

Velásquez Rodríguez v. Honduras. Interpretation of the Judgment of Reparations and Costs. Judgment of August 17, 1990. Series C No. 9 . . . 336, 337

Velasquez Rodriguez v. Honduras. Merits. Judgment of July 29, 1988. Series C No. 4 . . . 139, 141, 310, 311, 481

Velasquez Rodriguez v. Honduras. Preliminary Objections. Judgment of June 26, 1987. Series C No. 1 . . . 117, 324, 341

Velásquez Rodríguez v. Honduras. Provisional Measures. Order of the Inter-American Court of Human Rights of January 15, 1988 . . . 347

Velasquez Rodriguez v. Honduras. Reparations and Costs. Judgment of July 21, 1989. Series C No. 7 . . . 130, 146, 330, 487

Velez Loor v. Panama. Preliminary Objections, Merits, Reparations, and Costs. Judgment of November 23, 2010 Series C No. 218 . . . 136

Velez Restrepo and family v. Colombia. Preliminary Objection, Merits, Reparations, and Costs. Judgment of September 3, 2012. Series C No. 248 . . . 527

'White Van' (Paniagua Morales et al.) v. Guatemala. Merits. Judgment of March 8, 1998. Series C No. 37 . . . 310, 340

'White Van' (Paniagua Morales et al.) v. Guatemala. Reparations and Costs. Judgment of May 25, 2001. Series C No. 76 . . . 330

Wong Ho Wing v. Peru. Preliminary Objection, Merits, Reparations and Costs. Judgment of June 30, 2015. Series C No. 297 . . . 486

Xakmok Kasek Indigenous Community v. Paraguay. Merits, Reparations and Costs. Judgment of August 24, 2010. Series C No. 214 . . . 83, 493, 602

Xákmok Kásek Indigenous Community v. Paraguay. Monitoring Compliance with Judgment. Order of the Inter-American Court of Human Rights of May 14, 2019 . . . 335

Yakye Axa Indigenous Community v. Paraguay. Merits, Reparations, and Costs. Judgment of June 17, 2005. Series C No. 125 . . . 83, 493, 602, 603

Yakye Axa Indigenous Community v. Paraguay. Monitoring Compliance with Judgment. Order of the Inter-American Court of Human Rights of May 14, 2019 . . . 335

Yatama v. Nicaragua. Preliminary Objections, Merits, Reparations, and Costs. Judgment of June 23, 2005. Series C No. 127 . . . 143, 544

INTERNATIONAL CRIMINAL COURT (ICC)

The Prosecutor v. Ahmad Al Faqi Al Mahdi, ICC- 01/12-01/15 (27 September 2016) . . . 148

The Prosecutor v. Germain Katanga, ICC-01/04-01/07 (7 March 2014) . . . 148

The Prosecutor v. Thomas Lubanga Dyilo, ICC-01/04-01/06 (10 July 2012) . . . 148

INTERNATIONAL COURT OF JUSTICE (ICJ)

Accordance with International Law of the Unilateral Declaration of Independence in Respect of Kosovo, Advisory Opinion, I.C.J. Reports 2010, p. 403 . . . 595

Ahmadou Sadio Diallo (Republic of Guinea v. Democratic Republic of the Congo), Merits, Judgment, I.C.J. Reports 2010, p. 639 . . . 239

Allegations of Genocide under the Convention on the Prevention and Punishment of the Crime of Genocide (Ukraine v. Russian Federation), Order of Provisional Measures (16 March 2022) . . . 222

Application of the Convention on the Prevention and Punishment of the Crime of Genocide (Bosnia and Herzegovina v. Serbia and Montenegro), Judgment, I.C.J. Reports 2007, p. 43 . . . 159, 160, 161, 222, 223, 224

Application of the Convention on the Prevention and Punishment of the Crime of Genocide (Croatia v. Serbia), Judgment, I.C.J. Reports 2015, p. 3 . . . 218, 222, 223, 224

Application of the Convention on the Prevention and Punishment of the Crime of Genocide (The Gambia v. Myanmar), Order of Provisional Measures (23 January 2020) . . . 222

Application of the Convention on the Prevention and Punishment of the Crime of Genocide (The Gambia v. Myanmar), Preliminary Objections (22 July 2022) . . . 222

Application of the International Convention on the Elimination of All Forms of Racial Discrimination (Georgia v. Russian Federation), Preliminary Objections, Judgment, I.C.J. Reports 2011, p. 70 . . . 219, 247

Application of the International Convention on the Elimination of All Forms of Racial Discrimination (Qatar v. United Arab Emirates), Preliminary Objections, Judgment, I.C.J. Reports 2021, p. 21 . . . 219

Application of the International Convention for the Suppression of the Financing of Terrorism and of the International Convention on the Elimination of All Forms of Racial Discrimination (Ukraine v. Russian Federation), Preliminary Objections, Judgment, I.C.J. Reports 2019, p. 558 . . . 219, 247

Armed Activities on the Territory of the Congo (Democratic Republic of the Congo v. Uganda),

Judgment, I.C.J. Reports 2005, p. 168 . . . 156, 219

Armed Activities on the Territory of the Congo (New Application: 2002) (Democratic Republic of the Congo v. Rwanda), Jurisdiction and Admissibility, Judgment, I.C.J. Reports 2006, p. 6 . . . 134, 219

Avena and Other Mexican Nationals (Mexico v. United States of America), Judgment, I.C.J. Reports 2004, p. 12 . . . 220, 221

Barcelona Traction, Light and Power Company, Limited, Judgment, I.C.J. Reports 1970, p. 3 . . . 136, 219

Case concerning East Timor (Portugal v. Australia), Judgment, I.C.J. Reports 1995, p. 90 . . . 593

Case concerning the Temple of Preah Vihear (Cambodia v. Thailand), Merits, Judgment of 15 June 1962, I.C. J. Reports 1962, p. 6 . . . 108

Case concerning the Trial of Pakistani Prisoners of War (Pakistan v. India) . . . 222

Interpretation of the Agreement of 25 March 1951 between the WHO and Egypt, Advisory Opinion, I.C.J. Reports 1980, p. 7 . . . 149

Jadhav (India v. Pakistan), Judgment, I.C.J. Reports 2019, p. 418 . . . 221, 222

Ahmadou Sadio Diallo (Guinea v. Democratic Republic of the Congo), Merits, Judgment, I.C.J. Reports 2010, p. 639 . . . 92, 219, 220, 221

Judgment No. 2867 of the Administrative Tribunal of the International Labour Organization upon a Complaint Filed against the International Fund for Agricultural Development, Advisory Opinion, I.C.J. Reports 2012, p.10 . . . 218, 239

LaGrand (Germany v. United States of America), Judgment, I.C.J. Reports 2001, p. 466 . . . 220, 221

Legal Consequences of the Construction of a Wall in the Occupied Palestinian Territories, Advisory Opinion, I.C.J. Reports 2004 (9 July 2004) . . . 99, 154, 156, 191, 219, 239, 592, 593

Legal Consequences for States of the Continued Presence of South Africa in Namibia (South West Africa) notwithstanding Security Council Resolution 276 (1970), Advisory Opinion, I.C.J. Reports 1971, p. 16 . . . 109, 110, 117

Legal Consequences of the Separation of The Chagos Archipelago from Mauritius in 1965, Advisory Opinion, I.C.J. Reports 2019, p. 95 . . . 127, 129, 131, 592, 593, 595

Legality of the Threat or Use of Nuclear Weapons, Advisory Opinion, 1. C.J. Reports 1996, p. 226 . . . 127, 219

Legality of Use of Force (Serbia and Montenegro v. Belgium); Legality of Use of Force (Serbia and Montenegro v. Canada); Legality of Use of Force (Serbia and Montenegro v. France); Legality of Use of Force (Serbia and Montenegro v. Germany); Legality of Use of Force (Serbia and Montenegro v. Italy); Legality of Use of Force (Serbia and Montenegro v. Netherlands); Legality of Use of Force (Serbia and Montenegro v. Portugal); Legality of Use of Force (Yugoslavia v. Spain); Legality of Use of Force (Yugoslavia v. United States of America); Legality of Use of Force (Serbia and Montenegro v. United Kingdom) . . . 222

Legality of the Use by a State of Nuclear Weapons in Armed Conflict, Advisory Opinion, I.C.J. Reports 1996, p. 66 . . . 225, 226

Military and Paramilitary Activities in and against Nicaragua (Nicaragua v. United States of America) Merits, Judgment I.C.J. Reports 1986, p. 14 . . . 127, 159, 160

Nuclear Tests (Australia v. France), Judgment, I.C.J. Reports 1974, p. 253 . . . 224, 225

Nuclear Tests (New Zealand v. France), Judgment, I.C.J. Reports 1974, p. 45 . . . 224, 225

Obligations concerning Negotiations relating to Cessation of the Nuclear Arms Race and to Nuclear Disarmament (Marshall Islands v. United Kingdom), Preliminary Objections, Judgment, I.C.J. Reports 2016, p.833 . . . 218, 226, 227

Oil Platforms (Islamic Republic of Iran v. United States of America), Judgment, I.C.J. Reports 2003, p. 161 . . . 224

Pulp Mills on the River Uruguay (Argentina v. Uruguay), Judgment, I.C.J. Reports 2010, p. 14 . . . 224

Questions relating to the Obligation to Prosecute or Extradite (Belgium v. Senegal), Judgment, I.C.J. Reports 2012, p. 422 . . . 135, 219, 266, 495, 506

Request for Interpretation of the Judgment of 31 March 2004 in the Case concerning Avena and Other Mexican Nationals (Mexico v. United States of America), Judgment, I.C.J. Reports 2009, p. 3 . . . 220

Request for an Examination of the Situation in Accordance with Paragraph 63 of the Court's Judgment of 20 December 1974 in the Nuclear Tests (New Zealand v. France) Case, Order (22 September 1995) . . . 225

Reservations to the Convention on Genocide, Advisory Opinion, ICJ Reports 1951, p. 15 . . . 114, 120, 131, 134, 159, 219, 222

South West Africa, Second Phase, Judgment, I.C.J. Reports 1966, p. 6 . . . 218

Temple of Preah Vihear (Cambodia v. Thailand), ICJ Reports (1962), Pleadings, Oral Arguments, Documents, vol. II, pp 203 and 205 . . . 107

United States Diplomatic and Consular Staff in Tehran (United States of America v. Iran), Judgment, I.C.J. Reports 1980, p. 3 . . . 66, 219

Vienna Convention on Consular Relations (Paraguay v. United States of America), Provisional Measures, Order of 9 April 1998, I.C.J. Reports 1998, p. 248 . . . 220

INTERNATIONAL CRIMINAL TRIBUNAL FOR THE FORMER YUGOSLAVIA (ICTY)

Prosecutor v. Furundzija, Judgment, Case No. IT-95-17/1, Trial Chamber II (10 December 1998) (21 July 2000) . . . 30, 31, 135, 136, 495

Prosecutor v. Tadić. Case No.: IT-94-1-A (7 May 1997) (15 July 1999) . . . 161

PERMANENT COURT OF INTERNATIONAL JUSTICE (PCIJ)

Exchange of Greek and Turkish Populations, Advisory Opinion, Ser. B, No. 10 (21 February 1925) . . . 170

Greco-Bulgarian 'Communities'. Advisory Opinion (ser. B) No. 17 (31 July 1930) . . . 170, 354

S.S. Lotus (France v. Turkey), 1927 P.C.I.J. (ser. A) No. 10 (Sept. 7) . . . 126

Treatment of Polish Nationals and Other Persons of Polish Origin or Speech in the Danzig Territory. Advisory Opinion (ser. A/B) No. 44 (4 February 1932) . . . 170, 354

US SUPREME COURT (USSC)

Nardone v. United States, 308 U.S. 338 (1939) . . . 506

Silverthorne Lumber Co. v. United States, 251 U.S. 385 (1920) . . . 506

TABLE OF TREATIES

TREATIES

Additional Protocol to the Convention on Cybercrime, concerning the criminalization of acts of a racist and xenophobic nature committed through computer systems (adopted 28 January 2003, entered into force 1 March 2006), ETS No. 189 . . . 528

African Charter on Democracy, Elections and Governance (adopted 25 October 2011, entered into force 15 February 2012) . . . 430, 594

African Charter on Human and Peoples' Rights (ACHPR) (adopted 27 June 1981, entered into force 21 October 1986) OAU Doc. CAB/LEG/67/3 rev. 5, 21 I.L.M. 58 (1982) . . . 138, 220, 594, 595

preamble . . . 422, 426, 553
Art 1 . . . 138
Art 2 . . . 142, 543, 553, 560
Arts 2–17 . . . 167
Art 3 . . . 142, 543, 553
Art 4 . . . 477
Art 5 . . . 494
Art 6 . . . 427
Art 7 . . . 14
Art 8 . . . 427, 509, 604
Art 9 . . . 427, 523
Art 11 . . . 13
Art 12.2 . . . 13
Art 13 . . . 14, 427
Art 14 . . . 13, 86, 604
Arts 15–17 . . . 423
Arts 15–18 . . . 85
Art 16 . . . 86
Art 17 . . . 14, 425
Art 18 . . . 86
Art 19–24 . . . 85, 167, 423
Art 19 . . . 142, 543
Art 20–24 . . . 590
Art 21 . . . 85, 425, 604
Art 22 . . . 425, 604
Art 22.8–22.9 . . . 100
Art 26 . . . 86
Art 27 . . . 100, 426
Art 28 . . . 426
Art 29 . . . 426
Arts 31–32 . . . 437
Arts 33–34 . . . 437
Art 36 . . . 437
Art 41 . . . 437
Art 42 . . . 89, 437
Art 44 . . . 92, 437, 465
Art 45 . . . 92, 437
Arts 46–59 . . . 85
Arts 47–53 . . . 92
Art 48 . . . 468
Art 49 . . . 468
Art 52 . . . 459
Art 55 . . . 93, 166
Art 56 . . . 463
Art 56.5 . . . 463
Art 60 . . . 119
Art 62 . . . 85, 92
Art 63.2 . . . 108
Art 63.3 . . . 422

Protocol to the African Charter on Human and Peoples' Rights on the Establishment of an African Court on Human and Peoples' Rights (adopted 10 June 1998, entered into force 25 January 2004) . . . 86, 93, 422, 429, 444–7, 452, 457, 462, 473

Art 3 . . . 441
Art 4 . . . 466
Art 5 . . . 93, 166, 443
Art 5.1.a . . . 451
Art 5.3 . . . 444, 452
Art 6 . . . 456
Art 9 . . . 460
Art 11 . . . 440, 441
Arts 12–14 . . . 441
Art 12 . . . 456
Art 14 . . . 441
Art 15 . . . 441
Art 20 . . . 441
Art 21 . . . 441
Art 22 . . . 441
Art 26 . . . 453
Art 27 . . . 108, 453, 454, 458
Art 28.2 . . . 453
Art 28.3 . . . 453
Art 28.4 . . . 453
Art 28.5 . . . 453
Art 29 . . . 453, 457
Art 30 . . . 453
Art 34 . . . 93, 166, 440
Art 34.6 . . . 444, 445, 452
Art 65 . . . 422

TABLE OF TREATIES

Protocol to the African Charter on Human and Peoples' Rights on the Rights of Older Persons in Africa (adopted 28 January 2018, entered into force 11 September 2018) ... 429, 431
   Art 22 ... 430
Protocol to the African Charter on Human and Peoples' Rights on the Rights of Women in Africa (adopted 7 November 2003, entered into force 25 November 2005) ... 86, 480, 490, 568
   Art II ... 570
   Art II.2 ... 570
   Arts III–V ... 571
   Art VII ... 462
   Art XV ... 490
   Art XVI ... 490
   Art XXVI ... 429
   Art XXVII ... 429, 568
African Charter on the Rights and Welfare of the Child (adopted 11 July 1990, entered into force 29 November 1999) ... 430, 431, 443
   Preamble ... 431
   Art 1 ... 432
   Art 2 ... 431, 577
   Art 3 ... 434
   Art 4 ... 434, 588
   Art 5 ... 588
   Art 6 ... 432
   Art 11 ... 434, 588
   Art 14 ... 434, 588
   Art 16 ... 434, 588
   Art 21 ... 431, 432, 434, 588
   Art 22 ... 431, 432
   Art 27 ... 432
   Art 29 ... 588
   Art 29.b ... 588
   Art 30 ... 432, 436
   Art 31 ... 432, 436
   Art 32 ... 432, 578
   Arts 33–37 ... 432
   Art 37(1) ... 432
   Art 42 ... 432, 578
   Art 43 ... 433
   Art 44 ... 433
   Art 47 ... 468
   Art 47.3 ... 431
   Art 50 ... 468
   Art 52 ... 468
African Union Convention for the Protection and Assistance of Internally Displaced Persons in Africa (adopted 23 October 2009, entered into force 6 March 2020) ... 86, 87, 430
African Union Convention on Preventing and Combating Corruption (adopted 1 July 2003, entered into force 10 February 2020) ... 430
African Youth Charter (adopted 2 July 2006, entered into force 8 August 2009) ... 430
American Convention on Human Rights (ACHR) (adopted 22 November 1969, entered into force 18 July 1978) 1144 UNTS 123, OAS Treaty Series 36 ... 72, 81, 82, 89, 118, 121, 125, 138, 155, 156, 157, 168, 169, 302–4, 306–9, 313, 315, 320–2, 325, 327, 329, 330, 334, 339, 340, 346, 349, 350, 351, 354, 355, 357, 478, 543
   Art 1 ... 138, 142, 168, 543, 553
   Art 1.1 ... 154, 525, 560
   Art 2 ... 334, 525
   Art 4 ... 309, 333, 477, 489, 574
   Art 4.1 ... 478
   Art 4.2 ... 309, 483
   Art 4.3 ... 309, 483
   Art 4.4 ... 309, 483
   Art 4.5 ... 309, 484
   Art 4.6 ... 309, 484
   Art 5 ... 333, 489, 494, 509, 574
   Art 6.3.b ... 513
   Art 7 ... 311, 509, 574
   Art 8 ... 14, 333, 489, 574, 605
   Art 8.3 ... 509
   Art 11 ... 535
   Art 12 ... 509
   Art 12.3 ... 13, 510, 516
   Art 12.4 ... 511
   Art 13 ... 523, 527, 533
   Art 13.1 ... 524
   Art 13.2 ... 13, 525, 535
   Art 13.4 ... 13, 525
   Art 13.5 ... 524, 528
   Art 14 ... 523, 524
   Art 14.1 ... 525
   Art 14.3 ... 13
   Art 15 ... 13
   Art 16.2 ... 13
   Art 18 ... 168
   Art 19 ... 579
   Art 21 ... 605
   Art 21.2 ... 13
   Art 22 ... 168
   Art 22.3 ... 13
   Art 22.4 ... 13
   Art 23 ... 14
   Art 23.2 ... 13
   Art 24 ... 142, 543, 553
   Art 25 ... 489, 574, 605
   Art 26 ... 81, 82, 84, 309
   Art 27 ... 13, 135, 168, 427, 477, 495, 510, 524
   Art 27.1 ... 543
   Art 28 ... 155

TABLE OF TREATIES

Art 29 ... 118, 527, 533
Art 29.a ... 119
Art 29.b ... 118
Art 30 ... 13
Art 32.1 ... 425
Art 34 ... 313
Art 35 ... 313
Art 36 ... 313
Art 37 ... 314
Art 41 ... 314
Art 41.f ... 315
Art 41.g ... 316
Art 44 ... 166, 323
Art 45 ... 350
Art 46 ... 340
Art 46.1.d ... 340
Art 46.2 ... 341
Art 47 ... 340
Art 47.a ... 341
Art 47.b ... 341
Art 47.c ... 341
Art 48.1.f ... 324
Art 50 ... 325, 326, 339, 344
Art 51 ... 326
Art 52 ... 317
Art 53 ... 317
Art 54.1 ... 317
Art 62 ... 317, 339, 429
Art 64 ... 304, 317, 322
Art 64.1 ... 320
Art 65 ... 355
Art 66.2 ... 330
Art 63.1 ... 330
Art 65 ... 334, 336, 337
Art 67 ... 337
Art 68 ... 337
Art 78 ... 125, 339
Additional Protocol to the American Convention on Human Rights in the Area of Economic, Social and Cultural Rights (Protocol of San Salvador) (adopted 17 November 1988, entered into force 16 November 1999) OAS Treaty Series No. 69 ... 81, 82, 89, 92, 309
  Art 1 ... 81
  Art 12 ... 490
  Art 13 ... 14
  Art 19 ... 82, 309
  Art 19.7 ... 82
Protocol to the American Convention on Human Rights to Abolish the Death Penalty (adopted 6 August 1990), OAS Treaty Series No. 73
  Art 1 ... 310, 484
  Art 1.3 ... 310
  Art 2.1 ... 310, 484

Anti-War Treaty of Non-Aggression and Conciliation ('Saavedra-Lamas Pact') (adopted 10 October 1933, entered into force 13 November 1935) ... 300
Arab Charter on Human Rights (adopted 22 May 2004, entered into force 15 March 2008) ... 17, 72, 89, 125, 297
  Art 2 ... 17, 142, 543
  Art 3.1 ... 560
  Art 4 ... 135
  Arts 5–7 ... 477
  Art 7.2 ... 483
  Art 8–9 ... 494
  Art 25 ... 509
  Art 30 ... 509
  Art 32 ... 523
  Art 32.1 ... 524
  Art 32.2 ... 535
  Art 33 ... 17
  Arts 33–42 ... 79
  Art 34 ... 17
  Art 37 ... 17
  Art 41 ... 17
  Art 45 ... 89
  Art 48 ... 89
Charter for African Cultural Renaissance (adopted 25 January 2006, not yet in force) ... 430
Charter of the International Military Tribunal (adopted 8 August 1945), 280 UNTS 1951
  Art 6 ... 106
Charter of the Organization of African Unity (adopted 25 May 1963, entered into force 13 September 1963) 479 UNTS 39 ... 418
Charter of the Organization of American States (adopted 30 April 1948, entered into force 13 December 1951), OAS, Treaty Series, Nos. 1-C, 61, UN Registration No. 1609 Vol. 119 ... 301, 302, 303, 304, 305, 306
  Preamble ... 303
  Art 1 ... 299
  Art 3.j ... 303
  Art 3.l ... 303
  Art 13 ... 303
  Art 17 ... 303
  Art 67 ... 301, 305
  Art 68 ... 301
  Art 106 ... 303
  Art 112 ... 303
  Art 143 ... 301, 302
  Art 145 ... 303
  Art 150 ... 303
Charter of the United Nations (adopted 26 June 1945, entered into force 24 October 1945) ... 38, 53, 60, 65, 66, 133, 177, 178, 180, 193, 565, 591
  Ch XI ... 591

Ch XII ... 33, 591
Preamble ... 60, 177
Art 1 ... 60
Art 1(2) ... 591
Art 1(3) ... 60, 133, 177
Art 13 ... 60
Art 13(1)(b) ... 60, 177
Art 25 ... 133
Art 55 ... 60, 133, 591
Art 55(c) ... 65, 177
Art 56 ... 60, 65, 133
Art 62(2) ... 60, 177
Art 68 ... 60, 177, 178
Art 76 ... 177
Art 96 ... 218
Art 103 ... 132, 133
Constitutive Act of the African Union (adopted 11 July 2000, entered into force 26 May 2001) 2158 UNTS 3
　Art 3 ... 419
　Art 4 ... 419
　Protocol on Amendments to the Constitutive Act of the African Union (adopted 11 July 2003, entered into force 19 March 2018)
　　Art 11 ... 447
Convention for the Establishment of a Central American Court of Justice (adopted 20 December 1907) ... 165
Convention for the Protection of Cultural Property in the Event of Armed Conflict (adopted 14 May 1954, entered into force 7 August 1956) ... 30
Convention for the Protection of Human Rights and Dignity of the Human Being with regard to the Application of Biology and Medicine (adopted 4 April 1997, entered into force 1 December 1999) ... 365
Convention for the Protection of Human Rights and Fundamental Freedoms (adopted 4 November 1950, entered into force 3 September 1953) 213 UNTS 221 (ECHR, 'European Convention on Human Rights') ... 54, 72, 79, 88, 92, 125, 129, 138, 142, 149, 157, 159, 163, 169, 361
　Preamble ... 408
　Art 1 ... 138, 154, 157, 361
　Art 2 ... 382, 477, 574
　Art 2.1 ... 483
　Art 3 ... 118, 370, 382, 400, 401, 486, 494, 500, 501, 503, 504, 508, 574
　Art 4.3.(b) ... 513
　Art 5 ... 370, 400, 401, 411
　Art 6 ... 14, 80, 123, 370, 382, 393, 508
　Art 7 ... 407, 408
　Art 7.2 ... 130
　Art 8–11 ... 370, 412
　Art 8 ... 379, 393, 407, 412, 586
　Art 8.2 ... 13
　Art 9 ... 509
　Art 9.2 ... 13, 510, 516
　Art 10 ... 412, 523, 530, 532
　Art 10.1 ... 524
　Art 10.2 ... 13, 535
　Art 11 ... 387
　Art 11.2 ... 13
　Art 12 ... 259
　Art 13 ... 370, 401, 486
　Art 14 ... 142, 370, 379, 412, 543, 546, 553, 558, 560, 574
　Art 15 ... 13, 100, 135, 259, 370, 398, 400, 409, 410, 411, 412, 427, 477, 495, 524
　Art 16 ... 398, 416
　Art 17 ... 119, 530, 532
　Art 19 ... 362
　Art 20 ... 373
　Art 21.1 ... 373, 374
　Art 22 ... 373
　Art 23 ... 373
　Art 25 ... 96, 362
　Art 26.2 ... 396
　Art 26.3 ... 376
　Art 26.4 ... 396
　Art 26.5 ... 380
　Art 29.1 ... 377
　Art 29.2 ... 399
　Art 30 ... 379
　Art 31 ... 363
　Art 32 ... 363
　Art 33 ... 92, 399
　Art 34 ... 92, 166, 169, 382, 383
　Art 35 ... 384
　Art 35.1 ... 399
　Art 35.2.a ... 385
　Art 35.2.b ... 385, 387
　Art 35.3.a ... 387, 388
　Art 35.3.b ... 389, 396
　Art 36 ... 369
　Art 37 ... 378
　Art 38 ... 401
　Art 39.4 ... 376
　Art 41 ... 390
　Art 43 ... 379
　Art 43.2 ... 379
　Art 43.3 ... 379
　Art 44 ... 363
　Art 45 ... 363
　Art 46 ... 92, 362, 381, 392, 403, 404
　Art 46.1 ... 401
　Art 46.2 ... 401
　Art 47 ... 404, 405
　Art 48 ... 362, 363
　Art 50 ... 373, 390
　Art 56 ... 154, 363, 366

TABLE OF TREATIES

Art 58.1 ... 125
Art 58.2 ... 125
Art 59 ... 149
Art 76 ... 308
Protocol No. 1 to the Convention for the Protection of Human Rights and Fundamental Freedoms (adopted 20 March 1952, entered into force 18 May 1954) ETS No. 9 ... 363
  Art 1 ... 14, 159, 169, 395
  Art 2 ... 14, 546
Protocol No. 2 to the Convention for the Protection of Human Rights and Fundamental Freedoms, conferring upon the European Court of Human Rights competence to give advisory opinions (adopted 6 May 1963, entered into force 21 September 1970) ETS No. 44 ... 363, 404, 405
  Art 1 ... 404, 405
  Art 1.3 ... 405
  Art 2 ... 511
  Art 3 ... 405
Protocol No. 3 to the Convention for the Protection of Human Rights and Fundamental Freedoms (adopted 6 May 1963, entered into force 21 September 1970) ETS No. 45 ... 363
Protocol No. 4 to the Convention for the Protection of Human Rights and Fundamental Freedoms (adopted 16 September 1963, entered into force 2 May 1968) ETS No. 46 ... 363
  Art 4 ... 401
Protocol No. 5 to the Convention for the Protection of Human Rights and Fundamental Freedoms (adopted 20 January 1966, entered into force 20 December 1971) ETS No. 55 ... 363
Protocol No. 6 to the Convention for the Protection of Human Rights and Fundamental Freedoms concerning the Abolition of the Death Penalty (adopted 28 April 1983, entered into force 1 January 1985) ETS No. 114 ... 363, 484
Protocol No. 7 to the Convention for the Protection of Human Rights and Fundamental Freedoms (adopted 22 November 1984, entered into force 1 November 1988) ETS No. 117 ... 363
Protocol No 8 to the Convention for the Protection of Human Rights and Fundamental Freedoms (adopted 19 March 1985, entered into force 1 January 1990) ETS No. 118 ... 363
Protocol No. 9 to the Convention for the Protection of Human Rights and Fundamental Freedoms (adopted 6 November 1990, entered into force 1 October 1994) ETS No. 140 ... 363, 364

Protocol No. 10 to the Convention for the Protection of Human Rights and Fundamental Freedoms (adopted 25 March 1992) ETS No. 146 ... 363
Protocol No. 11 to the Convention for the Protection of Human Rights and Fundamental Freedoms, restructuring the control machinery established thereby (adopted 11 May 1994, entered into force 1 November 1998) ETS No. 155 ... 363, 364, 373, 390, 405
Protocol No. 12 to the Convention for the Protection of Human Rights and Fundamental Freedoms (adopted 4 November 2000, entered into force 1 April 2005) ETS No. 177 ... 142
  Art 1 ... 543, 553, 560
Protocol No. 13 to the Convention for the Protection of Human Rights and Fundamental Freedoms, concerning the Abolition of the Death Penalty in All Circumstances (adopted 3 May 2002, entered into force 1 July 2003) ETS No. 187 ... 363, 484, 485
Protocol No. 14 to the Convention for the Protection of Human Rights and Fundamental Freedoms, amending the control system of the Convention (adopted 13 May 2004, entered into force 1 June 2010) ETS No. 194 ... 149, 363, 364, 369, 377, 383, 389, 396, 397, 402, 416
  Preamble ... 396
  Art 6 ... 364, 396
  Art 7 ... 364
  Art 8 ... 364
  Art 12 ... 396
  Art 40 ... 373
Protocol No. 14bis to the Convention for the Protection of Human Rights and Fundamental Freedoms (adopted 25 May 2009, entered into force 1 October 2009) CETS No. 20 ... 363, 396
Protocol No. 15 amending the Convention for the Protection of Human Rights and Fundamental Freedom (adopted 24 June 2013) ETS No. 213 ... 17, 363, 373, 384, 389, 398, 408, 416, 417
  Art 2.1 ... 373
  Art 3 ... 379
  Art 5 ... 389
  Art 8.3 ... 384
Protocol No. 16 to the Convention for the Protection of Human Rights and Fundamental Freedoms (adopted 2 October 2013, entered into force 1 August 2018) CETS No. 214 ... 363, 369, 398, 404, 406, 416
  Art 1 ... 406
  Art 3 ... 369

Art 8 ... 406
Art 10 ... 406
Convention Governing Specific Aspects of Refugee Problems in Africa (adopted 10 September 1969, entered into force 20 June 1974) ... 430
Convention on Asylum (signed on 20 February 1928) ... 300
Convention on Contact concerning Children (ETS No. 192) (adopted 15 May 2003, entered into force 1 September 2005) ... 579
Convention on the Consent to Marriage, Minimum Age for Marriage, and Registration of Marriages (adopted on 10 December 1962, entered into force 9 December 1964), 521 UNTS 231 ... 260
Convention on the Nationality of Married Women (adopted 20 February 1957, entered into force 11 August 1958), 309 UNTS 65 ... 260, 565
Convention on the Political Rights of Women (adopted 31 March 1953, entered into force 7 July 1954), 193 UNTS 135 ... 260, 565
Convention on the Prohibition of Military or Any Other Hostile Use of Environmental Modification Techniques (adopted 10 December 1976, entered into force 5 October 1978) ... 30
Convention on the Prohibition of the Development, Production and Stockpiling of Bacteriological (Biological) and Toxin Weapons and on their Destruction (adopted 10 April 1972, entered into force 26 March 1975) ... 30
Protocol for the Prohibition of the Use of Asphyxiating, Poisonous or Other Gases, and of Bacteriological Methods of Warfare (adopted 17 June 1925, entered into force 8 February 1928) ... 30
Convention on Prohibitions or Restrictions on the Use of Certain Conventional Weapons which may be deemed to be Excessively Injurious or to have Indiscriminate Effects (adopted 10 October 1980, entered into force 2 December 1983) ... 30
Convention on Recognition and Enforcement of Decisions concerning Custody of Children and on Restoration of Custody of Children (ETS No. 105) (adopted 20 May 1980, entered into force 1 September 1983) ... 579
Convention Relating to the International Status of Refugees (adopted on 28 October 1933) League of Nations, Treaty Series Vol. CLIX No. 366 ... 31
Convention relating to the Status of Refugees (adopted 28 July 1951, entered into force 22 April 1954), 189 UNTS 137 ... 100, 103
Art 42(1) ... 124
Convention relative to the Rights of Aliens (signed on 29 January 1902) ... 300

Council of Europe Convention on Action against Trafficking in Human Beings (adopted 16 May 2005, entered into force 1 February 2008) ... 365
Council of Europe Convention on preventing and combating violence against women and domestic violence ('Istanbul Convention') (adopted 11 May 2011, entered into force 1 August 2014), CETS No. 210 ... 197, 365, 569
Art 12 ... 573
Convention on the Protection of Children against Sexual Exploitation and Sexual Abuse (CETS No. 201) (adopted 25 October 2007, entered into force 1 July 2010) ... 197, 365, 579
Covenant of the League of Nations (adopted 28 June 1919, entered into force 10 January 1920) ... 31, 33, 53
Preamble ... 31
Art 22 ... 33
European Charter for Regional or Minority Languages (adopted 5 November 1992, entered into force 1 March 1998) ETS No. 148 ... 365
European Convention for the Prevention of Torture and Inhuman or Degrading Treatment or Punishment (adopted 26 November 1987, entered into force 1 February 1987). ETS No. 126 ... 90, 365, 495
Art 1 ... 90
European Convention on the Adoption of Children (ETS No. 058) (adopted 24 April 1967, entered into force 26 April 1968) ... 579
European Convention on the Adoption of Children (ETS No. 202) (revised) (adopted 27 November 2008, entered into force 1 September 2011) ... 579
European Convention on the Exercise of Children's Rights (ETS No. 160) (adopted 25 January 1996, entered into force 1 July 2000) ... 365, 579
Art 1.1 ... 577
European Convention on the Legal Status of Children born out of Wedlock (ETS No. 085) (adopted 15 October 1975, entered into force 11 August 1978) ... 579
European Convention on the Legal Status of Migrant Workers (adopted 24 November 1977, entered into force 1 May 1983) ... 365
European Convention on the Non-Applicability of Statutory Limitation to Crimes against Humanity and War Crimes (adopted 25 January 1974, entered into force 27 June 2003) ... 365
European Social Charter (adopted 18 October 1961, entered into force 26 February 1965) ETS No. 035 ... 365, 366
Art 7 ... 579
Pt II, Art 20 ... 367

Art 34 . . . 366
Appendix . . . 366
Additional Protocol to the European Social Charter (adopted 5 May 1988, entered into force 4 September 1992) ETS No. 128, . . . 366
Appendix . . . 366
Additional Protocol to the European Social Charter Providing for a System of Collective Complaints (adopted 9 November 1995, entered into force 1 July 1995) ETS No. 158 . . . 79, 367
Protocol amending the European Social Charter (adopted 21 October 1991) ETS No. 142 . . . 366
European Social Charter (revised) (adopted 3 May 1996, entered into force 1 July 1999) ETS No. 163
　Part III, Art A . . . 367
　Art 17 . . . 579
　Appendix . . . 366
Framework Convention for the Protection of National Minorities (adopted 1 February 1995, entered into force 1 February 1998) ETS No. 15 . . . 365
Franco-Siamese Treaty (adopted 13 February 1904) . . . 108
Geneva Convention concerning Upper Silesia (adopted 15 May 1922) . . . 35, 165
　Art 64 . . . 36
Geneva Conventions (1949) . . . 469
　Convention (I) for the Amelioration of the Condition of the Wounded and Sick in Armed Forces in the Field (adopted 12 August 1949, entered into force 21 October 1950) . . . 29
　　Art 3 . . . 494
　　Art 12 . . . 494
　　Art 50 . . . 494
　Convention (II) for the Amelioration of the Condition of Wounded, Sick and Shipwrecked Members of Armed Forces at Sea (adopted 12 August 1949, entered into force 21 October 1950) . . . 29
　　Art 3 . . . 494
　　Art 12 . . . 494
　　Art 51 . . . 494
　Convention (III) relative to the Treatment of Prisoners of War (adopted 12 August 1949, entered into force 21 October 1950) . . . 29
　　Art 3 . . . 494
　　Art 12 . . . 102
　　Art 17 . . . 494
　　Art 87 . . . 494
　　Art 130 . . . 494
　Convention (IV) relative to the Protection of Civilian Persons in Time of War (adopted 12 August 1949, entered into force 21 October 1950) . . . 29, 162, 192
　　Art 3 . . . 494
　　Art 32 . . . 494
　　Art 147 . . . 494
　Protocol Additional to the Geneva Conventions of 12 August 1949, and relating to the Protection of Victims of International Armed Conflicts (Protocol I) (adopted 8 June 1977, entered into force 7 December 1978) . . . 29, 100, 102, 105, 469
　　Art 3 . . . 100, 105, 148
　　Arts 4–5 . . . 100
　　Art 75 . . . 100
　Protocol Additional to the Geneva Conventions of 12 August 1949, and relating to the Protection of Victims of Non-International Armed Conflicts (Protocol II) (adopted 8 June 1977, entered into force 7 December 1978) . . . 29, 105, 148
　　Art 3 . . . 100, 105, 148
　Protocol Additional to the Geneva Conventions of 12 August 1949, and relating to the Adoption of an Additional Distinctive Emblem (Protocol III) (adopted 8 December 2005, entered into force 14 January 2007) . . . 29, 30, 105, 148
　　Art 3 . . . 100, 105, 148
ILO Abolition of Forced Labour Convention (C105) (adopted on 25 June 1957, entered into force on 17 January 1959) . . . 32
ILO Discrimination (Employment and Occupation) Convention (C111) (adopted on 25 June 1958, entered into force on 15 June 1960) . . . 32
ILO Equal Remuneration Convention (C100) (adopted on 29 June 1951, entered into force on 23 May 1953) . . . 32
ILO Freedom of Association and Protection of the Right to Organize Convention (C087) (adopted on 9 July 1948, entered into force on 4 July 1950) . . . 32
ILO Forced Labour Convention, 1930 (C029) (adopted on 28 June 1930, entered into force on 1 May 1932) (and its 2014 Protocol, P029, adopted on 11 June 2014 and entered into force on 9 November 2016) . . . 32
ILO Indigenous and Tribal Peoples Convention (C169) (adopted 27 June 1989, entered into force 5 September 1991) ('ILO Convention C169')
　Art 3.1 . . . 599
　Art 4.1 . . . 599
　Art 6 . . . 603
　Arts 14–15 . . . 603
　Art 14.2 . . . 599
　Art 15.1 . . . 599

TABLE OF TREATIES

ILO Indigenous and Tribal Populations Convention (C107) (adopted on 26 June 1957, entered into force 2 June 1959) . . . 564
   Preamble . . . 598
   Art 1.1.b . . . 598
   Art 2.2.a . . . 598
   Art 2.2.b . . . 598
   Art 11 . . . 598
ILO Minimum Age Convention (Convention No. 138) (adopted on 26 June 1973, entered into force on 19 June 1976) . . . 32, 577, 578
ILO Occupational Safety and Health Convention (C155) (adopted on 22 June 1981, entered into force on 11 August 1983) . . . 32
ILO Promotional Framework for Occupational Safety and Health Convention (C187) (adopted on 15 June 2006, entered into force on 20 February 2009) . . . 32
ILO Right to Organize and Collective Bargaining Convention, (C098) (adopted on 9 July 1948, entered into force on 4 July 1950) . . . 32
ILO Worst Forms of Child Labour Convention (No. 182) (adopted on 17 June 1999, entered into force on 19 November 2000) . . . 32, 578
   Art 2 . . . 577
Inter-American Convention against all Forms of Discrimination and Intolerance (adopted 5 June 2013, entered into force 20 February 2020) . . . 89, 548
   Art 1.2 . . . 545
   Art 15 . . . 312
Inter-American Convention against Racism, Racial Discrimination and Related Forms of Intolerance (adopted 5 June 2013, entered into force 11 November 2013) UN Registration No. 54915 . . . 89, 548
   Art 15 . . . 312
Inter-American Convention on Protecting the Human Rights of Older Persons (adopted 15 June 2015, entered into force 11 January 2017) UN Registration No. 54318 . . . 81, 89
   Art 1 . . . 312
   Art 33 . . . 313
   Art 34 . . . 313
   Art 35 . . . 313
   Art 36 . . . 313
Inter-American Convention on the Elimination of All Forms of Discrimination against Persons with Disabilities (adopted 8 June 1999, entered into force 14 September 2001) . . . 312
   Art II . . . 312
   Art III . . . 312
   Art VI . . . 312
Inter-American Convention on the Forced Disappearance of Persons (adopted 9 June 1994, entered into force 28 March 1996) OAS, Treaty Series, No. 68 . . . 284, 310, 344
   Art I . . . 310, 481
   Art III . . . 310, 481
   Art IV . . . 310
   Art VII . . . 310
   Art XIII . . . 310, 344
   Art XIV . . . 310
Inter-American Convention on the Prevention, Punishment and Eradication of Violence against Women (adopted 9 June 1994, entered into force 5 March 1995) (Belém do Pará) . . . 89, 310, 568
   Art 1 . . . 311
   Art 2 . . . 311
   Art 6 . . . 573
   Art 7 . . . 311
   Art 8 . . . 311, 573
   Art 10 . . . 311
   Art 12 . . . 311
Inter-American Convention to Prevent and Punish Torture (adopted 9 December 1985, entered into force 28 February 1987) OAS Treaty Series 67 . . . 308, 495
   Art 1 . . . 310
   Art 2 . . . 497
   Art 3 . . . 310
   Art 4 . . . 310
   Art 5 . . . 310
   Art 6 . . . 310
   Art 9 . . . 310
International Convention against Apartheid in Sports (adopted 10 December 1985, entered into force 4 August 1993), 1728 UNTS 380 . . . 231, 287
International Convention for the Protection of All Persons from Enforced Disappearance (ICPPED) (adopted 20 December 2006, entered into force 23 December 2010) . . . 103, 125, 187, 232, 235, 244, 250, 482
   Preamble . . . 482
   Art 2 . . . 285, 481
   Art 5 . . . 482
   Art 8.1.(b) . . . 481
   Art 16 . . . 100, 103
   Art 17 . . . 287
   Art 18 . . . 287
   Art 20 . . . 287
   Art 21.1 . . . 241
   Art 26.1 . . . 234
   Art 26.2 . . . 234
   Art 26.4 . . . 234
   Art 27 . . . 286
   Art 29 . . . 235, 286
   Art 29.1 . . . 294

Art 31 . . . 93, 166, 240
Art 31.2 . . . 241
Art 31.4 . . . 108, 242
Art 32 . . . 240
Art 33 . . . 90, 244, 286, 287
Art 35 . . . 242
Art 42.2 . . . 241
International Convention for the Suppression of the Traffic in Women of Full Age (adopted on 11 October 1933, entered into force 24 August 1934) . . . 31, 564
International Convention for the Suppression of the Traffic in Women and Children (adopted on 30 September 1921, entered into force 15 June 1922), League of Nations TS vol. 9 p. 415 . . . 31, 564
International Convention on the Protection of the Rights of All Migrant Workers and Members of Their Families (ICRMW) (adopted 18 December 1990, entered into force 1 July 2003) . . . 72, 93, 197, 231, 232, 240
    Part III . . . 278
Art 1 . . . 142, 543
Art 7 . . . 142, 543
Art 18.1 . . . 142, 543
Art 25 . . . 142, 543
Art 27 . . . 142, 543
Art 28 . . . 142, 543
Art 42 . . . 240
Art 43 . . . 142, 543
Art 45.1 . . . 142, 543
Art 48 . . . 142, 543
Art 55 . . . 142, 543
Art 70 . . . 142, 543
Art 72.1.(b) . . . 234, 277
Art 72.2.(a) . . . 234
Art 72.2.(b) . . . 234
Art 72.4 . . . 234
Art 72.5.(a) . . . 234
Art 72.5.(c) . . . 234
Art 73 . . . 235
Art 73.1.a . . . 294
Art 73.1.b . . . 294
Art 74 . . . 277
Art 74.2 . . . 278
Art 74.5 . . . 277
Art 76 . . . 92, 240, 277
Art 77 . . . 93, 166, 240, 277
Art 77.2 . . . 242
Art 77.3.(a) . . . 241
Art 77.3.(b) . . . 241
Art 89 . . . 125
Art 92 . . . 240, 277
Art 92.2 . . . 241
International Convention on the Suppression and Punishment of the Crime of Apartheid (adopted 30 November 1973, entered into force 18 July 1976) . . . 231
Art VII . . . 289
Art VIII . . . 287
Art IX . . . 289
International Covenant on Civil and Political Rights (ICCPR) (adopted 16 December 1966, entered into force 23 March 1976) 999 UNTS 171 . . . 55, 59, 70, 72, 75, 76, 122, 125, 126, 129, 136, 138, 154, 155, 156, 168, 179, 184, 192, 197, 219, 220, 231–233, 245, 250–252, 477, 543
Art 1 . . . 55, 71, 76, 167, 590, 592, 595
Art 1.1 . . . 167, 592
Art 1.2 . . . 167, 592
Art 2 . . . 138, 142, 156, 543, 553
Art 2.1 . . . 75, 154, 560
Art 2.2 . . . 75
Art 2.3(a) . . . 75
Art 3 . . . 570
Art 4 . . . 13, 100, 135, 427, 477, 495, 510, 524
Art 4.1 . . . 543
Art 5.1 . . . 119
Art 6 . . . 477
Art 6.2 . . . 483
Arts 6.4–6.5 . . . 483
Art 7 . . . 254, 494
Art 8.3.(c).(ii) . . . 513
Art 12.3 . . . 13
Art 13 . . . 14
Art 14 . . . 14
Art 15.2 . . . 130
Art 17 . . . 535
Art 18 . . . 509
Art 18.3 . . . 13, 510, 516
Art 18.4 . . . 511
Art 19 . . . 523
Art 19.2 . . . 524
Art 19.3 . . . 13, 535
Art 20 . . . 13, 523, 524
Art 20.2 . . . 528
Art 21 . . . 13
Art 22.2 . . . 13
Art 25 . . . 14
Art 26 . . . 142, 543, 553, 557, 560
Art 28.2 . . . 234, 251
Art 28.3 . . . 234
Art 29.2 . . . 234
Art 30.4 . . . 234
Art 32.1 . . . 234
Art 38 . . . 234
Art 40 . . . 235
Art 40.1.a . . . 294
Art 40.1.b . . . 294
Art 40.4 . . . 251
Art 41 . . . 240, 251
Arts 41–43 . . . 92

Art 42 . . . 251
Art 50 . . . 155
First Optional Protocol to the International Covenant on Civil and Political Rights (ICCPR-OP1) (adopted 16 December 1966, entered into force 23 March 196) . . . 72, 126, 232, 244, 250, 251
  Arts 1–3 . . . 93, 166
  Art 1 . . . 242
  Art 2 . . . 241
  Art 3 . . . 242
  Art 5 . . . 93, 166
  Art 5.a . . . 241
  Art 5.b . . . 241
  Art 10 . . . 254
  Art 12 . . . 253
  Art 12.1 . . . 253
  Art 12.2 . . . 253
  Art 24 . . . 254
Second Optional Protocol to the International Covenant on Civil and Political Rights, aiming at the abolition of the death penalty (ICCPR-OP2) (adopted 15 December 1989, entered into force 11 July 1991) . . . 232, 250
  Art 1 . . . 484
  Art 2.1 . . . 484
International Covenant on Economic, Social and Cultural Rights (ICESCR) (adopted on 16 December 1966, entered into force 3 January 1976) 993 UNTS 3 . . . 72, 75, 77, 78, 81, 96, 98, 125, 155, 167, 179, 192, 197, 198, 231, 232, 245, 250, 251
  Art 1 . . . 590, 592, 595
  Art 1.1 . . . 167, 592
  Art 1.2 . . . 167, 592
  Art 2 . . . 75, 77
  Art 2.1 . . . 78
  Art 2.2 . . . 142, 543, 556, 560
  Art 3 . . . 77, 142, 543, 570
  Art 5.1 . . . 119
  Art 7.a.i . . . 77
  Art 10.3 . . . 77
  Art 11 . . . 490
  Art 11.1 . . . 490
  Art 12(a) . . . 216
  Art 13.2–13.4 . . . 77
  Art 15.3 . . . 77
  Arts 16–17 . . . 235
  Arts 16–22 . . . 76, 254
  Art 16 . . . 294
  Art 28 . . . 155
  Art 32 . . . 92
  Art 41 . . . 76
Optional Protocol to the International Covenant on Economic, Social and Cultural Rights (OP-ICESCR) (adopted 10 December 2008, entered into force 5 May 2013) . . . 78, 187, 232, 244
  Art 2 . . . 93, 166, 240, 241, 242
  Art 3.1 . . . 241
  Art 3.2 . . . 242
  Art 3.2.(a) . . . 241
  Art 4 . . . 258
  Art 7 . . . 242
  Art 10 . . . 92, 240, 257
  Art 11 . . . 244, 257, 287
International Convention on the Elimination of All Forms of Racial Discrimination (ICERD) (adopted on 21 December 1965, entered into force 4 January 1969) . . . 71, 72, 92, 124, 126, 169, 179, 198, 219, 231, 232, 240, 241, 242, 245, 246, 247, 248, 249, 262, 280, 294, 308
  Preamble . . . 550
  Art 1.1 . . . 246, 550
  Art 1.4 . . . 246
  Art 2 . . . 543
  Art 2.1.d . . . 144
  Art 2I . . . 142
  Art 4 . . . 249, 528
  Art 4.a . . . 524
  Art 8.1 . . . 234
  Art 8.2 . . . 234
  Art 8.4 . . . 234
  Art 8.5.a . . . 234
  Art 9 . . . 235
  Art 9.1.b . . . 294
  Art 9.2 . . . 238
  Arts 11–13 . . . 92, 247
  Art 11 . . . 240
  Art 14 . . . 93, 166, 240, 247
  Art 14.1 . . . 241
  Art 14.5 . . . 241
  Art 14.7.(a) . . . 241
  Art 20(2) . . . 124
  Art 21 . . . 125
  Art 22 . . . 240, 241, 247
Montevideo Convention on the Rights and Duties of States (adopted 26 December 1933) . . . 300
Rome Statute of the International Criminal Court (adopted 17 July 1998, entered into force 1 July 2002) 2187 UNTS 3 . . . 106, 496
  Preamble . . . 106
  Arts 5–8 . . . 106
  Arts 7–8 . . . 494
  Art 7.1.(i). . . . 482
  Art 126 . . . 106
Slavery Convention (adopted 25 September 1926, entered into force 9 March 1927) . . . 28, 32
Statute of the African Court of Justice and Human Rights (Annex to the 'Malabo Protocol') . . . 471

Art 4 . . . 471
Art 14 . . . 471
Art 16 . . . 470, 471
Art 22 . . . 471
Protocol on the Statute of the African Court of Justice and Human Rights (adopted on 1 July 2008) ('Merger Protocol') . . . 469, 470
  Art 3 . . . 470
  Art 6 . . . 470
  Art 16 . . . 470
  Art 18 . . . 470
  Art 21 . . . 470
  Art 28 . . . 470
  Art 29 . . . 470
  Art 30 . . . 470
  Art 53 . . . 470
Statute of the International Court of Justice (adopted 26 June 1945, entered into force 24 October 1945), 3 Bevans 1179
  Art 34 . . . 218
Statute of the Permanent Court of International Justice (adopted 16 December 1920) . . . 120
Treaty of Peace of Versailles (adopted 28 June 1919, entered into force 10 January 2020) . . . 31, 32
  Part XIII . . . 32, 577
  s I . . . 32
Treaty on the Non-Proliferation of Nuclear Weapons (adopted 1 July 1968, entered into force 5 March 1970) 729 UNTS 161 . . . 226
Treaty to Avoid or Prevent Conflicts between the American States ('Gondra Treaty') (adopted 3 May 1923) . . . 300
UN Convention against Torture and Other Cruel, Inhuman or Degrading Treatment or Punishment (adopted 10 December 1984, entered into force 26 June 1987) 1465 UNTS 85 (UNCAT) . . . 72, 98, 103, 179, 219, 231, 232, 245, 267, 268, 282, 495
  Art 1 . . . 496, 497
  Art 1.1 . . . 498
  Art 2 . . . 141
  Art 3 . . . 103
  Art 3.1 . . . 100
  Art 5 . . . 267
  Art 5.1 . . . 267
  Art 7 . . . 269
  Art 7.1 . . . 506
  Art 11 . . . 268
  Art 15 . . . 507
  Art 16 . . . 268
  Art 16.4 . . . 268
  Arts 17–19 . . . 268
  Art 17 . . . 268
  Art 17.1 . . . 234
  Art 17.2 . . . 234
  Art 17.3 . . . 234
  Art 17.5 . . . 234
  Art 19 . . . 235, 294
  Art 20 . . . 90, 244, 265, 266, 287
  Art 21 . . . 92, 240, 265
  Art 22 . . . 93, 240
  Art 22.1 . . . 241
  Art 22.4.(a) . . . 241
  Art 22.4.(b) . . . 241
  Art 27 . . . 265
  Art 28 . . . 244
  Art 30 . . . 240
  Art 30.2 . . . 241, 266
  Art 31 . . . 125
Optional Protocol to the Convention against Torture and Other Cruel, Inhuman or Degrading Treatment or Punishment (OPCAT) (adopted 18 December 2002, entered into force 22 June 2006) . . . 90, 91, 232, 234
  Art 1 . . . 90
  Art 6.1 . . . 234
  Art 11 . . . 90
UN Convention on the Elimination of All Forms of Discrimination against Women (CEDAW) (adopted 18 December 1979, entered into force 3 September 1981) . . . 72, 81, 89, 96, 98, 216, 231, 232, 238, 250, 442, 443, 490, 566
  Art 2 . . . 142, 543
  Art 2(a) . . . 573
  Art 2(b) . . . 573
  Art 2(e) . . . 144, 573
  Art 3 . . . 142, 543
  Arts 5–16 . . . 142, 543
  Art 5(a) . . . 570, 573
  Art 10(f) . . . 216
  Art 14.2.(h) . . . 490
  Art 16 . . . 573
  Art 17.1 . . . 234
  Art 17.2 . . . 234
  Art 17.4 . . . 234
  Art 17.5 . . . 234
  Art 18 . . . 235, 262, 294
  Art 20 . . . 262
  Art 29 . . . 240, 263
  Art 29.2 . . . 241
Optional Protocol to the Convention on the Elimination of All Forms of Discrimination against Women (OP-CEDAW) (adopted 6 October 1999, entered into force 22 December 2000) . . . 232, 262, 263
  Arts 1–2 . . . 93, 166
  Art 2 . . . 240, 241
  Art 4.1 . . . 241
  Art 4.2 . . . 242
  Art 4.2.(a) . . . 241
  Art 4.2.(c) . . . 242

Art 5 . . . 108, 242
Art 8 . . . 90, 244, 287
Art 10 . . . 244
UN Convention on the Non-applicability of Statutory Limitations to War Crimes and Crimes against Humanity (adopted 26 November 1968, entered into force 11 November 1970) . . . 179, 231
UN Convention on the Prevention and Punishment of the Crime of Genocide (adopted 9 December 1948, entered into force 12 January 1951 . . . 102, 120, 121, 134, 160, 161, 222, 223, 231, 287
Art VI . . . 104
Art VIII . . . 287
UN Convention on the Rights of Persons with Disabilities (UNCRPD) 2006 . . . 72, 187, 231–2, 490, 552
Preamble . . . 281, 552
Art 3 . . . 283
Art 4 . . . 283
Art 4.e . . . 144
Art 5 . . . 283, 543
Art 6 . . . 552
Art 12 . . . 543
Art 25 . . . 283
Art 26 . . . 283
Art 28 . . . 490
Art 33 . . . 282
Art 34.2 . . . 281
Art 34.3 . . . 234, 281
Art 34.4 . . . 281
Art 34.5 . . . 234
Art 34.7 . . . 234
Art 35 . . . 235, 281
Art 36 . . . 281
Art 39 . . . 281
Art 42 . . . 149
Art 48 . . . 125
Optional Protocol to the Convention on the Rights of Persons with Disabilities (OPCRPD) (adopted 13 December 2006, entered into force 3 May 2008) . . . 232, 279, 281–283
Art 1 . . . 93, 166, 169, 240, 282
Art 6 . . . 90, 244, 282, 287
Art 8 . . . 244
UN Convention on the Rights of the Child (adopted 20 November 1989, entered into force 2 September 1990) . . . 72, 179, 192, 197, 231, 232, 237, 238, 240, 241, 246–51, 430, 431, 490, 576
Preamble . . . 577
Art 1 . . . 431, 577
Art 2 . . . 142, 273, 543
Art 2.1 . . . 154
Art 2.1(a) . . . 169
Art 3 . . . 273, 585, 589
Art 4 . . . 270
Art 8 . . . 589
Art 10 . . . 585
Art 12 . . . 273, 585, 589
Art 20 . . . 589
Art 24 . . . 273
Art 25 . . . 273
Art 27 . . . 490
Art 28 . . . 273
Art 31 . . . 273
Art 37 . . . 589
Art 38 . . . 431
Art 43.2 . . . 232, 234, 270
Art 43.3 . . . 234
Art 43.5 . . . 234
Art 43.6 . . . 234
Art 44 . . . 235
Art 44.1.a . . . 294
Art 44.1. b . . . 294
Art 52 . . . 125
Optional Protocol to the Convention on the Rights of the Child on a communications procedure (OP3-CRC) (adopted 19 December 2011, entered into force 14 April 2014) . . . 198, 232, 271, 272, 578
Preamble . . . 272
Art 5 . . . 166, 240, 271
Art 7 . . . 241, 242
Art 9 . . . 242
Art 12 . . . 92, 240, 271
Art 13 . . . 90, 244, 271
Art 13.7 . . . 244
Optional Protocol to the Convention on the Rights of the Child on the involvement of children in armed conflict (adopted 25 May 2000, entered into force 12 February 2002) . . . 148, 270, 431, 578
Art 1 . . . 431
Art 2 . . . 431
Art 3 . . . 431
Art 41 . . . 148
Optional Protocol to the Convention on the Rights of the Child on the Sale of Children, Child Prostitution and Child Pornography (OP1-CRC) (adopted 25 May 2000, entered into force 18 January 2002) . . . 232, 270, 578
Vienna Convention on Consular Relations (adopted 24 April 1963, entered into force 19 March 1967) 596 UNTS 261 . . . 109, 111, 220, 221, 320
Vienna Convention on Diplomatic Relations (adopted 18 April 1961, entered into force 24 April 1964) 500 UNTS 95 . . . 134

Vienna Convention on the Law of Treaties (adopted 23 May 1969, entered into force 27 January 1980) ... 114, 115, 116, 120, 121, 124, 125, 133, 153, 446
  Preamble ... 115
  Art 2.1.d ... 120
  Art 19 ... 121
  Art 20(4) ... 121
  Art 27 ... 170, 324
  Art 28 ... 153
  Art 31 ... 116
  Art 53 ... 133
  Art 56.1 ... 125
  Art 60.5 ... 115
  Art 64 ... 133

OTHER INTERNATIONAL INSTRUMENTS

ACERWC, Revised Rules of Procedure of the African Committee of Experts on the Rights and Welfare of the Child (September 2020)
  Chapter XI ... 432
  r 19 ... 432
  r 70 ... 433
  rr 73–74 ... 433
  r 76 ... 432
ACHPR/Res. 194(L)2011 —Resolution Establishing a Working Group on Communications and Appointment of Members ... 450
ACHPR/Res. 225(LII)2012—Resolution on the Expansion of the Mandate of the Working Group on Communications and modifying its Composition ... 450
AHG/Res. 230 (XXX), para 4 ... 440
ACHPR/Res. 255(LIV)2013—Resolution on the Renewal of the Mandate of the Working Group on Communications ... 450
ACHPR/Res. 314(LVII)2015—Resolution on the Renewal of the Mandate and Reconstitution of the Working Group on Communications ... 450
ACHPR/Res. 361(LIX)2016 ... 444
ACHPR/Res. 385(LXI)2017—Resolution on the Renewal of the Mandate and Reconstitution of the Working Group on Communications ... 450
ACHPR/Res. 462 (LXVI) 2020—Resolution on the Renewal of the Mandate, Appointment of the Chairperson and Reconstitution of the Working Group on Communications ... 450
ACHPR, Rules of Procedure (adopted in February–March 2020)
  rr 12–15 ... 437
  r 26 ... 437
  rr 28–29 ... 437
  r 38 ... 447
  r 82 ... 438

r 100 ... 108, 458
r 100.3 ... 458
r 108.2 ... 468
r 108.4 ... 468
r 109.2 ... 468
r 112 ... 468
r 114 ... 468
r 115 ... 447
r 115.3.8 ... 448
r 116 ... 448
r 116.2 ... 448
r 117.1 ... 448
r 117.4 ... 448
r 119 ... 448
r 120.3 ... 448
r 121 ... 448
r 122 ... 448
r 123 ... 459
r 123.5.b ... 460
rr 123.6–123.7 ... 460
r 125.1 ... 448
r 125.8 ... 450, 468
r 127 ... 465
r 130 ... 448
r 138 ... 450, 468
ACtHPR, Rules of Court (1 September 2020)
  r 9.3 ... 441
  rr 16–21 ... 441
  rr 22–23 ... 441
  r 27 ... 453
  r 30 ... 453
  r 36.3 ... 452
  r 40 ... 453
  r 42 ... 453
  r 44 ... 453
  r 55 ... 453
  r 59.4 ... 459
  r 63 ... 454
  r 64 ... 460
  r 66 ... 472
  r 74 ... 453
  r 78 ... 454
  rr 77–79 ... 453
American Declaration of the Rights and Duties of Man (adopted 2 May 1948) ... 81, 82, 129, 156, 302, 303, 304, 306, 315, 323, 325, 339, 340, 425, 490, 598
  Art I ... 477
  Art III ... 509
  Art IV ... 523, 524
  Art XI ... 490
  Arts XXXIX–XXXVIII ... 425
American Declaration on the Rights of Indigenous Peoples (2016) ... 313
ASEAN Human Rights Declaration (adopted 18 November 2012)

Art 11 ... 477
Art 14 ... 494
Art 22 ... 509
Art 23 ... 523, 524
Arts 26–38 ... 79
Baguio Declaration (22 April 1999) ... 606
Bangkok Declaration, A/CONF.157/ASRM/8, A/CONF.157/PC/59
　preamble ... 95, 96
　para 3 ... 96
　para 7 ... 95, 96
　para 8 ... 96
Brighton Declaration, adopted by the High-Level Conference on the Future of the European Court of Human Rights, (19–20 April 2012), paras 12, 15 ... 398
CAT, Rules of Procedure, CAT/C/3/Rev.6
　r 98 ... 242
　r 113.(f) ... 241
　r 114 ... 108
CCPR, Rules of Procedure, CCPR/C/3/Rev.12
　r 76 ... 252
　r 83 ... 242
　r 94 ... 108, 242
　r 99.(c) ... 241
CED, Rules of Procedure, CED/C/1 (22 June 2012)
　r 56 ... 186
CERD, Rules of Procedure, CERD/C/35/Rev.3
　r 94 ... 109, 242
CRDP, Rules of Procedure, CRPD/C/1/Rev.1 (10 October 2016)
　Annex, para 17 ... 282
Charter of the International Military Tribunal for the Far East (19 January 1946)
　Art 5 ... 106
CHR, Analysis of Various Draft International Bills of Rights (Item 8 on the Agenda), E/CN.4/W.16 (23 January 1947) ... 212
CHR, Assistance to Somalia in the field of human rights, Resolution 1993/86 (10 March 1993) ... 190
CHR, Conscientious objection to military service, Resolution 1989/59 (8 March 1989), para 1 ... 513
CHR, Question of human rights in the territories occupied as a result of hostilities in the Middle East, Resolution 6 (XXV) (4 March 1969) ... 190, 201
CHR, Question of integrating the rights of women into the human rights mechanisms of the United Nations and the elimination of violence against women, E/CN.4/RES/1994/45 (4 March 1994) ... 572
CHR, Question of missing and disappeared persons, Resolution 20(XXXVI) (29 February 1980) ... 482
CHR, Question of the realization of the economic and social rights contained in the Universal Declaration of Human Rights and in the International Covenant on Economic, Social and Cultural Rights, and study of special problems relating to human rights in developing countries, Resolution 14 (XXV) (13 March 1969) ... 202
CHR, Question of the violation of human rights in the occupied Arab territories, including Palestine, Resolution 1993/2 (19 February 1993)
　para 4(a) ... 190
　para 4(a)–(c) ... 190
CHR, Report on the Thirty-Fourth Session, E/CN.4/1292 (1978), Resolution 24 (XXXIV), Regional arrangements for the promotion and protection of human rights ... 421
CHR, Report on the Twenty-Six Session, E/CN.4/1039 (1970), Resolution 6 (XXVI) ... 420
CHR, Resolution 2 (XXIII) (1967) ... 181, 201
CHR, Resolution 6 (XXIII) (16 March 1967) ... 420
CHR, Resolution 8 (XXIII) (1967) ... 181, 201
CHR, Resolution 1993/45 (5 March 1993) ... 524
CHR, Resolution 2000/82 (27 April 2000) ... 203
CHR, Situation of human rights in Cambodia, Resolution 1993/6 (19 February 1993) ... 190
CHR, Situation of human rights in Myanmar, Resolution 1992/58 (3 March 1992) ... 190
CHR, Summary of information regarding consideration by the United Nations organs of the question of the establishment of a post of United Nations High Commission for Human Rights, E/CN.4/Sub.2/1982/26 (30 July 1982) ... 212
CHR, The situation of human rights in Equatorial Guinea, Resolution 15 (XXXV) (13 March 1979) ... 201
Committee of Ministers, Resolution (99)50, On the Council of Europe Commissioner for Human Rights (7 May 1999)
　Art 1 ... 368
　Art 2 ... 368
　Art 3 ... 368
　Art 10 ... 368
　Art 11 ... 368
Committee of Ministers, Rules for the supervision of the execution of judgments and of the terms of friendly settlements (adopted 10 May 2006, and amended 18 January 2017)
　r 7 ... 401
　r 9 ... 369
　r 16 ... 402
　r 17 ... 401

TABLE OF TREATIES

Declaration by the United Nations (1 January 1942) ... 37
Declaration of Independence of the United States (adopted on 4 July 1776) ... 23, 25, 562
Declaration of Dakar (1967), Conclusions, Art VI.3 ... 419
Declaration of Principles on Freedom of Expression (2000) ... 313
Declaration of Santiago, Chile, adopted on the occasion of the Fifth Meeting of Consultation of Ministers of Foreign Affairs, Santiago, Chile, August 12 to 18, 1959, Final Act, Doc. OEA/Ser.C/II.5, Resolution VIII ... 305
Declaration of the Rights of Man and of the Citizen (26 August 1789) ... 23, 39, 50, 53
 Art 1 ... 24
Declaration on Human Rights Education and Training (2011) ... 211
Declaration on the Right to Peace (2016) ... 211
Declaration on the Rights and Welfare of the African Child (1979) ... 430
ECtHR, Rules of the Court
 r A1.1 ... 377
 r A1.2 ... 377
 r A1.3 ... 377
 r 17 ... 375
 r 18 ... 375
 r 18B ... 375
 r 26 ... 377
 r 25.2 ... 375
 r 27A ... 375
 r 32 ... 382
 r 39 ... 108, 381, 382
 r 46.d ... 399
 r 47 ... 385, 398
 r 47.4 ... 385
 r 49 ... 376
 r 49.2 ... 376
 r 51.2 ... 399
 r 52.1 ... 375
 r 52A.2 ... 376
 r 60 ... 390
 r 61 ... 394
 r 61.3 ... 394
 r 61.5 ... 394
 r 61.7 ... 394
 r 79 ... 381
 r 80 ... 381
 r 81 ... 381
ECOSOC, Disappeared Persons, Resolution 1979/38 (10 May 1979)
 para 1 ... 202
ECOSOC, Exploitation of labour though illicit and clandestine trafficking, Resolution 1706 (LIII) (28 July 1972)
 para 4 ... 275

ECOSOC, International Covenant on Economic, Social and Cultural Rights, Resolution 1987/5 (26 May 1987)
 para 9 ... 255
ECOSOC, Procedure for dealing with communications concerning human rights, Resolution 2000/3 (16 June 2000) ... 182
ECOSOC, Resolution 5(I), E/27 (22 February 1946) ... 60
ECOSOC, Resolution 2/11 (21 June 1946) ... 260, 565
ECOSOC, Resolution 350 (XII) (17 March 1951) ... 200
ECOSOC, Resolution 442 C (XIV) ... 524
ECOSOC, Resolution 728F (XXVIII), E/3290 (30 July 1959) ... 180
ECOSOC, Resolution 1235 (XLII), E/4393 (1967) ... 181, 199, 200
 para 1 ... 201
ECOSOC, Resolution 1503(XLVIII), E/4832/Add.1 (27 May 1970) ... 93, 181, 182
ECOSOC, Resolution 1982/34 (7 May 1982) ... 600
ECOSOC, Rationalization of the work of the Commission on Human Rights, Decision 1999/256 (27 July 1999) ... 184
ECOSOC, Review of the composition, organization and administrative arrangements of the Sessional Working Group of Governmental Experts on the Implementation of the International Covenant on Economic, Social and Cultural Rights, Resolution 1985/17 (28 May 1985) ... 76, 233, 255
 para (c) ... 255
Geneva Declaration of the Rights of the Child (adopted 26 September 1924) ... 31, 577
HRC, Combating defamation of religions, Resolution 7/19 (27 March 2008) ... 537
HRC, Combating intolerance, negative stereotyping and stigmatization of, and discrimination, incitement to violence and violence against, persons based on religion or belief, A/HRC/RES/16/18 (12 April 2011) ... 537
HRC, Elaboration of an international legally binding instrument on transnational corporations and other business enterprises with respect to human rights, A/HRC/RES/26/9 (14 July 2014) ... 231
HRC, Ensuring respect for international law in the Occupied Palestinian Territory, including East Jerusalem, Resolution S-21/1 (23 July 2014) ... 190
HRC, Follow-up to Human Rights Council resolution 5/1, Decision 6/102 (27 September 2007) ... 211

HRC, Follow-up to the Human Rights Council resolution 16/21 with regard to the universal periodic review, Decision 17/119 (19 July 2011)
  para 3 ... 195
HRC, From rhetoric to reality: a global call for concrete action against racism, racial discrimination, xenophobia and related intolerance, Resolution 48/18 (11 October 2021) ... 211
HRC, Human rights situation in the Occupied Palestinian Territory, Special session resolution S-1/1 (6 July 2006) ... 187, 190
HRC, Human rights violations emanating from Israeli military incursions in the Occupied Palestinian Territory, including the recent one in northern Gaza and the assault on Beit Hanoun, Resolution S-3/1 (15 November 2006) ... 190
HRC, Institution-building of the United Nations Human Rights Council, Resolution 5/1 (18 June 2007)
  Annex
    I.C ... 193
    II ... 200
    V.B ... 189
    para 1 ... 193
    para 2 ... 193
    para 3.(g) ... 193
    para 3.(h)–(i) ... 194
    para 4 ... 193
    para 15 ... 194
    para 18.(c) ... 195
    para 18.(d) ... 194
    para 19 ... 194
    paras 26–32 ... 195
    paras 29–31 ... 195
    para 31 ... 195
    paras 33–34 ... 195
    para 41 ... 200
    para 45 ... 200
    para 60 ... 202
    para 65 ... 210
    para 66 ... 210
    para 67 ... 211
    para 70 ... 211
    para 72 ... 211
    para 73 ... 210
    para 74 ... 211
    paras 75–76 ... 210
    para 77 ... 210
    para 79 ... 211
    paras 85–86 ... 208
    para 87 ... 208, 209
    paras 93–94 ... 208
    para 95 ... 209
    paras 96–97 ... 209
    para 98 ... 209
    para 101 ... 208
    para 104 ... 209
    para 108 ... 208
    para 109 ... 209
HRC, Israeli settlements in the Occupied Palestinian Territory, including East Jerusalem, and in the occupied Syrian Golan, Resolution 19/17 (22 March 2012) ... 190
HRC, Mandate of the Independent Expert on protection against violence and discrimination based on sexual orientation and gender identity, A/HRC/RES/41/18 (12 July 2019) ... 206
HRC, Mandate of Independent Expert on protection against violence and discrimination based on sexual orientation and gender identity, A/HRC/50/L.2 (30 June 2022) ... 206
HRC, Mandate of the Special Rapporteur on the promotion and protection of human rights in the context of climate change, Resolution 48/14 (8 October 2021) ... 211
HRC, Open-ended intergovernmental working group to consider the possibility of elaborating an international regulatory framework on the regulation, monitoring and oversight of the activities of private military and security companies, A/HRC/RES/15/26 (7 October 2010) ... 231
HRC, Open-ended Working Group on an optional protocol to the International Covenant on Economic, Social and Cultural Rights, Resolution 1/3 (29 June 2006)
  para 2 ... 257
HRC, Optional Protocol to the International Covenant on Economic, Social and Cultural Rights, Resolution 8/2 (18 June 2008) ... 257
HRC, Report of the Human Rights Council on its eighteenth session, A/HRC/18/2 (11 November 2011)
  para 210 ... 210
HRC, Report of the Human Rights Council on its seventh organizational meeting, A/HRC/OM/7/1 (4 April 2013) ... 196
HRC, Report of the open-ended intergovernmental working group on the review of the work and functioning of the Human Rights Council, A/HRC/WG.8/2/1 (4 May 2011) ... 188
HRC, Resolution 2001/57 (24 April 2001) ... 600
  para 1.b ... 601
HRC, Resolution 6/12 (28 September 2007) ... 600
  para 1.a ... 601
  para 1.c ... 601
HRC, Resolution 6/36 (14 December 2007) ... 600
HRC, Resolution 33/25 (30 September 2016), para 1 ... 600

TABLE OF TREATIES

HRC, The human right to a clean, healthy and sustainable environment, Resolution 48/13, A/HRC/48/L.23/Rev. 1 (5 October 2021) ... 590
HRC, Review of the work and functioning of the Human Rights Council, A/HRC/RES/16/21 (12 April 2011) ... 188, 196
   Annex, II ... 200
HRC, Situation of human rights in Eritrea, A/HRC/RES/21/1 (9 October 2021) ... 210
HRC, Situation of human rights in Kyrgyzstan, Decision 2/101 (2 October 2006) ... 209
HRC, Technical assistance and capacity building, A/HRC/6/L.29/Rev. 1 (26 September 2007) ... 187
HRC, The deteriorating human rights situation in Ukraine stemming from the Russian aggression, A/HRC/RES/S-34/1 (16 May 2022) ... 187
HRC, The Grave Attacks by Israeli Forces against the Humanitarian Boat Convoy, Resolution 14/1 (2 June 2010) ... 190
HRC, The grave violations of human rights in the Occupied Palestinian Territory, particularly due to the recent Israeli military attacks against the occupied Gaza Strip, Resolution S-9/1 (12 January 2009) ... 190
HRC, World Programme for Human Rights Education, Resolution 39/3 (3 October 2018) ... 187
HRC, Violations of international law in the context of large-scale civilian protests in the Occupied Palestinian Territory, including East Jerusalem, Resolution S-28/1 (18 May 2018) ... 190
IACHR, Rules of Procedure
   Art 11 ... 314
   Art 13 ... 314
   Art 18 ... 316
   Art 23 ... 339
   Art 25 ... 345
   Art 25.1 ... 108, 345
   Art 25.2 ... 345
   Art 26 ... 324
   Art 29 ... 324
   Art 30 ... 324
   Art 32.2 ... 342
   Art 36 ... 324
   Art 37 ... 324
   Art 40 ... 324
   Art 45 ... 325
   Art 46 ... 325
   Art 47 ... 326
   Art 48 ... 324, 326
   Art 50.1 ... 350
   Art 51 ... 339
   Art 59 ... 316
   Art 59.7 ... 316
   Art 59.10 ... 316
   Art 74 ... 326
   Art 74.3 ... 325
IACtHR, Rules of Procedure
   Art 3 ... 317
   Art 4 ... 317
   Art 6 ... 345
   Art 7 ... 318
   Art 16.4 ... 318
   Art 19 ... 318
   Art 22.2 ... 328
   Art 23 ... 328
   Art 27.6 ... 345
   Art 27.7 ... 346
   Art 28.2 ... 340
   Art 28.4 ... 341
   Art 28.5 ... 341
   Art 28.6 ... 341
   Art 37 ... 328
   Arts 39–41 ... 329
   Art 44.2 ... 328
   Art 51 ... 340
   Art 52 ... 340
   Art 65 ... 330
   Art 69 ... 335
   Art 76 ... 337
ILC, Responsibility of States for Internationally Wrongful Acts, A/56/10 (2001)
   Art 1 ... 354
   Art 2 ... 354
   Art 4 ... 354
   Arts 40–41 ... 137
Interlaken Declaration (19 February 2010) ... 374, 397
Mexico Declaration and Plan of Action to Strengthen the International Protection of Refugees in Latin America (16 November 2004) ... 100
   Preamble ... 100
San José Declaration on Refugees and Displaced Persons, (5–7 December 1994) ... 100
   Preamble ... 100
   para 3 ... 95
Statute of the Inter-American Commission on Human Rights (approved through Resolution No 447 adopted by the OAS General Assembly during its ninth period of sessions, held in La Paz, Bolivia, in October 1979) ... 314
   Art 12 ... 317
   Art 14 ... 318
   Art 18.g ... 314
   Art 19 ... 315
   Art 20 ... 315
   Art 21.3 ... 314

Art 22 ... 317
Art 23.2 ... 325
Art 23.3 ... 318
Statute of the International Criminal Tribunal for the Former Yugoslavia, adopted by UNSC Resolution 827 (25 May 1993)
Art 1 ... 105
Statute of the International Tribunal for Rwanda, adopted by UNSC Resolution 955 (8 November 1994)
Art 1 ... 105
UN Declaration on Principles of International Law concerning Friendly Relations and Cooperation among States (1971) ... 469
UNGA, 2005 World Summit Outcome, A/RES/60/1 (24 October 2005)
para 157 ... 185
UNGA, Affirmation of the principles of international law recognized by the Charter of the Nuremberg Tribunal, A/RES/95(1) (11 December 1946) ... 104
UNGA, Alternative approaches and ways and means within the United Nations system for improving the effective enjoyment of human rights and fundamental freedoms, A/RES/32/130 (16 December 1977) ... 74
UNGA, Combating defamation of religions, A/RES/62/154 (6 March 2008) ... 537
UNGA, Combating intolerance, negative stereotyping, stigmatization, discrimination, incitement to violence and violence against persons, based on religion or belief, A/RES/66/167 (27 March 2012) ... 537
UNGA, Comprehensive and integral international convention to promote and protect the rights and dignity of persons with disabilities A/RES/56/168 (19 December 2001) ... 280
UNGA, Declaration of the Rights of the Child, Resolution 1386 (XIV), A/4354 (20 November 1959) ... 179, 577
UNGA, Declaration on Principles of International Law concerning Friendly Relations and Co-operation among States in accordance with the Charter of the United Nations, A/RES/2625 (XXV) (24 October 1970) ... 596
UNGA, Declaration on the Elimination of All Forms of Intolerance and of Discrimination Based on Religion or Belief, Resolution 36/55 (25 November 1981) ... 179
Art 6 ... 510
UNGA, Declaration on the Elimination of Violence against Women, Resolution 48/104 (20 December 1993)
Preamble ... 499, 570
Art 1 ... 571
Art 4 ... 499, 572
UNGA, Declaration on the Granting of Independence to Colonial Countries and Peoples, Resolution 1514 (XV) (14 December 1960) ... 592, 596, 606
UNGA, Declaration on the Rights of Indigenous Peoples, A/RES/61/295 (2 October 2007) ... 132, 600, 601, 607
Art 3 ... 606
Art 29.1 ... 603
Art 46 ... 601
UNGA, Declaration on the Protection of All Persons from Being Subjected to Torture and Other Cruel, Inhuman or Degrading Treatment or Punishment Resolution 3452 (XXX) (9 December 1975) ... 265
Art 1 ... 494, 496, 497
Art 1.2 ... 501
UNGA, Declaration on the Protection of all Persons from Enforced Disappearance, Resolution 47/133 (18 December 1992) ... 284, 482
Preamble ... 482
Art 1.2 ... 481
Art 17.1 ... 481
UNGA, Declaration on the Right to Development, Resolution 41/128 (4 December 1986) ... 590
UNGA, Declaration on the Right to Peace, A/RES/71/189 (2 February 2017) ... 177, 590
UNGA, Declaration on the Rights of Disabled Person, A/RES/3447(XXX) (9 December 1975) ... 280
UNGA, Declaration on the Rights of Mentally Retarded Persons, A/RES/2856 (XXVI) (1971) ... 280
UNGA, Draft International Covenant on Humans Rights and Measures of Implementation: Future Work of the Commission on Human Rights, A/RES/421(V) (4 December 1950) ... 69
UNGA, Exploitation of labour though illicit and clandestine trafficking, Resolution 2920 (XXVII) (15 November 1972)
para 3 ... 275
UNGA, Disappeared Persons, Resolution 33/173 (20 December 1978)
para 2 ... 202
UNGA, Follow-up to the Second World Assembly on Ageing, A/RES/65/182 (4 February 2011) ... 231
UNGA, Further actions and initiatives to implement the Beijing Declaration and Platform for Action, A/RES/S-23/3 (16 November 2000) ... 567
UNGA, Human Rights Council, Resolution 60/251 (3 April 2006) ... 184
para 1 ... 188
para 2 ... 187

TABLE OF TREATIES

para 5.(e) ... 193
para 6 ... 208
para 7 ... 185, 186
para 8 ... 186
para 10 ... 187
para 16 ... 188
UNGA, High Commisioner for the promotion and protection of all human rights, A/RES/48/141 (20 December 1993) ... 211, 213
para 2 ... 212
para 5 ... 213
UNGA, Importance of the experience of the Ad Hoc Working Group on the Situation of Human Rights in Chile, A/RES/33/176 (20 December 1978) ... 201
UNGA, Measures to ensure the human rights and dignity of all migrant workers, Resolution 3449 (XXX) (9 December 1975) ... 275
UNGA, Measures to improve the situation and ensure the human rights and dignity of all migrant workers, Resolution 31/127 (16 December 1976) ... 275
UNGA, Measures to improve the situation and ensure the human rights and dignity of al migrant workers, Resolution 32/120 (16 December 1977) ... 275
UNGA, Measures to improve the situation and ensure the human rights and dignity of all migrant workers, Resolution 33/163 (20 December 1978) ... 275
UNGA, Measures to improve the situation and ensure the human rights and dignity of all migrant workers, Resolution 34/172 (17 December 1979)
UNGA, Measures to improve the situation of migrant workers, Resolution 3224 (XXIX) (6 November 1974) ... 275
UNGA, Principles relating to the Status of National Institutions (The Paris Principles), Resolution 48/134 (20 December 1993) ... 282
UNGA, Report of the ILC on the work of its forty-fourth session, A/RES/47/33 (9 February 1992), para 6 ... 105
UNGA, Reporting obligations of States parties to United Nations instruments on human rights, Resolution 42/105 (7 December 1987) ... 288
UNGA, Reporting obligations under the United Nations instruments on human rights, Resolution 41/121 (4 December 1986) ... 288
UNGA, Draft convention against torture and other cruel, inhuman or degrading treatment or punishment, Resolution 32/62 (8 December 1977) ... 265
UNGA, Draft declaration on the elimination of discrimination against women, Resolution 1921(XVIII) (5 December 1963) ... 260, 565

UNGA, Resolution 421 (V) of 4 December 1950 ... 592
UNGA, Preparation of two Drafts International Covenants on Human Rights, Resolution 543/VI (1951), A/RES/543(VI) ... 69
UNGA, Resolution 545 (VI) of 5 February 1952 ... 592
UNGA, Resolution 637 (VII) of 16 December 1952 ... 592
UNGA, Resolution 3452 (XXX) (9 December 1975) ... 494
UNGA, Regional arrangements for the promotion and protection of human rights, Resolution 32/127 (16 December 1977) ... 421
UNGA, Resolution Res.33/167 (20 December 1978) ... 421
UNGA, Resolution 37/194 (18 December 1982) ... 495
UNGA, Resolution 70/175, Annex (17 December 2015) ... 494
UNGA, Respect for an implementation of human rights in occupied territories, Resolution 2443(XXIII) (19 December 1968) ... 190
UNGA, Review of the Human Rights Council, A/RES/65/281 (20 July 2011) ... 188, 196
UNGA, Standard Rules on the Equalization of Opportunities for Persons with Disabilities Resolution 48/96 (20 December 1993) ... 280
UNGA, Strengthening and enhancing the effective functioning of the human rights treaty body system, A/RES/68/268 (21 April 2014)
para 1 ... 237
para 10 ... 234
para 11 ... 233
para 13 ... 234
paras 15–16 ... 236
paras 26–27 ... 234
UNGA, Suspension of the rights of membership of the Libyan Arab Jamahiriya in the Human Rights Council, A/RES/65/265 (3 March 2011) ... 186
UNGA, Suspension of the rights of membership of the Russian Federation in the Human Rights Council, A/RES/ES-11/3 (7 April 2022) ... 186
UNGA, Territorial Application of the International Covenant on Human Rights, A/RES/422(V) (4 December 1950) ... 70
UNGA, The Crime of Genocide, A/REWS/96(1) (11 December 1946) ... 104
UNGA, Transforming our world: the 2030 Agenda for Sustainable Development, A/RES/70/1 (21 October 2015) ... 567
UNGA, United Nations Standard Minimum Rules for the Treatment of Prisoners (Nelson Mandela Rules), A/RES/70/175 ... 132

UNGA, World Conference on Human Rights, A/RES/45/155 1990 (18 December 1990) . . . 95
UNGA, World Programme of Action concerning Disabled Persons, Resolution 37/52 (3 December 1982) . . . 280
Universal Declaration of Human Rights (UDHR) (adopted 10 December 1948) UNGA Res. 217.A(III) . . . 1, 4, 7, 14, 15, 16, 24, 38, 50, 54, 59, 62, 64, 66, 68–75, 81, 100, 104, 112, 114, 126, 128, 129, 151, 179, 193, 219, 292, 302, 418, 442, 565
  Preamble . . . 7, 54, 565
  Art 1 . . . 24, 50, 142, 478, 543
  Art 2 . . . 54
  Arts 2–21 . . . 69
  Art 3 . . . 50, 477
  Art 5 . . . 50, 494
  Art 10 . . . 14, 50, 565
  Art 11 . . . 14, 565
  Art 12 . . . 535, 565
  Art 13 . . . 565
  Art 14.1 . . . 100
  Art 15 . . . 565
  Art 17 . . . 565
  Art 18 . . . 509, 565
  Art 19 . . . 523, 524
  Art 21 . . . 14, 565
  Art 22–28 . . . 69
  Art 22 . . . 565
  Art 23 . . . 565
  Art 25 . . . 490, 565
  Art 25.2 . . . 577
  Art 26 . . . 14
  Art 29 . . . 565
Vienna Declaration and Programme of Action (1993) . . . 96, 97, 99
  para 1 . . . 97
  para 3 . . . 99
  para 6 . . . 97
  para 9 . . . 98
  para 13 . . . 96
  para 14 . . . 98
  para 15 . . . 97
  para 18 . . . 97
  para 20 . . . 97
  para 21 . . . 99
  para 23 . . . 99
  para 23–24 . . . 97
  para 25 . . . 98
  para 28–29 . . . 99
  para 38 . . . 96

We all live in time, which eventually consumes us all. Precisely because of this self-perception we have of ourselves as existing in time, each one of us seeks to envisage a life project. The term 'project' implies in itself a temporal dimension. The concept of life project has therefore an essentially existential value, grounded in the idea of complete personal achievement. In other words, within the framework of a transient life, people have the right to make the options they feel are best, of their own free will, in order to achieve their ideals. Therefore, endeavors to achieve a life project appear to have great existential value, and the potential to give meaning to each person's life.

I see no reason, in view of time going by, why one should exercise restraint in searching for meaning for one's life, for the life we know, for the world of those that are still alive; in fact, in my opinion, both the life project and the after-life hold fundamental values.

We are all bound together—rather than separated—in time. Remembrance is a duty of the living toward their dead; the dead need the remembrance from their surviving loved ones so that they do not cease to exist once and for all.

Separate opinion of Judge Antônio Augusto Cançado Trindade
IACtHR, *Gutiérrez Soler v. Colombia* (12 September 2005)

PART I

FOUNDATIONS, HISTORY, AND LEGAL FRAMEWORK

Part One provides an introduction to the international law of human rights across three chapters. **Chapter 1** covers three main topics. It begins with a discussion about the meaning and main characteristics of the idea of 'human rights', then explores one of the many possible histories of this concept. The final section of this chapter presents four different 'critiques' of human rights, providing theoretically grounded tools to query the definition and history presented. The selected critiques are those grounded on Marxist, feminist, postmodern, and postcolonial theories.

Chapter 2 provides a discussion of the temporal and substantive development of the international law of human rights, starting with the creation of the United Nations, where the history of human rights was left in **Chapter 1**. This chapter explores the process of adoption of the so-called International Bill of Human Rights—comprising the 1948 Universal Declaration of Human Rights and two significant treaties adopted in 1966—and of the mechanisms for the implementation of the protected rights. **Chapter 2** places special emphasis on the 'traditional' debate concerning the distinction between civil and political rights, on the one hand, and economic, social, and cultural rights, on the other, to conclude that such a dated differentiation of rights should be considered a relic of the past. The chapter then engages in further reflections on the development of the international law of human rights, focusing both on the convergence of different regimes for the international protection of individuals and on the meaning of time in the protection of rights.

Lastly, **Chapter 3** offers an important introduction to the normative framework of the protection of human rights under international law. This chapter is of particular relevance to those readers less acquainted with public international law as a discipline. It discusses the fundamental topics of sources, obligations, and subjects of international law, as applicable to the international law of human rights. The chapter concludes with an important reflection on the interaction between the international and domestic legal orders when dealing with the protection of rights.

1

HUMAN RIGHTS

1.1 THE MEANING OF HUMAN RIGHTS

The best-known definition of 'human rights' is the one that claims that these are *rights* inherent to all human beings by the mere fact of being *human* and, therefore, independent of any personal or contextual characteristic, such as nationality, ethnicity, gender, sexuality, religion, language, or any other status.[1] Human rights are, thus, characterized by their proclaimed universality, which is apparent in three different levels: every right, for every person, and everywhere. The idea that every person, irrespective of their personal characteristics or their geographic location, has a number of fundamental rights that are deserving of protection is certainly deeply attractive.[2] It has allowed human rights to become an invaluable tool for improving people's lives, being used in contemporary struggles against oppression, discrimination, deprivation, cruelty, and violence.[3]

In our days, the notion of human rights has acquired a central position in the fields of law and politics. The language of human rights has been accepted by governments and policy-makers, by academics and NGOs, by the media and wide sectors of the general population, and is seen by many as providing a framework for a progressive transformation of our social reality.[4] It can even be said that human rights are tantamount to a common language that allows victims of injustice to communicate their suffering in universally understandable terms.[5] They have been proclaimed the only political-moral idea that has received universal acceptance,[6]

---

[1] J. Donnelly, *The Concept of Human Rights* (Routledge 1985) 8; M. Ishay, *The History of Human Rights: From Ancient Times to the Globalization Era* (University of California Press 2004) 3; L. Hunt, *Inventing Human Rights: A History* (Norton and Company Press 2007) 20.

[2] A. Sen, 'Elements of a Theory of Human Rights' (2004) 32 *Philosophy and Public Affairs* 315, 315.

[3] V.S. Peterson and L. Parisi, 'Are Women Human? It's Not an Academic Question' in T. Evans (ed.) *Human Rights Fifty Years On: A Reappraisal* (Manchester University Press 1998) 132–160, 154; U. Baxi, *The Future of Human Rights* (2nd edn., OUP 2008) 3; D. Kennedy, 'The International Human Rights Movement: Part of the Problem?' (2002) 15 *Harvard Human Rights Journal* 101, 101.

[4] D. Chandler (ed.), *Rethinking Human Rights: Critical Approaches to International Politics* (Palgrave 2003) 1–4; C. Gearty, *Can Human Rights Survive?* (CUP 2006) 157; S. Benhabib, 'The Legitimacy of Human Rights' (2008) 137 *Daedalus* 94, 94.

[5] C. Beitz, *The Idea of Human Rights* (OUP 2009) 1.

[6] L. Henkin, *The Age of Rights* (Columbia University Press 1990) ix.

and even been declared the greatest legal invention of our civilization.[7] In short, human rights have become the ideology of our time.[8]

Human rights are conceived of as 'rights', which can be understood as significant interests that, in a given system, are granted priority over other interests, judged to be less important.[9] As such, they have been famously described as 'trumps'.[10] This means that rights would be usually conferred priority over other conflicting considerations, even though such priority is not absolute, and, under certain circumstances, rights might fail to trump conflicting interests at stake.[11] Importantly, the main function of rights is to give rise to regulated interactions by which the right-holder has an entitlement to a specific behaviour, either an action or inaction, from a duty-bearer.[12] In the case of human rights, every human is a right-holder, while States are the main duty-bearers.[13]

At present, it is quite unproblematic to affirm that human rights are *legal* rights. From 1948 onwards, with the adoption of the Universal Declaration of Human Rights, the international community began a seemingly unstoppable and ever-growing process of proclaiming human rights under international law.[14] Some authors have even claimed that it is only from the time at which the international community came to an agreement on the existence of individuals' rights that must be protected worldwide that we can properly speak of human rights[15]—a rather positivist approach.[16] Conversely, other authors believe human rights to be *pre*-legal; having an existence prior and independent of their legal acknowledgement.[17] Indeed, it is not uncommon for human rights to be described as 'moral' rights; namely, rights that are affirmed and justified following moral principles that determine what is right/wrong and just/unfair with regards to the treatment of human beings,[18] and which

---

[7] C.S. Nino, *The Ethics of Human Rights* (Clarendon Press 1993) 1.

[8] U. Baxi, 'Voices of Suffering and the Future of Human Rights' (1998) 8 *Transnational Law and Contemporary Problems* 125, 126; C. Douzinas, 'Humanity, Military Humanism and the New Moral Order' (2003) 32 *Economy and Society* 159, 161.

[9] J. Donnelly, *The Concept of Human Rights* (Routledge 1985) 5.

[10] R. Dworkin, *Taking Rights Seriously* (Harvard University Press 1977) xi.

[11] J. Donnelly, 'Human Rights and Human Dignity: An Analytic Critique of Non-Western Conceptions of Human Rights' (1982) 76 *American Political Science Review* 303, 305; J. Nickel, *Making Sense of Human Rights* (2nd edn., Blackwell 2007) 9.

[12] J. Donnelly, *The Concept of Human Rights* (Routledge 1985) 12; C.S. Nino, *The Ethics of Human Rights* (Clarendon Press 1993) 26–29.

[13] S. Besson, 'The Bearers of Human Rights' Duties and Responsibilities for Human Rights: A Quiet (R)Evolution?' (2015) 32 *Social Philosophy & Policy* 244, 248, 253, 267.

[14] This development, which we call the 'international law of human rights', is the focus of **Chapter 2**.

[15] M. Pinto, *Temas de Derechos Humanos* (Del Puerto 1997) 15–16; A. Buchanan, *The Heart of Human Rights* (OUP 2013) 11.

[16] A main tenet of legal positivism is the conviction that the validity of the law is determined by the process of its adoption, being 'posited' by the pertinent law-making authority, irrespective of its content and its relation to morality. See: C.S. Nino, 'Dworkin and Legal Positivism' (1980) 89 *Mind* 519, 519–520.

[17] G. Bidart Campos, 'La Interpretación del Sistema de Derechos Humanos' (1994) 19 *Revista IIDH* 11, 14.

[18] C.S. Nino, 'Sobre los Derechos Morales' (1990) 7 *Doxa: Cuadernos de Filosofía del Derecho* 311, 316; J. Raz, 'Human Rights in the Emerging World Order' (2010) 1 *Transnational Legal Theory* 31, 34; J. Tasioulas, 'On the Nature of Human Rights' in G. Ernst and J-C. Heilinger (eds.), *The Philosophy of Human Rights Contemporary Controversies* (De Gruyter 2012) 17–59, 27–28.

the law merely recognizes.[19] As will be further discussed in **Section 1.1.1.3**, scholars adopting a 'moral' conception of human rights share the belief that the justification for the existence of human rights is to be found outside the realm of the law, being independent from it, although the actual principles underpinning human rights would vary, depending on their moral and philosophical standpoint.

An undeniable advantage of moral approaches to human rights is that they provide grounds for employing the language of human rights to oppose social injustice and oppression even in the absence of concrete legal norms. Under such a gaze, an injustice could be criticized as a human rights violation, irrespective of whether a particular State has become Party to a specific treaty—or bound by a customary norm—or even in the absence of a specific right crafted in precise terms that would protect against such an injustice.[20] Following these approaches to human rights, the fact that a specific 'moral' right has been enshrined into positive law is not a requirement for its existence as a human right. However, even from a moral approach, the legal recognition of a human right would be seen as a convenient development, as it would make the respective moral right more certain and less controverted, while also providing means for legal redress.[21]

1.1.1 PHILOSOPHICAL EXPLORATIONS OF THE IDEA OF HUMAN RIGHTS

Whether or not human rights can be said to exist in the absence of legal recognition, the justification given either for their existence (if considered pre-legal) or for their (legal) adoption is important, providing us with reasons for their respect and protection that go beyond mere pragmatism, concerning adverse legal consequences for their breach. The main philosophical approaches to the foundation of human rights are provided by the so-called moral and political conceptions. As discussed in **Section 1.1.1.3**, these two conceptions need not be understood as truly competing approaches. They can also be thought of as schools of thought that focus on different aspects of the contemporary idea of human rights;[22] hence providing different explanations as to the foundation of rights, which could even be seen as complementary.

1.1.1.1 Moral conceptions of human rights

Moral conceptions of human rights are usually considered to be the 'orthodox' approach to the philosophical exploration of human rights. Within this school of thought, philosophers of human rights have developed different frameworks to ground rights

---

[19] C.S. Nino, *The Ethics of Human Rights* (Clarendon Press 1993) 10; S. Besson, 'Human Rights: Ethical, Political ... or Legal? First Steps in a Legal Theory of Human Rights' in D.E. Childres (ed.), *The Role of Ethics in International Law* (CUP 2011) 211–245, 219.

[20] C.S. Nino, *Ética y Derechos Humanos: Un Ensayo de Fundamentación* (2nd edn., Astrea 1989) 48; C. Beitz, *The Idea of Human Rights* (OUP 2009) 49.

[21] C.S. Nino, *Ética y Derechos Humanos: Un Ensayo de Fundamentación* (2nd edn., Astrea 1989) 24–25.

[22] L. Henkin, 'International Human Rights as "Rights"' (1981) 23 *Nomos* 257, 262; C. Beitz, 'Human Rights as a Common Concern' (2001) 95 *American Political Science Review* 269, 280.

in specific moral principles from which they could be derived. Given the universal character attributed to human rights, the philosophical foundations provided to them tend to begin with identifying characteristics universally shared by all human beings. Thus, human rights are 'derived' as necessary tools to protect or realize such important common human features.

These philosophical approaches differ on the specific grounds and reasons for the underlying principles identified. Hence, autonomy, dignity, equality, justice, inviolability, human capabilities, and individuals' needs have all been proposed either in isolation or in combination with one another as potential grounding principles from which human rights can be derived.[23] For instance, Carlos Nino founded his moral theory of human rights on the combination of three liberal principles: autonomy—individuals' ability to guide their lives according to their personal moral views; inviolability—the prohibition to treat individuals as means for ulterior ends; and dignity—the treatment of individuals according to their own decisions.[24] James Griffin developed a theory of rights based on his understanding of the principle of 'normative agency', which refers to individuals' capacity to conceive their own idea of a good life and to pursue this conception without external interference.[25] A somewhat different approach is the one adopted by Alan Gewirth, whose theory does not technically derive rights from underpinning moral principles but, in turn, presents the essential principle of 'human agency' as logically necessitating a minimum set of fundamental rights to secure its exercise by individuals.[26]

Moral theories of human rights have been confronted by two main lines of argument. The first proposes that the search for the foundation of rights could be abandoned, because human rights have become an unquestionable fact. The second—increasingly becoming the mainstream approach—suggests that the justification of human rights should not be searched for in their moral underpinnings, but in their significant political function as governing principles of the contemporary international community. Neither of these lines of argument present a strong attack against moral foundationalism in human rights *per se*, but they propose that the most important debates concerning human rights lie beyond contested moral principles.

1.1.1.2 The consensus approach to human rights

The first of the abovementioned arguments can be labelled the 'consensus' approach.[27] The focus of this theory is not on the human, as holder of rights, but on the rights

---

[23] See, among others: A. Gewirth, *Reason and Morality* (University of Chicago Press 1978); C.S. Nino, *The Ethics of Human Rights* (Clarendon Press 1993); M. Nussbaum, 'Capabilities and Human Rights' (1997) 66 *Fordham Law Review* 274; A. Sen, 'Elements of a Theory of Human Rights' (2004) 32 *Philosophy and Public Affairs* 315; J. Nickel, *Making Sense of Human Rights* (2nd edn., Blackwell 2007); J. Griffin, *On Human Rights* (OUP 2008); W. Talbott, *Human Rights and Human Well-Being* (OUP 2010); D. Miller, 'Grounding Human Rights' (2012) 15 *Critical Review of International Social and Political Philosophy* 407; J. Tasioulas, 'On the Foundations of Human Rights' in R. Cruft, S.M. Liao, and M. Renzo (eds.), *Philosophical Foundations of Human Rights* (OUP 2015) 45–70.
[24] C.S. Nino, *The Ethics of Human Rights* (Clarendon Press 1993), esp. Chapter 5.
[25] J. Griffin, *On Human Rights* (OUP 2008).
[26] A. Gewirth, *Reason and Morality* (University of Chicago Press 1978).
[27] Beitz refers to these as 'agreement theories'. See: C. Beitz, *The Idea of Human Rights* (OUP 2009), Chapter 4.

themselves. It affirms that in the aftermath of the genocide committed by Nazi Germany the world changed dramatically, including the emergence of a culture of human rights. This culture has evolved to become an undeniable fact of the world, thereby rendering the search for justifications for the existence of human rights 'outmoded'.[28] The legitimacy of human rights under international law would then be provided by the existence of an actual (or developing) consensus among States. This approach grounds the authority of human rights in the fact that the international community has actually reached the agreement that a certain number of human rights must be respected and protected, which can be confirmed by the large number of States Parties to multiple human rights treaties.[29] There are two possible versions of the 'consensus' theory. The first is a more restricted and pragmatic stance, which avoids drawing inferences from the consensus reached, beyond the fact that the international community has managed, for a plurality of reasons, to commit to the protection of these rights. A second more ambitious version, takes the level of consensus reached among States as evidence of the existence of a cross-cultural agreement in the actual values underpinning human rights.[30]

However, the pragmatic (and positivist) approach to human rights of the supporters of the consensus theory encounters different problems. First, the existence of a universal consensus could be questioned. It certainly did not exist at the time of the proclamation of the Universal Declaration of Human Rights by, what can be considered, a relatively small number of States—in comparison to what the UN Membership would become following the process of de-colonization. To overcome this objection, consensus theorists can, in turn, propose the notion of a developing, rather than universally agreed, consensus. According to this stance, human rights were not adopted as a reflection of universal consensus, but with the conviction and desire that such consensus would be reached. The actual language of the 1948 Declaration would certainly indicate this,[31] as the General Assembly adopted it as 'a common standard of achievement for all peoples and all nations'.[32] In other words, the idea of human rights would be based on values that are capable of being agreed upon by different cultures worldwide and their proclamation was geared towards reaching such a universal agreement.[33] This stance

---

[28] E. Rabossi, 'La Teoría de los Derechos Humanos Naturalizada' (1990) 5 *Revista del Centro de Estudios Constitucionales* 159; R. Rorty, 'Human Rights, Rationality and Sentimentality' in S. Shute and S. Hurley (eds.), *On Human Rights: The Oxford Amnesty Lectures* (Basic Books 1993) 111–134; N. Bobbio, *The Age of Rights* (Polity 1996) 12–31.

[29] N. Bobbio, *The Age of Rights* (Polity 1996) 13–15.

[30] Nonetheless, the stronger version of the 'consensus' theory could be said to lack of empirical support. As will be discussed in **Section 2.2.1**, even the rather small committee that drafted the Universal Declaration of Human Rights seemed to reach an agreement on the text, but not on its philosophical or moral foundations. See: J.P Humphrey, *Human Rights & the United Nations: a great adventure*(Transnational Publishers 1984) 66–67. See also: Human Rights: Comments and interpretations. A symposium edited by UNESCO, UNESCO/PHS/3(rev.), 25 July 1948, p. 1.

[31] C. Beitz, 'What Human Rights Mean' (2003) 132 *Daedalus* 36, 38.

[32] Universal Declaration of Human Rights (adopted 10 December 1948) UNGA Res 217 A(III) (UDHR), preamble.

[33] C. Gould, *Globalizing Democracy and Human Rights* (CUP 2004) 64–65; J. Cohen, 'Minimalism About Human Rights: The Most We Can Hope For?' (2004) 12 *Journal of Political Philosophy* 190, 194, 213.

could be reinforced by the fact that multiple human rights treaties adopted since the 1960s have received almost universal approval, even if the consensus on some of the rights could again be questioned, based on the reservations appended to them.

Another, perhaps more critical, problem the consensus approach can face is that while most of us would agree that the significance of human rights should not be questioned, that is certainly not enough to guarantee that views opposing human rights would not (continue to) emerge in the future. In fact, one of the most evident examples of attacks on some of the most incontrovertible rights, such as respect for personal integrity, enshrined in the absolute prohibition of torture, featured in policies and discourses from prominent political leaders and high-profile academics in the aftermath of the terrorist attacks in the United States on 11 September 2001.[34] Therefore, it can certainly be questioned whether debates about justifications for human rights are truly superfluous or outmoded.

1.1.1.3 Political conceptions of human rights

A different type of argument is the one that shifts the focus from the common characteristics of the right-holders or the existence of a human rights culture onto the behaviour of the duty-bearers, in search for justifications for the existence of human rights. This approach, usually referred to as the 'political' conception of human rights, is these days the main alternative view to the 'orthodox' school of thought. The political conception has led to the development of different political theories that provide grounds to justify counting human rights among the essential rules governing the international community of States.[35]

A well-known example of a political theory of human rights is the one proposed by John Rawls, following a similar pattern to the theory he developed to justify the adoption of principles of justice at the national level in his famous 1970s book *A Theory of Justice*.[36] His theory of human rights reproduced the previously developed ideas of the 'original position' and the 'veil of ignorance', applying them to the international sphere.[37] That is to say, human rights would be the rights that could be reasonably agreed upon by representatives of the different States of the international community if they were placed in a *position* in which they only knew that they were representing an independent State, but *ignored* the specific socio-economic, demographic, and political characteristics of their own State. The representatives in this fictional scenario are assumed to be rational actors that would be selecting prudently the basic rules to govern an international

---

[34] R. Gordon, *Mainstreaming Torture: Ethical Approaches in the Post-9/11 United States* (OUP 2014); R. Sanders, *Plausible Legality: Legal Culture and Political Imperative in the Global War on Terror* (OUP 2018).

[35] S. Besson, 'Human Rights: Ethical, Political . . . or Legal? First Steps in a Legal Theory of Human Rights' in D.E. Childres (ed.), *The Role of Ethics in International Law* (CUP 2011) 211–245, 223.

[36] J. Rawls, *A Theory of Justice* (Harvard University Press 1971); J. Rawls, *The Law of Peoples* (Harvard University Press 1999).

[37] In a nutshell, the book proposed a theory that could justify the principles of justice to be adopted in a liberal democratic State, based on the decisions that would be made by a group of rational individuals placed behind a hypothetical 'veil of ignorance' that inhibit them to know their own socio-economic status. See: J. Rawls, *A Theory of Justice* (Harvard University Press 1971) 11–22.

community, given the uncertainty of their State's own position. This theory proposes that the accepted rules would include some human rights standards.[38] In particular, this approach distances itself from 'consensus' theories, since the existence of a specific right is not a matter of empirical examination—the actual existence of a positive right under international law—but a matter of dialectic practice.[39]

Following Rawls, other authors have developed further political theories of human rights that build on the international practice developed by States.[40] For instance, Beitz proposed what he labelled a 'practical' conception of human rights, which is constructed from the observation of the doctrine and actual practice developed by States in global politics.[41] He understands human rights to be (urgent) individual interests that must be protected by States against predictable dangers and for which the international community acts as a guarantor, given their status as matters of international concern.[42]

While it is common to understand that the two mainstream philosophical approaches to human rights—'moral' and 'political'—as antagonistic, recent scholarship has explored their potential complementarity.[43] Even acknowledging that some versions of moral and political theories might be irreconcilable, this scholarship proposes that there is no fundamental reason why moral and political conceptions could not be made compatible.[44] As mentioned in **Section 1.1.1**, the main distinction between both conceptions is on their focus; one concerned with the foundation of these rights in the human (the right-holder), and the other focused on the role these rights perform in regulating the behaviour of States (the duty-bearers) within global politics. Consequently, it is not unthinkable that a combined approach could provide a more wholesome theory of human rights that explains both their nature and their international role.[45]

1.1.1.4 The emergent lists of rights

An important consequence of the conception of human rights we embrace is that the list of human rights that would emerge from such an approach would be different in kind

---

[38] J. Rawls, *The Law of Peoples* (Harvard University Press 1999).
[39] C. Beitz, *The Idea of Human Rights* (OUP 2009) 136–141.
[40] C. Beitz, *The Idea of Human Rights* (OUP 2009); A. Buchanan, *The Heart of Human Rights* (OUP 2013); S. Wheatley, *The Idea of International Human Rights Law* (OUP 2019).
[41] C. Beitz, *The Idea of Human Rights* (OUP 2009) 102.
[42] C. Beitz, *The Idea of Human Rights* (OUP 2009) 108–117.
[43] S.M. Liao and A. Etison, 'Political and Naturalistic Conceptions of Human Rights: A False Polemic?' (2012) 9 *Journal of Moral Philosophy* 327; S. Besson, 'Legal Human Rights Theory' in K. Lippert-Rasmussen, K. Brownlee, and D. Coady (eds.), *A Companion to Applied Philosophy* (Wiley 2016) 328–341, 334–335, 338–339; J. Nickel, 'Assigning Functions to Human Rights: Methodological Issues in Human Rights Theory' in A. Etison (ed.), *Human Rights: Moral or Political?* (OUP 2018) 145–159.
[44] S.M. Liao and A. Etison, 'Political and Naturalistic Conceptions of Human Rights: A False Polemic?' (2012) 9 *Journal of Moral Philosophy* 327, 343. See also: C. Beitz, 'Human Rights as a Common Concern' (2001) 95 *American Political Science Review* 269, 280; J. Raz, 'Human Rights Without Foundations', Oxford Legal Studies Research Paper No. 14/2007, 16.
[45] S.M. Liao and A. Etison, 'Political and Naturalistic Conceptions of Human Rights: A False Polemic?' (2012) 9 *Journal of Moral Philosophy* 327, 348–352; S. Besson, 'Legal Human Rights Theory' in K. Lippert-Rasmussen, K. Brownlee, and D. Coady (eds.), *A Companion to Applied Philosophy* (Wiley 2016) 328–341, 334–335, 338–339.

and length. While a 'consensus' stance would equate human rights to those consecrated in adopted international instruments, 'moral' approaches to human rights would derive rights from the moral principles that ground them, and 'political' theories would infer them from the practice of the international community. These different theoretical approaches have led to writings proclaiming various lists of rights considered to belong to the realm of human rights, some of which have been extensive, while others have been quite minimalistic.[46] The length of such lists has mainly depended on whether human rights are conceived of as a (limited) tool that imposes protection against the most fundamental threats faced by individuals' interests, or as encompassing idealistic views of a fair and just world.[47]

Although minimalistic conceptions are evidently problematic in that they would render the protection of multiple valuable human interests at the mercy of the will of individual States,[48] they have provided a warning worth considering as to the dangerous consequences of human rights 'inflation'.[49] Two problems are likely to arise from this phenomenon: the first is that more rights would normally translate into further resources being needed for their protection or, alternatively, in the existing resources being spread more thinly, to provide protection of more rights. A second related issue refers to the 'devaluation' of rights,[50] in the sense that the more rights we proclaim, the more mundane and, therefore, less powerful it becomes to assert a claim against social injustice in terms of a human rights violation. To clarify, the abovementioned warning need not lead to the embracing of a minimalist approach to human rights; quite the contrary. While it should mean that careful thought must be given to a continuous expansion of listed rights, securing that truly fundamental human interests achieve the significant standard of protection deserved by human rights, it should also lead to careful reflection on what political interests might lie behind the warnings about the dangers of expanding human rights.[51]

An important outcome of the above discussion is that there are many different ways to justify the existence, validity, and authority of human rights in the contemporary international legal order. Whichever line of justification we pick will bring attached particular advantages and will, certainly, be susceptible to criticism. We are fortunate

---

[46] M. Nussbaum, 'Capabilities and Human Rights' (1997) 66 *Fordham Law Review* 274; J. Rawls, *The Law of Peoples* (Harvard University Press 1999); W. Talbott, *Which Rights Should be Universal?* (OUP 2005); J. Nickel, *Making Sense of Human Rights* (2nd edn., Blackwell 2007); J. Griffin, *On Human Rights* (OUP 2008).

[47] M. Cranston, 'Are There Any Human Rights?' (1983) 112 *Daedalus* 1, 12–13; M. Ignatieff, *Human Rights as Politics and Idolatry* (Princeton University Press 2001) 56, 173; J. Nickel, *Making Sense of Human Rights* (2nd edn., Blackwell 2007) 3, 25–26; J. Tasioulas, 'Saving Human Rights from Human Rights Law' (2019) 52 *Vanderbilt Journal of Transnational Law* 1167, 1181.

[48] S. Benhabib, 'The Legitimacy of Human Rights' (2008) 137 *Daedalus* 94, 96.

[49] U. Baxi, *The Future of Human Rights* (2nd edn., OUP 2008) 112–113; A. Buchanan, *The Heart of Human Rights* (OUP 2013) 75.

[50] P. Alston, 'Conjuring Up New Human Rights: A Proposal for Quality Control' (1984) 78 *American Journal of International Law* 607, 614–615; J. Nickel, *Making Sense of Human Rights* (2nd edn., Blackwell 2007) 96–97.

[51] J. Theilen, 'The Inflation of Human Rights: A Deconstruction' (2021) 34 *Leiden Journal of International Law* 831, 848–850.

that, in our days, the international law of human rights provides us with the positive acknowledgement of rights in numerous international treaties, as well as through customary law and soft law instruments. However, as aforementioned, limiting our understanding of human rights to those enshrined in positive law, detached from meta-legal foundations, would leave us with a conception of rights *de lege lata* (of the law as it exists), depriving human rights of their radical power to denounce and oppose social injustice in circumstances in which existing laws have yet failed to raise to the challenge.

1.1.2 THE MAIN CHARACTERISTICS OF HUMAN RIGHTS

As discussed in **Section 1.1**, human rights can be understood as rights that every human being has by the mere fact of being human. Given the global reach of human rights, and even avoiding the pitfall of minimalistic approaches, it is evident that not all legal rights are human rights. Human rights protect individual interests that can be agreed to be of paramount importance;[52] hence, their power to trump other important socio-political considerations. Human rights are defined as *universal* rights, which are not only *inherent* to human beings, but also *inalienable*. Another important characteristic ascribed to human rights is their interdependence and indivisibility, in the sense that it is not possible to exercise a human right dissociated form the enjoyment of others—a topic that will be further discussed in **Chapter 2** of this book.

1.1.2.1 Inherent and inalienable

Human rights are conceived as inherent and inalienable. Both these characteristics of human rights are bound together, in a way that clearly determines that human rights cannot be taken away; not even renounced by the right-holders themselves. The first of these characteristics means that they are intrinsic to the person, due to our own 'humanity', rather than granted to us by an external source; human beings are understood to be born with these rights. This idea is a legacy of the Enlightenment (as discussed in **Section 1.2.1.1**), which had been enshrined into law by the eighteenth-century declarations of rights adopted by the North American colonies and in revolutionary France.[53] The inherence of rights appears (almost) explicitly from the onset of the 1948 Universal Declaration, which refers not to inherent but to inalienable rights, as well as to the dignity of all members of the human family, an idea that is complemented by the first article of this instrument stating that '[a]ll human beings

---

[52] M. Cranston, 'Are There Any Human Rights?' (1983) 112 *Daedalus* 1, 14; M. Nussbaum, 'Capabilities and Human Rights' (1997) 66 *Fordham Law Review* 274, 292; C. Beitz, *The Idea of Human Rights* (OUP 2009) 109–110.

[53] N. Bobbio, *The Age of Rights* (Polity 1996) 82; M. Ishay, *The History of Human Rights: From Ancient Times to the Globalization Era* (University of California Press 2004) 3, 18, 222; L. Hunt, *Inventing Human Rights: A History* (Norton and Company Press 2007) 17.

are born free and equal in dignity and rights'.[54] This conception of human rights being intrinsic and inextricable, belonging to all human beings from birth due to our own humanity, has been subsequently embraced by numerous binding international human rights instruments.[55]

The belief in human rights as inherent to all humans can be justified from any of the philosophical standpoints discussed earlier, even if more evidently associated with the moral conception. As moral approaches find the ultimate justification for human rights in universal characteristics common to all human beings, they encompass the idea of such fundamental characteristics being inherent themselves. However, the inherent character can also be supported by consensus theories, which can propose the innateness of human rights as one of the agreed upon qualities attached to these rights.[56] That is to say, the consensus reached concerning human rights is not just about which rights all humans have (or should have), but also on the fact that these rights are indissociable from being human. Ultimately, the main point of contention between moral and consensus theories that converge on the idea of the existence of inherent rights would be about whether this characteristic is a natural fact or a cultural construct.[57] That is to say, are human rights inherent because they derive from human nature or are they inherent because that was agreed when the idea of human rights was created? Political theories can also find the inherence of rights in the practice of the international community concerning human rights. As mentioned in **Section 1.1.1.3**, political theories do not necessarily oppose the existence of universal moral foundations of human rights, but focus their attention on a different aspect—the 'practice' of human rights—to infer these rights and to justify their relevance.[58]

The idea of inalienability of rights is closely connected to their inherence. It proposes that these rights are not just innate to the individuals, but also inseperable from them. This again fits neatly with moral theories that could easily justify that the agency, dignity, or humanity of the person is such an essential characteristic of humans that cannot be dissociated from them.[59] Similarly, the reasons provided earlier concerning inherence support the inalienability of human rights from both consensus and political approaches. However, it is important to highlight that the inalienable character of rights does not entail their absoluteness. The exercise of rights is subject to regulation, which

---

[54] S. Marks, 'From the "Single Confused Page" to the "Decalogue for Six Billion Persons": The Roots of the Universal Declaration of Human Rights in the French Revolution' (1998) 20 *Human Rights Quarterly* 459, 460, 486, 511; J. Morsink, *Inherent Human Rights: Philosophical Roots of the Universal Declaration* (PENN 2009) 17–24; A. Biletzki, 'Inherent Dignity: The Essence of Human Rights (or How to Get from Dignity to Political Power)' (2012) 57 *Diogenes* 21, 22.

[55] J. Morsink, *Inherent Human Rights: Philosophical Roots of the Universal Declaration* (PENN 2009) 45–46.

[56] As argued by Hannah Arendt, despite rhetoric, rather than being born equal, individuals become equals 'on the strength of our decision to guarantee ourselves mutually equal rights'. See: H. Arendt, *The Origins of Totalitarianism* (Harvest 1973) 301.

[57] J. Morsink, *Inherent Human Rights: Philosophical Roots of the Universal Declaration* (PENN 2009) 59.

[58] C. Beitz, *The Idea of Human Rights* (OUP 2009) 99–104.

[59] J. Donnelly, 'Human Rights and Human Dignity: An Analytic Critique of Non-Western Conceptions of Human Rights' (1982) 76 *American Political Science Review* 303, 306.

imposes common restrictions and even the possibility of suspending their exercise under extreme circumstances.[60] A question that, nonetheless, arises is whether inalienability implies the impossibility of individuals voluntarily renouncing these rights themselves. An objection to such a prescriptive view could be that the idea of human rights itself is about the protection of interests of the right-holder (the individual) through the behaviour of the duty-bearer (the State) and should not be turned into its obverse—an obligation upon the right-holder to hold a right that is unwanted. Nevertheless, the inalienable character could then subsist voluntary renunciation, if the system would, in principle, allow the right-holder to reclaim a renounced right, if so desired.

1.1.2.2 Universality

The idea of inherent rights is also linked to that of the universality of the rights. Rights conceived as inherent to all humans are, consequentially, universal, even if the universality of rights does not necessarily imply their inherent character—since universality, as a feature of rights, could also be consensually established. As with regards to the inherent character of human rights, the claim to the universality of these rights can be supported by different theories of rights for independent reasons. Moral theorists can see human rights as derived from the universal humanity of individuals; political theorists can take the claim of universality as one that exists in the current global practice of human rights; while consensus theorists can propose that such a feature has either been already agreed, as evidenced by the text of multiple (quasi-)universally-agreed upon treaties, or is capable of reaching such an agreement in time.

The universality of human rights means that all individuals, no matter their location in the world, are entitled to the enjoyment of all these rights. Universality is thus understood as covering every right, for everyone, and everywhere. Of course, this is a normative rather than empirical claim, given the sad reality that not everyone is able to enjoy all rights everywhere. However, the belief in universal human rights brings with it the powerful resort to the language of human rights to denounce the existence of a violation, when an individual does not have their rights respected in a given place.

Another usual objection to the universality of rights is linked to the moral conception of human rights. This states that the universality of human rights should also mean their eternal existence, as if these rights are held by humans by the mere fact of being human, then they would have existed since the beginning of humanity itself. This understanding is problematic, as certain human rights are time-bound.

---

[60] See, among many provisions: Convention for the Protection of Human Rights and Fundamental Freedoms (adopted 4 November 1950, entered into force 3 September 1953) 213 UNTS 221 ('European Convention on Human Rights'), Arts. 8.2, 9.2, 10.2, 11.2, 15; International Covenant on Civil and Political Rights (adopted 16 December 1966, entered into force 23 March 1976) 999 UNTS 171, Arts. 4, 12.3, 18.3, 19.3, 20, 21, 22.2; American Convention on Human Rights (adopted 22 November 1969, entered into force 18 July 1978) 1144 UNTS 123, OAS Treaty Series 36, Arts. 12.3, 13.2, 13.4, 14.3, 15, 16.2, 21.2, 22.3, 22.4, 23.2, 27, 30; African Charter on Human and Peoples' Rights (adopted 27 June 1981, entered into force 21 October 1986) OAU Doc. CAB/LEG/67/3 rev. 5, 21 I.L.M. 58 (1982), Arts. 11, 12.2, 14.

They could not have existed before certain factual conditions made them even feasible, and would perhaps cease to be relevant at some point in time, when specific factual circumstances are surpassed.[61] Clear examples are the way we conceive due process rights—such as the right to stand trial with certain minimum guarantees; political rights—such as the ability to vote and to stand for election for public office; or the right to education—such as an entitlement to receive formal education—which are rights that rely for their exercise on the existence of institutions that are not timeless.[62] Nevertheless, such an objection has been responded to by an argument based on the 'synchronic' universality of human rights.[63] The universal character of human rights need not have the meaning of eternal existence. If we claim that human rights have a beginning, even if pinpointing their genesis is not an easy task (as discussed in **Section 1.2**), then it is not a requirement for universal human rights to have had validity before such a time. Similarly, if we adopt an understanding of human rights as a developing idea, they can continue to exist, even if their specific content and scope evolves with time.

1.1.2.2.1 Critical debate: universality and cultural relativism

A further important objection to the universality of human rights concerns whether values that transcend all frontiers can even be said to exist. As will be discussed in **Section 2.2.1**, the Universal Declaration of Human Rights was drafted by the United Nations Commission on Human Rights between January 1947 and June 1948. In June 1947, while the drafting was taking place, the Executive Board of the American Anthropological Association submitted a statement to the Commission in which it warned against the dangers of writing up a 'universal' instrument that would only reflect the cultural values of the Western world.[64] This concern was not limited to highlighting the dangers of Western cultural imperialism—i.e. the imposition of Western values upon other cultures, a usual concern of 'postcolonial' critiques—but slid into what is usually referred to as 'cultural relativism'.

---

[61] C. Beitz, 'What Human Rights Mean' (2003) 132 *Daedalus* 36, 43.

[62] UDHR, Arts. 10, 11, 21, 26; European Convention on Human Rights (adopted 4 November 1950, entered into force 3 September 1953) 213 UNTS 221, Art. 6, A1P1 and A2P1; International Covenant on Civil and Political Rights (adopted 16 December 1966, entered into force 23 March 1976) 999 UNTS 171, Arts. 14, 25; International Covenant on Economic, Social and Cultural Rights (adopted 16 December 1966, entered into force 3 January 1976) 993 UNTS 3, Art. 13; American Convention on Human Rights (adopted 22 November 1969, entered into force 18 July 1978) 1144 UNTS 123, OAS Treaty Series 36, Arts. 8, 23; Additional Protocol to the American Convention on Human Rights in the Area of Economic, Social and Cultural Rights (Protocol of San Salvador) (adopted 17 November 1988, entered into force 16 November 1999) OAS Treaty Series No. 69, Art. 13; African Charter on Human and Peoples' Rights (adopted 27 June 1981, entered into force 21 October 1986) OAU Doc. CAB/LEG/67/3 rev. 5, 21 I.L.M. 58 (1982), Arts. 7, 13, 17.

[63] J. Raz, 'Human Rights in the Emerging World Order' (2010) 1 *Transnational Legal Theory* 31, 41; J. Tasioulas, 'On the Nature of Human Rights' in G. Ernst and J-C. Heilinger (eds.), *The Philosophy of Human Rights Contemporary Controversies* (De Gruyter 2012) 17–59, 35–36; R. Cruft, S.M. Liao, and M. Renzo, 'The Philosophical Foundations of Human Rights: An Overview' in R. Cruft, S.M. Liao, and M. Renzo (eds.), *Philosophical Foundations of Human Rights* (OUP 2015) 1–41, 7.

[64] American Anthropological Association, 'Statement on Human Rights' (1947) 49 *American Anthropologist* 539.

Cultural relativism can be defined as a view according to which moral standards and values are context-specific, with their validity stemming from the culture from which they themselves derive. That is to say, what is considered to be right/wrong or just/unfair would lack universal validity, but depend on the society that judges the specific behaviour.[65] Within the field of anthropology, cultural relativism actually developed as a reaction to 'cultural evolutionism'; a stance that viewed human cultures in a trend to progressively develop from 'primitive' to 'modern', with Western culture located at the apex of the scale of progress.[66] When applied to human rights, cultural relativism could mean that whether a specific State behaviour can be construed as a human rights violation would depend on the cultural context in which it has taken place.[67] The support for such a view was evident at multiple places of the American Anthropological Association's statement, which expressly argued that '[w]hat is held to be a human right in one society may be regarded as anti-social by another people'[68] and concluded by claiming that: 'Only when a statement of the right of men to live in terms of their own traditions is incorporated into the proposed Declaration, then, can the next step of defining the rights and duties of human groups as regards each other be set upon the firm foundation of the present-day scientific knowledge of Man.'[69] Over time, the American Anthropological Association came to distance itself from its 1947 stance,[70] but 'relativist' opposition to the universality of human rights has continued to emerge.

That the 'universal' rights proclaimed in 1948 were of Western provenance is not an uncommon assertion,[71] and this has led to different forms of backlash.[72] Claims of incompatibility of these rights with the values of particular cultures have included

---

[65] Jack Donnelly, 'Cultural Relativism and Universal Human Rights' (1984) 6 *Human Rights Quarterly* 400, 401; M. Freeman, 'Universalism of Human Rights and Cultural Relativism' in S. Sheeran and N. Rodley (eds.), *Routledge Handbook of International Human Rights Law* (Routledge 2013) 49–61, 51.

[66] A.A. An-Na'im, 'Problems of Universal Cultural Legitimacy for Human Rights' in A.A. An-Na'im and F. Deng (eds.), *Human Rights in Africa: Cross-Cultural Perspectives* (Brookings Institution 1990) 331–367, 339; M-B. Dembour, *Who Believes in Human Rights? Reflections on the European Convention* (CUP 2006) 157–158.

[67] F. Tesón, 'International Human Rights and Cultural Relativism' (1985) 25 *Virginia Journal of International Law* 869, 871.

[68] American Anthropological Association, 'Statement on Human Rights' (1947) 49 *American Anthropologist* 539, 542.

[69] American Anthropological Association, 'Statement on Human Rights' (1947) 49 *American Anthropologist* 539, 543.

[70] K. Engle, 'From Scepticism to Embrace: Human Rights and the American Anthropological Association from 1947–1999' (2001) 23 *Human Rights Quarterly* 536, 537, 559. See: American Anthropological Association, 'Statement on Human Rights' (June 1999); American Anthropological Association, 'Statement on Human Rights' (July 2020), available at: https://humanrights.americananthro.org/1999-statement-on-human-rights/; https://www.americananthro.org/ParticipateAndAdvocate/AdvocacyDetail.aspx?ItemNumber=25769 (accessed on 13 February 2023).

[71] V. Leary, 'The Effect of Western Perspectives on International Human Rights' in A.A. An-Na'im and F. Deng (eds.), *Human Rights in Africa: Cross-Cultural Perspectives* (Brookings Institution 1990) 15–30; A. Cassese, 'The General Assembly: Historical Perspective 1945–1989' in P. Alston (ed.), *The United Nations and Human Rights: A Critical Appraisal* (Clarendon Press 1992) 25–54, 31–32; M. Mutua, *Human Rights Standards: Hegemony, Law, and Politics* (State University of New York Press 2016) 18–19.

[72] The specific debate about the Western character of the 1948 Universal Declaration is discussed further in **Section 2.2.1.3**.

those articulated in terms of African, Asian, and Islamic values.[73] One of the earliest versions of such 'relativist' claims was expressed by Saudi Arabia, at the time of the adoption of the Universal Declaration, raising its concerns about the compatibility of this instrument with principles of Islamic law on which the State was founded. This led to Saudi Arabia becoming one of the eight States that abstained in the vote to adopt the Universal Declaration by the UN General Assembly.[74]

Similarly, discourses that opposed the applicability of human rights due to their incompatibility with 'Asian values' were prominent in the 1990s, with political leaders from Indonesia, Malaysia, and (especially) Singapore claiming that (individualistic) human rights should not become obstacles in a country's path to socio-economic development and political stability.[75] However, an important objection raised against claims based on shared regional values has been that they proclaim a homogeneity of societies that does not exist in reality, but is, instead, rhetorically constructed to justify political objectives of the ruling elites.[76] Furthermore, homogeneity claims tend to ignore the fact that cultures are not static, but involve practices, meanings, and understandings that change and evolve over time.[77]

Claims have also been made concerning 'African values', arguing that these rely on a worldview that emphasizes commonality over individuality and which prioritizes individuals' duties and group rights.[78] Indeed, the importance of duties and collective rights is reflected in the text of African Charter of Human and Peoples' Rights (discussed in **Chapter 8**), but has also been magnified and turned into an insurmountable conflict between human rights and traditional worldviews, especially by authoritarian rulers.[79]

---

[73] V. Leary, 'The Effect of Western Perspectives on International Human Rights' in A.A. An-Na'im and F. Deng (eds.), *Human Rights in Africa: Cross-Cultural Perspectives* (Brookings Institution 1990) 15–30, 20; A.A. An-Na'im, 'Problems of Universal Cultural Legitimacy for Human Rights' in A.A. An-Na'im and F. Deng (eds.), *Human Rights in Africa: Cross-Cultural Perspectives* (Brookings Institution 1990) 331–367, 350–352; Y. Ghai, 'Universalism and Relativism: Human Rights as a Framework for Negotiating Interethnic Claims' (2000) 21 *Cardozo Law Review* 1095, 1096.

[74] J. Humphrey, *Human Rights & the United Nations: a great adventure* (Transnational Publishers 1984) 73; J. Morsink, *Inherent Human Rights: Philosophical Roots of the Universal Declaration* (PENN 2009) 75–76.

[75] D. Bell, 'The East Asian Challenge to Human Rights: Reflections on an East West Dialogue' (1996) 18 *Human Rights Quarterly* 641, 644; A. Langlois, *The Politics of Justice and Human Rights* (CUP 2001) 159; R. Coomaraswamy, 'The Contemporary Challenges to International Human Rights' in S. Sheeran and N. Rodley (eds.), *Routledge Handbook of International Human Rights Law* (Routledge 2013) 127–139, 128–129.

[76] I. Tatsuo, 'Liberal Democracy and Asian Orientalism' in J. Bauer and D. Bell (eds.), *The East Asian Challenge for Human Rights* (CUP 1999) 27–59, 43; A. Langlois, *The Politics of Justice and Human Rights* (CUP 2001) 27–28; G.C. Spivak, 'Righting Wrongs' (2004) 103 *The South Atlantic Quarterly* 523, 526; J. Griffin, *On Human Rights* (OUP 2008) 138.

[77] A.A. An-Na'im, 'Toward a Cross-Cultural Approach to Defining International Standards of Human Rights: The Meaning of Cruel, Inhuman, or Degrading Treatment or Punishment' in A.A. An-Na'im (ed.) *Human Rights in Cross-Cultural Perspectives: A Quest for Consensus* (University of Pennsylvania Press 1992) 19–43, 27–28; Y. Ghai, 'Universalism and Relativism: Human Rights as a Framework for Negotiating Interethnic Claims' (2000) 21 *Cardozo Law Review* 1095, 1100; S. Marks, 'Four Human Rights Myths', LSE Legal Studies Working Paper No. 10/2012 (4 September 2012) 5.

[78] J.A.M. Cobbah, 'African Values and the Human Rights Debate: An African Perspective' (1987) 9 *Human Rights Quarterly* 309, 320, 326 and 331; B. Ibhawoh, *Human Rights in Africa* (CUP 2018) 38, 45, 48, 50.

[79] J. Donnelly, 'Cultural Relativism and Universal Human Rights' (1984) 6 *Human Rights Quarterly* 400, 412–414; B. Ibhawoh, *Human Rights in Africa* (CUP 2018) 50–51.

Therefore, whether these opinions have been articulated as legitimate expressions of concern or as a discursive subterfuge to justify restrictive political choices bears consideration.[80]

Strong relativist stances, which oppose the universal validity of basic ideas of justice, are incompatible with the idea of human rights itself, as rights would be rendered without any normative power if they could only be exercised within supporting cultural contexts. Nevertheless, the adoption of the aforementioned African Charter is a paradigmatic example of the possibility of reaching middle-ground solutions to the universalism/relativism debate.[81] Nuanced or moderate versions of cultural relativism and of universalism can be made compatible, for instance, by the understanding that even universal standards can be subject to interpretation and implementation in culturally specific ways.[82] Although some might find it surprising, the most evident example of a relativist approach to the protection of human rights comes from the most prominent Western monitoring body, the European Court of Human Rights. For decades now, the Court's jurisprudence has endorsed a doctrine called 'the margin of appreciation',[83] which, since August 2021, is even part of the preambular text of the European Convention on Human Rights.[84]

1.1.2.2.2 *The margin of appreciation*

The margin of appreciation is a doctrine of jurisprudential origin by which the European Court of Human Rights imposes self-restraint on its power of review.[85] The Court's case law has disclosed two main uses of this doctrine; the first one concerning the application of the Convention and the second its interpretation.[86] Regarding its main use, the margin of appreciation can be defined as a 'breadth of deference' which the Court allows to the domestic authorities of a State before finding their interference

---

[80] J. Donnelly, 'Cultural Relativism and Universal Human Rights' (1984) 6 *Human Rights Quarterly* 400, 411–413; N. Englehart, 'Rights and Culture in the Asian Values Argument: The Rise and Fall of Confucian Ethics in Singapore' (2000) *Human Rights Quarterly* 548, 549; A. Langlois, *The Politics of Justice and Human Rights* (CUP 2001) 25.

[81] To a similar degree, the Arab Charter of Human Rights could be thought of as expressing specific cultural values, for instance in the recognition of the rights to self-determination and development, as well as through the express restriction of the right to marry to same-sex couples, or in the limitation of rights to education and work to citizens. See: Arab Charter on Human Rights (adopted 22 May 2004, entered into force 15 March 2008), Arts. 2, 33, 34, 37, 41.

[82] U. Baxi, 'Voices of Suffering and the Future of Human Rights' (1998) 8 *Transnational Law and Contemporary Problems* 125, 154; M.-B. Dembour, *Who Believes in Human Rights? Reflections on the European Convention* (CUP 2006) 179–180; J. Donnelly, 'The Relative Universality of Human Rights' (2007) 29 *Human Rights Quarterly* 281, 299–300.

[83] E. Benvenisti, 'Margin of Appreciation, Consensus, and Universal Standards' (1999) 31 *New York University Journal of International Law and Politics* 843, 843–845.

[84] Protocol No. 15 amending the Convention for the Protection of Human Rights and Fundamental Freedom (adopted 24 June 2013, entered into force 1 August 2021) ETS No. 213.

[85] D. Spielmann, 'Allowing the Right Margin: The European Court of Human Rights and the National Margin of Appreciation Doctrine: Waiver or Subsidiarity of European Review?'(CELS Working Papers Series 2012) 2.

[86] J. Kratochvíl, 'The Inflation of the Margin of Appreciation by the European Court of Human Rights' (2011) 29 *Netherlands Quarterly of Human Rights* 324, 328.

with a substantive right to be incompatible with the obligations assumed under the Convention.[87] Hence, the Court will refrain from making a principled decision on the application (or interpretation) of the Convention, accepting that States might be in a better position to assess its application to the specific case. However, the extent of the discretion allowed to States under this tool of deference is different—wider or narrower—on each occasion, depending on multiple factors (as will be further discussed in **Section 7.7**).

The doctrine of the margin of appreciation was originally devised by the former European Commission of Human Rights,[88] but the Court adopted the idea of deference to the discretion of the domestic authorities from its early jurisprudence.[89] The *Handyside v. the United Kingdom* case is usually credited as the moment when the Court adopted the 'margin of appreciation' doctrine, given its explicit use within the reasoning of the judgment. The Court affirmed that: 'The Convention leaves to each Contracting State, in the first place, the task of securing the rights and liberties it enshrines.'[90] Then, it continued asserting that, due to 'their direct and continuous contact with the vital forces of their countries',[91] the domestic authorities, both legislative and judicial, are better positioned than the Court to decide and assess the regulation of human rights— freedom of expression, in this case—within the State. That is why the Court considered that, under the system of the Convention, States enjoy a 'margin of appreciation' to decide, in the first instance, whether their actions conform to the provisions of the Convention. Nonetheless, this degree of discretion granted to States is certainly not unlimited, and the supervisory role of the Court consists in examining whether the measures adopted by States remained within this breadth of deference.

ECtHR, *Handyside v. the United Kingdom*, 7 December 1976, Series A no. 24.

The case was brought to the European Commission of Human Rights by the owner of a publishing firm that had published the Danish book *The Little Red Schoolbook* in the United Kingdom. The book claimed to be a reference book and contained chapters on education, learning, teachers, pupils, and 'the system'. The chapter on pupils had a section on 'sex', including sub-sections on masturbation, orgasm, intercourse and petting, contraceptives, wet dreams, menstruation, child-molesters, pornography, impotence, homosexuality, venereal diseases, and abortion. Following a number of complaints, the publisher's premises were searched and

---

[87] H.C. Yourow, 'The Margin of Appreciation Doctrine in the Dynamics of European Human Rights Jurisprudence' (1987) 3 *Connecticut Journal of International Law* 111, 118; J. Kratochvíl, 'The Inflation of the Margin of Appreciation by the European Court of Human Rights' (2011) 29 *Netherlands Quarterly of Human Rights* 324, 330.

[88] ECHR, *Greece v the United Kingdom ('The Cyprus Case')*, App. no. 176/56, Report of the European Commission (Volume I) (1958).

[89] ECtHR, *Case 'relating to certain aspects of the laws on the use of languages in education in Belgium'* (merits), 23 July 1968, p. 31, § 10, Series A no. 6.

[90] ECtHR, *Handyside v. the United Kingdom*, 7 December 1976, § 48, Series A no. 24.

[91] ECtHR, *Handyside v. the United Kingdom*, 7 December 1976, § 48, Series A no. 24.

more than 1,000 copies of the book, advertising material, and the matrix used to print the book were seized. The publisher was prosecuted under the Obscene Publications Act (1964) and found guilty. In addition to a fine, the court made a forfeiture order for the destruction of the books. The publisher complained that the actions against him amounted to a violation of the rights to freedom of expression and to the peaceful enjoyment of possessions, both by themselves and in connection with the prohibition of discrimination, under the European Convention on Human Rights.

Neither the Commission nor the Court found a violation of the applicant's rights. The Court focused its main analysis on the interference with the applicant's freedom of expression. It assessed that the various measures challenged—the criminal conviction and the seizure and destruction of the matrix and of the books—were interferences by public authority that were prescribed by law. The Court proceeded to examine whether such interferences could be considered to be 'necessary in a democratic society' for the protection of morals, an aim that is allowed under the European Convention. To determine the 'necessity' of the interferences, the Court asserted that its role was merely to ensure that the domestic authorities had acted within the limits of the 'margin of appreciation' afforded to Contracting States. The Court emphasized that the domestic margin of appreciation went hand in hand with a European supervision, with the Court being empowered to give the final ruling on whether a 'restriction' was reconcilable with freedom of expression as protected by the Convention. The Court concluded that, even though many other States had allowed the publication and distribution of the book, the UK had still acted within the national margin of appreciation when deciding its censorship; hence, no violation had taken place.

1.2 THE HISTORIES OF HUMAN RIGHTS

There are multiple possible histories about the origin of our current notion of human rights.[92] Depending on the narrator, these histories can commence as early as hundreds of years before the Christian era or as recently as the middle of the twentieth century, if not even later.[93] Here, the intention is not to provide an authoritative history of the idea of human rights, but to discuss different elements that can be seen as significant for the emergence of the concept of human rights we use in our days. The reader is free to select which possible paths propose the most appealing genealogy of human rights—including those involving omitted elements. The suggested journey includes the ideas of natural law and natural rights, the eighteenth-century revolutions, the progressive prohibition of slavery, the development of international humanitarian law, the establishment of the League of Nations (and its dissolution), and the creation of

---

[92] P. Alston, 'Does the Past Matter? On the Origins of Human Rights' (2013) 126 *Harvard Law Review* 2043, 2077–2078; B. Ibhawoh, *Human Rights in Africa* (CUP 2018) 7, 9–10, 12.

[93] Moyn is probably the scholar who dates the beginning of the human rights movement in the most recent past, finding that 1977 was the 'year of human rights', beginning with a January speech of the then president of the USA and culminating in December of that year with Amnesty International being awarded the Nobel Peace Prize. See: S. Moyn, *The Last Utopia: Human Rights in History* (Harvard University Press 2010) 155.

the United Nations. However, these elements that provided inspiration for the creation of our current idea of human rights are not presented as a linear story of progress,[94] even if discussed in temporal succession.[95] It should not be forgotten that between the different elements discussed, there have been multiple other ideas and setbacks that also contributed to the formation of the concept of human rights.[96] This is especially true given that, as was discussed in **Section 1.1**, while a definition of human rights might be agreed upon, the underpinnings of such notion need not be.

1.2.1 NATURAL LAW

The development of a theory of 'natural law' (jusnaturalism) was an important element for the construction of the notion of universal rights. Jusnaturalism, as a theoretical standpoint, supports two main theses: first, the existence of universally valid principles of justice; and, second, that a legal system that fails to follow such principles should not be considered law.[97] As a theory, jusnaturalism has its roots in the ideas of natural law that have been developed throughout the centuries. A usual starting point for discussing natural law is Sophocles' tragedy *Antigone*, from the fifth century before the Christian era. In the play, Antigone defies what she believed to be an unjust edict from King Creon—her uncle—which forbade her from burying her brother, Polyneices. In breaching the injunction, she decries Creon's rule for lacking the authority to 'override the unwritten and unfailing statutes of heaven. For their life is not of today or yesterday, but from all time, and no man knows when they were first put forth.'[98]

This idea of an eternal law, which serves as a measure of what is right and wrong even in the absence of, or when contradicted by, human norms, appeared in the following century in the writings of Aristotle and in the doctrine of the Stoics.[99] The concept of a natural law was later defended by Cicero, during the Roman Republic, claiming the existence of an eternal and constant law that applies to all men. He understood this law to be distinct from positive law and to derive from reason (*recta ratio*), granted to all humans and in harmony with nature.[100] The concept of natural law even survived

---

[94] B. Ibhawoh, *Human Rights in Africa* (CUP 2018) 20–21.

[95] For a more linear and comprehensive history of human rights, see: M. Ishay, *The History of Human Rights: From Ancient Times to the Globalization Era* (University of California Press 2004).

[96] J-M. Barreto, 'Decolonial Strategies and Dialogue in the Human Rights Field: A Manifesto' (2012) 3 *Transnational Legal Theory* 1, 4; B. Ibhawoh, *Human Rights in Africa* (CUP 2018) 20–21; M. Koskenniemi, 'Rights, History, Critique' in A. Etison (ed.), *Human Rights: Moral or Political?* (OUP 2018) 41–60, 54.

[97] C.S. Nino, *The Ethics of Human Rights* (Clarendon Press 1993) 11.

[98] Sophocles, *Antigone* (R.C. Jebb trans. 442 BCE), available at: http://classics.mit.edu/Sophocles/antigone.html (accessed on 13 February 2023).

[99] I. Szabo, 'Historical Foundations of Human Rights and Subsequent Developments' in K. Vasak (ed.), *The International Dimensions of Human Rights* (UNESCO 1979) 9–38, 9–10; C. Douzinas, *The End of Human Rights: Critical Legal Thought at the Turn of the Century* (Hart 2000) 26–32.

[100] M.T. Cicero, *Republic* (N. Rudd trans, OUP 1998), Book III, 22. See: C. Douzinas, *The End of Human Rights: Critical Legal Thought at the Turn of the Century* (Hart 2000) 50–51; F. Llano Alonso, 'Cicero and Natural Law' (2012) 98 *Archives for Philosophy of Law and Social Philosophy* 157, 159–160; R. Rabinovich-Berkman, *¿Cómo se hicieron los derechos humanos? Volumen I* (Didot 2013) 261.

the Middle Ages, but it was redefined by Christian beliefs, through Thomas Aquinas' writings on the subject during the thirteenth century.[101] Aquinas proposed the existence of four different kinds of law: eternal—'God's plan'; divine—what had been revealed through the scriptures; natural—what reason allows people to know about eternal law; and human—positive law. According to Aquinas, the validity of human law was subject to its conformity not only with natural law, but also with the eternal and divine law.[102]

The slow detachment of natural law from strong religious dictates has been mediated by the work of religious legal scholars, especially those from the School of Salamanca,[103] such as Francisco de Vitoria[104] and Bartolomé de Las Casas.[105] This trend of secularization of natural law was also followed in the work of the Dutch legal scholar, Hugo Grotius, who is usually referred to as the father of modern international law by Western scholarship.[106] In his attempt to systematize the rules that governed the relations between sovereign States, Grotius proposed States being bound by both the law of nature—which might not even be subject to change by God themselves[107]—and by the law of nations.[108]

1.2.1.1 Natural rights

The belief in a law of nature that provides eternal principles of justice that must be abided by any valid positive law does not in itself prescribe the existence of inherent rights

---

[101] J. Donnelly, 'Natural Law and Right in Aquinas' Political Thought' (1980) 33 *Western Political Quarterly* 520, esp. 522–524; C. Douzinas, *The End of Human Rights: Critical Legal Thought at the Turn of the Century* (Hart 2000) 60; A. Pagden, 'Human Rights, Natural Rights, and Europe's Imperial Legacy' (2003) 31 *Political Theory* 171, 174.

[102] J. Donnelly, 'Natural Law and Right in Aquinas' Political Thought' (1980) 33 *Western Political Quarterly* 520, 520–521; E. Gelinas, 'The Natural Law according to Thomas Aquinas' (2011) 16 *Trinity Law Review* 13, 18–19; T. Jackson, 'Theology and Law Divorced and Reconciled: Aquinas, Luther, Rawls, and Us' (2017) 32 *Journal of Law and Religion* 71, 71–73.

[103] F. de Vitoria, 'On Law' in A. Pagden and J. Lawrence (eds.), *Vitoria: Political Writings* (CUP 1991) 153–204; G. Gordon, 'Natural Law in International Legal Theory: Linear and Dialectical Presentations' in A. Orford and F. Hoffmann (eds.), *The Oxford Handbook of the Theory of international law* (OUP 2016) 279–305, 282–285.

[104] The work of de Vitoria has also been significant for the development of the idea of 'natural rights', as he proposed, in opposition to canonical teachings, that the indigenous people who were being massacred at the time by the Western conquistadors were actually endowed with similar rights to those of the Christian invaders. However, revisionist approaches to his work have suggested that de Vitoria's humane approach was actually aimed at providing a more 'sophisticated' justification to the invasion and genocide ensuing in the Americas. See: F. de Vitoria, 'On the American Indians' in A. Pagden and J. Lawrence (eds.), *Vitoria: Political Writings* (CUP 1991) 231–292; A. Anghie, 'Francisco De Vitoria and the Colonial Origins of International Law' (1996) 5 *Social and Legal Studies* 321.

[105] In opposition to de Vitoria, de Las Casas elaborated on the idea of 'natural rights' to affirm the unity of the human race, decrying the massacre of the peoples of the Americas. See: J-M, Barreto, 'Imperialism and Decolonization as Scenarios of Human Rights History' in J-M. Barreto (ed.), *Human Rights from a Third World Perspective: Critique, History and International Law* (Cambridge Scholars 2013) 140–171, 153–154. See also: G. Sanderlin (ed.), *Witness: Writings of Bartolomé de Las Casas* (Orbis 1971).

[106] H. Lauterpacht, 'The Grotian Tradition in International Law' (1946) 23 *British Year Book of International Law* 1, 8, 27.

[107] As pointed out by Lauterpacht, Grotius affirmed, but then also detracted from, the idea of the existence of universal principles of justice that cannot even be changed by God. See: H. Lauterpacht, 'The Grotian Tradition in international law' (1946) 23 *British Year Book of International Law* 1, 8.

[108] H. Lauterpacht, 'The Grotian Tradition in International Law' (1946) 23 *British Year Book of International Law* 1, 17–21. See: S. Neff (ed.), *Hugo Grotius on the Law of War and Peace* (CUP 2012).

for individuals, but it is certainly linked to such a conception of 'natural rights'.[109] The construction of the idea of rights held inherently by the individual—although only by certain individuals, as will be discussed—is commonly attributed to the 'contractualist' philosophers of the Enlightenment period. Thinkers such as Hobbes, Locke, and Rousseau, to different extents, proposed that pre-social individuals possessed inherent rights, some of which they forsake in exchange for life in society; a process that takes the idealized form of the celebration of a 'social contract'.[110]

The idea of natural rights provides two fundamental elements to the notion of human rights we hold today: first, it presents the existence of individuals' rights that can be found in the (imaginary) 'state of nature' that pre-exists the State and, therefore, are not granted to individuals by a civil authority, but are inherent to the person. Second, these rights are not only pre-social, but actually become the reason for the existence of the State itself.[111] In social contract theory, the State is created by the association of individuals to protect themselves from the dangers they are exposed to in the 'state of nature'. While the outcome of the Hobbesian contract is that individuals forsake all inherent rights but for the preservation of their life, when they entered into society, Locke provided a picture of men in society that resembled more closely the idea of rights that we have in our days. According to Locke's account, the reason for the creation of the political community is the preservation of the rights of the individual, which are not only inherent, but also inalienable, and which include individuals' rights to life, liberty, property, and to rebel against arbitrary power.[112]

1.2.2 THE EIGHTEENTH-CENTURY DECLARATIONS

The idea of natural rights just discussed made appearances of fundamental importance in declarations of legal and political significance adopted towards the end of the eighteenth century in both the British colonies in the North of the American continent and in France.[113] The opening section of the first of these documents, the Virginia Declaration of Rights, adopted on 12 June 1776, provides a paradigmatic example of the embracement of the idea of natural rights. It stated:

> That all men are by *nature* equally free and independent and have certain *inherent rights*, of which, *when they enter into a state of society, they cannot, by any compact, deprive or divest their posterity*; namely, the enjoyment of life and liberty, with the means of acquiring and possessing property, and pursuing and obtaining happiness and safety.[114]

---

[109] C.S. Nino, *The Ethics of Human Rights* (Clarendon Press 1993) 10; C. Douzinas, *The End of Human Rights: Critical Legal Thought at the Turn of the Century* (Hart 2000) 61–68; J. Griffin, *On Human Rights* (OUP 2008) 9–10.

[110] See: T. Hobbes, *Leviathan* (Lerner 2018 (1651)), esp. Chapters XIII–XV; J. Locke, *Second Treatise of Government* (Wiley 1982 (1689)), esp. Chapter II; J.J. Rousseau, *The Social Contract and Discourses* (G. Cole trans, Dutton & Co. 1950(1762)), esp. 13–18.

[111] J. Waldron (ed.), *'Nonsense upon stilts': Bentham, Burke, and Marx on the Rights of Man* (Methuen 1987) 10.

[112] E. Clinton Gardner, 'John Locke: Justice and the Social Compact' (1992) 9 *Journal of Law and Religion* 347, 359. See: J. Locke, *Second Treatise of Government* (Wiley 1982 (1689)), Chapter XIX.

[113] J. Habermas, *Theory and Practice* (Beacon Press 1973) 86; M. Ishay, *The History of Human Rights: from Ancient Times to the Globalization Era* (University of California Press 2004) 94, 326.

[114] Virginia Declaration of Rights (12 June 1776), section 1 (emphasis added).

Similar inspiration was drawn upon in the drafting of the Declaration of Independence, adopted on 4 July 1776, by which the thirteen British colonies of the North of America declared their independence from Great Britain.[115] The second paragraph of the document also portrayed the philosophy of natural rights:

> We hold these truths to be self-evident, that *all men are created equal*; that they are endowed by their Creator with uncertain *unalienable rights*; that among these are life, liberty, and the pursuit of happiness. *That to secure these rights, governments are instituted among men*, deriving their just powers from the consent of the governed; that, whenever any form of government becomes destructive of these ends, it is the right of the people to alter or to abolish it, and to institute a new government, laying its foundation on such principles, and organizing its powers in such form, as to them shall seem most likely to effect their safety and happiness.[116]

The 1789 French Declaration of the Rights of Man and of the Citizen found its inspiration in the same philosophical ideas of the documents adopted in the previous decade by the American colonies, as well as on those texts. Indeed, the second article of the French Declaration clearly stated: 'The aim of every political association is the preservation of the natural and imprescriptible rights of Man. These rights are Liberty, Property, Safety and Resistance to Oppression.'[117]

Even if subsequent to the American texts, many scholars attribute to the French Declaration a more fundamental value in the genealogy of human rights, to the extent that the adoption of the Declaration by the National Assembly, on 26 August 1789, is not an uncommon moment for dating the creation of human rights.[118] The French Declaration proclaimed that a certain number of rights must be recognized to every 'man' for the simple reason of being born. That is to say, the mere fact of being born a 'man', rather than other metaphysical reasons, became the source of legal rights.[119] And

---

[115] Focus on the eighteenth-century declarations does not ignore the fact that many authors traced precursors of our notion of human rights to even older legal and political documents, such as the Magna Carta (1215) or the Habeas Corpus Act (1679) and English Bill of Rights (1689). As aforementioned, the present story about the creation of our notion of human rights does not attempt to provide an authoritative history of this concept, but a narrative of different plausible genealogies. See: M. Ishay, *The History of Human Rights: from Ancient Times to the Globalization Era* (University of California Press 2004) 85–86; H. Lauterpacht, *An International Bill of the Rights of Man* (OUP 2013) 55–59; R. Rabinovich-Berkman, *¿Cómo se hicieron los derechos humanos? Volumen II* (Didot 2017) 235–236.

[116] The United States Declaration of Independence (4 July 1776) (emphasis added).

[117] Declaration of the Rights of Man and of the Citizen (26 August 1789).

[118] C.S. Nino, *The Ethics of Human Rights* (Clarendon Press 1993) 1–2; S. Marks, 'From the "Single Confused Page" to the "Decalogue for Six Billion Persons": The Roots of the Universal Declaration of Human Rights in the French Revolution' (1998) 20 *Human Rights Quarterly* 459, 460, 486, 511; L. Hunt, *Inventing Human Rights: A History* (Norton and Company Press 2007) 17.

[119] While the idea of the existence of a deity is present in the French Declaration, with the National Assembly declaring the rights 'in the presence and under the auspices of the Supreme Being', this 'Supreme Being' did not become the source of the rights. The secular origin of rights clearly distinguishes the French Declaration from other political documents of the time, such as the Declaration of Independence of the United States in which the 'Creator' was constructed as the reason for recognising rights. See: H. Arendt, *On Revolution* (Penguin 1990) 45, 149; L. Hunt, *Inventing Human Rights: A History* (Norton and Company Press 2007) 15, 132.

even if these rights were 'declared' by the French National Assembly, which could give the impression of their pre-existence, the rights enunciated in the Declaration can be understood to be created by the document,[120] as individuals became entitled to these rights by virtue of the Declaration itself.[121]

Nonetheless, the 'rights of man' proclaimed by the French Declaration certainly lacked the universality we currently attribute to the idea of human rights. The actual 'man' of the Declaration was certainly not equivalent to the universal human of 'human rights', as only a relatively small number of individuals were entitled to the proclaimed rights. To be entitled to the rights of man, one had to be white, male, a French citizen, and a land-owner.[122] This reality led activist Olympe de Gouges to publish in 1790 the 'Declaration of the Rights of Woman'; a significant text addressed to the Queen, Marie-Antoinette, with a request for the National Assembly to adopt a new declaration, recognizing women as subjects of rights in equal terms to men.[123]

Despite the lack of universal character of the 'man' of the French Declaration, there is reasonable agreement within the academic literature that the Universal Declaration of Human Rights finds roots in the French document.[124] In fact, the 'human beings' to which the first article of the Universal Declaration makes reference can be seen as the universalized version of the 'men' that appeared in Article 1 of the French Declaration,[125] with the formula of both provisions being almost identical. While the French text affirmed that 'Men are born and remain free and equal in rights',[126] the Universal Declaration states that 'All human beings are born free and equal in dignity and rights.'[127] Thus, the human being of the Universal Declaration could be interpreted as a twentieth-century attempt at universalizing the subject of inherent rights, through the recognition that people that were excluded in 1789—such as the foreigner, the non-white, or the female—needed to be included in the protection of rights. However, the fact that those rights were originally conceived as rights that only belonged to wealthy white French men has raised concerns about their capacity to accommodate the needs

---

[120] C. Douzinas, *Human Rights and Empire: The Political Philosophy of Cosmopolitanism* (Routledge-Cavendish 2007) 92.

[121] This is certainly the opposite view to the one traditionally supported by the theorists of natural rights. See: T. Paine, 'Dissertation on First Principles of Government' in T. Paine, *Rights of Man, Common Sense, and Other Political Writings* (OUP 1995) 402.

[122] C. Douzinas, 'The End(s) of Human Rights' (2002) 26 *Melbourne University Law Review* 445, 455; M. Ishay, *The History of Human Rights: from Ancient Times to the Globalization Era* (University of California Press 2004) 8 and 108; L. Hunt, *Inventing Human Rights: A History* (Norton and Company Press 2007) 18.

[123] O. de Gouges, 'The Declaration of the Rights of Woman' in Darline G. Levy, Harriet B. Applewhite, and Mary D. Johnson (eds.), *Women in Revolutionary Paris 1789–1795* (University of Illinois Press 1979) 87–92.

[124] S. Marks, 'From the "Single Confused Page" to the "Decalogue for Six Billion Persons": The Roots of the Universal Declaration of Human Rights in the French Revolution' (1998) 20 *Human Rights Quarterly* 459, 460, 486, 511; M. Ishay, *The History of Human Rights: from Ancient Times to the Globalization Era* (University of California Press 2004) 3, 18, 222; L. Hunt, *Inventing Human Rights: A History* (Norton and Company Press 2007) 17; W.P. Simmons, *Human Rights Law and the Marginalized Other* (CUP 2011) 5.

[125] N. Bobbio, *The Age of Rights* (Polity 1996) 82.

[126] Declaration of the Right of Man and the Citizen (26 August 1789), Art. 1.

[127] UDHR, Art. 1.

and realities of those excluded. For instance, the critique that the situation of women remains belittled within the realm of rights is very persuasive and continues to have bite, despite the nominal inclusion of women within human rights language.[128]

Notwithstanding the evident limitations of the eighteenth-century declarations, these proclamations of rights helped to set in motion a developing trend of recognition of citizens' rights in domestic jurisdictions, although certainly not free from setbacks.[129] While the expansive recognition of (citizens') rights was taking place with the adoption of national constitutions that included specific lists of rights,[130] the creation of the international law of human rights would require the legal recognition of said rights beyond national frontiers and detached from the limitations set thereby, including those concerning citizenship, gender, and ethnicity.

1.2.3 THE EVOLVING PROHIBITION OF SLAVERY

Slavery, as a perverse political and economic system that allowed a person to be legally owned by another one, existed since ancient times in different societies.[131] While the eighteenth-century declarations proclaimed the natural rights of men, the system of slavery remained unaffected.[132] Slavery continued to be prevalent in the newly emerged United States of America for almost a century (until 1865) with even the drafter of the Declaration of Independence, Thomas Jefferson, being a slave-owner himself.[133] Similarly, slavery was only abolished temporarily in France in 1792 for metropolitan France, and in 1794 for the French colonial territories—to be re-established in 1802, until its re-abolition in 1848.[134] And, certainly, slavery was not only a lawful practice within States, but the slave trade that developed across the Atlantic, with enslaved

---

[128] H. Charlesworth, C. Chinkin, and S. Wright, 'Feminist Approaches to International Law' (1991) 85 *American Journal of International Law* 613, 628; S. Palmer, 'Critical Perspectives on Women's Rights: The European Convention on Human Rights and Fundamental Freedoms' in A. Bottomley (ed.), *Feminist Perspectives on the Foundational Subjects of Law* (Cavendish Publishing 1996) 223–259, 228; V. Spike Peterson and L. Parisi, 'Are Women Human? It's Not an Academic Question' in T. Evans (ed.) *Human Rights Fifty Years On: A Reappraisal* (Manchester University Press 1998) 132–160, 132, 147, 153–154; S. Baer, 'Citizenship in Europe and the Construction of Gender by Law in the European Charter of Fundamental Rights' in K. Knop (ed.), *Gender and Human Rights* (Oxford University Press 2004) 83–112, 105.

[129] The constitutions adopted throughout Latin-America during the nineteenth and early twentieth centuries are clear examples of this legal trend, see: H. Gros Espiell, 'El constitucionalismo latinoamericano y la codificación en el siglo XIX' (2002) 6 *Anuario Iberoamericano de Justicia Constitucional* 143; P. Carozza, 'From Conquest to Constitutions: Retrieving a Latin American Tradition of the Idea of Human Rights' (2003) 25 *Human Rights Quarterly* 281.

[130] L. Henkin, 'International Human Rights as "Rights"' (1981) 23 *Nomos* 257, 263.

[131] B. Ibhawoh, *Human Rights in Africa* (CUP 2018) 64, 74.

[132] M. Koskenniemi, 'Rights, History, Critique' in A. Etison (ed.), *Human Rights: Moral or Political?* (OUP 2018) 41–60, 54.

[133] C. Samson, *The Colonialism of Human Rights* (Polity Press 2020) 81–85.

[134] S. Marks, 'From the "Single Confused Page" to the "Decalogue for Six Billion Persons": the roots of the Universal Declaration of Human Rights in the French Revolution' (1998) 20 *Human Rights Quarterly* 459, 502; C. Douzinas, *The End of Human Rights: Critical Legal Thought at the Turn of the Century* (Hart 2000) 98–99.

African people taken forcibly to work and die in the European colonies in the Americas, was a prominent feature of the world's economy for over three centuries.[135]

Anti-slavery sentiments coming from the oppressed populations were mostly ignored elsewhere.[136] However, towards the end of the eighteenth century a slow but progressive transnational movement towards the abolition of slavery managed to emerge. The independence of Haïti (Ayiti), in 1804, is perhaps one of the best-known early achievements against slavery, as the country itself emerged from the rebellion of slaves against the brutal regime France was imposing on its colonial territory named Saint-Domingue.[137] In parallel, the claims of anti-slavery societies formed in different parts of the world denouncing the radical incoherence of philosophical proclamations of the inherent rights of man on the face of the legal right to own a person began to gain traction.[138] For instance, although the adopted Constitution of the newly independent United States of America provided for slavery to continue, different States in the north of the country proceeded to legislate against it.[139] Subsequently, the Federal Congress established a ban on the slave trade in 1807, effective from the following year—even though slavery would not be fully banned in the whole territory of the country until 1865.[140]

An important step towards an international ban on slavery also took place in 1807. The British Parliament passed the Abolition of the Slave Trade, which banned participation in the slave trade by British subjects and the importation of slaves to British colonies, although not slavery in the British territories itself, which would remain 'lawful' until the Slavery Abolition Act of 1833.[141] Nevertheless, the implications of the adoption of the 1807 legislation were significant, given that the British Empire was among the main international actors profiting from the transatlantic slave trade. The actual motivations behind the passing of the mentioned law are contested. These range from those who

---

[135] The transatlantic slave trade extended for over three centuries, starting at the beginning of the sixteenth century and lasting until 1867, and encompassed the enslavement of approximately 12,500,000 individuals. See: D. Eltis and D. Richardson, *Atlas of the Transatlantic Slave Trade* (Yale University Press 2010), Introduction.

[136] B. Ibhawoh, *Human Rights in Africa* (CUP 2018) 57 and 66; J.M. Barreto, 'Decolonial Thinking and the Quest for Decolonising Human Rights' (2018) 46 *Asian Journal of Social Science* 484, 497.

[137] C.L.R. James, *The Black Jacobins: Toussaint L'Ouverture and the San Domingo Revolution* (Penguin 2001 (1938)) 8; J. Martínez, *The Slave Trade and the Origins of International Human Rights Law* (OUP 2012) 23; L. Wood, 'Across Oceans and Revolutions: Law and Slavery in French Saint-Domingue and beyond' (2014) 39 *Law & Social Inquiry* 758, 759–760.

[138] Y. Onuma, 'When was the Law of International Society Born? An Inquiry of the History of International Law from an Intercivilizational Perspective' (2000) 2 *Journal of the History of International Law* 1, 43; J. Martinez, 'The Anti-Slavery Movement and the Rise of International Non-Governmental Organizations' in D. Shelton (ed.), *The Oxford Handbook of International Human Rights Law* (OUP 2013) 222–249, esp. 234–237.

[139] M. Ishay, *The History of Human Rights: from Ancient Times to the Globalization Era* (University of California Press 2004) 114; J. Martínez, *The Slave Trade and the Origins of International Human Rights Law* (OUP 2012) 38–40.

[140] M. Ishay, *The History of Human Rights: from Ancient Times to the Globalization Era* (University of California Press 2004) 127 and 158; J. Martínez, *The Slave Trade and the Origins of International Human Rights Law* (OUP 2012) 17, 43.

[141] W. de Gruyter, *The Epochs of International Law* (M. Byers trans., W de G 2000); M. Ishay, *The History of Human Rights: from Ancient Times to the Globalization Era* (University of California Press 2004) 157; J. Martínez, *The Slave Trade and the Origins of International Human Rights Law* (OUP 2012) 23.

conceptualize it as an example of the triumph of the philosophy of the rights of man, to those who consider its main rationale to derive from the fact that the continuation of the transatlantic slave trade had become politically and economically detrimental to the British Empire.[142] Likely, the multiple actors involved in the adoption of the law pursued different objectives. However, to make the legislation succeed, it required implementation at the international level, with other States also committing themselves to the end of the transatlantic slave trade.[143] Therefore, the abolition of the slave trade (but not of slavery itself) became part of Britain's international policy, which managed to persuade other States to celebrate bilateral treaties to this end, even establishing a regime of international courts to enforce these agreements.[144]

Moreover, on a multilateral front, Britain sought to obtain European consensus on the prohibition of the slave trade during the Congress of Vienna (1814–15), where representatives of the European powers gathered to peacefully settle the layout of the continent in the aftermath of the Napoleonic wars, creating a new European order.[145] Although it does not appear in full text in the Final Act,[146] at the Congress, British diplomacy obtained a 'Declaration of the Powers on the Abolition of the Slave Trade', which portrayed the slave trade as a 'scourge' that had 'afflicted humanity' and which was 'repugnant to the principles of humanity and universal morality'. Nonetheless, the declaration failed to contain any firm legal commitments from each State as to the time in which they would effectively abolish it.[147] A multilateral treaty on the subject would only be achieved in 1841, when Austria, Britain, France, Russia, and Prussia celebrated the Quintuple Treaty for the Suppression of the African Slave Trade.[148]

A trend towards the abolition of slavery itself began as well in other States, in particular in those in the Southern parts of the Americas. Starting in the early years of the nineteenth century, and following the complete abolition of the practice in the new State of Haïti (1804), Venezuela (1810), Argentina (1813), Chile (1823), and México (Mēxihco) (1829) proceeded to abolished slavery within their territories.[149] It would take up to 1833 for Britain to finally ban the practice in its colonial domains

---

[142] W. de Gruyter, *The Epochs of International Law* (M. Byers trans., W de G 2000) 554–558; Y. Onuma, 'When was the Law of International Society Born? – An Inquiry of the History of International Law from an Intercivilizational Perspective' (2000) 2 *Journal of the History of International Law* 1, 43; C. Tomuschat, *Human Rights: Between Idealism and Realism* (2nd edn., OUP 2008) 14.

[143] W. de Gruyter, *The Epochs of International Law* (M. Byers trans., W de G 2000) 557.

[144] W. de Gruyter, *The Epochs of International Law* (M. Byers trans., W de G 2000) 557–561; J. Martínez, *The Slave Trade and the Origins of International Human Rights Law* (OUP 2012) 28, 34–35.

[145] W. de Gruyter, *The Epochs of International Law* (M. Byers trans., W de G 2000) 451; J. Martínez, *The Slave Trade and the Origins of International Human Rights Law* (OUP 2012) 33.

[146] Hansard, The Parliamentary Debates from the Year 1803 to the Present Time, Volume 32 (1 February to 6 March 1816) (T.C. Hansard, 1816) 71–113, Art. CXVIII.

[147] W. de Gruyter, *The Epochs of International Law* (M. Byers trans., W de G 2000) 554; J. Martínez, *The Slave Trade and the Origins of International Human Rights Law* (OUP 2012) 33. See: Declaration of the Powers on the Abolition of the Slave Trade (1815).

[148] W. de Gruyter, *The Epochs of International Law* (M. Byers trans., W de G 2000) 561.

[149] M. Ishay, *The History of Human Rights: from Ancient Times to the Globalization Era* (University of California Press 2004) 157.

and up to 1865 for the United States to prohibit it in its whole territory. The trend of domestic legislations banning slavery continued to progress and, finally in 1926, a general multilateral treaty, the Convention to Suppress the Slave Trade and Slavery, was adopted under the auspices of the League of Nations. Through the ratification of this treaty, States Parties committed to bring about, as soon as possible, the complete abolition of slavery in all its forms.[150]

And yet, the progressive eradication of slavery did not translate into actual freedom for the people in colonial territories, but the suppression of the slave trade was used to legitimize the further expansion of European colonialism in Africa.[151] As illustrated by the Final Act of the Berlin Conference (1885), by which the European empires agreed on how the exploitation of the African continent and their people was to be divided among themselves, a new era of colonialism was to ensue.[152] This 'humanized' colonialism entailed the imperial powers' oversight of the suppression of slavery in Africa, as well as their efforts towards the 'conservation of the indigenous populations, and the amelioration of their moral and material conditions'.[153] The civilizing mission of colonialism brought attached the extension of some (but certainly not all) of the rights of the Enlightenment project to the colonized subjects,[154] together with a new impetus for the subjugation of peoples and the appropriation of lands and natural resources.

1.2.4 INTERNATIONAL HUMANITARIAN LAW

International humanitarian law is the body of norms that regulates the conduct of armed hostilities, dealing with a series of restrictions and prohibition of certain means and methods of warfare to protect the victims of armed conflicts. As a branch of international law that provides protection to the individual, its development was extremely influential for the emergence of the international law of human rights.[155] Given the recurrence of armed conflict in the history of civilization, a variety of rules regulating how hostilities could be conducted, distinguishing legitimate from illegitimate targets or enemies, and determining how and when hostilities were to

---

[150] Slavery Convention (adopted 25 September 1926, entered into force 9 March 1927), League of Nations, Treaty Series, vol. 60, p. 254.

[151] B. Ibhawoh, *Human Rights in Africa* (CUP 2018) 83 and 86.

[152] M. Mutua, 'Why Redraw the Map of Africa: A Legal and Moral Inquiry' (1995) 16 *Michigan Journal of International Law* 1113, 1127; D.C.J. Dakas, 'The Role of International Law in the Colonization of Africa: A Review in Light of Recent Calls for Re-colonization' (1999) 7 *African Yearbook of International Law* 85, 111–112; A. Anghie, 'Finding the Peripheries: Sovereignty and Colonialism in Nineteenth-Century International Law' (1999) 40 *Harvard International Law Journal* 1, 37–38, 58.

[153] General Act of the Berlin Conference on West Africa (26 February 1885), Art. 6.

[154] B. Ibhawoh, *Human Rights in Africa* (CUP 2018) 97.

[155] Within international law, the development of the institute of 'diplomatic protection'—by which a State can seek redress from another State for the harmed suffered by one of its nationals—is usually also considered significant in the emergence of the international law of human rights. See, for instance: A. Vermeer-Künzli, 'Diplomatic Protection as a Source of Human Rights Law' in D. Shelton (ed.), *The Oxford Handbook of International Human Rights Law* (OUP 2013) 250–274.

cease, existed from immemorial times.[156] However, a codified system of norms that, even during hostilities, outlaws certain behaviour considered to be inhumane has its origin in the nineteenth century.[157]

The (official) story leading to the beginning of the codification of the rules of humanitarian law is well known.[158] Witnessing the horrors of the aftermath of the battle of Solferino (1859), during the Italian War of Reunification, and especially the suffering and death of many former combatants, inspired Henry Dunant to found a committee for the assistance of wounded military men.[159] This committee, which years later would become the International Committee of the Red Cross, prompted the Swiss government to host a diplomatic conference in 1864, which ended in the adoption of the Convention for the Amelioration of the Condition of the Wounded in Armies in the Field.[160] This first treaty of international humanitarian law was a multilateral instrument, open to universal ratification, which codified rules of war protecting wounded and sick combatants and the medical personnel caring for them—to be identified with the symbol of a red cross on a white background.[161] But this was only a first step in the development of a codified system of rules of (almost) universal acceptance that regulates both the conduct of hostilities and the protection of different categories of individuals during armed conflicts—including civilians and prisoners of war. International humanitarian law as it exists today encompasses the rules codified in the four 1949 Geneva Conventions,[162] its two 1977 Additional Protocols,[163] a third 2005

---

[156] J. Kellenberger, 'Foreword' in J.-M. Henckaerts and L. Doswald-Beck, *Customary International Humanitarian Law: Volume I: Rules* (ICRC 2009) xv–xvii, xv; G. Oberleitner, 'Humanitarian Law as a Source of Human Rights Law' in D. Shelton (ed.), *The Oxford Handbook of International Human Rights Law* (OUP 2013) 275–294, 276.

[157] C. Tomuschat, *Human Rights: Between Idealism and Realism* (2nd edn., OUP 2008) 15; G. Oberleitner, 'Humanitarian Law as a Source of Human Rights Law' in D. Shelton (ed.), *The Oxford Handbook of International Human Rights Law* (OUP 2013) 275–294, 283–284.

[158] A. Alexander, 'A Short History of International Humanitarian Law' (2015) 26 *The European Journal of International Law* 109, 111.

[159] H. Dunant, *A Memory of Solferino* (ICRC 1959).

[160] J. Kellenberger, 'Foreword' in J.-M. Henckaerts and L. Doswald-Beck, *Customary International Humanitarian Law: Volume I: Rules* (ICRC 2009) xv–xvii, xv; A. Alexander, 'A Short History of International Humanitarian Law' (2015) 26 *The European Journal of International Law* 109, 112.

[161] Convention for the Amelioration of the Condition of the Wounded in Armies in the Field (adopted on 22 August 1864, entered into force on 22 June 1865).

[162] Convention (I) for the Amelioration of the Condition of the Wounded and Sick in Armed Forces in the Field (adopted 12 August 1949, entered into force 21 October 1950); Convention (II) for the Amelioration of the Condition of Wounded, Sick and Shipwrecked Members of Armed Forces at Sea (adopted 12 August 1949, entered into force 21 October 1950); Convention (III) relative to the Treatment of Prisoners of War (adopted 12 August 1949, entered into force 21 October 1950); Convention (IV) relative to the Protection of Civilian Persons in Time of War (adopted 12 August 1949, entered into force 21 October 1950).

[163] Protocol Additional to the Geneva Conventions of 12 August 1949, and relating to the Protection of Victims of International Armed Conflicts (Protocol I) (adopted 8 June 1977, entered into force 7 December 1978); Protocol Additional to the Geneva Conventions of 12 August 1949, and relating to the Protection of Victims of Non-International Armed Conflicts (Protocol II) (adopted 8 June 1977, entered into force 7 December 1978).

Protocol,[164] and a significant number of treaties concerning the use of certain weapons, the protection of the environment, and the protection of cultural property.[165]

As foreshadowed, the development of international humanitarian law acted as a significant precursor for the creation of an international law of human rights. Although the original aim of humanitarian law might appear to differ from that of human rights, with its focus on regulating the conduct of armed conflicts,[166] humanitarian law provided an earlier example of international law moving beyond the mere protection of traditional States' interests and into offering direct international legal protection to individuals. Moreover, if humanitarian law lent grounds for the emergence of an international law of human rights, the latter reciprocated, by supporting the development of a more humane law of war.[167] Ultimately, the symbiotic influence of these legal regimes is understandable, as they are guided by a basic identity of purpose, which is to provide international protection to the human person in all circumstances— as further discussed in **Section 2.5**.[168]

The protection of the human dignity of all individuals, as a convergent aim of both humanitarian and human rights law, has been affirmed by the International Criminal Tribunal for the Former Yugoslavia (ICTY); a tribunal created in 1993 to judge individuals for the commission of grave crimes, including serious violations of humanitarian law, in the territory of the former Yugoslavia from 1991. The ICTY has stated that:

> The essence of the whole corpus of international humanitarian law as well as human rights law lies in the protection of the human dignity of every person ... The general principle of respect for human dignity is the basic underpinning and indeed the very *raison d'être* of international humanitarian law and human rights law; indeed in modern times it has become of such paramount importance as to permeate the whole body of international law.[169]

---

[164] Protocol Additional to the Geneva Conventions of 12 August 1949, and relating to the Adoption of an Additional Distinctive Emblem (Protocol III) (adopted 8 December 2005, entered into force 14 January 2007).

[165] Such as: Protocol for the Prohibition of the Use of Asphyxiating, Poisonous or Other Gases, and of Bacteriological Methods of Warfare (adopted 17 June 1925, entered into force 8 February 1928); Convention for the Protection of Cultural Property in the Event of Armed Conflict (adopted 14 May 1954, entered into force 7 August 1956); Convention on the Prohibition of the Development, Production and Stockpiling of Bacteriological (Biological) and Toxin Weapons and on their Destruction (adopted 10 April 1972, entered into force 26 March 1975); Convention on the prohibition of military or any other hostile use of environmental modification techniques (adopted 10 December 1976, entered into force 5 October 1978); Convention on Prohibitions or Restrictions on the Use of Certain Conventional Weapons which may be deemed to be Excessively Injurious or to have Indiscriminate Effects (adopted 10 October 1980, entered into force 2 December 1983).

[166] D. Luban, 'Human Rights Thinking and the Laws of War' in J. Ohlin (ed.), *Theoretical Boundaries of Armed Conflicts and Human Rights* (CUP 2016) 45, 45; R. Kolb, G. Gaggioli, and P. Kilibarda, 'Introduction' in R. Kolb, G. Gaggioli, and P. Kilibarda (eds.), *Research Handbook on Human Rights and Humanitarian Law: Further Reflections and Perspectives* (Elgar 2022) 1–6, 1.

[167] T. Meron, 'The Humanization of Humanitarian Law' (2000) 94 *American Journal of International Law* 239; T. Meron, *The Humanization of International Law* (Nijhoff 2006), esp. chapter 1.

[168] C. Swinarski, *Principales Nociones e Institutos del Derecho Internacional Humanitario como Sistema Internacional de Protección de la Persona Humana* (IIDH 1990) 83–88.

[169] ICTY, *Prosecutor v. Furundzija*, Judgment, Case No. IT-95-17/1, Trial Chamber II (10 December 1998), para. 183.

> **ICTY (Trial Chamber),** *Prosecutor v. Anto Furundzija,* **Case No.: IT-95-17/1-T (10 December 1998) (21 July 2000).**
>
> The accused, Anto Furundzija, was the local commander of a special unit of the military police of the 'Croatian Defence Council'. He was prosecuted for serious violations of international humanitarian law: namely, torture and outrages upon personal dignity, including rape, as violations of the laws or customs of war. In 1998, the Trial Chamber found him guilty and sentenced him to ten years' imprisonment. While the accused appealed the judgment on many grounds, these were all rejected by the Appeals Chamber in 2000, which dismissed the appeal and confirmed the conviction and sentence.

1.2.5 THE LEAGUE OF NATIONS

Established in 1920, the League of Nations was an international organization created by one of the multilateral agreements encompassed by the 1919 Treaty of Versailles that put an end to the First World War.[170] Emerging from the horrors of the war, the League of Nations was founded with the aim of promoting international cooperation and achieving international peace and security.[171] Unfortunately, the League was unable to stop the tragic outbreak of the Second World War; a failure that marked the end of the organization and its replacement by the United Nations (UN).[172] Despite its relatively short history, a number of developments that were carried out under the auspices of the League of Nations helped shape the idea of human rights endorsed by its successor. For instance, a number of important international instruments for the protection of women, children, and refugees were drafted under the League of Nations.[173] These included the 1921 International Convention for the Suppression of the Traffic in Women and Children, the 1924 Geneva Declaration of the Rights of the Child, the 1933 International Convention for the Suppression of the Traffic in Women of Full Age, and the 1933 Convention Relating to the International Status of Refugees.[174] Arguably,

---

[170] Covenant of the League of Nations (adopted on 28 April 1919, entered into force on 10 January 1920).

[171] Covenant of the League of Nations (adopted on 28 April 1919, entered into force on 10 January 1920), preamble.

[172] L. Goodrich, 'From League of Nations to United Nations' (1947) 1 *International Organization* 3, 3; C. Tams, 'Experiments Great and Small: Centenary Reflections on the League of Nations' (2019) 62 *German Yearbook of International Law* 93, 94.

[173] M. Ishay, *The History of Human Rights: from Ancient Times to the Globalization Era* (University of California Press 2004) 235.

[174] International Convention for the Suppression of the Traffic in Women and Children (adopted on 30 September 1921, entered into force 15 June 1922), League of Nations TS vol. 9 p. 415; Geneva Declaration of the Rights of the Child (adopted on 26 September 1924); International Convention for the Suppression of the Traffic in Women of Full Age (adopted on 11 October 1933, entered into force 24 August 1934); Convention Relating to the International Status of Refugees (adopted on 28 October 1933) League of Nations, Treaty Series Vol. CLIX No. 3663.

the most important multilateral treaty celebrated under the League of Nations is the already discussed 1926 Slavery Convention.

1.2.5.1 The International Labour Organization

The creation of the International Labour Organization (ILO), also through the Peace Treaty of Versailles,[175] as an affiliated agency of the League of Nations, was a significant development towards the emergence of the international law of human rights.[176] This organization, which survived the League of Nations to become a specialized agency of the UN, was grounded on the idea that 'peace can be established only if it is based upon social justice'[177] and tasked with improving working conditions and living standards worldwide.[178] Within its framework, almost 200 international treaties have been adopted up to the end of 2022, with the first sixty-seven Conventions pre-dating the creation of the UN.[179] The main purpose of these treaties has been to improve general standards of work across the world, as well as to provide protection to specific categories of workers, such as women and children. Moreover, of the nearly 200 Conventions celebrated under the ILO regime, the organization has signalled eleven as 'fundamental', understanding that the rights recognized thereby must be protected by all Members States, irrespective of whether they are Parties to the specific treaties.[180]

1.2.5.2 The mandate system

The European imperial project continued under the League of Nations, with the important exception of the colonies controlled before the First World War by the defeated German and Ottoman Empires, which were placed under a newly created international regime:

---

[175] Treaty of Peace of Versailles (adopted 28 June 1919, entered into force 10 January 2020), Part XIII.

[176] J. Diller, 'Social Justice, Rights, and Labour' in D. Shelton (ed.), *The Oxford Handbook of International Human Rights Law* (OUP 2013) 295–324, 296.

[177] Treaty of Peace of Versailles (adopted 28 June 1919, entered into force 10 January 2020), Part XIII, Section I.

[178] J. Diller, 'Social Justice, Rights, and Labour' in D. Shelton (ed.), *The Oxford Handbook of International Human Rights Law* (OUP 2013) 295–324, 307–310; D. Maul, *The International Labour Organization: 100 Years of Global Social Policy* (De Gruyter 2019) 1–5.

[179] See ILO's website, available at: https://www.ilo.org/dyn/normlex/en/f?p=1000:12001:4864291437270::::P12001_INSTRUMENT_SORT:4 (accessed on 13 February 2023).

[180] These 11 fundamental treaties are: ILO, Forced Labour Convention, 1930 (C029) (adopted on 28 June 1930, entered into force on 1 May 1932) (and its 2014 Protocol, P029, adopted on 11 June 2014 and entered into force on 9 November 2016); ILO, Freedom of Association and Protection of the Right to Organize Convention (C087) (adopted on 9 July 1948, entered into force on 4 July 1950); ILO, Right to Organize and Collective Bargaining Convention, (C098) (adopted on 9 July 1948, entered into force on 4 July 1950); ILO, Equal Remuneration Convention (C100) (adopted on 29 June 1951, entered into force on 23 May 1953); ILO, Abolition of Forced Labour Convention (C105) (adopted on 25 June 1957, entered into force on 17 January 1959); ILO, Discrimination (Employment and Occupation) Convention (C111) (adopted on 25 June 1958, entered into force on 15 June 1960); ILO, Minimum Age Convention (C138) (adopted on 26 June 1973, entered into force on 19 June 1976); ILO, Occupational Safety and Health Convention (C155) (adopted on 22 June 1981, entered into force on 11 August 1983); ILO, Worst Forms of Child Labour Convention (C182) (adopted on 17 June 1999, entered into force on 19 November 2000); ILO, Promotional Framework for Occupational Safety and Health Convention (C187) (adopted on 15 June 2006, entered into force on 20 February 2009). See: ILO, 'Declaration on Fundamental Principles and Rights at Work and its Follow-up' (adopted at the 86th Session of the International Labour Conference (1998), and amended at the 110th Session (2022)).

the mandate system.[181] Three different types of mandates were established, with varying degree of control exercised by the mandatory power, depending on the 'stage of development' of the colonies.[182] The purported objective of the system was to protect the (approximately 13 million)[183] colonized peoples, promote their welfare, and guide them towards self-government or even independence, depending on the case.[184] Some of the ideas that underpinned the 'humanized' colonialism of the Berlin Conference reappeared in the Covenant of the League of Nations,[185] which portrayed the colonies as inhabited by people 'not yet able to stand by themselves under the strenuous conditions of the modern world'; hence, their well-being and development—'a sacred trust of civilization'—was to be entrusted to 'advanced nations', which were considered well-placed to undertake such a mission.[186] A Commission was created under the League, to receive and examine annual reports on the fulfilment, by the mandatory powers, of the obligations entailed by the mandates.[187] A system of international petitions was also set in place, allowing the inhabitants of mandates to submit complaints about grievances in the application of the mandate,[188] which, although far from successful,[189] can be counted as an important predecessor of the right of petition that exists under the international law of human rights.[190] With the creation of the UN, the mandate system was replaced by an international trusteeship regime established under the Charter.[191]

---

[181] M. Mutua, 'Why Redraw the Map of Africa: A Legal and Moral Inquiry' (1995) 16 *Michigan Journal of International Law* 1113, 1137–1138.

[182] M. Mutua, 'Why Redraw the Map of Africa: A Legal and Moral Inquiry' (1995) 16 *Michigan Journal of International Law* 1113, 1138; A. Anghie, 'Colonialism and the Birth of International Institutions: Sovereignty, Economy, and the Mandate System of the League of Nations' (2002) 34 *New York University Journal of International Law and Politics* 513, 525–526.

[183] D. Myers, 'The Mandate System of the League of Nations' (1921) 96 *Annals of the American Academy of Political and Social Science* 74, 76.

[184] A. Anghie, 'Colonialism and the Birth of International Institutions: Sovereignty, Economy, and the Mandate System of the League of Nations' (2002) 34 *New York University Journal of International Law and Politics* 513, 525, 562–563, and 568; B. Rajagopal, *International Law from Below: Development, Social Movements and Third World Resistance* (CUP 2003) 57.

[185] M. Mutua, 'Why Redraw the Map of Africa: A Legal and Moral Inquiry' (1995) 16 *Michigan Journal of International Law* 1113, 1138; B. Ibhawoh, *Human Rights in Africa* (CUP 2018) 95–96.

[186] Covenant of the League of Nations (adopted 28 June 1919, entered into force 10 January 1920), Art. 22.

[187] A. Anghie, 'Colonialism and the Birth of International Institutions: Sovereignty, Economy, and the Mandate System of the League of Nations' (2002) 34 *New York University Journal of International Law and Politics* 513, 527, 575.

[188] A.A. Cançado Trindade, 'Exhaustion of Local Remedies in International Law Experiments Granting Procedural Status to Individuals in the First Half of the Twentieth Century' (1977) 24 *Netherlands International Law Review* 373, 386–388; B. Rajagopal, *International Law from Below: Development, Social Movements and Third World Resistance* (CUP 2003) 67.

[189] A. Anghie, 'Colonialism and the Birth of International Institutions: Sovereignty, Economy, and the Mandate System of the League of Nations' (2002) 34 *New York University Journal of International Law and Politics* 513, 528 and 605; B. Rajagopal, International Law from Below: Development, Social Movements and Third World Resistance (CUP 2003) 70–71.

[190] B. Rajagopal, *International Law from Below: Development, Social Movements and Third World Resistance* (CUP 2003) 67–68; B. Ibhawoh, *Human Rights in Africa* (CUP 2018) 153–154.

[191] See: UN Charter, Chapter XII.

1.2.5.3 The system for the protection of minorities

One of the most significant contributions to the international protection of individuals carried out by the League of Nations itself was the development of a 'minority protection system'. A major political outcome of the First World War was the re-drawing of the European map, with the fall of some of the remaining empires, the emergence of new States, and the re-setting of national borders, mostly within the European continent, but also beyond.[192]

The important changes in European political borders meant that the territorial gains of many States led to their populations being ethnically, religiously, culturally, or linguistically diverse.[193] To engage with this situation, the League of Nations established a system for the protection of the minorities resident in a country; although, in practice, the system only applied to certain States, especially to the newly emerging States and to those defeated during the war.[194] The system began with the treaty signed between the victorious powers and Poland, which served as model for subsequent agreements concerning other States.[195]

The international obligations concerning the protection of the members of minorities extended to different rights, with both individual and collective dimensions. To begin, the member of a minority had the right to acquire the citizenship of the State in which they resided due to the newly established borders. The obligations also extended to the principle of equality before the law and to the right to use their own language. Collective rights were also contemplated, including the right to establish own educational and religious institutions. Moreover, in areas where a minority constituted a considerable proportion of the population, there was an obligation to provide elementary education in the minorities' own language, although the curriculum could include the requirement to learn the country's official one.[196] Importantly, the legal status of these obligations was that of 'fundamental law'; meaning that they could not be displaced by subsequent

---

[192] Some of the most important political changes included the collapse of the Austro-Hungarian, German, Ottoman, and Russian Empires; the consequential emergence of different new States, such as Armenia, Czechoslovakia, Estonia, Finland, Latvia, Lithuania, Poland, and Yugoslavia (officially, the Kingdom of Serbs, Croats, and Slovenes); and the creation of the 'mandate system' under the League of Nations to change control over territories formerly under the colonial domination of the fallen German and Ottoman Empires. See: L. Sondhaus, *World War I: the global revolution* (CUP 2011).

[193] S. Benhabib, 'International Law and Human Plurality in the Shadow of Totalitarianism: Hannah Arendt and Raphael Lemkin' (2009) 16 *Constellations* 331, 336; P. Hilpold, 'The League of Nations and the Protection of Minorities–Rediscovering a Great Experiment' (2013) 17 *Max Planck Yearbook of United Nations Law* 87, 89.

[194] P. Hilpold, 'The League of Nations and the Protection of Minorities–Rediscovering a Great Experiment' (2013) 17 *Max Planck Yearbook of United Nations Law* 87, 93; P. Kovács, 'The Protection of Minorities under the Auspices of the League of Nations' in D. Shelton (ed.), *The Oxford Handbook of International Human Rights Law* (OUP 2013) 325–342, 327.

[195] Treaty obligations were established with regards to Armenia, Austria, Bulgaria, Czechoslovakia, Finland, Germany (only regarding Upper Silesia), Greece, Hungary, Romania, Turkey, and Yugoslavia (the Serb-Croat-Slovene State), while similar obligations were assumed by the unilateral declaration of other States, including Albania, Estonia, Iraq, Latvia, and Lithuania. See: P. Thornberry, *International Law and the Rights of Minorities* (Clarendon Press 1992) 41–42.

[196] H. Rosting, 'Protection of Minorities by the League of Nations' (1923) 17 *American Journal of International Law* 641, 648–649; P. Thornberry, *International Law and the Rights of Minorities* (Clarendon Press 1992) 42–43; P. Hilpold, 'The League of Nations and the Protection of Minorities–Rediscovering a Great Experiment' (2013) 17 *Max Planck Yearbook of United Nations Law* 87, 94–95.

domestic legislation and could only be amended with the approval of the Council of the League of Nations, one of the main organs of the organization.[197]

The minority system established also contained innovative elements concerning procedural measures to deal with breaches of the assumed international obligations. The original provisions in this respect allowed for States that sat on the League's Council to bring to the attention of this organ the existence of an infraction of an obligation, or even a danger of infraction, and also to refer to the Permanent Court of International Justice, the main judicial body of the League, any questions concerning these obligations.[198] Given that this heavily politicized system proved to offer limited redress to the victims of breaches, it was subject to progressive reforms. A first change came about in 1920, allowing for individuals, members of a minority, to bring infractions (or the danger of an infraction) to the attention of the Council, although the role of the complainer was limited to presenting such a petition to the organ.[199] It was up to the Council to decide whether an investigation was deemed pertinent, which would be undertaken by a 'Minorities Committee'.[200] However, an investigation revealing a breach then required a unanimous decision of the Council for the League to take further actions, which rendered such a course of action politically difficult. Hence, the Minorities Committee and the League's Secretariat often tried to find an agreeable solution to receivable petitions.[201]

The demise of this system can be associated with Hitler's ascent to power in 1933 and the promulgation of racist legislation in Nazi Germany, even before the infamous 'Nuremberg Laws' of 1935. Racist legislation adopted in 1933 already restricted Jewish individuals in the practice of the medical and legal professions, ordered the retirement of Jewish staff from the civil service, and limited the number of Jewish students at schools.[202] The application of such racist laws to the region of Upper Silesia brought the issue within the scope of the minorities protection of the League of Nations, due to the 1922 Convention concerning Upper Silesia.[203] The consideration of the Nazi legislation by the League's Council took place thanks to a

---

[197] H. Rosting, 'Protection of Minorities by the League of Nations' (1923) 17 *American Journal of International Law* 641, 649; P. Kovács, 'The Protection of Minorities under the Auspices of the League of Nations' in D. Shelton (ed), *The Oxford Handbook of International Human Rights Law* (OUP 2013) 325–342, 329.

[198] H. Rosting, 'Protection of Minorities by the League of Nations' (1923) 17 *American Journal of International Law* 641, 653–655; P. Thornberry, *International Law and the Rights of Minorities* (Clarendon Press 1992) 44–46; P. Hilpold, 'The League of Nations and the Protection of Minorities–Rediscovering a Great Experiment' (2013) 17 *Max Planck Yearbook of United Nations Law* 87, 96–101.

[199] P. Hilpold, 'The League of Nations and the Protection of Minorities–Rediscovering a Great Experiment' (2013) 17 *Max Planck Yearbook of United Nations Law* 87, 97.

[200] J. Stone, 'The Legal Nature of the Minorities Petition' (1931) 12 *British Year Book of International Law* 76, 76–77.

[201] P. Hilpold, 'The League of Nations and the Protection of Minorities–Rediscovering a Great Experiment' (2013) 17 *Max Planck Yearbook of United Nations Law* 87, 99–100.

[202] 'Berheim Petition to the League of Nations', *American Jewish Year Book* (Review of the Year 5693), 74–78.

[203] The system of minorities' protection established under the 1922 Geneva Convention concerning Upper Silesia actually envisioned a multiplicity of remedies, granting individuals access to two controlling agencies, in addition to the League's Council: the Mixed Commission and the Arbitral Tribunal for dealing with a petition. See: A.A. Cançado Trindade, 'Exhaustion of Local Remedies in International Law Experiments Granting Procedural Status to Individuals in the First Half of the Twentieth Century' (1977) 24 *Netherlands International Law Review* 373, 380–381. See also: Geneva Convention concerning Upper Silesia (adopted on 15 May 1922).

petition lodged by Franz Bernheim, who claimed that the laws in question amounted to a breach of Germany's obligations with regards to the rights of the Jewish minority in Upper Silesia.[204] The violations entailed by the legislation were so outrageous that even the (politicized) Council managed to reach a unanimous decision, with the abstentions of both Germany and Italy.[205] Although Nazi Germany would soon after withdraw from the League of Nations, it remained under the treaty obligation to protect the minorities in Upper Silesia from discrimination until July 1937, as the 1922 Convention established German obligations concerning Upper Silesia for a fifteen-year period.[206] Surprisingly, this international obligation did provide a degree of protection to the Jewish population in Upper Silesia, with much of the ominously racist Nazi legislation not being applied to the region until 1937.[207]

Following Germany's withdrawal from the League, other States, such as Poland and Romania, raised objections to continuing to engage with the League's minorities protection system. These backlashes brought about a *de facto* termination of the system. The official demise of the minorities' regime materialized with the political refusal to continue such a system under the new international organization to be created, the United Nations.[208] Nevertheless, the minority system established under the League of Nations acted as a significant predecessor of the current systems of human rights petitions developed under the United Nations and regional organizations in Africa, the Americas, and Europe, which will be extensively discussed throughout this book.[209]

1.2.6 FROM THE LEAGUE OF NATIONS TO THE UNITED NATIONS

As mentioned in **Section 1.2.5**, the outbreak of the Second World War marked the demise of the League of Nations and led to the creation of a new international organization: the United Nations. The lengthy and difficult path that connects the point in time in which some of the most horrific crimes against human beings were committed, such as the genocide perpetrated by Nazi Germany, to the creation of a post-war world order that counts the protection of human rights as one of its founding pillars was mediated by a series of important political and legal developments.

One of these important developments was the 1941 declaration known as the 'Atlantic Charter',[210] in which it is possible to find a (timid) commitment to a future where human rights have become part of international policy. The 'Charter' was actually a

---

[204] 'Berheim Petition to the League of Nations', *American Jewish Year Book* (Review of the Year 5693) 78.
[205] 'Berheim Petition to the League of Nations', *American Jewish Year Book* (Review of the Year 5693) 98.
[206] Geneva Convention concerning Upper Silesia (adopted on 15 May 1922), Art. 64.
[207] B. Karch, 'A Jewish "Nature Preserve": League of Nations Minority Protections in Nazi Upper Silesia, 1933–1937' (2013) 46 *Central European History* 124.
[208] M. Mazower, 'The Strange Triumph of Human Rights, 1933–1950' (2004) 47 *The Historical Journal* 379, 388–390; P. Kovács, 'The Protection of Minorities under the Auspices of the League of Nations' in D. Shelton (ed.), *The Oxford Handbook of International Human Rights Law* (OUP 2013) 325–342, 335–336.
[209] P. Kovács, 'The Protection of Minorities under the Auspices of the League of Nations' in D. Shelton (ed.), *The Oxford Handbook of International Human Rights Law* (OUP 2013) 325–342, 339–340.
[210] Atlantic Charter (14 August 1941).

joint declaration of US President Roosevelt and UK Prime Minister Churchill, made before the USA's direct intervention in the Second World War, in which they expressed a number of common principles of national policy on which a better future for the world could be built after the end of the war.[211] The declaration encompassed eight principles, including: the denial of any desire to expand territorially; that territorial changes should be based on the wishes of the peoples concerned; that the form of government adopted should also be a choice of said peoples;[212] the importance of engaging in collaborations to improve labour standards and social security; that the use of force in international relations should be abandoned; and that peace, following the final destruction of the Nazi tyranny, should 'afford assurance that all the men in all lands may live out their lives in freedom from fear and want'.[213]

The above-mentioned principles were later subscribed to by twenty-six States that entered the war against the members of the Tripartite Pact (Germany, Italy, and Japan) in the 'Declaration by United Nations' signed on the first day of 1942—and then endorsed by nineteen further States.[214] This international instrument was a war declaration in which the signatories committed to make use of their full economic and military resources against their enemies. In this document, it is possible to find the actual term 'human rights', as part of the commitment of the warring States for the future world order. In the Declaration, the Allies stated their conviction that 'complete victory over their enemies [was] essential to defend life, liberty, independence, and religious freedom, and to preserve human rights and justice in their own lands as well as in other lands'.[215]

The 'United Nations' that signed the Declarations—and six additional States that had failed to do so[216]—were invited to the 1945 San Francisco Conference, where the United Nations Charter was adopted. For the most part, the foundations of the UN had already

---

[211] R. Russell, *A History of the United Nations Charter: The Role of the United States, 1940–1945* (Brookings Institution 1958) 39–40.

[212] However, Churchill was adamant about these ideas of self-determination not being applicable to the British colonies, and only to the European continent. See: A. Cassese, *Self-Determination of Peoples: A Legal Reappraisal* (CUP 1995) 37; B. Ibhawoh, *Human Rights in Africa* (CUP 2018) 130–131.

[213] The declaration echoed Roosevelt's famous 'Four Freedoms Speech', which he delivered to the US Congress earlier that year, which concluded by stating that 'Freedom means the supremacy of human rights everywhere' and in which he expressed his vision of a world founded on four essential freedoms: 'The first is freedom of speech and expression—everywhere in the world. The second is freedom of every person to worship God in his own way—everywhere in the world. The third is freedom from want—which, translated into world terms, means economic understandings which will secure to every nation a healthy peacetime life for its inhabitants—everywhere in the world. The fourth is freedom from fear—which, translated into world terms, means a world-wide reduction of armaments to such a point and in such a thorough fashion that no nation will be in a position to commit an act of physical aggression against any neighbor—anywhere in the world.' See: F.D. Roosevelt, State of the Union Address (6 January 1941), available at: https://millercenter.org/the-presidency/presidential-speeches/january-6-1941-state-union-four-freedoms.

[214] R. Russell, *A History of the United Nations Charter: The Role of the United States,* (Brookings Institution 1958) 51–52.

[215] Declaration by the United Nations (1 January 1942).

[216] Argentina, the Byelorussian Soviet Socialist Republic, Denmark, Lebanon, Syria, and the Ukrainian Soviet Socialist Republic. See: B. Conforti and C. Focarelli, *The Law and Practice of the United Nations* (5th edn., Brill 2016) 4.

been sketched by the negotiations between Roosevelt, Stalin, and Churchill, with the participation of the Republic of China, in meetings taking place between late 1943 and early 1945.[217] It was only after the most important aspects of the new organization had been settled that a meeting in which the other allied nations would participate was announced.[218]

As will be further discussed in **Section 4.1**, that human rights managed to obtain a significant place in the constitutive document of the organization was perhaps an unintended outcome for the political leaders that decided to host the 1945 San Francisco Conference.[219] The reticence of the big powers to provide a preponderant place for human rights in the text of the Charter—partly explained by their own flagrant behaviour regarding colonialism, racial discrimination, and political persecution[220]—meant that when delegations from other States arrived at San Francisco, only one small mention of human rights could be found in the draft Charter. Nevertheless, the final text ended up containing references to the respect and promotion of human rights in seven different places.[221] The adoption of the UN Charter on 26 June 1945, where international obligations towards the respect and promotion of human rights were adopted by fifty of the fifty-one founding Member States of the organization,[222] combined with the subsequent adoption of the Universal Declaration of Human Rights, on 10 December 1948, constitutes a moment of such historical significance to be considered by many as the true birth of human rights.[223]

1.3 HUMAN RIGHTS CRITIQUES

The proclamation that all individuals have inherent rights has been the subject of extensive opposition throughout its history. As discussed in **Section 1.1.2.2.1**, relativist objections were raised during the process of adoption of the 1948 Universal Declaration

---

[217] The Moscow Conference (1943), the Tehran Conference (1943), the Dumbarton Oaks Conversations (1944), and the Yalta Conference (1945). See: R. Russell, *A History of the United Nations Charter: The Role of the United States,* (Brookings Institution 1958).

[218] M.A. Glendon, 'The Forgotten Crucible: The Latin American Influence on the Universal Human Rights Idea' (2003) 16 *Harvard Human Rights Journal* 27, 27.

[219] M.A. Glendon, 'The Forgotten Crucible: The Latin American Influence on the Universal Human Rights Idea' (2003) 16 *Harvard Human Rights Journal* 27, 28; M. Mazower, 'The Strange Triumph of Human Rights, 1933–1950' (2004) 47 *The Historical Journal* 379, 392.

[220] P. Alston, 'The Commission on Human Rights' in P. Alston (ed.), *The United Nations and Human Rights: A Critical Appraisal* (Clarendon Press 1992) 126–210, 141; W. Osiatynski, 'On the Universality of the Universal Declaration of Human Rights' in A. Sajó (ed.), *Human Rights with Modesty: The Problem with Universalism* (Springer 2004) 33–50, 36; B. Ramcharan, 'Normative Human Rights Cascades, North and South' (2016) 37 *Third World Quarterly* 1234, 1238.

[221] M.A. Glendon, 'The Forgotten Crucible: The Latin American Influence on the Universal Human Rights Idea' (2003) 16 *Harvard Human Rights Journal* 27, 28.

[222] Poland was not represented at the San Francisco Conference, but signed the Charter later that year. See: C. Benedetto Conforti, *The Law and Practice of the United Nations* (5th edn., Brill 2016) 4 and 6.

[223] M. Pinto, *Temas de Derechos Humanos* (Del Puerto 1997) 15–16; A. Buchanan, *The Heart of Human Rights* (OUP 2013) 11.

of Human Rights, and to the expansive recognition of such rights in the middle and late-twentieth century. However, backlashes to the idea of universal rights can already be found in the late eighteenth and early nineteenth centuries, when natural rights were declared.

Among the most renowned intellectual opposition to the inherent rights proclaimed, especially, by the 1789 French Declaration, we can find both the conservative antagonism expressed by Edmund Burke and the positivist objections raised by Jeremy Bentham.[224] Although Burke's and Bentham's opposition to the idea of the inherent rights of man are grounded on different ideological standpoints, they reached a similar conclusion as to the validity of such rights. Burke's antagonism to the proclamation of rights by the French Declaration has been described as ferocious, revealing a clear concern about the risk of revolutionary sentiments crossing the Anglo-French border and destabilizing the British political order.[225] He chastised the French Declaration's cry for *égalité* as proclaiming a 'monstrous fiction' of human equality, which was only capable of inspiring hopeless expectations of overcoming real inequality.[226] On its part, Bentham coined the famous reference to natural rights as 'nonsense upon stilts'.[227] His positivist hostility to the idea of inherent rights to be found in natural law was grounded in the conviction that only positive law could provide for 'real rights'.[228] In his critical examination of the French Declaration, he affirmed: '*Right*, the substantive *right*, is the child of law: from *real* laws come *real* rights; but from *imaginary* laws, from laws of nature, fancied and invented by poets, rhetoricians, and dealers in moral and intellectual poisons, come *imaginary* rights, a bastard brood of monsters, "gorgons and chimæra dire".'[229]

Nonetheless, this section is not about criticisms of the idea of human rights, but an exploration of human rights *critiques*; a rather different concept. A 'critique' is not about expressing disagreement or stating that something is not right, but 'a matter of pointing out on what kinds of assumptions, what kinds of familiar unchallenged, unconsidered modes of thought, the practices that we accept rest'.[230] In other words, a critique is a type of analysis that focuses on generally held assumptions that underpin a given field or discipline, such as human rights,

---

[224] E. Burke, *Revolutionary Writings* (CUP 2014 (1790)); J. Bentham, 'A Critical Examination of the Declaration of Rights' in *The Works of Jeremy Bentham* (Simkin, Marshall & Co. 1843) 496–524.

[225] J. Waldron (ed.), '*Nonsense upon stilts*': *Bentham, Burke, and Marx on the Rights of Man* (Methuen 1987) 79, 81–82, 89.

[226] M. Cranston, 'Are There Any Human Rights?' (1983) 112 *Daedalus* 1, 4. See: E. Burke, *Revolutionary Writings* (CUP 2014 (1790)) 38.

[227] J. Bentham, 'A Critical Examination of the Declaration of Rights' in *The Works of Jeremy Bentham* (Simkin, Marshall & Co. 1843) 496–524, 501.

[228] J. Waldron (ed.), '*Nonsense upon stilts*': *Bentham, Burke, and Marx on the Rights of Man* (Methuen 1987) 34.

[229] J. Bentham, 'A Critical Examination of the Declaration of Rights' in *The Works of Jeremy Bentham* (Simkin, Marshall & Co. 1843) 496–524, 523.

[230] M. Foucault, 'Practicing Criticism' in L.D. Kritzman (ed.), *Politics, Philosophy, Culture: Interviews and Other Writings 1977–1984* (A. Sherdan trans., Routledge 1988) 155.

confronting them with either its own orthodox discourse or with external ones, to bring attention to problems, inconsistencies, conflicts, or ambiguitie that usually go unproblematized.[231] Critiques are not necessarily antagonistic to the subject of analysis—although they might be—but can be aimed at identifying problematic assumptions to be overcome. The following sub-sections will discuss four human rights critiques to illustrate how these theoretically underpinned examinations of human rights can contribute to questioning some aspects of the philosophical and historical grounds of human rights discussed in **Section 1.1.1** and **Section 1.2**. The selected critiques are those grounded in Marxist, feminist, postmodern, and postcolonial approaches to the field of human rights.

1.3.1 MARXIST CRITIQUES

Similar to Burke and Bentham, but for radically different reasons, Karl Marx found the proclamation of the rights of man during the French Revolution to be problematic. In his (controversial) essay *On the Jewish Question*, published in 1844, Marx criticized the individualistic nature of the rights proclaimed in France. His main contention was that the 'man'[232] conceived thereby was an egoistic man, isolated both from other men and from the community. Questioning what constitutes 'liberty', according to the rights of man, Marx claimed that 'the right of man to liberty is based not on the association of man with man, but on the separation of man from man. It is the right of this separation, the right of the restricted individual, withdrawn into himself . . . into the confines of his private interests and private caprice, and separated from the community.'[233] This understanding of men as isolated egoistic individuals was further confirmed by how civil society was thought of: as if existing for the sole purpose to 'guarantee to each of its members the preservation of his person, his rights, and his property . . . society, appears as a framework external to the individuals, as a restriction of their original independence. The sole bond holding them together is natural necessity, need and private interest, the preservation of their property and their egoistic selves.'[234] Consequently, Marx seemed to reach the conclusion that instead of providing emancipation from oppression, the rights of man could be seen as acting as an *ideology* that supported the creation of

---

[231] T. Heller, 'Structuralism and Critique' (1984) 36 *Stanford Law Review* 127, 132; A. Azmanova, 'Social Harm, Political Judgment, and the Pragmatics of Justification' in C. Corradetti (ed.), *Philosophical Dimensions of Human Rights: Some Contemporary Views* (Springer 2012) 107–123, 117; D. Otto, 'Feminist Approaches to International Law' in A. Orford and F. Hoffmann (eds.), *The Oxford Handbook of the Theory of International Law* (OUP 2016) 488–504, 494.

[232] As highlighted by Dembour, Marx's concern was indeed about men, not caring particularly in the essay about the rights of women. See: M-B. Dembour, *Who Believes in Human Rights? Reflections on the European Convention* (CUP 2006) 114.

[233] K. Marx, 'On the Jewish Question' in D. McLellan (ed.), *Karl Marx: Selected Writings* (2nd edn., OUP 2000) 46–64.

[234] K. Marx, 'On the Jewish Question' in D. McLellan (ed.), *Karl Marx: Selected Writings* (2nd edn., OUP 2000) 46–64.

a different form of regulatory regime.[235] With these rights, 'man was not freed from religion, he received religious freedom. He was not freed from property, he received freedom to own property. He was not freed from the egoism of business; he received freedom to engage in business.'[236]

Importantly, Marxist critiques of human rights did not end with Marx's own engagement with the rights of man—which was in itself a scarce topic in his overall intellectual production.[237] Marx was to become one of the most influential thinkers in history, giving birth to a whole range of 'Marxist approaches' that have embraced different aspects and ideas of his writings to produce critical analyses, inclusive of human rights, that remain relevant in our days. To clarify, as it happens with all the critiques explored in this chapter, Marxist critiques—in plural—can adopt different shapes and forms, not always coinciding with one another, depending on the elements of Marxist doctrine selected to guide the analysis.[238]

For instance, Robert Knox has developed an appealing Marxist critique of human rights that focuses on key elements of Marx's 'historical materialism', which predicates that social phenomena cannot be properly understood unless grounded in the 'material conditions of life'. That is to say, the examination of social phenomena needs to be contextualized in the relations of production entered by men and determined by society's economic structure, in which lies the foundations of all legal and political (super)structures of society—which, in turn, determine the consciousness of men.[239] Knox focuses on three elements of historical materialism to undertake his critique of human rights: class, ideology, and capitalism. He argues that, from a Marxist perspective, it is far from coincidental that the emergence of the 'rights of man' took place at the time of transition from the feudal to the capitalist system of production, as these rights could be seen as performing an ideological function of support that helps to maintain and reproduce this system. The selfish isolated man Marx described in his critique of the

---

[235] M-B. Dembour, *Who Believes in Human Rights? Reflections on the European Convention* (CUP 2006) 122; R. Knox, 'A Marxist Approach to *R.M.T. v. United Kingdom*' in D. Gonzalez-Salzberg and L. Hodson (eds.), *Research Methods for International Human Rights Law: Beyond the Traditional Paradigm* (Routledge 2019) 13–41, 16.

[236] K. Marx, 'On the Jewish Question' in D. McLellan (ed.), *Karl Marx: Selected Writings* (2nd edn., OUP 2000) 46–64.

[237] J. Waldron (ed.), *'Nonsense upon stilts': Bentham, Burke, and Marx on the Rights of Man* (Methuen 1987) 134–135.

[238] There is extensive critical literature about Marxism and human rights. See, among many: S. Lukes, 'Can a Marxist Believe in Human Rights?' (1981) 1 *Praxis International* 334; A. Buchanan, *Marx and Justice: The Radical Critique of Liberalism* (Rowman and Littlefield 1982), esp. Chapter 4; R. Cornell, 'Should a Marxist Believe in Rights?' (1984) 4 *Praxis International* 45; M-B. Dembour, *Who Believes in Human Rights? Reflections on the European Convention* (CUP 2006), Chapter 5; B. Roth, 'Marxian Insights for the Human Rights Project' in S. Marks (ed.), *International Law on the Left: Re-examining Marxist Legacies* (CUP 2008) 220–251; C. Boyd, 'Can a Marxist Believe in Human Rights?' (2009) 37 *Critique* 579; R. Knox, 'A Marxist Approach to *R.M.T. v. United Kingdom*' in D. Gonzalez-Salzberg and L. Hodson (eds.), *Research Methods for International Human Rights Law: Beyond the Traditional Paradigm* (Routledge 2019) 13–41.

[239] R. Knox, 'A Marxist Approach to *R.M.T. v. United Kingdom*' in D. Gonzalez-Salzberg and L. Hodson (eds.), *Research Methods for International Human Rights Law: Beyond the Traditional Paradigm* (Routledge 2019) 13–41, 13.

French Declaration seems to be the type of person that perfectly fits capitalism, where production is carried out for individual, rather than communal, profit.[240]

Class, in Marxist terms, refers to a group of individuals who share a common relationship towards the means of production and, consequently, to the creation and appropriation of wealth. In a given society, the different classes struggle with one another to realize their antagonistic interests.[241] Knox proposes that human rights provide yet another ambit in which the struggle between classes takes place, in which social conflict is re-cast in terms of individual rights; thereby, drawing attention away from the root causes of social problems.[242] Indeed, human rights appear functional to the relations of domination within capitalism, as the rights provided to individuals bring attached the reinforcement of the authority of the State and the capitalistic means of production. Human rights violations are framed as mere deviation from the norm, without questioning the real causes of injustice, such as exclusion and oppression, immanent to capitalism as a system.[243] Therefore, from such a Marxist perspective, human rights have become part of the (capitalist) problem, as they are engrained into the system, providing strong ideological support to the reproduction of capitalist social relations.

Does this mean that a Marxist standpoint must be antagonistic to human rights? Not necessarily.[244] On the one hand, human rights, as we conceive them today, can be seen to be much more than the (problematic) rights of man from the eighteenth century; consequently, a moderate Marxist stance could take solace in the fact that traditional individual rights have been expanded though the years, not only by recognizing their interdependence with socio-economic and group rights, but also by the understanding that even the most individualistic of rights is endowed with a collective dimension.[245] However, as highlighted by Knox, human rights discourse would need to change to adjust to Marxist demands, including the (misleadingly) pervasive idea of human rights as a politically neutral tool to fight against oppression.[246] On the other hand, a strong Marxist approach might be hard, if not impossible, to harmonize with the

---

[240] R. Knox, 'A Marxist Approach to *R.M.T. v. United Kingdom*' in D. Gonzalez-Salzberg and L. Hodson (eds.), *Research Methods for International Human Rights Law: Beyond the Traditional Paradigm* (Routledge 2019) 13–41, 18–19.

[241] R. Knox, 'A Marxist Approach to *R.M.T. v. United Kingdom*' in D. Gonzalez-Salzberg and L. Hodson (eds.), *Research Methods for International Human Rights Law: Beyond the Traditional Paradigm* (Routledge 2019) 13–41, 14.

[242] R. Knox, 'A Marxist Approach to *R.M.T. v. United Kingdom*' in D. Gonzalez-Salzberg and L. Hodson (eds.), *Research Methods for International Human Rights Law: Beyond the Traditional Paradigm* (Routledge 2019) 13–41, 18.

[243] R. Knox, 'A Marxist Approach to *R.M.T. v. United Kingdom*' in D. Gonzalez-Salzberg and L. Hodson (eds.), *Research Methods for International Human Rights Law: Beyond the Traditional Paradigm* (Routledge 2019) 13–41, 17.

[244] B. Roth, 'Marxian Insights for the Human Rights Project' in S. Marks (ed.), *International Law on the Left: Re-examining Marxist Legacies* (CUP 2008) 220–251, 221.

[245] C. Boyd, 'Can a Marxist Believe in Human Rights?' (2009) 37 *Critique* 579, 585.

[246] R. Knox, 'A Marxist Approach to *R.M.T. v. United Kingdom*' in D. Gonzalez-Salzberg and L. Hodson (eds.), *Research Methods for International Human Rights Law: Beyond the Traditional Paradigm* (Routledge 2019) 13–41, 38.

defence of human rights.[247] For instance, if human rights are understood to be deeply engrained in the capitalistic system, as part of the ideological toolkit that maintains and reproduces capitalism, it is difficult to see not only their role, but even their desirability in a post-capitalist society. Similarly, after capitalism, the State—a tool of domination of the ruling class[248]—is expected to 'wither away',[249] which would render our conception of human rights, in which the State acts as duty-bearer, meaningless and likely to die away with the disappearing State. Consequently, whether it would be possible to find a harmonizing association of human rights and Marxist ideas depends to a great extent on the standpoint adopted. Nevertheless, even if we reject the Marxist critiques of human rights, that does not render them devoid of relevance.[250] Understanding such critiques could be extremely important for the development of human rights in a manner that avoids some of the highlighted pitfalls—see, for instance, the applied Marxist critique to human rights that can be found in **Section 10.1.6**.

1.3.2 FEMINIST CRITIQUES

As was the case with Marxist approaches, feminist critiques of human rights can be traced back in history to the time of the proclamation of the rights of man in the late-eighteenth century. Indeed, the rights proclaimed in the Declarations adopted in the Americas and France were those of men, clearly excluding women as subjects of inherent rights. Two of the best-known documents that draw attention to the exclusion of women from the recognition of the inalienable rights of individuals are Olympe de Gouges' 1790 Declaration of the Rights of Woman and Mary Wollstonecraft's 1792 Vindication of the Rights of Women.[251] As discussed in **Section 1.2.2**, de Gouges' Declaration was a request for the French National Assembly to adopt an identical Declaration to that proclaimed in 1789, but this time in favour of women and the female citizen, recognizing women as subjects of rights in equal terms to men.[252] Sadly, de Gouges was persecuted due to her political activism and sentenced to the guillotine in November 1793.[253] Wollstonecraft's second treatise on rights—following her 1790 Vindication of the Rights of Man, which was written in reply to Edmund

---

[247] S. Lukes, 'Can a Marxist Believe in Human Rights?' (1981) 1 *Praxis International* 334, 343–344; A. Buchanan, *Marx and Justice: The Radical Critique of Liberalism* (Rowman and Littlefield 1982) 69.

[248] A. Buchanan, *Marx and Justice: The Radical Critique of Liberalism* (Rowman and Littlefield 1982) 70.

[249] F. Engels, *Socialism: Utopian and Scientific* (Pathfinder Books 2008) 91.

[250] B. Roth, 'Marxian Insights for the Human Rights Project' in S. Marks (ed.), *International Law on the Left: Re-examining Marxist Legacies* (CUP 2008) 220–251, 250–251; C. Boyd, 'Can a Marxist Believe in Human Rights?' (2009) 37 *Critique* 579, 600.

[251] Certainly, these were not the first documents in which authors have decried the subjugation of women under the law. See: A.S. Fraser, 'Becoming Human: The Origins and Developments of Women's Human Rights' 21 (1999) *Human Rights Quarterly* 853.

[252] O. de Gouges, 'The Declaration of the Rights of Woman' in Darline G. Levy, Harriet B. Applewhite, and Mary D. Johnson (eds.), *Women in Revolutionary Paris 1789–1795* (University of Illinois Press 1979) 87–92.

[253] M-B. Dembour, *Who Believes in Human Rights? Reflections on the European Convention* (CUP 2006) 188.

Burke[254]—was a reflection on the similar nature of women and men, including a challenge to the recognition of rights to men that were denied to women. She strongly asserted the need to foster women's autonomy and the essential role that education should play in achieving such a goal.[255] Wollstonecraft's second treatise is considered by many to be one of the founding texts of feminist theory.[256]

Defining feminism—or, more accurately, feminisms—is a rather complex task, as it refers to a multiplicity of both theoretical and socio-political movements.[257] However, for the purpose of this section, the adjective 'feminist' will be used to characterize all academic scholarship and socio-political activism that share the understanding that roughly half of the members of our societies (women) find themselves in a subordinated position to the other half (men), as well as a commitment that such a situation is an affront to the most basic idea of justice and should, therefore, be changed.[258] There are, nonetheless, multiple streams of feminism, each focusing on particular aspects of female subordination and providing a different theoretical standpoint, which leads to each having their own particular relationship with human rights.[259] For instance, while 'liberal' feminists can find in human rights a valuable tool to fight against women's oppression, 'radical' feminists might see in human rights yet another manifestation of *patriarchal* power,[260] and 'postmodern' feminists would be wary of the regulatory power of rights.

In historical terms, the original feminist critiques of rights were pursued by what is known as 'liberal' feminism; the leading feminist movement from the eighteenth to the mid-twentieth century, which continues to be extremely influential in our days, especially in its engagement with the law.[261] This stream of feminism is commonly labelled liberal, as it shares the basic tenets of political liberalism,[262] including the

---

[254] M. Wollstonecraft, *A Vindication of the Rights of Men* (Johnson 1790).

[255] M. Wollstonecraft, *A Vindication of the Rights of Woman: With Strictures on Political and Moral Subjects* (Johnson 1792).

[256] A. Jaggar, *Feminist Politics and Human Nature* (Rowman & Littlefield 1983) 36–37; P. Smith, 'Feminist Jurisprudence and the Nature of Law' in P. Smith (ed.), *Feminist Jurisprudence* (OUP 1993) 3–15, 4; L. Disch and M. Hawkesworth, 'Feminist Theory: Transforming the Known World' in L. Disch and M. Hawkesworth (eds.), *The Oxford Handbook of Feminist Theory* (OUP 2016) 1–15, 1.

[257] L. Hodson, 'A Feminist Approach to *Silva Pimentel Teixeira v Brazil*' in D. Gonzalez-Salzberg and L. Hodson (eds.), *Research Methods for International Human Rights Law: Beyond the Traditional Paradigm* (Routledge 2019) 42–68, 42.

[258] P. Smith, 'Feminist Jurisprudence and the Nature of Law' in P. Smith (ed.), *Feminist Jurisprudence* (OUP 1993) 3–15, 3–4; J. Halley, *Split Decisions: How and Why to Take a Break from Feminism* (Princeton University Press 2006) 4–5.

[259] For a comprehensive introductory book to feminist theories, see: R. Tong and T. Fernandes Botts, *Feminist Thought: A More Comprehensive Introduction* (5th edn., Routledge 2017).

[260] Within feminism, 'patriarchy' is the name usually given to the institutionalized system of domination that imposes control of the reproductive capacities of a group of individuals (women) by an opposite group lacking those capacities (men). The regulatory consequences of patriarchy are central to the feminist understanding of women as a subjugated group, and even as a group at all. See: G. Lerner, *The Creation of Patriarchy* (OUP 1986) 238–239; S. Jackson, *Heterosexuality in Question* (Sage 1999) 125.

[261] M-B. Dembour, *Who Believes in Human Rights? Reflections on the European Convention* (CUP 2006) 190.

[262] A. Jaggar, *Feminist Politics and Human Nature* (Rowman & Littlefield 1983) 27–28.

belief in the value of autonomy and equality, which should be guaranteed to both men and women by law, even if many liberal feminists would also support the need for differential treatment in the form of 'affirmative action', to rectify structural inequalities—a topic further discussed in **Section 10.1.1.1**. In short, a liberal feminist critique would highlight the inconsistencies between liberal proclamations and a reality in which women remain subordinated and demand for liberalism to be true to its fundamental tenets.[263] Among the different feminisms, liberal feminism is certainly the biggest supporter of human rights, given that these rights, as recognized from the mid-twentieth century, are predicated on the equal moral standing of men and women. Hence, for liberal feminism, engagement in human rights struggles can be a relevant path for achieving its goals.

Radical feminism is a much more recent phenomenon, and can be seen as spearheading a 'second wave' of feminisms, with origins in the second half of the twentieth century, especially in connection to the 1960s 'women's liberation' movement in the Western world.[264] Radical feminism, which in itself encompasses many different feminist approaches, can be characterized by a shared understanding that the solution to the subordination of women in society requires a 'radical'[265] change, in the sense that it must involve tackling the 'root' cause of the problem: the patriarchal system itself.[266] 'The personal is political' has been a main political slogan of radical feminism, which synthesizes the idea that the power relations that determine the subjugation of women are not only to be found in an unequal recognition of rights and opportunities, but in every aspect of life, including the most fundamental relations of women within the family. Radical feminism would draw attention to the need to go beyond the critiques of the State, the law, and the public subordination of women, and critically examine the problematic assumptions underpinning naturalized institutions, such as marriage, sexuality, and reproduction, as well as motherhood, since this would reveal their role in maintaining and reproducing the patriarchal system.[267]

Radical feminism's engagement with rights is much more complex than that of liberal feminism. Similar to the stance adopted by the more extreme Marxists, human rights can be seen as product of an inherently unjust system—in this case, a patriarchal order—and, therefore, cannot be trusted.[268] As a product of a patriarchal order, the creation of human rights itself can be understood as geared towards helping to reinforce the system to which they belong, addressing problems only

---

[263] A. Jaggar, *Feminist Politics and Human Nature* (Rowman & Littlefield 1983) 35–36; M-B. Dembour, *Who Believes in Human Rights? Reflections on the European Convention* (CUP 2006) 190.

[264] A. Jaggar, *Feminist Politics and Human Nature* (Rowman & Littlefield 1983) 83–84.

[265] A term that derives from the Latin *rādīx*, which means 'root'. See: Oxford English Dictionary at: https://www.oed.com/dictionary/radical_adj.

[266] A. Jaggar, *Feminist Politics and Human Nature* (Rowman & Littlefield 1983) 84 and 101.

[267] See: K. Millet, *Sexual Politics* (Rupert Hart-Davis 1971); A. Oakley, *Woman's Work: The Housewife, Past and Present* (Pantheon Books 1974); A. Rich, *Of Woman Born: Motherhood as Experience & Institution* (Norton 1976); S. Firestone, *The Dialectic of Sex: The Case for Feminist Revolution* (Quill 1993).

[268] C. MacKinnon, *Feminism Unmodified: Discourses on Life and Law* (Harvard University Press 1987) 48–51.

on a superficial level, while drawing attention away from their true root causes.[269] While moderate radical feminists might find in rights strategies a pragmatic tool for tackling women's subordination, uncompromising radical feminists would expect human rights to be brought to an end when the patriarchal system is finally overturned.

A third, more recently emerged, feminist strand is postmodern feminism, which draws on the ideas of postmodern thinking—discussed in **Section 1.3.3**—and applies them to the realm of the sex/gender system and the categories and knowledge it produces. Its postmodern approach means that it refuses to understand social categories as objective or universal, and instead questions generally accepted forms of knowledge as outputs of specific cultural systems,[270] fraught with incoherence and instability; a perception from which not even naturalized concepts such as 'sex', 'gender', 'sexuality', or even the identity categories of 'man' and 'woman', can escape. Thus, it would not be surprising that, for postmodern feminists, human rights cannot be seen as universal valid norms. To the contrary, the mere idea of rights is to be suspected, as a form of regulatory power; an exercise of power that is not 'juridical' in the Foucauldian understanding of being imposed through the threat of repression, but is instead 'disciplinary', as it encourages embracing a specific desire, and consequential behaviour, that has been constructed as appropriate.[271] That is to say, the exercise of a right, which is usually understood as a claim to obtain a desired interest, is, at the same time, a manifestation of regulatory power, by which our claim is an expression of adjustment to behaviour that is expected by the system.[272] This is not necessarily good or bad, but just a subtle way in which power is exercised and bodies are (self-)disciplined; a phenomenon that postmodern feminism would advise us to be aware of.

The above discussion provides but a snapshot of the engagements with human rights of only three of the many expressions of feminisms in existence. Overall, these and others feminisms have been able to produce extremely significant critiques of law,[273] and of

---

[269] N. Kim, 'Toward a Feminist Theory of Human Rights: Straddling the Fence between Western Imperialism and Uncritical Absolutism' (1993) 25 *Columbia Human Rights Law Review* 49, 54–55; K. Mahoney, 'Theoretical Perspectives on Women's Human Rights and Strategies for Their Implementation' (1996) 21 *Brooklyn Journal of International Law* 799, 814–815; B. Hernandez-Truyol, 'Crossing Borderlands of Inequality with International Legal Methodologies - The Promise of Multiple Feminisms' (2001) 44 *German Yearbook of International Law* 113, 147–150.

[270] D. Otto, Dianne Otto, 'Rethinking Universals: Opening Transformative Possibilities in International Human Rights Law' (1997) 18 *Australian Year Book of International Law* 1, 9; D. Otto, 'Rethinking the Universality of Human Rights Law' (1997) 29 *Columbia Human Rights Law Review* 1, 7–8.

[271] C. Smart, *Feminism and the Power of Law* (Routledge 1989) 6 and 162; C.F. Stychin, 'Same-Sex Sexualities and the Globalization of Human Rights Discourse' (2004) 49 *McGill Law Journal* 951, 967.

[272] D. Otto, 'Rethinking Universals: Opening Transformative Possibilities in International Human Rights Law' (1997) 18 *Australian Year Book of International Law* 1, 26–27, 33–34; R. Kapur, *Gender, Alterity and Human Rights: Freedom in a Fishbowl* (Elgar 2018) 4–5, 174–175.

[273] Among some of the most significant ones, see: C. MacKinnon, *Towards a Feminist Theory of the State* (Harvard University Press 1989); C. Smart, *Feminism and the Power of Law* (Routledge 1989); H. Charlesworth, C. Chinkin, and S. Wright, 'Feminist Approaches to International Law' (1991) 85 *American Journal of International Law* 613.

human rights in particular.[274] Such opportune critiques have ranged from denouncing the formal exclusion of women from the universal enjoyment of the rights of man, to highlighting how human rights are (mainly) a manifestation of men's own fears, and from drawing attention to the forgotten 'private sphere', where the subjugation of women is excluded from the State's intervention, to questioning how the embracing of the benevolent idea of human rights brings attached (unexpected) regulatory effects, as well as how it remains ineffective to radically change the patriarchal system. A feminist critique of how the fundamental prohibition of torture can be seen as a reflection of men's, rather than women's, fears can be found in **Section 9.2.2.1**.

1.3.3 POSTMODERN CRITIQUES

Postmodernity is a concept with different possible meanings; one of the reasons for this is that, by its very nature, it sits uncomfortably with being precisely defined. First, postmodernity can be said to have a historical meaning, in that the term can be construed as a period in time that begins after (or 'post') Modernity.[275] Although historians do not really agree on the start and end of Modernity—or even on whether it has come to an end—both the Industrial and the French Revolutions are commonly identified as defining hallmarks of Modernity—or, at least, of late-Modernity—while its (uncertain) end might have taken place with the world order emerging after the Second World War, or even after the fall of the Soviet Union. Most importantly, postmodernity refers to a form of thinking that aims at critically engaging with the traditional philosophy of the Enlightenment.[276] In particular, postmodern thinking can be characterized by an incredulity towards metanarratives; a scepticism as to the existence of universal 'truths'; a disbelief in history as a gradual journey of humanity towards a more developed end point; and an awareness of the role ideology plays in maintaining a specific world order.[277]

---

[274] See, among many: C. Bunch, 'Women's Rights are Human Rights: Toward a Re-vision of Human Rights' (1990) 12 *Human Rights Quarterly* 486; K. Engle, 'International Human Rights and Feminism: When Discourses Meet' (1992) 13 *Michigan Journal of International Law* 517; H. Charlesworth and C. Chinkin, 'The Gender of Jus Cogens' (1993) 15 *Human Rights Quarterly* 63; G. Binion, 'Human Rights: A Feminist Perspective' (1995) 17 *Human Rights Quarterly* 509; S. Palmer, 'Critical Perspectives on Women's Rights: The European Convention on Human Rights and Fundamental Freedoms' in A. Bottomley (ed.), *Feminist Perspectives on the Foundational Subjects of Law* (Cavendish Publishing 1996) 223–259; V.S. Peterson and L. Parisi, 'Are Women Human? It's Not an Academic Question' in T. Evans (ed.) *Human Rights Fifty Years On: A Reappraisal* (Manchester University Press 1998) 132–160; S. Baer, 'Citizenship in Europe and the Construction of Gender by Law in the European Charter of Fundamental Rights' in K. Knop (ed.), *Gender and Human Rights* (Oxford University Press 2004) 83–112; D. Otto, 'Lost in Translation: Re-scripting the Sexed Subjects of International Human Rights Law' in A. Orford (ed.), *International Law and Its Others* (CUP 2006) 318–356; L. Hodson, 'A Feminist Approach to *Silva Pimentel Teixeira v Brazil*' in D. Gonzalez-Salzberg and L. Hodson (eds.), *Research Methods for International Human Rights Law: Beyond the Traditional Paradigm* (Routledge 2019) 42–68.

[275] Z. Bauman, 'A Sociological Theory of Postmodernity' (1991) 29 *Thesis Eleven* 33, 33–34.

[276] Z. Bauman, 'A Sociological Theory of Postmodernity' (1991) 29 *Thesis Eleven* 33, 34–40; E. Meiksins Wood, 'Modernity, Postmodernity or Capitalism?' (1997) 4 *Review of International Political Economy* 539, 540–541.

[277] J.-F. Lyotard, *The Postmodern Condition: A Report on Knowledge* (G. Bennington and B. Massumi trans, University of Minnesota Press 1984) xxiv.

The work of many renowned contemporary thinkers can be identified as postmodern, such as that of Zygmunt Bauman, Gilles Deleuze, Jacques Derrida, Emmanuel Lévinas, Jean-François Lyotard, and Slavoj Žižek, but it is perhaps the writings of Michel Foucault that have provided the most influential foundations for postmodern critiques of human rights.[278] The significance of Foucault lies in the new understanding he proposed of the idea of power,[279] and, particularly, in how this notion re-conceptualizes the relationship between the individual and the State, which can be applied to human rights. The use of Foucauldian insights can lead to understanding that human rights are not just restraints on State power, but also instruments of power used to discipline, exclude, and control the subject of rights: the human.[280] In the first volume of the *History of Sexuality*, Foucault argued that in the West, since the seventeenth century, sovereign power over life experienced a drastic transformation. Power over the life and death of individuals increasingly became a life-administering power, a power that rather than threatening life was involved in its reinforcement, its control, and its administration.[281] This power over life, which he called 'bio-power', manifested itself in two different but interlinked forms: an anatomo-politics of the human body and a biopolitics of the population. On the one hand, the anatomo-politics was aimed at disciplining the individual body, a regulatory power that, at the same time, aimed at optimising both the capabilities of the subject and its docility. On the other hand, the biopolitics focused on the regulation of the body of the species, directed at controlling populations through the processes of birth, mortality, health, and longevity. This bio-power, aimed at taking charge of life, needed continuous regulatory and corrective mechanisms. The outcome of a technology of power centred on life was a normalizing society.[282]

The law of a normalizing society is, for the most part, not 'juridical', in the sense that it is not aimed at prohibiting and punishing, but is mainly normalizing: it promotes homogeneity,[283] seeking the docility of bodies (anatomo-politics) and

---

[278] For Foucauldian critiques of human rights see, among many: D. Otto, 'Everything is Dangerous: Some Poststructural Tools for Rethinking the Universal Knowledge Claims of Human Rights Law' (1999) 5 *Australian Journal of Human Rights* 17; T. Evans, 'International Human Rights Law as Power/Knowledge' (2005) 27 *Human Rights Quarterly* 1046; U. Soirila, 'The European Court of Human Rights, Islam and Foucauldian Biopower' (2012) *Helsinki Law Review* 365; B. Golder, *Foucault and the Politics of Rights* (Stanford University Press 2015); B. Sokhi-Bulley, *Governing (Through) Rights* (Hart 2016); B. Sokhi-Bulley, 'A Postmodern Approach to Elisabeta Dano v Jobcenter Leipzig' in D. Gonzalez-Salzberg and L. Hodson (eds.), *Research Methods for International Human Rights Law: Beyond the Traditional Paradigm* (Routledge 2019) 69–97.

[279] For instance: M. Foucault, *The History of Sexuality: An Introduction* (Penguin 1978); M. Foucault, *Discipline and Punish: The Birth of the Prison* (Penguin 1979); Michel Foucault, *The Birth of Biopolitics: Lectures at the Colleège de France, 1978–79* (Palgrave Macmillan 2008).

[280] C. Douzinas, *Human Rights and Empire: The Political Philosophy of Cosmopolitanism* (Routledge 2007) 111–113.

[281] M. Foucault, *The History of Sexuality: An Introduction* (Penguin 1978) 136.

[282] M. Foucault, *The History of Sexuality: An Introduction* (Penguin 1978) 136, 139, 144.

[283] M. Foucault, *The History of Sexuality: An Introduction* (Penguin 1978) 140; Michel Foucault, *Discipline and Punish: The Birth of the Prison* (Penguin 1979) 199.

the regulation of the population (biopolitics). From a Foucauldian perspective, the proclamation of the 'rights of man' was a consequence of a normalizing power and society: in his own words, 'The "Enlightenment", which discovered the liberties, also invented the disciplines.'[284] The liberal State that emerged in the West was both a producer and a consumer of freedom, with the production of freedom being, concomitantly, the production of procedures of control, as both exist as needed counterweights.[285] As a result, a (bio-)power that increases freedom also produces an increased control.

Following a Foucauldian analysis, it can be seen that this new system of (bio-)power that relied on life as a political object, on men as living beings, was resisted by forces that also relied on the 'bare life' of men.[286] The right to life was demanded from a system aimed at both protecting and controlling life. That is, a system of power that was focused on normalizing men through the regulation of life faced, as a political response, the proclamation of rights aimed at protecting life, health, and the basic needs of men.[287] This is referred to as the 'paradox of human rights', in that rights act as a protection of humans and their needs, while simultaneously appearing as an expression of bio-power and of the inexorable registration, classification, and control of individuals and populations.[288] The most evident example of the relation between bio-power and human rights can be seen in how the Modern State changed its methods for dealing with criminality. Foucault argued that the emerging restrictions on the applicability of capital punishment did not result from the awakening of humanitarianism, but were the logical result of a power, the function of which was to administer life, not to terminate it.[289] Similarly, a paradigmatic manifestation of bio-power would be the abandonment of torture in favour of imprisonment; a legal consequence that is aimed at disciplining, rather than punishing the subject, as a clear illustration of anatomo-politics.[290] Indeed, the rehabilitation of the criminal, rather than retribution, became the objective of the State's sanction, while the element of publicity concerning the punitive legal process was no longer focused on the punishment, but on the trial itself.[291] It seems far from accidental that, within this system, public attention was drawn away from the punishment of the criminal to the trial of the crime, as discipline can be learned through the public knowledge of the process in which individuals' conduct comes under analysis and sanctions are decided.[292]

---

[284] Michel Foucault, *Discipline and Punish: The Birth of the Prison* (Penguin 1979) 222.
[285] Michel Foucault, *Discipline and Punish: The Birth of the Prison* (Penguin 1979) 63–67.
[286] G. Agamben, *Homo Sacer: Sovereign Power and Bare Life* (Stanford University Press 1998) 75.
[287] M. Foucault, *The History of Sexuality: An Introduction* (Penguin 1978) 144–145.
[288] W. Brown, 'Suffering the Paradoxes of Rights' in W. Brown and J. Halley (eds.), *Left Legalism/Left Critique* (Duke University Press 2002) 420–434, 422, 427; C. Douzinas, *Human Rights and Empire: The Political Philosophy of Cosmopolitanism* (Routledge 2007) 129.
[289] M. Foucault, *The History of Sexuality: An Introduction* (Penguin 1978) 138.
[290] M. Foucault, *Discipline and Punish: The Birth of the Prison* (Penguin 1979) 261.
[291] L. Hunt, *Inventing Human Rights: A History* (Norton and Company Press 2007) 137, 139.
[292] M. Foucault, *Discipline and Punish: The Birth of the Prison* (Penguin 1979) 17–18, 113–115, 128.

Taking the Universal Declaration of Human Rights as the proof of the 'triumph' of human rights, it is possible to read its text through a Foucauldian lens and to trace clear elements of bio-power in the recognized rights. The 1948 Declaration begins by affirming that: 'All human beings are born free and equal in dignity and rights.'[293] Hence, the bare life of individuals, represented by the mere act of birth, becomes the foundation of universal rights.[294] Furthermore, emblematic examples of life-administrating power are clearly present in the Declaration, such as the restrictions on the death penalty and the absolute banning of torture, leading to the prohibition of the public spectacle of the punishment of the criminal, in favour of the public character of hearings before a court of law, as a right of the criminally accused, which might then be followed by the normalizing practice of imprisonment, if found guilty.[295]

Therefore, a postmodern/Foucauldian critique provides an abundance of reasons to be wary of human rights, given their regulatory power. Does that mean that postmodern approaches are antagonistic to human rights? As said earlier, with regard to Marxist critiques: it depends. Of course, uncompromising postmodernists might find the idea of rights too dangerous as a tool for fighting injustice; a 'double-edged sword' of a kind, given that claiming rights also involves embracing their regulatory effects. However, making use of rights in struggles against oppression can also be done without losing awareness of their regulatory effects. Human rights can be strategically deployed by postmodernists, even with their inherent imperfections, if their usefulness outweighs their disadvantages.[296] After all, are there any tools for political struggle devoid of regulatory effects? In turn, an understanding of the postmodern critique of rights could be valuable to keep us alert to the power relations that exist within strategies involving rights deployment, allowing for a continuous critical reflection on whether human rights constitute the appropriate device for the fight at stake.[297] For further illustration, see the postmodern analysis of freedom of expression in **Section 9.4.4**.

---

[293] UDHR, Art. 1.
[294] A claim made by Agamben regarding the similarly worded provision of the 1789 French Declaration. See: G. Agamben, *Homo Sacer: Sovereign Power and Bare Life* (Stanford University Press 1998) 75.
[295] UDHR, Arts. 3, 5, 10.
[296] B. Golder, *Foucault and the Politics of Rights* (Stanford University Press 2015) 116–117; D. Gonzalez-Salzberg, *Sexuality and Transsexuality under the European Convention on Human Rights: A Queer Reading of Human Rights Law* (Hart 2019) 22–23 and 186; B. Sokhi-Bulley, 'A Postmodern Approach to *Elisabeta Dano v Jobcenter Leipzig*' in D. Gonzalez-Salzberg and L. Hodson (eds.), *Research Methods for International Human Rights Law: Beyond the Traditional Paradigm* (Routledge 2019) 69–97, 72, 74.
[297] W. Brown, '"The Most We Can Hope For . . . ": Human Rights and the Politics of Fatalism' (2004) 103 *South Atlantic Quarterly* 451, 462; B. Golder, *Foucault and the Politics of Rights* (Stanford University Press 2015) 160–161; B. Sokhi-Bulley, 'A Postmodern Approach to *Elisabeta Dano v Jobcenter Leipzig*' in D. Gonzalez-Salzberg and L. Hodson (eds.), *Research Methods for International Human Rights Law: Beyond the Traditional Paradigm* (Routledge 2019) 69–97, 74.

1.3.4 POSTCOLONIAL CRITIQUES

By now, the statement that 'postcolonial theory'[298] is not a concept susceptible of easy definition, but one subject to multiple potential (often contested) meanings, should come as no surprise.[299] On the one hand, 'postcolonialism' has a historical meaning, referring to what comes after colonialism; in particular, connected to the process of de-colonization by which many States achieved political independence from the European imperial powers, especially after the Second World War. On the other hand, 'postcolonialism' also refers to a theoretical standpoint or, more precisely, to a collection of theories, ideas, and conceptual insights that share a common concern with critically engaging with the continuous effects of colonialism, even after its (official) end.[300] Hence, postcolonial critiques are concerned with reconsidering both the history of colonialism and its contemporary impact, adopting the perspective of those who suffered the oppression of this socio-economic and political phenomenon.[301]

The plural and (somehow) heterogenous approaches that fit under the umbrella of postcolonial theories can be partly explained by the polymorphous vastness of the European colonial enterprise, which resulted in different expressions of oppression and subjugation across the world with varying lasting effects.[302] The European colonial project extended for over half a millennium and has not yet reached its end. Starting with the invasion of the Americas by the Spanish conquistadors in 1492 of the Christian era, European colonialism encompassed the domination, by different means, of 90 per cent of the planet by the end of the First World War, with the British Empire controlling 20 per cent of the world's territory and one quarter of its population.[303] Following the creation of the UN, after the end of the Second World War, there was an important wave of States gaining their political independence from the European colonial powers,

---

[298] Whether the most appropriate term to define this approach should be hyphenated ('post-colonial') or not ('postcolonial') has been a subject of debate. The lack of hyphenation seems, perhaps, more suitable to highlight the long-lasting effects of colonialism, which do not end with the political de-colonization of territories and peoples. See: L. Gandhi, *Postcolonial Theory: A Critical Introduction* (2nd edn., Columbia University Press 2019) 3.

[299] H. Tiffin, 'Introduction' in I. Adam and H. Tiffin (eds.), *Past the Last Post: Theorizing Post-colonialism and Post-modernism* (Harvester Wheatsheaf 1991) vii–xv, vii; S. Sleman, S. 'Modernism's Last Post' in I. Adam and H. Tiffin (eds.), *Past the Last Post: Theorizing Post-colonialism and Post-modernism* (Harvester Wheatsheaf 1991) 1–11, 3.

[300] R. Young, *Postcolonialism: An Historical Introduction* (Wiley & Sons 2001) 64; A. Loomba, *Colonialism/Postcolonialism* (Routledge 2005) 16; A. Roy, 'Postcolonial Theory and Law: A Critical Introduction' (2008) 29 *Adelaide Law Review* 315, 316–317.

[301] S. Sleman, S. 'Modernism's Last Post' in I. Adam and H. Tiffin (eds.), *Past the Last Post: Theorizing Post-colonialism and Post-modernism* (Harvester Wheatsheaf 1991) 1–11, 3; R. Young, *Postcolonialism: An Historical Introduction* (Wiley & Sons 2001) 4.

[302] It has become usual to distinguish between two main forms of colonialism: the colonization of territories for the purpose of the settlement of populations (such as North America or Brazil), and the colonization of lands for the purpose of economic exploitation (such as India or the Philippines). See: R. Young, *Postcolonialism: An Historical Introduction* (Wiley & Sons 2001) 17.

[303] R. Young, *Postcolonialism: An Historical Introduction* (Wiley & Sons 2001) 2.

although such a process is yet to be completed, with numerous territories worldwide that remain under control of a colonial power.[304]

The emergence of postcolonial theories can be found in the second half of the twentieth century—a period marked by the process of de-colonization[305]—as a political and academic response to the violent historical interactions between the Western powers and the territories and populations of Africa, Asia, Oceania, and Latin-America and the Caribbean.[306] While the primary focus of postcolonial theories lies in the lasting effects of the Western project of colonial domination, its theoretical foundations benefited from existing critical movements, including Marxism, feminism, and postmodernism.[307] Although the direct engagement of postcolonial theories with the law was timid at the beginning, with time it has become one of the most influential approaches for undertaking a critique of the discipline. Postcolonial thinking allows questioning the role played by law during the colonial process, including how the law of European States could promote and support the colonial enterprise of domination, how these States imposed their law (either existent, or by enacting special 'colonial laws')[308] on those colonized, and how the ideological effects of colonial laws remain relevant in our days.[309]

But it is not just the domestic law of the European empires that comes under the gaze of postcolonial theories, but also international law and the international law of human rights.[310] It was the (Western) international law of the time that helped to foster colonialism, by legitimizing the domination of populations and the expropriation of lands and natural resources.[311] In the words of a renowned postcolonial legal scholar: 'Death, destruction, pillage, plunder and humiliation are the key words that best capture the relationship between third world peoples and international law in this period.'[312] In

---

[304] R. Young, *Postcolonialism: An Historical Introduction* (Wiley & Sons 2001) 3. See: https://www.un.org/dppa/decolonization/en/nsgt (accessed on 13 February 2023).

[305] Among the main theorists behind the emergence of a postcolonial critical movement it is essential to mention Frantz Fanon, Edward Said, Gayatri Chakravorty Spivak, and Homi Bhabha. See: F. Fanon, *Black Skin, White Masks* (Penguin 2021 (1952)); F. Fanon, *The Wretched of the Earth* (Penguin 2001 (1961)); E. Said, *Orientalism* (Pantheon 1978); G.C. Spivak, 'Can the Subaltern Speak?' in C. Nelson and L. Grossberg (eds.), *Marxism and the Interpretation of Culture* (University of Illinois Press 1988) 271–313; H. Bhabha, *The Location of Culture* (Routledge 1994).

[306] R. Young, *Postcolonialism: An Historical Introduction* (Wiley & Sons 2001) 58–59, 68; A. Roy, 'Postcolonial Theory and Law: A Critical Introduction' (2008) 29 *Adelaide Law Review* 315, 317.

[307] R. Young, *Postcolonialism: An Historical Introduction* (Wiley & Sons 2001) 67, 410; L. Gandhi, *Postcolonial Theory: A Critical Introduction* (2nd edn., Columbia University Press 2019), chapter 2.

[308] M. Koskenniemi, 'Colonial Laws: Sources, Strategies and Lessons?' (2016) 18 *Journal of the History of International Law* 248, esp. 251, 260, 263, 266, 269–270.

[309] A. Roy, 'Postcolonial Theory and Law: A Critical Introduction' (2008) 29 *Adelaide Law Review* 315, 316–324, 328.

[310] A postcolonial analysis of the right to self-determination of indigenous peoples can be found towards the end of this book, in **Section 10.4.2.3**.

[311] M. Bedjaoui, 'Poverty of the International Order' in R. Falk, F. Kratochwil, and S. Mendlovitz (eds.), *International Law: A Contemporary Perspective* (Westview 1985) 152–163, 153; M. Shaw, *Title to Territory in Africa: International Legal Issues* (Clarendon Press 1986), chapter 1.

[312] B.S. Chimni, 'The Past, Present and Future of International Law: A Critical Third World Approach' (2007) 8 *Melbourne Journal of International Law* 499, 501.

particular, international law provided different modes by which the European empires could validate their claims to foreign territories. These included: the acquisition of territories by conquest;[313] the occupation of territories considered to be *terra nullius* ('a territory belonging to no one'), a label that was applied to non-Western forms of relations of peoples with their lands;[314] and the cession of land by indigenous peoples, under circumstances that raise questions regarding the existence of the required free and valid consent.[315] It is not surprising then that the international law at the time of colonialism has been described as 'a set of rules with a geographical basis (it was a European law), a religious-ethical inspiration (it was a Christian law), and economic motivation (it was a mercantilist law) and political aims (it was an imperialist law)'.[316]

From a postcolonial perspective, the idea of human rights is not free from criticism either. The rights of man proclaimed in the late eighteenth century, irrespective of whether we consider them already human rights or merely a precursor of them, were extremely problematic. Akin to the feminist critique, postcolonialists would claim that, despite their proclaimed universal character, the rights of man were the rights of only certain individuals. The 'man' of the French Declaration was clearly less than universal, the subject being male, land-owner, and European.[317] These rights, a product of the Enlightenment, reproduced the hierarchies underpinning Western law, which recognized European men as subjects of rights, while excluding colonized people from such recognition. This process of exclusion, far from unexpected, follows the process by which all identities are constructed; a construction dependent on exclusion, through the creation of the 'other'.[318] Thus, the exclusion of the colonial subject from the rights of 'man' was needed to confirm the male European as the universal man.[319]

---

[313] Conquest as a mode of territorial acquisition by a State was only slowly and progressively outlawed by international law through a series of instruments and treaties that prohibited aggression, war, and the use of force, including the Covenant of the League of Nations (1919), the Briand-Kellogg Pact (1928) and the UN Charter (1945). See: M. Kohen, 'Conquest' in *Max Planck Encyclopedias of International Law* (2015), available at: https://opil.ouplaw.com/display/10.1093/law:epil/9780199231690/law-9780199231690-e275.

[314] M. Shaw, *Title to Territory in Africa: International Legal Issues* (Clarendon Press 1986) 31–33; D.C.J. Dakas, 'The Role of International Law in the Colonization of Africa: A Review in Light of Recent Calls for Re-colonization' (1999) 7 *African Yearbook of International Law* 85, 97, and 117. See: ICJ, *Western Sahara*, Advisory Opinion, 1.C.J. Reports 1975, p. 12, paras. 79–82.

[315] M. Shaw, *Title to Territory in Africa: International Legal Issues* (Clarendon Press 1986) 40–43; D.C.J. Dakas, 'The Role of International Law in the Colonization of Africa: A Review in Light of Recent Calls for Re-colonization' (1999) 7 *African Yearbook of International Law* 85, 92–94.

[316] M. Bedjaoui, 'Poverty of the International Order' in R. Falk, F. Kratochwil, and S. Mendlovitz (eds.), *International Law: A Contemporary Perspective* (Westview 1985) 152–63, 154.

[317] C. Douzinas, 'The End(s) of Human Rights' (2002) 26 *Melbourne University Law Review* 445, 455; L. Hunt, *Inventing Human Rights: A History* (Norton and Company Press 2007) 18.

[318] W. Connolly, *Identity/Difference: Democratic Negotiations of Political Paradox* (Cornell University Press 1991) 64.

[319] C. Douzinas, 'The End(s) of Human Rights' (2002) 26 *Melbourne University Law Review* 445, 449–450; M. Ishay, *The History of Human Rights: from Ancient Times to the Globalization Era* (University of California Press 2004) 8 and 108; S. Pahuja, 'The Postcoloniality of International Law' (2005) 46 *Harvard International Law Journal* 459, 460–461.

While the universality of human rights proclaimed in the twentieth century could have been expected to overcome the limitation of the rights of man, the Universal Declaration's stance on colonialism is problematic. On the one hand, the Declaration is set to apply, without discrimination, to all individuals, including those belonging to 'non-self-governing' territories—a euphemism to refer to people under colonial domination.[320] On the other hand, such an acknowledgement of colonialism without an express reference to its incompatibility with human rights, indicates its implicit acceptance.[321] Far from surprising, this reflected the understanding of the European empires, which did not consider their colonial subjects to be the holders of inherent universal human rights.[322] In fact, when the debate concerning the adoption of a human rights treaty to follow the 1948 Declaration began to take place at the United Nations, the European empires defended the inclusion of a 'colonial clause'—akin to the one included in the European Convention on Human Rights, as discussed in **Section 3.2.3**—to be exempted from complying with human rights obligations in the colonies.[323]

But postcolonial critiques of human rights go beyond the indisputable problem of allowing human rights to apply merely to those in the Empire's metropole; an idea impossible to reconcile with the most basic understanding of human rights universality. One of the leading voices within these critiques is that of Makau wa Mutua, who has proposed that the human rights enterprise itself reproduces the logic and hierarchies of the colonial project.[324] He found even the emergence of the international law of human rights, following the Second World War, to be problematic, stating that:

> Neither the enslavement of Africans, with its barbaric consequences and genocidal dimensions, nor the classic colonization of Asians, Africans, and Latin Americans by Europeans, with its bone-chilling atrocities, were sufficient to move the West to create the human rights movement. It took the genocidal extermination of Jews in Europe – a white people – to start the process of the codification and universalization of human rights norms.[325]

Mutua saw in the universalization of rights, yet another Western project through which the self-proclaimed superior West enforces its values to the 'subaltern':

> The historical pattern is undeniable. It forms a long queue of the colonial administrator, the Bible-wielding Christian missionary, the merchant of free enterprise, the exporter of

---

[320] UDHR, Preamble and Art. 2.

[321] A. Cassese, 'The General Assembly: Historical Perspective 1945–1989' in P. Alston (ed.), *The United Nations and Human Rights: A Critical Appraisal* (Clarendon Press 1992) 25–54, 31.

[322] S. Jensen, *The Making of International Human Rights: The 1960s, Decolonization and the Reconstruction of Global Values* (CUP 2016) 23; E. Stone Mackinnon, 'Declaration as Disavowal: The Politics of Race and Empire in the Universal Declaration of Human Rights' (2019) 47 *Political Theory* 57, 74; M. Duranti, 'Decolonizing the United Nations: Anti-colonialism and Human Rights in the French Empire', in A.D. Moses, M. Duranti, and R. Burke (eds.), *Decolonization, Self-Determination, and the Rise of Global Human Rights Politics* (CUP 2020) 54–78, 57–63.

[323] R. Burke, *Decolonization and the Evolution of International Human Rights* (PENN 2013) 40–41; J. Whyte, *The Morals of the Market: Human Rights and the Rise of Neoliberalism* (Verso 2019) 86–87.

[324] M. Mutua, *Human Rights: A Political and Cultural Critique* (PENN 2002) 7.

[325] M. Mutua, *Human Rights: A Political and Cultural Critique* (PENN 2002) 16.

political democracy, and now the human rights zealot. In each case the European culture has pushed the 'native' culture to transform. The local must be replaced with the universal – that is, the European.[326]

To clarify, Mutua does not suggest that human rights are equivalent to colonialism;[327] on the contrary, he accepts that the motives behind each of these phenomena are radically different, one driven by noble ideas while the other was certainly not. But he sees in human rights another Western project aimed at transforming non-Western people.[328]

Mutua has argued that human rights reproduce a three-dimensional metaphor of 'savages–victims–saviours', in which a State that lacks a cultural foundation in human rights is presented as barbaric, victimizing its citizens, who are powerless and innocent, but who could be saved by human rights, brought to them by the West—the UN, Western States, and NGOs.[329] Hence, the culture of human rights comes to reproduce the hierarchies of Western thinking, with its impulse to universalize Eurocentric norms, while subordinating ('othering') that which does not fit the European model.[330] Nonetheless, Mutua's response to the identified problems is not to reject human rights.[331] He claims that a true universal project of human rights is indeed possible; one that would tackle the real inequalities of the international order, particularly the imbalances between the Global South and North. Such a re-shaped legal corpus would require, however, for the human rights movement to abandon its hierarchical world view according to which the West leads and the rest of the world follows.[332] This new human rights project would need to be open to the different critiques that have been raised about human rights and re-think, in a more radical way, among other aspects, the legacies of colonialism and the relation between rights and the world economy (e.g. global capitalism).[333]

---

[326] M. Mutua, *Human Rights: A Political and Cultural Critique* (PENN 2002) 20.

[327] In fact, the language of human rights was strategically used, as universally understandable rhetoric, to decry the long-lasting European colonization. This can be appreciated in the commitment to human rights in the Final Communiqué of the 1955 'Bandung Conference', as well as by the inclusion of the right to self-determination in the 1966 International Covenants. See: R. Burke, *Decolonization and the Evolution of International Human Rights* (PENN 2013) 14–15; S. Jensen, *The Making of International Human Rights: The 1960s, Decolonization and the Reconstruction of Global Values* (CUP 2016) 43–44, 54–55; B. Ibhawoh, *Human Rights in Africa* (CUP 2018) 134. See also: Final Communiqué of the Asian-African conference of Bandung (adopted on 24 April 1955); International Covenant on Civil and Political Rights (adopted 16 December 1966, entered into force 23 March 1976) 999 UNTS 171, Art. 1; International Covenant on Economic, Social and Cultural Rights (ICESCR) (adopted on 16 December 1966, entered into force on 3 January 1976) 993 UNTS 3, Art. 1.

[328] M. Mutua, *Human Rights: A Political and Cultural Critique* (PENN 2002) 33.

[329] M. Mutua, *Human Rights: A Political and Cultural Critique* (PENN 2002) 10–11.

[330] M. Mutua, *Human Rights: A Political and Cultural Critique* (PENN 2002) 15.

[331] In this, he coincides with other postcolonial human rights scholars. See: R. Kapur, 'Human Rights in the 21st Century: Take a Walk on the Dark Side' (2006) 28 *Sydney Law Review* 665, 668, 682–683.

[332] M. Mutua, *Human Rights: A Political and Cultural Critique* (PENN 2002) 6–9.

[333] M. Mutua, *Human Rights: A Political and Cultural Critique* (PENN 2002) 156–157; M. Mutua, *Human Rights Standards: Hegemony, Law, and Politics* (State University of New York Press 2016) 176–177, 180. See also: B.S. Chimni, 'The Past, Present and Future of International Law: A Critical Third World Approach' (2007) 8 *Melbourne Journal of International Law* 499, 511–514.

1.4 CONCLUSION

In our days, we tend to accept, almost unproblematically, that human rights are rights that every person has by the mere fact of being human. These rights are so fundamentally important that we consider them inherent to the human person. Faced with human suffering caused by oppression, injustice, and discrimination, we readily construe them as human rights abuses, demanding the State to intervene to put an end to it and provide redress to the victims. However, even if we claim these rights to be inherent and universal, human rights have not always existed (and might not exist forever). Human rights are a human creation and, therefore, have a history or, perhaps, multiple histories. This chapter explored only some of the different (possible) elements that, through history, provided the building blocks for the creation of human rights; a concept that might be only as new as the past century, depending on the moment in which we believe the notion of human rights has finally emerged. But the historical components that led us to our conception of human rights brought attached their cultural and political baggage. Already from the time of the proclamation of the 'rights of man', in the eighteenth-century declarations, it was possible to perceive that not all individuals were entitled to the innate rights of man. Feminist and Marxist critiques were early to point out some fundamental shortcomings of the proclaimed rights.

The international law of human rights, emergent towards the middle of the twentieth century, reinvigorated the promise of the value of rights as legal means to protect individuals against abuses of State power. Nevertheless, the embracing of human rights as the universal ideology of the twentieth century also failed to deliver the end of State-sponsored human suffering. The promise of rights as an ideal tool to bring inequality and oppression to an end remains, sadly, unfulfilled, while a devotion to rights strategies to achieve these aims might even be hindering the power of imagination needed for the development of alternative tactics.[334] Hence, it is important to understand the intellectual explorations of human rights undertaken by the different critiques. The purpose of proposing such an exercise was certainly not to encourage the rejection of human rights. Far from it, a conviction in the value of human rights as the best tool we currently have to fight against injustice is embedded throughout this book. However, a belief in human rights cannot mean blindness as to the problems and shortfalls that both the idea of rights itself and the deployment of human rights strategies entail. If human rights are the best device we have to protect individuals from injustice and subjugation, then we should critically examine them to help make human rights the best tool they can be.[335] This commitment should be continuous and unwavering until a time at which an even better device is invented,[336] if that were to happen.

---

[334] D. Kennedy, 'The International Human Rights Movement: Part of the Problem?' (2002) 15 *Harvard Human Rights Journal* 101, 108; D. Kennedy, 'The International Human Rights Regime: Still Part of the Problem?' in R. Dickinson, *et al.* (eds.), *Examining Critical Perspectives on Human Rights* (CUP 2012) 19–34, 24, 33.

[335] D. Kennedy, 'The International Human Rights Movement: Part of the Problem?' (2002) 15 *Harvard Human Rights Journal* 101, 125.

[336] U. Baxi, *The Future of Human Rights* (2nd edn., OUP 2008) xxxv; D. Kennedy, 'The International Human Rights Regime: Still Part of the Problem?' in R. Dickinson *et al.* (eds.), *Examining Critical Perspectives on Human Rights* (CUP 2012) 19–34, 33–34.

FURTHER READING

Beitz, C., *The Idea of Human Rights* (OUP 2009).

Dembour, M-B., *Who Believes in Human Rights? Reflections on the European Convention* (CUP 2006).

Gonzalez-Salzberg, D. and Hodson, L. (eds.), *Research Methods for International Human Rights Law: Beyond the Traditional Paradigm* (Routledge 2019).

Hunt, L., *Inventing Human Rights: A History* (Norton and Company Press 2007).

Ibhawoh, B., *Human Rights in Africa* (CUP 2018).

Ishay, M., *The History of Human Rights: From Ancient Times to the Globalization Era* (University of California Press 2004).

Martínez, J., *The Slave Trade and the Origins of International Human Rights Law* (OUP 2012).

Mutua, M., *Human Rights: A Political and Cultural Critique* (PENN 2002).

Nino, C.S., *The Ethics of Human Rights* (Clarendon Press 1993).

Shelton, D. (ed.), *The Oxford Handbook of International Human Rights Law* (OUP 2013).

2
THE DEVELOPMENT OF THE INTERNATIONAL LAW OF HUMAN RIGHTS

2.1 THE INTERNATIONAL LAW OF HUMAN RIGHTS

The international law of human rights is the legal regime oriented towards the protection of the rights of the human person in all circumstances. It is essentially a system of norms recognized in a multiplicity of international sources, such as international treaties, customary norms, and resolutions from international bodies, which establishes rights and guarantees for the protection of the human person, especially in its relation with the State. At the operative level, this regime comprises a series of monitoring bodies, with the power to supervise the State's obligations to respect and protect the rights of individuals through different mechanisms, which include systems of communications, the elaboration of reports, and country visits for on-site observations.[1]

While the international law of human rights belongs to the domain of international law, it is endowed with its own specificity and logic. Instead of regulating the relations between States, it is concerned with legal interactions that take place within them and geared towards the protection of individuals. The international law of human rights is fundamentally a law of protection, inspired by considerations of a public order (*ordre public*) based upon the safeguard of human beings, irrespective of nationality or of any other condition or circumstance.[2] Nevertheless, these particularities of the international law of human rights should not be understood as a case of departure from public international law, but as a confirmation of the latter's ability to overcome dated ideas of State sovereignty.

The international law of human rights has experienced a remarkable process of development and expansion throughout the second half of the twentieth century; one

---

[1] A.A. Cançado Trindade, *Tratado de Direito Internacional dos Direitos Humanos: Volume I* (2nd edn., SAFE 2003) 71.

[2] IACtHR, *Blake v. Guatemala*. Reparations and Costs. Judgment of January 22, 1999. Series C No. 48, separate opinion of Judge Cançado Trindade para. 7.

that is perhaps unparalleled within the whole of the legal universe.[3] As discussed in **Section 1.2**, the roots of what we call today the international law of human rights can be found in different social and political movements, schools of thought, and legal doctrines that have appeared through the centuries. However, the legal formulation of human rights at the international level is relatively recent. Towards the mid-twentieth century, at a time in which the future of the world was still uncertain, a universal consensus on the value of human rights emerged, grounded on the belief in the inherent humanity of every individual worldwide.

The international protection of the human person received worldwide acceptance just seventy-five years ago, with the proclamation of the Universal Declaration of Human Rights by the United Nations General Assembly on 10 December 1948. From the moment of adoption of the Universal Declaration it is possible to affirm the emergence of universal human rights, to which every human being is entitled regardless of personal characteristics or geographic location, and which can be opposed to the public power of every State.[4] Since then, States with very different cultural, political, and religious traditions have increasingly proceeded to express their consent to be bound by international human rights treaties celebrated within the United Nations and within other international organizations. This can be clearly appreciated by the level of ratification reached by the most important United Nations human rights treaties (see **Chapter 5**), some of which have achieved almost universal acceptance.

The temporal and substantive development of the international law of human rights is the topic of this chapter. As will be discussed, the universality of human rights has been affirmed in what is known as the 'International Bill of Human Rights', composed of the 1948 Universal Declaration of Human Rights, the 1966 International Covenant on Civil and Political Rights (ICCPR),[5] and the 1966 International Covenant on Economic, Social and Cultural Rights (ICESCR),[6] and has been further reaffirmed at two World Conferences on Human Rights, celebrated in 1968 and 1993. Moreover, these rights that were proclaimed at the international level also extended to almost every domestic legislation, in similar terms to those contained in the Universal Declaration of Human Rights.[7] As mentioned in **Section 1.1**, it is possible to affirm that human rights have become the *ethos* of our time.[8]

---

[3] A.A. Cançado Trindade, *Tratado de Direito Internacional dos Direitos Humanos: Volume I* (2nd edn., SAFE 2003) 38–40.

[4] IACtHR, *Juridical Condition and Human Rights of the Child*. Advisory Opinion OC-17/02 of August 28, 2002. Series A no.17. Concurring opinion of Judge A.A. Cançado Trindade para. 49.

[5] International Covenant on Civil and Political Rights (adopted 16 December 1966, entered into force 23 March 1976) 999 UNTS 171.

[6] International Covenant on Economic, Social and Cultural Rights (ICESCR) (adopted on 16 December 1966, entered into force on 3 January 1976) 993 UNTS 3.

[7] T.J. Farer, 'The United Nations and Human Rights: More than a Whimper less than a Roar' (1987) 9 *Human Rights Quarterly* 550, 557; P.G. Lauren, *The Evolution of International Human Rights: Visions Seen* (3rd edn., PENN 2011) 200, 228.

[8] L. Henkin, *The Age of Rights* (Columbia University Press 1990) ix; C.S. Nino, *The Ethics of Human Rights* (Clarendon Press 1993) 1; A.A. Cançado Trindade, *Tratado de Direito Internacional dos Direitos Humanos: Volume I* (2nd edn., SAFE 2003) 82.

2.2 THE INTERNATIONAL LAW OF HUMAN RIGHTS: LEGISLATIVE STAGE

The idea that the United Nations should have an active role in the protection of the rights of individuals grew out of the atrocious human rights violations committed during the Second World War.[9] However, while the Charter of the United Nations, adopted on 26 June 1945, explicitly mentions human rights on multiple occasions,[10] it does not provide an indication of which are the rights to be protected, with the exception of the prohibition of discrimination, which can be inferred from its repetition in Articles 1, 13, and 55.[11] As discussed in **Section 4.1**, the inclusion of a catalogue of rights within the UN Charter, as well as of mechanisms for implementation, were proposed by different national delegations during the drafting process of the Charter, but these proposals failed, due to the strong opposition of some of the most powerful States.[12] Nonetheless, the closing speech of the San Francisco Conference, delivered by US President Harry Truman, expressed the conviction that an 'international bill of rights' should be adopted by the new organization.[13] In 1946, following its Charter mandate,[14] the Economic and Social Council (ECOSOC) created the UN Commission on Human Rights and charged it with the elaboration of proposals, recommendations, and reports regarding 'an International bill of rights'.[15]

2.2.1 THE UNIVERSAL DECLARATION OF HUMAN RIGHTS

The original Commission on Human Rights was established in February 1946 as a nucleus of nine members, appointed in their individual capacity,[16] initially tasked with proposing to ECOSOC the shape and characteristics a permanent Commission should

---

[9] T. Buergenthal, 'The Normative and Institutional Evolution of International Human Rights' (1997) 19 *Human Rights Quarterly* 703, 706; J. Morsink, *The Universal Declaration of Human Rights: Origins, Drafting, and Intent* (University of Pennsylvania Press 1999) 37–38.

[10] Charter of the United Nations (adopted 26 June 1945, entered into force 24 October 1945), 1 UNTS XVI, preamble and Arts. 1(3), 13(1)(b), 55(c), 56, 62(2), and 68.

[11] T. Buergenthal, 'The Normative and Institutional Evolution of International Human Rights' (1997) 19 *Human Rights Quarterly* 703, 707; M. Pinto, *Temas de Derechos Humanos* (Del Puerto 2009) 24.

[12] P.G. Lauren, 'First Principles of Racial Equality: History and the Politics and Diplomacy of Human Rights Provisions in the United Nations Charter' (1983) 5 *Human Rights Quarterly* 1, 18–20; T. Buergenthal, 'The Normative and Institutional Evolution of International Human Rights' (1997) 19 *Human Rights Quarterly* 703, 706–707.

[13] E. Schwelb, 'Entry into Force of the International Covenants on Human Rights and the Optional Protocol to the International Covenant on Civil and Political Rights' (1976) 70 *American Journal of International Law* 511, 511; T. Farer, 'The United Nations and Human Rights: More than a Whimper less than a Roar' (1987) 9 *Human Rights Quarterly* 550, 555–556.

[14] UN Charter, Art. 68.

[15] ECOSOC, Resolution 5(I), E/27 (22 February 1946), paras. 1–2. See: W. Schabas (ed.), *The Universal Declaration of Human Rights: The travaux préparatoires: vol. I* (CUP 2013).

[16] The members were: Paal Berg (Norway), Alexander Borisov (USSR), Dusan Brkish (Yugoslavia), René Cassin (France), Fernand Dehousse (Belgium), Victor Haya de la Torre (Perú), C.L. Hsia (China) (who replaced the originally nominated C.H. Wu), K.C. Neogi (India), and Eleanor Roosevelt (USA). However, for the initial meetings, the Soviet Union only sent a secretary from their embassy (Nicolai Kirukov) as an observer. See: E. Roosevelt, 'The Promise of Human Rights' (1948) 26 *Foreign Affairs* 470, 470. See also: ECOSOC, Resolution 5(I), E/27 (22 February 1946).

have.[17] The nuclear Commission recommended that the full Commission should be composed of eighteen members, chosen in their individual capacity.[18] However, ECOSOC decided that the permanent Commission was to encompass eighteen members, from various political and cultural backgrounds, although acting as representatives of their States.[19] This decision would allow the political will of States to be the driving force behind the shape and content of the UN's human rights agenda.[20] ECOSOC entrusted the new Commission with the elaboration of an International Bill of Human Rights, as well as with suggestions on the means for the effective implementation of human rights and fundamental freedoms.[21]

In January 1947, the Commission on Human Rights started to work on drafting an instrument that would articulate the protected rights. To begin the process, the Commission decided that a first draft was to be produced by an executive committee, composed of the chairperson and vice-chairperson of the Commission and a designated rapporteur, with the assistance of the Commission's Secretariat.[22] This meant that Eleanor Roosevelt, P.C. Chang, and Charles Malik—respectively elected chairperson, vice-chairperson, and rapporteur—were to start working together with John Humphrey—recently appointed Director of the UN's Division on Human Rights—to produce a draft of the planned human rights bill.[23] However, the dissatisfaction of a number of delegations with being left out of the initial preparation of the text led to the enlargement of the drafting committee to include the representatives of five additional delegations—Australia, Chile, France, the USSR, and the UK.[24]

It would be Humphrey who produced a lengthy 400-page first draft of the instrument,[25] making use of abundant material that different delegations, organizations,

[17] E. Roosevelt, 'The Promise of Human Rights' (1948) 26 *Foreign Affairs* 470, 470.
[18] E. Roosevelt, 'The Promise of Human Rights' (1948) 26 *Foreign Affairs* 470, 471; H. Tolley, 'Decision-Making at the United Nations Commission on Human Rights, 1979–82' (1983) 5 *Human Rights Quarterly* 27, 28. See: ECOSOC, 'Report of the Commission on Human Rights to the Second Session of the Economic and Social Council', E/38/Rev.1 (21 May 1946).
[19] The eighteen States to have a delegate in the Commission were: Australia, Belgium, Byelorussia, Chile, China, Egypt, France, India, Iran, Lebanon, Panamá, Philippines, the UK, the USA, the USSR, Ukraine, Uruguay, and Yugoslavia. See: CHR, Report of the Commission on Human Rights to the Economic and Social Council, E/259 (11 February 1947), paras. 1–2.
[20] This is further confirmed by the States' decisions on who to appoint as their delegates. For instance, the UK opted against appointing an important figure such as Lauterpacht—the author of *An International Bill of the Rights of Man*—to the Commission, as the Foreign Office considered him 'although a distinguished and industrious international lawyer ... a Jew fairly recently come from Vienna', whereas 'the representative of HMG on human rights must be a very English Englishman imbued throughout his life and hereditary to the real meaning of human rights as we understand them in this country'. See: K. Sellars, *The Rise and Rise of Human Rights* (Sutton Press 2002) 12.
[21] ECOSOC, 'Commission on Human Rights', E/56/Rev.2 (21 June 1946).
[22] CHR, Report of the Commission on Human Rights to the Economic and Social Council, E/259 (11 February 1947), para. 10.
[23] CHR, Summary Record of the First Meeting, E/CN.4/SR.1 (28 January 1947).
[24] J. Humphrey, *Human Rights & the United Nations: a great adventure* (Transnational Publishers 1984) 27–29; J. Morsink, *The Universal Declaration of Human Rights: Origins, Drafting, and Intent* (University of Pennsylvania Press 1999) 5; P.G. Lauren, *The Evolution of International Human Rights: Visions Seen* (3rd edn., PENN 2011) 216.
[25] J. Humphrey, *Human Rights & the United Nations: a great adventure* (Transnational Publishers 1984) 31–32; M.A. Glendon, *A World Made New: Eleanor Roosevelt and the Universal Declaration of Human Rights* (Random House 2001) 57–58; R. Normand and S. Zaidi, *Human Rights at the UN: The Political History of Universal Justice* (Indiana University Press 2008) 179–180.

and individuals had submitted to both the UN and the Commission.[26] Of paramount importance, as sources of inspiration for Humphrey's draft, were the proposed bills of rights that had been provided by Panamá and by Chile—the former produced by the American Law Institute and the latter by the Inter-American Juridical Committee.[27] The extensive length of the document produced by Humphrey is partly explained by the inclusion of indications of how different rights could be traced back to the domestic legislation of multiple UN Member States.[28]

The enlarged committee discussed the draft prepared by Humphrey and then appointed a three-person group to work on the text in light of their debate. This group asked the French delegate, René Cassin, to re-draft and re-arrange the long document produced by Humphrey,[29] with this new draft becoming the one used as the basis for discussion during the Commission's following session.[30] It was during the Commission's second session, in December of 1947, that the decision was made to split the planned international bill of human rights into three separate parts: a Declaration of rights—which would become the Universal Declaration of Human Rights—, one or more binding treaties on rights, and mechanisms for the implementation of those rights. Three working groups were then established, each focusing on a different aspect of the (now split) international bill.[31]

2.2.1.1 UNESCO's contribution

At the time the Commission on Human Rights was drafting the Universal Declaration, the United Nations Educational, Scientific and Cultural Organization (UNESCO) decided to conduct an examination of the principal theoretical and philosophical issues raised by the elaboration of such a declaration. UNESCO set up a 'Committee on the Theoretical Bases of Human Rights', recruiting a number of notable intellectuals.[32] The Committee prepared and circulated a questionnaire around the globe among important thinkers of the time in order to better comprehend their understanding

---

[26] These included drafts by Gustavo Gutierrez, Irving Isaacs, Wilfred Parsons, Rollin McNitt, Hersch Lauterpacht, H.G. Wells, the American Bar Association, the American Law Institute, the American Association for the United Nations, the American Jewish Committee, the World Government Association, the Institut de Droit International, and the editors of 'Free World'. See: CHR, Analysis of Various Draft International Bills of Rights, E/CN.4/W.16 (23 January 1947) pp. 9–11.

[27] J. Humphrey, *Human Rights & the United Nations: a great adventure* (Transnational Publishers 1984) 32. See also: Working Paper on an International Bill of Rights, E/CN.4/W.4 (13 January 1947).

[28] J. Humphrey, *Human Rights & the United Nations: a great adventure* (Transnational Publishers 1984) 32; J. Morsink, *The Universal Declaration of Human Rights: Origins, Drafting, and Intent* (University of Pennsylvania Press 1999) 7.

[29] J. Morsink, *The Universal Declaration of Human Rights: Origins, Drafting, and Intent* (University of Pennsylvania Press 1999) 6–9; M.A. Glendon, *A World Made New: Eleanor Roosevelt and the Universal Declaration of Human Rights* (Random House 2001) 63–66.

[30] J. Morsink, *The Universal Declaration of Human Rights: Origins, Drafting, and Intent* (University of Pennsylvania Press 1999) 9–10; S. Waltz, 'Reclaiming and Rebuilding the History of the Universal Declaration of Human Rights' (2002) 23 *Third World Quarterly* 437, 441.

[31] CHR, Summary Record of Twenty-ninth Meeting, E/CN.4/SR.29 (8 December 1947).

[32] M.A. Glendon, *A World Made New: Eleanor Roosevelt and the Universal Declaration of Human Rights* (Random House 2001) 51.

of the idea of human rights. The questionnaire asked about the relationship between individual and group rights in different societies and historical times, as well as about the relationship between individual freedoms and collective responsibilities.[33] While the Committee sent out about 150 questionnaires,[34] the number of responses received is uncertain. While Glendon claimed that there were more than seventy, Goodale affirmed there were fewer than sixty.[35] Whichever the exact number might be, they were numerous, but their provenance was mostly male and Western, with about 80 per cent of all responses coming from Western intellectuals and only one from a woman—Margery Fry.[36]

In contrast to the pool of repliers, the answers received to the questions were indeed diverse. While Aldous Huxley expressed concerns about industrial societies and the scarcity of resources, Teilhard de Chardin emphasized the importance of individual's freedom over those of the collective, and Jacques Maritain defended the foundations of human rights in jusnaturalism. Edward Carr claimed that the declaration should include the recognition of economic and social rights, and Quincy Wright highlighted not only the distinction between individual and social rights, but also their difference in terms of implementation. Levi Carneiro emphasized the need of a binding treaty to follow the planned declaration, while Haesaert considered that a declaration of universal scope should be as limited as possible, and Harold Laski adopted a particularly critical stance arguing that declarations of rights have tended to legitimize the rights of specific groups rather than those of all individuals.[37]

Once the replies were collected, the UNESCO Committee hosted a meeting in Paris, at the end of which it published a report entitled 'The Grounds of an International Declaration of Human Rights'. The Committee highlighted that while all UN Member States shared common convictions on which human rights rest, a universal declaration on rights would inevitably face difficulties and divergent interpretations given the different prevalent philosophical perspectives across the globe.[38] As expressed by Maritain, all members of the Committee agreed on a list of rights that could be proclaimed as an international declaration of human rights, but only 'on condition that no one asks why'.[39]

The UN Commission on Human Rights was not particularly receptive to the UNESCO report, which is perhaps unsurprising, given that the work of UNESCO

---

[33] M. Goodale (ed.), *Letters to the Contrary: A Curated History of the UNESCO Human Rights Survey* (Stanford University Press 2018) 47–53.

[34] P.G. Lauren, *The Evolution of International Human Rights: Visions Seen* (3rd edn., PENN 2011) 210.

[35] M.A. Glendon, *A World Made New: Eleanor Roosevelt and the Universal Declaration of Human Rights* (Random House 2001) 73; M. Goodale (ed.), *Letters to the Contrary: A Curated History of the UNESCO Human Rights Survey* (Stanford University Press 2018) 20.

[36] M. Goodale, 'The Myth of Universality: The UNESCO "Philosophers' Committee" and the Making of Human Rights' (2018) 43 *Law & Social Inquiry* 596, 605.

[37] M. Goodale (ed.), *Letters to the Contrary: A Curated History of the UNESCO Human Rights Survey* (Stanford University Press 2018).

[38] Report of the UNESCO Committee on the Philosophic Principles of the Rights of the Man to the Commission on Human Rights of the United Nations, Phil./10 (31 July 1947).

[39] UNESCO, Human Rights: Comments and interpretations, UNESCO/PHS/3(rev.) (25 July 1948), p. 1.

had not been conducted in coordination with that of the Commission.[40] In a private session, held at the end of December 1947, the Commission decided not to reproduce the UNESCO report for distribution to UN Member States.[41] However, it is possible to wonder whether the UNESCO report might have still influenced the drafting work of the Commission to some extent.[42]

2.2.1.2 The adoption of the Declaration

Politics and time constraints led the Commission,[43] towards mid-1948, to decide that it should focus first on completing a Declaration for adoption by the General Assembly that year, while its work towards the production of a binding convention and means of implementation could be differed until after that task was completed.[44] In June 1948, the UN Commission adopted the text of a draft Declaration and submitted it to ECOSOC for its consideration.[45] ECOSOC elevated the draft to the General Assembly, where it was reviewed at length during 81 meetings of its Third Committee (Social and Humanitarian), before being discussed at the Plenary Session of the General Assembly.[46] At the Third Committee, chaired by Charles Malik, the Commission's delegate from Lebanon (Lubnān), the draft was debated in detail on daily sessions over a two-month period, during which 168 amendments were proposed and discussed.[47] The final outcome was the adoption of the text—by a vote of 29 to 0, with seven abstentions—for its discussion to proceed to the General Assembly's plenary.[48] On 10 December 1948, the Universal Declaration of Human Rights was adopted and proclaimed by the United Nations General Assembly. Its adoption was decided by the affirmative vote of forty-eight of the (then) fifty-eight

---

[40] R. Normand and S. Zaidi, *Human Rights at the UN: The Political History of Universal Justice* (Indiana University Press 2008) 182–183; M. Goodale (ed.), *Letters to the Contrary: A Curated History of the UNESCO Human Rights Survey* (Stanford University Press 2018) 23.

[41] CHR, Summary Record of the twenty-sixth meeting (held in closed session), E/CN.4/SR/26 (3 December 1947).

[42] See: R. Cassin, 'La Déclaration Universelle et la mise en oeuvre des droits de l'homme' (1951) 79 *Recueil des Cours de l'Academie de Droit International* 237, 272.

[43] T.J. Farer, 'The United Nations and Human Rights: More than a Whimper less than a Roar' (1987) 9 *Human Rights Quarterly* 550, 556; M. Mazower, 'The Strange Triumph of Human Rights, 1933–1950' (2004) 47 *The Historical Journal* 379, 395–396.

[44] J. Morsink, *The Universal Declaration of Human Rights: Origins, Drafting, and Intent* (University of Pennsylvania Press 1999) 18–19; R. Normand and S. Zaidi, *Human Rights at the UN: The Political History of Universal Justice* (Indiana University Press 2008) 171–172.

[45] P.G. Lauren, *The Evolution of International Human Rights: Visions Seen* (3rd edn., PENN 2011) 219; W. Schabas, *The Universal Declaration of Human Rights: The travaux préparatoires: vol. I* (CUP 2013) civ–cv.

[46] J. Morsink, *The Universal Declaration of Human Rights: Origins, Drafting, and Intent* (University of Pennsylvania Press 1999) 11–12; W. Schabas, *The Universal Declaration of Human Rights: The travaux préparatoires: vol. I* (CUP 2013) cv–cix.

[47] J. Humphrey, *Human Rights & the United Nations: a great adventure* (Transnational Publishers 1984) 63; S. Waltz, 'Reclaiming and Rebuilding the History of the Universal Declaration of Human Rights' (2002) 23 *Third World Quarterly* 437, 442.

[48] J. Humphrey, *Human Rights & the United Nations: a great adventure* (Transnational Publishers 1984) 71; J. Morsink, *The Universal Declaration of Human Rights: Origins, Drafting, and Intent* (University of Pennsylvania Press 1999) 11.

UN Member States, with no votes against, and eight abstentions, while two Member States were not present at the vote.[49]

As mentioned in **Section 2.2.1**, the Declaration was conceived as merely the first part of an International Bill of Human Rights to be complemented by one or more international treaties, as well as by measures for their implementation. Nevertheless, almost eighteen years elapsed between the proclamation of the Universal Declaration and the adoption of the two international treaties on human rights, in 1966. Paradoxically, this prolonged period of time helped to increase the impact of the Declaration itself on the international protection of human rights, allowing for the elaboration of different theses that support the idea that (at least) some of the rights recognized in the Universal Declaration held a binding character, either as part of customary international law or as a manifestation of general principles of law.[50]

Moreover, the dynamic interaction of the Universal Declaration and the UN Charter provided further reasons to support its normative character. As discussed in **Section 2.2**, the Charter makes reference to human rights in different articles, as well as in its preamble. One of the purposes of the United Nations itself is to achieve international cooperation in promoting and encouraging respect for human rights for all without distinction as to race, sex, language, or religion, and the Charter clearly establishes international obligations upon both the Organization and its Member States concerning the protection of human rights. While Article 55(c) states that the Organization shall promote universal respect for, and observance of, human rights and fundamental freedoms for all without distinction as to race, sex, language, or religion, Article 56 establishes that all Members pledge themselves to take joint and separate action, in cooperation with the Organization, for the achievement of such purpose.[51] These two provisions of the Charter, jointly with the Universal Declaration, have been deployed by the United Nations as the grounds for international action aimed at promoting the respect for human rights.[52] The Universal Declaration of Human Rights has been used to provide meaning and content to the commitments concerning human

---

[49] In alphabetical order, the States voting in favour of its adoption were: Afghanistan, Argentina, Australia, Belgium, Bolivia, Brasil, Burma, Canada, Chile, China, Colombia, Costa Rica, Cuba, Denmark, Dominican Republic, Ecuador, Egypt, El Salvador, Ethiopia, France, Greece, Guatemala, Haïti, Iceland, India, Iran, Iraq, Lebanon, Liberia, Luxembourg, Mexico, the Netherlands, New Zealand, Nicaragua, Norway, Pakistan, Panamá, Paraguay, Perú, Philippines, Siam, Sweden, Syria, Turkey, the UK, the USA, Uruguay, and Venezuela. The States abstaining in the vote were: the Byelorussian Soviet Socialist Republic, Czechoslovakia, Poland, Saudi Arabia, the Ukrainian Soviet Socialist Republic, Union of South Africa, the Union of Soviet Socialist Republics, and Yugoslavia. The two UN Member States absent at the session were Honduras and Yemen. See: UNGA (3rd session), 183rd meeting, held at the Palais de Chaillot, Paris (10 December 1948), A/PV.183.

[50] L.B. Sohn, 'The Universal Declaration of Human Rights: a Common Standard of Achievement? – The Status of the Universal Declaration in International Law' (1967) 8 *Journal of the International Commission of Jurists* 17, 23–26; H. Hannum, 'The Status of the Universal Declaration of Human Rights in National and International Law' (1995–1996) 25 *Georgia Journal of International and Comparative Law* 287, 289–354; M. Pinto, *Temas de Derechos Humanos* (Del Puerto 2009) 33–37.

[51] M. Pinto, *Temas de Derechos Humanos* (Del Puerto 2009) 22–23.

[52] A.A. Cançado-Trindade, 'O Legado da Declaraçao Universal de 1948 e o Futuro da Proteçao Internacional dos Direitos Humanos' (1999) 14 *Anuario HispanoLuso-Americano de Derecho Internacional* 197.

rights contained in the Charter.[53] It seemed that René Cassin's statement that the Declaration 'could be considered as an authoritative interpretation of the Charter of the United Nations'[54] had been accepted by the Organization.[55] This was further confirmed by the International Court of Justice making explicit reference to the principles of the UN Charter in conjunction with the Universal Declaration, when deciding in 1980 the *Case Concerning United States Diplomatic and Consular Staff in Tehran*.[56]

ICJ, *United States Diplomatic and Consular Staff in Tehran (United States of America v. Iran)*, Judgment, I.C.J. Reports 1980, p. 3.

This well-known case was brought to the International Court of Justice by the United States against Iran (Īrān). It followed the occupation of the US Embassy in Tehran by Iranian militants in November 1979, holding US diplomatic and consular staff as hostages (paras. 17–19). The Court decided the case on 24 May 1980, at a time when the situation still persisted, despite provisional measures previously ordered by the Court in December 1979. The Court found Iran responsible for the continuous violation of several international norms the situation entailed (paras. 67, 76–79, and 90). It stated: 'Wrongfully to deprive human beings of their freedom and to subject them to physical constraint in conditions of hardship is in itself manifestly incompatible with the principles of the Charter of the United Nations, as well as with the fundamental principles enunciated in the Universal Declaration of Human Rights' (para. 91).

The ICJ affirmed that, in principle, the conduct of militants could not be attributed to the State (para. 58). However, in the case, Iran had done nothing to prevent the attack, stop it before it reached its completion, or force the militants to withdraw from the premises and release the hostages (paras. 61–68). Furthermore, the Court noted that certain organs of Iran had endorsed the acts of the militants and decided to perpetuate them, thereby transforming them into acts of the State (paras. 71–74). The Court decided that Iran was bound to secure the immediate release of the hostages, to restore the Embassy premises, and to make reparation for the injury caused to the United States Government (para. 95).

2.2.1.3 Critical debate: is the Universal Declaration truly 'universal'?

As mentioned in **Section 1.1.2.2.1**, there is an extensive controversy as to whether the Universal Declaration of Human Rights can be seen as the fruit of cross-cultural

---

[53] L. Henkin, *The Age of Rights* (Columbia University Press 1990) 19; T. Buergenthal, 'The Normative and Institutional Evolution of International Human Rights' (1997) 19 *Human Rights Quarterly* 703, 708; M. Nowak, UN Covenant on Civil and Political Rights: CCPR Commentary (2nd edn., Engel 2005) xx.

[54] Summary Record of the Ninety-Second Meeting [of the Third Committee], Held at the Palais de Chaillot, Paris, on Saturday, 2 October 1948, at 3:15pm (A/C.3/SR.92).

[55] A.A. Cançado-Trindade, 'Introductory Note', United Nations Audiovisual Library of International Law, available at: http://legal.un.org/avl/ha/udhr/udhr.html (accessed on 19 August 2022).

[56] ICJ, *United States Diplomatic and Consular Staff in Tehran (United States of America v. Iran)*, Judgment, I.C.J. Reports 1980, p. 3, para. 91.

agreement or if, conversely, it suffers from an entrenched Western provenance.[57] There is certainly no clear-cut answer to this debate. The story of the adoption of the Declaration reveals a complex political history, subject to different possible interpretations and, thus, underscored by multiple possible truths.[58]

On the one hand, the rather Western origins of the idea of human rights itself were discussed in **Section 1.2** and it would seem fitting to apply that history to the first main international instrument dedicated to the proclamation of these rights. In fact, the connection between the rights of the Declaration and the 'natural rights' of the Enlightenment, was affirmed multiple times during the drafting process, with delegates from the Commission even confirming the link between the rights included in the draft and those found in eighteenth-century declarations.[59] Another important hint of the Western provenance of the Declaration is the fact that, at the time of its adoption, the United Nations was an organization with Western prominence;[60] a consequence of a world in which roughly half of the population was living under colonial domination.[61] Unsurprisingly, the composition of the Commission itself was skewed westward.[62] Even its most prominent delegates from non-Western States—P.C. Chang from China and Malik from Lebanon—had been educated in the United States.[63] In fact, one of the eight States that abstained in the vote for adopting the Declaration, Saudi Arabia, argued that its abstention was based on concerns about the compatibility of this instrument with principles of Islam.[64]

On the other hand, there is increasing literature that seeks to draw attention to the multiple non-Western contributions that helped shape the text of the Declaration.[65]

---

[57] V. Leary, 'The Effect of Western Perspectives on International Human Rights' in A.A. An-Na'im and F. Deng (eds.), *Human Rights in Africa: Cross-Cultural Perspectives* (Brookings Institution 1990) 15–30; A. Cassese, 'The General Assembly: Historical Perspective 1945-1989' in P. Alston (ed.), *The United Nations and Human Rights: A Critical Appraisal* (Clarendon Press 1992) 25–54, 31–32; M. Mutua, *Human Rights Standards: Hegemony, Law, and Politics* (State University of New York Press 2016) 18–19.

[58] S. Waltz, 'Universalizing Human Rights: The Role of Small States in the Construction of the Universal Declaration of Human Rights' in J-M. Barreto (ed.), *Human Rights from a Third World Perspective: Critique, History and International Law* (Cambridge Scholars 2013) 353–387, 379.

[59] J. Humphrey, *Human Rights & the United Nations: a great adventure* (Transnational Publishers 1984) 66–67; J. Morsink, *The Universal Declaration of Human Rights: Origins, Drafting, and Intent* (University of Pennsylvania Press 1999) 281.

[60] J. Morsink, *The Universal Declaration of Human Rights: Origins, Drafting, and Intent* (University of Pennsylvania Press 1999) 96; R. Burke, *Decolonization and the Evolution of International Human Rights* (University of Pennsylvania Press 2010) 145.

[61] J. Morsink, *The Universal Declaration of Human Rights: Origins, Drafting, and Intent* (University of Pennsylvania Press 1999) 96; J. Whyte, 'Human Rights and the Collateral Damage of Neoliberalism' (2017) 20 *Theory & Event* 137, 145.

[62] R. Burke, *Decolonization and the Evolution of International Human Rights* (University of Pennsylvania Press 2010) 145; A. Clapham, 'The General Assembly' in F. Mégret and P. Alston (eds.), *The United Nations and Human Rights: A Critical Appraisal* (2nd edn., OUP 2020) 99–129, 107.

[63] A.A. An-Na'im, 'Problems of Universal Cultural Legitimacy for Human Rights' in A.A. An-Na'im and F. Deng (eds.), *Human Rights in Africa: Cross-Cultural Perspectives* (Brookings Institution 1990) 331–367, 350.

[64] J. Humphrey, *Human Rights & the United Nations: a great adventure* (Transnational Publishers 1984) 73; J. Morsink, *Inherent Human Rights: Philosophical Roots of the Universal Declaration* (PENN 2009) 75–76.

[65] See: Waltz, 'Reclaiming and Rebuilding the History of the Universal Declaration of Human Rights' (2002) 23 *Third World Quarterly* 437; J-M. Barreto (ed.), *Human Rights from a Third World Perspective: Critique, History and International Law* (Cambridge Scholars 2013); L.H. Liu, 'Shadows of Universalism: The Untold Story of Human Rights around 1948' (2014) 40 *Critical Inquiry* 385; R. Ramcharan and B. Ramcharan, *Asia and the Drafting of the Universal Declaration of Human Rights* (Palgrave 2019).

As mentioned in **Section 2.2.1**, the main documents used as inspiration to produce the first working draft of the Declaration were actually of Latin-American origin. Moreover, the lengthy document collated by Humphrey disclosed that the rights that were included found equivalence in multiple constitutions worldwide.[66] Some essential characteristics of the final text also came from contributions made by non-Western delegations. One of the most evident examples is the inclusion of social, economic, and cultural rights, which is due to the persistence of Latin-American delegations, with the support of the Soviet Union and Syria (Suriyah), with the specific right to food and clothing included thanks to the delegates from China and the Philippines (Pilipinas).[67] Similarly, the Soviet delegation has been credited for its insistence on the strong recognition of the prohibition of discrimination,[68] while the use of gender-neutral language—further discussed in **Section 10.2.2** — is due to the delegates from India (Bhārat) and the Dominican Republic (República Dominicana).[69]

On a more general level, it can be highlighted that, even if nations from Asia and Africa were greatly under-represented in the Commission that drafted the text and in the General Assembly that approved it, these bodies did include representation from numerous States from beyond the West.[70] To sum up, while it is perhaps not accurate to claim that, at the time of its adoption, the Universal Declaration was truly universal, as a negotiated text, it did include multiple contributions from more than fifty States;[71] hence, it is also difficult to affirm that it was merely a Western document.[72]

---

[66] S. Waltz, 'Universalizing Human Rights: The Role of Small States in the Construction of the Universal Declaration of Human Rights' in J-M. Barreto (ed.), *Human Rights from a Third World Perspective: Critique, History and International Law* (Cambridge Scholars 2013) 353–387, 368.

[67] S. Waltz, 'Reclaiming and Rebuilding the History of the Universal Declaration of Human Rights' (2002) 23 *Third World Quarterly* 437, 444; M. Pinto, 'Integralidad de los Derechos Humanos: Exigibilidad de los Derechos Colectivos y Acceso a la Justicia de las Personas en Condición de Pobreza' (2009) 50 *Revista IIDH* 53, 56; J. Whyte, 'Human Rights and the Collateral Damage of Neoliberalism' (2017) 20 *Theory & Event* 137, 143–144.

[68] S. Waltz, 'Universalizing Human Rights: The Role of Small States in the Construction of the Universal Declaration of Human Rights' in J-M. Barreto (ed.), *Human Rights from a Third World Perspective: Critique, History and International Law* (Cambridge Scholars 2013) 353–387, 371, 375; J. Whyte, 'Human Rights, Revolution and the "Good Society": The Soviet Union and the Universal Declaration of Human Rights' in K. Greenman et al. (ed.), *Revolutions in International Law: The Legacies of 1917* (CUP 2021) 401–427, 423.

[69] A.S. Fraser, 'Becoming Human: The Origins and Developments of Women's Human Rights' (1999) 21 *Human Rights Quarterly* 853, 888; S. Waltz, 'Reclaiming and Rebuilding the History of the Universal Declaration of Human Rights' (2002) 23 *Third World Quarterly* 437, 444.

[70] P.G. Lauren, *The Evolution of International Human Rights: Visions Seen* (3rd edn., PENN 2011) 219–220; J-M. Barreto, 'Decolonial Strategies and Dialogue in the Human Rights Field: A Manifesto' (2012) 3 *Transnational Legal Theory* 1, 12–13.

[71] S. Waltz, 'Universalizing Human Rights: The Role of Small States in the Construction of the Universal Declaration of Human Rights' in J-M. Barreto (ed.), *Human Rights from a Third World Perspective: Critique, History and International Law* (Cambridge Scholars 2013) 353–387, 366; Z. Kabasakal Arat, 'Forging a Global Culture of Human Rights: Origins and Prospects of the International Bill of Rights' in J-M. Barreto (ed.), *Human Rights from a Third World Perspective: Critique, History and International Law* (Cambridge Scholars 2013) 387–439, 394.

[72] The Declaration would then become the single most translated document in history, being now available in more than 500 different languages. See: https://www.ohchr.org/en/ohchr/node/16711/new-record-translations-universal-declaration-human-rights-pass-500 (accessed on 15 May 2023).

2.2.2 THE ADOPTION OF THE FIRST THREE CORE HUMAN RIGHTS TREATIES

With the adoption of the Universal Declaration of Human Rights, the Commission of Human Rights was able to turn back its attention to the missing components of the international bill of human rights: one or more binding instruments and means of implementation of human rights (see **Section 2.2.1**).[73] However, it would take until 1966 for this international bill to be completed, with the adoption by the General Assembly of the text of ICCPR, its first Optional Protocol, and ICESCR. The ideological and political conflicts of the so-called Cold War marked the drafting process of these treaties.[74]

The Commission made use of a draft prepared by the UK as the basis for its debate, but this instrument was rather anaemic in scope and substance, and lacked any protection of economic, social, and cultural rights.[75] Although the Universal Declaration had recognized both civil and political rights, as well as economic, social, and cultural rights,[76] the inclusion of the latter within the treaty to be drafted was one of the crucial points of disagreement during the lengthy process to adopt, finally, two separate treaties. Western States, such as the USA and the UK, considered that any treaty should only focus on civil and political rights, while the Soviet Union promoted the binding force of economic, social, and cultural rights; a stance that had strong support from the Latin-American States.[77] The absence of agreement within the Commission was taken, through ECOSOC, to the General Assembly, which asserted that civil and political rights and economic, social, and cultural rights were interconnected and interdependent, and that the 'Covenant on Human Rights' to be adopted should include both sets of rights.[78] And yet, only one year later, political pressure, especially from Western States, managed to change the Assembly's position, leading to the decision that two treaties, instead of one, were to be elaborated.[79]

Where the political interest of the divergent powerful States—the USA, the UK, and the USSR—actually converged was in their common stance against the adoption of

---

[73] M. Hertig Randall, 'The History of the Covenants: Looking Back Half a Century and Beyond' in D. Moeckli, H. Keller, and C. Heri (eds.), *The Human Rights Covenants at 50: Their Past, Present, and Future* (OUP 2018) 7–30, 10.

[74] R. Normand and S. Zaidi, *Human Rights at the UN: The Political History of Universal Justice* (Indiana University Press 2008) 199; M. Hertig Randall, 'The History of the Covenants: Looking Back Half a Century and Beyond' in D. Moeckli, H. Keller, and C. Heri (eds.), *The Human Rights Covenants at 50: Their Past, Present, and Future* (OUP 2018) 7–30, 10.

[75] M. Hertig Randall, 'The History of the Covenants: Looking Back Half a Century and Beyond' in D. Moeckli, H. Keller, and C. Heri (eds.), *The Human Rights Covenants at 50: Their Past, Present, and Future* (OUP 2018) 7–30, 16.

[76] UDHR, Arts. 2–21 and 22–28.

[77] P.G. Lauren, *The Evolution of International Human Rights: Visions Seen* (3rd edn., PENN 2011) 232; M. Hertig Randall, 'The History of the Covenants: Looking Back Half a Century and Beyond' in D. Moeckli, H. Keller, and C. Heri (eds.), *The Human Rights Covenants at 50: Their Past, Present, and Future* (OUP 2018) 7–30, 16.

[78] UNGA, 'Draft International Covenant on Humans Rights and Measures of Implementation: Future Work of the Commission on Human Rights', A/RES/421(V) (4 December 1950).

[79] F. Jhabvala, 'On Human Rights and the Socio-economic Context' (2009) 31 *Netherlands International Law Review* 149, 159, 175–176. See: UNGA, Resolution 543/VI (1951), 'Preparation of two Drafts International Covenants on Human Rights', A/RES/543(VI).

strong international mechanisms for the implementation of any type of rights.[80] This is unsurprising, when considering that Soviet gulags, British colonialism, and US racial policies could not withstand any serious international human rights scrutiny.[81] Consequently, the UK embraced a protracting policy towards the adoption of the international treaties, while the USA plainly decided not to become Party to any human rights treaty adopted by the UN—a policy that would not change until the 1990s.[82] Despite these drawbacks, the Commission on Human Rights managed to complete the draft of the two separate covenants in 1954, but the complex political scenario, marked by the East/West divide of the 'Cold War' and the incipient process of de-colonization of the world,[83] led to a delay of over a decade for the Third Committee of the General Assembly to conclude the work on the text of these treaties.

The process of de-colonization was to have fundamental and long-lasting effects on the UN's human rights politics. Between the date of adoption of the Universal Declaration and that of the 1966 Covenants, membership of the United Nations more than doubled, increasing from 58 to 117 States, the majority of which had emerged from the process of de-colonization.[84] This re-shaping of the world was to have a substantive impact on the elaboration of the Covenants, as well as on the adoption of another universal human rights treaty before them. With regard to the Covenants, the process of de-colonization provided an impetus within the Third Committee of the General Assembly to secure the absence of a 'colonial clause'[85] in these treaties,[86] which had managed to survive

---

[80] F. Jhabvala, 'The Soviet-Bloc's View of the Implementation of Human Rights Accords' (1985) 7 *Human Rights Quarterly* 461, 471; R. Normand and S. Zaidi, *Human Rights at the UN: The Political History of Universal Justice* (Indiana University Press 2008) 200–201; M. Hertig Randall, 'The History of the Covenants: Looking Back Half a Century and Beyond' in D. Moeckli, H. Keller, and C. Heri (eds.), *The Human Rights Covenants at 50: Their Past, Present, and Future* (OUP 2018) 7–30, 26–27.

[81] P. Alston, 'The Commission on Human Rights' in P. Alston (ed.), *The United Nations and Human Rights: A Critical Appraisal* (Clarendon Press 1992) 126–210, 141; W. Osiatynski, 'On the Universality of the Universal Declaration of Human Rights' in A. Sajó (ed.), *Human Rights with Modesty: The Problem with Universalism* (Springer 2004) 33–50, 36.

[82] M.A. Glendon, *A World Made New: Eleanor Roosevelt and the Universal Declaration of Human Rights* (Random House 2001) 200, 205; P.G. Lauren, *The Evolution of International Human Rights: Visions Seen* (3rd edn., PENN 2011) 195 and 233.

[83] J.B. Marie, *La Commission des Droits de l'Homme de l'ONU* (Pedone 1975) 168; V. Leary, 'The Effect of Western Perspectives on International Human Rights' in A.A. An-Na'im and F. Deng (eds.), *Human Rights in Africa: Cross-Cultural Perspectives* (Brookings Institution 1990) 15–30, 25.

[84] This was the case of: Algeria, Burundi, Cambodia, Cameroon, Central African Republic, Ceylon (Sri Lanka), Chad, Congo, Côte d'Ivoire, Cyprus, Dahomey (Bénin), Democratic Republic of Congo, Gabon, Gambia, Ghana, Guinea, Indonesia, Jamaica, Jordan, Kenya, Kuwait, Laos (Lao), Libya, Malagasy (Madagascar), Malawi, Malaya (Malaysia), Maldives, Mali, Malta, Mauritania, Mongolia, Morocco, Nepal, Niger, Nigeria, Rwanda, Senegal, Sierra Leone, Singapore, Somalia, Sudan, Tanganyika (Tanzania), Togo, Trinidad and Tobago, Tunisia, Uganda, Upper Volta (Burkina Faso), and Zambia.

[85] Like the one included in the European Convention on Human Rights, as discussed in **Section 3.2.3**.

[86] R. Burke, *Decolonization and the Evolution of International Human Rights* (University of Pennsylvania Press 2010) 40; L.H. Liu, 'Shadows of Universalism: The Untold Story of Human Rights Around 1948' (2014) 40 *Critical Inquiry* 385, 394–398. See: UNGA, 'Territorial Application of the International Covenant on Human Rights', A/RES/422(V) (4 December 1950).

the debates of the Commission on Human Rights.[87] Such a clause would have allowed European imperial powers to exempt the people in colonial territories from the protection of the human rights the Covenants were aimed to provide. Similarly, the process of de-colonization was crucial in securing the recognition of the right to self-determination (discussed in **Section 10.4.1**) in Article 1 of both Covenants;[88] a right that was not recognized by the Universal Declaration and which had been extremely controversial during the drafting of the text in the Commission.[89]

Moreover, while agreement for the adoption of the two human rights Covenants continued to be difficult to reach, another important development in the protection of human rights materialized. In 1962, a group of nine francophone African States presented a resolution calling for the drafting of a convention on racial discrimination;[90] an initiative that found strong support from Latin-American countries.[91] This resolution was adopted by the General Assembly in December 1962, and the International Convention on the Elimination of All Forms of Racial Discrimination (ICERD) was completed and (unanimously) adopted by the General Assembly only three years later.[92] As further discussed in **Section 5.4**, this Convention became the first human rights treaty within the United Nations system to recognize a right of individual petition to a monitoring body.[93]

The adoption of ICERD in 1965 contributed to breaking the impasse that was stopping the completion of the two Covenants. It came to prove that it was possible to create binding international human rights norms and mechanism of implementation, when the political will existed.[94] A further divisive issue, that of the mechanisms of implementation, was also finally resolved by reaching compromising agreements within the Third Committee

---

[87] J. Humphrey, *Human Rights & the United Nations: a great adventure* (Transnational Publishers 1984) 129; C. Roberts, *The Contentious History of the International Bill of Human Rights* (CUP 2014) 148–151. See: Report of the Commission on Human Rights, E/1721 (19 June 1950).

[88] V. Leary, 'The Effect of Western Perspectives on International Human Rights' in A.A. An-Na'im and F. Deng (eds.), *Human Rights in Africa: Cross-Cultural Perspectives* (Brookings Institution 1990) 15–30, 28; R. Burke, *Decolonization and the Evolution of International Human Rights* (University of Pennsylvania Press 2010) 37, 41; A. Anghie, 'International Human Rights Law and a Developing World Perspective' in S. Sheeran and N. Rodley (eds.), *Routledge Handbook of International Human Rights Law* (Routledge 2013) 109–125, 116.

[89] R. Normand and S. Zaidi, *Human Rights at the UN: The Political History of Universal Justice* (Indiana University Press 2008) 212–213; M. Hertig Randall, 'The History of the Covenants: Looking Back Half a Century and Beyond' in D. Moeckli, H. Keller, and C. Heri (eds.), *The Human Rights Covenants at 50: Their Past, Present, and Future* (OUP 2018) 7–30, 11, 14.

[90] 'Manifestations of racial prejudice and national and religious intolerance: preparation of an international convention on the elimination of racial discrimination' (A/C.3/L.1006) (25 October 1962). Proposed by the Central African Republic, Chad, Dahomey (Bénin), Guinea, Ivory Coast (Côte d'Ivoire), Mali, Mauritania, Niger, and Upper Volta (Burkina Faso).

[91] S.L.B. Jensen, *The Making of International Human Rights: The 1960s, Decolonization and the Reconstruction of Global Values* (CUP 2016) 105, 107.

[92] S.L.B. Jensen, *The Making of International Human Rights: The 1960s, Decolonization and the Reconstruction of Global Values* (CUP 2016) 108.

[93] S.L.B. Jensen, *The Making of International Human Rights: The 1960s, Decolonization and the Reconstruction of Global Values* (CUP 2016) 125; R. Burke, *Decolonization and the Evolution of International Human Rights* (University of Pennsylvania Press 2010) 71.

[94] P.G. Lauren, *The Evolution of International Human Rights: Visions Seen* (3rd edn., PENN 2011) 239.

of the General Assembly.[95] As further discussed in **Section 2.3**, the end result was that the International Covenant on Economic, Social and Cultural Rights was to be deprived of any substantive mechanism of implementation, besides a procedural obligation upon States to report to ECOSOC. Meanwhile, the International Covenant on Civil and Political Rights was to be monitored by a 'Human Rights Committee', which, in addition to State reports, would be competent to receive inter-State complaints—but only if States accepted such ability, and subject to reciprocity—as well as individual communications—but just in respect of States that decided to become Parties to an Optional Protocol.

The following year, the General Assembly finally adopted and opened for signature, ratification and accession the International Covenant on Economic, Social and Cultural Rights (by 105 affirmative votes and 0 against), the International Covenant on Civil and Political Rights (by a vote of 106–0), and the (First) Optional Protocol of the latter (by 66 affirmative votes, 2 against, and 38 abstentions). As a result, the International Bill of Human Rights was completed at last, comprising the 1948 Universal Declaration and both 1966 Covenants. However, yet another decade would elapse before it could be fully in place. After obtaining the necessary number of ratifications (thirty-five for each Covenant and ten for the Protocol), ICESCR entered into force in January 1976, while ICCPR and its Optional Protocol entered into force in March of the same year.

The adoption of ICERD in 1965 and the completion of the International Bill of Human Rights in 1966 were only the beginning of the standard-setting activity of the UN concerning the international protection of human rights, as will be discussed in **Chapter 4** and **Chapter 5**. The multiplication of human rights instruments, and of the systems of implementation they set in place, would lead to the expansion of the sphere of protection of the human person. The different norms and systems created are not hierarchically linked to one another, but the protection they offer to the individual is mutually reinforcing. Within the international law of human rights, it is not important which legal instrument or monitoring body safeguards the rights of the individual, but for such protection to be offered to the maximum degree possible. This phenomenon of complementarity is further highlighted by the fact that all subsequent human rights instruments find in the 1948 Universal Declaration a common source of inspiration.[96] This is not a far-fetched assumption, but can be confirmed by the repeated references to the Declaration in the multiple international human rights treaties adopted, such as in the preamble of all UN core human rights conventions and regional human rights treaties.[97]

---

[95] H. Gros Espiell, 'La Adopción por la Asamblea General de las Naciones Unidas, en 1966, de los Dos Pactos Internacionales de Derechos Humanos y del Protocolo Facultativo al de Derechos Civiles y Políticos: Recuerdos y Reflexiones' (1995) 21 *Revista IIDH*, 53–66, 63; M. Hertig Randall, 'The History of the Covenants: Looking Back Half a Century and Beyond' in D. Moeckli, H. Keller, and C. Heri (eds.), *The Human Rights Covenants at 50: Their Past, Present, and Future* (OUP 2018) 7–30, 25–26.

[96] M. Hinz, 'Human Rights Between Universalism and Cultural Relativism? The Need for Anthropological Jurisprudence in the Globalising World' in A. Bösl and J. Diescho (eds.), *Human Rights in Africa: Legal Perspectives on Their Protection and Promotion* (Konrad Adenauer 2009) 3–78, 4; P.G. Lauren, *The Evolution of International Human Rights: Visions Seen* (3rd edn., PENN 2011) 195, 225.

[97] See: ICERD, ICESCR, ICCPR, CEDAW, UNCAT, UNCRC, ICRMW, UNCRPD, ICPPED, ECHR; ACHR; African Charter; Arab Charter.

2.2.3 THE (FIRST) INTERNATIONAL HUMAN RIGHTS CONFERENCE (TEHRAN, 1968)

The first global assessment of the development of the international law of human rights took place two decades after the adoption and proclamation of the Universal Declaration of Human Rights. The (first) International Conference of Human Rights was held in 1968 in Tehran[98] and was attended by representatives of 84 states, as well as by non-governmental organizations.[99] The outcome of the Conference was the 'Proclamation of Tehran', together with twenty-nine resolutions on different topics.[100] Despite valid concerns about the human rights record of the host State and about the views some delegations expressed on the persistent value of the Universal Declaration of Human Rights,[101] the contribution of the 1968 Conference to the reappraisal and further expansion of the international law of human rights should be acknowledged.[102] Arguably, the Conference's most impactful contribution was the affirmation that all human rights are indivisible and interdependent, made less than two years after the adoption of two separate treaties in 1966.[103] The most evident support for such a view can be found in the Proclamation of Tehran, adopted by the Conference's plenary, which affirms: '*Since human rights and fundamental freedoms are indivisible, the full realization of civil and political rights without the enjoyment of economic, social and cultural rights is impossible*. The achievement of lasting progress in the implementation of human rights is dependent upon sound and effective national and international policies of economic and social development.'[104] Two decades after the adoption of the Universal Declaration, the 1968 Conference asserted the existence of a new agreed-upon understanding of human rights, a global perspective that emphasized the need for an integral view of all rights.[105] The Proclamation concluded by urging 'all peoples

---

[98] The choice of host was contentious, given that Iran under the Shah Reza Pahlavi was not an example of democracy and human rights—although neither were a large number of States that attended the conference. See: R. Burke, 'From Individual Rights to National Development: The First UN International Conference on Human Rights, Tehran, 1968' (2008) 19 *Journal of World History* 275; S.L.B. Jensen, *The Making of International Human Rights: The 1960s, Decolonization and the Reconstruction of Global Values* (CUP 2016) 186.

[99] A.A. Cançado Trindade, *Tratado de Direito Internacional dos Direitos Humanos: Volume I* (2nd edn., SAFE 2003) 78.

[100] Proclamation of Tehran, Final Act of the International Conference on Human Rights, UN Doc. A/CONF. 32/41 at 3 (1968).

[101] R. Burke, 'From Individual Rights to National Development: The First UN International Conference on Human Rights, Tehran, 1968' (2008) 19 *Journal of World History* 275, 285–286, 294–296; R. Burke, *Decolonization and the Evolution of International Human Rights* (University of Pennsylvania Press 2010), chapter 4.

[102] For a rather tempered view on the Declaration, see: M. Moskowitz, *International Concern with Human Rights* (Oceana 1974), chapter II.

[103] The Conference also confirmed the acquired binding character of the Universal Declaration of Human Rights by 1968. See: Proclamation of Tehran, Final Act of the International Conference on Human Rights, UN Doc. A/CONF. 32/41 at 3 (1968), para. 2.

[104] Proclamation of Tehran, Final Act of the International Conference on Human Rights, UN Doc. A/CONF. 32/41 at 3 (1968), para. 13 (emphasis added).

[105] Only a few years later, in 1975, thirty-five States from both the Western and Eastern blocs signed the Helsinki Final Act, in which they expressed their commitment to promote and encourage the effective exercise of civil, political, economic, social, and cultural rights, all of which were recognized to be essential for the free and full development of the human person. See: Conference on Security and Co-operation in Europe, Final Act (Helsinki 1975), principle VII.

and governments to dedicate themselves to the principles enshrined in the Universal Declaration of Human Rights and to redouble their efforts to provide for all human beings a life consonant with freedom and dignity and conducive to physical, mental, social and spiritual welfare'.[106]

The proclamation of the indivisible nature and interdependent character of all human rights was an important contribution to the subsequent development of the discipline, as can be attested by the multiple acknowledgements of these principles by the United Nations. It led the UN General Assembly to adopt a number of resolutions in which it affirmed the interrelation and indivisibility of all human rights.[107] The General Assembly even decided that the approach of the work of the whole system of the United Nations concerning human rights had to take into account the following principles: that '[a]ll human rights and fundamental freedoms of the human person and of peoples are inalienable'; that '[a]ll human rights and fundamental freedoms are indivisible and interdependent'; and that 'equal attention and urgent consideration should be given to the implementation, promotion and protection of both civil and political, and economic, social and cultural rights'.[108] In fact, the recognition that all human rights are inalienable, indivisible, and interdependent provides one of the founding pillars of the international law of human rights and the path to approach the urgent global challenges the international community has been facing since the adoption of the Universal Declaration, such as widespread extreme poverty, the capacity for mass destruction, and environmental degradation.[109]

2.3 CIVIL AND POLITICAL RIGHTS AND ECONOMIC, SOCIAL, AND CULTURAL RIGHTS

Although the 1968 Tehran Declaration proclaimed the indivisibility and interdependence of all human rights, the implementation of economic, social, and cultural rights has been particularly neglected in the past.[110] The roots of the distinction between two 'categories' of human rights, with civil and political rights, on the one hand, and economic, social, and cultural rights, on the other, can be traced back to the *legislative stage* of the international law of human rights. As mentioned in **Section 2.2.2**, by a marginal vote, in 1951 the UN General Assembly changed its earlier position and instructed the Commission to

---

[106] Proclamation of Tehraan Final Act of the International Conference on Human Rights, UN Doc. A/CONF. 32/41 at 3 (1968), Art. 19.

[107] A.A. Cançado Trindade, *Tratado de Direito Internacional dos Direitos Humanos: Volume I* (2nd edn., SAFE 2003) 84.

[108] UNGA, 'Alternative approaches and ways and means within the United Nations system for improving the effective enjoyment of human rights and fundamental freedoms', A/RES/32/130 (16 December 1977).

[109] T. Meron, 'Teaching Human Rights: An Overview' in T. Meron (ed.), *Human Rights in International Law: Legal and Policy Issues* (Clarendon Press 1984) 15–24, 17; A.A. Cançado Trindade, *Tratado de Direito Internacional dos Direitos Humanos: Volume I* (2nd edn., SAFE 2003) 84.

[110] J.E. Mendez, 'The 60th Anniversary of the UDHR' (2009) 30 *University of Pennsylvania Journal of International Law* 1157, 1162.

prepare two separate international human rights treaties to follow the 1948 Universal Declaration.[111] The distinction between the categories of rights to be enshrined in each of the two Covenants was a reflection of the deep ideological division the world was experiencing at the beginning of the 1950s.[112] While the 'Western bloc' favoured the recognition of civil and political rights, the 'Eastern bloc' gave prevalence to economic, social, and cultural rights. Therefore, despite the fact that the Universal Declaration proclaimed both civil and political rights and economic, social, and cultural rights, two treaties were adopted in 1966, each bestowed with differently phrased commitments and very distinct systems of implementation.

At the time, many presumed that civil and political rights were susceptible of immediate implementation, as they merely needed abstentions from the State in order to comply with them, while economic, social, and cultural rights required the adoption of positive measures and, therefore, could only be progressively realized.[113] Consequently, the International Covenant on Civil and Political Rights (ICCPR) established obligations that were clear and concrete. Every State Parties undertook 'to respect and to ensure to all individuals within [their] territory and subject to [their] jurisdiction the rights recognized in the present Covenant'.[114] Likewise, all States Parties to this Covenant agreed 'to adopt such laws or other measures as may be necessary to give effect to the rights recognized in the present Covenant'[115] and '[t]o ensure that any person whose rights ... are violated shall have an effective remedy'.[116] For its part, the equivalent provision of the International Covenant on Economic, Social, and Cultural Rights (ICESCR) stated that every State Parties undertook to '*take steps*, individually and through international assistance and co-operation, especially economic and technical, *to the maximum of [their] available resources, with a view to achieving progressively the full realization of the rights recognized in the present Covenant* by all appropriate means, including particularly the adoption of legislative measures'.[117]

Nonetheless, even at the time, it was possible to observe that the constructed dichotomy between two categories of rights was artificial, as ICCPR allowed for the progressive protection of certain rights, and ICESCR contained provisions that were susceptible of implementation in the short term. Moreover, the fundamental unity of human rights was evidenced by the fact that certain economic, social, and cultural rights could be realized through State abstentions (e.g. trade union rights or the right to strike), while civil and political rights also required States to adopt positive

---

[111] F. Jhabvala, 'On Human Rights and the Socio-economic Context' (2009) 31 *Netherlands International Law Review* 149, 175–176.

[112] E. Rabossi, 'Los Derechos Humanos Básicos y los Errores de la Concepción Canónica' (1993) 18 *Revista IIDH* 45, 48; F. Jhabvala, 'On Human Rights and the Socio-economic Context' (2009) 31 *Netherlands International Law Review* 149, 159.

[113] E. Rabossi, 'Los Derechos Humanos Básicos y los Errores de la Concepción Canónica' (1993) 18 *Revista IIDH* 45, 52–55; S. Liebenberg, 'The International Covenant on Economic, Social and Cultural Rights and Its Implications for South Africa' (1995) 11 *South African Journal on Human Rights* 359, 361–362.

[114] ICCPR, Art. 2.1.   [115] ICCPR, Art. 2.2.   [116] ICCPR, Art. 2.3(a).

[117] ICESCR, Art. 2 (emphasis added).

measures for their realization (e.g. due process of law or electoral rights).[118] Connected to this distinction was the myth that social, economic, and cultural rights are costly, while civil and political rights can be protected without financial resources. If merely consisting of abstentions, civil and political rights would be free to realize, while the positive obligations required for economic, social, and cultural rights might make them expensive. Such (problematic) reasoning underlies the abovementioned provision of ICESCR, that subjects the progressive realization of these rights to the availability of resources, while no similar restriction is imposed upon the rights protected by ICCPR. And yet, the fact that protection of all rights entails both negative and positive obligations from States serves to debunk any misguided ideas about civil and political rights being cost-free in any sort of way.[119] Hence, the confines of each of the 'categories' of rights was far from clear and the distinction between the legal obligations emergent from each of them could be seen as a matter of degree, rather than of kind.[120]

However, a legal consequence of the erroneous perspective on rights adopted, coupled with the convergent interest of powerful States, led to the political decision to adopt rather differential mechanisms for the implementation of, on the one hand, civil and political rights, and, on the other hand, economic, social, and cultural rights. As mentioned in **Section 2.2.2**, a reporting system was the only common procedure adopted for both Covenants. While ICCPR established a specific monitoring body to supervise compliance with the treaty, which was even capable of receiving inter-State and individual complaints—although subject to further consent from States [121]—ICESCR lacked any such specific monitoring organ, and the main supervisory functions were left to a political body: ECOSOC.[122] As will be discussed in **Section 5.6**, it was ECOSOC that in 1978 determined the creation of, originally, a Sessional Working Group on the Implementation of the International Covenant on Economic, Social and Cultural Rights to assist in the consideration of the reports submitted by the States Parties to the treaty,[123] later turned into the existing Committee on Economic, Social and Cultural Rights.[124]

---

[118] V. Abramovich and C. Courtis, 'Hacia la Exigibilidad de los Derechos Económicos, Sociales y Culturales. Estándares Internacionales y Criterios de Aplicación ante los Tribunales Locales' in M. Abregú and C. Courtis (eds.), *La Aplicación de los Tratados sobre Derechos Humanos por los Tribunales Locales* (CELS 1997) 283–350, 284–296; S. Holmes and C.R. Sunstein, *The Cost of Rights: Why Liberty Depends on Taxes* (Norton 1999) 35–49.

[119] S. Holmes and C.R. Sunstein, *The Cost of Rights: Why Liberty Depends on Taxes* (Norton 1999) 15–16, 28–29; A. Eide, 'Economic, Social and Cultural Rights as Human Rights' in A. Eide, C. Krause, and A. Rosas (eds.), *Economic, Social and Cultural Rights* (2nd edn., Nijhoff 2001) 9–28, 10.

[120] T.C. van Boven, 'Le Critères de Distinction des Droits de l'Homme' in K. Vasak (ed.), *Les Dimensions Internationales des Droits de l'Homme* (UNESCO 1978) 45–63, 55–58; P. Alston and G. Quinn, 'The Nature and Scope of States Parties' Obligations under the International Covenant on Economic, Social and Cultural Rights' (1987) 9 *Human Rights Quarterly* 156, 183–184.

[121] ICCPR, Art. 41; First Optional Protocol to ICCPR, Art. 1.   [122] ICESCR, Arts. 16 to 22.

[123] ECOSOC, Composition of the Sessional Working Group on the Implementation of the International Covenant on Economic, Social and Cultural Rights, Decision 1978/10 (3 May 1978).

[124] ECOSOC, Review of the composition, organization and administrative arrangements of the Sessional Working Group of Governmental Experts on the Implementation of the International Covenant on Economic, Social and Cultural Rights, Resolution 1985/17 (28 May 1985).

2.3.1 STATES' OBLIGATIONS UNDER ICESCR

It was the Committee on Economic, Social, and Cultural Rights that, in 1990, took upon itself the task of clarifying some of the basic obligations assumed by all States Parties following their ratification of, or accession to, the treaty.[125] It emphasized that the differences in the wording between both Covenants should not be mistaken with the absence of clear international obligations emerging from ICESCR. The Committee affirmed that 'while the Covenant provides for progressive realization and acknowledges the constraints due to the limits of available resources, it also imposes various obligations which are of immediate effect'.[126] It stressed that Article 2 clearly established the obligation of all States Parties to *take steps*, which means that:

> while the full realization of the relevant rights may be achieved progressively, steps towards that goal must be taken within a reasonably short time after the Covenant's entry into force for the States concerned. Such steps should be deliberate, concrete and targeted as clearly as possible towards meeting the obligations recognized in the Covenant.[127]

Furthermore, the obligation is to take steps 'with a view to achieving progressively the full realization of the rights', which actually imposes upon States 'an obligation to move as expeditiously and effectively as possible towards that goal' and determined that 'any deliberately retrogressive measures in that regard would require the most careful consideration and would need to be fully justified by reference to the totality of the rights provided for in the Covenant and in the context of the full use of the maximum available resources'.[128]

The Committee also affirmed that a number of provisions in the Covenant would be capable of immediate application by the organs of the States and that any suggestions of them not being self-executing would be rather difficult to support. Such was the case of the prohibition of gender discrimination in the enjoyment of economic, social, and cultural rights; the payment of equal remuneration for work of equal value; the right to form and join trade unions and the right to strike in accordance to domestic laws; the right of children to be subject to special protection; the right (and obligation) of everyone to access primary education; the right of parents to choose their children's school; the right to establish educational institutions; and scientific freedom.[129] The Committee concluded that, already in 1990, it was possible to affirm the existence of 'a minimum core obligation to ensure the satisfaction of, at the very least, minimum essential levels

---

[125] This general comment was heavily influenced by the 1986 Limburg Principles on the Implementation of the International Covenant on Economic, Social and Cultural Rights. See: OHCHR, Economic, Social and Cultural Rights: Handbook for National Human Rights Institutions (UN 2005), HR/P/PT/12, p. 7.

[126] CESCR, General Comment 3: The Nature of States Parties' Obligations, E/1991/23 (1990), para. 1.

[127] CESCR, General Comment 3: The Nature of States Parties' Obligations, E/1991/23 (1990), para. 2.

[128] CESCR, General Comment 3: The Nature of States Parties' Obligations, E/1991/23 (1990), para. 9.

[129] CESCR, General Comment 3: The Nature of States Parties' Obligations, E/1991/23 (1990), para. 5. See: ICESCR, Arts. 3, 7.a.i, 8, 10.3, 13.2–13.4, and 15.3.

of each of the rights',[130] meaning that 'a State party in which any significant number of individuals is deprived of essential foodstuffs, of essential primary health care, of basic shelter and housing, or of the most basic forms of education is, prima facie, failing to discharge its obligations under the Covenant.'[131]

Further elaboration on States' obligations under ICESCR was provided by the Committee in a later general comment, issued in 1998.[132] There, the Committee offered more details on the requirement imposed by the Covenant that effect to the protected rights be given 'by all appropriate means'.[133] It affirmed that this obligation entailed the States' duty to recognize these rights in appropriate ways in their domestic legal orders and to provide pertinent means of redress for their violation, including either judicial or administrative procedures to secure their enforcement, as well as the Government's accountability for their breach.[134]

As will be discussed in **Section 5.6**, it took until December 2008 for an Optional Protocol to ICESCR to be adopted, which empowered the Committee to receive both individual petitions and inter-State communications against States Parties to the Protocol.[135] In 2007, when the Human Rights Council had confirmed the decision to progress with the drafting of the Protocol, the Committee considered it timely to provide some further insights into the scope of the States' obligation to 'take steps' to the 'maximum of available resources'. It stated that even in times of severe resource constraints inaction in the field of economic, social, and cultural rights was not a valid alternative, but States remained obliged to 'protect the most disadvantaged and marginalized members or groups of society by adopting relatively low-cost targeted programmes'.[136] It added that States' failure to take steps towards the realization of social, economic, and cultural rights, or their adoption of retrogressive measures concerning these rights, would only be allowed in the exceptional circumstances in which States could demonstrate that 'such a course of action was based on the most careful consideration and . . . justified by reference to the totality of the rights provided for in the Covenant and by the fact that full use was made of available resources'.[137]

---

[130] CESCR, General Comment 3: The Nature of States Parties' Obligations, E/1991/23 (1990), para. 10.
[131] CESCR, General Comment 3: The Nature of States Parties' Obligations, E/1991/23 (1990), para. 10.
[132] CESCR, General Comment 9: The Domestic Application of the Covenant, E/C.12/1998/24 (3 December 1998).
[133] ICESCR, Art. 2.1.
[134] CESCR, General Comment 9: The Domestic Application of the Covenant, E/C.12/1998/24 (3 December 1998), paras. 1–2 and 4.
[135] Optional Protocol to the International Covenant on Economic, Social and Cultural Rights (adopted on 10 December 2008, entered into force on 5 May 2013) C.N.869.2009.TREATIES-34.
[136] CESCR, An evaluation of the obligation to take steps to the 'maximum of available resources' under an optional protocol to the Covenant, E/C.12/2007/1 (21 September 2007), para. 4.
[137] CESCR, An evaluation of the obligation to take steps to the 'maximum of available resources' under an optional protocol to the Covenant, E/C.12/2007/1 (21 September 2007), para. 9.

2.3.2 THE 'CATEGORIES' OF RIGHTS WITHIN REGIONAL HUMAN RIGHTS SYSTEMS

2.3.2.1 The European human rights system

The ideologically grounded distinction between civil and political rights, on the one hand, and economic, social, and cultural rights, on the other, was also to be found in international human rights treaties celebrated at the regional level.[138] The European Convention of Human Rights, adopted in 1950, did not include economic, social, and cultural rights in its text.[139] The right to education was timidly added to the catalogue of protected rights, together with the right to property and the right to free elections, through the First Protocol to the Convention in 1952. As to other economic, social, and cultural rights, the European Social Charter was adopted within the Council of Europe in 1961, as a (discrete) counterpart to the European Convention on Human Rights.[140] However, as further discussed in **Section 7.1.2.1**, the rights thereby recognized are not susceptible of individual claims to the European Court of Human Rights, but the Social Charter set up an international system of supervision based on State reports to be monitored by a committee. An Additional Protocol to the Social Charter, establishing a 'system of collective complaints', was adopted in 1995.[141] This system empowers certain national and international organizations of employers and trade unions, as well as national and international non-governmental organizations, to lodge collective complaints concerning the protection of the rights recognized by the Charter for them to be examined by a committee of experts (the European Committee of Social Rights).[142] This system is complementary to the original reporting system and confirmed that economic, social, and cultural rights remained mostly excluded from the jurisdiction of the European Court of Human Rights.[143]

Despite their formal exclusion, already in 1979, the European Court of Human Rights opposed the view of the existence of a clear distinction between civil and political rights

---

[138] A tendency that was reversed following the end of the 'Cold War', and even overcome before then, as later discussed with regard to the African System. See: Arab Charter, Arts. 33–42. See also: ASEAN Declaration, Arts. 26–38.

[139] C. Warbrick, 'Economic and Social Interests and the European Convention on Human Rights' in M. Baderin and R. McCorquodale (eds.), *Economic, Social, and Cultural Rights in Action* (OUP 2007) 241–256, 242.

[140] C. Warbrick, 'Economic and Social Interests and the European Convention on Human Rights' in M. Baderin and R. McCorquodale (ed.), *Economic, Social, and Cultural Rights in Action* (OUP 2007) 241–256, 242–243; V. Mantouvalou and P. Voyatzis, 'The Council of Europe and the Protection of Human Rights: A System in Need of Reform' in S. Joseph and A. McBeth (eds.), *Research Handbook on International Human Rights Law* (Elgar 2010) 326–352, 340.

[141] Additional Protocol to the European Social Charter Providing for a System of Collective Complaints (adopted on 9 November 1995, entered into force on 1 July 1995) ETS No. 158.

[142] R. Brillat, 'The European Social Charter' in G. Alfredsson et al. (eds.), *International Human Rights Monitoring Mechanisms: Essays in Honour of Jakob Th. Möller* (2nd edn., Nihoff 2009) 503–513, 509.

[143] As further discussed in **Section 7.1.2.1**, a 'revised' Social Charter was adopted in 1996.

and economic, social, and cultural rights. In its judgment in the *Airey v. Ireland* case, the Court affirmed:

> Whilst the Convention sets forth what are essentially civil and political rights, many of them have implications of a social or economic nature ... the mere fact that an interpretation of the Convention may extend into the sphere of social and economic rights should not be a decisive factor against such an interpretation; there is no water-tight division separating that sphere from the field covered by the Convention.[144]

Moreover, the Court emphasized that the protection of the rights recognized under the Convention sometimes requires the adoption of positive measures by States Parties. It affirmed that, in the protection of human rights, there is no room to distinguish between acts and omissions.[145] Since then, the Court has developed an important jurisprudence that demonstrates that the protection of certain economic, social, and cultural rights can be achieved through the appropriate broad interpretation of some of the rights recognized by the Convention, such as through the right to access to justice, the right to respect for private and family life, and the prohibition of discrimination.[146]

ECtHR, *Airey v. Ireland*, 9 October 1979, Series A no. 32.

The case was about the positive obligations a State may have concerning the provision of free legal aid under the right of access to court for the determination of civil rights (Article 6.1). Ms Airey was a victim of domestic violence who had been unsuccessful in obtaining a judicial decree of separation from her husband, due to the lack of funds to afford the costs involved in such legal proceedings and the inability to obtain legal aid. She claimed before the Court that the prohibitive costs of litigation prevented her from obtaining a judicial separation and that this situation amounted to a violation of her right of access to court. The Court affirmed that Article 6 'may sometimes compel the State to provide for the assistance of a lawyer when such assistance proves indispensable for an effective access to court either because legal representation is rendered compulsory, as is done by the domestic law of certain Contracting States for various types of litigation, or by reason of the complexity of the procedure or of the case' (para. 26). The Court considered that this was one such occasion, so it ruled that Mrs Airey had not enjoyed an effective right of access to court, which amounted to a breach of Article 6 of the Convention (para. 28).

---

[144] ECtHR, *Airey v. Ireland*, 9 October 1979, Series A no. 32, para. 26.
[145] ECtHR, *Airey v. Ireland*, 9 October 1979, Series A no. 32, para. 26.
[146] See, for instance: ECtHR, *Airey v. Ireland*, 9 October 1979, Series A no. 32; ECtHR, *Feldbrugge v. The Netherlands*, App 8562/79, 29 May 1986; ECtHR, *López-Ostra v. Spain* (ser. A) 303-C (1994); ECtHR, *Guerra v. Italy*, Reports of Judgments and Decisions 1998-I (1998); ECtHR, *P.B. and J.S. v. Austria*, App. no. 18984/02, 22 July 2010.

2.3.2.2 The Inter-American human rights system

Within the Americas, the 1948 American Declaration of the Rights and Duties of Man, adopted a few months prior to the proclamation of the Universal Declaration of Human Rights, contemplated a catalogue of rights that included both civil and political rights, as well as economic, social, and cultural rights. Nonetheless, at the time of the adoption of the American Convention on Human Rights, the proposals to include economic, social, and cultural rights within the treaty were mostly rejected,[147] with one exception: Article 26. This Article establishes that

> [t]he States Parties undertake to adopt measures, both internally and through international cooperation, especially those of an economic and technical nature, with a view to achieving progressively, by legislation or other appropriate means, the full realization of the rights implicit in the economic, social, educational, scientific, and cultural standards set forth in the Charter of the Organization of American States as amended by the Protocol of Buenos Aires.[148]

An important step was taken in 1988 with the adoption of the Additional Protocol to the American Convention on Human Rights in the Area of Economic, Social and Cultural Rights ('Protocol of San Salvador'), which can be seen as the realization, within the American continent, of the need for a more effective system for the protection of economic, social, and cultural rights.[149] Following similar wording to that of ICESCR, the Protocol of San Salvador established in its first article that States Parties:

> ... undertake to adopt the necessary measures, both domestically and through international cooperation, especially economic and technical, to the extent allowed by their available resources, and taking into account their degree of development, for the purpose of achieving progressively and pursuant to their internal legislations, the full observance of the rights recognized in this Protocol.[150]

Once again, a distinction between civil and political rights and economic, social, and cultural rights was established, the latter being subject to progressive realization depending on the availability of resources.

---

[147] M. Ventura-Robles, 'Jurisprudencia de la Corte Interamericana de Derechos Humanos en materia de derechos económicos, sociales y culturales' (2004) 40 *Revista IIDH* 87, 93–100.

[148] Interestingly, while the Spanish version of the text makes this obligation subject to the existence of available resources ('en la medida de los recursos disponibles'), such a limitation is absent in the English text. See: D. González-Salzberg, 'Economic and Social Rights within the Inter-American Human Rights System: Thinking New Strategies for Obtaining Judicial Protection' (2011) 18 *International Law: Revista Colombiana de Derecho Internacional* 117, 130–131.

[149] Moreover, as discussed in **Section 6.1.5**, newer treaties have further enriched the regime of protection of socio-economic rights within the continent, such as the 1999 Inter-American Convention on the Elimination of All Forms of Discrimination against Persons with Disabilities and the 2017 Inter-American Convention on Protecting the Human Rights of Older Persons.

[150] Additional Protocol to the American Convention on Human Rights in the Area of Economic, Social and Cultural Rights (Protocol of San Salvador), (adopted 17 November 1988, entered into force 16 November 1999) OAS Treaty Series No. 69, Art. 1.

Furthermore, the Protocol contemplates a monitoring system for the protection of these rights through different procedures: first, a system of periodic reports to be submitted by States Parties on the progressive measures adopted to ensure due respect for the protected rights, which would be examined by a series of Inter-American agencies;[151] second, two provisions actually allow for individual petitions under the machinery set in place by the American Convention: the right of workers to organize and join trade unions, and the right to education.[152] The new system in place was to function without prejudice to the faculties of the Inter-American Commission on Human Rights to examine States' compliance with economic, social, and cultural rights under the 1948 American Declaration of the Rights and Duties of Man (and Article 26 of the Convention), as it had been doing since the 1970s;[153] now, with the expanded ability to monitor implementation of the rights recognized in the Protocol of San Salvador in respect of the States Parties to the treaty.[154]

On its part, the Inter-American Court of Human Rights took it upon itself to advance the protection of economic, social, and cultural rights. Although it was not until 2017 that a Court's judgment declared an actual violation of Article 26,[155] the Court has provided for the protection of economic, social, and cultural rights through the evolutive interpretation of the Convention.[156] This has allowed the Court, for instance, to recognize that the right to life includes not only the right not to be arbitrarily deprived of one's life, but also the right to access the conditions that guarantee a dignified existence.[157] This progressive interpretation of the right to life has enabled the Court to affirm that one of the obligations that States must undertake is that of generating minimum living

---

[151] V. Gómez, 'Economic, Social, and Cultural Rights in the Inter-American System' in M. Baderin and R. McCorquodale (eds.), *Economic, Social, and Cultural Rights in Action* (OUP 2007) 167–194, 179–181; M. Pinto, 'Cumplimiento y exigibilidad de los derechos económicos, sociales y culturales en el marco del Sistema Interamericano' (2012) 56 *Revista IIDH* 157, 176–178.

[152] Protocol of San Salvador, Art. 19.

[153] V. Gómez, 'Economic, Social, and Cultural Rights in the Inter-American System' in M. Baderin and R. McCorquodale (eds.), *Economic, Social, and Cultural Rights in Action* (OUP 2007) 167–194, 178; M. Pinto, 'Cumplimiento y exigibilidad de los derechos económicos, sociales y culturales en el marco del Sistema Interamericano' (2012) 56 *Revista IIDH* 157, 158–160. See, among many: IACHR, Seventh Report on the Situation of Human Rights in Cuba, OEA/Ser.L/V/II.61, doc. 29 rev. 1 (1983); IACHR, Fourth Report on the Situation of Human Rights in Guatemala, OEA/Ser.L/V/II.83, doc. 16 (1993); IACHR, Third Report on the Situation of Human Rights in Paraguay, OEA/Ser. L/V/II.110, doc. 52 (2001); IACHR, Report No. 45/81, Case 4402 (Cuba), OEA/Ser.L/V/II.54, doc. 9 rev.1 (1980–1981); IACHR, Report No. 12/85, Case 7615 (Brazil), OEA/Ser.L/V/II.66, doc. 10 rev.1 (1985).

[154] Protocol of San Salvador, Art. 19.7.

[155] IACtHR, *Lagos del Campo v. Peru*. Preliminary Objections, Merits, Reparations, and Costs. Judgment of August 31, 2017. Series C No. 340.

[156] IACtHR, *Mayagna (Sumo) Awas Tingni Community v. Nicaragua*. Merits, Reparations, and Costs. Judgment of August 31, 2001. Series C No. 79, para. 146.

[157] IACtHR, *'Street Children' (Villagrán Morales et al.) v. Guatemala*. Merits. Judgment of November 19, 1999. Series C No. 63, para. 144 and joint concurring opinion of Judges Cançado Trindade and Abreu Burelli paras. 4, 7, and 8.

conditions that are compatible with the dignity of the human person.[158] On numerous occasions, the Court has ordered States to supply drinking water and sufficient quantity and quality of food to individuals living in conditions of extreme vulnerability.[159] It has even examined positive measures that had been adopted by States within this ambit, finding a violation of the right to life when the quantity and quality of the food and water provided were not enough to guarantee the average essential needs of an individual.[160] In fact, the Court has gone as far as to affirm that chronic poverty should be considered a deprivation of all human rights.[161]

Similarly, the Inter-American Court has developed an expansive interpretation of the right to property, understanding that it does not just refer to the right to individual private property,[162] but also includes the right of the members of indigenous communities to benefit from the communal property of their lands.[163] In its judgment in the case of the *Mayagna (Sumo) Awas Tingni Community v. Nicaragua*, the Court found the State in breach of the right to property for having failed to adopt effective measure to secure an indigenous community's enjoyment of communal property rights of its ancestral lands and natural resources.[164] One of the most memorable paragraphs of the Court's judgment reads:

> Among indigenous peoples there is a communitarian tradition regarding a communal form of collective property of the land, in the sense that ownership of the land is not centered on an individual but rather on the group and its community. Indigenous groups, by the fact of their very existence, have the right to live freely in their own territory; the close ties of indigenous people with the land must be recognized and understood as the fundamental basis of their cultures, their spiritual life, their integrity, and their economic survival. For indigenous communities, relations to the land are not merely a matter of possession and production but a material and spiritual element which they must fully enjoy, even to preserve their cultural legacy and transmit it to future generations.[165]

---

[158] IACtHR, *Yakye Axa Indigenous Community v. Paraguay*. Merits, Reparations, and Costs. Judgment of June 17, 2005. Series C No. 125, para. 162.

[159] IACtHR, *Yakye Axa Indigenous Community v. Paraguay*. Merits, Reparations, and Costs. Judgment of June 17, 2005. Series C No. 125, para. 221; IACtHR, *Sawhoyamaxa Indigenous Community v. Paraguay*. Merits, Reparations, and Costs. Judgment of March 29, 2006. Series C No. 146, separate opinion of Judge Cançado Trindade para. 230.

[160] IACtHR, *Xákmok Kásek Indigenous Community v. Paraguay*. Merits, Reparations and Costs. Judgment of August 24, 2010. Series C No. 214, paras. 196, 200, and 217.

[161] IACtHR, *Sawhoyamaxa Indigenous Community v. Paraguay*. Merits, Reparations, and Costs. Judgment of March 29, 2006. Series C No. 146, separate opinion of Judge Cançado Trindade para. 71.

[162] In the Spanish text this right is actually presented as the Right to Private Property ('Derecho a la Propiedad Privada'). See: Convención Americana sobre Derechos Humanos, Artículo 21.

[163] IACtHR, *Mayagna (Sumo) Awas Tingni Community v. Nicaragua*. Merits, Reparations, and Costs. Judgment of August 31, 2001. Series C No. 79, para. 148.

[164] IACtHR, *Mayagna (Sumo) Awas Tingni Community v. Nicaragua*. Merits, Reparations, and Costs. Judgment of August 31, 2001. Series C No. 79, paras. 153, 164, and operative paras. 3 and 4.

[165] IACtHR, *Mayagna (Sumo) Awas Tingni Community v. Nicaragua*. Merits, Reparations, and Costs. Judgment of August 31, 2001. Series C No. 79, para. 149.

> **IACtHR, *Mayagna (Sumo) Awas Tingni Community v. Nicaragua*. Merits, Reparations and Costs. Judgment of August 31, 2001. Series C No. 79.**
>
> The case was brought to the Inter-American system by the Awas Tingni community, after failing to find a solution to its complaints through the domestic judicial system of Nicaragua. The Awas Tingni community is an indigenous community of the Mayagna ethnic group, which was affected by the lack of protection of their ancestral lands and natural resources. The State had failed to perform the delimitation, demarcation, and titling of the community's lands. Moreover, the State had granted a corporation a concession to manage a forest, including the cutting down of trees, situated within the community's land. The Court ruled that Nicaragua had breached the right to property and the right to judicial protection of the members of the Awas Tingni community (paras. 139 and 155). It ordered the State to carry out the delimitation, demarcation, and titling of the ancestral lands of the community and to abstain from any acts that might affect the use or enjoyment of the property located in the geographic area where the members of the Awas Tingni community live and carry out their activities (para. 173).

> **IACtHR, *Lagos del Campo v. Peru*. Preliminary Objections, Merits, Reparations and Costs. Judgment of August 31, 2017. Series C No. 340.**
>
> The case concerned the dismissal of Mr Lagos del Campo following public statements made to a magazine, in which he affirmed that the company for which he worked was interfering with the 'industrial committee'—an employees' organization created under Peruvian law to represent the interests of the workers of industrial companies. Mr Lagos del Campo (a former union leader) was at the time of the magazine's interview the elected president of the company's industrial committee. Before the domestic judicial system, Mr Lagos del Campo claimed (unsuccessfully) that his dismissal amounted to a breach of several rights, including the right to job security, freedom of association, and freedom of expression. The Inter-American Court ruled that the arbitrary dismissal suffered by the victim and the lack of judicial protection provided to him in the domestic jurisdiction amounted to breaches of several human rights. In particular, it found that Mr Lagos del Campo had suffered the violation of the 'right to job security', which the Court considered implicitly protected by Article 26 of the American Convention (para. 166).

2.3.2.3 The African system of human and peoples' rights

Setting themselves apart from the prevailing trend at the time, the drafters of the 1981 African Charter on Human and Peoples' Rights opted to include in the text of the treaty the explicit recognition of economic, social, and cultural rights, as well as of 'peoples' rights'.[166] Furthermore, the Charter does not subject any right to their 'progressive' realization and established the jurisdiction of the African Commission on Human and Peoples' Rights over all protected human rights;[167] thus, dispersing any possible doubts as to their equal justiciability.[168] The Commission has taken advantage of this broad jurisdiction to interpret the obligations assumed by the States under the Charter, having affirmed that 'collective rights, environmental rights, and economic and social rights are essential elements of human rights in Africa'.[169]

Moreover, the Commission has also engaged in an expansive interpretation of the rights under the Charter, having found, in the *Ogoni* case, that the right to food and the right to housing, while absent in the text, could be considered implicit in the African Charter. Concerning the right to housing, the Commission asserted that it was 'the corollary of the combination of the provisions protecting the right to enjoy the best attainable state of mental and physical health . . . the right to property, and the protection accorded to the family'.[170] With regard to the right to food, the Commission found it to be 'inseparably linked to the dignity of human beings and . . . therefore essential for the enjoyment and fulfilment of such other rights as health, education, work and political participation.'[171]

ACHPR, ACHPR/COMM/A044/1, 27 May 2002, 155/96 *Social and Economic Rights Action Center (SERAC) and Center for Economic and Social Rights (CESR) v. Nigeria ('Ogoni case')*.

The case concerned the oil production by the military government of Nigeria (Nijeriya), in consortium with Shell Petroleum Development Corporation, in the territory of Ogoniland, with severe detrimental consequences for the Ogoni people. The case dealt with both the initial environmental harm experienced by the local communities, as well as with the armed

---

[166] C.A. Odinkalu, 'Analysis of Paralysis or Paralysis by Analysis? Implementing Economic, Social, and Cultural Rights under the African Charter on Human and Peoples' Rights' (2001) 23 *Human Rights Quarterly* 327, 330, 336; C. Mbazira, 'Enforcing the Economic, Social and Cultural Rights in the African Charter on Human and People's Rights: Twenty Years of Redundancy, Progression and Significant Strides' (2006) 6 *African Human Rights Law Journal* 333, 338–339 and 342. See: African Charter on Human and Peoples' Rights (adopted 27 June 1981, entered into force 21 October 1986) OAU Doc. CAB/LEG/67/3 rev. 5, 21 I.L.M. 58 (1982), Arts. 15–18 and 19–24.

[167] African Charter, Arts. 46–59 and 62.

[168] C.A. Odinkalu, 'Analysis of Paralysis or Paralysis by Analysis? Implementing Economic, Social, and Cultural Rights under the African Charter on Human and Peoples' Rights' (2001) 23 *Human Rights Quarterly* 327, 349; M. Ssenyonjo, 'Analysing the Economic, Social and Cultural Rights Jurisprudence of the African Commission: 30 Years since the Adoption of the African Charter' (2011) 29 *Netherlands Quarterly of Human Rights* 358, 359.

[169] ACHPR, *Social and Economic Rights Action Center (SERAC) and Center for Economic and Social Rights (CESR) v. Nigeria ('Ogoni case')*, ACHPR/COMM/A044/1 (27 May 2002), para. 68.

[170] ACHPR, *Social and Economic Rights Action Center (SERAC) and Center for Economic and Social Rights (CESR) v. Nigeria ('Ogoni case')*, ACHPR/COMM/A044/1 (27 May 2002), para. 60.

[171] ACHPR, *Social and Economic Rights Action Center (SERAC) and Center for Economic and Social Rights (CESR) v. Nigeria ('Ogoni case')*, ACHPR/COMM/A044/1 (27 May 2002), para. 65.

> attacks suffered by them, as a response to their protests against the damaging oil production. The Commission found several violations of rights in the case. The first one concerned the right of the Ogoni people to their health and to a clean environment (Articles 16 and 26 of the African Charter of Human and People's Rights). The Commission ruled that Nigeria had failed to adopt the necessary measures to protect the Ogoni people, given the way in which the oil production had been undertaken (para. 54). Closely linked to the violations, the Commission examined the breach of the Ogoni people's right to freely dispose of their wealth and natural resources (Article 21). It affirmed that: 'The destructive and selfish role played by oil development in Ogoniland, closely tied with repressive tactics of the Nigerian Government, and the lack of material benefits accruing to the local population, may well be said to constitute a violation of Article 21' (para. 55). Another violation declared by the Commission was that of the right to housing; a right constructed through the dynamic interpretation of the right to property, the right to health, and the protection of the family (Articles 14, 16, and 18). The Commission affirmed that the State 'has destroyed Ogoni houses and villages and then, through its security forces, obstructed, harassed, beaten and, in some cases, shot and killed innocent citizens who have attempted to return to rebuild their ruined homes' (paras. 60–62). The Commission found the State also responsible for the violation of the Right to Food—implicitly recognized by the rights to life, to health, and to economic, social, and cultural development—caused by the destructions of food sources, either directly by Nigerian security forces or by allowing private actors to do so, as well as by the general situation of 'terror' suffered by the Ogoni communities, which made it difficult for them to feed themselves (para. 66). Lastly, the Commission found clear violations of the right to life, due to killing of community members by the armed forces (para. 67).

When the African Court on Human and Peoples' Rights was established in 2006, following the entry into force of a Protocol to the Charter,[172] it followed the Commission's conviction in the enforceability of all Charter rights, which should be enjoyed in equal footing, rejecting the dated conception of the separation of rights into different categories (see **Chapter 8**).[173] Moreover, within Africa, an even wider framework of protection for economic, social, and cultural rights is now provided by the adoption of further human rights treaties, such as the Protocol to the African Charter on Human and Peoples' Rights on the Rights of Women in Africa, the African Union Convention for the Protection and Assistance of Internally Displaced

---

[172] Protocol to the African Charter on Human and Peoples' Rights on the Establishment of an African Court on Human and Peoples' Rights (adopted 10 June 1998, entered into force 25 January 2004).

[173] ACHPR, *Free Legal Assistance Group, Lawyers' Committee for Human Rights, Union Interafricaine des Droits de l'Homme, Les Témoins de Jehovah v. Zaire (Democratic Republic of Congo)*, Communications 25/89-47/90-56/91-100/93 (1995); ACHPR, *Social and Economic Rights Action Center (SERAC) and Center for Economic and Social Rights (CESR) v. Nigeria ('Ogoni case')*, ACHPR/COMM/A044/1 (27 May 2002); ACHPR, *Social and Economic Rights Action Center (SERAC) and Center for Economic and Social Rights (CESR) v. Nigeria*, Communication 155/96 (2001); ACtHPR, *African Commission on Human and Peoples' Rights v. Kenya* (merits) (2017) 2 AfCLR 9.

Persons, the Protocol on the Rights of Older Persons in Africa, and the African Charter on the Rights and Welfare of the Child.[174] As discussed in **Section 8.1.2.1**, the latter has even established a special Committee for monitoring compliance with children's rights, which has developed a rich protective jurisprudence, inclusive of socio-economic rights.[175]

This evolving interpretation of human rights norms performed by different international monitoring bodies, from different regions in the world, leaves no room for doubts as to the existent obligations upon States concerning the effective implementation of economic, social, and cultural rights. The existence of, at least, a minimum core obligation to satisfy basic levels of protection of each and every right has been accepted for decades now, as recognized in 1990 by the Committee on Economic, Social and Cultural Rights, and proclaimed even before then by the 1986 Limburg principles.[176] Furthermore, the appropriate hermeneutics of human rights treaties has revealed that the full realization of civil and political rights imposes the duty to protect the social and economic dimensions of these rights. In sum, the universality, indivisibility, and interdependence of all human rights cannot be denied. The idea of different categories of rights belongs to a past where the struggle between two political ideologies was given priority over the universal protection of human rights. In our days, discussions over categories of rights should be abandoned in favour of reflections upon strategies for the expansion and strengthening of the protection of all human rights.

2.4 THE INTERNATIONAL LAW OF HUMAN RIGHTS: IMPLEMENTATION STAGE

As discussed in **Section 2.2.1**, one of the three components planned for the international bill of rights was that of the means of implementation for the protected human rights. The process of adoption of ICERD in 1965 and of the two 1966 Covenants—examined in **Section 2.2.2**—allowed States to agree on a number of mechanisms for supervising their conduct towards the implementation of human rights. But even before then, other mechanisms were being established, including a reporting system under the Universal

---

[174] S.A. Yeshanew, 'Approaches to the Justiciability of Economic, Social and Cultural Rights in the Jurisprudence of the African Commission on Human and Peoples' Rights: Progress and Perspectives' (2011) 11 *African Human Rights Law Journal* 317, 359–360.

[175] See: ACERWC, *The Centre for Human Rights (University of Pretoria) and La Rencontre Africaine pour la Defense des Droits de l'Homme (Senegal) v. Senegal*. Decision 003/Com/001/2012 (15 April 2014); ACERWC, *Minority Rights Group International and SOS-Esclaves (on behalf of Said Ould Salem and Yarg Ould Salem) v. Mauritania*. Communication No. 007/Com/003/2015, Decision 003/2017 (15 December 2017); ACERWC, *Legal and Human Rights Centre and Centre for Reproductive Rights (on behalf of Tanzanian girls) v. Tanzania*. Communication No. 0012/Com/001/2019, Decision No. 002/2022.

[176] CESCR, General Comment 3: The Nature of States Parties' Obligations, E/1991/23 (1990); Note verbale dated 5 December 1986 from the Permanent Mission of the Netherlands to the United Nations Office at Geneva addressed to the Centre for Human Rights ('Limburg Principles'), E/CN.4/1987/17.

Declaration, created by the Commission on Human Rights in the 1950s;[177] the system of individual and inter-State communications, created under the European Convention of Human Rights, in force since the late 1950s; or the procedure of on-site visits, developed by the Inter-American Commission of Human Rights since the early 1960s.

2.4.1 MECHANISMS OF IMPLEMENTATION

The types of monitoring procedures established towards the mid-twentieth century were replicated in the multiple human rights treaties subsequently adopted both within the UN and in regional human rights systems. Thus, the elaboration of State reports, on-site investigations, and complaints procedures (both inter-State and for individuals), became the usual means for monitoring the implementation of human rights.[178] Through these different legal mechanisms, the plurality of monitoring bodies created have developed an expansive interpretation of human rights norms, contributing to the progressive expansion of the protection provided by them and facilitating the creation of an international public order, based upon the respect for human rights in all circumstances.[179]

2.4.1.1 Reporting system

The reporting system is the mechanism most frequently established for monitoring States' compliance with human rights obligations. There are different types of reporting procedures to monitor the implementation of human rights. For instance, States' duty to produce an initial report and then periodic ones on their compliance with the treaties to which they become parties is an essential procedural obligation imposed by the core human rights treaties adopted under the auspices of the United Nations (see **Section 5.3.1**). As further discussed in **Section 4.3.2**, with the establishment of the Human Rights Council, now all States Members of the United Nations have acquired a duty to report on the measures of implementation of their human rights obligations under the Universal Periodic Review, regardless of whether or not they are parties to specific human rights treaties.

At the regional level, the African Charter on Human and Peoples' Rights imposes upon States Parties the obligation to report on the measures adopted towards its

---

[177] A.A. Cançado Trindade, 'General Course on the International Protection of Human Rights' (1988) 7 *Revista IIDH* 5, 15–16; P. Alston, 'The Historical Origins of the Concept of "General Comments" in Human Rights Law' in L. Boisson de Chazournes and V. Gowland Debbas (eds.), *The International Legal System in Quest of Equity and Universality: Liber Amicorum Georges Abi-Saab* (Nijhoff 2001) 763–776, 770–771. See: CHR, Resolution 1(XII) (1956).

[178] K. Vasak, 'Le Droit International des Droits de l'Homme' (1974) 140 *Recueil des Cours de l'Acadimie de Droit International de La Haye* 333, 348–349, 361, 366, 411–412; A.A. Cançado Trindade, *Tratado de Direito Internacional dos Direitos Humanos: Volume I* (2nd edn., SAFE 2003) 98–99; M. Pinto, *Temas de Derechos Humanos* (Del Puerto 2009).

[179] A.A. Cançado Trindade, *International Law for Humankind: Towards a New Jus Gentium* (3rd edn., Nijhoff 2020) 431–432.

implementation.[180] Although the procedure for examining these reports was unclear in the text of the Charter, the African Commission was authorized by the Assembly of Heads of State and Government of the Organization of African Unity to act as the monitoring body for such a procedure.[181] Other African treaties, adopted to improve the protection of rights provided by the Charter, also contemplate the obligation of States Parties to report periodically on their implementation, as discussed in **Section 8.1.2**.[182] Similarly, the 2004 Arab Charter on Human Rights has established a State reporting system as supervisory mechanism for compliance with human rights obligations. States Parties are under the obligation to submit periodic reports to the Committee of Experts on Human Rights, created by the Charter.[183]

Within the Americas, no reporting obligation emanates from the American Convention, but as mentioned in **Section 2.3.2.2**, such a procedural obligation is imposed upon Parties by the Protocol of San Salvador, with regard to economic, social, and cultural rights. Additionally, other specialized regional treaties, adopted to complement the protection provided by the Convention, provide for a system of periodic reports, as will be discussed in **Section 6.1.5**.[184] Similarly, within Europe, the European Convention does not impose any reporting obligations upon States, but these were established with regard to the implementation of socio-economic rights by the European Social Charter, as discussed in **Section 2.3.2.1** and further explored in **Section 7.1.2.1**.

One of the main aims of the reporting mechanisms is to lead States Parties to treaties to adopt the needed domestic measures to fully comply with the obligations emerging from these international instruments. When evaluating the reports submitted by States Parties, the monitoring organ exercises a control *ex officio* of the compliance with treaty obligations. The monitoring bodies are not acting as judicial or quasi-judicial organs, but are in some way providing assistance to States to help them fulfil their assumed obligations. These processes are non-contentious and are under certain

---

[180] African Charter, Art. 42.
[181] D. Gaer, 'First Fruits: Reporting by States under the African Charter on Human and Peoples' Rights' (1992) 10 *Netherlands Quarterly of Human Rights* 29, 29–30; M. Evans, T. Ige, and R. Murray, 'The Reporting Mechanism of the African Charter on Human and Peoples' Rights' in M. Evans and R. Murray (eds.), *The African Charter on Human and Peoples' Rights: The System of Practice, 1986–2000* (CUP 2002) 39.
[182] African Charter on the Rights and Welfare of the Child (adopted 11 July 1990, entered into force 29 November 1999), OAU Doc.CAB/LEG/24.9/49 (1990); Protocol to the African Charter on Human and Peoples' Rights on the Rights of Women in Africa (adopted 7 November 2003, entered into force 25 November 2005); Protocol to the African Charter on Human and Peoples' Rights on the Rights of Older Persons in Africa (adopted 28 January 2018, entered into force 11 September 2018).
[183] Arab Charter on Human Rights (adopted 22 May 2004, entered into force 15 March 2008), Arts. 48 and 45.
[184] Inter-American Convention on the Prevention, Punishment and Eradication of Violence against Women (adopted 9 June 1994, entered into force 5 March 1995); Inter-American Convention on the Elimination of All Forms of Discrimination against Persons with Disabilities (adopted 8 June 1999, entered into force 14 September 2001); Inter-American Convention against Racism, Racial Discrimination and Related Forms of Intolerance (adopted 5 June 2013, entered into force 11 November 2013) UN Registration No. 54915; Inter-American Convention against all Forms of Discrimination and Intolerance (adopted 5 June 2013, entered into force 20 February 2020); Inter-American Convention on Protecting the Human Rights of Older Persons (adopted 15 June 2015, entered into force 11 January 2017) UN Registration No. 54318.

regimes presented as a 'dialogue' between the monitoring organs and the States, aimed at securing the highest possible degree of protection for the individual within their jurisdictions.[185]

2.4.1.2 On-site investigations

Fact-finding mechanisms are another usual procedure for international human rights implementation. As the reporting system, the mechanisms of fact-finding are not of a judicial (or quasi-judicial) nature, but aimed at gathering information and ascertaining facts. Within the international law of human rights, these mechanisms are particularly useful for the investigation of patterns of grave human rights violations, such as torture, extra-judicial or summary executions, forced disappearances, and arbitrary detentions.[186] Human rights fact-finding has been frequently used within the United Nations, with its likely origin in the *ad hoc* Committee on Forced Labour established by ECOSOC in 1951.[187] Nowadays, fact-finding can be counted as one of the principal monitoring functions exercised by the numerous special rapporteurs, independent experts, and working groups established by the Human Rights Council, as further examined in **Section 4.3.3**. As discussed in **Section 5.3.4**, five of the main committees created by UN core human rights treaties also have the ability to undertake on-site inquiries concerning serious violations.[188]

Moreover, both at the European and the universal levels it is possible to find specialized monitoring bodies entrusted with conducting on-site visits to places where people are deprived of their liberty, in order to prevent torture and other cruel, inhuman or degrading treatment or punishment.[189] The European Committee for the Prevention of Torture and Inhuman or Degrading Treatment or Punishment was established in 1989, by the 1987 European Convention for the Prevention of Torture and Inhuman or Degrading Treatment or Punishment.[190] As discussed in **Section 5.8.1**, the UN General Assembly adopted, in 2002, the Optional Protocol to the Convention against Torture and Other Cruel, Inhuman or Degrading Treatment or Punishment, which established

---

[185] A.A. Cançado Trindade, *Tratado de Direito Internacional dos Direitos Humanos: Volume I* (2nd edn., SAFE 2003) 122.

[186] D. Weissbrodt and J. McCarthy, 'Fact-Finding by International Nongovernmental Human Rights Organizations' (1981) 22 *Virginia Journal of International Law* 1, 38, 43, 64–65; O.F. Orentlicher, 'Bearing Witness: The Art and Science of Human Rights Fact-Finding' (1990) 3 *Harvard Human Rights Journal* 83, 94, and 108.

[187] E. Domínguez-Redondo, 'The History of the Special Procedures: A "Learning-by-Doing" Approach to Human Rights Implementation' in A. Nolan, R. Freedman, and T. Murphy (eds.), *The United Nations Special Procedures System* (Brill 2017) 23 (fn 40).

[188] These are: CESCR (OP-ICESCR, Art. 11), CAT (UNCAT, Art. 20), CEDAW Committee (OP-CEDAW, Art. 8), CRC (OP3-CRC, Art. 13), CRPD (OPCRPD, Art. 6), and CED (ICPPED, Art. 33).

[189] European Convention for the Prevention of Torture and Inhuman or Degrading Treatment or Punishment (adopted on 26 November 1987 and entered into force on 1 February 1989), ETS No. 126, Art. 1; Optional Protocol to the Convention against Torture and other Cruel, Inhuman or Degrading Treatment or Punishment (adopted on 18 December 2002 and entered into force on 22 June 2006), 2375 UNTS 237, Art. 1.

[190] European Convention for the Prevention of Torture and Inhuman or Degrading Treatment or Punishment (adopted 26 November 1987, entered into force 1 February 1987). ETS No. 126.

the Subcommittee on Prevention of Torture and Other Cruel, Inhuman or Degrading Treatment or Punishment.[191]

With a wider mandate, the Inter-American Commission of Human Rights has frequently undertaken country visits to different Member States of the Organization of American States to conduct in-depth examinations of the general situation of human rights in the respective State or to investigate specific situations. This extended practice started in 1961 and has usually led the Inter-American Commission to the elaboration of public Country Reports, which describe and evaluate the situation that was observed. On its part, the African Commission on Human and Peoples' Rights has also conducted different missions to States Parties of the Charter since 1995.[192] The African Commission has derived its ability to conduct on-site missions to States Parties from a general provision contained in the Charter,[193] which allows it to resort to 'any appropriate method of investigation'.[194]

The existence of multiple bodies with faculties that would allow them to conduct fact-finding missions over the same situation should not be considered problematic in itself. On the contrary, the existence of convergent mandates can provide a more effective protection for the human person in contexts where grave human rights violations are taking place. It has been the existence of overlapping procedures which allowed the investigation of certain situations in the past, as the pressure of multiple organs made it more difficult for governments to oppose *in loco* visits.[195] Even if on-site visits require the agreement of the State to be visited, the decision to investigate a given State by a monitoring body does not need such consent. In the past, when States under examination have refused access, monitoring bodies have searched for creative alternatives to still pursue their mission.[196] The system of fact-finding missions, together with that of States reporting, favours a continuous monitoring of the implementation of human rights worldwide, since these mechanisms are not dependent on the existence of a specific petition.

2.4.1.3 Complaints system

The third main supervisory mechanism under the international law of human rights is the system of complaints, which allows monitoring bodies to examine alleged violations of human rights brought either by States Parties to the treaties or by individuals under

---

[191] Optional Protocol to the Convention against Torture and Other Cruel, Inhuman or Degrading Treatment or Punishment (adopted 18 December 2002, entered into force 22 June 2006).

[192] ACHPR, Eighth Annual Activity Report (1994–1995), 238–239; ACHPR, Tenth Annual Activity Report (1996–1997), 4.

[193] Within the African system, the African Children's Committee can also undertake country visits, as discussed in **Section 8.1.2.1**.

[194] R. Murray, 'On-Site Visits by the African Commission on Human and Peoples' Rights: A Case Study and Comparison with the Inter-American Commission on Human Rights' (1999) 11 *African Journal of International and Comparative Law* 460, 461.

[195] A.A. Cançado Trindade, 'General Course on the International Protection of Human Rights' (1988) 7 *Revista IIDH* 5, 21; A.A. Cançado Trindade, *Tratado de Direito Internacional dos Direitos Humanos: Volume I* (2nd edn., SAFE 2003) 150–151.

[196] A. Shaheed and R.P. Richter, 'Coping Mechanisms for State Non-cooperation' in A. Nolan, R. Freedman, and T. Murphy (eds.), *The United Nations Special Procedures System* (Brill 2017) 155–187, 172–175.

the jurisdiction of such States. On the one hand, several human rights treaties contemplate the possibility of inter-State communications, enabling States to raise complaints concerning the breach of the treaty by another Party.[197] Although the procedure for dealing with such complaints differs from treaty to treaty, it often requires an express acceptance from States Parties, under condition of reciprocity,[198] although no special consent is needed under some treaties, such as ICERD, the European Convention, or the African Charter.[199] In quantitative terms, inter-State communications are far less significant than those brought by individuals. While in all regional systems States have resorted to this type of complaint, even if infrequently—see **Sections 6.6, Section 7.4**, and **Section 8.6**—at the global level only the Committee on the Elimination of All Forms of Racial Discrimination has so far been called to deal with inter-State complaints (see **Section 5.4**). Nevertheless, it is becoming increasingly frequent for cases concerning human rights violations under international law to be brought to the consideration of the International Court of Justice (see **Section 4.5**), which has not been a traditional forum for human rights disputes in the past.[200]

On the other hand, the access of individuals to the international systems of protection, allowing them to seek redress for breaches of their human rights, can be said to be one of the greatest victories achieved by the development of the international law of human rights.[201] This right of individual petition is now recognized in numerous international human rights treaties. This right has been a central element of the regional systems for the protection of human rights since its recognition in the original text of the European Convention, which allowed for individuals to bring claims against a State Party to the Convention—subject to an additional declaration—for examination by the (then existing) European Commission on Human Rights.[202] In our days, the right of petition remains a central feature of the European Convention, allowing individuals to have access to the (now) compulsory jurisdiction of the European Court.[203] It is also recognized by the American Convention, providing access to the Inter-American Commission on Human Rights and, through it, to the Inter-American Court.[204] Within the African system, the African Charter contemplates a right of petition to the African

---

[197] As further discussed in **Section 5.3.3**, only two of the nine main monitoring bodies of the core human rights treaties lack of the ability to examine this type of communications: the CEDAW Committee and the Committee on the Rights of Persons with Disabilities.

[198] See: ICCPR, Arts. 41–43; ACHR, Arts. 45 and 62; UNCAT, Art. 21; ICRMW, Art. 76; ICPPED, Art. 32; Optional Protocol to ICESCR, Art. 10; Third Optional Protocol to UNCRC, Art. 12.

[199] ICERD, Arts. 11–13; ECHR, Art. 33; ACHPR, Arts. 47–53.

[200] See, among others, ECtHR, *Ireland v. the United Kingdom*, 18 January 1978, Series A no. 25; IACHR, *Nicaragua v. Costa Rica*, Report 11/07 (8 March 2007); ACHPR, *Democratic Republic of Congo v. Burundi, Rwanda and Uganda*, Communication 227/99 (2003); CERD, *State of Qatar v. Kingdom of Saudi Arabia*, ICERD-ISC 2018/1 (14 December 2018); ICJ, *Ahmadou Sadio Diallo (Republic of Guinea v. Democratic Republic of the Congo)*, Merits, Judgment, I.C.J. Reports 2010, p. 639.

[201] A.A. Cançado Trindade, *Tratado de Direito Internacional dos Direitos Humanos: Volume I* (2nd edn., SAFE 2003) 100–101.

[202] See Arts. 25 and 46 of the original text of the Convention, available at: https://www.echr.coe.int/Documents/Archives_1950_Convention_ENG.pdf (accessed on 13 May 2023).

[203] ECHR, Art. 34.   [204] ACHR, Art. 44.

Commission on Human and Peoples' Rights, while access to the Court is provided by the 2004 Protocol to the African Charter that created the tribunal.[205]

At the global level, there is a right of petition to the monitoring bodies of all nine core human rights treaties, provided either by the treaties themselves or by optional protocols to them.[206] However, by the end of 2022, the right of petition is yet to become effective with regard to the 1990 International Convention on the Protection of the Rights of All Migrant Workers and Members of their Families, as not enough States Parties have made the required declaration accepting the jurisdiction of the Committee.[207] Moreover, already since 1970, all Member States of the United Nations are subject to an additional procedure of complaints, regardless whether they have become parties to a specific treaty. As discussed in **Section 4.3.4**, the Human Rights Council (and before it, the Commission on Human Rights) can receive complaints from individuals concerning consistent patterns of gross violations of human rights in any UN Member State.[208]

The international human rights treaties that recognize this right of individual petition condition its exercise to the fulfilment of a series of requirements, which differ to some extent in the different treaties. Nonetheless, a standard main requirement for the admissibility of individual petitions concerns the prior exhaustion of domestic remedies.[209] This requirement evidences the fact that international mechanisms for the protection of human rights are subsidiary, or rather 'complementary', to the protection of such rights by the State. In other words, the protection of human rights is a primordial role of the domestic organs of the State, and only when the State has failed to perform this obligation can individuals seek protection at the international level.[210] The rule of prior exhaustion of domestic remedies emphasizes that the main duty of protection of human rights lies on the State, within its domestic jurisdiction, and should not be misused to inhibit access to international protection when required. That is why, under the international law of human rights, international monitoring bodies should be more flexible than in other areas of public international law when interpreting the

---

[205] African Charter, Art. 55; Protocol on the Establishment of an African Court on Human and Peoples' Rights (adopted 9 June 1998, entered into force 25 January 2004), OAU Doc. OAU/LEG/EXP/AFCHPR/PROT(III), Arts. 5 and 34.

[206] ICERD, Art. 14; Optional Protocol to ICCPR, Arts. 1–3 and 5; UNCAT, Art. 22; ICRMW, Art. 77; Optional Protocol to CEDAW, Arts. 1–2; Optional Protocol to UNCRPD, Art. 1; ICPPED, Art. 31; Optional Protocol to ICESCR, Art. 2; 2011 Third Optional Protocol to UNCRC, Art. 5.

[207] See: Report of the Committee on the Protection of the Rights of All Migrant Workers and Members of Their Families, Thirty-second session (6–16 and 29–30 April 2021), A/76/48, p. 17.

[208] ECOSOC, Resolution 1503(XLVIII), E/4832/Add.1 (27 May 1970); HRC, Institution-building of the United Nations Human Rights Council, A/HRC/RES/5/1 (18 June 2007).

[209] A.A. Cançado Trindade, *Tratado de Direito Internacional dos Direitos Humanos: Volume I* (2nd edn., SAFE 2003) 110–111.

[210] M. Nowak, *UN Covenant on Civil and Political Rights: CCPR Commentary* (2nd edn., Engel 2005) 28; N. Ando, 'National Implementation and Interpretation' in D. Shelton (ed.), *The Oxford Handbook of International Human Rights Law* (OUP 2013) 698–718, 698; A.A. Cançado Trindade, 'Réaffirmation de l´ universalité nécessaire et inéluctable des droits inhérents à la personne humaine', Addresse au Séminaire à la CourEDH, Strasbourg (8 March 2018).

rather usual defence opposed by States appearing before them concerning the lack of exhaustion of domestic remedies.[211]

Because different mechanisms of protection have overlapping jurisdictions over the same situation, it is up to the person bringing a petition to the international level to decide to which body to submit their claim.[212] Such a decision would later inhibit the possibility of having the case considered by a different body, as another usual pre-requirement to the admissibility of a petition at the international level is for it not to be under consideration of, or not to have been decided by, another international monitoring body—rules usually known by the Latin terminology as *lis pendens* and *res judicata*.[213] Nevertheless, these admissibility criteria should also be evaluated by the pertinent international organ without losing sight of the ultimate aim of the system: the protection of the human person.[214]

The multiplicity of legal sources that set up different mechanisms for the protection of human rights is the result of the historical process of a decentralized international community of States. It has led, nonetheless, to providing individuals with multiple international resources for the protection of their rights. What was said in **Section 2.2.2**, regarding the existence of monitoring bodies with overlapping jurisdictions also applies to concomitant mechanisms of protection. In the domain of the international law of human rights it is rather unimportant whether an improved implementation of human rights by the State comes as a consequence of the observations on a State report, is the outcome of a fact-finding mission, or follows a communication brought against the State. What truly matters is the superior common interest of the international community in the protection of human rights in all circumstances.[215] The convergent action of different monitoring bodies and their different mechanisms serves the protection of the human person in an ever-changing world, progressively expanding the scope of the international law of human rights.[216]

---

[211] A.A. Cançado Trindade, *Tratado de Direito Internacional dos Direitos Humanos: Volume I* (2nd edn., SAFE 2003) 112–113; D.A. González-Salzberg, 'Do Preliminary Objections Truly Object to the Jurisdiction of the Inter-American Court of Human Rights? An Empirical Study of the Use and Abuse of Preliminary Objections in the Court's Case Law' (2012) 12 *Human Rights Law Review* 255, 272–273.

[212] D. Shelton, 'State Practice on Reservations to Human Rights Treaties' (1983) *Canadian Human Rights Yearbook* 205, 215; L. Helfer, 'Forum Shopping for Human Rights' (1999) 148 *University of Pennsylvania Law Review* 285, 290.

[213] D.A. González-Salzberg, 'Do Preliminary Objections Truly Object to the Jurisdiction of the Inter-American Court of Human Rights? An Empirical Study of the Use and Abuse of Preliminary Objections in the Court's Case Law' (2012) 12 *Human Rights Law Review* 255, 273–274.

[214] See: IACtHR, *Baena Ricardo et al. v. Panama*. Preliminary Objections. Judgment of November 18, 1999. Series C No. 61; IACtHR, *Saramaka People v. Suriname*. Preliminary Objections, Merits, Reparations, and Costs. Judgment of November 28, 2007 Series C No. 172; IACtHR, *Cepeda Vargas v. Colombia*. Preliminary Objections, Merits, Reparations, and Costs. Judgment of May 26, 2010. Series C No. 213.

[215] A.A. Cançado Trindade, 'Co-existence and Co-ordination of Mechanisms of International Protection of Human Rights (At Global and Regional Levels)' (1987) 202 *Recueil des Cours de l'Académie de Droit International de La Haye* 9, 408; A.A. Cançado Trindade, 'General Course on the International Protection of Human Rights' (1988) 7 *Revista IIDH* 5, 12.

[216] A.A. Cançado Trindade, 'Co-existence and Co-ordination of Mechanisms of International Protection of Human Rights (At Global and Regional Levels)' (1987) 202 *Recueil des Cours de l'Académie de Droit International de La Haye* 401; F. Salvioli, 'El desarrollo progresivo: elemento central de la perspectiva pro persona' (2020) 71 *Revista IIDH* 115, 152.

2.4.2 THE (SECOND) WORLD CONFERENCE ON HUMAN RIGHTS (VIENNA, 1993)

Just over two decades after the adoption of the Proclamation of Tehran, the UN General Assembly decided to convene, in 1993, a (second) World Conference on Human Rights.[217] The end of the Cold War marked a significant historical moment in which the political climate seemed inclined to the construction of a new global consensus based on the protection of human rights and democracy.[218] Among its objectives, the Conference was to assess the progress achieved within the field of human rights since the adoption of the Universal Declaration and to identify the best path to continue strengthening the implementation of human rights for all; to evaluate the UN mechanisms in the field of human rights and formulate proposals for improving their effectiveness; and to make recommendations to ensure the necessary financial means for the UN activities in the promotion and protection of human rights.[219]

2.4.2.1 Preparatory meetings

Three regional meetings were celebrated during the preparatory process of the World Conference: a regional meeting for Africa, held in Tunis in November 1992; a regional meeting for Latin-America and the Caribbean, held in San José in January 1993; and a regional meeting for Asia, held in Bangkok in March–April 1993.[220] The outcome of each of these meetings was a declaration in which the States expressed their regional understanding of the situation of human rights. While the declarations emerging from each meetings counted many positive elements, such as a firm agreement in the indivisibility and interdependence of all human rights, the African and Asian meetings revealed undeniable concerns about the universality of human rights.[221]

These concerns about the universal character of human rights were more timidly present in the 'Tunis Declaration', which combined a conviction in universal human rights with a belief in the importance of taking into account 'the historical and cultural realities of each nation and the traditions, standards and values of each people'.[222] On its part, the 'Bangkok Declaration' adopted a seemingly stronger relativistic approach, stating that 'while human rights are universal in nature, they must be considered in the context of a dynamic and evolving process of international norm-setting, bearing in mind the significance of national and regional particularities and various historical,

---

[217] UNGA, World Conference on Human Rights, A/RES/45/155 1990 (18 December 1990).
[218] A.A. Cançado Trindade, *Tratado de Direito Internacional dos Direitos Humanos: Volume I* (2nd edn., SAFE 2003) 165–166; R. Burke, 'The 1993 World Conference on Human Rights and the Retreat of a Redistributive Rights Vision' (2020) 8 *London Review of International Law* 233, 233.
[219] UNGA, World Conference on Human Rights, A/RES/45/155 1990 (18 December 1990), para. 1.
[220] A.A. Cançado Trindade, *Tratado de Direito Internacional dos Direitos Humanos: Volume I* (2nd edn., SAFE 2003) 177–190.
[221] Regional Meeting for Africa, 'Tunis Declaration (1992)', para. 6; San José Declaration, A/CONF.157/LACRM/15, A/CONF.157/PC/58, para. 3; Bangkok Declaration, A/CONF.157/ASRM/8, A/CONF.157/PC/59, preamble and para. 7.
[222] Regional Meeting for Africa, 'Tunis Declaration (1992)', paras. 2 and 5.

cultural and religious backgrounds'.[223] The Bangkok Declaration was the most critical of the three as to the international state of affairs with regard to human rights protection. It asserted that the creation of uniform international human rights norms must be accompanied by similar endeavours towards 'a just and fair world economic order'.[224] It further stressed the 'urgent need to democratize the United Nations system' and expressed a clear concern about 'double standards in the implementation of human rights and its politicization'.[225]

The World Conference was also preceded by a three-day world forum of non-governmental organizations, entitled 'All Human Rights for All'. The Forum made a series of concrete recommendations aimed at strengthening the implementation of human rights worldwide, including many endorsed by the Conference itself.[226] Among these, the NGO Forum supported the creation of the office of a High Commissioner for Human Rights within the ambit of the United Nations;[227] it encouraged the adoption of protocols to ICESCR and to the Convention on the Elimination of All Forms of Discrimination against Women (CEDAW), to provide for individual complaints; and it supported the creation of a permanent, independent, and impartial International Penal Court to prosecute gross violations of human rights and humanitarian law.[228] The celebration of the NGO Forum had clear positive repercussions in the main document adopted by the World Conference. The Vienna Declaration and Programme of Action specifically stated the need for 'States and international organizations, in cooperation with non-governmental organizations, to create favourable conditions at the national, regional and international levels to ensure the full and effective enjoyment of human rights'.[229] It also recognized the significant role played by non-governmental organizations in the 'promotion of all human rights and in humanitarian activities at national, regional and international levels' and emphasized 'the importance of continued dialogue and cooperation between Governments and non-governmental organizations'.[230]

2.4.2.2 The Vienna Declaration and Programme of Action

The 1993 Vienna Declaration should be distinguished from the one adopted in Tehran twenty-five years earlier; a difference that can be fully appreciated in their historical context. While the Tehran Declaration seemed to adopt a clear overarching idea, that of the indivisibility and interdependence of all human rights—in itself significant for

---

[223] Bangkok Declaration, A/CONF.157/ASRM/8, A/CONF.157/PC/59, para. 8.
[224] Bangkok Declaration, A/CONF.157/ASRM/8, A/CONF.157/PC/59, preamble.
[225] Bangkok Declaration, A/CONF.157/ASRM/8, A/CONF.157/PC/59, paras. 3 and 7.
[226] A.A. Cançado Trindade, *Tratado de Direito Internacional dos Direitos Humanos: Volume I* (2nd edn., SAFE 2003) 220–231. See also: R. Burke, 'The 1993 World Conference on Human Rights and the Retreat of a Redistributive Rights Vision' (2020) 8 *London Review of International Law* 233, 255–257.
[227] The post of High Commissioner for Human Rights, created by the General Assembly in December 1993, is a topic discussed in-depth in **Section 4.4**.
[228] Report by the General Rapporteur, Manfred Nowak, as adopted by the Final Plenary Session of the NGO-Forum, A/CONF.157/7.
[229] Vienna Declaration (25 June 1993), para. 13.   [230] Vienna Declaration (25 June 1993), para. 38.

being adopted during the context of the Cold War—the Vienna Declaration lacked of a clear driving principle.[231] Instead, the Vienna Declaration focused on the need to better coordinate the multiple international human rights mechanisms that had been established by 1993. If the Tehran Proclamation highlighted the need to conceive all human rights as indivisible and interrelated in a theoretical plane, the ambition of the Vienna Declaration was to achieve such universality in practice, through the strengthening of the mechanisms of implementation.[232]

The Vienna Declaration and Programme of Action adopted by the World Conference on Human Rights on 25 June 1993 had two operative parts, one being the Declaration and the other one the Programme. While taking into account the contributions made by the different preparatory meetings, the Declaration starts by stating that the universal nature of human rights was beyond question.[233] As the first-person narrative of Judge Cançado Trindade highlights, the categorical assertion of the universality of all human rights was only agreed by consensus of the drafting committee of the Conference on the night of 23 June.[234] At that point in time, paragraph 5 of the Declaration had already been adopted, which even though stated the universal, indivisible, interdependent, and interrelated nature of all human rights, also affirmed that the 'significance of national and regional particularities and various historical, cultural and religious backgrounds must be borne in mind'.[235] The adoption of this paragraph had caused a certain level of concern to the supporters of a universalistic approach to human rights as to whether the protection of these rights might become dependent on cultural relativism (a topic discussed in **Section 1.1.2.2.1**). Therefore, the adoption of the first paragraph of the Declaration came to affirm that cultural diversity should serve to enrich the universality of human rights, but cannot be used as an excuse to negate the enjoyment of all human rights everywhere and by everyone.

While concern for the respect of all human rights was emphatically expressed in the Declaration, especial attention was drawn towards the prohibition of discrimination, particularly racial discrimination, and onto the need to adopt measures to protect the members of vulnerable groups, such as women, children, indigenous people, asylum-seekers, and migrant workers.[236] The Declaration also made an explicit connection between human rights, development, and democracy, as mutually reinforcing phenomena,[237] asserting that 'least developed countries committed to the process of democratization and

---

[231] A.A. Cançado Trindade, *Tratado de Direito Internacional dos Direitos Humanos: Volume I* (2nd edn., SAFE 2003) 239–242.
[232] A.A. Cançado Trindade, *Tratado de Direito Internacional dos Direitos Humanos: Volume I* (2nd edn., SAFE 2003) 241.
[233] Vienna Declaration (25 June 1993), para. 1.
[234] A.A. Cançado Trindade, *Tratado de Direito Internacional dos Direitos Humanos: Volume I* (2nd edn., SAFE 2003) 243.
[235] Report of the Preparatory Committee, A/CONF.157/PC/98, 24 May 1993, para. 5.
[236] Vienna Declaration (25 June 1993), paras. 15, 18, 20, 23–24.
[237] Unsurprisingly, the topic of democracy was not prominent in the Tehran Proclamation or the resolutions adopted by the First International Conference, given that over two-thirds of the participating States were undemocratic at the time, including the host. See: R. Burke, 'From Individual Rights to National Development: The First UN International Conference on Human Rights, Tehran, 1968' (2008) 19 *Journal of World History* 275, 283.

economic reforms, many of which are in Africa, should be supported by the international community in order to succeed in their transition to democracy and economic development'.[238] Furthermore, the Declaration recognized extreme poverty and social exclusion as violations of human dignity, which inhibit the full and effective enjoyment of human rights, and stated that the immediate alleviation, and eventual elimination, of extreme poverty must be a high priority for the international community as a whole.[239]

The second part of the document adopted by the World Conference corresponded to the Programme of Action. The Programme is longer than the Declaration and began by highlighting the need for an increased coordination on human rights within the United Nations system. In strong terms, the Programme of Action reiterated the need for universal acceptance of all human rights treaties without reservations, calling for 'a concerted effort to encourage and facilitate the ratification of and accession ... to international human rights treaties and protocols adopted within the framework of the United Nations system'.[240] It also recognized 'the necessity for a continuing adaptation of the United Nations human rights machinery to the current and future needs in the promotion and protection of human rights'.[241] Concerning human rights mechanisms, and taking into account the need to improve their coordination, efficiency, and effectiveness, the Programme recommended the General Assembly, as a matter of priority, to consider the establishment of a High Commissioner for Human Rights for the promotion and protection of all human rights (see **Section 4.4**).[242]

Following this, the Programme contained a series of concrete recommendations for expanding and improving specific mechanisms for the implementation of human rights in different areas. These included issues of discrimination against the members of multiple vulnerable groups, such as racial and ethnic minorities, indigenous peoples, migrant workers, disable people, children, and women, as well as the topic of grave violations of human rights, such as torture and forced disappearances. The Programme recommended the adoption of optional protocols to some of the core human rights treaties, including protocols to ICESCR and CEDAW that would allow for individual communications, and a protocol to the 1984 Convention against Torture and Other Cruel, Inhuman or Degrading Treatment or Punishment (UNCAT) that would establish a preventive system of on-site visits to detention centres.[243] It also encouraged the International Law Commission to continue its work to support the creation of an international criminal court (see **Section 2.5.2**).

Notwithstanding the multiple reasons to praise the Vienna Declaration and Programme of Action, the debates that took place during the Conference revealed that the understanding of all human rights as universal, indivisible, and enforceable is an idea

---

[238] Vienna Declaration (25 June 1993), para. 9.
[239] Vienna Declaration (25 June 1993), paras. 14 and 25.
[240] Vienna Programme of Action (25 June 1994), para. 4.
[241] Vienna Programme of Action (25 June 1994), para. 17.
[242] Vienna Programme of Action (25 June 1994), paras. 17–18.
[243] Vienna Programme of Action (25 June 1994), paras. 40, 61, 75.

that might always find detractors. Furthermore, an opportunity was missed to adopt a final document which contained more concrete and precise State commitments in certain areas, such as those concerning the needed financial resources to support existing human rights mechanisms, or as to the exact measures to be adopted to strengthen and improve the coordination of the international systems for the protection of human rights. Despite these (rather important) shortcomings, the significance of the (second) World Conference on Human Rights should not be dismissed.[244] The adopted Declaration and Programme of Action are clear signs of the existence of a shared community of basic values embraced by all States and of a common interest in working cooperatively towards continuously strengthening the mechanism for human rights implementation across the world.

2.5 THE INTERNATIONAL PROTECTION OF THE HUMAN PERSON THROUGH THE EVOLVING CONVERGENCE OF LEGAL REGIMES

The Vienna Declaration and Programme of Action contained multiple references to the importance of the observance of international humanitarian law and international refugee law.[245] This is far from surprising, given that the evolving international protection of the human person, in all circumstances, is not just achieved by the development of the international law of human rights, but also through the increasing convergence of different international regimes of protection. Notwithstanding each of these international regimes having distinct historical origins and specific objects, with refugee law granting a minimum level of protection to those escaping their own States and humanitarian law being concerned with rules that regulate the conduct of armed hostilities to protect their victims (as discussed in **Section 1.2.4**), these legal systems are guided by the same basic identity of purpose as the international law of human rights: securing the protection of the human person.[246]

At the substantive level, it is easy to identify several aspects of interconnection among these branches of international law. Convergences between basic principles of the international law of human rights, which predicates the protection of every person in all circumstances, even in times of war,[247] and the 'law of Geneva', which establishes the

---

[244] A.A. Cançado Trindade, *Tratado de Direito Internacional dos Direitos Humanos: Volume I* (2nd edn., SAFE 2003) 250–251.

[245] Vienna Declaration, paras. 3, 21, 23, and 28–29; Vienna Programme of Action, paras. 38, 50, 56, 79, 82, and 96.

[246] C. Swinarski, *Principales Nociones e Institutos del Derecho Internacional Humanitario como Sistema Internacional de Protección de la Persona Humana* (IIDH 1990) 84; A.A. Cançado Trindade, *Tratado de Direito Internacional dos Direitos Humanos: Volume I* (2nd edn., SAFE 2003) 340–341.

[247] ICJ, *Legal Consequences of the Construction of a Wall in the Occupied Palestinian Territories*, Advisory Opinion, I.C.J. Reports 2004 (9 July 2004), para. 106; CCPR, General Comment 31: The Nature of the General Legal Obligation Imposed on States Parties to the Covenant, CCPR/C/21/Rev.1/Add. 13 (26 May 2004), para. 11; IACtHR, *Serrano Cruz Sisters v. El Salvador*. Preliminary Objections. Judgment of November 23, 2004. Series C No. 118, para. 114.

protection of people who are not (or are no longer) taking part in hostilities, are easy to find.[248] For instance, common Article 3 of the four 1949 Geneva Conventions, concerning non-international armed conflicts, recognizes basic fundamental rights to be applied even in times of war, while the two 1977 Additional Protocols to the Geneva Conventions acknowledge fundamental guarantees that must be respected.[249] Among the rights concomitantly protected by both regimes, it is possible to mention the prohibition of arbitrary deprivation of life, the prohibition of torture, the prohibition of slavery, the right to juridical personality, the general prohibition of discrimination, freedom of conscience and religion, and access to essential judicial guarantees, including the prohibition of collective penalties and the prohibition of punishment by retrospective laws.[250]

The interrelation between the protection of human rights and the protection of refugees is also widely accepted. Some of the rights universally recognized by different international human rights instruments are directly aimed at providing protection to refugees. Indeed, the Universal Declaration specifically enunciates the right to seek and enjoy asylum from persecution in other States,[251] with the 1951 UN Convention relating to the Status of Refugees finding roots in such a recognition.[252] Similarly, provisions emerging from International Refugee Law have found direct applicability within the international law of human rights. The most evident example is the acknowledgment within human rights treaties of the principle of *non-refoulement*—further discussed in **Section 2.5.1**.[253] Moreover, international instruments adopted for improving the protection of refugees have expressly recognized the convergence between the regimes of protection of the human person set forth in refugee law, humanitarian law, and human rights, such as the 1994 Declaration of San José on Refugees and Displaced Persons and the 2004 México Declaration and Plan of Action to Strengthen the International Protection of Refugees in Latin-America.[254] These declarations came to re-affirm that

---

[248] J. Moreillon, 'The Fundamental Principles of the Red Cross, Peace and Human Rights' (1980) 217 *International Review of the Red Cross* 171, 179–180; J-M. Henckaerts and L. Doswald-Beck, *Customary International Humanitarian Law: Volume I: Rules* (ICRC 2009) xxxii.

[249] R. Provost, *International Human Rights and Humanitarian Law* (CUP 2002) 6; A.A. Cançado Trindade, *Tratado de Direito Internacional dos Direitos Humanos: Volume I* (2nd edn., SAFE 2003) 341–342; P.G. Lauren, *The Evolution of International Human Rights: Visions Seen* (3rd edn., PENN 2011) 229. See: Protocol Additional to the Geneva Conventions of 12 August 1949, and relating to the Protection of Victims of International Armed Conflicts (Protocol I) (adopted 8 June 1977, entered into force 7 December 1978), Art. 75; Protocol Additional to the Geneva Conventions of 12 August 1949, and relating to the Protection of Victims of Non-International Armed Conflicts (Protocol II) (adopted 8 June 1977, entered into force 7 December 1978), Arts. 4–5.

[250] D. Schindler, 'The International Committee of the Red Cross and Human Rights' (1979) 208 *International Review of the Red Cross* 3, 5–7, and 15; T. Meron, *Human Rights in Internal Strife: Their International Protection* (CUP 1987) 10–11, 14, 26–27, 142. See: ECHR, Art. 15; ICCPR, Art. 4; ACHR, Art. 27.

[251] UDHR, Art. 14.1.

[252] UNHCR, 'Introductory Note', available at: https://www.unhcr.org/media/28185 (accessed on 12 May 2023).

[253] Convention relating to the Status of Refugees (adopted 28 July 1951, entered into force 22 April 1954) 189 UNTS 137, Art. 33.1; ACHR, Art. 22.8–22.9; UNCAT, Art. 3.1; ICPPED, Art. 16.

[254] San José Declaration on Refugees and Displaced Persons (5–7 December 1994), preamble and third and sixteenth (a) conclusions; Mexico Declaration and Plan of Action to Strengthen the International Protection of Refugees in Latin America (16 November 2004), preamble.

even in situations of grave emergency, such as the one of forced migratory fluxes, the protection of the human person is secured by law, setting aside any risks of a legal vacuum.[255]

The concomitant operation of the international law of human rights, international humanitarian law, and international refugee law has also become evident at the operative level. A paradigmatic illustration is provided by the mandate of the Special Rapporteur in the Palestine (Filasṭīn) occupied territories, created by the UN Commission on Human Rights (see **Section 4.3.1**). The mandate itself is explicitly based on the convergent applicability of human rights and humanitarian law.[256] Furthermore, following visits to the area subject to the mandate, including different refugee camps, rapporteurs have expressed their views on human rights violations, as well as on breaches of refugee and humanitarian law.[257] In particular, an area of convergence highlighted by both the rapporteurs and by the United Nations High Commissioner for Refugees is that of individuals within zones of armed conflict that have been denied the possibility of fleeing the area, in contravention of all three regimes of protection.[258]

In the Americas, the Inter-American Commission of Human Rights has performed an exemplary role with regard to the convergent application of the legal regimes for the international protection of the human person, especially when examining situations of forced displaced individuals, both within a State and across States' borders.[259] In the past, the Commission has globally assessed the situation of refugees, displaced persons, and repatriates and has stated that an international protection for uprooted populations is provided not only by refugee law, but also by international human rights and humanitarian law.[260] What matters is that the most beneficial norm for refugees, displaced persons, and repatriates is applied to the case, irrespective of its provenance.

---

[255] A.A. Cançado Trindade, *International Law for Humankind: Towards a New Jus Gentium* (3rd edn., Nijhoff 2020) 516–518.

[256] CHR, Question of the violation of human rights in the occupied Arab territories, including Palestine, E/CN.4/RES/1993/2 (19 February 1993).

[257] See, among many: Report of the Special Rapporteur of the Commission on Human Rights, Mr John Dugard, E/CN.4/2003/30 (17 December 2002); Report of the Special Rapporteur of the Commission on Human Rights, John Dugard, E/CN.4/2004/6/Add.1 (27 February 2004); Report of the Special Rapporteur of the Commission on Human Rights, John Dugard, A/61/470 (27 September 2006); Report of the Special Rapporteur on the situation of human rights in the Palestinian territories occupied since 1967, Makarim Wibisono, A/HRC/28/78 (22 January 2015).

[258] Report of the Special Rapporteur on the situation of human rights in the Palestinian territories occupied since 1967, Richard Falk, A/HRC/10/20 (11 February 2009); Report of the Special Rapporteur on the situation of human rights in the Palestinian territories occupied since 1967, Richard Falk, A/HRC/13/53 (15 January 2010); Statement from the UNHCR, António Guterres, on 6 January 2009, available at: https://www.unhcr.org/uk/news/briefing/2009/1/496355082/gaza-only-conflict-world-people-allowed-flee-high-commissioner-guterres.html (accessed on 12 May 2023).

[259] See, among many, IACHR, Annual Report 1981–1982, OEA/Ser.L/V/II.57, doc. 6 rev.1 (20 September 1982), chapter II.C; IACHR, Annual Report 1982–1983, OEA/Ser.L/V/II.61, Doc. 22 rev. 1 (27 September 1983), chapter V.E; IACHR, Annual Report 1986–1987, OEA/Ser.L/V/II.71, Doc. 9 rev. 1 (22 September 1987), chapter IV; IACHR, Report No. 51/96, Case 10.675 (United States) (13 March 1997).

[260] IACHR, Annual Report 1993, OEA/Ser.L/V.85, Doc. 9 rev. (11 February 1994), Chapter V.II.A.

To summarize, any potential compartmentalization of international obligations for the protection of the human person has been replaced by a convergent application of protective norms from different regimes. The convergence of the international law of human rights, international humanitarian law, and international refugee law provides protection to human beings in all and every circumstance. The 1993 World Conference on Human Rights was adamant in highlighting the convergence of these three legal regimes of protection, counting with the support of the International Committee of the Red Cross (ICRC) and the UN High Commissioner for Refugees in their interventions at the Conference;[261] a stance that is now increasingly endorsed by all international human rights monitoring bodies.

2.5.1 THE PRINCIPLE OF *NON-REFOULEMENT*

As mentioned in **Section 2.5**, there are fundamental principles that can be found at the convergence of the international legal regimes for the protection of the human person. Among these, it is possible to count the principle of equality and non-discrimination, the principle of the inviolability of the human person, the principle of the inalienability of fundamental rights, the principle of the security of the individual, and the principle of *non-refoulement*—the prohibition of expelling or returning a person to a State in which they might face serious threats to their life or freedom.[262] The latter, in particular, serves as a clear illustration of the effects of the convergence of the three mentioned regimes of protection. The first references to *non-refoulement* occurred in international practice in the inter-war period, mainly as from the 1930s;[263] but it was in the aftermath of the Second World War that the prohibition of *refoulement* appeared as a basic principle of international refugee law.[264] This principle was also recognized under international humanitarian law, which prohibits in absolute terms the transfer of a protected person to a State where they may face persecution,[265] while it is further encompassed by a wider provision that prohibits the transferring of both prisoners of war and protected persons to a Power that is not a Party to the Geneva conventions (or not able and willing to apply them).[266]

The convergence between international refugee law and the international law of human rights has led to the expansion of the normative content of the principle of *non-refoulement*. The original understanding of this principle as a prohibition of rejection

---

[261] A.A. Cançado Trindade, *Tratado de Direito Internacional dos Direitos Humanos: Volume I* (2nd edn., SAFE 2003) 344–345.

[262] A.A. Cançado Trindade, *International Law for Humankind: Towards a New Jus Gentium* (3rd edn., Nijhoff 2020) 520.

[263] G.S. Goodwin-Gill and J. McAdam, *The Refugee in International Law* (3rd edn., OUP 2007) 202–203.

[264] Refugee Convention, Art. 33.1.

[265] C. Droege, 'Transfers of Detainees: Legal Framework, Non-Refoulement and Contemporary Challenges' (2008) 871 *International Review of the Red Cross* 669, 674. See: Convention (IV) relative to the Protection of Civilian Persons in Time of War (1949), Art. 45.

[266] C. Droege, 'Transfers of Detainees: Legal Framework, Non-Refoulement and Contemporary Challenges' (2008) 871 *International Review of the Red Cross* 669, 674–675. See: Convention (III) relative to the Treatment of Prisoners of War (1949), Art. 12.

at frontier of somebody escaping persecution, is now indissociably linked with the absolute prohibition of torture and cruel, inhuman, or degrading treatment, as evidenced by its recognition in the Convention against Torture and Other Cruel, Inhuman or Degrading Treatment or Punishment (UNCAT).[267] Initially, it was the case law of the European Court of Human Rights that extended the protection against *refoulement* to circumstances not originally conceived by the 1951 Refugee Convention—or even UNCAT—expanding its preventive dimension to encompass situations involving a risk to be subjected to torture or to cruel, inhuman, or degrading treatment resulting from an extradition, deportation, or expulsion.[268] This approach was then followed by other international monitoring bodies, such as the Committee against Torture, the Human Rights Committee, and the Inter-American Court of Human Rights.[269] Additionally, the 2006 International Convention for the Protection of All Persons from Enforced Disappearance (ICPPED) has widened the scope of the principle, mandating its use to avoid individuals being put at risk of falling victim to the international crime of forced disappearance.[270]

Nowadays, the principle of *non-refoulement* not only applies to the benefit of refugees but to that of every individual, in cases of extradition, expulsion, deportation, or devolution, towards a State in which they may be at risk of being submitted to torture, inhuman or degrading treatment, or the practice of forced disappearance.[271] Consequently, the principle of *non-refoulement* has now become part of an irreducible minimum of protection of the rights of the human person to be found at the convergence of international refugee law, international humanitarian law, and the international law of human rights. Its importance is such, that it is considered to pertain to the realm of general customary law,[272] and has even been acknowledged as belonging to the domain of *jus cogens*.[273]

---

[267] W. Suntinger, 'The Principle of Non-Refoulement: Looking Rather to Geneva than to Strasbourg?' (1995) 49 *Austrian Journal of Public and International Law* 203, 203–208; G.S. Goodwin-Gill and J. McAdam, *The Refugee in International Law* (3rd edn., OUP 2007) 220. See: UNCAT, Art. 3.

[268] ECtHR, *Soering v. United Kingdom*, No. 14038/88, 7 July 1989; ECtHR, *Bader and Kanbor v. Sweden*, No. 13284/04, 8 November 2005; ECtHR, *Hirsi Jamaa and Others v. Italy*, No. 27765/09, 23 February 2012.

[269] CAT, *Mutombo vs. Switzerland case*, Communication No. 13/1993, UN Doc. A/49/44 at 45 (1994); CCPR, *Kaba v. Canada*, 21 May 2010, CCPR/C/98/D/1465/2006, paras. 10.3–10.4; IACtHR, *Matter of Haitians and Dominicans of Haitian-origin in the Dominican Republic regarding Dominican Republic*. Provisional Measures. Order of the Inter-American Court of Human Rights of August 18, 2000.

[270] International Convention for the Protection of All Persons from Enforced Disappearance (adopted 20 December 2006, entered into force 23 December 2010), Art. 16.

[271] A.A. Cançado Trindade, *International Law for Humankind: Towards a New Jus Gentium* (3rd edn., Nijhoff 2020) 523.

[272] S. Kanako, 'Genuine Protection of International Refugees: A Study of the Influence of Western States on the Mandate of the UNHCR' (2004) 11 *Asian Yearbook of International Law* 89, 96.

[273] Declaración de Cartagena sobre los Refugiados (22 November 1984), fifth conclusion; IACtHR, *Matter of Haitians and Dominicans of Haitian-origin in the Dominican Republic regarding Dominican Republic*. Provisional Measures. Order of the Inter-American Court of Human Rights of August 18, 2000, concurring opinion of Judge Cançado Trindade para. 7 (fn 5); IACtHR, *Juridical Condition and Rights of the Undocumented Migrants*. Advisory Opinion OC-18/03 of September 17, 2003. Series A no.18, concurring opinion of Judge Cançado Trindade paras. 21 and 72.

2.5.2 THE STRUGGLE AGAINST IMPUNITY: FROM STATE TO INDIVIDUAL RESPONSIBILITY

A further aspect of convergence between the international law of human rights and international humanitarian law can be found in their shared quest against impunity for grave violations of the norms of these legal orders. The efforts to create mechanisms for the realization of justice, when protection had failed, have extended beyond the regime of State responsibility, towards the creation of an international criminal jurisdiction. The fight against impunity for gross violations of the international law of human rights and international humanitarian law has led to the establishment of international tribunals aimed at determining the responsibility of the individual culprits for such serious breaches; in other words, to the criminalization of the grave violations of human rights and humanitarian law.[274]

The idea to bring the culprits of such serious violations of international law to an international jurisdiction finds important antecedents in the Nuremberg and Tokyo tribunals,[275] established in August 1945 and January 1946.[276] These international military tribunals were created by the main victorious powers of the Second World War to prosecute war criminals for the commission of crimes against peace, war crimes, and crimes against humanity.[277] The work of these historical tribunals inspired an important debate on the codification of basic rules of international criminal justice and the potential creation of a permanent international court, from the early years of the United Nations.[278] Even the 1948 Genocide Convention, adopted the day before the Universal Declaration of Human Rights, foresaw the potential creation of a permanent international penal tribunal.[279] Nevertheless, the political context of the Cold War meant that the project to create such a court was not to see the light for half a century. Although, throughout the years, the General Assembly established special committees and entrusted the International Law Commission (ILC)—a body of experts

---

[274] R. Provost, *International Human Rights and Humanitarian Law* (CUP 2002) 117; A.A. Cançado Trindade, *International Law for Humankind: Towards a New Jus Gentium* (3rd edn., Nijhoff 2020) 234–235.

[275] R. Provost, *International Human Rights and Humanitarian Law* (CUP 2002) 105; D. Bosco, *Rough Justice: The International Criminal Court in a World of Power Politics* (OUP 2014) 23; W.A. Schabas, *An Introduction to the International Criminal Court* (5th edn., CUP 2017) 5–6.

[276] And even before them, in the 1919 Commission on the Responsibilities of the Authors of War and on Enforcement of Penalties. See: M.C. Bassiouni, 'From Versailles to Rwanda in Seventy-Five Years: The Need to Establish a Permanent International Criminal Court' (1997) 10 *Harvard Human Rights Journal* 11, 14–21.

[277] M.C. Bassiouni, 'From Versailles to Rwanda in Seventy-Five Years: The Need to Establish a Permanent International Criminal Court' (1997) 10 *Harvard Human Rights Journal* 11, 25–26. See: Agreement for the prosecution and punishment of the major war criminals of the European Axis (signed on 8 August 1945), Charter of the International Military Tribunal, 280 UNTS 1951, Art. 6; Special Proclamation by the Supreme Commander for the Allied Powers (19 January 1946), Charter of the International Military Tribunal for the Far East, Art. 5.

[278] D. Bosco, *Rough Justice: The International Criminal Court in a World of Power Politics* (OUP 2014) 30. See: UNGA, 'Affirmation of the principles of international law recognized by the Charter of the Nuremberg Tribunal', A/RES/95(1) (11 December 1946); UNGA, 'The Crime of Genocide', A/REWS/96(1) (11 December 1946).

[279] Convention on the Prevention and Punishment of the Crime of Genocide (adopted 9 December 1948, entered into force 12 January 1951), Art. VI.

created by the Assembly to progressively develop international law—with the tasks of drafting a statute for an international criminal court and codifying legal principles for international criminal responsibility, those initiatives could not be brought to fruition for decades.[280] It would take until the 1980s for the appetite for an international criminal jurisdiction to reappear, becoming a priority in the early 1990s.[281]

At the time in which a draft statute for an international criminal tribunal was being produced, the United Nations Security Council, acting under the authority of Chapter VII of the UN Charter, created two *ad hoc* international tribunals. These two tribunals were established to determine the criminal responsibility of individuals for the grave crimes committed in the territory of the former Yugoslavia since 1991 and during the internal conflict in Rwanda in 1994.[282] The International Criminal Tribunal for the Former Yugoslavia (ICTY) had the ability to prosecute grave violations of the 1949 Geneva Conventions, breaches of the laws and customs of war, the crime of genocide, and crimes against humanity.[283] It operated from its establishment, in 1993, until the end of 2017, indicting a total of 161 individuals.[284] The International Criminal Tribunal for Rwanda (ICTR) had jurisdiction to establish individual criminal responsibility for the commission of genocide, crimes against humanity, and serious violations of common Article 3 to the 1949 Geneva Conventions and of its Additional Protocol II that took place in the territory of Rwanda during the year 1994, as well as for such violations if committed in the territory of neighbouring States by Rwandan citizens.[285] During its time of operation, between 1995 and the end of 2015, it indicted a total of ninety-three individuals.[286]

The work of the International Law Commission on a draft statute for an international criminal court was completed by 1993. Between 1995 and 1998, the General Assembly convened two different committees to produce a 'consolidated text' of the draft statute.[287] The end result was the creation of the permanent International Criminal Court (ICC); a tribunal with jurisdiction for judging

---

[280] D. Bosco, *Rough Justice: The International Criminal Court in a World of Power Politics* (OUP 2014) 30, 32; W.A. Schabas, *An Introduction to the International Criminal Court* (5th edn., CUP 2017) 8–9.

[281] D. Bosco, *Rough Justice: The International Criminal Court in a World of Power Politics* (OUP 2014) 34; W.A. Schabas, *An Introduction to the International Criminal Court* (5th edn., CUP 2017) 9–10. See: UNGA, Report of the ILC on the work of its forty-fourth session, A/RES/47/33 (9 February 1992), para. 6.

[282] W.A. Schabas, *An Introduction to the International Criminal Court* (5th edn., CUP 2017) 11–12; R. Dubler and M. Kalyk, *Crimes Against Humanity in the 21st Century: Law, Practice and Threats to International Peace and Security* (Brill 2018) 157.

[283] Statute of the International Criminal Tribunal for the Former Yugoslavia, adopted by UNSC Resolution 827 (25 May 1993), Art. 1.

[284] Document 'ICTY Facts and Figures', available at: http://www.icty.org/node/9590 (accessed on 12 May 2023).

[285] Statute of the International Tribunal for Rwanda, adopted by UNSC Resolution 955 (8 November 1994), Art. 1.

[286] Document 'Key Figures of ICTR cases', available at: http://unictr.irmct.org/sites/unictr.org/files/publications/ictr-key-figures-en.pdf (accessed on 12 May 2023).

[287] M.C. Bassiouni, 'Negotiating the Treaty of Rome on the Establishment of an International Criminal Court' (1999) 32 *Cornell International Law Journal* 443, 443–444; W.A. Schabas, *An Introduction to the International Criminal Court* (5th edn., CUP 2017) 16–17.

individuals for grave violations of the international law of human rights and of international humanitarian law. In July 1998, the United Nations Rome Conference approved the Statute of the ICC, which defined four categories of 'core crimes' under the jurisdiction of the Court: genocide, crimes against humanity, war crimes, and the crime of aggression.[288] However, the recognition of this fourth crime, a rather politically charged matter,[289] lacked a definition within the Statute until 2010.[290] The Rome Statute managed to obtain the necessary sixty ratifications or accessions in April 2002,[291] entering into force on 1 July 2002,[292] and leading to the establishment of the Court the following year.[293] The creation of this Court constituted an achievement of the international community as a whole,[294] giving a new impetus to its struggle against impunity.[295]

There is a clear complementarity between the international law of human rights and international criminal law. The international responsibility of both the State and the individual complement each other, contributing to the eradication of impunity for grave violations of human rights.[296] While the determination of the international responsibility of States is the competence of human rights bodies—such as the international courts established in Europe, Africa, and the Americas—the international criminal responsibility of individuals is, nowadays, within the jurisdiction of the International Criminal Court.[297]

---

[288] Rome Statute of the International Criminal Court (adopted 17 July 1998, entered into force 1 July 2002) 2187 UNTS 3, Arts. 5–8.

[289] A.A. Cançado Trindade, *International Law for Humankind: Towards a New Jus Gentium* (3rd edn., Nijhoff 2020) 608.

[290] Amendments to the Rome Statute of the International Criminal Court on the Crime of Aggression, (11/06/2010), C.N.651.2010.TREATIES-8.

[291] See: https://asp.icc-cpi.int/states-parties/states-parties-chronological-list (accessed on 12 May 2023).

[292] Rome Statute, Art. 126.

[293] E. Odio Benito, 'Diez años después' (2013) 58 *Revista IIDH* 81, 89.

[294] However, important criticisms of the Court's particular focus on Africa, and the potential neo-colonial implications of this approach, cannot be ignored. See, among others: N.J. Udombana, '"Can These Dry Bones Live?" In Search of a Lasting Therapy for AU and ICC Toxic Relationship' (2014) 1 *African Journal of International Criminal Justice* 57; P. Manirakiza, 'A Twail Perspective on the African Union's Project to Withdraw from the International Criminal Court' (2018) 23 *African Yearbook of International Law Online* 391; A.B. Rukooko and J. Silverman, 'The International Criminal Court and Africa: A Fractious Relationship Assessed' (2019) 19 *African Human Rights Law Journal* 85.

[295] M.C. Bassiouni, 'Challenges to International Criminal Justice and International Criminal Law' in W. Schabas (ed.), *The Cambridge Companion to International Criminal Law* (CUP 2015) 353–391, 380, 388; A.A. Cançado Trindade, *International Law for Humankind: Towards a New Jus Gentium* (3rd edn., Nijhoff 2020) 235.

[296] A.A. Cançado Trindade, *International Law for Humankind: Towards a New Jus Gentium* (3rd edn., Nijhoff 2020) 235. See: ICC Statute, preamble.

[297] In addition to the ICC's jurisdiction being complementary to that of States, it has been supplemented by the creation of 'hybrid' or 'internationalized' tribunals in different parts of the world to deal with specific situations, such as the Special Panels for East Timor, the Special Court for Sierra Leone, the Extraordinary Chambers of Cambodia, the UN-administered Courts of Kosovo, and the Extraordinary African Chambers of Senegal. See: R. Dubler and M. Kalyk, *Crimes Against Humanity in the 21st Century: Law, Practice and Threats to International Peace and Security* (Brill 2018), chapter 5.

2.6 FURTHER REFLECTIONS: TIME AND THE INTERNATIONAL LAW OF HUMAN RIGHTS

As this chapter reveals, the formation and expansion of the international law of human rights cannot be dissociated from its temporal dimension; this is especially evidenced by the development of innovative forms of protection of human beings as a response to the emergence of new threats. The search for new legal solutions presupposes knowledge of past approaches and of the historical evolution of the international law of human rights as an open and dynamic legal system. Nonetheless, the relationship between the law and time requires much more attention than that dispensed to it thus far.[298]

The evolving international law of human rights is infused by the major enigma that permeates the existence of all subjects of law: the passage of time.[299] In this respect, Paul Reuter, legal counsel to Cambodia (Kămpŭchéa) in the case of the *Temple of Preah Vihear* before the International Court of Justice, had stated:

> Time exerts in fact a powerful influence in the establishment and the consolidation of juridical situations ... First of all, the duration of the time depends on the matters. ... A second element ought to be taken into account, we would be prepared to call it 'the density' of time. The time of men is not the time of the stars. What makes the time of men, is the density of the real events or of the eventual events which may have occurred. And what makes the density of the human time as regarded at the juridical level, is the density, the multitude of the juridical acts that have occurred or that could have occurred.[300]

Reflecting on such a statement, within the context of a case before the Inter-American Court, Judge Cançado Trindade said:

> The time of human beings is certainly not the time of the stars, in more than one sense. The time of the stars – I would venture to add – besides being an unfathomable mystery which has always accompanied human existence from the beginning until its end, is indifferent to legal solutions devised by the human mind; and the time of human beings, applied to their legal solutions as an element which integrates them, not seldom leads to situations which defy their own logic ... One specific aspect, however, appears to suggest a sole point of contact, or common denominator, between them: the time of the stars is inexorable; the time of human beings, albeit only conventional, is, like that of the stars, implacable...[301]

---

[298] IACtHR, *Blake v. Guatemala*. Merits. Judgment of January 24, 1998. Series C No. 36, separate opinion of Judge Cançado Trindade para. 4.

[299] A.A. Cançado Trindade, *International Law for Humankind: Towards a New Jus Gentium* (3rd edn., Nijhoff 2020) 33.

[300] ICJ, *Temple of Preah Vihear (Cambodia v. Thailand), ICJ Reports (1962), Pleadings, Oral Arguments, Documents*, vol. II, pp. 203 and 205. Translated in IACtHR, *Blake v. Guatemala*. Merits. Judgment of January 24, 1998. Series C No. 36, separate opinion of Judge Cançado Trindade p. 3 (fn. 6).

[301] IACtHR, *Blake v. Guatemala*. Merits. Judgment of January 24, 1998. Series C No. 36, separate opinion of Judge Cançado Trindade para. 6.

> ICJ, *Case concerning the Temple of Preah Vihear (Cambodia v. Thailand)*, Merits, Judgment of 15 June 1962, I.C. J. Reports 1962, p. 6.
>
> The case of the Temple of Preah Vihear was about a territorial dispute between Cambodia and Thailand (Prathet Thai) concerning sovereignty over the territory surrounding the ruins of the Temple of Preah Vihear, an ancient sanctuary of pilgrimage and worship for Cambodians. The ICJ ruled in favour of Cambodia (p. 15), following the interpretation and application of the Franco-Siamese Treaty of 1904, which established the frontier between Cambodia and Thailand (then Siam). The Court afforded binding character to a map based on the work of a Mixed Delimitation Commission set up by the mentioned treaty, which showed the Temple on the Cambodian side of the boundary (pp. 23–27). Given that the ICJ found the Temple to be situated in Cambodian territory, it ordered Thailand to withdraw any military or police forces stationed in or around the temple, as well as to restore to Cambodia any objects removed from the ruins of the Temple since 1954 (p. 37).

But, while time might be unfathomable and mysterious, the international law of human rights has engaged with time in manifold ways. A paradigmatic illustration of the connection between time and this legal regime is the notion of the 'potential' victim.[302] A concept present in multiple decisions adopted by international monitoring bodies, where attention has been drawn to the possibility of harm which may appear in the future.[303] A clear example of potential victims appears when States have in place domestic legislation that is incompatible with their obligations under the international law of human rights. International bodies have ruled that the mere existence of such legislation entails a violation of States' human rights obligations, even if the contentious domestic norms have not been applied yet and caused direct harm.[304] Another important appearance of the notion of potential victim takes place when individuals face an imminent and real risk of serious and irreversible harm to their rights. Most international monitoring bodies are empowered to instruct States the adoption of urgent measures—called 'interim', 'precautionary', or 'provisional' measures—in those circumstances.[305] This protective power entails an order addressed at a State to take urgent action to avoid the materialization of

---

[302] IACtHR, *Blake v. Guatemala*. Merits. Judgment of January 24, 1998. Series C No. 36, separate opinion of Judge Cançado Trindade para. 4.

[303] A.A. Cançado Trindade, *International Law for Humankind: Towards a New Jus Gentium* (3rd edn., Nijhoff 2020) 34.

[304] See, among many: ECtHR, *Dudgeon v. the United Kingdom*, 22 October 1981, Series A no. 45; IACtHR, *Suárez Rosero v. Ecuador*. Merits. Judgment of November 12, 1997. Series C No. 35.

[305] CERD, Rules of Procedure, CERD/C/35/Rev.3, r. 94; CCPR, Rules of Procedure, CCPR/C/3/Rev.12, r. 94; CAT, Rules of Procedure, CAT/C/3/Rev.6, r. 114; OP-CEDAW, Art. 5; ICPPED, Art. 31.4; ECtHR, Rules of the Court (10 February 2023), r. 39; IACHR, Rules of Procedure, Art. 25.1; ACHR, Art. 63.2; ACHPR, Rules of Procedure, r. 100; African Court Protocol, Art. 27.

the imminent irreparable damage to the rights of the person, given the situation of extreme gravity and urgency.[306] Thus, the international law of human rights endeavours to be anticipatory in the regulation of social facts, attempting to avoid harm from even occurring, with a clear awareness of the relevance of the preventive dimension of law.[307]

A further significant link between time and the international law of human rights is evidenced by the convergent case law of regional human rights courts on the interpretation of human rights treaties as 'living instruments', which accompany the evolution of times and of the circumstances in which the protected rights are exercised—a topic further discussed in **Section 3.1.1.1**.[308] While the 'living instrument' doctrine has become best-known for its development by the European Court of Human Rights, its origin can be found in an *obiter dictum* of the International Court of Justice, in its 1971 advisory opinion on Namibia. There, in reference to the Covenant of the League of Nations, the Court affirmed that 'an international instrument has to be interpreted and applied within the framework of the entire legal system prevailing at the time of the interpretation'.[309] A paradigmatic illustration of the evolutive interpretation of human rights norms can be found in the advisory opinion rendered by the Inter-American Court when asked by México about minimum guarantees individuals have in foreign States, when facing judicial proceedings. Within the context of its opinion, the Court confirmed that the right to consular assistance held by a person when deprived of their liberty in a foreign State, provided by the 1963 Vienna Convention on Consular Relations, had evolved to become part of the right to a fair trial that assists every person worldwide under the international law of human rights.[310] As affirmed by Judge Cançado Trindade in the context of that opinion: 'The evolution of the international norms of protection has been, in its turn, fostered by new and constant valuations which emerge and flourish from the basis of human society, and which are naturally reflected in the process of the evolutive interpretation of human rights treaties.'[311]

---

[306] See, among many: ECtHR, *F.H. v. Sweden*, App. no. 32621/06, 20 January 2009; IACtHR, *Matter of James et al. regarding Trinidad and Tobago*. Provisional Measures. Order of the Inter-American Court of Human Rights of May 25, 1999.

[307] A.A. Cançado Trindade, *International Law for Humankind: Towards a New Jus Gentium* (3rd edn., Nijhoff 2020) 43.

[308] See, among many: ECtHR, *Tyrer v. the United Kingdom*, 25 April 1978, § 31, Series A no. 26; ECtHR, *Marckx v. Belgium*, 13 June 1979, § 41, Series A no. 31; ECtHR, *Airey v. Ireland*, 9 October 1979, § 26, Series A no. 32.

[309] ICJ, *Legal Consequences for States of the Continued Presence of South Africa in Namibia (South West Africa) notwithstanding Security Council Resolution 276 (1970)*, Advisory Opinion, I.C.J. Reports 1971, p. 16, para. 53.

[310] IACtHR, *The Right to Information on Consular Assistance in the Framework of the Guarantees of the due Process of Law*. Advisory Opinion OC-16/99 of October 1, 1999. Series A No.16.

[311] IACtHR, *The Right to Information on Consular Assistance in the Framework of the Guarantees of the due Process of Law*. Advisory Opinion OC-16/99 of October 1, 1999. Series A No.16, concurring opinion of Judge Cançado Trindade para. 15.

> **ICJ, *Legal Consequences for States of the Continued Presence of South Africa in Namibia (South West Africa) notwithstanding Security Council Resolution 276 (1970)*, Advisory Opinion, I.C.J. Reports 1971, p. 16.**
>
> To fully understand the Advisory Opinion rendered by the ICJ, it is essential to comprehend the context of its adoption. On 17 December 1920, the territory of South-West Africa (Namibia) was placed under the administration of South Africa by the Council of the League of Nations. While the Mandatory State (South Africa) was to have full power of administration over the territory under mandate, it was under the obligation to promote the well-being and social progress of the inhabitants of the territory. Despite the dissolution of the League of Nations in 1946, in a previous Advisory Opinion (of 11 July 1950), the ICJ had found that the administration of the territory was not to be considered terminated. It was on 27 October 1966 that the United Nations General Assembly decided the termination of the mandate for South-West Africa (Resolution 2145(XXI)). On its part, in 1969, the Security Council called upon South Africa to immediately withdraw its administration from the Territory (Resolution 264) and, in January 1970, declared that the continued presence of the South African authorities in Namibia was illegal and that all acts taken by South Africa concerning Namibia after the termination of the Mandate were illegal and invalid (Resolution 276).
>
> Later that year, the Security Council requested an Advisory Opinion of the ICJ regarding the legal consequences for States of the continued presence of South Africa in Namibia. The Court rendered its Advisory Opinion on 21 June 1971. It found that the continued presence of South Africa in Namibia was illegal and, therefore, South Africa was under an obligation to withdraw its administration immediately. It also affirmed that all UN Member States were under the obligation to recognize the illegality of South Africa's presence in Namibia, and the invalidity of its acts on behalf of or concerning Namibia. Consequently, States were to refrain from any acts implying recognition of the legality of, or lending support or assistance to, such presence and administration. The Court also stated that even States that were not Members of the UN should provide assistance to the actions of the organization with regard to Namibia.

It is in the nature of the international law of human rights to accompany the progress of society, adapting to provide protection to emerging needs of the individual. With its constant development, this branch of international law is expected to reflect the evolving fundamental values shared by the international community and to respond to the needs and aspirations of humankind as a whole.[312] However, this statement should not be confused with a belief in the existence of a predetermined path through which the law will evolve in time. On the contrary, as lucidly expressed by Antonio Machado: 'Wanderer, there is no path; the path is made as you wander.'[313] What can be argued is that the development of human rights norms, and of their interpretation, imposes upon States and monitoring bodies the duty to continuously advance the scope of the protection of human rights. Neither States nor supervisory bodies should allow

---

[312] A.A. Cançado Trindade, *International Law for Humankind: Towards a New Jus Gentium* (3rd edn., Nijhoff 2020) 51.

[313] Translation from the Spanish original: 'Caminante, no hay camino; se hace camino al andar'. See: A. Machado, *Poesías Completas* (Espasa-Calpe 1989) 575.

themselves to halt the progress of the international protection of human rights.[314] The aim of the international law of human rights is to provide, in time, and ever-increasing protection of individuals in all circumstances.

> **IACtHR, *The Right to Information on Consular Assistance in the Framework of the Guarantees of the due Process of Law*. Advisory Opinion OC-16/99 of October 1, 1999. Series A no. 16.**
>
> This Advisory Opinion was rendered by the Inter-American Court of Human Rights following a request from México. The application concerned the issue of minimum judicial guarantees and due process of law in cases dealing with the death penalty against foreign nationals, when the State had not informed the defendant of their right to communicate with and seek assistance from the consular authorities of the State of which they are nationals (para. 2). The twelve questions put to the Court involved the interpretation of six different international instruments, including the 1963 Vienna Convention on Consular Relations (para. 33), technically not a human rights treaty. Nevertheless, the Court affirmed that Article 36 of such Convention actually conferred rights upon detained foreign national (para. 87). The Court stated that the right to information on consular assistance established in such a provision should be considered part of the due process of law, when a foreign national is subject to criminal prosecution (paras. 122–124). Moreover, the Court emphasized that if the criminal trial of a foreign national carries the imposition of the death penalty and the right to consular assistance had not been provided, then complying with the sentence would amount to an arbitrary deprivation of life (para. 137).

2.7 CONCLUSION

The twentieth century has been marked by the tragic companionship of extraordinary scientific and technological progress with unparalleled destruction, cruelty, and deprivation.[315] It is within this context that the international law of human rights has emerged and developed. As asserted by Judge Cançado Trindade:

> it is certain that the twentieth century was the stage ... of cruelties perpetrated against the human person in an unprecedented scale, it is also certain that this has generated a reaction – likewise unprecedented – against those abuses, as a manifestation of the awakening of the universal juridical conscience to the urgent needs of protection of the human being.[316]

This chapter has traced the development experienced by the international protection of human rights throughout the second half of the twentieth century and the beginning

---

[314] IACtHR, *Sawhoyamaxa Indigenous Community v. Paraguay*. Merits, Reparations, and Costs. Judgment of March 29, 2006. Series C No. 146, separate opinion of Judge A.A. Cançado Trindade para. 71.

[315] See: B. Russell, 'Knowledge and Wisdom' in H. Peterson (ed.) *Essays in Philosophy* (2nd edn., Pocket Library 1960) 498–502; Z. Bauman, *Modernity and the Holocaust* (Cornell University Press 1992) 6–18; K. Popper, *The Lesson of This Century* (Routledge 1997) 51–55.

[316] A.A. Cançado Trindade, 'The International Law of Human Rights at the Dawn of the XXIst Century' (1999) 3 *Cursos Euromediterráneos Bancaja de Derecho Internacional* 145, 212–213.

of the twenty-first, starting with the debates surrounding the adoption of the Universal Declaration of Human Rights in 1948. It has shown that the recurrence of atrocities in the past few decades has not hindered the progress of the international law of human rights, but actually indicated a path to follow. The discussions about the need to improve the protection of the human person in all circumstances, ensued in worldwide stages in UN-sponsored conferences, provided visibility to the urgency of continuously improving human rights protection. As discussed in the chapter, this protection has evolved and expanded not only within the international law of human rights *stricto sensu*, but also through the convergence of other international law regimes. The horrors of the Second World War acted as a catalyst for the development and strengthening of different branches of international law that came to offer protection to the human person in times of peace and war. Furthermore, the atrocity of that war, and of others that followed, inspired the desire to continuously provide legal redress for the grave suffering caused to humans everywhere and the need to tackle impunity, bringing both States and individuals to justice to determine their respective accountability.

The frequent and successive abuses against human beings in different latitudes is forcing us to continuously reflect on how to contribute to the development of the protection of individuals worldwide. Hence, the chapter came to an end with some brief reflections about the interrelationship between time and the international law of human rights. Far from attempting to exhaust such an important topic, the discussion acted instead as an invitation to continue deepening the study of the complex connexions between time and law.

FURTHER READING

BURKE, R., *Decolonization and the Evolution of International Human Rights* (University of Pennsylvania Press 2010).

CANÇADO TRINDADE, A.A., *International Law for Humankind: Towards a New Jus Gentium* (3rd edn., Nijhoff 2020).

CANÇADO TRINDADE, A.A., *Tratado de Direito Internacional dos Direitos Humanos: Volume I* (2nd edn., SAFE 2003).

GLENDON, M.A., *A World Made New: Eleanor Roosevelt and the Universal Declaration of Human Rights* (Random House 2001).

GOODALE, M. (ed.), *Letters to the Contrary: A Curated History of the UNESCO Human Rights Survey* (Stanford University Press 2018).

HUMPHREY, J.P., *Human Rights & the United Nations: A Great Adventure* (Transnational Publishers 1984).

LAUREN, P.G., The Evolution of International Human Rights: Visions Seen (3rd edn., PENN 2011).

MORSINK, J., *The Universal Declaration of Human Rights: Origins, Drafting, and Intent* (University of Pennsylvania Press 1999).

NORMAND, R. and ZAIDI, S., *Human Rights at the UN: The Political History of Universal Justice* (Indiana University Press 2008).

PINTO, M., *Temas de Derechos Humanos* (2nd edn., Del Puerto 2009).

3

THE NORMATIVE FRAMEWORK OF HUMAN RIGHTS UNDER INTERNATIONAL LAW

3.1 SOURCES

As discussed in **Section 2.1**, the international law of human rights is a legal system that is endowed with its own autonomy and specificity, but which nonetheless belongs to the wide domain of public international law. Therefore, the so-called formal sources of the international law of human rights; that is, the means by which the norms of this legal system are created, modified, and replaced, are those of public international law and, as such, can be found enumerated in Article 38 of the Statute of the International Court of Justice (ICJ). This provision, virtually identical to the one originally drafted for the Statute of the Permanent Court of International Justice (PCIJ),[1] enumerates the sources to be used by the International Court of Justice when adjudging a dispute. Given that the provision expressly states that the Court's function is to decide the disputes submitted to it 'in accordance with international law',[2] it is generally accepted that those mentioned in the article are indeed the sources of international law. These sources are: international treaties; international custom; the general principles of law ('recognized by civilized nations'); and, as subsidiary means for determining rules of law, judicial decisions and the teachings of the most highly qualified publicists of the various nations.[3] However, as indicated by the International Court of Justice itself, this enumeration of formal sources is by no means exhaustive.[4]

---

[1] A.A. Cançado Trindade, *International Law for Humankind: Towards a New Jus Gentium* (3rd edn., Nijhoff 2020) 113.

[2] Statute of the International Court of Justice (adopted 26 June 1945, entered into force 24 October 1945) 33 UNTS 993.

[3] To this, Art. 38.2 of the Statute of the ICJ adds the power of the Court to decide a case *ex aequo et bono*, when the Parties to the dispute agree to that.

[4] A.A. Cançado Trindade, *International Law for Humankind: Towards a New Jus Gentium* (3rd edn., Nijhoff 2020) 116.

3.1.1 TREATIES

International treaties are, in quantitative terms, the principal source of obligations under the international law of human rights. Although the names of the treaties celebrated by States aimed at the international protection of human rights vary significantly—Conventions, Covenants, Protocols, Charters—they all designate international binding agreements concluded in writing between States and which are governed by international law, in the terms of the 1969 Vienna Convention of the Law of Treaties (VCLT).[5] Following their entry into force, States are bound to comply with the international obligations established by the treaties they have ratified—or acceded to, in the case of treaties whose text had already been adopted.

However, since treaty obligations are dependent on the willingness of States to become Parties to treaties, the strength of the protection they provide is based on the level of ratification of these international instruments. Furthermore, the actual degree of protection offered by a given treaty would also depend on the number and scope of the reservations States have appended when becoming Parties to the treaties. As further discussed in **Section 3.1.1.2**, when it comes to multilateral treaties, especially human rights ones, there is a clear tension between promoting participation and preserving the integrity of their obligations;[6] while a strict system of reservations can affect the level of participation, a flexible system could lead to widely ratified treaties at the expense of sacrificing the integrity of the obligations that spring from them.[7]

The proliferation of human rights treaties led to the creation of an international system for the protection of human rights with concrete obligations upon States concerning the treatment of individuals within their respective jurisdictions. As discussed in **Section 2.2.2**, following the proclamation of the 1948 Universal Declaration of Human Rights, a series of treaties were adopted under the auspices of the United Nations (UN), establishing what can be called the spine of a universal regime for the protection of the human person. As further explained in **Chapter 5**, nine of the treaties adopted within the framework of the UN instituted a system for supervising compliance with the obligations emanating from them through monitoring bodies. To this, we can add the development of regional human rights systems in the Americas, Europe, and Africa,[8] also established by constitutive treaties, which put in place international courts for supervising compliance with treaty obligations (see **Chapter 6**, **Chapter 7**, and **Chapter 8**).

---

[5] Vienna Convention on the Law of Treaties (adopted 23 May 1969, entered into force 27 January 1980) 1155 UNTS 331, Art. 2.1.a.

[6] ICJ, *Reservations to the Convention on Genocide*, Advisory Opinion, ICJ Reports 1951, p. 15.

[7] C. Redgwell, 'Universality or integrity? Some Reflections on Reservations to General Multilateral Treaties' (1993) 64 *British Year Book of International Law* 245, 279; A. Pellet, 'Reservations to Treaties and the Integrity of Human Rights' in S. Sheeran and N. Rodley (eds), *Routledge Handbook of International Human Rights Law* (Routledge 2013) 323–338, 323.

[8] And the incipient development of systems in other regions of the world, such as under the League of Arab States and the Association of Southeast Asian Nations.

Human rights treaties differ to some extent from traditional international treaties. As stated by the Inter-American Court of Human Rights:

> modern human rights treaties ... are not multilateral treaties of the traditional type concluded to accomplish the reciprocal exchange of rights for the mutual benefit of the contracting States. Their object and purpose is the protection of the basic rights of individual human beings irrespective of their nationality, both against the State of their nationality and all other contracting States. In concluding these human rights treaties, the States can be deemed to submit themselves to a legal order within which they, for the common good, assume various obligations, not in relation to other States, but towards all individuals within their jurisdiction.[9]

An important consequence of the particular character of human rights treaties is that States cannot invoke the breach of treaty obligations by another Party as a justification for suspending or terminating the operation of said treaty.[10] The prohibition of the invocation of reciprocity as a subterfuge for non-compliance with humanitarian conventional obligations is asserted in unequivocal terms by the 1969 VCLT.[11] This is further strengthened by the assertion, in the preamble of the VCLT,[12] of the principle of universal respect and observance of human rights, to be taken into account in the interpretation of the Vienna Convention itself.[13] Thus, it becomes evident that considerations of a superior general interest (or public order), which transcend the individual interests of Contracting Parties, should guide the interpretation and application of human rights treaties.[14] As emphasized by the European Court of Human Rights, human rights treaties impose upon the Parties 'objective obligations', allowing all Contracting States to require the observance of these obligations without having to justify an interest deriving, for example, from the fact that a measure they complain of has prejudiced one of their own nationals.[15] A new vision of the relations between public power and the human being underpins the application and interpretation of human rights treaties, which can be traced, ultimately, to the recognition that human beings are the *raison d'être* of the State, and not vice-versa.[16]

---

[9] IACtHR, 'Other treaties' subject to the consultative jurisdiction of the Court (Art. 64 American Convention on Human Rights). Advisory Opinion OC-1/82 of September 24, 1982. Series A no. 1, para. 29.

[10] IACtHR, *Caesar v. Trinidad and Tobago*. Merits, Reparations and Costs. Judgment of March 11, 2005. Series C No. 123, separate opinion of Judge A.A. Cançado Trindade para. 57.

[11] VCLT, Art. 60.5.   [12] VCLT, preamble.

[13] IACtHR, *Caesar v. Trinidad and Tobago*. Merits, Reparations and Costs. Judgment of March 11, 2005. Series C No. 123, separate opinion of Judge A.A. Cançado Trindade para. 65. See also: E. Schwelb, 'The Law of Treaties and Human Rights' in W.M. Reisman and B.H. Weston (eds.) *Toward World Order and Human Dignity: Essays in Honor of M.S. McDougal* (Free Press 1976) 262–290, 263, 265.

[14] IACtHR, *Caesar v. Trinidad and Tobago*. Merits, Reparations and Costs. Judgment of March 11, 2005. Series C No. 123, separate opinion of Judge A.A. Cançado Trindade para. 6. See also: A.A. Cançado Trindade, *A Proteção Internacional dos Direitos Humanos—Fundamentos Jurídicos e Instrumentos Básicos* (Saraiva 1991) 11–12.

[15] ECtHR, *Ireland v. the United Kingdom*, 18 January 1978, § 239, Series A no. 25.

[16] IACtHR, *Blake v. Guatemala*. Reparations and Costs. Judgment of January 22, 1999. Series C No. 48, separate opinion of Judge A.A. Cançado Trindade, para. 33.

3.1.1.1 Treaty interpretation

As with any other international treaty, when it comes to the interpretation of human rights treaties, the pertinent provisions of the 1969 VCLT appear as the first resource.[17] In Article 31, the VCLT details the general (and customary) rule for the interpretation of international treaties, which encompasses four elements to be applied simultaneously. According to this provision, a treaty shall be interpreted in good faith, in accordance with the ordinary meaning of its terms (literal interpretation) in their context (systemic interpretation), and in the light of the object and purpose of the treaty (teleological interpretation).[18] However, the process of interpretation of human rights treaties presents particular characteristics that distinguish it from that of traditional treaties, contributing to a phenomenon that can be labelled the *humanization* of the law of treaties.[19]

The different monitoring bodies established to supervise compliance with human rights treaties, from the regional courts to the United Nations treaty bodies, have developed a series of principles and methods aimed at the specific interpretation of this type of treaties. These guidelines take into account the special nature of human rights treaties discussed earlier and stress the need to seek the fulfilment of their object and purpose, which is the protection of the basic rights of individual human beings. The four main principles developed are the following: a) the principle of effective protection (or *effet utile*); b) the principle of 'autonomous meaning'; c) the principle of 'evolutive interpretation'; and d) the *pro homine* principle.[20]

The principle of effective interpretation establishes that, given the importance of the object and purpose of human rights treaties, the process of interpretation must place a special emphasis on ensuring the effective protection of these rights.[21] As affirmed by the European Court more than three decades ago: 'the object and purpose of the Convention as an instrument for the protection of individual human beings require that its provisions be interpreted and applied so as to make its safeguards practical and effective.'[22] Similarly, the Inter-American Court, in its first ruling in a contentious case

---

[17] M. Fitzmaurice, 'Interpretation of Human Rights Treaties' in D. Shelton (ed.), *The Oxford Handbook of International Human Rights Law* (OUP 2013) 739–771, 739, 757.

[18] VCLT, Art. 31. See also: M. Bos, 'Theory and Practice of Treaty Interpretation' (1980) 27 *Netherlands International Law Review* 1; A. Orakhelashvili, *The Interpretation of Acts and Rules in Public International Law* (OUP 2008), chapter 10.

[19] IACtHR, *Caesar v. Trinidad and Tobago*. Merits, Reparations and Costs. Judgment of March 11, 2005. Series C No. 123, separate opinion of Judge A.A. Cançado Trindade paras. 34 and 39. See also: M. Fitzmaurice, 'Interpretation of Human Rights Treaties' in D. Shelton (ed.), *The Oxford Handbook of International Human Rights Law* (OUP 2013) 739–771.

[20] IACtHR, *Blake v. Guatemala*. Reparations and Costs. Judgment of January 22, 1999. Series C No. 48, separate opinion of Judge A.A. Cançado Trindade para. 33; IACtHR, *Caesar v. Trinidad and Tobago*. Merits, Reparations and Costs. Judgment of March 11, 2005. Series C No. 123, separate opinion of Judge A.A. Cançado Trindade para. 7.

[21] A.A. Cançado Trindade, *International Law for Humankind: Towards a New Jus Gentium* (3rd edn., Nijhoff 2020) 429–430; L. Lixinski, 'Treaty Interpretation by the Inter-American Court of Human Rights: Expansionism at the Service of the Unity of International Law' (2010) 21 *European Journal of International Law* 585, 589.

[22] ECtHR, *Soering v. the United Kingdom*, 7 July 1989, § 87, Series A no. 161. See also: ECtHR, *Artico v. Italy*, 13 May 1980, § 33, Series A no. 37.

stated: 'The Convention must ... be interpreted so as to give it its full meaning and to enable the system for the protection of human rights entrusted to the Commission and the Court to attain its "appropriate effects".'[23]

Moreover, while the VCLT establishes that the terms of a treaty should be interpreted according to their ordinary meaning, the terms in a human rights treaty are assumed to have an 'autonomous meaning'. That is to say, the meaning of the terms employed by human rights is autonomous with respect to the meaning given to those terms by the domestic law of States.[24] There is strong agreement among different monitoring bodies on this point, from the Human Rights Committee to the European and Inter-American regional courts. Importantly, the principle of 'autonomous meaning' contributes to a harmonious interpretation of different human rights treaties; hence, establishing a common pattern of behaviour for the Contracting States in terms of the protection of rights under their respective jurisdictions.[25]

As famously proclaimed by the European Court of Human Rights in the *Tyrer v. United Kingdom* case, human rights treaties are 'living instruments' that 'must be interpreted in the light of present-day conditions',[26] so as to accompany the evolving social reality in which human rights are exercised by individuals.[27] This rule of dynamic or evolutive interpretation has become paramount when it comes to human rights treaties, having been subsequently endorsed by other human rights monitoring bodies.[28] It is possible to argue that the evolutive interpretation of human rights treaties actually imposes, upon both States Parties and monitoring bodies, the duty to continuously advance the scope of the protection of human rights. Following the dynamic interpretation of human rights treaties, supervisory bodies should not allow themselves to halt their own case law and lower the level of protection already reached. The international law of human rights is a legal system of protection and, as such, it should be considered incompatible with the idea of diminishing standards.[29]

---

[23] IACtHR, *Velásquez Rodríguez v. Honduras*. Preliminary Objections. Judgment of June 26, 1987. Series C No. 1, para. 30.

[24] A.A. Cançado Trindade, *Tratado de Direito Internacional dos Direitos Humanos: Volume II* (Sérgio A. Fabris ed. 1999) 32–33.

[25] ECtHR, *König v. Germany*, 28 June 1978, §§ 88–89, Series A no. 27; CCPR, *Van Duzen v. Canada*, CCPR/C/15/D/50/1979 (1982), para. 10.2; IACtHR, *The Word 'Laws' in Article 30 of the American Convention on Human Rights*. Advisory Opinion OC-6/86 of May 9, 1986. Series A no. 6, paras 19–20. See also: A.A. Cançado Trindade, *Tratado de Direito Internacional dos Direitos Humanos: Volume II* (Sérgio A. Fabris ed. 1999) 33, 35.

[26] ECtHR, *Tyrer v. the United Kingdom*, 25 April 1978, § 31, Series A no. 26.

[27] The origin of this doctrine can be found in the *obiter dictum* of the International Court of Justice in its 1971 Advisory opinion on Namibia, in which—in reference to the Covenant of the League of Nations—the Court affirmed that 'an international instrument has to be interpreted and applied within the framework of the entire legal system prevailing at the time of the interpretation'. See: ICJ, *Legal Consequences for States of the Continued Presence of South Africa in Namibia (South West Africa) notwithstanding Security Council Resolution 276 (1970)*, Advisory Opinion, I.C.J. Reports 1971, p. 16, para. 53.

[28] IACtHR, *Interpretation of the American Declaration of the Rights and Duties of Man within the Framework of Article 64 of the American Convention on Human Rights*. Advisory Opinion OC-10/89 of July 14, 1989. Series A no.10, para. 37.

[29] IACtHR, *Sawhoyamaxa Indigenous Community v. Paraguay*. Merits, Reparations and Costs. Judgment of March 29, 2006. Series C No. 146, separate opinion of Judge A.A. Cançado Trindade para. 71.

> **ECtHR, *Tyrer v. the United Kingdom*, 25 April 1978, Series A no. 26.**
>
> The case concerned the use of corporal punishment—three strokes of the birch—and whether it amounted to a violation of Article 3 ECHR. The applicant was a fifteen-year-old resident of the Isle of Man who pleaded guilty to unlawful assault occasioning actual bodily harm to another pupil of the same school. He was sentenced to three strokes of the birch, in accordance with the relevant legislation, his appeal to the sentence being dismissed by the High Court. The application of the punishment was carried out. The applicant was made to take down his trousers and underpants and bend over a table; he was held by two policemen whilst a third administered the punishment. Both the Commission and the Court found a violation of the prohibition of degrading treatment contained in Article 3 of the Convention. The Court held that the punishment at stake did not amount to torture or inhuman treatment, but it could be considered a degrading punishment, given the element of humiliation associated with the type of punishment (para. 35). The Court asserted that the Convention was a 'living instrument' which had to be interpreted 'in the light of present-day conditions'; hence, its conclusion was influenced by the developments and commonly accepted standards in the penal policy of the Member States of the Council of Europe in this field (para. 31).

3.1.1.1.1 The pro homine *principle*

According to the *pro homine* principle, in order to establish the scope of exercise of a right the interpretation that shall always prevail is the most favourable one for the right-holder, and this is regardless of whether the actual norm providing for a wider scope of protection is to be found in an international treaty or in the domestic legislation of the State.[30] Even more, the prevalence of the most favourable interpretation of human rights norms is not restricted to the relation between international treaties and domestic law, but also extends to the harmonious interpretation of the different treaties to which a State is Party.[31] For instance, the American Convention on Human Rights establishes in its Article 29 that:

> No provision of this Convention shall be interpreted as:
>
> ...
>
> b.   restricting the enjoyment or exercise of any right or freedom recognized by virtue of the laws of any State Party or by virtue of another convention to which one of the said states is a party.[32]

---

[30] M. Pinto, 'El principio *pro homine*. Criterios de hermenéutica y pautas para la regulación de los derechos humanos' in M. Abregú and C. Courtis (eds.), *La aplicación de los tratados sobre derechos humanos por los tribunales locales* (Del Puerto 2004) 163–172, 163; M. Nowak, *UN Covenant on Civil and Political Rights: CCPR Commentary* (2nd edn., Engel 2005) xxvii. See also: IACtHR, *Enforceability of the Right to Reply or Correction*. Advisory Opinion OC-7/85 of August 29, 1986. Series A no. 7, separate opinion of Judge Piza E. para. 36; IACtHR, *Gender identity, and equality and non-discrimination with regard to same-sex couples*. Advisory Opinion OC-24/17 of November 24, 2017. Series A no. 24, para. 70.

[31] See, for instance: IACtHR, *Compulsory Membership in an Association Prescribed by Law for the Practice of Journalism*. Advisory Opinion OC-5/85 of November 13, 1985. Series A no. 5, para. 52.

[32] ACHR, Art. 29.b.

Similarly, the African Charter on Human and Peoples' Rights instructs one of its monitoring bodies—the African Commission—that, when interpreting the Charter, it:

> shall draw inspiration from international law on human and peoples' rights, particularly from the provisions of various African instruments on Human and Peoples' Rights, the Charter of the United Nations, the Charter of the Organisation of African Unity, the Universal Declaration of Human Rights, other instruments adopted by the United Nations and by African countries in the field of Human and Peoples' Rights, as well as from the provisions of various instruments adopted within the Specialised Agencies of the United Nations of which the Parties to the present Charter are members.[33]

Another implication of the *pro homine* principle is that the provisions in a human rights treaty that limit the exercise of a guaranteed right or allow States to derogate from their assumed obligations of protection need to be restrictively interpreted,[34] as explicitly established in different human rights treaties.[35] Human rights provisions leave no room for 'implied limitations';[36] the only limitations or restrictions permissible are those for which the human rights treaty itself makes express provision and these should be interpreted in a restrictive manner. Furthermore, a State cannot make use of the restriction clauses provided by a human rights treaty on a given right if a different treaty to which the State is also Party allows for lesser restrictions on such a right.[37] Successive human rights treaties can improve and strengthen—but never weaken or undermine—the protection of recognized human rights.[38]

Moreover, the concomitant interpretative work of the multiple international supervisory organs has reinforced the influence that human rights treaties have on one another. The existence of similar provisions in different human rights treaties means that the interpretation and application of the provisions from one treaty are used as inspiration for the interpretation of corresponding provisions of others.[39] This phenomenon, which has been labelled 'cross-fertilization', favours an increasing protection of human rights in all corners of the world, as supervisory organs take advantage of the interpretation concerning the scope of human rights undertaken by other monitoring bodies, carrying the degree of protection even further forward. While some

---

[33] ACHPR, Art. 60.

[34] IACtHR, *Judicial Guarantees in States of Emergency*. Advisory Opinion OC-9/87 of October 6, 1987. Series A no. 9, para. 38; CCPR, General Comment 29: States of Emergency, CCPR/C/21/Rev.1/Add.11 (2001), para. 4; IACtHR, *Caesar v. Trinidad and Tobago*. Merits, Reparations and Costs. Judgment of March 11, 2005. Series C No. 123, separate opinion of Judge A.A. Cançado Trindade para. 12.

[35] ICCPR, Art. 5.1; ICESCR, Art. 5.1; ECHR, Art. 17; ACHR, Art. 29.a.

[36] ECtHR, *Golder v. the United Kingdom*, 21 February 1975, § 44, Series A no. 18.

[37] IACtHR, *Caesar v. Trinidad and Tobago*. Merits, Reparations and Costs. Judgment of March 11, 2005. Series C No. 123, separate opinion of Judge A.A. Cançado Trindade para. 13.

[38] A.A. Cançado Trindade, 'Co-existence and Co-ordination of Mechanisms of International Protection of Human Rights (At Global and Regional Levels)' (1987) 202 *Recueil des Cours de l'Académie de Droit International de La Haye* 401; F. Salvioli, 'El desarrollo progresivo: elemento central de la perspectiva pro persona' (2020) 71 *Revista IIDH* 115, 152.

[39] IACtHR, *Caesar v. Trinidad and Tobago*. Merits, Reparations and Costs. Judgment of March 11, 2005. Series C No. 123, separate opinion of Judge A.A. Cançado Trindade para. 61.

international monitoring bodies are somewhat restrained in their observation of the developing protective case law of others,[40] other bodies, such as the African Court on Human and Peoples' Rights and Inter-American Court of Human Rights, have been eager to engage with the jurisprudence of multiple supervisory organs. Through this reciprocal cross-referring, these bodies are cooperatively constructing an expansive interpretation of human rights norms; hence, facilitating the creation of an international public order, based upon the respect for human rights in all circumstances.[41]

3.1.1.2 Reservations

A reservation can be defined as a statement made by a State when expressing its consent to be bound by a treaty with the aim of excluding or modifying the legal effect of certain provision of the treaty in its application to the reserving State.[42] The current system of treaty reservations set in place by the 1969 VCLT is of clear voluntarist character.[43] This system is based on a 1951 Advisory Opinion rendered by the International Court of Justice in 1951,[44] in which this Court affirmed that compatibility with the object and purpose of a treaty was the main criterion for determining the validity of a reservation, as the silence of the text could not be equated with a prohibition to append reservations.[45] The stance adopted by the ICJ endorsed the so-called 'Pan-American practice' aimed at reaching a certain balance between the integrity of the text of the treaty and the universality of participation in it.[46]

> **ICJ, *Reservations to the Convention on Genocide*,**
> **Advisory Opinion, ICJ Reports 1951, p. 15.**
>
> The General Assembly asked the Court three questions concerning the position of a State which attached reservations to its ratification or accession to the Convention on Genocide if other States, Parties to the same Convention, objected to these reservations. The Assembly asked the Court whether a reserving State can be considered Party to the Convention if other Parties have objected to the reservation and, if so, what are the legal effects of such reservations between the reserving State and the other Parties. The Court asserted that even when a treaty contains no provision on the subject of reservations—as is the case with the

---

[40] L. Hennebel, 'The Human Rights Committee' in F. Mégret and P. Alston (eds.), *The United Nations and Human Rights: A Critical Appraisal* (2nd edn., OUP 2020) 339–391, 377.

[41] IACtHR, *Caesar v. Trinidad and Tobago*. Merits, Reparations and Costs. Judgment of March 11, 2005. Series C No. 123, separate opinion of Judge A.A. Cançado Trindade para. 7.

[42] VCLT, Art. 2.1.d.

[43] IACtHR, *Caesar v. Trinidad and Tobago*. Merits, Reparations and Costs. Judgment of March 11, 2005. Series C No. 123, separate opinion of Judge A.A. Cançado Trindade para. 21.

[44] ICJ, *Reservations to the Convention on Genocide*, Advisory Opinion, ICJ Reports 1951, p. 15.

[45] This Advisory Opinion marked the gradual passage, in the matter of reservations to treaties, from the rule of unanimous approval by States Parties to the test of its compatibility with the object and purpose of the treaty. See: I.M. Sinclair, 'Vienna Conference on the Law of Treaties' (1970) 19 *International and Comparative Law Quarterly* 47.

[46] ICJ, *Reservations to the Convention on Genocide*, Advisory Opinion, ICJ Reports 1951, p. 15, p. 24.

> Genocide Convention—it does not follow that they are prohibited. It is the compatibility of the reservation with the object and purpose of the treaty which should act as the main criterion for determining the validity of a reservation. Consequently, the Court declined to give an absolute answer to the question: the appraisal of a reservation and the effect of objections that might be made to it depend upon the particular circumstances of each individual case. This answer also led to an equivocal answer to the second question: whether a State Party considers a reserving State as Party to the Convention would be dependent on whether it considers such reservations to be compatible or not with the object and purpose of the Convention.

In a similar vein, the VCLT allows for reservations to treaties when not explicitly or implicitly banned by the treaty in question, and as long as they are not incompatible with the object and purpose of the treaty.[47] However, the system in place fails to identify 'who ultimately ought to determine the permissibility or otherwise of a reservation, or to pronounce on its compatibility or otherwise with the object and purpose of the treaty at issue'.[48] This system of reservation appears inadequate for treaties whose beneficiaries are human beings and not the Contracting Parties,[49] which can be confirmed by the fact that human rights treaties have been particularly susceptible to reservations.[50] This system undermines the integrity of human rights treaties, leaving to the discretion of States the extent of their international obligations.[51] Already in the early 1980s, the Inter-American Court of Human Rights highlighted the problems with a mere transposition from the general system of reservations of the VCLT into the domain of the international protection of human rights;[52] an opinion also supported by the Human Rights Committee.[53]

---

[47] VCLT, Art. 19.

[48] IACtHR, *Caesar v. Trinidad and Tobago*. Merits, Reparations and Costs. Judgment of March 11, 2005. Series C No. 123, separate opinion of Judge A.A. Cançado Trindade para. 25.

[49] D. Shelton, 'State Practice on Reservations to Human Rights Treaties' (1983) 1 *Canadian Human Rights Yearbook* 205, 234; B. Clark, 'The Vienna Convention Reservations Regime and the Convention on Discrimination against Women' (1991) 85 *American Journal of International Law* 281, 316–318; T. Meron, *The Humanization of International Law* (Nijhoff 2006) 227.

[50] B. Clark, 'The Vienna Convention Reservations Regime and the Convention on Discrimination against Women' (1991) 85 *American Journal of International Law* 281, 320; H. Charlesworth and C. Chinkin, *The Boundaries of International Law: A Feminist Analysis* (2nd edn., Manchester University Press 2022) 103.

[51] IACtHR, *Caesar v. Trinidad and Tobago*. Merits, Reparations and Costs. Judgment of March 11, 2005. Series C No. 123, separate opinion of Judge A.A. Cançado Trindade, para. 27.

[52] In its second Advisory Opinion the Court dismissed the postponement of the entry into force of the American Convention by application of Art. 20(4) of the 1969 Vienna Convention. In its third Advisory Opinion the Court affirmed that the question of reciprocity as related to reservations did not fully apply *vis-à-vis* human rights treaties. See: IACtHR, *The Effect of Reservations on the Entry into Force of the American Convention on Human Rights*. Advisory Opinion OC-2/82 of September 24, 1982. Series A no. 2, para. 34; IACtHR, *Restrictions to the Death Penalty*. Advisory Opinion OC-3/83 of September 8, 1983. Series A no. 3, paras. 62–65.

[53] CCPR, General Comment 24: Issues Relating to Reservations Made upon Ratification or Accession to the Covenant or the Optional Protocols thereto, or in Relation to Declarations under Article 41 of the Covenant, CCPR/C/21/Rev.1/Add.6 (11 November 1994), para. 17.

The uncertainties surrounding the VCLT's system of reservations led the International Law Commission (ILC) to engage with the subject from 1993. In 1997, the ILC's debates focused on the question of the applicability of this system of reservations to human rights treaties in particular,[54] and the Draft Guidelines it adopted in 2007 contained a specific provision on reservations to general human rights treaties, as well as one concerning reservations to non-derogable rights.[55] Although the 'Guide to Practice on Reservations to Treaties' finally adopted by the ILC in 2011 did not provide precise guidelines for human rights treaties, they came to reaffirm the competence of the monitoring bodies established by treaties to assess, within the scope of their functions, the permissibility of reservations made to a treaty.[56]

The practice of different treaty monitoring bodies had already established these organs as the appropriate authority to decide on the compatibility of reservations with the object and purpose of the respective treaties, even when the latter does not expressly confer such a function upon them.[57] In 1998, the European Court of Human Rights decided the *Belilos* case,[58] in which it considered that an 'interpretative declaration'[59] made by Switzerland when ratifying the Convention actually amounted to a reservation of a general character and ruled it incompatible with the object and purpose of the Convention.[60] Following the lead of the European Court, the Inter-American Court also confirmed its ability to assess the validity of reservations made to the American Convention, rejecting attempts of States Parties to limit their obligations.[61] Similarly, the Human Rights Committee affirmed its capacity, as monitoring body of the International Covenant on Civil and Political Rights (ICCPR), to decide on the compatibility of reservations made by States Parties with the object and purpose of the treaty.[62] In agreement with the stance adopted by the mentioned courts,[63] the Committee asserted that the legal consequence of a reservation found to be incompatible with the object and purpose of a human rights treaty was the severance of the reservation from the State's

---

[54] Report of the International Law Commission, forty-ninth session (1997), A/52/10, para. 47.
[55] Report of the International Law Commission, fifty-ninth Session (2007), A/62/10, para. 104.
[56] ILC, 'Guide to Practice on Reservations to Treaties', A/66/10 (2011), guideline 3.2.
[57] IACtHR, *Caesar v. Trinidad and Tobago*. Merits, Reparations and Costs. Judgment of March 11, 2005. Series C No. 123, separate opinion of Judge A.A. Cançado Trindade, para. 33.
[58] ECtHR, *Belilos v. Switzerland*, 29 April 1988, Series A no. 132. See also: ECtHR, *Weber v. Switzerland*, 22 May 1990, Series A no. 177.
[59] An 'interpretative declaration' can be defined as a 'unilateral statement, however phrased or named, made by a State or an international organization, whereby that State or that organization purports to specify or clarify the meaning or scope of a treaty or of certain of its provisions'. See: ILC, Guide to Practice on Reservations to Treaties, Yearbook of the International Law Commission, 2011, vol. II, Part Two, para. 75(1.2).
[60] ECtHR, *Belilos v. Switzerland*, 29 April 1988, § 38–60, Series A no. 132.
[61] IACtHR, *Hilaire v. Trinidad and Tobago*. Preliminary Objections. Judgment of September 1, 2001. Series C No. 80, paras. 78–98; IACtHR, *Boyce et al. v. Barbados*. Preliminary Objection, Merits, Reparations and Costs. Judgment of November 20, 2007. Series C No. 169, para. 13–17.
[62] CCPR, General Comment 24: Issues Relating to Reservations Made upon Ratification or Accession to the Covenant or the Optional Protocols thereto, or in Relation to Declarations under Article 41 of the Covenant, CCPR/C/21/Rev.1/Add.6 (11 November 1994), para. 18.
[63] ECtHR, *Belilos v. Switzerland*, 29 April 1988, § 60, Series A no. 132; IACtHR, *Hilaire v. Trinidad and Tobago*. Preliminary Objections. Judgment of 1 September 2001. Series C No. 80, paras. 78–98.

manifestation to be bound by the treaty,[64] making it operative for the State without the benefit of the reservation.[65] This understanding of the effect of an impermissible reservation came to be (only) partially confirmed by the mentioned Guidelines from the ILC, as these provisions set a rebuttable presumption that the reserving State continues to be Party to the treaty, without benefiting from the invalid reservation, unless its intention not to be bound can be clearly established.[66]

> **ECtHR, *Belilos v. Switzerland*, 29 April 1988, Series A no. 132.**
>
> The case concerned a Swiss student who was fined by the police for allegedly taking part in a demonstration that lacked the relevant permission. She denied having taken part in the demonstration, but the Police Board concluded otherwise, confirming a reduced fine. Her judicial appeals were dismissed and she complained before the European Commission and Court of a violation of her right to be tried by an independent and impartial tribunal with full jurisdiction to determine questions both of law and of fact under Article 6 ECHR. Both the Commission and the Court found breaches of Article 6. The Court found two separate violations of Article 6: first, due to the legitimate doubts the applicant could have as to the independence and organizational impartiality of the Police Board, and, second, based on the insufficient judicial revision available of the Board's decisions (paras. 70–73). The Court recalled that its case law had established that conferring the prosecution and punishment of minor offences on administrative authorities was not inconsistent with the Convention, provided that such decisions were subject to appeal before a tribunal that offered the guarantees of Article 6, making it possible for any deficiencies in the earlier proceedings to be remedied.
>
> However, before the Court could examine the merits of the case it had to decide on the validity of the 'interpretative declaration' made by Switzerland when ratifying the Convention, which aimed to remove certain categories of proceedings from the ambit of Article 6 and would, if valid, render the case beyond the Court's jurisdiction. The Court ruled that the so-called declaration actually amounted to a reservation of a general character—couched in terms too vague or broad for it to be possible to determine their exact meaning and scope—which was incompatible with the object and purpose of the Convention (paras. 50–60).

It seems only suitable that the supervisory organs established by a treaty are considered empowered to decide on the validity of the reservations made by States Parties. The practice of these organs confirming this position is commendable, but an express

---

[64] CCPR, General Comment 24: Issues Relating to Reservations Made upon Ratification or Accession to the Covenant or the Optional Protocols thereto, or in Relation to Declarations under Article 41 of the Covenant, CCPR/C/21/Rev.1/Add.6 (11 November 1994), para. 18.

[65] A stance that was not happily received by a number of States, including France, the UK, and the USA. See: E. Baylis, 'General Comment 24: Confronting the Problem of Reservations to Human Rights Treaties' (1999) 17 *Berkeley Journal of International Law* 277, 318; K. Korkelia, 'New Challenges to the Regime of Reservations under the International Covenant on Civil and Political Rights' (2002) 13 *European Journal of International Law* 437, 462; H. Charlesworth and C. Chinkin, *The Boundaries of International Law: A Feminist Analysis* (2nd edn., Manchester University Press 2022) 111.

[66] ILC, 'Guide to Practice on Reservations to Treaties', A/66/10 (2011), guidelines 4.5.1 to 4.5.3.

provision in future human rights treaties would be the ideal solution to clear any doubts.[67] Such a step would be one among others that need to be taken to improve the current system of reservations for human rights treaties.[68] For instance, it would be important that future treaties include an express indication of the provisions not susceptible to reservations,[69] including those providing protection for non-derogable rights,[70] as a minimum requirement to become Party to a human rights treaty.[71] A further positive move would be to establish an obligation for States Parties to rectify any reservation considered non-permissible or incompatible with the object and purpose of the treaty,[72] as well as to withdraw any reservations made as soon as the domestic legal order has been harmonized with the international obligations assumed by ratifying a treaty.[73] Future human rights treaties should also consider following the example set by the International Convention on the Elimination of All Forms of Racial Discrimination (ICERD),[74] which provides for a collective system for the objection to reservations, as a safeguard of the integrity of the treaty. Treaties can also attribute to their depositaries the ability to request, from reserving States, information about the reasons behind their refusal to withdraw reservations appended to treaties. These developments concerning the system of reservations for human rights treaties would foster the development of the current process of *humanization* of international law, encompassing the domain of treaty law, traditionally so vulnerable to manifestations of State voluntarism.[75]

3.1.1.3 Denunciation

A denunciation can be defined as the act by which a Party seeks to terminate its participation in a treaty.[76] The VCLT determines that a treaty which contains no provision on the matter is not subject to denunciation, unless it can be established that

---

[67] IACtHR, *Caesar v. Trinidad and Tobago*. Merits, Reparations and Costs. Judgment of March 11, 2005. Series C No. 123, separate opinion of Judge A.A. Cançado Trindade paras. 39–40.

[68] A.A. Cançado Trindade, *International Law for Humankind: Towards a New Jus Gentium* (3rd edn., Nijhoff 2020) 440–441.

[69] See, for instance: Convention relating to the Status of Refugees (adopted 28 July 1951, entered into force 22 April 1954), 189 UNTS 137, Art. 42(1).

[70] On the already heavier onus of justification of reservations to non-derogable rights in general, and absolute prohibition in the case of those with *jus cogens* status, see: CCPR, General Comment 24: Issues Relating to Reservations Made upon Ratification or Accession to the Covenant or the Optional Protocols thereto, or in Relation to Declarations under Article 41 of the Covenant, CCPR/C/21/Rev.1/Add.6 (11 November 1994), para. 10.

[71] C. Redgwell, 'Universality or Integrity? Some Reflections on Reservations to General Multilateral Treaties' (1993) 64 *British Yearbook of International Law* 245, 281; A.A. Cançado Trindade, *International Law for Humankind: Towards a New Jus Gentium* (3rd edn., Nijhoff 2020) 440.

[72] A. Pellet, Second report on reservations to treaties, A/CN.4/477 and Add.1 (1996), para. 252.

[73] A.A. Cançado Trindade, *International Law for Humankind: Towards a New Jus Gentium* (3rd edn., Nijhoff 2020) 440–441.

[74] A system of two-thirds of the States Parties is set forth in that Convention, see: ICERD, Art. 20(2).

[75] IACtHR, *Caesar v. Trinidad and Tobago*. Merits, Reparations and Costs. Judgment of March 11, 2005. Series C No. 123, separate opinion of Judge A.A. Cançado Trindade paras. 34 and 39.

[76] A. Aust, *Handbook of International Law* (2nd edn., CUP 2010) 93. For an in-depth discussion of denunciation of human rights treaties, see: Y. Tyagi, 'The Denunciation of Human Rights Treaties' (2008) 79 *British Yearbook of International Law* 86.

the Parties intended to admit the possibility of denunciation or that the latter 'may be implied by the nature of the treaty'.[77] At the regional level, the European Convention provides that denunciation of the treaty is possible, but can only take place after a five-year period from the date on which the denouncing State became a Party and after six months' notice.[78] Moreover, the denunciation does not release the denouncing Party from its obligations under the Convention in respect of 'any act which, being capable of constituting a violation of such obligations, may have been performed by it before the date at which the denunciation became effective'.[79] As discussed in **Section 7.1.3**, there has only been one case of denunciation of the Convention—that of Greece in 1969 (to later re-join in 1974), while in the recent case of Russia, the State has ceased to be a Party to the Convention due to the termination of its membership of the Council of Europe.

The provision of the American Convention concerning denunciation is similar to that of the European regional treaty. Article 78 also establishes that denunciation is not allowed for a five-year period after becoming a Party, but it increases the notice period from six months to one year. Like the European Convention, it mandates that the denouncing State remains obliged by the Convention for any violation committed prior to the date on which the denunciation becomes effective. As further discussed in **Section 6.1.4.1**, this second paragraph of the provision became quite important, as two States have denounced the Convention but have still been brought to the Inter-American Court following their withdrawal. These were the cases of Trinidad and Tobago and Venezuela, which denounced the Convention, respectively, in 1998 and 2012.

As to the nine UN core treaties, five of them contain provisions allowing their denunciation following a one-year notice period.[80] On their part, ICCPR, the International Covenant on Economic, Social and Cultural Rights (ICESCR), the Convention on the Elimination of All Forms of Discrimination Against Women (CEDAW), and the International Convention for the Protection of All Persons from Enforced Disappearance (ICPPED) are silent on the subject of denunciation, which coincides with the approach adopted by the drafters of the African Charter on Human and Peoples' Rights and of the Arab Charter on Human Rights. The Human Rights Committee had the opportunity to analyse the meaning of the silence on denunciation of ICCPR.[81] Following the provisions of the VCLT, it affirmed that the Covenant should not be considered subject to denunciation unless it could be established that the Parties intended to admit the possibility of denunciation. The Committee emphasized that the

---

[77] VCLT, Art. 56.1.   [78] ECHR, Art. 58.1.   [79] ECHR, Art. 58.2.
[80] ICERD, Art. 21; UNCRC, Art. 52; UNCAT, Art. 31; ICRMW, Art. 89 (which also establishes a five-year minimum for a State Party to denounce); UNCRPD, Art. 48.
[81] The General Comment was adopted by the Human Rights Committee following an attempt by the Democratic People's Republic of Korea to denounce the ICCPR on 23 August 1997. The opinion of the Committee was mostly coincidental with the 'Aide Memoire' issued by the UN Secretary General on 23 September 1997, which affirmed that withdrawal from ICCPR could only proceed if it had the consent of all States Parties, following the general rules of the 1969 VCLT. See: E. Evatt, 'Democratic People's Republic of Korea and the ICCPR: Denunciation as an Exercise of the Right of Self-defence?' (1999) 5 *Australian Journal of Human Rights* 215. See also: C.N.467.1997.TREATIES-10 (12 November 1997).

absence of a provision concerning denunciation was certainly not an oversight by the drafters, evidenced by the fact that its First Optional Protocol, adopted on the same day, and ICERD, adopted a year before, both contain a provision allowing denunciation.[82] Concerning the possibility of an implicit right to denunciation based on the nature of the treaty, the Committee affirmed that ICCPR is clearly not a treaty of temporary character. Rather, the rights contained therein could be seen as codification, in treaty form, of universal rights enshrined in the Universal Declaration of Human Rights.[83] Therefore, the Committee concluded that States Parties are not allowed to withdraw from ICCPR.[84]

3.1.2 CUSTOMARY INTERNATIONAL LAW

Norms that bind States do not necessarily have to be based on the consent of each State bound by the norm,[85] as evidenced by the recognition of customary law as a source of international law. International custom appears defined in Article 38 of the ICJ Statute as 'evidence of a general practice accepted as law'.[86] This definition refers to the existence of the two constitutive elements of international custom,[87] an objective element, represented by the international practice itself, and the subjective element, the *opinio juris sive necessitatis*, which is the belief that such practice is performed in accordance with law and accepted as such.[88] Customary law is a rather complex source of international obligations. On the one hand, it can be a rather helpful tool to limit State voluntarism in the ambit of human rights, as rights that have acquired the status of customary law would bind States not Parties to treaties and would limit States' ability

---

[82] CCPR, General Comment 26: continuity of obligations to the International Covenant on Civil and Political Rights, CCPR/C/21/Rev.1/Add.8/Rev. (8 December 1997), paras. 1–2.

[83] CCPR, General Comment 26: continuity of obligations to the International Covenant on Civil and Political Rights, CCPR/C/21/Rev.1/Add.8/Rev. (8 December 1997), para. 3.

[84] Conversely, the First Optional Protocol to ICCPR admits denunciation, imposing a three-month notice period. The two States Parties that have denounced this treaty are Jamaica and Trinidad and Tobago (twice). Guyana had also denounced the treaty, but only to re-accede to it on the same day with a reservation. Such a practice, denunciation followed by accession with a reservation, had also been resorted to by Trinidad and Tobago in 1998, when it first denounced the Protocol. However, Trinidad and Tobago later again denounced the Protocol, when the Human Rights Committee found its reservation to be incompatible with the object and purpose of the treaty. See CCPR, *Rawle Kennedy v. Trinidad and Tobago*, 2 November 1999, Communication No. 845/1999; UN Doc. CCPR/C/67/D/845/1999, paras 6.2, 6.6, 6.7, 7. See also: P.R. Ghandhi, 'The Human Rights Committee and Reservations to the Optional Protocol' (2001) 8 *Canterbury Law Review* 13; Y. Tyagi, 'The Denunciation of Human Rights Treaties' (2008) 79 *British Yearbook of International Law* 86, 170–177.

[85] C.G. Weeramantry, *Universalising International Law* (Brill 2004) 226; G.R. Bandeira Galindo and C. Yip, 'Customary International Law and the Third World: Do Not Step on the Grass' (2017) 16 *Chinese Journal of International Law* 251, 254.

[86] Statute of the International Court of Justice (adopted 26 June 1945, entered into force 24 October 1945) 33 UNTS 993, Art. 38.1.b.

[87] Sketched by the PCIJ, as early as 1927. See: PCIJ, *S.S. Lotus (France v. Turkey)*, 1927 P.C.I.J. (ser. A) No. 10 (Sept. 7), p. 28.

[88] A.A. Cançado Trindade, *International Law for Humankind: Towards a New Jus Gentium* (3rd edn., Nijhoff 2020) 116.

to append reservations on certain provisions when becoming Parties to a treaty.[89] On the other hand, it should not be forgotten that, historically, international custom as a source of law has been of a rather anti-democratic nature, as its formation has served the interests and needs of a selected group of powerful European States.[90] An invitation to adopt a healthy degree of scepticism when assessing customary norms has been posed by Mohammed Bedjaoui, who reminds us that a norm is not necessarily good or fair merely for having been in place from time immemorial.[91]

Nowadays, it is possible to affirm that a number of obligations towards human rights have acquired customary status under international law. However, a difficult issue behind the customary character of certain human rights is their determination. To establish the existence of State practice (the objective element) it is necessary to observe the behaviour of States both within the domestic and the international spheres. The adoption of legislation that protects certain rights or decisions of the judiciary in that direction can provide evidence of State practice. The same can be said concerning the manifestations of States within international organizations, such as their voting pattern concerning specific resolutions; their engagement with the drafting of treaties and the manifestation of their will to become Parties; the tenor of speeches pronounced within international organizations; or arguments made when appearing before instances of international dispute settlement.[92] Perhaps more difficult is to determine the existence of the subjective element (*opinio juris*); the conviction that a certain practice is being performed to comply with a legal obligation, either existing or emerging. To establish the existence of *opinio juris*, the International Court of Justice has resorted to the content, conditions of adoption, and specific wording of resolutions adopted within the United Nations,[93] in particular by the General Assembly.[94] It can be hoped that, in the future, the process of formation of international custom will increasingly rely less on the repetitive State practice and more on the emergence of an *opinio juris communis*—a common conviction of all subjects of international law, including States, international organizations, individuals, and

---

[89] CCPR, General Comment 24: Issues Relating to Reservations Made upon Ratification or Accession to the Covenant or the Optional Protocols thereto, or in Relation to Declarations under Article 41 of the Covenant, CCPR/C/21/Rev.1/Add.6 (11 November 1994), para. 8.

[90] M. Bedjaoui, *Towards a New International Economic Order* (UNESCO 1979) 135; B.S. Chimni, 'Customary International Law: A Third World Perspective' (2018) 112 *American Journal of International Law* 1, 12, 17.

[91] M. Bedjaoui, *Towards a New International Economic Order* (UNESCO 1979) 134.

[92] T. Meron, *The Humanization of International Law* (Nijhoff 2006) 361–362, 365; H. Charlesworth and C. Chinkin, *The Boundaries of International Law: A Feminist Analysis* (2nd edn., Manchester University Press 2022) 63–65.

[93] ICJ, *Military and Paramilitary Activities in and against Nicaragua (Nicaragua v. United States of America)*. Merits, Judgment. I.C.J. Reports 1986, p. 14, paras. 188, 191, 202; ICJ, *Legality of the Threat or Use of Nuclear Weapons*, Advisory Opinion, 1. C.J. Reports 1996, p. 226, paras 70–73; ICJ, *Legal Consequences of the Separation of The Chagos Archipelago from Mauritius in 1965*, paras. 150–153.

[94] It is worth noting that when the Assembly decides to designate a resolution as a 'declaration', there is a clear intent to confer to such instrument a solemnity reserved to rare occasions in which principles of great and lasting importance are enunciated and, consequently, maximum compliance is expected by Member States. See: Memorandum by the Office of Legal Affairs on the 'Use of the Terms "Recommendation" and "Declaration"' (1962) (E/CN.4/L.610).

humankind as a whole. General norms that emanate from a common conscience would contribute to the universalization of international law.[95]

The Universal Declaration of Human Rights is usually considered a paradigmatic example of a non-binding international instrument whose provisions have evolved into customary norms. Originally adopted as a resolution by the General Assembly, the rights proclaimed in the Declaration can be said to have acquired the status of binding law.[96] Support for the understanding of the Universal Declaration as customary law has grown even stronger since 2006, with the establishment of the Human Rights Council, as the Universal Declaration of Human Rights became an explicit standard to evaluate compliance with human rights by all United Nation Member States. The creation of a system of Universal Periodic Review (discussed in **Section 4.3.2**) that makes use of the Universal Declaration as one of the standards for determining the fulfilment of human rights obligations seems to have put beyond debate the binding character of all rights protected by the Declaration.[97]

3.1.3 GENERAL PRINCIPLES OF LAW

The acceptance of general principles of law as a formal source of international law crystallized in 1920, during the debates of the Advisory Committee of Jurists, entrusted with the drafting of the Statute of the Permanent Court of International Justice (PCIJ).[98] The inclusion of these principles responded to the essential need of avoiding *non liquet* (unclear) situations, providing solutions to cases in which there might not be applicable treaty law and where customary norms might not have yet formed.[99] Sadly, a rather telling expression was used by both the Statutes of the PCIJ and the ICJ when enumerating this source of international law, which is referred to as 'general principles of the law *recognized by civilized nations*'.[100] This problematic expression is not only a

---

[95] A.A. Cançado Trindade, *International Law for Humankind: Towards a New Jus Gentium* (3rd edn., Nijhoff 2020) 139, 144; ICJ, *Obligations concerning Negotiations relating to Cessation of the Nuclear Arms Race and to Nuclear Disarmament (Marshall Islands v. United Kingdom)*, Preliminary Objections, Judgment, I.C.J. Reports 2016, p. 833, dissenting opinion of Judge Cançado Trindade, paras. 193, 229, 305.

[96] E. Schwelb, *Human Rights and the International Community: The Roots and Growth of the Universal Declaration of Human Rights 1948–1963* (Quadrangle Books 1964), 36–37; L. Henkin, *The Age of Rights* (Columbia University Press 1990) ix; C.S. Nino, *The Ethics of Human Rights* (Clarendon Press 1993) 19.

[97] R. McCorquodale, 'A Future for Human Rights Law' in M. Ssenyonjo and M.A. Baderin (eds.), *International Human Rights Law: Six Decades after the UDHR and Beyond* (Routledge 2016) 541, 542; O. De Schutter, *International Human Rights Law: Cases, Materials, Commentary* (CUP 2019) 63.

[98] A.A. Cançado Trindade, *International Law for Humankind: Towards a New Jus Gentium* (3rd edn., Nijhoff 2020) 62; A.A. Cançado Trindade, *Princípios do Direito Internacional Contemporâneo* (2nd edn., de Gusmão 2017) 88.

[99] H. Charlesworth and C. Chinkin, *The Boundaries of International Law: A Feminist Analysis* (2nd edn., Manchester University Press 2022) 64–65. See also: PCIJ/Advisory Committee of Jurists, *Proces-Verbaux of the Proceedings of the Committee* (16 June-24 July 1920), p. 346, available at: https://www.icj-cij.org/public/files/permanent-court-of-international-justice/serie_D/D_proceedings_of_committee_annexes_16june_24july_1920.pdf (accessed on 22 March 2022).

[100] Statute of the International Court of Justice (adopted 26 June 1945, entered into force 24 October 1945) 33 UNTS 993, Art. 38.1(c); Statute of the Court (PCIJ), Series D. Acts and Documents concerning the Organization of the Court, Art. 38.3 (emphasis added).

clear vestige of colonialism,[101] but an acknowledgement that only certain legal systems were seen as relevant for determining the content of the law,[102] as the general principles of law are to be found within the domestic legal systems of States.[103] Conversely, it can be affirmed that there is no such a thing as a nation civilized by nature, but only those that behave in a 'civilized' manner to others, and in our days, the respect they profess for human rights should be a central element to evaluate such behaviour.[104]

The general principles are the fundamental principles that inspire and inform domestic legal systems, providing them with an axiological dimension on which their coherence and legitimacy are based.[105] To name only a few, it is generally accepted that these general principles include those of *bona fides* (good faith), *res judicata*, the prohibition of the abuse of rights, equality before the law, and the presumption of innocence.[106] This non-exhaustive enumeration already reveals a strong connection between human rights and the general principles of law. In fact, the notion of general principles of law, common to all nations, was discussed during the drafting of the Universal Declaration of Human Rights, influencing the debates of the drafting committee within the Commission on Human Rights, as well as those of the Third Committee of the General Assembly.[107] As many authors have proposed, both the 1948 broad declarations of rights, the American Declaration of the Rights and Duties of Man and the Universal Declaration of Human Rights, are themselves codification of general principles of law at least in part, if not in their entirety.[108]

The existence of general principles of law underpinning the protection human rights has been expressly recognized in the text of both the European Convention on Human Rights and ICCPR. When these treaties prohibit criminal prosecution based on retrospective laws, they exempt from constituting retroactive application of

---

[101] J. Barberis, 'Los principios generales del derecho como fuente del derecho internacional' (1991) 14 *Revista IIDH* 11, 33; L.H. Liu, 'Shadows of Universalism: The Untold Story of Human Rights around 1948' (2014) 40 *Critical Inquiry* 385, 390.

[102] B.S. Chimni, 'Customary International Law: A Third World Perspective' (2018) 112 *American Journal of International Law* 1, 15, 17.

[103] PCIJ/Advisory Committee of Jurists, *Proces-Verbaux of the Proceedings of the Committee* (16 June-24 July 1920), p. 335.

[104] ICJ, *Legal Consequences of the Separation of The Chagos Archipelago from Mauritius in 1965*, Separate Opinion of Judge Cançado Trindade paras. 294–296.

[105] IACtHR, *Juridical Condition and Rights of the Undocumented Migrants*. Advisory Opinion OC-18/03 of September 17, 2003. Series A no.18, concurring opinion of Judge A.A. Cançado Trindade para. 44. See also: PCIJ/Advisory Committee of Jurists, *Proces-Verbaux of the Proceedings of the Committee* (16 June–24 July 1920), pp. 318–319.

[106] A.A. Cançado Trindade, *International Law for Humankind: Towards a New Jus Gentium* (3rd edn., Nijhoff 2020) 63, 122.

[107] J. Morsink, *The Universal Declaration of Human Rights: Origins, Drafting, and Intent* (University of Pennsylvania Press 1999) 54–56, 221.

[108] J.P. Humphrey, *Human Rights and the United Nations: A Great Adventure* (Transnational Publishers 1984) 85; B. Simma and P. Alston, 'The Sources of Human Rights Law: Custom, Jus Cogens, and General Principles' (1989) 12 *Australian Year Book of International Law* 82, 104–106; T. Meron, *Human Rights and Humanitarian Norms as Customary Law* (Clarendon Press 1991) 88; M. Pinto, *Temas de Derechos Humanos* (Del Puerto 2009) 33–37.

criminal law the criminality of actions established by the 'general principles of law'.[109] This exception allows combating impunity for grave violations of human rights, such as genocide, slavery, war crimes, or crimes against humanity, by imposing the obligation to prosecute the individuals responsible for those crimes even when the specific crime is not included in the domestic legal order, as the principles underpinning the criminalization of such actions are common to the whole community of nations.[110]

Human rights monitoring bodies have extensively resorted to the general principles of law within their jurisprudence, as the source of both procedural and substantive rules. For instance, the European Court has acknowledged that the right of access to justice for civil claims and the principle of the independence of the judiciary can be regarded as general principles of law.[111] On its part, the Inter-American Court of Human Rights has made repeated use of general principles of law, such as *iura novit curia*—'the court knows the law'[112]—and estoppel—a principle that precludes an actor from changing a stance on a particular issue when a previous position created a legitimate expectation on another actor.[113]

3.1.4 OTHER SOURCES

As mentioned in **Section 3.1**, following the enumeration of the three 'main' sources of international law, Article 38 of the ICJ Statute enunciates that judicial decisions and the teachings of the most highly qualified publicists act as subsidiary means for determining rules of law. The reference to judicial decisions encompasses both those emanating from international tribunals, as well as those pronounced by national courts—when deciding on questions of international law.[114] When this provision was originally drafted in 1920, as part of the Statute of the PCIJ, it was not foreseen that the international judicial function was to grow exponentially, leading to the creation of a multiplicity of arbitral tribunals and permanent courts.[115] The extensive case law developed by the International Court

---

[109] ECHR, Art 7.2; ICCPR 15.2.

[110] M. Nowak, *UN Covenant on Civil and Political Rights: CCPR Commentary* (2nd edn., Engel 2005) 368. See: ECtHR, *Kolk and Kislyiy v. Estonia* (dec.), App. nos. 23052/04 and 24018/04, 17 January 2006, p. 9; see also: IACtHR, *Almonacid Arellano et al. v. Chile*. Preliminary Objections, Merits, Reparations and Costs. Judgment of September 26, 2006. Series C No. 154, para. 99.

[111] ECtHR, *Golder v. the United Kingdom*, 21 February 1975, § 35, Series A no. 18; ECtHR, *Baka v. Hungary* [GC], App. no. 20261/12, 23 June 2016, joint concurring opinion of judges Pinto de Albuquerque and Dedov, para. 19.

[112] IACtHR, *Velásquez Rodríguez v. Honduras*. Reparations and Costs. Judgment of July 21, 1989. Series C No. 7, para. 163; IACtHR, *Castillo Petruzzi et al. v. Peru*. Merits, Reparations and Costs. Judgment of May 30, 1999. Series C No. 52, para. 116; IACtHR, *Hilaire, Constantine and Benjamin et al. v. Trinidad and Tobago*. Merits, Reparations and Costs. Judgment of June 21, 2002. Series C No. 94, para. 110.

[113] IACtHR, *Neira Alegría et al. v. Peru*. Preliminary Objections. Judgment of December 11, 1991. Series C No. 13, para. 29; IACtHR, *Almonacid Arellano et al. v. Chile*. Preliminary Objections, Merits, Reparations and Costs. Judgment of September 26, 2006. Series C No. 154, para. 65.

[114] R.A. Falk, *The Role of Domestic Courts in the International Legal Order* (Syracuse University Press 1964), chapters III and VIII; F. Morgenstern, 'Judicial Practice and the Supremacy of International Law' (1950) 27 *British Yearbook of International Law* 90.

[115] A.A. Cançado Trindade, *International Law for Humankind: Towards a New Jus Gentium* (3rd edn., Nijhoff 2020) 124.

of Justice, together with that of the international human rights courts in the Americas, Europe, and Africa, as well as that of the international criminal tribunals—the International Criminal Tribunals for the former Yugoslavia and Rwanda and the International Criminal Court—has contributed to the creation of an international public order based upon the respect of human rights in all circumstances.[116] The jurisprudence developed by these courts has not only led to the identification of existing general principles of the law[117] and contributed to the development of international customary law,[118] but has also made it possible to ascertain the emergence of norms belonging to the realm of *jus cogens*, as discussed in **Section 3.1.5**.

When it comes to doctrinal work—'the teachings of the most highly qualified publicists of the various nations'—the historical provenance of the text also lends concerns about whose were the educated views the drafters had in mind, given that, especially in 1920, the field of international law was overwhelmingly male and Western.[119] Nowadays, this provision should not be understood as limited to the teachings of individual authors, but comprises as well the work emanated from collegiate organs within international organizations, such as the ILC, the OAS Inter-American Juridical Committee, or the Asian-African Legal Consultative Organization, all devoted to the codification and progressive development of international law, as well as from international scientific-academic institutes or associations, whose reports contain a wealth of materials that reflect the evolving doctrine of international law.[120]

In addition to all the listed sources of international law cited by the ICJ Statute, the international protection of human rights has evolved through the adoption of a multiplicity of non-binding instruments –usually referred to as 'soft law' in Anglo-American doctrine—such as the resolutions and declarations issued by the organs of international organizations, as well as the documents adopted by groups of human rights experts under the auspices of academic or political institutions.[121] Examples of the former are the 'Norms on the responsibilities of transnational corporations and other business enterprises with regard to human rights', adopted by the UN Sub-commission on the Promotion and Protection of Human Rights in 2003; the United Nations Declaration on the Rights of Indigenous Peoples, adopted by the UN General

---

[116] A.A. Cançado Trindade, *International Law for Humankind: Towards a New Jus Gentium* (3rd edn., Nijhoff 2020) 124.

[117] ICJ, *Reservations to the Convention on Genocide*, Advisory Opinion, ICJ Reports 1951, p. 15; IACtHR, *Neira Alegría et al. v. Peru*. Preliminary Objections. Judgment of December 11, 1991. Series C No. 13, para. 29.

[118] ICJ, *Legal Consequences of the Separation of The Chagos Archipelago from Mauritius in 1965*, paras. 148, 152, 155, 160; ECtHR, *Al-Saadoon and Mufdhi v. the United Kingdom*, App. no. 61498/08, § 120, ECHR 2010.

[119] B.S. Chimni, 'Customary International Law: A Third World Perspective' (2018) 112 *American Journal of International Law* 1, 25–26; H. Charlesworth and C. Chinkin, *The Boundaries of International Law: A Feminist Analysis* (2nd edn., Manchester University Press 2022) 70.

[120] A.A. Cançado Trindade, *International Law for Humankind: Towards a New Jus Gentium* (3rd edn., Nijhoff 2020) 126; H. Charlesworth and C. Chinkin, *The Boundaries of International Law: A Feminist Analysis* (2nd edn., Manchester University Press 2022) 65.

[121] H. Charlesworth and C. Chinkin, *The Boundaries of International Law: A Feminist Analysis* (2nd edn., Manchester University Press 2022) 66–67.

Assembly in 2007; and the United Nations Standard Minimum Rules for the Treatment of Prisoners (the 'Nelson Mandela Rules'), adopted by the General Assembly in 2015.[122] As to the latter, it is possible to mention the 1997 Maastricht Guidelines on Violations of Economic, Social and Cultural Rights, which followed the 1986 Limburg Principles on the Implementation of the International Covenant on Economic, Social and Cultural Rights; or the 2007 Yogyakarta Principles on the application of international human rights law in relation to sexual orientation and gender identity.[123]

All non-binding instruments are relevant for the evolution of the international law of human rights, as they specify the expected behaviour of States within a given area of the protection of human rights and States are under the obligation to, at least, regard them in good faith. In some cases, these instruments can even codify existing customary rules, while in others they can become essential to the progressive development of international norms.[124]

3.1.5 FURTHER REFLECTIONS: THE HIERARCHY OF INTERNATIONAL NORMS

The order in which the sources of international law are enumerated within Article 38 of the ICJ Statute does not imply the existence of a hierarchy of norms. It is broadly accepted that a treaty may overcome a pre-existing custom (leading to the formation of a new custom), just as a subsequent custom may overcome a treaty.[125] However, certain exceptions to this principle of equivalent hierarchy can be found under international law, which have particular importance within the international law of human rights. An incipient attempt at establishing a hierarchy of norms (or rather, the prevalence of certain international obligations over others) is grounded in Article 103 of the United Nations Charter, which states: 'In the event of a conflict between the obligations of the Members of the United Nations under the present Charter and their obligations under any other international agreement, their obligations under the present Charter shall

---

[122] UN Sub-commission on the Promotion and Protection of Human Rights, Norms on the responsibilities of transnational corporations and other business enterprises with regard to human rights (E/CN.4/Sub.2/2003/12/Rev.2); UNGA, Declaration on the Rights of Indigenous Peoples, A/RES/61/295 (2 October 2007); UNGA, United Nations Standard Minimum Rules for the Treatment of Prisoners (the Nelson Mandela Rules), A/RES/70/175 (17 December 2015).

[123] UN Commission on Human Rights, Note verbale dated 5 December 1986 from the Permanent Mission of the Netherlands to the United Nations Office at Geneva addressed to the Centre for Human Rights ('Limburg Principles'), 8 January 1987, E/CN.4/1987/17; International Commission of Jurists (ICJ), Maastricht Guidelines on Violations of Economic, Social and Cultural Rights, 26 January 1997; International Commission of Jurists (ICJ), *Yogyakarta Principles—Principles on the Application of International Human Rights Law in Relation to Sexual Orientation and Gender Identity*, March 2007.

[124] A.A. Cançado Trindade, *International Law for Humankind: Towards a New Jus Gentium* (3rd edn., Nijhoff 2020) 131; A. Clapham, 'The General Assembly' in F. Mégret and P. Alston (eds.), *The United Nations and Human Rights: A Critical Appraisal* (2nd edn., OUP 2020) 99–129, 113.

[125] A.A. Cançado Trindade, *International Law for Humankind: Towards a New Jus Gentium* (3rd edn., Nijhoff 2020) 115–116.

prevail.'[126] This provision was originally thought of in close connection to the actions of the UN Security Council, as its reference to Member States' obligations under the Charter links back to the States' agreement to 'carry out the decisions of the Security Council' under Article 25 of the Charter.[127] Nevertheless, it is certainly possible to claim that the protection of human rights is also an obligation of UN Member States under the Charter.[128] As discussed in **Section 2.2.1.2**, the joint operation of Articles 1.3, 55, and 56 of the Charter clearly imposes upon both the Organization and its Member States the obligation to promote universal respect for, and observance of, human rights and fundamental freedoms for all without distinction as to race, sex, language, or religion. Therefore, it can be argued that obligations concerning the protection of human rights should also take prevalence in case of any conflict with international duties emanating from international agreements other than the UN Charter.

Nonetheless, the main acknowledgment of hierarchy between norms within international law is that associated with the notion of *jus cogens* (peremptory norms). As defined by the 1969 VCLT, 'a peremptory norm of general international law is a norm accepted and recognized by the international community of States as a whole as a norm from which no derogation is permitted and which can be modified only by a subsequent norm of general international law having the same character'.[129] While this concept originally emerged in connection to the law of treaties, with the VCLT affirming that a treaty which conflicts with an existing (or emerging) peremptory norm would be void,[130] it would be a mistake to believe that the idea of *jus cogens* is restricted to treaty law. The sphere of *jus cogens* has expanded to encompass the whole of international law.[131]

Jus cogens should be understood as an open category, which expands itself in accordance with the necessity of protecting the rights of individuals in all situations.[132] International tribunals, as well as legal doctrine,[133] have paid extensive attention to the development of the domain of *jus cogens*, with the work of the former, in particular, being essential for the expansion of the material scope of *jus cogens*.

---

[126] Charter of the United Nations (adopted 26 June 1945, entered into force 24 October 1945) 1 UNTS XVI, Art. 103.

[127] C. Chinkin, 'Jus Cogens, Article 103 of the UN Charter and Other Hierarchical Techniques of Conflict Solution' (2006) 17 *Finnish Yearbook of International Law* 63, 71.

[128] C. Chinkin, 'Jus Cogens, Article 103 of the UN Charter and Other Hierarchical Techniques of Conflict Solution' (2006) 17 *Finnish Yearbook of International Law* 63, 74; O. De Schutter, *International Human Rights Law: Cases, Materials, Commentary* (CUP 2019) 72–73.

[129] VCLT, Art. 53.   [130] VCLT, Arts. 53, 64.

[131] IACtHR, *Juridical Condition and Rights of the Undocumented Migrants*. Advisory Opinion OC-18/03 of September 17, 2003. Series A no.18, concurring opinion of Judge A.A. Cançado Trindade para. 99.

[132] IACtHR, *Juridical Condition and Rights of the Undocumented Migrants*. Advisory Opinion OC-18/03 of September 17, 2003. Series A no.18, concurring opinion of Judge A.A. Cançado Trindade para. 68.

[133] A. Verdross, 'Jus dispositivum and Jus Cogens in International Law' (1966) 60 *American Journal of International Law* 55; J. Barberis, 'La liberté de traiter des États et le jus cogens' (1970) 30 *Zeitschrift für ausländisches öffentliches Recht und Völkerrecht* 19; G. Gaja, 'Jus Cogens beyond the Vienna Convention' (1981) 172 *Recueil des Cours de l'Académie de Droit International de La Haye* 279; H. Charlesworth and C. Chinkin, 'The Gender of Jus Cogens' (1993) 15 *Human Rights Quarterly* 63, 75.

For instance, the ICJ in its aforementioned 1951 Advisory Opinion (discussed in **Section 3.1.1.2**) pointed out that there were humanitarian principles underlying the 1948 Genocide Convention, which were recognized 'as binding on States, even without any conventional obligation'.[134] The undisputed *jus cogens* character of the prohibition of genocide was further reaffirmed by the ICJ, more than five decades later, when ruling in the *Case concerning Armed Activities on the Territory of the Congo*.[135] By then, other international courts were also contributing their opinion to the development of the material content of *jus cogens*.

ICJ, *Armed Activities on the Territory of the Congo (New Application: 2002) (Democratic Republic of the Congo v. Rwanda)*, Jurisdiction and Admissibility, Judgment, I.C.J. Reports 2006, p.6.

In June 1999, the Democratic Republic of the Congo (Republika ya Kôngo ya Dimokalasi or DRC) instituted proceedings against Burundi (Uburundi), Uganda, and Rwanda for acts of armed aggression, later discontinuing its action against Burundi and Rwanda. However, in 2002, the DRC submitted a new application against Rwanda. The Court delivered its ruling on the merits of the original case in 2005, finding Uganda's actions in violation of the prohibition of the use of force and the principle of non-intervention, as well as in breach of different obligations under the international law of human rights and international humanitarian law, due to the conduct of its armed forces.

Conversely, in 2006, the Court ruled it had no jurisdiction to entertain the application against Rwanda. It found that none of the treaties claimed by the DRC conferred jurisdiction on the Court to adjudicate on Rwanda's alleged acts of aggression because either Rwanda was not a Party to those treaties, it had appended reservations to them, or the requirements for seizing the Court under them had not been satisfied. The Court further asserted that the fact that the acts claimed by the DRC could amount to the violation of *jus cogens* norms did not provide alternative grounds for the Court to exercise its jurisdiction, which remains based on the consent of the parties (paras. 64 and 125).

Nonetheless, mindful of the similarity of this case to that already decided against Uganda, the Court thought appropriate to emphasize that a fundamental distinction must be drawn between the Court's ability to exercise jurisdiction over a given case and the existence of international responsibility for the violation of international obligations. It stated: 'Whether or not States have accepted the jurisdiction of the Court, they are required to fulfil their obligations under the United Nations Charter and the other rules of international law, including international humanitarian and human rights law, and they remain responsible for acts attributable to them which are contrary to international law.' (para. 127).

---

[134] ICJ, *Reservations to the Convention on Genocide*, Advisory Opinion, ICJ Reports 1951, pp. 15, 19.
[135] ICJ, *Armed Activities on the Territory of the Congo (New Application:2002)(Democratic Republic of the Congo v. Rwanda)*, Jurisdiction and Admissibility, Judgment, I.C.J. Reports 2006, p. 6, paras. 64, 125.

In 1993, the Inter-American Court of Human Rights confirmed that the prohibition of slavery had to be understood as a peremptory norm.[136] Half a decade later, the International Criminal Tribunal for the Former Yugoslavia (ICTY) affirmed, in the case of *Furundzija* (see **Section 1.2.4**), that the prohibition of torture, established in an absolute manner by both conventional and customary international law, had the character of a *jus cogens* norm.[137] According to the tribunal, the *jus cogens* nature of this prohibition rendered it 'one of the most fundamental standards of the international community', incorporating 'an absolute value from which no one should divert himself'.[138] The recognition of the prohibition of torture as part of the *jus cogens* was echoed by many others courts, including the ICJ,[139] the European Court,[140] and the Inter-American Court of Human Rights.[141] In fact, both regional human rights courts went further, stating that other violations of personal integrity that might not amount to torture, such as inhuman and degrading treatment, also contravene *jus cogens* prohibitions.[142] Moreover, in our days, there are many practices that are undoubtedly condemned by the universal juridical conscience, their prohibition firmly rooted within the realm of *jus cogens*.[143] The crime of forced disappearance of persons, that of summary and extra-legal executions, and all practices that could be labelled crimes against humanity, are certainly found in this category.[144]

The evolution of the international law of human rights, and its emphasis on the existence of a number of fundamental rights that admit no derogation, has acted as an irresistible force for further developing the material content of *jus cogens*.[145] Multiple human rights treaties provide for a nucleus of rights whose enjoyment cannot be suspended, even in times of public emergencies; so-called 'non-derogable rights'.[146]

---

[136] IACtHR, *Aloeboetoe v. Suriname (Reparations and Costs)*, Serie C 15 (1993), para. 57.

[137] ICTY (Trial Chamber), *Prosecutor v. Anto Furundzija*, Case No.: IT-95-17/1-T, 10 December 1998, paras. 137–139, 144, 154, 160.

[138] ICTY (Trial Chamber), *Prosecutor v. Anto Furundzija*, Case No.: IT-95-17/1-T, 10 December 1998, para. 154.

[139] ICJ, *Questions relating to the Obligation to Prosecute or Extradite (Belgium v. Senegal)*, Judgment, I.C.J. Reports 2012, p. 422, para. 99.

[140] ECtHR, *Al-Adsani v. the United Kingdom* [GC], App. no. 35763/97, § 61, ECHR 2001-XI; ECtHR, *Selmouni v. France* [GC], App. no. 25803/94, § 95, ECHR 1999-V.

[141] IACtHR, *Cantoral Benavides v. Peru*. Merits. Judgment of August 18, 2000. Series C No. 69, paras. 95–96; IACtHR, *Maritza Urrutia v. Guatemala*. Merits, Reparations and Costs. Judgment of November 27, 2003. Series C No. 103, para. 92.

[142] ECtHR, *Selmouni v. France* [GC], App. no. 25803/94, § 95, ECHR 1999-V; IACtHR, *Caesar v. Trinidad and Tobago*. Merits, Reparations and Costs. Judgment of March 11, 2005. Series C No. 123, para. 100; IACtHR, *Fermín Ramírez v. Guatemala*. Merits, Reparations and Costs. Judgment of June 20, 2005. Series C No. 126, para. 117.

[143] ILC, Fifth report on peremptory norms of general international law (*jus cogens*) by Dire Tladi, Special Rapporteur, A/CN.4/747 (24 January 2022), conclusion 23.

[144] IACtHR, *Gómez Paquiyauri Brothers v. Peru*. Merits, Reparations and Costs. Judgment of July 8, 2004. Series C No. 110, paras. 76, 128; IACtHR, *Goiburú et al. v. Paraguay*. Merits, Reparations and Costs. Judgment of September 22, 2006. Series C No. 153, para. 84; IACtHR, *Almonacid Arellano et al. v. Chile*. Preliminary Objections, Merits, Reparations, and Costs. Judgment of September 26, 2006. Series C No. 154, paras. 99, 153.

[145] IACHR, *Michael Domingues v. United States*, Report No. 62/02 (22 October 2002), paras. 49, 85.

[146] ECHR, Art. 15; ICCPR, Art. 4; ACHR, Art. 27; Arab Charter, Art. 4.

However, the Human Rights Committee has drawn an important distinction between non-derogable rights, on the one hand, and those belonging to the realm of *jus cogens*, on the other. While ICCPR exempts a number of its provisions from derogation, not all those provisions are considered by the Committee to contain peremptory norms, nor can be inferred that the listed provisions are the only ones recognising peremptory norms.[147] The Committee included the prohibition of arbitrary deprivation of life and the prohibition of torture, inhumane, and degrading treatment within the scope of *jus cogens*, while also stating that other provisions such as those prohibiting imprisonment for not fulfilling contractual obligations, or the right to freedom of thought, conscience, and religion, are considered to be non-derogable merely 'because it can never become necessary to derogate from these rights during a state of emergency'.[148] Moreover, the Committee mentioned the existence of peremptory norms beyond the non-derogable rights expressly recognized by the Covenant, such as the fundamental principles of fair trial, including the presumption of innocence.[149] To these, the Inter-American Court has added the general prohibition of discrimination and the right of access to justice,[150] while the African Court has also included the right of peoples to self-determination.[151]

The emergence of international norms that establish obligations belonging to the realm of *jus cogens* has conformed a regime of 'objective illegality', as it not possible to justify their breach under any circumstances. Such a regime imposes upon States obligations of *erga omnes* character;[152] obligations States have assumed towards the international community as a whole, as their compliance is of interest of the whole community of States.[153] The existence of *erga omnes* obligations was affirmed by the ICJ in a well-known *obiter dictum* in its 1970 judgment in the case of *Barcelona Traction*. In a non-exhaustive enumeration, the ICJ mentioned some *erga omnes* obligations, such as obligations that derive from the outlawing of acts of aggression, and of genocide, and also from the principles and rules concerning the basic rights of the human person, including the protection from slavery and racial discrimination.[154] It is important to

---

[147] CCPR, General Comment 29: States of Emergency, CCPR/C/21/Rev.1/Add.11 (2001), para. 4.
[148] CCPR, General Comment 29: States of Emergency, CCPR/C/21/Rev.1/Add.11 (2001), para. 4.
[149] CCPR, General Comment 29: States of Emergency, CCPR/C/21/Rev.1/Add.11 (2001), para. 4.
[150] IACtHR, *Juridical Condition and Rights of the Undocumented Migrants*. Advisory Opinion OC-18/03 of September 17, 2003. Series A no.18, paras. 112–113 and concurring opinion of Judge Cançado Trindade para. 14–15; IACtHR, *Vélez Loor v. Panama*. Preliminary Objections, Merits, Reparations, and Costs. Judgment of November 23, 2010 Series C No. 218, para. 101; IACtHR, *Goiburú et al. v. Paraguay*. Merits, Reparations and Costs. Judgment of September 22, 2006. Series C No. 153, para. 131.
[151] ACtHPR, *Bernard Anbataayela Mornah v. Benin, Burkina Faso, Côte d'Ivoire, Ghana, Mali, Malawi, Tanzania, and Tunisia*. Judgment, App. no. 028/2018 (22 September 2022), para. 298.
[152] ICTY (Trial Chamber), *Prosecutor v. Anto Furundzija*, Case No.: IT-95-17/1-T, 10 December 1998, para. 151.
[153] ICJ, *Barcelona Traction, Light and Power Company, Limited*, Judgment, I.C.J. Reports 1970, p. 3, paras. 33–34; IACtHR, *Juridical Condition and Rights of the Undocumented Migrants*. Advisory Opinion OC-18/03 of September 17, 2003. Series A no.18, concurring opinion of Judge A.A. Cançado Trindade para. 80.
[154] ICJ, *Barcelona Traction, Light and Power Company, Limited*, Judgment, I.C.J. Reports 1970, p. 3, paras. 33–34.

highlight that, by definition, all *jus cogens* norms generate obligations *erga omnes*; although, in turn, not all obligations *erga omnes* follow from *jus cogens* norms.[155]

> **ICJ, *Barcelona Traction, Light and Power Company, Limited*, Judgment, I.C.J. Reports 1970, p. 3.**
>
> Belgium brought a legal action against Spain, seeking reparation for damage caused to its nationals, shareholders in the Barcelona Traction, Light and Power Company, Ltd—a company incorporated under Canadian law—as the result of acts contrary to international law allegedly committed by various organs of the Spanish State. Spain filed four preliminary objections, two of which were rejected in an initial judgment of the ICJ in 1964, while the remaining two were joined to the merits. In its 1970 judgment, the Court found that Belgium lacked legal standing to exercise diplomatic protection of shareholders in a Canadian company, as there was nothing preventing Canada from granting such protection. It emphasized that the exercise of diplomatic protection on behalf of shareholders could lead to competing diplomatic claims, creating an atmosphere of confusion and insecurity in international economic relations. Therefore, based in considerations of equity, the Court rejected Belgium's claim.

Given their particular importance, there are special consequences that flow from the violation of *jus cogens* norms. However, the Articles on the Responsibility of States for Internationally Wrongful Acts, adopted by the ILC in 2001, only (timidly) asserted that a legal consequence arising from a gross or systematic breach of a peremptory norm is the general prohibition of all States to recognize such a situation as lawful, together with a duty to cooperate to bring such a serious breach to an end.[156] On its part, the international law of human rights has developed a regime of aggravated responsibility of the State for the violation of *jus cogens* norms, which encompasses more severe legal consequences, such as the need to adopt wider measures of reparation.[157] Stringent measures of reparation, associated with the aggravated responsibility of the State, not only seek to compensate the harm caused by the breach of *jus cogens* norms, but are also aimed at having an exemplary or dissuasive purpose, to avoid both impunity

---

[155] IACtHR, *Juridical Condition and Rights of the Undocumented Migrants*. Advisory Opinion OC-18/03 of September 17, 2003. Series A no.18, concurring opinion of Judge A.A. Cançado Trindade para. 80; ILC, Report of the Study Group on Fragmentation of International Law: Difficulties arising from the Diversification and Expansion of International Law, A/CN.4/L.676 (29 July 2005), para. 50.

[156] ILC, Responsibility of States for Internationally Wrongful Acts, A/56/10 (2001), Arts. 40–41.

[157] IACtHR, *Juridical Condition and Rights of the Undocumented Migrants*. Advisory Opinion OC-18/03 of September 17, 2003. Series A no.18, concurring opinion of Judge A.A. Cançado Trindade paras. 70–71; IACtHR, *Almonacid Arellano et al. v. Chile*. Preliminary Objections, Merits, Reparations, and Costs. Judgment of September 26, 2006. Series C No. 154, concurring opinion of Judge A.A. Cançado Trindade para. 19; IACtHR, *Gómez Paquiyauri Brothers v. Peru*. Merits, Reparations and Costs. Judgment of July 8, 2004. Series C No. 110, separate opinion of Judge A.A. Cançado Trindade paras. 37–40, 44.

for the violation committed and recidivism.[158] The Inter-American Court has even affirmed that a logical consequence of the peremptory character of the norms prohibiting the commission of certain crimes—such as torture or forced disappearance—is that the obligation upon States to investigate them and to prosecute those individuals responsible for their commission also holds *jus cogens* status.[159]

The recognition of the existence of obligations of protection that are owed to everyone, and to the international community as a whole—*erga omnes* obligations—, as well as of a hierarchy of legal norms through the idea of *jus cogens*, reveals the juridical expression of the fundamental principles and values which guide the international community as a whole.[160] This emergence and development are contributions to the creation of a true international public order based upon the respect for, and observance of, human rights, centred on the human person.[161]

3.2 THE NATURE AND SCOPE OF INTERNATIONAL HUMAN RIGHTS OBLIGATIONS

International human rights norms impose a series of obligations upon States. While these obligations emanate from all sources of international law, they have been more clearly indicated in international treaties. However, the different treaties enunciate the obligations held by States in different terms. The European Convention on Human Rights states that: 'The High Contracting Parties shall *secure* to everyone within their jurisdiction the rights and freedoms defined in Section I of this Convention',[162] while the ICCPR and the American Convention phrase the general obligations as duties to 'respect' and to 'ensure' the protected rights[163] and the African Charter refers to an obligation to 'recognize' the rights, duties, and freedoms enshrined in it.[164] Notwithstanding the different denominations given to the obligations emanating from human rights treaties, the nature of the duties they entail is the same.

In its first-ever judgment on the merits of a case, the Inter-American Court set out to clarify the meaning of the two general duties imposed by the American Convention— 'to respect' and 'to ensure'.[165] It affirmed that the duty 'to respect' the rights protected by the Convention establishes a clear limit to the exercise of public authority, delineating

---

[158] IACtHR, *Myrna Mack Chang v. Guatemala*. Merits, Reparations and Costs. Judgment of November 25, 2003. Series C No. 101, reasoned opinion of Judge A.A. Cançado Trindade paras. 45–47.

[159] IACtHR, *Perozo et al. v. Venezuela*. Preliminary Objections, Merits, Reparations, and Costs. Judgment of January 28, 2009. Series C No. 195, para. 298.

[160] IACtHR, *Perozo et al. v. Venezuela*. Preliminary Objections, Merits, Reparations, and Costs. Judgment of January 28, 2009. Series C No. 195, concurring opinion of Judge A.A. Cançado Trindade para. 73.

[161] IACtHR, *Perozo et al. v. Venezuela*. Preliminary Objections, Merits, Reparations, and Costs. Judgment of January 28, 2009. Series C No. 195, concurring opinion of Judge A.A. Cançado Trindade para. 81.

[162] ECHR, Art. 1 (emphasis added). [163] ICCPR, Art. 2; ACHR, Art. 1.
[164] ACHPR, Art. 1. [165] ACHR, Art. 1.

specific attributes of the individual that States cannot restrict.[166] On its part, the obligation 'to ensure' the rights:

> ... implies the duty of States Parties to organize the governmental apparatus and, in general, all the structures through which public power is exercised, so that they are capable of juridically ensuring the free and full enjoyment of human rights. As a consequence of this obligation, the States must prevent, investigate and punish any violation of the rights recognized by the Convention and, moreover, if possible attempt to restore the right violated and provide compensation as warranted for damages resulting from the violation.[167]

However, the most extended typology of obligations emanating from international human rights norms distinguishes among three types of duties States have to undertake to comply with the protection of human rights. These are: the obligations to respect, to protect, and to fulfil. This typology was developed in the 1980s by Asbjørn Eide, former Special Rapporteur on the Right to Adequate Food as a Human Right, in a series of reports to the UN Sub-Commission on Prevention of Discrimination and Protection of Minorities.[168] This layered approach to the nature of States' obligations has been expressly adopted by international monitoring bodies, such as the Committee on Economic, Social and Cultural Rights, the Committee on the Rights of the Child, and the African Commission on Human and People's Rights.[169] The primary level obligation ('to respect') imposes upon States the duty to refrain from interfering in the enjoyment of human rights; respecting the right-holders, their freedoms, autonomy, resources, and liberty of their action.[170] The secondary level obligation ('to protect') refers to the States' duty to adopt measures that will protect individuals from other actors that might interfere with the enjoyment of a right.[171] The last layered obligation ('to fulfil') means that States must adopt proactive measures to secure the realization of human rights by individuals. Following Eide's typology, the Committee on Economic, Social and Cultural Rights has proposed that the obligation to fulfil encompasses both a

---

[166] IACtHR, *Velásquez Rodríguez v. Honduras*. Merits. Judgment of July 29, 1988. Series C No. 4, para. 165.

[167] IACtHR, *Velásquez Rodríguez v. Honduras*. Merits. Judgment of July 29, 1988. Series C No. 4, para. 166.

[168] M. Sepúlveda, *The Nature of the Obligations Under the International Covenant on Economic, Social and Cultural Rights* (Intersentia 2003) 161–162. See, especially: A. Eide, Report on the right to adequate food as a human right, E/CN.4/Sub.2/1987/23 (7 July 1987), paras. 112–114.

[169] CESCR, General Comment 12: the Right to Adequate Food, E/C.12/1999/5 (12 May 1999), para. 15; CRC, General Comment 16: State obligations regarding the impact of the business sector on children's rights, CRC/C/GC/16 (17 April 2013), paras. 25–29; ACHPR, *Social and Economic Rights Action Center (SERAC) and Center for Economic and Social Rights (CESR) v. Nigeria*, Communication 155/96 (October 2001), paras. 44–47. See also: CESCR, General Comment 14: the right to the highest attainable standard of health, E/C.12/2000/4 (11 August 2000) and CESCR, General Comment 18: the Right to Work, E/C.12/GC/18 (6 February 2006).

[170] A. Eide, 'Economic, Social and Cultural Rights as Human Rights' in A. Eide, C. Krause, and A. Rosas (eds.), *Economic, Social and Cultural Rights: A Textbook* (2nd edn., Nijhoff 2001) 23–24; ACHPR, *Social and Economic Rights Action Center (SERAC) and Center for Economic and Social Rights (CESR) v. Nigeria*, Communication 155/96 (October 2001), para. 44.

[171] A. Eide, 'Economic, Social and Cultural Rights as Human Rights' in A. Eide, C. Krause, and A. Rosas (eds.), *Economic, Social and Cultural Rights: A Textbook* (2nd edn., Nijhoff 2001) 24; ACHPR, *Social and Economic Rights Action Center (SERAC) and Center for Economic and Social Rights (CESR) v. Nigeria*, Communication 155/96 (October 2001), para. 45.

duty for States 'to facilitate', adopting measures that would favour individuals' access to the needed resources to enjoy their rights, as well as a duty 'to provide' such resources when facilitating them proves to be insufficient, such as in the cases of individuals in particularly vulnerable situations.[172]

What becomes evident, following the previous discussion, is that compliance with the international law of human rights imposes upon States a number of essential obligations, which range from abstaining from directly breaching the rights of individuals to various positive steps to secure the required conditions for everyone to enjoy their rights. It is also worth highlighting that the duties imposed upon States do not allow for distinction among obligations concerning civil and political rights, on the one hand, and economic, social, and cultural rights, on the other. Recalling the discussion from **Section 2.3**, any rigid distinction between 'categories' of rights must be rejected. Although it is true that the normative frameworks historically adopted for the protection of rights have endowed different monitoring mechanisms with differential powers, based on the (anachronistic) idea of different types of rights, this is a relic of the past. No human right can be fully realized without States undertaking a number of both abstentions and positive measures.[173]

The international law of human rights imposes upon States the duty to undertake all necessary steps to give effect to human rights in the domestic order. These include essential positive duties, such as the adoption of legislative, judicial, administrative, educative, and other appropriate measures in order to fulfil their legal obligations.[174] This means that States are required to make such changes to domestic laws and practices as are needed to ensure their conformity with the international obligations assumed.[175] As clarified by the Inter-American and African Courts, this obligation encompasses the need to amend any domestic norm in contravention with the international law of human rights, which includes even the States' constitutions.[176]

Another essential positive obligation that derives from international human rights norms is the requirement that States make available to the individuals under their

---

[172] A. Eide, 'Economic, Social and Cultural Rights as Human Rights' in A. Eide, C. Krause, and A. Rosas (eds.), *Economic, Social and Cultural Rights: A Textbook* (2nd edn., Nijhoff 2001) 24; CESCR, General Comment 12: the Right to Adequate Food, E/C.12/1999/5 (12 May 1999), para. 15.

[173] F. Jhabvala, 'On Human Rights and the Socio-Economic Context' (1984) 31 *Netherlands International Law Review* 149, 161–162; M. Pinto, 'Integralidad de los derechos humanos. Exigibilidad de los derechos colectivos y acceso a la justicia de las personas en condición de pobreza' (2009) 50 *Revista IIDH* 53, 56–57; D. Shelton and A. Gould, 'Positive and Negative Obligations' in D. Shelton (ed.), *The Oxford Handbook of International Human Rights Law* (OUP 2013) 562–584, 564.

[174] CCPR, General Comment 31: the Nature of the General Legal Obligation Imposed on States Parties to the Covenant, CCPR/C/21/Rev.1/Add. 13 (26 May 2004), para. 7.

[175] CESCR, General Comment 9: the domestic application of the Covenant, E/C.12/1998/24 (3 December 1998), paras. 9 and 10; CCPR, General Comment 31: the Nature of the General Legal Obligation Imposed on States Parties to the Covenant, CCPR/C/21/Rev.1/Add. 13 (26 May 2004), para. 13; ECtHR, *Marckx v. Belgium*, 13 June 1979, § 31, Series A no. 31; IACtHR, *Loayza Tamayo v. Peru*. Reparations and Costs. Judgment of November 27, 1998. Series C No. 42, op. para. 5.

[176] IACtHR, *'The Last Temptation of Christ' (Olmedo Bustos et al.) v. Chile*. Merits, Reparations and Costs. Judgment of February 5, 2001. Series C No. 73; ACtHPR, *Jebra Kambole v. Tanzania*, App. 18/2018, Judgment (28 November 2019).

jurisdiction accessible and effective remedies to vindicate human rights, which includes both administrative and judicial mechanisms.[177] These domestic remedies need to be 'truly effective in establishing whether there has been a violation of human rights and in providing redress'.[178] In fact, the absence of such remedies or their lack of effectiveness would amount to an additional violation of human rights,[179] independent to the one that was sought to be redressed in the first place.[180]

In addition to the positive obligations to adequate domestic legislation and to provide administrative and judicial remedies, States have, under certain circumstances, the positive duties to 'prevent' violation from taking place,[181] to 'investigate' them when they have occurred, and to 'prosecute and punish' those individuals responsible for them. In the words of the Inter-American Court: 'The State has a legal duty to take reasonable steps to prevent human rights violations and to use the means at its disposal to carry out a serious investigation of violations committed within its jurisdiction, to identify those responsible, to impose the appropriate punishment and to ensure the victim adequate compensation.'[182] Of course, the mere fact that a particular violation has taken place does not, in itself, prove the State has failed to take preventive measures. The obligation to prevent is one of means, rather than of results, but it must be undertaken in a serious manner, and not as a mere formality preordained to be ineffective.[183] As to the actual measures encompassed by the duty to prevent, in a 2015 Report, the Office of the United Nations High Commissioner (OHCHR) stressed that prevention 'requires a proactive, continuing and systemic process of addressing risk factors and causes of human rights violations through a range of measures, including law, policy and practice, to ensure respect for and protection of all human rights for all those within the State's territory or jurisdiction'.[184]

As mentioned earlier, a further positive duty of States is to investigate when a violation of human rights has taken place. The Inter-American Court has been unequivocal, since its first judgment, in asserting that when a grave violation of human rights has taken place—a forced disappearance, in that case—the State is under a duty to investigate it, as well as to prosecute (and punish) the individuals responsible for it.[185] Even before

---

[177] CESCR, General Comment 9: the domestic application of the Covenant, E/C.12/1998/24 (3 December 1998), paras. 9 and 10; CCPR, General Comment 31: the Nature of the General Legal Obligation Imposed on States Parties to the Covenant, CCPR/C/21/Rev.1/Add. 13 (26 May 2004), para. 15.

[178] IACtHR, *Judicial Guarantees in States of Emergency (Arts. 27(2), 25 and (8) American Convention on Human Rights)*. Advisory Opinion OC-9/87 of October 6, 1987. Series A no. 9, para. 24.

[179] The Right to an Effective Remedies is expressly recognized as an autonomous right by different human rights treaties. See: ECHR, Art. 13; ACHR, Art. 25.

[180] CCPR, General Comment 31: the Nature of the General Legal Obligation Imposed on States Parties to the Covenant, CCPR/C/21/Rev.1/Add. 13 (26 May 2004), para. 15.

[181] UNCAT, Art. 2.

[182] IACtHR, *Velásquez Rodríguez v. Honduras*. Merits. Judgment of July 29, 1988. Series C No. 4, para. 174.

[183] IACtHR, *Velásquez Rodríguez v. Honduras*. Merits. Judgment of July 29, 1988. Series C No. 4, paras. 175–177.

[184] OHCHR, 'The Role of Prevention in the Promotion and Protection of Human Rights' (16 July 2015) A/HRC/30/20, para. 48.

[185] IACtHR, *Velásquez Rodríguez v. Honduras*. Merits. Judgment of July 29, 1988. Series C No. 4, paras. 166, 172, 176, 181.

the Inter-American Court's judgment, the Human Rights Committee had also begun to develop a jurisprudence according to which States are under a duty to investigate serious human rights violations.[186] Later on, the European Court of Human Rights would also reach this interpretation of the scope of States' positive obligations under the European Convention on Human Rights.[187] However, it is perhaps the Inter-American Court which has given this duty its widest interpretation, as its established case law is adamant that when a grave violation of human rights—such as forced disappearance, extra-judicial executions, or torture—has taken place, the State is under an obligation to refrain from adopting any measures—including amnesty laws, statutes of limitations, or presidential pardons—that might hinder the investigation of the crime or the prosecution and punishment of those individuals responsible for it.[188]

3.2.1 THE PROHIBITION OF DISCRIMINATION AS A GENERAL GUARANTEE

As Article 1 of the Universal Declaration of Human Rights reveals, the whole international system for the protection of the human person rests on the belief that all individuals are born equal in dignity and rights.[189] Consequently, there is an inseparable connection between the general obligations upon States concerning human rights and the principle of equality and non-discrimination, as States are obliged to respect, protect, and fulfil all human rights without discrimination.[190] The prohibition of discrimination has been established as a general guarantee for securing the enjoyment of human rights in the most important international human rights treaties,[191] meaning that it should be seen as one of the fundamental pillars of the international law of human rights, which permeates the whole structure of the system.[192] In fact, the constant jurisprudence

---

[186] CCPR, *Quinteros v. Uruguay*, Communication No. 107/1981 (21 July 1983), paras. 11, 15, 16.

[187] A. Mowbray, 'Duties of Investigation under the European Convention on Human Rights' (2002) 51 *International and Comparative Law Quarterly* 435.

[188] IACtHR, *El Amparo v. Venezuela*. Reparations and Costs. Judgment of September 14, 1996. Series C No. 28, op. para. 4; IACtHR, *Gómez Paquiyauri Brothers v. Peru*. Merits, Reparations and Costs. Judgment of July 8, 2004. Series C No. 110, para. 232; IACtHR, *Huilca Tecse v. Peru*. Merits, Reparations and Costs. Judgment of March 3, 2005. Series C No. 121, para. 108; IACtHR, *Moiwana Community v. Suriname*. Preliminary Objections, Merits, Reparations and Costs. Judgment of June 15, 2005. Series C No. 124, para. 206.

[189] UDHR, Art. 1. The prohibition of discrimination as a substantive human right is further discussed in **Section 10.1**.

[190] IACtHR, *Juridical Condition and Rights of the Undocumented Migrants*. Advisory Opinion OC-18/03 of September 17, 2003. Series A no.18, para. 85.

[191] ICERD, Art. 2I; CESCR, Arts. 2.2, 3; ICCPR, Arts. 2, 26; UNCRC, Art. 2; ICRMW, Arts. 1, 7, 18(1), 25, 27, 28, 43, 45(1), 48, 55, 70; CEDAW, Arts. 2, 3, 5–16; ECHR, Art. 14 and Protocol 12; ACHR, Arts. 1, 24; African Charter, Arts. 2, 3, 19; Arab Charter, Art. 2.

[192] IACtHR, *Proposed Amendments of the Naturalization Provisions of the Constitution of Costa Rica*. Advisory Opinion OC-4/84 of January 19, 1984. Series A no. 4, separate opinion of judge Rodolfo Piza E. para. 10; CCPR, General Comment 18: Non-discrimination (10 November 1989), paras. 1–2; IACtHR, *Juridical Condition and Rights of the Undocumented Migrants*. Advisory Opinion OC-18/03 of September 17, 2003. Series A no.18, paras. 100–101. See also: Y. Dinstein, 'Discrimination and International Human Rights' (1985) 15 *Israel Yearbook on Human Rights* 11.

of the Inter-American Court of Human Rights has gone as far as to affirm that the prohibition of discrimination belongs to the realm of *jus cogens*.[193]

Of course, not every distinction in treatment pertaining to human rights entails prohibited discrimination. An accepted definition of discrimination under the international law of human rights is the one proposed by the Human Rights Committee, following the reading of different human rights treaties.[194] According to the Committee, the term 'discrimination' should be 'understood to imply any distinction, exclusion, restriction or preference'[195] based on prohibited grounds—which include, but are not limited to, race, colour, sex, language, religion, political or other opinion, national or social origin, property, birth, or other status—and 'which has the purpose or effect of nullifying or impairing the recognition, enjoyment or exercise by all persons, on an equal footing, of all rights and freedoms'.[196] This general and broad character of the prohibition of discrimination has allowed for its use to provide an evolving protection of human rights both in terms of rights not explicitly acknowledged in the text of international treaties, as well as in favour of members of excluded groups whose characteristics might not be expressly mentioned in the treaties. As will be further discussed in **Section 10.1**, an example of this improved protection is the interpretation of the prohibition of discrimination, by different international monitoring bodies, to extend the protection of economic, social, and cultural rights to groups of individuals deprived of such rights.[197]

3.2.2 THE SCOPE OF INTERNATIONAL HUMAN RIGHTS OBLIGATIONS (PERSONAL DIMENSION)

The scope of the obligations concerning the respect, protection, and fulfilment of human rights extends across four different axes; namely, personal, material, temporal, and territorial. The personal axis refers to both the active and passive subjects of the obligations; in other words, who is the bearer of human rights obligations (the topic of this section), as well as who are the subjects entitled to benefit from them (to be further explored in **Section 3.3**). For their part, the material dimension concerns the sources of the legal obligations (as discussed in **Section 3.1**), while the temporal and territorial axes (covered in **Section 3.2.3**) refer, respectively, to the moment in which obligations arise and conclude and to the geographical extension of the obligations.

---

[193] IACtHR, *Juridical Condition and Rights of the Undocumented Migrants*. Advisory Opinion OC-18/03 of September 17, 2003. Series A no.18, paras. 100–101; IACtHR, *Yatama v. Nicaragua*. Preliminary Objections, Merits, Reparations, and Costs. Judgment of June 23, 2005. Series C No. 127, paras. 184–185; IACtHR, *Girls Yean and Bosico v. Dominican Republic*. Preliminary Objections, Merits, Reparations and Costs. Judgment of September 8, 2005. Series C No. 130, para. 141.

[194] CCPR, General Comment 18: Non-discrimination (10 November 1989), para. 7.

[195] CCPR, General Comment 18: Non-discrimination (10 November 1989), para. 7.

[196] CCPR, General Comment 18: Non-discrimination (10 November 1989), para. 7.

[197] CCPR, *Mr. Edward Young v. Australia*, Communication No. 941/2000, UN Doc. CCPR/C/78/D/941/2000 (2003); CCPR, *X v. Colombia*, Communication No. 1361/2005, CCPR/C/89/D/1361/2005 (2007); IACtHR, *Duque v. Colombia*. Preliminary Objections, Merits, Reparations and Costs. Judgment of February 26, 2016. Series C No. 310.

As discussed in **Section 1.1**, the international law of human rights is a legal regime that is (mostly) concerned with the relationship between individuals and the State. This legal system is based on the premise of the international legal personality of the State (the main duty-bearer) and that of the individual (the primary right-holder). The aim of the whole system is to protect individuals in all circumstances and this objective is pursued by norms that regulate the conduct of the State towards individuals, by imposing legal obligations that would lead to its international responsibility in case of a violation.

Given that the international protection of human rights is founded on States' obligations and responsibility, the rules of this legal regime do not tend to engage directly with the responsibility of non-State actors.[198] However, this logic should not be understood as implying impunity for human rights violations committed by non-State actors.[199] On the one hand, other branches of the law deal with the legal responsibility of non-State entities. On the other hand, the actions of non-State actors can, under certain circumstances, also give rise to the international responsibility of States. The international law of human rights imposes upon States obligations that extend to ensuring the protection of human rights when these are threatened by the actions of non-State actors. The norms concerning the protection of the human person mandate States to adopt measures to regulate, prevent, and redress human rights violations, even when these are not directly attributable to the State.

These obligations include the so-called horizontal effect of international human rights norms (or *Drittwirkung*). *Drittwirkung* is a doctrine originating in German jurisprudence which refers to the ability of individuals to invoke before the domestic courts the protection of their rights *vis-à-vis* third parties.[200] This horizontal applicability of human rights norms is expressly mandated in specific provisions of some international treaties, such as those that require States to adopt measures to eliminate discrimination by private individuals, groups, organizations, or enterprises.[201] The horizontal effect of human rights norms has been embraced by multiple monitoring bodies.[202] For instance, in the judgment in *X and Y v. the Netherlands*, the European Court of Human Rights has acknowledged the existence of positive obligations emanating from the European Convention, which may involve the adoption of measures designed to secure human rights even in the sphere of the relations of individuals between themselves.[203] Similarly, the Inter-American Court has specifically

---

[198] Although exceptions are increasingly appearing, as discussed in **Section 3.2.2.1**.

[199] An expression used to refer to a diversity of actors, including international organizations, non-governmental organizations, transnational corporations, and organized armed groups. See: D. Weissbrodt, 'Roles and Responsibilities of Non-State Actors' in D. Shelton (ed.), *The Oxford Handbook of International Human Rights Law* (OUP 2013) 719–736, 720.

[200] D. Xenos, *The Positive Obligations of the State under the European Convention of Human Rights* (Routledge 2012) 42–47.

[201] ICERD, Art. 2.1.d; CEDAW, Art. 2.e; UNCRPD, Art. 4.e.

[202] ECtHR, *Young, James and Webster v. the United Kingdom*, 13 August 1981, Series A no. 44; CCPR, General Comment 31: the Nature of the General Legal Obligation Imposed on States Parties to the Covenant, CCPR/C/21/Rev.1/Add. 13 (26 May 2004), para. 8.

[203] ECtHR, *X and Y v. the Netherlands*, 26 March 1985, § 23, Series A no. 91.

referred to the notion of *Drittwirkung* in its advisory opinion on undocumented migrants.[204] It affirmed that States are under the obligation to enact legislation that protects human rights within private relationships, as well as to provide appropriate judicial mechanisms for individuals to resort to in case of a breach of their rights.[205]

ECtHR, *X and Y v. the Netherlands*, 26 March 1985, Series A no. 91.

The case concerned the rape of a sixteen-year-old girl (Y) who had an intellectual disability, and the inability of both her and her father (X) to institute criminal proceedings against the offender. The rape had taken place within the privately run home in which Y lived, committed by the son-in-law of the directress, who lived in the premises. The following day, X filed a complaint at the police station, asking for criminal proceedings to be instituted. However, the public prosecutor decided not to pursue the case and X's appeal against such decision was dismissed by the Court of Appeal. On the one hand, the court considered it doubtful that a charge of rape could be proved and, on the other hand, the crime of sexual assault through the abuse of a dominant position could not be pursued as the law only allowed prosecution when the victim herself had taken action, the father's complaint being unable to substitute that of the victim. Mr X brought a claim to the European Commission and both the Commission and, subsequently, the Court found that the facts of the case revealed a violation of Article 8 ECHR against Y.

The Court recalled that 'although the object of [the Right to Respect for Private Life] is essentially that of protecting the individual against arbitrary interference by the public authorities, it does not merely compel the State to abstain from such interference: in addition to this primarily negative undertaking, there may be positive obligations inherent in an effective respect for private or family life... These obligations may involve the adoption of measures designed to secure respect for private life even in the sphere of the relations of individuals between themselves (para. 23). In the case, the Court considered that the domestic legislation failed to provide Y with practical and effective protection; hence, she was the victim of a violation of Article 8.

IACtHR, *Juridical Condition and Rights of the Undocumented Migrants*. Advisory Opinion OC-18/03 of September 17, 2003. Series A No.18.

México requested an Advisory Opinion on the international obligations of the American States concerning the labour rights of migrant workers. The Court structured its answers around four points: the nature of the principle of equality and non-discrimination; the application of this principle to migrants; the rights of undocumented migrant workers; and the States' international obligations in the determination of migratory policies.

The Court affirmed that the principle of equality and non-discrimination is essential for the safeguard of human rights in both international and domestic law, being of such

---

[204] ECtHR, *X and Y v. the Netherlands*, 26 March 1985, § 140, Series A no. 91.
[205] ECtHR, *X and Y v. the Netherlands*, 26 March 1985, § 140, Series A no. 91, paras. 147–153.

> a fundamental nature as to belong to the domain of *jus cogens*. It also affirmed that the prohibition of discrimination includes the migratory status of a person, which means that distinctions between documented and undocumented migrants or between migrants and nationals, must be reasonable, objective, proportionate, and not harm human rights.
>
> The Court also affirmed that the employment relationship originates rights, irrespective of the employee's regular or irregular migratory status in the State. Nonetheless, the Court distinguished between public and private employment. In the former, any violation of labour rights would entail the international responsibility of the State, while in the latter this responsibility only arises by the breach of the State's positive obligation to ensure the effectiveness of the protected rights by third parties.
>
> Lastly, the Court affirmed that the elaboration and implementation of migratory policies was not exempted from complying with human rights standards, including the prohibition of discrimination. Although it is licit for States to establish measures relating to the entry, residence, or departure of migrant workers, these should be compatible with the prohibition of discrimination, taking into account only the characteristics of the productive activity and the individual capability of the workers.

Similarly, the responsibility of the State for the acts of non-State actors impairing the enjoyment of human rights might arise due to a lack of prevention of such acts, or for the absence of appropriate investigation of the violations or prosecution of the individuals responsible for them, both of which amount to positive obligations of States, as discussed in **Section 3.2**.[206] It is possible to find numerous decisions of regional monitoring bodies in which States have been found in breach of human rights norms either due to the lack of prevention of a violation of human rights attributable to non-State actors, or due to the lack of investigation and criminal prosecution of private individuals responsible for serious human rights violations. As stated by the Inter-American Court:

> An illegal act which violates human rights and which is initially not directly imputable to a State (for example, because it is the act of a private person or because the person responsible has not been identified) can lead to international responsibility of the State, not because of the act itself, but because of the lack of due diligence to prevent the violation or to respond to it as required by the Convention.[207]

---

[206] CCPR, General Comment 31: the Nature of the General Legal Obligation Imposed on States Parties to the Covenant, CCPR/C/21/Rev.1/Add. 13 (26 May 2004), para. 8; CCPR, *Paul Arenz, Thomas Röder and Dagmar Röder v. Germany*, Communication No. 1138/2002, CCPR/C/80/D/1138/2002 (24 March 2004), para. 8.5; CEDAW, General Recommendation 19: Violence against Women (1992), paras. 9 and 24.a; CEDAW *A.T. v. Hungary*, Communication No. 2/2003, CEDAW/C/36/D/2/2003 (26 January 2005), paras 9.3, 9.4, 9.6; CESCR, General Comment 14: the right to the highest attainable standard of health, E/C.12/2000/4 (11 August 2000), para. 35; CESCR, General Comment 15: the Right to Water, E/C.12/2002/11 (20 January 2003), paras. 23–24, 44.b, 56; CRC, General Comment 16: State obligations regarding the impact of the business sector on children's rights, CRC/C/GC/16 (17 April 2013).

[207] IACtHR, *Velásquez Rodríguez v. Honduras*. Merits. Judgment of July 29, 1988. Series C No. 4, para. 172.

However, it took time for regional courts to start developing a consistent jurisprudence on the international responsibility of a State for actions carried out by non-State actors. In 2000, the European Court of Human Rights decided the case *Mahmut Kaya v. Turkey*, in which it found that the summary execution of two individuals by contra-guerrilla members gave rise to the international responsibility of the State. The grounds for the attribution of responsibility were two-fold: on the one hand, the State had failed to take reasonable measures to prevent a real and immediate risk to the life of one of the victims, when it should have been aware of the existence of such a risk;[208] on the other hand, the State was also liable because the investigations undertaken into the executions were found by the Court to be neither adequate nor effective.[209] Similarly, in 2006, the Inter-American Court of Human Rights found Colombia to be responsible for a massacre perpetrated by paramilitary groups against the inhabitants of Pueblo Bello with the result that forty-three people were arbitrarily deprived of their lives.[210] The Court found that although the crimes were committed by private actors, they entailed the international responsibility of the State, given the lack of preventive measures as well as the absence of a serious investigation leading to the prosecution and punishment of those criminally responsible for the massacre.[211]

3.2.2.1 Further reflections: the international responsibility of non-State actors

Under international law, there is an evolving recognition of the fact that State conduct is not the only source of injustice and individuals' suffering;[212] hence, attention is increasingly drawn to the actions of non-State actors—a vague concept used to refer to a variety of entities, as diverse as international organizations, non-governmental organizations, transnational corporations, or organized armed groups.[213] As discussed in **Section 3.2.2**, violations of human rights committed by non-State actors can, under certain circumstances, engage the international responsibility of States as the main duty bearers of human rights obligations. Moreover, in certain cases, international law even allows for the responsibility of non-State actors to arise due to human rights violations.[214] However, an important caveat should be borne in mind: international responsibility

---

[208] ECtHR, *Mahmut Kaya v. Turkey*, App. no. 22535/93, § 85–101, ECHR 2000-III.
[209] ECtHR, *Mahmut Kaya v. Turkey*, App. no. 22535/93, § 85–101, ECHR 2000-III, paras. 102–109.
[210] IACtHR, *Pueblo Bello Massacre v. Colombia*. Merits, Reparations and Costs. Judgment of January 31, 2006. Series C No. 140.
[211] IACtHR, *Pueblo Bello Massacre v. Colombia*. Merits, Reparations and Costs. Judgment of January 31, 2006. Series C No. 140, paras. 142–153.
[212] R. Coomaraswamy, 'The Contemporary Challenges to International Human Rights' in S. Sheeran and N. Rodley (eds), *Routledge Handbook of International Human Rights Law* (Routledge 2013) 127–139, 137.
[213] M. Goodhart, 'Human Rights and Non-State Actors: Theoretical Puzzles' in G. Andreopoulos, Z.F. Kabasakal Arat, and P. Juviler (eds.), *Non-State Actors in the Human Rights Universe* (Kumarian 2006) 23–41, 28; D. Weissbrodt, 'Roles and Responsibilities of Non-State Actors' in D. Shelton (ed.), *The Oxford Handbook of International Human Rights Law* (OUP 2013) 719–736, 720.
[214] J.G. Ruggie, *Just Business: Multinational Corporations and Human Rights* (Norton & Company 2013) 39.

does not automatically translate into accountability, as most international supervisory bodies lack jurisdiction to rule on the responsibility of entities other than States.[215]

An exception worth highlighting is that of the individual, which in addition to being the main right-holder under the international law of human rights, is also subject to obligations, such as clear prohibitions on engaging in serious violations of human rights. The notion that international responsibility for grave violations of human rights extends beyond the State is contemporaneous to the development of the international law of human rights itself, as confirmed by the creation of specific international tribunals to judge grave violations of human rights committed during the Second World War.[216] As discussed in **Section 2.5**, the progressive and convergent development of the international law of human rights, international humanitarian law, and international criminal law has even led to contemporary international criminal jurisdictions with the ability to establish the responsibility of individuals themselves, including a permanent International Criminal Court.[217]

The potential international responsibility for human rights breaches of the different non-State entities varies from case to case. For instance, armed groups that take part in a conflict that reaches a certain degree of intensity are indisputably bound by norms of international humanitarian law,[218] such as those contained in common Article 3 of the 1949 Geneva Conventions and their Second 1977 Additional Protocol,[219] but are also subject to international human rights norms. This is evidenced by the Optional Protocol to the Convention on the Rights of the Child on the involvement of children in armed conflict, which expressly forbids armed groups to recruit and use children during hostilities,[220] but extends beyond treaty obligations, encompassing customary norms pertaining to human rights.[221] Furthermore, the members of organized armed groups, as individuals, can be brought to justice themselves before the International Criminal Court;[222] a situation that is far from hypothetical, as evidenced by the first convictions rendered by the Court against Thomas Lubanga Dyilo, Germain Katanga, and Ahmad Al Faqi Al Mahdi.[223]

---

[215] A. Clapham, *Human Rights Obligations of Non-State Actors* (OUP 2006) 31.

[216] A. Clapham, *Human Rights Obligations of Non-State Actors* (OUP 2006) 561–562.

[217] Rome Statute of the International Criminal Court (adopted 17 July 1998, entered into force 1 July 2002).

[218] Armed groups involved in a conflict below the threshold—in itself a developing criterion not easily pinpointed—would be subject to the criminal law of the respective State. See: ICRC, 'How is the Term "Armed Conflict" Defined in International Humanitarian Law? Opinion Paper' (March 2008).

[219] R. Coomaraswamy, 'The Contemporary Challenges to International Human Rights' in S. Sheeran and N. Rodley (eds), *Routledge Handbook of International Human Rights Law* (Routledge 2013) 127–139, 137.

[220] Optional Protocol to the Convention on the Rights of the Child on the involvement of children in armed conflict (adopted 25 May 2000, entered into force 12 February 2002), Art. 41.

[221] Institut De Droit International, 'The Application of International Humanitarian Law and Fundamental Human Rights, in Armed Conflicts in which Non-State Entities are Parties' (August 1999).

[222] Rome Statute of the International Criminal Court (adopted 17 July 1998, entered into force 1 July 2002).

[223] ICC, *The Prosecutor v. Thomas Lubanga Dyilo*, ICC-01/04-01/06 (10 July 2012); ICC, *The Prosecutor v. Germain Katanga*, ICC-01/04-01/07 (7 March 2014); ICC, *The Prosecutor v. Ahmad Al Faqi Al Mahdi*, ICC-01/12-01/15 (27 September 2016).

The topic of the international responsibility of international organizations (IOs) has been the focus of mounting attention in recent years. In 2011, the International Law Commission adopted the 'Draft Articles on the Responsibility of International Organizations', which asserts that the international responsibility of IOs follows from any breaches of international obligations attributable to them under international law.[224] This was consistent with previous findings of international courts, such as the International Court of Justice and the European Court of Human Rights. While these courts were unable, due to their personal jurisdiction, to rule on the responsibility of IOs, they were clear as to the applicable legal rules. As affirmed by the ICJ: 'International organizations are subjects of international law and, as such, are bound by any obligations incumbent upon them under general rules of international law, under their constitutions or under international agreements to which they are parties.'[225] Therefore, IOs would be bound by any human rights treaty to which they become parties, as well as by any applicable general rule of international law, which includes customary norms and general principles of the law.[226] Although it is not common for IOs to be parties to human rights treaties—as these instruments are almost exclusively addressed at States[227]—it is possible to find exceptions. A clear example is the UN Convention on the Rights of Persons with Disabilities, which expressly allows for 'regional integration organizations' to become parties to the Convention[228] and which counts the European Union as a Party to it.[229] Moreover, it is planned that the European Union will also accede to the European Convention on Human Rights; thus, becoming subject to the jurisdiction of the European Court of Human Rights.[230]

Whether responsibility for a violation of human rights falls on an international organization or its Member States would depend on the rules governing the attribution of the wrongful act. The European Court of Human Rights has an interesting jurisprudence concerning this topic, which suggests that responsibility will fall on the international subject that exercises authority and (effective) control over the situation. In its diverse case law, the Court has found States responsible for breaches of the Convention, even when exercising authority and control with the approval of IOs,[231] and when undertaking actions to comply with an obligation that followed from their

---

[224] ILC, Draft articles on the responsibility of international organizations, Yearbook of the International Law Commission, 2011, vol. II, Part Two.

[225] ICJ, *Interpretation of the Agreement of 25 March 1951 between the WHO and Egypt*, Advisory Opinion, I.C.J. Reports 1980, p. 7, para. 37.

[226] See also: CJEU, Case C-308/06, *Intertanko* [2008] ECR I-4057, para. 51.

[227] P. Alston, 'The "Not-a-Cat" Syndrome: Can the International Human Rights Regime Accommodate Non-State Actors?' in P. Alston (ed), *Non-State Actors and Human Rights* (OUP 2005) 9.

[228] UNCRPD, Art. 42.

[229] OHCHR (authored by Israel de Jesús Butler), 'The European Union and International Human Rights Law' (2012).

[230] Current Art. 59, as amended by Protocol 14, provides the possibility of the EU's accession to the ECHR.

[231] ECtHR, *Al-Jedda v. the United Kingdom* [GC], App. no. 27021/08, ECHR 2011; ECtHR, *Jaloud v. the Netherlands* [GC], App. no. 47708/08, ECHR 2014.

membership to an international organization.[232] On other occasions, the European Court found itself lacking personal jurisdiction, as it considered the impugned actions to be under the authority and (effective) control of an international organization, even if taking place within the territory of a State Party.[233] As aforementioned, the answer to the question of the international responsibility of IOs does not solve the problem of accountability and enforcement, when IOs are not subject to the jurisdiction of international monitoring bodies.[234]

3.2.2.1.1 Transnational corporations

Among non-State actors, special attention has been increasingly drawn to the role of transnational corporations (TNCs) and their obligations towards human rights. This is certainly unsurprising, as TNCs can exercise more power and influence than many States, such power not necessarily being wielded for good, as exemplified by their implication in an array of human rights abuses.[235] A difference traditionally drawn between TNCs and some other non-State actors is that the former were not usually thought of as international legal subjects;[236] hence, avoiding scrutiny as to their direct responsible under international law for breaches of human rights norms.[237] However, this is a rather anachronistic approach, which is being progressively overcome by the development of international norms that impose human rights obligation onto TNCs.[238]

A strong interest in the international regulation of the behaviour of TNCs emerged in the 1960s, with concern from the Global South about the increasing influence TNCs had over the domestic politics of States.[239] Since the 1970s, different instruments have been adopted concerning the regulation of the behaviour of TNCs but, unfortunately, these

---

[232] ECtHR, *Nada v. Switzerland* [GC], App. no. 10593/08, § 195–198, ECHR 2012. The Human Rights Committee has followed a similar approach to that of the ECtHR, see: CCPR, *Sayadi and Vinck v. Belgium*, Communication No. 1472/2006, UN Doc. CCPR/C/94/D/1472/2006 (22 October 2008).

[233] ECtHR, *Behrami and Behrami v. France* and *Saramati v. France, Germany and Norway* (dec.) [GC], App. no. 71412/01 and 78166/01, 2 May 2007. See also: ECtHR, *Bède Djokaba Lambi Longa v. The Netherlands* (dec.), App. no. 33917/12, 9 October 2012.

[234] E. De Brabandere, 'Non-State Actors, State-Centrism and Human Rights Obligations' (2009) 22 *Leiden Journal of International Law* 191, 196.

[235] R. Chen, 'Organizational Irrationality and Corporate Human Rights Violations' (2009) 122 *Harvard Law Review* 1931, 1931; J-M. Barreto, 'Decolonial Strategies and Dialogue in the Human Rights Field: A Manifesto' (2012) 3 *Transnational Legal Theory* 1, 14–15; D. Weissbrodt, 'Roles and Responsibilities of Non-State Actors' in D. Shelton (ed.), *The Oxford Handbook of International Human Rights Law* (OUP 2013) 719–736, 726–727; J.G. Ruggie, *Just Business: Multinational Corporations and Human Rights* (Norton & Company 2013) 3–19.

[236] E. De Brabandere, 'Non-State Actors, State-Centrism and Human Rights Obligations' (2009) 22 *Leiden Journal of International Law* 191, 196.

[237] Important exceptions do exist, such as the conviction of German corporations by the Nuremberg International War Crimes Tribunal for their participation in genocide and crimes against humanity. See: U. Baxi, *The Future of Human Rights* (2nd edn., OUP 2008) 254.

[238] A. Clapham, *Human Rights Obligations of Non-State Actors* (OUP 2006) 76–80.

[239] D.M. Chirwa, 'The Long March to Binding Obligations of Transnational Corporations in International Human Rights Law' (2006) 22 *South African Journal on Human Rights* 76, 78; J. Gunderson, 'Multinational Corporations as Non-State Actors' in G. Andreopoulos, Z.F. Kabasakal Arat, and P. Juviler (eds.), *Non-State Actors in the Human Rights Universe* (Kumarian 2006) 77–91, 78.

are characterized by a lack of direct binding force.[240] Such is the case of the 1976 OECD Guidelines for Multinational Enterprises and the 1977 ILO Tripartite Declaration of Principles concerning Multinational Enterprises and Social Policy.[241] Further action concerning the regulation of TNCs in respect of human rights was adopted within the United Nations from the late 1990s.[242] In 1999, at the World Economic Forum in Davos, UN Secretary-General Kofi Annan proposed to the gathered business leaders 'a global compact of shared values and principles, which will give a human face to the global market'[243] in consortium with the United Nations. Those businesses that voluntarily opt into the UN Global Compact adhere to ten principles that deal with the protection of human rights, labour rights, the environment, and the fight against corruption.[244]

A further attempt at regulating the behaviour of TNCs in respect of human rights took place in 2003, when the Sub-Commission on the Promotion and Protection of Human Rights adopted the (draft) 'Norms on the responsibilities of transnational corporations and other business enterprises with regard to human rights'.[245] Notwithstanding their (technical) lack of binding force, even from the preamble, the 'norms' affirm the existence of international obligations upon TNCs concerning human rights, including their responsibility for 'promoting and securing the human rights set forth in the Universal Declaration of Human Rights' and their 'obligation' to respect generally recognized norms contained in the most important international human rights treaties.[246] Within the body of 'norms' themselves, the first provision contains a 'general obligation' upon TNCs to 'promote, secure the fulfilment of, respect, ensure respect of and protect' human rights within their 'respective spheres of activity and influence'[247] and the remaining provisions refer to the 'obligations' of TNCs with regard to specific

---

[240] O. De Schutter, 'The Challenge of Imposing Human Rights Norms on Corporate Actors' in O. De Schutter (ed.) *Transnational Corporations and Human Rights* (Hart 2006) 2–9; D.M. Chirwa, 'The Long March to Binding Obligations of Transnational Corporations in International Human Rights Law' (2006) 22 *South African Journal on Human Rights* 76, 79.

[241] OECD, Guidelines for Multinational Enterprises (1976); ILO, Tripartite Declaration of Principles concerning Multinational Enterprises and Social Policy (1977). Both of these documents have been amended through time, and the current versions are available in the websites of the respective organizations. See: http://mneguidelines.oecd.org/ and https://www.ilo.org/empent/areas/mne-declaration/lang--en/index.htm (accessed on 8 September 2022).

[242] O. De Schutter, 'The Challenge of Imposing Human Rights Norms on Corporate Actors' in O. De Schutter (ed.) *Transnational Corporations and Human Rights* (Hart 2006) 9–13; A. Clapham, *Human Rights Obligations of Non-State Actors* (OUP 2006) 218–225.

[243] Press Release (SG/SM/6881), Secretary-General Proposes Global Compact on Human Rights, Labour, Environment, in Address to World Economic Forum in Davos.

[244] UN Global Compact. See: https://www.unglobalcompact.org/what-is-gc/mission/principles (accessed on 8 September 2022).

[245] Sub-Commission on the Promotion and Protection of Human Rights, 'Norms on the responsibilities of transnational corporations and other business enterprises with regard to human rights' (26 August 2003) E/CN.4/Sub.2/2003/12/Rev.2.

[246] Sub-Commission on the Promotion and Protection of Human Rights, 'Norms on the responsibilities of transnational corporations and other business enterprises with regard to human rights' (26 August 2003) E/CN.4/Sub.2/2003/12/Rev.2, preamble.

[247] Sub-Commission on the Promotion and Protection of Human Rights, 'Norms on the responsibilities of transnational corporations and other business enterprises with regard to human rights' (26 August 2003) E/CN.4/Sub.2/2003/12/Rev.2, para. 1.

rights. Despite their normative language, in 2005 the Office of the High Commissioner for Human Rights produced a Report concerning the responsibility of TNCs with regard to human rights which identified the draft 'norms', together with the previously mentioned initiatives, as lacking binding legal character.[248]

Perhaps the most important step adopted within the framework of the United Nations towards advancing the international responsibility of TNCs has been the establishment of a Special Representative of the Secretary-General on the issue of human rights and transnational corporations and other business enterprises,[249] later replaced by a Working Group.[250] Professor John Ruggie acted as Special Representative from 2005 to 2011;[251] his mandate culminated with the adoption by the Human Rights Council of his proposed 'Guiding Principles on Business and Human Rights: Implementing the United Nations "Protect, Respect and Remedy" Framework'.[252] The principles adopted are based on three pillars: (i) the fact that the main responsibility to protect against human rights abuses lies upon States, and that this includes their duty to protect individuals from violations committed by business enterprises; (ii) the existence of an obligation upon business enterprises to respect human rights, which means that they should avoid infringing on the human rights of others and should address adverse human rights impacts with which they are involved;[253] and (iii) the availability of effective remedies, provided by the State, where a violation of human rights has taken place.

In addition to the duties of TNCs identified by the 2011 Guiding Principles, international law has continued to develop a framework leading to the international responsibility of TNCs, in particular with respect to their international criminal liability. At the time of the adoption of the Rome Statute, the topic of the international criminal responsibility of corporations was actually discussed,[254] although finally left aside,

---

[248] OHCHR, Report of the United Nations High Commissioner on Human Rights on the responsibilities of transnational corporations and related business enterprises with regard to human rights, E/CN.4/2005/91.

[249] J.G. Ruggie, *Just Business: Multinational Corporations and Human Rights* (Norton & Company 2013) xi–xii. See: CHR, 'Human rights and transnational corporations and other business enterprises', Resolution 2005/69 (20 April 2005).

[250] HRC, 'Human rights and transnational corporations and other business enterprises', A/HRC/RES/17/4 (6 July 2011).

[251] A comprehensive first-person narrative of the mandate can be found in: J.G. Ruggie, *Just Business: Multinational Corporations and Human Rights* (Norton & Company 2013).

[252] Report of the Special Representative of the Secretary-General on the issue of human rights and transnational corporations and other business enterprises, John Ruggie, Guiding Principles on Business and Human Rights: Implementing the United Nations 'Protect, Respect and Remedy' Framework (A/HRC/17/31) (21 March 2011).

[253] At a minimum, the human rights that should be respected are the ones expressed in the International Bill of Human Rights and the principles concerning fundamental rights set out in the International Labour Organization's Declaration on Fundamental Principles and Rights at Work. See: Report of the Special Representative of the Secretary-General on the issue of human rights and transnational corporations and other business enterprises, John Ruggie, Guiding Principles on Business and Human Rights: Implementing the United Nations 'Protect, Respect and Remedy' Framework (A/HRC/17/31) (21 March 2011), para. 12.

[254] A. Clapham, *Human Rights Obligations of Non-State Actors* (OUP 2006) 244–246; C. Chiomenti, 'Corporations and the International Criminal Court' in O. De Schutter (ed.) *Transnational Corporations and Human Rights* (Hart 2006) 287–312, 289–290.

revealing a lack of general acceptance of the idea of corporate criminal responsibility under international law.[255] However, there seems to be an emerging trend in that direction. An indication of this can be found in the 'Malabo Protocol' (further discussed in **Section 8.7**), which foresees the creation of a criminal chamber to a future African Court of Justice as Human Rights.[256] This future court would have jurisdiction over 'corporate criminal liability', under Article 46.c of the Protocol. Similarly, the 2019 Draft Articles on Crimes against Humanity elaborated by the International Law Commission recognizes the liability of legal persons (civil, administrative, and criminal) for the commission of crimes against humanity.[257] As foreshadowed by Clapham, a paradigm shift has clearly taken place; TNCs must be seen as having responsibility for breaches of their international obligations under international law.[258]

3.2.3 THE SCOPE OF INTERNATIONAL HUMAN RIGHTS OBLIGATIONS (TEMPORAL AND TERRITORIAL DIMENSIONS)

In addition to their material and personal scope, human rights obligations have temporal and territorial dimensions. With regard to the former, the 1969 VCLT codifies a customary norm which states the general rule that treaties do not apply retroactively—unless intended or established otherwise.[259] This means that human rights obligations contained in treaties only bind States Parties following their entry into force for the respective State. There is, nonetheless, an important exception to this general rule, which concerns the applicability of treaty provisions to situations that, although pre-existent to its entry into force, are of a continuous character. Unless expressly reserved at the time of ratification or accession, States are bound to comply with new treaty obligations in respect of ongoing situations that began before the State became a Party to a specific human rights treaty.[260]

On its part, the territorial scope of human rights obligations is perhaps the most controversial axis concerning the extent of obligations. The most basic understanding of the scope of human rights norms imposes upon States the duty to undertake their human rights obligations (to respect, to protect, and to fulfil) within the whole of their respective territories. The majority of human rights treaties use the concept of 'jurisdiction' to refer to the extent of the States' obligations, asserting that States should

---

[255] C. Chiomenti, 'Corporations and the International Criminal Court' in O. De Schutter (ed.) *Transnational Corporations and Human Rights* (Hart 2006) 287–312, 289–290; E. De Brabandere, 'Non-State Actors, State-Centrism and Human Rights Obligations' (2009) 22 *Leiden Journal of International Law* 191, 206–207.

[256] Protocol on Amendments to the Protocol on the Statute of the African Court of Justice and Human Rights (adopted 27 June 2014) ('Malabo Protocol').

[257] ILC, Draft Articles on Crimes against Humanity (A/CN.4/L.935), Seventy-first Session, Geneva, 29 April–7 June and 8 July–9 August 2019, Art. 6.8.

[258] A. Clapham, *Human Rights Obligations of Non-State Actors* (OUP 2006) 270.

[259] VCLT, Art. 28.

[260] D. Gonzalez-Salzberg, 'Do Preliminary Objections Truly Object to the Jurisdiction of the Inter-American Court of Human Rights? An Empirical Study of the Use and Abuse of Preliminary Objections in the Court's Case Law' (2012) 12 *Human Rights Law Review* 255–268.

ensure to all individuals within their 'jurisdiction' the protected rights.[261] While the idea of a State's jurisdiction is closely linked to that of its territory, they are not exactly the same.[262] ICCPR actually makes use of a formula that links territory and jurisdiction, by expressing that 'Each State Party ... undertakes to respect and to ensure to all individuals within its territory and subject to its jurisdiction the rights recognized in the present Covenant ... '.[263] The ambiguous drafting left room for interpreting the provision as either encompassing only individuals who are both present within a State's territory and subject to its jurisdiction, or as covering individuals subject to a State's jurisdiction both within and outside of a State's territory.[264] When interpreting this provision, both the Human Rights Committee and the International Court of Justice have been unequivocal that the correct understanding is that ICCPR provides human rights protection to any person within the jurisdiction of any State Party, even beyond the State's territory,[265] a topic further discussed in **Section 3.2.3.1**.

Conversely, other human rights treaties include the possibility of restricting their territorial scope of application. The most evident example of this is the European Convention, which continues to provide for a 'colonial clause',[266] enabling States Parties to declare whether the Convention 'shall extend to all or any of the territories for whose international relations it is responsible'.[267] This provision has allowed States to exclude the applicability of the Convention from territories under colonial administration; thereby exempting individuals in territories under the control of colonial powers from the international protection of their rights. The European Court of Human Rights has strengthened the colonialist effect of the clause, accepting that the absence of an explicit extension of the scope of the Convention to territories under colonial administration precludes the applicability of the Convention.[268] While the Court has disclosed a (rather timid) agreement with the arguments against the continued existence of a 'colonial clause' in the Convention—a relic from colonial times that should not be used as a tool for escaping international responsibility following a breach of human rights law[269]—it has confirmed its validity, stating that:

---

[261] ICCPR, Art 2.1; ECHR, Art. 1; ACHR, Art 1.1; CRC, Art. 2.1.
[262] ICJ, *Legal Consequences of the Construction of a Wall in the Occupied Palestinian Territory*, Advisory Opinion, I.C.J. Reports 2004, p. 136, para. 109.
[263] ICCPR, Art 2.1.
[264] ICJ, *Legal Consequences of the Construction of a Wall in the Occupied Palestinian Territory*, Advisory Opinion, I.C.J. Reports 2004, p. 136, para. 108.
[265] CCPR, General Comment 31: The Nature of the General Legal Obligation Imposed on States Parties to the Covenant, CCPR/C/21/Rev.1/Add. 13 (26 May 2004), para. 10; ICJ, *Legal Consequences of the Construction of a Wall in the Occupied Palestinian Territory*, Advisory Opinion, I.C.J. Reports 2004, p. 136, para. 109.
[266] L. Moor and A.W.B. Simpson, 'Ghosts of Colonialism in the European Convention on Human Rights', (2006) 76 *British Yearbook of International Law* 121.
[267] ECHR, Art. 56.
[268] ECtHR, *Yonghong v. Portugal* (dec.), App. no. 50887/99, ECHR 1999-IX, p. 4; ECtHR, *Quark Fishing Ltd v. the United Kingdom* (dec.), App. no. 15305/06, 19 September 2006.
[269] As argued by the applicant in the *Quark Fishing Ltd v. UK* case. ECtHR, *Quark Fishing Ltd v. the United Kingdom* (dec.), App. no. 15305/06, 19 September 2006.

'If the Contracting States wish to bring the declarations system to an end, this can only be possible through an amendment to the Convention.'[270]

Another example of provisions that could be interpreted as enabling States to restrict the territorial application of human rights treaties are 'federal clauses', such as the one contained in the American Convention.[271] Article 28 of the Convention states:

1. Where a State Party is constituted as a federal state, the national government of such State Party shall implement all the provisions of the Convention over whose subject matter it exercises legislative and judicial jurisdiction.
2. With respect to the provisions over whose subject matter the constituent units of the federal state have jurisdiction, the national government shall immediately take suitable measures, in accordance with its constitution and its laws, to the end that the competent authorities of the constituent units may adopt appropriate provisions for the fulfillment of this Convention.

However, according to the Inter-American Court, the correct interpretation of such a provision does not allow federal States to escape their international responsibility for violations committed by local authorities. On the contrary, the Court has affirmed that 'a State cannot plead its federal structure to avoid complying with an international obligation'.[272] This understanding is only consistent with the provisions of other human rights treaties, such as the ICCPR and ICESCR, which clearly indicate that their provisions 'extend to all parts of federal States without any limitations or exceptions'.[273]

3.2.3.1 Extra-territorial scope of human rights obligations

While the 'colonial' and the 'federal' clauses are provisions that can be utilized in attempts to justify a restriction on the territorial scope of human rights obligations, there has been a wealth of jurisprudence that engaged with extending such a scope beyond the territory of States. The topic of the extra-territorial scope of human rights obligations has been examined over many decades by various international monitoring bodies, as these supervisory organs have been called to decide whether State responsibility was engaged for acts or omissions that took place beyond the territory of State Parties. In July 1981, the Human Rights Committee dealt with this specific issue in two similar cases involving the abduction of individuals by State agents beyond the territory of that

---

[270] ECtHR, *Quark Fishing Ltd v. the United Kingdom* (dec.), App. no. 15305/06, 19 September 2006, p. 4.
[271] For an in-depth discussion of the origins and application of this provision, see: A. Dulitzky, 'Article 28 – Cláusula Federal' in C. Steiner and M-C. Fuchs (eds.), *Convención Americana: Comentario* (2nd edn., Konrad-Adenauer-Stiftung 2019) 847–868.
[272] IACtHR, *Garrido and Baigorria v. Argentina*. Reparations and Costs. Judgment of August 27, 1998. Series C No. 39, para. 46; IACtHR, *The Right to Information on Consular Assistance in the Framework of the Guarantees of the due Process of Law*, para. 139; IACtHR, *Matter of Urso Branco Prison regarding Brazil*. Provisional Measures. Order of the Inter-American Court of Human Rights of July 7, 2004, concurring opinion of Judge Cançado Trindade para. 15.
[273] ICCPR, Art. 50; ICESCR, Art. 28.

State Party.[274] The Committee was adamant that: 'the Covenant places an obligation upon a State party to respect and to ensure rights "to all individuals within its territory and subject to its jurisdiction", but it does not imply that the State party concerned cannot be held accountable for violations of rights under the Covenant which its agents commit upon the territory of another State'.[275] It further emphasized that: 'it would be unconscionable to so interpret the responsibility under article 2 of the Covenant as to permit a State party to perpetrate violations of the Covenant on the territory of another State, which ... it could not perpetrate on its own territory.'[276] Making reference to the mentioned decisions of the Committee, the International Court of Justice affirmed that 'while the jurisdiction of States is primarily territorial, it may sometimes be exercised outside the national territory. Considering the object and purpose of the International Covenant on Civil and Political Rights, it would seem natural that, even when such is the case, States parties to the Covenant should be bound to comply with its provisions.'[277] The ICJ further reaffirmed that the international law of human rights applies 'in respect of acts done by a State in the exercise of its jurisdiction outside its own territory', when finding Uganda responsible for violations of different international human rights instruments due to actions that took place in the territory of the Democratic Republic of Congo.[278]

In the 1980s the Inter-American Commission on Human Rights also took it upon itself to examine human rights violations committed by States Members of the Organization of American States within the territory of other Member States, affirming the extra-territorial scope of human rights obligations under the 1948 American Declaration of the Rights and Duties of Man. For instance, the Commission examined cases that concerned human rights violations committed by the US military operation in Grenada in 1983 and it also reported on extra-judicial executions carried out by Chilean agents in the territory of Argentina and the USA.[279] The Commission later confirmed that the scope of the human rights obligations under the American Convention on

---

[274] CCPR, *Sergio Euben Lopez Burgos v. Uruguay*, Communication No. R.12/52, UN Doc. Supp. No. 40 (A/36/40) at 176 (1981); CCPR, *Lilian Celiberti de Casariego v. Uruguay*, Communication No. R.13/56, UN Doc. Supp. No. 40 (A/36/40) at 185 (1981).

[275] CCPR, *Sergio Euben Lopez Burgos v. Uruguay*, Communication No. R.12/52, UN Doc. Supp. No. 40 (A/36/40) at 176 (1981), para. 12.3; CCPR, *Lilian Celiberti de Casariego v. Uruguay*, Communication No. R.13/56, UN Doc. Supp. No. 40 (A/36/40) at 185 (1981), para. 10.3.

[276] CCPR, *Sergio Euben Lopez Burgos v. Uruguay*, Communication No. R.12/52, UN Doc. Supp. No. 40 (A/36/40) at 176 (1981), para. 12.3; CCPR, *Lilian Celiberti de Casariego v. Uruguay*, Communication No. R.13/56, UN Doc. Supp. No. 40 (A/36/40) at 185 (1981), para. 10.3.

[277] ICJ, *Legal Consequences of the Construction of a Wall in the Occupied Palestinian Territory*, Advisory Opinion, I.C.J. Reports 2004, p. 136, paras. 109, 111.

[278] ICJ, *Armed Activities on the Territory of the Congo (Democratic Republic of the Congo v. Uganda)*, Judgment, I.C.J. Reports 2005, p.168, paras. 216–220, 345(2) and (3).

[279] IACHR, *Disabled Peoples International et al., against the United States*, App. no. 9213. Decision on Admissibility, September 22, 1987 in Annual Report of the Inter-American Commission on Human Rights 1986–1987, OEA/Ser.L/V/II.71. Doc. 9 rev. 1; IACHR, *Report on the Situation of Human Rights in Chile*, OEA/Ser.L/V/II.66, doc. 17, 1985 (referring to Letelier's assassination in Washington, D.C.). See also: IACHR, *Second Report on the Situation of Human Rights in Suriname*, OEA/Ser.L/V/II.66, doc. 21, rev. 1, 1985, which engaged with allegations that Surinamese citizens residing in the Netherlands had been harassed by agents of Suriname.

Human Rights also extends beyond the territory of States Parties. It affirmed that the term 'jurisdiction' under the Convention is not limited to or merely coextensive with national territory, but States Parties to the Convention can be found responsible 'for the acts and omissions of its agents which produce effects or are undertaken outside that state's own territory.'[280] According to the Commission, the attribution of State responsibility for violations caused by extra-territorial acts is not only consistent with, but actually required by, the pertinent rules of the international law of human rights.[281]

The body which has dealt most extensively with the topic of the extra-territorial scope of human rights obligations has been the European Court of Human Rights, having decided on multiple cases whether the acts of State agents undertaken outside the territory of their respective States could be attributed to said States under the European Convention.[282] The starting point within the Court's reasoning on the matter is the understanding that the concept of 'jurisdiction' contained in Article 1 of the Convention is a threshold criterion, as 'The exercise of jurisdiction is a necessary condition for a Contracting State to be able to be held responsible for acts or omissions imputable to it which give rise to an allegation of the infringement of rights and freedoms set forth in the Convention.'[283] Moreover, it is presumed that the exercise of a State's jurisdiction is primarily linked to the territory of the State, although exceptions to this presumption do exist, which means that under certain circumstances, the acts of Contracting States performed, or producing effects, outside their territories can constitute the exercise of jurisdiction.[284] The Court's case law has recognized a number of circumstances capable of giving rise to violations of human rights due to the exercise of jurisdiction by a Contracting State outside its own territorial boundaries. However, it should be mentioned that the Court's complex jurisprudence has raised a number of concerns about its overall consistency.

The Court laid down different circumstances that would lead to the extra-territorial application of the Convention and, therefore, to extending the scope of human rights obligations beyond the territory of States. The first of these would be acts of a State's authorities which produce effects outside the State's own territory.[285] A clear example of this are the actions and omissions of diplomatic and consular agents of the State.[286] A second scenario that entails the extra-territorial application of the Convention takes

---

[280] IACHR, *Saldano v. Argentina*, Report N° 38/99 (11 March 1999), para. 17.

[281] IACHR, *Coard et al. v. United States*, Report N° 109/99 (29 September 1999), para. 37; IACHR, *Armando Alejandre Jr, Carlos Costa, Mario De La Peña, and Pablo Morales v. Cuba*, Report N° 86/99 (29 September 1999), para. 23.

[282] For a discussion of the Court's extensive case law, see: K. da Costa, *The Extraterritorial Application of Selected Human Rights Treaties* (Nijhoff 2012), chapter 2.

[283] ECtHR, *Ilaşcu and Others v. Moldova and Russia* [GC], App. no. 48787/99, § 311, ECHR 2004-VII.

[284] ECtHR, *Banković and Others v. Belgium and Others* (dec.) [GC], App. no. 52207/99, § 67, ECHR 2001-XII; ECtHR, *Ilaşcu and Others v. Moldova and Russia* [GC], App. no. 48787/99, § 312, ECHR 2004-VII.

[285] ECtHR, *Drozd and Janousek v. France and Spain*, 26 June 1992, § 91, Series A no. 240; ECtHR, *Loizidou v. Turkey (preliminary objections)*, 23 March 1995, § 62, Series A no. 310.

[286] ECtHR, *Banković and Others v. Belgium and Others* (dec.) [GC], App. no. 52207/99, § 73, ECHR 2001-XII; ECtHR, *Al-Skeini and Others v. the United Kingdom* [GC], App. no. 55721/07, § 174, ECHR 2011.

place when a State exercises public powers within the territory of another State, such as executive or judicial functions, based on customary or treaty law, or other agreement between the authorities. In such cases, a State may be responsible for breaches of human rights obligations, as long as the acts in question are attributable to it rather than to the territorial State.[287] A third set of circumstances that extends the territorial scope of human rights obligations takes place when State agents operating outside their territory exercise authority and control over individuals, including the use of force.[288] The Court has encountered this scenario in different cases, where States were exercising physical power and control over persons,[289] both in the territory of foreign States, as well as on ships sailing in the high seas.[290] According to the Court, State responsibility in such situations stems from the fact that States cannot be allowed to perpetrate abroad human rights violations that could not perpetrate on its own territory—a similar reasoning to that of the Human Rights Committee, as mentioned earlier.[291]

3.2.3.1.1 Further reflections: The exercise of 'control'

Within the European Court's jurisprudence, the scenario that was most discussed regarding the extra-territorial scope of human rights obligations has been that of a State exercising control over the territory of another State as a consequence of military action—either lawful or unlawful.[292] This situation has been analysed in different judgments since the 1990s, with the criteria established by the Court for determining the existence of such control seeming to have changed over time.[293] When deciding the *Loizidou* case,[294] the Court found that Turkey could be found responsible for human rights violations that occurred in the northern part of Cyprus, as its army exercised '*effective overall control* over that part of the island'.[295] The Court confirmed the use of the 'effective overall control' criterion in the subsequent case of *Cyprus v. Turkey*, ruling that Turkey's level of control over northern Cyprus meant that it was to be found responsible for the human rights violations occurring not only as a consequence of the acts and omissions of its own soldiers and official, but also 'by virtue of the acts of the local administration which survives by virtue of Turkish military and other support'.[296]

---

[287] ECtHR, *Al-Skeini and Others v. the United Kingdom* [GC], App. no. 55721/07, § 137, ECHR 2011.
[288] ECtHR, *Issa and Others v. Turkey*, App. no. 31821/96, § 71, 16 November 2004.
[289] ECtHR, *Al-Skeini and Others v. the United Kingdom* [GC], App. no. 55721/07, § 136, ECHR 2011.
[290] ECtHR, *Öcalan v. Turkey* [GC], App. no. 46221/99, § 91, ECHR 2005-IV; ECtHR, *Issa and Others v. Turkey*, App. no. 31821/96, § 71, 16 November 2004; ECtHR, *Al-Jedda v. the United Kingdom* [GC], App. no. 27021/08, § 85, ECHR 2011; ECtHR, *Medvedyev and Others v. France* [GC], App. no. 3394/03, § 67, ECHR 2010; ECtHR, *Hirsi Jamaa and Others v. Italy* [GC], App. no. 27765/09, § 81, ECHR 2012.
[291] ECtHR, *Issa and Others v. Turkey*, App. no. 31821/96, § 71, 16 November 2004.
[292] ECtHR, *Issa and Others v. Turkey*, App. no. 31821/96, § 71, 16 November 2004, para. 138; ECtHR, *Catan and Others v. the Republic of Moldova and Russia* [GC], App. nos. 43370/04 and 2 others, § 106, ECHR 2012.
[293] K. da Costa, *The Extraterritorial Application of Selected Human Rights Treaties* (Nijhoff 2012) 110–115.
[294] ECtHR, *Loizidou v. Turkey (preliminary objections)*, 23 March 1995, Series A no. 310; ECtHR, *Loizidou v. Turkey (merits)*, 18 December 1996, Reports of Judgments and Decisions 1996-VI.
[295] ECtHR, *Loizidou v. Turkey (merits)*, 18 December 1996, § 56, Reports of Judgments and Decisions 1996-VI (emphasis added).
[296] ECtHR, *Cyprus v. Turkey* [GC], App. no. 25781/94, § 77, ECHR 2001-IV.

> ECtHR, *Loizidou v. Turkey (preliminary objections)*, 23 March 1995, Series A no. 310.
> ECtHR, *Loizidou v. Turkey (merits)*, 18 December 1996, Reports of Judgments and Decisions 1996-VI.
>
> The case concerned a Cypriot national who grew up in northern Cyprus, later relocating to Nicosia. She claimed to be the owner of land in northern Cyprus and that following the Turkish occupation she had been prevented from peacefully enjoying her property. She complained that the refusal of access to her property amounted to a breach of the ECHR. Following the decision of the European Commission finding no violations of the Convention, the Government of Cyprus submitted the case to the Court. Before proceeding to decide on the merits, the Court issued a separate ruling on two objections to its territorial jurisdiction interposed by Turkey (while joining an objection to its temporal jurisdiction to the merits); namely, that the Court lacked competence to consider the case due to the matters falling beyond Turkish jurisdiction and that, in any case, Turkey had restricted its recognition of the Commission's and Court's competence to acts and events taking place within its metropolitan territory. The Court rejected both preliminary objections: it found Turkey's declaration to be invalid and ruled that Turkey could be found responsible for human rights violations that occurred in northern Cyprus where its army exercises effective overall control (paras. 62 and 89). When examining the merits, the Court also rejected the objection to its temporal jurisdiction, which was based on the expropriation of the land taking place before Turkey became a Party to the ECHR. The Court affirmed that such a violation was of a continuing character; hence falling within its temporal jurisdiction (para. 47). Consequently, it found Turkey responsible for the ongoing breach of Article 1 of Protocol No. 1 due to the applicant's inability to enjoy the use of her land (para. 64).

The specific criterion utilized by the European Court, that of 'effective overall control', resembles an adaptation of the threshold test of 'effective control' developed by the International Court of Justice when deciding the *Nicaragua* case—and reiterated in the *Genocide* case[297]—to determine the attribution to the State of a conduct undertaken by non-State actors.[298] It is worth remembering that the 'effective control' test has so far established a rather high threshold of attribution,[299] which led the ICJ to rule that the conduct of the 'contras' in Nicaragua could not be attributed to the USA, despite the State having had a preponderant or decisive participation in the 'financing, organizing, training, supplying and equipping of the contras, the selection of its military or paramilitary targets,

---

[297] ICJ, *Military and Paramilitary Activities in und against Nicaragua (Nicaragua v. United States of America)*. Merits, Judgment. I.C.J. Reports 1986, p. 14; ICJ, *Application of the Convention on the Prevention and Punishment of the Crime of Genocide (Bosnia and Herzegovina v. Serbia and Montenegro)*, Judgment, I.C.J. Reports 2007, p. 43.
[298] ICJ, *Military and Paramilitary Activities in und against Nicaragua (Nicaragua v. United States of America)*. Merits, Judgment. I.C.J. Reports 1986, p. 14, para. 115.
[299] S. Talmon, 'The Responsibility of Outside Powers for Acts of Secessionist Entities' (2009) 58 *International and Comparative Law Quarterly* 493, 503.

and the planning of the whole of its operation'.[300] All said actions were still considered by the Court to be insufficient to reach the minimum threshold of 'effective control'. Similarly, this test determined that the genocide committed in Srebrenica by the armed forces of the Republika Srpska could not be attributed to Serbia, as there was a lack of State instructions in respect of the specific operation, despite the Court finding that the State 'was thus making its considerable military and financial support available to the Republika Srpska, and had it withdrawn that support, this would have greatly constrained the options that were available to the Republika Srpska authorities'.[301]

> **ICJ, *Military and Paramilitary Activities in and against Nicaragua (Nicaragua v. United States of America)*. Merits, Judgment. I.C.J. Reports 1986, p. 14.**
>
> In April 1984 Nicaragua instituted proceedings against the USA concerning its responsibility for military and paramilitary activities in and against Nicaragua. In November 1984, the Court ruled that it had jurisdiction to deal with the case. In January 1985 the USA announced its refusal to participate in any further proceedings in connection with the case; hence, the proceedings continue with its absence. The Court issued its judgment in June 1986.
>
> The Court ruled that the USA had violated the obligations imposed by customary international law not to intervene in the affairs of another State, by training, arming, equipping, financing, and supplying the contra forces (op. para. 3). However, it refused to find the violations of international law committed by the contra forces attributable to the USA (paras. 115–116). The Court did find the USA in breach of the prohibition of the use of force due to specific attacks on Nicaraguan territory in 1983–84 and by laying mines in the internal or territorial waters of Nicaragua (op. paras. 4, 6). The latter also amounted to violations of the principle of non-intervention, that of territorial sovereignty, and of the prohibition to interrupt peaceful maritime commerce. The Court also found the breach of certain obligations arising from a 1956 bilateral treaty.

> **ICJ, *Application of the Convention on the Prevention and Punishment of the Crime of Genocide (Bosnia and Herzegovina v. Serbia and Montenegro)*, Judgment, I.C.J. Reports 2007, p. 43.**
>
> In March 1993, Bosnia and Herzegovina instituted proceedings against the (then) Federal Republic of Yugoslavia in respect of a dispute concerning alleged violations of the 1948 Convention on the Prevention and Punishment of the Crime of Genocide. The final judgment of the Court in 2007 only concerned Serbia. This is because the FRY first assumed the name of 'Serbia and Montenegro' without change in its legal personality but, subsequently, Montenegro's independence led to Serbia accepting continuity with the previous State. On its part, Montenegro refused to give consent to the Court's jurisdiction (paras. 67–79).
>
> The main claim at stake was Serbia's international responsibility for breaches of the 1948 Genocide Convention, including the commission of genocide, complicity in genocide, aiding

---

[300] ICJ, *Military and Paramilitary Activities in and against Nicaragua (Nicaragua v. United States of America)*. Merits, Judgment. I.C.J. Reports 1986, p. 14, para. 115.

[301] ICJ, *Application of the Convention on the Prevention and Punishment of the Crime of Genocide (Bosnia and Herzegovina v. Serbia and Montenegro)*, Judgment, I.C.J. Reports 2007, p. 43, para. 241.

and abetting entities that committed genocide, failing to prevent genocide, and failing to punish genocide. Although the Court found that massive killings and other atrocities had been perpetrated throughout the territory of Bosnia and Herzegovina during the armed conflict, it considered that these acts were not accompanied by the specific intent that defines the crime of genocide, namely the intent to destroy, in whole or in part, the protected group.

A notable exception to this finding was that the killings in Srebrenica in July 1995 did amount to genocide, but the Court refused to find the acts of the army of the Republika Srpska attributable to Serbia under the international rules of State responsibility (paras. 388–415). Nevertheless, the Court ruled that Serbia had violated its obligation to prevent the Srebrenica genocide under the Genocide Convention. The Court observed that this obligation required States that are or should normally be aware of the serious danger that acts of genocide would be committed, to employ all means reasonably available to them to prevent genocide (paras. 432–438). Furthermore, the Court held that Serbia had violated its obligation to punish the perpetrators of genocide under the Genocide Convention, including its failure to fully cooperate with the ICTY (paras. 449–450).

Conversely, the European Court's 'effective overall control' criterion seemed to have inspired a lower threshold test, developed by the ICTY,[302] and then seemingly adopted by the Court itself. The 'overall control' test was advanced by the ICTY Appeal Chamber in its ruling in the *Tadić* case.[303] It established a (much) lower threshold than the 'effective control' test; one thought by the ICJ to be too low for the purpose of establishing State responsibility.[304] The ICTY Appeal Chamber proposed that in cases dealing with organized armed groups, for their actions to be attributed to the controlling State there is no need to reach the high threshold of (the ICJ's) 'effective control', but an 'overall control' of those actions should suffice. According to the Appeal Chamber, 'overall control' requires not only the equipping and financing of the group by the controlling State, but also the coordination or help in the general planning of its military activity.[305] However, such control does not extend to the point of requiring the issuance of specific orders or instructions relating to single military actions.[306]

ICTY, *Prosecutor v. Tadić*. Case No.: IT-94-1-A (7 May 1997) (15 July 1999).

This was the first case to go to trial at the ICTY. Duško Tadić, a Bosnian Serb, stood trial accused of thirty-one individual counts of serious violations of international humanitarian law committed in 1992. In 1997, the ICTY Trial Chamber found him guilty on eleven

---

[302] In fact, the judgment actually references the case law of the ECtHR. See: ICTY, *Prosecutor v. Tadić*. Case No.: IT-94-1-A (15 July 1999), para. 128.
[303] ICTY, *Prosecutor v. Tadić*. Case No.: IT-94-1-A (15 July 1999).
[304] ICJ, *Application of the Convention on the Prevention and Punishment of the Crime of Genocide (Bosnia and Herzegovina v. Serbia and Montenegro)*, Judgment, I.C.J. Reports 2007, p. 43, paras. 404–406.
[305] ICTY, *Prosecutor v. Tadić*. Case No.: IT-94-1-A (15 July 1999), paras. 122, 131.
[306] ICTY, *Prosecutor v. Tadić*. Case No.: IT-94-1-A (15 July 1999), paras. 122, 145.

> different counts, including the commission of crimes against humanity—acts of persecution, forced transfer, confinement, beatings, rape, and murder that took part within a widespread or systematic attack on the civilian population in furtherance of a policy to commit these acts—and of violations of the laws or customs of war—beatings and other grievous acts of violence against people not taking part in the hostilities. He was sentenced to twenty years' imprisonment, but both the defendant and the Prosecution appealed.
>
> In 1999, the Appeals Chamber denied Tadić's appeals, but allowed those of the Prosecution. The Appeals Chamber determined that the armed conflict at stake was of an international character and established the 'overall control' test for determining whether an individual's actions were part of the war when they were performed by a non–State actor (paras. 120, 131, 145). It held that the grave breaches regime of the Geneva Conventions applied and that the victims were protected persons under the Geneva Convention Relative to the Protection of Civilian Persons in Time of War. It further reversed other interpretations of the Trial Chamber: it held that acts carried out for purely personal motives can constitute crimes against humanity and that discriminatory intent is not required for all crimes against humanity, but only for such crimes relating to persecution (paras. 272, 305). It also found the accused guilty of crimes committed by other members of his group, which despite going beyond the common plan were foreseeable consequences of it. Consequently, the Appeals Chamber found the accused guilty on nine counts on which he had been acquitted, which led to a sentence of twenty-five years' imprisonment.

Following the mentioned cases concerning former Yugoslavia, the European Court's jurisprudence both expanded and restricted its previously established criteria. On the one hand, the Court developed the notion of the Convention's 'legal space' (*espace juridique*), which seemed to indicate that the scope of the human rights obligation assumed under the Convention was limited to the geographic area normally expected to be covered by the Convention, as a regional human rights treaty. In the Court's own words: 'The Convention was not designed to be applied throughout the world, even in respect of the conduct of Contracting States.'[307] Paradoxically, this notion was used as a justification to exclude the application of human rights obligations from the territory of the former Yugoslavia. On the other hand, the Court also resorted to the 'overall control' test—arguably a lower threshold than its own 'effective overall control' criterion—for determining the extra-territorial scope of human rights obligations.[308] The Court affirmed that the acts of non-State actors can be attributed to a non-territorial State when the latter exercises 'decisive influence' over them or when a given non-State actor 'survives by virtue of the military, economic, financial and political support given to it' by the non-territorial State.[309]

Yet, those later interpretations as to the extra-territorial applicability of the obligations assumed under the Convention seem to have been abandoned by the European

---

[307] ECtHR, *Banković and Others v. Belgium and Others* (dec.) [GC], App. no. 52207/99, § 80, ECHR 2001-XII.
[308] ECtHR, *Ilaşcu and Others v. Moldova and Russia* [GC], App. no. 48787/99, § 315–316, ECHR 2004-VII; ECtHR, *Issa and Others v. Turkey*, App. no. 31821/96, § 70, 16 November 2004.
[309] ECtHR, *Ilaşcu and Others v. Moldova and Russia* [GC], App. no. 48787/99, § 392, ECHR 2004-VII. It has been argued that this amounted to a lower threshold to that of the 'effective overall control' developed earlier. See: S. Joseph and S. Dipnall, 'Scope of Application' in D. Moeckli et al. (eds.) *International Human Rights Law* (3rd edn., OUP 2017) 121.

Court.[310] First, the idea of restricting the extra-territorial scope of the Convention to the European continent was soon left aside. It appeared to have been reshaped by the Court to understand that, when a Contracting State is exercising control over a territory, then the *'espace juridique'* of the Convention extends to cover such a territory.[311] Similarly, both the 'overall control' test and the 'effective overall control' test seemed to have been replaced by the Court, by the adoption of the 'effective control' test.[312] However, the actual meaning of 'effective control' under the case law of the European Court remains rather different to that of the ICJ.

When faced with the challenge that this adopted test seemed to establish a rather different threshold to the original 'effective control' one, the European Court dismissed such an objection. The Court argued that, unlike the ICJ, it was not making use of the control test to determine State responsibility, but merely to establish the extension of States' jurisdiction under the Convention. And added that the test for establishing the scope of jurisdiction 'has never been equated with the test for establishing a State's responsibility for an internationally wrongful act under international law'.[313] In other words, the meaning of 'jurisdiction' under the European Convention refers to the authority or control a State has over a territory and over individuals,[314] which acts as necessary (but not sufficient) condition to engage the responsibility of a State for the breach of human rights obligations. The additional element needed is that the actual conduct under examination amounts to a violation of the Convention.

According to the European Court, in order to determine the existence of 'effective control' and, thus, jurisdiction, a first indicator would be the strength of the State's military presence in the area.[315] Other relevant indicators will be 'the extent to which its military, economic and political support for the local subordinate administration provides it with influence and control over the region'.[316] Moreover, the Court confirmed that when such control over the territory has been established, 'it is not necessary to determine whether the [controlling] State exercises detailed control over the policies and actions of the subordinate local administration. The fact that the local

---

[310] K. da Costa, *The Extraterritorial Application of Selected Human Rights Treaties* (Nijhoff 2012) 250–253.

[311] ECtHR, *Issa and Others v. Turkey*, App. no. 31821/96, § 74, 16 November 2004; ECtHR, *Al-Skeini and Others v. the United Kingdom* [GC], App. no. 55721/07, § 142, ECHR 2011; ECtHR, *Pad and Others v. Turkey* (dec.), App. no. 60167/00, 28 June 2007, para. 53.

[312] ECtHR, *Al-Skeini and Others v. the United Kingdom* [GC], App. no. 55721/07, § 138-13974, ECHR 2011; ECtHR, *Catan and Others v. the Republic of Moldova and Russia* [GC], App. nos. 43370/04 and 2 others, § 106, ECHR 2012.

[313] ECtHR, *Catan and Others v. the Republic of Moldova and Russia* [GC], App. nos. 43370/04 and 2 others, § 115, ECHR 2012; ECtHR, *Mozer v. the Republic of Moldova and Russia* [GC], App. no. 11138/10, § 102, 23 February 2016.

[314] In this sense, the meaning of 'jurisdiction' differs to that more generally used under international law to designate the legal competence of States to make, apply, and enforce rules upon persons. See: A. Orakhelashvili, 'Restrictive Interpretation of Human Rights Treaties in the Recent Jurisprudence of the European Court of Human Rights' (2003) 14 *European Journal of International Law* 529, 539–540; A. Ruth and M. Trilsch, 'Bankovic v. Belgium (Admissibility)' (2003) 97 *American Journal of International Law* 168, 171.

[315] ECtHR, *Al-Skeini and Others v. the United Kingdom* [GC], App. no. 55721/07, § 139, ECHR 2011.

[316] ECtHR, *Al-Skeini and Others v. the United Kingdom* [GC], App. no. 55721/07, § 139, ECHR 2011; ECtHR, *Catan and Others v. the Republic of Moldova and Russia* [GC], App. nos. 43370/04 and 2 others, § 107, ECHR 2012.

administration survives as a result of [that] State's military and other support entails that State's responsibility for its policies and actions.'[317]

On their part, the Human Rights Committee and both the African and the Inter-American Commissions have adopted a similar approach to the one (currently) held by the European Court.[318] When it comes to examining the extra-territorial application of human rights obligations, all these bodies have made reference to 'effective control' as a threshold test.[319] However, it is fair to assume that the level of this test is the one established by the European Court of Human Rights, instead of the more stringent one from the ICJ, as the latter would be inappropriately onerous for application under the international law of human rights.[320]

3.3 THE PROTECTED SUBJECTS OF HUMAN RIGHTS

3.3.1 THE INDIVIDUAL

The international law of human rights is a legal regime grounded on the imperative of providing international protection to the rights of individuals. Its development during the second half of the twentieth century, through the proliferation of international instruments recognizing human rights and the creation of international monitoring bodies for the protection of such rights, came to confirm the individual as true subject of international law.[321] An ineluctable consequence of the recognition of the international legal personality of the individual is the procedural capacity to vindicate human rights at the international level.[322] However, the right of individual petition was the outcome of a rather lengthy process.

---

[317] ECtHR, *Al-Skeini and Others v. the United Kingdom* [GC], App. no. 55721/07, § 138, ECHR 2011; ECtHR, *Catan and Others v. the Republic of Moldova and Russia* [GC], App. nos. 43370/04 and two others, § 106, ECHR 2012.

[318] The Human Rights Committee seems to have gone even further, finding that the jurisdiction of a State might extend onto the high seas, even if not exercising effective control of a situation, when it has the capacity to protect the life of individuals at risk, but opts not to take any positive measures to that end. See: *CCPR, A.S., D.I., O.I. and G.D. v. Italy*, CCPR/C/130/D/3042/2017 (27 January 2021), paras. 8.5, 8.8.

[319] CCPR, General Comment 31: the Nature of the General Legal Obligation Imposed on States Parties to the Covenant, CCPR/C/21/Rev.1/Add. 13 (26 May 2004), paras. 10–11; ACHPR, *Mohammed Abdullah Saleh Al-Asad v. Djibouti*, Communication 383/10 (14 October 2014), para. 134; ACHPR, General Comment 3: on the African Charter on Human and Peoples' Rights: The Right to Life (Article 4) (November 2015), para. 14; ACHR, *Jose Isabel Salas Galindo and others v. United States*, Case 10.573, Report No. 121/18, OEA/Ser.L/V/II.169 Doc. 138 (5 October 2018), paras. 313, 318.

[320] In the particular case of the Inter-American Commission, this seems rather certain, given the extensive reference to the European Court's case law.

[321] The doctrinal support for such an idea was already mounting by the time of the adoption of the main international human rights treaties. See: H. Accioly, *Tratado de Direito Internacional Público: Vol. I* (Imprensa Nacional 1933) 71–75; P.C. Jessup, *A Modern Law of Nations: An Introduction* (Macmillan 1948) 41; H. Lauterpacht, *International Law and Human Rights* (Stevens 1950) 51, 61, 69.

[322] IACtHR, *'Five Pensioners' v. Peru*. Merits, Reparations and Costs. Judgment of February 28, 2003. Series C No. 98, concurring opinion of Judge A.A. Cançado Trindade, para. 24; A.A. Cançado Trindade, *The Access of Individuals to International Justice* (OUP 2011) 15–16.

Prior to the recognition of the international capacity of the individual, the protection of their rights at the international level could only be carried out though inter-State actions by resort to the institution of diplomatic protection; hence, it was essentially a prerogative of the State.[323] Only gradually, States began to establish mechanisms for dispute resolution that would allow for individuals to directly bring petitions at the international level.

Perhaps the oldest of these international jurisdictions was the one established within the international system on the navigation of the Rhine.[324] The 1815 Congress of Vienna provided for a Commission that exercised both administrative and judicial functions, which was set up by the Rhine States in 1816. This Commission acted as an appeal instance for navigation matters that could decide upon private disputes.[325] Another antecedent was the attempt of the II Hague Peace Conference of 1907 to establish an International Prize Court through the Hague Convention XII—even if this ended up being a failed attempt, as the treaty never entered into force.[326] An even more relevant precedent was the creation of the 'Corte de Justicia Centroamericana' (Central American Court of Justice) in 1907. Over the course of a decade, this Court provided access to both States and individuals to bring cases against any of its five Parties.[327]

As discussed in **Section 1.2.5.3**, a system for the protection of minorities was established under the League of Nations. This entitled the minority groups of certain European countries to petition the League about alleged infractions to 'minority treaties', which could be investigated by the League and submitted to a 'Minorities Committee' for examination.[328] Of the different minorities systems established under the League of Nations, the procedure created by the 1922 Geneva Convention concerning Upper Silesia is worth mentioning, as the system envisioned a multiplicity of remedies for dealing with a petition.[329] The individuals concerned could address a direct petition to the Council of the League of Nations, but also had resort to two controlling agencies set up by the Convention: the Mixed Commission and the Arbitral Tribunal.[330] Furthermore, the 'mandate system' also developed under the League of

---

[323] T. Meron, *The Humanization of International Law* (Nijhoff 2006) 301–306; A. Vermeer-Künzli 'Diplomatic Protection as a Source of Human Rights Law' in D. Shelton (ed.), *The Oxford Handbook of International Human Rights Law* (OUP 2013) 250–274.

[324] It is possible to add other opportunities for individuals to put forward petitions at ad hoc diplomatic conferences during the nineteenth century, such as those of Aix-la-Chapelle (1818), Berlin (1878), and the Peace Hague Conferences of 1899. See: A.A. Cançado Trindade, 'Exhaustion of Local Remedies in International Law Experiments Granting Procedural Status to Individuals in the First Half of the Twentieth Century' (1977) 24 *Netherlands International Law Review* 373, 373.

[325] A.A. Cançado Trindade, 'Exhaustion of Local Remedies in International Law Experiments Granting Procedural Status to Individuals in the First Half of the Twentieth Century' (1977) 24 *Netherlands International Law Review* 373–374.

[326] Convention (XII) relative to the Creation of an International Prize Court (adopted 18 October 1907).

[327] Convention for the Establishment of a Central American Court of Justice (adopted 20 December 1907).

[328] J. Stone, 'The Legal Nature of the Minorities Petition' (1931) 12 *British Year Book of International Law* 76, 76–77.

[329] Geneva Convention concerning Upper Silesia (adopted 15 May 1922).

[330] A.A. Cançado Trindade, 'Exhaustion of Local Remedies in International Law Experiments Granting Procedural Status to Individuals in the First Half of the Twentieth Century' (1977) 24 *Netherlands International Law Review* 373, 380–381.

Nations provided for mechanisms for individuals to petition under international law.[331] The inhabitants of territories under mandate could submit a petition through the mandatory power to be addressed by the Permanent Mandates Commission of the League. This system was succeeded by the trusteeship system under the United Nations, which also recognized the right to individual petition.[332]

These historical antecedents paved the way for the development, during the second half of the twentieth century, of the contemporary mechanisms of petitions pertaining to violations of human rights, both within the ambit of the United Nations and under the human rights treaties at global and regional levels.[333] As discussed in **Section 2.4.1.3**, nowadays, individuals have a right to international petition under numerous human rights treaties. It is an essential part of the regional human rights systems, which allow individuals to access the European Court of Human Rights,[334] the Inter-American Commission on Human Rights—and, through the Commission, the Inter-American Court of Human Rights—[335] as well as both the African Commission and Court on Human and Peoples' Rights.[336] As discussed in **Section 5.3.3**, at the global level, the right of petition has been recognized under the nine core UN treaty bodies, either by the treaty itself or by an optional protocol to it—even if not yet operative with respect to the 1990 International Convention on the Protection of the Rights of All Migrant Workers and Members of their Families.[337] Moreover, as examined in **Section 4.3.4**, all Member States of the United Nations are subject to an additional procedure of complaints, regardless of whether they have become Parties to a specific treaty. The Human Rights Council has succeeded the Commission on Human Rights in its ability to receive complaints from individuals concerning consistent patterns of gross violations of human rights in any Member State.[338]

To summarize, the protracted process of recognition of the legal personality of the individual under international law came to put an end to the archaic idea of the individual as a mere object of protection. The development of the international law of human rights has confirmed the notion of the individual as a subject of international law, endowed with legal capacity to vindicate human rights. The fundamental right of

---

[331] For a critical discussion of the 'mandate system', see: B. Rajagopal, *International Law from Below: Development, Social Movements, and Third World Resistance* (CUP 2003), chapter 3.

[332] A.A. Cançado Trindade, 'Exhaustion of Local Remedies in International Law Experiments Granting Procedural Status to Individuals in the First Half of the Twentieth Century' (1977) 24 *Netherlands International Law Review* 373, 386–388; B. Rajagopal, *International Law from Below: Development, Social Movements, and Third World Resistance* (CUP 2003) 67–68, 71.

[333] A.A. Cançado Trindade, *The Access of Individuals to International Justice* (OUP 2011) 20.

[334] ECHR, Art. 34.   [335] ACHR, Art. 44.

[336] ACHPR, Art. 55; Protocol to the African Charter on Human and Peoples' Rights on the Establishment of (Arts. 5 and 34) in respect to the African Court.

[337] ICERD, Art. 14; First Optional Protocol to ICCPR, Arts. 1–3 and 5; UNCAT, Art. 22; 1999 Optional Protocol to CEDAW, Arts. 1–2; Optional Protocol to UNCRPD, Art. 1; ICPPED, Art. 31; Optional Protocol to ICESCR, Art. 2; Third Optional Protocol to UNCRC, Art. 5; ICRMW, Art. 77.

[338] ECOSOC, 'Procedure for Dealing with Communications Relating to Violations of Human Rights and Fundamental Freedoms', Resolution 1503(XLVIII) (27 May 1970); HRC, 'Institution-building of the United Nations Human Rights Council', A/HRC/RES/5/1 (18 June 2007).

individual petition is a cornerstone of the international protection of human rights, allowing the juridical emancipation of the individual from their own State.[339]

3.3.2 PEOPLES

Human rights are mostly predicated upon the protection of the individual, with the vast majority of rights recognized in international human rights instruments aimed at protecting the interests of human beings in an individual capacity. However, there are clear expressions of recognition of rights that belong to a collective.[340] As further discussed in **Section 10.4**, perhaps the most evident illustration of a collective right is to be found in common Article 1 of ICCPR and ICESCR, which establishes that 'All peoples have the right of self-determination',[341] pursuant to which they have a collective right to freely determine their political status; pursue their economic, social, and cultural development; and dispose of their natural wealth and resources.[342] On its part, and as its designation indicates, the African Charter on Human and Peoples' Rights has gone further than other human rights treaties, constituting itself in an instrument of both individual's and peoples' rights.[343]

Although it is now generally accepted that 'peoples' can be the subjects of rights under international law, a difficulty that persists is to determine which groups of individuals qualify as 'peoples' for the purpose of collective rights.[344] There has been clear reticence to provide a definition of 'peoples' under international law. In a study completed in 1978, a Special Rapporteur of the Sub-Commission on Prevention of Discrimination and Protection of Minorities acknowledged the lack of an accepted definition of the term 'peoples', but proposed 'elements of a definition which have emerged from discussions on this subject in the United Nations'.[345] The elements the Special Rapporteur highlighted were that 'people' denotes a social entity possessing a clear identity and its own characteristics and that it 'implies a relationship with a territory, even if the people in question has been wrongfully expelled from it and

---

[339] IACtHR, *Castillo Petruzzi et al. v. Peru*. Preliminary Objections. Judgment of September 4, 1998. Series C No. 41, concurring opinion of Judge A.A. Cançado Trindade para. 5.

[340] CCPR, General Comment 31: the Nature of the General Legal Obligation Imposed on States Parties to the Covenant, CCPR/C/21/Rev.1/Add. 13 (26 May 2004), para. 9.

[341] ICCPR, Art. 1.1; ICESCR, Art. 1.1.   [342] ICCPR, Art. 1.1, 1.2; ICESCR Arts. 1.1, 1.2.

[343] African Charter, Arts. 2–17, 19–24.

[344] P. Baehr, *Human Rights: Universality in Practice* (Palgrave Macmillan 1999) 55; G. Alfredsson, 'Minorities, Indigenous and Tribal Peoples, and Peoples: Definitions of Terms as a Matter of International Law' in N. Ghanea and A. Xanthaki (eds), *Minorities, Peoples and Self-Determination: Essays in Honour of Patrick Thornberry* (Nijhoff 2005) 170; M. Nowak, *UN Covenant on Civil and Political Rights: CCPR Commentary* (2nd edn., Engel 2005) 19–22; J. Castellino, 'International Law and Self-Determination: Peoples, Indigenous Peoples, and Minorities' in C. Walter, A. von Ungern-Sternberg, and K. Abushov, *Self-Determination and Secession in International Law* (OUP 2014) 28.

[345] Special Rapporteur of the Sub-Commission on Prevention of Discrimination and Protection of Minorities (Aureliu Cristescu), The Right to Self-Determination Historical and Current Development on the Basis of United Nations Instruments, E/CN.4/Sub.2/404/Rev. 1 (1981), para. 279.

artificially replaced by another population'.[346] The study clarified that 'people' should not be confused with minorities (ethnic, religious, or linguistic), as the members of such groups are entitled to a different type of protection of their rights.[347]

In 1989, UNESCO held an 'International Meeting of Experts' on the rights of peoples, which issued a final report that also contained a list of characteristics that could be used to describe—but not to define, according to the report—the concept of 'peoples'. Following this final report, a 'people' would be 'a group of individual human beings who enjoy at least some of the following features: (a) a common historical tradition; (b) racial or ethnic identity; (c) cultural homogeneity; (d) linguistic unity; (e) religious or ideological affinity; (f) territorial connection; (g) common economic life'.[348] In addition to these characteristics, the group must be of a certain number, although there is no minimum quantity established; the group as a whole must have the will to be identified as a 'people' or the consciousness of being 'people'; and the group must have means of expressing its common characteristics and will for identity.[349] For those groups that succeed in being identified as 'people', international law recognizes certain rights, as further discussed in **Section 10.4**.

3.3.3 LEGAL ENTITIES

Technically speaking, only human beings are the bearers of human rights. Nevertheless, juridical persons, such as associations or corporations, are subjects of rights and obligations under domestic law and might be entitled to bring applications claiming the violation of their own rights before certain monitoring bodies. On the one hand, the Human Rights Committee, the Inter-American Court of Human Rights, and the African Court on Human and Peoples' Rights have excluded legal entities as subjects of the rights protected by ICCPR, the American Convention, and African Charter, respectively. The Committee has asserted that:

> The beneficiaries of the rights recognized by the Covenant are individuals. Although, with the exception of article 1, the Covenant does not mention the rights of legal persons or similar entities or collectivities, many of the rights recognized by the Covenant, such as the freedom to manifest one's religion or belief (article 18), the freedom of association (article 22) or the rights of members of minorities (article 27), may be enjoyed in community with others. The fact that the competence of the Committee to receive and consider communications is restricted to those submitted by or on behalf of individuals (article 1 of the Optional

---

[346] Special Rapporteur of the Sub-Commission on Prevention of Discrimination and Protection of Minorities (Aureliu Cristescu), The Right to Self-Determination Historical and Current Development on the Basis of United Nations Instruments, E/CN.4/Sub.2/404/Rev. 1 (1981), para. 279.

[347] Special Rapporteur of the Sub-Commission on Prevention of Discrimination and Protection of Minorities (Aureliu Cristescu), The Right to Self-Determination Historical and Current Development on the Basis of United Nations Instruments, E/CN.4/Sub.2/404/Rev. 1 (1981), para. 279.

[348] UNESCO, International Meeting of Experts on further study of the concept of the rights of peoples, SHS-89/CONF.602/7 (1989), para. 22.

[349] UNESCO, International Meeting of Experts on further study of the concept of the rights of peoples, SHS-89/CONF.602/7 (1989), para. 22.

Protocol) does not prevent such individuals from claiming that actions or omissions that concern legal persons and similar entities amount to a violation of their own rights.[350]

Similarly, the Inter-American Court has opined that legal entities are not the legal subjects of the rights protected under the American Convention,[351] but that indigenous and tribal communities, as well as trade unions can be.[352] Within the African System, whether legal entities, in addition to individuals and peoples, can be the subjects of rights has been contested. While, in the past, both the Commission and the Court have ruled on violations against legal persons,[353] more recently, the Court has affirmed that its jurisdiction excludes violations suffered by private- or public law entities.[354]

On the other hand, legal entities can be seen as bearing rights under the European Convention on Human Rights, which acknowledges that non-governmental organizations can be the victims of a violation of the rights protected by the Convention and its Protocols.[355] Consequently, the European Court of Human Rights has developed an extensive case law in which legal entities were granted legal standing to claim the breach of their own rights.[356] In the same way, the International Convention on the Elimination of All Forms of Racial Discrimination seems to extend certain degree of protection to legal entities, as it states that: 'Each State Party undertakes to engage in no act or practice of racial discrimination against persons, groups of persons or *institutions* and to ensure that all public authorities and public institutions, national and local, shall act in conformity with this obligation.'[357] Accordingly, the Committee on the Elimination of Racial Discrimination has expressly granted standing to legal entities that claim to be victims of discriminatory measures.[358]

---

[350] CCPR, General Comment 31: the Nature of the General Legal Obligation Imposed on States Parties to the Covenant, CCPR/C/21/Rev.1/Add. 13 (26 May 2004), para. 9.

[351] Conversely, the Inter-American Commission has accepted in the past that legal entities might be the subjects of human rights under the American Declaration of the Rights and Duties of Man. See: IACHR, *Jehovah's Witnesses v. Argentina*, Case 2.137 (18 November 1978), op. para. 1; IACHR, *ABC Color v. Paraguay*, Report No. 6/84 (17 May 1984), op. para. 1; IACHR, *Radio Ñandutí v. Paraguay*, Report No. 14/87 (28 March 1987), op. para. 1.

[352] IACtHR, *Entitlement of legal entities to hold rights under the Inter-American Human Rights System*. Advisory Opinion OC-22/16 of February 26, 2016. Series A no. 22, op. para. 2.

[353] ACHPR, *Zimbabwe Lawyers for Human Rights & Associated Newspapers of Zimbabwe v. Zimbabwe*, Communication 284/03 (2009), para. 179; ACtHPR, *Beneficiaries of late Norbert Zongo, Abdoulaye Nikiema alias Ablasse, Ernest Zongo, Blaise Ilboudo and Mouvement Burkinabe des Droits de l'Homme et des Peuples v. Burkina Faso* (reparations) (2015) 1 AfCLR 258, paras. 65–67.

[354] ACtHPR, *Gombert v. Côte d'Ivoire* (jurisdiction and admissibility) (2018) 2 AfCLR 270, para. 47.

[355] ECHR, Art. 34. See also: ECHR Protocol 1, Art. 1.

[356] See, among many: ECtHR, *The Sunday Times v. the United Kingdom (No. 1)*, 26 April 1979, Series A no. 30; ECtHR, *Observer and Guardian v. the United Kingdom*, 26 November 1991, Series A no. 216; ECtHR, *Open Door and Dublin Well Woman v. Ireland*, 29 October 1992, Series A no. 246-A; ECtHR, *Metropolitan Church of Bessarabia and Others v. Moldova*, App. no. 45701/99, ECHR 2001-XII; ECtHR, *Refah Partisi (the Welfare Party) and Others v. Turkey* [GC], App. nos. 41340/98 and 3 others, ECHR 2003-II.

[357] CERD, Art. 2.1(a) (emphasis added).

[358] CERD, *The Documentation and Advisory Centre on Racial Discrimination (DACRD) v. Denmark*, Decision on Admissibility, Communication No. 28/2003, UN Doc. CERD/C/63/D/28/2003 (19 August 2003), para. 6.4; CERD, *Jewish Community of Oslo v. Norway*, Communication No. 30/2003, UN Doc. CERD/C/67/D/30/2003 (15 August 2005), para. 7.4.

3.4 THE INTERACTION OF INTERNATIONAL AND DOMESTIC LAW IN THE PROTECTION OF HUMAN RIGHTS

The implementation of the international law of human rights is primarily a domestic matter.[359] The act of becoming Party to an international treaty, or the emergence of an international customary norm, determines States' duty to give effect to international obligations in its domestic legal order.[360] International law does not prescribe how States should implement these international obligations in the domestic sphere, but it does require States' compliance with international norms.[361] According to international law, the fulfilment of international obligations should take place even if these were to clash with domestic norms; in case of conflict between norms, international obligations should prevail.[362] In other words, international law places upon States the obligation to adapt their domestic legal orders to make them compatible with their assumed international obligations.[363]

Traditional legal doctrine has attempted to explain the relationship between international law and domestic law through the theories of 'monism' and 'dualism'.[364] For the former, international law and domestic laws conform a single legal system, with either international law or national law at its apex. This understanding avoids the need for 'incorporation' or 'transformation' of international norms, for their implementation within the domestic jurisdictions. In case of conflict between domestic and international obligations, each legal system will have its own rules as to which has prevalence, although from the perspective of international law the solution is clear, as aforementioned, international law should prevail. Conversely, according to 'dualism', international law and the domestic orders are separate legal systems. Each domestic system will establish its own rules to regulate the incorporation of international law into the domestic system, as well as the procedures to determine hierarchies and rules of interaction between norms.[365]

---

[359] M. Nowak, *UN Covenant on Civil and Political Rights: CCPR Commentary* (2nd edn., Engel 2005) 28; N. Ando, 'National Implementation and Interpretation' in D. Shelton (ed.), *The Oxford Handbook of International Human Rights Law* (OUP 2013) 698–718, 698.

[360] A.A. Cançado Trindade, *The Access of Individuals to International Justice* (OUP 2011) 84.

[361] A.A. Cançado Trindade, *The Access of Individuals to International Justice* (OUP 2011) 57; E. Denza, 'The Relationship between International Law and National Law' in M. Evans (ed.), *International Law* (4th edn., OUP 2018) 383.

[362] A rule clearly codified in Art. 27 of the 1969 VCLT. See also: PCIJ, *The Greco-Bulgarian 'Communities'*. Advisory Opinion (ser. B) No. 17 (31 July 1930), p. 32; PCIJ, *Treatment of Polish Nationals and Other Persons of Polish Origin or Speech in the Danzig Territory*. Advisory Opinion (ser. A/B) No. 44 (4 February 1932), p. 24.

[363] PCIJ, *Exchange of Greek and Turkish Populations*, Advisory Opinion, Ser. B, No. 10 (21 February 1925), p. 20.

[364] J. Jackson, 'Status of Treaties in Domestic Legal Systems: A Policy Analysis' (1992) 86 *American Journal of International Law* 310, 313–315; B.G. Ramcharan, *The Fundamentals of International Human Rights Treaty Law* (Nijhoff 2011) 14–16; E. Denza, 'The Relationship between International Law and National Law' in M. Evans (ed.), *International Law* (4th edn., OUP 2018) 383–409.

[365] J. Jackson, 'Status of Treaties in Domestic Legal Systems: A Policy Analysis' (1992) 86 *American Journal of International Law* 310, 316–319; E. Denza, 'The Relationship between International Law and National Law' in M. Evans (ed.), *International Law* (4th edn., OUP 2018) 383–409.

However, these theories are insufficient to explain the realities and complexities of the multiple possible interactions between international norms and domestic legal orders.[366] Breaking free from such debates, the international law of human rights challenges past dogmas that are based on an uncritical adoption of legal positivistic positions. On the one hand, on ratification of human rights treaties, States become obliged to give effect to the protected rights in their national system, making any changes to domestic laws and practices as are necessary to ensure their conformity with the assumed international obligations.[367] On the other hand, the international law of human rights affirms the human person as a subject of domestic and international law, endowed with legal personality and capacity in both ambits. From a perspective grounded in the international law of human rights, it is rather futile to argue about the prevalence of norms from either the international or the national sphere. International and domestic law act together, complementing each other, to secure the most effective protection of the human person.[368] This is a stance expressly adopted by many international human rights treaties, as well as by contemporary domestic constitutions, which state that what should prevail in all circumstances is the norm—either domestic or international—that better protects the human rights of the individual. As discussed in **Section 3.1.1.1.1**, it is through the application of the *pro homine* principle that any perceived conflict between norms pertaining to the protection of the human person should be resolved.[369]

3.5 CONCLUSION

This chapter offered a discussion of the fundamental issues that together provide the normative framework of the international law of human rights. It began with a reflection about the sources of this legal order; that is, the means whereby the law manifests itself and norms are created (custom, treaties, general principles of law, case law, doctrine). Then, it focused on the nature and scope of international human rights obligations,

---

[366] A.A. Cançado Trindade, *The Access of Individuals to International Justice* (OUP 2011) 84; E. Denza, 'The Relationship between International Law and National Law' in M. Evans (ed.), *International Law* (4th edn., OUP 2018) 389; M. Shaw, *International Law* (9th edn., CUP 2021) 113.

[367] CCPR, General Comment 31: the Nature of the General Legal Obligation Imposed on States Parties to the Covenant, CCPR/C/21/Rev.1/Add. 13 (26 May 2004), paras. 5, 13; CESCR, General Comment 9: the domestic application of the Covenant, E/C.12/1998/24 (3 December 1998), paras. 4, 5, 8; See also: IACtHR, *Loayza Tamayo v. Peru*. Reparations and Costs. Judgment of November 27, 1998. Series C No. 42; ACtHPR, *Jebra Kambole v. Tanzania*, App. 18/2018, Judgment (28 Nov. 2019).

[368] G. Bidart Campos, 'La interpretación del sistema de derechos humanos' (1994) 19 *Revista IIDH* 11, 30; S. Besson, 'Human Rights as Transnational Constitutional Law' in A. Lang and A. Wiener (eds.), *Handbook on Global Constitutionalism* (Elgar 2017) 234–247, 235; A.A. Cançado Trindade, 'Réaffirmation de l' universalité nécessaire et inéluctable des droits inhérents à la personne humaine', Addresse au Séminaire à la Cour EDH, Strasbourg (8 March 2018).

[369] A.A. Cançado Trindade, *Tratado de Direito Internacional dos Direitos Humanos: Volume I* (2nd edn., Fabris 2003) 544; M. Pinto, 'El principio *pro homine*. Criterios de hermenéutica y pautas para la regulación de los derechos humanos' in M. Abregú and C. Courtis (eds.), *La aplicación de los tratados sobre derechos humanos por los tribunales locales* (Del Puerto 2004) 163–172, 163.

reflecting on what types of duties are imposed by the international law of human rights, as well as on their extension across personal, temporal, and spacial dimensions. Lastly, the chapter succinctly engaged with the essential duties to implement these obligations with the domestic legal systems of States.

As discussed, the evolving nature of the international law of human rights means that the scope of the obligations concerning the protection of the human person necessarily expands through time. Human rights treaties are 'living instruments' that must be interpreted in the light of present-day conditions, so as to accompany the evolving social reality in which human rights are exercised. Furthermore, the concurrent interpretative work of the multiple international monitoring bodies reinforces the influence that human rights treaties have on one another and favours an increasing protection of human rights in all corners of the world. Consequently, the material scope of human rights obligations increases with time, due not only to the growing number of human rights treaties celebrated or to the emergence of new customary rules, but also to the developing interpretation of existing human rights treaties by their respective monitoring bodies. To this, we can add that the material content of *jus cogens* also expands with time, placing the protection of these rights beyond the scope of State voluntarism.

These developments of the obligations concerning the international protection of human rights coincide with what is arguably the most precious legacy of the international legal thinking of the second half of the twentieth century; the historical rescue of the human being as subject of international law.[370] Individuals are in our days undoubtedly subjects of rights and bearers of duties, which emanate directly from the international legal order. To such personality corresponds the legal capacity of individuals to act, and vindicate their rights, at the international level before multiple supervisory organs. However, it is not just the individual who has become a subject of rights under international law; collective entities, such as peoples, including indigenous and tribal communities, have also gained legal standing to bring claims on their own behalf as groups before international human rights bodies.

Conversely, the international law of human rights remains attached to its traditional structures that overwhelmingly focus on the accountability of States for human rights violations. However, our world's reality shows that other actors, especially powerful transnational corporations, have an ever-increasing role in the violation of the rights of individuals and peoples. In the mid-twentieth century, humankind recognized the need to reconstruct international law, placing restrictions on an unlimited State voluntarism, through the progressive adoption of norms capable of holding States responsible and accountable for the treatment of individuals under their jurisdiction.[371] The twenty-first century is then the time to extend this accountability beyond State-centric worldviews to protect individuals not only in all circumstances, but also from increasingly powerful actors that do not take the shape of a State.

---

[370] A.A. Cançado Trindade, *International Law for Humankind: Towards a New Jus Gentium* (3rd edn., Nijhoff 2020) 636.

[371] A.A. Cançado Trindade, *International Law for Humankind: Towards a New Jus Gentium* (3rd edn., Nijhoff 2020) 157, 635.

FURTHER READING

Cançado Trindade, A.A., *International Law for Humankind: Towards a New Jus Gentium* (3rd edn., Nijhoff 2020).

Cançado Trindade, A.A., *The Access of Individuals to International Justice* (OUP 2011).

Charlesworth, H., and Chinkin, C., *The Boundaries of International Law: A Feminist Analysis* (2nd edn., Manchester University Press 2022).

Clapham, A., *Human Rights Obligations of Non-State Actors* (OUP 2006).

da Costa, K., *The Extraterritorial Application of Selected Human Rights Treaties* (Nijhoff 2012).

Meron, T., *The Humanization of International Law* (Nijhoff 2006).

De Schutter, O. (ed.) *Transnational Corporations and Human Rights* (Hart 2006).

Nowak, M., *UN Covenant on Civil and Political Rights: CCPR Commentary* (2nd edn., N.P. Engel 2005).

Ruggie, J.G., *Just Business: Multinational Corporations and Human Rights* (Norton & Company 2013).

Shelton, D. (ed.), *The Oxford Handbook of International Human Rights Law* (OUP 2013).

PART II

THE UNIVERSAL SYSTEM

Part Two of this book extends across two chapters, both concerned with the universal protection of human rights under the United Nations. **Chapter 4** focuses on how human rights became one of the pillars of the United Nations since its creation in 1945. It engages with the bodies created under the UN Charter for the protection and promotion of human rights and the changes these have experienced throughout their history. This discussion covers the creation of the UN Commission on Human Rights, its replacement with the Human Rights Council (HRC), the mechanisms and organs developed under these bodies, as well as the creation of the Office of the UN High Commissioner for Human Rights (OHCHR). The chapter concludes with a reflection on the increasing role the International Court of Justice—the principal judicial organ of the United Nations—is adopting in the international protection of human rights and, in particular, on the contribution that Judge Antônio Augusto Cançado Trindade—co-author of this book—had in this respect during his tenure at the Court.

For its part, **Chapter 5** focuses on the so-called treaty bodies, supervisory organs created to monitor the implementation of each of the nine core human rights treaties adopted throughout time under the auspice of the UN. This chapter begins with an exploration of the main common functions of the treaty bodies, to then focus on each of these organs individually. The chapter concludes with important reflections on the long-debated need to reform the treaty body system, as well as with brief insights into the debate about the creation of a world human rights court.

4

UNITED NATIONS CHARTER-BASED BODIES

4.1 HUMAN RIGHTS UNDER THE UNITED NATIONS CHARTER

The promotion and protection of human rights is consistently identified as one of the founding pillars of the United Nations,[1] being recognized in multiple articles of the UN Charter.[2] As a pillar of the organization, human rights permeate multiple decisions adopted in all corners of the United Nations, from the Security Council to the International Court of Justice (ICJ), with the General Assembly having adopted, arguably, the most impactful international human rights instruments in existence.[3] However, this significant place gained by human rights in the constitutive document of the organization was an unexpected outcome for many of the political leaders that attended the 1945 San Francisco Conference, where the UN Charter was adopted.

The San Francisco meeting followed the 'Dumbarton Oaks Conversations' that took place in 1944, in which the USA, the UK, and the Soviet Union—then followed by meetings among the first two and China—laid down the foundations of the United Nations.[4] It was only after Roosevelt, Stalin, and Churchill had settled the most important aspects of the new organization that a meeting in which the other allied nations could participate was announced.[5] When delegations from fifty States arrived at San Francisco,[6] only one small mention of human rights could be found in the

---

[1] B. Boutros-Ghali, 'Foreword: The United Nations Family–Challenges of Law and Development' (1995) 36 *Harvard International Law Journal* 267, 267; N. Pillay, 'Strengthening the United Nations Human Rights Treaty Body System: A Report by the United Nations High Commissioner for Human Rights' (June 2012), 62; UNGA, Declaration on the Right to Peace, A/RES/71/189 (2 February 2017).

[2] Charter of the United Nations (adopted 26 June 1945, entered into force 24 October 1945), 1 UNTS XVI, preamble and Arts. 1(3), 13(1)(b), 55(c), 62(2), 68, 76.

[3] One of the main six committees of the Assembly—the Third Committee—is tasked with actively debating human rights issues, including the draft texts of resolutions and treaties to be adopted by the plenary of the body.

[4] S. Waltz, 'Reclaiming and Rebuilding the History of the Universal Declaration of Human Rights' (2002) 23 *Third World Quarterly* 437, 440; B. Conforti and C. Focarelli, *The Law and Practice of the United Nations* (5th edn., Brill 2016) 2.

[5] M.A. Glendon, 'The Forgotten Crucible: The Latin American Influence on the Universal Human Rights Idea' (2003) 16 *Harvard Human Rights Journal* 27, 27.

[6] B. Conforti and C. Focarelli, *The Law and Practice of the United Nations* (5th edn., Brill 2016) 4.

draft Charter.[7] A number of factors contributed to the promotion and protection of human rights achieving a much more significant place in the adopted Charter, gaining recognition in seven places of the text.[8] First, the Latin-American delegations that arrived at the conference had a strong commitment to making human rights a prevalent issue. Shortly before coming to San Francisco, nineteen Latin-American States (and the USA) had met in Chapultepec (México) for an Inter-American conference and converged in their desire to see the protection of human rights included in the UN Charter. These delegations even proposed the inclusion of a bill of rights into the Charter.[9] Second, the efforts from Latin-American States were echoed and amplified by the pressure of the representatives of more than forty non-governmental organizations (NGOs) that had been invited to the conference by the USA.[10] These organizations, due to their important role in channelling public support, managed to exert important pressure on the delegates at the conference.[11] An additional factor was the shock caused by photographs from the liberated concentration camps in Europe, made available at the conference,[12] which revealed the extent of the atrocities committed under the Nazi regime.[13] The reticence of the big powers to provide a preponderant place for human rights in the text of the Charter—partly explained by their own flagrant behaviour regarding colonialism, racial discrimination, and political persecution—was defeated by the aforementioned efforts.

Article 68 of the adopted Charter tasked the Economic and Social Council (ECOSOC) with establishing a commission for the promotion of human rights. This is the only commission whose creation is directly mandated by the Charter, revealing the status human rights managed to achieve within the final text.[14] As discussed in **Section 2.2**,

---

[7] M.A. Glendon, *A World Made New: Eleanor Roosevelt and the Universal Declaration of Human Rights* (Random House 2001) 6; P.G. Lauren, *The Evolution of International Human Rights: Visions Seen* (3rd edn., PENN 2011) 176.

[8] T. Farer, 'The United Nations and Human Rights: More than a Whimper less than a Roar' (1987) 9 *Human Rights Quarterly* 550, 555; A. Cassese, 'The General Assembly: Historical Perspective 1945-1989' in P. Alston (ed.), *The United Nations and Human Rights: A Critical Appraisal* (Clarendon Press 1992) 25–54, 26; M.A. Glendon, 'The Forgotten Crucible: The Latin American Influence on the Universal Human Rights Idea' (2003) 16 *Harvard Human Rights Journal* 27, 28.

[9] T. Farer, 'The United Nations and Human Rights: More than a Whimper less than a Roar' (1987) 9 *Human Rights Quarterly* 550, 555; M.A. Glendon, *A World Made New: Eleanor Roosevelt and the Universal Declaration of Human Rights* (Random House 2001) 15; S. Waltz, 'Reclaiming and Rebuilding the History of the Universal Declaration of Human Rights' (2002) 23 *Third World Quarterly* 437, 441.

[10] T. Farer, 'The United Nations and Human Rights: More than a Whimper less than a Roar' (1987) 9 *Human Rights Quarterly* 550, 554; J. Morsink, *The Universal Declaration of Human Rights: Origins, Drafting, and Intent* (University of Pennsylvania Press 1999) 2.

[11] P.G. Lauren, *The Evolution of International Human Rights: Visions Seen* (3rd edn., PENN 2011) 178–180.

[12] On the impact of visual images on human rights protection, see: G. Borradori, 'Tiny Sparks of Contingency. On the Aesthetics of Human Rights' in C. Corradetti (ed.), *Philosophical Dimensions of Human Rights: Some Contemporary Views* (Springer 2012) 157–172.

[13] M.A. Glendon, 'The Forgotten Crucible: The Latin American Influence on the Universal Human Rights Idea' (2003) 16 *Harvard Human Rights Journal* 27, 29–30.

[14] J. Morsink, *The Universal Declaration of Human Rights: Origins, Drafting, and Intent* (University of Pennsylvania Press 1999) 3.

the Commission on Human Rights was the body that drafted the International Bill of Human Rights. However, the contribution this organ has made to the promotion and protection of human rights extends beyond the drafting of those significant instruments.

4.2 THE UNITED NATIONS COMMISSION ON HUMAN RIGHTS

Starting work in early 1947, the Commission became the main UN body concerned with the promotion and protection of human rights[15] until its replacement with the Human Rights Council in 2006. It provided a forum for States, international organizations, UN agencies, and NGOs to voice concerns about human rights issues.[16] Although the Commission's functions changed radically throughout its history, for most of its existence the Commission can be seen as a technical rather than a political body, which is especially true for its first two decades of operation.[17] As discussed in **Section 2.2**, the Commission had a significant role in human rights standard-setting, acting as a drafting body for human rights international instruments adopted by the UN General Assembly. It was the Commission that completed the drafting of the Universal Declaration of Human Rights (UDHR) in less than two years (1947–1948) and the drafts of the two 1966 Covenants, the International Covenant on Economic, Social and Cultural Rights (ICESCR) and the International Covenant on Civil and Political Rights (ICCPR).[18] In addition to these, the Commission elaborated the drafts of both the 1984 Convention against Torture and Other Cruel, Inhuman or Degrading Treatment or Punishment (UNCAT) and the 1989 Convention on the Rights of the Child (UNCRC), while it was also involved in the drafting of other significant human rights instruments, including the 1959 Declaration on the Rights of the Child, the 1963 Declaration on the Elimination of all Forms of Racial Discrimination, the 1965 International Convention on the Elimination of All Forms of Racial Discrimination (ICERD), the 1967 Declaration on Territorial Asylum, the 1969 Convention on the Non-Applicability of Statutory Limitations to War Crimes and Crimes Against Humanity, and the 1981 Declaration on the Elimination of all Forms of Intolerance and of Discrimination Based on Religion or Belief.[19]

For almost two decades, the Commission's remarkable standard-setting activity was coupled with a lack of power to take action with regards to complaints concerning

---

[15] P. Alston, 'The Commission on Human Rights' in P. Alston (ed.), *The United Nations and Human Rights: A Critical Appraisal* (Clarendon Press 1992) 126–210, 126.

[16] Statement by High Commissioner for Human Rights to the Last Meeting of the Commission on Human Rights (27 March 2006).

[17] P. Alston, 'The Commission on Human Rights' in P. Alston (ed.), *The United Nations and Human Rights: A Critical Appraisal* (Clarendon Press 1992) 126–210, 130.

[18] However, the Commission was not involved in the drafting of either the 1948 Genocide Convention or the First Optional Protocol to ICCPR. See: P. Alston, 'The Commission on Human Rights' in P. Alston (ed.), *The United Nations and Human Rights: A Critical Appraisal* (Clarendon Press 1992) 126–210, 134–135.

[19] P. Alston, 'The Commission on Human Rights' in P. Alston (ed.), *The United Nations and Human Rights: A Critical Appraisal* (Clarendon Press 1992) 126–210, 133–136.

human rights; a stance usually referred to as the 'no power' doctrine.[20] From its earlier days, the Commission was the recipient of thousands of appeals, from individuals in every corner of the world, asking for help with human rights abuses they were suffering.[21] However, the States sitting at the Commission expressly instructed their delegates that the Commission had no power to take action on those petitions.[22] The 'no power' doctrine adopted by the Commission was endorsed by ECOSOC, which set in place a procedure by which the Commission would be merely informed of the human rights complaints received by the United Nations.[23] This practice was (only slightly) amended with time into a procedure consolidated by a new ECOSOC resolution,[24] which required the Secretary-General to compile a list of all communications received involving human rights, which were shared with the Commission and with the concerned States.[25] The Commission's 'no power' doctrine was adopted and maintained by an alliance of States, from both the Western and Eastern blocs, interested in securing that no serious system of petitions for human rights violations could be established under the UN Charter.[26] This was perhaps unsurprising given that the USA retained a system of racial discrimination in the south—known as the 'Jim Crow' laws—the European powers continued their colonial project, and the Soviet bloc's Stalinism could not but clash with the protection of human rights.[27]

The refusal to engage with violations was only abandoned in 1967, when a changing political context, with States in Asia and Africa emerging from the process of decolonization, led to an important shift in the membership of the United Nations.[28]

---

[20] P. Alston, 'The Commission on Human Rights' in P. Alston (ed.), *The United Nations and Human Rights: A Critical Appraisal* (Clarendon Press 1992) 126–210, 129–131, 139–140; U. Sundberg, 'Five Years of Working in the UN Commission on Human Rights: Some Reflections for the Future Work of the UN Human Rights Council' in G. Alfredsson et al. (ed.), *International Human Rights Monitoring Mechanisms Essays in Honour of Jakob Th. Möller* (2nd edn., Nijhoff 2009) 151–164, 153–154.

[21] As an illustration of the extraordinary volume of petitions sent to the Commission, the records of a 1952 meeting reveal that only within the previous year it had received 25,279 communications. See: CHR, Summary Record of the three hundred and thirty-second meeting, E/CN.4/SR.332 (27 June 1952) 2–3.

[22] B. Rajagopal, 'Lipstick on a Caterpillar? Assessing the New U.N. Human Rights Council through Historical Reflection' (2007) 13 *Buffalo Human Rights Law Review* 7, 8; P.G. Lauren, *The Evolution of International Human Rights: Visions Seen* (3rd edn., PENN 2011) 212.

[23] ECOSOC, 'Communications concerning Human Rights', E/CN.4/27 (23 October 1947).

[24] A procedure which will come to be described as 'the most elaborate wastepaper basket ever invented'. See: Humphrey, J.P., *Human Rights & the United Nations: a great adventure* (Transnational Publishers 1984) 28.

[25] H. Boekle, 'Western States, the UN Commission on Human Rights, and the 1235 Procedure: The Question of Bias Revisited' (1995) 13 *Netherlands Quarterly of Human Rights* 367, 377. See: ECOSOC, Resolution 728F (XXVIII), E/3290 (30 July 1959).

[26] P. Alston, 'The Commission on Human Rights' in P. Alston (ed.), *The United Nations and Human Rights: A Critical Appraisal* (Clarendon Press 1992) 126–210, 141.

[27] P. Alston, 'The Commission on Human Rights' in P. Alston (ed.), *The United Nations and Human Rights: A Critical Appraisal* (Clarendon Press 1992) 126–210, 141; W. Osiatynski, 'On the Universality of the Universal Declaration of Human Rights' in A. Sajó (ed.), *Human Rights with Modesty: The Problem with Universalism* (Springer 2004) 33–50, 36.

[28] H. Tolley, 'The Concealed Crack in the Citadel: The UN Commission on Human Rights' Response to Confidential Communications' (1984) 6 *Human Rights Quarterly* 420, 427; F. Cowell, 'The Evolution and Design of Powers at the UN Commission on Human Rights: The Complex Legacy of Anti-Apartheid Activism' (2019) 19 *Acta Universitatis Carolinae—Studia Territorialia* 67, 76.

Even the Commission's composition had been modified by then, with a small increase in membership already in 1961 (from eighteen to twenty-one Members) and a more significant enlargement, to thirty-two Members, in 1966, a majority of which (twenty of them) were from the Global South.[29] A first timid step towards the Commission assuming human rights monitoring functions had already been taken in 1956, with the adoption of a system of (triennial) State-reporting that lasted until 1981. Under this mechanism, all UN Member States were expected to report on the progress made in the protection of human rights for the Commission to make recommendations based on them.[30] Unfortunately, this little-known procedure did not prove to be very effective, with Alston characterizing it as a mechanism that 'wasted a great number of trees'.[31]

The two main procedures granting the Commission the power to supervise compliance with human rights were adopted, respectively, in 1967 and 1970, and were known after the resolutions that established them: the 1235 Procedure—created by ECOSOC's Resolution 1235 (XLII)—and the 1503 Procedure—adopted by Resolution 1503 (XLVIII). The 1235 Procedure allowed the Commission to study situations revealing gross or systematic human rights violations. Resolution 1235 empowered the Commission to debate these situations and to adopt resolutions, as well as to undertake thorough studies and produce reports, including recommendations, for consideration of ECOSOC.[32] The relevance of the 1235 Procedure subsists in our days, acting as the legal basis used by the Commission (and now the HRC) for appointing special rapporteurs and representatives, independent experts, and working groups to monitor human rights violations in particular States. The adoption of the 1235 Procedure was preceded by the Commission's apparent disavowal of its historic 'no power' doctrine, evidenced by the decisions to create, in March 1967, an Ad Hoc Working Group of Experts on the Situation of Human Rights in South Africa, together with the appointment of a Special Rapporteur on the Politics of Apartheid. These were followed by the Commission's express request to ECOSOC for the authorization to deal with human rights violations in the future.[33]

The second procedure (the 1503 Procedure) concerned the confidential examination of individual communications revealing a consistent pattern of gross

---

[29] The expansion of the Commission's membership continued, reaching forty-three Members in 1980 and fifty-three in 1992. See: P. Alston, 'The Commission on Human Rights' in P. Alston (ed.), *The United Nations and Human Rights: A Critical Appraisal* (Clarendon Press 1992) 126–210, 143, 194.

[30] A.A. Cançado Trindade, 'General Course on the International Protection of Human Rights' (1988) 7 *Revista IIDH* 5, 15–16; P. Alston, 'The Historical Origins of the Concept of "General Comments" in Human Rights Law' in L. Boisson de Chazournes and V. Gowland Debbas (eds.), *The International Legal System in Quest of Equity and Universality: Liber Amicorum Georges Abi-Saab* (Nijhoff 2001) 763–776, 770–771. See: CHR, Resolution 1(XII) (1956).

[31] P. Alston, 'The Commission on Human Rights' in P. Alston (ed.), *The United Nations and Human Rights: A Critical Appraisal* (Clarendon Press 1992) 126–210, 183–184.

[32] ECOSOC, Resolution 1235 (XLII), E/4393 (1967).

[33] P. Alston, 'The Commission on Human Rights' in P. Alston (ed.), *The United Nations and Human Rights: A Critical Appraisal* (Clarendon Press 1992) 126–210, 156; E. Domínguez-Redondo, 'The History of the Special Procedures: A "Learning-by-Doing" Approach to Human Rights Implementation' in A. Nolan, R. Freedman, and T. Murphy (eds.), *The United Nations Special Procedures System* (Brill 2017) 11–51, 23–24. See: CHR, Resolution 2 (XXIII) (1967); CHR, Resolution 8 (XXIII) (1967).

human rights violations. These communications were to be considered, in the first instance, by the Sub-Commission on Prevention of Discrimination and Protection of Minorities (discussed in **Section 4.2.2**),[34] which could refer them to the Commission.[35] The Commission could then keep the communication confidential, even appointing an *ad hoc* committee to conduct an investigation (subject to the consent of the concerned State), but was also empowered to transfer the communication to the public 1235 Procedure, allowing it to undertake an in-depth study and produce a report, including recommendations, to transmit to ECOSOC.[36] While the principle of confidentiality governs the examination of communications under the 1503 Procedure, from 1978, the Commission started to disclose the names of the States subject to examination.[37]

4.2.1 THE COMMISSION'S FALL INTO DISCREDIT

The replacement of the Commission by the HRC took place in 2006, at a time of reforms within the United Nations.[38] The Commission had fallen into discredit, with different criticisms raised by multiple actors, which casted doubts on its legitimacy.[39] As expressed by the UN Secretary-General, it was believed that many 'States have sought membership of the Commission not to strengthen human rights but to protect themselves against criticism or to criticize others'.[40] Problems with the Commission's membership gained particular notoriety in 2001,[41] when the USA failed to secure a seat at the Commission

---

[34] According to the former High Commissioner, Louise Arbour, at the time of its replacement by the Council the Commission was receiving an average number of communications close to 20,000 per year. See: Statement by High Commissioner for Human Rights to the Last Meeting of the Commission on Human Rights (27 March 2006).

[35] The Sub-Commission was replaced in this role by a Working Group on Communications and a Working Group on Situations in 2000. See: ECOSOC, 'Procedure for dealing with communications concerning human rights', Resolution 2000/3 (16 June 2000).

[36] ECOSOC, Resolution 1503 (XLVIII), UN Doc. E/4832/Add.1 (1970).

[37] H. Tolley, 'The Concealed Crack in the Citadel: The UN Commission on Human Rights' Response to Confidential Communications' (1984) 6 *Human Rights Quarterly* 420, 446–447; J. Donnelly, 'Human Rights at the United Nations 1955-85: The Question of Bias' (1988) 32 *International Studies Quarterly* 275, 294.

[38] UN Secretary-General, 'Strengthening of the United Nations: An Agenda for Further Change', A/57/38 (9 September 2002); UN Secretary-General, 'In Larger Freedom: Towards Development, Security and Human Rights for All', A/59/2005 (21 March 2005).

[39] N. Ghanea, 'From UN Commission on Human Rights to UN Human Rights Council: One Step Forwards or Two Steps Sideways?' (2006) 55 *International and Comparative Law Quarterly* 695, 695–699.

[40] UN Secretary-General, 'In Larger Freedom: Towards Development, Security and Human Rights for All', A/59/2005 (21 March 2005), para. 182.

[41] The Commission's membership was expected to reflect regional representation. With the creation of regional groups within the UN, in 1963, the Commission's membership was determined by the seats assigned to each of the five regional groups, with the election performed by the Members of ECOSOC, based on the candidacies presented by each group. The five UN regional groups are: Africa, Asia-Pacific, Eastern Europe, Latin-America and the Caribbean, and Western States and Others. See: F. Cowell, 'The Evolution and Design of Powers at the UN Commission on Human Rights: The Complex Legacy of Anti-Apartheid Activism' (2019) 19 *Acta Universitatis Carolinae—Studia Territorialia* 67, 73. See also: https://www.un.org/dgacm/en/content/regional-groups (accessed on 30 January 2023).

for the first time since 1947.[42] In 2001, the three seats available for the 'Western European and other States' regional group went to Austria, France, and Sweden, while Sudan (As-Sudan) was elected to sit at the Commission, as the 'African Group' presented a clean slate—a number of candidates equal to the number of available seats for the regional group.[43] The fact that the USA was left out of the Commission (for one year) while other States with questionable human rights records (in particular, Sudan) managed to secure a seat was portrayed, especially by US politicians and media outlets, as an illustration of the problems concerning the Commission's membership.[44] These concerns were exacerbated by the subsequent election of Libya to Chair the Commission in 2003—despite its poor human rights record and suspicions of supporting terrorism—and the re-election of Sudan in 2004—at a time when genocide was taking place within its jurisdiction.[45]

Nevertheless, the presence of States with appalling human rights records among the Commission's members was only one of the problems. The Commission's over-politicization was perhaps the most contentious issue, which included selective decisions, double standards, and obstructive regional divisions.[46] Even the most democratic of States would see their voting patterns on the condemnation of human rights violations change, depending on whether their vote could affect important relations with political allies.[47] Similarly, the selection of States placed under the Commission's gaze depended on political factors, at least, as much as on their own behaviour concerning human rights.[48] In fact, the General Assembly's resolution establishing the HRC expressly mentioned

---

[42] P. Alston, 'Reconceiving the UN Human Rights Regime: Challenges Confronting the New UN Human Rights Council' (2006) 7 *Melbourne Journal of International Law* 185, 191; C. Mallory, 'Membership and the UN Human Rights Council' (2013) 2 *Canadian Journal of Human Rights* 1, 7.

[43] L. Moss, 'Will the Human Rights Council Have Better Membership than the Commission on Human Rights?' (2006) 13 *Human Rights Brief* 5, 5; U. Sundberg, 'Five Years of Working in the UN Commission on Human Rights: Some Reflections for the Future Work of the UN Human Rights Council' in G. Alfredsson et al. (ed.), *International Human Rights Monitoring Mechanisms Essays in Honour of Jakob Th. Möller* (2nd edn., Nijhoff 2009) 151–164, 161–162.

[44] P. Alston, 'Reconceiving the UN Human Rights Regime: Challenges Confronting the New UN Human Rights Council' (2006) 7 *Melbourne Journal of International Law* 185, 191; L. Moss, 'Will the Human Rights Council Have Better Membership than the Commission on Human Rights?' (2006) 13 *Human Rights Brief* 5, 5. See: K. Roth, 'Despots Pretending to Spot and Shame Despots' *New York Times* (17 April 2001).

[45] P. Alston, 'Reconceiving the UN Human Rights Regime: Challenges Confronting the New UN Human Rights Council' (2006) 7 *Melbourne Journal of International Law* 185, 188–193; M. Kothari, 'From Commission to the Council: Evolution of UN Charter Bodies' in D. Shelton (ed.), *The Oxford Handbook of International Human Rights Law* (OUP 2013) 587–620, 590.

[46] L. Moss, 'Will the Human Rights Council Have Better Membership than the Commission on Human Rights?' (2006) 13 *Human Rights Brief* 5, 5; U. Sundberg, 'Five Years of Working in the UN Commission on Human Rights: Some Reflections for the Future Work of the UN Human Rights Council' in G. Alfredsson et al. (ed.), *International Human Rights Monitoring Mechanisms Essays in Honour of Jakob Th. Möller* (2nd edn., Nijhoff 2009) 151–164, 163.

[47] L. Moss, 'Will the Human Rights Council Have Better Membership than the Commission on Human Rights?' (2006) 13 *Human Rights Brief* 5, 5.

[48] J. Donnelly, 'Human Rights at the United Nations 1955-85: The Question of Bias' (1988) 32 *International Studies Quarterly* 275, 288; H. Boekle, 'Western States, the UN Commission on Human Rights, and the 1235 Procedure: The Question of Bias Revisited' (1995) 13 *Netherlands Quarterly of Human Rights* 367, 401; Amnesty International, 'Meeting the Challenge: Transforming the Commission on Human Rights into a Human Rights Council', IOR 40/008/2005 (26 April 2005), p. 5.

'the elimination of double standards and politicization' among the rationale for the creation of the new body.[49] The Commission's political selectivity can be appreciated in some clear examples. For instance, in 2002, all States under the 1503 Procedure were from Africa, although gross human rights violations were also taking place in other latitudes.[50] Likewise, the Commission ignored large-scale human rights violations taking place in Iraq (Al-'Iraq) during the late 1980s, only finding the will to take action with the change of political mores following Iraq's invasion of Kuwait (Al Kuwayt) in 1991, while also deciding to put an end to the mandate to monitor Iraq's human rights situation following the US-led invasion of the country.[51]

4.2.2 THE SUB-COMMISSION ON PREVENTION OF DISCRIMINATION AND PROTECTION OF MINORITIES

Created in 1947, the Sub-Commission on Prevention of Discrimination and Protection of Minorities—renamed Sub-Commission on the Promotion and Protection of Human Rights in 1999—[52] was a subsidiary body of the Commission on Human Rights. Unlike the Commission, the membership of the Sub-Commission was made of independent experts,[53] who were tasked with undertaking studies on issues pertaining to minorities and discrimination (later extended to comprise any issues concerning human rights) and with making recommendations to the Commission.[54] The membership of the Sub-Commission, as that of the Commission, expanded through time. It was initially composed of twelve members, but it counted twenty-six experts by the time of its replacement by the Human Rights Council's Advisory Committee in 2006 (discussed in **Section 4.3.5**).

The Sub-Commission had an important role in the Commission's standard-setting activity, with significant contributions concerning the prohibition of discrimination under the UDHR, and the protection of minorities under ICCPR and, more generally, with regard to the International Convention on the Elimination of All Forms of Racial Discrimination (ICERD).[55] Moreover, the Sub-Commission was

[49] UNGA, 'Human Rights Council', Resolution 60/251 (3 April 2006).
[50] U. Sundberg, 'Five Years of Working in the UN Commission on Human Rights: Some Reflections for the Future Work of the UN Human Rights Council' in G. Alfredsson et al. (ed.), *International Human Rights Monitoring Mechanisms Essays in Honour of Jakob Th. Möller* (2nd edn., Nijhoff 2009) 151–164, 156.
[51] Amnesty International, 'Meeting the Challenge: Transforming the Commission on Human Rights into a Human Rights Council', IOR 40/008/2005 (26 April 2005), p. 5; U. Sundberg, 'Five Years of Working in the UN Commission on Human Rights: Some Reflections for the Future Work of the UN Human Rights Council' in G. Alfredsson et al. (ed.), *International Human Rights Monitoring Mechanisms Essays in Honour of Jakob Th. Möller* (2nd edn., Nijhoff 2009) 151–164, 157.
[52] ECOSOC, 'Rationalization of the work of the Commission on Human Rights', Decision 1999/256 (27 July 1999).
[53] Even if the actual independence of its members has been called into question. See: Humphrey, J.P., *Human Rights & the United Nations: a great adventure* (Transnational Publishers 1984) 21.
[54] Humphrey, J.P., *Human Rights & the United Nations: a great adventure* (Transnational Publishers 1984) 310; A. Eide, 'The Sub-Commission on Prevention of Discrimination and Protection of Minorities' in P. Alston (ed.), *The United Nations and Human Rights: A Critical Appraisal* (Clarendon Press 1992) 211–264, 211–213.
[55] Humphrey, J.P., *Human Rights & the United Nations: a great adventure* (Transnational Publishers 1984) 310; A. Eide, 'The Sub-Commission on Prevention of Discrimination and Protection of Minorities' in P. Alston (ed.), *The United Nations and Human Rights: A Critical Appraisal* (Clarendon Press 1992) 211–264, 242–243.

given a primary role in the 1503 Procedure, as a Working Group of its members was charged with considering the admissibility of all communications received, while the Sub-Commission, in plenary, was tasked with deciding whether to refer to the Commission those situations that revealed a consistent pattern of gross human rights violations.[56]

4.3 THE HUMAN RIGHTS COUNCIL (HRC)

The decision to create the HRC to replace the Commission was adopted as part of the package of reforms agreed upon at the 2005 World Summit.[57] It followed a proposal made by former Secretary-General, Kofi Annan, who believed that if the United Nations was to 'take the cause of human rights as seriously as those of security and development—then Member States should agree to replace the Commission on Human Rights with a smaller standing Human Rights Council'.[58] The creation of the Council was decided by an overwhelming majority of UN Member States, with 170 voting in favour and only four against—Israel, the Marshall Islands, Palau, and the USA— with three abstentions—Belarus, Iran, and Venezuela.[59] Arguably, the establishment of the Council was one the most significant outcomes of the institutional reform process generated by the UN's sixtieth anniversary.[60] While the hopes that the new main human rights body would become a principal organ of the UN, through a Charter amendment,[61] did not come to fruition, the Council can be seen as having a higher status than its predecessor, as a subsidiary organ of the General Assembly, instead of ECOSOC.[62] Like the old Commission, the Council is an inter-governmental body composed of State representatives, although the number of Members was reduced from fifty-three to forty-seven.[63]

---

[56] In 2000, the Sub-Commission's role under the 1503 Procedure was removed, while preserving that of its Working Group. See: CHR, 'Enhancing the effectiveness of the mechanisms of the Commission on Human Rights', E/CN.4/DEC/2000/109 (26 April 2000).

[57] UNGA, '2005 World Summit Outcome', A/RES/60/1 (24 October 2005), para 157.

[58] Secretary-General, 'In Larger Freedom: Towards Development, Security and Human Rights for All', A/59/2005 (21 March 2005), para 183.

[59] D. Etone, *The Human Rights Council: The Impact of the Universal Periodic Review in Africa* (Routledge 2020) 27. See: UNGA, A/60/PV.72 (15 March 2006) 5–6.

[60] K. Boyle, 'The United Nations Human Rights Council: Origins, Antecedents, and Prospects' in K. Boyle (ed.), *New Institutions for Human Rights Protection* (OUP 2009) 11–47, 11–12; H. Charlesworth and E. Larking, 'Introduction: the regulatory power of the Universal Periodic Review' in H. Charlesworth and E. Larking (eds.), *Human Rights and the Universal Periodic Review: Rituals and Ritualism* (CUP 2014) 2.

[61] Secretary-General, 'In Larger Freedom: Towards Development, Security and Human Rights for All. Addendum: Human Rights Council', A/59/2005/Add.1 (23 May 2005), para. 14.

[62] K. Boyle, 'The United Nations Human Rights Council: Origins, Antecedents, and Prospects' in K. Boyle (ed.), *New Institutions for Human Rights Protection* (OUP 2009) 11–47, 12; O. de Frouville, 'Building a Universal System for the Protection of Human Rights: The Way Forward' in M. Cherif Bassiouni and W. Schabas (eds.), *New Challenges for the UN Human Rights Machinery: What Future for the UN Treaty Body System and the Human Rights Council Procedures?* (Intersentia 2011) 241–266, 246.

[63] UNGA, 'Human Rights Council', Resolution 60/251 (3 April 2006), para. 7.

The election of Members to sit at the Council differs quite substantially from that of the Commission. Members are to be elected, directly and individually, by secret ballot by the majority of the (193) Members of the General Assembly rather than by the fifty-four Members sitting at ECOSOC. To secure equitable geographical membership of the Council, the distribution of seats is determined based on the UN's regional grouping, with thirteen seats for the African Group, thirteen seats for Asia-Pacific, eight seats for Latin-America and the Caribbean (GRULAC), seven seats for the Western Group (WEOG), and six seats for Eastern Europe.[64] When electing Council Members, States should consider 'the contribution of candidates to the promotion and protection of human rights and their voluntary pledges and commitments made thereto',[65] a requirement that was intended to avoid the election of States with egregious human rights records into the Council. However, the practice of regional groups presenting 'clean slates' remains a common (although not universal) practice, rendering the actual process of pledge and election meaningless to some extent.[66]

Elected Members sit at the Council for a three-year period and, to avoid the permanent presence of certain States—a usual occurrence at the Commission—,[67] are only eligible once for immediate re-election.[68] Moreover, in case of gross and systematic violations of human rights by a Council Member, the General Assembly is empowered to suspend their membership, by a two-thirds majority of the present Members,[69] as it occurred with Libya in 2011 and Russia in 2022.[70] In June 2018, for the first time in the body's history, a State voluntarily stopped its membership of the Council by withdrawing from its seat. A day after the UN High Commissioner for Human Rights gave a speech at the Council criticizing the practice of forcibly separating undocumented families entering the country, the USA, then under the Trump administration, decided to abandon the Council. The withdrawal was public and done in extremely strong terms, such as referring to the Council as a 'hypocritical and self-serving organization that makes a mockery of human rights'.[71] In addition to leaving the body, the USA also expressed its intention to de-fund the Council, by decreasing its contribution to the UN budget.[72] Nevertheless, despite its 2018 withdrawal, the USA still engaged in its third Universal

---

[64] UNGA, 'Human Rights Council', Resolution 60/251 (3 April 2006), para. 7.

[65] UNGA, 'Human Rights Council', Resolution 60/251 (3 April 2006), para 8.

[66] C. Mallory, 'Membership and the UN Human Rights Council' (2013) 2 *Canadian Journal of Human Rights* 1, 33, 35; A. Clapham, 'The General Assembly' in F. Mégret and P. Alston (eds.), *The United Nations and Human Rights: A Critical Appraisal* (2nd edn., OUP 2020) 99–129, 126.

[67] K. Boyle, 'The United Nations Human Rights Council: Origins, Antecedents, and Prospects' in K. Boyle (ed.), *New Institutions for Human Rights Protection* (OUP 2009) 11–47, 14.

[68] UNGA, 'Human Rights Council', Resolution 60/251 (3 April 2006), para. 7.

[69] UNGA, 'Human Rights Council', Resolution 60/251 (3 April 2006), para. 8.

[70] UNGA, 'Suspension of the rights of membership of the Libyan Arab Jamahiriya in the Human Rights Council', A/RES/65/265 (3 March 2011); UNGA, 'Suspension of the rights of membership of the Russian Federation in the Human Rights Council', A/RES/ES-11/3 (7 April 2022).

[71] AJIL, 'United States Withdraws from the UN Human Rights Council, Shortly after Receiving Criticism about its Border Policy' (2018) 112 *American Journal of International Law* 745, 747.

[72] AJIL, 'United States Withdraws from the UN Human Rights Council, Shortly after Receiving Criticism about its Border Policy' (2018) 112 *American Journal of International Law* 745, 751.

Periodic Review (UPR) in November 2020 and, in 2021, put itself forward for election to the Council, regaining a seat from 2022.

The Council is required to meet for ten weeks per year, over at least three sessions, which amounts to an increased meeting time compared to the six-week annual session of the Commission.[73] This gives the Council a semi-permanent status, which added to the possibility of holding special sessions if requested by a third of its membership,[74] enables it to respond to emergency situations more effectively.[75] The extended meeting time is partly explained by the need to perform the most important new faculty attributed to the Council: the UPR of the fulfilment by every UN Member State of its human rights obligations (discussed in **Section 4.3.2**). The Council was established by the General Assembly with the main responsibility of 'promoting universal respect for the protection of all human rights and fundamental freedoms for all without distinction of any kind and in a fair and equal manner'.[76] To fulfil its fundamental mandate, the Council was entrusted to undertake a multiplicity of functions, which include: to promote human rights education;[77] to provide advisory services, technical assistance, and capacity-building to States;[78] to serve as a forum for dialogue on any issues concerning human rights; to make recommendations to the General Assembly for the progressive development of the international law of human rights;[79] to make recommendations concerning the promotion and protection of human rights; to cooperate with the plurality of stakeholders in the field of human rights; to respond promptly to human rights emergencies;[80] to maintain a complaint procedure, as the Commission had; to continue the system of special procedures created under the Commission; and to undertake the aforementioned UPR.

While the array of the Council's functions seems impressive, the truth is that the scope of its powers remains restricted. Like most UN organs, the Council lacks the legal power to adopt binding measures. Even if it has been empowered to respond to human rights emergencies and to engage with complaints concerning human rights violations, the Council is limited as to the measures it can take, which include adopting

---

[73] Secretary-General, 'In Larger Freedom: Towards Development, Security and Human Rights for All. Addendum: Human Rights Council', A/59/2005/Add.1 (23 May 2005), para. 4.

[74] UNGA, 'Human Rights Council', Resolution 60/251 (3 April 2006), para. 10.

[75] M. Viegas e Silva, 'The United Nations Human Rights Council: Six Years On' (2013) 18 *SUR–International Journal of Human Rights* 97, 101.

[76] UNGA, 'Human Rights Council', Resolution 60/251 (3 April 2006), para. 2.

[77] See, for instance: HRC, 'World Programme for Human Rights Education', Resolution 39/3 (3 October 2018).

[78] See, for instance: HRC, 'Technical assistance and capacity building', A/HRC/6/L.29/Rev. 1 (26 September 2007).

[79] The Council has produced the draft texts of the 2006 Convention on the Rights of Persons with Disabilities, the 2006 International Convention for the Protection of All Persons from Enforced Disappearance, and the 2008 Optional Protocol to the International Covenant on Economic, Social and Cultural Rights (all discussed in **Chapter 5**).

[80] For instance, the Council can hold 'urgent debates' or call for 'special sessions' to swiftly proceed to discuss human rights emergencies and adopt measures in consequence, such as the appointment of fact-finding missions and their dispatchment to the concerned area. See: HRC, 'Human rights situation in the Occupied Palestinian Territory', Special session resolution S-1/1 (6 July 2006); HRC, 'The deteriorating human rights situation in Ukraine stemming from the Russian aggression', A/HRC/RES/S-34/1 (16 May 2022).

resolutions expressing its repudiation of human rights violations, the hosting of special sessions to discuss human rights emergencies, or the dispatchment of investigative missions—commissions of inquiry or fact-finding missions. In fact, the main output of the Council's sessions is a series of resolutions (and decisions),[81] which are adopted following negotiation among Member States.

The HRC was also tasked with reviewing its own work and operation five years after its establishment and with reporting back to the General Assembly, which was to review the Council's status within that timeframe.[82] To fulfil such a task, in 2009, the Council set up an inter-governmental working group, which produced a report with a number of proposals for improvement. The proposals included, among others, extending to four and a half years the cycle of the UPR, changing the process for the nomination of candidates as special procedure mandate-holders, strengthening the Council's interaction with its Advisory Committee, and enhancing accessibility to the Council's work and its mechanisms for people with disabilities.[83] The proposals were endorsed by both the Council and the Assembly; the latter also decided to maintain the status of the Council as its subsidiary organ and to revisit the issue again in ten to fifteen years.[84]

4.3.1 CRITICAL DEBATES: ISRAEL AND THE HUMAN RIGHTS COUNCIL

As discussed in **Section 4.2.1**, putting an end to politicization and double standards in the protection of human rights by the United Nations was among the chief motives for replacing the Commission on Human Rights with the new HRC. However, there are reasons to question whether such a goal has been achieved. Politicization refers to the use of political discretion to trump the objective application of pertinent standards, such as when action is taken against the reproachable behaviour of a State while ignoring similar conduct of another, based on the strategic relationship held towards one State and the other.[85] If the Council is seen as continuing the pattern of political selectivity that existed under its predecessor, a loss of legitimacy and qualms about its capacity to protect human rights worldwide are likely outcomes.[86]

---

[81] Interestingly, there are no clear criteria that allow determining when a certain action should be adopted through a 'resolution' or a 'decision' or to clearly determine a different standing of one output over the other. While resolutions are the main form in which the Council takes action, decisions tend to be used for more procedural issues and are usually more succinct and linked to previous actions already adopted by the Council. See: E. Tistounet, *The UN Human Rights Council: A Practical Anatomy* (Elgar 2020) 228–230.

[82] UNGA, 'Human Rights Council', Resolution 60/251, A/RES/60/251 (3 April 2006), paras. 1, 16.

[83] HRC, 'Report of the open-ended intergovernmental working group on the review of the work and functioning of the Human Rights Council', A/HRC/WG.8/2/1 (4 May 2011).

[84] HRC, 'Review of the work and functioning of the Human Rights Council', A/HRC/RES/16/21 (12 April 2011); UNGA, 'Review of the Human Rights Council', A/RES/65/281 (20 July 2011).

[85] V. Carraro, 'The United Nations Treaty Bodies and Universal Periodic Review' (2017) 39 *Human Rights Quarterly* 943, 948; R. Terman and J. Byun, 'Punishment and Politicization in the International Human Rights Regime' (2022) 116 *American Political Science Review* 385, 385.

[86] V. Carraro, 'The United Nations Treaty Bodies and Universal Periodic Review' (2017) 39 *Human Rights Quarterly* 943, 944–945.

The uneasy relationship between the Council and Israel can shed some light on the degree of credibility the abovementioned concerns might deserve. The academic literature has, at large, identified a clear bias against Israel in the practice of the old Commission, evidenced by the exacerbated level of attention placed on Israel, in contrast with the stark lack of action against other offenders, even in the face of abhorrent human rights violations taking place during the same period.[87] On its part, the Council's intention to provide special attention to Israel can already be found in its early days of operation. In 2007, during its fifth session, the Council decided to include as a regular agenda item, for discussion in each regular session, the 'Human rights situation in Palestine and other occupied Arab territories' (Item 7), thus making it the only country situation that features as a permanent item in the Council's order of the day.[88]

But the permanent agenda item is not the only means by which the Council lends attention to the situation concerning Israel. Since its inception and until the end of 2022, the Council has held thirty-five special sessions, nine of which had been on Israel. This degree of consideration was only followed by that placed on Syria, which had been involved in an armed conflict lasting over a decade and causing more than 100,000 deaths, to which the Council has dedicated five special sessions.[89] The Council's enhanced focus on Israel is also evidenced by the number of condemnatory resolutions it issues annually when compared to those focusing on other UN Member States.[90] According to the database collected by UN Watch (a Swiss-based NGO), between its creation and the end of 2022, the Council has issued 449 Resolutions, of which 266 were critical of the human rights record of countries. From those, 37 per cent concerned Israel (99 resolutions), while just under 63 per cent dealt with the other 192 UN Members. The comparison might be more staggering when the number of critical resolutions on Israel is compared to those received by other States with problematic human rights records, such as Syria (forty-one resolutions), Myanmar (Myanma) (twenty-eight

---

[87] T.M. Franck, 'Of Gnats and Camels: Is there a Double Standard at the United Nations?' (1984) 78 *The American Journal of International Law* 811, 824–825; J. Donnelly, 'Human Rights at the United Nations 1955–85: The Question of Bias' (1988) 32 *International Studies Quarterly* 275, 290–291; Y. Roznai and I. Tzang, 'The United Nations Human Rights Council and Israel: Sour Old Wine in a New Bottle' (2014) 5 *Human Rights and Globalization Law Review* 25, 30–39.

[88] R. Freedman, 'The United Nations Human Rights Council: More of the Same' (2013) 31 *Wisconsin International Law Journal* 208, 228–233; S. Joseph and E. Jenkin, 'The United Nations Human Rights Council: Is the United States Right to Leave This Club?' (2019) 35 *American University International Law Review* 75, 112. See: HRC, 'Institution-building of the United Nations Human Rights Council', Resolution 5/1 (18 June 2007), Annex, V.B.

[89] S. Joseph and E. Jenkin, 'The United Nations Human Rights Council: Is the United States Right to Leave This Club?' (2019) 35 *American University International Law Review* 75, 88. For a discussion of the first six special sessions on Israel, see: R. Freedman, 'New Mechanisms of the UN Human Rights Council' (2011) 29 *Netherlands Quarterly of Human Rights* 289, 313–323.

[90] Nossel and C.L. Broecker, 'The High Commissioner and the UN Human Rights Council' in F.D. Gaer and C.L. Broecker (eds.), *The United Nations High Commissioner for Human Rights: Conscience for the World* (Brill 2013) 221–244, 224–225; S. Joseph and E. Jenkin, 'The United Nations Human Rights Council: Is the United States Right to Leave This Club?' (2019) 35 *American University International Law Review* 75, 113.

resolutions), Belarus (fifteen resolutions), North Korea (fifteen resolutions), Iran (thirteen resolutions), or Eritrea (Ertra) (twelve resolutions).[91]

The Council has also decided to continue the country-specific mandate on the Occupied Palestinian Territory, created by the Commission in 1993;[92] one of the longest-lasting mandates, only comparable to those of Myanmar, Cambodia, and Somalia (Soomaaliya), which have been ongoing since 1992 (Myanmar) and 1993 (Cambodia and Somalia).[93] While the importance of this mandate has been highlighted in **Section 2.5**, it does present two distinctive features. First, unlike most country mandates, it is not subject to a yearly vote to determine its renewal, but it is to last until the Israeli occupation comes to an end. Second, only Israel's behaviour is under examination, shielding from scrutiny the actions of other actors, such as the Palestinian authorities or even Hamas.[94] When the continuation of the Commission's mandates was debated at the Council, the retention of the one on Israel was supported even by States that traditionally object to the mere existence of country mandates.[95]

In addition to the country mandate, over the years, the Council has also decided the deployment of numerous urgent fact-finding missions to investigate specific human rights violations by Israel.[96] These have included, among others, missions following the arrest of Palestinian officials in 2006, the military operation in Beit Hanoun in 2006,

---

[91] See: https://unwatch.org/database/ (accessed on 30 January 2023).

[92] As discussed in **Section 2.5**, the second-ever country-specific mandate instituted by the Commission was a Working Group to investigate alleged violations of the 1949 Geneva Convention relative to the Protection of Civilian Persons in Time of War in the territories occupied by Israel, which was established in 1969 and extended for two years. This mandate overlapped to some degree with the Special Committee created by the General Assembly, in late 1968, to 'Investigate Israeli Practices Affecting the Human Rights of the Palestinian People and Other Arabs of the Occupied Territories', although the composition of the latter is made of State representatives, rather than independent experts. See: UNGA, 'Respect for an implementation of human rights in occupied territories', Resolution 2443(XXIII) (19 December 1968); CHR, 'Question of human rights in the territories occupied as a result of hostilities in the Middle East', Resolution 6 (XXV) (4 March 1969).

[93] CHR, 'Situation of human rights in Myanmar', Resolution 1992/58 (3 March 1992); CHR, 'Question of the violation of human rights in the occupied Arab territories, including Palestine', Resolution 1993/2 (19 February 1993), para 4(a); CHR, 'Situation of human rights in Cambodia', Resolution 1993/6 (19 February 1993); CHR, 'Assistance to Somalia in the field of human rights', Resolution 1993/86 (10 March 1993).

[94] S. Joseph and E. Jenkin, 'The United Nations Human Rights Council: Is the United States Right to Leave This Club?' (2019) 35 *American University International Law Review* 75, 91. See: CHR, 'Question of the violation of human rights in the occupied Arab territories, including Palestine', Resolution 1993/2 (19 February 1993), para. 4(a)–(c).

[95] R. Freedman, 'The United Nations Human Rights Council: More of the Same' (2013) 31 *Wisconsin International Law Journal* 208, 233–238.

[96] HRC, 'Human rights situation in the Occupied Palestinian Territory', Resolution S-1/1 (6 July 2006); HRC, 'Human rights violations emanating from Israeli military incursions in the Occupied Palestinian Territory, including the recent one in northern Gaza and the assault on Beit Hanoun', Resolution S-3/1 (15 November 2006); HRC, 'The grave violations of human rights in the Occupied Palestinian Territory, particularly due to the recent Israeli military attacks against the occupied Gaza Strip', Resolution S-9/1 (12 January 2009); HRC, 'The Grave Attacks by Israeli Forces against the Humanitarian Boat Convoy', Resolution 14/1 (2 June 2010); HRC, 'Israeli settlements in the Occupied Palestinian Territory, including East Jerusalem, and in the occupied Syrian Golan', Resolution 19/17 (22 March 2012); HRC, 'Ensuring respect for international law in the Occupied Palestinian Territory, including East Jerusalem', Resolution S-21/1 (23 July 2014); HRC, 'Violations of international law in the context of large-scale civilian protests in the Occupied Palestinian Territory, including East Jerusalem', Resolution S-28/1 (18 May 2018).

the Gaza conflict (late 2008 and early 2009), the attack on the ship flotilla in Gaza in 2010, and the attacks on demonstrations that took place in the Gaza strip throughout 2018. Despite their political selectivity, some of these fact-finding missions produced renowned reports that shed light on important aspects of the situation.[97]

To summarize, it would be unthinkable for anyone to justify the violations of human rights perpetrated by Israel in the territories it unlawfully occupies,[98] some of which had even been sanctioned by the ICJ in its 2004 Advisory Opinion. Certainly, there should be no call for the Council to lessen its concerns about the human rights violations committed by Israel. However, it would help the Council's credibility and legitimacy, as well as its effectiveness in pursuing its main role of protecting and promoting human rights worldwide, to provide an equal amount of attention to that lent to Israel to the other grave and serious human rights violations ensuing in all corners of the world and committed by other UN Members. In the end, the Council only has a finite amount of resources to carry out its work and allowing a single situation to monopolize its attention necessarily detracts from its ability to engage with others, which might entail equally grave or even graver violations—as warned by UN Secretary-General Kofi Annan at the third session of the Council.[99] In other words, the Council's bias against Israel is counter-productive; it leaves the Council open to empirically grounded charges of selectivity and politicization, damaging its legitimacy, which does little to help the effective protection of human rights worldwide.[100]

ICJ, *Legal Consequences of the Construction of a Wall in the Occupied Palestinian Territory*, Advisory Opinion, I.C.J. Reports 2004, p. 136.

This Advisory Opinion of the ICJ was requested by the UN General Assembly in late 2003. The Assembly asked the Court to provide an 'urgent' opinion on the legal consequences arising from the construction of the wall by Israel in the Occupied Palestinian Territory, considering the rules and principles of international law, including the Fourth Geneva Convention of 1949, and relevant Security Council and General Assembly resolutions.

The ICJ asserted that the wall constructed by Israel, and its associated regime, were contrary to many norms of international law. For instance, the ICJ assessed that the construction of the wall encompassing Israeli settlements in Occupied Palestine Territory amounted to a 'de

---

[97] From these, the so-called 'Goldstone Report' from 2009 on the Gaza conflict is probably the best-known, in part due to the controversies that arose after publication, including the head of the mission expressing regrets about potential inaccuracies of the report. See: Report of the United Nations Fact-Finding Mission on the Gaza Conflict, A/HRC/12/48 (25 September 2009); R. Goldstone, 'Reconsidering the Goldstone Report on Israel and War Crimes', *Washington Post* (1 April 2009).

[98] S. Joseph and E. Jenkin, 'The United Nations Human Rights Council: Is the United States Right to Leave This Club?' (2019) 35 *American University International Law Review* 75, 113–114.

[99] Secretary-General, 'Message to the Human Rights Council, Cautions against Focusing on Middle East at Expense of Darfur and other Grave Crises', SG/SM/10769-HR/4907 (29 November 2006).

[100] S. Joseph and E. Jenkin, 'The United Nations Human Rights Council: Is the United States Right to Leave This Club?' (2019) 35 *American University International Law Review* 75, 116.

facto' annexation of Palestine territory, in breach of the Fourth 1949 Geneva Convention, relative to the Protection of Civilian Persons in Time of War, which prohibits the transferring of population into territories occupied by an Occupying Power (paras. 119–121). Similarly, the Court examined how the construction of the wall, the Israeli settlements, and the whole régime in place, interfere with the right of Palestinians to self-determination, finding Israel's actions responsible for it—although failing to expressly linked this particular violation with Israel's obligations under ICCPR and ICESCR (para. 122).

The Court also examined the situation under ICCPR, ICESCR, and UNCRC, as the wall and its associated regime interfere with several human rights of the inhabitants of the Occupied Palestinian Territory. The ICJ confirmed that these human rights treaties applied to the situation, both because they apply extra-territorially when a State Party exercises jurisdiction beyond its own frontiers and due to their continuous applicability even in times of war, concurrently with international humanitarian law (paras. 106, 109, and 111–112). The Court affirmed that several human rights protected by these treaties were breached by the construction of the wall and the attached regime enforced, including the right to free movement (under ICCPR), and the rights to work, health, education, and an adequate standard of living (under ICESCR and UNCRC) (paras. 134 and 136–137).

The Court examined whether the aforementioned violations could be justified as acts of self-defence—an argument it rejected after succinct consideration—and whether the wrongfulness of those breaches could be precluded by their adoption under a 'state of necessity'—a defence also dismissed by the Court (paras. 139–142).

Lastly, the ICJ analysed the legal consequences of its findings. It, first, affirmed that Israel was under an obligation to put an end to the identified violations of international law, which included: to cease the works of construction of the wall in the Occupied Palestinian Territory; to dismantle the structure already constructed in those territories; and to render ineffective the régime in place. Second, given that the construction of the wall entailed the requisition and destruction of property, including homes and businesses, the Court stated that Israel had to proceed to make reparation for the damages caused, by returning the property in question or by paying compensation, if restitution was materially impossible (paras. 150–153). Third, the ICJ examined the obligations of other States with regards to the situation. Given that many of the obligations breached by Israel were of an *erga omnes* character—owed to the international community as a whole—it affirmed that all States were under the obligation not to recognize the unlawful situation created and not to assist in any way in maintaining such situation (paras. 155 and 159). Lastly, the Court called on the General Assembly and Security Council to consider what further actions were needed to bring to an end the situation at stake, as well as the outstanding problems that have impeded the existence side-by-side of the States of Israel and Palestine in a regional context of peace and security for all (paras. 160 and 162).

4.3.2 THE UNIVERSAL PERIODIC REVIEW (UPR)

The UPR is the most significant new power the General Assembly attributed to the Council. In its resolution establishing the Council, the Assembly mandated this new body to undertake a UPR of the fulfilment by each UN Member State of its human rights obligations and commitments. The review of all States is envisioned as a cooperative mechanism based on objective and reliable information, counting with the full involvement of the State concerned and having due consideration of its capacity-building needs.[101] The UPR is to be conducted ensuring universality of coverage and equal treatment with respect to all States,[102] in a clear sign that the Council was to avoid repeating the political selectivity and bias attributed to its predecessor.[103] Although presenting some similarities to the State-reporting mechanism under treaty bodies (discussed in **Section 5.3.1**), such as the review taking the form of an 'interactive dialogue' between the State and the monitoring body, the procedure was expected to complement, rather than duplicate, the work of treaty bodies.[104]

The review is not only universal with respect to the States subject to it, covering all UN Members,[105] but also has an extremely wide substantive scope, as it examines States' compliance with the obligations assumed under multiple sources: the UN Charter and the UDHR, all human rights treaties to which the State is Party, voluntary pledges, and commitments undertaken by the State—including those made when presenting its candidature for election to the Council and in previous reviews—as well as applicable international humanitarian law.[106] Overall, the main objective of the UPR is to improve the human rights situation on the ground, which is to be achieved by bettering States' fulfilment of their human rights obligations; enhancing States' capacity for complying with such international obligations; and further developing States' cooperation in this area both among themselves and with the pertinent monitoring bodies.[107]

---

[101] UNGA, 'Human Rights Council', Resolution 60/251, A/RES/60/251 (3 April 2006), para. 5(e).

[102] UNGA, 'Human Rights Council', Resolution 60/251, A/RES/60/251 (3 April 2006), para. 5(e). See also: HRC, 'Institution-building of the United Nations Human Rights Council', Resolution 5/1 (18 June 2007), Annex, para. 3(g).

[103] H. Charlesworth and E. Larking, 'Introduction: The Regulatory Power of the Universal Periodic Review' in H. Charlesworth and E. Larking (eds.), *Human Rights and the Universal Periodic Review: Rituals and Ritualism* (CUP 2014) 1.

[104] Concerns as to whether the UPR manages to complement the work of treaty bodies rather than conflict with it have been raised by the academic literature. See: N. Bernaz, 'Reforming the UN Human Rights Protection Procedures: A Legal Perspective on the Establishment of the Universal Periodic Review' in K. Boyle (ed.), *New Institutions for Human Rights Protection* (OUP 2009) 75–92, 87–91; O. de Frouville, 'Building a Universal System for the Protection of Human Rights: The Way Forward' in M. Cherif Bassiouni and W. Schabas (eds.), *New Challenges for the UN Human Rights Machinery: What Future for the UN Treaty Body System and the Human Rights Council Procedures?* (Intersentia 2011) 241–266, 250–253; H. Collister, 'Rituals and Implementation in the Universal: Periodic Review and the Human Rights Treaty Bodies' in H. Charlesworth and E. Larking (eds.), *Human Rights and the Universal Periodic Review: Rituals and Ritualism* (CUP 2015) 109–125, 119.

[105] The order in which States were to be reviewed was determined by a combination of requirements, such as the need to review the Member States of the Council during their tenure, but also securing a mix of both member and observer States and respecting an equitable geographic distribution. The final order came from States volunteering for review and the drawing of lots from each regional group. See: E. Domínguez Redondo, 'The Universal Periodic Review of the UN Human Rights Council: An Assessment of the First Session' (2008) 7 *Chinese Journal of International Law* 721, 725; HRC, 'Institution-building of the United Nations Human Rights Council', Resolution 5/1 (18 June 2007), Annex, I.C.

[106] HRC, 'Institution-building of the United Nations Human Rights Council', Resolution 5/1 (18 June 2007), Annex, paras. 1, 2.

[107] HRC, 'Institution-building of the United Nations Human Rights Council', Resolution 5/1 (18 June 2007), Annex, para. 4.

Each review undergoes different phases: the gathering and collating of information about the State under review; the actual review of the human rights situation in the State; the elaboration of a draft outcome report; the adoption of the final report; the implementation of recommendations accepted by the States during the review; and the monitoring of the implementation of recommendations during subsequent UPR cycles.[108] The review is based on information from three sources: a 'national report', produced by the reviewed State, which could be either oral or written; a compilation of UN information on the State, including reports from treaty bodies and special procedures, prepared by the Office of the High Commissioner for Human Rights (OHCHR); and, lastly, a summary of 'credible and reliable' information from stakeholders—also prepared by the OHCHR—including the contributions received from a range of civil society actors, such as NGOs and academic institutions, as well as national human rights institutions.[109] To ensure that the procedure does not become overly burdensome to either States or the Council, and does not absorb a disproportionate amount of time, human, and financial resources,[110] the submission of information is heavily regulated, with strict page limits on the written material provided.[111]

The review itself is facilitated by a group of three States from different regional groups (known as the 'troika')[112] and takes the form of an 'interactive dialogue' between the State under review and other UN Member States during a meeting of the Working Group on the UPR (composed of all forty-seven States of the Council). All UN Member States can pose questions and make comments or recommendations, not just those sitting at the Council. States who intend to intervene should provide notice of this intention beforehand, allowing the troika to group issues or questions to ensure that the dialogue ensues in a smooth and orderly manner.[113] Unsurprisingly, politics plays a big part in these interventions, with allies and foes providing praise or criticism to the State under review based on political affinities, more than on actual human rights track records. Strategies consisting of large numbers of allies signing up to deliver

---

[108] D. Etone, *The Human Rights Council: The Impact of the Universal Periodic Review in Africa* (Routledge 2020) 19–21. See also: H. Charlesworth and E. Larking, 'Introduction: The Regulatory Power of the Universal Periodic Review' in H. Charlesworth and E. Larking (eds.), *Human Rights and the Universal Periodic Review: Rituals and Ritualism* (CUP 2014) 4.

[109] Doubts have been raised both about the reliability and independence of intervening NGOs and as to whether their concerns appear reflected in the summary prepared by the OHCHR. See: D. Etone, *The Human Rights Council: The Impact of the Universal Periodic Review in Africa* (Routledge 2020) 14–15.

[110] HRC, 'Institution-building of the United Nations Human Rights Council', Resolution 5/1 (18 June 2007), Annex, para. (h)–(i).

[111] The State report, if presented in writing, cannot exceed twenty pages, and the limit for the ones prepared by the OHCHR is ten pages. See: HRC, 'Institution-building of the United Nations Human Rights Council', Resolution 5/1 (18 June 2007), Annex, para. 15.

[112] The reviewed State can request that one of the three States belongs to its own regional group and also that one of the members of the troika be substituted. See: HRC, 'Institution-building of the United Nations Human Rights Council', Resolution 5/1 (18 June 2007), Annex, paras. 18(d), 19.

[113] H. Charlesworth and E. Larking, 'Introduction: The Regulatory Power of the Universal Periodic Review' in H. Charlesworth and E. Larking (eds.), *Human Rights and the Universal Periodic Review: Rituals and Ritualism* (CUP 2014) 5; J. Cowan and J. Billaud, 'Between Learning and Schooling: The Politics of Human Rights Monitoring at the Universal Periodic Review' (2015) 36 *Third World Quarterly* 1175, 1178.

'friendly' recommendations means that criticism must be crowded in the remaining time available for interventions.[114] While the time allocated for each review was three hours during the first UPR cycle, it has been extended to three hours and thirty minutes from the second one.[115] Other stakeholders, including NGOs with consultative status with ECOSOC, can attend the review. They may not take the floor but can make general comments before the adoption of the outcome report by the Council.[116]

The outcome report is drafted by the troika, with input from the State under review and assistance from the OHCHR. It summarizes the interactive dialogue that ensued, including the questions, comments, and recommendations made to the reviewed State, as well as its responses to these, such as the voluntary commitments and pledges made. The report should identify the recommendations that count with the 'support' of the State and those that lack such support, which are merely 'noted'.[117] The adoption of the outcome report by the plenary of the Council takes place in the Council's following session, months later.[118] Before its adoption, the reviewed State and all States involved in the review are allowed to express their views on the outcome of the review, while other stakeholders, such as NGOs, are given an opportunity to make general comments about the report.[119] Once the outcome report is adopted, it becomes the primary responsibility of the reviewed State to implement the recommendations it has accepted and to report on the progress made in the following review,[120] although different States have also decided to provide a mid-cycle report, indicating which recommendation they had already implemented.[121]

---

[114] J. Cowan and J. Billaud, 'Between Learning and Schooling: The Politics of Human Rights Monitoring at the Universal Periodic Review' (2015) 36 *Third World Quarterly* 1175, 1180–1181; R. Terman and J. Byun, 'Punishment and Politicization in the International Human Rights Regime' (2022) 116 *American Political Science Review* 385, 390–391.
[115] HRC, 'Follow-up to the Human Rights Council resolution 16/21 with regard to the universal periodic review', Decision 17/119 (19 July 2011), para. 3.
[116] HRC, 'Institution-building of the United Nations Human Rights Council', Resolution 5/1 (18 June 2007), Annex, paras. 18.(c), 31.
[117] H. Charlesworth and E. Larking, 'Introduction: The Regulatory Power of the Universal Periodic Review' in H. Charlesworth and E. Larking (eds.), *Human Rights and the Universal Periodic Review: Rituals and Ritualism* (CUP 2014) 5. See: HRC, 'Institution-building of the United Nations Human Rights Council', Resolution 5/1 (18 June 2007), Annex, paras. 26–32.
[118] M. Kothari, 'From Commission to the Council: Evolution of UN Charter Bodies' in D. Shelton (ed.), *The Oxford Handbook of International Human Rights Law* (OUP 2013) 587–620, 604; J. Cowan & J. Billaud, 'Between Learning and Schooling: The Politics of Human Rights Monitoring at the Universal Periodic Review' (2015) 36 *Third World Quarterly* 1175, 1178.
[119] HRC, 'Institution-building of the United Nations Human Rights Council', Resolution 5/1 (18 June 2007), Annex, paras. 29–31.
[120] H. Charlesworth and E. Larking, 'Introduction: The Regulatory Power of the Universal Periodic Review' in H. Charlesworth and E. Larking (eds.), *Human Rights and the Universal Periodic Review: Rituals and Ritualism* (CUP 2014) 6. See: HRC, 'Institution-building of the United Nations Human Rights Council', Resolution 5/1 (18 June 2007), Annex, paras. 33–34.
[121] J. Cowan & J. Billaud, 'Between learning and schooling: the politics of human rights monitoring at the Universal Periodic Review' (2015) 36 *Third World Quarterly* 1175, 1184; D. Etone, *The Human Rights Council: The Impact of the Universal Periodic Review in Africa* (Routledge 2020) 21.

The first full cycle of reviews was completed within four years, from 2008 to 2011, but from the second cycle onwards, these have been extended to last four and a half years.[122] The second cycle was conducted between 2012 and 2016, and the third between 2016 and 2022. The fourth cycle commenced at the end of 2022 and will extend until early 2027. The fact that, so far, all Member States have participated in their reviews, even if that required postponing the original date of review,[123] should most definitely be considered a success.[124] Nevertheless, concerns as to the actual efficiency of the UPR have been raised. Mere participation does not mean a true intention of constructively engaging with the process and, ultimately, implementation of even accepted recommendations depends on the goodwill of States.[125] Moreover, even when such an intention exists, poorer States might face institutional and financial limitations in implementing large numbers of recommendations, with postcolonial States still addressing the heavy legacy colonialism has left on their economies, institutions, and laws.[126] While comprehensive data has not yet been produced, reports published by the Swiss NGO 'UPR Info' reveal a rather promising picture of implementation of States' engagement with the recommendations received, disclosing implementation rates ranging from 40 per cent to 55 per cent for accepted recommendations and levels between 15 per cent and 19 per cent for rejected ones.[127]

4.3.2.1 Further reflections: The UK and the UPR

Like all States, by the end of 2022, the UK has completed three cycles of UPR, with its reviews taking place in April 2008, May 2012, and May 2017. In line with the development of the UPR system, the number of recommendations received after each of these cycles has increased[128] from 28 in the first review, to 132 in the second, to 227

---

[122] HRC, 'Review of the work and functioning of the Human Rights Council', A/HRC/RES/16/21 (12 April 2011); UNGA, 'Review of the Human Rights Council', A/RES/65/281 (20 July 2011).

[123] This was the case of Israel during the second cycle. See: HRC, 'Report of the Human Rights Council on its seventh organizational meeting', A/HRC/OM/7/1 (4 April 2013).

[124] D. Etone, 'African States: Themes Emerging from the Human Rights Council's Universal Periodic Review' (2018) 62 *Journal of African Law* 201, 209; E. Tistounet, *The UN Human Rights Council: A Practical Anatomy* (Elgar 2020) 12.

[125] O. de Frouville, 'Building a Universal System for the Protection of Human Rights: The Way Forward' in M. Cherif Bassiouni and W. Schabas (eds.), *New Challenges for the UN Human Rights Machinery: What Future for the UN Treaty Body System and the Human Rights Council Procedures?* (Intersentia 2011) 241–266, 253–254; W. Kälin, 'Ritual and Ritualism at the Universal Periodic Review: A Preliminary Appraisal' in H. Charlesworth and E. Larking (eds.), *Human Rights and the Universal Periodic Review: Rituals and Ritualism* (CUP 2014) 25–41, 31.

[126] J. Cowan & J. Billaud, 'Between learning and schooling: the politics of human rights monitoring at the Universal Periodic Review' (2015) 36 *Third World Quarterly* 1175, 1186–1187.

[127] UPR Info, 'On the Road to Implementation' (2012), pp. 5 and 10–13; UPR Info, 'Beyond Promises' (2014) pp. 5, 29–30.

[128] In fact, the number of recommendations was already gradually increasing through the very first cycle of reviews, with States reviewed in 2008 receiving an average of twenty-seven recommendations, while those reviewed in 2011 counted an average of 143. See: R. Chauville, 'The Universal Periodic Review's First Cycle: Successes and Failures' in H. Charlesworth and E. Larking (eds.), *Human Rights and the Universal Periodic Review: Rituals and Ritualism* (CUP 2014) 87–108, 97.

in the last one (although this total number includes overlapping recommendations).[129] During the UK's most recent interactive dialogue with the UPR Working Group, ninety-four delegations actively participated. From the 227 recommendations received, the UK opted to support 96—that is, it has either already implemented them or intends to do so—and to merely 'note' 131 of them—that is, not planning to (fully) implement them.[130] Some of the most important recommendations, together with the stance adopted by the UK towards them are summarized below.

> **HRC, United Nations Universal Periodic Review: United Kingdom, British Overseas Territories and Crown Dependencies, Annex to the response to the recommendations received on 4 May 2017 (29 August 2017)**
>
> In the third cycle of the UPR the UK received a total of 227 recommendations, but many overlapped with one another. A number of recommendations concerned the need to accede to international human rights treaties the UK is not Party to, such as: the International Convention on the Protection of all Migrant Workers and Members of Their Families (ICRMW), the optional protocols to core treaties (ICCPR, ICESCR, and UNCRC) establishing communication procedures, the ILO Conventions 169 (on Indigenous and Tribal People) and 189 (on domestic workers), the Council of Europe Conventions on Protection of Children against Sexual Exploitation and Sexual Abuse (Lanzarote Convention) and on Preventing and Combating Violence against Women and Domestic Violence (Istanbul Convention), and the Kampala Amendments to the Rome Statute of the International Criminal Court relating to the crime of aggression (recommendations 134.2–134.3, 134.6–134.10, 134.13–134.14, 134.16–134.21, 134.23–134.50, 134.52).
>
> Except for the recommendations regarding the Istanbul Convention, which the UK 'supported', the reaction to these was to merely 'note' them. With respect to ICRMW, the UK stated that the rights of migrant workers were already protected in domestic legislation, including the Human Rights Act (1998) and the Equality Act (2010), and that migrants who are legally working in the UK enjoy the full protection of UK employment law. Therefore, the UK Government was unclear about the benefits of ratifying this Convention, and it had no plans to do so (response to 134.10). Similarly, the recommendations made regarding the acceptance of the right of individual petition under all core human rights treaties (recommendations 134.1, 134.9–134.14, 134.16–134.21) were 'noted', with the UK stating that it had already considered that issue and concluded that the benefits of these communication procedures remained unclear. It affirmed that as a Party to the European Convention on Human Rights, individuals had access to the European Court of Human Rights (response to 134.1).

---

[129] HRC, Report of the Working Group on the Universal Periodic Review: United Kingdom of Great Britain and Northern Ireland, A/HRC/8/25 (23 May 2008); HRC, Report of the Working Group on the Universal Periodic Review: United Kingdom of Great Britain and Northern Ireland, A/HRC/21/9 (6 July 2012); HRC, Report of the Working Group on the Universal Periodic Review: United Kingdom of Great Britain and Northern Ireland, A/HRC/36/9 (14 July 2017).

[130] HRC, Report of the Working Group on the Universal Periodic Review: United Kingdom of Great Britain and Northern Ireland, A/HRC/36/9 (14 July 2017).

Different recommendations also questioned the reservations and interpretative declarations the UK had appended to certain human rights treaties, and suggested the importance of withdrawing such limitations to the UK's international obligations (134.4–134.5, 134.15, 134.22). The UK supported the general recommendation to keep under review its appended reservations to UN human rights treaties, but merely 'noted' the recommendations that call for withdrawing specific reservations, such as those appended to ICERD, ICESCR, and the Optional Protocol to UNCRC on the involvement of children in armed conflict.

Numerous recommendations focused on the potential repeal of the Human Rights Act and its replacement with a 'Bill of Rights', encouraging the Government to provide reassurance that such a change would not bring attached a reduced protection of human rights (recommendations 134.66–134.78). In response, the UK asserted that it had no plans of withdrawing from the European Convention on Human Rights for the duration of the current Parliament (response to 134.66).

The UK also received a range of communications concerning combating 'hate speech' against minority groups (recommendations 134.84–134.85, 134.99, 134.111–134.112, 134. 123). It supported these recommendations and provided a detailed response, with measures that it had adopted to tackle 'hate speech'. It asserted that it had a strong legislative framework in place, including 'criminal offences of inciting hatred on the grounds of race, religion and sexual orientation, specific racially . . . and religiously aggravated offences and enhanced sentencing for crimes that are motivated by the race, religion, sexual orientation, disability or [gender] identity of the victim' (response to 134.84).

A number of recommendations focused on the need to improve the protection of girls and women against violence (recommendations 134.180–134.188). The UK supported these recommendations and provided a lengthy explanation of the different measures undertaken to strengthen the protection against gender-based violence. Among many, these measures included introducing new laws to ensure the prosecution of perpetrators, such as the criminalization of forced marriages, new stalking offences, a new offence of domestic abuse (which covered controlling and coercive behaviour), and strengthening the law on female genital mutilation (FGM). It also pledged to increase funding by £100 million for combating gender-based violence between 2017 and 2020 (response to 134.180).

The UK also received a number of recommendations concerning minors and the criminal legal system, including raising the age of criminal responsibility and abolishing the life sentence as a punishment for children (recommendations 134.203–134.208). It 'noted' these recommendations. With regard to the minimum age of criminal responsibility, the Government affirmed that it considered 'that children aged 10 are able to differentiate between bad behaviour and serious wrongdoing', so they should be held accountable for their actions. Nonetheless, it accepted that criminal prosecution was not always the best response to youth offending, and should be avoided whenever possible. Moreover, at the time of the review, the age of criminal responsibility in Scotland was eight, but the Government asserted that the Scottish Parliament was to increase it to twelve—as finally happened in December 2021 (response to 134.205). With respect to life imprisonment, the UK asserted that a life sentence did not mean that young offenders would be in custody for life. The courts set an initial tariff which the offender must serve in custody, but after such time had elapsed the offender is considered for release on licence (response to 134.203).

The last two recommendations concerned the remainder of the UK's imperialistic policies. The second to last recommendation, from Mauritius, related to the completion of the decolonization process of the Chagos Islands, and the last one, from Syria, concerned the need to apologize and provide due compensation to the peoples of the States that the UK had colonized or attacked. Both recommendations were 'noted' (recommendations 134.226–134.227). As to the first, the UK 'expressed its sincere regret about the manner in which the Chagossians were removed from the British Indian Ocean Territory in the late 1960s and early 1970s' (response to 134.226). However, it stated that in 2016, the UK Government decided against resettlement, despite the aspirations of some Chagossians, 'on the grounds of feasibility and cost, as well as incompatibility with continuing defence and security interests' (response to 134.226). It concluded by stating that this was not a matter of decolonization—a misconception debunked by the 2019 ICJ's Advisory Opinion, discussed in **Section 10.4.1.1**. Concerning Syria's recommendation, the UK affirmed that it enjoys good relations with the independent States that emerged from the British Empire, many of which 'are members of the Commonwealth, an association of States based on equality and a shared attachment to common values, including of human rights, democracy and the rule of law' (response to 134.227).

4.3.3 SPECIAL PROCEDURES

The system of 'special procedures' that currently exists under the orbit of the HRC is an (unexpected) product of Resolution 1235, adopted by ECOSOC in 1967,[131] which was discussed in **Section 4.2**. The 1235 Procedure endowed the Commission (and the Sub-Commission) with the power to undertake thorough studies of situations that revealed gross or systematic human rights violations and to elaborate reports on them, including recommendations.[132] This resolution became the legal basis on which the Commission developed a system of experts to study and report on human rights from either a thematic or country-specific perspective. The former, mandates experts to investigate and advise on a specific issue concerning human rights, which could be a particular right or type of violation, with a worldwide territorial scope, while the latter are mandates that cover the overall human rights situation of one specific State (or region within a State). The mandates can be undertaken by an individual, usually designated as Special Rapporteur or Independent Expert,[133] or by a 'Working Group' of five experts—one from each UN

---

[131] E. Domínguez-Redondo, 'The History of the Special Procedures: A "Learning-by-Doing" Approach to Human Rights Implementation' in A. Nolan, R. Freedman, and T. Murphy (eds.), *The United Nations Special Procedures System* (Brill 2017) 11–51, 12.

[132] ECOSOC, Resolution 1235 (XLII), E/4393 (1967).

[133] Other designations have also been used in the past, such as Special Representative or Special Envoy. See: E. Domínguez-Redondo, 'The History of the Special Procedures: A "Learning-by-Doing" Approach to Human Rights Implementation' in A. Nolan, R. Freedman, and T. Murphy (eds.), *The United Nations Special Procedures System* (Brill 2017) 11–51, 12–13.

regional group.[134] The denomination given to the mandate is not really linked to the attributions of the mandate-holder, but seems to be motivated to denote the political relevance of the issue at stake, with the title of Special Rapporteur (apparently) reserved for the most serious cases.[135] Importantly, the mandate-holders should be 'highly qualified individuals who possess established competence, relevant expertise, and extensive professional experience in the field of human rights'[136] and in the exercise of the mandate act in their personal capacity and not in representation of their State of nationality. The tenure of mandate-holders cannot exceed a period of six years.[137] The process of selection of the individual experts to undertake mandates has changed quite drastically throughout the years, gaining transparency and favouring independence.[138] The selection remains a political decision that falls on the Council's Presidency, with approval of the Council, following a process of shortlisting of candidates undertaken by a Consultative Group from the poll of individuals who had applied or been nominated for the mandate.[139]

The origin of these mandates can be found in earlier UN fact-finding missions, such as the 'ad hoc Committee on Forced Labour' established by ECOSOC in 1951 to investigate the use of forced labour as a form of punishment of political dissidents, which was followed, in 1963, by the General Assembly's establishment of a fact-finding mission to South Viet Nam to investigate alleged human rights violations to the detriment of the Vietnamese Buddhist community.[140] As mentioned in **Section 4.2**, the first two mandates established by the UN Commission on Human Rights, in 1967, were the

---

[134] Larger groups have been appointed in the past, such as the 15-person Working Group on the Right to Development created in 1993. See: H.M. Cook, 'International Human Rights Mechanisms. The Role of the Special Procedures in the Protection of Human Rights: The Way Forward After Vienna' (1993) 50 *International Commission of Jurists: The Review* 31, 35.

[135] H.M. Cook, 'International Human Rights Mechanisms. The Role of the Special Procedures in the Protection of Human Rights: The Way Forward After Vienna' (1993) 50 *International Commission of Jurists: The Review* 31, 43–44; E. Domínguez-Redondo, 'The History of the Special Procedures: A "Learning-by-Doing" Approach to Human Rights Implementation' in A. Nolan, R. Freedman, and T. Murphy (eds.), *The United Nations Special Procedures System* (Brill 2017) 11–51, 12–13.

[136] HRC, 'Institution-building of the United Nations Human Rights Council', Resolution 5/1 (18 June 2007), Annex, para. 41.

[137] HRC, 'Institution-building of the United Nations Human Rights Council', Resolution 5/1 (18 June 2007), Annex, para. 45.

[138] M. Viegas e Silva, 'The United Nations Human Rights Council: Six Years On' (2013) 18 *Sur–International Journal of Human Rights* 97, 104; E. Domínguez-Redondo, *In Defense of Politicization of Human Rights: The UN Special Procedures* (OUP 2020) 162–164.

[139] E. Domínguez-Redondo, *In Defense of Politicization of Human Rights: The UN Special Procedures* (OUP 2020) 163–164. See: HRC, 'Institution-building of the United Nations Human Rights Council', Resolution 5/1 (18 June 2007), Annex, II; HRC, 'Review of the work and functioning of the Human Rights Council', Resolution 16/21 (12 April 2011), Annex, II.

[140] R. Miller, 'United Nations Fact-Finding Missions in the Field of Human Rights' (1975) 5 *Australian Year Book of International Law* 40, 40; E. Domínguez-Redondo, 'The History of the Special Procedures: A "Learning-by-Doing" Approach to Human Rights Implementation' in A. Nolan, R. Freedman, and T. Murphy (eds.), *The United Nations Special Procedures System* (Brill 2017) 11–51, 23. See: ECOSOC, Resolution 350 (XII) (17 March 1951); UNGA, 'Report of the United Nations Fact-Finding Mission to South Viet-Nam', Document A/5630 (1963).

'Ad Hoc Working Group of Experts on the Situation of Human Rights in South Africa' and a Special Rapporteur on the Politics of Apartheid, both in 1967.[141] These were followed, in 1969, by the creation of a Working Group to investigate alleged violations of the 1949 Geneva Convention relative to the Protection of Civilian Persons in Time of War in the territories occupied by Israel as a result of the 1967 'Six Day War'.[142]

However, it was the creation of the following mandate, that of the Working Group on the Situation of Human Rights in Chile, that truly cemented the Commission's power to create special procedures. While the situations concerning South Africa (iNingizimu Afrika or uMzantsi Afrika) and the Occupied Palestine Territories had been the focus of extensive political condemnation, including the adoption of measures by both the General Assembly and the Security Council, the situation of Chile differed from these to some extent. Although still the subject of international condemnation, the situation of Chile did not concern violations expressly recognized under Resolution 1235 as those capable of triggering procedures of this type.[143] The appointment of a special procedure for Chile was an indisputable signal that violations of human rights could no longer be claimed to belong to the realm of States' internal affairs, but could actually be the focus of a Commission's investigation, provided that the political will existed.[144] The mandate on Chile led to the creation of other country-specific procedures; these included mandates the Commission entrusted directly to the UN Secretary-General— including Cyprus in 1975, Kampuchea in 1978, and Nicaragua in 1979,[145]—as well as the appointment of a Special Rapporteur on Equatorial Guinea (Guinea Ecuatorial) in 1979.[146] Moreover, in December 1978, the Commission's ability to establish special procedures, when it had identified consistent patterns of gross human rights violations, received the express endorsement of the General Assembly.[147]

But, as mentioned earlier, special procedures are not limited to country-specific investigations and can also take the form of thematic mandates entrusted to study

---

[141] P. Alston, 'The Commission on Human Rights' in P. Alston (ed.), *The United Nations and Human Rights: A Critical Appraisal* (Clarendon Press 1992) 126–210, 156; E. Domínguez-Redondo, *In Defense of Politicization of Human Rights: The UN Special Procedures* (OUP 2020) 20–21. See: CHR, Resolution 2 (XXIII) (1967); CHR, Resolution 8 (XXIII) (1967).

[142] CHR, 'Question of human rights in the territories occupied as a result of hostilities in the Middle East', Resolution 6 (XXV) (4 March 1969).

[143] ECOSOC, Resolution 1235 (XLII), E/4393 (1967), para. 1.

[144] P. Alston, 'The Commission on Human Rights' in P. Alston (ed.), *The United Nations and Human Rights: A Critical Appraisal* (Clarendon Press 1992) 126–210, 158; A.L. Jernow, 'Ad Hoc and Extra-Conventional Means for Human Rights Monitoring' (1996) 28 *New York University Journal of International Law and Politics* 785, 790; E. Domínguez-Redondo, 'The History of the Special Procedures: A "Learning-by-Doing" Approach to Human Rights Implementation' in A. Nolan, R. Freedman, and T. Murphy (eds.), *The United Nations Special Procedures System* (Brill 2017) 11–51, 27.

[145] E. Domínguez-Redondo, *In Defense of Politicization of Human Rights: The UN Special Procedures* (OUP 2020) 25.

[146] CHR, 'The situation of human rights in Equatorial Guinea', Resolution 15 (XXXV) (13 March 1979).

[147] E. Domínguez-Redondo, 'The History of the Special Procedures: A "Learning-by-Doing" Approach to Human Rights Implementation' in A. Nolan, R. Freedman, and T. Murphy (eds.), *The United Nations Special Procedures System* (Brill 2017) 11–51, 28. See: UNGA, 'Importance of the experience of the Ad Hoc Working Group on the Situation of Human Rights in Chile', A/RES/33/176 (20 December 1978).

and report on the situation of a specific issue concerning human rights worldwide. An incipient thematic mandate was created by the Commission in 1969, appointing a Special Rapporteur to conduct a study on economic, social, and cultural rights.[148] However, the institutionalization of the system of thematic mandates is usually found in the creation of the Working Group on Enforced or Involuntary Disappearances in 1980; a monitoring mechanism that continues to operate in our days. The establishment of this thematic procedure was intrinsically linked to the egregious human rights situation under the military dictatorship governing Argentina since 1976, where the systematic practice of forced disappearances had been well-documented.[149] Following increasing pressure from civil society organizations, both the General Assembly and ECOSOC requested the Commission to focus its attention on the issue of enforced disappearances.[150] Although, at the time, Argentina was the subject of the Commission's scrutiny under the confidential 1503 Procedure, the diplomatic tactics of the Argentine dictatorship managed to obstruct the establishment of a country-specific mandate.[151] A different strategy was then adopted by the Commission, with the proposed mandate on Argentina transformed into a thematic Working Group on enforced disappearances.[152]

These original country-specific and thematic mandates were followed over the years by the creation of numerous special procedures. While the length of these mandates varied, over the years the practice that developed was the appointment of country mandates for one-year terms and thematic ones for three years, with the possibility of renewing the mandate before the end of the term.[153] Authors disagree on labelling as 'special procedure' all the different situations placed under study by the Commission (and later the Council),[154] but a tentative list of country mandates established should include, in chronological order: Bolivia (Wuliwya) (1981), El Salvador (1981), Guatemala (1982), Poland (1982), Afghanistan (1984), Iran (1984), Haïti (1987), Cuba (1988), Romania (1989), Iraq (1991), Kuwait (1991), former Yugoslavia (1992), Myanmar (1992), Cambodia (1993), Somalia (1993), Sudan (1993), Rwanda (1994), Democratic

---

[148] CHR, 'Question of the realization of the economic and social rights contained in the Universal Declaration of Human Rights and in the International Covenant on Economic, Social and Cultural Rights, and study of special problems relating to human rights in developing countries', Resolution 14 (XXV) (13 March 1969).

[149] IACHR, Report on the Situation of Human Rights in Argentina, OEA/Ser.L/V/II.49 doc. 19 corr.1 (11 April 1980); CONADEP, *Nunca Más: The Report of the Argentine Commission on the Disappeared* (FSG 1986).

[150] UNGA, 'Disappeared Persons', Resolution 33/173 (20 December 1978), para. 2; ECOSOC, 'Disappeared Persons', Resolution 1979/38 (10 May 1979), para. 1.

[151] N. Rodley, 'The Evolution of the United Nations Chater-based Machinery of the Protection of Human Rights' (1997) 1 *European Human Rights Law Review* 4, 6; E. Domínguez-Redondo, 'The History of the Special Procedures: A "Learning-by-Doing" Approach to Human Rights Implementation' in A. Nolan, R. Freedman, and T. Murphy (eds.), *The United Nations Special Procedures System* (Brill 2017) 11–51, 31.

[152] E. Domínguez-Redondo, 'The History of the Special Procedures: A "Learning-by-Doing" Approach to Human Rights Implementation' in A. Nolan, R. Freedman, and T. Murphy (eds.), *The United Nations Special Procedures System* (Brill 2017) 11–51, 31.

[153] HRC, 'Institution-building of the United Nations Human Rights Council', Resolution 5/1 (18 June 2007), Annex, para. 60.

[154] The most comprehensive list of special procedures seems to be the one compiled by Limon and Power. See: M. Limon and H. Power, 'History of the United Nations Special Procedures Mechanisms: Origins, Evolution and Reform' (Universal Rights Group 2014).

Republic of Congo (DRC) (1994), Papua New Guinea (Papua Niugini) (1994), Burundi (1995), Nigeria (1997), Liberia (2003), North Korea (2004), Chad (Tšād) (2004), Belarus (2007), Cote D'Ivoire (2011), Syria (2011), Eritrea (2012), Mali (2013), and Central African Republic (Bêafrîka) (2013). Most of these mandates have been discontinued with time, although some have been then re-established, such as those on Afghanistan, Iran, or Burundi. As the list evidences, the needed political agreement for the creation of country mandates had been achieved with more ease when it concerns Latin-American and African States, while Western States have escaped examination under this type of mechanism.

In addition to this type of mandate, the HRC has also developed the practice of dispatching independent commissions of inquiry, on an *ad hoc* basis, to undertake fact-finding missions when especially serious situations concerning human rights arise.[155] While not all bodies have had the same structure or mandate, they have mostly been composed of independent international experts and tasked with establishing the facts and circumstances of the violations at stake, reporting back to the Council.[156] Since its inception the Council has appointed this type of fact-finding missions on more than thirty occasions,[157] including numerous ones to the Occupied Palestinian Territory (as discussed in **Section 4.3.1**), as well as to Lebanon (2006), Sudan (2006), Libya (2011, 2015, 2020), Cote d'Ivoire (2011), Syria (2011), North Korea (2013), Central African Republic (2013), Sri Lanka, (2014), Eritrea (2014), Iraq (2014), South Sudan (Paguot Thudän) (2015, 2016), Burundi (2015, 2016, 2017), Myanmar (2017, 2018), DRC (2017, 2018), Yemen (Al-Yaman) (2017), Venezuela (2019), Ethiopia (Ityop'ia) (2021), Nicaragua (2022), and Ukraine (2022).

Concerning thematic procedures, following the original one on forced disappearances in 1980, the created mandates have been on: massive exoduses (1981), extrajudicial, summary or arbitrary executions (1982), torture and other cruel, inhuman or degrading treatment or punishment (1985), freedom of religion or belief (1986), mercenaries (1987), the sale and sexual exploitation of children, including child prostitution, child pornography, and other child sexual abuse material (1990), arbitrary detention (1991), the right to property (1991), freedom of opinion and expression (1993), contemporary forms of racism, racial discrimination, xenophobia, and related intolerance (1993), the right to development (1993), independence of judges and lawyers (1994), violence against women (1994), management and disposal of hazardous substances and wastes (1995), structural adjustment policies (1997), effects of foreign debt on the full enjoyment of human rights (1998),[158] extreme poverty (1998), the right to education (1998), the human

---

[155] B. Ramcharan, *The Law, Policy and Politics of the UN Human Rights Council* (Brill 2015) 207; E. Tistounet, *The UN Human Rights Council: A Practical Anatomy* (Elgar 2020) 16–17.

[156] E. Tistounet, *The UN Human Rights Council: A Practical Anatomy* (Elgar 2020) 17.

[157] See: https://www.ohchr.org/en/hr-bodies/hrc/list-hrc-mandat (accessed on 8 September 2022).

[158] Originally, the mandate was focused on economic, social, and cultural rights, but the scope was expanded in 2000 when it was merged with the mandate on structural adjustment policies. See: M. Limon and H. Power, 'History of the United Nations Special Procedures Mechanisms: Origins, Evolution and Reform' (Universal Rights Group 2014) 41. See also: CHR, Resolution 2000/82 (27 April 2000).

rights of migrants (1999), the right to food (2000), adequate housing (2000), human rights defenders (2000), the rights of indigenous people (2001), people of African descent (2002), the right to health (2002), trafficking in persons, especially women and children (2004), internally displaced persons (2004), counter-terrorism (2005), minority issues (2005), international solidarity (2005), contemporary forms of slavery (2007), the rights to safe drinking water and sanitation (2008), transnational corporations and other business enterprises (2011), cultural rights (2009), freedom of peaceful assembly and of association (2010), discrimination against women and girls (2010), the promotion of a democratic and equitable international order (2011), truth, justice, reparation, and guarantees of non-recurrence (2011), the enjoyment of a safe, clean, healthy, and sustainable environment (2012), the enjoyment of all human rights by older persons (2013), the rights of persons with disabilities (2014), the negative impact of unilateral coercive measures on the enjoyment of human rights (2014), the enjoyment of human rights by persons with albinism (2015), the right to privacy (2015), violence and discrimination based on sexual orientation and gender identity (2016), the elimination of discrimination against persons affected by leprosy and their family members (2017), and climate change (2021). As mentioned with regards to country mandates, many thematic mandates have been discontinued, and some subsequently re-established. Towards the end of 2022, there were a total of fourteen country mandates and forty-five thematic mandates in operation. A full list of current mandates can be found on the website of the OHCHR.[159]

The system of special procedures has been characterized by former Secretary-General Kofi Annan as the 'jewel in the crown' of the UN human rights system.[160] Although when the first mandates were adopted it was almost unthinkable to conceive the handful of procedures as a 'system', the situation has changed through the years. The 'evolving collection of these procedures and mechanisms now clearly constitutes and functions as a system of human rights protection'.[161] The specificity of each mandate is defined by the Council's resolution establishing it, but mandate-holders are usually tasked with similar functions, which are, nonetheless, increasing with time. Among others, these functions include undertaking in-person country visits to examine the situation pertinent to the mandate (with the consent of the State); receiving information from both public authorities and civil society; making recommendations to governmental authorities with regards to the situation observed and how to improve it—including through an 'urgent appeal' to the State authorities, when the situation is serious and time-sensitive—and reporting back to the HRC and the General Assembly on the findings of the mandate.[162] Moreover, whether expressly avowed in the resolution creating a mandate

---

[159] See:https://www.ohchr.org/en/special-procedures-human-rights-council/current-and-former-mandate-holders-existing-mandates (accessed on 18 October 2022).

[160] UN Secretary-General, 'Message to the Human Rights Council: Cautions against Focusing on Middle East at Expense of Darfur, Other Grave Crises', SG/SM/10769-HR/4907 (29 November 2006).

[161] Joint declaration of the independent experts responsible for the special procedures for the protection of human rights, A/CONF.157/9 (18 June 1993) 3.

[162] E. Domínguez-Redondo, *In Defense of Politicization of Human Rights: The UN Special Procedures* (OUP 2020) 99–100 and Chapter 5. See: Manual of Operations of the Special Procedures of the Human Rights Council (August 2008) pp. 11–21.

or not, the reports produced by mandate-holders make an important contribution to human rights standard-setting with respect of the issues covered by the mandate.[163]

4.3.3.1 Further reflections: The Independent Expert on protection against violence and discrimination based on sexual orientation and gender identity

Undoubtedly, one of the most contested mandates of special procedures created by the HRC was that of the independent expert on protection against violence and discrimination based on sexual orientation and gender identity (IE-SOGI).[164] The mandate was originally established in June 2016 by a rather tight majority of twenty-three Members voting in favour, eighteen against, and six abstentions.[165] Similar in scope to other thematic mandates, the independent expert was tasked with: assessing the implementation of international human rights norms concerning violence and discrimination against the members of the lesbian, gay, bisexual, trans, queer, and intersex (LGBTQI) collective and with cooperating with States to improve compliance; raising awareness of violence and discrimination based on sexual orientation and gender identity, while identifying and addressing the root causes of such practices; engaging in dialogue with all relevant stakeholders; and with providing advisory services, technical assistance, capacity-building, and international cooperation in support of national efforts to combat violence and discrimination against LGBTQI persons.[166]

Following the creation of the three-year mandate, Vitit Muntarbhorn from Thailand was appointed as the first independent expert. However, soon after this appointment, a group of African States moved to halt the mandate during consideration of the HRC's Report by the General Assembly, first at the Assembly's Third Committee and, subsequently, at the Assembly's plenary.[167] The amendment proposed by the African Group aimed at suspending the mandate until further (re-)consideration of its scope by the Council, the following year. The proposal was defeated, although once again by a slim majority. This time, with all UN Members voting, eighty-four voted against

---

[163] P. Alston, 'Hobbling the Monitors: Should U.N. Human Rights Monitors Be Accountable?' (2011) 52 *Harvard International Law Journal* 561, 580; M. Kothari, 'From Commission to the Council: Evolution of UN Charter Bodies' in D. Shelton (ed.), *The Oxford Handbook of International Human Rights Law* (OUP 2013) 587–620, 610–611.

[164] M.J. Voss, 'Contesting Sexual Orientation and Gender Identity at the UN Human Rights Council' (2018) 19 *Human Rights Review* 1, 9–10; E. Domínguez-Redondo, *In Defense of Politicization of Human Rights: The UN Special Procedures* (OUP 2020) 174.

[165] HRC, 'Protection against violence and discrimination based on sexual orientation and gender identity', A/HRC/RES/32/2 (30 June 2016). The voting reflected a very clear ideological/geographic split, with the following States voting in favour: Albania, Belgium, Bolivia, Cuba, Ecuador, El Salvador, France, Georgia, Germany, Latvia, México, Mongolia, Netherlands, Panamá, Paraguay, Portugal, Republic of Korea, Slovenia, Switzerland, the former Yugoslav Republic of Macedonia, the UK, Venezuela, and Viet Nam. The following States opposed: Algeria, Bangladesh, Burundi, China, Congo, Côte d'Ivoire, Ethiopia, Indonesia, Kenya, Kyrgyzstan, Maldives, Morocco, Nigeria, Qatar, Russian Federation, Saudi Arabia, Togo, and United Arab Emirates. While six States abstained: Botswana, Ghana, India, Namibia, Philippines, and South Africa.

[166] HRC, 'Protection against violence and discrimination based on sexual orientation and gender identity', A/HRC/RES/32/2 (30 June 2016), para. 3.

[167] Botswana's draft resolution, A/C.3/71/L.46 (3 November 2016); Report of the Third Committee, A/71/479 (5 December 2016); Burkina Faso's amendment, A/71/L.45 (15 December 2016).

the suspension, seventy-seven in favour, and seventeen abstained.[168] Sadly, just over a year after taking on the mandate, Muntarbhorn resigned due to health-related issues.[169] This led to the appointment of the second independent expert to the mandate, Victor Madrigal-Borloz from Costa Rica, who began his tenure in January 2018. The Council voted on the renewal of the mandate for three more years in July 2019—by a majority of 27 to 12 and seven abstentions[170]—and once again in June 2022, this time with an even narrower majority of twenty-three Members in favour and seventeen against, with seven abstentions.[171]

During the first six years of the mandate, the experts adopted a total of twelve reports, covering a range of relevant topics that included the legal recognition of gender identity and de-pathologization; data collection; social inclusion; so-called conversion therapies; the impact of Covid-19; gender theory; peace and security; and the right to health. From these, the 2020 Report of the independent expert presented to the HRC on 'conversion therapy' is further discussed below.

Report of the Independent Expert on protection against violence and discrimination based on sexual orientation and gender identity, 'Practices of so-called "conversion therapy"', A/HRC/44/53 (1 May 2020).

The Report of the independent expert (IE-SOGI) defined 'conversion therapy' as an umbrella term that describes a wide range of interventions that are premised on the belief that individuals' sexualities and gender identities not only can, but should, be modified when they do not match those that are considered normative and desirable by a given society at a specific time (para. 17). These 'therapies' are particularly used to target individuals who identify as lesbian, gay, bisexual, trans, or gender diverse, aimed at changing non-heterosexual and trans or gender diverse conducts and identities to fit heteronormative expectations.[172] The Report explained that practices of 'conversion therapy' rely on the medically false pathologization of sexualities and gender identities, with historical origins in nineteenth-century ideas that characterized as illness behaviours that social mores considered unacceptable (paras. 20 and 22).

Conversely, far from providing a positive health effect, these 'therapies' entail interventions that inflict severe pain and suffering that result in psychological and physical damage

---

[168] UNGA, 'Reports of the Third Committee' (official records), A/71/PV.65 (19 December 2016), pp. 7–18.

[169] V. Muntarbhorn, Resignation letter (September 2017), available at: https://apcom.org/wp-content/uploads/2017/09/IE-SOGIE-Resignation-Letter.pdf (accessed on 9 September 2022).

[170] HRC, 'Mandate of the Independent Expert on protection against violence and discrimination based on sexual orientation and gender identity', A/HRC/RES/41/18 (12 July 2019).

[171] HRC, 'Mandate of Independent Expert on protection against violence and discrimination based on sexual orientation and gender identity', A/HRC/50/L.2 (30 June 2022).

[172] For a discussion of heteronormativity, see: C. Ingraham, 'The Heterosexual Imaginary: Feminist Sociology and the Theories of Gender' (1994) 12 *Sociological Theory* 203, 204; L. Berlant and M. Warner, 'Sex in Public' (1998) 24 *Critical Inquiry* 547, 548; D. Gonzalez-Salzberg, *Sexuality and Transsexuality under the European Convention on Human Rights: A Queer Reading of Human Rights Law* (Hart 2019) 20–21.

(paras. 20, 38, 43, and 55). As affirmed by the Report, these practices are inherently humiliating, demeaning, and discriminatory, and can have a serious detrimental impact on individuals, including significant loss of self-esteem, anxiety, depression, self-hatred, shame and guilt, sexual dysfunction, suicidality, and post-traumatic stress disorder (paras. 55–56).

Despite their harmful character, 'conversion therapies' are documented to continue taking place in, at least, sixty-eight States across the world, in many of which are performed by health professionals and sanctioned by law (paras. 24, 27–28, and 32–33). Given the known stance of many religions with regards to sexual and gender diversity, it is not surprising that faith-based organizations and religious authorities also appear as common providers of these 'therapies', which, in turn, represent a lucrative source of income (paras. 30–31).

The IE-SOGI undertook an assessment of 'conversion therapy' practices, reaching important conclusions as to their incompatibility with the international law of human rights, and discussed their violation of several rights. For instance, these practices must be considered themselves to amount to prohibited discrimination, as they target a specific group on the basis of sexual orientation and gender identity, with the aim of interfering with their personal integrity and autonomy (para. 59). They also amount to a breach of the right to health, as these practices inhibit the enjoyment of the highest attainable standard of health by individuals, which encompasses the right to sexual and reproductive health in accordance with one's sexual orientation and gender identity (para. 60). The practices involved in 'conversion therapy' are also a manifest violation of the right to personal integrity. They follow the assumption that sexualities and genders that divert from the (hetero-)norm are somehow inferior and should, therefore, be amended; constructing individuals subject to them as lesser human beings, which is degrading in itself. Moreover, the means and mechanisms employed to pursue such objective tend to be inhuman and cruel in their very essence and can even reach the threshold of torture, depending on the severity of the pain they inflict (paras. 62–65).

The IE-SOGI's Report highlighted the particular vulnerability of children to conversion practices, who could be subjected to such 'therapies' by the will of their own parents, often influenced by conservative beliefs that identify gender and sexual diversity with the violation of religious or moral tenets. The subjection of children to practices that aimed at modifying their perceived sexual or gender identity was considered by the IE-SOGI as a clear failure of States' international obligation to protect children from violence and from cruel, inhuman, and degrading treatment and to respect children's right to their identity and their personal integrity; and to entail the violation of the core principle of the best interests of the child as a primary consideration in all matters that affect them (paras. 71–73).

The Report concluded with a range of significant recommendations for States to adopt. These included: to repeal all legislation that enables or encourages practices of 'conversion therapy', such as those criminalizing sexual and gender diversity; to adopt legislation banning 'conversion therapy', including prohibiting its advertisement and implementing a system of sanctions for non-compliance; to take urgent measures to protect children and young people from becoming victims of 'conversion therapy', given their special vulnerability; to facilitate health-care and other public services related to the free exploration and development of individuals' sexual orientation and gender identity; to ensure the de-pathologization of diversity in sexual orientation and gender identity in medical classifications; and to adopt measures to eliminate any social stigma associated with sexual and gender diversity, including education campaigns (paras. 87–88).

4.3.4 COMPLAINT PROCEDURE

The General Assembly's resolution creating the Council clearly stated that it was to maintain a complaint procedure, while authorizing the Council to review, improve, and rationalize the mechanism existent under the Commission.[173] The complaint procedure adopted follows closely the main characteristics of that of its predecessor, retaining, in particular, its confidential character.[174] On the one hand, the procedure has a substantive scope limited to 'consistent patterns of gross ... violations of ... human rights'; thus, much more restrictive than the systems of petitions before treaty bodies or regional courts (discussed in **Chapter 5**, **Chapter 6**, **Chapter 7**, and **Chapter 8**). On the other hand, its personal and territorial scope is extremely wide, as it allows for complaints regarding violations taking place in any part of the world under the jurisdiction of any UN Member State.

The complaints can be submitted by any person or group of persons claiming to be victims of gross violations of human rights, but also by other individuals or NGOs that have direct and reliable knowledge of the violations—not merely based on media reports.[175] The complaint can be sent to the Council by both postal and electronic mail and can be written in any of the six official languages of the United Nations (Arabic, Chinese, English, French, Russian, or Spanish). Given the serious character of the violations at stake, the complainants have a right to request their identities be kept confidential.[176] Complaints are received by a Working Group on Communications, composed of five members of the Council's Advisory Committee (discussed in **Section 4.3.5**), one from each regional group. An initial screening of the complaints is undertaken by the Chairperson of this Working Group, together with the secretariat, to determine whether the complaint *prima facie* satisfies the admissibility criteria, before it is transmitted to the State concerned to obtain its views on the violations alleged.[177] The State is expected to have a cooperative attitude throughout the procedure, making every effort to provide substantive replies.[178] The Working Group should then decide whether the complaint fulfils the admissibility criteria.[179] These include: containing

---

[173] UNGA, 'Human Rights Council', Resolution 60/251, A/RES/60/251 (3 April 2006), para. 6.

[174] M. Viegas e Silva, 'The United Nations Human Rights Council: Six Years On' (2013) 18 *Sur—International Journal on Human Rights* 97, 104. See: HRC, 'Institution-building of the United Nations Human Rights Council', Resolution 5/1 (18 June 2007), Annex, paras. 85–86.

[175] HRC, 'Institution-building of the United Nations Human Rights Council', Resolution 5/1 (18 June 2007), Annex, para. 87.

[176] HRC, 'Institution-building of the United Nations Human Rights Council', Resolution 5/1 (18 June 2007), Annex, para. 108.

[177] HRC, 'Institution-building of the United Nations Human Rights Council', Resolution 5/1 (18 June 2007), Annex, paras. 93–94.

[178] HRC, 'Institution-building of the United Nations Human Rights Council', Resolution 5/1 (18 June 2007), Annex, para. 101.

[179] The admissibility criteria seem to have been eased in comparison to that under the 1503 Procedure, although it is not possible to know how strict the scrutiny is, given the confidential character of the mechanism. See: M. Viegas e Silva, 'The United Nations Human Rights Council: Six Years On' (2013) 18 *Sur—International Journal on Human Rights* 97, 105.

a factual description of the alleged violation, including the rights violated; not being politically motivated, nor phrased in abusive language; not having been dealt with by another international complaint procedure, including those of regional courts, treaty bodies, or special procedures; and the prior exhaustion of domestic remedies, unless such remedies appear to be ineffective or unreasonably prolonged.[180] Complaints that are found admissible and which (alone or in combination with others) reveal the existence of a consistent pattern of gross and reliably attested violations of human rights are transmitted to the Working Group on Situations.[181]

The Working Group on Situations is also composed of five individuals, each appointed by a regional group, with due consideration of gender balance. Although appointed individuals should serve in the Working Group on Situations in their personal capacity, they are selected from among the representatives of Member States sitting at the Council.[182] It is up to this Working Group to present to the Council a report on consistent patterns of gross and reliably attested violations of human rights, including recommendation for action, based on the information received from the Working Group on Communications.[183] This report is examined by the Council in a confidential manner, unless it decides otherwise, for instance, in case of manifest and unequivocal lack of cooperation from the State.[184]

If, following the examination of the complaint, the Council finds that there is merit to the allegations, there are three pathways of action: it can appoint an independent expert to monitor the situation and report back to the Council; it can wave confidentiality and take up public consideration of the situation; or it can recommend the OHCHR to provide technical cooperation, capacity-building assistance, or advisory services to the State concerned.[185] It should be noted that the complaints procedure would not, therefore, provide specific redress to the individual victims of the violations. During its first decade of operation, the Council itself has examined complaints brought against Kyrgyzstan, Iran, Uzbekistan, Turkmenistan, the Maldives (Dhivehi Raajje), the DRC, Guinea (Gine), Tajikistan, Iraq, Eritrea, and Cameroon. While most of these were ultimately discontinued, the Council adopted further measures in some. In the case of Kyrgyzstan, it decided to make its decision public;[186] concerning DRC, it recommended

---

[180] HRC, 'Institution-building of the United Nations Human Rights Council', Resolution 5/1 (18 June 2007), Annex, para. 87.
[181] HRC, 'Institution-building of the United Nations Human Rights Council', Resolution 5/1 (18 June 2007), Annex, para. 95.
[182] HRC, 'Institution-building of the United Nations Human Rights Council', Resolution 5/1 (18 June 2007), Annex, paras. 96–97.
[183] HRC, 'Institution-building of the United Nations Human Rights Council', Resolution 5/1 (18 June 2007), Annex, para. 98.
[184] HRC, 'Institution-building of the United Nations Human Rights Council', Resolution 5/1 (18 June 2007), Annex, para. 104.
[185] HRC, 'Institution-building of the United Nations Human Rights Council', Resolution 5/1 (18 June 2007), Annex, para. 109.
[186] HRC, 'Situation of human rights in Kyrgyzstan', Decision 2/101 (2 October 2006).

the OHCHR to provide technical cooperation and assistance;[187] and, with respect to Eritrea, it not only decided to make its decision public, but also requested the Special Rapporteur on the situation of human rights in Eritrea to investigate the allegations contained in the complaints.[188]

4.3.5 THE HUMAN RIGHTS COUNCIL ADVISORY COMMITTEE

Created in 2007 as a subsidiary body of the new Council,[189] the Advisory Committee is an organ composed of eighteen independent experts, aimed at functioning as a 'think-tank' for the Council.[190] The main function of the Advisory Committee is to provide expert advice to the Council, which should be grounded on research and oriented towards implementation, when requested to do so by the Council.[191] The Committee is banned from adopting resolutions and decisions and may only make suggestions on topics for further research within the field of human rights for the Council's consideration.[192] If compared to the powers of the former Sub-Commission (discussed in **Section 4.2.2**), those of the Advisory Committee are clearly curtailed.[193]

The seats on the Committee are established based on geographic distribution,[194] and the election of experts takes place in two stages.[195] In the first stage, States can propose (or endorse) candidates from their respective regional groups. When proposing a candidate, States are required to 'consult their national human rights institutions and civil society organizations'.[196] Candidates should be of high moral standing,

---

[187] HRC, Report of the Human Rights Council on its eighteenth session, A/HRC/18/2 (11 November 2011), para. 210.
[188] HRC, 'Situation of human rights in Eritrea', A/HRC/RES/21/1 (9 October 2021).
[189] It held its first session in August 2008. See: G. Sweeney and Y. Saito, 'An NGO Assessment of the New Mechanisms of the UN Human Rights Council' (2009) 9 *Human Rights Law Review* 209, 221.
[190] HRC, 'Institution-building of the United Nations Human Rights Council', Resolution 5/1 (18 June 2007), Annex, para. 65.
[191] HRC, 'Institution-building of the United Nations Human Rights Council', Resolution 5/1 (18 June 2007), Annex, paras. 75–76.
[192] HRC, 'Institution-building of the United Nations Human Rights Council', Resolution 5/1 (18 June 2007), Annex, paras. 77.
[193] G. Sweeney and Y. Saito, 'An NGO Assessment of the New Mechanisms of the UN Human Rights Council' (2009) 9 *Human Rights Law Review* 209, 220; O. de Frouville, 'Building a Universal System for the Protection of Human Rights: The Way Forward' in M. Cherif Bassiouni and W. Schabas (eds.), *New Challenges for the UN Human Rights Machinery: What Future for the UN Treaty Body System and the Human Rights Council Procedures?* (Intersentia 2011) 241–266, 245; L. Boisson de Chazournes and A. Gadkowski, 'A Critical Appraisal of the Human Rights Council Advisory Committee' in F. Mégret and P. Alston (eds.), *The United Nations and Human Rights: A Critical Appraisal* (2nd edn., OUP 2020) 239–252, 242.
[194] Five for the African Group, five for the Asia-Pacific Group, three for the Latin-American and Caribbean Group, three for the Western Europe and Other States Group, and two for the Eastern Europe Group. See: HRC, 'Institution-building of the United Nations Human Rights Council', Resolution 5/1 (18 June 2007), Annex, para. 73.
[195] L. Boisson de Chazournes and A. Gadkowski, 'A Critical Appraisal of the Human Rights Council Advisory Committee' in F. Mégret and P. Alston (eds.), *The United Nations and Human Rights: A Critical Appraisal* (2nd edn., OUP 2020) 239–252, 243–244.
[196] HRC, 'Institution-building of the United Nations Human Rights Council', Resolution 5/1 (18 June 2007), Annex, para. 66.

independent and impartial, and have recognized competence and experience in the field of human rights.[197] In the second stage, the Council elects, by majority vote, in secret ballot, the experts to sit at the Committee, having due consideration to gender balance and appropriate representation of the world cultures and legal systems.[198] Elected experts serve in the Committee for a three-year period, with the possibility of only one re-election.[199]

The Committee does not sit year-round but holds up to two annual sessions for up to a maximum of ten working days, and only with the Council's approval can convene additional sessions.[200] Since its inception, the Committee has been mandated by the Council to undertake studies on multiple topics pertaining to human rights, which have included, among many others, terrorism, corruption, vulture funds, the right to food, the right to peace, and human rights education.[201] Important achievements of these mandates are the 2011 Declaration on Human Rights Education and Training and the 2016 Declaration on the Right to Peace, for which the Committee prepared the initial drafts.[202] More recently, the Council has tasked the Committee with the elaboration of studies on racial justice and equality and on the impact of new technologies for climate protection on the enjoyment of human rights.[203]

4.4 THE HIGH COMMISSIONER FOR HUMAN RIGHTS

The post of the High Commissioner for Human Rights was created by the General Assembly on 20 December 1993.[204] Despite its relatively recent creation, the idea to appoint a UN high-level official to take responsibility for the promotion and protection of human rights was not new. It had already been discussed during the drafting of the Universal Declaration of Human Rights, was subsequently the subject of a number of

---

[197] HRC, 'Institution-building of the United Nations Human Rights Council', Resolution 5/1 (18 June 2007), Annex, paras. 70, 72. Some of these criteria were further clarified by the Council, see: HRC, 'Follow-up to Human Rights Council resolution 5/1', Decision 6/102 (27 September 2007).

[198] HRC, 'Institution-building of the United Nations Human Rights Council', Resolution 5/1 (18 June 2007), Annex, para. 67.

[199] HRC, 'Institution-building of the United Nations Human Rights Council', Resolution 5/1 (18 June 2007), Annex, para. 74.

[200] HRC, 'Institution-building of the United Nations Human Rights Council', Resolution 5/1 (18 June 2007), Annex, para. 79.

[201] A full list of the Committee's mandates is available at: https://www.ohchr.org/en/hr-bodies/hrc/advisory-committee/mandates (accessed on 1 May 2022).

[202] L. Boisson de Chazournes and A. Gadkowski, 'A Critical Appraisal of the Human Rights Council Advisory Committee' in F. Mégret and P. Alston (eds.), *The United Nations and Human Rights: A Critical Appraisal* (2nd edn., OUP 2020) 239–252, 250.

[203] HRC, 'Mandate of the Special Rapporteur on the promotion and protection of human rights in the context of climate change', Resolution 48/14 (8 October 2021); HRC, 'From rhetoric to reality: a global call for concrete action against racism, racial discrimination, xenophobia and related intolerance', Resolution 48/18 (11 October 2021).

[204] UNGA, 'High Commissioner for the promotion and protection of all human rights', A/RES/48/141 (20 December 1993).

proposals to the General Assembly by different States, and was even studied by the Commission on Human Rights at the initiative of its Sub-Commission.[205] However, it was only in the early 1990s, with the end of the Cold War, that the idea of a Human Rights Commissioner managed to come to fruition.[206]

As mentioned in **Section 2.4.2.2**, the 1993 World Conference on Human Rights gave a significant nudge towards the creation of this post, with its Programme of Action recommending to the General Assembly to 'begin, as a matter of priority, consideration of the question of the establishment of a High Commissioner for Human Rights for the promotion and protection of all human rights'.[207] In December 1993, the General Assembly created the role of High Commissioner for Human Rights; thereby, assigning to a high-level UN official (who is given the rank of Under-Secretary-General) the principal responsibility for the coordination of the human rights promotion and protection activities of the organization. While the creation of this anticipated post lent reasons to celebrate,[208] the use of the very title of 'high commissioner'—a clear vestige of British colonialism[209]—was, perhaps, not the most appropriate choice.

The High Commissioner is appointed by the UN Secretary-General, with approval from the General Assembly. The selected person must be 'of high moral standing and personal integrity' and possess both expertise in the field of human rights and 'the general knowledge and understanding of diverse cultures necessary for impartial, objective, non-selective, and effective performance of the duties'.[210] The appointment is made for a (once renewable) four-year term and must have due consideration of geographic rotation. In chronological order, the High Commissioners to date have been from Ecuador (José Ayala-Lasso), Ireland (Mary Robinson), Brazil (Sergio Vieira de Mello), Guyana (Bertrand Ramcharan),[211] Canada (Louise Arbour), South Africa (Navanethem Pillay), Jordan (Zeid Ra'ad Al Hussein), Chile (Michelle Bachelet), and

---

[205] R.S. Clark, *A United Nations High Commissioner for Human Rights* (Nijhoff 1972) 39–59; J. Humphrey, 'A United Nations High Commissioner for Human Rights: The Birth of an Initiative' (1973) 11 *Canadian Yearbook of International Law* 220, 220–225; A. Clapham, 'Creating the High Commissioner for Human Rights: The Outside Story' (1994) 5 *European Journal of International Law* 556, 556–557. See: CHR, 'Analysis of Various Draft International Bills of Rights (Item 8 on the Agenda)', E/CN.4/W.16 (23 January 1947); CHR, 'Summary of information regarding consideration by the United Nations organs of the question of the establishment of a post of United Nations High Commission for Human Rights', E/CN.4/Sub.2/1982/26 (30 July 1982).

[206] T. van Boven, 'The United Nations High Commissioner for Human Rights: The History of a Contested Project' (2007) 20 *Leiden Journal of International Law* 767, 774, 783; A. Clapham, 'The High Commissioner for Human Rights' in F. Mégret and P. Alston (eds.), *The United Nations and Human Rights: A Critical Appraisal* (2nd edn., OUP 2020) 667–707, 668–669.

[207] Vienna Programme of Action, UN Doc. A/CONF.157/24 (1993), para. 18.

[208] K. Boyle, 'Marking Another Birthday: Ten Years of the United Nations High Commissioner for Human Rights' (2004) 22 *Netherlands Quarterly of Human Rights* 301, 311; F.D. Gaer and C.L. Broecker, 'Introduction' in F.D. Gaer and C.L. Broecker (eds.), *The United Nations High Commissioner for Human Rights: Conscience for the World* (Brill 2013) 1–32, 31.

[209] B. Boutros-Ghali, *Unvanquished: A U.S.–U.N. Saga* (Random House 1999) 167.

[210] UNGA, 'High Commissioner for the promotion and protection of all human rights', A/RES/48/141 (20 December 1993), para. 2.

[211] Bertrand Ramcharan was acting High Commissioner (from August 2003 to July 2004), following the assassination of High Commissioner Vieira de Mello in an attack on the UN headquarters in Baghdad (Iraq).

Austria (Volker Türk). The High Commissioner for Human Rights performs their functions under the direction and authority of the Secretary-General and must also report annually both to the HRC (as successor of the Commission on Human Rights) and, through ECOSOC, to the General Assembly.[212]

The High Commissioner was initially tasked with supervising the UN Centre for Human Rights and with rationalizing, strengthening, and streamlining the UN human rights machinery to improve its efficiency and effectiveness.[213] In 1997, the High Commissioner and the UN Centre for Human Rights were consolidated into a single unit, called the Office of the High Commissioner for Human Rights (OHCHR), as part of the process to improve coordination and efficiency of the UN human rights activities.[214] The OHCHR is led by the High Commissioner, together with a Deputy High Commissioner and an Assistant Secretary-General for Human Rights, and counts more than 1,000 staff members in our days.[215] The specific functions to be performed by the OHCHR were clarified by a Secretary-General's bulletin, issued in September 1997 by Kofi Annan. Among many, the functions of the OHCHR include supporting the work of other human rights organs, including the HRC, its special procedures, and the treaty monitoring bodies,[216] responding to serious violations of human rights, adopting preventive human rights action, promoting the establishment of national human rights infrastructures, deploying human rights field activities and operations, and providing advisory services and technical assistance in the field of human rights.[217]

Although some mandate-holders have been more vocal than others, it is an essential function of the High Commissioner to denounce and bring international attention to grave violations of human rights occurring anywhere in the world.[218] While publicly

---

[212] UNGA, 'High Commissioner for the promotion and protection of all human rights', A/RES/48/141 (20 December 1993), para. 5.

[213] UNGA, 'High Commissioner for the promotion and protection of all human rights', A/RES/48/141 (20 December 1993).

[214] F.D. Gaer and C.L. Broecker, 'Introduction' in F.D. Gaer and C.L. Broecker (eds.), *The United Nations High Commissioner for Human Rights: Conscience for the World* (Brill 2013) 1–32, 6; A. Clapham, 'The High Commissioner for Human Rights' in F. Mégret and P. Alston (eds.), *The United Nations and Human Rights: A Critical Appraisal* (2nd edn., OUP 2020) 667–707, 671–672. See: Secretary-General, 'Reviewing the United Nations: A Programme for Reform', A/51/1950 (14 July 1997), paras. 79 and 198.

[215] A. Clapham, 'The High Commissioner for Human Rights' in F. Mégret and P. Alston (eds.), *The United Nations and Human Rights: A Critical Appraisal* (2nd edn., OUP 2020) 667–707, 677–679.

[216] H.H. Koh, 'The UN High Commissioner: From the Personal to the Institutional' in F.D. Gaer and C.L. Broecker (eds.), *The United Nations High Commissioner for Human Rights: Conscience for the World* (Brill 2013) 45–61, 55–57; M. O'Flaherty, 'The High Commissioner and the Treaty Bodies' in F.D. Gaer and C.L. Broecker (eds.), *The United Nations High Commissioner for Human Rights: Conscience for the World* (Brill 2013) 101–119, 118; F.D. Gaer, 'The High Commissioner and the Special Procedures: Colleagues and Competitors' in F.D. Gaer and C.L. Broecker (eds.), *The United Nations High Commissioner for Human Rights: Conscience for the World* (Brill 2013) 133–156, 154.

[217] Secretary-General, 'Organization of the Secretariat of the United Nations', ST/SGB/1997/10 (15 September 1997), section 2.

[218] K. Boyle, 'Marking Another Birthday: Ten Years of the United Nations High Commissioner for Human Rights' (2004) 22 *Netherlands Quarterly of Human Rights* 301, 307; F.D. Gaer and C.L. Broecker, 'Introduction' in F.D. Gaer and C.L. Broecker (eds.), *The United Nations High Commissioner for Human Rights: Conscience for the World* (Brill 2013) 1–32, 6.

decrying human rights violations entails pointing metaphorical fingers at specific governments and, consequently, becoming the target of political criticisms from governmental officials of the concerned States, this is one of the main functions of the High Commissioner, who should be able to enjoy the needed political independence from all governments to address human rights violations irrespective where in the world they are taking place. Thus, different mandate-holders made the news headlines by denunciating grave human rights violations, including those occurring in Kosovo, Chechnya, Guantánamo Bay, and Gaza.[219] That the High Commissioner is capable of publicly speaking without fear or favour became an essential element for the credibility of the human rights activities of the whole of the United Nations.[220]

Another important role of the OHCHR is in the rapid response to human rights emergencies, including the deployment of field operations, such as inquiry commissions or even the establishment of a country office, like those in Colombia, Cambodia, Sudan, and Tunisia (Tūns).[221] While the deployment of UN operational human rights activities on the ground precedes the creation of the OHCHR, under the High Commissioner for Human Rights there was an increase in such activities, especially in what regards to technical assistance to and cooperation with States.[222] The mandate of each field presence of the OHCHR is unique to the specific situation and requires a delicate negotiation process to reach an agreement with the host State that, simultaneously, satisfies the government, ensures that the presence of the OHCHR is capable of balancing the needed activities of human rights monitoring, protection, and technical cooperation, while is also perceived by local human rights defenders as a positive contribution towards improving the country situation.[223] These field missions have the potential to enhance the protection of human rights in the ground, making a positive impact on the everyday lives of those affected by grave human rights violations.[224]

---

[219] F.D. Gaer and C.L. Broecker, 'Introduction' in F.D. Gaer and C.L. Broecker (eds.), *The United Nations High Commissioner for Human Rights: Conscience for the World* (Brill 2013) 1–32, 7–17; A. Clapham, 'The High Commissioner for Human Rights' in F. Mégret and P. Alston (eds.), *The United Nations and Human Rights: A Critical Appraisal* (2nd edn., OUP 2020) 667–707, 684–696.

[220] A. Clapham, 'The High Commissioner for Human Rights' in F. Mégret and P. Alston (eds.), *The United Nations and Human Rights: A Critical Appraisal* (2nd edn., OUP 2020) 667–707, 691.

[221] At the end of 2022, the OHCHR has seventeen country offices and two stand-alone offices located in: Burkina Faso, Cambodia, Chad, Colombia, Guatemala, Guinea, Honduras, Liberia, Mauritania, México, Niger, Palestine, Syria (based in Beirut), Sudan, Tunisia, Uganda, and Yemen, plus one field-based structure in Seoul that covers the Democratic People's Republic of Korea (DPRK) and the Human Rights Monitoring Mission in Ukraine. See: https://www.ohchr.org/en/about-us/where-we-work (accessed on 12 May 2023).

[222] K. Boyle, 'Marking Another Birthday: Ten Years of the United Nations High Commissioner for Human Rights' (2004) 22 *Netherlands Quarterly of Human Rights* 301, 309.

[223] C.L. Broecker, 'Protection through Presence: The Office of the High Commissioner for Human Rights in the Field' in F.D. Gaer and C.L. Broecker (eds.), *The United Nations High Commissioner for Human Rights: Conscience for the World* (Brill 2013) 157–174, 171–172.

[224] C.L. Broecker, 'Protection through Presence: The Office of the High Commissioner for Human Rights in the Field' in F.D. Gaer and C.L. Broecker (eds.), *The United Nations High Commissioner for Human Rights: Conscience for the World* (Brill 2013) 157–174, 170–171.

4.4.1 FURTHER REFLECTIONS: ASSESSING IMPLEMENTATION OF HUMAN RIGHTS NORMS

Among the many significant actions the OHCHR has taken since its inception, drawing attention to the importance of developing adequate tools for evaluating the implementation of international norms and the progressive realization of human rights is one that deserves highlighting.[225] Prompted by an increasing interest from treaty bodies in the use of indicators to monitor compliance with human rights treaties, the OHCHR embarked in a project to develop a set of indicators to measure the implementation of the obligations emerging from core human rights treaties.[226] The ultimate goal was to create indicators that would contribute to tackling two important interconnected challenges faced by treaty bodies: first, to translate the rather broad and vague legal obligations imposed by treaties into measurable benchmarks and, second, to encourage States to collect and provide the required information that would allow assessing their compliance with such targets.[227] Building on the expertise of a small group of human rights lawyers, development economists, and statisticians—mostly from the Global North[228]—the OHCHR produced two very important documents on human rights indicators: a background paper in 2006—which was updated in 2008—and a 2012 'Guide', aimed at all stakeholders engaged in monitoring national implementation of human rights, from State agencies to UN bodies and civil society organizations.[229]

As explained in the documents produced, human rights indicators are specific information on the state of an event, activity, or outcome that can be related to human rights norms and standards and which can be used to assess the level of implementation of such norms and standards and, in turn, for developing policies to strengthen human rights protection.[230] Although indicators are mostly thought of as quantitative,

---

[225] Although a healthy degree of scepticism and caution about the growing 'scientism' of human rights discourse has also been advised. See: U. Baxi, *The Future of Human Rights* (2nd edn., OUP 2008) 113–114.

[226] F. López-Bermúdez, 'Creating and Applying Human Rights Indicators' in D. Shelton (ed.), *The Oxford Handbook of International Human Rights Law* (OUP 2013) 873–892, 881, 886–887; S.E. Merry, *The Seductions of Quantification: Measuring Human Rights, Gender Violence, and Sex Trafficking* (University of Chicago Press 2016) 162–163, 175–177. See: CESCR General Comment 1: Reporting by States Parties, E/1989/22 (27 July 1981), para. 6; Twelfth meeting of chairpersons of the human rights treaty bodies, HRI/MC/2000/3 (16 June 2000), para. 22.

[227] S.E. Merry, *The Seductions of Quantification: Measuring Human Rights, Gender Violence, and Sex Trafficking* (University of Chicago Press 2016) 165–166.

[228] S.E. Merry, *The Seductions of Quantification: Measuring Human Rights, Gender Violence, and Sex Trafficking* (University of Chicago Press 2016) 163, 204.

[229] OHCHR, 'Report on Indicators for Monitoring Compliance with International Human Rights Instruments', HRI/MC/2006/7 (11 May 2006); OHCHR, 'Report on Indicators for Promoting and Monitoring the Implementation of Human Rights', HRI/MC/2008/3 (6 June 2008); OHCHR, 'Human Rights Indicators: A Guide to Measurement and Implementation' HR/PUB/12/5 (2012).

[230] OHCHR, 'Report on Indicators for Monitoring Compliance with International Human Rights Instruments', HRI/MC/2006/7 (11 May 2006), para. 7; OHCHR, 'Human Rights Indicators: A Guide to Measurement and Implementation' HR/PUB/12/5 (2012) 16.

indicating in numbers, percentages, or indices the magnitude of a given fact—such as ratifications of treaties, enrolment rates for school-age children, the proportion of seats held by women in parliament, or reported number of enforced disappearances[231]—they can also be qualitative, such as the perception of fairness of the electoral process in a country, the impression of the level of government corruption, or the satisfaction with the impartiality of the judiciary. Many human rights treaties already resort to indicators to specify the scope of certain obligations assumed by States. For instance, ICESCR mandates that the full realization of the right to health requires the adoption of the necessary steps for '[t]he provision for the reduction of the stillbirth-rate and of infant mortality'.[232] Similarly, CEDAW stipulates that gender equality in the field of education requires State Parties to adopt all appropriate measures to ensure '[t]he reduction of female student drop-out rates'.[233]

The construction of indicators is a complex task and requires de-constructing the legal standard of protection into a number of aspects or characteristics of the specific right that can be more easily measured. It is possible to distinguish between structural, process, and outcome indicators, depending on the aspect of the right that they aim to measure. Structural indicators capture the initial will of the State in protecting the right at stake by the commitments adopted, such as ratifying treaties, adapting domestic legislation, and setting-up needed organs or institutions. Process indicators are concerned with the concrete measures States adopt regarding implementation, including appropriate policies and programmes and the respective budgetary allocations. Lastly, outcome indicators relate to the actual achievements of the State that reflect the realization of the right under its jurisdiction.[234] To illustrate this discussion, it is possible to focus on the right to life. Structural indicators for monitoring the protection of this right by a given State can include the number of international treaties protecting the right to life ratified, as well as the adoption or amendment of domestic legislation concerning this right, while process indicators could be the number of complaints concerning this right received by the pertinent national organ or by specific international monitoring bodies, and the proportion redressed; and outcome indicators could be the rate of homicides in the country, as

---

[231] OHCHR, 'Report on Indicators for Monitoring Compliance with International Human Rights Instruments', HRI/MC/2006/7 (11 May 2006), para. 8; OHCHR, 'Human Rights Indicators: A Guide to Measurement and Implementation' HR/PUB/12/5 (2012) 17.

[232] OHCHR, 'Report on Indicators for Monitoring Compliance with International Human Rights Instruments', HRI/MC/2006/7 (11 May 2006), para. 10; OHCHR, 'Human Rights Indicators: A Guide to Measurement and Implementation' HR/PUB/12/5 (2012), pp. 24–25. See: ICESCR, art. 12(a).

[233] OHCHR, 'Report on Indicators for Monitoring Compliance with International Human Rights Instruments', HRI/MC/2006/7 (11 May 2006), para. 10; OHCHR, 'Human Rights Indicators: A Guide to Measurement and Implementation' HR/PUB/12/5 (2012), pp. 24–25. See: CEDAW, art. 10(f).

[234] OHCHR, 'Report on Indicators for Monitoring Compliance with International Human Rights Instruments', HRI/MC/2006/7 (11 May 2006), paras. 14–20; OHCHR, 'Report on Indicators for Promoting and Monitoring the Implementation of Human Rights', HRI/MC/2008/3 (6 June 2008), paras. 17–22; OHCHR, 'Human Rights Indicators: A Guide to Measurement and Implementation' HR/PUB/12/5 (2012) 34–38.

well as the proportion of perpetrators of crimes concerning the right to life that have been prosecuted and convicted in a given timeframe.[235]

Nevertheless, while indicators can be essential tools for monitoring progress in the fulfilment of human rights obligations and contribute to identifying shortcomings for future improvement, they are far from perfect.[236] For instance, on a theoretical level, indicators reduce complex human rights obligations to proxy measurements, which necessarily neglect different dimensions of rights. On a practical level, experience shows that data collection and processing are susceptible to political manipulation by States; a mischief that can then be hidden behind a veil of apparent numerical objectivity.[237] To achieve their desired goal, indicators must be methodologically sound and relevant for their purpose, and follow appropriate and transparent means for data collection and processing that allows obtaining data that is valid, reliable, and verifiable.[238] Moreover, collected data should be subject to disaggregation by personal characteristics, such as gender, age, ethnicity, religion, socioeconomic status, disability, or sexuality, to help measure inequality and discrimination against members of vulnerable groups and, consequently, devise meaningful strategies for implementation of human rights policies.[239] The inevitable shortcomings of the process of translating complex social facts into measurable data must be acknowledged, with the use of quantitative indicators complemented by resort to other evaluative criteria, including judicial assessment and qualitative indicators, to enable a more holistic and accurate assessment of social reality.[240]

As to the impact of the indicators produced by the OHCHR, the results are mixed. Some States, especially from Latin-America and Europe, have taken on the use of indicators for reporting on the implementation of certain human rights obligations. Similarly, although the use of indicators has been promoted and endorsed by human rights treaty bodies, only some of these organs have enthusiastically adopted them into their reporting guidelines and mechanisms of examination.[241] Therefore, the OHCHR's indicators project has not (yet) managed to make the significant contribution to expediting and standardizing the process of monitoring the implementation of human rights treaties that it can hopefully make.[242]

---

[235] OHCHR, 'Human Rights Indicators: A Guide to Measurement and Implementation' HR/PUB/12/5 (2012) 101.

[236] OHCHR, 'Human Rights Indicators: A Guide to Measurement and Implementation' HR/PUB/12/5 (2012) iii.

[237] S.E. Merry, *The Seductions of Quantification: Measuring Human Rights, Gender Violence, and Sex Trafficking* (University of Chicago Press 2016) 42, 171.

[238] OHCHR, 'Human Rights Indicators: A Guide to Measurement and Implementation' HR/PUB/12/5 (2012) 45.

[239] OHCHR, 'Human Rights Indicators: A Guide to Measurement and Implementation' HR/PUB/12/5 (2012) 68–70.

[240] S.E. Merry, *The Seductions of Quantification: Measuring Human Rights, Gender Violence, and Sex Trafficking* (University of Chicago Press 2016) 220–221.

[241] S.E. Merry, *The Seductions of Quantification: Measuring Human Rights, Gender Violence, and Sex Trafficking* (University of Chicago Press 2016) 199–203.

[242] S.E. Merry, *The Seductions of Quantification: Measuring Human Rights, Gender Violence, and Sex Trafficking* (University of Chicago Press 2016) 203, 205.

4.5 THE INTERNATIONAL COURT OF JUSTICE AND THE INTERNATIONAL PROTECTION OF HUMAN RIGHTS: A TRIBUTE TO JUDGE ANTÔNIO AUGUSTO CANÇADO TRINDADE

Individuals do not have access to the ICJ.[243] The Statute of the Court only grants legal standing to bring contentious cases to States,[244] while advisory opinions may only be requested by the Security Council, by the General Assembly, or by any UN organ or specialized agency authorized by the Assembly.[245] Yet, the Court has the power to become a truly significant actor with regards to the international protection of human rights, as many of its decisions in both contentious cases and advisory opinions entailed the interpretation and application of the international law of human rights. Judge Cançado Trindade, who had been a Judge and President of the Inter-American Court of Human Rights, made an especially relevant contribution to the Court's positive involvement with human rights during his tenure at the ICJ. Such a contribution can be attested by his appended individual opinions, some of them in disagreement with the majority of the Court. This section will examine some of the most relevant engagements the ICJ has had with human rights, with a special focus on Judge Cançado Trindade's important reflections on the issues at stake in those cases.

As stated earlier, the ICJ has the potential to be a significant adjudicator of disputes concerning international human rights norms, a standing that should not be measured by the number of cases it decides but by the scope and relevance of its authority. And yet, the Court has been historically unwilling to adopt a proactive approach in its judgments engaging with human rights. Different authors have discussed in depth the Court's jurisprudence and the many aspects in which it relates to human rights,[246] mostly agreeing that the rather conservative approach many times adopted by the Court may be linked to the (political) constraints in which it operates, as the main judicial body of the United Nations.[247]

---

[243] A topic thoroughly criticized by Judge Cançado Trindade in his separate opinions during his tenure at the Court. See, for instance: ICJ, *Judgment No. 2867 of the Administrative Tribunal of the International Labour Organization upon a Complaint Filed against the International Fund for Agricultural Development*, Advisory Opinion, I.C.J. Reports 2012, p. 10, separate opinion of Judge Cançado Trindade, paras. 70–75.

[244] Statute of the International Court of Justice (adopted 26 June 1945, entered into force 24 October 1945), 3 Bevans 1179, Art. 34.

[245] Charter of the United Nations (adopted 26 June 1945, entered into force 24 October 1945), 1 UNTS XVI, Art. 96.

[246] See: S.R.S. Bedi, *The Development of Human Rights Law by the Judges of the International Court of Justice* (Hart 2007); S. Sivakumaran, 'The International Court of Justice and Human Rights' in S. Joseph and A. McBeth (eds.), *Research Handbook on International Human Rights Law* (Elgar 2010) 299–325; B. Simma, 'Human Rights Before the International Court of Justice: Community Interest Coming to Life?' in C.J. Tams and J. Sloan (eds.), *The Development of International Law by the International Court of Justice* (OUP 2013) 301–326.

[247] See, for instance: ICJ, *South West Africa*, Second Phase, Judgment, I.C.J. Reports 1966, p. 6; ICJ, *East Timor (Portugal v. Australia)*, Judgment, I.C.J. Reports 1995, p. 90; ICJ, *Application of the Convention on the Prevention and Punishment of the Crime of Genocide (Croatia v. Serbia)*, Judgment, I.C.J. Reports 2015, p. 3; ICJ, *Obligations concerning Negotiations relating to Cessation of the Nuclear Arms Race and to Nuclear Disarmament (Marshall Islands v. United Kingdom)*, Preliminary Objections, Judgment, I.C.J. Reports 2016, p. 833.

In **Chapter 2** and **Chapter 3**, we discussed some of the earlier significant references to human rights made by the Court, such as the recognition of the 1948 UDHR as enunciating fundamental principles of international law in the *Case Concerning United States Diplomatic and Consular Staff in Tehran*,[248] and the assertion of the existence of certain international obligations that are *erga omnes* in character—which States have towards the international community as a whole—including the principles and rules concerning the basic rights of the human person, such as the prohibition of slavery and racial discrimination, as expressed in the *Barcelona Traction* case.[249] Additionally, we highlighted the contributions made by the World Court in cementing the expansion of the material scope of the realm of *jus cogens* norms pertaining to the international protection of individuals, by confirming that the prohibition of certain international crimes had become peremptory norms.[250]

With the passing of time, the ICJ also had the opportunity to engage with actual claims concerning the violation of human rights norms, both consuetudinary and conventional ones, with the Court, arguably, taking advantage of some of these opportunities more than others. For instance, States have brought claims to the ICJ alleging the violation of obligations held under some of the UN core human rights treaties, including ICERD,[251] ICCPR, and UNCAT.[252] However, it was not until 2010 when the Court declared a violation of a human rights treaty for the first time in a contentious case.[253] The case of *Diallo* was brought to the Court by Guinea, in exercise of diplomatic protection, claiming that the DRC committed serious violations of international law, including of human rights norms, against its national, who had been deprived of his property by the State, unjustly imprisoned, and then expelled from the DRC's territory. The ICJ

---

[248] ICJ, *United States Diplomatic and Consular Staff in Tehran (United States of America v. Iran)*, Judgment, I.C.J. Reports 1980, p. 3, para. 91.

[249] ICJ, *Barcelona Traction, Light and Power Company, Limited*, Judgment, I.C.J. Reports 1970, p. 3, paras. 33–34.

[250] ICJ, *Armed Activities on the Territory of the Congo (New Application: 2002)(Democratic Republic of the Congo v. Rwanda)*, Jurisdiction and Admissibility, Judgment, I.C.J. Reports 2006, p. 6, paras. 64, 125; ICJ, *Questions relating to the Obligation to Prosecute or Extradite (Belgium v. Senegal)*, Judgment, I.C.J. Reports 2012, p. 422, para. 99; ICJ, *Legality of the Threat or Use of Nuclear Weapons*, Advisory Opinion, I.C.J. Reports 1996, p. 257, para. 79.

[251] The Court's engagement with the cases concerning ICERD, all dismissed as inadmissible, are discussed in **Section 5.4**. See: ICJ, *Application of the International Convention on the Elimination of All Forms of Racial Discrimination (Georgia v. Russian Federation)*, Preliminary Objections, Judgment, I.C.J. Reports 2011; ICJ, *Application of the International Convention for the Suppression of the Financing of Terrorism and of the International Convention on the Elimination of All Forms of Racial Discrimination (Ukraine v. Russian Federation)*, Preliminary Objections, Judgment, I.C.J. Reports 2019, p. 558; ICJ, *Application of the International Convention on the Elimination of All Forms of Racial Discrimination (Qatar v. United Arab Emirates)*, Preliminary Objections, Judgment, I.C.J. Reports 2021, p. 71.

[252] The case concerning UNCAT is discussed in **Section 5.8**. See: ICJ, *Questions relating to the Obligation to Prosecute or Extradite (Belgium v. Senegal)*, Judgment, I.C.J. Reports 2012, p. 422.

[253] Although not the first time in which the Court found violations of human rights, see: ICJ, *Legal Consequences of the Construction of a Wall in the Occupied Palestinian Territory*, Advisory Opinion, I.C.J. Reports 2004, p. 136, para. 163; ICJ, *Armed Activities on the Territory of the Congo (Democratic Republic of the Congo v. Uganda)*, Judgment, I.C.J. Reports 2005, p. 168, para. 345; ICJ, *Ahmadou Sadio Diallo (Republic of Guinea v. Democratic Republic of the Congo)*, Merits, Judgment, I.C.J. Reports 2010, p. 639, para. 165.

examined the circumstances of Mr Diallo's detention and expulsion and found that these had amounted to a breach of rights protected under both ICCPR and the African Charter of Human and Peoples' Rights (ACHPR), ruling that the DRC was to pay compensation to Guinea for the consequences of the violations.[254]

Although *Diallo* became the ICJ's first judgment in which a violation of human rights treaties was declared, over the years, there are two issues pertaining to the field of human rights that have been the most developed by the Court's jurisprudence: the protection of life and the self-determination of peoples. As the Court's contribution to the latter is addressed in **Section 10.4.1.1**, here I will delve into the former. The Court's engagement with the international protection of the life of individuals appears in a significant number of cases. My focus will be on the jurisprudence that engages with three main aspects of the topic: the death penalty, the crime of genocide, and the use of nuclear weapons. The following sub-sections will also place special emphasis on the opinions rendered on these issues by Judge Cançado Trindade and are presented as a tribute to him.

4.5.1 DEATH PENALTY CASES

The ICJ's saga of cases on the death penalty is well-known, involving three cases against the USA and one against Pakistan. The cases against the USA were brought, respectively, by Paraguay (Paraguái), Germany, and México, as nationals of those countries had been prosecuted, tried, and sentenced to death in the USA without the appropriate notification of their right to consular assistance, provided for by the 1963 Vienna Convention on Consular Relations. While the first case was discontinued by Paraguay, following provisional measures ordered by the ICJ,[255] the other two cases led to judgments on the merits issued by the Court in 2001 and 2004.[256] In both cases, the Court found that the USA had breached its obligations under the pertinent Convention by not informing the foreign nationals of their right to consular assistance and by not proceeding to review the convictions imposed in violation of the mentioned right.[257] Notwithstanding such finding, the Court refused to construct the breach at stake as a violation of 'human' rights, as requested by both Germany and México, stating that

---

[254] As the Parties to the case failed to reach an agreement as to the amount of compensation due, in 2012, the Court rendered its (second-ever) judgment in which it quantified compensation and ordered the payment of USD 95,000 to redress both the material and non-material harm experienced by Diallo. See: ICJ, *Ahmadou Sadio Diallo (Republic of Guinea v. Democratic Republic of the Congo)*, Compensation, Judgment, I.C.J. Reports 2012, p. 324.

[255] ICJ, *Vienna Convention on Consular Relations (Paraguay v. United States of America)*, Provisional Measures, Order of 9 April 1998, I.C.J. Reports 1998, p. 248.

[256] ICJ, *LaGrand (Germany v. United States of America)*, Judgment, I.C.J. Reports 2001, p. 466; ICJ, *Avena and Other Mexican Nationals (Mexico v. United States of America)*, Judgment, I.C.J. Reports 2004, p. 12.

[257] Furthermore, in both cases, the Court found the USA's international responsibility engaged for failing to follow its previous decisions: in *LaGrand*, for executing Walter LaGrand after the ICJ had ordered provisional measures and, in *Avena*, for executing José Ernesto Medellín Rojas following the judgment on the merits. See: ICJ, *LaGrand (Germany v. United States of America)*, Judgment, I.C.J. Reports 2001, p. 466, para. 128(5); ICJ, *Request for Interpretation of the Judgment of 31 March 2004 in the Case concerning Avena and Other Mexican Nationals (Mexico v. United States of America)*, Judgment, I.C.J. Reports 2009, p. 3, para. 61(2).

such characterization was not needed,[258] and further refused to consider the right of consular assistance as an element of the right to due process of law,[259] as argued by México—following the precedent set by the Inter-American Court of Human Rights (discussed in **Section 2.6**).[260]

A similar story unfolded in the most recent judicial episode of the 'death penalty' saga before the ICJ, which concerned the case of Mr Kulbhushan Sudhir Jadhav, an Indian national who, in April 2017, had been sentenced to death by a military court in Pakistan. The authorities had failed to inform Mr Jadhav of his right to consular assistance, and while they informed the Indian Consulate of the arrest three weeks after it had taken place, they did not allow for Indian consular staff to have access to Mr Jadhav. Unsurprisingly, the ICJ found Pakistan to be in breach of its international duties under the Vienna Convention on Consular Relations and ordered the State to stay the execution and to undertake an effective review and reconsideration of the conviction and sentence of Mr Jadhav.[261] However, once again, despite India's claims, the Court refused to engage with the argument that the right to consular assistance pertains to the domain of human rights, as an integral element of the due process of law, when a foreign national faces criminal proceedings and, even more so, when the consequences could entail the imposition of the death penalty.

This conservative stance of the ICJ was rightfully criticized by Judge Cançado Trindade, first in his separate opinion in *Diallo* and, then again, in his vote in *Jadhav*. In the former, Judge Cançado Trindade asserted that: 'the right to information on consular assistance belongs to the conceptual universe of human rights, and non-compliance with it ineluctably affects judicial guarantees vitiating the due process of law',[262] to later emphasize that ignoring the contribution made by other contemporary international tribunals to the progressive development and humanization of international law resembles an 'attempt to avoid the penetrating sunlight with a fragile blindfold'.[263] In his opinion in *Jadhav*, Judge Cançado Trindade again regretted the reactionary approach adopted by the Court.[264] In particular, he argued that the Court's decision that Pakistan

---

[258] ICJ, *LaGrand (Germany v. United States of America)*, Judgment, I.C.J. Reports 2001, p. 466, para. 126; ICJ, *Avena and Other Mexican Nationals (Mexico v. United States of America)*, Judgment, I.C.J. Reports 2004, p. 12, para. 124.

[259] ICJ, *Avena and Other Mexican Nationals (Mexico v. United States of America)*, Judgment, I.C.J. Reports 2004, p. 12, para. 124.

[260] IACtHR, *The Right to Information on Consular Assistance in the Framework of the Guarantees of the Due Process of Law*. Advisory Opinion OC-16/99 of October 1, 1999. Series A no.16.

[261] ICJ, *Jadhav (India v. Pakistan)*, Judgment, I.C.J. Reports 2019, p. 418.

[262] ICJ, *Ahmadou Sadio Diallo (Republic of Guinea v. Democratic Republic of the Congo)*, Merits, Judgment, I.C.J. Reports 2010, p. 639, separate opinion of Judge Cançado Trindade, para. 187.

[263] ICJ, *Ahmadou Sadio Diallo (Republic of Guinea v. Democratic Republic of the Congo)*, Merits, Judgment, I.C.J. Reports 2010, p. 639, separate opinion of Judge Cançado Trindade, para. 188.

[264] I remember visiting Antônio at the Court the day after the adoption of the provisional measures in the case, to which he had appended a concurring opinion emphasizing the need to appreciate the right to consular assistance as belonging to the international law of human rights, with an unwavering hope that the Court would come to embrace such an interpretation in a future judgment on the merits. It was our conversation about this topic, and others connected, that prompted the idea to write this book together.

must review and reconsider the conviction and penalty imposed in breach of the human rights of Mr Jadhav was insufficient, as it left open the possibility of a new trial that, once again, led to a death sentence. He affirmed the existence of an evolving *opinio juris communis* on the prohibition of the death penalty as a lawful form of punishment and argued that the ICJ, as the principal judicial organ of the United Nations, should have ruled in line with the progressive development of international law in this respect.[265]

4.5.2 THE GENOCIDE CASES

A second relevant aspect of the protection of the right to life by the ICJ concerns its engagement with the prohibition of the international crime of genocide, which has ranged from the Court's early days' 1951 Advisory Opinion on *Reservations to the Convention on the Prevention and Punishment of the Crime of Genocide* (discussed in **Section 3.1.1.2**)[266] to ongoing cases, such as the ones instituted by The Gambia against Myanmar in 2019 and by Ukraine against Russia in 2022.[267] Up to the end of 2022, the Court ruled on the merits of two contentious cases concerning the crime of genocide,[268] the ones filed, respectively, by Bosnia and Herzegovina and by Croatia.[269] As discussed in **Section 3.2.3.1.1**, the first of these cases concerned the international responsibility of Serbia (as successor of the Federal Republic of Yugoslavia) for breaches of the 1948 Genocide Convention. Although the Court found that massive killings had been perpetrated throughout the territory of Bosnia and Herzegovina during the armed

---

[265] ICJ, *Jadhav (India v. Pakistan)*, Judgment, I.C.J. Reports 2019, p. 418, separate opinion of Judge Cançado Trindade, paras. 87–91, 105.

[266] ICJ, *Reservations to the Convention on Genocide*, Advisory Opinion, ICJ Reports 1951, p. 15.

[267] ICJ, *Application of the Convention on the Prevention and Punishment of the Crime of Genocide (The Gambia v. Myanmar)*, Order of Provisional Measures (23 January 2020); ICJ, *Application of the Convention on the Prevention and Punishment of the Crime of Genocide (The Gambia v. Myanmar)*, Preliminary Objections (22 July 2022); ICJ, *Allegations of Genocide under the Convention on the Prevention and Punishment of the Crime of Genocide (Ukraine v. Russian Federation)*, Order of Provisional Measures (16 March 2022).

[268] Other cases involving allegations of breaches of the Genocide Convention have been instituted before the Court but did not reach the stage of merits, including a claim brought by Pakistan against India (discontinued in 1973), a claim brought by the DRC against Rwanda (rejected by the Court in 2006), and the series of applications brought by the Federal Republic of Yugoslavia against ten Member States of NATO, due to the bombing in Kosovo in 1999, which were all dismissed (either summarily in 1999 or in judgments on preliminary objections in 2004). See: ICJ, *Case concerning the Trial of Pakistani Prisoners of War (Pakistan v. India)*; ICJ, *Armed Activities on the Territory of the Congo (New Application: 2002)(Democratic Republic of the Congo v. Rwanda)*, Jurisdiction and Admissibility, Judgment, I.C.J. Reports 2006, p. 6; ICJ, *Legality of Use of Force (Yugoslavia v. Spain)*; *Legality of Use of Force (Yugoslavia v. United States of America)*; *Legality of Use of Force (Serbia and Montenegro v. Belgium)*; *Legality of Use of Force (Serbia and Montenegro v. Canada)*; *Legality of Use of Force (Serbia and Montenegro v. France)*; *Legality of Use of Force (Serbia and Montenegro v. Germany)*; *Legality of Use of Force (Serbia and Montenegro v. Italy)*; *Legality of Use of Force (Serbia and Montenegro v. Netherlands)*; *Legality of Use of Force (Serbia and Montenegro v. Portugal)*; *Legality of Use of Force (Yugoslavia v. Spain)*; *Legality of Use of Force (Yugoslavia v. United States of America)*; *Legality of Use of Force (Serbia and Montenegro v. United Kingdom)*.

[269] ICJ, *Application of the Convention on the Prevention and Punishment of the Crime of Genocide (Bosnia and Herzegovina v. Serbia and Montenegro)*, Judgment, I.C.J. Reports 2007, p. 43; ICJ, *Application of the Convention on the Prevention and Punishment of the Crime of Genocide (Croatia v. Serbia)*, Judgment, I.C.J. Reports 2015, p. 3.

conflict, it only identified one specific episode of genocide—that of Srebrenica in July 1995—understanding, otherwise, a lack of the specific intent that defines the crime, namely the intent to destroy, in whole or in part, the protected group. Even so, the Court refused to find the acts of the Republika Srpska's army attributable to Serbia by applying a rather high threshold for attribution of international responsibility. Conversely, the Court ruled that Serbia had violated the Genocide Convention on two counts: first, by failing to prevent the Srebrenica genocide, as it considered that Serbia should, at least, have been aware of the serious risk that acts of genocide would be committed and failed to employ all reasonable means available to prevent it; and, second, due to the lack of punishment of the perpetrators of the genocide.[270] While the Court's ruling on the violation of the 1948 Genocide Convention, for the first time in its history, could be seen as a positive development, the endorsement of such a high threshold for the attribution of the actions of non-State actors to a State has been subject to some acute academic criticism.[271]

The Court revisited the potential violation of the Genocide Convention in the case instituted by Croatia against the (then) FRY—succeeded by Serbia at the time of the Court's judgment on the merits. Croatia claimed that genocide had been committed in its territory during the armed conflict that extended from 1991 to 1995 following its declaration of independence. However, the main finding of the Court was that the commission of genocide had not been proved by Croatia. The ICJ understood that the large number of atrocities committed lacked the 'dolus specialis' required for the crime; the intent to destroy, in whole or in part, the Croat group.[272] Hence, the Court not only found that the commission of this crime could not be attributed to Serbia but also that neither the issue of prevention nor that of punishment, arose in the case, unlike in the one brought by Bosnia and Herzegovina.[273]

Judge Cançado Trindade was the only permanent member of the Court to disagree with the Court's ruling, drafting a 179-page-long dissenting opinion to justify his disagreement. A fundamental question raised by his dissent was whether the Court was applying the right standards for the assessment of proof, a concern that has been recurrently raised by other judges and academic literature. Indeed, it is not a secret that the Court has been thought of as not the most consistent of tribunals when it comes to determining the level of proof required in a given case to satisfy a Party's respective

---

[270] ICJ, *Application of the Convention on the Prevention and Punishment of the Crime of Genocide (Bosnia and Herzegovina v. Serbia and Montenegro)*, Judgment, I.C.J. Reports 2007, p. 43, para. 471.

[271] M. Gibney, 'Genocide and State Responsibility' (2007) 4 *Human Rights Law Review* 760; A.M. Weisburd, *Failings of the International Court of Justice* (OUP 2016) 226–231.

[272] ICJ, *Application of the Convention on the Prevention and Punishment of the Crime of Genocide (Croatia v. Serbia)*, Judgment, I.C.J. Reports 2015, p. 3, paras. 440–441.

[273] ICJ, *Application of the Convention on the Prevention and Punishment of the Crime of Genocide (Croatia v. Serbia)*, Judgment, I.C.J. Reports 2015, p. 3, para. 524.

burden or even when assessing the evidence presented.[274] In this judgment, as it had in the previous *Genocide* case, the Court decided that the severity of the allegations imposed the requirement of a truly high standard of proof, which it called 'fully conclusive'.[275] Conversely, Judge Cançado Trindade argued that a comprehensive, rather than atomized, assessment of the evidence, in line with the lower threshold of proof adopted by other international courts when examining grave breaches of human rights, such as genocide, should have led the Court to infer the existence of the required special intent, based on the widespread and systematic pattern of destruction and extreme violence of the case, which encompassed massive killings, torture, sexual crimes, systematic expulsions, and the destruction of culture.[276] Therefore, if the Court's 2007 judgment left concerns as to the threshold for attributing to the State crimes by non-State actors, the 2015 ruling led to similar worries with regard to the high standard of proof the Court required to determine the existence of a grave violation of human rights, such as genocide. It can only be hoped that the Court will continue to reflect on these essential elements of the law of State responsibility when it deals with cases concerning grave violations of human rights in the future.

4.5.3 NUCLEAR WEAPONS

A final aspect of the protection of human life in the Court's jurisprudence that deserves attention is that of the use of nuclear weapons, an issue that not only threatens the life of individuals but the actual survival of humankind and life on the planet more generally. The topic of nuclear weapons is recurrent before the ICJ. In 1974, the Court rendered judgments on cases brought up by both Australia and New Zealand (Aotearoa) against France regarding atmospheric tests of nuclear weapons planned to be carried out in the South Pacific region, with risk of radioactive fall-out in Australia and New Zealand.[277] It is well-known that the Court avoided providing a decision on the merits of those cases by granting binding effect to the unilateral declarations made by the French

---

[274] ICJ, *Oil Platforms (Islamic Republic of Iran v. United States of America)*, Judgment, I.C.J. Reports 2003, p. 161, separate opinion of Judge Higgins para. 33; ICJ, *Oil Platforms (Islamic Republic of Iran v. United States of America)*, Judgment, I.C.J. Reports 2003, p. 161, separate opinion of Judge Buergenthal para. 41; ICJ, *Pulp Mills on the River Uruguay (Argentina v. Uruguay)*, Judgment, I.C.J. Reports 2010, p. 14, joint dissenting opinion Judges Al-Khasawneh and Simma paras. 2, 3. See also: K. Del Mar, 'The International Court of Justice and Standards of Proof' in K. Bannelier, T. Christakis, and S. Heathcote (eds.), *The ICJ and the Evolution of International Law: The Enduring Impact of the Corfu Channel Case* (Routledge 2012) 98–123, 123; R. Kolb, *The International Court of Justice* (Hart 2013) 944–945; A.M. Weisburd, *Failings of the International Court of Justice* (OUP 2016) 191–192, 227–231.

[275] ICJ, *Application of the Convention on the Prevention and Punishment of the Crime of Genocide (Bosnia and Herzegovina v. Serbia and Montenegro)*, Judgment, I.C.J. Reports 2007, p. 43, para. 209; ICJ, *Application of the Convention on the Prevention and Punishment of the Crime of Genocide (Croatia v. Serbia)*, Judgment, I.C.J. Reports 2015, p. 3, paras. 178–179.

[276] ICJ, *Application of the Convention on the Prevention and Punishment of the Crime of Genocide (Croatia v. Serbia)*, Judgment, I.C.J. Reports 2015, p. 3, dissenting opinion of Judge Cançado Trindade paras. 459–471.

[277] ICJ, *Nuclear Tests (New Zealand v. France)*, Judgment, I.C.J. Reports 1974, p. 45; ICJ, *Nuclear Tests (Australia v. France)*, Judgment, I.C.J. Reports 1974, p. 253.

President, outside the context of the actual case, in which he had declared that nuclear tests were to cease.[278] The Court, therefore, found that the dispute between the parties had disappeared, as the claims no longer had an object.[279] A further pronouncement on nuclear weapons was also avoided by the Court on procedural ground when, in 1993, the World Health Organization (WHO) submitted a request for an Advisory Opinion on the following question: 'In view of the health and environmental effects, would the use of nuclear weapons by a State in war or other armed conflict be a breach of its obligations under international law including the WHO Constitution?'[280] The Court considered that the question was beyond the scope of the activities of the requesting agency, the WHO, as it did not truly concern the effects of the use of nuclear weapons on health, but the legality of the use of these weapons.[281]

Following that decision, the UN General Assembly requested of the Court an Advisory Opinion on a related question: 'Is the threat or use of nuclear weapons in any circumstance permitted under international law?'[282] This question ICJ could not avoid answering. The Court opined that international law, either conventional or customary, neither authorizes the use or threat of nuclear weapons, nor prohibits such use or threat in any comprehensive and universal manner. Therefore, in a split (7 to 7) decision, with the President casting the deciding vote, the Court asserted that: 'the threat or use of nuclear weapons would generally be contrary to the rules of international law applicable in armed conflict, and in particular the principles and rules of humanitarian law[.] However, in view of the current state of international law, and of the elements of fact at its disposal, the Court cannot conclude definitively whether the threat or use of nuclear weapons would be lawful or unlawful in an *extreme circumstance of self-defence, in which the very survival of a State would be at stake*'.[283] Paraphrasing, the Court reached the compromised decision that the use or threat of nuclear weapons is undoubtedly prohibited under international law, with the only potential exception when the very survival of the State is at risk.

In reaching this contested decision, the Court made some important contributions to the protection of the right to life under international law. For instance, it recognized that the operation of the international law of human rights does not stop in circumstances

---

[278] ICJ, *Nuclear Tests (New Zealand v. France)*, Judgment, I.C.J. Reports 1974, p. 45, para. 53; ICJ, *Nuclear Tests (Australia v. France)*, Judgment, I.C.J. Reports 1974, p. 253, para. 51.

[279] ICJ, *Nuclear Tests (New Zealand v. France)*, Judgment, I.C.J. Reports 1974, p. 45, para. 65; ICJ, *Nuclear Tests (Australia v. France)*, Judgment, I.C.J. Reports 1974, p. 253, para. 62. Furthermore, a request for the re-examination of the situation, submitted by New Zealand in 1995 due to the announcement by French authorities that new nuclear tests were to be carried out in the region, was dismissed by the Court. See: ICJ, *Request for an Examination of the Situation in Accordance with Paragraph 63 of the Court's Judgment of 20 December 1974 in the Nuclear Tests (New Zealand v. France) Case*, Order (22 September 1995).

[280] ICJ, *Legality of the Use by a State of Nuclear Weapons in Armed Conflict*, Advisory Opinion, I.C.J. Reports 1996, p. 66.

[281] ICJ, *Legality of the Use by a State of Nuclear Weapons in Armed Conflict*, Advisory Opinion, I.C.J. Reports 1996, p. 66, para. 31.

[282] ICJ, *Legality of the Threat or Use of Nuclear Weapons*, Advisory Opinion, I.C.J. Reports 1996, p. 226.

[283] ICJ, *Legality of the Threat or Use of Nuclear Weapons*, Advisory Opinion, I.C.J. Reports 1996, p. 226, para. 105 (emphasis added).

of armed conflict and that to suspend the exercise of certain rights requires following specific rules of derogation, which do not allow for the suspension of the protection of the right to life.[284] The Court also acknowledged that many of the rules of humanitarian law are 'so fundamental to the respect of the human person' that they constitute 'intransgressible principles of international customary law', suggesting that they form part of the material realm of *jus cogens*.[285] Moreover, the ICJ recognized the importance of protecting the environment, which would be catastrophically affected by further use of nuclear weapons, and which 'represents the living space, the quality of life and the very health of human beings, including [of future] generations'.[286] In sum, in a decision that stopped short from providing the widest possible legal protection to the right to life, the Court managed to make relevant contributions to its protection under international law.

Furthermore, in that Advisory Opinion, the Court unanimously agreed that States were under the 'obligation to pursue in good faith, and bring to a conclusion, negotiations leading to nuclear disarmament in all its aspects';[287] a duty that provided grounds for nine applications brought before the Court by the Marshall Islands in 2014. The Marshall Islands instituted proceedings against China, North Korea (Chosŏn), France, India, Israel, Pakistan, Russia, the UK, and the USA, accusing them of failing to comply with their obligations concerning nuclear disarmament. Given that only the UK, India, and Pakistan had consented to the Court's jurisdiction, those were the only claims examined by the ICJ. The claim against the UK involved its obligations under the 1968 Treaty on the Non-Proliferation of Nuclear Weapons (NPT),[288] as well as under customary law, while the remaining claims only concerned international custom, as neither India nor Pakistan are Parties to the NPT. Nevertheless, in October 2016, the Court dismissed all three cases, affirming that no dispute existed between the Parties. The cases against India and Pakistan were dismissed by a majority of 9 to 7, while the case against the UK required the President's casting vote to break the 8-to-8 split decision.[289] In the opinion of the (slight) majority of the Court, there was no 'dispute' in these cases, as there was no actual conflict of legal views, facts, or of interests between the Parties, at the time the applications were submitted.[290]

---

[284] ICJ, *Legality of the Threat or Use of Nuclear Weapons*, Advisory Opinion, I.C.J. Reports 1996, p. 226, para. 25.
[285] ICJ, *Legality of the Threat or Use of Nuclear Weapons*, Advisory Opinion, I.C.J. Reports 1996, p. 226, para. 79.
[286] ICJ, *Legality of the Threat or Use of Nuclear Weapons*, Advisory Opinion, I.C.J. Reports 1996, p. 226, para. 29.
[287] ICJ, *Legality of the Threat or Use of Nuclear Weapons*, Advisory Opinion, I.C.J. Reports 1996, p. 226, para. 105.
[288] Treaty on the Non-Proliferation of Nuclear Weapons (adopted 1 July 1968, entered into force 5 March 1970) 729 UNTS 161.
[289] Interestingly, six of the eight judges that voted to dismiss the cases were nationals of 'nuclear-weapons' States: Abraham (France); Greenwood (UK), Xue (China), Donoghue (USA), Bhandari (India), and Gevorgian (Russia).
[290] ICJ, *Obligations concerning Negotiations relating to Cessation of the Nuclear Arms Race and to Nuclear Disarmament (Marshall Islands v. India)*, Jurisdiction and Admissibility, Judgment, I.C.J. Reports 2016, p. 255, paras. 34, 38–40, 56; ICJ, *Obligations concerning Negotiations relating to Cessation of the Nuclear Arms Race and to Nuclear Disarmament (Marshall Islands v. Pakistan)*, Jurisdiction and Admissibility, Judgment, I.C.J. Reports 2016, p. 552, paras. 34, 38–40, 55; ICJ, *Obligations concerning Negotiations relating to Cessation of the Nuclear Arms Race and to Nuclear Disarmament (Marshall Islands v. United Kingdom)*, Preliminary Objections, Judgment, I.C.J. Reports 2016, p. 833, paras. 37, 41–43, 59.

In all three cases, at least five of the permanent judges and the *ad hoc* judge dissented with the majority of the Court and voted for the examination of the merits of the case.[291] Counting himself among the dissenting judges, Judge Cançado Trindade delivered a 122-page-long opinion that went further than merely reasoning why the case should have been admitted and into how it should have been decided on the merits.[292] Judge Cançado Trindade cogently argued that, in our days, it is possible to identify the existence of a general rule of international customary law that mandates all States, and not just the Parties to the NPT, to negotiate in good faith on effective measures relating to nuclear disarmament.[293] Characterizing the existence of nuclear weapons as one of the global tragedies of our age,[294] he affirmed that all weapons of mass destruction need to be understood as unlawful under international law and, even more, such prohibition must be seen as *jus cogens*.[295] He stated that weapons with the capacity to destroy humankind as a whole offend the universal juridical conscience, ultimate material source of the law, given that securing the survival of humankind must be among the most fundamental aims of justice.[296] And indeed, it is as difficult to disagree with the reflections from Judge Cançado Trindade as it is upsetting to see that the ICJ had once again missed an opportunity to affirm the illegality of weapons that cannot be reconciled with the most fundamental protection of human rights.

4.6 CONCLUSION

The United Nations has maintained a specific body tasked with the promotion and protection of human rights worldwide (almost) since the very creation of the organization itself. From 1947 until its replacement in 2006, the Commission on Human Rights had a noteworthy role in international standard-setting, with a more modest monitoring function developed in 1967. Created to replace a body that held such a task for six decades, the HRC continues to face the dual challenge of measuring to the Commission's achievements, such as the drafting of the International Bill of Human Rights and the creation of the system of special procedures, while also avoiding falling

---

[291] These were: Judges Bennouna, Cançado Trindade, Sebutinde, Robinson, Crawford, and *ad hoc* Judge Bedjaoui, with Vice-President Yussuf also voting with the minority in the case against the UK.

[292] See also the interest reflections in the last section of Judge *ad hoc* Bedjaoui (paras. 70–91).

[293] ICJ, *Obligations concerning Negotiations relating to Cessation of the Nuclear Arms Race and to Nuclear Disarmament (Marshall Islands v. United Kingdom)*, Preliminary Objections, Judgment, I.C.J. Reports 2016, p. 833, dissenting opinion of Judge Cançado Trindade, paras. 63, 83, 147, 322.

[294] ICJ, *Obligations concerning Negotiations relating to Cessation of the Nuclear Arms Race and to Nuclear Disarmament (Marshall Islands v. United Kingdom)*, Preliminary Objections, Judgment, I.C.J. Reports 2016, p. 833, dissenting opinion of Judge Cançado Trindade, para. 206.

[295] ICJ, *Obligations concerning Negotiations relating to Cessation of the Nuclear Arms Race and to Nuclear Disarmament (Marshall Islands v. United Kingdom)*, Preliminary Objections, Judgment, I.C.J. Reports 2016, p. 833, dissenting opinion of Judge Cançado Trindade, para. 229.

[296] ICJ, *Obligations concerning Negotiations relating to Cessation of the Nuclear Arms Race and to Nuclear Disarmament (Marshall Islands v. United Kingdom)*, Preliminary Objections, Judgment, I.C.J. Reports 2016, p. 833, dissenting opinion of Judge Cançado Trindade, paras. 152, 228.

into the same pitfalls that led to the demise of its predecessor, especially the political bias behind the adoption of measures allegedly aimed at the protection of universal values (all rights, everywhere, for everyone). However, as discussed in particular regarding the tense relationship between the Council and Israel, impartiality does not seem to feature as one of the main strengths of the new body.

At the same time, the Council has been granted an important new tool in terms of the universal coverage of its monitoring functions—the UPR—which might not avoid political bias but at least reduces selectivity, as all States are subject to it.[297] This mechanism has opened up new possibilities in terms of supervising the protection of human rights worldwide, with all UN Members States engaging in the procedure, both as reviewee and as reviewers, making it the only (almost) universal human rights monitoring mechanism in existence.[298] In fact, taking part in other States' reviews, even if merely for the politically motivated reason of criticizing a State in a public international forum, brings attached the (unintended and positive) consequence of contributing to the reinforcement of the legal obligations highlighted, and perhaps helping with the formation of *opinio juris*,[299] as an element of customary norms.[300]

Moreover, part of the rationale of the UPR itself relies on its political character. While its outcome lacks binding legal force, its potential success in affecting States' behaviour, leading to the improvement of their human rights records, depends, at least in part, on the political pressure the body can exercise over the States under review.[301] Although States under review can even reject all the recommendations made to them,[302] the fact that every single UN Member State must participate in the process and that this mechanism can evaluate compliance with all their assumed human rights obligations, lends reasons for (cautious) hope in the progressive protection of human rights worldwide.[303] At the end, the real test of the UPR's effectiveness will be the evidence of

---

[297] K. Boyle, 'The United Nations Human Rights Council: Politics, Power and Human Rights' (2009) 60 *Northern Ireland Legal Quarterly* 121, 130.

[298] Almost universal in the sense that not all States in the world are UN Members.

[299] The conviction that a certain practice is being performed to comply with a legal obligation, as discussed in **Section 3.1.2**.

[300] W. Kälin, 'Ritual and Ritualism at the Universal Periodic Review: A Preliminary Appraisal' in H. Charlesworth and E. Larking (eds.), *Human Rights and the Universal Periodic Review: Rituals and Ritualism* (CUP 2014) 25–41, 35–36.

[301] K. Boyle, 'The United Nations Human Rights Council: Politics, Power and Human Rights' (2009) 60 *Northern Ireland Legal Quarterly* 121, 133.

[302] Following North Korea's first UPR, the French delegate interpreted that all recommendations had been rejected. See: W. Kälin, 'Ritual and ritualism at the Universal Periodic Review: A Preliminary Appraisal' in H. Charlesworth and E. Larking (eds.), *Human Rights and the Universal Periodic Review: Rituals and Ritualism* (CUP 2014) 25–41, 31. See also: HRC, Report of the Human Rights Council on its thirteenth session, A/HRC/13/56 (8 February 2011), paras. 642, 644–645.

[303] Although, as mentioned earlier, this hopeful stance is not necessarily universally shared. See: O. de Frouville, 'Building a Universal System for the Protection of Human Rights: The Way Forward' in M. Cherif Bassiouni and W. Schabas (eds.), *New Challenges for the UN Human Rights Machinery: What Future for the UN Treaty Body System and the Human Rights Council Procedures?* (Intersentia 2011) 241–266.

implementation of the accepted recommendation by States, which remains subject to their own commitment in advancing the cause of human rights.[304]

The development of the system of special procedures—the 'jewel in the crown' of the UN human rights system—is another essential part of the regimen of international protection of human rights under the UN Charter. The decision to maintain and strengthen this system of mandates under the Council was undoubtedly correct, as these independent experts have provided an invaluable contribution to both the protection of human rights in the field, holding governments accountable for their human rights violations, as well as to the development of the normative understanding of international human rights.[305] Additionally, complementing the special procedures regime with that of urgent commissions of inquiry was a laudable move that can improve the UN's ability to respond to human rights emergencies. However, the system presents issues that require further serious consideration. Examples of these are the existence of budgetary constraints, which could endanger the level of support the special procedures system requires,[306] as well as the politicization of the decisions that identify where the most pressing emergencies are located, which can lead to questions as to whether victims of human rights violations do receive equal and fair protection worldwide.

Lastly, the creation of the post of the High Commissioner for Human Rights provided an additional significant element to the mechanisms for the promotion and protection of human rights under the Charter. In addition to improving the coordination and efficiency of the organization's human rights activities, the OHCHR came to provide a leading voice and put a human face to the United Nations' efforts in the area of human rights.[307] The existence of a high-profile person that can bring international attention to serious violations of human rights and has the authority to speak truth to power without fear of political backlash plays a significant role in identifying and shedding light on human rights violations, irrespective of where in the world they are taking place.[308]

---

[304] K. Boyle, 'The United Nations Human Rights Council: Politics, Power and Human Rights' (2009) 60 *Northern Ireland Legal Quarterly* 121, 132–133.

[305] P. Alston, 'Hobbling the Monitors: Should U.N. Human Rights Monitors Be Accountable?' (2011) 52 *Harvard International Law Journal* 561, 565, 572, 578.

[306] M. Limon and H. Power, 'History of the United Nations Special Procedures Mechanisms: Origins, Evolution and Reform' (Universal Rights Group 2014) 20–22; J. Connors, 'Special Procedures: Independence and Impartiality' in A. Nolan, R. Freedman, and T. Murphy (eds.), *The United Nations Special Procedures System* (Brill 2017) 52–86, 77–80; E. Domínguez-Redondo, *In Defense of Politicization of Human Rights: The UN Special Procedures* (OUP 2020) 171–173.

[307] H.H. Koh, 'A Job Description for the U.N. High Commissioner for Human Rights' (2004) 35 *Columbia Human Rights Law Review* 493, 495; K. Boyle, 'Marking Another Birthday: Ten Years of the United Nations High Commissioner for Human Rights' (2004) 22 *Netherlands Quarterly of Human Rights* 301, 307.

[308] A. Clapham, 'The High Commissioner for Human Rights' in F. Mégret and P. Alston (eds.), *The United Nations and Human Rights: A Critical Appraisal* (2nd edn., OUP 2020) 667–707, 684 and 690.

FURTHER READING

Bedi, S.R.S., *The Development of Human Rights Law by the Judges of the International Court of Justice* (Hart 2007).

Boyle, K. (ed.), *New Institutions for Human Rights Protection* (OUP 2009).

Charlesworth, H., and Larking, E. (eds.), *Human Rights and the Universal Periodic Review: Rituals and Ritualism* (CUP 2014).

Domínguez-Redondo, E., *In Defense of Politicization of Human Rights: The UN Special Procedures* (OUP 2020).

Etone, D., *The Human Rights Council: The Impact of the Universal Periodic Review in Africa* (Routledge 2020).

Gaer, F.D., and Broecker, C.L. (eds.), *The United Nations High Commissioner for Human Rights: Conscience for the World* (Brill 2013).

Mégret, F., and Alston, P. (eds.), *The United Nations and Human Rights: A Critical Appraisal* (2nd edn., OUP 2020).

Merry, S.E., *The Seductions of Quantification: Measuring Human Rights, Gender Violence, and Sex Trafficking* (University of Chicago Press 2016).

Nolan, A., Freedman, R., and Murphy, T. (eds.), *The United Nations Special Procedures System* (Brill 2017).

Tistounet, E., *The UN Human Rights Council: A Practical Anatomy* (Elgar 2020).

5

UNITED NATIONS TREATY (MONITORING) BODIES

5.1 THE UN CORE HUMAN RIGHTS TREATIES

Since its inception, the United Nations has provided an invaluable forum for debating, drafting, and adopting numerous human rights treaties of envisioned universal participation. Among these treaties, nine are recognized as the core international human rights instruments,[1] each monitored as to its compliance and implementation by so-called treaty bodies.[2] The nine core human rights treaties are: the 1965 International Convention on the Elimination of All Forms of Racial Discrimination (ICERD), the 1966 International Covenant on Economic, Social and Cultural Rights (ICESCR), the 1966 International Covenant on Civil and Political Rights (ICCPR), the 1979 Convention on the Elimination of All Forms of Discrimination against Women (CEDAW), the 1984 Convention against Torture and Other Cruel, Inhuman or Degrading Treatment or Punishment (UNCAT), the 1989 Convention on the Rights of the Child (UNCRC), the 1990 International Convention on the Protection of the Rights of All Migrant Workers and Members of Their Families (ICRMW), the 2006 Convention

---

[1] Other human rights treaties adopted under the auspices of the UN include: Convention on the Prevention and Punishment of the Crime of Genocide (adopted 10 December 1948, entered into force 12 January 1951), 78 UNTS 277; Convention on the Non-applicability of Statutory Limitations to War Crimes and Crimes against Humanity (adopted 26 November 1968, entered into force 11 November 1970), 754 UNTS 73; International Convention on the Suppression and Punishment of the Crime of Apartheid (adopted 30 November 1973, entered into force 18 July 1976) 1015 UNTS 243; International Convention against Apartheid in Sports (adopted 10 December 1985, entered into force 4 August 1993), 1728 UNTS 380.

[2] The adoption of further UN human rights treaties is an ongoing topic of discussion, including potential treaties on the rights of older persons, the regulation of the activities of private military and security companies, and the activities of transnational corporations and other business enterprises with respect to human rights. See: HRC, 'Open-ended intergovernmental working group to consider the possibility of elaborating an international regulatory framework on the regulation, monitoring and oversight of the activities of private military and security companies', A/HRC/RES/15/26 (7 October 2010); UNGA, 'Follow-up to the Second World Assembly on Ageing', A/RES/65/182 (4 February 2011); HRC, 'Elaboration of an international legally binding instrument on transnational corporations and other business enterprises with respect to human rights', A/HRC/RES/26/9 (14 July 2014).

on the Rights of Persons with Disabilities (UNCRPD), and the 2006 International Convention for the Protection of All Persons from Enforced Disappearance (ICPPED).[3]

Moreover, five of these nine core treaties have been complemented, either substantively or procedurally, by the adoption of optional protocols.[4] Protocols to the ICCPR, CEDAW, UNCRPD, ICESCR, and UNCRC have established procedures for individual petitions under the respective committees.[5] A second protocol to ICCPR was aimed at achieving the complete abolition of the death penalty (discussed in **Section 9.1.3**).[6] Two further protocols to UNCRC, adopted in 2000, concerned the prohibition of child prostitution and child pornography, and the regulation of children's participation in armed conflicts.[7] Lastly, an Optional Protocol to UNCAT (OPCAT) created an additional monitoring body, the Subcommittee on Prevention of Torture and Other Cruel, Inhuman or Degrading Treatment or Punishment (SPT), tasked with a rather preventive function to be undertaken through on-site visits to places of detention, as further discussed in **Section 5.8.1**.[8]

---

[3] International Convention on the Elimination of All Forms of Racial Discrimination (adopted 21 December 1965, entered into force 4 January 1969), International Covenant on Economic, Social and Cultural Rights (adopted 16 December 1966, entered into force 3 January 1976), International Covenant on Civil and Political Rights (adopted 16 December 1966, entered into force 23 March 1976), Convention on the Elimination of All Forms of Discrimination against Women (adopted 18 December 1979, entered into force 3 September 1981), Convention against Torture and Other Cruel, Inhuman or Degrading Treatment or Punishment (adopted 10 December 1984, entered into force 26 June 1987), Convention on the Rights of the Child (adopted 20 November 1989, entered into force 2 September 1990), International Convention on the Protection of the Rights of All Migrant Workers and Members of Their Families (adopted 18 December 1990. entered into force 1 July 2003), Convention on the Rights of Persons with Disabilities (adopted 13 December 2006, entered into force 3 May 2008), International Convention for the Protection of All Persons from Enforced Disappearance (adopted 20 December 2006, entered into force 23 December 2010).

[4] The original text of UNCRC has also been amended to increase the number of Committee members from ten to eighteen, while amendments proposed to the text of ICERD, UNCAT, and CEDAW have not received the necessary number of acceptances to enter into force. See: Amendment to Art. 43(2) of the Convention on the Rights of the Child (12 December 1995), CRC/SP/1995/L.1/Rev. 1.

[5] Optional Protocol to the International Covenant on Civil and Political Rights (ICCPR-OP1) (adopted 16 December 1966, entered into force 23 March 196); Optional Protocol to the Convention on the Elimination of All Forms of Discrimination against Women (OP-CEDAW) (adopted 6 October 1999, entered into force 22 December 2000); Optional Protocol to the Convention on the Rights of Persons with Disabilities (OPCRPD) (adopted 13 December 2006, entered into force 3 May 2008); Optional Protocol to the International Covenant on Economic, Social and Cultural Rights (OP-ICESCR) (adopted 10 December 2008, entered into force 5 May 2013); Optional Protocol to the Convention on the Rights of the Child on a communications procedure (OP3-CRC) (adopted 19 December 2011, entered into force 14 April 2014).

[6] Second Optional Protocol to the International Covenant on Civil and Political Rights, aiming at the abolition of the death penalty (ICCPR-OP2) (adopted 15 December 1989, entered into force 11 July 1991).

[7] Optional Protocol to the Convention on the Rights of the Child on the Sale of Children, Child Prostitution and Child Pornography (OP1-CRC) (adopted 25 May 2000, entered into force 18 January 2002); Optional Protocol to the Convention on the Rights of the Child on the Involvement of Children in Armed Conflict (OP2-CRC) (adopted 25 May 2000, entered into force 12 February 2002).

[8] Optional Protocol to the Convention against Torture and Other Cruel, Inhuman or Degrading Treatment or Punishment (OPCAT) (adopted 18 December 2002, entered into force 22 June 2006).

5.2 TREATY (MONITORING) BODIES

Treaty bodies are supervisory organs composed of human rights experts created to monitor the implementation of each of the nine core human rights treaties. The creation of this system of human rights treaty bodies has been labelled 'one of the greatest achievements in the efforts of the international community to promote and protect human rights'.[9] However, while we tend to refer to the network of the created bodies as a system, the reality is that the existence of the current number of committees was not a planned enterprise, but rather one that evolved haphazardly over time.[10] Currently, the system is composed of nine committees and the aforementioned Subcommittee. Eight of these nine committees have been directly created by the treaty they monitor, the exception being the Committee on Economic, Social and Cultural Rights (CESCR), which was created by ECOSOC in 1978, originally as a Sessional Working Group to assist in the consideration of State reports submitted by the Parties to the treaty.[11] The monitoring powers of the treaty bodies have expanded through the years. As discussed in **Section 5.3**, the main functions of the committees comprise the evaluation of State reports, the examination of communications, the elaboration of interpretative guidelines for the respective treaty, and the undertaking of inquiries.

5.2.1 THE COMPOSITION OF TREATY BODIES

The committees are comprised of independent experts nominated and elected by the States Parties to the respective treaty. The number of experts sitting in each body ranges from ten to twenty-three, following the provisions of the treaty, with an even larger number of experts (twenty-five) sitting on SPT. The election of committee experts takes place every two years at meetings of the 'Conference of States Parties' to the pertinent treaty, with the exception of CESCR, whose members are (still) elected by ECOSOC.[12] The usual process of election of committee members is by secret ballot from a list of candidates nominated by the States Parties from among their nationals. While most treaties only allow for each State to nominate one candidate, ICCPR and OPCAT allow

---

[9] N. Pillay, 'Strengthening the United Nations human rights treaty body system: A report by the United Nations High Commissioner for Human Rights' (June 2012), p. 8.

[10] S. Egan, 'Reform of the UN Human Rights Treaty Body System' in F. Mégret and P. Alston (eds.), *The United Nations and Human Rights: A Critical Appraisal* (2nd edn., OUP 2020) 645–664, 646.

[11] ECOSOC, 'Composition of the Sessional Working Group on the Implementation of the International Covenant on Economic, Social and Cultural Right', Decision 1978/10 (3 May 1978); ECOSOC, 'Review of the composition, organization and administrative arrangements of the Sessional Working Group of Governmental Experts on the Implementation of the International Covenant on Economic, Social and Cultural Rights', Resolution 1985/17 (28 May 1985).

[12] The General Assembly has recommended that ECOSOC considers replacing this procedure with a meeting of States Parties to ICESCR, in line with the procedure for other treaty bodies. See: UNGA, 'Strengthening and enhancing the effective functioning of the human rights treaty body system', A/RES/68/268 (21 April 2014), para. 11.

for two.[13] Candidates who receive the largest number of votes and an absolute majority of the votes of States Parties present and voting, are elected, with quorum for the election set at two-thirds of States Parties.[14] For the election of committee members States are expected to give due consideration to geographical diversity,[15] the representation of the different legal systems of the world, balanced gender representation, and the participation of experts with disabilities.[16]

Committee members should be individuals of high moral standing and recognised competence and expertise in the field of human rights and, in particular, in the sub-field of the respective treaty.[17] Although it has been common for experts to have a legal background, this is not a requirement and, over the years, committees have benefited from an inter-disciplinary composition.[18] Once elected, members serve on the treaty body in their personal capacity and not as representatives of their State of nationality.[19] Their term of tenure at the committees is four years, with the possibility of re-election.[20]

5.3 THE COMMITTEES' MAIN FUNCTIONS

Committees do not operate year-round but instead hold sessions twice or thrice yearly. Nowadays, their annual meeting time is established by the General Assembly, using a mathematical formula based on fixed weekly workload targets that take into account the number of State reports and individual communications received by each committee in the previous four years.[21] Conversely, the Office of the United Nations High Commissioner for Human Rights (discussed in **Section 4.4**), which provides administrative and logistical support to the treaty bodies, does operate on a permanent basis. As mentioned in **Section 5.2**, the main functions these bodies perform involve

---

[13] ICERD, Art. 8.2; ICCPR, Art. 29.2; CEDAW, Art. 17.2; UNCAT, Art. 17.2; UNCRC, Art. 43.3; ICRMW, Art. 72.2.(a); ICPPED, Art. 26.2; ICRPD, Art. 34.5; OPCAT, Art. 6.1. UNCAT also suggests States consider nominating candidates to its committee who are also members of the Human Rights Committee. See: UNCAT, Art. 17.1.

[14] ICERD, Arts. 8.2, 8.4; ICCPR, Arts. 29.2, 30.4; CEDAW, Arts. 17.2, 17.4; CAT, Arts. 17.2, 17.3; CRC, Arts. 43.3, 43.5; ICRMW, Arts. 72.2.(a), 72.4; ICPPED, Art. 26.2; ICRPD, Art. 34.5.

[15] However, only in the election of members to CESCR are rules of geographic distribution based on regional groups strictly adhered to, as the election is performed by ECOSOC and the electoral rules for UN organs apply.

[16] UNGA, 'Strengthening and enhancing the effective functioning of the human rights treaty body system', A/RES/68/268 (21 April 2014), paras. 10, 13.

[17] ICERD, Art. 8.1; ICCPR, Art. 28.2; CEDAW, Art. 17.1; CAT, Art. 17.1; CRC, Art. 43.2; ICRMW, Art. 72.1.(b); ICPPED, Art. 26.1; ICRPD, Art. 34.3.

[18] ICCPR expressly refers to the usefulness of some of its members having legal experience. See: ICCPR, Art. 28.2.

[19] ICERD, Art. 8.1; ICCPR, Arts. 28.3, 38; CEDAW, Art. 17.1; ICRMW, Arts. 72.1.(b), 72.2.(b); ICPPED, Art. 26.1; ICRPD, Art. 34.3.

[20] ICERD, Art. 8.5.a; ICCPR, Art. 32.1; CEDAW, Art. 17.5; CAT, Art. 17.5; CRC, Art. 43.6; ICRMW, Arts. 72.5.(a), 72.5.(c); ICPPED, Art. 26.4; ICRPD, Art. 34.7. The possibility of re-election is explicitly limited to two consecutive terms in the cases of ICPED, ICRPD, and OPCAT.

[21] AGNU, 'Strengthening and enhancing the effective functioning of the human rights treaty body system', A/RES/68/268 (21 April 2014), paras. 26–27.

the evaluation of State reports, the examination of communications, the elaboration of interpretative guidelines, and the undertaking of inquiries.

5.3.1 STATE-REPORTING SYSTEM

All nine core human rights treaties impose upon States Parties the obligation to report on the measures taken to implement the provisions of the relevant treaty within their jurisdiction.[22] This system of State-reporting finds important antecedents in the mechanism instituted under the Constitution of the International Labour Organisation and in the 1956 ECOSOC resolution requesting UN Member States to submit (triennial) reports on the progress achieved in the field of human rights.[23] The obligation to report to treaty bodies is undertaken by the submission of an initial report within one or two years of ratification or accession to the treaty, followed by periodic reports submitted on set intervals, which range from two to five years, depending on the treaty.[24] The increasing number of core treaties adopted over the years brought attached a consequential increase in the demands on States to report on their implementation. In turn, this has led numerous States to experience difficulties and delays in complying with their reporting obligations.[25] In fact, the relatively low level of States' compliance with their reporting duties has led to different proposals for harmonizing reporting procedures across committees in order to improve the efficiency of the system as a whole.[26]

The reporting process places great emphasis on the activities States undertake at the domestic level, given that it is within that sphere that the implementation of their international obligations takes place—as discussed in **Section 3.4**.[27] As observed by CESCR, more than three decades ago, the reporting procedure has a plurality of interconnected objectives, aimed at assisting States Parties to fulfil their obligations under the respective treaty.[28] These objectives encompass encouraging States to undertake a comprehensive review of their domestic legal order; to guarantee the fullest possible

---

[22] ICERD, Art. 9; ICESCR, Arts. 16–17; ICCPR, Art. 40; CEDAW, Art. 18; UNCAT, Art. 19; UNCRC, Art. 44; ICRMW, Art. 73; ICPPED, Art. 29; ICRPD, Art. 35.

[23] W. Kälin, 'Examination of State Reports' in H. Keller and G. Ulfstein (eds.), *UN Human Rights Treaty Bodies: Law and Legitimacy* (CUP 2012) 16–72, 18, 46.

[24] ICPPED is the only core treaty that establishes no obligation to report periodically, but to provide information on implementation as requested by the Committee. See: ICPPED, Art. 29.

[25] N. Pillay, 'Strengthening the United Nations human rights treaty body system: A report by the United Nations High Commissioner for Human Rights' (June 2012), p. 9. See also: W. Kälin, 'Examination of State Reports' in H. Keller and G. Ulfstein (eds.), *UN Human Rights Treaty Bodies: Law and Legitimacy* (CUP 2012) 16–72, 18, 46.

[26] UN Secretary-General, 'Strengthening of the United Nations: An Agenda for Further Change', A/57/38 (9 September 2002), para. 54; UN Secretary-General, 'In Larger Freedom: Towards Development, Security and Human Rights for All', A/59/2005 (21 March 2005), para. 147; N. Pillay, 'Strengthening the United Nations human rights treaty body system: A report by the United Nations High Commissioner for Human Rights' (June 2012), p. 9.

[27] P. Alston, 'The Committee on Economic, Social and Cultural Rights' in F. Mégret and P. Alston (eds.), The United Nations and Human Rights: A Critical Appraisal (2nd edn., OUP 2020) 439–475, 446.

[28] CESCR, General Comment 1: Reporting by States parties (1989).

conformity with their treaty obligations; ensuring that States monitor the human rights situation within their jurisdiction on a regular basis, providing States with essential knowledge on which to base the elaboration of public policies; allowing for public scrutiny of States' human rights policies by various social actors, laying the grounds on which both States and treaty bodies can evaluate the progress made towards the effective realization of human rights; and enabling States and committees to better understand the problems and shortcomings encountered in the protection of human rights.[29]

The process of periodic reporting is not fully harmonized across committees but seems to be in a state of transition towards enhanced coordination. Common characteristics can, nonetheless, be found. For instance, State-reporting now takes the form of two reports to be submitted to each committee: a common core document, identical for every committee, and a treaty-specific report.[30] The common document provides general and factual information relating to the State's political structure and legal system and of the legal framework for the implementation of the human rights treaties to which the reporting State is Party. Meanwhile, the treaty-specific document contains information relating to the implementation of the pertinent treaty, including responses to issues raised by the committee in previous observations on State reports. Reports should include sufficient information to provide each treaty body with a comprehensive understanding of the implementation of the relevant treaty by the State. The reports should address the implementation, both *de jure* and *de facto*, of the treaty, including relevant statistical data that would allow the committee to assess the impact of the measures adopted.[31] To encourage the harmonization of the reporting system and enhance its overall effectiveness, the General Assembly has established maximum word limits for each of these reports and for the documents produced by the treaty bodies themselves, in line with the UN practice in other areas.[32]

The consideration of State reports takes place during a plenary session of the treaty body and consists of a 'constructive dialogue' in which the committee engages with the delegation of the State Party. Before the session in which the report is scheduled to be examined, the committee draws up a 'list of issues' for the State, requesting any additional information that it deems important. The submitted report and the State's reply to the 'list of issues' constitute the basis of the interactive dialogue, but treaty bodies can also receive information from different sources, including UN agencies, other inter-governmental organizations, national human rights institutions, NGOs, professional groups, and

---

[29] CESCR, General Comment 1: Reporting by States parties (1989).

[30] The system of two reports, one common to all core treaties, has been implemented since 1991. See: M. Kjærum, 'State Reports' in G. Alfredsson et al. (ed.), *International Human Rights Monitoring Mechanisms Essays in Honour of Jakob Th. Möller* (2nd edn., Nijhoff 2009) 20.

[31] UN Secretary-General, 'Compilation of Guidelines on the Form and Content of Reports to be Submitted by States Parties to the International Human Rights Treaties', HRI/GEN/2/Rev.6 (3 June 2009), paras. 24–29.

[32] Documents issued by treaty bodies cannot exceed 10,700 words, while State reports have word limits of 42,400 (core documents), 31,800 (initial reports), and 21,200 (treaty-specific reports). See: UNGA, 'Strengthening and enhancing the effective functioning of the human rights treaty body system', A/RES/68/268 (21 April 2014), paras. 15–16.

academic institutions. Committees can even allocate time to hear submissions from UN agencies and civil society organizations when examining State reports.

After the public discussion, the committee meets in closed session to discuss the adoption of 'concluding observations'. These observations would normally recognize the progress made by the State in the implementation of the treaty, as well as highlight further action that is required to improve compliance.[33] When submitting their subsequent periodic report, States are expected to inform the committee of all measures adopted to implement concluding observations. Since 2001, almost all committees have also set up their own procedures to monitor compliance with concluding observations,[34] requesting States to submit follow-up reports on certain issues within a year or two of the adoption of the observations.[35]

An alternative simplified procedure for State reporting emerged in 2007 following an initiative of the Committee against Torture (CAT). In this new optional procedure, the committee prepares the 'list of issues' prior to the State report to assist the State with its elaboration. This simplified procedure has already been adopted by other treaty bodies, and the General Assembly has encouraged all committees to offer it as an alternative to States.[36] Given that this new procedure dispenses with a entire step of the traditional process, its adoption could help expedite and simplify the reporting system as a whole.

As aforementioned, the relatively low level of timely reporting has been a consistent problem in the monitoring of compliance with human rights treaties by States.[37] When a State fails to submit reports over a long period of time and refuses to respond to the request to produce them, committees can decide to evaluate their situation in the absence of a report; a process known as the 'review procedure'. This procedure was developed by the Committee on the Elimination of Racial Discrimination (CERD) in 1991 and later adopted by other treaty bodies. It allows committees to review the human rights situation of all States Parties, elaborating their observations on all information available to them, including exchanges with the State and submissions by UN agencies, national human rights institutions, and NGOs.[38]

---

[33] W. Kälin, 'Examination of State Reports' in H. Keller and G. Ulfstein (eds.), *UN Human Rights Treaty Bodies: Law and Legitimacy* (CUP 2012) 16–72, 26.

[34] At the end of 2022, CRC was the only committee without a follow-up mechanism between periodic reports. See: https://www.ohchr.org/en/treaty-bodies/follow-concluding-observations (accessed on 12 May 2023).

[35] M. Kjærum, 'State Reports' in G. Alfredsson et al. (eds.), *International Human Rights Monitoring Mechanisms Essays in Honour of Jakob Th. Möller* (2nd edn., Nijhoff 2009) 22; N. Pillay, 'Strengthening the United Nations human rights treaty body system: A report by the United Nations High Commissioner for Human Rights' (June 2012), p. 80.

[36] N. Pillay, 'Strengthening the United Nations human rights treaty body system: A report by the United Nations High Commissioner for Human Rights' (June 2012), pp. 47–48; UNGA, 'Strengthening and enhancing the effective functioning of the human rights treaty body system', A/RES/68/268 (21 April 2014), para. 1.

[37] S. Egan, 'Transforming the UN Human Rights Treaty System: A Realistic Appraisal' (2020) 42 *Human Rights Quarterly* 762, 774.

[38] OHCHR, 'Report on the working methods of the human rights treaty bodies relating to the State party reporting process', HRI/ICM/2010/2 (10 May 2010), para. 85.

5.3.2 GENERAL COMMENTS/RECOMMENDATIONS

Committees have developed the ability to issue 'general comments'—called 'general recommendations' by CERD and the Committee on the Elimination of Discrimination against Women (CEDAW Committee). These comments allow treaty bodies to clarify the content and scope of States' international obligations, providing an authoritative interpretation of the monitored treaty. The practice of elaborating general comments/recommendations was initiated by CERD in 1972[39] on the basis of a treaty provision that empowered it to 'make suggestions and general recommendations based on the examination of the reports and information received from the States Parties'.[40] Initially, the elaboration of these comments was closely connected with the committees' role in the State-reporting procedure,[41] but with time, it became a distinctive aspect of their functions as monitoring bodies.[42]

As explained by CESCR, more than two decades ago, the elaboration of general comments pursues multiple essential aims, which include:

> to make the experience gained ... through the examination of States' reports available for the benefit of all States parties in order to assist and promote their further implementation of the Covenant; to draw the attention of the States parties to insufficiencies disclosed by a large number of reports; to suggest improvements in the reporting procedures; and to stimulate the activities of the States parties, international organizations and the specialized agencies concerned in achieving progressively and effectively the full realization of the rights recognized in the Covenant.[43]

Over the years, the general comments adopted by treaty bodies have evolved in length and complexity, providing detailed and comprehensive commentaries on specific rights, issues, and treaty provisions.[44] The need for evolving and progressive protection

---

[39] OHCHR, 'Report on the working methods of the human rights treaty bodies relating to the State party reporting process', HRI/ICM/2010/2 (10 May 2010), para. 120.

[40] ICERD, Art. 9.2.

[41] The origin of this faculty can be traced back to the power of the UN Commission on Human Rights to issue recommendations and comments of a general character under a reporting mechanism adopted between 1953 and 1956. See: P. Alston, 'The Historical Origins of the Concept of "General Comments" in Human Rights Law' in L. Boisson de Chazournes and V. Gowland Debbas (eds.), *The International Legal System in Quest of Equity and Universality: Liber Amicorum Georges Abi-Saab* (Nijhoff 2001) 763–776, 770–771.

[42] P. Alston, 'The Historical Origins of the Concept of "General Comments" in Human Rights Law' in L. Boisson de Chazournes and V. Gowland Debbas (eds.), *The International Legal System in Quest of Equity and Universality: Liber Amicorum Georges Abi-Saab* (Nijhoff 2001) 763–776, 775–776; E. Klein and D. Kretzmer, 'The UN Human Rights Committee: The General Comments—The Evolution of an Autonomous Monitoring Instrument' (2015) 58 *German Yearbook of International Law* 189, 190. See: CCPR, Report of the Human Rights Committee, A/36/40 (1981), Annex IV, 101–103.

[43] CESCR Committee, Report on the Twentieth and Twenty-first Sessions (26 April–14 May 1999, 15 November–3 December 1999), E/2000/22, E/C.12/1999/11 (2000), para. 51.

[44] OHCHR, 'Report on the working methods of the human rights treaty bodies relating to the State party reporting process', HRI/ICM/2010/2 (10 May 2010), para. 120.

of human rights has also led to the revision of earlier general comments on given topics and their replacement with recent ones.[45]

The elaboration of a general comment can be proposed by any committee member at any time. Although this process presents variations across the different treaty bodies, it usually involves the elaboration of a draft by one or more committee members; a wide range of consultation with specialized agencies, NGOs, academics, and other human rights treaty bodies; the debate and revision of the draft, paragraph-by-paragraph, at committee sessions; and the formal adoption of the (revised) draft by consensus in a plenary session.[46] In recent years, some general comments have been adopted jointly by two committees, focusing on topics of relevance for the implementation of both treaties.[47]

The legal nature of general comments is contested. While, technically, these are not directly binding on States Parties,[48] the comments provide the authoritative interpretation of the treaty by the pertinent monitoring body.[49] Hence, general comments clarify the content and scope of the international obligations that have been assumed by States under the treaty.[50] The increasing reliance on general comments for the interpretation of treaty obligations by other international bodies, including the International Court of Justice (ICJ),[51] further supports the fundamental legal character of general comments.

---

[45] See, for instance: CCPR, General Comment 6: Right to life (1982); CCPR, General Comment 14: Right to life; CCPR, General Comment No. 36: Right to life, CCPR/C/GC/36 (3 September 2019); CEDAW Committee, General Recommendation 19: Violence against Women, A/47/38; CEDAW Committee, General Recommendation 35: on gender-based violence against women (updating General Recommendation 19), CEDAW/C/GC/35 (26 July 2017).

[46] OHCHR, 'Report on the working methods of the human rights treaty bodies relating to the State party reporting process', HRI/ICM/2010/2 (10 May 2010), paras. 122, 124; Consultation process for the elaboration of treaty body general comments, HRI/MC/2015/4 (15 May 2015). See also: F. Salvioli, 'Observaciones generales de los órganos de tratados de Derechos Humanos de las Naciones Unidas' (2022) 76 *Revista IIDH* 137, 149–160.

[47] CEDAW and CRC, Joint General Recommendation No. 31/General Comment No. 18, CEDAW/C/GC/31-CRC/C/GC/18 (14 November 2014); CMW and CRC, Joint General Comment Nos. 3, 22: on the general principles regarding the human rights of children in the context of international migration, CMW/C/GC/3-CRC/C/GC/22 (16 November 2017); CMW and CRC, Joint General Comment Nos. 4, 23: on State obligations regarding the human rights of children in the context of international migration in countries of origin, transit, destination, and return, CMW/C/GC/4-CRC/C/GC/23 (16 November 2017).

[48] H. Keller and L. Grover, 'General Comments of the Human Rights Committee and Their Legitimacy' in H. Keller and G. Ulfstein (eds.), *UN Human Rights Treaty Bodies: Law and Legitimacy* (CUP 2012) 116–198, 129; S. Liebenberg, 'Between Sovereignty and Accountability: The Emerging Jurisprudence of the United Nations Committee on Economic, Social and Cultural Rights Under the Optional Protocol' (2020) 42 *Human Rights Quarterly* 48, 55.

[49] CCPR, General Comment 33: Obligations of States parties under the Optional Protocol to the International Covenant on Civil and Political Rights, 25 June 2009, CCPR/C/GC/33, para. 13; ICJ, *Ahmadou Sadio Diallo (Republic of Guinea v. Democratic Republic of the Congo)*, Merits, Judgment, I.C.J. Reports 2010, p. 639, para. 66.

[50] F. Salvioli, 'Observaciones generales de los órganos de tratados de Derechos Humanos de las Naciones Unidas' (2022) 76 *Revista IIDH* 137, 166–167.

[51] ICJ, *Legal Consequences of the Construction of a Wall in the Occupied Palestinian Territory*, Advisory Opinion, I.C.J. Reports 2004, p. 136, para. 136; ICJ, *Ahmadou Sadio Diallo (Republic of Guinea v. Democratic Republic of the Congo)*, Merits, Judgment, I.C.J. Reports 2010, p. 639, paras. 66, 77; ICJ, *Judgment No. 2867 of the Administrative Tribunal of the International Labour Organization upon a Complaint Filed against the International Fund for Agricultural Development*, Advisory Opinion, I.C.J. Reports 2012, p. 10, para. 39.

5.3.3 COMMUNICATIONS: INTER-STATE AND INDIVIDUAL

The ability to receive and examine communications concerning breaches of treaty obligations by States Parties is envisioned under all committees. These communications can be of two kinds: those submitted by a State Party regarding the failure of another Party to duly comply with the treaty and those of individuals claiming a violation of human rights attributable to a State Party. With the sole exception of inter-State communications under ICERD, the committees' jurisdiction to receive complaints is subject to the explicit consent of States Parties through either an express declaration or the ratification of, or accession to, an optional protocol.[52] Seven of the nine committees are empowered, either by the core treaty or by an optional protocol, to receive inter-States complaints, with the CEDAW Committee and the Committee on the Rights of Persons with Disabilities (CRPD) lacking such faculty. The possibility of individual communications is foreseen under all committees, although it has not yet entered into force with respect to the International Convention on the Protection of the Rights of All Migrant Workers and Members of their Families (ICRMW), as the required minimum number of States to accept such a procedure has not been reached.[53]

5.3.3.1 Inter-State disputes

Although seven committees are empowered to receive inter-States communications, as at the end of 2022 these types of complaints have only been brought under ICERD. CERD has received three communications: two from Qatar—against Saudi Arabia and the United Arab Emirates—and one from Palestine—against Israel. While the proceedings initiated by Qatar were terminated by agreement of the parties,[54] the communication against Israel has been declared admissible, with the appointment of a conciliation commission that would offer its good offices to attempt reaching an amicable solution to the dispute.[55]

Five of the core treaties also provide for an alternative procedure for the settlement of disputes between States Parties concerning the interpretation and application of the treaty.[56] Unlike inter-States communications, this dispute settlement mechanism is provided by the treaties as an opt-out clause, enabling States to exclude themselves from it by an express declaration—the exception being again ICERD, which does not allow

---

[52] ICERD, Arts. 11, 14; ICCPR, Art. 41 and OP-ICCPR1; OP-ICESCR, Arts. 2, 10; UNCAT, Arts. 21, 22; OP-CEDAW, Art. 2; OP3-CRC, Arts. 5, 12; ICRMW, Arts. 76, 77; OPCRPD, Art. 1; ICPPED, Arts. 31, 32.

[53] At the end of 2022, only four of the needed ten States Parties have accepted this competence of the Committee (Ecuador, El Salvador, Mexico, and Uruguay). See: ICRMW, Art. 77.

[54] CERD, Decision of the *ad hoc* Conciliation Commission on the termination of the proceedings concerning the interstate communication *Qatar v. the Kingdom of Saudi Arabi* (19 January 2022); CERD, Decision of the *ad hoc* Conciliation Commission on the termination of the proceedings concerning the interstate communication *Qatar v. the United Arab Emirates* (26 January 2023).

[55] CERD, Decision on the admissibility of the inter-State communication submitted by the State of Palestine against Israel, CERD/C/103/R.6 (20 May 2021).

[56] ICERD, Art. 22; CEDAW, Art. 29; UNCAT, Art. 30; ICRMW, Art. 92; ICPPED, Art. 42.

for opting-out.[57] Under four of the treaties, this dispute settlement mechanism does not involve the committees themselves, but might lead to the intervention of the ICJ.[58] Disputes should initially be addressed by negotiation between States, with resort to arbitration if negotiation proves unsuccessful. Only if States Parties fail to agree on the terms of arbitration, and after a six-month timeframe, can they submit the issue to the consideration of the ICJ. This dispute settlement mechanism has been resorted to in a few instances, as discussed in **Section 5.4** and **Section 5.8**.

5.3.3.2 Individual communications

While the system of inter-State communications under the treaty bodies has not experienced a high degree of engagement, that is not the case for individual communications. The system of individual communications is usually referred to as 'quasi-judicial', given its similarities to the proceedings before domestic tribunals and regional human rights courts. In fact, the admissibility of individual complaints is subject to similar requirements to those of the applications to regional human rights courts—discussed in **Chapter 6**, **Chapter 7**, and **Chapter 8**. Although admissibility requirements vary to some degree among the different treaty bodies, all include the need to previously exhaust domestic remedies—unless these are unduly prolonged or unlikely to provide an effective relief[59]—as well as the lack of existence of *lis pendes* and *res judicata*—that is, the same matter being under the examination of, or having been decided by, another procedure of international investigation or settlement.[60] The procedure before CERD, CESCR, and the Committee on the Rights of the Child (CRC) is also subject to time-sensitive deadlines from the moment at which domestic remedies have been exhausted—six months with regards to CERD, and one year in the other two—although exceptions are allowed.[61]

Communications can be submitted by a person or group of persons whose rights have been affected under the respective treaty,[62] although these can also be submitted by a third person on behalf of an alleged victim when the latter is unable to act—a possibility that is particularly important in cases of arbitrary detentions or forced disappearances.[63] Communications should not be anonymous—although it could be

---

[57] ICERD, Art. 22; CEDAW, Art. 29.2; UNCAT, Art. 30.2; ICRMW, Art. 92.2; ICPPED, Art. 42.2.
[58] The procedure is somehow different under ICERD and will be discussed in **Section 5.4**.
[59] ICERD, Art. 14.7.(a); ICCPR-OP1, Art. 5.b.; UNCAT, Art. 22.4.(b); OP-CEDAW, Art. 4.1; IRCMW, Art. 77.3.(b); OP-ICESCR, Art. 3.1; ICPPED, Art. 31.2; OPCRPD, Art. 2; OP3-CRC, Art. 7.
[60] ICCPR-OP1, Art. 5.a.; UNCAT, Art. 22.4.(a); OP-CEDAW, Art. 4.2.(a); IRCMW, Art. 77.3.(a); ICPPED, Art. 31.2; OPCRPD, Art. 2; OP3-CRC, Art. 7.
[61] While not stated in the text of the treaties, other committees would also reject a communication when an unreasonably long period of time has elapsed between the exhaustion of domestic remedies and the submission of the communication. See: ICERD, Art. 14.5; OP-ICESCR, Art. 3.2.(a); OP3-CRC, Art. 7; CCPR, Rules of Procedure, CCPR/C/3/Rev.12, r. 99.(c); CAT, Rules of Procedure, CAT/C/3/Rev.6, r. 113.(f).
[62] In exceptional cases, a communication can be filed before a violation has taken place if it can be considered imminent and sufficiently certain. See: O. De Schutter, *International Human Rights Law: Cases, Materials, Commentary* (CUP 2019) 901.
[63] ICERD, Art. 14.1; ICCPR-OP1, Art. 2; OP-CEDAW, Art. 2; UNCAT, Art. 22.1; ICPPED, Art. 21.1.

requested that the victim's identity be anonymized by the committee—and should not amount to an abuse of the right to submit a complaint.[64] The current system for the submission of communications expresses a strong preference for submissions by email and requires them to be written in one of only four of the official languages of the UN: English, French, Russian, or Spanish.[65]

Communications must fall within the jurisdiction of the respective committee, which encompasses different elements, such as: to be against a State that is not only Party to the respective treaty but which has also accepted the treaty body's competence to receive individual complaints; to be based on facts that have occurred after this acceptance of competence took place—with the exception of cases of ongoing violations[66]—and to be compatible with the provisions of the respective treaty.[67] Communications that are manifestly ill-founded, or nor sufficiently substantiated, would be found inadmissible by the pertinent committee.[68]

Once a communication has been received, the committee submits it to the respondent State, which has an opportunity to provide written observations on both the admissibility and the merits of the complaint. The State's observations are then transmitted to the author of the communication for their own views on them. In situations of urgency, where potentially irreparable consequences to the rights invoked might occur, the committee can request the respondent State to adopt 'interim measures' necessary to avoid such harm from taking place. This request can be made at any point of the proceedings, even before determining the admissibility of the communication.[69]

If the committee finds the complaint admissible, it will issue its 'views'—called 'opinion' under ICERD—as to whether the State has breached its obligations under the pertinent treaty to the detriment of the alleged victim and, if so, concerning measures that should be adopted to redress such violations. The committee's decision is adopted in closed session, by consensus, based on the written information provided by the parties. Before the adoption of views, most committees have the power to offer their good offices to the parties of the dispute with a view to reaching an amicable solution to the case.[70] The committee's decision is final and not subject to appeal and, once adopted, is transmitted to the parties to the case and made public. Any committee member who

---

[64] OP-CEDAW, Art. 4.2; IRCMW, Art. 77.2; OP-ICESCR, Art.3.2; OPCRPD, Art. 2; OP3-CRC, Art. 7.

[65] See: https://www.ohchr.org/en/documents/tools-and-resources/form-and-guidance-submitting-individual-communication-treaty-bodies (accessed on 7 February 2023).

[66] On this point, while the crime of forced disappearance is one of the most paradigmatic examples of a continuous human rights violation, ICCPED (Art. 35) expressly excludes from the Committee's temporal jurisdiction the examination of forced disappearances that have commenced before the respective State became Party to the treaty. However, such exclusion does not necessarily apply to the examination of States' compliance with other ongoing obligations that can be breached by their acts and omissions following the treaty's entry into force. It would be expected that the Committee's case law will confirm this interpretation.

[67] ICCPR-OP1, Arts. 1, 3; OP-CEDAW, Art. 4.2.(c); OP-ICESCR, Art. 3.2; OPCRPD, Art.2; OP3-CRC, Art. 7.

[68] OP-CEDAW, Art. 4.2.(c); OP-ICESCR, Art. 3.2; OPCRPD, Art.2; OP3-CRC, Art. 7.

[69] CERD, Rules of Procedure, CERD/C/35/Rev.3, r. 94; CCPR, Rules of Procedure, CCPR/C/3/Rev.12, r. 94; CAT, Rules of Procedure, CAT/C/3/Rev.6, r. 114; OP-CEDAW, Art. 5; ICPPED, Art. 31.4.

[70] CCPR, Rules of Procedure, CCPR/C/3/Rev.12, r. 83; CAT, Rules of Procedure, CAT/C/3/Rev.6, r. 98; OP-CEDAW, Art. 5; ICPPED, Art. 31.4; OP-ICESCR, Art. 7; OP3-CRC, Art. 9.

disagrees with the decision or who, even in agreement, wishes to present their own reasons for reaching such a decision can append a separate opinion.

As aforementioned, when violations of the treaty are found, the committee provides recommendations to the respondent State to redress the situation. The recommendations tend to be rather diverse, and are designed to provide full reparation to the victims, including restitution, compensation, rehabilitation, satisfaction, and measures to avoid recidivism.[71] The measures of reparation recommended have included: the restoration of the victim's rights, to the extent possible, as well as measures of rehabilitation, such as providing medical and psychological treatment; the need to adopt legislative and judicial measures to put an end to the violation and avoid its repetition in the future; measures of satisfaction, such as the State's acknowledgment of wrongdoing, accompanied by a public apology; and, certainly, the payment of compensation, to redress the damages experienced by the victim, even if the committees—unlike regional human rights courts—do not determine the quantum of the award.[72] The committee would then invite the State to provide information, within a set timeframe—usually 180 days—on the measures taken to implement the recommendations. This follow-up procedure should remain in place until satisfactory measures have been adopted.[73]

The committee's decisions, while not technically binding—unlike the judgments of regional human rights courts[74]—present some of the relevant features of a judicial decision. Over a decade ago the Human Rights Committee (CCPR) elaborated on the reasons why States should comply with committees' views on communications. As asserted by CCPR, the views of the committees are adopted in a 'judicial spirit, including the impartiality and independence of [c]ommittee members, the considered interpretation of the language of the [respective treaty], and the determinative character of the decisions'.[75] Committees' views are not only a product of the monitoring body entrusted by the treaty itself with its interpretation, but they also bring attached the State's duty to cooperate, in good faith, with the committee in the realization of the rights

---

[71] CCPR, Guidelines on measures of reparation under the Optional Protocol to the International Covenant on Civil and Political Rights, CCPR/C/158 (30 November 2016).

[72] See, for instance: CEDAW, *Fatma Yildirim (deceased) v. Austria*, Communication No. 6/2005, CEDAW/C/39/D/2005 (1 October 2007); CESCR, *Ben Djazia and Bellili v. Spain*, Communication 5/2015, E/C.12/61/D/5/2015 (2017); CCPR, *Sonia Yaker*, Communication 2747/2016, CCPR/C/123/D/2747/2016 (17 July 2018); CRC, *Y.B. and N.S. v. Belgium*, CRC/C/79/D/12/2017 (5 November 2018). See also: CCPR, Guidelines on measures of reparation under the Optional Protocol to the International Covenant on Civil and Political Rights, CCPR/C/158 (30 November 2016).

[73] N. Rodley, 'The Role and Impact of Treaty Bodies' in D. Shelton (ed.), *The Oxford Handbook of International Human Rights Law* (OUP 2013) 621–648, 639.

[74] European Commission for Democracy through Law (Venice Commission), Report on the Implementation of International Human Rights Treaties in Domestic Law and the Role of Courts, CDL-AD(2014)036 (December 2014), para. 78; K. Fox Principi, 'Implementation of UN Treaty Body Decisions: A Brief Insight for Practitioners', (2020) 12 *Journal of Human Rights Practice* 185, 188.

[75] CCPR, General Comment 33: Obligations of States parties under the Optional Protocol to the International Covenant on Civil and Political Rights, 25 June 2009, CCPR/C/GC/33, para.11.

protected by the treaty.[76] Unfortunately, this opinion on the legal implications of views was followed by observations from twenty-one States, with the most explicit objections to the CCPR's interpretation coming from Western States, including the USA—which is not even a Party to the Optional Protocol to the ICCPR.[77] It is, therefore, unsurprising that the overall level of compliance with committees' views remains rather low, with a recent empirical study finding that satisfactory compliance with treaty bodies' views was at a level of around 24 per cent.[78]

5.3.4 INQUIRY PROCEDURES

Five of the nine committees—as well as SPT—have the power to undertake confidential inquiries concerning serious, grave, or systematic violations of the respective treaty by a State Party.[79] As with the communications procedures, the one concerning inquiries is also subject to the acceptance of States Parties, with the notable exception of ICPPED, which establishes the compulsory jurisdiction of the Committee for conducting inquiries over all Parties.[80] However, the competence to undertake inquiries is usually conceived in opt-out terms, requiring States to expressly exclude themselves from the committees' inquisitorial power at the time of ratification or accession;[81] the exception being the Optional Protocol to ICESCR (OP-ICESCR), which requires an express declaration of States Parties—which can, nonetheless, be withdrawn at any time.[82]

Inquiries can take place when the treaty body receives reliable information indicating the existence of grave, serious, or systematic human rights violations by a State Party that has accepted the committee's competence. The treaty body then invites the State to cooperate with the examination of the information received by providing its observations. On the basis of all the information gathered, the treaty body decides whether to designate one or more of its members to conduct an inquiry, which may include a visit to the State, subject to its consent. The whole procedure is confidential and ensues with the cooperation of the State.[83] The findings of the inquiry are examined by the treaty body in plenary and communicated to the concerned State, together with any pertinent recommendations, and with a request to submit further observations within a set timeframe including, if appropriate, an indication of any measures adopted in response to the inquiry.

---

[76] CCPR, General Comment 33: Obligations of States parties under the Optional Protocol to the International Covenant on Civil and Political Rights, 25 June 2009, CCPR/C/GC/33, paras.13, 15.

[77] V. Shikhelman, 'Implementing Decisions of International Human Rights Institutions—Evidence from the United Nations Human Rights Committee' (2019) 30 *European Journal of International Law* 753, 761.

[78] K. Fox Principi, Implementation of Decisions under Treaty Body Complaints Procedures—Do States Comply? How Do They Do It?, UN Office of the High Commissioner for Human Rights (January 2017), p. 9.

[79] These are: CESCR (OP-ICESCR, Art. 11), CAT (UNCAT, Art. 20), CEDAW Committee (OP-CEDAW, Art. 8), CRC (OP3-CRC, Art. 13), CRPD (OPCRPD, Art. 6), and CED (ICPPED, Art. 33).

[80] ICPPED, Art. 33.   [81] UNCAT, Art. 28; OP-CEDAW, Art. 10; OP3-CRC, Art. 13.7; OPCRPD, Art. 8.

[82] OP-ICESCR, Art. 11.

[83] Under ICPPED, there is no requirement for confidentiality of the inquiry, unlike under the other treaties.

5.4 THE COMMITTEE ON THE ELIMINATION OF RACIAL DISCRIMINATION (CERD)

CERD is the body of eighteen independent experts that monitors the implementation of the 1965 ICERD. As discussed in **Section 2.2.2**, this Convention was the first core treaty adopted within the United Nations at a time when political divides between the Eastern and Western blocs were making the adoption of ICCPR and ICESCR a rather difficult process. Conversely, thanks to the impetus of States from the Global South, a binding international instrument denouncing racial discrimination materialized in just over three years (December 1962–December 1965)[84] in a unanimously adopted Convention,[85] which reached the needed level of ratification to enter into force only three years later (January 1969)[86] and counted 182 States Parties by the end of 2022.[87]

This overwhelming level of consensus discloses the particular importance that States attributed to the fight against racial discrimination within the context of the international protection of human rights.[88] It is beyond dispute that the prohibition of racial discrimination holds the status of *jus cogens* norm,[89] which means that the prohibition of racial discrimination admits no derogation of any kind and that the obligations emanating from this essential provision are of an *erga omnes* character—owed to the international community as a whole[90]—as discussed in **Section 3.1.5**. As asserted by CERD, building upon the jurisprudence of both the European and Inter-American Courts of Human Rights,[91] ICERD is a special type of treaty, even among human rights treaties, because it protects a rather fundamental norm, that of the absolute prohibition of racial discrimination.[92] With its entry into force, the Convention became the main international instrument to provide an explicit ban on racial discrimination, confirming that a world without racial discrimination was a fundamental aim of the United Nations and its Member States.[93]

---

[84] Although early drafts of the Convention can be traced back to the work carried out by the Sub-Commission on Prevention of Discrimination and Protection of Minorities (see **Section 4.2.2**). See: J. Humphrey, *Human Rights & the United Nations: a great adventure* (Transnational Publishers 1984) 102.

[85] P. Thornberry, *The International Convention on the Elimination of All Forms of Racial Discrimination: A Commentary* (OUP 2016) 1.

[86] A.A. Cançado Trindade, 'Exhaustion of Local Remedies under the United Nations International Convention on the Elimination of All Forms of Racial Discrimination' (1979) 22 *German Yearbook of International Law* 374, 374. See: UNGA, Resolution 1780 (XVII), Preparation of a draft declaration and a draft convention on the elimination of all forms of racial discrimination (7 December 1962); International Convention on the Elimination of All Forms of Racial Discrimination (adopted on 21 December 1965, entered into force 4 January 1969) 660 UNTS 195.

[87] See: https://indicators.ohchr.org/ (accessed on 7 February 2023).

[88] N. Lerner, *The UN Convention on the Elimination of All Forms of Racial Discrimination* (Brill 2014) 11; P. Thornberry, *The International Convention on the Elimination of All Forms of Racial Discrimination: A Commentary* (OUP 2016) 1.

[89] ILC, 'Draft Articles on the Responsibility of States for Wrongful Acts, with commentaries' (2001) 2(2) Yearbook of the International Law Commission 31, 85 para 5; ILC, 2019 Annual Report, A/74/10, p. 147.

[90] ICJ, *Barcelona Traction, Light and Power Company, Limited*, Judgment, I.C.J. Reports 1970, p. 3, paras. 33–34.

[91] CERD, *Palestine v. Israel*, CERD/C/100/5 (12 December 2019), paras. 3.26–3.30.

[92] CERD, *Palestine v. Israel*, CERD/C/100/5 (12 December 2019), paras. 3.36–3.37.

[93] T. Meron, 'The Meaning and Reach of the International Convention on the Elimination of All Forms of Racial Discrimination' (1985) 79 *American Journal of International Law* 283, 283.

The Convention provides a broad definition of 'racial discrimination',[94] which is to be understood as:

> [A]ny distinction, exclusion, restriction or preference based on race, colour, descent, or national or ethnic origin which has the purpose or effect of nullifying or impairing the recognition, enjoyment or exercise, on an equal footing, of human rights and fundamental freedoms in the political, economic, social, cultural or any other field of public life.[95]

Importantly, measures that entail a distinction or preference based on race but which are adopted by the State for the purpose of improving structural situations of racial inequality—usually referred to as 'affirmative action'—are not only allowed but actually required under the Convention,[96] as will be further discussed in **Section 10.1.1.1**.

Following the Convention's entry into force, CERD became the first treaty body to be established. The election of its first members took place in 1969 and the Committee's first meeting was held in January 1970 at the UN headquarters.[97] As mentioned in **Section 5.3.2**, it was this Committee that originated the treaty body's practice of adopting general recommendations, elaborating the first ones in 1972.[98] Up to the end of 2022, the Committee has issued thirty-six general recommendations, aimed at providing guidance to States Parties in the interpretation of the Convention's provisions and, therefore, in implementing to the fullest possible extent the international obligations assumed under ICERD.[99] Among its guidance, the Committee has clarified that, in principle, the belonging to a specific racial or ethnic group is a matter of individual self-identification.[100] It has also confirmed that the existence of racial discrimination requires neither the State's intention to discriminate, nor its direct involvement.[101] From 2000 onwards, the Committee has started drafting lengthier and more detailed general recommendations; a practice that has been coupled with the holding of 'thematic discussions' on issues concerning racial discrimination, in which States Parties, and inter-governmental and non-governmental organizations, are invited to take part. More recently, CERD has also begun to invite stakeholders to provide their input on general recommendations once a first draft has been adopted.[102]

---

[94] The adopted wording of the definition was discussed at length during the drafting process. See: N. Lerner, *The UN Convention on the Elimination of All Forms of Racial Discrimination* (Brill 2014) 30–37.

[95] ICERD, Art. 1.1.   [96] ICERD, Art. 1.4.

[97] T. Buergenthal, 'Implementing the Racial Convention' (1977) 12 *Texas International Law Journal* 187, 187; N. Lerner, *The UN Convention on the Elimination of All Forms of Racial Discrimination* (Brill 2014) 147.

[98] CERD, General Recommendation I concerning States parties' obligations (Art. 4 of the Convention), A/87/18 (1972); CERD, General Recommendation II: concerning States parties' obligations, A/87/18 (1972).

[99] CERD, Guidelines on the elaboration of general recommendations, CERD/C/504 (10 September 2021), para. 1.

[100] CERD, General Recommendation VIII: concerning the interpretation and application of Art. 1, paras. 1, 4 of the Convention, A/45/18 (1990).

[101] CERD, General Recommendation XIV: on Art. 1, para. 1, of the Convention 1, A/48/18 (1993); CERD, General Recommendation XIX: on Art. 3 of the Convention, A/50/18 (1995).

[102] P. Thornberry, 'The Committee on the Elimination of Racial Discrimination (CERD)' in F. Mégret and P. Alston (eds.), *The United Nations and Human Rights: A Critical Appraisal* (2nd edn., OUP 2020) 209–338, 318. See: CERD, Guidelines on the elaboration of general recommendations, CERD/C/504 (10 September 2021), para. 13.

As highlighted in **Section 5.3.3.1**, CERD has also been the pioneering Committee in dealing with inter-State complaints, having received three up to the end of 2022.[103] This is perhaps unsurprising, as ICERD is the only core treaty to provide a compulsory mechanism for inter-State communications since the same States that supported the inclusion of this mechanism in this Convention opposed it when it concerned other treaties.[104] Under ICERD, if a State considers that another Party is not giving effect to the obligations assumed under the treaty, it can bring the matter to the attention of CERD. Negotiations are the means for resolving the dispute in the first instance, but if these were to fail—and after confirming that domestic resources have been exhausted—the Committee can appoint an *ad hoc* conciliation commission, which would produce recommendations for reaching an amicable solution.[105]

Additionally, ICERD is one of the five core treaties to provide for access to the ICJ in case of disputes between States Parties with respect to its interpretation or application.[106] Whether prior negotiations or the use of the Convention's conciliation procedure are prerequisites for submitting a case to the ICJ has been examined by the Court itself. Unfortunately, a restrictive interpretation of ICERD led the Court (by a 10 to 6 majority) to decide that either negotiations or conciliation are required for the admissibility of a case.[107] Conversely, an 84-page-long dissent of Judge Cançado Trindade proposed that greater emphasis on the realization of the object and purpose of the Convention, so as to secure the protection of human beings, leads to the understanding that resort to the ICJ should not be subjected to exhausting the usual procedure for inter-State complaints before the Committee.[108]

While inter-State complaints were made a compulsory mechanism under ICERD, the Committee's faculty to receive individual communications is subject to an express declaration from States Parties recognizing the competence of CERD.[109] Up to the end

---

[103] CERD, Decision of the *ad hoc* Conciliation Commission on the request for suspension submitted by Qatar concerning the interstate communication *Qatar v. the Kingdom of Saudi Arabia* (15 March 2021); CERD, Decision of the *ad hoc* Conciliation Commission on the request for suspension submitted by Qatar concerning the interstate communication *Qatar v. the United Arab Emirates* (15 March 2021); CERD, Decision on the admissibility of the inter-State communication submitted by the State of Palestine against Israel, CERD/C/103/R.6 (20 May 2021).

[104] D. Keane, 'Mapping the International Convention on the Elimination of All Forms of Racial Discrimination as a Living Instrument' (2020) 20 *Human Rights Law Review* 236, 261.

[105] ICERD, Arts. 11–13. For a discussion of the different stages of the procedure, see: E. Schwelb, 'The International Convention on the Elimination of All Forms of Racial Discrimination' (1966) 15 *International and Comparative Law Quarterly* 996, 1037–1041.

[106] ICERD, Art. 22.

[107] ICJ, *Application of the International Convention on the Elimination of All Forms of Racial Discrimination (Georgia v. Russian Federation)*, Preliminary Objections, Judgment, I.C.J. Reports 2011, p. 70. Later confirmed in ICJ, *Application of the International Convention for the Suppression of the Financing of Terrorism and of the International Convention on the Elimination of All Forms of Racial Discrimination (Ukraine v. Russian Federation)*, Preliminary Objections, Judgment, I.C.J. Reports 2019, p. 558, para. 113.

[108] ICJ, *Application of the International Convention on the Elimination of All Forms of Racial Discrimination (Georgia v. Russian Federation)*, Preliminary Objections, Judgment, I.C.J. Reports 2011, p. 70, dissenting opinion of Judge Cançado Trindade.

[109] ICERD, Art. 14.

of 2022, only 59 of the 182 States Parties have accepted the Committee's jurisdiction.[110] In fact, CERD has not been among the most active treaty bodies with regard to individual communications, due to the relative low number of complaints received.[111] According to its 2022 Report, between 1984 and 2022, the Committee had only registered eighty-one complaints, adopting opinions as to the merits in forty of them.[112]

Although not explicitly provided for by ICERD, since 1993, CERD has adopted the proactive approach to intervene to prevent serious violations of the Convention.[113] Two specific types of preventive measures were foreseen by the Committee to address serious violations in an urgent manner: 'early warning measures', to intervene when structural problems could escalate into conflicts; and 'urgent procedures', to respond to issues that require immediate attention to prevent or reduce the scale (or the number) of serious violations of ICERD.[114] The Committee has developed a varied range of criteria for determining the adoption of measures under these mechanisms. Among many scenarios, the following can trigger CERD's early warning and urgent action procedures: the existence of a significant and persistent pattern of racial discrimination, evidenced by social and economic indicators; the presence of escalating racist hatred and violence, or of racist propaganda; the adoption of discriminatory legislation; a significant flow of refugees or internally displaced persons, especially when involving members of specific racial or ethnic groups; the encroachment on the traditional lands of indigenous peoples or their forced removal from these lands; and the undertaking of polluting or hazardous activities that reflect a pattern of discrimination affecting specific groups.[115] There is a range of measures that CERD can adopt under its early warning and urgent action procedures, which include: requesting a State to urgently submit information on a given situation; expressing concern about the situation and issuing recommendations to address it; and offering to undertake a visit to the concerned State to provide technical assistance with the setting of infrastructure or the implementation of international standards.[116] Over the years, the Committee has made use of these procedures on numerous occasions, having adopted measures on a large number of situations concerning multiple States Parties from all regions of the world.[117]

---

[110] See: https://indicators.ohchr.org/ (accessed on 27 March 2022).

[111] P. Thornberry, 'The Committee on the Elimination of Racial Discrimination (CERD)' in F. Mégret and P. Alston (eds.), *The United Nations and Human Rights: A Critical Appraisal* (2nd edn., OUP 2020) 209–338, 336.

[112] CERD Report, 104th session (9–25 August 2021), 105th session (15 November–3 December 2021), 106th session (11–29 April 2022), A/77/18, para. 61.

[113] CERD Report, A/48/18 (15 September 1993), Annex III, para. 7.

[114] CERD Report, A/48/18 (15 September 1993), Annex III, paras. 7–8.

[115] CERD Report, A/62/18, 70th session (19 February–9 March 2007) and 71st session (30 July–17 August 2007), Annex III, para. 12.

[116] CERD Report, A/62/18, 70th session (19 February–9 March 2007) and 71st session (30 July–17 August 2007), Annex III, para. 14.

[117] The information on these procedures is available on CERD's website: https://www.ohchr.org/en/treaty-bodies/cerd/decisions-statements-and-letters (accessed on 21 March 2022).

CERD, *The Jewish community of Oslo; the Jewish community of Trondheim; Rolf Kirchner; Julius Paltiel; the Norwegian Antiracist Centre; and Nadeem Butt v. Norway*, Communication No. 30/2003 (15 August 2005).

The case concerned the organisation of a march in commemoration of a Nazi leader (Rudolf Hess) by a neo-Nazi group in Norway. The event took place in Askim in August 2000; it lasted for roughly five minutes, and included a speech by one of the organizers, Terje Sjolie, in which he praised Hess for 'his brave attempt to save Germany and Europe from Bolshevism and Jewry during the Second World War' (para. 2.1). He stated: 'Every day immigrants rob, rape and kill Norwegians, every day our people and country are being plundered and destroyed by the Jews, who suck our country empty of wealth and replace it with immoral and un-Norwegian thoughts' (para. 2.1), and he encouraged the thirty-something people listening to follow in Hitler's footsteps to fight for a State built upon National Socialism.

Following the march, Sjolie was prosecuted under the criminal prohibition of 'threatening, insulting, or subjecting to hatred, persecution or contempt, any person or group of persons because of their creed, race, colour or national or ethnic origin'. He was acquitted in first instance, but convicted on appeal. Ultimately, in 2002, the Supreme Court overturned the conviction, considering it to encroach on Sjolie's freedom of expression, characterizing the speech as nothing more than Nazi rhetoric.

The authors—three individuals and three organizations—brought a complaint before CERD, contending that the Supreme Court's decision amounted to a violation of Norway's obligations under ICERD, as they had not been afforded protection against the dissemination of discriminatory and hateful ideas and the incitement to racist acts. The authors affirmed their status as 'victims', given that the State proved unable to protect them from the dissemination of anti-Semitic and racist propaganda and that the Supreme Court's decision placed them at risk of being exposed to the effects of the dissemination of these ideas.

The Committee accepted the authors' status as (potential) victims, including that of the three organizations, given the nature of their activities and the people they represented (paras. 7.3–7.4). It went on to examine whether the Supreme Court's ruling had amounted to a breach of Article 4 of ICERD, which imposes upon States Parties obligations towards the condemnation of all propaganda and all organizations based on ideas of racial superiority or which attempt to justify or promote racial hatred and discrimination in any form, including the criminalization of such propaganda and organizations.

The CERD considered that the speech in question contained ideas of racial superiority or hatred and that the reference to Hitler should have been interpreted as an incitement to, at least, racial discrimination, if not to violence (para. 10.4). It affirmed that, under ICERD, freedom of expression has been afforded a lower level of protection when it contains racist or hate speech, which leads to the compatibility of the prohibition of ideas based upon racial superiority or hatred with the protection of this right. Consequently, the CERD decided that, due to the exceptionally offensive character of Mr Sjolie's speech, his acquittal by the Supreme Court gave rise to a violation of ICERD (para. 10.5). The Committee then recommended the State to take measures to ensure that statements such as those made by Mr Sjolie were not protected under domestic law and requested the State to inform, within six months, about the measures taken in light of the Committee's opinion (paras. 10.12–10.13).

5.5 THE HUMAN RIGHTS COMMITTEE (CCPR)

The history of the ICCPR and its monitoring treaty body, the Human Rights Committee (CCPR), was discussed in **Section 2.2.2**. To recap, the drafting of a binding treaty of human rights that was to complement the 1948 Universal Declaration on Human Rights started in 1947 within the UN Commission on Human Rights.[118] However, this projected treaty became two separate ones, as decided by the UN General Assembly in 1951, in a complex political context marked by divergent positions, especially between the Eastern and Western blocs, that supported the dated conception of categories of rights. From the twin Covenants adopted by the General Assembly in 1966, the ICCPR was favoured, with States' obligations phrased in stronger terms with regard to immediateness and justiciability, and with the creation of a specific monitoring body to supervise compliance with the treaty. In addition, an Optional Protocol to ICCPR (ICCPR-OP1) was adopted together with the two Covenants, endowing the Committee with the ability to receive individual communications against States Parties concerning violations of the treaty. Although adopted in December 1966, it took almost a decade for ICCPR to enter into force, in March 1976, after receiving its thirty-fifth ratification.

At the end of 2022, the ICCPR counted 173 States Parties, and as discussed in **Section 3.1.1.3**, is one of the four core treaties that do not include a provision allowing for denunciation—the others are the ICESCR, CEDAW, and ICPPED. Following the second attempt of a State Party at withdrawing from the treaty,[119] that of the Democratic People's Republic of Korea in 1997,[120] the Human Rights Committee affirmed that the absence of a denunciation clause should be interpreted as a prohibition for States Parties to withdraw from the treaty,[121] which means that Parties to the Covenant can only increase with time. As to the mentioned ICCPR-OP1, it entered into force the same date as ICCPR after receiving its tenth ratification and has reached 117 States Parties by the end of 2022. A second Protocol to ICCPR concerning the abolition of the death penalty (further discussed in **Section 9.1.3**) was adopted in December 1989 and, nowadays, counts ninety States Parties.

The Human Rights Committee was established in 1977, following the election of its first members in September 1976, making it the second treaty body to be created, after CERD.[122] The Committee is composed of eighteen experts, nationals of the States Parties to ICCPR, who should be 'persons of high moral character and recognized

---

[118] E. Schwelb, 'The International Measures of Implementation of the International Covenant on Civil and Political Rights and of the Optional Protocol' (1977) 12 *Texas International Law Journal* 141, 143; M.J. Bossuyt, *Guide to the 'Travaux Préparatoires' of the International Covenant on Civil and Political Rights* (Nijhoff 1987) xix.

[119] The first one had been the attempt made by the Federal Republic of Yugoslavia in 1995. See: Y. Tyagi, 'The Denunciation of Human Rights Treaties' (2008) 79 *British Yearbook of International Law* 86, 163–167.

[120] E. Evatt, 'Democratic People's Republic of Korea and the ICCPR: Denunciation as an Exercise of the Right of Self-Defence?' (1999) 5 *Australian Journal of Human Rights* 215.

[121] CCPR, General Comment No. 26: Continuity of obligations to the International Covenant on Civil and Political Rights, CCPR/C/21/Rev. 1/Add.8/Rev. (8 December 1997), para. 1.

[122] M. Nowak, *UN Covenant on Civil and Political Rights: CCPR Commentary* (2nd edn., Engel 2005) xxiv.

competence in the field of human rights, consideration being given to the usefulness of the participation of some persons having legal experience'.[123] There is an expectation that besides their expertise, the candidates to sit in the Committee will have a devotion to the cause of protecting human rights.[124] Such an expectation is well-founded, as both the Committee and ICCPR occupy a rather significant position in the realm of the international protection of human rights: the Human Rights Committee has become one of the most innovative and prolific supervisory bodies, while the Covenant has been proclaimed one of the most important human rights treaties in the world.[125] Notwithstanding the significance of the Committee, its designation as the 'Human Rights Committee' is misleading,[126] setting it apart from that of all other treaty bodies, which receive their names from the designation of their respectively monitored treaty.[127] Certainly, it would have been preferable to name it the 'Committee on Civil and Political Rights'; thus acknowledging the existence of another human rights treaty body (CERD), the potential creation of more in the future, and the equal standing of other human rights, such as those enshrined in ICESCR.

The main monitoring functions granted to the Committee by ICCPR are the examination of State periodic reports and inter-State communications, while ICCPR-OP1 conferred upon the Committee the ability to receive individual communications. The Committee's power to issue general comments was inspired by the practice initiated by CERD and found grounds in a treaty provision that uses such an expression with regards to the study of State reports.[128] Both communication mechanisms are optional for States; that of inter-State complaints depends on States declaring their acceptance of the Committee's competence, while the system of individual petitions only applies with respect to States Parties to ICCPR-OP1.

Articles 41 and 42 of ICCPR detail the procedure for inter-State complaints,[129] which encompasses the stages of bilateral exchanges (including the use of domestic remedies), the Committee's good offices, and the potential appointment of an *ad hoc* Conciliation Commission. According to the Committee's 2021 Report,

---

[123] ICCPR, Art. 28.2.

[124] Y. Tyagi, *The UN Human Rights Committee: Practice and Procedure* (CUP 2011) 75.

[125] T. Buergenthal, 'The U.N. Human Rights Committee' (2001) 5 *Max Planck Yearbook of United Nations Law* 341, 341–342; S. Joseph and M. Castan, *The International Covenant on Civil and Political Rights: Cases, Materials, and Commentary* (3rd edn., OUP 2013) 3–4; L. Hennebel, 'The Human Rights Committee' in F. Mégret and P. Alston (eds.), *The United Nations and Human Rights: A Critical Appraisal* (2nd edn., OUP 2020) 339–391, 342.

[126] M Bossuyt, Guide to the 'Travaux Préparatoires' of the International Covenant on Civil and Political Rights (Nijhoff 1986) 502.

[127] L. Hennebel, 'The Human Rights Committee' in F. Mégret and P. Alston (eds.), *The United Nations and Human Rights: A Critical Appraisal* (2nd edn., OUP 2020) 339–391, 340.

[128] ICCPR, Art. 40.4.

[129] Both Schwelb and Nowak provide extensive discussions of the drafting history of these provisions and the political compromises they entailed. See: E. Schwelb, 'The International Measures of Implementation of the International Covenant on Civil and Political Rights and of the Optional Protocol' (1977) 12 *Texas International Law Journal* 141, 160–177; M. Nowak, *UN Covenant on Civil and Political Rights: CCPR Commentary* (2nd edn., Engel 2005) 753–786.

fifty States Parties have accepted CCPR's jurisdiction to intervene in inter-State communications;[130] nonetheless, a single communication is yet to reach the Committee. Conversely, CCPR has been the most prolific of the treaty bodies in its engagement with individual communications. Since receiving its first petition in 1977, it has developed a rich jurisprudence on the interpretation of the different rights protected under ICCPR.[131] According to its 2021 Report, the Committee has received 3,727 communications up to March 2021, having adopted views on the merits of 1,737 of them, from which 1,289 disclosed the existence of human rights violations.[132]

The Committee has also been very productive in the elaboration of general comments, having adopted a total of thirty-seven between July 1981 and the end of 2022. These comments have provided a progressive codification of its interpretation of particular treaty provisions based on past communications and concluding observations.[133] The topics of general comments have been decided by the Committee and aimed at assisting States Parties in fulfilling their international obligations. As per its current Rules of Procedure, once a preliminary draft of a comment is produced, it is circulated for observations among States Parties and other relevant stakeholders, such as UN bodies, NGOs, and national human rights institutions, before its formal adoption.[134] The comments have addressed a range of issues, which can be divided between those engaging with general obligations of States and those focusing on specific rights. As to the former, the Committee has produced, among others, comments on State-reporting obligations;[135] on the domestic implementation of the Covenant;[136] on reservations to the treaty;[137] and on the nature of the obligations assumed under ICCPR.[138] Concerning rights, CCPR has issued comments, among

---

[130] CCPR Report, 129th session (29 June–24 July 2020), 130th session (12 October–6 November 2020), 131st session (1–26 March 2021), A/76/44 (2021), para. 2.

[131] S. Joseph and M. Castan, *The International Covenant on Civil and Political Rights: Cases, Materials, and Commentary* (3rd edn., OUP 2013) 4, 27, 54.

[132] CCPR Report, 129th session (29 June–24 July 2020), 130th session (12 October–6 November 2020), 131st session (1–26 March 2021), A/76/44 (2021), para. 21.

[133] G.L. Neuman, 'Giving Meaning and Effect to Human Rights: The Contributions of Human Rights Committee Members' in D. Moeckli and H. Keller (eds.), *The Human Rights Covenants: Their Past, Present, and Future* (OUP 2018) 31–47, 35.

[134] CCPR, Rules of Procedure, CCPR/C/3/Rev.12 (4 January 2021), r. 76.

[135] CCPR, General Comment No. 1: Reporting obligation (1981); CCPR, General Comment No. 2: Reporting guidelines (1981); CCPR, General Comment No. 30: Reporting Obligations of States parties under Art. 40 of the Covenant, CCPR/C/21/Rev.2/Add. 12 (16 July 2002).

[136] CCPR, General Comment No. 3: Art. 2 (Implementation at the national level) (1981). See also: CCPR, General Comment No. 31: The Nature of the General Legal Obligation Imposed on States Parties to the Covenant, CCPR/C/21/Rev.1/Add. 13 (29 March 2004).

[137] CCPR, General comment No. 24: Issues relating to reservations made upon ratification or accession to the Covenant or the Optional Protocols thereto, or in relation to declarations under Art. 41 of the Covenant, CCPR/C/21/Rev.1/Add. 6 (11 November 1994).

[138] CCPR, General Comment No. 31: The Nature of the General Legal Obligation Imposed on States Parties to the Covenant, CCPR/C/21/Rev.1/Add. 13 (29 March 2004).

others, on gender equality and the prohibition of discrimination;[139] the right to life;[140] personal integrity;[141] freedom of opinion and expression;[142] and freedom of thought, conscience, and religion.[143] While the Committee's initial comments were rather brief, since the late—1980s they have become much more sophisticated, detailed, and extensive.[144] Furthermore, to ensure that the interpretation of the Covenant remains relevant and adapts to contemporary challenges, the Committee has updated older comments, through the elaboration of newer ones on the same topics; thus, earlier comments on personal integrity, gender equality, and the right to life, produced in the 1980s, have all been updated by newer comments.[145]

CCPR, *Damian Thomas v. Jamaica*, Communication No. 800/1998, UN Doc. CCPR/C/65/D/800/1998 (26 May 1999).

As aforementioned, ICCPR is not susceptible of denunciation. However, that is not the case of ICCPR-OP1, which established the system of individual complaints. Article 12 of ICCPR-OP1 stipulates that denunciations take effect three months after their notification is received, but do not affect the ability of the Committee to examine petitions submitted before the denunciation took effect (Articles 12.1 and 12.2).

The temporal validity of a denunciation of ICCPR-OP1 was put to the test in this case, which concerned the alleged violations of human rights suffered by a minor, imprisoned within the Jamaican penal system. In his original petition, submitted in August 1997, the author complained against his imprisonment with adult inmates. Additionally, in a letter dated 11 May 1998, the author claimed that during his detention he had been the victim of

---

[139] CCPR, General Comment No. 4: Equal right of men and women to the enjoyment of all civil and political rights (1981); CCPR, General Comment No. 18: Non-discrimination (1989); CCPR, General Comment No. 28: The equality of rights between men and women (29 March 2000).

[140] CCPR, General Comment No. 6: Right to life (1982); CCPR, General Comment No. 14: Right to life; CCPR, General Comment No. 36: Right to life, CCPR/C/GC/36 (3 September 2019).

[141] CCPR, General Comment No. 7: Prohibition of torture or cruel, inhuman or degrading treatment or punishment (30 May 1982); CCPR, General Comment No. 20: Prohibition of torture, or other cruel, inhuman or degrading treatment or punishment (1992).

[142] CCPR, General Comment No. 10: Freedom of opinion (1983); CCPR, General Comment 11: Art. 20 (1983); CCPR, General Comment No. 34: Freedoms of opinion and expression, CCPR/C/GC/34 (12 September 2011).

[143] CCPR, General Comment No. 22: Freedom of thought, conscience or religion, CCPR/C/21/Rev. 1/Add. 4 (20 July 1993).

[144] E. Klein and D. Kretzmer, 'The UN Human Rights Committee: The General Comments—The Evolution of an Autonomous Monitoring Instrument' (2015) 58 *German Yearbook of International Law* 189, 192.

[145] CCPR, General Comment No. 7: Prohibition of torture or cruel, inhuman or degrading treatment or punishment (30 May 1982); CCPR, General Comment No. 20: Prohibition of torture, or other cruel, inhuman or degrading treatment or punishment (1992); CCPR, General Comment No. 4: Equal right of men and women to the enjoyment of all civil and political rights (1981); CCPR, General Comment No. 28: The equality of rights between men and women (29 March 2000); CCPR, General Comment No. 6: Right to life (1982); CCPR, General Comment No. 14: Right to life; CCPR, General comment No. 36: Right to life, CCPR/C/GC/36 (3 September 2019).

several physical attacks by prison wardens, which had taken place between November 1996 and December 1997.

The admissibility of the case was partially challenged by Jamaica, as it had denounced ICCPR-OP1, with its denunciation coming into force on 23 January 1998. The Committee accepted the objection posed by the State and declared the complaints regarding ill-treatment inadmissible, as they were communicated after 23 January 1998. Conversely, the complaints concerning the author's imprisonment in adult centres were declared admissible, which led CCPR to find the violation of Articles 10 and 24, which establish the State's obligation to provide segregated penal facilities for minors and adults, as well as the duty to adopt measures of protection towards minors (para. 7). Consequently, the Committee recommended the State to place the author in a juvenile institution, to provide compensation, and to ensure that similar violations did not take place again (para. 8).

An important dissenting opinion was appended to the Committee's decision by the Argentine member (Mr Solari Yrigoyen). He affirmed that the communication should had been declared admissible as a whole, given that the reported incidents of ill-treatment preceded the denunciation of the Protocol taking effect, even if communicated afterwards. He argued that the relevant provision of ICCPR-OP1 establishes that it continues to apply to any communications received before the denunciation becomes effective and, in this case, the original communication was submitted before the denunciation took effect. Therefore, he claimed that the Committee should have also found the violation of Article 7 of ICCPR, which prohibits torture and cruel, inhuman, and degrading treatment.

5.6 THE COMMITTEE ON ECONOMIC, SOCIAL AND CULTURAL RIGHTS (CESCR)

As discussed in **Section 2.2.2**, both ICCPR and ICESCR were adopted by the General Assembly on 16 December 1966, but it took almost a decade for them to reach the needed thirty-five ratifications to enter into force. ICESCR was the first to obtain them, entering into force in January 1976 and, even if ratifications were not easy to come by in the earlier days, by the end of 2022 ICESCR counts 171 States Parties.[146] However, while ICCPR established a specific monitoring body to supervise its compliance, ICESCR was silent about the creation of a similar organ and the main supervisory functions were left to the UN Economic and Social Council (ECOSOC).[147] In 1978, ECOSOC decided to establish a Sessional Working Group on the Implementation of ICESCR, to assist in the consideration of the reports submitted by States Parties,[148] but this body was composed of representatives from States. Widespread criticism led to this monitoring

---

[146] See: https://indicators.ohchr.org/ (accessed on 27 March 2022).   [147] ICESCR, Arts. 16–22.
[148] ECOSOC, Decision 1978/10, Composition of the Sessional Working Group on the Implementation of the International Covenant on Economic, Social and Cultural Rights, 3 May 1978.

system being changed into a Sessional Working Group of Governmental Experts.[149] It was only in 1986 that ECOSOC decided on the creation of an independent committee to operate similarly to the existing CERD and CCPR: the Committee on Economic, Social and Cultural Rights (CESCR).[150]

The CESCR is composed of eighteen independent experts, but unlike the members of other committees, they are elected by ECOSOC and not by a Conference of States Parties. Although only States Parties to ICESCR can nominate experts, all fifty-four members of ECOSOC, whether Parties or not, have a vote in the election.[151] Originally, ICESCR only contemplated the mechanism of State-reporting as its mode of supervision. Nevertheless, in February 1988, following a suggestion from ECOSOC,[152] the new Committee decided to emulate the practice of CERD and CCPR with respect to the elaboration of general comments.[153]

General comments became the main means for CESCR to define the normative content of ICESCR.[154] The Committee became very prolific in the production of these comments, having elaborated twenty-six by the end of 2022. Many of the Committee's general comments have been extremely influential, such as the ones on State-reporting and on the nature of States Parties' obligations,[155] two separate comments on the right to adequate housing,[156] and general comments on the enjoyment of economic, social, and cultural rights by members of vulnerable groups, including elderly people and persons with disabilities.[157] From 1999 onwards, CESCR has implemented a specific detailed structure for its comments, presenting longer reflections in each of them.[158] Since then, it has adopted important comments on different rights, including the rights to food and

---

[149] P. Alston, 'The Committee on Economic, Social and Cultural Rights' in F. Mégret and P. Alston (eds.), *The United Nations and Human Rights: A Critical Appraisal* (2nd edn., OUP 2020) 439–475, 440–441.

[150] ECOSOC, Resolution 1985/17, Review of the composition, organization and administrative arrangements of the Sessional Working Group of Governmental Experts on the Implementation of the International Covenant on Economic, Social and Cultural Rights.

[151] ECOSOC, Review of the composition, organization and administrative arrangements of the Sessional Working Group of Governmental Experts on the Implementation of the International Covenant on Economic, Social and Cultural Rights, Resolution 1985/17 (28 May 1985), para. (c).

[152] ECOSOC, 'International Covenant on Economic, Social and Cultural Rights', Resolution 1987/5 (26 May 1987), para. 9.

[153] P. Alston, 'Second Session of the UN Committee on Economic, Social and Cultural Rights' (1988) 82 *American Journal of International Law* 603, 606.

[154] D. Moeckli, 'Interpretation of the ICESCR: Between Morality and State Consent' in D. Moeckli and H. Keller (eds.), The Human Rights Covenants: Their Past, Present, and Future (OUP 2018) 48–74, 50.

[155] CESCR, General Comment No. 1: Reporting by States parties, E/1989/22 (1989); CESCR, General Comment 3: The nature of States parties' obligations (Art. 2, para. 1, of the Covenant), E/1991/23 (1990).

[156] CESCR, General Comment No. 4: The right to adequate housing (Art. 11 (1) of the Covenant), E/1992/23 (1991); CESCR, General Comment No. 7: The right to adequate housing (Art. 11 (1) of the Covenant): Forced evictions, E/1998/22 (1997).

[157] CESCR, General Comment No. 5: Persons with disabilities, E/1995/22 (1994); CESCR, General Comment No. 6: The economic, social and cultural rights of older persons, E/1996/22 (1995).

[158] P. Alston, 'The Committee on Economic, Social and Cultural Rights' in F. Mégret and P. Alston (eds.), The United Nations and Human Rights: A Critical Appraisal (2nd edn., OUP 2020) 439–475, 453–454. See: CESCR, Report on the 20th and 21st Sessions (26 April–14 May 1999, 15 November–3 December 1999), E/C.12/1999/11 (2000), Annex IX.

to water,[159] the rights to health and to sexual and reproductive health,[160] and the rights to work and to social security.[161] In addition to the adoption of general comments, the Committee has developed the practice of issuing 'statements'; these are used to express shorter opinions, which do not require attachment to the more formal procedure of general comments.[162] These statements have covered a wide variety of topical issues, such as poverty, the world food crisis, public debt and austerity measures, and access to vaccination against Covid-19.[163]

No mechanism for communications, either individual or inter-State, was provided for under ICESCR. In 1990, the Committee started the discussion of the drafting of an optional protocol, similar to ICCPR-OP1, to allow for the examination of individual communications.[164] During the following years, the Committee's Chairperson, Philip Alston, prepared detailed reports on the convenience of adopting such a protocol, and even prepared a draft text of a protocol.[165] In 1996, CESCR submitted a revised draft protocol for consideration of the UN Commission on Human Rights, which eventually appointed an independent expert to examine the idea of a draft protocol.[166] The appointed expert, Hatem Kotrane, was in favour of the adoption of a protocol,

---

[159] CESCR, General Comment No. 12: The right to adequate food (Art. 11), E/C.12/1999/5 (12 May 1999); CESCR, General Comment No. 15: The right to water (Arts. 11 and 12), E/C.12/2002/11 (20 January 2003).

[160] CESCR, General Comment No. 14: The right to the highest attainable standard of health (Art. 12), E/C.12/2000/4 (11 August 2000); CESCR, General Comment No. 22: on the right to sexual and reproductive health (Art. 12), E/C.12/GC/22 (2 May 2016).

[161] CESCR, General Comment No. 18: The right to work (Art. 6), E/C.12/GC/18 (24 November 2005); CESCR, General Comment No. 19: The right to social security (Art. 9), E/C.12/GC/19 (23 November 2007); CESCR, General Comment No. 23 (2016) on the right to just and favourable conditions of work (Art. 7 of the International Covenant on Economic, Social and Cultural Rights), E/C.12/GC/23 (27 April 2016).

[162] P. Alston, 'The Committee on Economic, Social and Cultural Rights' in F. Mégret and P. Alston (eds.), *The United Nations and Human Rights: A Critical Appraisal* (2nd edn., OUP 2020) 439–475, 459–460.

[163] CESCR, 'Substantive Issues Arising in the Implementation of the International Covenant on Economic, Social and Cultural Rights: Poverty and the International Covenant on Economic, Social and Cultural Rights', E/C.12/2001/10 (4 May 2001); CESCR, 'The World Food Crisis', E/C.12/2008/1 (20 May 2008); CESCR, 'Public debt, austerity measures and the International Covenant on Economic, Social and Cultural Rights', E/C.12/2016/1 (22 July 2016); CESCR, 'Statement on universal and equitable access to vaccines for the coronavirus disease (COVID-19)', E/C.12/2020/2 (15 December 2020); CESCR, 'Statement on universal affordable vaccination against coronavirus disease (COVID-19), international cooperation and intellectual property', E/C.12/2021/1 (23 April 2021).

[164] CESCR, Report on the 5th session (26 November–14 December 1990), E/1991/23, E/C.12/1990/8, para. 285.

[165] T.J. Melish, 'Introductory Note to the Optional Protocol to the International Covenant on Economic, Social and Cultural Rights' (2009) 48 *International Legal Materials* 256, 257; P. Alston, 'The Committee on Economic, Social and Cultural Rights' in F. Mégret and P. Alston (eds.), *The United Nations and Human Rights: A Critical Appraisal* (2nd edn., OUP 2020) 439–475, 456–457.

[166] C. de Albuquerque, 'Chronicle of an Announced Birth: The Coming into Life of the Optional Protocol to the International Covenant on Economic, Social and Cultural Rights—The Missing Piece of the International Bill of Human Rights' (2010) 32 *Human Rights Quarterly* 144, 150–154; P. Alston, 'The Committee on Economic, Social and Cultural Rights' in F. Mégret and P. Alston (eds.), *The United Nations and Human Rights: A Critical Appraisal* (2nd edn., OUP 2020) 439–475, 457.

supporting the creation of a working group for this purpose.[167] However, the politics surrounding the protocol led to important compromises, with the establishment of the working group delayed until 2003 and its mandate limited to considering the options regarding the elaboration of a protocol.[168] The working group met throughout the years 2003, 2004, and 2005, without reaching consensus as to the elaboration of a protocol, until the creation of the Human Rights Council (HRC) in 2006 brought new impetus to this initiative.[169] The Council changed the working group's mandate, instructing it to actually elaborate an optional protocol to ICESCR. It further requested the Group's Chairperson, Catarina de Albuquerque, to prepare a draft protocol based on past discussions to act as the basis for negotiating the text of the treaty.[170] In April 2008, the final draft was submitted for consideration of the HRC,[171] which approved it in June 2008,[172] leading to its adoption by the General Assembly on 10 December 2008. Nevertheless, it took until 2013 for OP-ICESCR to enter into force, and it only counts twenty-six States Parties at the end of 2022.[173]

OP-ICESCR came to establish a system of both individual and inter-State communications under CESCR, thus rectifying the thirty-year-old asymmetries in the protection of human rights provided under the 1966 Covenants.[174] OP-ICESCR also contemplates the Committee's ability to undertake inquiries, in case of grave or systematic violations of ICESCR by a State Party. Both the system of inter-State complaints and that of inquiries require an additional declaration of acceptance by States Parties,[175] even though this requirement with regards to inquiries appears at

---

[167] Report of the independent expert on the question of a draft optional protocol to the International Covenant on Economic, Social and Cultural Rights, E/CN.4/2002/57 (12 February 2002), para. 56; Report by Mr Hatem Kotrane, independent expert on the question of a draft optional protocol to the International Covenant on Economic, Social and Cultural Rights, E/CN.4/2003/53 (13 January 2003), paras. 75–76.

[168] C. de Albuquerque, 'Chronicle of an Announced Birth: The Coming into Life of the Optional Protocol to the International Covenant on Economic, Social and Cultural Rights—The Missing Piece of the International Bill of Human Rights' (2010) 32 *Human Rights Quarterly* 144, 155–156; A. Vandenbogaerde and W. Vandenhole, 'The Optional Protocol to the International Covenant on Economic, Social and Cultural Rights: An Ex Ante Assessment of Its Effectiveness in Light of the Drafting Process' (2010) 10 *Human Rights Law Review* 207, 237.

[169] C. de Albuquerque, 'Chronicle of an Announced Birth: The Coming into Life of the Optional Protocol to the International Covenant on Economic, Social and Cultural Rights—The Missing Piece of the International Bill of Human Rights' (2010) 32 *Human Rights Quarterly* 144, 165.

[170] HRC, 'Open-ended Working Group on an optional protocol to the International Covenant on Economic, Social and Cultural Rights', Resolution 1/3 (29 June 2006), para. 2.

[171] T.J. Melish, 'Introductory Note to the Optional Protocol to the International Covenant on Economic, Social and Cultural Rights' (2009) 48 *International Legal Materials* 256, 258.

[172] C. de Albuquerque, 'Chronicle of an Announced Birth: The Coming into Life of the Optional Protocol to the International Covenant on Economic, Social and Cultural Rights—The Missing Piece of the International Bill of Human Rights' (2010) 32 *Human Rights Quarterly* 144, 176. See: HRC, 'Optional Protocol to the International Covenant on Economic, Social and Cultural Rights', Resolution 8/2 (18 June 2008).

[173] See: https://indicators.ohchr.org/ (accessed on 7 February 2023).

[174] L. Chenwi, 'Correcting the Historical Asymmetry between Rights: The Optional Protocol to the International Covenant on Economic, Social and Cultural Rights' (2009) 9 *African Human Rights Law Journal* 23, 51; T.J. Melish, 'Introductory Note to the Optional Protocol to the International Covenant on Economic, Social and Cultural Rights' (2009) 48 *International Legal Materials* 256, 256.

[175] OP-ICESCR, Arts. 10, 11.

odds with how the mechanism has been conceived under other treaties.[176] So far, these optional procedures have only been accepted by a handful of States.[177]

Concerning the system of individual complaints, the political resistance to OP-ICESCR, with concerns as to the potential thousands of complaints that could be brought to the Committee, led to the inclusion of an admissibility requirement absent for communications before other treaty bodies. The delegations of Canada, New Zealand, and the UK put forward a criterion that emulates admissibility under the European Convention on Human Rights (see **Section 7.3.7.4**),[178] allowing the Committee to reject a communication when it considers that it does not reveal a clear disadvantage suffered by the author unless the communication raises a 'serious issue of general importance'.[179] However, due to the extremely low number of Parties to OP-ICESCR, the number of individual communications remains relatively low. The Committee's 2021 Annual Report reveals the registration of only 230 communications, with CESCR adopting a total of eleven decisions on the merits.[180]

CESCR, *S.C. and G.P. v. Italy*, Communication No. 22/2017 (7 March 2019).

The vast majority of the complaints decided by CESCR up to date were brought against Spain and concerned the right to adequate housing, such as the case discussed in **Section 9.1.5**. However, other topics are beginning to come under the gaze of CESCR, raising innovative questions for it to address. Such is the case of *S.C. and G.P. v. Italy*, which concerned the regulation of *in vitro* fertilization under Italian law.

The authors, an Italian couple, had sought assistance to conceive a child from a private clinic specialized in assisted reproductive technology. S.C. underwent two in vitro fertilization cycles. In the first one, the authors requested that at least six embryos be produced; that those embryos be subject to pre-implantation genetic diagnosis to identify possible 'genetic disorders'—given that S.C. suffered from a hereditary disorder (multiple osteochondrimas)— and that the embryos with such disorders not be transferred into S.C.'s uterus. The clinic replied that such requests were not authorized under the law, which established that only

---

[176] D.J. Sullivan, 'The Inquiry Procedure' in M. Langford (ed.), *The Optional Protocol to the International Covenant on Economic, Social and Cultural Rights: A Commentary* (PULP 2016) 77–146, 89.

[177] Up to the end of 2022, the following five States Parties have declared their acceptance of both optional mechanisms: Belgium, El Salvador, Finland, San Marino, and Portugal. See: https://treaties.un.org/Pages/ViewDetails.aspx?src=TREATY&mtdsg_no=IV-3-a&chapter=4&clang=_en (accessed on 27 March 2022).

[178] C. Mahon, 'Progress at the Front: The Draft Optional Protocol to the International Covenant on Economic, Social and Cultural Rights' (2008) 8 *Human Rights Law Review* 617, 635–636; C. Courtis and J. Rossi, 'Individual Complaints Procedure' in M. Langford (ed.), *The Optional Protocol to the International Covenant on Economic, Social and Cultural Rights: A Commentary* (PULP 2016) 37–75, 58–61.

[179] CESCR has interpreted that this is not technically an admissibility requirement but rather a discretionary power conferred to administer its resources on best discharging its functions. See: OP-ICESCR, Art. 4; CESCR, *Ben Djazia and Bellili v. Spain*, Communication 5/2015, E/C.12/61/D/5/2015 (2017), para. 11.5.

[180] CESCR, Report on the 69th (15 February–5 March 2021) and 70th sessions (27 September–15 October 2021), E/C.12/2021/3 (2022), para. 81.

three embryos could be produced per cycle; prohibited pre-implantation genetic diagnosis; and mandated the transfer into the uterus of all embryos, regardless of their viability or genetic disorders. The authors resorted to the domestic courts, which ordered the genetic testing of the three embryos produced. The testing revealed the presence of the genetic disorder in them and were, therefore, not implanted.

A judgment of the Constitutional Court declared the limit of three embryos per cycle to be unconstitutional, which prompted the authors to undertake a second *in vitro* fertilization cycle. Ten embryos were produced, but only one was free from hereditary multiple osteochondromas and this one was graded as being of 'average quality', which meant that it had a low chance of nesting. While S.C. declined to have the embryo transferred into her uterus, under the law she could not waive her consent to transfer the embryo, and was threatened with a lawsuit if she refused. S.C. felt compelled to agree to have the embryo transferred, but she subsequently suffered a miscarriage. Moreover, the remaining nine embryos (affected by the hereditary condition) had been cryopreserved, so the authors requested that the clinic surrender them to donate them for scientific research. However, the clinic refused, as the law prohibited research on embryos.

The authors resorted to the courts again. On the one hand, they requested an order for the embryos to be donated for research. On the other hand, they sought compensation for the implantation of the 'average quality' embryo that led to the miscarriage. They were unsuccessful in the domestic courts, which found that the claim about the refusal to have an embryo transferred was moot, as it had already taken place, and that the issue concerning research on embryos had multiple ethical and legal implications that were up to the legislator to decide.

Following the adverse rulings from the courts, the authors brought the complaint to CESCR, arguing the violation of different provisions under ICESCR. Among these, they claimed the violation of S.C.'s right to health (Article 12), as she had been forced to endure transfer into her uterus of an embryo against her will and not given the opportunity to withdraw her consent. As well, they claimed the breach of their rights under Article 15, to participate in scientific research and to enjoy the benefits of scientific progress. They argued that the legal prohibition of research on embryos interfered with scientific progress, slowing down the search for a cure for various diseases, including the one affecting S.C.

The authors' claim under Article 15 was found inadmissible by CESCR, considering that they had not sufficiently substantiated their status as victims. The reasons were three-fold: first, the authors failed to provide sufficient evidence of the link between the donation of embryos and the development of better treatments for the disease that would benefit them personally; second, whether the mere donation of an embryo consisted in itself of scientific research was not duly substantiated; and third, the authors were not undertaking any research themselves (paras. 6.13–6.19).

Conversely, the claim under Article 12 was declared admissible and the Committee found a violation of S.C.'s right to health. CESCR emphasized that the right to sexual and reproductive health entails 'the right to make free and responsible decisions and choices, free of violence, coercion and discrimination, regarding matters concerning one's body and sexual and reproductive health' (para. 8.1). The Committee affirmed that 'the right to health includes the right to make free and informed decisions concerning any medical treatment a person might be subjected to. Thus, laws and policies that prescribe involuntary, coercive or forced

> medical interventions violate the State's responsibility to respect the right to health' (para. 10.1). Therefore, CESCR asserted that forcing a woman to have an embryo transferred into her uterus clearly constituted a forced medical intervention, in violation of her right to health, both by itself and in conjunction with the prohibition of gender discrimination (paras. 10.1 and 10.3).
>
> Consequently, CESCR recommended the State to provide the authors with an effective remedy, which should include: enabling the authors' right to access *in vitro* fertilization, with the guarantee that the right to withdraw their consent would be respected; and awarding S.C. adequate compensation for the physical, psychological, and moral damages suffered. As a general measure, CESCR also recommended the State to amend its domestic legislation regulating this issue.

5.7 THE COMMITTEE ON THE ELIMINATION OF DISCRIMINATION AGAINST WOMEN (CEDAW COMMITTEE)

In 1946, in addition to the Commission on Human Rights, ECOSOC created a Commission on the Status of Women (CSW), with a mandate that included the elaboration of reports and recommendations on the promotion of women's rights in political, economic, civil, social, and educational fields.[181] Over the years, the work of CSW led to the adoption of important instruments,[182] but significant gaps subsisted in the protection of women's rights under international law.[183] In 1963, the General Assembly tasked CSW with the elaboration of a draft declaration on discrimination against women, which would compile in a single instrument the international standards that articulated the equal rights of men and women.[184] The outcome was the 1967 Declaration on the Elimination of Discrimination against Women, in itself a fundamental step towards the elaboration of a binding treaty on the topic.[185] In 1972, CSW requested the UN Secretary-General to call upon UN Member States to provide their views on the adoption of a convention and, the following year, a working group was appointed to consider the elaboration of such an instrument. Three drafts were

---

[181] Initially created as a Sub-Commission, it was quickly granted status as a Commission. See: ECOSOC, Resolution 2/11 (21 June 1946).

[182] See: Convention on the Political Rights of Women (adopted on 31 March 1953, entered into force 7 July 1954), 193 UNTS 135; Convention on the Nationality of Married Women (adopted on 20 February 1957, entered into force 11 August 1958), 309 UNTS 65; Convention on the Consent to Marriage, Minimum Age for Marriage, and Registration of Marriages (adopted on 10 December 1962, entered into force 9 December 1964), 521 UNTS 231.

[183] M. Campbell, *Women, Poverty, Equality: The Role of CEDAW* (Hart 2018) 35.

[184] UNGA, Resolution 1921(XVIII) 'Draft declaration on the elimination of discrimination against women' (5 December 1963).

[185] A.S. Fraser, 'Becoming Human: The Origins and Developments of Women's Human Rights' 21 (1999) *Human Rights Quarterly* 853, 893–894.

submitted to the working group—one from the Philippines, one from the Soviet Union, and a joint Philippines USSR draft—which were combined into one document.[186] The CSW worked on the text of the convention until 1976 and, between 1977 and 1979, the text was finalized by the Third Committee of the UN General Assembly.[187] Undoubtedly, the adoption of the Convention on the Elimination of Discrimination against Women (CEDAW), in December 1979, marked a turning point in the history of the protection of women's rights under international law—as further discussed in **Section 10.2.2**.[188] By the end of 2022, there are 189 States Parties to CEDAW, making it the core human rights treaty with the second highest number of Parties.

While the entry into force of CEDAW in 1981 was a remarkable achievement, this success was partly marred by two shortcomings: the number of reservations of a general character appended to the treaty and the limited powers initially conferred upon the Committee. As to the former, the volume of reservations of a general character or effect exceeded that of other core treaties,[189] including reservations aimed at subordinating significant treaty obligations to the State's domestic law, customary practices, or religious law.[190] The Committee has taken an active role in questioning the validity of these reservations,[191] both in concluding observations to State reports and general recommendations,[192] given their incompatibility with the object and purpose of CEDAW. Concerning the Committee's powers, although CEDAW provided for the creation of a monitoring body to supervise compliance with treaty obligations, it

---

[186] M. Campbell, *Women, Poverty, Equality: The Role of CEDAW* (Hart 2018) 36.

[187] CEDAW, 'Progress Achieved in the Implementation of the Convention on the Elimination of All Forms of Discrimination against Women', A/CONF.177/7 (21 June 1995), para. 12.

[188] L. Reanda, 'Human Rights and Women's Rights: The United Nations Approach' (1981) 3 *Human Rights Quarterly* 11, 12; H. Charlesworth and C. Chinkin, *The Boundaries of International Law: A Feminist Analysis* (2nd edn., Manchester University Press 2022) 216–217.

[189] A. Byrnes, 'The Other Human Rights Treaty Body: The Work of the Committee on the Elimination of Discrimination against Women' (1989) 14 *Yale Journal of International Law* 1, 51–52; R.J. Cook, 'Reservations to the Convention on the Elimination of All Forms of Discrimination against Women' (1990) 30 *Virginia Journal of International Law* 643, 643–644; B. Clark, 'The Vienna Convention Reservations Regime and the Convention on Discrimination against Women' (1991) 85 *American Journal of International Law* 281, 283, 318.

[190] R.J. Cook, 'Reservations to the Convention on the Elimination of All Forms of Discrimination against Women' (1990) 30 *Virginia Journal of International Law* 643, 687–707; A. Byrnes, 'The Committee on the Elimination of Discrimination Against Women' in F. Mégret and P. Alston (eds.), *The United Nations and Human Rights: A Critical Appraisal* (2nd edn., OUP 2020) 393–438, 420.

[191] This was a matter of concern even raised at the 1993 World Conference of Human Rights, with the Vienna Declaration and Programme of Action calling on reserving States to withdraw their reservations. See: Vienna Programme of Action, UN Doc. A/CONF.157/24 (1993), para. 39.

[192] B. Clark, 'The Vienna Convention Reservations Regime and the Convention on Discrimination against Women' (1991) 85 *American Journal of International Law* 281, 287, 318; Byrnes, 'The Committee on the Elimination of Discrimination Against Women' in F. Mégret and P. Alston (eds.), *The United Nations and Human Rights: A Critical Appraisal* (2nd edn., OUP 2020) 393–438, 421–422; R. Vijeyarasa, 'Quantifying CEDAW: Concrete Tools for Enhancing Accountability for Women's Rights' (2021) 34 *Harvard Human Rights Journal* 37, 61–63. See, for instance: CEDAW, General Recommendation No. 21: Equality in marriage and family relations, A/49/38 (1994), paras. 41–47; CEDAW, General Recommendation No. 23: Political and public life, A/52/38 (1997), para. 44; CEDAW, General Recommendation No. 28: on the Core Obligations of States Parties under Art. 2 of the Convention on the Elimination of All Forms of Discrimination against Women, CEDAW/C/2010/47/GC.2 (19 October 2010), paras. 41–42.

only granted the Committee the faculty to receive and examine State reports.[193] The inclusion of a procedure for individual communications, akin to that envisioned under ICERD and ICCPR-OP1, was considered during the drafting of the treaty, but ultimately rejected.[194] It would take strong advocacy from multiple actors for the limitations on the Committee's abilities to be redressed, through the adoption of an optional protocol.

The call for the adoption of a procedure for individual complaints before the CEDAW Committee was well-received at the 1993 World Conference on Human Rights. As mentioned in **Section 2.4.2.2**, the Vienna Declaration and Programme of Action called on CSW and the CEDAW Committee to study the possibility of drafting an optional protocol that would include an individual right of petition.[195] The Committee took a proactive approach to the adoption of a protocol, suggesting CSW to convene an expert group meeting to prepare a draft. Despite the inaction of CSW, an independent group of experts, which included three members of the CEDAW Committee, met at the Maastricht Centre for Human Rights in 1994 and adopted the 'Maastricht draft', which foresaw the creation of a procedure of individual communications—but not an inter-State one—as well as a mechanism for inquiries into allegations of serious and systematic violations.[196] The draft was submitted to the CEDAW Committee, which endorsed its substantive elements through the adoption of a 'suggestion' transmitted to CSW.[197] In 1996, CSW recommended that the UN Secretary-General requested the views of States, inter-governmental organizations, and NGOs on the adoption of a protocol to CEDAW.[198] A working group was established, which worked on the draft protocol until 1999, when it was submitted for its adoption first by CSW, then ECOSOC, and finally the UN General Assembly. The Optional Protocol (OP-CEDAW), providing the Committee with the power to receive individual communications and undertake inquiries, was adopted in October 1999, and entered into force on 22 December 2000.[199] By the end of 2022, it has reached 115 States Parties.[200]

---

[193] CEDAW, Arts. 18, 20.

[194] C. Flinterman and G. Liu, 'CEDAW and the Optional Protocol: First Experiences' in G. Alfredsson et al. (ed.), *International Human Rights Monitoring Mechanisms Essays in Honour of Jakob Th. Möller* (2nd edn., Nijhoff 2009) 91–97, 92; M.A. Freeman, C. Chinkin, and B. Rudolf (eds.), *The UN Convention on the Elimination of All Forms of Discrimination against Women: A Commentary* (OUP 2012) 614–615.

[195] Vienna Programme of Action, UN Doc. A/CONF.157/24 (1993), para. 40.

[196] M.A. Freeman, C. Chinkin, and B. Rudolf (eds.), *The UN Convention on the Elimination of All Forms of Discrimination against Women: A Commentary* (OUP 2012) 618.

[197] Report of the Committee on the Elimination of Discrimination against Women (fourteenth session) (1996). A/50/38, Suggestion 7.

[198] A. Byrnes, 'Slow and Steady Wins the Race? The Development of an Optional Protocol to the Women's Convention' (1997) 91 *Proceedings of the Annual Meeting (American Society of International Law)*, 383, 384; M.A. Freeman, C. Chinkin, and B. Rudolf (eds.), *The UN Convention on the Elimination of All Forms of Discrimination against Women: A Commentary* (OUP 2012) 6188.

[199] M.A. Freeman, C. Chinkin, and B. Rudolf (eds.), *The UN Convention on the Elimination of All Forms of Discrimination against Women: A Commentary* (OUP 2012) 619–620.

[200] See: https://indicators.ohchr.org/ (accessed on 27 March 2022).

All States Parties to OP-CEDAW agree that individual communications can be brought against them to the Committee.[201] However, the number of these complaints has been relatively low, with the Committee reporting to have received 155 individual communications during the first two decades of this procedure being in force.[202] Concerning the inquiries mechanism, OP-CEDAW allows for States Parties to opt out of such a monitoring procedure, but only a handful of Parties have done so.[203] From its first inquiry, the one concerning México (discussed below), and up to the end of 2022, the Committee has completed a handful of inquiries.

While the Committee has only acquired the power to engage in inquiries and individual complaints in 2000, it has been operating since 1982, following CEDAW's entry into force. At the time, it was the treaty body with the largest number of members (twenty-three) until the membership of SPT was enlarged to twenty-five. The Committee is the only treaty body that has had a consistent majority of women members throughout its history.[204] Another distinctive feature of the CEDAW Committee is that for many years it did not share the site in Geneva with other treaty bodies but convened its sessions in either Vienna or New York and was supported in its work by the Division for the Advancement of Women, rather than by the Office for the High Commissioner for Human Rights.[205] Only in 2008 was the Committee relocated to Geneva.[206]

The Committee has been quite prolific in the elaboration of general recommendations, having adopted a total of thirty-nine between 1986 and the end of 2022.[207] From the early 1990s, the Committee began to elaborate lengthier and more sophisticated recommendations, focusing on a range of substantive topics under CEDAW.[208] In 1997, the Committee adopted an even more structured procedure,

---

[201] No mechanism of inter-State complaints has been included in the OP-CEDAW. However, CEDAW is one of the five core treaties providing a procedure for inter-State disputes on the interpretation or application of the Convention to be submitted to the ICJ, as discussed in **Section 5.3.3.1**. See: CEDAW, Art. 29.

[202] CEDAW, 'Status of Communications Registered by CEDAW under the Optional Protocol, information as of 28 January 2020', available at: https://www.ohchr.org/Documents/HRBodies/CEDAW/StatisticalSurvey.xls (accessed on 27 March 2022).

[203] The status of ratifications, including reservations, is available at: https://treaties.un.org/pages/ViewDetails.aspx?src=TREATY&mtdsg_no=IV-8-b&chapter=4&clang=_en (accessed on 27 March 2022).

[204] M.A. Freeman, C. Chinkin, and B. Rudolf (eds.), *The UN Convention on the Elimination of All Forms of Discrimination against Women: A Commentary* (OUP 2012) 508; Byrnes, 'The Committee on the Elimination of Discrimination Against Women' in F. Mégret and P. Alston (eds.), *The United Nations and Human Rights: A Critical Appraisal* (2nd edn., OUP 2020) 393–438, 400.

[205] M. Bustelo, 'The Committee on the Elimination of Discrimination against Women at the Crossroads' in P. Alston and J. Crawford (eds.), *The Future of UN Human Rights Treaty Monitoring* (CUP 2000) 79–111, 81–83; H. Schopp-Schilling, 'Treaty Body Reform: The Case of the Committee on the Elimination of Discrimination against Women' (2007) 7 *Human Rights Law Review* 201, 218–219.

[206] A. Byrnes, 'The Committee on the Elimination of Discrimination Against Women' in F. Mégret and P. Alston (eds.), *The United Nations and Human Rights: A Critical Appraisal* (2nd edn., OUP 2020) 393–438, 397.

[207] E. Evatt, 'Finding a Voice for Women's Rights: The Early Days of CEDAW' (2002) 34 *George Washington International Law Review* 515, 535–537.

[208] M. Bustelo, 'The Committee on the Elimination of Discrimination against Women at the Crossroads' in P. Alston and J. Crawford (eds.), *The Future of UN Human Rights Treaty Monitoring* (CUP 2000) 79–111, 96; Byrnes, 'The Committee on the Elimination of Discrimination Against Women' in F. Mégret and P. Alston (eds.), *The United Nations and Human Rights: A Critical Appraisal* (2nd edn., OUP 2020) 393–438, 414.

providing opportunities for specialized agencies and civil society to intervene in the adoption of recommendations.[209] These recommendations have engaged, among other topics, with gender-based violence, women and health, the right to education, political rights, access to justice, equality within marriage and the economic consequences of marriage and its dissolution, older women, women migrant workers, and rural women.[210]

CEDAW, Report on México produced by the Committee on the Elimination of Discrimination against Women under Article 8 of the Optional Protocol to the Convention, CEDAW/C/2005/OP.8/MEXICO (27 January 2005).

The inquiry was initiated due to information received by the Committee in 2002, from two NGOs, concerning the abduction, rape, and murder of women in and around Ciudad Juárez, México. The information received led the Committee to organize a visit of two of its members to the area to conduct interviews with public authorities, as well as with victims' organisations. The information they obtained revealed that between 1993 and 2003 over 300 women had been murdered in the area, within the context of a widespread pandemic of gender-based violence. The victims were mostly poor working women, who had been victims of abduction, sexual violence, and then murder, with the response from the public authorities being extremely inadequate in both preventing the crimes and investigating and prosecuting the perpetrators.

Based on all the information collected, the Committee concluded that the situation disclosed a pattern of grave and systematic violations of CEDAW, of the United Nations Declaration on the Elimination of Violence against Women, and of the Committee's General Recommendation 19 on gender-based violence. The Committee expressed its concerns over the fact that the serious and systematic violations of women's rights had extended for over 10 years, without the State being able to put an end to them, punish the perpetrators, and provide the victims' families with due measures of redress.

---

[209] Byrnes, 'The Committee on the Elimination of Discrimination Against Women' in F. Mégret and P. Alston (eds.), *The United Nations and Human Rights: A Critical Appraisal* (2nd edn., OUP 2020) 393–438, 416. See: Report of the Committee on the Elimination of Discrimination against Women (16th and 17th sessions), A/52/38/Rev.1 (1997), para. 480.

[210] CEDAW, General Recommendation No. 14: Female circumcision, A/45/38 (1990); CEDAW, General Recommendation No. 19: Violence against Women, A/47/38; CEDAW and CRC, Joint General Recommendation No. 31/General Comment No. 18: on harmful practices, CEDAW/C/GC/31-CRC/C/GC/18 (14 November 2014); CEDAW, General Recommendation No. 35: on gender-based violence against women (updating General Recommendation No. 19), CEDAW/C/GC/35 (26 July 2017); CEDAW, General Recommendation No. 24: women and health, A/54/38/Rev. 1, chap. I. (1999); CEDAW, General Recommendation No. 36: on the right of girls and women to education, CEDAW/C/GC/36 (27 November 2017); CEDAW, General Recommendation No. 23: Political and public life, A/52/38 (1997); CEDAW, General Recommendation No. 33: on women's access to justice, CEDAW/C/GC/33 (3 August 2015); CEDAW, General Recommendation No. 21: Equality in marriage and family relations, A/49/38 (1994); CEDAW, General Recommendation No. 29: on economic consequences of marriage, family relations and their dissolution, CEDAW/C/GC/29 (30 October 2013); CEDAW, General Recommendation No. 27: on older women and protection of their human rights, CEDAW/C/GC/27 (16 December 2010); CEDAW, General Recommendation No. 26: on women migrant workers, CEDAW/C/2009/WP.1/R (5 December 2008); CEDAW, General Recommendation No. 34: on the rights of rural women, CEDAW/C/GC/34 (7 March 2016).

> Consequently, the Committee issued a number of recommendations for the State to adopt. These included: to incorporate a gender perspective into the investigation of the crimes and the policies to combat gender-based violence; to maintain a close relationship of cooperation with civil society in the implementation of measures to redress the situation; to investigate not only the serious crimes committed, but also the negligence and complicity of public authorities, prosecuting the public officials involved; to establish early-warning mechanisms for cases of missing women in Ciudad Juárez; and to ensure that the victims' relatives are treated with due respect and compassion for their grief (paras. 268, 270, 274, 276, and 280).

5.8 THE COMMITTEE AGAINST TORTURE (CAT)

In December 1977, the UN General Assembly requested the Commission on Human Rights to draft the text of an international convention against torture and other cruel, inhuman, or degrading treatment or punishment, to translate into indisputably binding terms the principles embodied in the 1975 Declaration on the Protection of All Persons from Being Subjected to Torture and Other Cruel, Inhuman or Degrading Treatment or Punishment.[211] A few months later, the Commission set up a working group to undertake this task, including the consideration of the draft texts already produced by Sweden and by the International Association of Penal Law.[212] The draft convention elaborated was transmitted by the Commission, through ECOSOC, to the General Assembly in 1984, which unanimously adopted it in December of that year.[213] The Convention against Torture and Other Cruel, Inhuman or Degrading Treatment or Punishment (UNCAT) entered into force on 26 June 1987, after it obtained its twentieth ratification.[214] At the end of 2022, there were 173 States Parties to the treaty.[215] Nonetheless, as discussed in **Section 3.1.5**, the actual prohibition of torture belongs to the realm of *jus cogens*, being a non-derogable norm under general international law that applies to every State, regardless of their status as party to UNCAT.

The Convention established the Committee Against Torture (CAT), a body of ten independent experts tasked with monitoring the implementation of UNCAT by States Parties, which started its work in 1988. The Committee has the ability to receive both inter-State and individual complaints but requires States Parties to expressly accept CAT's competence for these.[216] Up to the end of 2022, sixty-nine States Parties have made the declaration accepting the Committee's jurisdiction for receiving individual

---

[211] UNGA, Resolution 32/62, 'Draft convention against torture and other cruel, inhuman or degrading treatment or punishment' (8 December 1977).

[212] M. Nowak, M. Birk, and G. Monina, *The United Nations Convention Against Torture and its Optional Protocol: A Commentary* (2nd edn., OUP 2019) 3.

[213] M. Nowak, M. Birk, and G. Monina, *The United Nations Convention Against Torture and its Optional Protocol: A Commentary* (2nd edn., OUP 2019) 4–5.

[214] UNCAT, Art. 27.   [215] See: https://indicators.ohchr.org/ (accessed on 7 February 2023).

[216] UNCAT, Arts. 20, 21.

complaints. According to CAT's 2022 Report, it had received a total of 1,126 individual complaints, having adopted final decisions on the merits of 445 of them.[217]

Conversely, just over one-third of States Parties have accepted CAT's jurisdiction to intervene in inter-States complaints, and no such case has yet reached the Committee. However, the dispute settlement provision under Article 30 of UNCAT has been used in the past.[218] This article allows States Parties to refer any dispute regarding the interpretation or application of UNCAT to the ICJ if the dispute cannot be settled through negotiation or arbitration.[219] Making use of this provision, Belgium brought a case to the ICJ in 2012, claiming the violation of UNCAT by Senegal (Senegaal). The case concerned the duty to either prosecute or extradite former Chad's dictator Hissène Habré, who was residing in Senegal and had been indicted in Belgium for gross and systematic human rights violations, including torture. The ICJ ruled that, indeed, Senegal's refusal to either prosecute or extradite Habré had amounted to the violation of UNCAT.[220] As discussed in **Section 5.8.1**, a case on this matter has also been decided by CAT, in the context of individual complaints.

Like other treaty bodies, CAT has the ability to elaborate general comments. However, it has not been very active in this respect, having produced four general comments up to the end of 2022, which focused on the implementation of three treaty provisions: the one concerning prevention, the one dealing with extradition, expulsion, and *refoulement*, and the one on redress.[221] Moreover, CAT was the first treaty body endowed with the power to undertake confidential inquiries (discussed in **Section 5.3.4**).[222] An inquiry can take place when CAT receives reliable information that torture is being systematically practised in the territory of a State Party.[223] States have the ability to opt out of this mechanism, although only twenty-four States have decided to do so. At the end of 2022, CAT had completed inquiries with regards to ten States Parties.[224]

---

[217] Report of the Committee against Torture, 71st session (12–30 July 2021), 77nd session (8 November–3 December 2021), 73rd session (19 April–13 May 2022), A/77/44, para. 50.

[218] ICJ, *Questions relating to the Obligation to Prosecute or Extradite (Belgium v. Senegal)*, Judgment, I.C.J. Reports 2012, p. 422.

[219] ICJ, *Questions relating to the Obligation to Prosecute or Extradite (Belgium v. Senegal)*, Judgment, I.C.J. Reports 2012, p. 422, para. 63.

[220] ICJ, *Questions relating to the Obligation to Prosecute or Extradite (Belgium v. Senegal)*, Judgment, I.C.J. Reports 2012, p. 422, para. 122.

[221] CAT, General Comment No. 1: Implementation of Art. 3 of the Convention in the context of Art. 22, A/53/44 (21 November 1997); CAT, General Comment No. 2: Implementation of Art. 2 by States parties, CAT/C/GC/2 (24 January 2008); CAT, General Comment No. 3: Implementation of Art. 14 by States parties, CAT/C/GC/3 (13 December 2012); CAT, General Comment No. 4: on the implementation of Art. 3 of the Convention in the context of Art. 22, CAT/C/GC/4 (4 September 2018).

[222] A. Byrnes, 'The Committee against Torture and the Subcommittee for the Prevention of Torture' in F. Mégret and P. Alston (eds.), *The United Nations and Human Rights: A Critical Appraisal* (2nd edn., OUP 2020) 478–517, 492.

[223] UNCAT, Art. 20.

[224] See: https://tbinternet.ohchr.org/_layouts/15/TreatyBodyExternal/Inquiries.aspx (accessed on 2 March 2022).

5.8.1 THE SUBCOMMITTEE ON PREVENTION OF TORTURE AND OTHER CRUEL, INHUMAN OR DEGRADING TREATMENT OR PUNISHMENT (SPT)

The protective regime established by UNCAT was complemented in 2002 by the adoption of an Optional Protocol (OPCAT), which came to establish an additional supervisory body, the Subcommittee for the Prevention of Torture (SPT). SPT is composed of twenty-five experts, and its main task consists of undertaking regular visits to places where people are deprived of their liberty, to prevent torture and other cruel, inhuman, or degrading treatment or punishment.[225] The membership of SPT is expected to be somehow different to that of the other treaty bodies, as instead of expertise on human rights OPCAT places a decisive emphasis on proven experience in the fields of criminal law and prison and police administration.[226]

The adoption of a preventive mechanism, such as the one established by OPCAT, was already discussed at the time of the negotiation of UNCAT. Such a proposal had been submitted by Costa Rica, based on an idea developed by Jean-Jacques Gautier, but while it had the support of the International Commission of Jurists and the Swiss Committee against Torture, it failed to obtain the needed political traction to be adopted.[227] The Protocol entered into force in 2006, leading to the establishment of SPT in 2007. At the end of 2022, OPCAT counted ninety-one States Parties.[228]

By becoming Party to OPCAT, States agree to allow SPT to undertake visits to their territory,[229] as well as to provide SPT with almost unrestricted access to all places of detention, the relevant information it requests, and the individuals it decides to interview.[230] Following a visit, SPT elaborates a report and submits it to the concerned State, including recommendations to which the State is expected to respond, indicating

---

[225] The initial membership of SPT was ten experts, which was to increase to twenty-five following the fiftieth ratification or accession to the treaty. See: OPCAT, Art. 5.1.

[226] K. Buchinger, 'Art. 5: Size and Composition of the Subcommittee on Prevention' in M. Nowak, M. Birk, and G. Monina, The United Nations Convention Against Torture and its Optional Protocol: A Commentary (2nd edn., OUP 2019) 755–765, 763. See: OPCAT, Art. 5.

[227] R. Bank, 'Country-oriented Procedures under the Convention against Torture: Towards a New Dynamism' in P. Alston and J. Crawford (eds.), The Future of UN Human Rights Treaty Monitoring (CUP 2000) pp. 145–174, 145; M. Evans and C. Haenni-Dale, 'Preventing Torture—The Development of the Optional Protocol to the UN Convention against Torture' (2004) 4 Human Rights Law Review 19, 20–24.

[228] See: https://indicators.ohchr.org/ (accessed on 7 February 2023).

[229] In recent years, SPT has decided to suspend visits when the authorities have restricted its access to places of detention, individuals, or information, as happened in Rwanda in 2017 and Australia in 2022. See: https://www.ohchr.org/en/press-releases/2017/10/prevention-torture-un-human-rights-body-suspends-rwanda-visit-citing; https://www.ohchr.org/en/press-releases/2022/10/un-torture-prevention-body-suspends-visit-australia-citing-lack-co-operation (accessed on 12 May 2023).

[230] S. Egan, 'The Optional Protocol to the Convention against Torture: Paying the Price for Prevention' (2009) 44 Irish Jurist 182, 188–189; A. Byrnes, 'The Committee against Torture and the Subcommittee for the Prevention of Torture' in F. Mégret and P. Alston (eds.), The United Nations and Human Rights: A Critical Appraisal (2nd edn., OUP 2020) 478–517, 514.

the measures taken for their implementation.[231] SPT's report to the State is, in principle, confidential but the State can proceed to publish it or request its publication by SPT. A report can also be made public by CAT when the concerned State fails to adopt any meaningful measures to implement SPT's recommendations.[232]

Another significant feature of OPCAT is that it places upon States Parties the obligation to set up independent National Preventive Mechanisms (NPMs) to examine the treatment of people in detention and to advise the government on how to improve the treatment and the conditions of persons deprived of their liberty, including by analysing existent or proposed domestic legislation.[233] SPT is tasked with providing assistance and advice to the NPMs.[234] In particular, it is entrusted with offering training and technical assistance to NPMs upon their creation, which OPCAT mandates should be no longer than one year from the State becoming Party to the treaty.[235] To fulfil this mandate, SPT has created four regional task forces in charge of liaising with the NPMs of the respective world region.[236] Furthermore, even since its first annual report, SPT has started to produce guidelines to provide assistance with the creation and operation of the NMPs.[237] In its annual reports, which SPT is required to submit to CAT,[238] SPT has developed the practice of exploring different themes concerning the implementation of its mandate,[239] setting views on a range of topics that have included: indigenous justice and the prevention of torture, the relation between petty corruption and torture and other ill-treatment, LGBTQI persons and the prevention of torture and ill-treatment, and the detention of migrants and asylum seekers.[240]

---

[231] K. Buchinger, 'Art. 11: Mandate of the Subcommittee' in M. Nowak, M. Birk, and G. Monina, *The United Nations Convention Against Torture and its Optional Protocol: A Commentary* (2nd edn., OUP 2019) 803–819, 816; A. Byrnes, 'The Committee against Torture and the Subcommittee for the Prevention of Torture' in F. Mégret and P. Alston (eds.), *The United Nations and Human Rights: A Critical Appraisal* (2nd edn., OUP 2020) 478–517, 514–515.

[232] OPCAT, Art. 16.

[233] M. Evans and C. Haenni-Dale, 'Preventing Torture—The Development of the Optional Protocol to the UN Convention against Torture' (2004) 4 *Human Rights Law Review* 19, 20. See: OPCAT, Arts. 17–19.

[234] OPCAT, Art. 11.   [235] OPCAT, Art. 17.

[236] K. Buchinger, 'Art. 11: Mandate of the Subcommittee' in M. Nowak, M. Birk, and G. Monina, *The United Nations Convention Against Torture and its Optional Protocol: A Commentary* (2nd edn., OUP 2019) 803–819, 814–815; A. Byrnes, 'The Committee against Torture and the Subcommittee for the Prevention of Torture' in F. Mégret and P. Alston (eds.), *The United Nations and Human Rights: A Critical Appraisal* (2nd edn., OUP 2020) 478–517, 515.

[237] E. Steinerte, 'The Changing Nature of the Relationship between the United Nations Subcommittee on Prevention of Torture and National Preventative Mechanisms: In Search for Equilibrium' (2013) 31 *Netherlands Quarterly of Human Rights* 132, 149–150; K. Buchinger, 'Art. 11: Mandate of the Subcommittee' in M. Nowak, M. Birk, and G. Monina, *The United Nations Convention Against Torture and its Optional Protocol: A Commentary* (2nd edn., OUP 2019) 803–819, 813.

[238] OPCAT, Art. 16.4.

[239] A. Byrnes, 'The Committee against Torture and the Subcommittee for the Prevention of Torture' in F. Mégret and P. Alston (eds.), *The United Nations and Human Rights: A Critical Appraisal* (2nd edn., OUP 2020) 478–517, 515–516.

[240] SPT, Sixth Annual Report, CAT/C/50/2 (23 April 2013), paras. 81–94; SPT, Seventh Annual Report, CAT/C/52/2 (20 March 2014), paras. 94–100; SPT, Ninth Annual Report, CAT/C/57/4 (22 March 2016), paras. 48–82; SPT, Eleventh Annual Report, CAT/C/63/4 (26 March 2018), paras. 47–51.

> **CAT, *Suleymane Guengueng et al. v. Senegal*, Communication No. 181/2001, CAT/C/36/D/181/2001 (19 May 2006).**
>
> The complainants were seven Chadian nationals who claimed to have suffered torture by Chadian agents under Hissène Habré's regime (1982–1990), during which 40,000 political murders and systematic torture have been reported. They claimed the violation of UNCAT by Senegal, to their detriment, due to the State's unwillingness to either prosecute Habré, who had resided in Senegal since 1990, or to extradite him to Belgium, where he could be tried.
>
> The facts of the case can be summarized as follows: in July 2000, the judiciary of Senegal had dismissed the charges against Habré for acts of torture, stating that it lacked jurisdiction to judge torture committed abroad; a ruling that was upheld by the Court of Cassation the following year. Five years later, in September 2005, the Belgian judiciary issued an international arrest warrant against Habré, charging him with genocide, crimes against humanity (including torture), and war crimes, and requested his extradition from Senegal. The request was rejected by the Senegalese judiciary in November 2005, also on the grounds of lack of jurisdiction. Soon after, the Minister for Foreign Affairs announced that the case of Habré was to be brought to the attention of the Summit of Heads of State and Government of the African Union. In January 2006, the Assembly of the AU decided to appoint a committee of eminent African jurists to advise on the situation of Habré.
>
> The case was brought to the CAT before the AU adopted any further measures on the situation. Ultimately, in 2012, the AU and Senegal agreed to the creation of Extraordinary African Chambers to bring to justice the perpetrators of the serious international crimes committed during Habré's regime. Habré was convicted of torture, crimes against humanity, and war crimes, and sentenced to life in prison in 2016.
>
> Deciding the case in 2006, CAT found two clear breaches of UNCAT. First, under Article 5.2, States Parties are obliged to adopt all necessary measures to exercise jurisdiction over acts of torture when the alleged perpetrator is under their jurisdiction. The Committee found that Senegal had failed to comply with this obligation. Second, Article 7 provides States Parties with a path to avoid their international responsibility for the lack of prosecution of torture when an extradition request exists. The assumed obligation of international cooperation against impunity for the crime of torture translates into the duty to either prosecute or extradite (*aut dedere aut judicare*) those individuals, under the jurisdiction of the State suspected of having committed torture. Consequently, Senegal incurred another breach of UNCAT, that of Article 7, for refusing to extradite Habré to Belgium, while refusing to exercise jurisdiction itself (paras. 9.5–9.9 and 10).

5.9 THE COMMITTEE ON THE RIGHTS OF THE CHILD (CRC)

UNCRC is the international human rights treaty with the largest number of State Parties—196 up to the end of 2022— which includes all UN Member States with the sole exception of the USA.[241] The number of Parties illustrates the overwhelming consensus amongst States on the importance of providing due protection and legal recognition

---

[241] See: https://indicators.ohchr.org/ (accessed on 27 March 2022).

to children everywhere.[242] In the words of a former member of the Committee on the Rights of the Child (CRC): 'It is difficult to be an opponent to the goal of making a better world for children'.[243]

The adoption of the Convention in 1989 was an undeniable milestone in the development of the protection of children's rights under the international law of human rights,[244] but international law's concern for the protection of children neither started with UNCRC nor finished therewith, as further discussed in **Section 10.3**.[245] The Convention came to confirm the recognition of children as subjects of rights, rather than as mere objects of international protection, imposing upon States Parties clear obligations in terms of the respect and promotion of children's rights, encompassing civil, political, social, economic, and cultural rights.[246] Although an apparent scepticism about the immediate effect of economic, social, and cultural rights transpires from Article 4 of UNCRC, which subjects their implementation to the availability of resources, such a limitation should be interpreted quite restrictively.

The Convention entered into force only months after its adoption,[247] setting in place the CRC to monitor compliance with the treaty. The CRC, which held its first meeting in 1991, was initially composed of ten independent experts, but its membership was expanded to eighteen through an amendment of the treaty that entered into force in 2002.[248] Like the CEDAW Committee, the main monitoring power granted to the CRC was the consideration of State periodic reports[249]—a deficit only addressed by a 2011 protocol, as discussed below.

In 2000, the substantive content of UNCRC was augmented by the adoption of two optional protocols.[250] The first one concerned the prohibition of child prostitution

---

[242] R. Shackel, 'The United Nations Convention on the Rights of the Child—A Review of Its Successes and Future Directions' (2003) *Australian International Law Journal* 21, 22.

[243] L. Smith, 'Monitoring the CRC' in G. Alfredsson et al. (eds.), *International Human Rights Monitoring Mechanisms Essays in Honour of Jakob Th. Möller* (2nd edn., Nijhoff 2009) 109–116, 109.

[244] Y. Lee, 'Communications Procedure under the Convention on the Rights of the Child: 3rd Optional Protocol' (2010) 18 *International Journal of Children's Rights* 567, 568; C. Evans, 'The Committee on the Rights of the Child' in F. Mégret and P. Alston (eds.), *The United Nations and Human Rights: A Critical Appraisal* (2nd edn., OUP 2020) 519–545, 519.

[245] R. Shackel, 'The United Nations Convention on the Rights of the Child - A Review of Its Successes and Future Directions' (2003) *Australian International Law Journal* 21, 24–26; W. Vandenhole, G. Türkelli, and S. Lembrechts, *Children's Rights: A Commentary on the Convention on the Rights of the Child and its Protocols* (Elgar 2019) 2–3.

[246] Y. Lee, 'Communications Procedure under the Convention on the Rights of the Child: 3rd Optional Protocol' (2010) 18 *International Journal of Children's Rights* 567, 567; W. Vandenhole, G. Türkelli, and S. Lembrechts, *Children's Rights: A Commentary on the Convention on the Rights of the Child and its Protocols* (Elgar 2019) 6.

[247] C.P. Cohen and S. Kilbourne, 'Jurisprudence of the Committee on the Rights of the Child: A Guide for Research and Analysis' (1998) 19 *Michigan Journal of International Law* 633, 634.

[248] Amendment to Art. 43(2) of the Convention on the Rights of the Child (12 December 1995), CRC/SP/1995/L.1/Rev.1; CRC, Report on the 32nd Session (Geneva, 13–31 January 2003), CRC/C/124 (23 June 2003), para. 4.

[249] W. Vandenhole, G. Türkelli, and S. Lembrechts, *Children's Rights: A Commentary on the Convention on the Rights of the Child and its Protocols* (Elgar 2019) 467.

[250] OP1-CRC; OP2-CRC.

and child pornography, and the second one focused on the regulation of children's participation in armed conflicts. Both protocols entered into force in 2002 and had obtained a large number of ratifications and accessions up to the end of 2022: 172 and 178, respectively.[251] The scope of the rights entrenched in the Convention has also been enriched by the general comments produced by CRC. By the end of 2022, the Committee has elaborated twenty-five general comments, all produced within the past two decades, as it did not adopt any during its first ten years of existence. CRC has developed a rather inclusive procedure for the elaboration of general comments, encompassing the preparation of an initial draft, usually in consultation with experts, and then inviting comments from other experts, UN agencies, States, and NGOs. It has also started undertaking consultations with children from different countries.[252] CRC's general comments have covered a wide range of issues. These included the different needs of children depending on their stages of development, focusing both on early childhood (below the age of eight years) and adolescence (between ten and eighteen years of age),[253] as well as the special measures of protection that should be adopted to protect children and how these should be tailored to target the multifaceted and intersectional discrimination experienced by, for instance, indigenous children, disabled children, or migrant children—and, in particular, girls—as their intersecting characteristics make them especially vulnerable.[254]

A third Optional Protocol (OP3-CRC) was adopted in 2011, entering into force in 2014, aimed at strengthening the operational capacities of the Committee. This third protocol empowered CRC to receive individual communications from victims of human rights violations under UNCRC (or its optional protocols) against any State Party to OP3-CRC.[255] The Protocol also allows for inter-State communications, but only if States Parties expressly consent to the CRC's competence in this regard.[256] Additionally, OP3-CRC endows the Committee with the ability to undertake inquiries, if it receives reliable information indicating grave or systematic violations of CRC or its protocols by a State Party.[257]

While support for OP3-CRC is still relatively low, with only fifty States Parties by the end of 2022,[258] its adoption is truly significant. By providing children with explicit legal standing to seek protection of their rights at the international level, it came to

---

[251] See: https://indicators.ohchr.org/ (accessed on 7 February 2023).

[252] C. Evans, 'The Committee on the Rights of the Child' in F. Mégret and P. Alston (eds.), *The United Nations and Human Rights: A Critical Appraisal* (2nd edn., OUP 2020) 519–545, 537.

[253] CRC, General Comment No. 7: Implementing child rights in early childhood, CRC/C/GC/7/Rev.1 (20 September 2006); CRC, General Comment No. 20: On the implementation of the rights of the child during adolescence, CRC/C/GC/20 (6 December 2016).

[254] CRC, General Comment No. 9: The rights of children with disabilities, CRC/C/GC/9 (27 February 2007), paras. 8, 10, 79; CRC, General Comment No. 11: Indigenous children and their rights under the Convention, CRC/C/GC/11 (12 February 2009), paras. 5, 29; CMW and CRC, Joint General Comment Nos. 3, 22: On the general principles regarding the human rights of children in the context of international migration, CMW/C/GC/3-CRC/C/GC/22 (16 November 2017), paras. 16, 18, 23.

[255] OP3-CRC, Art. 5.   [256] OP3-CRC, Art. 12.   [257] OP3-CRC, Art. 13.

[258] See: https://indicators.ohchr.org/ (accessed on 7 February 2023).

reaffirm the status of children as subjects of the international law of human rights.[259] However, concerns have been voiced as to whether children would be able to access CRC by themselves, given that this would require not only an awareness of their rights and knowledge of the UNCRC system, but also having effective access to exhausting domestic judicial remedies.[260] The creation of national mechanisms that could provide advice, assistance, and representation to children in domestic courts would appear as a requirement to render the exercise of their procedural capacity a reality.[261] Similarly, the lack of a 'public defender' figure under OP3-CRC, which could assist children in their communications before CRC, enhances the difficulties of bringing a claim at the international sphere by themselves.[262] Despite these important shortcomings, the system of individual communications before CRC is proving to be quite successful in quantitative terms, with the Committee reporting to have 116 registered cases already by March 2020.[263] Conversely, the inquiries procedure that came into force at the same time has so far been less resorted to by CRC. Up to the end of 2022, CRC has only undertaken one inquiry, which concerned the situation of children in residential care in Chile.[264]

CRC, Inquiry concerning Chile under Article 13 of the Optional Protocol to the Convention on the Rights of the Child on a communications procedure, CRC/C/CHL/IR/1 (6 May 2020).

This was the first inquiry procedure undertaken by CRC and concerned the situation of children deprived of a family environment who live in residential centres under the (direct or indirect) control of the National Service for Minors in Chile. Following information it received, CRC decided to undertake a country visit in 2018, in which the experts visited four of the centres in question and met with a range of public authorities, civil society organizations, and people who as children had lived in the centres under examination.

---

[259] C. Evans, 'The Committee on the Rights of the Child' in F. Mégret and P. Alston (eds.), *The United Nations and Human Rights: A Critical Appraisal* (2nd edn., OUP 2020) 519–545, 542. See: OP3-CRC, preamble.

[260] R. Smith, 'The Third Optional Protocol to the UN Convention on the Rights of the Child—Challenges Arising Transforming the Rhetoric into Reality' (2013) 21 *International Journal of Children's Rights* 305; G. de Beco, 'The Optional Protocol to the Convention on the Rights of the Child on a Communications Procedure: Good News' (2013) 13 *Human Rights Law Review* 367; W. Vandenhole, G. Türkelli, and S. Lembrechts, *Children's Rights: A Commentary on the Convention on the Rights of the Child and its Protocols* (Elgar 2019) 471–472.

[261] R. Smith, 'The Third Optional Protocol to the UN Convention on the Rights of the Child—Challenges Arising Transforming the Rhetoric into Reality' (2013) 21 *International Journal of Children's Rights* 305, 321.

[262] R. Smith, 'The Third Optional Protocol to the UN Convention on the Rights of the Child—Challenges Arising Transforming the Rhetoric into Reality' (2013) 21 *International Journal of Children's Rights* 305, 315.

[263] Report of the Committee on the Rights of the Child, 78th session (14 May–1 June 2018), 79th session (17 September–5 October 2018), 80th session (14 January–1 February 2019), 81st session (13–31 May 2019), 82nd (9–27 September 2019), 83rd session (20 January–7 February 2020), Extraordinary 84th session (2–6 March 2020), A/75/41, para. 43.

[264] CRC, Inquiry concerning Chile under Art. 13 of the Optional Protocol to the Convention on the Rights of the Child on a communications procedure, CRC/C/CHL/IR/1 (6 May 2020).

The centres subject of the inquiry numbered more than 250; of these only eleven were directly run by the State while the vast majority were run privately but subsidized and monitored by the State. More than 14,000 children lived in those centres, the majority of whom were from poor backgrounds.

Based on the information collected, the CRC was of the view that a grave and systematic violation of the rights of children in residential centres existed. The Committee found the violations to be attributable to the State, regardless of whether these were committed in the centres under its direct control or in centres run by partner organizations, as the latter should be considered State agents, since the State had delegated to them the responsibilities assumed under UNCRC.

The Committee found multiple violations of UNCRC. Among many others, these violations included the breach of Article 2 (prohibition of discrimination), given that the State was placing children into the residential system due to the financial hardship experienced by their families instead of providing the needed material support to the families to allow them to adequately care for their children. The CRC also determined multiple violations of Article 3 (best interests of the child), due to the poor condition of the centres and their inadequate infrastructure, their chronic overcrowding, the limited training of staff, and the insufficient number of specialized professionals (paras. 32, 33, 35, and 40). It also found the combined breaches of Articles 3 and 25 (the right of children in care to a periodic review of their treatment) on several grounds, including the use of residential centres over other forms of intervention, such as placing children with extended family or with other families, and the placing of siblings in separate homes. The same violations were found due to the lack of clear criteria for placing children in residential care and due to the absence of periodic independent reviews for monitoring the length of time children spent therein (paras. 23–25, 30, and 59).

The Committee also found the violation of Article 4 (duty to amend the domestic legal order), because of the failure to allocate sufficient resources to the centres in operation and due to the absence of comprehensive domestic legislation on children that provided a legal framework for public institutions (para. 51). Breaches of Article 12 (the right to be heard) were found on the basis that the State had failed to provide adequate information to all children so that their opinion was respected within the process leading to their admission to centres, and also due to its failure to ensure that children had access to a judge and a lawyer in the process (para. 69).

The violation of Article 24 (highest attainable standard of health) was grounded, among other reasons, on the limited availability of mental health services and on the lack of plans for the care of children and adolescents with mental health problems or psychiatric or neurological disorders, or those who use alcohol or drugs (para. 86). CRC also found the breach of Article 34 (protection from sexual exploitation and abuse), due to the State's failure to prevent sexual violence, both among peers and by adults against the children under their protection; the failure to act in a timely and effective manner when sexual violence was reported; and the lack of staff training in the prevention of sexual abuse (para. 102).

The breach of Article 28 (right to education) was found given the inadequate preparation of teachers and staff to deal with the physical, emotional, and psychological vulnerability of children in the residential system and the absence of due measures to ensure they could access education on an equal footing with other children and adolescents (para. 90). CRC was also of the view that the State breached Article 31 (right to rest and leisure), as it did not provide children living in institutions with full opportunities to engage in recreational activities appropriate to their age, including artistic expression (para. 94).

The Committee characterized the violations as grave and systematic: grave, because they were likely to produce substantial harm to the victims, taking into consideration the scale, prevalence, nature, and impact of the violations. These violations have affected thousands of children over an extensive period of time and were likely to produce long-term effects. The violations were also considered systematic, due to the persistence of the State's inaction and its failure to change laws, policies, and practices that had led to continued infringements of the rights of children and adolescents in the State's care (paras. 111–114).

Given the critical nature of the assessed situation, CRC made a number of important recommendations to the State. These included: to proceed with the immediate closure of one to the centres; to urgently adopt legislation that would provide comprehensive protection to children in need of alternative care, in line with the obligations assumed under UNCRC; to provide assistance to families in the fulfilment of parental responsibilities, in order to reduce the need for alternative care; to prioritize foster care—either through the extended family or in another family—over residential care; to allocate sufficient resources (human, technical, and financial) to the residential care system; to provide training programmes for personnel working in the system; and to establish effective control mechanisms (paras. 117, 122, 124, and 128).

5.10 THE COMMITTEE ON THE PROTECTION OF THE RIGHTS OF ALL MIGRANT WORKERS AND MEMBERS OF THEIR FAMILIES (CMW)

International migration is a heavily politicized topic. The imminent threat posed by the dangerous migrant—a frightful figure that inhabits the collective imaginary—is regularly featured in political discourses and reports from media outlets, despite the actual figure of international migrants equating to roughly 3.6 per cent of the global population.[265] As stated in the 2022 World Migration Report of the International Organization for Migration (IOM), while disinformation may be an age-old phenomenon, it certainly thrives in our digital age.[266] The social panic about (im)migration, fed and exploited by certain actors, offers a significant contextual background to understanding why the 1990 International Convention on the Protection of the Rights of All Migrant Workers and Members of Their Families (ICRMW) remains the core human rights treaty with the lowest level of States Parties, more than two decades after its adoption.[267]

---

[265] M. McAuliffe and A. Triandafyllidou (eds.), World Migration Report 2022, International Organization for Migration (2022), p. 21.

[266] M. McAuliffe and A. Triandafyllidou (eds.), World Migration Report 2022, International Organization for Migration (2022), p. 217.

[267] V. Chetail, 'The Committee on the Protection of the Rights of All Migrant Workers and Members of Their Families' in F. Mégret and P. Alston (eds.), *The United Nations and Human Rights: A Critical Appraisal* (2nd edn., OUP 2020) 601–644, 601–602.

Although the protection of migrant workers had been the focus of ILO conventions and recommendations, these instruments have been far from comprehensive, leaving multiple areas of weak or absent protection.[268] This was the conclusion reached by ECOSOC in 1972. Following an incident that involved the illegal trafficking of twenty-eight individuals from Mali to France,[269] ECOSOC issued a resolution instructing the Commission on Human Rights to evaluate the issue of illegal trafficking of migrants and to prepare recommendations for the adoption of further action.[270] Echoing ECOSOC's resolution, the General Assembly recommended the Commission to consider the question of the exploitation of workers and illegal trafficking as a matter of priority.[271] Throughout the 1970s, this call was followed by a number of resolutions,[272] until the General Assembly decided to create a working group to elaborate an 'international convention on the protection of the rights of all migrant workers and their families' in 1979.[273]

The drafting process of the convention extended for a decade, from the establishment of the working group in 1980 until its adoption in 1990. México and Morocco (Al Maghrib), two important States of origin for migrant workers, had a particular leading role at the onset of the drafting process—and even before, in campaigning for the elaboration of such a treaty.[274] However, it was a group of seven Mediterranean and Scandinavian States—which formed the MESCA group—that had the biggest influence in driving the negotiating process and, therefore, in the final structure and content of the Convention.[275]

---

[268] S. Hune, 'Drafting an International Convention on the Protection of the Rights of All Migrant Workers and Their Families' (1985) 19 *International Migration Review* 570, 570–571. See: ILO, Convention concerning Migration for Employment (C097) (adopted 1 July 1949, entered into force 22 January 1952); ILO, Migrant Workers (Supplementary Provisions) (C143) (adopted 24 June 1975, entered into force 9 December 1978).

[269] G. Battistella, 'Migration and Human Rights: The Uneasy but Essential Relationship' in R. Cholewinski, P. De Guchteneire, and A. Pécoud (eds.), *Migration and Human Rights: The United Nations Convention on Migrant Workers' Rights* (CUP 2009) 47–69, 51–52.

[270] ECOSOC, 'Exploitation of labour though illicit and clandestine trafficking', Resolution 1706 (LIII) (28 July 1972), para. 4.

[271] UNGA, 'Exploitation of labour though illicit and clandestine trafficking', Resolution 2920 (XXVII) (15 November 1972), para. 3.

[272] V. Chetail, 'The Committee on the Protection of the Rights of All Migrant Workers and Members of Their Families' in F. Mégret and P. Alston (eds.), The United Nations and Human Rights: A Critical Appraisal (2nd edn., OUP 2020) 601–644, 604. See: UNGA, 'Measures to improve the situation of migrant workers', Resolution 3224 (XXIX) (6 November 1974); UNGA, 'Measures to ensure the human rights and dignity of all migrant workers', Resolution 3449 (XXX) (9 December 1975); UNGA, 'Measures to improve the situation and ensure the human rights and dignity of all migrant workers', Resolution 31/127 (16 December 1976); UNGA, 'Measures to improve the situation and ensure the human rights and dignity of al migrant workers', Resolution 32/120 (16 December 1977); UNGA, 'Measures to improve the situation and ensure the human rights and dignity of all migrant workers', Resolution 33/163 (20 December 1978).

[273] UNGA, 'Measures to improve the situation and ensure the human rights and dignity of all migrant workers', Resolution 34/172 (17 December 1979), para. 3.

[274] P. De Guchteneire and A. Pécoud, 'Introduction: The UN Convention on Migrant Workers' Rights' in R. Cholewinski, P. De Guchteneire and A. Pécoud (eds.), *Migration and Human Rights: The United Nations Convention on Migrant Workers' Rights* (CUP 2009) 1–44, 7.

[275] R. Bohning, 'The ILO and the New UN Convention on Migrant Workers: The Past and Future' (1991) 25 *The International Migration Review* 698, 701–702; J. Lonnroth, 'The International Convention on the Rights of All Migrant Workers and Members of Their Families in the Context of International Migration Policies: An Analysis of Ten Years of Negotiation' (1991) 25 *The International Migration Review* 710, 712, 730.

The adoption of ICRMW by the General Assembly was a significant achievement, especially with regard to its symbolic meaning, recognizing that migrant workers are indeed subjects of rights under the international law of human rights.[276] Nevertheless, the Convention could be seen as essentially compiling and restating international norms of protection for migrant workers that were already set in place by other instruments;[277] a fact that makes the rather low level of ratification and accession to the Convention particularly puzzling. While adopted in 1990, ICRMW only managed to reach the twenty ratifications needed to enter into force in 2003 and merely counts fifty-eight States Parties by the end of 2022.[278] Unsurprisingly, the overwhelming majority of Parties are countries (traditionally) of origin for migrant workers, with Argentina as the main exception to this trend.[279] Despite the Convention being a rather European-drafted instrument, as aforementioned, not a single State from the Global North has yet decided to accede to the treaty.[280] The resistance to ICRMW can be seen as grounded on misconceptions, such as the belief that the Convention imposes obligations upon States that would restrict their overall migration policy, or that it creates new rights concerning migrants in irregular situation.[281] However, those are both false impressions, which allows wondering whether the reluctance of States from the Global North to become Parties to ICRMW could actually be grounded on either ideological opposition to the values underpinning the Convention—at odds with the liberal values purportedly

---

[276] S. Hune, 'Migrant Women in the Context of the International Convention on the Protection of the Rights of All Migrant Workers and Members of Their Families' (1991) 25 *International Migration Review* 800, 807–808; P. De Guchteneire and A. Pécoud, 'Introduction: The UN Convention on Migrant Workers' Rights' in R. Cholewinski, P. De Guchteneire, and A. Pécoud (eds.), Migration and Human Rights: The United Nations Convention on Migrant Workers' Rights (CUP 2009) 1–44, 1.

[277] G. Battistella, 'Migration and Human Rights: The Uneasy but Essential Relationship' in R. Cholewinski, P. De Guchteneire, and A. Pécoud (eds.), *Migration and Human Rights: The United Nations Convention on Migrant Workers' Rights* (CUP 2009) 47–69, 57; V. Chetail, 'Human Rights of Migrants in General International Law' (2013) 28 *Georgetown Immigration Law Journal* 225, 237.

[278] See: https://indicators.ohchr.org/ (accessed on 7 February 2023).

[279] P. De Guchteneire and A. Pécoud, 'Introduction: The UN Convention on Migrant Workers' Rights' in R. Cholewinski, P. De Guchteneire, and A. Pécoud (eds.), *Migration and Human Rights: The United Nations Convention on Migrant Workers' Rights* (CUP 2009) 1–44, 13–14; G. Battistella, 'Migration and Human Rights: The Uneasy but Essential Relationship' in R. Cholewinski, P. De Guchteneire, and A. Pécoud (eds.), *Migration and Human Rights: The United Nations Convention on Migrant Workers' Rights* (CUP 2009) 47–69, 59.

[280] This lack of commitment towards the protection of migrants' rights from States from the Global North is also illustrated by the low number of ratifications and accessions of the aforementioned ILO Conventions 97 and 143, with fifty-three and twenty-eight Parties, respectively by the end of 2022. See: P. De Guchteneire and A. Pécoud, 'Introduction: The UN Convention on Migrant Workers' Rights' in R. Cholewinski, P. De Guchteneire, and A. Pécoud (eds.), *Migration and Human Rights: The United Nations Convention on Migrant Workers' Rights* (CUP 2009) 1–44, 12. See also: https://www.ilo.org/dyn/normlex/en/f?p=1000:11300:0::NO:11300:P11300_INSTRUMENT_ID:312242; https://www.ilo.org/dyn/normlex/en/f?p=NORMLEXPUB:11300:0::NO:11300:P11300_INSTRUMENT_ID:312288:NO (accessed on 7 February 2023).

[281] G. Battistella, 'Migration and Human Rights: The Uneasy but Essential Relationship' in R. Cholewinski, P. De Guchteneire, and A. Pécoud (eds.), *Migration and Human Rights: The United Nations Convention on Migrant Workers' Rights* (CUP 2009) 47–69, 58, 63; V. Chetail, 'The Committee on the Protection of the Rights of All Migrant Workers and Members of Their Families' in F. Mégret and P. Alston (eds.), *The United Nations and Human Rights: A Critical Appraisal* (2nd edn., OUP 2020) 601–644, 643.

supported by those States—or even on politically motivated fears as to how voters would perceive politicians' support for this treaty.

The Committee on the Protection of the Rights of All Migrant Workers and Members of their Families (CMW) is the monitoring body of ICRMW and was established in 2004 following the entry into force of the Convention. It was originally composed of ten independent experts, a number raised to fourteen after ICRMW reached forty-one States Parties.[282] As other committees, its main monitoring function is exercised through the examination of State periodic reports.[283] Nonetheless, following the practice of other committees, CMW also elaborates general comments to clarify the interpretation and scope of the provisions of ICRMW. Up to the end of 2022, CMW has produced five general comments, including a significant comment concerning migrant workers in an irregular situation—discussed later—and two general comments elaborated jointly with the Committee on the Rights of the Child.[284]

The Convention contemplates, as opt-in procedures, that CMW could receive both individual and inter-States communications.[285] However, for each of these mechanisms to enter into force, it is required for ten States Parties to make a declaration of their acceptance. Up to the end of 2021, only five States had accepted the Committee's competence to receive individual communications,[286] while merely four had recognised its jurisdiction for inter-State complaints.[287] Similar to other core human rights treaties, ICRMW also contemplates as a mechanism for international dispute settlement that States Parties could submit a dispute concerning the interpretation or application of the treaty to the ICJ if they fail to solve it by negotiation or arbitration. This procedure is established as an opt-out clause, requiring the State's declaration to not be subject to the mechanism at the time of ratifying or acceding to the Convention.[288]

A particularity of ICRMW is that it attributes specific consultative roles to the International Labour Organisation (ILO) with regard to the work of the Committee. The Convention establishes that the ILO's permanent secretariat—the International Labour Office—will be invited by CMW to appoint representatives to participate in the Committee's meetings in a consultative capacity.[289] Additionally, the ILO's permanent secretariat is tasked with providing comments on State periodic reports, to assist

---

[282] ICRMW, Art. 72.(b).   [283] ICRMW, Art. 74.

[284] CMW, General Comment No. 2: The rights of migrant workers in an irregular situation and members of their families, CMW/C/GC/2 (28 August 2013); CMW and CRC, Joint General Comment Nos. 3, 22: on the general principles regarding the human rights of children in the context of international migration, CRC/C/GC/22 – CMW/C/GC/3 (16 November 2017); CMW and CRC, Joint General Comment Nos. 4, 23: on State obligations regarding the human rights of children in the context of international migration in countries of origin, transit, destination and return, CMW/C/GC/4-CRC/C/GC/23 (16 November 2017).

[285] ICRMW, Arts. 76, 77.

[286] Ecuador, El Salvador, Guatemala, México, and Uruguay. See: Report of the Committee on the Protection of the Rights of All Migrant Workers and Members of Their Families, 33rd and 34th session (27 September–8 October 2021 and 28 March–8 April 2022), A/77/48, p. 20.

[287] Ecuador, El Salvador, Guatemala, and Guinea-Bissau. See: Report of the Committee on the Protection of the Rights of All Migrant Workers and Members of Their Families, 33rd and 34th session (27 September–8 October 2021 and 28 March–8 April 2022), A/77/48, p. 20.

[288] ICRMW, Art. 92.   [289] ICRMW, Art. 74.5.

CMW in their examination.[290] This collaborative approach among agencies adopted by ICRMW seems to be fruitful and constructive, with the Committee having expressed its appreciation for the support provided by the ILO to its work.[291]

> **CMW, *General Comment 2: on the rights of migrant workers in an irregular situation and members of their families*, CMW/C/GC/2 (28 August 2013).**
>
> In 2013, CMW produced its second general comment, which was on the rights of migrant workers in an irregular situation and of their family members. This general comment was of extreme significance as it came not only to clarify the minimum standard of protection that States Parties to ICRMW must afford to migrant workers who are undocumented or in an irregular situation, but also to challenge the stigmatizing use of the term 'illegal immigrant' that has been popularized by political discourse and the media.
>
> The comment started by providing some contextual information, such as the estimated number of migrants in an irregular situation being approximately 10 to 15 per cent of the total number of migrants worldwide, although acknowledging that reliable data might be difficult to gather given the very nature of the situation (para. 1). It also expressed concern about how States are increasingly resorting to repressive measures, including criminalization, administrative detentions, and expulsion, as frequent answers to the problem of irregular migration. In particular, the Committee highlighted that the criminalization of irregular migration promotes a public perception of migrant workers as 'illegal', second-class individuals, or unfair competitors for jobs and social benefits, fuelling anti-immigration rhetoric, discrimination, and xenophobia (para. 2). CMW asserted the rather important opinion that the use of the term 'illegal' to refer to migrant workers that are undocumented or in an irregular situation is inappropriate, as it stigmatizes individuals by associating them with criminality. The appropriate expressions to refer to migrants that lack of the authorization to enter and stay in a country or to engage in remunerated activity therein are 'non-documented' or 'in an irregular situation' (para. 4).
>
> The Committee expressed that Part III of ICRMW protects the rights of all migrant workers and the members of their family, irrespective of their situation, and that most of the rights provided therein are already protected in other human rights treaties, such as ICCPR and ICESCR, which guarantee such rights without discrimination (paras. 6 and 8). CMW was careful in clarifying that while the Convention provides minimum standards of rights protection, it does not entail an obligation upon States Parties to regularize the situation of migrant workers or their relatives, even if that is likely to be the most effective measure applicable to the situation (paras. 15 and 16). Then, the Committee focused on specific rights and the scope of their protection. This included the obligation upon States to protect migrant workers in an irregular situation from violence at the hands of both public and private actors (para. 21).
>
> Importantly, the Committee affirmed that irregularly crossing a State's border, or overstaying a stay permit, cannot constitute a crime, but could amount to an administrative offence. Linked to this, CMW argued that custodial measures against this type of offence should be

---

[290] ICRMW, Art. 74.2.
[291] V. Chetail, 'The Committee on the Protection of the Rights of All Migrant Workers and Members of their Families' in F. Mégret and P. Alston (eds.), *The United Nations and Human Rights: A Critical Appraisal* (2nd edn., OUP 2020) 601–644, 627–628.

used as a last resort and only applied when the circumstances of the particular case can justify such measures (paras. 24–27). When a custodial measure is adopted, the individual should be notified without delay of their right to consular assistance and the pertinent authorities notified of the detention (para. 30). Moreover, the conditions of detention must meet the minimum international standards, including adequate sanitary and shower facilities; adequate and appropriate food and drinking water; the right to communicate with relatives and friends; access to medical attention; and opportunities to practise one's faith (para. 36).

Migrants in an irregular situation should also be protected from arbitrary and collective expulsions. All cases for expulsion should be examined on their individual merits and include due procedural guarantees (including exercising the right to access consular protection), as well as a right to request a review by the competent authority (paras. 51, 53, and 59). If a decision of expulsion is adopted, the individual subject to it should be provided with the opportunity to settle any claims for due wages (para. 55). The costs of legal proceedings and detention should be afforded by the State, although under certain circumstances States can require the individual to pay for the costs of travel (para. 57).

The Committee also asserted that States Parties are under the obligation to provide migrant workers in an irregular situation with protection against labour exploitation. While the State can refuse access to the labour market, if an irregular employment relationship is established, undocumented migrant workers are entitled to fair and equal conditions of employment (para. 62).

Of extreme significance was the opinion rendered by CMW concerning access to both urgent medical care and education. As to the former, the Committee accepted that medical care need not necessarily be free, but it stated that the principle of equality imposes that the same rules for payment should apply to migrant workers (and their families) and to nationals, and that States are banned from either refusing attention to migrant workers in an irregular situation, or from charging them excessive fees, as well as from demanding immediate payment before attention is provided. In particular, CMW affirmed that health care providers cannot be made instruments of immigration control by requesting them to report individuals or share immigration status of patients to immigration authorities and that States Parties must not conduct immigration enforcement operations near medical care providers (paras. 73 and 74).

A similar assessment was made concerning the right to education. The Committee argued that States must provide free and compulsory primary education to the children of migrant workers, irrespective of their migration status, as well as access to secondary education in equal terms to those for children who are nationals. To guarantee the enjoyment of the right to education States Parties cannot require education institutions to report to, or share data on the migration status of pupils or their parents with, immigration authorities, nor conduct immigration enforcement operations near school premises (paras. 75 and 77).

5.11 COMMITTEE ON THE RIGHTS OF PERSONS WITH DISABILITIES (CRPD)

UNCRPD and its Optional Protocol (OPCRPD) were adopted by the General Assembly on 13 December 2006. Thus, UNCRPD became the first core human rights treaty adopted in the new millennium, coming to provide both recognition and protection under the international law of human rights to what has been labelled by the United Nations as the world's largest minority.[292] The Convention and its Protocol were the product of the four-year work of an Ad Hoc Committee established in 2002 by the UN General Assembly—at the initiative of México—for the specific purpose of elaborating a treaty to promote and protect the rights and dignity of persons with disabilities.[293] Although the official drafting process of these instruments took only four years, they were the fruit of nearly two decades of activism by individuals, NGOs, and governments.[294] The two treaties built on previous instruments adopted by the United Nations,[295] but came to fill the important legal gap left by the absence of binding norms concerning the protection of people with disabilities.[296]

Unlike ICERD or CEDAW, UNCRPD is not a convention that centres on the prohibition of discrimination and how it applies to disabilities. While containing strong provisions on the meaning and scope of the prohibition of discrimination,[297] UNCRPD follows more closely the model of UNCRC as a substantive treaty that articulates human rights obligations across civil, political, economic, social, and cultural rights,[298] blurring the dated distinction about categories of human rights.[299] Importantly, UNCRPD entailed a paradigm shift. It abandoned the outmoded medicalized and charitable approach to disabilities, embracing an understanding of persons with disabilities instead as true subjects of rights, active, and essential members of society who are capable of making autonomous decisions about their

---

[292] G. Quinn, 'A Short Guide to the United Nations Convention on the Rights of Persons with Disabilities' (2009) 1 *European Yearbook of Disability Law* 89, 89; A.S. Kanter, 'Do Human Rights Treaties Matter: The Case for the United Nations Convention on the Rights of People with Disabilities' (2019) 52 *Vanderbilt Journal of Transnational Law* 577, 594. See: UN Department of Economic and Social Affairs, 'Factsheet on Persons with Disabilities', available at: https://www.un.org/development/desa/disabilities/resources/factsheet-on-persons-with-disabilities.html (accessed on 5 April 2022).

[293] UNGA, 'Comprehensive and integral international convention to promote and protect the rights and dignity of persons with disabilities' A/RES/56/168 (19 December 2001).

[294] A.S. Kanter, 'The Promise and Challenge of the United Nations Convention on the Rights of Persons with Disabilities' (2007) 34 *Syracuse Journal of International Law and Commerce* 287, 288.

[295] These included: UNGA, Declaration on the Rights of Mentally Retarded Persons, A/RES/2856 (XXVI) (1971); UNGA, Declaration on the Rights of Disabled Person, A/RES/3447(XXX) (9 December 1975); UNGA, World Programme of Action concerning Disabled Persons, Resolution 37/52 (3 December 1982); Human Rights and Disabled Persons, Special Rapporteur Leandro Despouy, ST/HR(05)/H852/no.6 (1993); UNGA, Standard Rules on the Equalization of Opportunities for Persons with Disabilities Resolution 48/96 (20 December 1993).

[296] M.A. Stein and J.E. Lord, 'Future Prospects for the United Nations Convention on the Rights of Persons with Disabilities' in O.M., Arnardóttir and G. Quinn, (eds.) *The UN Convention on the Rights of Persons with Disabilities: European and Scandinavian Perspectives* (Brill 2009) 17–40, 22.

[297] A. Lawson, 'The United Nations Convention on the Rights of Persons with Disabilities: New Era or False Dawn' (2007) 34 *Syracuse Journal of International Law and Commerce* 563, 595–599; F. Mégret and D. Msipa, 'Global Reasonable Accommodation: How the Convention on the Rights of Persons with Disabilities Changes the Way We Think about Equality' (2014) 30 *South African Journal on Human Rights* 252.

[298] S. Tromel, 'A Personal Perspective on the Drafting History of the United Nations Convention on the Rights of Persons with Disabilities' (2009) 1 *European Yearbook of Disability Law* 115, 118; J.E. Lord and M.A. Stein, 'The Committee on the Rights of Persons with Disabilities' in F. Mégret and P. Alston (eds.), *The United Nations and Human Rights: A Critical Appraisal* (2nd edn., OUP 2020) 547–578, 550–551.

[299] G. de Beco, 'The Indivisibility of Human Rights and The Convention on the Rights of Persons with Disabilities' (2019) 68 *International and Comparative Law Quarterly* 140, 154, 159–160.

lives.[300] As stated in the Convention's preamble, a disability is not to be found in the person, but in the 'interaction between persons with impairments and attitudinal and environmental barriers that hinders their full and effective participation in society on an equal basis with others'.[301]

The Convention entered into force in 2008 and counted 186 Parties by the end of 2022,[302] which are not just limited to States, since UNCRPD is the first UN human rights treaty to be open to regional integration organizations.[303] While OPCRPD was adopted on the same date as UNCRPD, it has received the ratification or accession of only 103 States.[304] The Convention established CRPD, currently a body of eighteen independent experts,[305] tasked with monitoring compliance and implementation of UNCRPD by its Parties. The selection of the experts should not only take into account an equitable geographical distribution and the representation of the principal world's legal systems but also the existence of a balanced gender representation and the participation of experts with disabilities.[306] Even more, when nominating candidates, States Parties are expected to consult with, and actively involve, persons with disabilities and disability organizations.[307] As a result, over the years, the majority of the experts of CRPD have been people with disabilities, which challenged the shortcomings of the United Nations as seat of the Committee, since the organization proved to be sadly unprepared. The UN headquarters in New York and Geneva had to be made accessible for wheelchair use, websites had to be made accessible for visually impaired persons, sign language interpreters and captioning had to be provided, and travel rules had to be changed to allow for personal assistants.[308]

Under the text of the Convention, the main monitoring function of CRPD was to consist of the examination of State periodic reports.[309] Nevertheless, following the existing practice of other treaty bodies, the Committee was not to limit its recommendations to the concluding observations on State reports, but also has taken to elaborate general comments, to clarify the interpretation and scope of States' obligations under UNCRPD.[310] Up to the end of 2022, the Committee has produced eight general comments, covering different issues under UNCRPD, such as equality and non-discrimination,[311] women and girls with disabilities,[312] and the rights to inclusive

---

[300] A.S. Kanter, 'The Promise and Challenge of the United Nations Convention on the Rights of Persons with Disabilities' (2007) 34 *Syracuse Journal of International Law and Commerce* 287, 291; R. Kayess and P. French, 'Out of Darkness into Light—Introducing the Convention on the Rights of Persons with Disabilities' (2008) 8 *Human Rights Law Review* 1, 3–7.

[301] UNCRPD, preamble.   [302] See: https://indicators.ohchr.org/ (accessed on 7 February 2023).

[303] The European Union became a Party to UNCRPD in 2010.

[304] See: https://indicators.ohchr.org/ (accessed on 7 February 2023).

[305] The original number of Committee members was twelve, which was to be increased to eighteen after sixty accessions were received following the entry into force of the Convention. See: UNCRPD, Art. 34.2.

[306] UNCRPD, Art. 34.4.   [307] UNCRPD, Art. 34.3.

[308] T. Degener, '10 Years of Convention on the Rights of Persons with Disabilities' (2017) 35 *Netherlands Quarterly of Human Rights* 152, 153.

[309] UNCRPD, Arts. 35, 36.   [310] UNCRPD, Art. 39.

[311] CRPD, General Comment No. 1: Art. 12: Equal recognition before the law, CRPD/C/GC/1 (19 May 2014); CRPD, General Comment No. 6: on equality and non-discrimination, CRPD/C/GC/6 (26 April 2018).

[312] CRPD, General Comment No. 3: on Art. 6—women and girls with disabilities, CRPD/C/GC/3 (25 November 2016).

education and to independent living.[313] On its part, OPCRPD granted the Committee the power to receive and examine individual communications on alleged violations of the rights protected by UNCRPD against Parties to the Protocol, as well as to undertake inquiries, upon reception of reliable information indicating grave or systematic violations of the Convention—a procedure from which Parties can opt out at the time of ratification or accession.[314] Although the number of individual complaints received by the Committee has not been very high, CRPD has started to develop a rather interesting jurisprudence and is seemingly setting the grounds for an expansive interpretation of UNCRDP.[315]

Another distinctive aspect of UNCRPD, inspired by a similar feature included under OPCAT, is the obligation upon States Parties to have in place independent mechanisms to promote and monitor the implementation of the Convention at the domestic level. Civil society and, in particular, persons with disabilities and disability organizations should be involved and participate fully in this monitoring process.[316] However, unlike OPCAT, the Convention provided scarce details as to the characteristics and the functioning of the national mechanisms. The only guidance offered was an explicit reference to the Principles Relating to the Status and Functioning of National Institutions for Protection and Promotion of Human Rights ('Paris Principles').[317] Although UNCRPD does not mandate that National Human Rights Institutions (NHRIs) need to become themselves the domestic mechanisms for monitoring the implementation of the Convention,[318] it does provide that similar principles to those governing NHRIs should guide the establishment and operation of the mechanisms in place.[319] This is an important provision, as it helps delineate some essential functions the national mechanisms must perform. These include making recommendations to the government on the promotion of UNCRPD and the protection of the rights it enshrines; promoting the harmonization of domestic legislation and practices with the State's obligations under UNCRDP; and contributing to the State periodic reports to be submitted to CRPD.[320]

---

[313] CRPD, General Comment No. 4: on Art. 24—the right to inclusive education, CRPD/C/GC/4 (25 November 2016); CRPD, General Comment No. 5: on Art. 19—the right to live independently and be included in the community, CRPD/C/GC/5 (27 October 2017).

[314] OP-CRPD, Arts. 1, 6.

[315] See: I. Mgijima-Konopi, 'The Jurisprudence of the Committee on the Rights of Persons with Disabilities and Its Implications for Africa' (2016) 4 *African Disability Rights Yearbook* 269.

[316] UNCRDP, Art. 33.

[317] A. Bruce, 'Negotiating the Monitoring Mechanism for the Convention on the Rights of Persons with Disabilities: Two Steps Forward, One Step Back' in G. Alfredsson et al. (ed.), *International Human Rights Monitoring Mechanisms Essays in Honour of Jakob Th. Möller* (2nd edn., Nijhoff 2009) 133–148, 145–146.

[318] Nevertheless, the Committee's Rules of Procedure do encourage States to designate their NHRI as part of their monitoring mechanism. See: CRDP, Rules of Procedure, CRPD/C/1/Rev.1 (10 October 2016), Annex, para. 17.

[319] G. de Beco, 'Article 33(2) of the UN Convention on the Rights of Persons with Disabilities: Another Role for National Human Rights Institutions' (2011) 29 *Netherlands Quarterly of Human Rights* 84, 106.

[320] UNGA, Principles relating to the Status of National Institutions (The Paris Principles), Resolution 48/134 (20 December 1993).

> CRPD, *H.M. v. Sweden*, CRPD/C/7/D/3/2011 (19 April 2012).
>
> This was the first case decided by CRPD. The author of the communication was a Swedish national who had a chronic connective tissue disorder (Ehlers-Danlos Syndrome), which had led her strictly bedridden for two years, suffering from severe chronic pain. The only rehabilitation that could help her was hydrotherapy, which required the building of an indoor pool in her property. For that purpose, the author had required building permission to create an extension, which was rejected. After a series of judicial appeals, the denial of her request was final, as the authorities did not consider her situation merited making an exception to the 'development plan', to allow for the building of the extension.
>
> She complained before CRPD that the denial of her request amounted to a violation of a range of provisions under UNCRDP, in particular the prohibition of discrimination (Articles 3 and 5), the right to health (Article 25), and the State's obligations concerning rehabilitation (Article 26). The Committee agreed with the author's claims. It found that the author's health condition was critical and access to a hydrotherapy pool at home was essential, as it was the only effective means to meet her health needs. It noted that the State's legislation actually allowed for departures from the development plan in exceptional circumstances and considered that such an exception should have been made in this case to accommodate her request (para. 8.5). CRPD considered that the refusal to accommodate the author's health needs amounted to discrimination, as it entailed the denial of reasonable accommodation (para. 8.4). This had a discriminatory effect that adversely affected the author's access, as a person with disability, to the health care and rehabilitation required for her specific health condition. Therefore, the Committee concluded that the actions of the State amounted to the breach of Articles 5, 25, and 26 of the Convention, both alone and in conjunction with the State's general obligations under Articles 3 and 4 (para. 8.8).
>
> The Committee recommended Sweden to proceed to remedy the violation of the author's rights under UNCRPD, including by reconsidering her application for a building permit for a hydrotherapy pool (para. 9.1). It also stated that the State was under the obligation to take steps to prevent similar violations in the future, by ensuring its legislation to be applied consistently with the obligations under UNCRPD (para. 9.2).

5.12 COMMITTEE ON ENFORCED DISAPPEARANCES (CED)

ICPPED was adopted by the UN General Assembly on 20 December 2006, merely a week after the adoption of UNCRPD and OPCRPD. While the official drafting history of ICPPED is rather short, the struggle to achieve a universal and comprehensive binding framework to deal with the heinous crime of forced disappearances was actually much lengthier. The impetus for the elaboration of international binding norms could be traced back to the early 1980s with activists, NGOs, and family members of disappeared individuals working towards the adoption of such norms, both at the international and regional levels.[321] The unyielding efforts of these groups produced some earlier results towards the end of the decade, with the OAS General Assembly requesting the Inter-American Commission of Human Rights to elaborate a draft convention in 1987 and with the UN Sub-commission on Prevention of Discrimination and Protection of Minorities engaging in the debate of a draft declaration on 'unrecognized detentions' during the second half of the 1980s.[322] While the latter was ultimately not further pursued, the OAS draft convention was much more successful. First, it was used as the basis for the discussion of a universal instrument, which became the UN Declaration on the Protection of All Persons from Enforced Disappearance, adopted by the General Assembly on 18 December 1992.[323] Moreover, it managed to obtain the required regional support to become the 1994 Inter-American Convention on the Forced Disappearance of Persons, which is further discussed in **Section 6.1.5**.

Following the adoption of the 1992 UN Declaration, discussions began within the UN and beyond as to the need for a universal binding instrument. A sessional working group (on the administration of justice) of the UN Sub-commission on Prevention of Discrimination and Protection of Minorities, chaired by Louis Joinet, adopted a draft convention in 1998, which was transmitted to the UN Commission on Human Rights for its consideration.[324] For two years, the draft was circulated for comments among States, but no serious consensus for the adoption of a convention seemed to exist at the time.[325] In 2001, the Commission on Human Rights took two important steps towards it: first, it established a working group to elaborate a legally binding instrument on forced disappearances; and, second, it appointed an independent expert to evaluate the international legal framework for the protection of persons from enforced disappearance, and to identify whether relevant gaps existed.[326] Manfred Nowak, the appointed expert, produced a report which affirmed that there were many gaps, disputed questions, and uncertainties in the existent international framework, including the absence of a universally agreed-upon definition of the crime of forced disappearance and of concrete international obligations concerning preventive measures and effective

---

[321] W. Tayler, 'Background to the Elaboration of the Draft International Convention for the Protection of All Persons from Forced Disappearance' (2001) 62–3 *International Commission of Jurists: The Review* 63, 65.

[322] W. Tayler, 'Background to the Elaboration of the Draft International Convention for the Protection of All Persons from Forced Disappearance' (2001) 62–3 *International Commission of Jurists: The Review* 63, 66–67.

[323] W. Tayler, 'Background to the Elaboration of the Draft International Convention for the Protection of All Persons from Forced Disappearance' (2001) 62–3 *International Commission of Jurists: The Review* 63, 67.

[324] Report of the sessional working group on the administration of justice, E/CN.4/Sub.2/1998/19 (19 August 1998); Sub-Commission on Prevention of Discrimination and Protection of Minorities, Resolution 1998/25 (26 August 1998).

[325] S. McCrory, 'International Convention for the Protection of All Persons from Enforced Disappearance' (2007) 7 *Human Rights Law Review* 545, 548; O. de Frouville, 'The Committee on Enforced Disappearances' in F. Mégret and P. Alston (eds.), *The United Nations and Human Rights: A Critical Appraisal* (2nd edn., OUP 2020) 579–599, 580–581.

[326] O. de Frouville, 'The Committee on Enforced Disappearances' in F. Mégret and P. Alston (eds.), *The United Nations and Human Rights: A Critical Appraisal* (2nd edn., OUP 2020) 579–599, 581.

remedies.[327] He proposed that a binding instrument should be adopted to remedy the reported shortcomings, but that this instrument could take different forms, from that of a new convention to that of an optional protocol to either ICCPR or UNCAT.[328] Following the recommendations from Nowak's report, the working group created in 2001 finally met for the first time in 2003. Between 2003 and 2005, the group drafted the text of a convention, which led to its adoption in 2006, first by the recently created HRC and then by the General Assembly.[329] ICPPED entered into force 23 December 2010, after receiving its twentieth ratification. With the accession of South Korea in January 2023, it has reached seventy States Parties.[330]

The Convention came to fill the gaps identified by the independent expert. First, it provided a clear definition of 'enforced disappearance' as follows:

> [the] arrest, detention, abduction or any other form of deprivation of liberty by agents of the State or by persons or groups of persons acting with the authorization, support or acquiescence of the State, followed by a refusal to acknowledge the deprivation of liberty or by concealment of the fate or whereabouts of the disappeared person, which place such a person outside the protection of the law.[331]

Moreover, the Convention set in place the needed comprehensive legal framework, imposing upon States Parties obligations with regards to prevention, reparations, and individual criminal responsibility.[332] With the entry into force of ICPPED, the practice of forced disappearance was undoubtedly established under the international law of human rights as an international crime whose prohibition is of an absolute character, belonging to the realm of *jus cogens*.

The establishment of a new treaty body to monitor compliance with ICPPED was a contentious topic during the negotiation of the Convention. On the one hand, potential conflicts with the existing Working Group on Enforced or Involuntary Disappearances, created by the Commission on Human Rights (as discussed in **Section 4.3.3**), were raised. These concerns were mostly dispersed, as the new Committee would lack universal reach unless such a level of ratification or accession to ICPPED was achieved, while the competence of both bodies would differ, with the Working Group having a

---

[327] Report submitted by Mr Manfred Nowak, independent expert charged with examining the existing international criminal and human rights framework for the protection of persons from enforced or involuntary disappearances, E/CN.4/2002/71 (8 January 2002), para. 96.

[328] Report submitted by Mr Manfred Nowak, independent expert charged with examining the existing international criminal and human rights framework for the protection of persons from enforced or involuntary disappearances, E/CN.4/2002/71 (8 January 2002), paras. 97–102.

[329] K. Anderson, 'How Effective Is the International Convention for the Protection of All Persons from Enforced Disappearance Likely to Be in Holding Individuals Criminally Responsible for Acts of Enforced Disappearance' (2006) 7 *Melbourne Journal of International Law* 245, 266; S. McCrory, 'International Convention for the Protection of All Persons from Enforced Disappearance' (2007) 7 *Human Rights Law Review* 545, 548.

[330] See: https://indicators.ohchr.org/ (accessed on 7 February 2023).

[331] ICPPED, Art. 2.

[332] N. Kyriakou, 'The International Convention for the Protection of All Persons from Enforced Disappearance and Its Contributions to International Human Rights Law, With Specific Reference to Extraordinary Rendition' (2012) 13 *Melbourne Journal of International Law* 424, 450.

more humanitarian mandate. Second, the proliferation of treaty bodies was already a concern for many actors, some of which were lobbying for their unification into one main organ, as discussed in **Section 5.13**. A compromise was reached by including a 'sunset clause' within ICPPED.[333] Article 27 stipulated that between four and six years following the entry into force of the Convention, a Conference of the States Parties would evaluate the functioning of the Committee and decide whether to transfer the monitoring of ICPPED onto another body.

The Committee on Enforced Disappearances (CED) was established in 2011 as a body composed of ten independent experts—the same number of members as CAT—and, in December 2016, the aforementioned Conference of States Parties decided that CED was to continue monitoring compliance with ICPPED.[334] Like other Committees, CED has the power to evaluate State periodic reports,[335] as well as to elaborate general comments on the interpretation of ICPPED.[336] By the end of 2022, CED was in the process of adopting its first general comment, but it had already issued short 'substantive statements', clarifying certain aspects of States' obligations assumed under ICPPED.[337] The Convention also provides for (opt-in) mechanisms for both individual and inter-State communications. However, as indicated in CED's 2022 Annual Report, only twenty-six States Parties to the Convention had recognized the Committee's competence to receive and consider either individual or inter-State communications.[338] Up to the end of 2022, CED had only adopted views on two cases.[339]

Furthermore, following the precedent established by other treaties, CED was also empowered with the ability to undertake inquiries, allowing it to conduct visits to States Parties, with the consent of the State, when it receives reliable information indicating serious violations of the Convention.[340] The inquiries procedure also works on the basis of States Parties' acceptance of the Committee's competence, with sixty-four of them having made such a declaration by February 2023.[341] The inquiries procedure under ICCPED seems to present some particularities, compared to its regulation under other

---

[333] O. de Frouville, 'The Committee on Enforced Disappearances' in F. Mégret and P. Alston (eds.), *The United Nations and Human Rights: A Critical Appraisal* (2nd edn., OUP 2020) 579–599, 583–585.

[334] Report of the Conference of the States Parties to the International Convention for the Protection of All Persons from Enforced Disappearance on its first session, CED/CSP/2016/4 (18 January 2017).

[335] ICPPED, Art. 29.

[336] CED, Rules of Procedure, CED/C/1 (22 June 2012), r. 56.

[337] CED, Statement on Enforced Disappearance and Military Jurisdiction (13 February 2015); CED, Statement on the *ratione temporis* element in the review of reports submitted by States Parties under the International Convention for the Protection of All Persons from Enforced Disappearance (13 November 2013).

[338] CED, Report of the Committee on Enforced Disappearances, 21st session (13–24 September 2021), 22nd session (28 March–8 April 2022), A/77/56, para. 1.

[339] CED, *Yrusta v. Argentina*, CED/C/10/D/1/2013 (11 March 2016); CED, *E.L.A. v. France*, CED/C/19/D/3/2019 (25 September 2020).

[340] ICPPED, Art. 33.

[341] R. Sunga II, 'The Committee on Enforced Disappearances and Its Monitoring Procedures' (2012) 17 *Deakin Law Review* 151, 175–176; O. de Frouville, 'The Committee on Enforced Disappearances' in F. Mégret and P. Alston (eds.), *The United Nations and Human Rights: A Critical Appraisal* (2nd edn., OUP 2020) 579–599, 598.

treaties. First, the procedure has not been characterized as confidential under ICPPED. Second, the threshold for CED to undertake inquiries appears to be lower than for other committees, not requiring the existence of a 'systematic' practice of the crime.[342]

In line with the practice developed by CERD, ICPPED explicitly contemplates an 'urgent action' procedure. This enables CED to request of States Parties that a disappeared person should be sought and found as a matter of urgency if it receives reliable information of their disappearance from the person's relatives or legal representative or any other individual having a legitimate interest. The admissibility requirements for such a request are much less burdensome than for an individual complaint and still allow the Committee to issue recommendations to the State Party, including the urgent adoption of measures to locate and protect the person concerned.[343]

Lastly, ICPPED has also been endowed with an additional mechanism: a referral procedure. This empowers the Committee to urgently bring to the attention of the UN General Assembly, through the Secretary-General, the existence of a situation in which enforced disappearance is being practised on a widespread or systematic basis in the territory under the jurisdiction of a State Party, after seeking from the respective State all relevant information on the situation.[344] Such a mechanism is absent under any of the other core human rights instruments, but resembles the ability of States Parties conferred by other human rights treaties, such as the 1948 Genocide Convention and the 1973 Apartheid Convention.[345]

CED, *Yrusta v. Argentina*, CED/C/10/D/1/2013 (11 March 2016).

This was the first case decided by CED. The authors of the communication were the sisters of an inmate who was disappeared while in prison. They claimed the violation of multiple provisions under ICPPED, both against their brother and on their behalf.

The case concerned Mr Yrusta, who was serving a custodial sentence for aggravated robbery in prison in the province of Córdoba (Argentina), where he claimed to have been subjected to torture and ill-treatment. He requested a transfer to a prison in a different province (Santiago del Estero) to be close to relatives, but was transferred instead to a different prison in another province (Santa Fé). At arrival, he was placed in isolation in punishment cells and information

---

[342] Compare Art. 33 of ICCPED to the equivalent provision in UNCAT (Art. 20), OP-CEDAW (Art. 8), OPCRPD (Art. 6) and OP-ICESCR (Art. 11). See: R. Sunga II, 'The Committee on Enforced Disappearances and Its Monitoring Procedures' (2012) 17 *Deakin Law Review* 151, 173; O. de Frouville, 'The Committee on Enforced Disappearances' in F. Mégret and P. Alston (eds.), *The United Nations and Human Rights: A Critical Appraisal* (2nd edn., OUP 2020) 579–599, 594–595.

[343] CED, Art. 30.   [344] CED, Art. 34.

[345] Convention on the Prevention and Punishment of the Crime of Genocide (adopted on 9 December 1948, entered into force 12 January 1951), 78 UNTS 277, Art. VIII; International Convention on the Suppression and Punishment of the Crime of Apartheid (adopted on 30 November 1973, entered into force 18 July 1976), 1015 UNTS 243, Art. VIII.

of his whereabouts was denied to his family members on a number of occasions. This situation lasted over seven days and constituted the factual grounds for the violations claimed in the case. Nevertheless, four months before he was due for release on parole, the prison service staff notified the family that Mr Yrusta had committed suicide in his cell.

The Committee found that Mr Yrusta had been subjected to enforced disappearance during the period in which he could not communicate with his family, given that the authorities refused to acknowledge and inform whether he had been transferred, despite the requests from his relatives (para. 10.4). As affirmed by CED, an enforced disappearance does not need to begin as an illegal detention, but could commence as lawful imprisonment and take place in an official prison. Neither does it have a minimum temporal requirement (paras. 10.2–10.3).

According to CED, the situation gave rise to multiple violations of ICPPED, both against Mr Yrusta and his sisters, including the prohibition on being held in secret detention (Article 17) and the obligation to provide information of a person's whereabouts to their relatives (Articles 18 and 20). Consequently, CED recommended the State, among other measures of reparation, to recognize the authors' status as victims, allowing them to play an effective part in the investigations into the death and enforced disappearance of their brother; to ensure that the investigation into the case was not confined to Mr Yrusta's death, but also includes an impartial investigation of his disappearance; to prosecute, judge, and punish the persons responsible for the violations that had been committed; and to provide the authors with adequate compensation (para. 12).

5.13 FURTHER REFLECTIONS: IMPROVING THE TREATY BODY SYSTEM

Discussions within the United Nations about the need to improve the treaty body system can already be found shortly after the creation of the first committees in the 1970s and continue into our days. Over the years, the growth in the number of core human rights treaties and the number of States Parties to each treaty meant that both States and treaty bodies experienced an increasing burden on their respective obligations, which also translated into an increased financial burden on the United Nations itself.[346] The problems faced by States regarding their reporting duties and by treaty bodies concerning their limited human and financial resources to undertake their supervisory role have been a concern for a range of UN bodies for decades.[347]

---

[346] H. Keller and G. Ulfstein, 'Conclusions' in H. Keller and G. Ulfstein (eds.), *UN Human Rights Treaty Bodies: Law and Legitimacy* (CUP 2012) 414–425, 418.

[347] See, among many: Report of Meeting of Chairpersons, A/39/484 (20 September 1984); UNGA, Reporting obligations under the United Nations instruments on human rights, Resolution 41/121 (4 December 1986); UNGA, Reporting obligations of States parties to United Nations instruments on human rights, Resolution 42/105 (7 December 1987); CHR, 'Effective functioning of bodies established pursuant to United Nations human rights instruments', Resolution 1989/47, E/CN.4/RES/1989/47 (6 March 1989).

In 1989,[348] a report by Philip Alston, commissioned by the UN Secretary-General, highlighted, among different issues, the importance of increasing the committees' budget and their meeting time, as well as of rationalizing the treaty body system, including the harmonization of working procedures and normative standards across committees.[349] Subsequently updated, the report reiterated some of the relevant difficulties, including the chronic delinquency of States in their reporting obligations, which was characterized (ironically) as a contributing factor to making the committees' workload manageable, given that they were understaffed, underfinanced, and lacked the needed meeting time to fulfil all their duties.[350] The state of affairs was described as unsustainable, calling for systemic solutions to rationalize the treaty body system, such as increased human and budgetary resources, as well as the re-thinking of the periodic reporting procedure.[351] Alston's reports also raised the critical question of the reduction in the number of treaty bodies; a topic that would continue to be discussed throughout the years.[352]

The need to streamline and harmonize procedures among treaty bodies was highlighted by the UN Secretary-General in its comprehensive review of the work of the UN in the late 1990s and early 2000s. In a 2002 Report, the Secretary-General suggested two measures to help solve the existing shortcomings: a more coordinated work of the committees, including the standardization of reporting requirements, and the possibility of States producing a unified report for all committees.[353] The Secretary-General's call was (partly) followed by the treaty bodies, which in 2006 adopted harmonized guidelines on State-reporting for all committees, including clear guidelines as to the content of a common core document and treaty-specific documents.[354]

---

[348] At the time, there were already five treaty bodies, in addition to the discontinued Special Committee on Apartheid. See: S. Egan, 'Transforming the UN Human Rights Treaty System: A Realistic Appraisal' (2020) 42 *Human Rights Quarterly* 762, 765; International Convention on the Suppression and Punishment of the Crime of Apartheid (adopted 30 November 1973, entered into force 18 July 1976) 1015 UNTS 243, Arts. VII, IX.

[349] UN Secretary-General, Effective implementation of international instruments on human rights, including reporting obligations under international instruments on human rights', A/44/668 (8 November 1989).

[350] Interim report on updated study by Philip Alston, A/CONF.157/PC/62/Add.11/Rev.1 (22 April 1993), paras. 13–14.

[351] Interim report on updated study by Philip Alston, A/CONF.157/PC/62/Add.11/Rev.1 (22 April 1993); Final report on enhancing the long-term effectiveness of the United Nations human rights treaty system, E/CN.4/1997/74 (27 March 1997).

[352] UN Secretary-General, Effective implementation of international instruments on human rights, including reporting obligations under international instruments on human rights', A/44/668 (8 November 1989), paras. 179–183; Final report on enhancing the long-term effectiveness of the United Nations human rights treaty system, E/CN.4/1997/74 (27 March 1997), para. 94.

[353] UN Secretary-General, 'Strengthening of the United Nations: An Agenda for Further Change', A/57/38 (9 September 2002), para. 54. The Secretary-General's call for a unified report was reiterated in its 2005 Report, see: Secretary-General, 'In Larger Freedom: Towards Development, Security and Human Rights for All', A/59/2005 (21 March 2005), para. 147.

[354] Report of the Inter-Committee Technical Working Group, Harmonized guidelines on reporting under the international human rights treaties, including guidelines on a common core document and treaty-specific documents, HRI/MC/2006/3 (10 May 2006).

Also in 2006, the High Commissioner for Human Rights, Louis Arbour, elaborated a proposal for the consolidation of the (then seven) committees into one unified standing treaty body.[355] The proposal emphasized the shortcomings of the system, including the 'steep increase in the workload of the treaty bodies and the Secretariat, backlogs in the consideration of reports and individual complaints, and increasing resource requirements', within a context in which 'treaty bodies have been under-resourced, and their meeting time has been insufficient to handle their workload'.[356] This situation was expected to worsen, as the mechanisms for individual complaints remained underutilized, with their increased use potentially leading to further delays in the processing of complaints—which were already averaging over thirty months.[357] Ultimately, the idea to consolidate the different treaty bodies into one main committee did not succeed.[358] The project itself was subject to different objections,[359] to which could be added that the political will require to overcome the legal complexities to set such a mechanism in place, with amendments to different treaties or the adoption of an overarching procedural protocol,[360] made it seem unviable.[361]

In 2009, the incoming High Commissioner for Human Rights, Navanethem Pillay, opted for a different approach to the reform of the treaty body system. It began with undertaking extensive consultations with relevant stakeholders, including States Parties, committee experts, NGOs, and national human rights institutions.[362] The outcome of this process was a report published in 2012, which made several concrete proposals for strengthening the treaty body system. Many of these proposals were focused on the State-reporting procedure, such as the creation of a coordinated calendar of reports in a five-year cycle, limiting the number of State reports to a maximum of two per year;

---

[355] The idea was already foreshadowed in her 2005 Plan of action. See: 'Plan of action submitted by the United Nations High Commissioner for Human Rights', A/59/2005/Add.3 (26 May 2005).

[356] Concept Paper on the High Commissioner's Proposal for a Unified Standing Treaty Body, HRI/MC/2006/2 (22 March 2006), para. 18.

[357] Concept Paper on the High Commissioner's Proposal for a Unified Standing Treaty Body, HRI/MC/2006/2 (22 March 2006), para. 18.

[358] Nonetheless, the idea of reducing the number of treaty bodies has continued to be raised, such as at the time of the adoption of ICPPED and OP-ICESCR. See: M. Scheinin, 'The Proposed Optional Protocol to the Covenant on Economic, Social and Cultural Rights: A Blueprint for UN Human Rights Treaty Body Reform—Without Amending the Existing Treaties' (2006) 6 *Human Rights Law Review* 131; O. de Frouville, 'The Committee on Enforced Disappearances' in F. Mégret and P. Alston (eds.), *The United Nations and Human Rights: A Critical Appraisal* (2nd edn., OUP 2020) 579–599.

[359] F.J. Hampson, 'An Overview of the Reform of the UN Human Rights Machinery' (2007) 7 *Human Rights Law Review* 7, 12–14; M. O'Flaherty and C. O'Brien, 'Reform of UN Human Rights Treaty Monitoring Bodies: A Critique of the Concept Paper on the High Commissioner's Proposal for a Unified Standing Treaty Body' (2007) 7 *Human Rights Law Review* 141, 165–172.

[360] Concept Paper on the High Commissioner's Proposal for a Unified Standing Treaty Body, HRI/MC/2006/2 (22 March 2006), para. 64.

[361] For an analysis on the needed legal reform and its complexities, see: M. Bowman, 'Towards a Unified Treaty Body for Monitoring Compliance with UN Human Rights Conventions? Legal Mechanisms for Treaty Reform' (2007) 7 *Human Rights Law Review* 225.

[362] S. Egan, 'Strengthening the United Nations Human Rights Treaty Body System' (2013) 13 *Human Rights Law Review* 209, 210, 213.

the imposition of strict lengths for the reports; the use of CAT's 'simplified reporting procedure' by all committees; and the adoption of an aligned methodology for the constructive dialogue between committees and States.[363] Further proposals focused on other aspects of the treaty body system, including some dealing with the selection process for committee members, to ensure their independence and expertise, and others concerning individual communications.[364]

Shortly before the publication of the High Commissioner's 2012 Report, the General Assembly, at the initiative of the Russian Federation and a group of 'like-minded' States,[365] adopted a resolution launching an inter-governmental negotiation process on 'how to strengthen and enhance the effective functioning of the human rights treaty body system'.[366] The process was concluded in 2014 with a resolution from the General Assembly that endorsed only some of the proposals made by the High Commissioner's Report.[367] It was this resolution that established the formula to be used to determine the meeting time for each committee, and the corresponding financial and human resources for conducting such meetings, discussed in **Section 5.3**.[368] The General Assembly tasked the Secretary-General with reporting on the implementation of the 2014 resolution on a biennial basis, setting a review of the state of the treaty bodies to take place no later than in 2020.[369]

In April 2020, the General Assembly appointed two co-facilitators to lead the process of consideration of the state of the treaty body system, which led to the elaboration of a report that supported the adoption of many of the proposals under discussion since 2012, such as the streamlining and harmonization of the committees' working methods; the implementation of a coordinated fixed calendar for State-reporting; further use of the simplified reporting procedure; the adoption of an aligned methodology for the constructive dialogue with States; and an improved selection process for committee experts.[370] The report was well-received by the

---

[363] N. Pillay, 'Strengthening the United Nations human rights treaty body system: A report by the United Nations High Commissioner for Human Rights' (June 2012) 37–57.

[364] N. Pillay, 'Strengthening the United Nations human rights treaty body system: A report by the United Nations High Commissioner for Human Rights' (June 2012).

[365] C. Broecker and M. O'Flaherty, 'The Outcome of the General Assembly's Treaty Body Strengthening Process: An Important Milestone on a Longer Journey' (June 2014), p. 14; S. Egan, 'Reform of the UN Human Rights Treaty Body System' in F. Mégret and P. Alston (eds.), *The United Nations and Human Rights: A Critical Appraisal* (2nd edn., OUP 2020) 645–664, 657.

[366] UNGA, 'Intergovernmental process of the General Assembly on strengthening and enhancing the effective functioning of the human rights treaty body system', A/RES/66/295 (12 February 2012).

[367] UNGA, 'Strengthening and enhancing the effective functioning of the human rights treaty body system', A/RES/68/268 (21 April 2014), paras. 1–3, 5–6, 10, 13, 15–16, 35.

[368] UNGA, 'Strengthening and enhancing the effective functioning of the human rights treaty body system', A/RES/68/268 (21 April 2014), paras. 26–28.

[369] UNGA, 'Strengthening and enhancing the effective functioning of the human rights treaty body system', A/RES/68/268 (21 April 2014), paras. 40–41. See also: Secretary General, 'Status of the human rights treaty body system', A/71/118 (18 July 2016); Secretary General, 'Status of the human rights treaty body system', A/73/309 (6 August 2018); A/73/309.

[370] Report on the process of the consideration of the state of the United Nations human rights treaty body system, A/75/601 (17 November 2020).

General Assembly, which requested all stakeholders to continue working towards the implementation of its 2014 resolution and the Secretary-General to continue to report on implementation on a biennial basis.[371]

5.13.1 CRITICAL DEBATES: A WORLD HUMAN RIGHTS COURT?

The idea of creating a world human rights court with the power to adjudicate disputes brought by individuals against States is not a novel one. It had been proposed by Australia in February 1947, when the UN Commission on Human Rights was debating potential mechanisms for the implementation of human rights—a topic discussed in **Section 2.2.1**.[372] However, the political will to create such a court was clearly absent at the time.[373] Over the years, the idea to establish a universal human rights court resurged from time to time,[374] but it was in the new millennium that it managed to gain further momentum.[375]

At the sixtieth anniversary of the adoption of the Universal Declaration of Human Rights, the Swiss government sponsored an initiative called 'Protecting Dignity', aimed at setting an agenda of targets to be achieved concerning human rights. A convened panel of experts selected the creation of a world court of human rights as one of the agenda items.[376] Manfred Nowak, a member of the panel and one of the strongest supporters of the creation of a world court, took a leading role on the initiative.[377] In collaboration with Julia Kozma, the panel drafted a proposal for the creation of a world court; a task also undertaken by Martin Scheinin.[378] Following the elaboration of both drafts, the Swiss-sponsored panel requested their consolidation into one document, which was published in 2010.[379]

---

[371] UNGA, 'Human rights treaty body system', A/RES/75/174 (28 December 2020).

[372] Draft Resolution for an International Court of Human Rights, E/CN.4/15 (5 February 1947).

[373] International Commission of Jurists, 'Towards a world court of human rights: questions and answers' (December 2011), pp. 3–4.

[374] A.J. Goldberg, 'The Need for a World Court of Human Rights' (1965) 11 *Howard Law Journal* 621; W. Weinstein, 'Africa's Approach to Human Rights at the United Nations' (1976) 6 *Issue: A Quarterly Journal of Africanist Opinion* 14, 15. See: Final Act of the International Conference on Human Rights (1968), Haiti: draft resolution, Annex V, p. 46 (A/CONF.32/L.14 and Corr.1).

[375] J. Morsink, *The Universal Declaration of Human Rights: Origins, Drafting, and Intent* (University of Pennsylvania Press 1999) 15–16; International Commission of Jurists, 'Towards a world court of human rights: questions and answers' (December 2011), pp. 3–4.

[376] M. Robinson, P. Pinheiro et al., 'Protecting Dignity: An Agenda for Human Rights' (2011).

[377] M. Nowak, 'The Need for a World Court of Human Rights' (2007) 7 *Human Rights Law Review* 251; M. Nowak, 'Eight Reasons Why We Need a World Court of Human Rights' in G. Alfredsson et al. (ed.), *International Human Rights Monitoring Mechanisms Essays in Honour of Jakob Th. Möller* (2nd edn., Nijhoff 2009) 697–706.

[378] M. Scheinin, 'International Organizations and Transnational Corporations at a World Court of Human Rights' (2012) 3 *Global Policy* 488, 489; M. Nowak, 'The Right of Victims of Human Rights Violations to a Remedy: The Need for a World Court of Human Rights' (2014) 32 *Nordic Journal of Human Rights* 3, 11.

[379] J. Kozma, M. Nowak, and M. Scheinin, 'A World Court of Human Rights: Consolidated Draft Statute and Commentary' (May 2010). Available at: https://www.eui.eu/Documents/DepartmentsCentres/Law/Professors/Scheinin/ConsolidatedWorldCourtStatute.pdf (accessed on 2 February 2022).

The proposed world court could be created without the legal complexities surrounding the unification of treaty bodies, not requiring the amendment of existing treaties but the drafting of a new one. The proposed court would have material jurisdiction over all core human rights treaties and their protocols, although allowing States accepting the court's jurisdiction to restrict such a wide substantive scope. Moreover, the proposed court would not only have personal jurisdiction over States, but inter-governmental organizations, transnational corporations, and other 'entities' would also be allowed to voluntarily subject themselves to the court's jurisdiction.[380]

Nevertheless, the idea of a world human rights court has not been free from antagonism.[381] One of the most notable voices raised against it has been that of Philip Alston. He opined that not only might the creation of a world court be untimely and politically and economically unfeasible, but the 'very idea fundamentally misconceives the nature of the challenges confronting an international community dedicated to eliminating major human rights violations.'[382] Alston questioned the belief that a selected group of judges could offer hope to resolving complex and continued serious human rights violations, arguing that this might actually detract both attention and resources from more pressing and fundamental issues.[383]

That the creation of a world court of human rights has the potential to positively impact the international protection of human rights seems a safe assumption to make. What is certainly a matter for academic and political debate is whether the establishment of a world court would be the wisest way to allocate resources, bearing in mind the existence of multiple serious human rights violations that ensue on a daily basis. However, what can be affirmed is that the current political context makes the prospect of creating such a court unfeasible, at least in the foreseeable future.

5.14 CONCLUSION

By the end of 2022, all UN Members were Parties to at least two core human rights treaties and their protocols, with only 10 of the 193 Members having ratified or acceded to fewer than six.[384] The UN human rights treaty system, nowadays comprising ten treaty bodies—nine committees and one sub-committee—created by the core human rights treaties and their optional protocols, is considered one of the United Nations'

---

[380] M. Nowak, 'The Need for a World Court of Human Rights' (2007) 7 *Human Rights Law Review* 251, 255–256; M. Scheinin, 'International Organizations and Transnational Corporations at a World Court of Human Rights' (2012) 3 *Global Policy* 488, 489.

[381] S. Trechsel, 'A World Court for Human Rights?' (2003) 1 *Northwestern University Journal of International Human Rights* 1, 19; P. Alston, 'Against a World Court for Human Rights' (2014) 28 *Ethics & International Affairs* 197; F.D. Gaer, 'The Institutional Future of the Covenants: A World Court for Human Rights?' in D. Moeckli and H. Keller (eds), *The Human Rights Covenants: Their Past, Present, and Future* (OUP 2018) 334–356, 354–355.

[382] P. Alston, 'Against a World Court for Human Rights' (2014) 28 *Ethics & International Affairs* 197, 197, 205.

[383] P. Alston, 'Against a World Court for Human Rights' (2014) 28 *Ethics & International Affairs* 197, 206, 211.

[384] These are: Tonga (2), Tuvalu and Palau (3), Bhutan (4), Brunei Darussalam, Malaysia, Micronesia, Nauru, Singapore, and the USA (5).

biggest achievements. Over the years, the work of the treaty bodies has managed to have a direct impact in improving the protection of the human rights of individuals, both by shaping the domestic law and policy of States, and by providing redress for individual victims of violations.[385]

Nevertheless, the system is in need of improvement, as has been discussed throughout most of its history. Among the many proposals discussed in the past few years, the one aimed at rationalizing State-reporting obligations for the benefit of both States and monitoring bodies and the one highlighting the need to secure that committee members have the right level of independence and expertise appear as two of the most pressing. With regard to reporting obligations, the treaties themselves vary as to the required timing of these reports, but after the initial report, the usual minimum timeframe for the submission of periodic reports is that of four years,[386] subject to the decision of the respective treaty body.[387] These treaty requirements allow for the adoption of a uniform reporting calendar across committees, as proposed in 2012 by the OHCHR, which could be based on a five-year cycle with a maximum of two reports per annum for States Parties to all core treaties.[388] This would be a relatively low-cost reform, which could have a significant impact on the efficiency of the whole treaty body system.[389]

As to strengthening the selection process of candidates for the committees, that is a measure that remains in the hands of States Parties and their willingness to listen to civil society organizations. The authority that treaty bodies command is contingent on the level of actual and perceived expertise and impartiality of their members.[390] On the one hand, States should avoid selecting candidates whose independence and impartiality could be seen as compromised by their political proximity to the executive branch of the State.[391] On the other hand, States could easily adopt competitive national selection procedures that allow for public scrutiny of potential candidates and which could help secure that independence and expertise become the main criteria for the selection of candidates to sit at the committees. This would also be a rather low-cost measure, which could lead to an improved protection of human rights worldwide.

---

[385] Secretary-General, 'In Larger Freedom: Towards Development, Security and Human Rights for All', A/59/2005 (21 March 2005), para. 95. See also: G. de Burca, 'Human Rights Experimentalism' (2017) 111 *American Journal of International Law* 277, 303–304.

[386] ICERD is the only treaty that establishes a periodicity of two years, but CERD has allowed for merging two reports into one, turning the prescribed periodicity into that of four years. See: ICERD, Art. 9.1.b.

[387] ICCPR, Arts. 40.1.a–b.; ICESCR, Art. 16; UNCAT, Art. 19; CEDAW, Art. 18; UNCRC, Arts. 44.1.a–b; ICRMW, Arts. 73.1.a–b; ICPPED, Art. 29.1.

[388] N. Pillay, 'Strengthening the United Nations human rights treaty body system: A report by the United Nations High Commissioner for Human Rights' (June 2012), pp. 37–46.

[389] A predictable reporting cycle would also allow for strengthening the engagement of national NGOs with the reporting system, enabling the development of planned advocacy strategies. See: H. Collister, 'Rituals and implementation in the Universal: Periodic Review and the human rights treaty bodies' in H. Charlesworth and E. Larking (eds.), *Human Rights and the Universal Periodic Review: Rituals and Ritualism* (CUP 2015) 109–125, 121–122.

[390] N. Pillay, 'Strengthening the United Nations human rights treaty body system: A report by the United Nations High Commissioner for Human Rights' (June 2012), p. 74.

[391] Guidelines on the independence and impartiality of members of the human rights treaty bodies ('the Addis Ababa guidelines'), A/67/222 (2012), para. 12.

FURTHER READING

ARNARDÓTTIR, O.M., and QUINN, G. (eds.), *The UN Convention on the Rights of Persons with Disabilities: European and Scandinavian Perspectives* (Nijhoff 2009).

CHOLEWINSKI, R., DE GUCHTENEIRE, P., and PÉCOUD, A. (eds.), *Migration and Human Rights: The United Nations Convention on Migrant Workers' Rights* (CUP 2009).

FREEMAN, M.A., CHINKIN, C., and RUDOLF, B. (eds.), *The UN Convention on the Elimination of All Forms of Discrimination against Women: A Commentary* (OUP 2012).

JOSEPH, S., and CASTAN, M., *The International Covenant on Civil and Political Rights: Cases, Materials, and Commentary* (3rd edn., OUP 2013).

KELLER, H., and ULFSTEIN, G. (eds.), *UN Human Rights Treaty Bodies: Law and Legitimacy* (CUP 2012).

LANGFORD, M. (ed.), *The Optional Protocol to the International Covenant on Economic, Social and Cultural Rights: A Commentary* (PULP 2016).

LERNER, N., *The UN Convention on the Elimination of All Forms of Racial Discrimination* (Brill 2015).

MÉGRET, F., and ALSTON, P. (eds.), *The United Nations and Human Rights: A Critical Appraisal* (2nd edn., OUP 2020).

NOWAK, M., BIRK, M., and MONINA, G., *The United Nations Convention Against Torture and its Optional Protocol: A Commentary* (2nd edn., OUP 2019).

THORNBERRY, P., *The International Convention on the Elimination of All Forms of Racial Discrimination: A Commentary* (OUP 2016).

VANDENHOLE, W., TÜRKELLI, G., and LEMBRECHTS, S., *Children's Rights: A Commentary on the Convention on the Rights of the Child and its Protocols* (Elgar 2019).

PART III

REGIONAL SYSTEMS

Part Three of this book encompasses three chapters, each dealing with a specific regional human rights system, presented in order of inception. Each chapter covers the system's historical development from their creation to their current institutional design, as well as some planned potential developments in the case of the African system. The chapters also engage with the main organs created under the respective regional regimes and the principal functions attributed to each of them. Particular focus is placed on how individuals can bring claims concerning the violation of their rights under each regime, discussing the potential life of a petition or case before the systems' main bodies. Additionally, key challenges faced by each of the systems have been selected for discussion. However, the following chapters only focus on the Inter-American, European, and African human rights systems; hence, some clarifications are needed in order to explain the exclusion of other regional regimes from the discussion.

On the one hand, the three mentioned regional systems are not the only ones that exist in our days. Within the past decades, important developments in other regions have taken place, as illustrated by repeated mentions throughout this book of the protection of human rights provided by the 2004 Arab Charter on Human Rights and the 2012 Human Rights Declaration of the Association of Southeast Asian Nations (ASEAN). Concerning the former, States Parties to the Arab Charter have the duty to submit reports to a Committee of Experts on Human Rights, established in 2009, while in 2014, the Arab League adopted a Statute for a future Arab Court of Human Rights—although this treaty is yet to achieve the needed ratifications to enter into force. With regard to ASEAN, an Inter-governmental Commission on Human Rights was created in 2009, following the mandate of the 2007 ASEAN Charter. It was this inter-governmental body that drafted the 2012 Human Rights Declaration adopted by the organization. In addition to these, the CIS Convention on Human Rights and Fundamental Freedoms was adopted in 1995 by the Commonwealth of Independent States—an international organization created in 1991 by post-Soviet States. This treaty even provided for an inter-governmental Commission with the power to receive complaints, even though, decades later, this body is yet to be established. Nonetheless, all these human rights systems are still in rather early stages of development, so devoting specific chapters to them would have led to a significantly uneven engagement compared to the attention paid to the three well-established regional human rights systems.

On the other hand, the protection of human rights is increasingly becoming an important consideration under other regional integration organizations, such as those pursuing more comprehensive forms of economic and political integration. While the best-known illustrations of these types of organizations are probably the European Union and the African Union, other relevant sub-regional examples exist, including the Andean Community, the Caribbean Community (CARICOM), the East African Community, the Economic Community of West African States (ECOWAS), the Gulf Cooperation Council, the Southern African Development Community (SADC), or the Southern Common Market (MERCOSUR). Some of these systems have established their own courts of justice, which have taken up a significant role in the protection of human rights. A main example of this phenomenon is the Court of Justice of the European Union—with its parent organization even adopting its own Charter of Fundamental Rights—but other regional tribunals have also been progressively active in rendering decisions concerning human rights, such as the ECOWAS Court of Justice, the East African Court of Justice, or the Caribbean Court of Justice. Nevertheless, it is essential to distinguish between those systems that pertain to the international law of human rights, created under international law for the purpose of supervising compliance with human rights obligations—discussed in the following chapters—and those regimes that, while also established by international treaties, pursue wider objectives in terms of regional integration. These latter regimes tend to be endowed with a different logic and often operate by developing their own community or supra-national law, hence exceeding the scope of this book.

6

THE INTER-AMERICAN HUMAN RIGHTS SYSTEM

6.1 THE CREATION AND DEVELOPMENT OF THE INTER-AMERICAN SYSTEM

The Inter-American human rights system was created within the framework provided by the Organization of American States (OAS), an international organization established by the States of the Americas with, among others, the purposes of strengthening the peace and security of the continent; promoting and consolidating representative democracy; eradicating extreme poverty; and defending the sovereignty, territorial integrity, and independence of the American States.[1] The OAS was founded in Bogotá (Colombia) in 1948 with the adoption of the organization's Charter by twenty-one States.[2] In the years to follow, these original Members were joined by fourteen others;[3] a consequence of the process of de-colonization of many Caribbean States.

The history of the OAS and the Inter-American system created within its framework can be traced back to the end of the nineteenth century, more precisely, to the period between October 1889 and April 1890, when the first International Conference of American States was held in Washington DC, setting a precedent of periodic meetings to forge a common system of norms and institutions for the American States.[4] This Conference created 'The International Union of American Republics' (later renamed

---

[1] Charter of the Organization of American States (adopted 30 April 1948, entered into force 13 December 1951) (hereinafter 'OAS Charter'), OAS, Treaty Series, Nos. 1-C, 61, UN Registration No. 1609 Vol. 119, Art. 1.

[2] These were: Argentina, Bolivia, Brasil, Chile, Colombia, Costa Rica, Cuba, Dominican Republic, Ecuador, El Salvador, Guatemala, Haïti, Honduras, México, Nicaragua, Panamá, Paraguay, Perú, the USA, Uruguay, and Venezuela.

[3] In chronological order, these were: Trinidad and Tobago (1967), Barbados (1967), Jamaica (1969), Grenada (1975), Suriname (1977), Dominica (1979), Saint Lucia (1979), Antigua and Barbuda (1981), Saint Vincent and the Grenadines (1981), Bahamas (1982), Saint Kitts and Nevis (1984), Canada (1989), Belize (1991), and Guyana (1991).

[4] Some authors have traced the origins of the Inter-American system even further, pointing to the 1826 Congress of Panama, called by Simón Bolívar, to consider establishing a Confederation of Latin American States. See: C.B. Casey, 'The Creation and Development of the Pan American Union' (1933) 13 *The Hispanic American Historical Review* 437, 437; T. Buergenthal and D. Shelton, *Protecting Human Rights in the Americas: Cases and Materials* (4th edn., IIHR 1995) 37.

the 'Union of American Republics'),[5] which was aimed at the collection and distribution of commercial information.[6] The text of an agreement on arbitration was also drafted at the Conference, which provided for compulsory arbitration in all matters, except where a nation's independence was at stake, and which proclaimed that in the Americas all rights of conquest were denied. Although the adoption of this treaty was not followed by its ratification, the relevance of the peaceful settlement of disputes within the Americas was revisited in subsequent conferences.[7]

This initial Conference was followed by periodic ones that took place in México (1901–1902), Brasil (1906), Argentina (1910), Chile (1923), Cuba (1928), Uruguay (1933), Perú (1938), Colombia (1948), and Venezuela (1954). Over the years, these regular conferences, supplemented by special meetings,[8] led to the adoption of numerous agreements that established the essential principles on which the reciprocal relations of the American States were to be based, such as the sovereign equality of all States, the principle of non-intervention, and the peaceful settlement of disputes.[9] This international cooperation also extended to the establishment of different agencies, including the Pan American Health Organization (1902), the Permanent Commission of Jurists (1906),[10] the Inter-American Children's Institute (1927), and the Inter-American Commission of Women (1928).

The interest of the American States in the international protection of human rights can be observed in their adoption of different treaties[11] and resolutions through the years.[12] Nonetheless, it was at the 1945 Inter-American Conference on Problems of War and Peace (the 'Chapultepec Conference') that a regional programme for the protection of human rights started taking shape. At this Conference, the American States adopted a resolution titled 'International Protection of the Essential Rights of Man'[13] which, in its preamble, asserted that the effective protection of the fundamental rights of man required the definition of these rights 'in a declaration to be adopted as a convention by the States'. After proclaiming the 'adherence of the American

---

[5] Resolution 'Reorganization of the "Union of American Republics"' (adopted by the Fourth International American Conference at Buenos Aires on 11 August 1910).

[6] C.B. Casey, 'The Creation and Development of the Pan American Union' (1933) 13 *The Hispanic American Historical Review* 437, 439.

[7] S.G. Inman, 'Pan-American Conferences and their Results' (1923) 4 *The Southwestern Political and Social Science Quarterly* 238, 245.

[8] T. Buergenthal and D. Shelton, *Protecting Human Rights in the Americas: Cases and Materials* (4th edn., IIHR 1995) 37–38.

[9] See: Treaty to Avoid or Prevent Conflicts between the American States ('Gondra Treaty') (adopted 3 May 1923); Anti-War Treaty of Non-Aggression and Conciliation ('Saavedra-Lamas Pact') (adopted 10 October 1933); Montevideo Convention on the Rights and Duties of States (adopted 26 December 1933).

[10] This Commission can be seen as a predecessor of the Inter-American Juridical Committee. See: J.O. Murdock and H.J. Gobbi, 'The Inter-American Juridical Committee' (1960) 9 *The American Journal of Comparative Law* 596.

[11] See: Convention relative to the Rights of Aliens (signed on 29 January 1902); Convention on Asylum (signed on 20 February 1928).

[12] See, for instance, a series of resolutions adopted by the Eighth International Conference of American States in 1938, including: 'Freedom of Association and Freedom of Expression for Workers' (Resolution VIII), 'Defense of Human Rights' (Resolution XVI), and the 'Lima Declaration in Favor of Women's Rights' (Resolution XX).

[13] Resolution XL (Final Act of the Inter-American Conference of Problems of War and Peace 1945).

Republics to the principles established by international law for safeguarding the essential rights of man', the resolution tasked the Inter-American Juridical Committee[14] with the elaboration of a draft 'Declaration of the International Rights and Duties of Man'.[15] Notwithstanding the apparent intention to elaborate a regional human rights treaty, the draft international instrument produced by the Inter-American Juridical Committee, and submitted for discussion to the Ninth International Conference of American States, became a 'declaration' of rights by decision of the States at the conference.[16]

6.1.1 CRITICAL DEBATE: THE CONTENTIOUS MEMBERSHIP OF THE OAS

Membership of the OAS is open to the 35 States of the Americas. However, membership to the organization has not been free from conflict, a claim best illustrated by the situation of Cuba, Venezuela, and Nicaragua. Concerning Cuba, its government was excluded from participation in the OAS system in 1962, when the Meeting of Consultation of Ministers of Foreign Affairs found Cuba's adherence to Marxism-Leninism ideology to be incompatible with the principles and objectives of the organization.[17] It was not until 2009 that the OAS General Assembly revoked such a decision, allowing Cuba's participation to resume through a process of dialogue to be initiated at Cuba's request.[18] So far, Cuba has not taken up the invitation to resume its active participation in the OAS. Despite the exclusion of the government, the OAS has continued to consider the State of Cuba an OAS Member, which has allowed the Inter-American Commission on Human Rights to exercise its monitoring faculties concerning the protection of human rights.

More recently, in April 2017, the Government of Venezuela gave notice of denunciation of the OAS Charter, set to become effective two years later, withdrawing Venezuela from the organization.[19] However, in January 2019, the OAS Permanent

---

[14] This Committee had been established in 1942 (replacing the Inter-American Committee on Neutrality) and tasked with the work of codifying international law and with the ability to formulate recommendations to the States. While the original text of the OAS Charter (original Art. 68) made it a subsidiary body of the then-created Inter-American Council of Jurists (original Art. 67), the 'Protocol of Buenos Aires' abolished the latter and made the Inter-American Juridical Committee a principal agency of the OAS (current Chapter XIV). See: J.O. Murdock and H.J. Gobbi, 'The Inter-American Juridical Committee' (1960) 9 *The American Journal of Comparative Law* 596, 596; A.A. Cançado Trindade, 'The Inter-American Juridical Committee: An Overview' (1982) 38 *The World Today* 437.

[15] R.K. Goldman, 'History and Action: The Inter-American Human Rights System and the Role of the Inter-American Commission on Human Rights' (2009) 31 *Human Rights Quarterly* 856, 858.

[16] Novena Conferencia Internacional Americana, Actas y Documentos, vol. II (Ministerio de Relaciones Exteriores de Colombia 1953) 137–138. See: R.K. Goldman, 'History and Action: The Inter-American Human Rights System and the Role of the Inter-American Commission on Human Rights' (2009) 31 *Human Rights Quarterly* 856, 860.

[17] Resolution VI, 'Exclusion of the Present Government of Cuba from Participation in the Inter-American System' (adopted by the Eighth Meeting of Consultation of Ministers of Foreign Affairs, held in Punta del Este in January 1962).

[18] AG/RES. 2438 (XXXIX-O/09), 'Resolution on Cuba' (approved during the third plenary session on 3 June 2009).

[19] Note from the Permanent Mission of the Bolivarian Republic of Venezuela Enclosing a Copy of the Letter Denouncing the Charter of the OAS pursuant to Art. 143 and Initiating the Permanent Withdrawal of the Bolivarian Republic of Venezuela from the Organization (28 April 2017), OEA/Ser.G/CP/INF. 7707/17.

Council disavowed the legitimacy of Nicolas Maduro's new term of office as Venezuela's president,[20] recognizing instead the authority of Juan Guaidó as interim president of the country.[21] In March 2019, this recognized interim government annulled the 2017 notice of denunciation,[22] leaving a complex political scenario with regard to Venezuela's effective participation within the OAS. Moreover, with an increasing number of OAS Members changing their stance on the legitimacy of Guaidó's authority, the National Assembly that had appointed him interim president decided his removal at the end of 2022. The complexity of Venezuela's situation extends also onto its uncertain status as Party to the American Convention on Human Rights—a topic further discussed in **Section 6.1.4.1**.[23]

Lastly, in November 2021, the government of Nicaragua notified the OAS Secretary General of its decision to denounce the Charter, while accusing the Organization of acting as a hegemonic tool of the USA.[24] This would lead to the withdrawal of the State from the OAS with effect from 21 November 2023, two years after the notification was received.[25] Unlike the case of Venezuela, Ortega's government has not (so far) followed the denunciation of the Charter with actions against the American Convention on Human Rights and, therefore, Nicaragua should continue to be bound by the human rights obligations imposed by this treaty.[26]

6.1.2 THE AMERICAN DECLARATION OF THE RIGHTS AND DUTIES OF MAN

The American Declaration on the Rights and Duties of Man was proclaimed at the Ninth International Conference of American States, held in Bogotá in 1948, the same Conference in which the OAS Charter was adopted. This 1948 Declaration can be described as the world's first major international instrument on human rights, adopted a few months prior to the proclamation of the Universal Declaration of Human Rights. It encompasses a catalogue of human rights, including civil and political rights, as well as economic, social, and cultural rights.[27] The adoption of the American Declaration

---

[20] CP/RES. 1117 (2200/19), 'Resolution on the Situation in Venezuela' (adopted by the Permanent Council at its special meeting held on January 10, 2019).

[21] OAS General Secretariat, 'Statement of the OAS General Secretariat on the Situation in Venezuela', E-116/20 (5 January 2020).

[22] Available on the OAS website at: http://www.oas.org/en/sla/dil/docs/a-41_note_Juan_Guaido_03-7-2019.pdf (accessed on 29 March 2023).

[23] Instrument of ratification (31 July 2019), available at: http://www.oas.org/es/sla/ddi/docs/B-32_venezuela_RA_7-31-2019.pdf (accessed on 29 March 2023).

[24] Available on the OAS website at: https://www.oas.org/es/sla/ddi/docs/A-41_carta_denucia_Nicaragua_11-19-2021.pdf (accessed on 29 March 2023).

[25] OAS Charter, Art. 143.

[26] IACtHR, Denunciation of the American Convention on Human Rights and the Charter of the Organization of American States and the consequences for State human rights obligations. Advisory Opinion OC-26/20, November 9, 2020. Series A no. 26, op. para. 3.

[27] With respect to social rights, the Conference also adopted the Inter-American Charter of Social Guarantees, a 39-articles-long declaration that details essential labour rights and working conditions. Unfortunately, this document, which counted with the express objection of the USA at the time of its adoption, did not manage to obtain the recognition or legal status of the American Declaration. See: L.J. LeBlanc, 'Economic, Social, and Cultural Rights and the Interamerican System' (1977) 19 *Journal of Interamerican Studies and World Affairs* 61, 69–70.

marked the inception of the Inter-American human rights system, a system that would be consolidated and strengthened through the years.

While the American Declaration was originally adopted as a non-binding instrument, it is inconceivable to deny its binding force in our days. The legal basis for the binding character of the Declaration can be found in different sources of international law. For instance, it can be seen as a reflection of general principles of Inter-American law since most of the rights proclaimed in the Declaration could already be found in the majority of the constitutions of the American States at the time of its adoption.[28] The Declaration can also be considered part of regional customary law, given the praxis of the Inter-American Commission on Human Rights of routinely identifying breaches of the Declaration as violations of human rights and the acceptance of this practice by the American States; a practice even reaffirmed by progressively widening the Commission's faculties.[29]

The Declaration's binding force can also be found in treaty law by reference to the OAS Charter. From its preamble, the Charter reveals a concern for the protection of human rights, expressing that 'the true significance of American solidarity and good neighborliness can only mean the consolidation on this continent, within the framework of democratic institutions, of *a system of individual liberty and social justice based on respect for the essential rights of man*'.[30] This commitment is further confirmed by other Charter's provisions, such as the one identifying 'the fundamental rights of the individual without distinction as to race, nationality, creed, or sex' (original Article 3.j, now Article 3.l) as a principle underpinning the foundation of the organization, and the one asserting the respect of 'the rights of the individual and the principles of universal morality' as one of the fundamental duties of the State (original Article 13, now Article 17). The first amendment of the Charter,[31] through the adoption of the 'Protocol of Buenos Aires', strengthened this concern about the protection of human rights. As discussed in **Section 6.1.3**, the amended Charter gave recognition to the Inter-American Commission on Human Rights as one of the OAS main organs, entrusted with the promotion and protection of human rights in the Americas.[32] Furthermore, a 'transitory provision' stipulated that until a future Inter-American Convention on Human Rights was in force, the existing Inter-American Commission would 'keep vigilance over the observance of human rights'.[33] However, the text of the Charter failed to define these 'human rights' whose promotion and protection was tasked to

---

[28] M. Pinto, *Temas de Derechos Humanos* (Del Puerto 2009) 37.
[29] P. Nikken, 'La Declaración Universal y la Declaración Americana: La Formación del Moderno Derecho Internacional de los Derechos Humanos' (1989) *Revista IIDH* 65, 86–95.
[30] OAS Charter, Preamble (emphasis added).
[31] The OAS Charter has been modified by four Protocols of Amendment: the 'Protocol of Buenos Aires' (1967), the 'Protocol of Cartagena de Indias' (1985), the 'Protocol of Washington' (1992), and the 'Protocol of Managua' (1993).
[32] OAS Charter, Art. 112 following the amendment of the 'Protocol of Buenos Aires' (with changes, current Art. 106).
[33] OAS Charter, Art. 150 following the amendment of the 'Protocol of Buenos Aires' (with changes, current Art. 145).

the Commission.[34] This led the Inter-American Court of Human Rights to confirm that those 'rights are none other than those enunciated and defined in the American Declaration'.[35] The Inter-American Court affirmed that: '... by means of an authoritative interpretation, the member states of the Organization have signaled their agreement that the Declaration contains and defines the fundamental human rights referred to in the Charter'.[36] It concluded by reaffirming that: 'For the member states of the Organization, the Declaration is the text that defines the human rights referred to in the Charter ... the American Declaration is for these States a source of international obligations related to the Charter of the Organization.'[37]

> IACtHR, *Interpretation of the American Declaration of the Rights and Duties of Man within the Framework of Article 64 of the American Convention on Human Rights*. Advisory Opinion OC-10/89 of July 14, 1989. Series A no. 10.
>
> The Opinion originated in a question from Colombia as to whether the American Declaration of the Rights and Duties of Man, which is not a treaty, could be the subject of an Advisory Opinion of the Court, considering that the Convention expressly refers to the interpretation of the American Convention or of 'other treaties concerning the protection of human Rights' (Article 64). The Court asserted that the Convention authorizes the Court to render advisory opinions interpreting the American Declaration, provided that in doing so the Court is acting within its jurisdiction in relation to a treaty, such as the OAS Charter or the American Convention, which make express reference to the Declaration. In such a context, the interpretation of the Declaration might actually be required, to provide an interpretation of the treaties at stake. It was within this Advisory Opinion that the Court confirmed the binding character of the American Declaration.

6.1.3 THE CREATION OF THE INTER-AMERICAN COMMISSION ON HUMAN RIGHTS

The development of the system of regional human rights protection within the framework of the OAS was staggered and not free from setbacks. Together with the OAS Charter and the American Declaration, the 1948 Conference adopted a resolution that tasked the Inter-American Juridical Committee with the elaboration of a draft statute for the creation and functioning of an Inter-American Court to guarantee the rights

---

[34] T. Buergenthal, 'The Revised OAS Charter and the Protection of Human Rights' (1975) 69 *American Journal of International Law* 828, 835.

[35] IACtHR, Interpretation of the American Declaration of the Rights and Duties of Man within the Framework of Article 64 of the American Convention on Human Rights. Advisory Opinion OC-10/89 of July 14, 1989. Series A no. 10, para. 41.

[36] IACtHR, Interpretation of the American Declaration of the Rights and Duties of Man within the Framework of Article 64 of the American Convention on Human Rights. Advisory Opinion OC-10/89 of July 14, 1989. Series A no. 10, para. 43.

[37] IACtHR, Interpretation of the American Declaration of the Rights and Duties of Man within the Framework of Article 64 of the American Convention on Human Rights. Advisory Opinion OC-10/89 of July 14, 1989. Series A no. 10, para. 45.

of man.[38] However, the Committee advised that a treaty creating such an international tribunal should precede the adoption of its statute.[39] The matter was revisited at the Tenth International Conference in 1954, leading to the adoption of a resolution titled 'Inter-American Court for the Protection of Human Rights', while the substantive consideration of the topic was referred to the Eleventh Inter-American Conference; a conference that never took place.[40]

It was a 1959 Meeting of Consultation of Ministers of Foreign Affairs that triggered the development of the regional human rights system. This meeting was hosted in Santiago (Chile), prompted by the need to address the situation of political unrest in the Caribbean, in particularly in the Dominican Republic.[41] A very significant resolution, titled 'human rights' (Resolution VIII), tasked the Inter-American Council of Jurists[42] with preparing the drafts of, at least, two conventions; first, a 'Convention on Human Rights' and, in addition, one or more conventions concerning the creation of an 'Inter-American Court for the Protection of Human Rights' and of other appropriate organizations for the protection of such rights. The same resolution created the Inter-American Commission on Human Rights, a body composed of seven members, elected as individuals (as opposed to in representation of their governments), entrusted with furthering the respect for human rights.[43] Thus, the Inter-American Commission, one of the two main organs nowadays in charge of the international protection of human rights in the Americas, was not the outcome of a treaty negotiated among States, but of a resolution adopted by a Meeting of Consultation of Ministers of Foreign Affairs.[44]

The Commission started operating in 1960 after the OAS Council adopted its Statute and elected its first members. According to the 1960 Statute, the Commission is an autonomous entity of the OAS with a mandate restricted to promoting respect for human rights among the American States, lacking any explicit powers of protection. Proposals that would have conferred broader powers upon the Commission, such

---

[38] Ninth International Conference of American States (Bogotá, Colombia, 1948), Resolution XXXI ('Inter-American Court to Protect the Rights of Man').

[39] R.K. Goldman, 'History and Action: The Inter-American Human Rights System and the Role of the Inter-American Commission on Human Rights' (2009) 31 *Human Rights Quarterly* 856, 860.

[40] The eleventh Conference, planned for 1959 and then postponed to 1960, was to take place in Ecuador but never happened. These regular conferences were then replaced by the sessions of the OAS General Assembly from 1970. See: M.J. Reid Martz, 'Ecuador and the Eleventh Inter-American Conference' (1968) 10 *Journal of Inter-American Studies* 306; OAS, Basic Documents Pertaining to Human Rights in the Inter-American System, OEA/Ser.L.V/II.82, doc. 6 Rev.1 (1992).

[41] D. Forsythe, 'Human Rights, the United States and the Organization of American States' (1991) 13 *Human Rights Quarterly* 66, 81–82.

[42] The Inter-American Council of Jurists was created by the OAS Charter to serve as an advisory body to the Organization on juridical matters, as well as to promote the development and codification of international law and, to a certain extent, uniformity in the legislation of the American States (OAS Charter, original Art. 67). It was to be assisted in its functions by the existing Inter-American Juridical Committee as its permanent committee. The Council was abolished by the 'Protocol of Buenos Aires', which made the Inter-American Juridical Committee its principal agency (see *supra* note 14).

[43] Declaration of Santiago, Chile, adopted on the occasion of the Fifth Meeting of Consultation of Ministers of Foreign Affairs, Santiago, Chile, August 12 to 18, 1959, Final Act, Doc. OEA/Ser.C/II.5, Resolution VIII.

[44] A.A. Cançado Trindade, 'The Evolution of the Organisation of American States (OAS) System of Human Rights Protection: An Appraisal' (1982) 25 *German Yearbook of International Law* 498, 499.

as allowing it to receive and process individual petitions or State communications, were considered but failed to receive enough support for their adoption by the OAS Council.[45] Nevertheless, once created, the Commission endeavoured to enlarge its own competence. From its first session, the Commission interpreted its authority rather broadly as allowing it to make recommendations to the American States on measures to adopt in their domestic jurisdictions. Similarly, the Commission determined that, although not empowered to rule on individual petitions alleging human rights violations, it was entitled to receive such petitions by way of information.[46] The Commission went on to request the OAS Council to amend its Statute to provide it with explicit powers of protection, including the ability to process individual communications and to elaborate reports with recommendations for States.[47] The Commission's appeals proved to be fruitful and, in 1962, the Eighth Meeting of Consultation of Ministers of Foreign Affairs adopted a resolution that recommended the amendment of the Commission's Statute to broaden and strengthen the Commission's faculties.

In 1965, the Second Special Inter-American Conference, held in Rio de Janeiro (Brazil), amended the Commission's Statute, empowering it to receive petitions concerning violations of human rights, as well as to request any information deemed pertinent from the government of any American State, and to make recommendations to States with the aim of improving the observance of human rights.[48] Moreover, with the first amendment of the OAS Charter, through the 1967 'Protocol of Buenos Aires' (in force in 1970), the Commission was established as one of the principal organs of the OAS, providing a conventional basis to its mandate not only of promotion, but also protection of human rights.[49] Meanwhile, the American Convention on Human Rights would provide the Commission with wider powers and its status as one of the two main bodies in the regional human rights system in the Americas.

6.1.4 THE AMERICAN CONVENTION ON HUMAN RIGHTS

As mentioned in **Section 6.1**, the idea of an international human rights instrument to be adopted as a convention by the American States was discussed at the 1945 'Chapultepec Conference', leading to the adoption of the 1948 American Declaration instead of a treaty. However, the project of a binding treaty was not abandoned and

---

[45] H. Faúndez Ledesma, *The Inter-American System for the Protection of Human Rights: Institutional and Procedural Aspects* (3rd edn., IIDH 2008) 31; R.K. Goldman, 'History and Action: The Inter-American Human Rights System and the Role of the Inter-American Commission on Human Rights' (2009) 31 *Human Rights Quarterly* 856, 862.

[46] A.A. Cançado Trindade, 'The Evolution of the Organisation of American States (OAS) System of Human Rights Protection: An Appraisal' (1982) 25 *German Yearbook of International Law* 498, 500.

[47] P. Nikken, 'El Sedicente "Fortalecimiento" del Sistema Interamericano de Derechos Humanos y sus Dobles Estándares frente a las Obligaciones Internacionales de los Estados Americanos' (2012) 56 *Revista IIDH* 73, 91.

[48] A.A. Cançado Trindade, 'The Evolution of the Organisation of American States (OAS) System of Human Rights Protection: An Appraisal' (1982) 25 *German Yearbook of International Law* 498, 500.

[49] A.A. Cançado Trindade, 'The Evolution of the Organisation of American States (OAS) System of Human Rights Protection: An Appraisal' (1982) 25 *German Yearbook of International Law* 498, 500; H. Faúndez Ledesma, *The Inter-American System for the Protection of Human Rights: Institutional and Procedural Aspects* (3rd edn., IIDH 2008) 44.

resurged in the 1959 resolution adopted by the Fifth Meeting of Consultation of Ministers of Foreign Affairs that created the Inter-American Commission, as this resolution also mandated the elaboration of a 'Convention on Human Rights'.

The Inter-American Council of Jurists prepared a draft convention and submitted it to the OAS Council in 1959. This draft was to be considered by the American States at the Eleventh Inter-American Conference, which—as aforementioned—did not take place; hence, its debate was postponed until the Second Special Inter-American Conference held in 1965. The Governments of Chile and Uruguay also sent draft conventions for consideration at the conference, and the decision was made to refer all three drafts to the OAS Council, which would receive views on the texts from the Inter-American Commission and other interested bodies to then prepare a final draft for consideration by the American States at a subsequent specialized conference. The Inter-American Commission returned its views to the OAS Council, including proposals for amendments, but the consideration of the convention was again postponed as doubts arose as to whether the adoption of the 1966 UN Covenants could lead to potential conflicts between the universal and the regional systems of human rights protection.[50]

Following a consultation among the American States, only two (Argentina and Brasil) opposed the coexistence of both systems, while ten other States were in favour of the coordination of a universal and regional regime, as was the case in Europe.[51] Consequently, the OAS Council requested the Inter-American Commission to prepare a final text of the draft convention for its adoption at a Special Inter-American Conference to be held in 1969 in San José (Costa Rica).[52] It was this conference that adopted the American Convention on Human Rights, which entered into force in 1978 after receiving its eleventh ratification.[53]

6.1.4.1 States Parties to the American Convention

Since its adoption in 1969, twenty-five OAS Member States have become Parties to the American Convention, although three of those States—Dominica, Grenada, and Jamaica—have not yet recognized the jurisdiction of the Inter-American Court.[54] Conversely, ten American States have consistently resisted becoming Parties to the Convention.[55] Of these, the USA, under the Carter Administration, took concrete

---

[50] D. Zovatto, 'Antecedentes de la Creación de la Corte Interamericana de Derechos Humanos', in *La Corte Interamericana de Derechos Humanos: Estudios y Documentos* (IIDH 1986) 207–254, 214–228; R.K. Goldman, 'History and Action: The Inter-American Human Rights System and the Role of the Inter-American Commission on Human Rights' (2009) 31 *Human Rights Quarterly* 856, 864.

[51] D. Zovatto, 'Antecedentes de la Creación de la Corte Interamericana de Derechos Humanos', in *La Corte Interamericana de Derechos Humanos: Estudios y Documentos* (IIDH 1986) 207–254, 227; R.K. Goldman, 'History and Action: The Inter-American Human Rights System and the Role of the Inter-American Commission on Human Rights' (2009) 31 *Human Rights Quarterly* 856, 864.

[52] Conferencia Especializada Interamericana sobre Derechos Humanos, San José, Costa Rica, 7–22 de noviembre de 1969, Actas y Documentos (OEA/Ser.K/XVI/1.2) 1–3; S. García-Ramírez, *Los Derechos Humanos y la Jurisdicción Interamericana* (UNAM 2002) 62–63.

[53] American Convention on Human Rights (adopted 22 November 1969, entered into force 18 July 1978) 1144 UNTS 123, OAS Treaty Series 36.

[54] These are: Dominica, Grenada, and Jamaica.

[55] These are: the USA and Canada in North America, Belize in Central America, Guyana in South America, and the Caribbean States of Antigua y Barbuda, Bahamas, Cuba, St. Kitts & Nevis, St. Lucia, St. Vincent & Grenadines.

action towards mending such a deficit, proceeding to the signing of the Convention in 1977, but this was not followed by its ratification.

Furthermore, two States, Trinidad and Tobago in 1998 and Venezuela in 2012, have denounced the Convention pursuant to Article 78, which allows for denunciation after a five-year period from the date of its entry into force, providing a one-year notice. However, as mentioned in **Section 6.1.1**, the situation with Venezuela is rather complex, leading to potential controversies as to whether the State can be considered a Party to the Convention. This is because, in July 2019, Guaidó's recognized interim government deposited a new instrument of accession to the American Convention, stipulating its retrospective effect to the date in which the earlier denunciation of the Convention had become effective.[56] Although, in numerous judgments, the Court has considered the 2012 denunciation to have had effect as of September 2013,[57] this validation had no real impact on those cases, as the facts preceded such a date. Only in the near future will the Court have to truly engage with the validity of the 2019 ratification instrument when deciding on the admissibility of cases based on alleged violations that occurred after September 2013.[58] To add to the complexity of the situation, irrespective of the validity of Venezuela's denunciation, it will remain under the jurisdiction of the Inter-American monitoring bodies, as it continues to be Party to five of the additional Inter-American human rights treaties adopted.[59]

6.1.5 ADDITIONAL REGIONAL HUMAN RIGHTS INSTRUMENTS

The entry into force of the American Convention on Human Rights and the creation of the Inter-American Court of Human Rights gave new impetus to the consolidation and development of the regional human rights system. This was followed through the years by the adoption of two Protocols to the Convention and an increasing number of additional Inter-American treaties. Unlike the multiple amendments experienced by the European Convention on Human Rights (discussed in **Section 7.1.1**), the original

---

[56] Instrument of ratification (31 July 2019), available at: http://www.oas.org/es/sla/ddi/docs/B-32_venezuela_RA_7-31-2019.pdf (accessed on 29 March 2023).

[57] IACtHR, *Álvarez Ramos v. Venezuela*. Preliminary Objection, Merits, Reparations and Costs. Judgment of August 30, 2019. Series C No. 380, para. 16; IACtHR, *Díaz Loreto et al. v. Venezuela*. Preliminary Objections, Merits, Reparations and Costs. Judgment of November 19, 2019. Series C No. 392, para. 13; I/A Court H. R., *Olivares Muñoz et al. v. Venezuela*. Merits, Reparations and Costs. Judgment of November 10, 2020. Series C No. 415, para. 16; IACtHR, *Mota Abarullo et al. v. Venezuela*. Merits, Reparations and Costs. Judgment of November 18, 2020. Series C No. 417, para. 12; IACtHR, *Guerrero, Molina et al. v. Venezuela*. Merits, Reparations and Costs. Judgment of June 3, 2021. Series C No. 424, para. 13; IACtHR, *González et al. v. Venezuela*. Merits and Reparations. Judgment of September 20, 2021. Series C No. 436, para. 13.

[58] See, for instance: IACHR, *Chirinos Salamanca and others v. Venezuela*, Case No. 14.143 (16 February 2022); IACHR, *Lares Rángel and others v. Venezuela*, Case No. 14.170 (6 July 2022).

[59] These are: the Inter-American Convention to Prevent and Punish Torture (*infra* note 71, ratified on 26 August 1991), the Protocol to Abolish the Death Penalty (*infra* note 63, ratified on 9 July 1994), the Convention of Belem do Pará (*infra* note 75, ratified on 3 February 1995), the Inter-American Convention on the Forced Disappearance of Persons (*infra* note 74, ratified on 19 January 1999), and the Inter-American Convention on the Elimination of All Forms of Discrimination against Persons with Disabilities (*infra* note 81, ratified on 28 September 2006).

text of the American Convention remains in force. Article 76 of the Convention provides for the possibility of proposals of amendment to be submitted to the OAS General Assembly, either directly by any State Party of the Convention or through the OAS Secretary General by the Commission or the Court. However, until now, the proposals presented to the General Assembly for amending the Convention's text have been unsuccessful.[60]

The first additional protocol to the Convention was the 'Protocol of San Salvador', adopted in 1988.[61] This new treaty came to fill the normative gap vis-a-vis economic, social, and cultural rights, as the Convention contained only one general provision on the progressive development of these rights (Article 26). As discussed in **Section 2.3.2.2**, the Protocol contemplates a monitoring system for the protection of economic, social, and cultural rights through different procedures: first, a system of periodic reports on the progressive measures adopted to ensure due respect for the protected rights and, second, allowing individual petitions under the judicial machinery set in place by the American Convention for two of its provisions: the right of workers to organize and join trade unions and the right to education.[62]

A second protocol on the abolition of the death penalty was adopted in 1990.[63] The protocol complements the regime of limitation of capital punishment established by Article 4 of the American Convention. The original text of the Convention did not completely forbid the applicability of the death penalty, but set a number of clear restrictions 'designed to delimit strictly its application and scope, in order to reduce the application of the penalty to bring about its gradual disappearance'.[64] These included: an absolute prohibition of the death penalty to be re-established in States that have abolished it;[65] an absolute prohibition on the extension of the death penalty,[66] meaning that a State cannot apply it to crimes for which such a penalty was not provided for under its domestic law at the time of becoming Party to the Convention;[67] a material limitation, stating that in countries that have not abolished it, the death penalty could only be imposed for the most serious crimes;[68] personal restrictions, indicating that capital punishment cannot be imposed upon persons who, at the time the crime was

---

[60] J.M. Arrighi, 'El Procedimiento para la Adopción de Enmiendas a la Convención Americana sobre Derechos Humanos' in Secretaría de La Corte Interamericana de Derechos Humanos, *Liber Amicorum: Héctor Fix-Zamudio*, vol. I (Corte IDH 1998) 329–340; A.A. Cançado Trindade, Bases para un Proyecto de Protocolo a la Convención Americana sobre Derechos Humanos, para Fortalecer Su Mecanismo de Protección, vol. II (2nd edn., Corte IDH 2003).

[61] Additional Protocol on Human Rights in the Area of Economic, Social, and Cultural Rights (adopted 17 November 1988, entered into force 16 November 1999) OAS, Treaty Series, No. 69.

[62] Protocol of San Salvador, Art. 19.

[63] Protocol to the American Convention on Human Rights to Abolish the Death Penalty (adopted 8 June 1990, entry into force on the date of the deposit of the instrument of ratification) OAS, Treaty Series, No. 73.

[64] IACtHR, *Restrictions to the Death Penalty*. Advisory Opinion OC-3/83 of September 8, 1983. Series A no. 3, para. 57.

[65] ACHR, Art. 4.3.

[66] IACtHR, *Restrictions to the Death Penalty*. Advisory Opinion OC-3/83 of September 8, 1983. Series A no. 3, op. para. 3.a.1.

[67] ACHR, Art. 4.2.   [68] ACHR, Art. 4.4.

committed, were under eighteen or over seventy years of age; and temporal constraints, prohibiting the application of this penalty to pregnant women or to anyone who has applied for amnesty, pardon, or commutation of sentence, while the petition is pending decision.[69] The protocol came to establish an absolute prohibition of the death penalty under the jurisdiction of States Parties, only allowing the possibility of appending a reservation concerning its applicability 'in wartime in accordance with international law, for extremely serious crimes of a military nature'.[70]

Besides the two additional protocols, a series of Inter-American conventions have been adopted, supplementing the existing regional human rights regime. The first of these was the 1985 Inter-American Convention to Prevent and Punish Torture,[71] which came to confirm the States' obligation to prevent and punish torture under their jurisdiction, including the duty to impose criminal responsibility upon the perpetrators of this crime, as well as the right of the victim to obtain suitable compensation.[72] Although the supervisory mechanisms originally foreseen by the treaty seemed rather weak—limited to the States' duty to inform the Inter-American Commission of any measures adopted in application of the Convention—the Inter-American Court decided that it has jurisdiction to rule on the international responsibility of States Parties for breaches of the Convention.[73]

In 1994, the American States adopted the text of two further conventions, the Inter-American Convention on the Forced Disappearance of Persons[74] and the Inter-American Convention on the Prevention, Punishment and Eradication of Violence against Women (best known as 'Convention of Belém do Pará').[75] The first of these came to codify a definition for the international crime of forced disappearance—a crime that had been categorized as a multiple and continuous violation of human rights by the Inter-American Court from its first judgment on the merits of a case.[76] The Convention provides for the international responsibility of the State, as well as the individual responsibility of the perpetrators of the crime, as did the Inter-American Convention against Torture. It also establishes the principle of universal jurisdiction over the crime and its imprescriptibility as a matter of principle.[77] As to its international supervision, the Convention expressly refers to the jurisdiction of both the Inter-American Commission and Court.[78] The other treaty adopted was the 'Convention of

---

[69] ACHR, Arts. 4.5, 4.6.

[70] Protocol to the American Convention on Human Rights to Abolish the Death Penalty, Arts. 1 and 2.1.

[71] Inter-American Convention to Prevent and Punish Torture (adopted 9 December 1985, entered into force 28 February 1987) OAS, Treaty Series, No. 67.

[72] Inter-American Convention to Prevent and Punish Torture, Arts. 1, 3, 4, 5, 6, 9.

[73] IACtHR, 'White Van' (Paniagua Morales et al.) v. Guatemala. Merits. Judgment of March 8, 1998. Series C No. 37, para. 136 and op. para. 3; IACtHR, 'Street Children' (Villagrán Morales et al.) v. Guatemala. Merits. Judgment of November 19, 1999. Series C No. 63, paras. 247–252.

[74] Inter-American Convention on the Forced Disappearance of Persons (adopted 9 June 1994, entered into force 28 March 1996) OAS, Treaty Series, No. 68.

[75] Inter-American Convention on the Prevention, Punishment and Eradication of Violence against Women (adopted 9 June 1994, entered into force 5 March 1995).

[76] IACtHR, Velásquez Rodríguez v. Honduras. Merits. Judgment of July 29, 1988. Series C No. 4, paras. 155–158.

[77] Inter-American Convention on the Forced Disappearance of Persons, Arts. I, III, IV, VII.

[78] Inter-American Convention on the Forced Disappearance of Persons, Arts. XIII, XIV.

Belém do Pará', to address the pandemic of violence against women in the Americas. The Convention specifically emphasizes its applicability both in the public and private spheres and the obligation of States Parties to adopt measures without delay to prevent, punish, and eradicate all forms of violence against women. It also acknowledges that radical structural changes within American societies are needed, including modifying cultural gender patterns, to put an end to the pandemic of gender violence.[79] The Convention establishes a double system of international supervision. On the one hand, it provides for a State's duty to report to the Inter-American Commission of Women on measures adopted to prevent and prohibit violence against women and those aimed at assisting the victims. On the other hand, a breach of Article 7, the provision establishing the main obligations of States concerning the prevention and eradication of violence and the punishment of perpetrators, is subject to the individual complaints procedure to the Inter-American Commission and Court.[80]

IACtHR, *Velásquez Rodríguez v. Honduras*. Merits. Judgment of July 29, 1988. Series C No. 4.

This was the first case the Court decided on the merits. It concerned the forced disappearance of a Honduran student, Angel Manfredo Velásquez Rodríguez, victim of the systematic practice of this crime that existed in the State from 1981 to 1984. The Court ruled that the crime of forced disappearance amounted to the multiple and continuing violation of several human rights, including the arbitrary deprivation of liberty and the right to appropriate resources to review the legality of the arrest, while the prolonged isolation of the victim and the deprivation of communication amounts to cruel and inhuman treatment, harmful to the psychological and moral integrity of the person (paras. 155–156). It also affirmed that this crime often involves the secret execution of the victim, followed by the concealment of the body to eliminate any material evidence of the crime and to ensure the impunity of the perpetrators, which entails a flagrant violation of the right to life (para. 157).

Moreover, the Court clarified the scope of the general obligations assumed by States under the Convention: they are not limited to the respect of the rights protected, by not taking actions to breach them, but also encompass an obligation to 'ensure' them, which 'implies the duty of States Parties to organize the governmental apparatus and, in general, all the structures through which public power is exercised, so that they are capable of juridically ensuring the free and full enjoyment of human rights. As a consequence of this obligation, the States must prevent, investigate, and punish any violation of the rights recognized by the Convention and, moreover, if possible attempt to restore the right violated and provide compensation as warranted for damages resulting from the violation' (para. 166).

As a result of its assessment, the Court found Honduras responsible for the violation of multiple Convention rights. Consequently, it ordered the State to pay compensation to the victim's next-of-kin.

---

[79] Convention of Belem do Pará, Arts. 1, 2, 7, 8.   [80] Convention of Belem do Pará, Arts. 10, 12.

In 1999, the Inter-American Convention on the Elimination of All Forms of Discrimination against Persons with Disabilities was adopted.[81] The Convention's main aims are to prevent and eliminate all forms of discrimination against persons with disabilities and to promote their full integration into society, imposing upon States Parties the duty to adopt the legislative, social, educational, labour-related, or any other measures needed to reach the mentioned objectives. The treaty provides for the creation of a specific supervisory committee to examine periodic reports submitted by States Parties on the measures adopted pursuant to the Convention and on any progress made in eliminating discrimination against persons with disabilities.[82]

Two inter-connected treaties were adopted in 2013: the Inter-American Convention against Racism, Racial Discrimination and Related Forms of Intolerance and the Inter-American Convention against all Forms of Discrimination and Intolerance.[83] Both treaties aimed at strengthening the general prohibition of discrimination established in the American Convention, imposing upon States Parties a broad duty to prevent, eliminate, prohibit, and punish, all acts and manifestations of racism, discrimination, and intolerance. These conventions provide for the same two mechanisms of supervision: first, the creation of a common committee to evaluate State periodic reports and, second, the possibility of individual petitions to the Inter-American Commission. Furthermore, the conventions contemplate optional clauses for States Parties to recognize the Commission's jurisdiction for inter-State communications, as well as to recognize the Court's jurisdiction.[84]

The most recent Inter-American treaty on human rights adopted to date is the 2015 Inter-American Convention on Protecting the Human Rights of Older Persons.[85] The purpose of the Convention is 'to promote, protect and ensure the recognition and the full enjoyment and exercise, on an equal basis, of all human rights and fundamental freedoms of older persons, in order to contribute to their full inclusion, integration, and participation in society'.[86] It contains a detailed catalogue of protected rights, including civil, political, economic, social, and cultural rights, which the States Parties undertake to safeguard in favour of older people. The Convention provides for the existence of three supervisory mechanisms. Following the regime established by the 2013 conventions on discrimination, it foresees the creation of a Committee of Experts

---

[81] Inter-American Convention on the Elimination of All Forms of Discrimination against Persons with Disabilities (adopted 8 June 1999, entered into force 14 September 2001).

[82] Inter-American Convention on the Elimination of All Forms of Discrimination against Persons with Disabilities, Arts. II, III, VI.

[83] Inter-American Convention against Racism, Racial Discrimination and Related Forms of Intolerance (adopted 5 June 2013, entered into force 11 November 2013) UN Registration No. 54915; Inter-American Convention against all Forms of Discrimination and Intolerance (adopted 5 June 2013, entered into force 20 February 2020).

[84] Inter-American Convention against Racism, Racial Discrimination and Related Forms of Intolerance, Art. 15; Inter-American Convention against all Forms of Discrimination and Intolerance, Art. 15.

[85] Inter-American Convention on Protecting the Human Rights of Older Persons (adopted 15 June 2015, entered into force 11 January 2017) UN Registration No. 54318.

[86] Inter-American Convention on Protecting the Human Rights of Older Persons, Art. 1.

to perform a technical review of State periodic reports, and it establishes the possibility of individual petitions to the Inter-American Commission, as well as optional clauses concerning the Commission's jurisdiction for inter-State communications and the Court's jurisdiction. Additionally, the Convention indicates the 'Conference of States Parties' as its principal supervisory organ, which is tasked not only with monitoring States' progress with the implementation of the Convention but also with monitoring the activities of the Committee of Experts.[87]

In addition to the aforementioned treaties, numerous international instruments aimed at the protection of human rights have been adopted by the OAS through the years. Among others, these include the 2000 Declaration of Principles on Freedom of Expression, the 2001 Inter-American Democratic Charter, the 2008 Principles and Best Practices on the Protection of Persons Deprived of Liberty in the Americas, the 2012 Social Charter of the Americas, and the 2016 American Declaration on the Rights of Indigenous Peoples.

6.2 THE INTER-AMERICAN COMMISSION ON HUMAN RIGHTS: COMPOSITION AND STRUCTURE

As aforementioned, pursuant to the 'Protocol of Buenos Aires', the Inter-American Commission on Human Rights became a Charter-based main organ of the OAS. The amended Charter stated that the structure and competence of the Commission were to be determined by a convention. The American Convention on Human Rights came to confirm that the Commission was to be composed of seven members, persons of high moral character and recognized competence in the field of human rights,[88] not limited to the discipline of law. While the Commission, as an organ of the OAS, represents all Member States, the Commissioners themselves are elected in a personal capacity.[89] This election takes place through a secret ballot by the OAS General Assembly from a list of candidates proposed by Member States.[90] Each State may propose up to three candidates, nationals of any State of the OAS, but if a slate of three is proposed, then at least one of them needs to be a national of a State other than the proposing one.[91]

---

[87] Inter-American Convention on Protecting the Human Rights of Older Persons, Arts. 33, 34, 35, 36.
[88] ACHR, Art. 34.   [89] ACHR, Arts. 35, 36.
[90] The process of nomination and election of the system's commissioners and judges has been the subject of needed extensive reflection by different actors aimed at promoting the implementation of more transparent procedures that would lead to the election of the best possible candidates. See, among many: CEJIL, 'Aportes para el proceso de selección de miembros de la Comisión y la Corte Interamericanas de Derechos Humanos', Documento de Coyuntura (2005); J. Schönsteiner, 'Alternative Appointment Procedures for the Commissioners and Judges in the Inter-American System of Human Rights' (2007) 46 *Revista IIDH* 195; CEJIL, 'The selection process of the Inter-American Commission and Court on Human Rights: Reflections on necessary reforms', Position Paper 10 (2014); L. Burgorgue-Larsen, 'Between Idealism and Realism: A Few Comparative Reflections and Proposals on the Appointment Process of the Inter-American Commission and Court of Human Rights Members' (2015) 5 *Notre Dame Journal of International & Comparative Law* 29.
[91] ACHR, Art. 36.

The candidates who obtain the largest number of votes and an absolute majority of the votes of the Member States are elected.[92] The mandate of each Commissioner lasts four years, with the membership of the organ partially renewed in biennial elections. Commissioners can be re-elected once, but no two nationals of the same State can be members of the Commission at a given time.[93]

The functions of the Commission are assisted by a permanent Secretariat under the direction of an Executive Secretary. The role of the Secretary is of extreme importance, considering that the Commission is not a permanent body.[94] The Secretariat is in charge of the Commission's general administration: it prepares the draft reports, resolutions, studies, and any other work entrusted to it by the Commission, and receives and processes the correspondence, petitions, and communications addressed to the Commission.[95] The Executive Secretary is an official of the General Secretariat of the OAS, selected by the Commission, but appointed by the Secretary General of the Organization.[96] The Commission's Rules of Procedure, amended in 2011, set the procedure followed by the Commission to 'identify the best qualified candidate' and forward their name to the OAS Secretary General for their appointment. This is an open and public procedure that provides an opportunity to gather observations from civil society on a final list of candidates interviewed for the post.[97]

6.2.1 THE FUNCTIONS OF THE INTER-AMERICAN COMMISSION

According to the American Convention, the main function of the Commission is to promote respect for and defence of human rights. In order to pursue this mandate, the Commission has an extensive range of powers that include, among others, the ability to prepare studies and reports concerning the situation of human rights within the Americas; the faculty to request the governments of the OAS Member States the information it considers pertinent on the measures adopted by them in matters concerning human rights; as well as the capacity to make recommendations to the governments of the Member States for the adoption of measures aimed at improving the protection of human rights within their jurisdictions.[98] Pursuant to its Statute, the Commission has the explicit power to conduct on-site observations in a State, with the consent or at the invitation of the government in question.[99] Moreover, the Commission has jurisdiction to receive

---

[92] Statute of the Inter-American Commission on Human Rights (approved through Resolution No 447 adopted by the OAS General Assembly during its ninth period of sessions, held in La Paz, Bolivia, in October 1979), Art. 5.

[93] ACHR, Art. 37.

[94] The Rules of Procedure establish that the Commission should hold regular sessions at least twice a year, although the practice in recent years has been to hold four sessions yearly. See: Rules of Procedure of The Inter-American Commission on Human Rights (approved by the Commission at its 137th regular period of sessions, held from 28 October to 13 November 2009, modified in September 2011 and March 2013).

[95] IACHR, Rules of Procedure, Art. 13.   [96] IACHR, Statute, Art. 21.3.
[97] IACHR, Rules of Procedure, Art. 11.   [98] ACHR, Art. 41.   [99] IACHR, Statute, Art. 18.g.

and take action on petitions that claim a violation of human rights. This jurisdiction encompasses the rights enshrined in the American Convention with respect to the States Parties to it[100] but is limited to the rights recognized by the 1948 American Declaration with respect to OAS Member States that are not Parties to the treaty.[101] As mentioned in **Section 6.1.5**, the Commission's jurisdiction to receive petitions has been expanded by additional Inter-American conventions, with regards to the Parties to such treaties.

6.2.1.1 The Commission's reporting system

The Commission produces three distinct types of reports: country, annual, and thematic reports. Country reports are aimed at examining the overall situation of human rights in a particular OAS Member State, making recommendations to the government of the country.[102] The elaboration of country reports was one of the Commission's earliest methods of monitoring compliance with human rights.[103] Although it was unclear whether the Commission had been granted such faculties by its original Statute, it took upon itself to conduct studies on the situation of human rights in Cuba, the Dominican Republic, and Haïti, which were published during its earlier years of work.[104] This reporting practice of the Commission was assisted by a wide interpretation of its original Statute that would allow it to conduct visits to Member States to examine the situation of human rights on-site.[105] Once the Commission decides to investigate the situation in a specific country, it communicates confidentially with the authorities of the State, urging them to invite it for a country visit.[106] While refusing to invite the Commission is a State's prerogative, the lack of an invitation does not put an end to an investigation, as the Commission can produce

---

[100] ACHR, 41.f; IACHR, Statute, Art. 19.   [101] IACHR, Statute, Art. 20.

[102] W.M. Reisman, 'Practical Matters for Consideration in the Establishment of a Regional Human Rights Mechanism: Lessons from the Inter-American Experience' (1995) *St. Louis-Warsaw Transatlantic Law Journal* 89, 92–93; C. Medina, 'The Role of Country Reports in the Inter-American System of Human Rights' in D. Harris and S. Livingstone (eds.), *The Inter-American System of Human Rights* (Clarendon Press 1998) 115–132, 121–122.

[103] C. Cerna, 'The Inter-American Commission on Human Rights: Its Organisation and Examination of Petitions and Communications' in D. Harris and S. Livingstone (eds.), *The Inter-American System of Human Rights* (Clarendon Press 1998) 65–114, 67.

[104] T. Farer, 'The Rise of the Inter-American Human Rights Regime: No Longer a Unicorn, Not Yet an Ox' in D. Harris and S. Livingstone (eds.), *The Inter-American System of Human Rights* (Clarendon Press 1998) 31–64, 49; D. Forsythe, 'Human Rights, the United States and the Organization of American States' (1991) 13 *HumanRights Quarterly* 66, 83. See: IACHR, Report on the Situation of Human Rights in Cuba, OEA/Ser.L/V/II.4, doc. 2 (20 March 1962); IACHR, Report on the Situation of Political Prisoners and their Families in Cuba, OEA/Ser.L/V/II.7, doc. 4 (17 May 1963); IACHR, Report on the Situation of Human Rights in Cuba, OEA/Ser.L/V/II.17, doc. 4 (7 April 1967); IACHR, Report of the IACHR on its Activities in Dominican Republic, OEA/Ser.L/V/II.13, doc. 14 Rev. (15 October 1965); IACHR, Report of the IACHR on its Activities in Dominican Republic, OEA/Ser.L/V/II.15, doc. 6 Rev. (28 October 1966); IACHR, Report on the Situation of Human Rights in Haiti, OEA/Ser.L/V/II.21, doc. 6 Rev. (21 May 1969).

[105] C. Medina, 'The Role of Country Reports in the Inter-American System of Human Rights' in D. Harris and S. Livingstone (eds.), *The Inter-American System of Human Rights* (Clarendon Press 1998) 115–132, 115–116.

[106] T. Farer, 'The Rise of the Inter-American Human Rights Regime: No Longer a Unicorn, Not Yet and Ox' in D. Harris and S. Livingstone (eds.), *The Inter-American System of Human Rights* (Clarendon Press 1998) 31–64, 50.

country reports despite the refusal to allow an on-site visit.[107] Since the publication of the first country report in 1962 (on Cuba),[108] the Commission has published over eighty country reports up to the end of 2022.[109]

The Commission's examination of the human rights situation of a specific State is also a rather controversial feature of its annual report. According to the American Convention, the Commission must submit an annual report of its activities to the OAS General Assembly.[110] The structure and content of this report are set in clear terms in the Commission's Rules of Procedure.[111] The most contentious part of the annual report is Chapter IV.B,[112] which contains special reports regarding the situation of human rights in specific Member States. The decision to include a State in this section requires an absolute majority vote of the Commissioners (instead of the usual majority of present members)[113] and should be based on the existence of at least one of four criteria: the unlawful suspension of the exercise of human rights; the existence of massive, serious, and widespread violations of human rights; the presence of structural situations that seriously affect the enjoyment of fundamental rights; or a serious breach of the core institutions of representative democracy.[114]

In addition to its country and annual reports, the Commission has adopted the practice of elaborating thematic reports. From 1990, the Commission began creating thematic and special *rapporteurships* to devote attention to historically vulnerable groups, communities, and peoples, as well as to specific issues.[115] The rapporteurships are distributed among the Commissioners themselves, although some of these are assigned to external experts, such as the Special Rapporteurship on Freedom of Expression, created in 1997, and the Special Rapporteurship on Economic, Social, Cultural, and Environmental Rights, established in 2017. The Commission's thematic reports have covered topics of regional interest including, among many others, the rights of women (1998, 2011, 2015, 2019), indigenous people (2000, 2009, 2016, 2017, 2019, 2021), children's rights (2008, 2009, 2017, 2021), and the rights of LGBTQI persons (2015, 2019). These reports have the potential to address situations involving collective or structural problems and to set regional standards on the covered issues.[116]

---

[107] C. Medina, 'The Role of Country Reports in the Inter-American System of Human Rights' in D. Harris and S. Livingstone (eds.), *The Inter-American System of Human Rights* (Clarendon Press 1998) 115–132, 120; D. Harris, 'Regional Protection of Human Rights: The Inter-American Achievement' in D. Harris and S. Livingstone (eds.), *The Inter-American System of Human Rights* (Clarendon Press 1998) 1–29, 20.

[108] IACHR, Report on the Situation of Human Rights in Cuba, OEA/Ser.L/V/II.4, doc. 2 (20 March 1962).

[109] See the IACHR's website: http://www.oas.org/en/iachr/reports/country.asp (accessed on 29 March 2023).

[110] ACHR, Art. 41.g.   [111] IACHR, Rules of Procedure, Art. 59.

[112] C. Medina, 'The Role of Country Reports in the Inter-American System of Human Rights' in D. Harris and S. Livingstone (eds.), *The Inter-American System of Human Rights* (Clarendon Press 1998) 115–132, 127–129.

[113] IACHR, Rules of Procedure, Arts. 18, 59.7.

[114] Prior to the publication of Chapters IV.B and V (on follow-up recommendations) of the Annual Report, the Commission transmits a preliminary copy of the Report to the concerned States, which have the right to send a reply. See: IACHR, Rules of Procedure, Art. 59.10.

[115] J.L. Cavallaro et al., *Doctrine, Practice, and Advocacy in the Inter-American Human Rights System* (OUP 2019) 199.

[116] V. Abramovich, 'From Massive Violations to Structural Patterns: New Approaches and Classic Tensions in the Inter-American Human Rights System' (2009) 11 *Sur International Journal on Human Rights* 7, 12.

6.3 THE INTER-AMERICAN COURT OF HUMAN RIGHTS: COMPOSITION AND STRUCTURE

The Inter-American Court of Human Rights is an autonomous judicial organ established by the American Convention on Human Rights and tasked with its interpretation and application.[117] Unlike the Commission, the Court is technically not an organ of the OAS but the judicial organ of the Inter-American system of protection of human rights.[118] The Inter-American Court is endowed by the Convention with both adjudicatory and advisory functions.[119] The former involves the Court's power to adjudicate contentious cases relating to charges that a State Party has violated the Convention, while the latter refers to the ability to render opinions on the interpretation of the Convention and of other treaties concerning the protection of human rights in OAS Member States.[120]

Following the entry into force of the Convention in 1978, the States Parties elected the Court's first judges at the Seventh Special Session of the General Assembly, held on 22 May 1979. The judges first met in June 1979 at the OAS headquarters before San José (Costa Rica) was adopted as the Court's seat later that year.[121] The Court is composed of seven judges, nationals of the OAS Member States—irrespective of their status as Parties to the Convention—although no more than one judge of a given nationality can sit at the Court at a time. Judges are elected in an individual capacity from among jurists of the highest moral authority and of recognized competence in the field of human rights, who possess the qualifications required for the exercise of the highest judicial functions in conformity with the law of their State of nationality or of the State that proposes them as candidates.[122] The composition of the Court is partially renewed every three years. The election takes place in the OAS General Assembly through secret ballot by an absolute majority vote of the States Parties to the Convention. Each State Party can propose up to three candidates, but if a slate of three is proposed, at least one of the candidates shall be a national of an OAS State other than the proposing one. Judges are elected for a six-year term and may be re-elected once.[123]

The Court is not a permanent institution. Its Statute indicates that the Court shall hold the regular periods of sessions necessary for the exercise of its functions, with the ability to convene extraordinary sessions.[124] The Court elects its president and vice-president from among its members for two-year periods, although their re-election is permitted. The president directs the work of the Court, represents it, regulates the disposition of matters brought before the Court, presides over its sessions, and presents to the Court a biannual report on the activities carried out during their presidency.[125]

---

[117] A.A. Cançado Trindade, 'The Operation of the Inter-American Court of Human Rights' in D. Harris and S. Livingstone (eds.), *The Inter-American System of Human Rights* (Clarendon Press 1998) 133–149, 133.

[118] IACtHR, *'Other treaties' subject to the consultative jurisdiction of the Court*. Advisory Opinion OC-1/82 of September 24, 1982. Series A no. 1, para. 19.

[119] ACHR, Arts. 62, 64.

[120] A.A. Cançado Trindade, 'The Operation of the Inter-American Court of Human Rights' in D. Harris and S. Livingstone (eds.), *The Inter-American System of Human Rights* (Clarendon Press 1998) 133–149, 141–142.

[121] A.A. Cançado Trindade, 'The Operation of the Inter-American Court of Human Rights' in D. Harris and S. Livingstone (eds.), *The Inter-American System of Human Rights* (Clarendon Press 1998) 133–149, 133.

[122] ACHR, Art. 52.   [123] ACHR, Arts. 53, 54.1.   [124] IACtHR, Statute, Art. 22.

[125] IACtHR, Statute, Art. 12; IACtHR, Rules of Procedure, Arts. 3, 4.

The president also has the right to cast the deciding vote in the event of a tie.[126] To assist its functions, the Court has a Secretariat that works under the authority of the Secretary, who is elected by the Court for a term of five years and may be re-elected.[127] The functions of the Secretary are extensive and refer to the administration of the Court, pursuant to the instructions of the Presidency, directing and coordinating the work of the Court's personnel; currently more than sixty members of staff, including almost twenty lawyers.

6.3.1 AD HOC JUDGES

Whether judges can hear cases against their State of nationality and whether States Parties to a case have the right to appoint an *ad hoc* judge, when none of the sitting judges are nationals of the State, are topics that have experienced a radical change in the Court's history. Traditionally, the Court had interpreted Article 55 of the Convention to mean that judges of the nationality of a State Party to a case before the Court retained their right to hear the case. Similarly, it had been understood that when a State Party to a case did not have a sitting national judge, it had the right to appoint an *ad hoc* judge. While the first of these rules did not seem problematic, given that judges are appointed in an individual capacity, the State's prerogative to appoint *ad hoc* judges in individual cases did not seem particularly appropriate.[128] The Court reversed its interpretation in a 2009 Advisory Opinion,[129] which was followed by the amendment of its Rules of Procedure. Now, in individual cases, a judge who is a national of the respondent State cannot participate in the hearing of the case,[130] and the faculty of States to appoint an *ad hoc* judge is restricted to inter-State cases, none of which has yet reached the Court.[131]

> **IACtHR, 'Article 55 of the American Convention on Human Rights'. Advisory Opinion OC-20/09 of September 29, 2009. Series A no. 20.**
>
> The request for an Advisory Opinion was made by Argentina with regards to Art. 55 of the Convention, which in its pertinent paragraphs states:
>
> 1. If a judge is a national of any of the States Parties to a case submitted to the Court, [they] shall retain [their] right to hear that case.
>
> ...

---

[126] IACtHR, Statute, Art. 23.3; IACtHR, Rules of Procedure, Art. 16.4.
[127] IACtHR, Statute, Art. 14; IACtHR, Rules of Procedure, Art. 7.
[128] H. Faúndez Ledesma, *The Inter-American System for the Protection of Human Rights: Institutional and Procedural Aspects* (3rd edn., IIDH 2008) 181. See also: IACtHR, *Paniagua Morales et al. Case.* Order of September 11, 1995, separate opinion of Judge Cançado Trindade.
[129] IACtHR, 'Article 55 of the American Convention on Human Rights'. Advisory Opinion OC-20/09 of September 29, 2009. Series A no. 20.
[130] IACtHR, Rules of Procedure, Art. 19.
[131] IACtHR, 'Article 55 of the American Convention on Human Rights'. Advisory Opinion OC-20/09 of September 29, 2009. Series A no. 20, op. para. 1.

3. If among the judges called upon to hear a case none is a national of any of the States Parties to the case, each of the latter may appoint an *ad hoc* judge.

Two questions were posed to the Court: the first, concerning the institution of the judge *ad hoc* in cases arising from an individual petition, and the second, also concerning individual petitions, whether judges should be allowed to sit in cases against their State of nationality. The Court acknowledged that its practice had been that so-called national judges retain the right to sit in cases against their State of nationality and that when a State in a case did not have a national judge sitting at the Court it was allowed to appoint an *ad hoc* judge.

However, the Court decided to change its interpretation of the Convention, understanding that the possibility for States to appoint an *ad hoc* judge in a case to which they are parties, when there is no judge of their nationality sitting at the Court, should be restricted to cases originating in inter-State communications. That followed from the interpretation of Art. 55, which explicitly refers to the States Parties to the case, in the plural form (para. 66). Moreover, following a similar understanding, the Court resolved that the national judge of the respondent State of a case can no longer participate in the hearing of individual cases. It considered that its new interpretation helped to strengthen the perceived impartiality of the Court (para. 84).

6.3.2 THE COURT'S ADVISORY JURISDICTION

As aforementioned, the Inter-American Court is endowed with both adjudicatory and advisory jurisdiction. Since its first ever Advisory Opinion, rendered in 1982, the Court acknowledged that, compared to other courts, its advisory jurisdiction was particularly broad.[132] The Convention allows both OAS Member States, irrespective of whether Party to the American Convention or not, and OAS organs,[133] within their respective spheres of competence,[134] to seek advisory opinions, thus, creating a parallel system to that of judicial adjudication in contentious cases. This advisory procedure was described as 'an alternate judicial method of a consultative nature, which is designed to assist states and organs to comply with and to apply human rights treaties without subjecting them to the formalism and the sanctions associated with the contentious judicial process'.[135] The advisory opinions rendered by the Court have undoubtedly led

---

[132] IACtHR, *'Other treaties' subject to the consultative jurisdiction of the Court*. Advisory Opinion OC-1/82 of September 24, 1982. Series A no. 1, para. 17.

[133] These include: the General Assembly; the Meeting of Consultation of Ministers of Foreign Affairs; the Councils; the Inter-American Juridical Committee; the Inter-American Commission on Human Rights; the General Secretariat; the Specialized Conferences; and the Specialized Organizations.

[134] The situation of the Inter-American Commission should be distinguished from that of other organs since it enjoys, as a practical matter, an absolute right to request opinions. See: IACtHR, *The Effect of Reservations on the Entry into Force of the American Convention on Human Rights*. Advisory Opinion OC-2/82 of September 24, 1982. Series A no. 2, para. 16.

[135] IACtHR, *Restrictions to the Death Penalty*. Advisory Opinion OC-3/83 of September 8, 1983. Series A no. 3, para. 43.

to the conceptual evolution of the international law of human rights.[136] A paradigmatic example of this development can be found in the Court's Advisory Opinion 18/03 (discussed in **Section 3.2.2**), which asserted the expansion of the material realm of *jus cogens* to include the general prohibition of discrimination.[137]

The scope of the Court's advisory jurisdiction is not limited to the interpretation of the American Convention but extends to 'other treaties concerning the protection of human rights in the American states'.[138] It was elucidating the precise meaning of this provision that led to the first request of an opinion from the Court. The Court affirmed that its advisory jurisdiction extends to the interpretation of 'any provision dealing with the protection of human rights set forth in any international treaty applicable in the American States, regardless of whether it be bilateral or multilateral, whatever be the principal purpose of such a treaty, and whether or not non-Member States of the Inter-American system are or have the right to become parties thereto'.[139] That is to say, the Court's advisory jurisdiction not only extends to human rights treaties to which at least one American State is party to, but also to provisions dealing with the protection of human rights in other type of treaties. Perhaps the most evident illustration of this broad interpretation is to be found in Advisory Opinion 16/99 (discussed in **Section 2.6**), in which the Court interpreted, among others, a provision from the 1963 Vienna Convention on Consular Relations.[140] Furthermore, the Court considered its advisory jurisdiction to include the ability to interpret the American Declaration of the Rights and Duties of Man, which is technically not a treaty—as discussed in **Section 6.1.2**.[141]

In addition to the Court's ability to issue advisory opinions on the interpretation of the American Convention and of other international human rights provisions, the Convention confers upon the Court the power to deliver, at the request of a Member State of the OAS, advisory opinions on the compatibility of any of its domestic laws with the American Convention or other treaties concerning human rights protection.[142] When asked for the first time to render an advisory opinion of this type, the Court clarified that the expression 'any of its domestic laws' had to be understood as comprehensive of

---

[136] T. Buergenthal, 'The Advisory Practice of the Inter-American Human Rights Court' (1985) 79 *American Journal of International Law* 1, 2 and 18; J-M. Pasqualucci, 'Advisory Practice of the Inter-American Court of Human Rights: Contributing to the Evolution of International Human Rights Law' (2002) 38 *Stanford Journal of International Law* 241, 287.

[137] IACtHR, *Juridical Condition and Rights of the Undocumented Migrants*. Advisory Opinion OC-18/03 of September 17, 2003. Series A no. 18, paras. 112–113 and concurring opinion of Judge A.A. Cançado Trindade, paras. 14–15.

[138] ACHR, Art. 64.1.

[139] IACtHR, *The Effect of Reservations on the Entry into Force of the American Convention on Human Rights*. Advisory Opinion OC-2/82 of September 24, 1982. Series A no. 2, para. 52.

[140] IACtHR, *The Right to Information on Consular Assistance in the Framework of the Guarantees of the Due Process of Law*. Advisory Opinion OC-16/99 of October 1, 1999. Series A no. 16.

[141] IACtHR, *Interpretation of the American Declaration of the Rights and Duties of Man within the Framework of Article 64 of the American Convention on Human Rights*. Advisory Opinion OC-10/89 of July 14, 1989. Series A no. 10, para. 48.

[142] A.A. Cançado Trindade, 'The Operation of the Inter-American Court of Human Rights' in D. Harris and S. Livingstone (eds.), *The Inter-American System of Human Rights* (Clarendon Press 1998) 133–149, 142.

'all national legislation and legal norms of whatsoever nature, including provisions of the national constitution',[143] as well as inclusive of proposed legislation, not yet adopted as law.[144] Up to the end of 2022, Costa Rica has been the only State to request the Court's opinion on the compatibility of its own legislation with its international commitments concerning human rights.[145]

While the Court's ability to issue advisory opinions remains of particular importance in our days,[146] it was of even more relevance in the early days of the life of the Convention. The Court had already rendered eight opinions before it delivered its first judgment on the merits of a case in July 1988. Up to the end of 2022, the Court has issued twenty-eight advisory opinions;[147] twenty of them requested by States and eight by the Inter-American Commission.[148] These opinions have covered a wide range of truly important issues including, among others, the effects of reservations and of the denunciation of the Convention on States' human rights obligations;[149] the scope of certain powers granted by the American Convention to the Inter-American Commission;[150] and the scope of the protection under the Convention of the rights of particularly vulnerable groups, such as children, undocumented migrants, refugees, and LGBTQI persons.[151]

---

[143] IACtHR, *Proposed Amendments of the Naturalization Provisions of the Constitution of Costa Rica*. Advisory Opinion OC-4/84 of January 19, 1984. Series A no. 4, para. 14.

[144] IACtHR, *Proposed Amendments of the Naturalization Provisions of the Constitution of Costa Rica*. Advisory Opinion OC-4/84 of January 19, 1984. Series A no. 4, paras. 26–28.

[145] Costa Rica has submitted five requests, but two of these have been rejected. See: IACtHR, *Compatibility of Draft Legislation with Article 8(2)(h) of the American Convention on Human Rights*. Advisory Opinion OC-12/91 of December 6, 1991. Series A no. 12, para. 28; IACtHR, *Rejection to the Request of an Advisory Opinion submitted by Costa Rica*. Order of the IACtHR of May 10, 2005.

[146] J. Contesse, 'The Rule of Advice in International Human Rights Law' (2021) 115 *American Journal of International Law* 367, 369.

[147] Although, on May 2022, the Court issued Advisory Opinion 29/2022, it has actually only rendered twenty-eight opinions, as Advisory Opinion 12/1991 was actually a rejection of the Court to render an opinion requested by Costa Rica.

[148] The only other OAS organ to have sought an opinion was the Secretary-General, whose request was rejected in 2016. See: IACtHR, *Rejection to the Request of an Advisory Opinion submitted by the Secretary General of the Organization of American States*. Order of the IACtHR of June 23, 2016.

[149] IACtHR, *The Effect of Reservations on the Entry into Force of the American Convention on Human Rights*. Advisory Opinion OC-2/82 of September 24, 1982. Series A no. 2; I/A Court HR. IACtHR, *Denunciation of the American Convention on Human Rights and the Charter of the Organization of American States and the consequences for State human rights obligations*. Advisory Opinion OC-26/20 of November 9, 2020. Series A no. 26.

[150] IACtHR, *Certain Attributes of the Inter-American Commission on Human Rights*. Advisory Opinion OC-13/93, of July 16, 1993. Series A no. 13; IACtHR, *Reports of the Inter-American Commission on Human Rights*. Advisory Opinion OC-15/97 of November 14, 1997. Series A no. 15; IACtHR, *Control of due process in the exercise of the powers of the Inter-American Commission on Human Rights*. Advisory Opinion OC-19/05 of November 28, 2005. Series A no. 19.

[151] IACtHR, *Juridical Condition and Human Rights of the Child*. Advisory Opinion OC-17/02 of August 28, 2002. Series A no. 17; IACtHR, *Juridical Condition and Rights of the Undocumented Migrants*. Advisory Opinion OC-18/03 of September 17, 2003. Series A no.18; IACtHR, *Rights and guarantees of children in the context of migration and/or in need of international protection*. Advisory Opinion OC-21/14 of August 19, 2014. Series A no. 21; IACtHR, *Gender identity, and equality and non-discrimination with regard to same-sex couples*. Advisory Opinion OC-24/17 of November 24, 2017. Series A no. 24; IACtHR, *The institution of asylum, and its recognition as a human right under the Inter-American System of Protection*. Advisory Opinion OC-25/18 of May 30, 2018. Series A no. 25.

Notwithstanding their designation as 'advisory' opinions, when the Inter-American Court exercises its jurisdiction under Article 64, it makes use of its faculties to state what the law is (*juris dictio*). On different occasions, the Court seemingly toned down the legal effects of its advisory opinions by asserting that these 'lack the same binding force' as the decisions in contentious cases,[152] but it has also affirmed that its opinions have an undeniable legal effect.[153] It is undisputable that through advisory opinions the Court provides the authoritative interpretation of the American Convention,[154] clarifying the extent of the States' international obligations. One of the most evident legal effects of these opinions is that States' behaviour in contravention of such an authoritative interpretation would amount to a violation of the Convention, engaging the international responsibility of the State.

> **IACtHR, 'Other treaties' subject to the consultative jurisdiction of the Court (Art. 64 American Convention on Human Rights). Advisory Opinion OC-1/82 of September 24, 1982. Series A no. 1.**
>
> The Opinion originated in a question posed by Perú concerning the scope of the Court's jurisdiction regarding advisory opinions. Specifically, it assessed which treaties could be subject to such an interpretation by the Court, considering that Art. 64, in its pertinent part, makes reference to 'the interpretation of this Convention or of other treaties concerning the protection of human rights in the American states'. The Court undertook an extensive interpretation of the provision at stake and affirmed that, under its advisory jurisdiction, it can provide interpretations of 'any provision dealing with the protection of human rights set forth in any international treaty applicable in the American States ... whatever be the principal purpose of such a treaty, and whether or not non-Member States of the inter-American system are or have the right to become parties thereto' (para. 52).

> **IACtHR, *Proposed Amendments of the Naturalization Provisions of the Constitution of Costa Rica*. Advisory Opinion OC-4/84 of January 19, 1984. Series A no. 4.**
>
> The request was submitted by Costa Rica, asking the Court to examine the compatibility of proposed reforms to its Constitution with its obligations under the Convention. The Court had to first elucidate whether it could provide an opinion regarding the compatibility of

---

[152] IACtHR, *'Other treaties' subject to the consultative jurisdiction of the Court*. Advisory Opinion OC-1/82 of September 24, 1982. Series A no. 1, para. 51; IACtHR, *Restrictions to the Death Penalty*. Advisory Opinion OC-3/83 of September 8, 1983. Series A no. 3, paras. 22, 32.

[153] IACtHR, *Reports of the Inter-American Commission on Human Rights*. Advisory Opinion OC-15/97 of November 14, 1997. Series A no. 15, para. 26.

[154] P. Nikken, 'La Función Consultiva de la Corte Interamericana de Derechos Humanos' in A.A. Cançado Trindade (ed.), *Memoria del Seminario 'El sistema interamericano de protección de los derechos humanos en el umbral del siglo XXI': Vol. 1* (CorteIDH 1999) 161–181, 176; H. Faúndez Ledesma, *The Inter-American System for the Protection of Human Rights: Institutional and Procedural Aspects* (3rd edn., IIDH 2008) 921–925.

> legislation not yet in force, as the Convention refers to opinions regarding the compatibility of domestic laws with international human rights obligations. The Court decided to admit the request, considering that this would provide the State with better assistance to comply with its international obligations, as it could help avoid the adoption of legislation in conflict with the Convention (paras. 26 and 30). As to the proposed constitutional amendments, they referred to the right to acquire citizenship of the State. The Court found most of the provisions to be compatible with the Convention, even those that provided preferential treatment to the nationals of certain States over others (requiring shorter periods of residence to qualify for citizenship). However, the Court did consider that granting preferential treatment for the purpose of citizenship to women who marry Costa Rican citizens, over men, would amount to discrimination (para. 67).

6.4 THE INDIVIDUAL AND THE INTER-AMERICAN HUMAN RIGHTS SYSTEM

As discussed in **Section 6.1.3**, within the Americas, the individual was first granted a right of petition to the Inter-American Commission in 1965. This right extends to every individual within the jurisdiction of any of the thirty-five OAS Member States covering alleged violations of the human rights set forth in the 1948 American Declaration. With the entry into force of the American Convention, the right of individual petition was further developed and provided with a conventional basis. Article 44 of the Convention entitles any person, group of persons, or non-governmental organization (NGO) legally recognized in at least one of the OAS Member States to lodge petitions with the Commission containing complaints of violation of the Convention by a State Party. This right of petition can also include claims of violations of other Inter-American treaties, with respect to States Parties to these. The Inter-American human rights system adopted a rather liberal stance on legal standing to lodge petitions with the Commission, dispensing of any specific link between petitioners and victim—not even requiring the latter's consent.[155] Any person, group of persons, or recognized NGO can lodge a petition in favour of a victim of a human rights violation. The main requirement is for the alleged victim of a violation of the American Convention to be a physical person, even though exceptions are made on behalf of indigenous and tribal communities and trade unions (as discussed in **Section 3.3**).[156] Petitions to the Commission can be submitted electronically, through the Commission's website, and must be written in one of the official languages of the OAS (English, French, Portuguese, or Spanish).[157]

---

[155] H. Faúndez Ledesma, *The Inter-American System for the Protection of Human Rights: Institutional and Procedural Aspects* (3rd edn., IIDH 2008) 231; A.A. Cançado Trindade, *The Access of Individuals to International Justice* (OUP 2011) 130. See: IACHR, Resolución 59/81, Caso 1954 (Uruguay) (16 October 1981), Annual Report 1981–1982 (Spanish), OEA/Ser.L/V/II.57, doc. 6 Rev.1 (20 September 1982).

[156] IACtHR, *Entitlement of legal entities to hold rights under the Inter-American Human Rights System*. Advisory Opinion OC-22/16 of February 26, 2016. Series A no. 22, op. paras. 2, 3, 4.

[157] See: https://www.oas.org/en/IACHR/jsForm/?File=/en/iachr/mandate/petitions.asp (accessed on 29 March 2023).

Once a petition is lodged, the Commission's Executive Secretariat is in charge of its study and its initial processing to ascertain whether the admissibility requirements are fulfilled.[158] The Registry undertakes an initial review of the petition, which could lead to either its expedited rejection, to a request for additional information, or to the opening of the petition for processing.[159] Only a small percentage of the petitions received satisfy this initial scrutiny.[160] Although petitions are usually studied in the order they are received, the examination of petitions can be expedited under certain circumstances. These include when the passage of time would deprive the petition of its effectiveness; when the alleged victims are persons deprived of their liberty; when the State expresses its intention to enter into a friendly settlement process; or when the resolution of the case could have a wide impact, such as affecting a serious structural situation or by promoting changes in legislation that would avoid the lodging of multiple similar petitions.[161]

Petitions that *prima facie* satisfy admissibility requirements are forwarded to the concerned State to submit a response within three months. The Commission's decision on admissibility is adopted once it has had the opportunity to consider the positions of both parties.[162] The Commission's current practice is to place itself at the disposal of the parties with a view to reaching a friendly settlement of the matter from the moment in which the processing of a petition begins, even before deciding on its admissibility.[163] Although the Commission enjoys a degree of discretion to decide in each case whether the friendly settlement procedure would be a suitable way of resolving the dispute,[164] only in exceptional cases, and based on substantive reasons, can the Commission omit the friendly settlement procedure.[165] If a settlement is reached, it is up for the Commission to approve it, ensuring that is based on the respect of human rights. The Commission is also entrusted with the adoption of follow-up measures to verify compliance with the terms of a settlement.[166] According to the data provided by the Commission, between 1985 and 2017, it approved a total of 137 friendly settlements.[167]

---

[158] IACHR, Rules of Procedure, Arts. 26, 29.

[159] D. Shelton, 'The Rules and the Reality of Petition Procedures in the Inter-American Human Rights System' (2015) 5 *Notre Dame Journal of International & Comparative Law* 1, 9, 11. See also: IACHR, Digest of the Inter-American Commission on Human Rights on its Admissibility and Competence Criteria, OEA/Ser.L/V/II.175, doc. 20 (4 March 2020), para. 1.

[160] A 2011 study found that only 10%–13% of petitions pass the initial scrutiny of the Secretariat. See: Human Rights Clinic, University of Texas, School of Law, 'Maximizing Justice, Minimizing Delay: Streamlining Procedures of the Inter-American Commission on Human Rights' (2011), p. 25. Available at: https://law.utexas.edu/clinics/2015/04/24/iachr-study-on-the-pace-of-adjudication-of-the-inter-american-commission-on-human-rights-fall-2010-to-the-present/ (accessed on 29 March 2023).

[161] IACHR, Rules of Procedure, Art. 29.   [162] IACHR, Rules of Procedure, Arts. 30, 36.

[163] ACHR, Art. 48.1.f; IACHR, Rules of Procedure, Arts. 37, 40; IACHR, 'Impact of the Friendly Settlement Procedure (Second Edition)', OEA/Ser.L/V/II.167, doc. 31 (1 March 2018), para. 65.

[164] IACtHR, *Velásquez Rodríguez v. Honduras*. Preliminary Objections. Judgment of June 26, 1987. Series C No. 1, para. 45; IACtHR, *Godínez Cruz v. Honduras*. Preliminary Objections. Judgment of June 26, 1987. Series C No. 3, para. 48.

[165] IACtHR, *Caballero Delgado and Santana v. Colombia*. Preliminary Objections. Judgment of January 21, 1994. Series C No. 17, para. 27.

[166] IACHR, Rules of Procedure, Art. 48.

[167] IACHR, 'Impact of the Friendly Settlement Procedure (Second Edition)', OEA/Ser.L/V/II.167, doc. 31 (1 March 2018), paras. 1, 265.

If a friendly settlement is not reached,[168] and the petition is found admissible, the Commission has a period of 180 days to draw up a report on the merits of the case (known as 'Article 50 Report'), setting forth the facts and stating its conclusions.[169] If the report establishes violations of the American Convention—or of the American Declaration for States not Party to the Convention—it should include recommendations for the State to address them. This report is then transmitted to the State, setting a deadline—shorter than three months—by which it must inform the Commission on the measures adopted to comply with the recommendations. This report is confidential and cannot be published.[170] If the State concerned is a Party to the Convention and has accepted the Court's jurisdiction, the Commission gives the petitioner one month to present their opinion on whether the case should be submitted to the Court.

Pursuant to Article 51 of the Convention, the Commission enjoys a three-month timeframe to decide whether to submit the case to the Court, which starts from the moment of the transmission of the Article 50 Report to the State. While the Court has interpreted that such a time limit is not peremptory and may be extended,[171] the Commission has adopted the practice of granting States a short period to address its recommendations so as to have enough time to decide on the submission of the case to the Court within the three-month deadline.[172] This three-month time limit can be suspended when the State shows willingness to implement the Commission's recommendations and if it waives the right to file preliminary objections regarding compliance with the time limit in the event that the matter is later referred to the Court.[173]

If the State in question has accepted the Court's jurisdiction and the Commission considers that the State has not complied with the recommendations of its Article 50 Report, it shall refer the case to the Court unless there is a reasoned decision by an absolute majority of the commissioners to the contrary.[174] Conversely, if the concerned State has not accepted the Court's jurisdiction, or if the Commission decides not to submit the case, the Commission has the power to issue a final report, containing its

---

[168] If a friendly settlement is not reached during the initial stages of processing a petition, it can be agreed at later stages, even after a case has been submitted to the Court. See: IACtHR, Rules of Procedure, Art. 63. See also: IACtHR, *Maqueda v. Argentina*. Preliminary Objections. Order of January 17, 1995. Series C No. 18; IACtHR, *Gómez Murillo et al. v. Costa Rica*. Judgment of November 29, 2016. Series C No. 326.

[169] ACHR, Art. 50; IACHR, Statute, Art. 23.2.

[170] The Commission can only proceed to publish the Art. 50 Report if and when the case is submitted to the jurisdiction of the Court. See: IACHR, Rules of Procedure, Art. 74.3.

[171] IACtHR, *Neira Alegría et al. Case*. Preliminary Objections. Judgment of December 11, 1991. Series C No. 13, para. 34; IACtHR, *Cayara v. Peru*. Preliminary Objections. Judgment of February 3, 1993. Series C No. 14, para. 39; IACtHR, *Certain Attributes of the Inter-American Commission on Human Rights*. Advisory Opinion OC-13/93 of July 16, 1993. Series A no. 13, para. 51.

[172] H. Faúndez Ledesma, *The Inter-American System for the Protection of Human Rights: Institutional and Procedural Aspects* (3rd edn., IIDH 2008) 450. Faúndez Ledesma also questions the legal grounds for the Court's interpretation that a precise period of time established by the text of the Convention could be extended by a decision of the Commission (p. 463).

[173] IACHR, Rules of Procedure, Art. 46.   [174] IACHR, Rules of Procedure, Art. 45.

conclusions and recommendations. This report is transmitted to both parties and can be published by the Commission. The Commission is also charged with monitoring compliance with the recommendations issued,[175] which are usually not limited to the payment of compensation but cover a wide range of measures to be adopted by States, such as the amendment of domestic laws, the release of people unfairly imprisoned, the investigation of the violations that took place, and the prosecution of those responsible for them.[176]

As per the current Rules of Procedure, when the Commission decides to bring a case before the Court, it shall submit a copy of the Article 50 Report, a copy of the case file, and a note of referral, which may include an appraisal of the degree of State's compliance with its recommendations.[177] Although States are also entitled to submit a case to the Court themselves, the general practice within the system has been for cases to be submitted by the Commission. A rare exception to this general trend took place in 1981,[178] when Costa Rica decided to present a case directly to the Court, bypassing the procedure before the Commission, a practice that was found inadmissible.[179] **Figure 6.1** shows the process of individual petitions (by a person, group of persons, or NGO) before the Inter-American human rights system.

> **IACtHR, *In the matter of Viviana Gallardo et al.* Series A no. 101.**
>
> The matter of Viviana Gallardo and others concerned a submission of a formal request by Costa Rica for the Court to examine the death in prison of Viviana Gallardo and the wounding of two other individuals, to determine whether these amounted to violations of the American Convention. In its submission, the State waived the requirement of the exhaustion of domestic remedies, as well as the proceedings before the Commission. However, the Court decided it could not admit the case, as it considered that the proceedings before the Commission were a mandatory step in the processing of a case that could not be waived by the State. Therefore, it decided to refer the matter to the Inter-American Commission.

---

[175] ACHR, Art. 51; IACHR, Rules of Procedure, Arts. 47, 48.

[176] IACHR, Case 1944 (Haiti) (27 May 1977), Annual Report 1978, OEA/Ser.L/V/II.43, doc. 21 corr. 1 (20 April 1978); IACHR, Resolution 12/80, Case 3358 (Argentina) (9 April 1980), Annual Report 1979–1980; IACHR, Case 11.010, Report 15/95 (*Hildegard María Feldman v. Colombia*), OEA/Ser.L/V/II.91, doc. 7 at 57 (28 February 1996); IACHR, Report 96/19, Case 11.726 (*Norberto Javier Restrepo v. Colombia*), OEA/Ser.L/V/II, doc. 105 (14 June 2019).

[177] IACHR, Rules of Procedure, Art. 74.

[178] The *Lori Berenson Mejía case* could be considered another exception, as Perú submitted a 'petition' to the Court regarding it, although, days before, the Commission had already submitted the case for consideration. See: IACtHR, *Lori Berenson Mejía v. Peru.* Merits, Reparations and Costs. Judgment of November 25, 2004. Series C No. 119.

[179] IACtHR, In the matter of Viviana Gallardo et al. Series A no. 101.

6 THE INTER-AMERICAN HUMAN RIGHTS SYSTEM 327

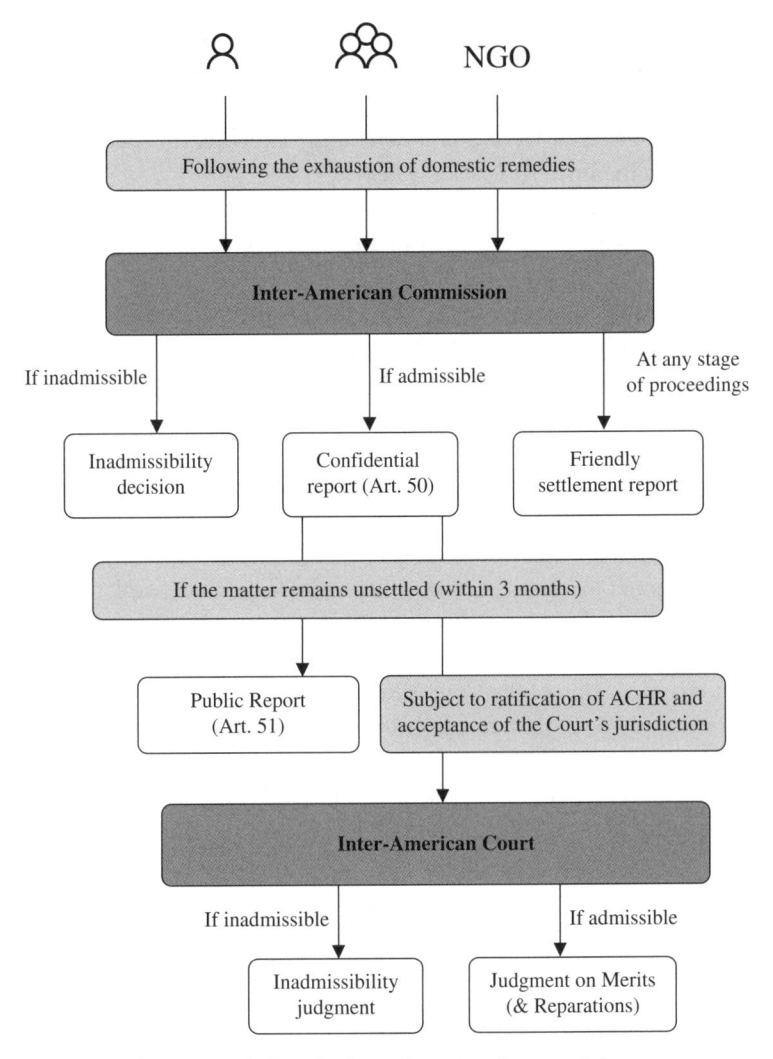

Figure 6.1 Process of a petition before the Inter-American human rights system

6.4.1 THE EVOLVING ROLE OF THE INDIVIDUAL BEFORE THE COURT

The role of the individual before the Court has evolved through time. In the early years, the Inter-American Commission and the respondent State were considered to be the parties in the case, as the Convention determines that only they have the right to submit a case to the Court. The legal representatives of the victims were integrated into the delegation of the Commission with the designation of 'assistants' to the latter.[180]

---

[180] A.A. Cançado Trindade, *The Access of Individuals to International Justice* (OUP 2011) 37.

This situation was certainly at odds with the prior stage of the case before the Commission, where the parties are the individual complainants and the respondent State. The Commission thus found itself in an ambiguous role at a time defending the interests of the alleged victims and defending, likewise, the 'public interest' as a *Ministère Public* of the Inter-American system.[181]

The amendment of the Court's Rules of Procedure in 1991 foresaw, in rather oblique terms, a timid participation of the victims or their representatives in the procedure before the Court, in particular in the stage of reparations and when requested by the latter.[182] A more significant step took place in 1996 with the adoption of new Court's Rules, which asserted that 'at the stage of reparations, the representatives of the victims or of their next of kin may independently submit their own arguments and evidence'.[183] The incipient procedural standing was further developed by the 2000 Rules of the Court, which secured the legal standing of the individual in all stages of the proceedings before the Court.[184] These Rules provided that when the application had been admitted, the alleged victims, their next-of-kin, or their duly accredited representatives may submit their requests, arguments, and evidence, autonomously, throughout the proceedings.[185] This was confirmed by the further amendment of the Rules in 2003, which provided a small tweak to the provision, stating that, once the application had been admitted, the alleged victims could submit their 'pleadings, motions and evidence', autonomously, throughout the proceedings.[186]

The most recent version of the Court's Rules was adopted in 2009. One of the main reforms introduced concerns the role of the Commission in the proceedings before the Court. The Rules accord greater prominence to litigation between the respondent State and the representatives of the alleged victims, allowing the Commission to play its role as guarantor of the 'public interest' of the proceedings under the Convention.[187] The new Rules established the figure of the Inter-American Defender, to secure that all alleged victims in the proceedings have legal representation. A defender may be appointed by the Court, on its own motion, in cases where alleged victims lack duly accredited representation.[188] Unlike under the previous Rules, the Commission can no longer assume the representation of alleged victims that lack legal representation. Another contemporary development adopted to strengthen the individuals' right of petition was the creation of the 'Legal Assistance Fund to the Inter-American human rights system' to facilitate access to both the Commission and the Court to individuals with scarce economic resources.[189] The rules for the operation of the Fund allow the Court, when delivering a judgment, to order respondent States found in breach of the

---

[181] A.A. Cançado Trindade, *The Access of Individuals to International Justice* (OUP 2011) 42.
[182] IACtHR, Rules of Procedure (1991), Arts. 44.2, 22.2.
[183] IACtHR, Rules of Procedure (1996), Art. 23.
[184] A.A. Cançado Trindade, *The Access of Individuals to International Justice* (OUP 2011) 43.
[185] IACtHR, Rules of Procedure (2000), Art. 23.   [186] IACtHR, Rules of Procedure (2003), Art. 23.
[187] IACtHR, Second Statement of Reasons to Modify the Rules of Procedure (November 2009), available at: https://www.corteidh.or.cr/reglamento.cfm?lang=en#tab4 (accessed 29 March 2023).
[188] IACtHR, Rules of Procedure, Art. 37.
[189] AG/RES. 2426 (XXXVIII-O/08), Establishment of the Legal Assistance Fund of the Inter-American Human Rights System (3 June 2008).

Convention to reimburse any disbursements made in favour of the victims, in order to secure the sustainability of the Fund.[190]

The progressive recognition of the individual's legal standing before the Court contributes to the 'jurisdictionalization' of protection, bringing an end to the ambiguity of the Commission's functions, which is not a 'party' in the process but rather a guardian of the correct application of the Convention.[191] It can be hoped that this progress will continue in the future, leading to the concession of full legal standing to the individual, inclusive of the right of direct access to the Court.[192] This would not entail the disappearance of the Inter-American Commission on Human Rights—as it happened with its European counterpart—since in the Americas the Commission performs multiple vital functions besides its intervention in contentious cases before the Court. This development would, nonetheless, require the adoption for the first time of a Protocol of Reform to the American Convention, such as the one proposed two decades ago by the then President of the Court Cançado Trindade.[193] The recognition of the individuals' legal standing would be the logical consequence of a system of protection purported to guarantee individual rights at the international level, as it is not reasonable to conceive of rights without the procedural capacity to vindicate them.[194]

6.4.2 THE CASE BEFORE THE COURT

When the Commission submits a case to the Court (see **Figure 6.1**), both the alleged victim and the State are notified by the Court's Secretary. The alleged victims are given a two-month period to submit their brief containing pleadings, motions, and evidence. Then, the respondent State shall assert its position on the case, including whether it accepts the facts and claims—those not expressly controverted can be taken as accepted by the Court—and provide its legal arguments, and evidence.[195] The State is also entitled to file preliminary objections in its response—a topic further discussed in **Section 6.4.5**. Unlike the European Court of Human Rights, the normal practice of the Inter-American Court is to hold oral hearings.[196] These provide an opportunity for the Commission to present the case and for the alleged victims and the respondent State to present their oral arguments. The Court's current practice is to deliver a single judgment encompassing admissibility, merits, and reparations. The judgment indicates

---

[190] Rules for the Operation of the Victims' Legal Assistance Fund of the Inter-American Court of Human Rights (4 February 2010).
[191] A.A. Cançado Trindade, *The Access of Individuals to International Justice* (OUP 2011) 37.
[192] IACtHR, *Castillo Petruzzi et al. v. Peru*. Preliminary Objections. Judgment of September 4, 1998. Series C No. 41, concurring opinion of Judge A.A. Cançado Trindade paras. 42–43.
[193] A.A. Cançado Trindade, Bases para un Proyecto de Protocolo a la Convención Americana sobre Derechos Humanos, para Fortalecer Su Mecanismo de Protección, vol. II (2nd edn., Corte IDH 2003) 3–64.
[194] A.A. Cançado Trindade, *The Access of Individuals to International Justice* (OUP 2011) 42.
[195] IACtHR, Rules of Procedure, Arts. 39–41.
[196] On the importance of the Court conducting this type of hearings, see: A.A. Cançado Trindade, *El Ejercicio de la Función Judicial Internacional: Memorias de la Corte Interamericana de Derechos Humanos* (3rd edn., Del Rey 2013) 137–142.

whether the respondent State is found responsible for the violation of any provisions of the American Convention or any other Inter-American treaty to which the State is Party, as well as the pertinent reparations and costs. Any Judge who has taken part in the consideration of the case is entitled to append a separate reasoned opinion to the judgment, concurring or dissenting.[197]

6.4.3 REPARATIONS AND COMPLIANCE

The American Convention entrusts the Court with the power to order that any violation of the rights protected therein be remedied. Article 63.1 establishes that when there has been breach of the Convention, the Court shall rule that the violation be brought to an end, that fair compensation be paid to the victim, and 'that the consequences of the measure or situation that constituted the breach of such right or freedom be remedied'.[198] The provision shows the extensive remedial competence conferred upon the Court, not limited to ordering the payment of compensation, which has allowed it to devise a wide range of non-monetary remedies through the years.[199]

From its earliest judgments, the Court has affirmed that under international law, reparation should ideally consist of full restitution (*restitutio in integrum*), which includes the restoration of the prior situation, the reparation of the consequences of the violation, and the award of compensation.[200] However, in cases of human rights violations, full restitution is usually impossible, and this has led the Court to order a comprehensive series of measures as means of reparation.[201] The Court normally orders the payment of a monetary award to compensate both the pecuniary and the non-pecuniary damage suffered by the victims. While pecuniary damage refers to the financial consequences of the violation—including the loss of income suffered by the victim, the expenses incurred by their next-of-kin, and any consequential damage showing a direct causal connection with the violation[202]—non-pecuniary damage covers the harmful effects of the violation that are not immediately financial, such as the suffering and distress caused to the victim and their close relatives, and the impairment of values that are highly significant to them.[203] Given the particular difficulty of translating non-pecuniary damage into precise monetary terms, the Court establishes the amount of compensation for non-pecuniary damage on the 'reasonable

---

[197] ACHR, Art. 66.2; IACtHR, Rules of Procedure, Art. 65.   [198] ACHR, Art. 63.1.
[199] D. Shelton, *Remedies in International Human Rights Law* (OUP 2015) 228.
[200] IACtHR, *Velásquez Rodríguez v. Honduras*. Reparations and Costs. Judgment of July 21, 1989. Series C No. 7, para. 26.
[201] IACtHR, '*White Van*' *(Paniagua Morales et al.) v. Guatemala*. Reparations and Costs. Judgment of May 25, 2001. Series C No. 76, para. 76; IACtHR, *Bulacio v. Argentina*. Merits, Reparations and Costs. Judgment of September 18, 2003. Series C No. 100, para. 72; IACtHR, *Barrios Altos v. Peru*. Reparations and Costs. Judgment of November 30, 2001. Series C No. 87, para. 25.
[202] IACtHR, *Myrna Mack Chang v. Guatemala*. Merits, Reparations and Costs. Judgment of November 25, 2003. Series C No. 101, para. 250; IACtHR, *Cantoral Huamaní and García Santa Cruz v. Peru*. Preliminary Objection, Merits, Reparations and Costs. Judgment of July 10, 2007. Series C No. 167, para. 140.
[203] IACtHR, '*Street Children*' *(Villagrán Morales et al.) v. Guatemala*. Reparations and Costs. Judgment of May 26, 2001. Series C No. 77, para. 84.

exercise of judicial discretion'[204] and on the 'principle of equity'.[205] A recent empirical study of the Court's practice concerning the monetization of its awards for non-pecuniary damage revealed that the most important factors the Court uses to quantify these are the severity of the violation and the vulnerability of the victim.[206]

Moreover, the Court normally adopts a wide range of measures aimed at repairing to the fullest possible extent the violation committed and avoiding recidivism. It is almost impossible to specify all the different types of measures the Court has ordered through the years, but the following can provide a relevant illustration of the degree of originality in its practice. The Court has ordered measures aimed at the restitution of the right that has been violated, whenever possible, such as nullifying a criminal conviction imposed in violation of the Convention,[207] or reinstating a person to their job.[208] It has also indicated measures aimed at the rehabilitation of the victims, such as the provision of medical and psychological treatment,[209] or at improving their livelihoods, such as the award of a scholarship to continue or pursue studies.[210] Since 2001, the Court has also consistently ordered measures of satisfaction, including the need to celebrate acts of public apology,[211] the publication of certain parts of the judgment,[212]

---

[204] IACtHR, *19 Merchants v. Colombia*. Merits, Reparations and Costs. Judgment of July 5, 2004. Series C No. 109, para. 244; IACtHR, *Plan de Sánchez Massacre v. Guatemala*. Reparations. Judgment of November 19, 2004. Series C No. 116, para. 80.

[205] IACtHR, *'Street Children' (Villagrán Morales et al.) v. Guatemala*. Reparations and Costs. Judgment of May 26, 2001. Series C No. 77, para. 84; IACtHR, *Cantoral Benavides v. Peru*. Reparations and Costs. Judgment of December 3, 2001. Series C No. 88, paras. 57, 62.

[206] D.A. Gonzalez-Salzberg, 'Non-pecuniary Damage under the American Convention on Human Rights: An Empirical Analysis of 30 Years of Case Law' (2021) 34 *Harvard Human Rights Journal* 81, 103.

[207] IACtHR, *Castillo Petruzzi et al. v. Peru*. Merits, Reparations and Costs. Judgment of May 30, 1999. Series C No. 52, op. para. 7; IACtHR, *Cesti Hurtado v. Peru*. Reparations and Costs. Judgment of May 31, 2001. Series C No. 78, op. para. 8.

[208] IACtHR, *Loayza Tamayo v. Peru*. Reparations and Costs. Judgment of November 27, 1998. Series C No. 42, op. para. 1; IACtHR, *Apitz Barbera et al. ('First Court of Administrative Disputes') v. Venezuela*. Preliminary Objection, Merits, Reparations and Costs. Judgment of August 5, 2008. Series C No. 182, op. para. 17.

[209] IACtHR, *19 Merchants v. Colombia*. Merits, Reparations and Costs. Judgment of July 5, 2004. Series C No. 109, op. para. 9; IACtHR, *Mapiripán Massacre v. Colombia*. Merits, Reparations and Costs. Judgment of September 15, 2005. Series C No. 134, op. para. 10; *Cantoral Huamaní and García Santa Cruz v. Peru*. Preliminary Objection, Merits, Reparations and Costs. Judgment of July 10, 2007. Series C No. 167, op. para. 13.

[210] IACtHR, *Escué Zapata v. Colombia*. Merits, Reparations and Costs. Judgment of July 4, 2007. Series C No. 165, op. para. 11; IACtHR, *Valle Jaramillo et al. v. Colombia*. Merits, Reparations and Costs. Judgment of November 27, 2008. Series C No. 192, op. para. 19.

[211] IACtHR, *Cantoral Benavides v. Peru*. Reparations and Costs. Judgment of December 3, 2001. Series C No. 88, op. para. 7; IACtHR, *Caracazo v. Venezuela*. Reparations and Costs. Judgment of August 29, 2002. Series C No. 95, op. para. 5; IACtHR, *Bámaca Velásquez v. Guatemala*. Reparations and Costs. Judgment of February 22, 2002. Series C No. 91, op. para. 3; IACtHR, *Myrna Mack Chang v. Guatemala*. Merits, Reparations and Costs. Judgment of November 25, 2003. Series C No. 101, op. para. 7; IACtHR, *Durand and Ugarte v. Peru*. Reparations and Costs. Judgment of December 3, 2001. Series C No. 89, op. para. 4.

[212] IACtHR, *Durand and Ugarte v. Peru*. Reparations and Costs. Judgment of December 3, 2001. Series C No. 89, op. para. 4; IACtHR, *Cantoral Benavides v. Peru*. Reparations and Costs. Judgment of December 3, 2001. Series C No. 88, op. para. 7; IACtHR, *Molina Theissen v. Guatemala*. Reparations and Costs. Judgment of July 3, 2004. Series C No. 108, op. para. 4; IACtHR, *Gómez Paquiyauri Brothers v. Peru*. Merits, Reparations and Costs. Judgment of July 8, 2004. Series C No. 110, op. para. 11; IACtHR, *Ricardo Canese v. Paraguay*. Merits, Reparations and Costs. Judgment of August 31, 2004. Series C No. 111, op. para. 8.

and the duty to memorialize the victims through monuments in cases of grave violations of human rights.[213]

Furthermore, measures aimed at putting an end to the situation of impunity surrounding a violation and avoiding recidivism have featured heavily in the Court's case law. Since 1996,[214] the Court's constant jurisprudence has established that in cases concerning grave human rights violations, such as those involving forced disappearances, extrajudicial killings, or torture, States are under the obligation to investigate the violations committed and prosecute and convict the individuals responsible for them.[215] The State must abstain from resorting to domestic measures that would prevent criminal prosecution and from those that would suppress the effects of a criminal conviction.[216] The jurisprudence on the incompatibility of amnesty laws, presidential pardons, and statutes of limitation with the obligations assumed under the American Convention is one of the best-known legacies of the Court. Similarly, its case law has clearly established that the American Convention sets a general obligation upon States Parties to adapt their domestic legislation to the provisions of this treaty in order to guarantee the rights protected thereby. This includes the obligation to suppress legislation not conforming to the Convention and the duty to adopt legislation leading to the effective observance of the protected human rights.[217] The Court has indicated that such an obligation applies to the whole of the domestic legal order, having ordered States to reform their constitutions to align them with the international obligations emerging from the Convention.[218]

This innovative system of reparations developed by the Inter-American Court displays multiple praiseworthy qualities.[219] The wide range of measures ordered to address the violations of the American Convention is certainly innovative and has become a source

---

[213] IACtHR, *Pueblo Bello Massacre v. Colombia*. Merits, Reparations and Costs. Judgment of January 31, 2006. Series C No. 140, op. para. 14; IACtHR, *Las Dos Erres Massacre v. Guatemala*. Preliminary Objection, Merits, Reparations and Costs. Judgment of November 24, 2009. Series C No. 211, op. para. 15; IACtHR, *Kawas Fernández v. Honduras*. Merits, Reparations and Costs. Judgment of April 3, 2009. Series C No. 196, op. para. 12.

[214] IACtHR, *El Amparo v. Venezuela*. Reparations and Costs. Judgment of September 14, 1996. Series C No. 28, op. para. 4.

[215] IACtHR, *Juan Humberto Sánchez v. Honduras*. Preliminary Objection, Merits, Reparations and Costs. Judgment of June 7, 2003. Series C No. 99, op. para. 10; IACtHR, *Bulacio v. Argentina*. Merits, Reparations and Costs. Judgment of September 18, 2003. Series C No. 100, op. para. 4; IACtHR, *Myrna Mack Chang v. Guatemala*. Merits, Reparations and Costs. Judgment of November 25, 2003. Series C No. 101, op. para. 5.

[216] IACtHR, *Gómez Paquiyauri Brothers v. Peru*. Merits, Reparations and Costs. Judgment of July 8, 2004. Series C No. 110, para. 232; IACtHR, *Huilca Tecse v. Peru*. Merits, Reparations and Costs. Judgment of March 3, 2005. Series C No. 121, para. 108; IACtHR, *Moiwana Community v. Suriname*. Preliminary Objections, Merits, Reparations and Costs. Judgment of June 15, 2005. Series C No. 124, para. 206.

[217] IACtHR, *Loayza Tamayo v. Peru*. Reparations and Costs. Judgment of November 27, 1998. Series C No. 42, op. para. 5; IACtHR, *Lori Berenson Mejía v. Peru*. Merits, Reparations and Costs. Judgment of November 25, 2004. Series C No. 119, para. 220.

[218] IACtHR, '*The Last Temptation of Christ*' *(Olmedo Bustos et al.) v. Chile*. Merits, Reparations and Costs. Judgment of February 5, 2001. Series C No. 73, para. 85; IACtHR, *Boyce et al. v. Barbados*. Preliminary Objection, Merits, Reparations and Costs. Judgment of November 20, 2007. Series C No. 169, op. para. 8.

[219] L. Burgorgue-Larsen and A. Úbeda de Torres, *The Inter-American Court of Human Rights: Case Law and Commentary* (OUP 2011) 224; J-M. Pasqualucci, *The Practice and Procedure of the Inter-American Court of Human Rights* (2nd edn., CUP 2013) 444; D. Shelton, *Remedies in International Human Rights Law* (OUP 2015) 222.

of inspiration for other international courts.[220] At the same time, some of these measures have been found by States to be more cumbersome, or at least to require a lengthier period of time, to comply with, compared to the mere payment of compensation. This partly explains the apparently low level of compliance with the Court's judgments.

> IACtHR, *El Amparo v. Venezuela*. Merits. Judgment of January 18, 1995. Series C No. 19; *El Amparo v. Venezuela*. Reparations and Costs. Judgment of September 14, 1996. Series C No. 28.
>
> The case concerned the summary execution of fourteen fishermen by security forces of Venezuela. The Commission found the State responsible for the violation of the right to life of the victims, as well as for the breach of the right to humane treatment, to a fair trial, and to judicial protection of two survivors of the attack, and decided to submit the case to the Court. Before the Court, the State acknowledged its international responsibility for the mentioned violations, which was accepted by the Court. Consequently, the Court ordered the payment of compensation to the surviving victims and to the deceased victims' next-of-kin and, for the first time, it ordered the State to continue the investigations into the events of the case, and to punish those responsible for the violations committed.

> IACtHR, *Boyce et al. v. Barbados*. Preliminary Objection, Merits, Reparations and Costs. Judgment of November 20, 2007. Series C No. 169.
>
> The case concerned four individuals who had been sentenced to the death penalty in Barbados, although the conviction of three of them had been subsequently commuted. The applicants claimed that the domestic legislation contemplating the mandatory death sentence for those convicted of murder amounted to a violation of the Convention. The Commission found violations of Articles 4 (right to life) and 8 (right to a fair trial), relating to the mandatory nature of the death penalty imposed upon the alleged victims, as well as of Article 5 (right to personal integrity), due to the conditions of detention and the method of execution. Given the failure of the State to comply with its recommendations, the Commission submitted the case to the Court.
>
> Following its earlier jurisprudence, the Court ruled that the existence of mandatory death sentences for a specific crime, depriving the judiciary of the authority to fully assess the circumstances of the case, amounted to a violation of the prohibition of arbitrary deprivation of life under the Convention (para. 62). The Court also found the conditions of detention, including the lack of privacy, adequate lighting and ventilation, contact with the outside world, and exercise, amounted to inhuman and degrading treatment (paras. 94 and 102). The Court went on to examine the compatibility of the domestic legislation of Barbados with the American Convention. It analysed not only the Offences Against the Person Act, which imposed the mandatory death sentence for murder, but also the National Constitution, which banned judges from declaring the unconstitutionality of laws in effect from before the Constitution was adopted, such as the norm at stake. The Court concluded that the interaction of these norms amounted to a

---

[220] D.A. Gonzalez-Salzberg, 'Non-pecuniary Damage under the American Convention on Human Rights: An Empirical Analysis of 30 Years of Case Law' (2021) 34, *Harvard Human Rights Journal* 81, 109.

violation of Article 2 of the Convention, which requires States to amend their domestic legislation to bring it in conformity with their obligations under the Convention (para. 80).

The Court ordered the State to commute the only death penalty still in force, and to amend its domestic legislation, both the statute that imposed the mandatory death penalty for the crime of murder, as well as the constitutional provision that deprived judges of their ability to assess the constitutionality of certain norms.

6.4.3.1 Monitoring compliance

The topic of compliance with the Court's judgments has been the object of academic interest for many years, with a number of empirical studies analysing States' behaviour following judgments against them.[221] This is hardly surprising, as the Inter-American human rights system would be rendered illusory without the States' effective compliance with judgments.[222] Unlike the European system, where the Convention provides for a specific political body to monitor compliance with the Court's rulings (discussed in **Section 7.5**), the American Convention is silent on the matter of supervision of judgments.[223] This silence was filled by the Court through a comprehensive analysis of the Convention, which imposes upon it the duty to submit to the OAS General Assembly an annual report of its work, specifying the cases in which States have not complied with its judgments and making recommendations on the matter.[224] The Court considered that such a report could not be produced without knowledge of the degree of compliance with its own decisions; hence, only by monitoring compliance could this mandate be fulfilled.[225] Nowadays, the Court's authority to monitor compliance does not only follow from the above interpretation of the Convention, but has also become grounded in customary law, through the practice adopted by the Court and accepted by the States.[226]

Therefore, within the Inter-American system, the Court has assumed the task of monitoring compliance since its earliest judgments,[227] although the monitoring process has changed through time. The current Rules of the Court set a procedure based on written reports submitted by the State concerned, with observations on said reports by

---

[221] D.A. Gonzalez-Salzberg, 'The Effectiveness of the Inter-American Human Rights System: A Study of the American States' Compliance with the Judgments of the Inter-American Court of Human Rights' (2010) 15 *International Law: Revista Colombiana de Derecho Internacional* 115; F. Basch et al., 'The Effectiveness of the Inter-American System of Human Rights Protection: A Quantitative Approach to its Functioning and Compliance with its Decisions' (2010) 12 *Sur—International Journal of Human Rights* 9; D. Hawkins and W. Jacoby, 'Partial Compliance: A Comparison of the European and Inter-American Courts of Human Rights' (2011) 6 *Journal of International Law and International Relations* 35.

[222] D.A. Gonzalez-Salzberg, 'Do States Comply with the Compulsory Judgments of the Inter-American Court of Human Rights? An Empirical Study of the Compliance with 330 Measures of Reparation' (2014) 13 *Revista do Instituto Brasileiro de Direitos Humanos* 93, 95.

[223] IACtHR, *Baena Ricardo et al. v. Panama*. Competence. Judgment of November 28, 2003. Series C No. 104, paras. 87–88.

[224] ACHR, Art. 65.

[225] IACtHR, *Baena Ricardo et al. v. Panama*. Competence. Judgment of November 28, 2003. Series C No. 104, paras. 90, 101.

[226] IACtHR, *Baena Ricardo et al. v. Panama*. Competence. Judgment of November 28, 2003. Series C No. 104, para. 102.

[227] IACtHR, Annual Report 1991, p. 9; IACtHR, Annual Report 1996, p. 18; IACtHR, Annual Report 1997, p. 13; IACtHR, Annual Report 1998, p. 30.

the victims, and with the Commission submitting its opinion on both. The Court is, nonetheless, entitled to convene hearings when it deems it appropriate, which could even be joint proceedings for the supervision of compliance with multiple judgments issued with respect to a single State if the decisions are closely related.[228] The Court can also carry out visits to States to monitor compliance with specific measures.[229]

Whether the degree of compliance with the Court's judgments is seen as high or low depends partly on the criteria used to measure it. Given the diversity of measures the Court orders, it does take a rather lengthy period of time for States to fully comply with judgments. This means that if the focus is on the ratio of cases fully complied with, it would seem that the Court's judgments have a rather low degree of compliance.[230] Conversely, if the focus is on States' behaviour and whether actions are taken towards complying with the different measures ordered by the Court, it is possible to observe that States do obey the Court's rulings. Empirical studies focusing on compliance with different measures, rather than with each judgment as a whole, have revealed that the Court is quite effective, with some of the measures of reparation being complied with in over 60 per cent of cases.[231] In particular, reparation orders that entail the payment of compensation or those that could be directly fulfilled by the executive branch of power, such as acts of public apology or the publication of judgments, are complied with by States in shorter times and to a higher degree.[232] On the contrary, compliance with certain measures demands a lengthier time from States, for instance, those that require action from the legislature and might need

---

[228] IACtHR, Rules of Procedure, Art. 69. See: IACtHR, *Joint Monitoring Compliance of 11 cases v. Guatemala*. Monitoring Compliance with Judgment of the Inter-American Court of Human Rights of August 21, 2014; IACtHR, *Cases of the Río Negro Massacres and Gudiel Álvarez et al. v. Guatemala*. Monitoring Compliance with Judgment. Order of the Inter-American Court of Human Rights of August 21, 2014; IACtHR, *Cases of Fernández Ortega et al. and Rosendo Cantú and other v. México*. Monitoring Compliance with Judgment. Order of the Inter-American Court of Human Rights of November 21, 2014.

[229] IACtHR, *Cases of the Yakye Axa, Sawhoyamaxa and Xákmok Kásek Indigenous Communities v. Paraguay*. Monitoring Compliance with Judgment. Order of the President of the Inter-American Court of Human Rights of September 1, 2016; IACtHR, *Xákmok Kásek Indigenous Community v. Paraguay*. Monitoring Compliance with Judgment. Order of the Inter-American Court of Human Rights of May 14, 2019; IACtHR, *Yakye Axa Indigenous Community v. Paraguay*. Monitoring Compliance with Judgment. Order of the Inter-American Court of Human Rights of May 14, 2019.

[230] D.A. Gonzalez-Salzberg, 'The Effectiveness of the Inter-American Human Rights System: A Study of the American States' Compliance with the Judgments of the Inter-American Court of Human Rights' (2010) 15 *International Law: Revista Colombiana de Derecho Internacional* 115, 122; D.A. Gonzalez-Salzberg 'Do States Comply with the Compulsory Judgments of the Inter-American Court of Human Rights? An Empirical Study of the Compliance with 330 Measures of Reparation' (2014) 13, *Revista do Instituto Brasileiro de Direitos Humanos* 93, 93.

[231] D.A. Gonzalez-Salzberg, 'The Effectiveness of the Inter-American Human Rights System: A Study of the American States' Compliance with the Judgments of the Inter-American Court of Human Rights' (2010) 15 *International Law: Revista Colombiana de Derecho Internacional* 115, 129; D.A. Gonzalez-Salzberg 'Do States Comply with the Compulsory Judgments of the Inter-American Court of Human Rights? An Empirical Study of the Compliance with 330 Measures of Reparation' (2014) 13 *Revista do Instituto Brasileiro de Direitos Humanos* 93, 107.

[232] D.A. Gonzalez-Salzberg, 'The Effectiveness of the Inter-American Human Rights System: A Study of theAmerican States' Compliance with the Judgments of the Inter-American Court of Human Rights' (2010) 15 *International Law: Revista Colombiana de Derecho Internacional* 115, 129; D.A. Gonzalez-Salzberg 'Do States Comply with the Compulsory Judgments of the Inter-American Court of Human Rights? An Empirical Study of the Compliance with 330 Measures of Reparation' (2014) 13, *Revista do Instituto Brasileiro de Direitos Humanos* 93, 107.

reaching political compromises in the domestic sphere, such as the amending of domestic legislation, and those that depend on the judiciary, such as prosecuting perpetrators of human rights violations with due legal guarantees.

The Court has adopted a series of measures to improve compliance with its judgments, such as imposing the payment of interest in case of arrears with regards to pecuniary measures.[233] Moreover, in order to preserve the purchasing power of the amounts of compensation awarded, since its earliest case law,[234] the Court developed the practice of determining the sums of compensation in United States dollars, as the use of a hard currency helps to preserve the value of the amounts awarded against inflation and the devaluation of volatile currencies.[235] Within the past few years,[236] the Court has also become more active in making use of its ability to bring to the attention of the OAS General Assembly those cases in which States have failed to comply with a judgment.[237] The increased use of such a power by the Court is an important step towards the collective enforcement of its rulings, seeking the help of a political body to guarantee the practical effects of the American Convention and to prevent the whole system from being at the discretion of the internal organs of a State.[238] However, whether the OAS General Assembly can gather the political will to take an active role in the process of enforcing compliance with the Court's judgments is an issue that has raised certain degree of concern.[239]

> **IACtHR, *Baena Ricardo et al. v. Panama*. Competence. Judgment of November 28, 2003. Series C No. 104.**
>
> In the *Baena and others* case, the Court had found Panamá in breach of the Convention due to the dismissal of 270 government employees who had participated in a demonstration for labour rights, and it ordered the State to reinstate the victims to their jobs and to pay

---

[233] The Court started ordering the payment of interest when deciding reparations in the *El Amparo* case in 1996. See: IACtHR, *El Amparo v. Venezuela*. Reparations and Costs. Judgment of September 14, 1996. Series C No. 28, para. 49.

[234] IACtHR, *Velásquez Rodríguez v. Honduras*. Interpretation of the Judgment of Reparations and Costs. Judgment of August 17, 1990. Series C No. 9, para. 31.

[235] Exceptionally, the Court has also ordered the payment of compensation in euros. See: IACtHR, *Tibi v. Ecuador*. Preliminary Objections, Merits, Reparations and Costs. Judgment of September 7, 2004. Series C No. 114, op. paras. 14–16.

[236] IACtHR, Annual Report 2012, p. 62; IACtHR, Annual Report 2015, pp. 68–71; IACtHR, Annual Report 2019, p. 81; IACtHR, Annual Report 2020, p. 74; IACtHR, Annual Report 2021, p. 80.

[237] ACHR, Art. 65.

[238] A.A. Cançado Trindade, *El Ejercicio de la Función Judicial Internacional: Memorias de la Corte Interamericana de Derechos Humanos* (3rd edn., Del Rey 2013) 38–41; D.A. Gonzalez-Salzberg 'Do States Comply with the Compulsory Judgments of the Inter-American Court of Human Rights? An Empirical Study of the Compliance with 330 Measures of Reparation' (2014) 13 *Revista do Instituto Brasileiro de Direitos Humanos* 93, 108.

[239] V. Gómez, 'The Interaction between the Political Actors of the OAS, the Commission and the Court' in D. Harris and S. Livingstone (eds.), *The Inter-American System of Human Rights* (Clarendon Press 1998) 173–211, 197, 200; H. Faúndez Ledesma, *The Inter-American System for the Protection of Human Rights: Institutional and Procedural Aspects* (3rd edn., IIDH 2008) 940; J-M. Pasqualucci, *The Practice and Procedure of the Inter-American Court of Human Rights* (2nd edn., CUP 2013) 28–30.

them compensation. During the stages of monitoring compliance with the judgment, the State actually challenged the Court's ability to monitor compliance, which the Court ratified in its ruling on 'competence'. The Court provided different strong arguments to support its decision. For instance, that Article 65 imposes upon the Court the duty to submit to the OAS General Assembly an annual report of its work, specifying the cases in which States have not complied with its judgments. Certainly, such a report could not be produced without the Court having the knowledge of the degree of compliance with its own decisions. Therefore, only by monitoring compliance with its judgments can the Court fulfil the mandate of Article 65 (paras. 100–101). Moreover, the Court's authority to monitor compliance is also grounded in international customary law. This is a practice undertaken by the Court for over a decade and which undeniably encountered the acquiescence of the States that have engaged in the monitoring process (para. 102). In addition, the Court's power to monitor compliance has been confirmed by the OAS General Assembly, which has considered that the State reports on compliance with the Court's decisions should be submitted to the Court itself (para. 114).

6.4.4 INTERPRETATION, RECTIFICATION, AND REVISION OF JUDGMENTS

The judgments rendered by the Court are final and not subject to appeal, and States are bound to comply with them.[240] The Court may, nonetheless, on its own motion or at the request of any of the parties to a case, rectify obvious mistakes, clerical errors, or errors in calculation.[241] Moreover, in case of disagreement as to the meaning or scope of a judgment, the parties can request an interpretation from the Court, within ninety days from the date of its notification.[242] This type of request is rather frequent, having been made by States numerous times, ever since the Court's first rulings on reparations in contentious cases.[243] The Court has cautioned that a request for interpretation should not be used as a means of challenging a judgment, seeking its amendment or nullification, but must be made for the sole purpose of finding out the meaning of the decision, when one of the parties maintains that the text is unclear or imprecise, and provided that the parts subject to interpretation actually affect the operative parts of the ruling.[244] However, the Court has not been inflexible in its interpretations and has amended its orders when relevant arguments have been presented through an interpretation request.[245]

---

[240] ACHR, Arts. 67, 68.   [241] IACtHR, Rules of Procedure, Art. 76.   [242] ACHR, Art. 67.

[243] IACtHR, *Velásquez Rodríguez v. Honduras*. Interpretation of the Judgment of Reparations and Costs. Judgment of August 17, 1990. Series C No.9; IACtHR, *Godínez Cruz v. Honduras*. Interpretation of the Judgment of Reparations and Costs. Judgment of August 17, 1990. Series C No. 10.

[244] IACtHR, *Neira Alegría et al. Case*. Requests of Review and Interpretation of the Judgment on Preliminary Objections of December 11, 1991. Order of July 3, 1992, para. 23; IACtHR, *Loayza Tamayo v. Peru*. Interpretation of the Judgment of Merits. Order of the Court of March 8, 1998. Series C No. 47, para. 16.

[245] For instance, see: IACtHR, *Miguel Castro Castro Prison v. Peru*. Interpretation of the Judgment on Merits, Reparations and Costs. Judgment of August 2, 2008 Series C No. 181, para. 57; IACtHR, *Escher et al v. Brazil*. Monitoring Compliance with Judgment. Order of the Inter-American Court of Human Rights of June 19, 2012 para. 21; IACtHR, *Mapiripán Massacre v. Colombia*. Monitoring compliance with Judgment. Order of the Inter-American Court of Human Rights of November 23, 2012, op. paras. 3, 4.

Furthermore, the silence of the Convention—and of the Court's Statute and Rules—as to the possibility of the revision of a judgment should not be interpreted as amounting to a legal vacuum, with the consequence of the inadmissibility of such a remedy. On the contrary, both the application of the principle *jura novit curia* (which means that the court knows the law) and the powers inherent to the Court's judicial function give grounds to the admissibility of applications for revision.[246] Nevertheless, for the revision of a judgment to proceed there should be exceptional circumstances that justify it, such as the emergence of evidence that was unknown at the time of the judgment; the existence of prevarication, bribery, violence, or fraud; or the revelation that facts assumed to be true were indeed false.[247]

6.4.5 FURTHER REFLECTIONS: THE ADMISSIBILITY OF INDIVIDUAL PETITIONS AND CASES

Within the Inter-American system, both the Inter-American Commission and Court exercise the ability to determine the admissibility of petitions (the former) and cases (the latter) brought before them. For a petition to be processed by the Commission, it should fulfil the admissibility criteria set out by the Convention and fit within its jurisdictional competence. As to the latter, the Commission's competence depends on the intervening persons (jurisdiction *ratione personae*), the subject matter of the case (jurisdiction *ratione materiae*), the time when the facts of the case took place (jurisdiction *ratione temporis*), and the place where the facts have occurred (jurisdiction *ratione loci*). The Commission's personal jurisdiction encompasses who can submit a petition, who can be the victim of such a complaint, and who can be held responsible for the violation contained in the petition. As to the first aspect, it was discussed in **Section 6.4** that the American Convention embraces a rather generous stance on standing to lodge petitions, as it does not require a specific link between petitioners and victims. Any person, group of persons or recognized NGO can lodge a petition in favour of a victim of a human rights violation. As to the second aspect, the Inter-American system requires the alleged victim of a violation of the American Convention to be a physical person, with exceptions made on behalf of indigenous and tribal communities and trade unions. Lastly, while any OAS Member State could be found responsible for the violation of the American Declaration, petitions concerning the American Convention (or other Inter-American treaties) would only be admissible against States Parties.

Concerning its temporal jurisdiction, the general rule is that the Commission lacks the competence to examine any petition that concerns facts that took place before it

---

[246] IACtHR, *Genie Lacayo v. Nicaragua*. Application for Judicial Review of the Judgment of Merits, Reparations and Costs. Order of the Court of September 13, 1997. Series C No. 45, separate opinion of Judge A.A. Cançado Trindade paras. 6–7.

[247] IACtHR, *Genie Lacayo v. Nicaragua*. Application for Judicial Review of the Judgment of Merits, Reparations and Costs. Order of the Court of September 13, 1997. Series C No. 45, paras. 10, 12.

was granted the power to receive petitions in 1965.[248] Moreover, when the petition is based on the American Convention or other Inter-American treaty, it calls for the facts on which the petition is based to have taken place following the State's ratification of, or accession to, the respective instrument, as international treaties do not apply retrospectively. An exception to this general rule concerns ongoing violations, which allow for the admissibility of cases in which the breach precedes ratification or accession as long as it continues after the time of ratification or accession.[249] Furthermore, the denunciation of the Convention by a State Party does not have the effect of releasing the State concerned from its obligations with respect to any act that may constitute a violation and that has taken place prior to the denunciation coming into effect, which is a year after the notice of denunciation is addressed to the OAS Secretary General.[250]

The Commission's material jurisdiction requires the alleged violation to concern a right protected by the American Declaration, the American Convention, or any of the Inter-American human rights treaties that grant it jurisdiction.[251] As to the Commission's territorial jurisdiction, it extends to the whole territory of the States, but can also extend beyond it, when State agents are exercising authority and control of individuals abroad—a topic discussed in **Section 3.2.3.1**.[252] Moreover, both the Commission and Court can see their jurisdiction restricted by reservations to the text of the Convention (or other Inter-American treaty) appended by a State Party at the time of ratification or accession. Nevertheless, given that the object and purpose of these treaties is the protection of the essential rights of the individual, any reservations to their text should be restrictively interpreted.[253]

The Court's jurisdiction operates in similar ways to that of the Commission, except for the following differences. The first is that only the Commission or a State Party to the Convention can bring a case to the Court (and only within the three-month period from the Commission's adoption of the Article 50 Report). However, for a State Party to be subject to the Court's jurisdiction, it is also required, pursuant to Article 62 of the Convention, for it to have made a declaration to that effect. This optional clause also affects the Court's temporal jurisdiction, as violations of the Convention that took place following the State ratification or accession but before the aforementioned declaration, although entail the

---

[248] IACHR, Report 48/15 (Admissibility), Petition 79-06 (*Yaqui People v. Mexico*), OEA/Ser.L/V/II.155, doc. 28 (28 July 2015), para. 45.

[249] IACHR, Report 65/05 (Admissibility), Petition 777-01 (*Rosendo Radilla Pacheco v. Mexico*), OEA/Ser.L/V/II.124, doc. 5 (27 February 2006), para. 16; IACHR, Report 66/16 (Admissibility), Petition 824-12 (*Tamara Mariana Adrián Hernández v. Venezuela*), OEA/Ser.L/V/II.159, doc. 75 (6 December 2016), para. 28.

[250] ACHR, Art. 78.   [251] IACHR, Rules of Procedure, Arts. 23, 51.

[252] IACHR, Report 112/10 (Admissibility), *Franklin Guillermo Aisalla Molina and family*, Inter-State Petition IP-02 (Ecuador—Colombia) (21 October 2012), paras. 90, 99; IACHR, Report 153/11 (Admissibility), Petition 189-03 (*Danny Honorio Bastidas Meneses and others v. Ecuador*) (2 November 2011), para. 21; IACHR, Report 21/16 (Admissibility), Petition 419-08 (*Khaled El-Masri v. United States*) (15 April 2016), para. 24.

[253] IACtHR, *The Effect of Reservations on the Entry into Force of the American Convention on Human Rights*. Advisory Opinion OC-2/82 of September 24, 1982. Series A no. 2, paras. 66, 69; IACtHR, *Boyce et al. v. Barbados*. Preliminary Objection, Merits, Reparations and Costs. Judgment of November 20, 2007. Series C No. 169, paras. 15–17.

responsibility of the State under international law, fall outside of the Court's jurisdiction. Of course, the exception to this exclusion is the authority of the Court to examine ongoing violations that continue to be committed after the acceptance of its jurisdiction.[254]

A further difference between the jurisdiction of the Commission and that of the Court is that the latter cannot rule on violations of the American Declaration on the Rights and Duties of Man,[255] but only on breaches of the American Convention and other Inter-American treaties that granted it jurisdiction.[256] Although the Court can interpret the States' international obligations concerning other treaties and the American Declaration under its advisory jurisdiction,[257] and even use other legal sources to interpret the scope of the provisions of the American Convention within the context of contentious cases,[258] it is not empowered to find violations of other international legal norms beyond the aforementioned ones.[259]

In addition to the question of jurisdiction of both the Commission and Court, petitions (and, therefore, cases) also need to fulfil the admissibility criteria set out in Articles 46 and 47 of the Convention.[260] Petitions should contain the name, nationality, profession, domicile, and signature of the person or persons or of the legal representative of the entity lodging the petition,[261] as well as an indication of whether they wish to keep their identity withheld from the State and the reasons for this.[262] Petitions should provide an account of the facts denounced, specifying the alleged human rights violations, and indicate the State considered responsible. If possible, they should also contain the name of the alleged victim and of any

---

[254] IACtHR, *Moiwana Community v. Suriname*. Preliminary Objections, Merits, Reparations and Costs. Judgment of June 15, 2005. Series C No. 124, para. 39; IACtHR, *Heliodoro Portugal v. Panama*. Preliminary Objections, Merits, Reparations and Costs. Judgment of August 12, 2008. Series C No. 186, para. 25; IACtHR, *Radilla Pacheco v. Mexico*. Preliminary Objections, Merits, Reparations and Costs. Judgment of November 23, 2009. Series C No. 209, paras. 22–24.

[255] IACtHR, *Moiwana Community v. Suriname*. Preliminary Objections, Merits, Reparations and Costs. Judgment of June 15, 2005. Series C No. 124, para. 63; IACtHR, *Bueno Alves v. Argentina*. Merits, Reparations and Costs. Judgment of May 11, 2007. Series C No. 164, paras. 54–60.

[256] IACtHR, *'White Van' (Paniagua Morales et al.) v. Guatemala*. Merits. Judgment of March 8, 1998. Series C No. 37, para. 136 and op. para. 3; IACtHR, *Gómez Palomino v. Peru*. Merits, Reparations and Costs. Judgment of November 22, 2005. Series C No. 136, op. para. 5; IACtHR, *González et al. ('Cotton Field') v. Mexico*. Preliminary Objection, Merits, Reparations and Costs. Judgment of November 16, 2009. Series C No. 205, op. paras. 4, 5.

[257] IACtHR, Interpretation of the American Declaration of the Rights and Duties of Man within the Framework of Article 64 of the American Convention on Human Rights. Advisory Opinion OC-10/89 of July 14, 1989. Series A No.10; IACtHR, The Right to Information on Consular Assistance in the Framework of the Guarantees of the due Process of Law. Advisory Opinion OC-16/99 of October 1, 1999. Series A no.16.

[258] IACtHR, *'Street Children' (Villagrán Morales et al.) v. Guatemala*. Merits. Judgment of November 19, 1999. Series C No. 63, paras. 194–198; IACtHR, *Raxcacó Reyes v. Guatemala*. Merits, Reparations and Costs. Judgment of September 15, 2005. Series C No. 133, para. 99; IACtHR, *Santo Domingo Massacre v. Colombia*. Preliminary Objections, Merits and Reparations. Judgment of November 30, 2012. Series No. 259, paras. 24–25.

[259] IACtHR, *Las Palmeras v. Colombia*. Preliminary Objections. Judgment of February 4, 2000. Series C No. 67, para. 33; IACtHR, *Bámaca Velásquez v. Guatemala*. Merits. Judgment of November 25, 2000. Series C No. 70, paras. 208–209; IACtHR, *Radilla Pacheco v. Mexico*. Preliminary Objections, Merits, Reparations and Costs. Judgment of November 23, 2009. Series C No. 209, para. 43; IACtHR, *Santo Domingo Massacre v. Colombia*. Preliminary Objections, Merits and Reparations. Judgment of November 30, 2012. Series No. 259, para. 24.

[260] The Commission applies the same criteria for petitions brought under the American Declaration. See: IACtHR, Rules of Procedure, Arts. 51, 52.

[261] ACHR, Art. 46.1.d.   [262] IACtHR, Rules of Procedure, Art. 28.2.

public authority who has taken cognizance of the situation denounced.[263] The Commission's Executive Secretary would declare a petition inadmissible when the stated facts are not capable to establish *prima facie* a violation of protected human rights, or if the petition is considered to be manifestly groundless or obviously out of order.[264] Petitions would be declared 'manifestly groundless' when, following an initial examination, it becomes obvious that the acts that gave rise to the complaint do not amount to a violation of protected human rights, such as when they fit within the legitimate restriction of a right, or when the disclosed facts no longer subsists.[265]

6.4.5.1 The exhaustion of domestic remedies and the six-month rule

The first two admissibility requirements provided for the Convention are the prior exhaustion of domestic remedies and the six-month rule—the requirement for petitions to be lodged with the Commission within six months from the date of the notification of the decision exhausting national remedies. As the Commission and the Court's supervisory roles are complementary to that of the national systems of the States, only after the national courts have failed to redress the alleged violation can a petition be brought to the Inter-American system. However, the Convention provides three exceptions to the need to exhaust domestic remedies—and, consequently, to the six-month rule. These are: when the State's domestic legislation does not afford due process of law for the protection of the rights that have been allegedly violated; when the person claiming a violation has been denied access to the remedies under domestic law or has been prevented from exhausting them; and when there has been an unwarranted delay in rendering a final judgment under the aforementioned remedies.[266] When a petition is brought to the Inter-American system claiming that an exception to the need to exhaust domestic remedies applies, it is for the State objecting to the admissibility of the petition to specify the domestic remedies that remain to be exhausted and to demonstrate that such remedies were at the claimant's disposal and were appropriate, suitable, and effective; they should be capable of both addressing the infringement of the right in question and of producing the results for which they were designed.[267] The Court's jurisprudence has established that objections concerning the lack of exhaustion of domestic remedies need to be filed in a timely fashion, before the Commission, as otherwise it would be assumed that the State has waived its right to object.[268]

---

[263] IACtHR, Rules of Procedure, Art. 28.4, 28.5, 28.6.   [264] ACHR, Art. 47.a, 47.b, 47.c.

[265] H. Faúndez Ledesma, *The Inter-American System for the Protection of Human Rights: Institutional and Procedural Aspects* (3rd edn., IIDH 2008) 342–343.

[266] ACHR, Art. 46.2.

[267] IACtHR, *Velásquez Rodríguez v. Honduras*. Preliminary Objections. Judgment of June 26, 1987. Series C No. 1, para. 88; IACtHR, *Durand and Ugarte v. Peru*. Preliminary Objections. Judgment of May 28, 1999. Series C No. 50, para. 33; IACtHR, *Moiwana Community v. Suriname*. Preliminary Objections, Merits, Reparations and Costs. Judgment of June 15, 2005. Series C No. 124. para. 49.

[268] D.A. Gonzalez-Salzberg, 'Do Preliminary Objections Truly Object to the Jurisdiction of the Inter-American Court of Human Rights? An Empirical Study of the Use and Abuse of Preliminary Objections in the Court's Case Law' (2012) 12 *Human Rights Law Review* 255, 272.

The second aforementioned criterion refers to the timeframe within which a petition can be submitted to the Commission, following the exhaustion of the domestic remedies, normally referred to as the 'six-month rule'. This requirement is closely related to the previous one, as the six-month period to present the petition is counted from the moment of the notification of the decision exhausting national remedies. That is why States that object to the admissibility of a petition based on the lack of exhaustion of domestic remedies are barred from also claiming a lack of compliance with the six-month rule since they contradict each other.[269] When a petition is brought claiming an exception to the exhaustion of domestic remedies rule, then it should be presented within a 'reasonable period of time',[270] which will be assessed by the Commission, considering the date in which the alleged violation took place and the circumstances of the case.

6.4.5.2 Duplicity of proceedings and *res judicata*

Read jointly, Articles 46.c and 47.d of the Convention establish that a petition should be found inadmissible if its subject matter is pending settlement in other international proceedings (*lis pendens*) or if it is substantially the same as a petition previously studied by the Commission or by another international organization (*res judicata*). The Court's interpretation is that the questions of *lis pendens* and *res judicata* require deciding whether two cases are actually identical. For this, the presence of three elements is needed: the same parties, both the defendant and the victims; the same object, an identical factual basis and claims; and the same legal grounds, the allegation of the identical infringement of rights.[271] The Court has gone as far as to affirm that a decision adopted by an international monitoring organ that is not a court, could not be considered identical to a compulsory judgment issued by an international tribunal and, therefore, lead to the case being considered already settled.[272] The use of such strict criteria would suggest that it might not be possible for a petition to be rejected on the grounds of the existence of *res judicata*, unless it had already been decided by the organs of the Inter-American system.[273] The Commission and the Court had declared the admissibility of petitions and cases despite aspects of them being already dealt with by the International Court of Justice,[274] the ILO's Committee on Freedom of

---

[269] IACtHR, *Neira Alegría et al. v. Peru*. Preliminary Objections. Judgment of December 11, 1991. Series C No. 13, para. 29.

[270] IACHR, Rules of Procedure, Art. 32.2.

[271] D.A. Gonzalez-Salzberg, 'Do Preliminary Objections Truly Object to the Jurisdiction of the Inter-American Court of Human Rights? An Empirical Study of the Use and Abuse of Preliminary Objections in the Court's Case Law' (2012) 12 *Human Rights Law Review* 273.

[272] IACtHR, *Baena Ricardo et al. v. Panama*. Preliminary Objections. Judgment of November 18, 1999. Series C No. 61, para. 57; IACtHR, *Saramaka People v. Suriname*. Preliminary Objections, Merits, Reparations and Costs. Judgment of November 28, 2007 Series C No. 172, para. 54.

[273] D.A. Gonzalez-Salzberg, 'Do Preliminary Objections Truly Object to the Jurisdiction of the Inter-American Court of Human Rights? An Empirical Study of the Use and Abuse of Preliminary Objections in the Court's Case Law' (2012) 12 *Human Rights Law Review* 255, 274.

[274] IACHR, Report 73/12 (Admissibility), Petition 15–12 (*Edgar Tamayo Arias v. United States*) (17 July 2012), para. 44.

Association,[275] the reporting system of treaty-bodies,[276] the early warning procedure of the Committee on the Elimination of Racial Discrimination,[277] the United Nations Human Rights Council,[278] the UN Working Group on Enforced Disappearances,[279] the UN Working Group on Arbitrary Detentions,[280] and the UN Special Rapporteur on Extrajudicial, Summary, or Arbitrary Executions.[281]

6.4.5.3 Objections based on the Commission's proceedings

Whether the Court should revisit the decision of admissibility adopted by the Commission has been a contentious topic. Judge Cançado Trindade proposed that the requirements of admissibility before the Commission should not be engaged with by the Court but considered settled in a definitive manner, as it is the case with decisions on inadmissibility.[282] Unfortunately, the Court has rejected that approach, reaffirming its power to re-open the discussion of admissibility of petitions. However, a comprehensive empirical study of the first twenty-five years of the Court's practice revealed that it had examined a total of 246 preliminary objections, including ninety-one objections concerning the admissibility of petitions, and that not a single one of those ninety-one objections had been accepted by the Court.[283]

Conversely, the Court must engage with challenges to the admissibility of cases when based on objections regarding the Commission's processing of the petition or the submission of the case to the Court.[284] For instance, the Court has the power to assess whether due process of law has been followed during the proceedings before the

---

[275] IACtHR, *Baena Ricardo et al. v. Panama*. Preliminary Objections. Judgment of November 18, 1999. Series C No. 61, para. 57; IACHR, Report 15/15 (Admissibility), Petition 374-05 (*Members of the Trade Union of Workers of the National Federation of Coffee Growers of Colombia v. Colombia*) (24 March 2015), para. 49; IACHR, Report 41/16 (Admissibility), Petition 142-04 (*José Tomás Tenorio Morales and others v. Nicaragua*) (11 September 2016), para. 53.

[276] IACtHR, *Saramaka People v. Suriname*. Preliminary Objections, Merits, Reparations and Costs. Judgment of November 28, 2007 Series C No. 172, para. 54.

[277] IACtHR, *Saramaka People v. Suriname*. Preliminary Objections, Merits, Reparations and Costs. Judgment of November 28, 2007 Series C No. 172, para. 54.

[278] IACHR, Report 33/15 (Admissibility), Petition 11.754 (*U'wa People v. Colombia*) (22 July 2015), para. 42.

[279] IACHR, Report 78/16 (Admissibility), Petition 1170-09 (*Almir Muniz Da Silva v. Brazil*) (30 December 2016), para. 37.

[280] IACHR, Report No. 67/15 (Admissibility), Petition 211-07 (*Jorge Marcial Tzompaxtle Tecpile and others v. Mexico*) (27 October 2015), para. 35.

[281] IACHR, Report 22/05 (Admissibility), Petition 12.270 (Johan Alexis Ortiz Hernández v. Venezuela) (25 February 2005), para. 41.

[282] IACtHR, *Gangaram Panday v. Suriname*. Preliminary Objections. Judgment of December 4, 1991. Series C No. 12, concurring opinion of Judge A.A. Cançado Trindade para. 6; IACtHR, *Loayza Tamayo v. Peru*. Preliminary Objections. Judgment of January 31, 1996. Series C No. 25, separate opinion of Judge A.A. Cançado Trindade paras. 2, 7.

[283] D.A. Gonzalez-Salzberg, 'Do Preliminary Objections Truly Object to the Jurisdiction of the Inter-American Court of Human Rights? An Empirical Study of the Use and Abuse of Preliminary Objections in the Court's Case Law' (2012) 12 *Human Rights Law Review* 255, 257, 271.

[284] D.A. Gonzalez-Salzberg, 'Do Preliminary Objections Truly Object to the Jurisdiction of the Inter-American Court of Human Rights? An Empirical Study of the Use and Abuse of Preliminary Objections in the Court's Case Law' (2012) 12 *Human Rights Law Review* 255, 271.

Commission in relation to the processing of matters that are submitted to the Court.[285] In the past, the Court has admitted an objection based on the breach of the State's right of defence during the proceedings before the Commission, when a change in the object of the procedure barred the State from challenging the admissibility of certain claims.[286] Concerning objections to the submission of the case to the Court, these have appeared in the case law since early days. In the past, the Court has dismissed an entire case when the Commission had submitted it after the expiration of the three-month period following the adoption of its Article 50 Report.[287]

6.4.6 MEASURES OF PROTECTION: PRECAUTIONARY AND PROVISIONAL MEASURES

Both the Inter-American Commission and the Inter-American Court are empowered to issue urgent measures of protection aimed at preventing irreparable harm to persons who are in a situation of extreme gravity and urgency. These types of measures are denominated 'precautionary measures' when issued by the Commission and 'provisional measures' when ordered by the Court. As discussed in **Section 2.6**, the prevention of irreparable harm to the human person is one of the areas in which the international law of human rights has considerably evolved in recent times. The purpose of these urgent measures is twofold. On the one hand, they have an essentially preventive character, aimed at the preservation of the *status quo*, avoiding irremediable situations that would make compliance with a final decision illusory.[288] On the other hand, these measures are endowed with a truly tutelary character, in so far as they seek to avoid harm from even occurring, effectively protecting individuals' fundamental rights.[289]

The Commission has historically required States to adopt urgent measures regarding certain violations; an ability expressly acknowledged by its inclusion in the Commission's Rules of Procedure in 1980.[290] Moreover, since the adoption of the 1994 Inter-American Convention on the Forced Disappearance of Persons, the Commission's competence to adopt this type of measures counts with a conventional basis with respect to the processing of cases alleging the forced disappearance of

---

[285] IACtHR, Control of due process in the exercise of the powers of the Inter-American Commission on Human Rights. Advisory Opinion OC-19/05 of November 28, 2005. Series A no.19, op. para. 3.

[286] IACtHR, *Grande v. Argentina*. Preliminary Objections and Merits. Judgment of August 31, 2011. Series C No. 231, para. 61.

[287] IACtHR, *Cayara v. Peru*. Preliminary Objections. Judgment of February 3, 1993. Series C No. 14.

[288] H. Faúndez Ledesma, *The Inter-American System for the Protection of Human Rights: Institutional and Procedural Aspects* (3rd edn., IIDH 2008) 501.

[289] IACtHR, *Constitutional Court v. Peru*. Provisional Measures. Order of the President of the Inter-American Court of Human Rights of April 7, 2000, para. 11; IACtHR, *Matter of the Peace Community of San José de Apartadó regarding Colombia*. Provisional Measures. Order of the Inter-American Court of Human Rights of November 24, 2000, para. 12.

[290] F. González, 'Urgent Measures in the Inter-American Human Rights System' (2010) 13 *Sur— International Journal on Human Rights* 50, 52.

persons.[291] While certain OAS Member States have questioned the Commission's power to adopt precautionary measures—such as Ecuador, the USA, and Venezuela[292]—the Commission's ability has been confirmed by the Court,[293] and even the binding nature of these measures has been strongly affirmed by the international legal doctrine.[294]

Pursuant to its current Rules, the Commission may, on its own initiative or at the request of a party, request that a State adopts precautionary measures. These measures need not be linked to an existing petition and can be ordered against any of the thirty-five OAS Member States, regardless of their status as Parties to the American Convention. Precautionary measures must concern serious and urgent situations that present a risk of irreparable harm to individuals or to the subject matter of a case pending before the Inter-American system.[295] As further explained by the Commission's Rules, the seriousness of the situation concerns the gravity of the impact that an action or omission can have on a protected right or the eventual effect on a pending decision in a case, while its urgency refers to the imminent character of the risk or threat, which would require an immediate preventive or protective action. As to the requirement of an 'irreparable harm', this involves an injury to rights which, due to their nature, would not be susceptible to reparation, restoration, or adequate compensation.[296] Given these requirements, it is not surprising that the vast majority of measures adopted by the Commission have encompassed the protection of the right to life and the right to personal integrity.[297] Precautionary measures may be issued to protect both a person or group of persons, as long as the beneficiaries are determined or susceptible of determination due to their geographic location or their membership of, or association with, a group, people, community, or organization.[298]

Unlike the Commission's precautionary measures, the provisional measures ordered by the Court are clearly endowed with a conventional basis. The

---

[291] Inter-American Convention on the Forced Disappearance of Persons, Art. XIII.

[292] H. Faúndez Ledesma, *The Inter-American System for the Protection of Human Rights: Institutional and Procedural Aspects* (3rd edn., IIDH 2008) 372; F. González, 'Urgent Measures in the Inter-American Human Rights System' (2010) 13, *Sur—International Journal on Human Rights* 50, 52; C. Burbano-Herrera and Y. Haeck, 'The Impact of Precautionary Measures in Persons Deprived of their Liberty in the Americas' in P. Engstrom (ed.), *The Inter-American Human Rights System: Impact beyond Compliance* (Palgrave 2019) 89–113, 91.

[293] IACtHR, *Matter of James et al. regarding Trinidad and Tobago*. Provisional Measures. Order of the Inter-American Court of Human Rights of November 26, 2001; IACtHR, *Matter of the Mendoza Prisons regarding Argentina*. Provisional Measures. Order of the Inter-American Court of Human Rights of November 22, 2004.

[294] H. Faúndez Ledesma, *The Inter-American System for the Protection of Human Rights: Institutional and Procedural Aspects* (3rd edn., IIDH 2008) 361; D. Rodríguez-Pinzón, 'Precautionary Measures of the Inter-American Commission on Human Rights: Legal Status and Importance' (2013) 20 *Human Rights Brief* 13, 14–15; C. Burbano-Herrera and Y. Haeck, 'The Impact of Precautionary Measures in Persons Deprived of their Liberty in the Americas' in P. Engstrom (ed.), *The Inter-American Human Rights System: Impact beyond Compliance* (Palgrave 2019) 89–113, 93.

[295] IACHR, Rules of Procedure, Art. 25.1. [296] IACHR, Rules of Procedure, Art. 25.2.

[297] F. González, 'Urgent Measures in the Inter-American Human Rights System' (2010) 13 *Sur—International Journal on Human Rights* 50, 61; C. Burbano-Herrera and F. Viljoen, 'Interim Measures Before the Inter-American and African Human Rights Commissions: Strengths and Weaknesses' in Y. Haeck and E. Brems, *Human Rights and Civil Liberties in the 21st Century* (Springer 2014) 157–177, 166.

[298] IACHR, Rules of Procedure, Art. 25.

Convention empowers the Court to order any provisional measures of protection that it considers necessary, in cases of extreme gravity and urgency, in order to avoid irreparable damage to individuals. The Court can exercise this ability in relation to cases pending before it, at the request of a party or on its own motion, and also with regard to cases which have not yet been submitted to it, upon the Commission's request.[299] However, only States Parties to the Convention that have accepted the Court's jurisdiction can be subject to this type of measures, as the authority to order them derives from the text of the Convention itself.[300] When the Court is not in session, the President, in consultation with the Permanent Commission,[301] might call upon a State to adopt such 'urgent measures' as needed to ensure the effectiveness of any provisional measures that may be ordered by the Court during its subsequent period of sessions.[302]

The essential requirements for the adoption of provisional measures are akin to those of the Commission's precautionary measures: situations encompassing the extreme gravity of a threat that may cause irreparable damage to individuals, which would require the adoption of urgent measures to prevent it.[303] Irreparable damage may not only be the result of a violation of the rights to life or physical integrity, but taking into account the indivisibility of all human rights, such measures can be applied in relation to all rights protected by the American Convention, so long as the aforementioned requirements are met.[304] On numerous occasions, the Court has ordered provisional measures aimed at protecting different Convention rights, usually in addition to the rights to life or personal integrity, including the right to personal liberty, the right to a fair trial, freedom of expression, freedom of movement and residency, the right to nationality, the right to property, and the rights of the family.[305] As with precautionary

---

[299] A.A. Cançado Trindade, *The Access of Individuals to International Justice* (OUP 2011) 119.

[300] T. Buergenthal, 'The Inter-American Court of Human Rights' (1982) 76 *American Journal of International Law* 231, 241; A.A. Cançado Trindade, *Tratado de Direito Internacional dos Direitos Humanos: Volume III* (Fabris ed. 2003) 55, 81.

[301] The Court's Permanent Commission is appointed to assist the president in the exercise of their functions, and it is composed of the president, the vice-president, and any other judges that the president deems appropriate to appoint. See: IACtHR, Rules of Procedure, Art. 6.

[302] IACtHR, Rules of Procedure, Art. 27.6.

[303] H. Faúndez Ledesma, *The Inter-American System for the Protection of Human Rights: Institutional and Procedural Aspects* (3rd edn., IIDH 2008), 508–509.

[304] IACtHR, *Matter of Haitians and Dominicans of Haitian-origin in the Dominican Republic*. Provisional Measures. Order of the Inter-American Court of Human Rights of August 18, 2000, concurring opinion of Judge A.A. Cançado Trindade para. 14.

[305] IACtHR, *Gutiérrez Soler v. Colombia*. Provisional Measures. Order of the Inter-American Court of Human Rights of March 11, 2005; IACtHR, *Ivcher Bronstein v. Peru*. Provisional Measures. Order of the Inter-American Court of Human Rights of November 23, 2000; IACtHR, *Matter of 'Globovisión' Television Station regarding Venezuela*. Provisional Measures. Order of the Inter-American Court of Human Rights of September 4, 2004; IACtHR, *Matter of Kichwa Indigenous People of Sarayaku regarding Ecuador*. Provisional Measures. Order of the Inter-American Court of Human Rights of July 6, 2004; IACtHR, *Matter of Haitians and Dominicans of Haitian-origin in the Dominican Republic*. Provisional Measures. Order of the Inter-American Court of Human Rights of May 26, 2001; IACtHR, *Mayagna (Sumo) Awas Tingni Community v. Nicaragua*. Provisional Measures. Order of the Inter-American Court of Human Rights of September 6, 2002; IACtHR, *Matter of L.M. regarding Paraguay*. Provisional Measures. Order of the Inter-American Court of Human Rights of July 1, 2011.

measures, the beneficiaries of provisional measures need not be individualized, but susceptible to identification.[306] For instance, in the case of the *Community of Peace of San José of Apartadó*, the Inter-American Court ratified the urgent measures ordered by its President in favour of a 'community of peace' in Colombia, instructing the adoption of urgent measures for the protection of the life and personal integrity of more than 1,000 persons, which included not only all the members of the said 'peace community', but also the people which they helped.

Provisional measures of protection ordered by the Court are, by definition, of a temporary character. Nevertheless, if their prerequisites persist in time, so would the measures. Sadly, it is not at all surprising that, in a region where the conditions of vulnerability of the fundamental rights of individuals are pathologically prolonged in time, provisional measures have been frequently maintained in time.[307] The monitoring of urgent or provisional measures is carried out through the submission of State reports, the observations on said reports by the beneficiaries of the measures, and the submission of the Commission's opinion on both the report and the observations.[308] This procedure enables the Court to exert a continuous monitoring of the compliance, on the part of the States, with the measures it has ordered.[309]

While there is a certain degree of dispute as to the legal effect of the Commission's precautionary measures, the Court's provisional measures are undoubtedly binding.[310] This is confirmed by the high degree of compliance with these measures by the States.[311] Since their adoption for the first time in 1988 to protect the witnesses that had appeared and would be appearing within the proceedings of the first three contentious cases against Honduras—and prompted by the murder of two witnesses to these cases[312]— the Court has ordered measures to provide urgent protection to tens of thousands of individuals.[313]

---

[306] IACtHR, *Matter of the Peace Community of San José de Apartadó regarding Colombia*. Provisional Measures. Order of the Inter-American Court of Human Rights of November 24, 2000, para. 7 and op. para. 3.

[307] A.A. Cançado Trindade, 'The Evolution of Provisional Measures of Protection under the Case-Law of the Inter-American Court of Human Rights (1987–2002)' (2003) 24 *Human Rights Law Journal* 162, 168.

[308] IACtHR, Rules of Procedure, Art. 27.7.

[309] A.A. Cançado Trindade, *The Access of Individuals to International Justice* (OUP 2011) 158.

[310] IACtHR, *Matter of James et al. regarding Trinidad and Tobago*. Provisional Measures. Order of the Inter-American Court of Human Rights of August 29, 1998, para. 7; IACtHR, *Constitutional Court v. Peru*. Provisional Measures. Order of the Inter-American Court of Human Rights of August 14, 2000, para. 14.

[311] C. Burbano-Herrera, *Provisional Measures in the Case Law of the Inter-American Court of Human Rights* (Intersentia 2010) 3.

[312] IACtHR, *Velásquez Rodríguez v. Honduras*. Provisional Measures. Order of the Inter-American Court of Human Rights of January 15, 1988.

[313] IACtHR, *Kawas Fernandez v. Honduras*. Provisional Measures. Order of the Inter-American Court of Human Rights of July 5, 2011, concurring opinion of Judges Diego García-Sayán, Leonardo A. Franco, Manuel Ventura Robles, Margarette May Macaulay, and Rhadys Abreu Blondet, para. 24.

6.5 CRITICAL DEBATES: BACKLASHES AND LACK OF FINANCIAL SUPPORT

The financial situation of the Inter-American system has been critical since its inception, with a protracted history of underfunding affecting the activities of both the Commission and the Court.[314] This translates into a reduced number of permanent staff working for each of these bodies and the impossibility of ever achieving a Commission and a Court operating on a permanent basis, which would be desirable, especially considering the continuously increasing number of petitions, contentious cases, and requests for urgent measures.[315] For many years now, the limited budget received from the OAS has made both the Commission and the Court rely on voluntary contributions coming from States (both OAS Member States and non-Members), international organizations, and even foundations and academic institutions.[316]

The situation reached particularly high notoriety in 2016 when the Commission issued a press release explaining that unless additional funds were urgently confirmed, it would not be able to renew the work contract of 40 per cent of its staff. It further highlighted that beyond the immediate financial crisis it was experiencing, the Commission suffered from a 'structural, systematic lack of funds that must be addressed and resolved', asserting that there was a deep discrepancy between the mandate given to the Commission and the financial resources allocated to it.[317] The imminent financial debacle of 2016 was finally overcome, thanks to voluntary contributions,[318] and in 2017, the OAS General Assembly decided that over a three-year period it would double the regular funds allocated to both the Commission and Court.[319] Although the decision to substantially increase the budget of these organs is to be welcome, the enlarged budgets are still sub-optimal for the correct functioning of these bodies.[320]

---

[314] V. Gómez, 'The Interaction between the Political Actors of the OAS, the Commission and the Court' in D. Harris and S. Livingstone (eds.), *The Inter-American System of Human Rights* (Clarendon Press 1998) 173–211, 201–203; R.K. Goldman, 'History and Action: The Inter-American Human Rights System and the Role of the Inter-American Commission on Human Rights' (2009) 31 *Human Rights Quarterly* 856, 882–883; A. Dulitzky, 'The Inter-American Human Rights System Fifty Years Later: Time for Changes' (2011) *Quebec Journal of International Law* 127, 133.

[315] A.A. Cançado Trindade, *The Access of Individuals to International Justice* (OUP 2011) 40; A. Dulitzky, 'The Inter-American Human Rights System Fifty Years Later: Time for Changes' (2011) *Quebec Journal of International Law* 127, 151–156; J-M. Pasqualucci, *The Practice and Procedure of the Inter-American Court of Human Rights* (2nd edn., CUP 2013) 24–26.

[316] A. Dulitzky, 'The Inter-American Human Rights System Fifty Years Later: Time for Changes' (2011) *Quebec Journal of International Law* 127, 133–134; R. Cetra and J. Nascimento, 'Counting Coins: Funding the Inter-American Human Rights System' in *The Inter-American Human Rights System: Changing Times, Ongoing Challenges* (Due Process of Law Foundation 2016) 53–94, 57, 64.

[317] IACHR, Press Release 069/16 (23 May 2016), available at: https://www.oas.org/en/iachr/media_center/PReleases/2016/069.asp (accessed on 29 March 2023).

[318] IACHR, Press Release 145/16 (30 September 2016), available at: https://www.oas.org/en/iachr/media_center/PReleases/2016/145.asp (accessed on 29 March 2023).

[319] AG/RES. 2908 (XLVII-O/17), 'Promotion and Protection of Human Rights' (Adopted at the third plenary session, held on 21 June 2017), xvi.1.

[320] See: 'Inter-American Court of Human Rights, Financial Requirements', Presentation by the Secretary of the Inter-American Court of Human Rights, Dr Pablo Saavedra, OEA/Ser.G, CAAP/GT/RVPP-60/10 (11 May 2010); CEJIL, 'Aportes de CEJIL sobre el Adecuado Financiamiento del Sistema Interamericano de Derechos Humanos' Documento de Coyuntura 11 (2018), 13–15.

Certainly, the financial hardship experienced by the Commission and Court is a reflection of the States' level of commitment to a strong and independent regional human rights system, given that allocating enough economic resources to this particular objective of the OAS is a matter of political will. In fact, political backlashes against the Inter-American system have not been uncommon through the years. Some paradigmatic illustrations of these were the denunciation of the American Convention by Trinidad and Tobago in 1998 and Venezuela in 2012, and the attempt of Perú at withdrawing from the jurisdiction of the Court in 1999.[321] Even the process for 'strengthening the inter-American human rights system' set by the OAS General Assembly in 2011 has been perceived by many commentators as a political reaction to a number of decisions adopted by the Inter-American Commission that had not been well-received by the governments of different Member States.[322]

By 2011, a varied range of expressions of hostility towards the two main organs of the Inter-American system had been voiced by a number of governments of OAS Members. Perhaps the most vocal of these had been the repeated public manifestations of the former President of Venezuela, Hugo Chávez, accusing both the Commission and the Court of acting as imperialistic tools of the USA.[323] This led to Venezuela's denunciation of the American Convention; a decision notified to the OAS Secretary General through a thirty-three-page-long notice in which Venezuela charged the Commission and Court with infringing the American Convention and with adopting interventionist measures in contravention with the principle of State sovereignty.[324]

Ecuador had been another State that voiced its discontent with the Inter-American Commission, threatening to imitate Venezuela in its withdrawal from the Convention.[325] Ecuador's grievance was particularly aimed at the Commission's Special Rapporteur for Freedom of Expression following two press releases the Rapporteur issued in 2011.[326]

---

[321] IACtHR, *Ivcher Bronstein v. Peru*. Competence. Judgment of September 24, 1999. Series C No. 54; IACtHR, *Constitutional Court v. Peru*. Competence. Judgment of September 24, 1999. Series C No. 55.

[322] P. Nikken, 'El Sedicente "Fortalecimiento" del Sistema Interamericano de Derechos Humanos y sus Dobles Estándares frente a las Obligaciones Internacionales de los Estados Americanos' (2012) 56 *Revista IIDH* 73, 87; A. Anaya-Muñoz and N. Saltalamacchia-Ziccardi, 'El Proceso de Reforma al Sistema Interamericano de Derechos Humanos (2011–2013): Crónica Reciente y Desafíos Futuros' (2013) 38 *Pensamiento Propio* 13, 14–15; D. Cassel, 'The Perfect Storm: Count and Balance' (2014) 19 *Aportes DPLF* 20, 20–22.

[323] P. Nikken, 'El Sedicente "Fortalecimiento" del Sistema Interamericano de Derechos Humanos y sus Dobles Estándares frente a las Obligaciones Internacionales de los Estados Americanos' (2012) 56 *Revista IIDH* 73, 78–79, 123–124.

[324] Text of Venezuela's notice of denunciation (10 September 2012), pp. 5, 9, 12, 16, available at: http://www.oas.org/DIL/Nota_Rep%C3%BAblica_Bolivariana_Venezuela_to_SG.English.pdf (accessed on 29 March 2023).

[325] A.R. Oquendo, 'The Politicization of Human Rights: Within the Inter-American System and Beyond' (2018) 50 *NYU Journal of International Law and Politics* 1, 4–5.

[326] O. Ruiz-Chiriboga, 'Is Ecuador That Wrong? Analyzing the Ecuadorian Proposals concerning the Special Rapporteurship on Freedom of Expression of the Inter-American Commission on Human Rights' (2013) 20 *Human Rights Brief* 1, 5–6. See: Special Rapporteur for Freedom of Expression, 'Office of the Special Rapporteur Expresses Profound Concern Regarding Conviction of Journalist, Directors and Media Outlet in Ecuador', OAS Press Release R72/11 (21 July 2011); Special Rapporteur for Freedom of Expression, 'Office of the Special Rapporteur Expresses Concern Regarding Confirmation of Conviction Against Journalist, Directors and Media Outlet in Ecuador', OAS Press Release R104/11 (21 September 2011).

In the first of these, the Rapporteur expressed, in rather strong terms, concerns about a judicial ruling against a newspaper issued the day before, going as far as to consider the judgment to be contrary to the regional standards on freedom of expression.[327] Brasil had also expressed its disagreement with the Commission in 2011. The Commission's adoption of precautionary measures, requesting Brazil to suspend the construction of a hydroelectric plant in Belo Monte to prevent irreparable damage to the life and personal integrity of the members of the neighbouring indigenous communities,[328] led the government to recall its ambassador to the OAS, suspend the payment of its annual financial contribution, and forego proposing a candidate to integrate the Commission.[329]

While the process of reform initiated in 2011 officially came to an end in 2013, with a proposal for amendments to the Commission's Rules of Procedure—especially with regards to precautionary measures, the processing of petitions, and the request of provisional measures to the Court[330]—the political backlashes against the Inter-American system have continued. The Dominican Republic provides a clear example of this lasting trend, with ongoing challenges to the authority of the Inter-American Court. In 2014, only two months after the Court ruled against the State in a case concerning the citizenship rights of individuals of Haitian descent,[331] the Dominican Constitutional Court ruled against the validity of the State's acceptance of the Court's jurisdiction from 1999. The domestic court decided that such an acceptance had been unconstitutional, as it lacked Congressional approval.[332]

More recently, in April 2019, the Governments of Argentina, Brasil, Chile, Colombia, and Paraguay presented the Executive Secretary of the Commission with a brief joint 'declaration' aimed at 'perfecting the operability, functionality and efficacy of the Inter-American human rights system'.[333] In this document, the aforementioned States highlighted the relevance of the principle of subsidiarity; the importance of the strict adherence to the sources of the international law of human rights and the

---

[327] Press Release, Special Rapporteur for Freedom of Expression, Office of the Special Rapporteur Expresses Profound Concern Regarding Conviction of Journalist, Directors and Media Outlet in Ecuador, OAS Press Release R72/11 (21 July 2011).

[328] IACHR, PM 382/10—Indigenous Communities of the Xingu River Basin, Pará, Brazil

[329] P. Nikken, 'El Sedicente "Fortalecimiento" del Sistema Interamericano de Derechos Humanos y sus Dobles Estándares frente a las Obligaciones Internacionales de los Estados Americanos' (2012) 56 *Revista IIDH* 73, 79–80; A.R. Oquendo, 'The Politicization of Human Rights: Within the Inter-American System and Beyond' (2018) 50 *NYU Journal of International Law and Politics* 1, 19.

[330] AG/RES. 1 (XLIV-E/13), Results of the Process of Reflection on the Workings of the Inter-American Commission on Human Rights with a View to Strengthening the Inter-American Human Rights System (22 March 2013). See also: OEA/Ser.G CP/doc.4824/13 (20 February 2013), Draft Amendments to the Rules of Procedure, Policies, and Practices of The Inter-American Commission on Human Rights (IACHR) that were Open for Public Consultation this Past February 15.

[331] IACtHR, *Expelled Dominicans and Haitians v. Dominican Republic*. Preliminary Objections, Merits, Reparations and Costs. Judgment of August 28, 2014. Series C No. 282, op. paras. 19, 20.

[332] J. Contesse, 'Resisting the Inter-American Human Rights System' (2018) 44 *Yale Journal of International Law* 179, 199–204.

[333] Original text in Spanish available on the website of the Foreign Affairs Ministry of Paraguay at: https://www.mre.gov.py/index.php/noticias-de-embajadas-y-consulados/gobiernos-de-argentina-brasil-chile-colombia-y-paraguay-se-manifiestan-sobre-el-sistema-interamericano-de-derechos-humanos (accessed on 29 March 2023).

acknowledgement of the 'margin of appreciation of States'; and the need for the measures of reparation imposed upon States to respect the principle of proportionality and the Rule of Law. This document, signed by five States Parties to the Convention, reveals that the backlashes against the Inter-American system are far from over and that the claims for wider deference in favour of States present in the most recent process of reform of the European human rights system, are also making an appearance in the Americas.

6.6 INTER-STATE CASES

The American Convention also contemplates the possibility of cases arising from inter-State communications. Article 45 provides for States Parties to recognize the competence of the Commission to receive and examine communications in which a State Party alleges that another Party has committed a violation of human rights. This type of communication operates on the basis of reciprocity, so it can only be submitted by a State that recognizes the Commission's competence under the abovementioned provision.[334] By the end of 2022, only eleven States Parties to the Convention have accepted the Commission's competence to receive inter-State communications.[335] This includes Jamaica, despite not having accepted the Court's jurisdiction, and Venezuela, if the 2019 accession to the Convention by Juan Guaidó is considered valid.

So far, no inter-State case has reached the Court, but the Commission has had the opportunity to engage with inter-State communications on rare occasions. The first time was in a communication brought by Nicaragua against Costa Rica in 2006. Nicaragua claimed that Costa Rica had breached multiple provisions of the American Convention due to the failure to protect the human rights of the Nicaraguan migrant population under its jurisdiction. Nicaragua identified six individual victims of serious violations, in addition to the claim that all Nicaraguan migrant population in Costa Rica was subject to a general situation of discrimination and xenophobia.[336] The Commission declared the communication inadmissible, as Nicaragua had failed to exhaust the domestic remedies of Costa Rica.[337]

The following inter-State communication received by the Commission was submitted by Ecuador in 2009. It alleged that Colombia had violated the American Convention when a military operation of its armed forces bombarded a camp of the 'Revolutionary Armed Forces of Colombia' located in Ecuador, killing an Ecuadorian citizen. The Commission found the communication to be admissible, confirming the extra-territorial application of the American Convention when the

---

[334] IACHR, Rules of Procedure, Art. 50.1.
[335] The eleven States are: Argentina (1984), Bolivia (1993), Chile (1990), Colombia (1985), Costa Rica (1980), Ecuador (1984), Jamaica (1978), Nicaragua (2006), Perú (1981), Uruguay (1985), and Venezuela (1977 and 2019). See: https://www.cidh.oas.org/basicos/english/Basic4.Amer.Conv.Ratif.htm (accessed on 29 March 2023).
[336] IACHR, Report 11/07, Inter-State Case 01/06 (*Nicaragua v. Costa Rica*), 8 March 2007, paras. 186, 207.
[337] IACHR, Report 11/07, Inter-State Case 01/06 (*Nicaragua v. Costa Rica*), 8 March 2007, paras. 308–309.

alleged victims were subjected to the authority and control of State agents operating within the territory of another State.[338] Although domestic remedies had not been exhausted, the Commission considered that there had been an unwarranted delay in the criminal investigation, amounting to one of the exceptions from this general requirement.[339] Following the admissibility of the communication, negotiations between the parties led to an agreement and, consequently, to the withdrawal of the claim by Ecuador.[340]

6.7 FURTHER REFLECTIONS: THE 'MARGIN OF APPRECIATION' AND THE 'CONVENTIONALITY CONTROL' DOCTRINES

As discussed in **Section 1.1.2.2.2**, the European human rights system has developed the 'margin of appreciation' doctrine. This is essentially a doctrine of self-restraint by which the European Court refrains from making principled decisions on the application or interpretation of the European Convention, accepting that States might be in a better position to assess the application of the Convention to the specific case or to determine the meaning or scope of the provision or term in question. Despite the political pressure to which the Inter-American system has been subjected from different Member States, the doctrine of the margin of appreciation has only found reception within the Inter-American Court's case law in rare instances.[341] For example, the doctrine was used by the Court in its early days, when adopting its fourth Advisory Opinion; asserting that States enjoy a certain margin of appreciation when determining the requirements needed for acquiring citizenship.[342] It was also briefly referenced by the Court, when discussing the domestic regulation of the right to appeal a judgment to a higher court,[343] and has been

---

[338] IACHR, Report 112/10 (Admissibility), Inter-State Petition IP-02 (*Franklin Guillermo Aisalla Molina*) (Ecuador—Colombia), OEA/Ser.L/V/II.140, doc. 10 (21 October 2010), paras. 98–103.

[339] IACHR, Report 112/10 (Admissibility), Inter-State Petition IP-02 (*Franklin Guillermo Aisalla Molina*) (Ecuador—Colombia), OEA/Ser.L/V/II.140, doc. 10 (21 October 2010), para. 160.

[340] IACHR, Report No. 96/13, *Franklin Guillermo Aisalla Molina and family*, Inter-State Case 12.779 (Ecuador—Colombia), Decision to Archive, 4 November 2013.

[341] The Inter-American Commission has also made use of it in exceptional cases. See: IACHR, *Ríos Montt v. Guatemala*, Case 10.804, Report No. 30/93, OEA/Ser.L/V/II.85, doc. 9 Rev. at 206 (1994), para. 24. See also: IACHR, *Aylwin Azócar*, Report No. 137/99, OEA/Ser.L/V/II.106, doc. 6 Rev. (1999), para. 99; IACHR, *Statehood Solidarity Comm. v. U.S.*, Case 11.204, Report No. 98/03, OEA/Ser.L/V/II.118, doc. 5 Rev. 2 (2003), para. 88.

[342] IACtHR, *Proposed Amendments of the Naturalization Provisions of the Constitution of Costa Rica*. Advisory Opinion OC-4/84 of January 19, 1984. Series A no. 4, paras. 58, 62.

[343] IACtHR, *Herrera Ulloa v. Costa Rica*. Preliminary Objections, Merits, Reparations and Costs. Judgment of July 2, 2004. Series C No. 107, para. 161; IACtHR, *Barreto Leiva v. Venezuela*. Merits, Reparations and Costs. Judgment of November 17, 2009. Series C No. 206, para. 90. The Court can be seen making use of the 'margin of appreciation' doctrine, although avoiding such a denomination, in a handful of other cases, for instance, with regards to the regulation of 'political rights'. See: IACtHR, *Castañeda Gutman v. Mexico*. Preliminary Objections, Merits, Reparations and Costs. Judgment of August 6, 2008. Series C No. 184, paras. 204–205.

resorted to by dissenting judges in attempts to stop the Court from adopting progressive stances with regard to both LGBTQI and reproductive rights.[344]

Conversely, the Court has developed a doctrine it denominates 'conventionality control', which, far from being grounded in States' deference, is focused on States' compliance with the Court's jurisprudence.[345] The notion of a 'conventionality control' highlights the duty of the domestic judicial authorities, within their respective spheres of competence, to exercise an *ex officio* examination to ensure that the domestic norms they apply are in line with the American Convention, taking into account not only the text of the treaty but also its interpretation by the Inter-American Court.[346] The 'conventionality control' doctrine made its first appearance in the Court's judgments in the case of *Almonacid Arellano v. Chile*,[347] although it can be found even before then in the separate opinions of a former President of the Court.[348] Since its adoption by the Court in 2006, references to this doctrine have featured recurrently in the case law.[349]

---

[344] IACtHR, *Atala Riffo and daughters v. Chile*. Merits, Reparations and Costs. Judgment of February 24, 2012. Series C No. 239, partially dissenting opinion of Judge Alberto Pérez Pérez paras. 23–24; IACtHR, *Duque v. Colombia*. Preliminary Objections, Merits, Reparations and Costs. Judgment of February 26, 2016. Series C No. 310, partially dissenting opinion of Judge Eduardo Vio Grossi p. 9; IACtHR, *Gender identity, and equality and non-discrimination with regard to same-sex couples*. Advisory Opinion OC-24/17 of November 24, 2017. Series A no. 24, separate opinion of Judge Eduardo Vio Grossi paras. 5, 114, 163; IACtHR, *Gómez Murillo et al. v. Costa Rica*. Judgment of November 29, 2016. Series C No. 326, individual dissenting vote of Judge Vio Grossi p. 5.

[345] The topic has certainly raised much academic interest. See, among many: J.C. Hitters, 'El Control de Convencionalidad y el Cumplimiento de las Sentencias de la Corte Interamericana' (2012) 10 *Estudios Constitucionales* 535; E. Ferrer MacGregor, 'The Constitutionalization of International Law in Latin America: Conventionality Control—The New Doctrine of the Inter-American Court of Human Rights' (2015) *AJIL Unbound* 93; A. Dulitzky, 'An Inter-American Constitutional Court? The Invention of the Conventionality Control by the Inter-American Court of Human Rights' (2015) 50 *Texas International Law Journal* 45; J. Contesse, 'The International Authority of the Inter-American Court of Human Rights: A Critique of the Conventionality Control Doctrine' (2018) 22 *International Journal of Human Rights* 1168.

[346] IACtHR, *Almonacid Arellano et al. v. Chile*. Preliminary Objections, Merits, Reparations and Costs. Judgment of September 26, 2006. Series C No. 154, para. 124; IACtHR, *Dismissed Congressional Employees (Aguado Alfaro et al.) v. Peru*. Preliminary Objections, Merits, Reparations and Costs. Judgment of November 24, 2006. Series C No. 158, para. 128; IACtHR, *Furlan and family v. Argentina*. Preliminary Objections, Merits, Reparations and Costs. Judgment of August 31, 2012. Series C No. 246, para. 303.

[347] IACtHR, *Almonacid Arellano et al. v. Chile*. Preliminary Objections, Merits, Reparations and Costs. Judgment of September 26, 2006. Series C No. 154, para. 124.

[348] IACtHR, *Myrna Mack Chang v. Guatemala*. Merits, Reparations and Costs. Judgment of November 25, 2003. Series C No. 101, reasoned concurring opinion of Judge Sergio García Ramírez para. 27. See also: IACtHR, *Tibi v. Ecuador*. Preliminary Objections, Merits, Reparations and Costs. Judgment of September 7, 2004. Series C No. 114, separate concurring opinion of Judge Sergio García Ramírez para. 3; IACtHR, *López Álvarez v. Honduras*. Merits, Reparations and Costs. Judgment of February 1, 2006. Series C No. 141, concurring opinion of Judge Sergio Garcia Ramirez para. 30.

[349] See, among many: IACtHR, *Dismissed Congressional Employees (Aguado Alfaro et al.) v. Peru*. Preliminary Objections, Merits, Reparations and Costs. Judgment of November 24, 2006. Series C No. 158, para. 128; IACtHR, *Radilla Pacheco v. Mexico*. Preliminary Objections, Merits, Reparations and Costs. Judgment of November 23, 2009. Series C No. 209, para. 339; IACtHR, *Furlan and family v. Argentina*. Preliminary Objections, Merits, Reparations and Costs. Judgment of August 31, 2012. Series C No. 246, para. 303.

> **IACtHR,** *Almonacid Arellano et al. v. Chile.* **Preliminary Objections, Merits, Reparations and Costs. Judgment of September 26, 2006. Series C No. 154.**
>
> The case was brought to the Inter-American system by the next-of-kin of Mr Almonacid-Arellano and it concerned the alleged failure to investigate his extra-legal execution, during the Pinochet regime, as well as the consequential lack of punishment of the individuals responsible for it, due to the enactment of an amnesty law in 1978. While the actual deprivation of life happened before Chile acceded to the Convention, the Commission considered that the lack of investigation of the facts and prosecution and conviction of the wrongdoers amounted to the violation of the rights to a fair trial and judicial protection of the deceased's next-of-kin. Given the lack of adoption of measures by the State, following its Report, the Commission decided to submit the case to the Court.
>
> The Court ruled that, despite the extra-legal execution of Almonacid-Arellano taking place before the State's accession to the Convention, a number of actions concerning the investigation of the crime where adopted following Chile's accession to the Convention, which had affected the rights of the victim's next-of-kin. These actions fitted within the Court's temporal jurisdiction (paras. 49–50). The Court decided that the adopted amnesty law, which was providing impunity for perpetrators of crimes against humanity, was incompatible with the Convention and that the lack of investigation of the crime, due to the application of said law, amounted to a breach of the rights of the next-of-kin of Almonacid-Arellano (para. 128). It ordered the State to ensure that the amnesty law did not continue to hinder the investigation, prosecution, and conviction of the individuals responsible for this crime and for similar violations committed (op. paras. 5–6).

Notwithstanding the pre-eminence this doctrine has acquired in the Court's jurisprudence and, in particular, bearing in mind the backlashes experienced by the Inter-American system (as highlighted in **Section 6.5**), it is important to emphasize that the idea of a 'conventionality control' exercised by the organs of the States Parties to the American Convention is not truly a creation of the Inter-American Court. As discussed in **Section 3.4**, the implementation of the international law of human rights is primarily a domestic matter. When a State becomes Party to an international treaty, it is bound to give effect to the acquired international obligations in its domestic legal order. International law imposes upon States the duty to comply with international obligations, even if these were to clash with domestic norms, given that in case of conflict between norms, international obligations should prevail.[350] Any action or omission of an organ of the State, whether it exercises legislative, executive, judicial, or any other functions, is attributable to the State under international law and would entail its responsibility if in breach of an international obligation.[351] The Inter-American Court has acknowledged the mentioned principles of international law in its jurisprudence, repeatedly asserting

---

[350] A rule clearly codified in Art. 27 of the 1969 Vienna Convention on the Law of Treaties. See: PCIJ, *The Greco-Bulgarian 'Communities'*. Advisory Opinion (ser. B) No. 17 (31 July 1930), p. 32; PCIJ, *Treatment of Polish Nationals and Other Persons of Polish Origin or Speech in the Danzig Territory*. Advisory Opinion (ser. A/B) No. 44 (4 February 1932), p. 24. See also: Vienna Convention on the Law of Treaties (adopted 23 May 1969, entered into force 27 January 1980) 1155 UNTS 331, Art. 27.

[351] ILC, Draft Articles on Responsibility of States for Internationally Wrongful Acts, November 2001, Supplement No. 10 (A/56/10), chp.IV.E.1, Arts. 1, 2, 4.

that the principle of *pacta sunt servanda* requires States to ensure that the provisions of a treaty—in this case the American Convention—have an *effet utile* in their domestic law.[352] Such measures are only effective when States adjust their actions (i.e. the actions of all its organs) to the rules established by the Convention.

It follows from the aforementioned general rules of international law that the national judiciary of each State Party to the American Convention should apply not only domestic law but also the international law of human rights. When deciding a case, these organs should exercise an *ex officio* control of compliance of the applicable domestic norms with the State Constitution, as well as with the international treaties to which the State is Party—not limited to the American Convention. In particular, in the domain of the protection of the human person, international and national norms should always be considered together, as both legal systems are in constant interaction to offer the widest possible protection to the individual.[353] The Inter-American Court should not be blamed for developing a 'new doctrine' that encroaches on the constitutional sphere of States and the attributions of their judiciary. If anything, it gave a memorable designation to an obligation clearly established under general international law.

6.8 TESTIMONIAL: REFLECTIONS FROM A FORMER JUDGE AND PRESIDENT OF THE COURT (JUDGE ANTÔNIO AUGUSTO CANÇADO TRINDADE)

I was a judge of the Inter-American Court of Human Rights for twelve years (1995–2006), exercising the Presidency of the Court for almost half a decade (1999–2004). My time in Costa Rica actually started before my election as a full member of the Court for the 1995–2000 term of office, since in 1990, I was appointed by the Government of Suriname to sit as judge *ad hoc* in the cases of *Aloeboetoe and others* and *Gangaram Panday*. Similarly, my time as an Inter-American judge did not truly finish when my official term of office came to an end, as the Statute and the Rules of the Court establish that judges continue to hear the cases that are still pending at the expiration of their terms. Thus, I continued to intervene in cases until August 2008, when I participated in the adoption of the judgment of interpretation of the ruling on merits and reparations of the case of the *Castro Castro Prison v. Peru*, to which I appended the last of the more than one hundred separate opinions I delivered during my time as a full judge of the Inter-American Court—a judicial record that I will discuss further.

My time as an Inter-American judge was marked by the consolidation of the Court as the main judicial body of the Inter-American human rights system and by an expansive

---

[352] IACtHR, *'The Last Temptation of Christ' (Olmedo Bustos et al.) v. Chile*. Merits, Reparations and Costs. Judgment of February 5, 2001. Series C No. 73, para. 87; IACtHR, *Bulacio v. Argentina*. Merits, Reparations and Costs. Judgment of September 18, 2003. Series C No. 100, para. 117; IACtHR, *Gómez Paquiyauri Brothers v. Peru*. Merits, Reparations and Costs. Judgment of July 8, 2004. Series C No. 110, para. 151.

[353] IACtHR, *Dismissed Congressional Employees (Aguado Alfaro et al.) v. Peru*. Preliminary Objections, Merits, Reparations and Costs. Judgment of November 24, 2006. Series C No. 158, separate opinion of Judge A.A. Cançado Trindade para. 3.

interpretation of the human rights enshrined in the American Convention on Human Rights and other Inter-American treaties. However, this important period in the history of the system was certainly not free from obstacles and difficulties. For instance, soon after I assumed the Presidency of the Court in 1999, we suffered what was one of the strongest backlashes of the Court's history. This came from the Fujimori regime, which was finally coming to an end in Perú. At that time, Perú was the State with the largest number of adverse rulings from the Court. The government launched a strong misinformation campaign against the Court and its judges and attempted to withdraw, with immediate effect, the State's acceptance of the Court's jurisdiction. The Court resisted these attacks and affirmed, in two historic rulings, that it was the master of its own jurisdiction and that the withdrawal attempt by Perú was incompatible with the American Convention on Human Rights. This outcome was not well-received by the Fujimori regime, which sought the support of other States to remove the judges of the Court. Both the Court and the judges received strong support from multiple institutions, including the European Court of Human Rights, the African Commission on Human and Peoples' Rights, the International Committee of the Red Cross, the United Nations High Commissioner for Refugees, and numerous NGOs (including Peruvian ones). Unfortunately, the OAS General Secretary, from whom I sought assurances, opted to remain neutral in the situation to avoid antagonizing the State of Perú.

In the subsequent session of the OAS General Assembly, which took place in Canada in 2000, I presented the Court's Annual Report, including a request for the General Assembly to adopt measures under Article 65 against Perú due to its manifest unwillingness to comply with the Court's judgments; thus, protecting the Court's institutional role as a guardian of the enjoyment of human rights in the Americas. In the end, the OAS General Assembly thanked the Court for its work during that year. It took the opportunity to emphasize that the Court's judgments are final and that States subject to them are under the international obligation to comply with them, and it urged the States that have denounced the Convention—in reference to Trinidad and Tobago—and those that have withdrawn their recognition of the binding jurisdiction of the Court—in clear reference to Perú—to reconsider such decisions. The State of Perú changed government shortly afterwards, and the relationship between the Court and the State became normalized. Moreover, the States Parties to the Convention provided clear signals of support to the Court and its judges. Instead of being removed from the Court, together with two other incumbent judges, I was re-elected by acclamation to sit at the Inter-American Court for another term of office.

It is important to remember that, far from being antagonistic, the relationship of the Court with many of the States Parties to the Convention is one of friendship and cooperation. The Court is, after all, a mechanism for the peaceful settling of disputes under international law. In connection with this spirit of cooperation, a truly valuable practice developed by the American States, which is worth highlighting, is that it has become rather usual for them to acknowledge their wrongdoing before the Court and to accept their international responsibility, even providing apologies and guarantees of non-repetition to the victims and their families. I was fortunate enough to be present on the first occasion a State acknowledged its international responsibility before the Court. It was in the case of *Aloeboetoe and others*, in which the Government of Suriname had appointed me as *ad hoc* judge. On that occasion, given the tragic nature of the case, involving the summary execution of seven individuals, members of the Saramaka people, Suriname offered a full acknowledgement of its international responsibility, which was pioneering in international law and went on to establish, an example to be followed by other States in numerous cases. Moreover, many States would even add to their acknowledgement of responsibility a plea for forgiveness to the victims and their relatives. This quest and request for forgiveness is an essential element for social reconciliation, especially when serious violations of human rights have taken place. The act of forgiveness, which requires true repentance from the wrongdoer and ample generosity from the victim, could allow for reconciliation and set the grounds for a brighter future.

The quest for forgiveness is also extremely powerful because it reminds us that the victims of human rights violations are the reason for the existence (*la raison d'être*) of the Inter-American human rights system. In fact, I believe that one of my most important contributions to the system during my years as judge was my efforts towards the recognition of the victims as the true complainant party before the Court. In 1995, when I started my term as full judge of the Court, the Inter-American Commission and the State were considered to be the parties in a case, with the legal representatives of the victims only integrated into the delegation of the Commission as its so-called 'assistants'. I felt I had no option but to rebel against such a state of affairs. In 1996, during the public hearing of the reparations stage of the case *El Amparo v. Venezuela*, I manifested that, at the very least at the reparations phase of the case, there could be no doubt that the representatives of the victims were the true complainant, and I began to address questions directly to them. This understanding was confirmed by the adoption of the 1996 Rules of the Court, for which I was the original draft's *rapporteur*. This stance was further affirmed in the 2000 Rules of Procedure, for which I was also *rapporteur*, recognizing the victims (or their representatives) as the true parties in all stages of the proceedings before the Inter-American Court. Fortunately, the most recent version of the Court's Rules, adopted in 2009, reinforced the role of the victims during the proceedings before the Court, even establishing the role of the 'Inter-American Defender', which could ensure that all victims have access to legal representation. I hope that this significant evolution continues further in the future, with the required amendments to the Convention that would allow individuals direct access to the Court. Two decades ago, I proposed a Protocol of Reform to the American Convention to that effect, which was, unfortunately, not adopted at the time.

Nevertheless, I know that probably my best-known contribution to the Court is my more than one hundred separate opinions. I have often been asked what motivated me to spend so many hours drafting opinions when, most of the time, I agreed with the final rulings adopted by the Court, as only a small percentage of these opinions had been dissents. The truth is that I always believed that the judgments of the Inter-American Court should not only settle the dispute between the parties and provide redress to the victims, but they should be didactic as well. They should not merely instruct the parties how to act but also persuade them that the solution found by the Court represents the dictates of justice, what the law truly demands. When the parties are not persuaded that the Court is correct in its ruling, problems with compliance are more likely to arise. Because of this needed element of persuasion is that often I had to seek the answers to cases beyond the field of law, since the legal universe can be conceptually restrictive. It is the domain of the arts that frequently helped me provide reasons for the opinions I rendered in a case. I had resorted to philosophy, literature, and poetry—from Sophocles to Jorge Luis Borges and from Seneca to T.S. Eliot—to try to find the right explanations as to why a particular decision should be adopted in a case.

Having just mentioned the importance of States' compliance with judgments, I will finish these reflections by briefly referring to what I identify as one of the main shortcomings of the Inter-American system; the lack of an appropriate system for supervising States' execution of the judgments rendered against them by the Court. The topic of compliance with the Court's judgments has attracted extensive attention from the world of academia and NGOs over the past decade, given that the system continues to suffer from compliance deficits. During my years as President of the Court, I insisted on the need to create a new mechanism for supervising the execution of judgments. My idea was for the OAS to establish a permanent committee, under the Committee on Juridical and Political Affairs (CAJP), composed of a small number of representatives from the States Parties to the American Convention on Human Rights—and only from States Parties—on a rotation basis. This nuclear committee would evaluate States' compliance, or otherwise, with the judgments of the Court and communicate its findings to the OAS Permanent Council, which would, in turn, report to the General Assembly. Although my proposal was under examination by the OAS political organs for quite some time—many years, actually—no decision was adopted to create such a mechanism. Even in our days, the Court is still monitoring compliance with its own decisions, adding to the heavy workload and busy schedule of a Court that still only operates part-time.

In my opinion, the absence of a permanent political procedure for monitoring States' compliance with the Court's judgments—similar to the one in operation within the Council of Europe—truly undermines the mechanism of collective guarantee underpinning the entire Inter-American human rights system, which binds States to act both individually and in cooperation with one another towards securing the enjoyment of the rights enshrined in the American Convention of Human Rights. Sadly, there can be no enjoyment of rights when States do not effectively comply with the judgments issued against them by the Court. Human rights would be rendered illusory if States Parties could be free to refuse, or forever delay, complying with the compulsory judgments of the Court because only compliance allows for the materialization of justice for the specific case. There is, indeed, no justice without the States' factual and full compliance with the Court's judgments.

6.9 CONCLUSION

The chapter has engaged at length with the Inter-American human rights system, the regional system for the protection of human rights created within the Americas. With origins in the foundation of the OAS in 1948 but with roots that can be traced back to the end of the nineteenth century, the system has experienced a remarkable development over the years. Notwithstanding this progress, there are different aspects of the system that remain in need of improvement. One of these concerns the lack of universal ratification of the American Convention on Human Rights (and of the additional regional treaties) by all OAS Member States, including their acceptance of the Court's jurisdiction. The Inter-American system has an important deficit in its membership, with States that have consistently refused to fully join in and others that have decided to leave. This lack of full support for the system is also reflected in the severe financial problems experienced by both the Commission and the Court throughout their history. These shortcomings are depriving millions of individuals within the Americas of more effective protection of their human rights.

Nevertheless, in a continent historically characterized by human rights violations, democratic deficit, and some of the greatest levels of inequality worldwide, the Inter-American Commission and Court have acted as beacons of hope, contributing to the creation of a regional public order grounded in the protection of the most essential rights of the individual. These bodies have provided a legal limit to State voluntarism and helped to strengthen the position of the individual as the centre of a regime of international protection. Looking into the future, the system is in need of reforms. A priority among these should be securing enough funds and political will to transform both the Commission and Court into permanent bodies. A permanent Court should have compulsory jurisdiction over all States Parties to the American Convention and allow for the direct access of individuals. The recognition of the legal standing of the individual before the Court is nothing but the logical consequence of a system of protection aimed at guaranteeing human rights at the international level. Such a reform should be complemented by the creation of a new system for monitoring compliance with the Court's judgments, as the expected increase in the number of cases would require releasing the permanent Court from additional functions. The proposed reform would also entail a substantial change in the Commission's role, as this body would become detached from processing individual cases. However, unlike the European experience, it would be unthinkable to suggest the suppression of the Commission in the Americas. A permanent Commission should continue to perform its essential role of monitoring the respect of human rights in all OAS Member States.

FURTHER READING

BURBANO-HERRERA, C., *Provisional Measures in the Case Law of the Inter-American Court of Human Rights* (Intersentia 2010).

BURGORGUE-LARSEN, L. and ÚBEDA DE TORRES, A., *The Inter-American Court of Human Rights: Case Law and Commentary* (OUP 2011).

CANÇADO TRINDADE, A.A., *El Ejercicio de la Función Judicial Internacional: Memorias de la Corte Interamericana de Derechos Humanos* (3rd edn., Del Rey 2013).

CAVALLARO, J.L. et al., *Doctrine, Practice, and Advocacy in the Inter-American Human Rights System* (OUP 2019).

ENGSTROM, P. (ed.), *The Inter-American Human Rights System: Impact beyond Compliance* (Palgrave 2019).

FAÚNDEZ LEDESMA, H., *The Inter-American System for the Protection of Human Rights: Institutional and Procedural Aspects* (3rd edn., IIDH 2008).

HARRIS, D. and LIVINGSTONE, S. (eds.), *The Inter-American System of Human Rights* (Clarendon Press 1998).

PASQUALUCCI, J-M., *The Practice and Procedure of the Inter-American Court of Human Rights* (2nd edn., CUP 2013).

7

THE EUROPEAN HUMAN RIGHTS SYSTEM

7.1 THE CREATION OF THE EUROPEAN HUMAN RIGHTS SYSTEM

The European human rights system was established in the aftermath of the Second World War. The creation of a regional system for the protection of human rights was thought to fulfil two main aims: to avoid the repetition of the horrors experienced in Europe in the recent past, as well to protect European democracies from the perceived threat of the spread of communism.[1] The system was set in place within the framework provided by the Council of Europe, an international organization founded on 5 May 1949 by ten European States—Belgium, Denmark, France, Ireland, Italy, Luxemburg, the Netherlands, Norway, Sweden, and the UK—which nowadays consists of forty-six Member States,[2] following Russia's withdrawal in March 2022.[3] Moving beyond the Declarations of rights adopted in 1948, both in the Americas and by the United Nations, there was a clear intention within the Council of Europe to establish procedures for the collective enforcement of human rights.[4]

The seminal moment for the adoption of a binding international instrument for the protection of human rights to be enforced by an international judicial body can be traced back to May 1948. The International Committee of Movements for European Unity (later renamed 'European Movement') convened the Congress of Europe in The Hague. The Congress culminated with its plenary session adopting a 'Message to Europeans'. The message contained a pledge of the desire for a Charter of Human Rights that

---

[1] E. Bates, 'The Birth of the European Convention on Human Rights—and the European Court of Human Rights' in J. Christoffersen and M.R. Madsen (eds.), *The European Court of Human Rights between Law and Politics* (OUP 2011) 17–42, 18.

[2] The Council of Europe should not be confused with the European Union (EU). As discussed in the introduction to **Part III**, the legal developments that have taken place under the latter exceed the scope of the present book.

[3] Committee of Ministers, Resolution CM/Res(2022)2 on the cessation of the membership of the Russian Federation to the Council of Europe (16 March 2022).

[4] A.A. Cançado Trindade, *Tratado de Direito Internacional dos Direitos Humanos: Volume III* (Sérgio A. Fabris (ed.) 2003) 120.

would guarantee certain fundamental rights, such as the liberties of thought, assembly, expression, and to form a political opposition, as well as for the creation of a Court of Justice with the power to impose sanctions for the lack of implementation of the rights contained in the Charter.[5] This desired Charter and Court were to become the Convention for the Protection of Human Rights and Fundamental Freedoms (better known as the 'European Convention on Human Rights')[6] and the European Court of Human Rights.

On 12 July 1949, the European Movement submitted to the Council of Europe a set of documents containing drafts of a proposed Convention and Court's Statute, together with carefully crafted explanatory notes for such documents.[7] These were discussed within the Council during the drafting process of the European Convention on Human Rights. Initially, it was the Consultative Assembly (later renamed 'Parliamentary Assembly') that made use of the European Movement's drafts to prepare an outline of the Convention, recommending the Committee of Ministers 'to cause a draft Convention to be drawn up as early as possible, providing a collective guarantee, and designed to ensure the effective enjoyment of all persons residing within their territories of the rights and fundamental freedoms referred to in the Universal Declaration'.[8] The enforcement mechanism outlined followed the proposal contained in the European Movement's drafts, composed of both a Court of Justice and a Commission, the later acting as a first port of call for the regional system of protection. The Commission was to have the power to decide on the admissibility of petitions filed by individuals or States, to investigate the facts of the complaints, and to provide an opportunity to reach a friendly solution to the claim.[9] Although the inclusion of the idea of establishing a Court, as the main supervisory body of the regional system, in the proposal to be sent to the Committee of Ministers proved to be controversial, a motion to suppress this recommendation was put to a vote within the Assembly and was defeated.[10]

After receiving the recommendation from the Assembly, the Committee of Ministers decided to convene a Committee of Legal Experts to prepare the first drafts of the

---

[5] Council of Europe, Explanatory Report to Protocol No. 11 to the Convention for the Protection of Human Rights and Fundamental Freedoms, restructuring the control machinery established thereby, ETS 155 (Strasbourg, 11 May 1994) 3.

[6] Convention for the Protection of Human Rights and Fundamental Freedoms (adopted 4 November 1950, entered into force 3 September 1953) 213 UNTS 221 ('European Convention on Human Rights').

[7] A.W.B. Simpson, *Human Rights and the End of Empire: Britain and the Genesis of the European Convention* (OUP 2004) 659–660; E. Bates, *The Evolution of the European Convention on Human Rights: From Its Inception to the Creation of a Permanent Court of Human Rights* (OUP 2010) 51–52; Council of Europe, Preparatory Working Paper Drafted by the Directorate of Human Rights CDH(59)1 (Strasbourg, 16 February 1959); Council of Europe, Explanatory Report to Protocol No. 11 to the Convention for the Protection of Human Rights and Fundamental Freedoms, restructuring the control machinery established thereby, ETS 155 (Strasbourg, 11 May 1994) 3.

[8] Parliamentary Assembly, Recommendation 38 (1949)—Human Rights and Fundamental Freedoms, Art. 1.

[9] Council of Europe, Explanatory Report to Protocol No. 11 to the Convention for the Protection of Human Rights and Fundamental Freedoms, restructuring the control machinery established thereby, ETS 155 (Strasbourg, 11 May 1994) 3; E. Bates, 'The Birth of the European Convention on Human Rights—and the European Court of Human Rights' in J. Christoffersen and M.R. Madsen (eds.), *The European Court of Human Rights between Law and Politics* (OUP 2011) 17–42, 20.

[10] E. Bates, *The Evolution of the European Convention on Human Rights: From Its Inception to the Creation of a Permanent Court of Human Rights* (OUP 2010) 72.

Convention, which started work in the early months of 1950.[11] The political nature of some of the central aspects of the treaty led the Committee of Ministers to convene a 'Conference of high officials, under instructions from their Governments' to agree on the more sensitive features of the Convention.[12] The most controversial issues were the recognition of a right of individual petition and the creation of a Court, as well as whether these should be compulsory or optional traits of the Convention.[13] The final decision, embodied in the original text of the Convention, was to establish a Court and include a right to petition, but it would be for States Parties to opt into these.[14]

On 4 November 1950, at the Palazzo Barberini in Rome, the governments of thirteen States signed the final text of the European Convention on Human Rights. These were Belgium, Denmark, France, Germany, Iceland, Ireland, Italy, Luxemburg, the Netherlands, Norway, Turkey, the UK, and Saarland (later to rejoin Germany).[15] It is believed that the President of the Consultative Assembly of the Council of Europe, Paul-Henri Spaak, marked the occasion with an expression that cast strong reservations as to the future success of the Convention: 'It is not a very good Convention, but it is a lovely Palace!'[16] Seven decades later, the Convention and the system of protection it set in place proved to be one of the major developments in European legal history, perhaps even in the history of all law.[17]

7.1.1 THE EVOLUTION OF THE EUROPEAN HUMAN RIGHTS SYSTEM

The European Convention on Human Rights entered into force on 3 September 1953, when Luxemburg became the tenth State to ratify it.[18] As aforementioned, the original institutional framework for the protection of human rights set in place by the

---

[11] E. Bates, 'The Birth of the European Convention on Human Rights—and the European Court of Human Rights' in J. Christoffersen and M.R. Madsen (eds.), *The European Court of Human Rights between Law and Politics* (OUP 2011) 17–42, 27.

[12] E. Bates, 'The Birth of the European Convention on Human Rights—and the European Court of Human Rights' in J. Christoffersen and M.R. Madsen (eds.), *The European Court of Human Rights between Law and Politics* (OUP 2011) 17–42, 27–28.

[13] A.W.B. Simpson, *Human Rights and the End of Empire: Britain and the Genesis of the European Convention* (OUP 2004) 712; E. Bates, 'The Birth of the European Convention on Human Rights—and the European Court of Human Rights' in J. Christoffersen and M.R. Madsen (eds.), *The European Court of Human Rights between Law and Politics* (OUP 2011) 17–42, 25–29.

[14] European Convention on Human Rights, Arts. 25, 46, 48 of the original text. Available at: https://www.echr.coe.int/Documents/Archives_1950_Convention_ENG.pdf (accessed on 29 March 2023).

[15] A.W.B. Simpson, *Human Rights and the End of Empire: Britain and the Genesis of the European Convention* (OUP 2004) 1; E. Bates, 'The Birth of the European Convention on Human Rights—and the European Court of Human Rights' in J. Christoffersen and M.R. Madsen (eds.), *The European Court of Human Rights between Law and Politics* (OUP 2011) 17–42, 28.

[16] J. Christoffersen and M.R. Madsen (eds.), *The European Court of Human Rights between Law and Politics* (OUP 2011) 6.

[17] M. O'Boyle, 'On Reforming the Operation of the European Court of Human Rights' (2008) *European Human Rights Law Review* 1, 1; R.S. Kay, 'The European Convention on Human Rights and the Control of Private Law' (2005) *European Human Rights Law Review* 466, 479.

[18] In chronological order, the ten original parties to the Convention were: the UK (08/03/1951), Norway (15 January 1952), Sweden (04 February 1952), Germany (05 December 1952), Saarland (14 January 1953), Ireland (25 February 1953), Greece (28 March 1953), Denmark (13 April 1953), Iceland (29 June 1953), and Luxemburg (03 September 1953). For the full list of ratifications and accessions, see: https://www.coe.int/en/web/conventions/full-list/-/conventions/treaty/005/signatures?p_auth=yHtxuCUj (accessed on 29 March 2023).

Convention comprised two main organs: the European Commission of Human Rights and the European Court of Human Rights,[19] with the Committee of Ministers exercising quasi-judicial powers when a case was not referred to the Court by the Commission.[20] The Commission was established in 1954 and the following year gained the power to receive individual petitions alleging the violation of Convention rights, as five States made the optional declaration to allow for individual petitions against them. Since then, the Commission has been able to investigate the complaints lodged by individuals and, unless a friendly settlement could be reached, elaborate a Report stating its opinion as to whether a breach of the Convention had taken place.[21] Until the establishment of the Court in 1959, the Commission could only submit the mentioned Report to the respondent State and the Committee of Ministers. It was up to the Committee of Ministers (by a two-thirds majority) to determine whether the State was responsible for breaching the Convention.[22] The Court was finally established in 1959, following the eighth recognition of its optional jurisdiction.[23] However, individuals could not yet bring applications directly to the Court, but only to the Commission. The Commission and the State Parties were the only ones with access to the Court until 1994, when the entry into force of Protocol 9 granted the individual legal standing before the Court.[24]

The system designed in 1950 has experienced a number of amendments through the decades. Up to the end of 2022, States Parties to the Convention have adopted a total of seventeen Protocols to this effect, counting Protocol 10—which never entered into force—and provisional Protocol 14bis. Seven of these Protocols (Nos. 3, 5, 8, 9, 11, 14, 14bis, 15) amended the actual text of the Convention,[25] producing institutional changes to the European Human Rights System. The remaining nine Protocols did not affect the Convention's text but were aimed at providing enhanced protection of individuals' rights or, in the case of Protocols 2 and 16, at conferring upon the Court its abilities to issue advisory opinions (a topic discussed in **Section 7.6**). Through the adoption of the additional Protocols, States Parties have extended the protection provided by the Convention to include, for instance, the right to property, the right to education, and political rights (Protocol 1); freedom of movement (Protocol 4); a strict prohibition of the death penalty (Protocols 6 and 13); the right to appeal in criminal matters and the principle of *non bis in idem* (Protocol 7); and a general prohibition of discrimination (Protocol 12).

---

[19] ECHR, Art. 19 (original text).

[20] When following the elaboration of a Report the Commission did not refer a case to the Court, it was up to the Committee of Ministers by a two-thirds majority to determine the existence of a violation of the Convention. This competence of the Committee of Ministers was abolished by Protocol 11. See: ECHR, Art. 32 (original text); Protocol No. 11 to the Convention for the Protection of Human Rights and Fundamental Freedoms, restructuring the control machinery established thereby (adopted 11 May 1994, entered into force 1 November 1998) ETS No. 155.

[21] ECHR, Art. 31 (original text).

[22] This would have become a simple majority if Protocol 10 had entered into force. See: ECHR, Art. 32 (original text); Protocol No. 10 to the Convention for the Protection of Human Rights and Fundamental Freedoms (adopted 25 March 1992) ETS No. 146.

[23] ECHR, Art. 56 (original text).

[24] ECHR, Arts. 44, 45, 48 (original text); Protocol No. 9 to the Convention for the Protection of Human Rights and Fundamental Freedoms (adopted 6 November 1990, entered into force 1 October 1994) ETS No. 140.

[25] Protocols 9 and 14bis only amended the text of the Convention with respect to the States Parties to them.

Arguably, it has been Protocols 9, 11, and 14, the ones that have brought the most radical changes to the original system of protection set in place in the 1950s. As mentioned earlier, Protocol 9 empowered the individual applicant to bring a case before the Court, following a decision adopted by the Commission, provided that the respondent State had declared its acceptance of the Court's jurisdiction.[26] Protocol 11, which entered into force in 1998, completely reshaped the enforcement machinery of the regional system, by establishing a permanent Court, which resulted from the merger of the original Court and the Commission. The suppression of the Commission as a monitoring body meant that individuals gained the right to bring claims directly to the new Court.

As to Protocol 14, the main rationale for its adoption was the strong concern about the continuing increase in the Court's caseload—a topic further discussed in **Section 7.3.9**. The reform of the control system planned by this Protocol was considered essential to preserve its sustainability.[27] The changes brought up by Protocol 14 do not concern the structure but rather the functioning of the system;[28] in particular, the Court's capacity to deal with the high volume of manifestly unmeritorious applications and with repetitive cases. While Protocol 11 had already provided for the Court to sit in three different formations—three-judge Committees, seven-judge Chambers, and seventeen-judge Grand Chamber—Protocol 14 added the possibility of individual judges declaring the inadmissibility of individual applications when it is considered that such a decision can be taken without further examination.[29] In addition to the faculties invested on the single-judge formation, three-judge Committees were empowered by Protocol 14 to decide (by unanimity) on the merits of a case, but only when the underlying question has already been the subject of the Court's well-established case law.[30]

7.1.2 NORMATIVE FRAMEWORK

The evolution of the system created by the European Convention on Human Rights did not take place in a vacuum but was surrounded by the development of a complex normative and institutional framework. While the European Convention remains the

---

[26] Protocol 9 (1990).

[27] Council of Europe, Explanatory Report to Protocol No. 14 to the Convention for the Protection of Human Rights and Fundamental Freedoms, amending the control system of the Convention, ETS No. 194 (13 May 2004), para. 9.

[28] Council of Europe, Explanatory Report to Protocol No. 14 to the Convention for the Protection of Human Rights and Fundamental Freedoms, amending the control system of the Convention, ETS No. 194 (13 May 2004), para. 35.

[29] Protocol No. 14 to the Convention for the Protection of Human Rights and Fundamental Freedoms, amending the control system of the Convention (adopted 13 May 2004, entered into force 1 June 2010) ETS No. 194, Arts. 6, 7; Council of Europe, Explanatory Report to Protocol No. 14 to the Convention for the Protection of Human Rights and Fundamental Freedoms, amending the control system of the Convention, ETS No. 194 (13 May 2004), paras. 36–38.

[30] Protocol No. 14 to the Convention for the Protection of Human Rights and Fundamental Freedoms, amending the control system of the Convention (adopted 13 May 2004, entered into force 1 June 2010) ETS No. 194, Arts. 6, 8; Council of Europe, Explanatory Report to Protocol No. 14 to the Convention for the Protection of Human Rights and Fundamental Freedoms, amending the control system of the Convention, ETS No. 194 (13 May 2004), para. 40.

main treaty concerning the protection of human rights celebrated within the framework of the Council of Europe, more than two hundred treaties have been adopted by the Member States since the creation of the organization in 1949. The list of treaties includes: the 1961 European Social Charter (discussed in **Section 2.3.2.1**), the 1974 European Convention on the Non-Applicability of Statutory Limitation to Crimes against Humanity and War Crimes, the 1977 European Convention on the Legal Status of Migrant Workers, the 1987 European Convention for the Prevention of Torture and Inhuman or Degrading Treatment or Punishment, the 1992 European Charter for Regional or Minority Languages, the 1995 Framework Convention for the Protection of National Minorities, the 1996 European Convention on the Exercise of Children's Rights, the 1997 Convention for the protection of Human Rights and Dignity of the Human Being with regard to the Application of Biology and Medicine ('Convention on Human Rights and Biomedicine'), the 2005 Council of Europe Convention on Action against Trafficking in Human Beings, the 2007 Council of Europe Convention on the Protection of Children against Sexual Exploitation and Sexual Abuse, and the 2011 Council of Europe Convention on preventing and combating violence against women and domestic violence ('Istanbul Convention').

Some of these treaties have established specific bodies in order to monitor their compliance, such as the Committee of Experts of the European Charter for Regional or Minority Languages, the Group of Experts on Action against Trafficking in Human Beings, and the Advisory Committee on the Framework Convention for the Protection of National Minorities. As mentioned in **Section 2.4.1.2**, that is also the case of the European Committee for the Prevention of Torture and Inhuman or Degrading Treatment or Punishment, established by the 1987 European Convention for the Prevention of Torture and Inhuman or Degrading Treatment or Punishment, which has the power to conduct *in loco* visits to places of detention within Europe, to assess how persons deprived of their liberty are treated, strengthening their protection from torture, and inhuman or degrading treatment. A European Committee on Social Rights has also been created under the European Social Charter—as mentioned in **Section 2.3.2.1**—endowed with the ability to monitor State reports and to adopt decisions concerning collective complaints, which is further discussed below.

7.1.2.1 The European Social Charter

As discussed in **Section 2.3**, the ideological distinction between the so-called civil and political rights, on the one hand, and economic, social, and cultural rights, on the other, which permeated the negotiations of human rights treaties within the United Nations, can also be found in international human rights treaties adopted at the European regional level. The European Convention on Human Rights did not include economic, social, or cultural rights in its original text, with the right to education timidly added to the catalogue of protected rights in 1952, together with the right to property and the right to free elections, through the First Protocol to the Convention. Other socioeconomic rights were recognized through the European Social Charter,[31]

---

[31] European Social Charter (adopted 18 October 1961, entered into force 26 February 1965) ETS No. 035.

adopted within the Council of Europe in 1961, as a (poorer) counterpart of the European Convention; its rights excluded from the jurisdiction of the European Court.[32] Instead, the European Social Charter set up an international system of supervision based on biennial State reports monitored by a Committee of Independent Experts. This was certainly not a surprising outcome, as the uneven degree of institutional protection of the separated sets of rights followed a similar pattern to that adopted within the United Nations, as well as later on in the Americas.[33]

Another restriction that distinguishes the Social Charter not only from the European Convention but also from most human rights treaties is its limited personal scope of application.[34] In addition to providing for a 'colonial clause', like the European Convention,[35] the Charter allows for the exclusion of most foreigners from the protection of rights, making this European treaty a rather 'Europeans' treaty'. The Appendix to the Charter, which has survived amendments, permits the protection of socioeconomic rights to be limited to the nationals of Contracting Parties, who are lawfully resident or working regularly within the territory of the State.[36] Even if evolving interpretations of the treaty have attempted to overcome such limitations, the text of the Charter remains extremely problematic.[37]

Furthermore, while the 1988 Additional Protocol to the European Social Charter expanded the rights protected under the treaty,[38] it also acted as a confirmation of the States' will to leave economic, social, and cultural rights outside the system of protection established by the European Convention on Human Rights, by ratifying the monitoring of obligations by the procedure created by the Charter. An attempt at strengthening the Charter's monitoring mechanism was made in 1991, with the adoption of a Protocol to the Charter aimed at streamlining the reporting procedure.[39] However, more than three decades later, the Protocol is yet to reach the needed number of ratifications to enter into force; a deficit only partly overcome by some of the amendments being made effective by the Committee of Ministers.[40]

---

[32] The unequal standing of both treaties is also evidenced by the fact that while being a Party to the ECHR is required for membership to the Council of Europe, no similar requisite exists with regards to the Social Charter. See: V. Mantouvalou and P. Voyatzis, 'The Council of Europe and the Protection of Human Rights: A System in Need of Reform' in S. Joseph and A. McBeth (eds.), *Research Handbook on International Human Rights Law* (Elgar 2010) 326–352, 340.

[33] P. Alston, 'Assessing the Strengths and Weaknesses of the European Social Charter's Supervisory System' in G. de Búrca and B. de Witte (eds.), *Social Rights in Europe* (OUP 2005) 45–67, 47; V. Mantouvalou and P. Voyatzis, 'The Council of Europe and the protection of human rights: a system in need of reform' in S. Joseph and A. McBeth (eds.), *Research Handbook on International Human Rights Law* (Elgar 2010) 326–352, 336.

[34] J-F. Akandji-Kombé, 'The Material Impact of the Jurisprudence of the European Committee of Social Rights' in G. de Búrca and B. de Witte (eds.), *Social Rights in Europe* (OUP 2005) 89–108, 94–95.

[35] European Social Charter, Art. 34; ECHR, Art. 56.

[36] European Social Charter, Appendix; Additional Protocol to the European Social Charter (adopted 5 May 1988, entered into force 4 September 1992) ETS No. 128, Appendix; European Social Charter (revised) (adopted 3 May 1996, entered into force 1 July 1999) ETS No. 163, Appendix.

[37] J-F. Akandji-Kombe, 'The Material Impact of the Jurisprudence of the European Committee of Social Rights' in G. de Burca and B. de Witte (eds.), *Social Rights in Europe* (OUP 2005) 89–108, 96–99.

[38] Additional Protocol (1988).

[39] Protocol amending the European Social Charter (adopted 21 October 1991) ETS No. 142.

[40] V. Mantouvalou and P. Voyatzis, 'The Council of Europe and the protection of human rights: a system in need of reform' in S. Joseph and A. McBeth (eds.), *Research Handbook on International Human Rights Law* (Elgar 2010) 326–352, 338.

Further improvement of the monitoring mechanisms for the rights enshrined in the Charter came in 1995, with the adoption of the Additional Protocol to the European Social Charter Providing for a System of Collective Complaints.[41] This new treaty established a mechanism of collective complaints to enhance the enforcement of the socioeconomic rights guaranteed by the Charter. Although the new procedure does not provide legal standing to individuals to submit complaints concerning the violation of their rights, it allows for certain national and international organizations of employers and trade unions, as well as for certain national and international NGOs,[42] to lodge collective complaints concerning the protection of the rights recognized by the Charter. The complaints are examined by the European Committee of Social Rights (formerly, the Committee of Independent Experts), which has the ability to make decisions on the merits of the complaint, which are then forwarded to the concerned parties and the Committee of Ministers in a report to be made public.[43] This system is complementary to the reporting system established by the Charter and, while a clear step forward towards the protection of socioeconomic rights, it also confirmed their main exclusion from the jurisdiction of the European Court.

A 'revised' Charter was adopted in 1996,[44] aimed at eventually replacing the old one, through the Parties of the original treaty becoming Parties to the revised version.[45] This goal is being progressively realized, as the 1996 Charter already counts thirty-five States Parties by the end of 2022.[46] The Revised Charter has updated and enlarged the protected rights, but, as the original one, stipulates a formula for the obligations to be assumed by States. While the 1961 Charter required States Parties to accept at least five out of the seven so-called 'core' articles and another ten articles or forty-five numbered paragraphs, the Revised Charter mandates States to accept at least six (out of the nine) 'core' articles and a number of other rights or paragraphs provided that the total number is at least sixteen articles or sixty-three numbered paragraphs.[47] Proposals for the further improvement of the monitoring mechanisms of the Social Charter have been made, even by the Parliamentary Assembly of the Council of Europe. These have included allowing the true international judicialization of these rights, either through providing access of individuals to bring claims to the European Court or by creating a specific Court for the monitoring of the Charter, but have so far been unsuccessful.[48]

---

[41] Additional Protocol to the European Social Charter Providing for a System of Collective Complaints (adopted 9 November 1995, entered into force 1 July 1995) ETS No. 158.

[42] R. Brillat, 'The European Social Charter' in G. Alfredsson et al. (eds.), *International Human Rights Monitoring Mechanisms: Essays in Honour of Jakob Th. Möller* (2nd edn., Nijhoff 2009) 503–513, 509.

[43] R. Brillat, 'The Supervisory Machinery of the European Social Charter: Recent Developments and their Impact' in G. de Búrca and B. de Witte (eds.), *Social Rights in Europe* (OUP 2005) 31–43, 34.

[44] Revised European Social Charter (1996).

[45] R. Brillat, 'The European Social Charter' in G. Alfredsson et al. (eds.), *International Human Rights Monitoring Mechanisms: Essays in Honour of Jakob Th. Moller* (2nd edn., Nijhoff 2009) 503–513, 503.

[46] See: https://www.coe.int/en/web/conventions/full-list?module=signatures-by-treaty&treatynum=163 (accessed on 29 March 23).

[47] V. Mantouvalou and P. Voyatzis, 'The Council of Europe and the protection of human rights: a system in need of reform' in S. Joseph and A. McBeth (eds.), *Research Handbook on International Human Rights Law* (Elgar 2010) 326–352, 337. See: 1961 European Social Charter, Part II, Art. 20; Revised European Social Charter, Part III, Art. A.

[48] PACE, Recommendation 1354 (1998), 'Future of the European Social Charter'; PACE, Recommendation 1415 (1999), 'Additional Protocol to the European Convention on Human Rights Concerning Fundamental Social Rights.'

7.1.2.2 The Commissioner for Human Rights

The development of the system of human rights protection for Europe was further complemented by the creation of an array of bodies to monitor the situation of human rights within its Member States. Among a long list, these included: the Steering Committee on Anti-discrimination, Diversity and Inclusion, the Steering Committee for the Rights of the Child, the Gender Equality Commission, the European Commission against Racism and Intolerance, an *ad hoc* Committee of Experts on Roma and Traveller Issues, an *ad hoc* Committee of Experts on the Rights of Persons with Disabilities, and a Special Representative of the Secretary General on Migration and Refugees.

Perhaps the most prominent of the monitoring systems created by the Council is the Commissioner for Human Rights, established in 1999 to promote awareness of and respect for human rights in the Member States of the Council of Europe.[49] The Commissioner is an independent and impartial organ with the broad mandate to promote education in, awareness of, and respect for human rights.[50] To perform this ample mandate, the Commissioner is tasked with providing advice and information on the protection of human rights and the prevention of human rights violations, facilitating the activities of national ombudspersons, and identifying shortcomings in the domestic systems of the Member States concerning compliance with human rights and assisting them to remedy such deficits.[51]

The Commissioner is elected by the Parliamentary Assembly by a majority vote from a list of three candidates drawn up by the Committee of Ministers, following the submission of candidates from Member States. The candidates must be 'eminent personalities of a high moral character having recognized expertise in the field of human rights, a public record of attachment to the values of the Council of Europe and the personal authority necessary to discharge the mission of the Commissioner effectively'.[52] The Commissioner's term of office lasts six years and is non-renewable.[53] Since its creation, the mandate has been exercised by Álvaro Gil-Robles (Spain), Thomas Hammarberg (Sweden), Nils Muižnieks (Latvia), and Dunja Mijatović (Bosnia).

The Commissioner lacks any powers to adopt binding or enforceable decisions upon States, but their role entails constructively cooperating with the national authorities of Member States by suggesting practical solutions and encouraging their implementation.[54]

---

[49] Nonetheless, proposals for the creation of this organ can already be found in 1972. See: D. Mijatovic and A. Weber, 'The Council of Europe Commissioner for Human Rights and the European Court of Human Rights: An Ever-Closer Relationship' (2020) 33 *Revue Quebecoise de Droit International* 79, 81.

[50] Committee of Ministers, Resolution (99)50, 'On the Council of Europe Commissioner for Human Rights' (7 May 1999), Arts. 1, 2.

[51] Committee of Ministers, Resolution (99)50, 'On the Council of Europe Commissioner for Human Rights' (7 May 1999), Art. 3.

[52] Committee of Ministers, Resolution (99)50, 'On the Council of Europe Commissioner for Human Rights' (7 May 1999), Art. 10.

[53] Committee of Ministers, Resolution (99)50, 'On the Council of Europe Commissioner for Human Rights' (7 May 1999), Art. 11.

[54] T. Hammarberg and J. Dalhuisen, 'The Council of Europe Commissioner for Human Rights' in G. Alfredsson et al. (eds.), *International Human Rights Monitoring Mechanisms: Essays in Honour of Jakob Th. Möller* (2nd edn., Nijhoff 2009) 515–521, 516–517.

As the resolution that created the organ provided little indication on the precise activities the Commissioner should perform, or the procedures to follow, it allowed an important degree of flexibility for the mandate-holders.[55] Thus, Commissioners have undertaken their activities by conducting visits to the different Member States, including targeting areas under crisis, followed by the elaboration of country reports that contained recommendations. They have also gathered information leading to the elaboration of thematic reports, issue papers, and policy recommendations, raising awareness of specific issues of concern to different Council of Europe Member States.[56] From 2006, the Commissioners also started producing shorter opinions on relevant topics, known as 'viewpoints' or 'human rights comments'.[57] Moreover, the Commissioner can also be requested by other organs of the Council of Europe to provide comments on human rights issues.

With the entry into force of Protocols 14 and 16 to the European Convention, the Commissioner has gained a role in cases before the Court.[58] These include the ability to submit written comments to the Court, as third-party intervener, in both contentious cases and advisory opinions, as well as to take part in hearings before the Chamber and Grand Chamber.[59] The Committee of Ministers has also assigned them a role in the process of monitoring the execution of judgments, as the Commissioner is entitled to address communications to the Committee about them.[60]

7.1.3 CRITICAL DEBATE: MEMBERSHIP AND BACKLASHES

In 2022, Russia became the second State to ever leave the Council of Europe, since its creation in 1949. Until then, the only State that had left to later re-join was Greece. The ten States that founded the Council in 1949 had more than doubled in thirty years and more than quadrupled in fifty. In fact, between 1949 and 2022, the Council saw its membership steadily enlarge through the years, with the consequential increase in the number of Parties to the European Convention, given that becoming a Party to the treaty is a requirement for membership of the Council. With the accession of Montenegro in 2007, the membership of the Council extended to all European States, with the sole exception of Belarus.

---

[55] T. Hammarberg and J. Dalhuisen, 'The Council of Europe Commissioner for Human Rights' in G. Alfredsson et al. (eds.), *International Human Rights Monitoring Mechanisms: Essays in Honour of Jakob Th. Möller* (2nd edn., Nijhoff 2009) 518.

[56] T. Hammarberg and J. Dalhuisen, 'The Council of Europe Commissioner for Human Rights' in G. Alfredsson et al. (eds.), *International Human Rights Monitoring Mechanisms: Essays in Honour of Jakob Th. Möller* (2nd edn., Nijhoff 2009) 519–520.

[57] T. Hammarberg, 'Contribution from the Commissioner for Human Rights of the Council of Europe' (2010) 2 *European Yearbook of Disability Law* 153, 154.

[58] D. Mijatovic and A. Weber, 'The Council of Europe Commissioner for Human Rights and the European Court of Human Rights: An Ever-Closer Relationship' (2020) 33 *Revue Quebecoise de Droit International* 79, 86–96.

[59] ECHR, Art. 36; Protocol 16, Art. 3.

[60] Committee of Ministers, Rules for the supervision of the execution of judgments and of the terms of friendly settlements (adopted 10 May 2006, and amended 18 January 2017), r. 9.

As mentioned, Greece had been the only State to withdraw from the Council in December 1969[61] to avoid its expulsion, following the lengthy Report rendered by the European Commission of Human Rights in the renowned *Greek* case.[62] At the time, Greece was under the dictatorial government of a military junta, which had seized power in 1967 and implemented a regime characterized by extensive human rights abuses. Only after the recovery of democracy in 1974, Greece was re-admitted to the Council.[63]

ECHR, *The Greek case* (1969), application nos. 3321/67, 3322/67, 3323/67, and 3344/67.

In September 1967, Denmark, Norway, and Sweden submitted identical applications to the Commission, claiming the violation of numerous Convention rights by Greece. A week later, the Netherlands made a similar application and the four of them were joined by the Commission. As a result of a coup d'état that took place in April 1967, the Government of Greece had been seized by a military junta, which had decided to derogate, under Article 15, from its Convention obligations under Articles 5, 6, 8 to 11, 13, and 14. Whether the derogation was compatible with the Convention was one of the main issues to be decided by the Commission. Another issue was the allegation of breaches of Article 3, a non-derogable right, which was submitted by the three Scandinavian States in 1968 as an extension of their original claims. The Commission's Report was adopted in 1969 concluding that Greece's derogation under Article 15 had not been justified, as the circumstances did not amount to a public emergency threatening the life of the nation. Consequently, the Commission found multiple violations of the provisions Greece attempted to derogate from. Moreover, it also found that torture had been inflicted in a number of cases and such repetition and its official tolerance demonstrated that it had amounted to an administrative practice. Therefore, the Commission found a violation of Article 3. Following the adoption of the Commission's Report, in December 1969, Greece proceeded to denounce the Convention, becoming the first State to have ever withdrawn from the European human rights system. It later re-joined, nonetheless, acceding to the Convention on 28 November 1974.

In the more than seven decades of the Council's existence, criticisms and backlashes have not been alien to the system, particularly regarding its main judicial organ, the European Court of Human Rights. While it is possible to find criticisms of the European human rights system in each of the Parties to the Convention, the strength and extent of such opposition varies widely among them.[64] Weighty political backlashes have surged,

---

[61] Government of Greece, 'Note Verbale' (12 December 1969).
[62] European Commission of Human Rights, *The Greek case* (1969), application no. 3321/67 (*Denmark v. Greece*), application no. 3322/67 (*Norway v. Greece*), application no. 3323/67 (*Sweden v. Greece*), application no. 3344/67 (*Netherlands v. Greece*); J. Becket, 'The Greek Case before the European Human Rights Commission of Human Rights' (1970) 1 *Human Rights* 91, 107, 113.
[63] Committee of Ministers, 'Readmission of Greece to the Council of Europe' CM(74)261 rev. (22 November 1974).
[64] The different types and degrees of criticism from fifteen States Parties are discussed in a collection edited by Popelier, Lambrecht, and Lemmens. See: P. Popelier, S. Lambrecht, and K. Lemmens (eds.), *Criticism of the European Court of Human Rights: Shifting the Convention System: Counter-dynamics at the National and EU Level* (Intersentia 2016).

at times, in many States Parties, including France, Hungary, the Netherlands, Norway, Switzerland, and Turkey.[65] However, it is the UK and Russia that have truly stood out as the main critics of the Court.[66]

In the UK, it is not uncommon to see the Court portrayed as a foreign threat to national sovereignty by tabloids and politicians from the political right, resembling the discourse many of those same actors used during the 'Brexit' campaign with regard to the EU, and which led to the UK's withdrawal from the EU.[67] The Conservative government, in power since 2010, has continuedly threatened to water down the legal status of the European Convention on Human Rights, if not its outright denunciation.[68] Conservative political leaders have publicly and repeatedly manifested their repudiation of the regional system of human rights protection in renown political episodes, which ranged from a Prime Minister stating in Parliament that certain Court judgments made him 'physically ill'[69] to another who, in a public speech during her time as Home Secretary, blamed a pet cat and the European Convention for her inability to deport a person.[70] The proposals to tackle the situation have ranged from a desire to denounce the European Convention to an impoverished protection of human rights through the replacement of the Human Rights Act 1998—the legislative act that incorporates the Convention into domestic law—with a new Bill of Rights that would empower domestic courts to ignore the European Court's rulings—although would certainly not avoid the State's international liability for doing so, unless coupled with the actual denunciation of the treaty.

However, not even the UK's strong antagonistic stance under the Conservative government compares to the situation of Russia. Russia only joined the Council of Europe in 1996 and ratified the European Convention in 1998, but its relationship with the Council was tumultuous from the earlier years. Soon after acceding to the

[65] In the mentioned collection (*supra* note 64), see, in particular, the chapters by Blay-Grabarczyk and Maubernard, Polgáry, Gerards, Altwicker, Akbulut, and Lambrecht.

[66] M. Madsen, 'The Challenging Authority of the European Court of Human Rights: From Cold War legal Diplomacy to the Brighton Declaration and Backlash' (2016) 79 *Law and Contemporary Problems* 141, 170; P. Popelier, S. Lambrecht, and K. Lemmens, 'Introduction' in P. Popelier, S. Lambrecht, and K. Lemmens (eds.), *Criticism of the European Court of Human Rights: Shifting the Convention System: Counter-dynamics at the National and EU Level* (Intersentia 2016) 3–22, 10.

[67] R. Masterman, 'The United Kingdom: From Strasbourg Surrogacy towards a British Bill of Rights?' in P. Popelier, S. Lambrecht, and K. Lemmens (eds.), *Criticism of the European Court of Human Rights: Shifting the Convention System: Counter-dynamics at the National and EU Level* (Intersentia 2016) 449–478, 451; M. Madsen, 'From Boom to Backlash? The European Court of Human Rights and The transformation of Europe' in H. Aust and E. Demir-Gürsel (eds.), *The European Court of Human Rights: Current Challenges in Historical Perspective* (Elgar 2021) 21–42, 37.

[68] M. Madsen, 'The challenging authority of the European Court of Human Rights: From Cold War legal diplomacy to the Brighton declaration and backlash' (2016) 79 *Law and Contemporary Problems* 141, 174, 176; P. Popelier, S. Lambrecht, and K. Lemmens, 'Introduction' in P. Popelier, S. Lambrecht, and K. Lemmens (eds.), *Criticism of the European Court of Human Rights: Shifting the Convention System: Counter-dynamics at the National and EU Level* (Intersentia 2016) 3–22, 6–7.

[69] A. Aldridge, 'Can "physically ill" David Cameron find a cure for his European law allergy?', The Guardian (6 May 2011). Available at: https://www.theguardian.com/law/2011/may/06/david-cameron-european-law-allergy (accessed on 29 March 2023).

[70] A. Wagner, 'Catgate: another myth used to trash human rights', The Guardian (4 October 2011). Available at: https://www.theguardian.com/law/2011/oct/04/theresa-may-wrong-cat-deportation (accessed on 29 March 2023).

Convention, Russia became the source of the highest number of applications among all States.[71] And yet, Russia's refusal to ratify Protocol 14 was the main reason for its delayed entry into force, despite the Protocol being specifically aimed at tackling the Court's backlog of pending cases.[72] Moreover, Russia's practice of partial compliance with the Court's rulings increased the tensions with the Council, with its relation with the Court further deteriorating after its Constitutional Court ruled that compliance with the judgments from Strasbourg would only take place when these were considered compatible with Russia's Constitution.[73] To these, it should be added that Russia's unlawful use of force, in its 1999 military campaign in Chechnya and its annexation of Crimea in 2014, led to its voting rights being suspended at the Parliamentary Assembly.[74]

Hence, it is not surprising that, on different occasions, Russia has both been threatened with expulsion from the Council as well as threatened to leave by itself.[75] However, it was Russia's unlawful invasion of Ukraine that finally led to the termination of Russia's membership of the Council. Russia began the invasion of Ukraine on 24 February 2022. On the same day, the Committee of Ministers urged it to cease its military operation immediately and, the following day, with the agreement of the Parliamentary Assembly, it proceeded to suspend Russia from the Council.[76] On 15 March 2022, at the request of the Committee of Ministers, the Parliamentary Assembly rendered the opinion that Russia could no longer be a Member State of the organization, given the severity of the violations committed.[77] That day, Russia notified its withdrawal from the Council of Europe, which became effective the following day.

---

[71] R. Provost, 'Teetering on the Edge of Legal Nihilism: Russia and the Evolving European Human Rights Regime' (2015) 37 *Human Rights Quarterly* 289, 290. See: ECtHR, Annual Report 2003, p. 108; ECtHR, Annual Report 2005, p. 124.

[72] R. Provost, 'Teetering on the Edge of Legal Nihilism: Russia and the Evolving European Human Rights Regime' (2015) 37 *Human Rights Quarterly* 289, 326; A. Matta and A. Mazmanyan, 'Russia: In Quest for a European Identity' in P. Popelier, S. Lambrecht, and K. Lemmens (eds.), *Criticism of the European Court of Human Rights: Shifting the Convention System: Counter-dynamics at the National and EU Level* (Intersentia 2016) 481–502, 491; M. Madsen, 'The challenging authority of the European Court of Human Rights: From Cold War legal diplomacy to the Brighton declaration and backlash' (2016) 79 *Law and Contemporary Problems* 141, 169.

[73] R. Provost, 'Teetering on the Edge of Legal Nihilism: Russia and the Evolving European Human Rights Regime' (2015) 37 *Human Rights Quarterly* 289, 313; A. Matta and A. Mazmanyan, 'Russia: In Quest for a European Identity' in P. Popelier, S. Lambrecht, and K. Lemmens (eds.), *Criticism of the European Court of Human Rights: Shifting the Convention System: Counter-dynamics at the National and EU Level* (Intersentia 2016) 481–502, 481, 501; M. Madsen, 'From boom to backlash? The European Court of Human Rights and the transformation of Europe' in H. Aust and E. Demir-Gursel (eds.), *The European Court of Human Rights: Current Challenges in Historical Perspective* (Elgar 2021) 21–42, 36.

[74] A. Matta and A. Mazmanyan, 'Russia: In Quest for a European Identity' in P. Popelier, S. Lambrecht, and K. Lemmens (eds.), *Criticism of the European Court of Human Rights: Shifting the Convention System: Counter-dynamics at the National and EU Level* (Intersentia 2016) 481–502, 481, 486.

[75] M. Madsen, 'The challenging authority of the European Court of Human Rights: From Cold War legal diplomacy to the Brighton declaration and backlash' (2016) 79 *Law and Contemporary Problems* 141, 172.

[76] Committee of Ministers, 'Situation in Ukraine' CM/Del/Dec(2022)1426bis/2.3 (24 February 2022); Committee of Ministers, 'Situation in Ukraine' CM/Del/Dec(2022)1426ter/2.3 (25 February 2022).

[77] PACE, Opinion 300 (2022), 'Consequences of the Russian Federation's aggression against Ukraine' (15 March 2022); Committee of Ministers, Resolution CM/Res (2022) 2, 'on the cessation of the membership of the Russian Federation to the Council of Europe' (16 March 2022).

7.2 THE EUROPEAN COURT OF HUMAN RIGHTS: COMPOSITION AND STRUCTURE

The Court consists of a total of forty-six judges,[78] as there must be an equal number of judges to that of States Parties to the Convention.[79] The election of judges is done by the Parliamentary Assembly (by a majority vote) from a list of three candidates nominated by each Contracting Party.[80] Although it is not a requirement, the judges are typically nationals of the State that nominates them. Nonetheless, in the performance of their judicial duties, they are expected to be independent from their State of nationality, sitting on the Court in their individual capacity.[81] Currently, judges serve for nine years without the possibility of re-election.[82] Under Protocol 11, their term of office also expired if they reached the age of seventy;[83] a restriction that was certainly difficult to understand, with the Protocol's Explanatory Report merely stating that 'it was deemed appropriate to introduce an age limit, as exists in most domestic legal systems'.[84] The entry into force of Protocol 15 confirmed the existence of an age restriction, only slightly amending it. Now, nominated candidates could be no older than sixty-five years of age 'at the date by which the list of three candidates has been requested by the Parliamentary Assembly';[85] hence enabling all judges to serve the full nine-year term of office for which they are elected.[86]

The procedure for the election of judges is triggered by a letter from the Secretary General of the Assembly inviting the respective State to submit a list of three candidates about a year before the intended election date to allow for enough time to complete the procedure.[87] Before Member States submit the list of three candidates to the Assembly, the candidates are assessed by an Advisory Panel of Experts, created by the Committee of Ministers in 2010,[88] which provides a confidential opinion on the quality of the nomination to both the nominating State and the Parliamentary Assembly. The purpose of the Advisory Panel's intervention is to evaluate whether all potential

---

[78] With the termination of its membership to the Council of Europe in March 2022, Russia ceased to be Party to the European Convention six months later by operation of Art. 50 of the Convention; hence, the office of a judge in respect of the State also ceased to exist. See: ECtHR, Resolution (5 September 2022).

[79] ECHR, Art. 20.   [80] ECHR, Art. 22.   [81] ECHR, Art. 21.2.

[82] The current term of office (nine years, no possible re-election) was established by Protocol 14, as the original text of the Convention envisioned a nine-year term with possible re-election (Art. 40), which had been reduced to a six-year term with possible re-election by Protocol 11.

[83] ECHR, Art. 23.

[84] Council of Europe, Explanatory Report to Protocol No. 11 to the Convention for the Protection of Human Rights and Fundamental Freedoms, restructuring the control machinery established thereby, ETS 155 (Strasbourg, 11 May 1994), para. 63.

[85] Protocol No. 15 amending the Convention for the Protection of Human Rights and Fundamental Freedom (adopted 24 June 2013) ETS No. 213, Art. 2.1.

[86] Council of Europe, Explanatory Report to Protocol No. 15 amending the Convention for the Protection of Human Rights and Fundamental Freedoms, ETS No. 213 (24 June 2013), para. 12.

[87] Memorandum prepared by the Secretary General of the Assembly, Procedure for the election of judges to the European Court of Human Rights as of 15 April 2019, para. 4.

[88] Committee of Ministers, Resolution CM/Res(2010)26 on the establishment of an Advisory Panel of Experts on Candidates for Election as Judge to the European Court of Human Rights (10 November 2010).

candidates satisfy the criteria for office. The main requirements established by the Convention are that 'judges shall be of high moral character and must either possess the qualifications required for appointment to high judicial office or be jurisconsults of recognised competence'.[89] However, the Member States and the pertinent organs of the Council of Europe have added more specific prerequisites.[90] For instance, when adopting the 2010 Interlaken Declaration, States have agreed that knowledge of public international law and of the national legal systems, as well as proficiency in at least one official language of the Council of Europe (English or French), should be requirements to sit on the Court.[91] In addition, the Parliamentary Assembly, through a series of resolutions adopted since 2004, established that the lists of candidates from a Member State should, as a general rule, contain at least one candidate of each sex, unless the sex of the candidates on the list is under-represented on the Court.[92] As discussed in **Section 7.6**, in its first ever advisory opinion, the Court confirmed the validity of the gender-balance rule for the list of candidates, but only as long as States were allowed to derogate from it in exceptional circumstances.[93]

While States are expected to act in accordance with the Advisory Panel's recommendation, they are not legally bound to do so and can submit their original list to the Parliamentary Assembly, despite the Panel's views.[94] Once the Assembly has received the list of candidates, it is the Committee on the Election of Judges that, first, scrutinizes the national procedure used to select the candidates and then interviews each of them in person.[95] If the Committee finds that all conditions are met, it issues a recommendation to the Assembly indicating which candidate or candidates are deemed to be the strongest. Alternatively, it can recommend that the State be asked to submit a new list. Judges are then elected by the Parliamentary Assembly through a secret ballot. The candidate that obtains an absolute majority of the votes cast is elected to serve as a judge in the Court. If no candidate reaches such a majority, a second round is held, and the candidate with the most votes is elected.[96]

---

[89] ECHR, Art. 21.1.

[90] Both the Parliamentary Assembly and the Committee of Ministers have developed further the required qualities established by the Convention. See: K. Dzehtsiarou and A. Schwartz, 'Electing Team Strasbourg: Professional Diversity on the European Court of Human Rights and Why it Matters' (2020) 21 *German Law Journal* 621, 625.

[91] Interlaken Declaration, adopted by the High-Level Conference on the Future of the European Court of Human Rights Interlaken Declaration, at the initiative of the Swiss Chairmanship of the Committee of Ministers of the Council of Europe (19 February 2010), para. 8.a.

[92] Parliamentary Assembly, Resolution 1366 (2004), Candidates for the European Court of Human Rights (30 January 2004); Parliamentary Assembly, Resolution 1426 (2005), Candidates for the European Court of Human Rights (18 March 2005); Parliamentary Assembly, Resolution 1627 (2008), Candidates for the European Court of Human Rights (30 September 2008); Parliamentary Assembly, Resolution 1841 (2011) (7 October 2011); Guidelines of the Committee of Ministers on the selection of candidates for the post of judge at the European Court of Human Rights, CM(2012)40-final (29 March 2012), paras. II.4, II.5, II.8.

[93] ECtHR, Advisory Opinion (No. 1) on certain legal questions concerning the lists of candidates submitted with a view to the election of judges to the European Court of Human Rights (12 February 2008).

[94] Memorandum prepared by the Secretary General of the Assembly, Procedure for the election of judges to the European Court of Human Rights as of 15 April 2019, para. 6.

[95] Memorandum prepared by the Secretary General of the Assembly, Procedure for the election of judges to the European Court of Human Rights as of 15 April 2019, para. 13.

[96] Memorandum prepared by the Secretary General of the Assembly, Procedure for the election of judges to the European Court of Human Rights as of 15 April 2019, para. 28.

The Court itself is organized through Sections set for three-year periods, with each judge allocated to a specific Section. There are currently five Sections, and the composition of each is determined taking into account the existence of geographic and gender balance, as well as representation of the different legal systems among the States Parties to the Convention.[97] Individual applications lodged before the Court are assigned to a Section, ensuring a fair distribution of cases between them.[98] The Chambers of seven judges are constituted from the judges of the Section to which the case is allocated. Three-judge Committees are also set up within each Section, organized for twelve-month periods by rotation of the judges assigned to the respective Section. Single judges are also appointed for twelve-month periods by the President of the Court, who is in charge of deciding the number of single judges needed to be appointed.[99]

7.3 THE INDIVIDUAL AND THE EUROPEAN COURT OF HUMAN RIGHTS

The Court exercises adjudicatory and advisory jurisdiction, with the former encompassing both inter-State cases and individual applications.[100] The topics of advisory opinions and inter-State cases will be discussed in **Section 7.6** and **Section 7.4**, respectively, while the present section engages with individual applications, which are the ones that originate the overwhelming majority of the Court's caseload. Individual cases before the Court commence with a complete application form sent by post to the Registrar of the Court. The Registrar is tasked with assisting the Court in the performance of its functions and is responsible for the organization and activities of the Court's Registry.[101] The members of the Registry are the ones that process applications and prepare them for adjudication.[102] The Court's Registry consists of Section Registries, equal in number to the Sections of the Court,[103] each providing legal and administrative support to the respective Court's Section.[104] Since June 2009, the Court has established a 'priority policy' aimed at providing more expedited decisions in cases that are especially important, serious or urgent. There are currently seven categories of priority available,

---

[97] ECtHR, Rules of the Court (10 February 2023), r. 25.2.
[98] ECtHR, Rules of the Court (10 February 2023), r. 52.1.
[99] ECtHR, Rules of the Court (10 February 2023), r. 27A.
[100] The discussion in this section greatly benefited from very helpful exchanges with Dr Pieter Cannoot, Prof Kanstantsin Dzehtsiarou, and Judge Paul Lemmens.
[101] ECtHR, Rules of the Court (10 February 2023), r. 17.
[102] D. Harris, M. O'Boyle, E. Bates and C. Buckley, *Harris, O'Boyle and Warbrick: Law of the European Convention on Human Rights* (4th ed., OUP 2018) 117.
[103] Within the Registry, the Court has created the figure of the 'Jurisconsult' to assist the Court and its members with ensuring the quality and consistency of the case law, by providing opinions and information to them. See: ECtHR, Rules of the Court, r. 18.
[104] The Registry is composed of more than 600 staff members, including lawyers, translators, and clerical staff. See: D. Harris, M. O'Boyle, E. Bates, and C. Buckley, *Harris, O'Boyle and Warbrick: Law of the European Convention on Human Rights* (4th edn., OUP 2018) 117.

which range from 'urgent cases concerning vulnerable applicants (Category I) to clearly inadmissible cases dealt with by a single judge (Category VII)'.[105]

Regarding the processing of applications, Rule 49 states that 'where the material submitted by the applicant is on its own sufficient to disclose that the application is inadmissible or should be struck out of the list, the application shall be considered by a single-judge formation'. As discussed in **Section 7.1.1**, an individual judge, assisted by a non-judicial rapporteur from the Registry, only has the power to reject cases as inadmissible, having to refer the application to a Committee or a Chamber in the alternative.[106] It can be clarified, nonetheless, that the single judge cannot decide an application lodged against the State in respect of which they have been elected.[107] If the examination of the application by a Committee or a Chamber seems justified, the President of the Section to which the case has been assigned designates a judge as 'Judge Rapporteur' to proceed to its examination.[108] Since 2019, the Court has adopted a new procedure applicable to most cases that are not manifestly inadmissible, dividing their proceedings into two distinctive twelve-week phases: a friendly settlement phase and the contentious phase.[109]

7.3.1 FRIENDLY SETTLEMENT PHASE

The Convention states that the Court may place itself at the disposal of the parties at any stage of the proceedings, with a view to securing a friendly settlement of the matter. Based on this provision, the Court has now allocated the first twelve weeks of *prima facie* admissible cases for encouraging the parties to reach a friendly settlement. During this phase, the Registry acts as a conduit for the parties to reach an agreement, usually encompassing the payment of a sum of money. If an agreement is reached, the Court would normally consider the matter resolved and, consequently, strike the case of the list.[110] This Court's decision is transmitted to the Committee of Ministers for supervising the execution of the terms of the agreement.[111]

When a settlement proposal is rejected by the applicant, the State has the possibility of submitting to the Court a unilateral declaration in which it acknowledges its international responsibility for breaching the Convention and offers to pay compensation, and is for the Court to decide whether to strike out the application.[112] There are multiple relevant factors the Court needs to take into consideration before accepting a unilateral declaration. These include the nature of the complaint; whether the issues raised are

---

[105] The Court has made available a document explaining its priority policy on its website. See: https://www.echr.coe.int/Documents/Priority_policy_ENG.pdf (accessed on 29 March 2023).
[106] ECtHR, Rules of the Court, r. 52A.2. [107] ECHR, Art. 26.3.
[108] ECtHR, Rules of the Court, r. 49.2.
[109] ECtHR, Press Release, ECHR 437(2018) (18 December 2018).
[110] D. Harris, M. O'Boyle, E. Bates and C. Buckley, *Harris, O'Boyle and Warbrick: Law of the European Convention on Human Rights* (4th ed., OUP 2018) 134.
[111] ECHR, Art. 39.4.
[112] D. Harris, M. O'Boyle, E. Bates and C. Buckley, *Harris, O'Boyle and Warbrick: Law of the European Convention on Human Rights* (4th ed., OUP 2018) 135–136.

similar to those examined in previous cases; the nature and scope of the actual measures taken by the State when complying with judgments delivered in any such previous cases; whether the facts are in dispute between the parties; as well as the measures of redress proposed by the State and whether these would be capable of eliminating the effects of the acknowledged violation.[113]

7.3.2 CONTENTIOUS PHASE

If the case could not be settled during the non-contention phase, it enters the contentious stage, with the Court proceeding to its consideration through the assigned formation. This would be a Committee when the issue is the subject of the Court's well-established case law. By unanimity of the three judges, a Committee can either reject an application as inadmissible or rule on the merits of the case.[114] Since Committees can only adopt decisions by unanimity, the failure to reach such an agreement on the matter means that the case has to be referred to a Chamber.

When an application is neither clearly inadmissible nor the subject of well-established case law, it would normally be dealt with by a seven-judge Chamber. Both the aforementioned 'Judge Rapporteur' and the judge elected in respect of the State Party involved in the case will sit in such Chamber.[115] The entry into force of Protocol 14 reversed the general norm governing the Court's practice, which means that deciding jointly on admissibility and merits has become the rule.[116] If the Chamber finds the application to be admissible—a topic further discussed in **Section 7.3.7**—it proceeds to the examination of the merits of the case. Usually, the facts of the case would have been established by the domestic courts, but the Chamber has the power to adopt, at the request of a party or of its own motion, investigative measures that it considers capable of clarifying the facts.[117] Among these measures, the Chamber 'may invite the parties to produce documentary evidence and decide to hear as a witness or expert . . . any person whose evidence or statements seem likely to assist it in carrying out its tasks'.[118] The Chamber may also invite any person or institution to provide an opinion or report it considers relevant to the case,[119] and can appoint a judge as its delegate 'to conduct an inquiry, carry out an on-site investigation or take evidence in some other manner'.[120] The proceedings before a Chamber are almost always conducted in writing, but exceptionally the Chamber might decide to hold oral hearings if some novel point of law is involved in the case.[121] The judgment of the Chamber will determine whether there has been a violation of the Convention

---

[113] ECtHR, *Tahsin Acar v. Turkey (preliminary issue)* [GC], App. no. 26307/95, § 76, ECHR 2003-VI.
[114] As an additional measure to combat its backlog of cases, from September 2021 and for a two-year trial period, the Court has decided that the rulings of the Committees must be drafted in a more concise manner, with a strict 2,000-word length-limit. See: ECtHR, 2021 Annual Report, p. 176.
[115] ECtHR, Rules of the Court, r. 26. [116] ECHR, Art. 29.1.
[117] ECtHR, Rules of the Court, r. A1.1. [118] ECtHR, Rules of the Court, r. A1.1.
[119] ECtHR, Rules of the Court, r. A1.2. [120] ECtHR, Rules of the Court, r. A1.3.
[121] D. Harris, M. O'Boyle, E. Bates and C. Buckley, *Harris, O'Boyle and Warbrick: Law of the European Convention on Human Rights* (4th ed., OUP 2018) 145.

(and/or its Protocols) and if 'just satisfaction' is due. The judgment of the Chamber becomes final after three months unless any of the parties request a referral to the Grand Chamber, discussed in **Section 7.3.4**.[122]

7.3.3 STRIKING OUT APPLICATIONS

The Convention empowers the Court to strike an application out of its list of cases at any stage of the proceedings, provided that the circumstances have led the Court to the conclusion that: the applicant does not intend to continue pursuing the application; the matter has been resolved, including redressing the effects of the violation,[123] such as through a friendly settlement; or even when, for any other reason, the Court considers it no longer justified to continue the examination of the case.[124] As acknowledged by the Court, it has been given a rather wide degree of discretion for striking out applications.[125] And indeed, the Court has used such an ample discretion to strike out applications for a variety of reasons, such as on the basis of a unilateral declaration by the respondent State, even against the wishes of the applicant;[126] when the applicant had reached a settlement with the domestic authorities, satisfying the demands made under the Convention;[127] following the death of an applicant without next-of-kin expressing an interest in pursuing the proceedings;[128] or in light of a lack of diligence on the part of the applicant.[129] However, even if the aforementioned conditions are present, the Court can decide to continue the examination of an application if respect for human rights so requires.[130] As stated by the Court in its ruling in the *Karner v. Austria* case: 'Although the primary purpose of the Convention system is to provide individual relief, its mission is also to determine issues on public-policy grounds in the common interest, thereby raising the general standards of protection of human rights and extending human rights jurisprudence throughout the community of Convention States.'[131]

---

[122] The judgment also becomes final when the parties declare that they will not request a referral or when such a referral is rejected.
[123] ECtHR, *El Majjaoui and Stichting Touba Moskee v. the Netherlands (striking out)* [GC], App. no. 25525/03, § 30, 20 December 2007.
[124] ECHR, Art. 37.
[125] ECtHR, *Association SOS Attentats and De Boëry v. France* (dec.) [GC], App. no. 76642/01, para. 37.
[126] ECtHR, *Tahsin Acar v. Turkey (preliminary issue)* [GC], App. no. 26307/95, § 75–77, ECHR 2003-VI; ECtHR, *Akman v. Turkey (striking out)*, App. no. 37453/97, ECHR 2001-VI; ECtHR, *Haran v. Turkey*, App. no. 25754/94, 26 March 2002; ECtHR, *Meriakri v. Moldova (striking out)*, App. no. 53487/99, 1 March 2005; ECtHR, *Van Houten v. the Netherlands (striking out)*, App. no. 25149/03, ECHR 2005-IX.
[127] ECtHR, *Calì and Others v. Italy (striking out)*, App. no. 52332/99, 19 May 2005; ECtHR, *La Rosa and Alba v. Italy (striking out)*, App. no. 58274/00, 28 June 2005.
[128] ECtHR, *Gładkowski v. Poland (striking out)*, App. no. 29697/96, 14 March 2000; ECtHR, *Sevgi Erdoğan v. Turkey (striking out)*, App. no. 28492/95, 29 April 2003.
[129] ECtHR, *Hun v. Turkey (striking out)*, App. no. 5142/04, 10 November 2005; ECtHR, *Mürrüvet Küçük v. Turkey (striking out)*, App. no. 21784/04, 10 November 2005.
[130] ECHR, Art. 37.
[131] ECtHR, *Karner v. Austria*, App. no. 40016/98, § 26, ECHR 2003-IX.

> **ECtHR, *Karner v. Austria*, App. no. 40016/98, ECHR 2003-IX.**
>
> The applicant, Mr Karner, had had his request to succeed to a tenancy agreement after the death of his same-sex partner refused by the domestic courts, as Austrian legislation only provided such a right for surviving different-sex partners. Before the European Court, he claimed that such a differential treatment, based on the sexuality of individuals, was in breach of Article 14 (prohibition of discrimination) of the Convention taken in conjunction with Article 8 (right to respect for private and family life). Prior to examining the merits of the case, the Court had to address a request from Austria to have the case struck out, since the applicant had died and there were no heirs interested in pursuing the claim further. However, the Court decided to proceed with the case, asserting that the subject matter of the application—the difference in treatment based on sexuality as regards to succession to tenancies under domestic law—involved an important question of general interest not only for Austria, but also for other States Parties to the Convention. Therefore, it concluded that respect for human rights, as defined in the Convention, required a continuation of the examination of the case (paras. 27–28).
>
> The Court analysed whether the differential treatment the law afforded to the surviving partner of same-sex and different-sex couples was compatible with the Convention. It first affirmed that the case fell 'within the ambit' of a Convention right (the right to respect for the applicant's home, under Article 8). Then, the Court accepted that the 'protection of the family in the traditional sense' might be a legitimate aim of the State, but it asserted that when a differential treatment was based on sexual orientation the State was only afforded a narrow margin of appreciation to justify the distinction. Consequently, particularly serious reasons by way of justification needed to be given by the State to prove that the measure adopted was necessary to achieve the legitimate aim (paras. 40–42). The Court held that no compelling reason had been advanced to justify the distinction in treatment between same-sex and different-sex partners and, therefore, there had been a violation of Article 14 in conjunction with Article 8 of the Convention.

7.3.4 THE GRAND CHAMBER

There are two paths to access the Grand Chamber: a referral requested by any of the parties of a case decided by a Chamber and a relinquishment of jurisdiction from a Chamber.[132] Concerning the former, the decision as to whether to accept such a request is made by a panel of five judges and based on whether the case raises a serious question affecting the interpretation or application of the Convention or a serious issue of general importance.[133] If the panel decides to accept the request, the Grand Chamber must issue a judgment on the case.[134] As to the relinquishment of jurisdiction by the Chamber, this can take place when a case raises a serious question affecting the interpretation of the Convention or when 'the resolution of a question before the Chamber might have a result inconsistent with a judgment previously delivered by the Court'.[135]

---

[132] ECHR, Arts. 30, 43.   [133] ECHR, Art. 43.2.   [134] ECHR, Art. 43.3.
[135] The ability of the parties to the case to object to the relinquishment of jurisdiction by the Chamber was suppressed by Protocol 15. See: ECHR, Art. 30; Protocol No. 15 amending the Convention for the Protection of Human Rights and Fundamental Freedom (adopted 24 June 2013) ETS No. 213, Art. 3.

The Grand Chamber is composed of seventeen judges, including the President of the Court, the Vice-Presidents, the Presidents of the Chambers, and the judge who sits in respect of the State Party involved. If the case comes to the Grand Chamber following a referral, it should not include any of the Chamber judges, with the exception of the President and the 'national judge'.[136] Even if the case arrives through a referral, the Grand Chamber retains the full powers of the Court. It is able to re-examine admissibility issues, approve friendly settlements, and re-assess the facts of the case.[137] The judgment issued by the Grand Chamber is final. **Figure 7.1** shows the process of an individual application (by a person, group of persons, or NGO) to the ECtHR.

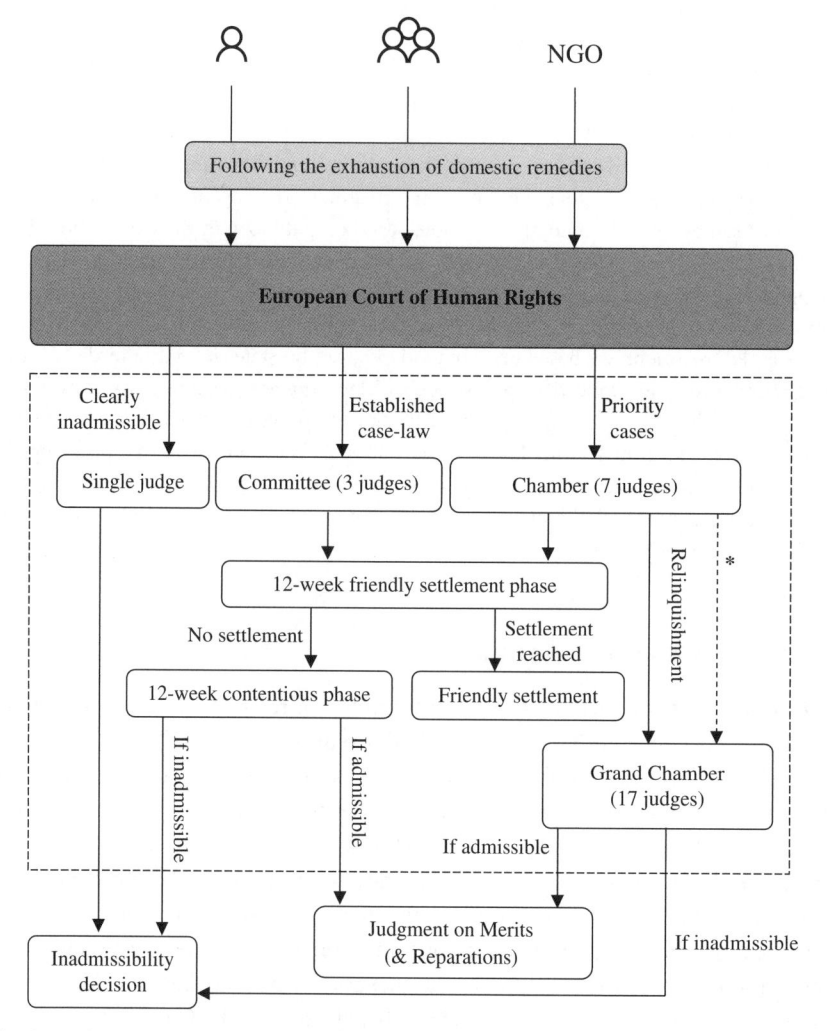

*Referrals can be requested by any of the parties to the case, within 3 months following a Chamber's ruling.

Figure 7.1 Process of an individual application to the European Court of Human Rights

---

[136] ECHR, Art. 26.5.

[137] D. Harris, M. O'Boyle, E. Bates and C. Buckley, *Harris, O'Boyle and Warbrick: Law of the European Convention on Human Rights* (4th ed., OUP 2018) 132.

7.3.5 RECTIFICATION, REVISION, AND INTERPRETATION OF JUDGMENTS

The judgments and decisions rendered by the Court are final and not subject to appeal, except for the aforementioned referral procedure. Nonetheless, certain circumstances allow for the rectification of errors, an interpretation of the judgment, or even its revision. Within one month of the delivery of a ruling, the Court may, of its own motion or at the request of a party, rectify clerical errors, errors in calculation, or obvious mistakes.[138] Concerning a revision of the judgment, this can only be requested by a party to the case within a six-month period from 'the discovery of a fact which might by its nature have a decisive influence and which, when a judgment was delivered, was unknown to the Court and could not reasonably have been known to that party'.[139] Lastly, there are two grounds for requesting an interpretation of the judgment. First, within a year from the delivery of the judgment, any party may request the interpretation of specific points of the operative provisions of a judgment.[140] Second, the Committee of Ministers may, by a two-thirds majority vote, request a ruling on interpretation from the Court when it considers that its role in the supervision of the execution of a judgment is hindered by a problem of interpretation.[141]

7.3.6 INTERIM MEASURES (RULE 39)

In exceptional cases, the Court may issue binding interim measures if it considers that the applicant faces a real risk of serious and irreversible harm were the measures not adopted.[142] The purpose of an interim measure is to preserve and protect the rights of the applicant pending the Court's decision on the compatibility of the acts of the State with its obligations under the Convention.[143] In practice, the Court adopts interim measures 'only if there is an imminent risk of irreparable damage',[144] usually concerning the right to life, the right not to be subjected to torture or inhuman treatment and, exceptionally, other rights, such as the right to respect for private and family life or the right to a fair trial.[145] Interim measures can consist of abstentions,[146] such as to abstain from extraditing an applicant to a State in which they will face risk of torture, but also of positive measures, such as to provide medical treatment to an applicant.[147]

---

[138] ECtHR, Rules of the Court, r. 81.
[139] ECtHR, Rules of the Court, r. 80.
[140] ECtHR, Rules of the Court, r. 79.
[141] ECHR, Art. 46.
[142] ECtHR, Rules of the Court, r. 39.
[143] D. Harris, M. O'Boyle, E. Bates and C. Buckley, *Harris, O'Boyle and Warbrick: Law of the European Convention on Human Rights* (4th ed., OUP 2018) 146.
[144] ECtHR, *Mamatkulov and Askarov v. Turkey* [GC], App. nos. 46827/99, 46951/99, § 104, ECHR 2005-I.
[145] ECtHR, *Mamatkulov and Askarov v. Turkey* [GC], App. nos. 46827/99, 46951/99, § 104, ECHR 2005-I.
[146] While these are usually addressed to the respondent State, they can exceptionally be indicated to applicants. See the case of *Ilaşcu and Others v. the Republic of Moldova and Russia*, where the Court's President urged an applicant to stop a hunger-strike. ECtHR, *Ilaşcu and Others v. Moldova and Russia* [GC], App. no. 48787/99, § 11, ECHR 2004-VII.
[147] ECtHR, *Mamatkulov and Askarov v. Turkey* [GC], App. nos. 46827/99, 46951/99, ECHR 2005-I; ECtHR, *Paladi v. Moldova* [GC], App. no. 39806/05, 10 March 2009.

Given the urgency of the matter, requests for interim measures should be made immediately after the final domestic decision has been adopted, to enable the Court and its Registry to have sufficient time to examine the matter. They can even be made without the need to wait for such a decision, when the final domestic ruling is imminent and there is a risk of immediate enforcement, especially in extradition or deportation cases.[148] Since October 2022, interim measures can be requested electronically, via a specific website created by the Court exclusively for 'Rule 39' measures (https://www.echr.coe.int/rule-39).[149] The decision to indicate interim measures is made by one of the duty judges of the Court, appointed by the President to deal with this type of request.[150] The binding character of interim measures has been confirmed by the Grand Chamber, which in its judgment in *Mamatkulov and Askarov v. Turkey* explained that 'by virtue of Article 34 of the Convention Contracting States undertake to refrain from any act or omission that may hinder the effective exercise of an individual applicant's right of application. A failure by a Contracting State to comply with interim measures is to be regarded as preventing the Court from effectively examining the applicant's complaint and as hindering the effective exercise of his or her right and, accordingly, as a violation of Article 34'.[151]

> **ECtHR, *Mamatkulov and Askarov v. Turkey* [GC], App. nos. 46827/99 and 46951/99, ECHR 2005-I.**
>
> The case concerned two Uzbek nationals arrested in Turkey under an international arrest warrant. While Uzbekistan requested their extradition, the applicants requested interim measures to the European Court, under Rule 39, to stop the extradition from taking place. Although the Court granted the interim measures, Turkey handed the applicants to the Uzbek authorities. Following their extradition, the Uzbek Supreme Court found the applicants guilty of the offences charged—which included homicide, injuries caused by a bomb explosion, and an attempted attack on the President of Uzbekistan—and sentenced them to 11 and 20 years of prison. The applicants complained that their extradition had entailed the violation of Articles 2 (right to life), 3 (prohibition of torture), 6 (right to a fair trial), and 34 (individual applications) of the Convention. The case was initially heard by a Chamber, which found no violation of any of the substantive rights claimed, but ruled that Turkey had breached its obligations under Article 34, by failing to comply with the Court's interim measures. Following a request from Turkey, the case was referred to the Grand Chamber, which delivered its judgment in 2005. The Grand Chamber also found no violation of the substantive provisions claimed, but ruled that Turkey's failure to comply with the Court's interim measures hindered the effective exercise of the applicant's right of individual application, which amounted to a breach of Article 34 of the Convention (paras. 128–129).

---

[148] Practice direction issued by the President of the Court in accordance with Rule 32 of the Rules of Court (5 March 2003, amended on 16 October 2009 and on 7 July 2011), Requests for interim measures (Rule 39), III.

[149] ECtHR, 2022 Annual Report, p. 136.

[150] D. Harris, M. O'Boyle, E. Bates and C. Buckley, *Harris, O'Boyle and Warbrick: Law of the European Convention on Human Rights* (4th ed., OUP 2018) 150.

[151] ECtHR, *Mamatkulov and Askarov v. Turkey* [GC], App. nos. 46827/99, 46951/99, § 128, ECHR 2005-I.

7.3.7 FURTHER REFLECTIONS: THE ADMISSIBILITY OF APPLICATIONS

The system of protection of human rights established by the Convention is based on the principle of complementarity—many times misconceived as subsidiarity.[152] This means that ensuring the respect of human rights falls primarily on the States Parties to the Convention and that the Court's role is to intervene when States have failed to comply with their international obligations. As will be discussed in **Section 7.3.9**, the Court receives an extremely large volume of applications yearly. Nevertheless, the overwhelming majority of these applications (above 90 per cent of them) are rejected without being examined on the merits for failure to satisfy one of the admissibility criteria laid down by the Convention.[153]

Article 34 of the Convention establishes that the Court may receive applications from individuals, groups of individuals, and NGOs claiming to be the victim of a violation of the rights protected by the Convention or its Protocols that is attributable to one of its States Parties. For an application to be admissible by the Court, it has to fit within its jurisdiction, which depends on the intervening persons (jurisdiction *ratione personae*), the subject matter of the case (jurisdiction *ratione materiae*), the time when the facts of the case took place (jurisdiction *ratione temporis*), and the place where the facts have occurred (jurisdiction *ratione loci*). The Court's jurisdiction *ratione personae* refers to both the legal standing to be brought before the Court as defendant—only the States Parties to the Convention or the respective Protocol—and the legal standing to submit a case—the individual, individuals, or NGO that can be considered to be the 'victim' of the alleged violation. An applicant would be considered a victim of a violation if their rights have been directly affected by the measure complained of, regardless of whether they have suffered any damage.[154] The Court's jurisdiction *ratione materiae* requires the alleged violation to concern a right protected by the Convention or a Protocol to which the respondent State is Party. As to the jurisdiction *ratione temporis*, it calls for the facts of the case to have taken place after the State had ratified or acceded to the Convention (or the respective Protocol), with the exception of ongoing violations, which allow bringing a case to the Court even if the breach started before ratification or accession, as long as it subsists after such a time.[155] Lastly, the Court's jurisdiction *ratione*

---

[152] A.A. Cançado Trindade, 'Réaffirmation de l' universalité nécessaire et inéluctable des droits inhérents à la personne humaine', Addresse au Séminaire à la CourEDH, Strasbourg (8 March 2018).

[153] Council of Europe, Explanatory Report to Protocol No. 14 to the Convention for the Protection of Human Rights and Fundamental Freedoms, amending the control system of the Convention, ETS No. 194 (13 May 2004), para. 7; Directorate of the Jurisconsult of the European Court of Human Rights, Practical Guide on Admissibility Criteria, p. 7.

[154] For a comprehensive discussion of the status of 'victim' under the ECHR, see: D. Harris, M. O'Boyle, E. Bates and C. Buckley, *Harris, O'Boyle and Warbrick: Law of the European Convention on Human Rights* (4th ed., OUP 2018) 87–98.

[155] The continuous character of the violation can also extend to procedural omissions, such as the lack of investigation of violations that took place before the State had ratified or acceded to the Convention. See: ECtHR, *Šilih v. Slovenia* [GC], App. no. 71463/01, § 152, 159, 162–163, 167, 9 April 2009.

loci normally extends to the whole territory of the States Parties to the Convention, although—as discussed in **Section 3.2.3**—might be subject to restrictions based on the (anachronistic) 'colonial clause', as well as extended beyond the States' territory in cases of extra-territorial application of the Convention.

7.3.7.1 The exhaustion of domestic remedies and the four-month rule

Article 35 begins by establishing two fundamental procedural grounds for admissibility: the prior exhaustion of domestic remedies and the 'four-month rule'—previously the 'six-month rule', until the entry into force of Protocol 15. These two admissibility criteria not only apply to individual applications, but need to be satisfied as well for the admissibility of inter-State cases.[156] As aforementioned, the Court's supervision of the protection of human rights is complementary to that of the national systems; hence, domestic courts should have the opportunity to determine, in the first instance, the compatibility of the measures complained about with the Convention. Only after the national courts have failed to redress the alleged violation is the applicant allowed to resort to the international protection provided by the Court. If the State's domestic law provides for several remedies in different fields of law, applicants only need to make use of one of these remedies to comply with this requirement. They are, nonetheless, required to appeal to the highest possible court of the Contracting Party to be considered to have exhausted domestic remedies.[157] Certainly, there are possible exceptions to the rule of prior exhaustion of domestic remedies and the Court has shown flexibility when assessing compliance with this criterion.[158] It has reiterated that applicants are only obliged to exhaust domestic remedies that are available and effective; that is to say, are accessible, are capable of providing redress in respect of the complaint at stake, and offer a reasonable prospect of success.[159] Furthermore, where the respondent State claims non-exhaustion of domestic remedies, it bears the burden of proving that the applicant has not used a remedy that was both effective and available.[160]

The second aforementioned criterion refers to the timeframe within which an application should be submitted to the Court, following the exhaustion of domestic remedies. With the entry into force of Protocol 15, the longstanding 'six-month rule' has been shortened to four months.[161] The time-limit marks the moment beyond which

---

[156] D. Harris, M. O'Boyle, E. Bates and C. Buckley, *Harris, O'Boyle and Warbrick: Law of the European Convention on Human Rights* (4th ed., OUP 2018) 69.

[157] D. Harris, M. O'Boyle, E. Bates and C. Buckley, *Harris, O'Boyle and Warbrick: Law of the European Convention on Human Rights* (4th ed., OUP 2018) 55–59.

[158] ECtHR, *Akdivar and Others v. Turkey*, 16 September 1996, § 69, Reports of Judgments and Decisions 1996-IV; ECtHR, *Sejdovic v. Italy* [GC], App. no. 56581/00, § 44, ECHR 2006-II.

[159] ECtHR, *Akdivar and Others v. Turkey*, 16 September 1996, § 68, Reports of Judgments and Decisions 1996-IV; ECtHR, *Sejdovic v. Italy* [GC], App. no. 56581/00, § 46, ECHR 2006-II.

[160] ECtHR, *Akdivar and Others v. Turkey*, 16 September 1996, § 68, Reports of Judgments and Decisions 1996-IV; ECtHR, *Sejdovic v. Italy* [GC], App. no. 56581/00, § 46, ECHR 2006-II.

[161] The introduction of the new time limit allowed for a transitional six-month period following the entry into force of Protocol 15 and did not apply retroactively. See: Council of Europe, Explanatory Report to Protocol No. 15 amending the Convention for the Protection of Human Rights and Fundamental Freedoms, ETS No. 213 (24 June 2013), para. 22; Protocol No. 15 amending the Convention for the Protection of Human Rights and Fundamental Freedom (adopted 24 June 2013) ETS No. 213, Art. 8.3.

the international supervision of the acts of the State by the regional Court is no longer possible.[162] The existence of a time-limit for the submission of cases to the Court has a number of aims: 'Its primary purpose is to maintain legal certainty by ensuring that cases raising issues under the Convention are examined within a reasonable time, and to prevent the authorities and other persons concerned from being kept in a state of uncertainty for a long period of time ... It also affords the prospective applicant time to consider whether to lodge an application and, if so, to decide on the specific complaints and arguments to be raised ... and facilitates the establishment of facts in a case, since with the passage of time, any fair examination of the issues raised is rendered problematic.'[163] The time limit starts to run on the day following the date on which the final decision has been pronounced in public or on which the applicant was notified of it, and expires four calendar months later, regardless of the actual duration of those calendar months and despite the *dies ad quem* falling on a non-working day.[164] According to the Court's Rules, a duly completed application containing all of the information requested in the relevant parts of the application form available at the Court's website,[165] and accompanied by copies of the relevant supporting documents, must be sent to the Court within the time limit.[166]

7.3.7.2 Anonymous applications and duplicity of proceedings

Applications submitted by an individual cannot be anonymous.[167] However, applicants 'who do not wish their identity to be disclosed to the public' can request this to the Court, indicating the reasons that would justify 'such a departure from the normal rule of public access to information in proceedings before the Court'.[168] If the Court grants the request, the applicant will be designated by their initials or simply by a letter. In exceptional circumstances, such as when the life or personal integrity of the applicants or of their next of kin may be at risk if their identities are disclosed, the Court might consider preserving the anonymity of the applicant even from the State.[169]

An individual application would be found inadmissible if it is either substantially the same as a matter that has already been examined by the Court (*res judicata*) or has already been submitted to another procedure of international investigation or settlement (*lis pendens*), unless it contains relevant new information.[170] The purpose of the principle of *res judicata* is to provide legal certainty, as a fundamental element of the rule of law, so that when the Court has finally determined an issue, its ruling is not called into question.[171]

---

[162] ECtHR, *Sabri Güneş v. Turkey* [GC], App. no. 27396/06, § 40, 29 June 2012.
[163] ECtHR, *Sabri Güneş v. Turkey* [GC], App. no. 27396/06, § 39, 29 June 2012.
[164] ECtHR, *Otto v. Germany* (dec.), App. no. 21425/06, 10 November 2009, pp. 3–4; ECtHR, *Sabri Güneş v. Turkey* [GC], App. no. 27396/06, § 61–62, 29 June 2012.
[165] See: https://www.echr.coe.int/Pages/home.aspx?p=applicants&c (accessed on 29 March 2023).
[166] For the purposes of complying with the time-limit, the date of the postmark is considered the date of introduction of the application. See: ECtHR, Rules of the Court, r. 47; ECtHR, *Malysh and Ivanin v. Ukraine*, App. nos. 40139/14, 41418/14, 9 September 2014, p. 6.
[167] ECHR, Art. 35.2.a. [168] ECtHR, Rules of the Court, r. 47.4.
[169] *Shamayev and Others v. Georgia and Russia* (dec.), App. no. 36378/02, 16 September 2003, pp. 37–38; ECtHR, *Shamayev and Others v. Georgia and Russia*, App. no. 36378/02, § 275, ECHR 2005-III. See also: F. de Londras and K. Dzehtsiarou, *Great Debates on the European Convention on Human Rights* (Palgrave 2018) pp. 65–66.
[170] ECHR, Art. 35.2.b.
[171] ECtHR, *Harkins v. the United Kingdom* (dec.) [GC], App. no. 71537/14, § 54, 15 June 2017.

Nonetheless, for this principle to apply, the cases have to share the same persons, the same facts, and the same complaints.[172] These extremes can be considered met even when the Court has struck the previous application out of the list of cases following a friendly settlement between the parties,[173] but would not be met if a substantially similar case is brought to the Court through both inter-State and individual applications.[174] An exception to the inadmissibility of a case due to *res judicata* takes place when the application contains relevant new information, which would actually modify the factual basis of the case.[175] However, the Court has considered that the development of its own jurisprudence, leading to a change of criteria that could have affected the evaluation of the facts of the case, does not amount to 'relevant new information' under the Convention.[176]

Concerning the duplicity of international proceedings (*lis pendens*), its purpose is to avoid the situation where different international bodies would be simultaneously dealing with applications that are substantially the same,[177] which could potentially lead to contradictory decisions. As with *res judicata*, cases would be considered 'substantially the same' only if involving the same persons, facts, and complaints.[178] Nevertheless, in the past, the Court has declared an application inadmissible, despite the applicants not being substantially the same, when it considered that a case brought by a trade union to the Committee on Freedom of Association of the International Labour Organization was identical to the one submitted to the Court jointly by the trade union and two of its officials on their own behalf.[179] As to what types of international procedures would be capable of precluding the Court from exercising its jurisdiction over a case, these would be those judicial or quasi-judicial proceedings similar to those set up by the Convention.[180] While the Court would assess 'the nature of the supervisory body, the procedure followed thereby and the effects of its decisions',[181] it has considered that the decisions of monitoring bodies lacking the power to issue binding judgments might be sufficient to object to the jurisdiction of the Court based on the duplicity of proceedings. Consequently, an application pending decision from a UN treaty-body seems to be

---

[172] ECtHR, *Folgerø and Others v. Norway* (dec.), App. no. 15472/02, 14 February 2006, p. 13; ECtHR, *Verein gegen Tierfabriken Schweiz (VgT) v. Switzerland (no. 2)* [GC], no. 32772/02, § 63, ECHR 2009; ECtHR, *Vojnović and Vojnović v. Croatia* (dec.), App. no. 4819/10, 26 June 2012, para. 28.

[173] ECtHR, *Kezer and Others v. Turkey* (dec.), App. no. 58058/00, 5 October 2004, pp. 3–4.

[174] ECtHR, *Varnava and Others v. Turkey* [GC], App. nos. 16064/90 and eight others, § 118, ECHR 2009.

[175] ECtHR, *Kafkaris v. Cyprus* (dec.), App. no. 9644/09, 21 June 2011, para. 68; ECtHR, *Harkins v. the United Kingdom* (dec.) [GC], App. no. 71537/14, § 50, 15 June 2017.

[176] ECtHR, *Harkins v. the United Kingdom* (dec.) [GC], App. no. 71537/14, § 56, 15 June 2017.

[177] ECtHR, *Smirnova and Smirnova v. Russia* (dec.), App. nos. 46133/99, 48183/99, 3 October 2002, p. 10; ECtHR, *OAO Neftyanaya Kompaniya Yukos v. Russia*, App. no. 14902/04, § 520, 20 September 2011; ECtHR, *The Professional Trades Union for Prison, Correctional and Secure Psychiatric Workers and Others (POA and Others) v. the United Kingdom* (dec.), App. no. 59253/11, 21 May 2013, para. 27.

[178] ECtHR, *Karoussiotis v. Portugal*, App. no. 23205/08, § 63, ECHR 2011; ECtHR, *Savda v. Turkey*, App. no. 42730/05, § 68, 12 June 2012; ECtHR, *Gürdeniz v. Turkey* (dec.), App. no. 59715/10, 18 March 2014, para. 41.

[179] ECtHR, *The Professional Trades Union for Prison, Correctional and Secure Psychiatric Workers and Others (POA and Others) v. the United Kingdom* (dec.), App. no. 59253/11, 21 May 2013, paras. 32–33.

[180] ECtHR, *Karoussiotis v. Portugal*, App. no. 23205/08, § 68, ECHR 2011.

[181] ECtHR, *Karoussiotis v. Portugal*, App. no. 23205/08, § 68, ECHR 2011; ECtHR, *OAO Neftyanaya Kompaniya Yukos v. Russia*, App. no. 14902/04, § 522, 20 September 2011.

sufficient for the Court to reject the admissibility of a petition.[182] The same can be said for proceedings before the ILO Committee on Freedom of Association, as mentioned earlier,[183] as well as for individual communications submitted to certain UN Special Procedures, such as the UN Working Group on Arbitrary Detention.[184] Conversely, the Court has ruled that neither proceedings before the Working Group on Enforced or Involuntary Disappearances nor a compliant under the '1503 procedure' of the former UN Commission on Human Rights—currently, the Human Rights Council—would lead to the inadmissibility of an application based on the principle of *lis pendens*.[185]

> **ECtHR, *The Professional Trades Union for Prison, Correctional and Secure Psychiatric Workers and Others (POA and Others) v. the United Kingdom* (dec.), App. no. 59253/11, 21 May 2013.**
>
> This was an application brought to the Court by a trade union—the Professional Trades Union for Prison, Correctional and Secure Psychiatric Workers—and two of its members. The complaint was based on the existence of an outright statutory ban on industrial action by all prison officers and prison custody officers, which the applicants considered to be an unjustified restriction on the exercise of their right to freedom of association (Article 11). However, the application failed on admissibility grounds. The Court ruled that the application should be considered to be substantially the same as a complaint already submitted by the trade union to the Committee on Freedom of Association of the International Labour Organization on the same subject matter, containing no new information (paras. 32–33). Therefore, the Court ruled that the application failed to satisfy the admissibility criteria pursuant to Article 35.2(b).

7.3.7.3 Abuse of right and 'manifestly ill-founded' applications

An application would also be declared inadmissible if it amounts to an abuse of the right of individual application.[186] The Court has clarified that the term 'abuse' should be understood in its ordinary meaning as the 'harmful exercise of a right by its holder in a manner that is inconsistent with the purpose for which such right is granted'.[187] For this provision to be applied, it is required 'not only manifest inconsistency

---

[182] ECtHR, *Smirnova and Smirnova v. Russia* (dec.), App. nos. 46133/99 and 48183/99, 3 October 2002, pp. 10–11; ECtHR, *Folgerø and Others v. Norway* (dec.), App. no. 15472/02, 14 February 2006, p. 13.

[183] ECtHR, *The Professional Trades Union for Prison, Correctional and Secure Psychiatric Workers and Others (POA and Others) v. the United Kingdom* (dec.), App. no. 59253/11, 21 May 2013, paras. 32–33; ECtHR, *Fédération Hellénique des Syndicats des Employés du Secteur Bancaire v. Greece* (dec.), App. no. 72808/10, 6 December 2011, paras. 44–45.

[184] ECtHR, *Peraldi v. France* (dec.), App. no. 2096/05, 7 April 2009, paras. 12–13 ECtHR, *Gürdeniz v. Turkey* (dec.), App. no. 59715/10, 18 March 2014, para. 39; ECtHR, *Hilal Mammadov v. Azerbaijan*, App. no. 81553/12, § 106, 4 February 2016.

[185] ECtHR, *Malsagova and Others v. Russia* (dec.), App. no. 27244/03, 6 March 2008, p. 13; ECtHR, *Mikolenko, v. Estonia* (dec.), App. no. 16944/03, 5 January 2006, p. 12.

[186] ECHR, Art. 35.3.a.

[187] ECtHR, *S.A.S. v. France* [GC], App. no. 43835/11, § 66, ECHR 2014; ECtHR, *Miroļubovs and Others v. Latvia*, App. no. 798/05, § 62, 15 September 2009.

with the purpose of the right of application but also some hindrance to the proper functioning of the Court or to the smooth conduct of the proceedings before it'.[188] The Court has resorted to this criterion to declare applications inadmissible in different situations, such as when an application had been based on misleading information, including untrue facts, falsified documents, or the failure to inform the Court of essential items of evidence;[189] when an applicant had resorted to vexatious, threatening or provocative expressions in the correspondence with the Court;[190] when the applicant had breached the confidentiality of negotiations of a friendly settlement;[191] and when the applicant had 'repeatedly sent quibbling and manifestly ill-founded applications resembling an application they had previously lodged that had been declared inadmissible'.[192]

Furthermore, the Convention allows the Court to declare the inadmissibility of a case even when all the formal admissibility conditions have been met, by finding the application to be 'manifestly ill-founded'.[193] The expression used by the Convention appears to indicate that an application would only be rejected on these grounds if it was clearly and evidently lacking foundation. However, the Court has interpreted this admissibility criterion rather broadly, using it for the rejection of cases it would have seemed appropriate to examine on the merits—including some that might have encompassed breaches of Convention rights.[194] An application can be found 'manifestly ill-founded' when a preliminary examination of its substance does not disclose any appearance of a violation of the Convention or when it reveals a lack of evidence for a breach to be proven. Sometimes, in order to reach such a conclusion, the Court would invite observations from the parties and might provide a detailed reasoning for its decision.[195]

7.3.7.4 Significant disadvantage

Protocol 14 introduced a new admissibility criterion, which was hardened by the entry into force of Protocol 15. This criterion allows the Court to reject an otherwise admissible application when 'the applicant has not suffered a significant disadvantage'.[196]

---

[188] ECtHR, *S.A.S. v. France* [GC], App. no. 43835/11, § 67, ECHR 2014; ECtHR, *Miroļubovs and Others v. Latvia*, App. no. 798/05, § 65, 15 September 2009.

[189] ECtHR, *S.A.S. v. France* [GC], App. no. 43835/11, § 67, ECHR 2014; ECtHR, *Varbanov v. Bulgaria*, App. no. 31365/96, § 36, ECHR 2000-X; ECtHR, *Jian v. Romania* (dec.), no. 46640/99, 30 March 2004; ECtHR, *Al-Nashif v. Bulgaria*, App. no. 50963/99, § 89, 20 June 2002; ECtHR, *Predescu v. Romania*, App. no. 21447/03, §§ 25–27, 2 December 2008.

[190] ECtHR, *S.A.S. v. France* [GC], App. no. 43835/11, § 67, ECHR 2014; ECtHR, *Řehák v. the Czech Republic* (dec.), App. no. 67208/01, 18 May 2004.

[191] ECtHR, *S.A.S. v. France* [GC], App. no. 43835/11, § 67, ECHR 2014; ECtHR, *Hadrabová and Others v. the Czech Republic* (dec.), App. nos. 42165/02, 466/03, 25 September 2007.

[192] ECtHR, *S.A.S. v. France* [GC], App. no. 43835/11, § 67, ECHR 2014; ECtHR, *Vieira & Filhos LDA and Ferreira da Costa LDA v. Portugal* (dec.), App. nos. 980/12, 28385/12, 13 November 2012.

[193] ECHR, Art. 35.3.a.

[194] ECtHR, *Dahlab v. Switzerland* (dec.), App. no. 42393/98, 15 February 2001; ECtHR, *Courten v. the United Kingdom* (dec.), App. 4479/06, 4 November 2008; ECtHR, *Manenc v. France* (dec.), App. no. 66686/09, 21 September 2010.

[195] Directorate of the Jurisconsult of the European Court of Human Rights, Practical Guide on Admissibility Criteria, paras. 254–255, 282.

[196] ECHR, Art. 35.3.b.

Nevertheless, a safeguard clause follows the general criterion,[197] stating that an application should not be considered inadmissible when 'respect for human rights requires an examination of the application on the merits'. This admissibility criterion is a reflection of the principle *de minimis non curat praetor*,[198] meaning that the Court should not deal with unimportant cases. As explained by the Court: 'the new criterion hinges on the idea that a violation of a right, however real from a purely legal point of view, should attain a minimum level of severity to warrant consideration by an international court.'[199]

To determine whether this minimum level of severity has been reached, the Court should take into account all the circumstances of the case, including both the applicant's subjective perception and what is objectively at stake.[200] Importantly, the Court has been adamant that the pecuniary interest involved in the case is not the only important element to determine whether the applicant has suffered a 'significant disadvantage', since a violation of the Convention may concern important questions of principle, and thus cause a significant disadvantage, without it amounting to any relevant financial harm.[201] The level of severity should be established considering different factors, including 'the nature of the right allegedly violated, the seriousness of the impact of the alleged violation on the exercise of a right and/or the possible effects of the violation on the applicant's personal situation'.[202] Moreover, if the Court considers that the applicant has not suffered a significant disadvantage, it then has to evaluate whether the case should still be found admissible due to the application of the safeguard clause. Therefore, the Court must ponder whether, despite the absence of a significant disadvantage, the case should be examined on the merits because it is so required by the respect for human rights, such as when it raises 'serious questions affecting the application or the interpretation of the Convention or important questions concerning national law'.[203]

7.3.8 REPARATIONS ('JUST SATISFACTION')

Current Article 41 of the Convention establishes: 'If the Court finds that there has been a violation of the Convention or the Protocols thereto, and if the internal law of the High Contracting Party concerned allows only partial reparation to be made,

---

[197] A second safeguard that stipulated that a case should not be rejected if it had not been duly considered by a domestic authority was removed by Protocol 15. See: Protocol No. 15 amending the Convention for the Protection of Human Rights and Fundamental Freedom (adopted 24 June 2013) ETS No. 213, Art. 5.

[198] ECtHR, *Korolev v. Russia* (dec.), App. no. 25551/05, 1 July 2010, p. 4; ECtHR, *Ladygin v. Russia* (dec.), App. no. 35365/05, 3 August 2011, p. 4.

[199] ECtHR, *Korolev v. Russia* (dec.), App. no. 25551/05, 1 July 2010, p. 4; ECtHR, *Ladygin v. Russia (dec.)*, App. no. 35365/05, 3 August 2011, p. 4.

[200] ECtHR, *Korolev v. Russia* (dec.), App. no. 25551/05, 1 July 2010, p. 4; ECtHR, *Ladygin v. Russia* (dec.), App. no. 35365/05, 3 August 2011, p. 4.

[201] ECtHR, *Korolev v. Russia* (dec.), App. no. 25551/05, 1 July 2010, p. 4; ECtHR, *Živić v. Serbia*, App. no. 37204/08, § 40, 13 September 2011.

[202] ECtHR, *Giusti v. Italy*, App. no. 13175/03, § 34, 18 October 2011; ECtHR, *Gagliano Giorgi v. Italy*, App. no. 23563/07, § 56, ECHR 2012.

[203] ECtHR, *Finger v. Bulgaria*, App. no. 37346/05, § 72, 10 May 2011; ECtHR, *Maravić Markeš v. Croatia*, App. no. 70923/11, § 51, 9 January 2014.

the Court shall, if necessary, afford just satisfaction to the injured party.'[204] In practice, after finding a violation of the Convention, the Court does not require the applicant to resort to domestic proceedings to seek reparation, but it establishes itself whether 'just satisfaction' is to be awarded in the case.[205]

It follows from a Court's judgment finding a breach of the Convention that the State is under the legal obligation to adopt, in its domestic legal order, the necessary measures to put an end to the violation declared and to redress its effects in such a way as to restore, as far as possible, the situation existing before the breach.[206] Consequently, the Court's ruling finding a violation of the Convention is in itself a form of reparation and, on some occasions, the Court might refrain from ordering additional measures.[207] However, most frequently, when the State is found responsible for a breach of the Convention, the Court would order as just satisfaction the payment of compensation and, in rare cases, it might even order further measures of reparation to be adopted.[208]

According to the Court's Rules, an applicant who wishes to be awarded just satisfaction must make a specific claim to that effect within the time-limit for the submission of the observations on the merits, and should detail the specific claims for which compensation is requested, together with supporting evidence for such claims.[209] Exceptionally, the Court had made awards of just satisfaction, even in the absence of an applicant's claim, when it considered that compelling reasons existed for doing so, taking into account the particular gravity and impact of the violation of the Convention.[210] However, the 2022 amendment of the Court's Practice Directive on the topic now states that the Court would not award more than what an applicant has claimed (*ne ultra petita* principle).[211]

The purpose of the Court's award of just satisfaction is to compensate the applicant for the harm actually suffered as a consequence of a violation of their rights.[212] This means, on the one hand, that a clear causal link must exist between the violation found and the ascertained damage and, on the other hand, that awarded damages are not intended to punish the respondent State.[213] The awards ordered by the Court consist

---

[204] Current Art. 41 is a simplified version of the original article 50 of the Convention. Council of Europe, Explanatory Report to Protocol No. 11 to the Convention for the Protection of Human Rights and Fundamental Freedoms, restructuring the control machinery established thereby, ETS 155 (Strasbourg, 11 May 1994), para. 97.

[205] D. Harris, M. O'Boyle, E. Bates and C. Buckley, *Harris, O'Boyle and Warbrick: Law of the European Convention on Human Rights* (4th ed., OUP 2018) 164.

[206] ECtHR, *Papamichalopoulos and Others v. Greece (Article 50)*, 31 October 1995, pp. 58–59 § 34, Series A no. 330-B; ECtHR, *Scozzari and Giunta v. Italy* [GC], App. nos. 39221/98, 41963/98, § 249, ECHR 2000-VIII.

[207] Practice direction issued by the President of the Court in accordance with Rule 32 of the Rules of Court (28 March 2007, amended on 9 June 2022), Just satisfaction claim, para. I.4.

[208] ECtHR, *Assanidze v. Georgia* [GC], App. no. 71503/01, § 202–203, ECHR 2004-II; ECtHR, *Ilaşcu and Others v. Moldova and Russia* [GC], App. no. 48787/99, § 490, ECHR 2004-VIII.

[209] ECtHR, Rules of the Court, r. 60.

[210] ECtHR, *Nagmetov v. Russia* [GC], App. no. 35589/08, § 74–92, 30 March 2017.

[211] Practice direction issued by the President of the Court in accordance with Rule 32 of the Rules of Court (28 March 2007, amended on 9 June 2022), Just satisfaction claim, para. II.A.7.

[212] Practice direction issued by the President of the Court in accordance with r. 32 of the Rules of Court (28 March 2007, amended on 9 June 2022), Just satisfaction claim, para. I.2.

[213] Practice direction issued by the President of the Court in accordance with r. 32 of the Rules of Court (28 March 2007, amended on 9 June 2022), Just satisfaction claim, paras. I.2 and II.A.5.

of the payment of monetary sums to redress the losses suffered under three categories: pecuniary damage, non-pecuniary damage, and the costs and expenses incurred by the victim.[214] Pecuniary damage refers to the actual financial harm experienced by the victim due to the violation declared by the Court. The general principle governing the determination of this type of damage is that of *restitutio in integrum*. As far as possible, the applicant should be placed in the position in which they would have been had the violation not occurred. Therefore, the compensation for pecuniary damage should comprise both the loss actually suffered (*damnum emergens*), as well as any future loss or diminished gain (*lucrum cessans*).[215] The Court would also normally award the reimbursement of the costs and expenses that the applicant has incurred, both at the domestic and the international level, in trying to prevent the violation from taking place and in trying to obtain redress for it.[216]

As to non-pecuniary damage, this refers to any suffering and harm experienced by the victim that is non-financial in nature. Given that the determination of compensation for non-pecuniary damage is not susceptible of precise calculation, the Court tends to make these awards based on equity, having due consideration of the standards emerging from its jurisprudence, as well as the particular circumstances of the case.[217] The amended Court's Directive affirms that among the 'factors considered by the Court to determine the value of such awards are the nature and gravity of the violation found, its duration and effects; whether there have been several violations of the protected rights; whether a domestic award has already been made or other measures have been taken by the respondent State that could be regarded as constituting the most appropriate means of redress; [and] any other context or case-specific circumstances that need to be taken into account'.[218] These amounts are also adjusted based on the cost of living in the respondent State to take into account the purchasing power of the award.[219] Since 2002,[220] the Court's awards of compensation are normally set in

---

[214] How the Court quantifies its monetary awards is a topic of increasing academic interest. See: S. Altwicker-Hámori, T. Altwicker, and A. Peters, 'Measuring Violations of Human Rights: An Empirical Analysis of Awards in Respect of Non-Pecuniary Damage under the European Convention on Human Rights' (2016) 76 *Heidelberg Journal of International Law* 1; V. Fikfak, 'Changing State Behaviour: Damages before the European Court of Human Rights' (2019) 29 *European Journal of International Law* 1091.

[215] Practice direction issued by the President of the Court in accordance with r. 32 of the Rules of Court (28 March 2007, amended on 9 June 2022), Just satisfaction claim, para. II.B.8.

[216] Practice direction issued by the President of the Court in accordance with r. 32 of the Rules of Court (28 March 2007, amended on 9 June 2022), Just satisfaction claim, para. II.D.15.

[217] Practice direction issued by the President of the Court in accordance with r. 32 of the Rules of Court (28 March 2007, amended on 9 June 2022), Just satisfaction claim, para. II.C.11, II.C.12.

[218] Practice direction issued by the President of the Court in accordance with r. 32 of the Rules of Court (28 March 2007, amended on 9 June 2022), Just satisfaction claim, para. II.C.13.

[219] Practice direction issued by the President of the Court in accordance with Rule 32 of the Rules of Court (28 March 2007, amended on 9 June 2022), Just satisfaction claim, para. II.C.14; D. Harris, M. O'Boyle, E. Bates and C. Buckley, *Harris, O'Boyle and Warbrick: Law of the European Convention on Human Rights* (4th ed., OUP 2018) 163; O. Ichim, *Just Satisfaction under the European Convention on Human Rights* (CUP 2015) 159–160.

[220] D. Harris, M. O'Boyle, E. Bates and C. Buckley, *Harris, O'Boyle and Warbrick: Law of the European Convention on Human Rights* (4th ed., OUP 2018) 165; O. Ichim, *Just Satisfaction under the European Convention on Human Rights* (CUP 2015) 229.

euros, to be converted into the national currency of the State at the official exchange rate on the date of payment.[221] The Court tends to order the payment of these awards to take place within a three-month period from the moment the judgment becomes final, setting a default interest rate to be paid in case of arrears.[222]

The practice of the Court concerning the award of compensation has been subjected to a certain level of academic criticism for being unclear and inconsistent.[223] However, the Court has created a specific Division within its Registry to advise on the level of awards in similar cases. It is believed that this Division has produced tables adopted by the Court, which set out the method for calculating compensation for non-pecuniary damage in respect of the different protected rights, indicating a minimum and a maximum sum of award.[224] Unfortunately, these reported tables seem to be internal documents of the Court and have not been made public.[225]

As aforementioned, the Court only order measures of reparation beyond the payment of compensation in exceptional circumstances. According to the Court's jurisprudence: 'its judgments are essentially declaratory in nature and that, in general, it is primarily for the State concerned to choose the means to be used in its domestic legal order to discharge its legal obligation under Article 46 of the Convention, provided that such means are compatible with the conclusions set out in the Court's judgment'.[226] Nonetheless, there are instances in which the nature of the violation leaves no real choice as to the measures required to remedy it.[227] In those occasions, the Court may decide to identify either individual or general measures the State is bound to adopt to redress the violation of the Convention. A clear example of an individual measure of this kind can be found in cases when the applicant has been found to be the victim of an ongoing illegal detention, given that the failure to release them from prison would entail a continuation of the violation.[228] As to general measures, in cases in which the

---

[221] Practice direction issued by the President of the Court in accordance with r. 32 of the Rules of Court (28 March 2007, amended on 9 June 2022), Just satisfaction claim, paras. IV.26.

[222] Practice direction issued by the President of the Court in accordance with r. 32 of the Rules of Court (28 March 2007, amended on 9 June 2022), Just satisfaction claim, paras. IV.27.

[223] A. Mowbray, 'The European Court of Human Rights' Approach to Just Satisfaction' (1997) *Public Law* 647, 650, 658–6759; D. Harris, M. O'Boyle, E. Bates and C. Buckley, *Harris, O'Boyle and Warbrick: Law of the European Convention on Human Rights* (4th ed., OUP 2018) 162–164; O. Ichim, *Just Satisfaction under the European Convention on Human Rights* (CUP 2015) 45–46, 128, 172, 236, 258, 271.

[224] D. Harris, M. O'Boyle, E. Bates and C. Buckley, *Harris, O'Boyle and Warbrick: Law of the European Convention on Human Rights* (4th ed., OUP 2018) 163; O. Ichim, *Just Satisfaction under the European Convention on Human Rights* (CUP 2015) 121.

[225] D. Harris, M. O'Boyle, E. Bates and C. Buckley, *Harris, O'Boyle and Warbrick: Law of the European Convention on Human Rights* (4th ed., OUP 2018) 163–164; O. Ichim, *Just Satisfaction under the European Convention on Human Rights* (CUP 2015) 160–161.

[226] ECtHR, *Assanidze v. Georgia* [GC], App. no. 71503/01, § 202, ECHR 2004-II; ECtHR, *Kavala v. Turkey*, no. 28749/18, § 238, 10 December 2019.

[227] ECtHR, *Assanidze v. Georgia* [GC], App. no. 71503/01, § 202, ECHR 2004-II; ECtHR, *Kavala v. Turkey*, App. no. 28749/18, § 239, 10 December 2019.

[228] ECtHR, *Assanidze v. Georgia* [GC], App. no. 71503/01, § 202–203, ECHR 2004-II; ECtHR, *Ilaşcu and Others v. Moldova and Russia* [GC], App. no. 48787/99, § 490, ECHR 2004-VIII; ECtHR, *Kavala v. Turkey*, App. no. 28749/18, § 240, 10 December 2019.

Court identifies the existence of structural problems, it can order the State to adopt changes to its domestic legal order to put an end to the violations found. For instance, in *Oleksandr Volkov v. Ukraine*, after ruling that the process of dismissal of a Supreme Court Judge was in breach of the Convention, the Court stressed the need to reform the domestic system of judicial discipline—in addition to ordering the State to reinstate the application to its post.[229] Similarly, in *Sinan Işık v. Turkey*, after ruling that stating individuals' religions in personal documents, such as civil registers and identity cards, breached the freedom not to disclose one's religion, the Court specified that the removal of the religion box in identity cards would constitute an appropriate form of redress to put an end to the breach it had found.[230]

ECtHR, *Oleksandr Volkov v. Ukraine*, App. no. 21722/11, ECHR 2013.

The applicant had been a judge of the Ukrainian Supreme Court until his dismissal in 2010. He claimed that the process leading to his destitution entailed an array of breaches to Article 6 (right to a fair trial), including: that the case had not been considered by an 'independent and impartial tribunal'; that the proceedings had been unfair; and that Parliament had decided its dismissal by abusing the electronic voting system. The applicant also argued that his irregular dismissal amounted to a violation of his right to respect for his private life (Article 8). The Court found that the applicant was dismissed in violation of fundamental principles of procedural fairness enshrined in Article 6, such as the independence and impartiality of tribunals, legal certainty, and the right to be heard by a tribunal established by law. The dismissal was also found to be incompatible with the requirements of lawfulness of restrictions adopted under Article 8.

When assessing how the State should redress the violations committed, the Court reflected that its judgment imposed upon States not only a legal obligation to pay compensation, but also the duty to adopt individual and general measures to put an end to the violations and to repair their consequences so as to restore, as far as possible, the situation that existed before the breach (para. 193). The Court considered that the case disclosed serious systemic problems in the functioning of the Ukrainian judiciary, as the dismissal of a Supreme Court's judge in manifest disregard of the discussed Conventional principles could be viewed as a threat to the independence of the judiciary as a whole. Therefore, for the appropriate execution of the judgment, the Court affirmed that Ukraine would be required to take a number of general measures that would reform the system of judicial discipline, including needed legislative reforms to restructure the institutional basis of the system (paras. 199–200). It also affirmed that the very exceptional circumstances of the case and the urgent need to put an end to the violations required the State to secure the applicant's reinstatement to its post at the Supreme Court at the earliest possible date (para. 208). This, in addition to the payment of compensation for the pecuniary and non-pecuniary damage suffered and the payment of costs and expenses.

---

[229] ECtHR, *Oleksandr Volkov v. Ukraine*, App. no. 21722/11, § 200, 208, ECHR 2013.
[230] ECtHR, *Sinan Işık v. Turkey*, App. no. 21924/05, § 60, ECHR 2010.

> **ECtHR, *Sinan Işık v. Turkey*, App. no. 21924/05, ECHR 2010.**
>
> The application was brought to the Court by a Turkish citizen, member of the Alevi religious community. He argued that the obligation to disclose a religion on his Turkish identity card, which contained a 'religion' box, amounted to a breach of the right to freedom of religion and conscience (Article 9). He also complained of the refusal to have the word 'Islam' replaced on his identity card by the indication of his faith as 'Alevi', which he understood as a further breach of Article 9. By the time the Court examined the case, the domestic legislation had been amended, allowing individuals the choice to leave the 'religion' box of their identity cards blank. The Court considered that, despite the amendment, when identity cards have a religion box, leaving that box blank inevitably has a specific connotation. Bearers of identity cards which do not contain information concerning religion would stand out, against their will, from those who have an identity card indicating their religious beliefs (para. 51). The Court found that situation to be incompatible with the principle of freedom not to manifest one's religion or belief, protected under Article 9. It further considered that the removal of the religion box would constitute an appropriate form of redress, to put an end to the breach found (para. 60).

7.3.8.1 Pilot judgments

The indication of general measures to redress the existence of a recurrent or systematic problem has become a central issue in the adoption of 'pilot judgments'. The pilot judgment procedure was created by the Court as a technique of identifying structural or systemic problems underlying repetitive applications.[231] It allows the Court to select one or more of these repeated applications for priority treatment, while adjourning the remaining ones for a period of time on the condition that the government acts promptly to adopt the measures required to solve the root cause of the applications.[232] The purpose of a pilot judgment is not just to rule on a violation of the Convention, but also to provide the respondent State with clear indications of the type of remedial measures needed to solve the systemic or structural problem identified.[233] The Court may also reserve the question of 'just satisfaction' pending the adoption by the respondent State of the measures specified in the pilot judgment.[234] If the parties to the pilot case reach a friendly-settlement agreement, such agreement shall comprise a declaration on the implementation of the general measures identified, as well as the redress to be afforded to the remaining (actual or potential) applicants.[235]

Although the pilot judgment procedure was only added to the Rules of the Court in 2011, the procedure was used for the first time already in 2004 in the *Broniowski v. Poland* case.[236] The case concerned the lack of due compensation of the repatriated Polish citizens who had abandoned their properties situated in the territories beyond the Bug River that became part of Ukraine, Belarus, or Lithuania when Poland's

---

[231] ECtHR, Press Unit, Pilot judgment—Fact sheet.   [232] ECtHR, Rules of the Court, r. 61.
[233] ECtHR, Rules of the Court, r. 61.3.   [234] ECtHR, Rules of the Court, r. 61.5.
[235] ECtHR, Rules of the Court, r. 61.7.
[236] ECtHR, *Broniowski v. Poland* [GC], App. no. 31443/96, ECHR 2004-V.

eastern border was redrawn in the aftermath of the Second World War.[237] This lack of compensation, a breach of the right to the peaceful enjoyment of possessions under Article 1 of Protocol 1, disclosed a structural problem affecting approximately 80,000 people. The Court requested Poland to adopt appropriate domestic measures to ensure the enjoyment of the property rights of the repatriated citizens or their successors.[238] The State actually complied with the pilot judgment by adopting a new law that afforded compensation for properties abandoned beyond the Bug River. With the assistance from the Court's Registry, the State reached a friendly settlement with the applicant, which not only provided him with compensation for the damages suffered, but also included the State's commitment to offer redress to all remaining claimants. This led the Court to strike out hundreds of similar applications that had been adjourned.[239]

7.3.9 CRITICAL DEBATE: THE CASELOAD OF THE EUROPEAN COURT OF HUMAN RIGHTS

Since its creation in the 1950s the European human rights system has developed beyond expectations. Originally aimed at providing supranational protection of core human rights within a group of Western European States, it now offers the compulsory supervision of a permanent Court to the hundreds of millions of people in forty-six European States.[240] A natural consequence of such an expansion was the exponential increment in the number of cases brought to the Court on a daily basis. The substantial number of applications, which led to an important backlog of cases, has been a recurrent concern within the Council of Europe for at least two decades.[241] During the 2000s, the Court experienced an enormous backlog of cases, which continued to grow significantly year after year.[242] At the end of 2009, a Report by the Secretary General of the Council of Europe, Thorbjørn Jagland, affirmed: 'The Court is now in a desperate situation. Its backlog of pending cases has broken the 100,000 barrier. As a result, the Court is no longer able to function as it should, despite its laudable efforts to improve efficiency and internal procedures and the considerable increase in its output of decisions and judgments. Applications are taking much too long to process.'[243] Some commentators have actually proposed that the Court should be turned into a Europe-wide

---

[237] ECtHR, *Broniowski v. Poland* [GC], App. no. 31443/96, ECHR 2004-V, § 10–12.
[238] ECtHR, *Broniowski v. Poland* [GC], App. no. 31443/96, ECHR 2004-V, § 192–194.
[239] ECtHR, *Broniowski v. Poland (friendly settlement)* [GC], App. no. 31443/96, ECHR 2005-IX.
[240] L.R. Helfer, 'Redesigning the European Court of Human Rights: Embeddedness as a Deep Structural Principle of the European Human Rights Regime' (2008) 19 *European Journal of International Law* 125, 126; Memorandum of the President of the European Court of Human Rights to the States with a View to Preparing the Interlaken Conference (2009) p. 1.
[241] E. Bates, *The Evolution of the European Convention on Human Rights: From Its Inception to the Creation of a Permanent Court of Human Rights* (OUP 2010) 3.
[242] E. Bates, *The Evolution of the European Convention on Human Rights: From Its Inception to the Creation of a Permanent Court of Human Rights* (OUP 2010) 480; Memorandum of the President of the European Court of Human Rights to the States with a View to Preparing the Interlaken Conference (2009) p. 2.
[243] Contribution of the Secretary General of the Council of Europe to the Preparation of the Interlaken Ministerial Conference (SG/Inf(2009)20) (18 December 2009), para. 15.

constitutional court,[244] which could focus on providing 'fully reasoned and authoritative judgments in cases which raise substantial or new and complex issues of human rights law, are of particular significance for the State concerned or involve allegations of serious human rights violations and which warrant a full process of considered adjudication.'[245] The idea of such a dramatic change in the Court's role, depriving it of its power to deliver individual justice to those who have suffered a violation of their human rights, has (so far) been rejected. Nonetheless, the system has been subjected to numerous changes through the years to address the high volume of applications.

The continuing increase in the Court's workload was one of fundamental reasons behind the reform of the system through Protocol 14.[246] The Preamble of the Protocol states that it is adopted due to 'the urgent need to amend certain provisions of the Convention in order to maintain and improve the efficiency of the control system for the long term, mainly in the light of the continuing increase in the workload of the European Court of Human Rights and the Committee of Ministers of the Council of Europe'.[247] As discussed in **Section 7.1.1**, Protocol 14 put in place important changes to the Court's formations, establishing the possibility of individual judges dealing with the rejection of clearly inadmissible applications and empowering three-judge Committees to rule on the merits of cases concerning issues subject to the Court's well-established case law.[248] The Protocol also added a new admissibility criterion, allowing the Court to declare an application inadmissible if the applicant has not suffered a 'significant disadvantage'.[249] Moreover, the same year that Protocol 14 was adopted, the Court implemented another essential tool for managing the increasing volume of cases: the pilot judgment procedure—discussed in **Section 7.3.8.1**.

Although adopted in 2004, Protocol 14 required ratification by the (then) forty-five States Parties to the Convention to enter into force and it took the Russian Federation until 18 February 2010 to ratify it. This extended delay motivated the adoption of Protocol 14bis, aimed at allowing the introduction of the single-judge formation and the extended competence of three-judge Committees to have effect among the Parties to the interim Protocol, as these were seen as the elements most likely to have an important effect on

---

[244] L. Wildhaber, 'A Constitutional Future for the European Court of Human Rights?' (2002) 23 *Human Rights Law Journal* 161, 163–164; P. Mahoney, 'New Challenges for the European Court of Human Rights Resulting from the Expanding Case Load and Membership' (2002) 21 *Penn State International Law Review* 101, 104–106; S. Greer, *The European Convention on Human Rights: Achievements, Problems and Prospects* (CUP 2006) 165–175; F. de Londras, 'Dual Functionality and the Persistent Frailty of the European Court of Human Rights' (2013) *European Human Rights Law Review* 38, 46.

[245] Evaluation Group, Report of the Evaluation Group to Examine Possible Means of Guaranteeing the Effectiveness of the European Court of Human Rights (EG Court (2001)1) (27 September 2001), para. 98.

[246] Council of Europe, Explanatory Report to Protocol No. 14 to the Convention for the Protection of Human Rights and Fundamental Freedoms, amending the control system of the Convention, ETS No. 194 (13 May 2004), para. 9.

[247] Protocol No. 14 to the Convention for the Protection of Human Rights and Fundamental Freedoms, amending the control system of the Convention (adopted 13 May 2004, entered into force 1 June 2010) ETS No. 194, preamble.

[248] The Protocol also allows the Court to request that the Committee of Ministers to reduce the number of judges of the Chambers from seven to five. Protocol No. 14 (2004), Art. 6; ECHR, Art. 26.2.

[249] Protocol No. 14 (2004), Art. 12; ECHR, Art. 35.3.b.

the Court's case-processing capacity.[250] The delay also provided impetus for the Member States to engage in discussions on the need to further reform the European human rights system. At the opening of the 2009 judicial year, the then President of the Court, Jean-Paul Costa, called upon the Governments of the States Parties to the Convention to come together around a major formal conference, aimed at reaffirming the Court's legitimacy and clarifying its mandate.[251] This call led to the celebration of a High-Level Conference on the Future of the Court in February 2010. The Interlaken Conference was actually the first of a series of conferences focused on reforms to achieve long-term effectiveness of the Convention system. While the increasing caseload—and the consequential backlog of cases—was not the only challenge faced by the Court, it certainly provided the overall background against which five high-level conferences were hosted.[252] The Declaration adopted in Interlaken stressed 'the need for effective measures to reduce the number of clearly inadmissible applications, the need for effective filtering of these applications and the need to find solutions for dealing with repetitive applications'.[253]

The entry into force of Protocol 14 in 2010, following Russia's awaited ratification, allowed for all the aforementioned amendments to be implemented. In order to make the most effective use of the powers of the new single-judge formation, the Court set up a 'Filtering Section' within its Registry to centralize the handling of application coming from five of the States Parties with the highest case-count—Russia, Turkey, Romania, Ukraine, and Poland—as the applications against those States accounted, at the time, for over half of the pending cases.[254] The Filtering Section started to operate at the beginning of 2011, sifting incoming application to ensure their placement on the appropriate procedural track, whether submitted to an individual judge for prompt decision or sent to await examination by a Committee or Chamber, in accordance with the Court's priority policy. Both the short- and longer-term numbers seem to indicate

[250] Council of Europe, Explanatory Report to Protocol No. 14bis to the Convention for the Protection of Human Rights and Fundamental Freedoms, ETS No. 204 (27 May 2009), para. 7.

[251] J.P. Costa, 'Speech given on the occasion of the opening of the judicial year, 30 January 2009, by Jean-Paul Costa, President of the European Court of Human Rights' Dialogue between judges: Fifty Years of the European Court of Human Rights Viewed by its Fellow International Courts (Strasbourg, 2009) 69.

[252] L.R. Glas, 'From Interlaken to Copenhagen: What Has Become of the Proposals Aiming to Reform the Functioning of the European Court of Human Rights?' (2020) 20 *Human Rights Law Review* 121, 124–125. The 2010 Interlaken Conference was followed by the Izmir Conference (26–27 April 2011), the Brighton Conference (18–20 April 2012), the Brussels Conference (26–27 March 2015), and the Copenhagen Conference (12–13 April 2018).

[253] Interlaken Declaration, adopted by the High-Level Conference on the Future of the European Court of Human Rights at the initiative of the Swiss Chairmanship of the Committee of Ministers of the Council of Europe (19 February 2010), para. 6.

[254] It could be highlighted that while four of those States are consistently among the States with the highest number of pending applications, over the past twenty-five years, Poland has consistently been behind Italy in that category. See: ECtHR, 2022 Annual Report, p. 140; ECtHR, 2021 Annual Report, p. 180; ECtHR, 2020 Annual Report, p. 156; ECtHR, 2019 Annual Report, p. 128; ECtHR, 2018 Annual Report, p. 168; ECtHR, 2017 Annual Report, p. 164; ECtHR, 2016 Annual Report, p. 192; ECtHR, 2015 Annual Report, p. 188; ECtHR, 2014 Annual Report, p. 166; ECtHR, 2013 Annual Report, p. 192; ECtHR, 2012 Annual Report, p. 150; ECtHR, 2011 Annual Report, p. 152; ECtHR, 2010 Annual Report, p. 152; ECtHR, 2009 Annual Report, p. 140; ECtHR, 2008 Annual Report, p. 128.

that the procedural changes introduced during 2010 and 2011 have had a substantial effect on the backlog of cases.[255]

At the third High-level Conference, celebrated in Brighton in 2012, the States agreed on further reforms to the system aimed at tackling the Court's caseload, to be put in place through the drafting of two Protocols; one that amended the Convention, hardening the admissibility criteria for applications (Protocol 15), and a further one empowering the Court to deliver advisory opinions requested by domestic courts (Protocol 16).[256] Protocol 16 was the first one to enter into force and, as discussed in **Section 7.6**, it allows the highest courts and tribunals of the States Parties to the Protocol to request the Court to render advisory opinions on questions of principle relating to the interpretation or application of Convention rights in the context of a case pending before them.[257] This procedure should allow the domestic courts to decide their cases in a manner consistent with the authoritative interpretation of the Convention, thereby preventing certain cases to reach the Court in the future.

Protocol 15 obtained its final ratification in April 2021, entering into force on 1 August 2021. The changes introduced by this Protocol are further discussed in **Section 7.3.7** and **Section 7.7**. As mentioned in **Section 7.3.7**, the hardening of two of the admissibility criteria—by reducing the timeframe to submit an application to the Court and by removing one of the safeguards accompanying the criterion of 'significant disadvantage'—was aimed at increasing the number of cases rejected as inadmissible. In line with the reduction of the time-limit for lodging applications, the Court amended its Rules, setting a stricter approach to the institution of proceedings (amended Rule 47), and introduced a new application form that simplifies the work of the Registry in determining the nature and scope of each new application.[258] Furthermore, Protocol 15 led to the inclusion of the 'principle of subsidiarity' and the concept of the 'margin of appreciation' into the text of the Convention—albeit into its Preamble—which was also envisioned to have an effect on the workload of the Court, restricting the examination of issues that had already been considered and decided by the domestic authorities.[259]

---

[255] ECtHR, Filtering Section speeds up processing of cases from highest case-count countries (2011); ECtHR, Analysis of Statistics 2022 (January 2023).

[256] Brighton Declaration, adopted by the High-Level Conference on the Future of the European Court of Human Rights, (19–20 April 2012), paras. 12, 15.

[257] This process of 'dialogue' between domestic high courts and the European Court of Human Rights was further complemented by the creation, in 2015, of the 'Superior Courts Network'; an initiative aimed at enriching and ensuring the effective exchange of information among the member courts, by which the European Court explains its developing jurisprudence and national courts provide it with insights into their own jurisdictions. The Court's Jurisconsult has been entrusted to manage the network. See: ECtHR, 2015 Annual Report, pp. 11–12; ECtHR, 'Operational Rules of the Superior Courts Network' (13 April 2018).

[258] L.R. Glas, 'From Interlaken to Copenhagen: What Has Become of the Proposals Aiming to Reform the Functioning of the European Court of Human Rights?' (2020) 20 *Human Rights Law Review* 121, 129.

[259] L.R. Glas, 'From Interlaken to Copenhagen: What Has Become of the Proposals Aiming to Reform the Functioning of the European Court of Human Rights?' (2020) 20 *Human Rights Law Review* 121, 134–136.

7.4 INTER-STATE CASES

Although the vast majority of cases that reach the Court are brought by individual applicants, the Convention allows for State Parties to refer to the Court any alleged breach of the Convention or its Protocols by another Party.[260] When bringing a case against another State, the applicant State is not required to justify any special connection to the alleged violation, as States can bring cases before the Court in exercise of their role in the 'collective enforcement' of the Convention.[261] However, the applicant State is required to fulfil two admissibility requirements. First, inter-State complaints are not exempted from resorting to the domestic courts of the State allegedly in breach of the Convention and, second, the application needs to be filled with the Court within the four-month time-limit following the exhaustion of domestic remedies.[262] In principle, inter-State cases should be heard by a Chamber, with the judges elected in respect of both the applicant and respondent States sitting as *ex officio* members,[263] although this type of cases are potential candidates for the relinquishment of jurisdiction in favour of the Grand Chamber.[264] In contrast to individual applications, in inter-State cases the general rule is that admissibility and merits should be decided at different stages of the proceedings.[265]

Up to the end of 2022, there have been just over thirty inter-State cases brought under the European Convention on Human Rights, many of which are still pending before the Court. Ten of those cases were dealt with by the former Commission and the Committee of Ministers, including the famous *Greek case* that led to Greece's withdrawal from the Convention system back in December 1969 (see **Section 7.1.3**).[266] So far, only nine inter-State cases have been subject to a final ruling of the Court. Four of these cases were struck out of the list either following the approval of a friendly settlement reached by the Parties or due to the decision of the applicant State not to pursue the application further,[267] on one occasion the Court found it lacked jurisdiction to decide on the matter,[268] while on the four opportunities in which the Court ruled on the merits of the case, it found the respondent States responsible for multiple breaches of the Convention.[269]

---

[260] ECHR, Art. 33.
[261] ECtHR, *Ireland v. the United Kingdom*, 18 January 1978, § 239, Series A App. no. 25.
[262] ECHR, Art. 35.1; ECtHR, Rules of the Court, r. 46.d.
[263] ECtHR, Rules of the Court, r. 51.2.
[264] D. Harris, M. O'Boyle, E. Bates and C. Buckley, *Harris, O'Boyle and Warbrick: Law of the European Convention on Human Rights* (4th ed., OUP 2018) 123.
[265] ECHR, Art. 29.2.
[266] European Commission of Human Rights, *The Greek case* (1969), Application No. 3321/67 (*Denmark v. Greece*), Application No. 3322/67 (*Norway v. Greece*), Application No. 3323/67 (*Sweden v. Greece*), Application No. 3344/67 (*Netherlands v. Greece*); J. Becket, 'The Greek Case before the European Human Rights Commission of Human Rights' (1970) 1 *Human Rights* 91, 107, 113.
[267] ECtHR, *Denmark v. Turkey*, App. no. 34382/97, ECHR 2000-IV; ECtHR, *Georgia v. Russia (III) (striking out)*, App. no. 61186/09, 16 March 2010; ECtHR, *Ukraine v. Russia (III) (striking out)*, App. no. 49537/14, 1 September 2015; ECtHR, *Latvia v. Denmark*, App. no. 9717/20, 16 June 2020.
[268] ECtHR, *Slovenia v. Croatia* [GC], App. no. 54155/16, 18 November 2020.
[269] ECtHR, *Ireland v. the United Kingdom*, 18 January 1978, § 239, Series A App. no. 25; ECtHR, *Cyprus v. Turkey* [GC], App. no. 25781/94, ECHR 2001-IV; ECtHR, *Georgia v. Russia (I)* [GC], App. no. 13255/07, ECHR 2014; ECtHR, *Georgia v. Russia (II)* [GC], App. no. 38263/08 (21 January 2021).

ECtHR, *Ireland v. the United Kingdom*, 18 January 1978, Series A App. no. 25.

This application, lodged by Ireland with the Commission in 1971, became the first judgment issued by the Court in an inter-State case. Within the context of the conflict in Northern Ireland in the early 1970s, the case concerned the policy of arrest, detention, and internment, without trial, of individuals suspected of serious terrorist activities and the use of five specific 'techniques of interrogation' during such extrajudicial detention by British security forces. These five interrogation 'methods' were: (a) wall-standing (forcing the detainees to remain for hours in 'stress positions'); (b) hooding (putting a bag over the detainees' heads at all times except during interrogation); (c) subjection to continuous loud and hissing noise; (d) sleep deprivation; and (e) food and drink deprivation (para. 96). Among other findings, the Commission considered that the powers of detention and internment without trial were not in conformity with Article 5 (Right to Liberty and Security), but were strictly required by the exigencies of the situation in Northern Ireland, within the meaning of Article 15 of the Convention, which allows derogation of certain obligations in times of emergency. Conversely, the Commission found the combined use of the five techniques to constitute inhuman treatment and torture in breach of Article 3.

Following the Commission's report, Ireland referred the case to the Court. The Court agreed with the Commission's findings that the situation in Northern Ireland amounted to a public emergency threatening the life of the nation, within the meaning of Article 15, and that the legislation providing for extrajudicial deprivation of liberty entailed permissible derogations (para. 224). As to the interrogation 'techniques', the Court agreed with the Commission in that the use of these methods constituted a practice of inhuman and degrading treatment, in breach of Article 3, but unlike the Commission, it considered that these techniques did not constitute a practice of torture (paras. 167 and 174).

In 2014, Ireland requested a revision of the judgment. It informed the Court that it had obtained new evidence, which might have had a decisive influence on the 1978 judgment, had it been known at the time, with regard to the understanding of the five 'techniques' as torture. However, the Court dismissed Ireland's request. It highlighted that its judgments were final; hence, the possibility of revision (introduced by the Court's Rules) was an exceptional procedure, subjected to strict scrutiny. The Court was unconvinced that the documents submitted contained sufficient evidence of any new facts that could have had a decisive influence on the findings in the original judgment.

ECtHR, *Georgia v. Russia (I)* [GC], App. no. 13255/07, ECHR 2014.

The case originated in an application by Georgia against the Russian Federation in 2007. It concerned the arrest, detention, and expulsion of thousands of Georgian nationals from Russia, in a four-month period. Georgia claimed that the increase in expulsions followed a governmental policy targeting specifically Georgian nationals. To support its allegations, Georgia submitted to the Court a number of official Russian documents, but Russia challenged their veracity, while refusing to provide copies of official documents on the grounds that they were classified as 'State secret'. Given Russia's reticence to assist the Court in establishing the facts of the case, the Court found it in breach of Article 38 of the Convention (para. 109). This also led the Court to the strong presumption of the credibility of Georgia's claims concerning the content of the documents ordering the expulsion of Georgian nationals (para. 140).

After examining the facts, the Court found that a pattern of collective expulsions clearly emerged. It emphasized that under Article 4 of Protocol No. 4 'collective expulsion' encompassed any measure compelling aliens, as a group, to leave a country, unless this measure was adopted following, and on the basis of, a reasonable and objective examination of the case of each person (para. 167). The Court concluded that the expulsions of Georgian nationals had amounted to an administrative practice in breach of Article 4 of Protocol No. 4 (para. 178). It also found that the arrests and detentions of Georgian nationals, during the period in question, were part of an arbitrary policy, in breach of Article 5 (right to liberty and security), and that the conditions of detention in which Georgian nationals were held (e.g. overcrowding, inadequate sanitary and health conditions) amounted to a violation of the prohibition of inhuman and degrading treatment (Article 3) (paras. 187–188 and 205). In addition, the Court found violations of Article 13 (right to an effective remedy), as there were no effective and accessible remedies for the Georgian nationals against the arrests, detentions, and expulsion orders, or against the conditions of detention they suffered (paras. 214 and 216).

7.5 COMPLIANCE WITH THE COURT'S JUDGMENTS

The Court's judgments are binding on the respondent States. This clearly transpires from current Article 46.1 of the Convention, which reads: 'The High Contracting Parties undertake to abide by the final judgment of the Court in any case to which they are parties.' It is the role of the Committee of Ministers of the Council of Europe to supervise the execution of judgments and of friendly settlements.[270] The Committee invites every State subject to a judgment finding a violation of the Convention to inform, through an 'action plan', of the measures it has taken or intends to take to comply with the payment of just satisfaction and with any other individual or general measure following from the judgment.[271] The cases pending execution remain under the Committee's continued supervision (entrusted to its Secretariat) until their closure;[272] once all measures to abide by the judgment are complied with by the State.[273] Since 2011, the Committee of Ministers has adopted a 'twin-track' approach to the supervision of compliance with judgments. Certain cases are placed under a procedure of 'enhanced' supervision,

---

[270] ECHR, Art. 46.2.
[271] Committee of Ministers, Rules of the Committee of Ministers for the supervision of the execution of judgments and of the terms of friendly settlements (adopted 10 May 2006 at the 964th meeting of the Ministers' Deputies and amended 18 January 2017 at the 1275th meeting of the Ministers' Deputies), r. 6.
[272] Committee of Ministers, Rules for the supervision of the execution of judgments and of the terms of friendly settlements (adopted 10 May 2006 and amended 18 January 2017), r. 7; ECtHR, *Ilgar Mammadov v. Azerbaijan (infringement proceedings)* [GC], App. no. 15172/13, § 100, 29 May 2019.
[273] Committee of Ministers, Rules for the supervision of the execution of judgments and of the terms of friendly settlements (adopted 10 May 2006 and amended on 18 January 2017), r. 17.

in order to closely follow progress of the execution of the judgment and to facilitate exchanges with the national authorities in charge of the execution.[274] This procedure is reserved for cases that require the adoption of urgent individual measures, for those that reveal important structural or complex problems, for pilot judgments, and for inter-State cases.[275] The Committee holds special human rights meetings,[276] hosted at least four times a year,[277] which are reserved for the examination of specific cases under the enhanced procedure. In these sessions, the Committee can adopt interim resolutions to express concern or make suggestions with respect to the execution.[278]

The Committee of Ministers normally relies on 'peer pressure and effective political leverage' to encourage States to comply with the individual and general measures required in response to the Court's judgments.[279] This can entail singling out cases for debate, requesting States to explain and defend their lack of compliance.[280] While the Committee has more coercive faculties under the Statute of the Council of Europe, such as the possibility of suspending a Member State's voting rights in the Committee of Ministers or even its expulsion from the organization, these extreme powers seem counter-productive for inducing compliance with a Court's judgment.[281] Protocol 14 entrusted the Committee of Ministers with further abilities to encourage Member States to comply with the Court's judgments. Article 46 now empowers the Committee of Ministers to bring infringement proceedings before the Court when a State refuses to abide by a final judgment. These proceedings require a qualified two-thirds majority vote of the Committee of Ministers and, for initiating them, the concerned State needs to be served with notice to comply. The infringement procedure does not reopen the question of the existence of a violation, already established by the original ruling, but

---

[274] Committee of Ministers, Supervision of the execution of the judgments and decisions of the European Court of Human Rights: implementation of the Interlaken Action Plan—Outstanding issues concerning the practical modalities of implementation of the new twin track supervision system (CM/ln f/D H (2010)45 final) (7 December 2010).

[275] Committee of Ministers, Supervision of the execution of the judgments and decisions of the European Court of Human Rights: implementation of the Interlaken Action Plan—Outstanding issues concerning the practical modalities of implementation of the new twin track supervision system (CM/ln f/D H (2010)45 final) (7 December 2010); ECtHR, *Ilgar Mammadov v. Azerbaijan (infringement proceedings)* [GC], App. no. 15172/13, § 101, 29 May 2019.

[276] Committee of Ministers, Rules for the supervision of the execution of judgments and of the terms of friendly settlements (adopted 10 May 2006 and amended 18 January 2017), r. 2.1.

[277] Committee of Ministers, Rapporteur Group on Human Rights, Supervision of the execution of judgments of the European Court of Human Rights: procedure and working methods for the Committee of Ministers' Human Rights meetings (GR-H(2016)2-final) (30 March 2016), para. 4.

[278] Committee of Ministers, Rules for the supervision of the execution of judgments and of the terms of friendly settlements (adopted 10 May 2006 and amended 18 January 2017), r. 16.

[279] Committee of Ministers, Supervision of the Execution of Judgments and Decisions of The European Court of Human Rights, 13th Annual Report (2019), p. 15.

[280] B. Çali and A. Koch, 'Foxes Guarding the Foxes? The Peer Review of Human Rights Judgments by the Committee of Ministers of the Council of Europe' (2014) 14 *Human Rights Law Review* 301, 318, 321.

[281] Council of Europe, Explanatory Report to Protocol No. 14 to the Convention for the Protection of Human Rights and Fundamental Freedoms, amending the control system of the Convention, ETS No. 194 (13 May 2004), para. 100.

submits to the Court's assessment whether the State has failed to fulfil its obligations under the judgment.[282]

The first infringement procedure took place in the *Ilgar Mammadov v. Azerbaijan* case. In the original judgment from 2014, the Court found several violations of Convention rights concerning the criminal charges brought against Mr Mammadov—an Azerbaijani opposition leader and activist—and his subsequent pre-trial detention. The Court concluded that the applicant's detention was not grounded on the 'reasonable suspicion' of having committed a criminal offence; his actions were prejudged by the intervening authorities, in breach of his presumption of innocence; he had not been afforded appropriate judicial review of the lawfulness of his detention; and the Court even found that the actual purpose of the restriction of the applicant's liberty was to silence or punish him for criticizing the government.[283] The judgment ordered the payment of compensation for the non-pecuniary damage experienced by the applicant, rejected the claim for pecuniary damage, and was silent about any additional particular measures that needed to be adopted for complying with the judgment, such as the release of the applicant from prison.[284] Despite this silence, when the Committee of Ministers examined the execution of the judgment, at the end of 2014, it called upon the State 'to ensure the applicant's release without delay'.[285] Given the reticence of the Azerbaijani authorities to comply with the release of Mr Mammadov, the Committee continued to examine the execution of the case in each meeting, issuing a number of interim resolutions and decisions insisting on the need for the immediate release of the applicant. In October 2017, almost three years after its first examination of the execution of the judgment, the Committee of Ministers decided to put Azerbaijan on formal notice of failure to comply with the Court's judgment and, in December of that same year, referred the case back to the Court for it to rule on whether Azerbaijan had failed to comply with the 2014 judgment.[286]

By the time the Court delivered its judgment, in May 2019, the applicant had been released.[287] Consequently, the Court had to determine which was the relevant date for assessing the State's alleged failure to comply with the judgment; whether it was the time of the Committee's referral or the time of the adoption of the judgment.[288]

---

[282] ECHR, Art. 46.
[283] ECtHR, *Ilgar Mammadov v. Azerbaijan*, no. 15172/13, § 99–101, 118–119, 126–128, 143–144, 22 May 2014.
[284] ECtHR, *Ilgar Mammadov v. Azerbaijan*, no. 15172/13, § 148, 22 May 2014.
[285] ECtHR, *Ilgar Mammadov v. Azerbaijan (infringement proceedings)* [GC], App. no. 15172/13, § 45, 29 May 2019.
[286] ECtHR, *Ilgar Mammadov v. Azerbaijan (infringement proceedings)* [GC], App. no. 15172/13, § 66–67, 29 May 2019; Committee of Ministers, Interim Resolution CM/ResDH(2017)379 (25 October 2017), adopted at the 1298th meeting of the Ministers' Deputies; Committee of Ministers, Interim Resolution CM/ResDH(2017)429 (5 December 2017), adopted at the 1302nd meeting of the Ministers' Deputies.
[287] ECtHR, *Ilgar Mammadov v. Azerbaijan (infringement proceedings)* [GC], no. 15172/13, § 133, 29 May 2019.
[288] ECtHR, *Ilgar Mammadov v. Azerbaijan (infringement proceedings)* [GC], no. 15172/13, § 169, 29 May 2019.

The Court picked the former and, therefore, examined whether the State's refusal to release the applicant by 5 December 2017 amounted to a failure to comply with the original judgment.[289] The Court acknowledged that its 2014 ruling had not explicitly indicated how the judgment should be executed. It highlighted that the ultimate choice of the measures to be taken to comply with a judgment always remains with the State concerned, under the supervision of the Committee of Ministers, provided that the adopted measures are compatible with the conclusions and spirit set out in the Court's ruling.[290] The Court affirmed that '[a]n approach which limited the supervision process to the Court's explicit indications would remove the flexibility needed by the Committee of Ministers to supervise, on the basis of the information provided by the respondent State and with due regard to the applicant's evolving situation, the adoption of measures that are feasible, timely, adequate and sufficient' to comply with the Court's judgments.[291]

The Court also stated that: 'It follows from well-established case-law under Article 46 of the Convention that the State must take individual measures in its domestic legal order to put an end to the violation found by the Court and to redress its effects. The aim is to put the applicant, as far as possible, in the position he would have been in had the requirements of the Convention not been disregarded. In exercising their choice of individual measures, the Government must bear in mind their primary aim of achieving *restitutio in integrum*'.[292] The Court found that, following from the 2014 ruling, the State was obliged to lift or annul the charges against the applicant that were found in breach of the Convention and end his pre-trial detention.[293] Therefore, the Court ruled that Azerbaijan had failed to fulfil its obligation to abide by the *Ilgar Mammadov v. Azerbaijan* judgment of 22 May 2014.[294]

7.6 THE COURT'S ADVISORY JURISDICTION

While, in our days, there are two separate grounds under which the Court can issue advisory opinions (Article 47 of the Convention and Protocol 16), the original text of the Convention did not envision the Court to have an advisory jurisdiction. This competence was initially granted to the Court by Protocol 2 (adopted in 1963 and entered into force in 1970), which empowered it to provide 'advisory opinions on legal questions concerning the interpretation of the Convention and the Protocols thereto'[295]

---

[289] ECtHR, *Ilgar Mammadov v. Azerbaijan (infringement proceedings)* [GC], no. 15172/13, § 170–171, 29 May 2019.
[290] ECtHR, *Ilgar Mammadov v. Azerbaijan (infringement proceedings)* [GC], no. 15172/13, § 182, 29 May 2019.
[291] ECtHR, *Ilgar Mammadov v. Azerbaijan (infringement proceedings)* [GC], no. 15172/13, § 184, 29 May 2019.
[292] ECtHR, *Ilgar Mammadov v. Azerbaijan (infringement proceedings)* [GC], no. 15172/13, § 191.
[293] ECtHR, *Ilgar Mammadov v. Azerbaijan (infringement proceedings)* [GC], no. 15172/13, § 192–195.
[294] ECtHR, *Ilgar Mammadov v. Azerbaijan (infringement proceedings)* [GC], no. 15172/13, § 218.
[295] Protocol No. 2 to the Convention for the Protection of Human Rights and Fundamental Freedoms, conferring upon the European Court of Human Rights competence to give advisory opinions (adopted 6 May 1963, entered into force 21 September 1970) ETS No. 44, Art. 1.

at the request of the Committee of Ministers.[296] However, these opinions could not deal with any question relating to the content or scope of Convention rights or with any other question that could be the subject of a future contentious case before the Court.[297] There was a clear intention for the Court's advisory jurisdiction to complement its adjudicatory competence and not to encroach on existing or potential contentious proceedings.[298] As expected, it remained within the jurisdiction of the Court itself to determine whether a request for an advisory opinion submitted by the Committee of Ministers fell within the (restrictive) consultative competence established by the Protocol.[299] Protocol 11 brought the advisory jurisdiction into the text of the Convention itself (current Article 47), ratifying that the new permanent Court would retain such a competence. Given that Protocol 2 had envisioned the advisory jurisdiction to be exercised by the Plenary of the Court,[300] the new Court was to perform this function as a Grand Chamber.[301]

The Court's (limited) ability to issue advisory opinions under Article 47 has not been widely exercised. In 2004, the Court rejected the first request it received, and it later rendered two opinions in 2008 and 2010, respectively. The first request concerned the coexistence of the European Convention on Human Rights and the Convention on Human Rights and Fundamental Freedoms of the Commonwealth of Independent States—a regional treaty adopted in 1995 by post-Soviet States. The Court was asked to provide an opinion as to whether an application submitted or examined by the monitoring body envisioned by the 1995 Convention—the CIS Commission—would produce the effect of *lis pendens* or *res judicata* susceptible to affect the admissibility of a claim before the Court. Given the nature of the question, the Court found that it lacked of competence to provide an advisory opinion, as it considered that the request related to a question which the Court might have to consider in the future within the framework of a contentious case.[302]

The two advisory opinions actually rendered by the Court, under Article 47, concerned the process of selection of judges.[303] The first one was about the rule adopted by the Parliamentary Assembly establishing that lists of candidates would not be considered unless they included at least one candidate of the sex under-represented at the Court. The question arose due to the list of candidates submitted in 2006 by the

---

[296] While Protocol 2 required a two-thirds majority vote for the Committee of Ministers to proceed to a request, Protocol 11 changed this to a simple majority of the representatives entitled to sit on the Committee. Protocol No. 2 (1963), Art. 1.3; Protocol No. 11 (1994); Council of Europe, Explanatory Report to Protocol No. 11 to the Convention for the Protection of Human Rights and Fundamental Freedoms, restructuring the control machinery established thereby, ETS 155 (Strasbourg, 11 May 1994).

[297] Protocol No. 2 (1963), Art. 1.

[298] ECtHR, *Decision on the Competence of the Court to Give an Advisory Opinion* (2 June 2004), para. 28.

[299] Protocol No. 2 (1963), Art. 2; Council of Europe, Explanatory Report to Protocol No. 2 to the Convention for the Protection of Human Rights and Fundamental Freedoms, conferring upon the European Court of Human Rights competence to give advisory opinions (Strasbourg, 6 May 1963).

[300] Protocol No. 2 (1963), Art. 3.   [301] Protocol No. 11 (1994).

[302] ECtHR, *Decision on the Competence of the Court to Give an Advisory Opinion* (2 June 2004), para. 35.

[303] ECtHR, *Advisory opinion on certain legal questions concerning the lists of candidates submitted with a view to the election of judges to the European Court of Human Rights* [GC], 12 February 2008; ECtHR, *Advisory opinion on certain legal questions concerning the lists of candidates submitted with a view to the election of judges to the European Court of Human Rights (No. 2)* [GC], 22 January 2010.

Government of Malta, which was composed of only male candidates.[304] The Court affirmed that even though the aim of ensuring gender balance in the composition of the lists of candidates was legitimate, it could not be pursued without provision being made for some exceptions.[305] It then asserted that the Assembly's practice of not allowing for exceptions to the rule was not compatible with the Convention and that a list of candidates could not be rejected solely on the grounds of a lack of gender balance, if the State had taken all the necessary steps to ensure that the list contained at least one candidate of the under-represented sex, especially, when an open and transparent procedure had been followed.[306] The second advisory opinion concerned the possibility of States to withdraw and replace a list of candidates for election as judges, once it had been submitted to the Parliamentary Assembly. The Court opined that States can indeed withdraw their lists and submit a new list of candidates, but only up until the deadline set by the Assembly for the submission of the list, so the election process can take place.[307]

Protocol 16, which entered into force in August 2018 when it reached its tenth ratification,[308] has now expanded the Court's competence for delivering advisory opinions. The Protocol establishes that the highest courts and tribunals designated by the Sates Parties to the Protocol are entitled to request the Court to give advisory opinions on questions of principle relating to the interpretation or application of Convention rights in the context of a case pending before them.[309] The advisory opinion would be delivered by the Grand Chamber, but only after a panel of five judges decides that the request should be accepted. The judge elected on behalf of the State Party concerned would sit both on the five-judge panel and the Grand Chamber when delivering the opinion. By the end of 2022, the Court has delivered five advisory opinions under the provisions of Protocol 16, following requests from France, Armenia, and Lithuania,[310] while it has declined to provide one, requested by Slovakia, and has accepted to rendered another, requested by Finland.

---

[304] ECtHR, *Advisory opinion on certain legal questions concerning the lists of candidates submitted with a view to the election of judges to the European Court of Human Rights* [GC], § 8–14, 12 February 2008.

[305] ECtHR, *Advisory opinion on certain legal questions concerning the lists of candidates submitted with a view to the election of judges to the European Court of Human Rights* [GC], § 53, 12 February 2008.

[306] ECtHR, *Advisory opinion on certain legal questions concerning the lists of candidates submitted with a view to the election of judges to the European Court of Human Rights* [GC], § 54, 12 February 2008.

[307] ECtHR, *Advisory opinion on certain legal questions concerning the lists of candidates submitted with a view to the election of judges to the European Court of Human Rights* [GC], § 48, 50, 57, 12 February 2008.

[308] Protocol No. 16 (2013), Art. 8.   [309] Protocol No. 16 (2013), Arts. 1, 10.

[310] ECtHR, *Advisory opinion concerning the recognition in domestic law of a legal parent-child relationship between a child born through a gestational surrogacy arrangement abroad and the intended mother* [GC], request no. P16-2018-001, French Court of Cassation, 10 April 2019; ECtHR, *Advisory opinion concerning the use of the 'blanket reference' or 'legislation by reference' technique in the definition of an offence and the standards of comparison between the criminal law in force at the time of the commission of the offence and the amended criminal law* [GC], request no. P16-2019-001, Armenian Constitutional Court, 29 May 2020; ECtHR, *Advisory opinion on the assessment, under Article 3 of Protocol No. 1 to the Convention, of the proportionality of a general prohibition on standing for election after removal from office in impeachment proceedings* [GC], Request no. P16-2020-002, Lithuanian Supreme Administrative Court, 8 April 2022; ECtHR, *Advisory opinion on the applicability of statutes of limitation to prosecution, conviction and punishment in respect of an offence constituting, in substance, an act of torture* [GC], Request no. P16-2021-001, Armenian Court of Cassation, 26 April 2022; ECtHR, *Advisory opinion on the difference in treatment between landowners' associations 'having a recognised existence on the date of the creation of an approved municipal hunters' association' and landowners' associations set up after that date* [GC], Request no. P16-2021-002, French Conseil d'État, 13 July 2022.

ECtHR, *Advisory opinion concerning the recognition in domestic law of a legal parent–child relationship between a child born through a gestational surrogacy arrangement abroad and the intended mother* [GC], request no. P16-2018-001, French Court of Cassation, 10 April 2019.

The French Court of Cassation requested this advisory opinion within the context of a case in which the registration of two children born abroad through gestational surrogacy had been annulled. Under French law, the mother of the children could not be recognized as their 'legal mother' if she did not share a biological link to them. The Court examined, first, whether the refusal of the registration of the child's mother as their legal mother in France amounted to a breach of Article 8 and, then, whether the State was under the obligation to automatically register the details of the foreign birth certificate or if it could subject the legal recognition of the mother–child bond to its domestic procedures.

The Court recalled that its case law had already established that Article 8 requires that domestic law allows for the recognition of the legal relationship between a child born through a surrogacy arrangement abroad and their father, where he is the 'biological father'. As to whether the mother should be recognized as the 'legal mother' when she does not share a biological link to the child, the Court affirmed that two factors carry particular weight: the child's best interests and the scope of the State's margin of appreciation (para. 37). It affirmed that, evidently, the lack of recognition of a legal bond between a child born through a surrogacy arrangement carried out abroad and their mother has a negative impact on several aspects of that child's right to respect for their private life. Therefore, an absolute impossibility of obtaining recognition of the mother–child relationship was incompatible with the child's best interests (para. 42). The Court concluded that, considering the narrow margin of appreciation left to the State in this area, Article 8 requires that domestic law allows for the recognition of a parent–child relationship between the child and their mother (para. 46). Nevertheless, it asserted that this did not necessarily require the recognition to take the form of an entry in the register of births, marriages, and deaths of the details of the foreign birth certificate; other means, such as the adoption of the child by their mother, may be used, provided that the procedure can be implemented promptly and effectively (para. 55).

ECtHR, *Advisory opinion concerning the use of the 'blanket reference' or 'legislation by reference' technique in the definition of an offence and the standards of comparison between the criminal law in force at the time of the commission of the offence and the amended criminal law* [GC], request no. P16-2019-001, Armenian Constitutional Court, 29 May 2020.

The request was submitted by the Armenian Constitutional Court and concerned the interpretation of Article 7 of the Convention (no punishment without law). The Court provided answers to two main questions: the first, concerning the use of the technique of 'blanket reference'—whereby provisions of criminal law, when setting out the constituent elements of a criminal offence, refer to legal provisions outside criminal law—and the second, regarding the standards to be used for comparing criminal legislation in the light of the principle of non-retroactivity of criminal law. The Court accepted the use of 'blanket reference', so long as the criminal law defining an offence by making use of that technique was sufficiently precise, accessible, and foreseeable in its application. According to the Court, the referencing and the referenced provisions, taken together, had to enable the individual concerned to foresee, if need be with the help of appropriate legal advice, what conduct would make them criminally liable (para. 74). As to the other question, the Court stated that to establish whether a law passed after an offence had allegedly been committed was more or less favourable to the accused than the law that had been in force at the time of the alleged commission of the offence, regard had to be had to the specific circumstances of the case (the principle of concretization). If the application of the subsequent law would entail more severe punishment than that of the law that had been in force at the time of the alleged commission of the offence, its application would breach Article 7 of the Convention (para. 92).

7.7 FURTHER REFLECTIONS: THE 'MARGIN OF APPRECIATION' DOCTRINE

As aforementioned, Protocol 15 incorporated the 'principle of subsidiarity' and the concept of the 'margin of appreciation' into the Preamble of the Convention. The principle of subsidiary—best understood as 'complementarity'[311]—refers to the seminal idea underpinning the whole of the international law of human rights: it is the States that assume the commitment to guarantee the full enjoyment of human rights within their domestic jurisdictions and, therefore, are under the obligation to effectively resolve any violations at the national level.[312] The role of the international bodies of supervision, such as the European Court, is to act as a safeguard when States have failed to redress such a violation at the domestic level. A clear manifestation of the principle of subsidiarity is to be found in the criteria for admissibility of cases by the Court; in particular, in the requirement of prior exhaustion of domestic remedies—a topic discussed in **Section 7.3.7.1**.[313]

On its part, the doctrine of the 'margin of appreciation'[314] is also closely connected to the idea of the subsidiary character of the regional system.[315] The margin of appreciation

---

[311] A.A. Cançado Trindade, 'Réaffirmation de l' universalité nécessaire et inéluctable des droits inhérents à la personne humaine', Addresse au Séminaire à la CourEDH, Strasbourg (8 March 2018).

[312] P.G. Carozza, 'Subsidiarity as a Structural Principle of International Human Rights Law' (2003) 97 *American Journal of International Law* 38, 57–58; D. Tsarapatsanis, 'The Margin of Appreciation Doctrine: A Low-Level Institutional View' (2015) 35 *Legal Studies* 675, 686–687.

[313] L.R. Helfer, 'Redesigning the European Court of Human Rights: Embeddedness as a Deep Structural Principle of the European Human Rights Regime' (2008) 19 *European Journal of International Law* 125, 128; D. Tsarapatsanis, 'The margin of appreciation doctrine: a low-level institutional view' (2015) 35 *Legal Studies* 675, 686.

[314] The margin of appreciation doctrine has been the subject of extensive academic discussion. See, among others: H.C. Yourow, *The Margin of Appreciation Doctrine in the Dynamics of the European Court of Human Rights Jurisprudence* (Nijhoff 1996); E. Brems, 'The Margin of Appreciation Doctrine in the Case-law of the European Court of Human Rights' (1996) 56 *Heidelberg Journal of International Law* 240; Y. Arai-Takahashi, *The Margin of Appreciation Doctrine and the Principle of Proportionality in the Jurisprudence of the European Court of Human Rights* (Intersentia 2002); G. Letsas, *A Theory of Interpretation of the European Convention on Human Rights* (OUP 2007), chapter 4.

[315] P.G. Carozza, 'Subsidiarity as a Structural Principle of International Human Rights Law' (2003) 97 *American Journal of International Law* 38, 40; D. Spielmann, 'Allowing the Right Margin: The European Court of Human Rights and the National Margin of Appreciation Doctrine: Waiver or Subsidiarity of European Review?' (CELS Working Papers Series 2012) 2.

is a doctrine of jurisprudential origin by which the Court imposes self-restraint on its power of review.[316] As discussed in **Section 1.1.2.2.2**, the Court's case law has disclosed two main uses of this doctrine; the first one concerning the application of the Convention and the second one its interpretation.[317] Regarding its main use, the margin of appreciation can be defined as a 'breadth of deference' the Court allows to the domestic authorities before finding their interference with a substantive Convention right to be incompatible with the obligations assumed under the Convention.[318] As to the doctrine's second use, it concerns the interpretation of a right (or of another term of the Convention), including the delimitations of its scope.[319] In both instances, the Court will refrain from making a principled decision on the application or interpretation of the Convention, accepting that States might be in a better position to assess the application of the Convention to the specific case or to determine the meaning or scope of the provision or term in question. However, as discussed in **Section 7.7.1**, the extent of the discretion allowed to States under this tool of deference would be different—wider or narrower—on each occasion, depending on multiple factors.

The doctrine of the margin of appreciation was originally devised by the former European Commission of Human Rights in 1958. In its decision of the inter-State case *Greece v. the United Kingdom* (concerning Cyprus), the Commission referred to the ability of States to exercise a certain 'measure of discretion' when assessing the strict necessity of the measures adopted derogating from the Convention in time of public emergency.[320] The Commission gave the name of 'margin of appreciation' to this idea of a State's degree of discretion in its Report in the *Lawless v. the United Kingdom* case— the first case to ever reach the Court—referring again to the power of States under Article 15 to determine the existence of a public emergency which threatens the life of the nation and, therefore, allowing derogation from the normal obligations under the Convention.[321] The Court adopted the idea of deference to the discretion of the domestic authorities from its early jurisprudence. In 1968, when deciding for the first time on a case concerning the prohibition of discrimination, the Court affirmed: 'The national authorities remain free to choose the measures which they consider appropriate in those matters which are governed by the Convention. Review by the Court concerns only the conformity of these measures with the requirements of the

---

[316] D. Spielmann, 'Allowing the Right Margin the European Court of Human Rights and the National Margin of Appreciation Doctrine: Waiver or Subsidiarity of European Review?' (CELS Working Papers Series 2012) 2.

[317] J. Kratochvíl, 'The Inflation of the Margin of Appreciation by the European Court of Human Rights' (2011) 29 *Netherlands Quarterly of Human Rights* 324, 328.

[318] H.C. Yourow, *The Margin of Appreciation Doctrine in the Dynamics of the European Court of Human Rights Jurisprudence* (Nijhoff 1996) 118; J. Kratochvíl, 'The Inflation of the Margin of Appreciation by the European Court of Human Rights' (2011) 29 *Netherlands Quarterly of Human Rights* 324, 330.

[319] J. Kratochvíl, 'The Inflation of the Margin of Appreciation by the European Court of Human Rights' (2011) 29 *Netherlands Quarterly of Human Rights* 324, 330; S. Greer, 'The Margin of Appreciation: Interpretation and Discretion under the European Convention on Human Rights' (Council of Europe 2000) 14–15.

[320] European Commission of Human Rights, *Greece v. the United Kingdom* ('The Cyprus Case'), App. no. 176/56, Report of the European Commission (Volume I) (1958), p. 152, para. 143.

[321] European Commission of Human Rights, *Lawless v. Ireland*, App. no. 332/57, Report of the Commission, 19 December 1959, p. 85, para. 90.

Convention.'[322] Nevertheless, it is the *Handyside v. the United Kingdom* case that is usually credited as the moment when the Court adopted the 'margin of appreciation' doctrine, given its explicit use within the reasoning of the judgment. The Court affirmed that: 'The Convention leaves to each Contracting State, in the first place, the task of securing the rights and liberties it enshrines.'[323] Then, it continued asserting that, due to 'their direct and continuous contact with the vital forces of their countries',[324] the domestic authorities, both legislative and judicial, are better positioned than the Court to decide and assess the regulation of human rights—freedom of expression, in this case—within the State. That is why the Court considered that, under the system of the Convention, States enjoy a 'margin of appreciation' to decide in the first instance whether their actions conform to the provisions of the Convention. Nonetheless, this degree of discretion granted to States is certainly not unlimited and the supervisory role of the Court consists of examining whether the measures adopted by States remained within this breadth of deference.

ECHR, *Greece v. the United Kingdom* ('The Cyprus Case'), App. no. 176/56, Report of the European Commission (Volume I) (1958).

In May 1965 the Greek Government brought an application to the Commission alleging the violation of several Convention rights attributable to the United Kingdom and taking place in Cyprus. In particular, Greece contended that the adoption of measures of derogation under Article 15 had been incompatible with the Convention and that under such framework the United Kingdom had adopted measures that amounted to multiple violations of the Convention, including the whipping of individuals, the use of collective punishment— through the imposition of curfew, collective fines, and the destruction of buildings and plantations—, the arrest of individuals without warrants, and the deportation of four individuals for detention in the Seychelles Islands.

The Commission examined whether the requirements of Article 15 could be considered satisfied in the case. In October 1955 the United Kingdom had notified the Secretary General of the Council of Europe of its intention to adopt measures derogating from its obligations under Article 5 of the Convention within (the Colony of) Cyprus, due to the existence of a public emergency within the meaning of Article 15. Article 15 allows measures derogating from Article 5, such as in time of war or other public emergency threatening the life of the nation. However, such measures need to be strictly required by the exigencies of the situation and not inconsistent with other obligations under international law.

The Commission affirmed that the Government retains, within certain limits, its 'discretion in appreciating' whether a threat to the life of the nation exists, within the meaning of Article 15,

---

[322] ECtHR, *Case 'relating to certain aspects of the laws on the use of languages in education in Belgium'* (merits), 23 July 1968, p. 31, § 10, Series A no. 6.
[323] ECtHR, *Handyside v. the United Kingdom*, 7 December 1976, § 48, Series A App. no. 24.
[324] ECtHR, *Handyside v. the United Kingdom*, 7 December 1976, § 48, Series A App. no. 24 ibid.

and it considered that such limits had not been exceeded in the case (para. 136). Similarly, it asserted that the Government should be able to exercise a 'certain measure of discretion' in its assessment as to whether the measures adopted in consequence of the derogation could be considered strictly required by the exigencies of the situation and it was for the Commission to examine if such discretion had been exceeded (para. 143). When examining each of the claims submitted by Greece, the Commission found the various measures adopted to be justified as necessary within the context of the public emergency and the State's power under Article 15. It did acknowledge, nonetheless, that the emergency legislation that had allowed punishment by whipping and collective punishment had been abolished.

ECHR, *Lawless v. Ireland*, App. no. 332/57, Report of the Commission, 19 December 1959.

The case was submitted to the Commission by the applicant, Mr Lawless, alleging that his detention for almost six months in a military detention camp in Ireland amounted to a violation of his Convention rights. To reach its conclusion, the Commission examined whether this detention had taken place under special powers of arrest and detention that could be considered compatible with the exercise of the right to derogate under Article 15 of the Convention. The Commission went on to analyse: first, whether Ireland had provided appropriate notice to derogate from Convention obligations; second, whether the circumstances existent in Ireland could be considered to amount to a 'public emergency threatening the life of the nation' within the meaning of Article 15; and, third, whether the special powers of arrest and detention allowed by the adopted legislation could be seen as 'strictly required by the exigencies of the situation' (para. 90). Satisfied that Ireland had provided appropriate notice, the Commission examined whether the circumstance amounted to a situation of public emergency as required by the Convention. On this point, the opinion of five Commissioners was that: 'it is evident that a certain discretion—a certain margin of appreciation—must be left to the Government in determining whether there exists a public emergency which threatens the life of the nation and which must be dealt with by exceptional measures derogating from its normal obligations under the Convention.' Lastly, the Commission concluded that the measures of arrest and detention adopted by Ireland could be considered strictly required by the situation (para. 105). The case went on to become the first ever case decided by the European Court of Human Rights. In its judgment from 1961, the Court agreed with the Commission's opinion in that the applicant's detention was founded on the right of derogation duly exercised by the Irish Government in pursuance of Article 15.

7.7.1 THE SCOPE OF THE MARGIN OF APPRECIATION

As aforementioned, the extent of the margin of appreciation varies according to the circumstances. The Court has identified a number of factors that influence its scope, which include: the nature of the Convention right at stake, as well as the importance of the particular issue; the nature, object, and scope of the State's interference; and the level of European consensus on the matter.[325] These factors determine whether the Court allows the State a wide or narrow margin of appreciation and, consequently, the burden of argumentation and proof the State needs to satisfy to convince the Court that its actions had remained within its margin of discretion. When the Court determines the existence of a wide margin of appreciation, it seems to only require the State to demonstrate that its actions were reasonable or, even more, that they were not 'manifestly unreasonable' for the Court to be satisfied that the degree of discretion had not been exceeded.[326] Conversely, if the Court finds that the circumstances allow for a narrow margin of appreciation, it seems to set a presumption of incompatibility, which the State must rebut if it is to prevail.[327] In those occasions, the State will be required to provide 'very weighty reasons' to convince the Court that its actions were compatible with the Convention.

The first factor identified as determinant for the scope of the State's margin of appreciation concerns the nature of the right at stake. As discussed in **Section 7.7**, this doctrine was originally formulated by the Commission in cases concerning derogations under Article 15 of the Convention,[328] but was then adopted by the Court when deciding cases under Articles 8, 10, and 14.[329] Nowadays, the examination of cases concerning so-called qualified rights—those enshrined in Articles 8 to 11 of the Convention—always involves an analysis of the margin of appreciation left to the State, but it is possible to find references to the margin of application in cases concerning any Convention right,[330] including aspects of non-derogable rights.[331] Although the Court has affirmed that the nature of the right itself is determinant to the scope of the margin of appreciation in a given case, and it can be expected such a margin to be narrow when dealing with non-derogable rights, it is difficult to know how this factor alone affects

---

[325] ECtHR, *S. and Marper v. the United Kingdom* [GC], App. nos. 30562/04, 30566/04, § 102, ECHR 2008.

[326] J. Kratochvíl, 'The Inflation of the Margin of Appreciation by the European Court of Human Rights' (2011) 29 *Netherlands Quarterly of Human Rights* 324, 348, 350.

[327] J. Kratochvíl, 'The Inflation of the Margin of Appreciation by the European Court of Human Rights' (2011) 29 *Netherlands Quarterly of Human Rights* 324, 350.

[328] European Commission of Human Rights, *Greece v. the United Kingdom* ('The Cyprus Case'), App. no. 176/56, Report of the European Commission (Volume I) (1958), p. 152, para. 143; European Commission of Human Rights, *Lawless v. Ireland*, App. no. 332/57, Report of the Commission, 19 December 1959, p. 85, para. 90.

[329] ECtHR, *De Wilde, Ooms and Versyp v. Belgium*, 18 June 1971, § 93, Series A App. no. 12; ECtHR, *Handyside v. the United Kingdom*, 7 December 1976, § 48, Series A no. 24; ECtHR, *Case 'relating to certain aspects of the laws on the use of languages in education in Belgium'* (merits), 23 July 1968, p. 31, § 10, Series A App. no. 6.

[330] ECtHR, *Luberti v. Italy*, 23 February 1984, § 27, Series A App. no. 75; ECtHR, *Petkoski and Others v. the former Yugoslav Republic of Macedonia*, no. 27736/03, § 41, 8 January 2009; ECtHR, *Konstantin Markin v. Russia* [GC], App. no. 30078/06, § 44, ECHR 2012; ECtHR, *X and Others v. Austria* [GC], App. no. 19010/07, § 98, ECHR 2013.

[331] ECtHR, *Vo v. France* [GC], App. no. 53924/00, § 82, ECHR 2004-VIII; ECtHR, *Lambert and Others v. France* [GC], App. no. 46043/14, § 82, ECHR 2015; ECtHR, *Budayeva and Others v. Russia*, nos. 15339/02 and four others, § 134–135, 156, ECHR 2008; ECtHR, *Valiulienė v. Lithuania*, App. no. 33234/07, § 85, 26 March 2013; ECtHR, *M.C. v. Bulgaria*, App. no. 39272/98, § 154–155, ECHR 2003-XII.

the analysis, as the extent of the margin of appreciation not only depends on the affected right but also, as regards each right, on the actual interest concerned.[332]

The importance of the specific issue at stake is another factor that affects the width of the State's margin of appreciation. For instance, when dealing with the protection of the right to respect for private and family life, the Court has repeated numerous times that '[w]here a particularly important facet of an individual's existence or identity is at stake, the margin allowed to the State will be restricted'.[333] This interpretation has been applied by the Court with regards to different aspects of individuals' lives, including matters of gender identity, sexuality, knowledge of one's parentage, or the confidential character of medical information.[334] Similarly, when it concerns freedom of expression, the Court has affirmed that the type of expression at stake influences the scope of the State's discretion. For example, while political speech or expressions concerning questions of public interest would be specially protected, the margin of appreciation afforded to the State will be wider when it comes to the regulation of commercial speech.[335]

A further factor that influences the breadth of the margin of appreciation concerns both the nature and the purpose of the State's interference with the applicant's Convention right. The interest pursued by the State must be balanced against the seriousness of the interference adopted.[336] On the one hand, this means that stringent measures of restriction would be subject to a stricter scrutiny by the Court to determine whether the interference amounts to curtailing the enjoyment of the right in question.[337] On the other hand, the Court will widen the margin of appreciation afforded to the State when it comes to general measures of economic or social strategy,[338] as well as when the measures are adopted to strike a balance between competing Convention rights.[339] Regarding the latter, a recent trend in the Court's case law indicates that when the balance between competing rights has been

---

[332] ECtHR, *Jäggi v. Switzerland*, App. no. 58757/00, § 37, ECHR 2006-X.

[333] ECtHR, *Evans v. the United Kingdom* [GC], App. no. 6339/05, § 77, ECHR 2007-I; ECtHR, *S. and Marper v. the United Kingdom* [GC], App. nos. 30562/04, 30566/04, § 102, ECHR 2008; ECtHR, *Hämäläinen v. Finland* [GC], App. no. 37359/09, § 67, ECHR 2014.

[334] ECtHR, *Dudgeon v. the United Kingdom*, 22 October 1981, § 52, Series A App. no. 45; ECtHR, *Z v. Finland*, 25 February 1997, § 95–96, Reports of Judgments and Decisions 1997-I; ECtHR, *Jäggi v. Switzerland*, App. no. 58757/00, § 37, ECHR 2006-X; ECtHR, *Hämäläinen v. Finland* [GC], App. no. 37359/09, § 67, ECHR 2014.

[335] ECtHR, *Wingrove v. the United Kingdom*, 25 November 1996, § 58, Reports of Judgments and Decisions 1996-V; ECtHR, *Sürek v. Turkey (no. 1)* [GC], App. no. 26682/95, § 61, ECHR 1999-IV; ECtHR, *Animal Defenders International v. the United Kingdom* [GC], App. no. 48876/08, § 102, ECHR 2013; ECtHR, *markt intern Verlag GmbH and Klaus Beermann v. Germany*, 20 November 1989, § 33, Series A no. 165; ECtHR, *Jacubowski v. Germany*, 23 June 1994, § 26, Series A App. no. 291-A.

[336] ECtHR, *Leander v. Sweden*, 26 March 1987, § 59, Series A App. no. 116.

[337] ECtHR, *Observer and Guardian v. the United Kingdom*, 26 November 1991, § 60, Series A App. no. 216.

[338] ECtHR, *Stec and Others v. the United Kingdom* (dec.) [GC], nos. 65731/01 and 65900/01, § 52, ECHR 2005-X; ECtHR, *National & Provincial Building Society, Leeds Permanent Building Society and Yorkshire Building Society v. the United Kingdom*, 23 October 1997, § 80, Reports of Judgments and Decisions 1997-VII.

[339] ECtHR, *Wingrove v. the United Kingdom*, 25 November 1996, § 58, Reports of Judgments and Decisions 1996-V; ECtHR, *Odièvre v. France* [GC], App. no. 42326/98, § 40–49, ECHR 2003-III; ECtHR, *Eweida and Others v. the United Kingdom*, App. nos. 48420/10 and three others, § 106, ECHR 2013.

examined by the superior domestic courts in a manner consistent with the Court's jurisprudence, particularly strong reasons would be needed for the Court to substitute its view for that of the domestic courts.[340]

Lastly, one of the main factors the Court uses for determining the extent of the margin of appreciation is the existence, or lack thereof, of a 'European consensus'.[341] Although, in our days, the expression 'European consensus' appears quite frequently in the Court's rulings, it seems to have only been adopted by the Court within the last two decades.[342] Nevertheless, the Court's interest in the existence of a common approach to the regulation of Convention rights among Contracting Parties can be found in much earlier cases,[343] under multiple different denominations.[344] It is important to highlight, however, that the Court's idea of consensus does not seem to refer to a level of agreement that is general or even clearly majoritarian between Contracting States,[345] but 'consensus' appears to mean something of a lesser degree,[346] satisfied by the existence of a clear trend among the practice of the States of the Council of Europe.[347] This 'European consensus' the Court searches for presents two interconnected aspects; first, it refers to the interpretation and scope of a Convention right itself, including the relative importance of the interest at stake; and, second, it concerns how the particular situation under examination is actually regulated across the different Member States of

---

[340] D. Spielmann, 'Allowing the Right Margin the European Court of Human Rights and the National Margin of Appreciation Doctrine: Waiver or Subsidiarity of European Review?' (CELS Working Papers Series 2012) 23–24. See: ECtHR, *Palomo Sánchez and Others v. Spain* [GC], App. nos. 28955/06 and three others, § 57, ECHR 2011; ECtHR, *Von Hannover v. Germany (no. 2)* [GC], App. nos. 40660/08, 60641/08, § 107, ECHR 2012.

[341] Nonetheless, the idea of 'European consensus', as a form of legal reasoning, is also used by the Court independently of the margin of appreciation. See: J. Theilen, *European Consensus between Strategy and Principle: The Uses of Vertically Comparative Legal Reasoning in Regional Human Rights Adjudication* (Nomos 2021) 300.

[342] ECtHR, *Marlow v. the United Kingdom* (dec.), App. no. 42015/98, 5 December 2000, p. 11; ECtHR, *S.L. v. Austria* (dec.), App. no. 45330/99, 22 November 2001, p. 8.

[343] ECtHR, *The Sunday Times v. the United Kingdom (no. 1)*, 26 April 1979, § 59, Series A App. no. 30; ECtHR, *Dudgeon v. the United Kingdom*, 22 October 1981, § 60, Series A App. no. 45; ECtHR, *Soering v. the United Kingdom*, 7 July 1989, § 102, Series A App. no. 161.

[344] J.A. Brauch, 'The Dangerous Search for an Elusive Consensus: What the Supreme Court Should Learn from the European Court of Human Rights' (2009) 52 *Howard Law Journal* 277, 282; K. Dzehtsiarou, *European Consensus and the Legitimacy of the European Court of Human Rights* (CUP 2015) 11; P. Mahoney and R. Kondak, 'Common Ground: A Starting Point or Destination for Comparative-Law Analysis by the European Court of Human Rights?' in M. Adenas and D. Fairgrieve (eds.) *Courts and Comparative Law* (OUP 2015) 121.

[345] L.R. Helfer, 'Consensus, Coherence and the European Convention on Human Rights' (1993) 26 *Cornell International Law Journal* 133, 140; J. Theilen, *European Consensus between Strategy and Principle: The Uses of Vertically Comparative Legal Reasoning in Regional Human Rights Adjudication* (Nomos 2021) 176–177.

[346] And yet, it has been lucidly characterized as 'too much of a compromise'. See: J. Theilen, *European Consensus between Strategy and Principle: The Uses of Vertically Comparative Legal Reasoning in Regional Human Rights Adjudication* (Nomos 2021) 19.

[347] K. Dzehtsiarou, *European Consensus and the Legitimacy of the European Court of Human Rights* (CUP 2015) 12–13; P. Mahoney and R. Kondak, 'Common Ground: A Starting Point or Destination for Comparative-Law Analysis by the European Court of Human Rights?' in M. Adenas and D. Fairgrieve (eds.) *Courts and Comparative Law* (OUP 2015) 121.

the Council of Europe.[348] When the Court finds that a European consensus exists on a particular issue, it narrows the margin of appreciation afforded to the State, restricting the leeway the national decision-maker has to regulate the issue at stake. On the contrary, the absence of consensus leads to a wider margin of appreciation, meaning that a broader diversity of States' measures can be found in ostensive conformity with the Convention.[349] Nonetheless, it should be highlighted that the Court's search for consensus and the use of such findings to determine the scope of the margin of appreciation have been subject to criticism, including from members of the Court.[350] This might not be surprising, since it is possible to identify numerous cases in which either the existence or the absence of consensus have led to conclusions that departed from the principles governing the Court's case law.[351]

Coming back to the margin of appreciation itself, the doctrine has been the subject of numerous academic analyses and—as with European consensus—it has also been the focus of an important degree of criticism, even from within the Court.[352] Perhaps one of the biggest critics of the doctrine was former Judge De Meyer who in a partly dissenting opinion in 1997 expressed his conviction that the Court should banish the concept of the margin of appreciation from its reasoning, 'recanting the relativism it implies'. He affirmed: 'where human rights are concerned, there is no room for a margin of appreciation which would enable the States to decide what is acceptable and what is not'.[353] In a slightly less critical tone, Judge Rozakis, in a concurring opinion rendered in 2009, stated that 'if the concept of the margin of appreciation has any meaning whatsoever in the present-day conditions of the Court's case-law, it should

---

[348] ECtHR, *Stec and Others v. the United Kingdom* [GC], App. nos. 65731/01, 65900/01, § 63–64, ECHR 2006-VI; ECtHR, *Alekseyev v. Russia*, App. nos. 4916/07 and two others, § 83–84, 21 October 2010; 83–84; Stec (2006) 63–64; ECtHR, *A, B and C v. Ireland* [GC], App. no. 25579/05, § 235, ECHR.

[349] ECtHR, *X, Y and Z v. the United Kingdom*, 22 April 1997, § 44, Reports of Judgments and Decisions 1997-II; ECtHR, *Schalk and Kopf v. Austria*, App. no. 30141/04, § 92, ECHR 2010; ECtHR, *Bayatyan v. Armenia* [GC], App. no. 23459/03, § 122–123, ECHR 2011.

[350] J.A. Brauch, 'The Dangerous Search for an Elusive Consensus: What the Supreme Court Should Learn from the European Court of Human Rights' (2009) 52 *Howard Law Journal* 277, 287–288. See: ECtHR, *Van der Heijden v. the Netherlands* [GC], App. no. 42857/05, joint dissenting opinion of Judges Casadevall and López Guerra para. 7 and joint dissenting opinion of Judges Tulkens, Vajić, Spielmann, Zupančič and Laffranque para. 5; ECtHR, *X and Others v. Austria* [GC], App. no. 19010/07, ECHR 2013, joint partly dissenting opinion of Judges Casadevall, Ziemele, Kovler, Jočienė, Šikuta, de Gaetano and Sicilianos, paras. 12–15.

[351] ECtHR, *Fretté v. France*, no. 36515/97, § 41, ECHR 2002-I; ECtHR, *A, B and C v. Ireland* [GC], no. 25579/05, § 234–236, ECHR; ECtHR, *S.H. and Others v. Austria* [GC], App. no. 57813/00, § 96–97, ECHR 2011; ECtHR, *Sitaropoulos and Giakoumopoulos v. Greece* [GC], App. no. 42202/07, § 66, 74–75, ECHR 2012.

[352] C.S. Feingold, 'The Doctrine of Margin of Appreciation and the European Convention on Human Rights' (1978) 53 *Notre Dame Law Review* 90, 96; R. Higgins, 'Derogations under Human Rights Treaties' (1978) 48 *British Yearbook of International Law* 281, 315; N. Lavender, 'The Problem of the Margin of Appreciation' (1997) *European Human Rights Law Review* 380, 380; O. Gross and F. Ní Aoláin, 'From Discretion to Scrutiny: Revisiting the Application of the Margin of Appreciation Doctrine in the Context of Article 15 of the European Convention on Human Rights' (2001) 23 *Human Rights Quarterly* 625, 635; O. Bakircioglu, 'The Application of the Margin of Appreciation Doctrine in Freedom of Expression and Public Morality Cases' (2007) 8 *German Law Journal* 711, 712.

[353] ECtHR, *Z v. Finland*, 25 February 1997, Reports of Judgments and Decisions 1997-I, partly dissenting opinion of Judge De Meyer.

only be applied in cases where, after careful consideration, it establishes that national authorities were really better placed than the Court to assess the "local" and specific conditions which existed within a particular domestic order, and, accordingly, had greater knowledge than an international court in deciding how to deal, in the most appropriate manner, with the case before them. Then, and only then, should the Court relinquish its power to examine, in depth, the facts of a case, and limit itself to a simple supervision of the national decisions, without taking the place of national authorities, but simply examining their reasonableness and the absence of arbitrariness.'[354] He concluded that the use of the doctrine should be limited to cases in which its applicability better serves the interests of justice and the protection of human rights.[355] Nevertheless, as aforementioned, far from its dismissal by the Court, the doctrine of the margin of appreciation has become a textual part of the Convention with the entry into force of Protocol 15.

7.8 CONCLUSION

The chapter has engaged at length with the European human rights system, which is usually seen as the original regional system for the protection of human rights, given that its rapid institutional development has acted as an inspiration for the creation and development of other regional supervisory mechanisms, including those adopted in the Americas and Africa. The main focus of the chapter was on the European Court of Human Rights; the longest standing and most prolific human rights court, which has delivered over 25,000 rulings in its six decades of existence.[356] The Court has been characterized as a world-leading authority in the protection of human rights, with its jurisprudence becoming a source of reference for both international and domestic courts alike. Indeed, the regional system as a whole can be seen as a success story, with the number of Member States growing significantly through the decades, from its creation by a relatively small number of Western European States to the forty-six Members it counts in our days, following the recent withdrawal of Russia from the Council of Europe.

At the same time, the very success achieved by this regional system also contributed to the Court becoming overwhelmed by a hardly manageable caseload. This situation acted as the main rationale for the most recent changes to the system brought about by the adoption of the latest Protocols, in search for means to reduce the sheer volume of cases dealt with by the Court on a daily basis. Protocols 14, 15, and 16 were not only aimed at strengthening the filtering capacity of the Court, but also at identifying alternative procedures that can stop future cases from reaching the Court. This includes

---

[354] ECtHR, *Egeland and Hanseid v. Norway*, App. no. 34438/04, 16 April 2009, concurring opinion of Judge Rozakis.

[355] ECtHR, *Egeland and Hanseid v. Norway*, App. no. 34438/04, 16 April 2009, concurring opinion of Judge Rozakis.

[356] ECtHR, Overview 1959–2021 (Feb. 2022) p. 3; ECtHR, 2022 Annual Report, p. 141, 147.

the possibility of advisory opinions that can confirm the authoritative interpretation of Convention rights (Protocol 16), as well as the emphasis on the 'subsidiary' character of the international mechanisms of human rights adjudication, especially the Court (Protocol 15).

The adoption of the later Protocols also indicates the outcome of the academic debate over the 'appropriate' role of the Court, between providing individual justice to a population of hundreds of millions and the re-shaping of the Court into a European constitutional tribunal. The adopted approach—confirming the Court as an international mechanism that provides individual justice—is undoubtedly correct and in line with the recognition of the individual as a subject of rights under international law, therefore endowed with the legal capacity to act and vindicate such rights at the international level. The problem of the volume of applications that reach the Court, undisputedly real, needs to be addressed by the correct understanding of what the subsidiarity principle entails. This principle should not be construed as a further impediment for allowing access to the Court, an imminent risk brought to the forefront by the entry into force of Protocol 15 in 2021, but rather as a reinforcement of the notion of States as the main duty-bearers when it comes to the respect and protection of human rights. It is through securing the protection of human rights within domestic jurisdictions that States can contribute to the reduction of the volume of applications that reach the Court day after day.

FURTHER READING

BATES, E., *The Evolution of the European Convention on Human Rights: From Its Inception to the Creation of a Permanent Court of Human Rights* (OUP 2010).

CHRISTOFFERSEN, J. and MADSEN, M.R., (eds.), *The European Court of Human Rights between Law and Politics* (OUP 2011).

DZEHTSIAROU, K., *European Consensus and the Legitimacy of the European Court of Human Rights* (CUP 2015).

HARRIS, D., O'BOYLE, M., BATES, E., and BUCKLEY, C., *Harris, O'Boyle and Warbrick: Law of the European Convention on Human Rights* (4th edn., OUP 2018).

ICHIM, O., *Just Satisfaction under the European Convention on Human Rights* (CUP 2015).

POPELIER, P., LAMBRECHT, S., and LEMMENS, K. (eds.), *Criticism of the European Court of Human Rights: Shifting the Convention System: Counter-dynamics at the National and EU Level* (Intersentia 2016).

SIMPSON, A.W.B., *Human Rights and the End of Empire: Britain and the Genesis of the European Convention* (OUP 2004).

THEILEN, J., *European Consensus between Strategy and Principle: The Uses of Vertically Comparative Legal Reasoning in Regional Human Rights Adjudication* (Nomos 2021).

8

THE AFRICAN HUMAN RIGHTS SYSTEM

8.1 ORIGINS AND DEVELOPMENT OF THE AFRICAN HUMAN RIGHTS SYSTEM

The African human rights system is the third regional system for the protection of human rights ever created. Although inspired by the other regional systems, the African one presents many unique characteristics shaped by the historical background in which it emerged. The history of Africa has been signed by the exploitation of its people and its material resources by the European imperial powers through the practices of slavery and colonialism, leaving behind imposed political limits and a problematic legacy of structural extreme poverty.[1] Sadly, Africa's reality continued to be signed by widespread human rights violations after the end of political colonialism, including the apartheid regime and several dictatorial governments across the continent.[2] Within this context, in 1963, the independent States of Africa established the Organization of African Unity (OAU), a pan-African inter-governmental organization, with, among others, the purpose of promoting the unity and solidarity of all African States; defending their independence; and eradicating all forms of colonialism from the continent. Even if the promotion and protection of human rights was not originally conceived as an explicit aim of the organization, its main purposes did include the promotion of international cooperation, 'having due regard to the Charter of the United Nations and the Universal Declaration of Human Rights'.[3]

---

[1] M. Mutua, 'The Banjul Charter and the African Cultural Fingerprint: An Evaluation of the Language of Duties' (1995) 35 *Virginia Journal of International Law* 339, 342–343; M. Ssenyonjo, 'Responding to Human Rights Violations in Africa: Assessing the Role of the African Commission and Court on Human and Peoples' Rights (1987–2018)' (2018) 7 *International Human Rights Law Review* 1, 2; H. Alisigwe and C. Obodo, 'Three Decades of the African Charter on Human and Peoples' Rights: An Appraisal of the Normative and Institutional Enforcement Regime' (2019) 1 *International Review of Law and Jurisprudence* 158, 159.

[2] S. Keetharuth, 'Major African Legal Instruments' in A. Bösl and J. Diescho, *Human Rights in Africa: Legal Perspectives on their Protection and Promotion* (Konrad Adenauer 2009) 163–231, 166–167; H. Alisigwe and C. Obodo, 'Three decades of the African Charter on Human and Peoples' Rights: an appraisal of the normative and institutional enforcement regime' (2019) 1 *International Review of Law and Jurisprudence* 158, 159.

[3] Charter of the Organization of African Unity (adopted 25 May 1963, entered into force 13 September 1963) 479 UNTS 39.

The creation of the African human rights system took place under the auspices of the OAU, to later continue its development under its successor, the African Union (AU).[4] The inception of the system can be found in the adoption of the African Charter on Human and Peoples' Rights,[5] which is known as the 'Banjul Charter', as its text was agreed during two conferences held in Banjul in 1980 and 1981.[6] Notwithstanding the birth of the African system dating from 1981, the idea of developing a regional system of human rights protection can be traced back to the 1960s, preceding even the creation of the OAU.[7] A series of conferences, seminars, and expert meetings organized by the International Commission of Jurists and the United Nations can be counted as important steps towards the formation of the system.

The first of these took place in Lagos in January 1961, when the International Commission of Jurists organized an 'African Conference on the Rule of Law' attended by almost 200 legal scholars.[8] This conference adopted a declaration entitled 'Law of Lagos' in which the participants called on the 'African Governments to study the possibility of adopting an African Convention of Human Rights in such a manner that the Conclusions of [the] Conference will be safeguarded by the creation of a court of appropriate jurisdiction and that recourse thereto be made available for all persons under the jurisdiction of the signatory States'.[9] The International Commission of Jurists continued to promote the creation of an African human rights system, sponsoring conferences on the topic, including two events in Dakar in 1967 and 1978.[10] The participants in the later conference, which included governmental officials, legal scholars, and social scientists, set up a committee to follow the implementation of the conclusions adopted. Their follow-up activity led to the commitment of the (then) President of Senegal, Léopold Sedar Senghor, to introduce a resolution on the establishment of a regional human rights commission for consideration by the OAU Assembly of Heads of State and Government.[11]

---

[4] The promotion and protection of human and peoples' rights was made one of the purposes of the AU, while the respect of human rights became one of its principles. See: Constitutive Act of the African Union (adopted 11 July 2000, entered into force 26 May 2001) 2158 UNTS 3, Arts. 3, 4.

[5] African Charter (adopted on 27 June 1981, entered into force 21 October 1986), OAU Doc. CAB/LEG/67/3 rev. 5, 21 I.L.M. 58 (1982) [hereinafter 'African Charter'].

[6] R. Gittleman, 'The African Charter on Human and Peoples' Rights: A Legal Analysis' (1982) 22 *Virginia Journal of International Law* 667, 668–669; G. Baricako, 'The African Charter and African Commission on Human and Peoples' Rights' in M. Evans and R. Murray, *The African Charter of Human and Peoples' Rights: The System in Practice, 1986–2006* (2nd edn., CUP 2008) 1–19, 7–8.

[7] D.C. Turack, 'The African Charter on Human and Peoples' Rights: Some Preliminary Thoughts' (1984) 17 *Akron Law Review* 365, 366; G. Baricako, 'The African Charter and African Commission on Human and Peoples' Rights' in M. Evans and R. Murray, *The African Charter of Human and Peoples' Rights: The System in Practice, 1986–2006* (2nd edn., CUP 2008) 1–19, 1.

[8] C.S. Rhyne, 'Law in Africa: A Report on the Lagos Conference' (1961) 47 *American Bar Association Journal* 685, 685.

[9] International Commission of Jurists, African Conference on the Rule of Law (3–7 January 1961), p. 11.

[10] G. Baricako, 'The African Charter and African Commission on Human and Peoples' Rights' in M. Evans and R. Murray, *The African Charter of Human and Peoples' Rights: The System in Practice, 1986–2006* (2nd edn., CUP 2008) 1–19, 2. See: Declaration of Dakar (1967), Conclusions, Art. VI.3. Available in: Bulletin of the International Commission of Jurists, No. 29 (1967); International Commission of Jurists, Report on Activities: 1977–1980 (1980) pp. 4–5.

[11] G. Baricako, 'The African Charter and African Commission on Human and Peoples' Rights' in M. Evans and R. Murray, *The African Charter of Human and Peoples' Rights: The System in Practice, 1986–2006* (2nd edn., CUP 2008) 1–19, 4–5.

The United Nations also provided strong support to the creation of an African human rights system, organizing a number of seminars and expert meetings during the 1960s.[12] These included a 1969 conference held in Cairo, which concluded with the participants' call on the UN Secretary-General to provide support for the creation of a Commission on Human Rights for Africa, including a request to the UN Commission on Human Rights to engage in consultations with the OAU with a view to the creation of such a regional monitoring mechanism.[13] Further meetings on the creation of an African system were organized by the United Nations during the 1970s,[14] culminating in a seminar hosted in Monrovia, in 1979,[15] which resulted in the adoption of the 'Monrovia Proposal for the Setting up of an African Commission on Human Rights'; a document that was to be sent for consideration to the OAU through the UN Secretary-General.[16]

Besides the organization of seminars, the United Nations encouraged the creation of an African human rights system through the adoption of a range of measures by the Commission on Human Rights and the General Assembly. A draft resolution on the establishment of a human rights commission in Africa, submitted by Nigeria in 1967, was adopted by the Commission on Human Rights and led to the creation of an *ad hoc* 'Study Group' to examine the establishment of regional commissions on human rights in areas where such bodies did not exist—such as in Africa—and to produce recommendations on the matter.[17] Following the Study Group's report, the UN Commission on Human Rights requested the Secretary-General to arrange for consultation and information exchange between the Commission and the OAU concerning the creation of a regional human rights commission.[18] In 1977, the General

---

[12] For instance, a 1966 seminar on human rights in developing countries discussed the adoption of an African human rights treaty without reaching a consensus on the issue. See: 'Seminar on Human Rights in Developing Countries', Dakar, Senegal, 8–22 February 1966, UN Doc. ST/TAO/HR/25 (1966).

[13] R. Gittleman, 'The African Charter on Human and Peoples' Rights: A Legal Analysis' (1982) 22 *Virginia Journal of International Law* 667, 671; G. Baricako, 'The African Charter and African Commission on Human and Peoples' Rights' in M. Evans and R. Murray, *The African Charter of Human and Peoples' Rights: The System in Practice, 1986–2006* (2nd edn., CUP 2008) 1–19, 2-3. See: 'Seminar on Regional Commissions on Human Rights with Special Reference to Africa', UN Doc. ST/TAO/HR/38 (1970); Commission on Human Rights, Report on the Twenty-Six Session, E/CN.4/1039 (1970) pp. 27–31.

[14] F. Ouguergouz, *African Charter of Human and People's Rights: A Comprehensive Agenda for Human Dignity and Sustainable Democracy in Africa* (Nijhoff 2003) 30–31. See: Report of the conference of African jurists on African legal process and the individual (Addis Ababa, 19–23 April 1971), UN Doc. E/CN.14/521; Seminar Series on the Creation of Regional Commissions on Human Rights with regard to Africa, UN Doc. ST/TAO/HR/38, 1970 (23 October–5 November 1973).

[15] N. Udombana, 'Toward the African Court on Human and Peoples' Rights: Better Late than Never' (2000) 3 *Yale Human Rights & Development Law Journal* 45, 59; G. Baricako, 'The African Charter and African Commission on Human and Peoples' Rights' in M. Evans and R. Murray, *The African Charter of Human and Peoples' Rights: The System in Practice, 1986–2006* (2nd edn., CUP 2008) 1–19, 4–5.

[16] Seminar on the Establishment of Regional Commissions on Human Rights with Special Reference to Africa, UN Doc. ST/HR/SER.A/4 (1979), Annex I.

[17] W. Weinstein, 'Human Rights in Africa: A Long-Awaited Voice' (1980) 78 *Current History* 97, 100; F. Ouguergouz, *African Charter of Human and People's Rights: A Comprehensive Agenda for Human Dignity and Sustainable Democracy in Africa* (Nijhoff 2003) 27; G. Baricako, 'The African Charter and African Commission on Human and Peoples' Rights' in M. Evans and R. Murray, *The African Charter of Human and Peoples' Rights: The System in Practice, 1986–2006* (2nd edn., CUP 2008) 1–19, 3. See: Commission on Human Rights, Resolution 6 (XXIII) of 16 March 1967.

[18] Commission on Human Rights, Report on the Twenty-Six Session, E/CN.4/1039 (1970), Resolution 6 (XXVI), 'Question of the establishment of commissions on human rights'.

Assembly echoed the Commission's assessment on the importance of creating regional human rights mechanisms in areas where such arrangements did not yet exist;[19] an appeal that was followed by a call on the Secretary-General to provide the OAU with assistance to facilitate the creation of a commission on human rights for Africa.[20]

Only a few months before the aforementioned Monrovia seminar, the OAU Assembly of Heads of State and Government adopted a decisive step towards the creation of the African human rights system.[21] It requested the OAU Secretary-General to convene (as soon as possible) a 'meeting of highly qualified experts to prepare a preliminary draft of an "African Charter on Human and Peoples' Rights" providing inter alia for the establishment of bodies to promote and protect human and peoples' rights'.[22] Following this call, a gathering of African experts took place in Dakar towards the end of 1979, aimed at preparing a first draft of the proposed African treaty. The objective was to formulate a regional human rights treaty grounded on African legal philosophy and responsive to African needs; thus distinct from the previously adopted European and American Conventions.[23] This was made evident by the opening words of the meeting by the (then) President of Senegal, Léopold Sedar Senghor, who expressed his desire to see a treaty that would draw inspiration from African traditions, reflecting the values of African civilization and considering the needs of Africa.[24]

The committee of experts, presided by Kéba Mbaye—at the time, President of both Senegal's Supreme Court and of the International Commission of Jurists—completed a draft text containing sixty-five articles in only ten days.[25] The draft was then to be considered by a conference of plenipotentiaries organized by the OAU Secretary-General in March 1980, but said conference did not take place due to a lack of quorum.[26] Instead, the draft was initially discussed at the OAU Council of Ministers of Justice,

---

[19] UNGA, Resolution 32/127, 'Regional arrangements for the promotion and protection of human rights' (16 December 1977).

[20] CHR, Report on the Thirty-Fourth Session, E/CN.4/1292 (1978), Resolution 24 (XXXIV), 'Regional arrangements for the promotion and protection of human rights'; UNGA, Resolution 33/167 (20 December 1978).

[21] N. Udombana, 'Toward the African Court on Human and Peoples' Rights: Better Late than Never' (2000) 3 *Yale Human Rights & Development Law Journal* 45, 59; G. Baricako, 'The African Charter and African Commission on Human and Peoples' Rights' in M. Evans and R. Murray, *The African Charter of Human and Peoples' Rights: The System in Practice, 1986–2006* (2nd edn., CUP 2008) 1–19, 5.

[22] AHG/Dec.115 (XVI) Rev. 1 1979.

[23] R. Gittleman, 'The African Charter on Human and Peoples' Rights: A Legal Analysis' (1982) 22 *Virginia Journal of International Law* 667, 668.

[24] N. Udombana, 'Toward the African Court on Human and Peoples' Rights: Better Late than Never' (2000) 3 *Yale Human Rights & Development Law Journal* 45, 60; G. Baricako, 'The African Charter and African Commission on Human and Peoples' Rights' in M. Evans and R. Murray, *The African Charter of Human and Peoples' Rights: The System in Practice, 1986–2006* (2nd edn., CUP 2008) 1–19, 6. See: OAU Doc. CAB/LEG/67/5.

[25] G. Baricako, 'The African Charter and African Commission on Human and Peoples' Rights' in M. Evans and R. Murray, *The African Charter of Human and Peoples' Rights: The System in Practice, 1986–2006* (2nd edn., CUP 2008) 1–19, 6.

[26] G. Baricako, 'The African Charter and African Commission on Human and Peoples' Rights' in M. Evans and R. Murray, *The African Charter of Human and Peoples' Rights: The System in Practice, 1986–2006* (2nd edn., CUP 2008) 1–19, 6. See: Council of Ministers, 'Report of the Secretary-General on the Draft of an African Charter on Human and Peoples' Rights' (June 1981), OAU Doc. CM/1149 (XXXVII).

held in Banjul in June 1980, at which only a fraction of the draft was examined.[27] A subsequent Ministerial Meeting was held in Banjul in January 1981, which concluded with the adoption of the text of a treaty with sixty-eight articles.[28] The text was submitted for consideration of the OAU Council of Ministers—where there was no agreement on the draft Charter—and, subsequently, to the Assembly of Heads of State and Government, which adopted it without debate.[29]

The Charter was adopted on 27 June 1981 and entered into force on 21 October 1986, three months after the OAU Secretary-General received the twenty-sixth instrument of ratification,[30] which amounted to its ratification by the majority of the OAU Member States.[31] By the end of 2022, all Member States of the AU, with the exception of Morocco, are Parties to the African Charter; meaning that this treaty counts fifty-four States Parties.[32] Unlike the European and American predecessors, the African Charter did not provide for a regional court. The main monitoring body set in place was the African Commission on Human and Peoples' Rights, which began operating in 1987 and has its seat in Banjul. The absence of a court—with the power to adopt binding rulings against States—from the institutional structure of the system was not surprising, given that at the time of the Charter's adoption, only a handful of African States could be labelled democratic.[33] It was the normative development of the system that led to the adoption of further treaties, including the one creating a regional court. The first additional protocol to the African Charter, the Protocol Establishing an African Court on Human and Peoples' Rights ('African Court Protocol'), was adopted in June 1998 and entered into force in January 2004.[34] In April 2023, there are

---

[27] D.C. Turack, 'The African Charter on Human and Peoples' Rights: Some Preliminary Thoughts' (1984) 17 *Akron Law Review* 365, 372; G. Baricako, 'The African Charter and African Commission on Human and Peoples' Rights' in M. Evans and R. Murray, *The African Charter of Human and Peoples' Rights: The System in Practice, 1986–2006* (2nd edn., CUP 2008) 1–19, 7.

[28] D.C. Turack, 'The African Charter on Human and Peoples' Rights: Some Preliminary Thoughts' (1984) 17, *Akron Law Review* 365, 372; G. Baricako, 'The African Charter and African Commission on Human and Peoples' Rights' in M. Evans and R. Murray, *The African Charter of Human and Peoples' Rights: The System in Practice, 1986–2006* (2nd edn., CUP 2008) 1–19, 7.

[29] G. Baricako, 'The African Charter and African Commission on Human and Peoples' Rights' in M. Evans and R. Murray, *The African Charter of Human and Peoples' Rights: The System in Practice, 1986–2006* (2nd edn., CUP 2008) 1–19, 8.

[30] By the time Niger deposited its ratification instrument, on 21 July 1986, the following twenty-five States had deposited theirs. In chronological order: Mali, Guinea, Senegal, Togo, Liberia, Congo, Tunisia, Gambia, Nigeria, Rwanda, Sierra Leone, Zambia, Tanzania, Egypt, Burkina Faso, Bénin, Guinea-Bissau, Sudan, Somalia, Sahrawi Arab Democratic Republic, Uganda, Zimbabwe, Gabon, Mauritania, Comoros.

[31] As established by Art. 63.3 of the African Charter.

[32] The status of ratifications is available on the AU's website: https://au.int/treaties/african-charter-human-and-peoples-rights (accessed on 29 March 2023).

[33] M. Mutua, 'The African Human Rights Court: A Two-Legged Stool?' (1999) 21 *Human Rights Quarterly* 342, 345; H. Alisigwe and C. Obodo, 'Three decades of the African Charter on Human and Peoples' Rights: an appraisal of the normative and institutional enforcement regime' (2019) 1 *International Review of Law and Jurisprudence* 158, 159.

[34] Protocol on the Establishment of an African Court on Human and Peoples' Rights (adopted 9 June 1998, entered into force 25 January 2004), OAU Doc. OAU/LEG/EXP/AFCHPR/PROT(III) [hereinafter 'African Court Protocol'].

thirty-four States Parties to the Protocol,[35] following Zambia's deposit of its instrument of accession in January 2023.[36]

8.1.1 THE AFRICAN CHARTER ON HUMAN AND PEOPLE'S RIGHTS

The absence of a court as part of the planned architecture of the system in the original text of the African Charter is not the only distinctive feature of this regional human rights treaty. Among the main characteristics that distinguish the Charter from other regional and universal human rights treaties, it is possible to mention its grounding in regional philosophical values,[37] partly reflected in the place the text grants to both socioeconomic and collective rights and to individual duties, as well as the peculiar rules the Charter sets for regulating the exercise of rights, including numerous claw-back clauses and an absence of a derogation provision.[38] Another important characteristic that distinguishes the African Charter from other regional treaties is that it does not provide for the possibility of denunciation.[39] The absence of such a provision can allow inferring the impossibility of States Parties to withdraw from the treaty,[40] which would avoid the regrettable occurrences of withdrawal experienced in the two other regional systems (as discussed in **Section 6.1.4.1** and **Section 7.1.3**).

8.1.1.1 African values and their implications

As aforementioned, the idea that an African human rights treaty needed to embrace African values was apparent in the different conferences and meetings that led to the adoption of the Charter.[41] Arguably, the most evident element of African cosmovision embraced by the Charter is the understanding of the individual bearer of rights as one with the community, in contrast to the traditional Western conception of individualistic rights.[42] The Bantu concept of 'ubuntu'—which exists, under different

---

[35] See: https://au.int/treaties/protocol-african-charter-human-and-peoples-rights-establishment-african-court-human-and (accessed on 23 March 2022).
[36] African Court Protocol, Art. 65.   [37] African Charter, preamble.
[38] M. Mutua, 'The African Human Rights Court: A Two-Legged Stool?' (1999) 21 *Human Rights Quarterly* 342, 343–344; S. Keetharuth, 'Major African legal instruments' in A. Bösl and J. Diescho, *Human Rights in Africa: Legal Perspectives on their Protection and Promotion* (Konrad Adenauer 2009) 163–231, 166; H. Alisigwe and C. Obodo, 'Three decades of the African Charter on Human and Peoples' Rights: an appraisal of the normative and institutional enforcement regime' (2019) 1, *International Review of Law and Jurisprudence* 158, 161–162.
[39] N.S. Rembe, *The System of Protection of Human Rights under the African Charter on Human and Peoples' Rights: Problems and Prospects* (ISAS 1991) 18–19; K.O. Kufuor, *The African Human Rights System: Origin and Evolution* (Palgrave 2010) 52.
[40] ACtHPR, *Ingabire Victoire Umuhoza v. Rwanda* (jurisdiction) (2016) 1 AfCLR 562, individual opinion of Judge Ouguergouz paras. 26–27. See also: F. Ouguergouz, *African Charter of Human and People's Rights: A Comprehensive Agenda for Human Dignity and Sustainable Democracy in Africa* (Nijhoff 2003) 789–790.
[41] M. Mutua, 'The Banjul Charter and the African Cultural Fingerprint: An Evaluation of the Language of Duties' (1995) 35 *Virginia Journal of International Law* 339, 359-360; B. Winks, 'A covenant of compassion: African humanism and the rights of solidarity in the African Charter on Human and Peoples' Rights' (2011) 11 *African Human Rights Law Journal* 447, 454–455.
[42] T. Metz, 'African Values, Human Rights and Group Rights: A Philosophical Foundation for the Banjul Charter' in A. Bösl and J. Diescho, *Human Rights in Africa: Legal Perspectives on their Protection and Promotion* (Konrad Adenauer 2009) 131–151, 136–138; B. Winks, 'A covenant of compassion: African humanism and the rights of solidarity in the African Charter on Human and Peoples' Rights' (2011) 11 *African Human Rights Law Journal* 447, 459; O. Okafor and G. Dzah 'The African human rights system as "norm leader": Three case studies' (2021) 21 *African Human Rights Law Journal* 669, 676.

designations, in different African languages—is central for understanding the Charter's conception of personhood as a social phenomenon that cannot be conceived but in the interdependence of the individual with the other members of their community.[43] This foundational idea helps understand the Charter's most distinctive characteristic;[44] the prominent place afforded to both socioeconomic rights—such as the rights to work, health, and education[45]—and collective rights, including the rights to development, peace, own natural resources, and a healthy environment.[46] Importantly, both the African Commission and Court have been firm in the conviction of the enforceability of all Charter rights, which should be enjoyed in equal footing, rejecting the dated conception of the separation of rights into different generations.[47]

ACHPR, *Purohit and Moore v. The Gambia*, Communication 241/2001 (2003)

The case was brought to the African Commission by mental health advocates on behalf of patients detained at a specific Unit, but also on behalf of potential future patients. It challenged the legislation of The Gambia governing mental health (the 'Lunatics Detention Act') and its implementation. Despite the lack of exhaustion of domestic remedies, the Commission admitted the case, ruling that it was not realistic to expect the category of people represented in the communication—commonly picked up from the street and those from poor backgrounds, to exhaust domestic remedies before bringing a communication to the Commission (paras. 37–38).

The Commission found that both the legislation at stake and its implementation amounted to multiple breaches of the African Charter. For instance, the Commission found that under the domestic legislation, persons suffering from mental illness were branded as 'lunatics' and 'idiots'; terms that dehumanise and deny them any form of dignity, in contravention of the Charter (para. 59). The Commission also found serious violations of the right to health. It stated that the enjoyment of the right to health was vital to all aspects of a person's life and well-being, and crucial to the realization of all other fundamental human rights. It affirmed that this right encompasses the right to access health facilities, goods, and services without discrimination, and that mental health patients should be provided with special measures of protection that would enable them to attain and sustain an optimum level of independence (paras. 80–81).

The Commission stated that: 'millions of people in Africa are not enjoying the right to health maximally because African countries are generally faced with the problem of poverty which renders them incapable to provide the necessary amenities, infrastructure and resources that facilitate the full enjoyment of this right'. (para. 84). Having regard to this state of affairs, which it characterized as 'depressing but real', the Commission asserted that

---

[43] B. Winks, 'A covenant of compassion: African humanism and the rights of solidarity in the African Charter on Human and Peoples' Rights' (2011) 11 *African Human Rights Law Journal* 447, 456–457.

[44] F. Ouguergouz, *African Charter of Human and People's Rights: A Comprehensive Agenda for Human Dignity and Sustainable Democracy in Africa* (Nijhoff 2003) 57–58, 203.

[45] African Charter, Arts. 15–17.   [46] African Charter, Arts. 19–24.

[47] ACHPR, *Free Legal Assistance Group, Lawyers' Committee for Human Rights, Union Interafricaine des Droits de l'Homme, Les Témoins de Jehovah v. Zaire (Democratic Republic of Congo)*, Communications 25/89-47/90-56/91-100/93 (1995); ACHPR, *Social and Economic Rights Action Center (SERAC) and Center for Economic and Social Rights (CESR) v. Nigeria*, Communication 155/96 (2001); ACtHPR, *African Commission on Human and Peoples' Rights v. Kenya* (merits) (2017) 2 AfCLR 9.

it would like to read into the Charter the obligation of States Parties to take concrete steps to ensure that the right to health is fully realized in all its aspects without discrimination, taking full advantage of their available resources (para. 84). Consequently, the Commission strongly urged the State to replace the existing legislation; to create an expert body to review the cases of the people detained under the impugned legislation; and to provide adequate medical care to those suffering from mental health problems within the State.

ACtHPR, *African Commission on Human and Peoples' Rights v. Kenya* (merits) (2017) 2 AfCLR 9.

The case was about the eviction of an indigenous group, the Ogieks, from their ancestral lands in the Mau Forest by Kenya, which the Court considered to entail the violation of a range of individual and group rights protected under the African Charter. The Court began its analysis of the case by confirming that the Ogieks should be considered as an indigenous population, with a strong attachment to their ancestral land and natural environment, whose survival depends on unhindered access to their ancestral home, and who also exhibit 'a voluntary perpetuation of cultural distinctiveness', including their self-identification as a distinct group, as well as their own language, social organization, and religious, cultural, and spiritual values (paras. 107–112). The Court found that the Ogieks' lack of recognition by the State as an indigenous population had deprived them of the enjoyment of rights that were granted to similar tribes so recognized, which amounted to discrimination (paras. 141–142 and 146).

The Court also confirmed that the Ogieks should be recognized as 'people', entitled to the collective rights protected by the Charter (paras. 196–199). It asserted the Ogieks' collective right to property over their ancestral lands (paras. 123–124), which was breached by the State by their expulsion from such lands against their will (para. 131). Similarly, the Court held that such expulsion also amounted to a violation of their collective right to dispose of their wealth and natural resources (Article 21), since they had been deprived of the food produced by their ancestral lands, as well as of their right to development (Article 22), as their economic, social, and cultural development had been adversely impacted (paras. 201 and 210–211).

The Court also found that the expulsion had deprived them of access to their ancestral lands for the purpose of practicing their religion, which amounted to a violation of freedom of religion (paras. 163–165 and 169). Moreover, the Court found that the situation entailed the violation of the right to culture (Article 17), in both its individual and collective dimensions (paras. 177–182 and 190). It affirmed that 'culture should be construed in its widest sense encompassing the total way of life of a particular group, including the group's languages, symbols such as dressing codes and the manner the group constructs shelters; engages in certain economic activities, produces items for survival; rituals such as the group's particular way of dealing with problems and practicing spiritual ceremonies; identification and veneration of its own heroes or models and shared values of its members which reflect its distinctive character and personality'. (para. 179).

Moreover, the understanding of individuals as indissociable parts of their communities shapes another distinguishing aspect of the African Charter; the level of detail of the duties it foresees on individuals towards their families (understood as extending beyond the nuclear family),[48] the community, and the State.[49] As Mutua explains, the philosophy of the group-centred individual materializes in the entanglement of rights and responsibilities, which serves to enhance solidarity—by connecting the needs of the individual with the needs of others—and secure the survival of the community.[50] This is a feature absent from the European Convention and limited to a short provision in the American one.[51] Conversely, under the African Charter, individuals' duties seem to extend much further, being encompassed within three different articles. The first of these provisions generically states the existence of duties towards one's family, society, State, and the international community, while the second one aims at fostering respect and equality among individuals.[52] On its part, the third provision is extensive and details a list of obligations:

The individual shall also have the duty:

1. To preserve the harmonious development of the family and to work for the cohesion and respect of the family; to respect his parents at all times, to maintain them in case of need;
2. To serve his national community by placing his physical and intellectual abilities at its service;
3. Not to compromise the security of the State whose national or resident he is;
4. To preserve and strengthen social and national solidarity, particularly when the latter is threatened;
5. To preserve and strengthen the national independence and the territorial integrity of his country and to contribute to its defence in accordance with the law;
6. To work to the best of his abilities and competence, and to pay taxes imposed by law in the interest of the society;
7. To preserve and strengthen positive African cultural values in his relations with other members of the society, in the spirit of tolerance, dialogue, and consultation and, in general, to contribute to the promotion of the moral well being of society;
8. To contribute to the best of his abilities, at all times and at all levels, to the promotion and achievement of African unity.[53]

Notwithstanding the concern expressed by some commentators about this extensive reference to duties in a human rights treaty and its potential abuse to subordinate the enjoyment of rights to the fulfilment of duties,[54] others have supported their inclusion.

---

[48] M. Mutua, 'The Banjul Charter and the African Cultural Fingerprint: An Evaluation of the Language of Duties' (1995) 35 *Virginia Journal of International Law* 339, 373.

[49] M. Mutua, *Human Rights: A Political and Cultural Critique* (University of Pennsylvania Press 2002) 71, 82–84; N. Udombana, 'Between Promise and Performance: Revisiting States' Obligations under the African Human Rights Charter' (2004) 40 *Stanford Journal of International Law* 105, 111; G. Naldi, 'The African Union and the Regional Human Rights System' in M. Evans and R. Murray, *The African Charter of Human and Peoples' Rights: The System in Practice, 1986–2006* (2nd edn., CUP 2008) 20–48, 28–29.

[50] M. Mutua, 'The Banjul Charter and the African Cultural Fingerprint: An Evaluation of the Language of Duties' (1995) 35 *Virginia Journal of International Law* 339, 361, 363.

[51] Conversely, the idea of duties features heavily in the 1948 American Declaration of the Rights and Duties of Man, encompassing a whole Chapter that extends through ten different Articles. See: ACHR, Art. 32.1; American Declaration, Arts. XXXIX–XXXVIII.

[52] African Charter, Arts. 27, 28.   [53] African Charter, Art. 29.

[54] R. Cohen, 'Endless Teardrops: Prolegomena to the Study of Human Rights in Africa' in R. Cohen, G. Hyden, and W. Nagan (eds.), *Human Rights and Governance in Africa* (University Press of Florida 1993) 3–38, 15; H. Okoth-Ogendo, 'Human and Peoples' Rights: What Point is Africa Trying to Make' in R. Cohen, G. Hyden, and W. Nagan (eds.), *Human Rights and Governance in Africa* (University Press of Florida 1993) 74–86, 78–79.

For instance, Mutua proposes that it is important to grasp the inspiration for the different types of duties. He explains that some Charter duties are actually general obligations citizens have towards every State worldwide, such as paying taxes and not compromising the State's security. Conversely, many duties are grounded in African philosophy, which assumes that individual development depends on the awareness of how one's actions impact others, such as the duty to strengthen social and national solidarity, while the rationale for other duties can be found in Africa's tragic history of foreign domination,[55] such as requiring individuals to defend the State's independence and integrity.[56]

8.1.1.2 Claw-back clauses and (lack of) derogation provision

Another particularity of the Charter, extensively discussed by the academic literature, is the fact that it contains no provision allowing States to derogate from their obligations during emergencies, at the same time that many of its provisions contain so-called 'claw-back clauses',[57] which seemingly provide a rather broad power to States to restrict protected rights to the extent determined by domestic law. For instance, the articles protecting the right to liberty, the freedoms of religion, expression, association, and movement, as well as political rights, are all phrased in a language that appears to make their enjoyment contingent on their exercise being 'subject to law and order',[58] 'within the law',[59] 'in accordance with the provisions of the law',[60] or susceptible to restrictions 'for reasons and conditions previously laid down by law'.[61] The broad character of such claw-back clauses is particularly worrying within the African context, given that many domestic laws are a legacy of its repressive colonial past and are, consequently, highly draconian.[62] Fortunately, the African Commission has been careful to clarify

---

[55] In fact, the duty to achieve the total liberation of Africa and the elimination of colonialism, neo-colonialism, and apartheid—as well as 'zionism'—appear in the Charter's preamble among the agreed principles on which the African Charter was grounded. Nonetheless, the specific reference to zionism—apparently introduced by Libya during the drafting process—has been called into question, as it entailed the problematic importation of a truly non-African issue into the grounding principles of the Charter. See: R. Gittleman, 'The African Charter on Human and Peoples' Rights: A Legal Analysis' (1982) 22 *Virginia Journal of International Law* 667, 675 (fn 43). See also: African Charter, preamble.

[56] M. Mutua, 'The Banjul Charter and the African Cultural Fingerprint: An Evaluation of the Language of Duties' (1995) 35 *Virginia Journal of International Law* 339, 370, 378.

[57] Among others: R. Gittleman, 'The African Charter on Human and Peoples' Rights: A Legal Analysis' (1982) 22 *Virginia Journal of International Law* 667; M. Mutua, 'The African Human Rights Court: A Two-Legged Stool?' (1999) 21 *Human Rights Quarterly* 342; F. Ouguergouz, *African Charter of Human and People's Rights: A Comprehensive Agenda for Human Dignity and Sustainable Democracy in Africa* (Nijhoff 2003) chapter VI; L. Sermet, 'The absence of a derogation clause from the African Charter on Human and Peoples' Rights: A critical discussion' (2007) 7 *African Human Rights Law Journal* 142; S. Keetharuth, 'Major African legal instruments' in A. Bösl and J. Diescho, *Human Rights in Africa: Legal Perspectives on their Protection and Promotion* (Konrad Adenauer 2009) 163–231; M. Tolera, 'Absence of Derogation Clause under the African Charter and the Position of the African Commission' (2014) 4 *Bahir Dar University Journal of Law* 229; A. Enabulele, 'Incompatibility of national law with the African Charter on Human and Peoples' Rights: Does the African Court on Human and Peoples' Rights have the final say?' (2016) 16 *African Human Rights Law Journal* 1; H. Alisigwe and C. Obodo, 'Three decades of the African Charter on Human and Peoples' Rights: an appraisal of the normative and institutional enforcement regime' (2019) 1 *International Review of Law and Jurisprudence* 158.

[58] African Charter, Art. 8. [59] African Charter, Art. 9.
[60] African Charter, Art. 13. [61] African Charter, Art. 6.
[62] M. Mutua, 'The African Human Rights Court: A Two-Legged Stool?' (1999) 21 *Human Rights Quarterly* 342, 358.

the appropriate interpretation of such clauses. Through a series of decisions, the Commission has asserted that the Charter's references to the legal regulations of rights do not allow national law to set aside the rights in question, as this would render the Charter's protection of rights ineffective.[63] In fact, both the Commission and Court have followed the jurisprudence of other monitoring bodies, interpreting that the restrictions placed by domestic law on the enjoyment of rights must pursue a legitimate interest and be necessary, in a democratic society, for achieving such an aim.[64]

Lastly, unlike other human rights treaties, such as the European and American Conventions and the International Covenant on Civil and Political Rights (ICCPR),[65] the African Charter contains no provision allowing States to temporarily derogate from their obligations during a public emergency. While the absence of a derogation provision can be seen as an innovative development, although certainly not unheard of,[66] its absence can also provide reasons for concern. In fairness, derogation clauses should not be seen as an excuse for States to exempt themselves from complying with their international human rights obligations but as provisions that set the requirements and limitations under which States are allowed, in truly exceptional circumstances and only for a limited time, to suspend the enjoyment of certain rights (and not of others) in order to tackle a particularly serious situation.[67] Importantly, the restrictive measures adopted by States during the time of emergency remain the subject of international supervision by the pertinent monitoring body of the instrument under which the measures of suspension are adopted.[68]

With regards to the meaning and implications of the absence of an express provision on derogations, the practice of the Commission has been called into question for lacking consistency.[69] On the one hand, within the context of communications, the Commission has clearly affirmed that the absence of such a provision meant that States were not allowed to derogate from their obligations under any circumstances.[70] On

---

[63] ACHPR, *Media Rights Agenda and Others v. Nigeria*, Communications 105/93, 128/94, 130/94, 152/96 (1998), para. 66.

[64] ACHPR, *Scanlen and Holderness v. Zimbabwe*, Communication 297/2005 (2009), para. 112; ACtHPR, *Tanganyika Law Society, Legal and Human Rights Centre and Reverend Christopher R. Mtikila v. Tanzania* (merits) (2013) 1 AfCLR 34, paras. 106–107.

[65] ECHR, Art. 15; ACHR, Art. 27; ICCPR, Art. 4.

[66] Such a clause is absent in other human rights treaties, such as ICESCR and UNCRC. See: L. Sermet, 'The absence of a derogation clause from the African Charter on Human and Peoples' Rights: A critical discussion' (2007) 7 *African Human Rights Law Journal* 142, 143; F. Viljoen, *International Human Rights Law in Africa* (2nd edn., OUP 2012) 334.

[67] R. Gittleman, 'The African Charter on Human and Peoples' Rights: A Legal Analysis' (1982) 22 *Virginia Journal of International Law* 667, 692; B. Kombo, 'Missed Opportunity? Derogation and the African Court Case of APDF and IHRDA v. Mali' (2020) 20 *African Human Rights Law Journal* 756, 758.

[68] R. Gittleman, 'The African Charter on Human and Peoples' Rights: A Legal Analysis' (1982) 22 *Virginia Journal of International Law* 667, 707.

[69] M. Tolera, 'Absence of Derogation Clause under the African Charter and the Position of the African Commission' (2014) 4 *Bahir Dar University Journal of Law* 229, 250, 261; B. Kombo, 'Missed Opportunity? Derogation and the African Court Case of APDF and IHRDA v. Mali' (2020) 20 *African Human Rights Law Journal* 756, 762, 765.

[70] ACHPR, *Commission Nationale Des Droits De l'Homme Et Des Liberté v. Chad*, Communication 74/92 (1995), para. 21; ACHPR, *Media Rights Agenda and Other v. Nigeria*, Communications 105/93, 128/94, 130/94, 152/96 (1998), para. 67; ACHPR, *Article 19 v. Eritrea*, Communication 275/2003 (2007), para. 98.

the other hand, during the examination of State reports that disclosed the adoption of measures of suspension of rights due to emergencies, the Commission had been silent on the validity of such actions.[71] Conversely, the Court seems to have adopted a more nuanced stance, interpreting the absence of a derogation provision within the broader regulation of the matter under the international law of human rights. Although still failing to provide an unambiguous position, the Court resorted to the application of the requirements under the derogation clause of ICCPR for determining the validity of the suspension of elections during the Covid-19 pandemic, as well as for the restriction of other rights, to prevent widespread Covid-19 transmissions, if elections were to be held.

> **ACtHPR, *The right to participate in the government of one's country in the context of an election held during a public health emergency or a pandemic, such as the Covid-19 crisis.* Advisory Opinion No. 1/2020 (2021).**
>
> The request for this Advisory Opinion was made by the Pan African Lawyers Union. The questions submitted concerned different aspects of the hosting of elections during the Covid-19 pandemic and their compatibility with rights emanating from both the African Charter on Human and Peoples' Rights and the African Charter on Democracy, Elections and Governance. The questions concerned three main aspects: whether States had discretion in deciding on holding or postponing planned elections, given the context of public emergency created by the pandemic; what types of measures were States to adopt, if they decided to carry on with holding elections; and what type of obligations existed upon States that decided to postpone elections.
>
> The Court responded that States did enjoy discretion on whether planned elections should go ahead or not; however, such a decision should be made following consultation with the health authorities and involved political actors, including representatives from the civil society (para. 54). Moreover, the Court affirmed that its role was not to produce policy guidelines as to how elections should be conducted under the pandemic, but to state the legal requirements to be applied to the restriction of rights under such a public emergency, applicable both to the restriction of electoral rights, by the postponement of elections, as well as to the restrictions of rights to protect public health, if elections were to be held.
>
> The Court opined that any measure that involved the restriction of rights should be adopted by law, pursue a legitimate aim in a proportionate manner, not undermine the essential content of the restricted rights, avoid discrimination, and—given the absence of a derogation clause in the African Charter—avoid derogation from the rights considered non-derogable under ICCPR (para. 76). Moreover, for States that decide to postpone elections, the Court affirmed that it was their domestic law that should regulate the situation of the expiration of mandates without elections taking place, due to a public emergency, until elections could be held (para. 105).

8.1.2 NORMATIVE FRAMEWORK

In addition to the African Court Protocol, two protocols have been adopted to complement the African Charter, aimed at reinforcing the protection of individuals belonging to particularly vulnerable groups, such as women and elderly people. The 2003 Protocol on the Rights of Women in Africa ('Maputo Protocol') is aimed at ensuring that

---

[71] M. Tolera, 'Absence of Derogation Clause under the African Charter and the Position of the African Commission' (2014) 4 *Bahir Dar University Journal of Law* 229, 258.

women's rights are promoted, realized, and protected in Africa to enable women to fully enjoy all human rights.[72] It established a legal framework for the protection of women in Africa, including a two-folded system of supervision of States Parties' obligations. On the one hand, the Maputo Protocol imposes upon States Parties the obligation to inform the African Commission of the measures adopted to achieve the full realization of the protected rights through the periodic report mechanism contemplated in the African Charter.[73] On the other hand, the Protocol allows for resort to the African Court with regards to its interpretation arising from its application or implementation by States Parties.[74] However, a contextual reading of the Protocol suggests that the Commission can also be seized in matters concerning its interpretation and application.[75]

The 2018 Protocol on the Rights of Older Persons in Africa was aimed at providing a legal framework for the protection of elderly people, detailing an extensive catalogue of rights that must be protected by States Parties.[76] This Protocol also imposes upon States the duty to report periodically, and unlike the Maputo Protocol, it expressly confers on the Commission the mandate to interpret its provision. It also entitles the Commission to refer to the Court 'matters of interpretation and enforcement or any dispute arising from [the Protocol's] application or implementation'.[77] In addition to these two substantive Protocols, other treaties have been adopted under the auspices of the AU (and its predecessor, the OAU) to supplement the protection of human rights provided by the African Charter. These include the 1969 OAU Convention Governing Specific Aspects of Refugee Problems in Africa and the 2009 AU Convention for the Protection and Assistance of Internally Displaced Persons in Africa ('Kampala Convention'); the 1990 African Charter on the Rights and Welfare of the Child and the 2009 African Youth Charter; the 2003 AU Convention on Preventing and Combating Corruption and the 2011 African Charter on Democracy, Elections and Governance; as well as the 2006 Charter for African Cultural Renaissance.[78]

8.1.2.1 Further reflections: The African Charter on the Rights and Welfare of the Child

The African Charter on the Rights and Welfare of the Child ('African Children's Charter') was adopted in July 1990,[79] making the African human rights system the first regional

---

[72] African Court Protocol, preamble.   [73] Maputo Protocol, Art. XXVI; ACHR, Art. 62.
[74] Maputo Protocol, Art. XXVII.
[75] F. Viljoen, *International Human Rights Law in Africa* (2nd edn., OUP 2012) 313.
[76] Protocol to the African Charter on Human and Peoples' Rights on the Rights of Older Persons in Africa (adopted 28 January 2018, entered into force 11 September 2018).
[77] Protocol to the African Charter on Human and Peoples' Rights on the Rights of Older Persons in Africa, Art. 22.
[78] Convention Governing Specific Aspects of Refugee Problems in Africa (adopted 10 September 1969, entered into force 20 June 1974); AU Convention for the Protection and Assistance of Internally Displaced Persons in Africa (adopted 23 October 2009, entered into force 6 March 2020); African Charter on the Rights and Welfare of the Child (adopted 1 July 1990, entered into force 29 November 1999); African Youth Charter (adopted 2 July 2006, entered into force 8 August 2009); AU Convention on Preventing and Combating Corruption (adopted 1 July 2003, entered into force 10 February 2020); African Charter on Democracy, Elections and Governance (adopted 25 October 2011, entered into force 15 February 2012); Charter for African Cultural Renaissance (adopted 25 January 2006, not yet in force).
[79] African Charter on the Rights and Welfare of the Child (adopted 11 July 1990, entered into force 29 November 1999), OAU Doc.CAB/LEG/24.9/49 (1990).

system to have a specific treaty focused on the protection of children; a topic that had been in the African agenda for years, as illustrated by the 1979 Declaration on the Rights and Welfare of the African Child.[80] The adoption of this Charter, to complement the 1989 United Nations Convention on the Rights of the Child (UNCRC), adopted only months before, could be explained by different reasons, including the limited influence African States had in the drafting of the UN Convention.[81] Feelings of frustration with the drafting process of the UNCRC led the African Network for the Prevention and Protection Against Child Abuse and Neglect (ANPPCAN) and UNICEF to convene a meeting in 1988, to analyse the existent draft of UNCRC and evaluate its ability to address the specific needs of African children. A main outcome of the meeting was to recommend the OAU to set up a group of African experts to draft a regional treaty.[82]

The drafting of the African Children's Charter was completed in a rather short period of time, with its text adopted by consensus in 1990. However, it took over nine years for the Charter to obtain the needed fifteen ratifications to enter into force.[83] The reasons behind the reluctance of African States to ratify the Charter are unknown, especially considering that African States amounted to the largest number of original Parties to UNCRC.[84] Certainly, the content of the Charter is unlikely to have acted as a deterrence, illustrated by the rather low number of reservations States have appended to it when finally becoming Parties.[85] By the end of 2022, the Charter counts fifty States Parties, out of the fifty-five AU Members,[86] although why the five missing States remain reluctant to sign into the Charter, while being Parties to UNCRC, remains a mystery.

Similar to UNCRC, the Charter details a catalogue of children's rights that should be protected by State Parties, but it presents important differences to the UN treaty, given its specific concern over the 'cultural heritage, historical background and the values of the African civilization'.[87] For instance, the Charter establishes at eighteen the

---

[80] A. Lloyd, 'Evolution of the African Charter on the Rights and Welfare of the Child and the African Committee of Experts: Raising the Gauntlet' (2002) 10 *International Journal of Children's Rights* 179, 179; A. Lloyd, 'The African Regional System for the Protection of Children's Rights' in J. Sloth-Nielsen (ed.), *Children's Rights in Africa: A Legal Perspective* (Ashgate 2008) 33–52, 34. See: AHG/ST.4 Rev. l.

[81] R. Barsh, 'The Draft Convention on the Rights of the Child: A Case of Eurocentrism in Standard Setting' (1989) 58 *Nordic Journal of International Law* 24, 24; A. Lloyd, 'Evolution of the African Charter on the Rights and Welfare of the Child and the African Committee of Experts: Raising the Gauntlet' (2002) 10 *International Journal of Children's Rights* 179, 182; F. Viljoen, *International Human Rights Law in Africa* (2nd edn., OUP 2012) 392.

[82] F. Viljoen, 'Supra-National Human Rights Instruments for the Protection of Children in Africa: The Convention on the Rights of the Child and the African Charter on the Rights and Welfare of the Child' (1998) 31 *The Comparative and International Law Journal of Southern Africa* 199, 206–207; B. Mezmur, 'Happy 18th Birthday to the African Children's Rights Charter: Not Counting Its Days But Making Its Days Count' (2017) 1 *African Human Rights Yearbook* 125, 128; A. Johnson and J. Sloth-Nielsen, 'Child Protection, Safeguarding and the Role of the African Charter on the Rights and Welfare of the Child: Looking Back and Looking Ahead' (2020) 20 *African Human Rights Law Journal* 643, 647.

[83] African Children's Charter, Art. 47.3.

[84] B. Mezmur, 'Happy 18th birthday to the African Children's Rights Charter: not counting its days but making its days count' (2017) 1 *African Human Rights Yearbook* 125, 129.

[85] B. Mezmur, 'Happy 18th birthday to the African Children's Rights Charter: not counting its days but making its days count' (2017) 1 *African Human Rights Yearbook* 125, 130.

[86] The exceptions are: Morocco, Sahrawi Arab Democratic Republic, Somalia, South Sudan, and Tunisia. See: https://au.int/treaties/african-charter-rights-and-welfare-child (accessed on 14 March 2023).

[87] African Children's Charter, preamble.

minimum age of adulthood, in opposition to the UNCRC, which allows for majority to be attained earlier under domestic law.[88] The Charter also imposes upon States the duty to take all possible measures to stop harmful social and cultural practices, such as child marriage, while the Convention is silent on the topic.[89] Moreover, the Charter contains an absolute prohibition on the recruitment of child soldiers, while the UN Convention only prohibits this for children under the age of 15,[90] and even the pertinent Optional Protocol to the UNCRC—Optional Protocol to the Convention on the Rights of the Child on the involvement of children in armed conflict[91]—failed to impose an absolute prohibition on child soldiers.[92] Another important difference is that, in consonance with the African Charter on Human and Peoples' Rights, the African Children's Charter states that, in addition to rights, children have responsibilities, 'towards their families and societies, to respect their parents, superiors and elders, to preserve and strengthen African cultural values in their relation with other members of their communities'.[93]

The Charter established a 'Committee of Experts on the Rights and Welfare of the Child', tasked with the promotion and protection of children's rights and with monitoring the implementation of the treaty.[94] The Committee is comprised of eleven members, who need to be nationals of the States Parties to the Charter and are elected by the AU Assembly for a five-year period,[95] following nominations by States Parties.[96] Although the Charter was adopted in 1990, under the auspices of the OAU, the Committee has now been incorporated into the AU, and it reports to the Assembly and Executive Council on an annual basis.[97] The AU is also responsible for providing the Committee's budget.[98]

As the monitoring body of the African Children's Charter, the Committee has a rather broad mandate.[99] Like treaty bodies (discussed in **Chapter 5**), it has the power to issue authoritative interpretations of the provisions of the Charter through general

---

[88] African Children's Charter, Art. 2; CRC, Art. 1.   [89] African Children's Charter, Art. 21.

[90] African Children's Charter, Art. 22; CRC, Art. 38.

[91] Optional Protocol to the Convention on the Rights of the Child on the involvement of children in armed conflict (adopted on 25 May 2000, entered into force 12 February 2002).

[92] The Optional Protocol only prohibits in absolute terms child soldiers' participation in direct hostilities and their compulsory recruitment and imposes an obligation on States Parties to raise the age of voluntary recruitment to over fifteen years. See: Optional Protocol to the Convention on the Rights of the Child on the involvement of children in armed conflict, Arts. 1, 2, 3.

[93] African Children's Charter, Art. 31.   [94] African Children's Charter, Arts. 32 and 42.

[95] Although the mandate of the members was originally non-renewable, the Charter was amended in 2015 to allow for the possibility of one re-election. See: Decision on the Amendment of Article 37(1) of the African Charter on the Rights and Welfare of the Child, Assembly/AU/Dec.548(XXIV) (31 January 2015).

[96] African Children's Charter, Arts. 33–37.

[97] AU Assembly, Decision on the Interim Period, ASS/AU/Dec.1(I), para. xi.

[98] ACERWC, Revised Rules of Procedure of the African Committee of Experts on the Rights and Welfare of the Child (September 2020), r. 19.

[99] D. Olowu, 'Protecting Children's Rights in Africa: Critique of the African Charter on the Rights and Welfare of the Child' (2002) 10 *International Journal of Children's Rights* 127, 131; A. Lloyd, 'The African Regional System for the Protection of Children's Rights' in J. Sloth-Nielsen (ed.), *Children's Rights in Africa: A Legal Perspective* (Ashgate 2008) 33–52, 44–45.

comments.[100] These interpretations can originate in a request from a State Party, an AU institution, or any person or institution recognized by the AU, or on a decision of the Committee itself.[101] Up to the end of 2022, the Committee has issued seven general comments, respectively, on children of incarcerated parents and caregivers (Article 30); on birth registration, name, and nationality (Article 6); on ending child marriage (Article 21) (issued jointly with the African Commission); on the responsibilities of the child (Article 31); on States' obligations (Article 1); on children in situations of conflict (Article 22); and on sexual exploitation (Article 27).[102]

Pursuant to its Rules of Procedure, the Committee has also developed the practice of assigning specific mandates both to its individual members (Special Rapporteurs) and to groups of its members (Working Groups) concerning thematic areas deemed of special interest.[103] These mechanisms are aimed at setting standards and developing strategies to better promote and protect children's rights. The created mandates have covered, among others, the issues of violence against children; health, welfare, and development; child marriage; the right to education; children and armed conflict; children's rights and business; and climate change.[104]

Furthermore, the Committee's task to supervise States' compliance with their obligations under the African Children's Charter is undertaken through two main procedures: State reporting and the reception of communications. As to the reporting mechanism, following an initial report to be submitted within two years of becoming Parties to the Charter, States are under the obligation to submit reports to the Committee every three years, explaining the measures adopted to make the Charter's provisions effective, as well as the progress made in the enjoyment of these rights under their jurisdiction.[105] The examination of these reports involves a dialogue with the incumbent State,[106] followed by 'concluding observations' from the Committee, which also has the power to undertake follow-up missions to monitor the implementations of its observations.[107]

8.1.2.1.1 Communications before the African Children's Committee

Communications concerning violations of the Charter can be submitted to the Committee by individuals, NGOs recognized by the AU, AU Member States, and even the United Nations.[108] These communications can be presented on behalf of a child victim without their agreement, as long as it is shown that the action is taken in

---

[100] African Charter, Art. 42.   [101] ACERWC, Rules of Procedure, r. 76.
[102] ACERWC, General Comment No. 1: children of incarcerated and imprisoned parents and primary caregivers (Art. 30) (2013); ACERWC, General Comment No. 2: right to birth registration, name, and nationality (Art. 6) (2014); ACHPR and ACERWC, Joint General Comment: ending child marriage (2017); ACERWC, General Comment No. 4: responsibilities of the child (Art. 31) (2017); ACERWC, General Comment No. 5: State Party obligations and systems strengthening for child protection (Art. 1) (2018); ACERWC, General Comment No. 6: children in situations of conflict (Art. 22) (2020); ACERWC, General Comment No. 7: sexual exploitation (Art. 27) (2021).
[103] ACERWC, Rules of Procedure, Chapter XI.
[104] See: http://www.acerwc.africa/page/about-special-mechanisms (accessed on 29 March 2023).
[105] African Children's Charter, Art. 43.   [106] ACERWC, Rules of Procedure, r. 70.
[107] ACERWC, Rules of Procedure, rr. 73–74.   [108] African Children's Charter, Art. 44.

the child's best interests.[109] The requirements for the admissibility of communications are similar to those under other treaties, including its compatibility with both the Children's Charter and with the AU Constitutive Act; its grounding in reliable information; the prior exhaustion of domestic remedies and the submission taking place within a reasonable time thereafter; the issue not having been decided (or being pending decision) before another international body; and the avoidance of disparaging or insulting language.[110]

Within the context of communications, the Committee is empowered to deploy a range of tools, including the adoption of provisional measures and the undertaking of on-site investigations.[111] The Committee, on its own initiative or at the request of any of the parties, can also promote the amicable settlement of cases, guided by the best interests of the child and on the basis of the mutual consent of the parties.[112] For this purpose, the Committee can appoint one or more of its members to render their good offices to facilitate negotiations between the parties.[113] When a settlement is not reached, the Committee proceeds to decide on the merits of the case and, if it finds breaches to the Charter, it provides recommendations on actions to remedy the violations. The diversity of the recommendations issued by the Committee in the cases in which it has found violations is an aspect worth highlighting. Up to the end of 2022, the Committee has decided on seven communications and has overseen two amicable settlements.

> **ACERWC, *Legal and Human Rights Centre and Centre for Reproductive Rights (on behalf of Tanzanian girls) v. Tanzania*. Communication No. 0012/Com/001/2019, Decision No. 002/2022.**
>
> The case was brought on behalf of all Tanzanian girls, due to the existence of a policy of forced exclusion of married and pregnant girls from school. The policy was enforced through pregnancy testing, at school and before admission to school, of primary and secondary school girls, and was leading to the exclusion of thousands of girls from education yearly. While Education Regulations did provide for marriage as a cause for expulsion of girls from school,

---

[109] ACERWC, 'Revised Guidelines for Consideration of Communications and Monitoring Implementation of Decisions by the African Committee of Experts on the Rights and Welfare of the Child', section I.iii.

[110] ACERWC, 'Revised Guidelines for Consideration of Communications and Monitoring Implementation of Decisions by the African Committee of Experts on the Rights and Welfare of the Child', section IX.

[111] A peculiar feature among the working methods of the Committee is that it has taken to conducting field visits before deciding on the merits of communications. See: B. Mezmur and M. Kahbila, 'Follow-up as a "Choice-less Choice": Towards Improving the Implementation of Decisions on Communications of the African Children's Committee' (2018) 2 *African Human Rights Yearbook* 200, 206.

[112] The first amicable settlement reached before the Committee obtained widespread attention, as it led to the reform of Malawi's constitution which, in contravention of the Children's Charter, considered childhood to finish at 16—with the consequential effect of allowing marriage from that age. See: ACERWC, *Institute for Human Rights and Development in Africa v. Malawi*. Communication 004/Com/001/2014; B. Mezmur, 'No Second Chance for First Impressions: The First Amicable Settlement under the African Children's Charter' (2019) 19 *African Human Rights Law Journal* 62, 83.

[113] ACERWC, 'Revised Guidelines for Consideration of Communications and Monitoring Implementation of Decisions by the African Committee of Experts on the Rights and Welfare of the Child', section XIII.

they did not prescribe such sanction for pregnancy, which was being interpreted as an 'offence against morality' to make pregnant girls susceptible to expulsion.

Before the Committee, the applicants claimed that the enforcement of mandatory pregnancy testing in schools; the expulsion of pregnant and married girls and the denial of their re-admission; as well as the failure to provide children with reproductive and sexual health information services, all amounted to violations of a range of rights protected under the Charter, including the prohibition of discrimination (Article 3), the best interests of the child (Article 4), the rights to education (Article 11), to health (Article 14), and to be protected from cruel, inhuman, and degrading treatment (Article 16) and from harmful social practices and stereotypes (Article 21).

Unsurprisingly, the Committee found that the expulsion of pregnant and married girls, their denial to re-enter education, and the forceful testing to which students were subjected, amounted to clear violations of the right to education (para. 49). The coercive testing was also considered to amount to cruel, inhuman, and degrading treatment, in detriment of the child's best interests, and to risk subjecting possible victims of sexual violence to further trauma (paras. 37 and 74). These policies were considered by the Committee to amount to discriminatory treatment, based on gender, health status, and marital status (para. 59).

Furthermore, in determining the violation of the right to health of Tanzanian girls, the Committee assessed not only the above policy, but also the state of sexual reproductive health services and sexuality education for children and adolescents in Tanzania. It asserted that: 'The relevant criteria for measuring the performance and implementation of healthcare obligations are availability, accessibility, acceptability, and quality. These criteria are implicated differently in the context of the provision of child-friendly services and extend to include the provision of safe, and confidential abortion services' (para. 79). The Committee considered that the lack of sexual reproductive health services and a comprehensive sexual education for children and adolescents in Tanzania were responsible for the prevalence of teenage pregnancy among school girls and that the lack of sexual reproductive health services—as well as a draconian legislation on the interruption of pregnancies—was forcing girls to resort to unsafe abortions, further endangering their lives, survival, and development (para. 87).

The Committee ruled that the actions of the respondent State were in breach of multiple Charter provisions, such as the prohibition of discrimination, the best interests of the child, the rights to education, privacy, and health, and the rights to be protected from child abuse and from harmful social practices. The Committee issued a range of recommendations to bring the ongoing violations committed to an end. These included: to immediately prohibit mandatory pregnancy testing in schools; to prevent the expulsion of pregnant and married girls from school and to re-admit those who had been expelled; to provide special support to students re-admitted after their unfair expulsion, to compensate for the lost years; to provide sexual education for adolescents at school, and child-friendly sexual reproductive and health services; to adopt proactive measures towards the elimination of child marriage; to develop an effective referral mechanism for survivors of sexual violence, including child marriage, and provide psychosocial support, rehabilitation, and reintegration services for the survivors (para. 109).

The practice of the Committee is to allow States 180 days to implement its decisions, after which they should submit a report on the measures taken towards implementation. When a report submitted is unsatisfactory or lacks clarity, the Committee can call a hearing on the implementation of recommendations, which the

Committee has done in the past.[114] Compliance with recommendations is monitored by a rapporteur, who is tasked with reporting back to the Committee on the progress on implementation in each ordinary session. The examination of State periodic reports is also an important opportunity for the Committee to assess the implementation of its decisions, providing a space for constructive dialogue between the Committee and the State on the measures taken and any obstacles concerning compliance.[115] As part of the Committee's repertoire of measures to follow-up on implementation, the Committee has also undertaken on-site visits to States, in which members of the Committee engaged with different stakeholders to better understand the measures effectively adopted by the State.[116]

In the event of non-compliance with its decision, the Committee is empowered to draw the attention of the AU Permanent Representatives Committee and the Executive Council on the matter,[117] which the Committee has in effect done in the past.[118] However, the AU political bodies have, so far, been hesitant in adopting any serious enforcement measures against States for non-compliance.[119] This had led the Committee to explore the recourse to the African Court to seek enforcement of its decisions. Whether this was a possibility allowed by the African system was the focus of the first advisory opinion rendered by the African Court in 2014.[120] After careful examination of the provisions on legal standing under the African Court Protocol, the Court was of the opinion that while the Children's Committee enjoys legal standing to requests advisory opinions, it lacks such standing for the purpose of submitting contentious cases. Nevertheless, the Court expressed its view that it would be 'highly desirable' for the Committee to be granted direct access to the Court also in contentious proceedings.[121] An amendment to allow for this change has been discussed by the AU,[122] and a provision providing the

---

[114] V. Ayeni and A. von Staden, 'Monitoring Second-order Compliance in the African Human Rights System' (2022) 6 *African Human Rights Yearbook* 3, 14.

[115] V. Ayeni and A. von Staden, 'Monitoring Second-order Compliance in the African Human Rights System' (2022) 6 *African Human Rights Yearbook* 3, 18.

[116] B. Mezmur and M. Kahbila, 'Follow-up as a "choice-less choice": towards improving the implementation of decisions on communications of the African Children's Committee' (2018) 2 *African Human Rights Yearbook* 200, 215; V. Ayeni and A. von Staden, ' Monitoring second-order compliance in the African human rights system' (2022) 6 *African Human Rights Yearbook* 3, 17.

[117] ACERWC, 'Revised Guidelines for Consideration of Communications and Monitoring Implementation of Decisions by the African Committee of Experts on the Rights and Welfare of the Child', section XXII.

[118] B. Mezmur and M. Kahbila, 'Follow-up as a "choice-less choice": towards improving the implementation of decisions on communications of the African Children's Committee' (2018) 2 *African Human Rights Yearbook* 200, 219.

[119] V. Ayeni and A. von Staden, 'Monitoring second-order compliance in the African human rights system' (2022) 6 *African Human Rights Yearbook* 3, 22.

[120] ACtHPR, *Request for Advisory Opinion by the African Committee of Experts on the Rights and Welfare of the Child on the Standing of the African Commission of Experts on the Rights and Welfare of the Child before the African Court on Human and Peoples' Rights*, Request 2/2013 (4 December 2014).

[121] ACtHPR, *Request for Advisory Opinion by the African Committee of Experts on the Rights and Welfare of the Child on the Standing of the African Commission of Experts on the Rights and Welfare of the Child before the African Court on Human and Peoples' Rights*, Request 2/2013 (4 December 2014), para. 100.

[122] B. Mezmur and M. Kahbila, 'Follow-up as a "choice-less choice": towards improving the implementation of decisions on communications of the African Children's Committee' (2018) 2 *African Human Rights Yearbook* 200, 221.

Committee with legal standing before the Court appears in the Protocol that envisions the creation of the African Court of Justice and Human Rights—a topic discussed in **Section 8.7**.

8.2 THE AFRICAN COMMISSION ON HUMAN AND PEOPLES' RIGHTS

The African Commission on Human and People's Rights was created by the African Charter as its main monitoring body and tasked with the promotion and protection of human and peoples' rights in Africa.[123] Although the Commission started to operate in 1987 in Addis Ababa, since 1989, it has had its permanent seat in Banjul.[124] It is composed of eleven members who should be 'chosen from amongst African personalities of the highest reputation, known for their high morality, integrity, impartiality and competence in matters of human and peoples' rights', with particular consideration to their legal experience.[125] They are elected through secret ballot by the AU Assembly, from a list of candidates nominated by the States Parties to the African Charter. Each State Party can nominate up to two candidates for election, although only one could be of the nationality of the nominating State.[126] Despite the fact that commissioners serve in their personal capacity,[127] the Commission can sit at a given time no more than one member of a given nationality. Commissioners are elected for a six-year period, with the possibility of re-election.[128] From among its members, the Commission elects its Chairperson and Vice-Chairperson for (renewable) two-year periods.[129]

The Commission does not sit on a permanent basis, with its 2020 Rules of Procedure establishing that it shall hold four ordinary sessions annually, with the ability to hold additional extraordinary sessions.[130] The Commission's work is assisted by its Secretariat, which operates year-round. The AU is responsible for appointing the Commission's Secretary (head of the Secretariat), as well as for providing the staff, services, and facilities for the Commission's operation.[131] Nevertheless, it should be highlighted that

---

[123] African Charter, Art. 30.
[124] G. Baricako, 'The African Charter and African Commission on Human and Peoples' Rights' in M. Evans and R. Murray, *The African Charter of Human and Peoples' Rights: The System in Practice, 1986–2006* (2nd edn., CUP 2008) 1–19, 11.
[125] African Charter, Art. 31.
[126] African Charter, Arts. 33–34.   [127] African Charter, Arts. 31–32.
[128] African Charter, Arts. 33 and 36.
[129] African Charter, Art. 42; ACHPR, Rules of Procedure (adopted by the African Commission on Human and Peoples' Rights during its 27th Extra-Ordinary Session held in Banjul (The Gambia) from 19 February to 04 March 2020), rr. 12–15.
[130] ACHPR, Rules of Procedure, rr. 28–29. The previous Rules indicated a minimum of two annual ordinary sessions. See: Rules of Procedure of the African Commission (2010), r. 26.
[131] African Charter, Arts. 41, 44.

the Commission and its Secretariat have suffered from a lack of adequate resources and budgetary deficits for many years, forcing it to resort to outside voluntary funders.[132]

The African Charter lays down the main functions of the Commission, which are to ensure the protection of human and peoples' rights; to interpret the African Charter's provisions; to promote human and peoples' rights, including undertaking studies, organizing dissemination events, making recommendations to governments, formulating rules for governments to base their legislation upon, and cooperating with other human rights institutions; as well as to perform any other tasks entrusted to it by the AU Assembly of Heads of State and Government.[133]

8.2.1 STATE REPORTING MECHANISM

The African Charter imposes upon States Parties the obligation to submit biannual reports of the measures adopted to give effect to the rights protected by the treaty. Although the Charter is silent as to who is entitled to receive and review such reports, the Commission took it upon itself to fill that gap. The Commission asserted that it was the appropriate organ of the (then) OAU for studying State periodic reports and for providing observations on them; hence, in 1988, it requested the OAU to mandate it with the power to examine them.[134] The Assembly of Heads of State and Government accepted the recommendation and even entrusted the Commission with elaborating guidelines on the form and content the periodic reports should assume.[135] The Commission adopted guidelines for the reporting procedure in 1988, emphasizing that the mechanism should be aimed at creating a 'channel for constructive dialogue between the states and itself on human and peoples' rights'.[136] These guidelines suggest that the States must produce an initial report of general character, describing the basic conditions prevailing in the States and the programmes and institutions relevant to the rights and duties covered in the Charter, which is then to be followed every two years by more detailed reports on the measures adopted to comply with their obligations under each provision of the Charter.[137] As discussed in **Section 8.1.2**, the reporting duties of States also extend to obligations assumed under further treaties, such as the Maputo Protocol and the Protocol of the Rights of Older Persons in Africa.

---

[132] G. Baricako, 'The African Charter and African Commission on Human and Peoples' Rights' in M. Evans and R. Murray, *The African Charter of Human and Peoples' Rights: The System in Practice, 1986-2006* (2nd edn., CUP 2008) 1-19, 13. M. Hansungule, 'African courts and the African Commission on Human and Peoples' Rights' in A. Bösl and J. Diescho, *Human Rights in Africa: Legal Perspectives on their Protection and Promotion* (Konrad Adenauer 2009) 233-271, 252-253; F. Viljoen, *International Human Rights Law in Africa* (2nd edn., OUP 2012) 293-294.

[133] African Charter, Art. 45.

[134] M. Evans and R. Murray, 'The State Reporting Mechanism of the African Charter' in M. Evans and R. Murray, *The African Charter of Human and Peoples' Rights: The System in Practice, 1986-2006* (2nd edn., CUP 2008) 49-75, 52.

[135] M. Evans and R. Murray, 'The State Reporting Mechanism of the African Charter' in M. Evans and R. Murray, *The African Charter of Human and Peoples' Rights: The System in Practice, 1986-2006* (2nd edn., CUP 2008) 49-75, 52.

[136] ACHPR, Guidelines for National Periodic Reports (1988), para. 3.

[137] ACHPR, Guidelines for National Periodic Reports (1988).

Following the submission of a report, States are invited to attend the following session of the Commission for the examination of the report in open session.[138] Unfortunately, only a small number of States Parties have duly fulfilled their reporting obligations, with the vast majority of them having overdue reports.[139] An additional difficulty with the reporting process is that States which have submitted a report may then fail to attend the session for its debate. Faced with the latter problem, the Commission has decided that, following two unsuccessful notifications requesting the presence of the State, the Commission would proceed to examine the report in its absence.[140] After the examination, the Commission formulates 'concluding observations', which are transmitted to the respective State and made public through the Commission's website.[141] Nonetheless, it has been pointed out that, in the past, the Commission has been less than consistent with publicizing its observations on State reports.[142]

8.2.2 SPECIAL MECHANISMS

Over the years, the Commission has created a number of 'special mechanisms', including special rapporteurs, working groups, and committees, to deal with thematic issues concerning the protection of human and peoples' rights, as well as with its internal work. These have included six special rapporteurs, seven working groups, and four committees.[143] Although the actual reasons behind the initial decision to create special mandates are unknown, speculations have led to the belief that each mandate has been a reaction to important political issues in the continent that were not duly addressed by existing procedures. For instance, the creation of the first rapporteurship in 1994 on extrajudicial executions is believed to have been triggered by the egregious Rwandan genocide.[144]

The mandates of the special rapporteurs, who are themselves commissioners, have focused on extrajudicial executions; prisons and conditions of detention and policing in Africa; women's rights; freedom of expression; human rights defenders; and refugees,

---

[138] M. Evans and R. Murray, 'The State Reporting Mechanism of the African Charter' in M. Evans and R. Murray, *The African Charter of Human and Peoples' Rights: The System in Practice, 1986–2006* (2nd edn., CUP 2008) 49–75, 53.

[139] M. Evans and R. Murray, 'The State Reporting Mechanism of the African Charter' in M. Evans and R. Murray, *The African Charter of Human and Peoples' Rights: The System in Practice, 1986–2006* (2nd edn., CUP 2008) 49–75, 54; M. Ssenyonjo, 'Responding to human rights violations in Africa: assessing the role of the African Commission and Court on Human and Peoples' Rights (1987–2018)' (2018) 7 *International Human Rights Law Review* 1, 30. See the statistics of the Commission on compliance with report submission: https://achpr.au.int/sessions-statistics-table (accessed on 17 March 2023).

[140] M. Evans and R. Murray, 'The State Reporting Mechanism of the African Charter' in M. Evans and R. Murray, *The African Charter of Human and Peoples' Rights: The System in Practice, 1986–2006* (2nd edn., CUP 2008) 49–75, 55.

[141] ACHPR, Rules of Procedure, r. 82.

[142] M. Evans and R. Murray, 'The State Reporting Mechanism of the African Charter' in M. Evans and R. Murray, *The African Charter of Human and Peoples' Rights: The System in Practice, 1986–2006* (2nd edn., CUP 2008) 49–75, 67–68.

[143] See: https://achpr.au.int/special-mechanisms (accessed on 14 March 2023).

[144] K. Kariseb, 'Understanding the Nature, Scope and Standard Operating Procedures of the African Commission's Special Procedure Mechanisms (2021) 21 *African Human Rights Law Journal* 149, 152–153.

asylum seekers, internally displaced persons, and migrants in Africa.[145] Under these mandates, rapporteurs can analyse States' domestic legislation; conduct investigative missions to State Parties and make recommendations; undertake promotional visits; elaborate guidelines to improve human rights protection; and produce reports.

Working groups and committees have a similar mandate to that of rapporteurs, but this is exercised collectively, with their membership not limited to commissioners but including independent experts as well.[146] Two different types of working groups/committees have so far been created; those dealing with substantive issues, and those focused on matters pertaining to the Commission's working methods. Among the first, it is possible to count the ones on indigenous communities and minorities; economic, social, and cultural rights; the prevention of torture; death penalty, arbitrary killings, and enforced disappearances; the rights of elderly persons and people with disabilities; extractive industries and environment; and the rights of people living with HIV. As to those focused on internal mechanisms, the Commission has created groups on issues pertaining to its work, budget, communications, and resolutions.

8.2.3 MISSIONS (PROMOTIONAL AND PROTECTIVE)

The Commission is empowered to undertake on-site visits to States Parties to the Charter, subject to the States' consent. These visits can be for different reasons. Those with a protective purpose tend to follow the reception of a number of communications against the State and be aimed at investigating the context surrounding these communications, but can also be undertaken to examine a State's general situation, regardless of the existence of formal communications against it.[147] Moreover, the African Commission is expressly entitled to undertake 'promotional visits'. These visits chiefly aim at engaging in a dialogue with government officials about the Commission's role and the importance of the protection of human and peoples' rights by States, including fulfilling their reporting duties.[148] The importance of promotional visits also lies in spreading awareness of the existence of the regional system and the Commission's work, as limited knowledge about the system and its work has a detrimental effect on its effectiveness.[149] On occasions, both types of visits have also been used by the Commission to obtain information about measures adopted to implement decisions on communications against the State.[150]

---

[145] R. Murray, 'The Special Rapporteurs in the African System' in M. Evans and R. Murray, *The African Charter of Human and Peoples' Rights: The System in Practice, 1986–2006* (2nd edn., CUP 2008) 344–378, 344–345. See: https://www.achpr.org/specialmechanisms (accessed on 29 March 2023).

[146] K. Kariseb, 'Understanding the nature, scope and standard operating procedures of the African Commission's special procedure mechanisms' (2021) 21 *African Human Rights Law Journal* 149, 159, 161.

[147] F. Viljoen, *International Human Rights Law in Africa* (2nd edn., OUP 2012) 344–345.

[148] F. Viljoen, *International Human Rights Law in Africa* (2nd edn., OUP 2012) 379.

[149] M. Ssenyonjo, 'Responding to human rights violations in Africa: assessing the role of the African Commission and Court on Human and Peoples' Rights (1987–2018)' (2018) 7 *International Human Rights Law Review* 1, 42.

[150] R. Murray and D. Long, 'Monitoring the implementation of its own decisions: What role for the African Commission on Human and Peoples' Rights?' (2021) 21 *African Human Rights Law Journal* 836, 845.

8.3 THE AFRICAN COURT ON HUMAN AND PEOPLES' RIGHTS

As aforementioned, unlike the constitutive treaties of the European and Inter-American human rights systems, the African Charter only envisioned the Commission as its monitoring body. It took almost two decades for the creation of a court to be decided through the adoption of the African Court Protocol in 1998.[151] The official drafting process of the African Court Protocol began in 1994, with the OAU Assembly of Heads of State and Government adopting a resolution that requested the organization's Secretary-General to convene an expert meeting to consider the creation of an African Court of Human and Peoples' Rights.[152] Nevertheless, draft texts of such a treaty have already been sketched by legal experts under the auspices of the International Commission of Jurists.[153] The first official draft Protocol was produced in 1995 at a Government Legal Experts' meeting held in Cape Town, which was followed by two further drafts adopted at meetings held in 1997, respectively, in Nouakchott and Addis Ababa.[154] In 1998, the Council of Ministers approved the text of the Protocol and sent it to the Assembly for its adoption.[155] The Protocol entered into force in 2004, following the required thirty-day period after the deposit of the fifteenth instrument of ratification,[156] but it would not be until January 2006 that the election of the first judges took place. While the Court commenced its operation in July 2006 in Addis Ababa, in 2007, its seat was relocated to Arusha, where another international tribunal—the International Criminal Tribunal for Rwanda—had its seat between 1995 and 2015.[157]

The Court consists of eleven judges, elected in an individual capacity from among jurists of high moral character and recognized practical, judicial or academic competence and experience in the field of human and peoples' rights.[158] They should be nationals of Member States of the AU, but only one national of a given State can sit at the Court during a term of office, which lasts for six years—with the possibility of one re-election.[159] Only States Parties to the African Court Protocol can nominate candidates (up to three candidates, from which at least two should be nationals of the nominating State), but the election is by secret ballot by the AU Assembly,[160] which means that States that are not Parties to the Protocol have the right to participate in the election of the Court's judges. This peculiar feature has been the subject of criticisms,

---

[151] African Court Protocol. [152] African Court Protocol, preamble. See: AHG/Res. 230 (XXX), para. 4.
[153] J. Harrington, 'The African Court on Human and People's Rights' in M. Evans and R. Murray, *The African Charter of Human and Peoples' Rights: The System in Practice, 1986–2000* (CUP 2002) 305–334, 315.
[154] African Court Protocol, preamble.
[155] J. Harrington, 'The African Court on Human and People's Rights' in M. Evans and R. Murray, *The African Charter of Human and Peoples' Rights: The System in Practice, 1986–2000* (CUP 2002) 305–334, 315.
[156] F. Viljoen, *International Human Rights Law in Africa* (2nd edn., OUP 2012) 413. See: Protocol to the African Charter on the Establishment of an African Court on Human and Peoples' Rights, Art. 34.
[157] F. Viljoen, *International Human Rights Law in Africa* (2nd edn., OUP 2012) 413.
[158] African Court Protocol, Art. 11.
[159] African Court Protocol, Arts. 11, 15. Similar to the now-adopted practice of the Inter-American Court (see **Section 6.3.1**), judges of the nationality of a State party to a case cannot take part in the hearing of that case. See: African Court Protocol, Art. 20.
[160] African Court Protocol, Arts. 12–14.

including that the requirement to become a Party to the Protocol to gain the right to participate in the election of judges could act as an incentive for increasing the number of States subject to the Court's jurisdiction.[161] Although judges perform their functions in their personal capacity, they are excluded from sitting in cases against their State of nationality,[162] or against the State that nominated them for election.[163]

It is the responsibility of each nominating State to give adequate consideration to gender representation in the nomination process and of the Assembly to ensure that the outcome of the election leads to gender balance and due representation of the main regions and legal traditions of Africa in the Court's composition.[164] Elected judges do not sit at the Court on a permanent basis, which the exception of the Court's President, who performs its functions full-time and is required to reside at the seat of the Court. The Court's President and a Vice-President are elected by the Court for two-year periods and can be re-elected once.[165] The Court holds four ordinary sessions yearly, each lasting for at least four weeks. It is also entitled to hold extraordinary sessions, convened at the President's initiative or at the request of a majority of the judges.[166] The functions of the Court are assisted by a full-time Registry composed of a Registrar, a Deputy-Registrar, and other required staff, all appointed by the Court. The Registry assists the Court in the exercise of its functions and is in charge of its daily administrative tasks.[167]

Like its sister regional courts in Europe and the Americas, the African Court has both advisory and contentious jurisdiction. As will be further discussed in **Section 8.5**, pursuant to the African Court Protocol, the Court may provide an opinion on any legal matter pertaining to the Charter or any other relevant human rights instrument at the request of an AU Member State, the AU or any of its organs, or any other African organization recognized by the AU. The Court's contentious jurisdiction is also truly wide, covering all cases and disputes submitted to it concerning the interpretation and application of the Charter; the Court's constitutive Protocol; and, unlike other regional courts, any other relevant human rights treaty ratified by the State concerned.[168] Consequently, the African Court has on different occasions ruled on breaches of human rights treaties adopted within the framework of the United Nations, such as ICCPR and the Convention on the Elimination of all Forms of Discrimination Against Women (CEDAW),[169] and even on the violation of the Universal Declaration on Human Rights (UDHR), which it confirmed belongs to the realm of customary international law.[170] This

---

[161] E. de Wet, 'The present control machinery under the European Convention on Human Rights: Its future reform and the possible implications for the African Court on Human Rights' (1996) 29 *The Comparative and International Law Journal of Southern Africa* 338, 356–357.

[162] African Court Protocol, Art. 22.   [163] ACtHPR, Rules of Court (1 September 2020), r. 9.3.

[164] African Court Protocol, Arts. 12 and 14.   [165] African Court Protocol, Art. 21.

[166] ACtHPR, Rules of Court, rr. 22–23.   [167] ACtHPR, Rules of Court, rr. 16–21.

[168] African Court Protocol, Art. 3.

[169] ACtHPR, *Lohé Issa Konaté v. Burkina Faso*, (merits) (2014) 1 AfCLR 314, op. paras. 3–8; ACtHPR, *Alex Thomas v. Tanzania* (merits) (2015) 1 AfCLR 465, op. para. vii; ACtHPR, *Mohamed Abubakari v. Tanzania* (merits) (2016) 1 AfCLR 599, op. para. ix.

[170] ACtHPR, *Robert John Penessis v. Tanzania*, App. 13/2015, Judgment (28 November 2019), paras. 85–87 and op. para. v.

ample material jurisdiction has been the source of some concern, as it allows the Court to interpret and apply international treaties that have their own monitoring bodies, such as those adopted under the auspices of the United Nations, which can lead to potential conflicting interpretations of the obligations under such international instruments.[171]

> ACtHPR, *Lohe Issa Konaté v. Burkina Faso* (merits) (2014) 1 AfCLR 314; (reparations) (2016) 1 AfCLR 346.
>
> The case concerned the criminal conviction of a journalist for defamation, public insult, and contempt of court, due to the publication of a series of articles in which a prosecutor was accused of corruption. The applicant was sentenced to a year of imprisonment and the payment of fines equivalent to 3,000 USD and damages in an amount equivalent to 9,000 USD, while the newspaper that had published the articles was suspended for a six-month period. Before the African Court, the applicant alleged that his conviction entailed a breach of freedom of expression, protected under both the African Charter and ICCPR, as well as of the obligation to protect the rights of journalists assumed by the State under the Revised Treaty of the Economic Community of West African States (ECOWAS treaty).
>
> The Court ruled that the conviction imposed was disproportionate to the aim pursued— the protection of the rights and reputation of a public prosecutor—hence, amounted to the violation of freedom of expression as protected under the African Charter, ICCPR, and the ECOWAS treaty (para. 170). In fact, it considered that each of the elements of the conviction—the imprisonment, the fine and damages, and the suspension of publication— entailed different breaches of freedom of expression. Similarly, it ruled that the domestic legislation allowing for the imposition of custodial sentences for the offence of defamation was in itself incompatible with freedom of expression and ordered the State to amend its legislation accordingly (para. 164 and op. para. 8). In its separate judgment on reparations, the Court also ordered Burkina Faso to expunge from the applicant's judicial records the imposed criminal conviction; to revise downwards the amount of fines and damages imposed; and to pay compensation for the material and moral damage suffered by him and his family.

> ACtHPR, *Association pour le Progrès et la Défense des Droits des Femmes Maliennes and the Institute for Human Rights and Development in Africa v. Mali* (merits) (2018) 2 AfCLR 380.
>
> The case concerned the Family Code adopted by Mali in 2011. This important piece of legislation was the outcome of a complex political process, set in motion in the late 1990s with the aim of amending the domestic law to make it comply with Mali's international commitments. However, the draft Code approved by the National Assembly in 2009 was not promulgated by the Executive, due to widespread protests by Islamic movements in opposition to this piece of legislation. The Code finally adopted, in 2011, reflected this religious pressure. Human rights organisations impugned the adopted 2011 Code, considering it in breach of a number of international obligations assumed by Mali, including under the African Children's Charter, the Maputo Protocol, and CEDAW.

---

[171] C. Heyns, 'The African regional human rights system: In need of reform?' (2001) 2 *African Human Rights Law Journal* 155, 166–169; F. Viljoen, *International Human Rights Law in Africa* (2nd edn., OUP 2012) 435–439.

> The Court agreed with the applicants. In particular, it considered that the Code by setting the marriage age for girls at 16, and even allowing marriage at 15 with the consent of the girl's father, was in contravention with the age of 18 set by the Maputo Protocol and with the State's obligation to eliminate practices and traditions harmful towards women and children, under the Children's Charter, the Maputo Protocol, and CEDAW (para. 78). Similarly, by allowing religious marriages in which no procedure was in place to verify the existing consent to marry, the Code breached the State's duties under both the Maputo Protocol and CEDAW to adopt measures to secure that marriage is carried out with the full and free consent of the parties (para. 95). Lastly, by allowing the application of customary and religious law in matters of inheritance, which provided lesser inheritance rights for women and none for those born out of wedlock, the Code was in breach of the right to inheritance for women and natural children, as protected by both the Maputo Protocol and the African Children's Charter (paras. 112 and 115).
>
> Consequently, the Court ordered the State to amend the 2011 Code, bringing it in harmony with the international obligations it breached. It also ordered the State to inform on the implementation of the judgment in a period no longer than two years.

The Court's jurisdiction is not just broad in its material aspect, but legal standing to submit a case to it is also ample.[172] Pursuant to Article 5 of the African Court Protocol, a case can be submitted by the African Commission; a State Party that has lodged a complaint to the Commission; the State Party against which the complaint has been lodged with the Commission; the State Party whose citizen is a victim of a human rights violation; and African Intergovernmental Organizations. The wording of the provision has led to doubts as to whether inter-governmental organizations and State Parties claiming a violation of the rights of their citizens have been granted direct access to the Court without the need to first bring the case to the Commission. While Viljoen has claimed the answer to be in the affirmative with regard to inter-governmental organizations, but in the negative regarding States, which would only be allowed to submit a case to the Court on behalf of their citizens if the Commission had found a violation of rights,[173] the Court's website seems to indicate that both States and inter-governmental organizations would be able to submit cases directly to the Court.[174]

Additionally, the African Court Protocol provides that individuals and NGOs with observer status before the Commission may also institute cases directly before the Court,[175] but only in respect of States Parties that have made a special declaration to

---

[172] O.C. Okafor, *The African Human Rights System, Activist, Forces, and International Institutions* (CUP 2007) 86–87.

[173] F. Viljoen, *International Human Rights Law in Africa* (2nd edn., OUP 2012) 433–434.

[174] See: https://www.african-court.org/wpafc/how-to-file-a-case/ (accessed on 29 March 2023).

[175] To gain observe status before the Commission, NGOs must work in the field of human rights in Africa, have objectives and activities in consonance with the fundamental principles and objectives enunciated in the AU Constitutive Act, the preamble to the African Charter, and the Maputo Protocol; and they should declare their financial resources in their application to the Commission. Moreover, this legal standing is strictly interpreted and does not extend, for example, to trade unions. See: ACHPR, 'Resolution on the Criteria for Granting and Maintaining Observer Status to Non-Governmental Organizations working on Human and Peoples' Rights in Africa', ACHPR/Res. 361(LIX)2016. See also: ACtHPR, *Confederation Syndicale des Travailleurs du Mali v. Mali* (jurisdiction), 25 June 2021.

this effect.[176] In fact, the validity of the Protocol's clause that subordinates individuals and NGOs direct access to the Court to a special declaration has been the subject of unsuccessful litigation before the Court.[177] Over the years, only twelve States Parties have made the declaration allowing direct access to the Court,[178] but four of them had subsequently withdrawn their declaration—Rwanda, in 2016, Tanzania, in 2019, and both Bénin and Côte d'Ivoire in 2020. In the absence of any express provisions within the African Court Protocol regulating the withdrawal of these declarations, the Court was called to rule on their validity when Rwanda first adopted this measure in the context of the *Ingabire Umuhoza v. Rwanda* case. While it accepted the validity of unilateral withdrawals, the Court asserted that these would only take effect after one year following the deposit of the notice of withdrawal.[179]

ACtHPR, *Femi Falana v. African Union* (jurisdiction) (2012) 1 AfCLR 118.

This application was brought to the Court by a Nigerian lawyer. He claimed that the provision of the African Court Protocol subjecting the right to individual petition to the making of an express declaration by States, combined with Nigeria's failure to make such declaration, were depriving him of the enjoyment of rights protected by the African Charter, including the right to a fair hearing and the prohibition of discrimination. Falana requested the Court to declare that Article 34(6) of the African Court Protocol was null and void, as it contravened the letter and spirit of the African Charter. He considered the African Union to be responsible for this situation, as successor of the Organization for African Unity (OAU), the organization under which both the Charter and the African Court Protocol had been adopted.

The Court rejected the case—by a 7-3 majority—affirming that it lacked personal jurisdiction to deal with the matter at stake. The Court explained that its personal jurisdiction only extends to cases brought against States, which need to be Parties to both the Charter and the African Court Protocol, and which must also have made the challenged declaration, when the application is submitted by individuals or NGOs (para. 73).

Conversely, the joint dissenting opinion of Judges Akuffo, Ngoepe, and Thomson, affirmed the Court's personal jurisdiction in the case, but not its material competence to declare a provision of the African Court Protocol null and void. Concerning the Court's jurisdiction *ratione persone*, the dissenting judges affirmed that given that the AU has the right to bring international claims before the Court, a natural legal consequence would be the capacity to also

---

[176] African Court Protocol, Arts. 5.3, 34.6.
[177] ACtHPR, *Femi Falana v. African Union* (jurisdiction) (2012) 1 AfCLR 118; ACtHPR, *Atabong Denis Atemnkeng v. African Union* (jurisdiction) (2013) 1 AfCLR 182.
[178] In chronological order: Burkina Faso (1998), Malawi (2008), Mali (2010), Tanzania (2010), Ghana (2011), Rwanda (2013), Cote d'Ivoire (2013), Bénin (2014), Tunisia (2017), Gambia (2018), Niger (2021), and Guinea Bissau (2021). See: https://www.african-court.org/wpafc/declarations/ (accessed on 29 March 2023).
[179] ACtHPR, *Ingabire Victoire Umuhoza v. Rwanda* (jurisdiction) (2016) 1 AfCLR 562, paras. 67–69.

be sued before it,[180] and as the Charter imposes upon the AU the duty to protect human and peoples' rights, its lack of enforcement would render it moot (dissenting opinion para. 8.1.1).

The dissent further agreed with the applicant that by conditioning access to the Court to an optional declaration by States, Article 34(6) restricts individuals' direct access to the Court, in contravention of the objective, language, and spirit of the Charter; hence, far from enhancing the protection of human rights, it does the very opposite (dissenting opinion para. 16). Nevertheless, the dissenting judges accepted that the Court is a creature of the Protocol and, consequently, the scope of its competence derives from it, which does not empower the Court to declare its provisions null and void. Therefore, the dissent stopped short from declaring Article 34(6) null and void, despite it being in apparent contravention with the Charter (dissenting opinion paras. 17–18).[181]

ACtHPR, *Ingabire Victoire Umuhoza v. Rwanda* (jurisdiction) (2016) 1 AfCLR 562.

The case concerned a Hutu Rwandan politician who, after living abroad for nearly seventeen years, returned to Rwanda to register an opposition political party to participate in upcoming elections. Upon her return, she gave public speeches and interviews in which she spoke about problems with reconciliation and ethnic violence. The authorities considered that her expressions amounted to the crime of minimizing genocide, propagating the ideology of genocide, and threatening State security. She was prosecuted and convicted on charges of spreading the ideology of genocide, as well as on an array of charges against national security, including terrorist related offences. She was initially convicted to eight years of imprisonment, increased to fifteen years on appeal.

The applicant resorted directly to the African Court of Human and People's Rights, as Rwanda had at the time accepted the direct access of individuals. The judgment on merits is further discussed in **Section 9.4.2.1**, but what is relevant here is Rwanda's decision to withdraw its declaration accepting the direct access of individuals to the Court, which it had made on 22 June 2013. Within the context of the application, the Court called for hearings to be held in March 2016, but days before such a date, Rwanda notified the Court that it had withdrawn its declaration and requested the suspension of the planned hearing. The Court decided to proceed with the hearing, which Rwanda did not attend, and later on, allowed the parties to file submissions on the validity of Rwanda's withdrawal.

After confirming that it had jurisdiction to rule on the matter, as master of its own jurisdiction, the Court considered that three main issues needed to be decided concerning Rwanda's withdrawal of its declaration: First, whether it was valid; second, what conditions apply to such a withdrawal; and, third, what were its legal effects (paras. 48 and 52). The

---

[180] While strong supporters of the automatic access of individuals and NGOs to international jurisdictions, we cannot help but find this interpretation of the dissenting judges problematic for a variety of reasons, including that the same logic would lead to finding the Court to have also been granted jurisdiction to find individuals responsible for human rights violations.

[181] The same dissenting judges actually went ahead and pronounced themselves in favour of declaring the provision null and void in an almost identical case decided by the Court the following year. See: ACtHPR, *Atabong Denis Atemnkeng v. African Union* (jurisdiction) (2013) 1 AfCLR 182, dissenting opinion of Judges Akuffo, Ngoepe, and Thomson para. 11.

Court decided that Rwanda was entitled to withdraw its declaration; it considered that while legally based in the African Court Protocol—which does not provide for denunciation—the declaration was a discretionary unilateral act that is separable from it and susceptible to withdrawal (paras. 57–59). However, the Court affirmed that the discretionary character of the withdrawal was not absolute, especially since such a declaration had created a right to access the Court for individuals and groups. Therefore, a withdrawing State should be required to provide prior notice of its intention to deprive individuals of such a right (paras. 60–64).

As to the period of notice, the Court came up with the term of one year, which was based both on a peculiar reading of a paragraph from a ruling of the Inter-American Court of Human Rights—more specifically, from a submission made by the Inter-American Commission, which was not endorsed by the Court[182]—as well as from the provision of treaty denunciation of the 1969 Vienna Convention on the Law of Treaties, which the Court was applying by analogy to the unilateral withdrawal (paras. 63–66).

Consequently, the Court ruled that Rwanda's withdrawal was to have effect following the expiration of the one-year period (i.e. from 1 March 2017) and was not to affect cases pending before it (paras. 67–68). Although the Court might have failed to be strictly clear on the matter, it meant cases pending on 1 March 2017, as the acceptance of the direct access to the Court was to be valid until then.

8.4 THE INDIVIDUAL AND THE AFRICAN HUMAN RIGHTS SYSTEM

Within the African system, individual applications concerning human and peoples' rights violations against States Parties to the African Charter can be submitted to both the Commission and the Court. However, as discussed in **Section 8.3**, individual cases to the Court can only proceed against States that are Parties to the African Court Protocol and have also made the express declaration to this effect.

8.4.1 COMMUNICATIONS BEFORE THE COMMISSION

Although the Charter did not provide the Commission with an explicit mandate to consider individual communications, the Commission confirmed its authority to receive and examine this type of complaints when drafting its Rules of Procedure.[183] Since 1988, when the first individual communication was sent to the Commission, this body has

---

[182] It might seem surprising that the Court supported this conclusion with reference to a ruling of the Inter-American Court in which the latter rejected the possibility of withdrawing unilateral declarations without denouncing the Convention itself. However, a stark distinction between the American Convention and both the African Charter and the African Court Protocol is that the former provides for its denunciation, while the African treaties are silent on the matter. See: ACtHPR, *Ingabire Victoire Umuhoza v. Rwanda* (jurisdiction) (2016) 1 AfCLR 562, para. 63; IACtHR, *Ivcher Bronstein v. Peru*. Competence. Judgment of September 24, 1999. Series C No. 54, paras. 36, 39–40.

[183] R. Murray, 'Decisions by the African Commission on Individual Communications under the African Charter on Human and Peoples' Rights' (1997) 46 *International and Comparative Law Quarterly* 412, 413. See also: Communication 147/95–149/96, *Sir Dawda K. Jawara v. Gambia* (The), 11 May 2000, para. 42.

received more than 600 communications and rendered more than 150 decisions on merits.[184] The legal standing for submitting a communication to the Commission is rather broad, as it can be submitted by the victim(s), by other individual(s) on their behalf, or by any NGO. All communication must be written and addressed to the Commission's Secretary in one of the working languages of the AU, which include Arabic, English, French, Kiswahili, Portuguese, Spanish, and any other African language.[185] Given that the Charter protects not only human rights but also peoples' rights, the Commission has also admitted communications in the public interest (as *actio popularis*).[186]

A successful communication progresses through four different stages: seizure, admissibility, merits, and remedies.[187] The initial seizure of a communication by the Commission is to determine whether it, *prima facie*, reveals a violation of the Charter.[188] This is a role mainly undertaken by the Commission's Secretary.[189] It is for the Secretary to ensure that communications contain the name, nationality, address, and signature of the person(s) submitting them; the name of the victim(s), if different from the complainant(s), and an account of the alleged violations, including the State allegedly responsible for them. The Secretary has sixty days from receipt of a complaint to communicate, in writing, the decision on seizure to the parties.[190] Then, it would request the complainant to submit their arguments and evidence on the admissibility and merits and, within sixty days and upon reception of this submission, transfer the communication to the State for a reply.[191] The State also has sixty days to submit its reply to the communication, but only thirty days to submit any preliminary objections to its admissibility,[192] which would be considered by the Commission before any other matter relating to the communication.[193]

The following stage is the examination of the admissibility of the communication, which is usually decided on the written claims.[194] Interestingly, before deciding on admissibility, the Commission could opt to refer the case directly to the Court, subject

---

[184] C. Okoloise, 'Circumventing Obstacles to the Implementation of Recommendations by the African Commission on Human and Peoples' Rights' (2018) 18 *African Human Rights Law Journal* 27, 44; V. Ayeni, 'The African Human Rights Architecture: Reflections on the Instruments and Mechanisms within the African Human Rights System' (2019) 10 *Beijing Law Review* 302, 308; V. Ayeni and A. von Staden, 'Monitoring second-order compliance in the African human rights system' (2022) 6 *African Human Rights Yearbook* 3, 8.

[185] ACHPR, Rules of Procedure, r. 38; Protocol on Amendments to the Constitutive Act of the African Union (adopted 11 July 2003, entered into force 19 March 2018), Art. 11.

[186] F. Viljoen, *International Human Rights Law in Africa* (2nd edn., OUP 2012) 305. See: ACHPR, *Social and Economic Rights Action Center (SERAC) and Center for Economic and Social Rights (CESR) v. Nigeria*, Communication 155/96 (2001).

[187] F. Viljoen, 'Communications under the African Charter: procedure and admissibility' in M. Evans and R. Murray, *The African Charter of Human and Peoples' Rights: The System in Practice, 1986–2006* (2nd edn., CUP 2008) 76–138, 77.

[188] F. Adolu, 'A View from the Inside: the role of the Secretariat' in M. Evans and R. Murray, *The African Charter of Human and Peoples' Rights: The System in Practice, 1986–2006* (2nd edn., CUP 2008) 316–343, 329. See: ACHPR, *African Freedom of Expression Exchange & 15 Others (Represented by FOI Attorneys) v. Algeria & 27 Others*, Communication 742/20, para. 42.

[189] ACHPR, Rules of Procedure, r. 115.

[190] ACHPR, Rules of Procedure, r. 115.3.8. [191] ACHPR, Rules of Procedure, r. 116.

[192] ACHPR, Rules of Procedure, rr. 116.2 and 117.1. [193] ACHPR, Rules of Procedure, r. 117.4.

[194] R. Murray, *The African Charter on Human and Peoples' Rights: A Commentary* (OUP 2019) 685.

to the respondent State being Party to the African Court Protocol and consenting to the referral of the case.[195] Alternatively, the Commission, or a working group of its members, decides on whether the Commission should examine the merits of the communication. Pursuant to the Commission's Rules, its decision on the admissibility or inadmissibility of a communication is subject to review upon the emergence of a new fact, provided that the discovered fact is decisive and was not known to the party seeking the review—and that such lack of knowledge was not due to negligence.[196]

When a communication is found admissible, the Commission proceeds to the examination of the merits, which takes place at a different session. While the Commission's main source of evidence remains written materials,[197] the holding of a hearing before the adoption of a decision has become usual practice.[198] According to its current Rules, '[t]he Commission shall decide on a communication within one year from the time the [c]ommunication becomes ripe for a decision on the merits'.[199] Over the years, the decisions of the Commission have become longer, and the reasoning more sophisticated.[200] As with admissibility, the Commission's decision on merits is subject to review upon the emergence of a new fact, provided the fact is decisive and was not known to the party seeking the review—and that such a lack of knowledge was not due to negligence.[201]

The Commission can defer the issue of reparations to a subsequent session and is entitled to invite the parties to make additional written submissions or to hold a separate oral hearing to this end.[202] The Commission's practice on reparations has certainly evolved through time. In its early years, the Commission was silent on the question of remedies, and only later started to recommend respondent States to adopt the necessary measures to comply with their obligations under the Charter, but without specifying these measures. More recently, the Commission began to adopt more detailed remedial orders,[203] including the need to amend domestic legislation to bring it in conformity with the Charter;[204] the duty to investigate violations and prosecute

---

[195] ACHPR, Rules of Procedure, r. 130.

[196] The timeframes for the review of admissibility decisions vary depending on whether the decision was the admissibility of the communication—up to sixty days from the transmission of the decision—or its inadmissibility—up to 180 days from the discovery of the fact, but no more than three years from the transmission of the decision. See: ACHPR, Rules of Procedure, r. 119.

[197] F. Viljoen, *International Human Rights Law in Africa* (2nd edn., OUP 2012) 322.

[198] R. Murray, *The African Charter on Human and Peoples' Rights: A Commentary* (OUP 2019) 673.

[199] ACHPR, Rules of Procedure, r. 120.3.

[200] F. Viljoen, *International Human Rights Law in Africa* (2nd edn., OUP 2012) 336.

[201] The review can be sought up to 180 days from the discovery of the new fact and no later than three years from when the decision was transmitted to the parties. See: ACHPR, Rules of Procedure, r. 122.

[202] ACHPR, Rules of Procedure, r. 121.

[203] F. Viljoen, 'Communications under the African Charter: procedure and admissibility' in M. Evans and R. Murray, *The African Charter of Human and Peoples' Rights: The System in Practice, 1986–2006* (2nd edn., CUP 2008) 76–138, 79–80; F. Viljoen, *International Human Rights Law in Africa* (2nd edn., OUP 2012) 337–339; M. Ssenyonjo, 'Responding to human rights violations in Africa: assessing the role of the African Commission and Court on Human and Peoples' Rights (1987–2018)' (2018) 7 *International Human Rights Law Review* 1, 12–14.

[204] ACHPR, *Scanlen and Holderness v. Zimbabwe*, Communication 297/05 (2009), para. 125.

the wrongdoers;[205] or the obligation to pay compensation to the victims,[206] having even started to quantify the awards to be paid.[207] When a Commission's decision requests the respondent State to adopt specific measures, the parties to the case should inform the Commission, within 180 days, of all action taken to implement the decision.[208]

It is worth emphasizing that the Commission's decision should be considered legally binding,[209] despite certain resistance on the matter.[210] The compulsory character of the Commission's decisions can be derived from the fact that States are bound to comply with their obligations under the Charter, as interpreted by its monitoring body in individual cases.[211] To this, Viljoen has added that the binding nature of the Commission's decision also follows from the legal status granted to them by the AU Assembly, when approving the Commission's Activity Report.[212] Unfortunately, the African Court did not seem to endorse this stance, having referred in the past to the Commission's recommendations as not binding.[213]

8.4.1.1 Implementation of recommendations

Despite the compulsory character of the Commission's decisions, their implementation by States remains one of the main challenges of the regional system. Although the Commission has not provided specific data, it has asserted for years that the level of compliance with its recommendations is low.[214] This can be explained by different factors, such as the lack of political will of certain States to comply with the Commission's decisions, the concurrent absence of a will in the political organs of the AU to adopt measures to promote compliance, as well as the Commission's historically suboptimal regime of monitoring implementation.[215]

The mechanisms for monitoring implementation of the Commission's decisions have been an *ad hoc* development of this body, making recourse to some of its existing procedures, such as the State reporting mechanism and on-site country visits, as well as to the sending

---

[205] ACHPR, *Movement Burkinabé des Droits de l'Homme et des Peuples v. Burkina Faso*, Communication 204/97 (2001).

[206] ACHPR, *Mekongo v. Cameroon*, Communication 59/91 (2000); ACHPR, *Movement Burkinabé des Droits de l'Homme et des Peuples v. Burkina Faso*, Communication 204/97 (2001).

[207] ACHPR, *Jean-Marie Atangana Mebara v. Cameroon*, Communication 416/12 (2015); ACHPR, *Institute for Human Rights and Development in Africa and Others v. Democratic Republic of Congo*, Communication 393/10 (2016).

[208] ACHPR, Rules of Procedure, r. 125.1.

[209] Resolution on the Importance of the Implementation of the Recommendations of the African Commission on Human and Peoples' Rights, adopted at the Commission's 40th session, November 2006 (Final Communiqué of the 40th session).

[210] The reaction of Botswana to one of the Commission's decisions is well-known, including a diplomatic note stating: 'the Government has made its position clear; that it is not bound by the decision of the Commission'. See: ACHPR, 'Combined 32nd and 33rd Activity Report', EX.CL/782(XXII) Rev. 2 (2013), p. 9.

[211] V. Ayeni, 'The African Human Rights Architecture: Reflections on the Instruments and Mechanisms within the African Human Rights System' (2019) 10 *Beijing Law Review* 302, 309.

[212] F. Viljoen, *International Human Rights Law in Africa* (2nd edn., OUP 2012) 339.

[213] ACtHPR, *Johnson v. Ghana* (jurisdiction and admissibility) (2019) 3 AfCLR 99, para. 54.

[214] See, among many: ACHPR, 41st Activity Report (2016) 11; 42nd Activity Report (2017) 14; 45th Activity Report (2018) 13; 47th Activity Report (2019) 11; 48th and 49th Activity Report (2020) 16.

[215] M. Ssenyonjo, 'Responding to human rights violations in Africa: assessing the role of the African Commission and Court on Human and Peoples' Rights (1987–2018)' (2018) 7 *International Human Rights Law Review* 1, 20.

of letters to States enquiring about the measures adopted and, occasionally, even holding hearings on implementation.[216] A specific follow-up mechanism was finally enshrined in the Commission's 2010 Rules[217] and, as mentioned in **Section 8.2.2**, in 2011 the Commission also created a Working Group on Communications.[218] The Working Group is composed of a number of commissioners—which has fluctuated from three to seven over the years—the Commission's Secretary, and four legal officers.[219] Among its tasks, this Group is in charge of coordinating the follow-up of the Commission's decisions and with collecting information on the status of decisions' implementation, to inform the Commission about it at each ordinary session.[220] Unfortunately, the Working Group has highlighted that the lack of actual information on implementation provided by the States makes it extremely difficult to duly assess the level of compliance with the Commission's decisions.[221]

The lack of compliance with its recommendations allows the Commission to refer the matter to the attention of the competent organs of the AU, with a request for the adoption of the necessary measures for the implementation of the decisions.[222] However, the AU Executive Council merely encourages Member States, in rather generic terms, to comply with the decisions of the Commission;[223] encouragement that does not seem to be enough to improve implementation.[224] This has led to pleas for a paradigm shift in the relation between the Commission and the AU political bodies.[225] While the former

---

[216] R Murray, 'Confidentiality and the implementation of the decisions of the African Commission on Human and Peoples' Rights' (2019) 19 *African Human Rights Law Journal* 1, 18–19; V. Ayeni and A. von Staden, 'Monitoring second-order compliance in the African human rights system' (2022) 6 *African Human Rights Yearbook* 3, 8–9.

[217] Commission's Rules of Procedure (2010), r. 112.

[218] Resolution Establishing a Working Group on Communications and Appointment of Members—ACHPR/Res. 194(L)2011.

[219] Resolution on the Expansion of the Mandate of the Working Group on Communications and modifying its Composition—ACHPR/Res. 225(LII)2012; Resolution on the Renewal of the Mandate of the Working Group on Communications—ACHPR/Res. 255(LIV)2013; Resolution on the Renewal of the Mandate and Reconstitution of the Working Group on Communications—ACHPR/Res. 314(LVII)2015; Resolution on the Renewal of the Mandate and Reconstitution of the Working Group on Communications—ACHPR/Res. 385(LXI)2017; Resolution on the Renewal of the Mandate, Appointment of the Chairperson and Reconstitution of the Working Group on Communications—ACHPR/Res. 462 (LXVI) 2020.

[220] Resolution on the Expansion of the Mandate of the Working Group on Communications and modifying its Composition—ACHPR/Res. 225(LII)2012.

[221] R. Murray and D. Long, 'Monitoring the implementation of its own decisions: What role for the African Commission on Human and Peoples' Rights?' (2021) 21 *African Human Rights Law Journal* 836, 843.

[222] ACHPR, Rules of Procedure, rr. 125.8, 138.

[223] AU Executive Council, 'Decision on the Activities of the African Commission on Human and Peoples' Rights' EX.CL/Dec.948(XXX) (2017), para. 4; AU Executive Council, 'Decision on the Activities of the African Commission on Human and People's Rights' EX.CL/Dec.1089(XXXIII) (2018), para. 9; AU Executive Council, 'Decision on the Activities of the African Commission on Human and People's Rights' EX.CL/Dec.113(XXXVIII) (2021), para. 8; AU Executive Council, 'Decision on the Activities of the African Commission on Human and Peoples' Rights' EX.CL/Dec.1154(XL) (2022), para. 8.

[224] C. Okoloise, 'Circumventing Obstacles to the Implementation of Recommendations by the African Commission on Human and Peoples' Rights' (2018) 18 *African Human Rights Law Journal* 27, 50; V. Ayeni and A. von Staden, 'Monitoring second-order compliance in the African human rights system' (2022) 6 *African Human Rights Yearbook* 3, 22.

[225] C. Okoloise, 'Circumventing Obstacles to the Implementation of Recommendations by the African Commission on Human and Peoples' Rights' (2018) 18 *African Human Rights Law Journal* 27, 47–49.

needs to improve its recourse to the latter, in the many cases of non-compliance, the AU political bodies should start adopting serious measures to promote implementation of the Commission's decisions.

Alternatively, the widespread non-compliance with the Commission's decisions could lead the Commission to submit at least some of these cases to the African Court when the respective States are Parties to the African Court Protocol. For unknown reasons, this is a largely unexplored avenue. In fact, the Commission's unwillingness to refer cases to the Court has led to a case against it before the Court,[226] which was, nonetheless, swiftly rejected due to evident deficiencies with jurisdictional matters.[227]

ACtHPR, *Femi Falana v. African Commission on Human and Peoples' Rights* (jurisdiction) (2015) 1 AfCLR 499

The application was submitted by the same Nigerian lawyer who brought the case against the AU (see **Section 8.3**). He claimed that despite the widespread and systematic violations of human rights taking place in Burundi, the African Commission was failing to bring communications lodged against the State to the Court. He, therefore, requested the Court to order the Commission to submit to it a particular communication, which had been initiated before the Commission in May 2010.

The Court, unanimously, rejected the case for lack of personal jurisdiction. It ruled that the respondent was an entity that is not a State Party to the Charter and Protocol; hence, the Court had no jurisdiction *ratione personae* over it. Furthermore, the Court decided to clarify that the Commission and Court are independent, yet mutually reinforcing, partner institutions; thus, one does not have the power to compel the other to adopt any measures.

In his separate opinion, Judge Ouguergouz felt compelled to emphasize that this was the fourth occasion on which the Court rendered an actual judgment under circumstances in which it was evident that it lacked personal jurisdiction, given that they were brought against non-State actors. He proposed that, in the future, this type of decision could be dismissed by way of a letter from the Registry to preserve the Court's limited human and financial resources to deal with the increasing number of cases it receives.

The African Court Protocol is clear in that the Commission enjoys legal standing to submit cases to the Court.[228] The Commission's current Rules include a whole Part that regulates its relation with the Court, but unlike its 2010 Rules, they are silent as to the conditions that govern the referral of a case. The Commission's 2010 Rules envisioned four specific scenarios for referral to the Court: cases of non-compliance with the Commission's

---

[226] ACtHPR, *Femi Falana v. African Commission on Human and Peoples' Rights* (jurisdiction) (2015) 1 AfCLR 499.

[227] While technically unsuccessful, the case had been said to achieve the intended purpose of drawing attention to the existent problems involving compliance with the Commission's decisions and the lack of use of the Court to improve the situation. See: C. Okoloise, 'Circumventing Obstacles to the Implementation of Recommendations by the African Commission on Human and Peoples' Rights' (2018) 18 *African Human Rights Law Journal* 27, 55.

[228] African Court Protocol, Art. 5.1.a.

recommendations; cases of non-compliance with its provisional measures; cases of serious violations of human rights; as well as whenever the Commission deemed it 'necessary'.[229] Surprisingly, thus far, the Commission has only submitted three cases to the Court, and none of these concerned the lack of compliance with its recommendations.[230] The fact that many States against which recommendations had been adopted were not Parties to the African Court Protocol only provides a partial explanation to the Commission's reluctance to submitting cases to the Court in circumstances that reveal clear non-compliance.[231] The Commission's actual lack of knowledge as to the level of compliance with its own recommendations provides further clarifications on the matter.[232]

Certainly, strengthening the system demands the reversal of this situation, with the Commission beginning to take advantage of the Court's existence to improve the level of compliance with human rights obligations by the States Parties to the African Court Protocol. While an objection to this has been raised by Murray and Long, suggesting that the referral of cases with unfulfilled recommendations entails an acknowledgement of the Commission's own weakness, we reject such an interpretation.[233] A Commission and Court working in cooperation to enhance compliance with international human rights obligations would be nothing but a clear sign of healthy synergy, in a regional human rights system that counts more than one monitoring body. Concordantly, the silence of the Commission's current Rules as to the conditions for submitting a case to the Court should be replaced by clear criteria under which the Commission will seize the Court.

8.4.2 THE CASE BEFORE THE COURT

As discussed in **Section 8.3**, different actors can bring cases to the Court. These include the African Commission,[234] both the State Party engaged in the case before the Commission and the State Party whose citizen is found to be a victim of a human rights violation by the Commission, and African Intergovernmental Organizations. Yet, the vast majority of cases have been brought to the Court by individuals and NGOs, in respect of the dozen States Parties that have made the needed special declaration to this effect.[235]

---

[229] Commission's Rules of Procedure (2010), r. 118.

[230] The first case against Libya concerned serious violations and was struck out due to the Commission's own inaction, and both subsequent cases involved the lack of compliance with provisional measures. See: ACtHPR, *African Commission on Human and Peoples' Rights v. Libya* (order) (2013) 1 AfCLR 21, para. 1; ACtHPR, *African Commission on Human and Peoples' Rights v. Libya* (merits) (2016) 1 AfCLR 153; ACtHPR, *African Commission on Human and Peoples' Rights v. Kenya* (merits) (2017) 2 AfCLR 9, paras. 4–5.

[231] M. Ssenyonjo, 'Responding to human rights violations in Africa: assessing the role of the African Commission and Court on Human and Peoples' Rights (1987–2018)' (2018) 7 *International Human Rights Law Review* 1, 38.

[232] R. Murray and D. Long, 'Monitoring the implementation of its own decisions: What role for the African Commission on Human and Peoples' Rights?' (2021) 21 *African Human Rights Law Journal* 836, 849–850.

[233] R. Murray and D. Long, 'Monitoring the implementation of its own decisions: What role for the African Commission on Human and Peoples' Rights?' (2021) 21 *African Human Rights Law Journal* 836, 850.

[234] Unfortunately, when a case is brought to the Court by the Commission, this body is considered to be acting as the applicant, with the consequential loss of legal standing by the individual or NGO who submitted the original communication. See: F. Viljoen, *International Human Rights Law in Africa* (2nd edn., OUP 2012) 441–444; ACtHPR, Rules of Court, r. 36.3.

[235] African Court Protocol, Arts. 5.3, 34.6.

The Court's website provides a form for individual cases that can be completed in any of the Court's official languages—Arabic, English, French, Kiswahili, Portuguese, Spanish, and any other African language[236]—and which can be sent to the Court by post, courier, email, or fax.[237] The procedure before the Court is mainly written. Upon reception of an application, the Court's Registrar transfers it to the respondent State, which has ninety days to submit its pleadings covering admissibility, merits, and reparations. Following this, the applicant is granted forty-five days to file a reply.[238] The Court is entitled to order the production of any evidence that it considers conducive, including the holding of hearings to hear the parties (or their representatives), witnesses, or experts.[239] It can also request any person or institution of its choice to express an opinion or submit a report to it. The Court may, as well, assign one or more judges to conduct an enquiry, carry out an on-site visit, or take evidence in any other manner.[240]

The Court conducts a preliminary examination of its jurisdiction and the admissibility of the application. Only if the Court finds that it has jurisdiction over the matter and considers the case to fulfil all admissibility requirements, can it proceed to decide on the merits of the case. The Court's decision should be reasoned and indicate whether violations of human or peoples' rights have been found and the legal grounds for these. If the Court finds there have been violations, it should also make appropriate orders to remedy them, including the payment of fair compensation.[241] The Court's judgment is final and binding on the respondent State, which undertakes to comply with the judgment and guarantee its execution.[242] The judgment should be read in open court—or, under exceptional circumstances, in a virtual manner[243]—and is also notified both to the parties and to the AU Executive Council (formerly, the Council of Ministers), which should monitor its execution.[244]

Notwithstanding the impossibility of appeal against the Court's judgments,[245] these are subject to rectification, interpretation, and review.[246] A rectification may proceed due to clerical errors and can be pursued by the Court of its own motion or at the request of a party.[247] Requests for interpretation of a judgment should be aimed at the clarification of aspects considered essential for the execution of the decision, and hence should be focused on the operative provisions of the judgment.[248] The review of a judgment only proceeds when a party discovers a new fact or evidence, susceptible of having a decisive influence in the decision, and which was unknown to said party— and could not have been known with due diligence—at the time of the adoption of the

---

[236] ACtHPR, Rules of Court, rr. 27, 40.
[237] See: https://www.african-court.org/wpafc/how-to-file-a-case/ (accessed on 29 March 2023).
[238] ACtHPR, Rules of Court, rr. 42, 44.
[239] African Court Protocol, Art. 26; ACtHPR, Rules of Court, rr. 30, 55.
[240] ACtHPR, Rules of Court, r. 55.   [241] African Court Protocol, Art. 27.
[242] African Court Protocol, Arts. 28.2, 30.
[243] African Court Protocol, Arts. 28.5; ACtHPR, Rules of Court, r. 74.
[244] African Court Protocol, Art. 29.   [245] African Court Protocol, Arts. 28.2.
[246] African Court Protocol, Arts. 28.3, 28.4; ACtHPR, Rules of Court, rr. 77–79.
[247] A party's request for rectification should be submitted within a month from the date of the notification of the judgment. See: ACtHPR, Rules of Court, r. 79.
[248] A request for interpretation should be submitted within twelve months from the date of notification. See: ACtHPR, Rules of Court, r. 77.

judgment.[249] Moreover, the Court's 2020 Rules introduced a new provision that applies to judgments rendered by the Court in default—with a party failing to appear before the Court. This innovation is a clear response to the backlashes experienced by the Court in recent years, with certain States refusing to engage with cases against them—a trend chiefly illustrated by Rwanda, following the withdrawal of its declaration concerning direct access to individuals and NGOs to the Court.[250] Under this new rule, the Court can set aside a judgment rendered in default if, within a year from the notification of the decision, the defaulting party shows 'good cause' for their lack of appearance.[251]

Figure 8.1 shows the process of an individual communication or case before the African Commission and the African Court of Human and Peoples' Rights lodged by a person, group of persons, or NGO.

8.4.2.1 Reparations

Similar to that of the Inter-American Court on Human Rights (discussed in **Section 6.4.3**), the African Court has been given a wide remedial power. Indeed, Article 27 of the African Court Protocol is rather explicit as to the Court's reparations not being limited to the payment of compensation but extending to all 'appropriate orders to remedy the violation'. The Court's interpretation of this provision has led it to affirm that its measures of reparations should be 'adequate, effective and comprehensive; be proportional to the gravity of the violations and the harm suffered; and address all of the kinds of harm suffered by the victim'.[252]

In the exercise of its broad remedial faculties, the Court has ordered States to adopt a range of measures of reparation, to redress both the pecuniary and non-pecuniary damage suffered by the victims, including measures of restitution, rehabilitation, satisfaction, and guarantees of non-repetition.[253] For instance, having found criminal convictions imposed in breach of the African Charter, the Court has ordered the immediate release of a victim still in prison,[254] the expunging of criminal convictions,[255] and the partial rehearing of cases.[256] Similarly, having found domestic legislation, including the State's constitution, to be incompatible with the obligations emerging

---

[249] A request for review should be submitted within six months after the requesting party acquires knowledge of the fact or evidence, which in no case can be more than five years after the delivery of the decision. See: ACtHPR, Rules of Court, r. 78.

[250] A Rachovitsa, 'The judicial function of the African Court on Human and Peoples' Rights in default judgments: the developments set forth in the Léon Mugesera case' (2022) 6 *African Human Rights Yearbook* 343, 349–350.

[251] ACtHPR, Rules of Court, r. 63.

[252] ACtHPR, 'Comparative Study on the Law and Practice of Reparations for Human Rights Violations' (September 2019) p. 2.

[253] ACtHPR, 'Comparative Study on the Law and Practice of Reparations for Human Rights Violations' (September 2019) pp. 1–3.

[254] ACtHPR, *Robert John Penessis v. Tanzania*, App. 13/2015, Judgment (28 November 2019), op. para. xii.

[255] ACtHPR, *Lohé Issa Konaté v. Burkina Faso* (reparations) (2016) 1 AfCLR 346, op. para. i.

[256] ACtHPR, *Ally Rajabu and others v. Tanzania*, App. 7/2015, Judgment (28 November 2019), op. para. xvi.

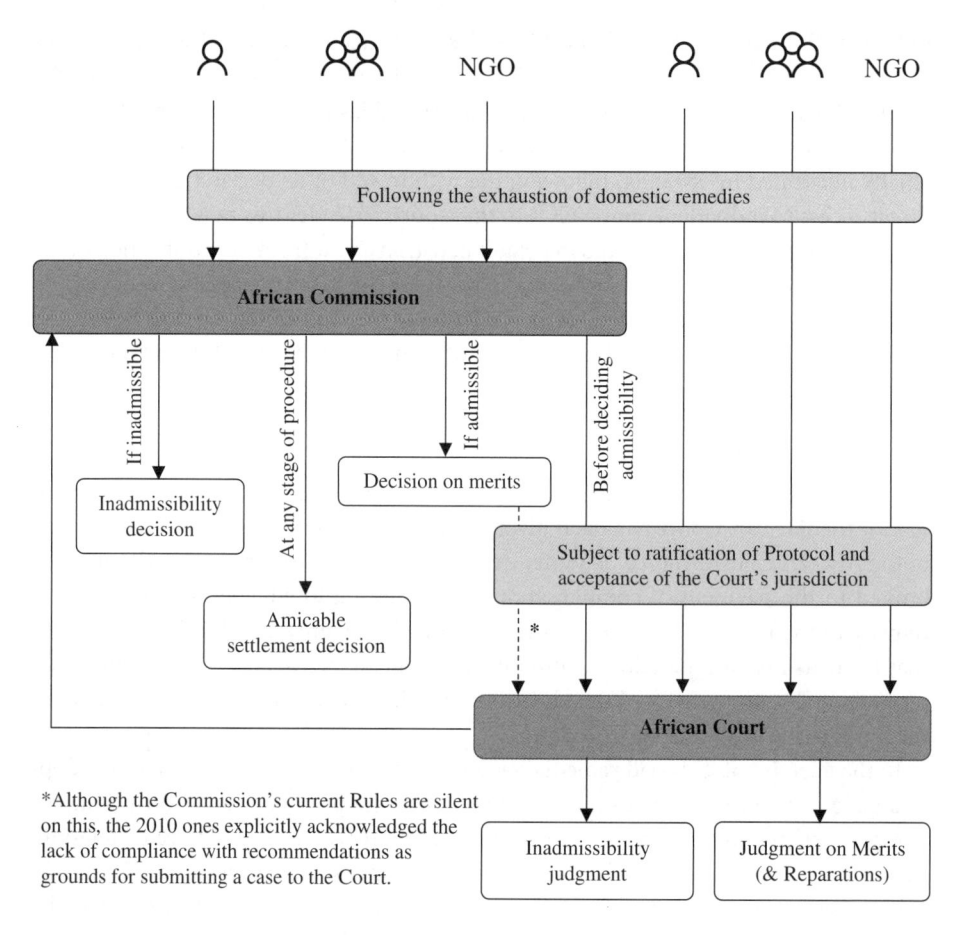

Figure 8.1 Process of an individual communication/case before the African Commission and the African Court of Human and Peoples' Rights

from the Charter, the Court has instructed States to amend such norms.[257] Moreover, in cases of impunity surrounding serious human rights violations, the Court has ordered the reopening of criminal investigations with a view to apprehend, prosecute, and bring to justice the perpetrators of such crimes.[258] In addition to these, and following the established case law of the Inter-American Court, the African Court has imposed upon States the duty to publicize its findings, by publishing its judgment (or a summary of it) on official governmental websites.[259]

---

[257] ACtHPR, *Tanganyika Law Society, Legal and Human Rights Centre and Reverend Christopher R. Mtikila v. Tanzania* (merits) (2013) 1 AfCLR 34, para. 126.3; ACtHPR, *Ally Rajabu and others v. Tanzania*, App. 7/2015, Judgment (28 November 2019), op. para. xv; ACtHPR, *Jebra Kambole v. Tanzania*, App. 18/2018, Judgment (28 November 2019), op. para. viii.

[258] ACtHPR, *Beneficiaries of Late Norbert Zongo Abdoulaye Nikiema, Ernest Zongo and Blise Ilboudo & the Burkinabe Movement on Human and Peoples' Rights v. Burkina Faso* (reparations), 1 AfCLR 258, para. 109 and op. para. ix.

[259] ACtHPR, *Lohé Issa Konaté v. Burkina Faso* (reparations) (2016) 1 AfCLR 346, op. para. viii; ACtHPR, *Ally Rajabu and others v. Tanzania*, App. 7/2015, Judgment (28 November 2019), op. para. xvii; ACtHPR, *Jebra Kambole v. Tanzania*, App. 18/2018, Judgment (28 November 2019), op. para. ix.

ACtHPR, *Robert John Penessis v. Tanzania*, Judgment (28 November 2019).

The case concerned an individual claiming to be a national of Tanzania who had been arrested, detained, and convicted for illegal entry and presence in the territory of the respondent State. Following legal proceedings, he was sentenced to a hefty fine (80,000 Tanzanian Shillings) or, in default, to two years imprisonment and ten strokes of the cane; a sentence upheld by two higher courts, with the exception of the physical punishment aspect, which was set aside.

The African Court ruled that the applicant's right to nationality had been breached. It asserted that even though the Charter does not explicitly provide protection for such a right, it is recognized by the UDHR, which has international customary law status, and could also be considered implicitly protected by the right to dignity, which is recognized by the African Charter (paras. 84–87 and 103). Following said finding, the Court ruled that the applicant's arrest, conviction, and imprisonment all became unlawful, which it found in breach of his right to liberty and freedom of movement (Articles 6 and 12). Consequently, the Court ordered the respondent State to proceed to the immediate release of the victim, in addition to the payment of compensation, to him and his mother, for the moral damage suffered by them due to the violations.

ACtHPR, *Jebra Kambole v. Tanzania*, Judgment (15 July 2020)

The case concerned the compatibility of a constitutional provision of Tanzania with the African Charter—in particular, with the prohibition of discrimination and the right to a fair trial—in that it prohibited the domestic courts from inquiring into the election of a presidential candidate after the Electoral Commission had declared a winner.

The Court considered the provision at stake to be at odds with the prohibition of discrimination, since it treated citizens that may wish to challenge a presidential election differently (and less favourably) to citizens with grievances other than those concerned with such matters, and the distinction did not appear to be necessary and reasonable in a democratic society (paras. 76–77 and 82–83). The Court also found the constitutional provision to be in breach of the right to a fair trial, given that it ousted the jurisdiction of the domestic courts to consider challenges to a presidential election after a winner had been declared (paras. 103–104). Consequently, the Court ordered the respondent State to amend its Constitution in accordance with its judgment within a two-year period.

8.4.2.2 Compliance with the Court's judgments

By the end of 2022, the Court had received a total of 330 cases and finalized 172 of them.[260] However, one of the major challenges faced by the Court is the lack of States' cooperation in implementing its judgments, with some States failing to comply at all with the decisions rendered, and some openly indicating that they do not intend to comply.[261] Pursuant to the African Court Protocol, the Court must submit to each regular session of the AU Assembly, a report on its annual work, specifying the cases

---

[260] See: https://www.african-court.org/cpmt/statistic (accessed on 29 March 2023).
[261] ACtHPR, Activity Report of the African Court on Human and Peoples' Rights (2021), EX.CL/1258(XXXVIII), pp. 13–14.

in which a State has not complied with a judgment,[262] while the Council of Ministers (now, the Executive Council) is charged with monitoring the execution of judgments on behalf of the Assembly.[263] Sadly, neither the Executive Council nor the AU Assembly has taken any serious enforcement measures against non-complying States.[264]

It has taken until 2018 for actions to be set in motion for the adoption of an appropriate mechanism to assist the Executive Council in fulfilling its monitoring task. To address the relatively poor level of compliance with the Court's judgments, the Council instructed the Court, in collaboration with the Commission and the Permanent Representatives Committee, to undertake an in-depth study on mechanisms that would enable the Council to monitor more effectively the execution of judgments.[265] Following such a request, the Court elaborated a 'Draft Framework for Reporting and Monitoring Execution of Judgments and other Decisions of The African Court on Human and Peoples' Rights'. This framework of implementation envisions the creation of a 'Compliance Monitoring Unit' within the Court's Registry tasked with monitoring the implementation of its decisions. It also proposes a process for undertaking this task, including the possibility of monitoring hearings and on-site visits, and it foresees the involvement of the Permanent Representative Committee and, subsequently, the Executive Council and the Assembly in the political supervision of States' compliance.[266] While the adoption of this framework would be a positive step towards improving the implementation of the Court's decisions, it is fundamentally needed for this mechanism to be supported by a serious commitment from States to comply with the judgments against them and from the political organs of the AU to adopt the necessary measures to enforce such judgments in case of non-compliance.

8.4.3 PROVISIONAL MEASURES

The African Charter is silent as to the prerogative of its established monitoring body—the Commission—to adopt urgent protective measures. However, the Commission's Rules have filled such a silence, stating that it has the power to issue, at any time after the

---

[262] To fulfil its reporting mandate, the Court has developed the practice of requiring States to submit a report on the measures taken to ensure compliance with its judgments. See: ACtHPR, *Lohé Issa Konaté v. Burkina Faso* (reparations) (2016) 1 AfCLR 346, op. para. ix; ACtHPR, *Ally Rajabu and others v. Tanzania*, App. 7/2015, Judgment (28 November 2019), op. para. xviii; ACtHPR, *Robert John Penessis v. Tanzania*, App. 13/2015, Judgment (28 November 2019), op. para. xiv.

[263] African Court Protocol, Art. 29.

[264] M. Ssenyonjo, 'Responding to human rights violations in Africa: assessing the role of the African Commission and Court on Human and Peoples' Rights (1987–2018)' (2018) 7 *International Human Rights Law Review* 1, 42; S. Adjolohoun, 'A crisis of design and judicial practice? Curbing state disengagement from the African Court on Human and Peoples' Rights' (2020) 20 *African Human Rights Law Journal* 1, 21; V. Ayeni and A. von Staden, 'Monitoring second-order compliance in the African human rights system' (2022) 6, *African Human Rights Yearbook* 3, 11, 22.

[265] AU Executive Council, Decision on the Activity Report of the African Court on Human and Peoples' Rights, Doc. EX.CL/1088(XXXIII).

[266] ACtHPR, Activity Report of the African Court on Human and Peoples' Rights (2019), EX.CL/1126(XXXIV), Annex 1.

reception of a communication, urgent provisional measures to prevent irreparable harm to the victim of an alleged violation of human rights, on its own initiative or at the request of the claimant.[267] When the Commission is not in session, provisional measures can be adopted by the Commission's Chairperson, following consultation with the Working Group on Communications.[268] Unfortunately, States Parties have not been diligent in complying with the Commission's provisional measures.[269] To make matters worse, the initial stance adopted by the Commission, stating that its orders of provisional measures were legally binding on States Parties,[270] seems to have changed. In the Commission's opinion, failure to comply with its provisional measures might no longer amount to a breach of the State's obligations under the Charter.[271] Moreover, under its previous Rules of Procedure, the Commission was explicitly entitled to submit a case to the Court when an order of provisional measures was not complied with by a State and, concordantly, the Rules of the Court recognized the Commission's entitlement to request it to issue provisional measures.[272] These provisions have now been replaced in the current Rules of both organs, casting doubts as to the Commission's power to request the Court to issue provisional measures, when their own have not been complied with.

For its part, the African Court has been explicitly granted the power to adopt provisional measures in cases of extreme gravity and urgency to avoid irreparable harm caused to persons.[273] The adoption of such measures can be requested by an alleged victim of a violation or can be decided *motu proprio* by the Court. For the most part, the Court's practice seems to reveal a generosity in its approach. For instance, it has taken an ample interpretation of what might amount to an 'irreparable harm', granting provisional measures to protect a broad range of rights, not limited to situations endangering life and personal integrity, but also encompassing cases concerning property rights and the holding of elections.[274] At the same time, the Court's practice reveals a certain lack of rigour and consistency.[275] This has been reflected, for example, in the adoption of seemingly incongruous decisions in rather similar situations,[276] as well as in failing to examine the adoption of this type of measures within the required urgency.[277] However, the Court's

---

[267] ACHPR, Rules of Procedure, r. 100.   [268] ACHPR, Rules of Procedure, r. 100.3.

[269] F. Viljoen, *International Human Rights Law in Africa* (2nd edn., OUP 2012) 306.

[270] ACHPR, *International Pen and Others v. Nigeria*, Communications 137/94, 139/94, 154/96, 161/97 (1998), paras. 103, 114, 116.

[271] F. Viljoen, *International Human Rights Law in Africa* (2nd edn., OUP 2012) 308. See: ACHPR, *Interights et al. (on behalf of Mariette Sonjaleen Bosch) v. Botswana*, Communication 240/01 (2003), para. 55.

[272] Commission's Rules of Procedure (2010), r. 118.2; Rules of the Court (2010), r. 51.1.

[273] African Court Protocol, Art. 27.

[274] ACtHPR, *Woyome v. Ghana* (provisional measures) (2017) 2 AfCLR 213, op. para. i; ACtHPR, *Ajavon v. Benin* (provisional measures) (2020) 4 AfCLR 123, op. para. 4.

[275] Z. Teferra, 'Provisional measures in international human rights law: the practice of the African Court on Human and Peoples' Rights' (2022) 6 *African Human Rights Yearbook* 28, 44, 50–51, 62.

[276] Z. Teferra, 'Provisional measures in international human rights law: the practice of the African Court on Human and Peoples' Rights' (2022) 6 *African Human Rights Yearbook* 28, 44, 51.

[277] ACtHR, *African Commission on Human and Peoples' Rights v. Libya* (provisional measures) (2013) 1 AfCLR 145, separate opinion of Judge Ouguergouz. See also: T. Makunya 'Decisions of the African Court on Human and Peoples' Rights during 2020: Trends and lessons' (2021) 21 *African Human Rights Law Journal* 1230, 1243.

more recent decisions appear to disclose a more careful and stricter analysis of the needed conditions for the granting of provisional measures.[278] This is further confirmed by a lower percentage of provisional measures ordered by the Court in recent years.[279] Notwithstanding a certain level of resistance some States have shown in complying with provisional measures issued against them,[280] the Court's orders of provisional measures are binding on States.[281] States' lack of compliance with them can lead the Court to finding an additional violation, when assessing the merits of a case, and can also prompt the Court to request the AU Assembly to adopt measures against the concerned State.[282]

8.4.4 AMICABLE SETTLEMENTS

The African Charter mandates the Commission to attempt all appropriate means to reach an 'amicable solution based on the respect of Human and Peoples' rights' when dealing with inter-State communications.[283] Nonetheless, the Commission's Rules have stipulated that it may offer its good offices to facilitate an amicable settlement, at any stage of the proceedings, on its own initiative or at the request of any of the parties, not limiting this procedure to inter-State cases.[284] The amicable settlement mechanism can only proceed with the consent of the parties and may be terminated by the Commission if it considers the matter not to be susceptible to amicable resolution or when any of the parties does not display the willingness to reach such an agreement. When a friendly settlement is reached by the parties, the Commission has to ensure that the agreement is in compliance with the respect of the rights enshrined in the African Charter and other human rights instruments.[285] If satisfied with the agreement reached by the parties, the Commission prepares a decision containing a brief statement of the facts and a description of the settlement reached. However, the Commission's practice concerning friendly settlements has been a source of concern over the years. Failures from the Commission to duly consider the best interests of applicants and to redress evident power imbalances between the parties have led to agreements in which the interests of the States had apparently prevailed.[286] To this, the lack of transparency of the procedures added yet another layer of doubts as to whether the mechanisms

---

[278] Z. Teferra, 'Provisional measures in international human rights law: the practice of the African Court on Human and Peoples' Rights' (2022) 6 *African Human Rights Yearbook* 28, 34, 62.

[279] Z. Teferra, 'Provisional measures in international human rights law: the practice of the African Court on Human and Peoples' Rights' (2022) 6 *African Human Rights Yearbook* 28, 35.

[280] Z. Teferra, 'Provisional measures in international human rights law: the practice of the African Court on Human and Peoples' Rights' (2022) 6 *African Human Rights Yearbook* 28, 35 (fn 36).

[281] ACtHPR, *African Commission on Human and Peoples' Rights v. Libya* (provisional measures 2) (2015) 1 AfCLR 150, para. 10; ACtHPR, *Noudehouenou v. Benin*, App. 003/2020, Order (provisional measures) (5 May 2020), para. 46.

[282] ACtHPR, Rules of Court, r. 59.4.   [283] African Charter, Art. 52.

[284] ACHPR, Rules of Procedure, r. 123.   [285] ACHPR, Rules of Procedure, r. 123.5.b.

[286] I. Zarifis, 'The settlement option: friend or foe to human rights protection in Africa?' (2019) 3 *African Human Rights Yearbook* 221, 226; V. Ayeni and T. Ibraheem, 'Amicable Settlement of Disputes and Proactive Remediation of Violations under the African Human Rights System' (2019) 10 *Beijing Law Review* 406, 412–414.

were leading to appropriate outcomes.[287] Consequently, the improvement of this settlement mechanism through the adoption of a more robust procedure and clear criteria is paramount, bearing in mind that the Commission's confirmation of a settlement amounts to a decision requiring implementation on the same footing as the Commission's decisions on the merits of a communication.[288]

On its part, the Court is empowered, but not compelled, to assist the parties in a case before it to reach an amicable settlement of the matter.[289] This can take place following a request from the parties or due to the Court's own decision. If a settlement is reached, the Court would still render a judgment, limited only to the facts agreed upon and the solution adopted. Importantly, the Court has asserted that settlements need not be limited to an agreement on the payment of compensation but may also include a wide variety and number of reparation measures.[290] Moreover, in the interest of justice or to preserve public interest or order, the Court can decide to proceed with a case, notwithstanding the parties reaching an amicable settlement.[291]

8.4.5 FURTHER REFLECTIONS: THE ADMISSIBILITY OF COMMUNICATIONS BEFORE THE COMMISSION AND CASES BEFORE THE COURT

Both the Commission and the Court are empowered to assess whether applications submitted to them are to be admitted, fulfilling all admissibility requirements stated by the African Charter and fitting within their respective jurisdictions. As discussed in **Section 6.4.5** and **Section 7.3.7**, with regard to other regional bodies, jurisdiction encompasses four dimensions: material, personal, temporal, and territorial. For a communication to fit within the Commission's jurisdiction, it should engage a provision of the African Charter or one of its Protocols (jurisdiction *ratione materiae*);[292] allege the responsibility of a State Party to the Charter or pertinent Protocol (jurisdiction *ratione personae*); the alleged violation should have occurred after the State became Party to the treaty, unless it concerns a continuous violation (jurisdiction *ratione temporis*);[293] and it

---

[287] I. Zarifis, 'The settlement option: friend or foe to human rights protection in Africa?' (2019) 3 *African Human Rights Yearbook* 221, 227; V. Ayeni and T. Ibraheem, 'Amicable Settlement of Disputes and Proactive Remediation of Violations under the African Human Rights System' (2019) 10 *Beijing Law Review* 406, 413.

[288] ACHPR, Rules of Procedure, rr. 123.6–123.7.   [289] African Court Protocol, Art. 9.

[290] ACtHPR, 'Comparative Study on the Law and Practice of Reparations for Human Rights Violations' (September 2019) p. 101.

[291] ACtHPR, Rules of Court, r. 64.

[292] In principle, the Commission's material jurisdiction, unlike the Court's, does not extend beyond those regional treaties that have expressly granted it jurisdiction over them. However, in the past, the Commission has ruled on the violation of instruments beyond the Charter and its Protocols, such as the UN Basic Principles on the Independence of the Judiciary. See: ACHPR, *Luke Munyandu Tembani and Benjamin John Freeth (represented by Norman Tjombe) v. Angola and Thirteen Others*, Communication 409/12 (2013), para. 131. See also: ACHPR, *Media Rights Agenda v. Nigeria*, Communications 224/98 (2000).

[293] ACHPR, *Malawi African Association and others v. Mauritania*, Communications 54/91, 61/91, 98/93, 164–196/97, 210/98 (2002), para. 91; *Mgwanga Gunme v. Cameroon*, Communication 266/2003 (2009), para. 97; ACHPR, *J.E. Zitha & P.J.L .Zitha (represented by Prof. Dr Liesbeth Zegveld) v. Mozambique*, Communication 361/08 (2011) para. 94.

should have taken place within the territory of the State or otherwise under its control (jurisdiction *ratione loci*).[294]

With regard to the Court, the personal, material, and temporal aspects of its jurisdiction are somehow different to those aforementioned. The Court's personal jurisdiction requires the respondent State to be Party not only to the African Charter but also to the African Court Protocol, as well as to have made the discussed declaration if brought by an individual or NGO.[295] It also requires the case to be brought by one of the actors with legal standing to do so, as discussed in **Section 8.3** and **Section 8.4.2**, and on behalf of a natural person or group. Whether legal entities can be 'victims' under the African system has not been clearly settled. While both the Commission and the Court have, in the past, ruled on violations against legal persons,[296] more recently, the Court has affirmed its competence to exclude violations suffered by private or public law entities.[297] Concerning the Court's territorial jurisdiction, as that of the Commission, it extends beyond States' political boundaries and onto actions or omissions taking place under their control extraterritorially.[298]

Regarding the Court's material jurisdiction, as discussed in **Section 8.3**, this is particularly wide, allowing the finding of violations not only of the African Charter and its Protocols but also of other human rights treaties.[299] The main requirement is for the respondent State to be legally bound by the relevant instrument, being Party to the specific treaty.[300] Nevertheless, whether a specific international instrument can be considered a human rights treaty subject to the Court's jurisdiction is not always evident.[301] The Court has affirmed that: 'in determining whether a convention is a human rights instrument, it is necessary to refer in particular to the purposes of

---

[294] F. Viljoen, 'Communications under the African Charter: procedure and admissibility' in M. Evans and R. Murray, *The African Charter of Human and Peoples' Rights: The System in Practice, 1986–2006* (2nd edn., CUP 2008) 76–138, 107–108. See: Communication 383/10, *Mohammed Abdullah Saleh Al- Asad v. The Republic of Djibouti*, 14 October 2014, para. 134.

[295] Therefore, the Court has rejected applications brought against the African Commission on Human and Peoples' Rights and the African Union. See: ACtHPR, *Femi Falana v. The African Commission on Human and Peoples' Rights* (jurisdiction), 20 November 2015, 1 AfCLR 499; ACtHPR, *Femi Falana v. African Union* (jurisdiction), 26 June 2012, 1 AfCLR 118; ACtHPR, *Atabong Denis Atemnkeng v. African Union* (jurisdiction) (2013) 1 AfCLR 182.

[296] ACHPR, *Zimbabwe Lawyers for Human Rights & Associated Newspapers of Zimbabwe v. Zimbabwe*, Communication 284/03 (2009), para. 179; ACtHPR, *Beneficiaries of late Norbert Zongo, Abdoulaye Nikiema alias Ablasse, Ernest Zongo, Blaise Ilboudo and Mouvement Burkinabe des Droits de l'Homme et des Peuples v. Burkina Faso* (reparations) (2015) 1 AfCLR 258, paras. 65–67.

[297] ACtHPR, *Gombert v. Côte d'Ivoire* (jurisdiction and admissibility) (2018) 2 AfCLR 270, para. 47.

[298] ACtHPR, *Bernard Anbataayela Mornah v. Benin, Burkina Faso, Côte d'Ivoire, Ghana, Mali, Malawi, Tanzania, and Tunisia*. Judgment, App. No. 028/2018 (22 September 2022), paras. 149 and 155.

[299] Protocol to the African Charter on Human and Peoples' Rights on the Rights of Women in Africa (adopted 7 November 2003, entered into force 25 November 2005), Art. 7.

[300] As discussed in **Section 8.3**, the Court has ruled on the violation of the ICCPR on different occasions, as well as on the violation of CEDAW, and has even applied the Universal Declaration of Human Rights, finding it legally binding as part of international customary law. See: ACtHPR, *Lohé Issa Konaté v. Burkina Faso* (merits) (2014) 1 AfCLR 314, op. paras. 3–8; ACtHPR, *Alex Thomas v. Tanzania* (merits) (2015) 1 AfCLR 465, op. para. vii; ACtHPR, *Association pour le Progrès et la Défense des Droits des Femmes Maliennes and the Institute for Human Rights and Development in Africa v. Mali* (merits) (2018) 2 AfCLR 380, op. paras. Viii, ix; ACtHPR, *Robert John Penessis v. Tanzania*, App. 13/2015, Judgment (28 November 2019), paras. 85–87 and op. para. v.

[301] A. Rudman, 'The African Charter: Just one treaty among many? The development of the material jurisdiction and interpretive mandate of the African Court on Human and Peoples' Rights' (2021) 21 *African Human Rights Law Journal* 699, 707.

such convention. Such purposes are reflected either by an express enunciation of the subjective rights of individuals or groups of individuals, or by mandatory obligations on State Parties for the consequent enjoyment of the said rights'.[302] However, it has been highlighted that the Court has so far failed to develop a systematic approach to determine whether specific treaty provisions fall within its jurisdiction and that its jurisprudence on the matter reveals a severe lack of rigour.[303]

The scope of the Court's temporal jurisdiction presents a contentious aspect as to its precise starting point, since it could be argued that the critical date is either the day on which the African Charter entered into force for the respective State or the day on which it deposited the instrument ratifying the African Court Protocol. The Court has endorsed the understanding that its jurisdiction over a case can only commence with the entry into force of the Protocol,[304] even if such interpretation was not always clearly articulated.[305] The same doubt can arise concerning direct applications by individuals or NGOs, and whether the critical date should be any of the aforementioned or even the date of the State's declaration accepting direct submissions. We agree with Viljoen in that, again, the date the Protocol entered into force would be the appropriate one.[306] Of course, exceptions should be made for ongoing violations that have started before the critical date but continue thereafter, which would fall within the Court's temporal jurisdiction.[307]

8.4.5.1 Admissibility requirements

In addition to satisfying the jurisdictional requirements, the application must fulfil the admissibility criteria established in Article 56 of the Charter. These requirements are the same for communications to the Commission and cases to the Court, even if these bodies have interpreted them differently to some extent. Some of these requirements are rather usual, such as the inadmissibility of matters already adjudged (*res judicata*), as well as the need for the prior exhaustion of local remedies and for applications to be submitted within a 'reasonable period' thereafter. As to the first of these requirements, unlike other treaties, the African Charter does not seem to ban the examination of cases pending before other international bodies, but only the admission of settled cases.[308]

---

[302] ACtHPR, *Actions pour la Protection des Droits de l'Homme (APDH) v. Côte d'Ivoire* (2016) 1 AfCLR 668, para. 57.

[303] G. Waschefort, 'The subject-matter jurisdiction and interpretive competence of the African Court on Human and Peoples' Rights in relation to international humanitarian law' (2020) 20 *African Human Rights Law Journal* 41, 67. See also: A. Rudman, 'The African Charter: Just one treaty among many? The development of the material jurisdiction and interpretive mandate of the African Court on Human and Peoples' Rights' (2021) 21 *African Human Rights Law Journal* 699, 714, 717–718.

[304] ACtHPR, *Beneficiaries of Late Norbert Zongo Abdoulaye Nikiema, Ernest Zongo and Blise Ilboudo & the Burkinabe Movement on Human and Peoples' Rights v. Burkina Faso* (preliminary objections) (2013) 1 AfCLR 197, para. 68; ACtHPR, *Kouadio Kobena Fory v. Républic of Côte d'Ivoire* (judgment) (2 December 2021), para. 32.

[305] ACtHPR, *Urban Mkandawire v. Malawi* (admissibility) (2013) 1 AfCLR 283, para. 32 and joint dissenting opinion of Judges Gerard Niyungeko and El Hadji Guisse, para. 8.

[306] F. Viljoen, *International Human Rights Law in Africa* (2nd edn., OUP 2012) 435–439.

[307] ACtHPR, *Beneficiaries of Late Norbert Zongo Abdoulaye Nikiema, Ernest Zongo and Blise Ilboudo & the Burkinabe Movement on Human and Peoples' Rights v. Burkina Faso* (preliminary objections) (2013) 1 AfCLR 197, para. 77.

[308] F. Viljoen, 'Communications under the African Charter: procedure and admissibility' in M. Evans and R. Murray, *The African Charter of Human and Peoples' Rights: The System in Practice, 1986–2006* (2nd edn., CUP 2008) 76–138, 126–127. See: ACHPR, *Interights (on behalf of Pan African Movement and Citizens for Peace in Eritrea) v. Ethiopia*, Communication 233/99 (2003), paras. 60–61.

Under this requirement, a matter would be considered settled when there is already a decision on the merits of a case that involves both the same parties and claims.[309] For assessing whether a case can be considered settled, the Court has accepted decisions made by organs without the power to issue binding rulings, such as treaty bodies. Moreover, in cases of public interest, it has not been required for the claimants to be the same. Lastly, for the claims to be considered identical, they need not be based on the exact same international instrument, so long as the rights at stake are the same.[310]

Concerning the rule of prior exhaustion of domestic remedies, this is a rather common condition for accessing regional monitoring mechanisms, as discussed in **Section 6.4.5.1** and **Section 7.3.7.1**. Similar to the rules of other regional bodies, there are exceptions to the need to exhaust domestic remedies, such as when the domestic proceedings are 'unduly prolonged'.[311] Moreover, only ordinary judicial remedies that are in fact available, effective, and sufficient need to be exhausted.[312] For this purpose, a remedy would be considered available if it can be pursued without impediment, it would be deemed effective if it offers a prospect of success, and it would be found sufficient if it is capable of redressing the complaint.[313] If an application claims that remedies are unavailable, inadequate, or insufficient, the burden is on the respondent State to prove that such allegations are untrue.[314] Furthermore, circumstances in which it has been possible to assume that local remedies need not be exhausted included contexts of widespread serious human rights violations;[315] situations in which the jurisdiction of the courts had been ousted;[316] as well as when indigence had made it practically impossible for the victim to access the courts system.[317]

As to the timeframe for the submission of an application, the Charter does not establish a set time limit, unlike the six-month rule of the American Convention or the (now)

---

[309] ACtHPR, *Johnson v. Ghana* (jurisdiction and admissibility) (2019) 3 AfCLR 99, para. 48; ACtHPR, *Gombert v. Côte d'Ivoire* (jurisdiction and admissibility) (2018) 2 AfCLR 270, para. 45.

[310] ACtHPR, *Johnson v. Ghana* (jurisdiction and admissibility) (2019) 3 AfCLR 99, paras. 52–54; ACtHPR, *Emil Touray and Others v. Gambia* (ruling), 24 March 2022, para. 43; ACtHPR, *Tike Mwambipile and Equality Now v. Tanzania* (ruling), 1 December 2022, paras. 49–50.

[311] African Charter, Art. 56.5. See: ACtHPR, *Beneficiaries of Late Norbert Zongo Abdoulaye Nikiema, Ernest Zongo and Blise Ilboudo & the Burkinabe Movement on Human and Peoples' Rights v. Burkina Faso* (merits) (2014) 1 AfCLR 219, paras. 88–106.

[312] F. Viljoen, 'Communications under the African Charter: procedure and admissibility' in M. Evans and R. Murray, *The African Charter of Human and Peoples' Rights: The System in Practice, 1986–2006* (2nd edn., CUP 2008) 76–138, 117–118.

[313] ACHPR, *Sir Dawda K Jawara v. The Gambia*, Communications 147/95 and 149/96 (11 May 2000), para. 32; ACtHPR, *Lohé Issa Konaté v. Burkina Faso* (merits) (2014) 1 AfCLR 314, paras. 96 and 108; ACtHPR, *Ajavon v. Benin* Judgment (2020) 4 AfCLR 133, para. 86.

[314] F. Viljoen, 'Communications under the African Charter: procedure and admissibility' in M. Evans and R. Murray, *The African Charter of Human and Peoples' Rights: The System in Practice, 1986–2006* (2nd edn., CUP 2008) 76–138, 112–113. See: ACHPR, *Ilesanmi v. Nigeria*, Communication 268/2003 (2005), para. 46.

[315] ACHPR, *Free Legal Assistance Group and Others v. Zaire*, Communications 25/89, 47/90, 56/91, 100/93 (1995), para. 37; ACHPR, *Organisation Mondiale Contre La Torture v. Rwanda*, Communications 27/89, 46/91, 49/91, 99/93 (1996), para. 17.

[316] ACHPR, *Constitutional Rights Project v. Nigeria*, Communication 60/91 (1995), paras. 10–11; ACHPR, *The Constitutional Rights Project v. Nigeria*, Communication 87/93 (1995), paras. 8–9; ACHPR, *Media Rights Agenda and Other v. Nigeria*, Communications 105/93, 128/94, 130/94, 152/96 (1998), paras. 49–52.

[317] ACHPR, *Purohit and Moore v. The Gambia*, Communication 241/2001 (2003) paras. 37–38.

four-month rule of the European system, but only requires the submission to take place within a 'reasonable period' following the exhaustion of local remedies. While the Commission seems to have adopted six months as a standard to measure the reasonability of the delay,[318] the Court has adopted a rather flexible approach, admitting cases submitted years after the exhaustion of local remedies.[319] The Court has been duly aware of the many difficulties experienced by applicants and conscientious of existing structural problems in the continent. In particular, it has identified a range of circumstances as justification for its flexible approach to the issue, such as the violation being a continuous one; the applicants being indigent, illiterate, deprived of their freedom, or lacking legal assistance; and the generally poor level of awareness of the existence of the Court.[320] Nevertheless, it should be mentioned that the Court's practice for assessing both the requirement to exhaust domestic remedies and the timeframe for the submission of a case has been the subject of criticisms, as it appears to be inconsistent.[321]

The Charter also establishes some less usual admissibility requirements, such as the need to avoid the use of 'disparaging or insulting language'. Although this explicit requirement is unique to the African Charter,[322] the use of abusive language is also grounds for the inadmissibility of petitions in other systems, as discussed in **Section 7.3.7.3**. In the Court's own words: 'In determining whether language is derogatory or insulting, the Court must satisfy itself that the language used has intentionally violated the dignity, reputation or integrity of a public official or judicial body. The terms must be aimed at undermining the integrity and status of the institution and discrediting it.'[323] Moreover, the Court highlighted that 'public figures including those who hold the highest government positions are legitimately exposed to criticism such that for remarks to be regarded as being disparaging to them, the remarks must be of extreme gravity and manifestly affect their reputation'.[324] Therefore, for language against public officials to be considered disparaging and insulting, it 'must be offensive seeking to belittle and undermine their integrity and reputation'.[325]

An additional requirement is that the application be grounded on evidence beyond news reports, a condition that also exists for complaints to the Human Rights Council, as discussed in **Section 4.3.4**. This prerequisite does not rule out the use of media

---

[318] F. Viljoen, *International Human Rights Law in Africa* (2nd edn., OUP 2012) 320.

[319] ACtHPR, *Mango v. Tanzania* (merits) (2018) 2 AfCLR 314, para. 55; *Evarist v. Tanzania* (merits) (2018) 2 AfCLR 402, para. 45.

[320] ACtHPR, *Alex Thomas v. Tanzania* (merits) (2015) 1 AfCLR 465, para. 92; ACtHPR, *Mohamed Abubakari v. Tanzania* (merits) (2016) 1 AfCLR 599, para. 92; ACtHPR, *Harold Mbalanda Munthali v. Malawi* (merits) 23 June 2022, para. 63.

[321] S. Adjolohoun, 'A crisis of design and judicial practice? Curbing state disengagement from the African Court on Human and Peoples' Rights' (2020) 20 *African Human Rights Law Journal* 1, 26–27; M. Nkhata, 'What counts as a "reasonable period"? An analytical survey of the jurisprudence of the African Court on Human and Peoples' Rights on reasonable time for filing applications' (2022) 6 *African Human Rights Yearbook* 129, 148, 151.

[322] F. Viljoen, *International Human Rights Law in Africa* (2nd edn., OUP 2012) 314. See: ACHPR, *Ligue Camerounaise des Droits de l'Homme v. Cameroon*, Communication 65/92 (1997), para. 13; ACHPR, *Ilesanmi v. Nigeria*, Communication 268/03 (2005), paras. 37–40.

[323] ACtHPR, *Sissoko & 74 Others v. Mali* (judgment) (2020) 4 AfCLR 641, para. 28.

[324] ACtHPR, *Ajavon v. Benin* (merits) (2019) 3 AfCLR 130, para. 73.

[325] ACtHPR, *Sissoko & 74 Others v. Mali* (judgment) (2020) 4 AfCLR 641, para. 29.

reports to support an application but requires that these are not the only basis for the allegations.[326] Certainly, all the aforementioned requirements for the admissibility of an application to the Commission and Court are 'conjunctive', meaning that if any of them is missing, the application will be declared inadmissible.[327]

8.5 ADVISORY OPINIONS

The African Commission and Court have been conferred by their constitutive treaties the competence to provide advice. The Commission has the power to interpret the provisions of the African Charter at the request of a State Party, an organ of the AU, or an African organization recognized by the AU. The Commission can also decide *motu proprio* to undertake research and studies on African problems in the field of human and peoples' rights and provide opinions and recommendations to States Parties to the Charter, as well as to formulate principles and rules aimed at solving legal problems relating to human and peoples' rights upon which African governments may base their legislation.[328] Within the purview of these abilities, the Commission has elaborated a series of guidelines and principles;[329] has produced six general comments (up to the end of 2022);[330] and has issued an Advisory Opinion on the UN Declaration on the Rights of Indigenous Peoples, to support a common position for African States during the negotiation of this instrument (discussed in **Section 10.4.2.1**).[331]

Pursuant to the African Court Protocol, the Court may provide an opinion on any legal matter relating to the Charter or any other relevant human rights instruments at the request of an AU Member State, the African Union, or any of its organs—including the African

---

[326] ACHPR, *Sir Dawda K. Jawara v. The Gambia*, Communications 147/95 and 149/96 (2000), para. 24; ACtHPR, *Laurent Munyandilikirwa v. Rwanda*, App. no. 23/2015 (2 December 2021), para. 63.

[327] ACHPR, *Article 19 v. The State of Eritrea*, Communication 275/2003 (2007).

[328] F. Ouguergouz, *African Charter of Human and People's Rights: A Comprehensive Agenda for Human Dignity and Sustainable Democracy in Africa* (Nijhoff 2003) 565–566. See: ACHPR, Art. 45; ACHPR, Rules of Procedure, r. 127.

[329] See: ACHPR, Guidelines and Measures for the Prohibition and Prevention of Torture, Cruel, Inhuman or Degrading Treatment or Punishment in Africa (2002); ACHPR, Principles and Guidelines on the Right to a Fair Trial and Legal Assistance in Africa (2003); ACHPR, Guidelines and Principles on Economic, Social and Cultural Rights in the African Charter on Human and Peoples' Rights (2011); ACHPR, Guidelines on the Conditions of Arrest, Police Custody and Pre-Trial Detention in Africa (2015); ACHPR, Guidelines on Freedom of Association and Assembly in Africa (2017); ACHPR, Guidelines on Combating Sexual Violence and its Consequences in Africa (2017); ACHPR, Principles on the Decriminalisation of Petty Offences in Africa (2018).

[330] ACHPR, General Comments No. 1 on Art. 14 (1) (d), (e) of the Protocol to the African Charter on Human and Peoples' Rights on the Rights of Women in Africa (6 November 2012); ACHPR, General Comment No. 2 on Art. 14.1 (a), (b), (c), (f) and Art. 14. 2 (a) and (c) of the Protocol to the African Charter on Human and Peoples' Rights on the Rights of Women in Africa (28 November 2014); ACHPR, General Comment No. 3 On The African Charter On Human And Peoples' Rights: The Right To Life (Art. 4) (12 December 2015); ACHPR, General Comment No. 4: The Right to Redress for Victims of Torture and Other Cruel, Inhuman or Degrading Punishment or Treatment (Art. 5) (4 March 2017); ACHPR, General Comment No. 5 on the African Charter on Human and Peoples' Rights: The Right to Freedom of Movement and Residence (Art. 12(1)) (10 November 2019); ACHPR, General Comment No. 6 On The Protocol To The African Charter on Human And Peoples Right on the Rights of Women in Africa (Maputo Protocol): The Right To Property During Separation, Divorce Or Annulment Of Marriage (Art. 7(D)) (4 March 2020).

[331] ACHPR, *Advisory Opinion of The African Commission on Human and Peoples' Rights on The United Nations Declaration on the Rights of Indigenous Peoples* (2007).

Commission, despite it not being listed as an AU organ[332]—or any other African organization recognized by the AU. As to the latter, the Court has had to examine, within the context of a request for an advisory opinion, what type of organizations would be encompassed by the provision. The Court affirmed that both non-governmental and inter-governmental bodies are included. Concerning NGOs in particular, their 'African' character is given by their registration in an African State but also requires the performance of activities beyond the territory of the State of registration. As to the requirement of recognition by the AU, such acknowledgement must emanate from the Executive Council of the AU itself, it not being sufficient for the recognition to be provided by other AU organs.[333]

The main substantive restriction to the extent of the exercise of the Court's advisory jurisdiction is for the material subject of the requested opinion to be unrelated to a matter being examined by the Commission.[334] Up to the end of 2022, the Court has answered fifteen requests of opinions, with only three of them leading to the adoption of advisory opinions.[335] In its first advisory opinion (discussed in **Section 8.1.2.1.1**), the Court confirmed that the African Committee of Experts on the Rights and Welfare of the Child enjoys legal standing to requests advisory opinions to the Court, but it lacks such standing for the purpose of submitting contentious cases;[336] while in the third one (discussed in **Section 8.1.1.2**) it examined the complexities of both holding and postponing elections during the Covid-19 pandemic.[337] For its part, the second advisory opinion, rendered by the Court in 2020, assessed the (in)compatibility of 'vagrancy laws' with the international protection of human rights.[338]

> **ACtHPR, *The Compatibility of Vagrancy Laws with the African Charter on Human and Peoples' Rights and other Human Rights Instruments Applicable in Africa*. Advisory Opinion 1/2018 (2020).**
>
> The request for an Advisory Opinion was made by the Pan African Lawyers Union, an African organisation recognized by the AU. The questions submitted concerned the compatibility of 'vagrancy laws'—legislation that criminalizes poor, homeless, or unemployed individuals, instead of specific reprehensible acts—with the African Charter on Human and Peoples' Rights, the African Charter on the Rights and Welfare of the Child, and the Protocol to the African Charter on Human and Peoples' Rights on the Rights of Women in Africa.
>
> The Court responded to all submitted questions in the affirmative. It considered that the existence and the application of 'vagrancy laws' amounted to multiple violations of the

---

[332] F. Viljoen, *International Human Rights Law in Africa* (2nd edn., OUP 2012) 447.

[333] Request for Advisory Opinion by the Socio-Economic Rights and Accountability Project (SERAP), No. 001/2013 Advisory Opinion 26 May 2017, paras. 46, 48, 62.

[334] African Court Protocol, Art. 4.

[335] The Court's Advisory Opinions are available on its website: https://www.african-court.org/cpmt/advisory-finalised (accessed on 29 March 2023).

[336] ACtHPR, *Request for Advisory Opinion by the African Committee of Experts on the Rights and Welfare of the Child on the Standing of the African Commission of Experts on the Rights and Welfare of the Child before the African Court on Human and Peoples' Rights*, Request 2/2013 (4 December 2014).

[337] ACtHPR, *Request for Advisory Opinion by the Pan African Lawyers Union (PALU) on the right to participate in the government of one's country in the context of an election held during a public health emergency or a pandemic, such as the Covid-19 crisis*. Advisory Opinion No. 1/2020 (16 July 2021).

[338] ACtHPR, *Request for Advisory Opinion by the Pan African Lawyers Union (PALU)*, Advisory Opinion No. 1/2018 (4 December 2020).

human rights instruments at stake and, consequently, entailed the obligation of States Parties to amend or repeal such legislation. In particular, the Court found that such laws, which criminalize the status of individuals, rather than the commission of specific acts, entailed the discrimination against those already underprivileged and marginalized (paras. 70 and 73). Furthermore, the Court considered that arrests carried out in application of such laws, and lacking a warrant, amounted to the breach of multiple human rights, including the right to human dignity, liberty and security, and freedom of movement (paras. 74–75, 82, and 87).

8.6 INTER-STATE COMMUNICATIONS

As is the case with other regional human rights systems, inter-State communications are a rare occurrence in the African system.[339] Nonetheless, the African Charter foresees two distinctive types of inter-State communications. On the one hand, under Article 47, any State Party that considers that another Party has breached the Charter can submit a 'communication-negotiation' addressed to the respective State, the AU Secretary-General, and the Commission's Chairperson. This communication should contain a comprehensive statement of facts and the Charter provisions allegedly breached.[340] Within three months, the State to which the communication is addressed should provide the enquiring State with a written explanation of the situation, including the actions adopted and any redress provided.[341] The resolution of the matter does not technically involve the Commission,[342] as its Secretary is merely requested to demand the parties to keep the Commission informed of developments which could arise within their negotiation.[343]

On the other hand, Charter Articles 48 and 49, provide for the possibility of States Parties to submit against one another 'communications-complaints'. These could arise from the failure to settle a 'communication-negotiation' within three months or by the direct referral to the Commission of an alleged breach of the Charter. Admissibility of inter-State communications depends on the prior exhaustion of domestic remedies unless these do not exist or exhausting them would be unduly prolonged.[344] The State submitting the communication should also indicate any measures taken to exhaust regional or international procedures of settlement or good offices, as well as any other procedure of international investigation or settlement to which the States Parties have resorted.[345]

If the Commission finds an inter-State communication to be admissible, it must place its good offices at the disposal of the parties to reach an amicable settlement

---

[339] Only in 1999 did the Commission examine its first inter-State case on the merits, when the DRC submitted a communication against Burundi, Rwanda, and Uganda. While Harrington reports an initial inter-State communication submitted by Libya against the USA in the late 1980s—found inadmissible *ratione personae*—in 2013, the Commission decided not to be seized in a communication submitted by Sudan against South Sudan, but, in 2019, has declared admissible one submitted by Djibouti against Eritrea. See: R. Murray, *The African Charter on Human and Peoples' Rights: A Commentary* (OUP 2019) 656; J. Harrington, 'The African Court on Human and People's Rights' in M. Evans and R. Murray, *The African Charter of Human and Peoples' Rights: The System in Practice, 1986–2000* (CUP 2002) 305–334, 330.

[340] ACHPR, Rules of Procedure, r. 108.2.   [341] African Charter, Art. 47.
[342] R. Murray, *The African Charter on Human and Peoples' Rights: A Commentary* (OUP 2019) 658.
[343] ACHPR, Rules of Procedure, r. 108.4.
[344] African Charter, Art. 50.   [345] ACHPR, Rules of Procedure, r. 109.2.

based on respect for human and peoples' rights.[346] Should the parties reach such an agreement, the Commission would issue a decision containing a brief description of the facts and of the agreed settlement, which should be complied with by the parties. Conversely, if no settlement is reached, the Commission should request the parties to make submissions regarding the merits of the case and, after deliberation, adopt its decision, communicating it to the parties and the AU Assembly.[347] Compliance with the decision should be monitored by the Commission, and non-compliance could lead to the matter being referred to the attention of the competent organs of the AU with a request for the adoption of the necessary measures of implementation.[348]

> ACHPR, *Democratic Republic of Congo v. Burundi, Rwanda and Uganda*, Communication 227/99 (2003).
>
> The communication brought by the DRC against Burundi, Rwanda, and Uganda was the first inter-State case decided by the African Commission. It concerned the multiple violations of general international law, international human rights law, and international humanitarian law committed by the respondent States while occupying border provinces of the DRC in the eastern part of the country. Notwithstanding the fact that Rwanda and Uganda only engaged with the case during the stage of admissibility, while Burundi plainly refused to take part in the proceedings, the Commission found all three States responsible for multiple serious violations of the African Charter.
>
> The DRC alleged grave and systematic violations of human and peoples' rights committed by the armed forces of the three respondent States in the territory under occupation. These included a series of massacres of unarmed soldiers and civilian population; the systematic rape of girls and women by HIV-positive soldiers, aimed at propagating AIDS within the population; the deportation of civilians to 'concentration camps' in the territory of Rwanda; the systematic looting of the possessions of the population; and the besieging of a hydroelectric plant, which caused the disruption of energy supply to a hospital and the subsequent death of patients.
>
> The Commission found multiple breaches of the African Charter, encompassing, among others, the right to life; human dignity; the right to health; the right to property; the right to self-determination; and the right to peace. It made use of multiple sources of international law to interpret the scope of the rights under the African Charter, including the 1971 UN Declaration on Principles of International Law concerning Friendly Relations and Cooperation among States, and the four 1949 Geneva Conventions and its First Additional Protocol. As to its recommendations, it urged the three respondent States to abide by its obligations under international law and to pay compensation to the DRC for, and on behalf of, the victims of human rights violations.

8.7 CRITICAL DEBATES: TOWARDS A NEW AFRICAN COURT

The transformation of the OAU into the AU in the early 2000s led to envisioning the creation of several new organs for the incipient organization, including a Court of Justice of the AU.[349] In 2003, a Protocol creating this new court was adopted, which

---

[346] African Charter, Art. 52; ACHPR, Rules of Procedure, r. 112.
[347] ACHPR, Rules of Procedure, r. 114. [348] ACHPR, Rules of Procedure, rr. 125.8, 138.
[349] I. Kane and A.C. Motala, 'The Creation of a New African Court of Justice and Human Rights' in M. Evans and R. Murray, *The African Charter of Human and Peoples' Rights: The System in Practice, 1986–2006* (2nd edn., CUP 2008) 406–440, 409.

entered into force in 2009, and counted nineteen States Parties by the end of 2022—with the latest ratification received in 2020.[350] However, in 2004, the AU Assembly decided—apparently due to financial reasons—that instead of proceeding with the creation of a new court, the existing African Court of Human and Peoples' Rights would be integrated with the proposed Court of Justice, leading to the existence of only one court: the African Court of Justice and Human Rights.[351] The decision was surprising, and seemed abrupt, given that the idea of the existence of only one court had already been discussed at large, and dismissed, during the drafting of the Court of Justice Protocol.[352]

In 2005, the AU Assembly decided to proceed with drafting a protocol establishing a merged African Court of Justice and Human Rights (the 'Merger Protocol'). This new Protocol was to replace the 1998 and 2003 Protocols, which envisioned two separate courts.[353] The Court intended by the Merger Protocol would be composed of sixteen judges, half serving in the general affairs section and the other half in the human rights one. States nominating candidates to integrate the Court would need to indicate the section for which their candidate was proposed.[354] The Court would also be able to deal with cases as a Full Court of sixteen judges through the referral of a case by any of the sections.[355] The Court would have a rather wide substantive jurisdiction, encompassing all legal disputes concerning the interpretation and application of the AU Constitutive Act, any AU treaty and measures adopted by the organs of the Union, the African Charter on Human and Peoples' Rights, any human rights treaty ratified by States Parties, and any question of international law.[356] Legal standing before the Court would also be ample, especially when concerning human rights disputes. The draft Statute grants standing for any dispute to the States Parties to the Protocol, the AU Assembly and Parliament—and any other AU organ authorized by the Assembly—and to AU staff members under certain conditions regarding staff rules and regulations.[357] However,

---

[350] Information available on the AU's website, see: https://au.int/treaties/1164; https://au.int/treaties/protocol-court-justice-african-union (accessed on 14 March 2023).

[351] I. Kane and A.C. Motala, 'The Creation of a New African Court of Justice and Human Rights' in M. Evans and R. Murray, *The African Charter of Human and Peoples' Rights: The System in Practice, 1986–2006* (2nd edn., CUP 2008) 406–440, 409–410; V. Nmehielle, 'Financing and Sustaining the African Court of Justice and Human and Peoples' Rights' in C.C. Jalloh, K.M. Clarke, and V.O. Nmehielle (eds.), *The African Court of Justice and Human and Peoples' Rights in Context: Development and Challenges* (CUP 2019) 1057–1058. See: Decision on the seats of the Organs of the African Union, Decisions and Declarations, Assembly of the African Union, Third Ordinary Session, 6–8 July 2004, Addis Ababa, Ethiopia, Assembly/AU/Dec.45(III).

[352] I. Kane and A.C. Motala, 'The Creation of a New African Court of Justice and Human Rights' in M. Evans and R. Murray, *The African Charter of Human and Peoples' Rights: The System in Practice, 1986–2006* (2nd edn., CUP 2008) 406–440, 410–413; M. Hansungule, 'African courts and the African Commission on Human and Peoples' Rights' in A. Bösl and J. Diescho, *Human Rights in Africa: Legal Perspectives on their Protection and Promotion* (Konrad Adenauer 2009) 233–271, 236.

[353] Protocol on the Statute of the African Court of Justice and Human Rights (adopted on 1 July 2008) ('Merger Protocol'). The Protocol is set to enter into force thirty days after the deposit of fifteen ratifications (Art. 9). By the end of 2022, it had received eight ratifications. See: https://au.int/en/treaties/protocol-statute-african-court-justice-and-human-rights (accessed on 14 March 2023).

[354] Statute of the African Court of Justice and Human Rights (Annex to the 'Merger Protocol'), Arts. 3, 6, 16.

[355] Statute of the African Court of Justice and Human Rights, Arts. 18, 21.

[356] Statute of the African Court of Justice and Human Rights, Art. 28.

[357] Statute of the African Court of Justice and Human Rights, Art. 29.

when it concerns human rights cases, legal standing is conferred upon States Parties; the African Commission on Human and Peoples' Rights; the African Committee of Experts on the Rights and Welfare of the Child; African inter-governmental organizations accredited to the AU; African National Human Rights Institutions; as well as to individuals and NGOs, but in this case, subject to the respondent State having made a declaration to that effect.[358] Conversely, standing for requesting the Court to issue an advisory opinion is restricted to AU organs.[359]

Nevertheless, in February 2009, before the merged court could come into existence, the AU Assembly decided that the AU Commission, in consultation with the African Commission and Court, should examine the possibility of the envisioned new court having additional jurisdiction to judge grave international crimes, such as genocide, war crimes, and crimes against humanity.[360] This decision led to the drafting of a 'Protocol on Amendments to the Protocol on the Statute of the African Court of Justice and Human Rights' ('Malabo Protocol'), adopted in June 2014.[361] Although an important impulse behind the decision to create a regional criminal court to prosecute international crimes seemed to lie in the growing political tension between the AU and the International Criminal Court (ICC),[362] the desire of African States for the prosecution of such crimes can already be found in the 1970s, during the debates on the African Charter on Human and Peoples' Rights.[363]

Under the 2014 Protocol, the (yet-to-be-established) African Court of Justice and Human Rights would be composed of three sections instead of two, adding a criminal law section with jurisdiction to try individuals and corporations for the commission of international crimes.[364] The total number of judges remains sixteen, with the general

---

[358] Statute of the African Court of Justice and Human Rights, Art. 30. The 'Malabo Protocol', discussed later, envisions replacing the standing of individuals and NGOs as provided by the 'Merger Protocol', by restricting direct access only to 'African individuals' and 'African' NGOs with observer status before the AU or its organs, and only with respect to States that have made a special declaration allowing for direct access. See: 'Malabo Protocol', Art. 16.

[359] Statute of the African Court of Justice and Human Rights, Art. 53.

[360] G. Werle and M. Vormbaum, 'Creating an African Criminal Court' in G. Werle and M. Vormbaum (eds.), *The African Criminal Court: A Commentary on the Malabo Protocol* (Asser Press 2017) 3–9, 3. See: AU Assembly, Decision on the Implementation of the Assembly Decision on the Abuse of the Principle of Universal Jurisdiction, Assembly/AU/Dec.213(XII), para. 9.

[361] 'Protocol on Amendments to the Protocol on the Statute of the African Court of Justice and Human Rights' (adopted 27 June 2014).

[362] C.B. Murungu, 'Towards a Criminal Chamber in the African Court of Justice and Human Rights' (2011) 9 *Journal of International Criminal Justice* 1067, 1068–1069; N. Udombana, 'Can These Dry Bones Live? In Search of Lasting Therapy for AU and ICC Toxic Relationship' (2014) *African Journal of International Criminal Justice* 57, 62–66, 71–76; K.M. Clarke, C.C. Jalloh, and V. Nmehielle, 'Origins and Issues of the African Court of Justice and Human and Peoples' Rights in the Prosecution of Serious Crimes in Africa' in C.C. Jalloh, K.M. Clarke, and V.O. Nmehielle (eds.), *The African Court of Justice and Human and Peoples' Rights in Context: Development and Challenges* (CUP 2019) 1–53, 9.

[363] A. Abass 'Historical and Political Background to the Malabo Protocol' in G. Werle and M. Vormbaum (eds.), *The African Criminal Court: A Commentary on the Malabo Protocol* (Asser Press 2017) 11–28, 15–16; C.C. Jalloh, 'The Place of the African Court of Justice and Human and Peoples' Rights' in C.C. Jalloh, K.M. Clarke, and V.O. Nmehielle (eds.), *The African Court of Justice and Human and Peoples' Rights in Context: Development and Challenges* (CUP 2019) 57–108, 74.

[364] Statute of the African Court of Justice and Human Peoples' Rights (Annex to the 'Malabo Protocol'), Arts. 14, 22.

affairs and human rights sections sitting five judges each—instead of the envisioned eight—and the remaining six judges assigned to the criminal law section.[365] The criminal law section would have an ambitious jurisdiction encompassing fourteen international crimes, ranging from genocide, war crimes, and crimes against humanity to corruption, money laundering, and the illicit exploitation of natural resources.[366] However, at the end of 2022, no State had ratified the Malabo Protocol.[367]

The adoption of the Malabo Protocol has provoked strong reactions. Some of these are in favour, stressing the potential contributions the Court's criminal jurisdiction could make to comprehensively addressing, in a single legal forum, both State and individual responsibility following grave violations of human rights. However, other reactions towards the envisioned Court have been negative, perceiving it as an attempt to undermine the authority of the ICC instead of as a mechanism that would complement the latter's jurisdiction—since it was never intended, in any case, for the ICC to be the sole institutional response to atrocious international crimes.[368] Whichever the case might be, if created, the envisioned regional Court would be the first in the world to encompass general international law, international human rights law, and international criminal law jurisdiction in one singular judicial institution.

8.8 CONCLUSION

The African human (and peoples') rights system might be the youngest of the established regional systems for the protection of human rights, but it has come a long way since its inception in the 1980s. In our days, the system comprises an operating Commission and Court, which have taken seriously their mission to promote and protect human and peoples' rights within the African continent. Unfortunately, the development of the regional system has not been free from important challenges and shortcomings, including certain criticism of the Commission and Court for their lack of consistency in important aspects of their work, as discussed throughout this chapter.[369]

Arguably, the biggest challenge faced by the African system is the rather poor level of compliance with the decisions of its monitoring bodies. Although failing to provide

---

[365] Statute of the African Court of Justice and Human and Peoples' Rights (Annex to the 'Malabo Protocol'), Arts. 4, 16.

[366] Statute of the African Court of Justice and Human and Peoples' Rights (Annex to the 'Malabo Protocol'), Art. 14.

[367] Status of ratifications available on the AU's website, see: <https://au.int/en/treaties/1164 (accessed on 14 March 2023).

[368] P. Manirakiza, 'A TWAIL Perspective on the African Union's Project to Withdraw from the International Criminal Court' (2018) 23 *African Yearbook of International Law Online* 391, 422–423; K.M. Clarke, C.C. Jalloh, and V. Nmehielle, 'Origins and Issues of the African Court of Justice and Human and Peoples' Rights in the Prosecution of Serious Crimes in Africa' in C.C. Jalloh, K.M. Clarke, and V.O. Nmehielle (eds.), *The African Court of Justice and Human and Peoples' Rights in Context: Development and Challenges* (CUP 2019) 1–53, 13–15.

[369] The inclusion of the pilot-judgment procedure in the Court's Rules, inspired by the practice of the European Court (see **Section 7.3.8.1**), is a welcome addition that might not only have a positive effect in the preservation of the Court's limited resources, but which can also provide consistency in the decision of multiple similar cases. See: ACtHPR, Rules of Court, r. 66.

any specific data, the Commission has for years asserted that the level of compliance with the recommendations it adopts on communications is low.[370] It has also reported that only a handful of States—six, in the Commission's 2020 Report[371]—are up-to-date on their reporting obligations, while twenty States Parties have more than three outstanding reports, and six States have not even submitted their initial report.[372] The Court's 2020 and 2021 Reports present a similar appraisal of the situation. In these, the Court emphasized that one of the major problems it faces is the lack of cooperation from States in complying with its decisions, stating an overall poor level of compliance. Only a handful of States—namely, Burkina Faso, Côte d'Ivoire, and Tanzania—have adopted serious measures to comply with the more than one hundred judgments and orders the Court had rendered. Conversely, other States, such as Bénin, Libya, and Rwanda, have plainly failed to inform the Court of any measures adopted to comply with its judgments, when not openly indicating their intention not to comply.[373]

Another worrying situation is the overwhelming refusal of the majority of States to make the declaration under the African Court Protocol, allowing individuals and NGOs direct access to the Court. These include the five biggest contributors to the AU's budget—Algeria (Al Jaza'ir or Dzayer), Egypt (Misr), Morocco,[374] Nigeria, and South Africa.[375] To make matters worse, between 2016 and 2020, four States that had made the optional declaration—Rwanda, Tanzania, Bénin, and Côte d'Ivoire—proceeded to withdraw it, in a move that left more than one hundred million people with diminished protection of their human rights. This situation poses the risk of further worsening if such a decision was to be mimicked by the other States that have accepted direct access to the Court for individual cases.[376]

The lack of an adequate level of both human and financial resources has been another problem experienced by both main organs of the system.[377] The Commission has consistently raised its concerns about this problem through the years and has had to rely on contributions from external funders—including foreign governments and international organizations—for undertaking some of its activities. The Court has also raised the scarcity of funding as a problem limiting its operational capacity, and usually benefits from

---

[370] See, among many: ACHPR, 41st Activity Report (2016) 11; 42nd Activity Report (2017) 14; 45th Activity Report (2018) 13; 47th Activity Report (2019) 11; 48th and 49th Activity Report (2020) 16.

[371] Benin, Cameroon, Malawi, Mauritius, Niger, and Zimbabwe. See: 48th and 49th Activity Report (2020) 8.

[372] Comoros, Equatorial Guinea, Guinea Bissau, Sao Tome and Principe, Somalia, and South Sudan. See: 48th and 49th Activity Report (2020) 8.

[373] ACtHPR, Activity Report of the African Court on Human and Peoples' Rights (2021), EX.CL/1258(XXXVIII), pp. 13–14; ACtHPR, Activity Report of the African Court on Human and Peoples' Rights (2022), EX.CL/1323(XL), Annex II.

[374] Morocco being also the only AU State not even Party to the African Charter.

[375] S. Adjolohoun, 'A crisis of design and judicial practice? Curbing state disengagement from the African Court on Human and Peoples' Rights' (2020) 20 *African Human Rights Law Journal* 1, 3.

[376] ACtHPR, Activity Report of the African Court on Human and Peoples' Rights (2021), EX.CL/1258(XXXVIII), p. 14.

[377] F. Adolu, 'A View from the Inside: the role of the Secretariat' in M. Evans and R. Murray, *The African Charter of Human and Peoples' Rights: The System in Practice, 1986–2006* (2nd edn., CUP 2008) 316–343, 339–343; R. Murray, *The African Charter on Human and Peoples' Rights: A Commentary* (OUP 2019) 616–620; ACtHPR, Activity Report of the African Court on Human and Peoples' Rights (2021), EX.CL/1258(XXXVIII), p. 15.

external funders to carry out its tasks.[378] As highlighted, the scarcity of financial resources was the essential reason claimed in 2004 for the decision of the AU Assembly to merge the proposed Court of Justice with the African Court of Human and Peoples' Rights. However, this envisioned Court, further extended by the Malabo Protocol to encompass a third section exercising criminal jurisdiction, will require substantial additional resources.[379] Although it is not really clear when (or even if) the Malabo Protocol will come into force—which is unlikely to happen in the near future[380]—the work of a court with such a unique and comprehensive jurisdiction would require a strong commitment from the AU and its Member States to provide the adequate level of resources for its operation. Considering the financial difficulties experienced by the existent regional human rights bodies, whether a truthful will exists to provide the needed resources remains uncertain.

FURTHER READING

BÖSL, A. and DIESCHO, J., *Human Rights in Africa: Legal Perspectives on their Protection and Promotion* (Konrad Adenauer 2009).

EVANS, M. and MURRAY, R., *The African Charter of Human and Peoples' Rights: The System in Practice, 1986–2006* (2nd edn., CUP 2008).

JALLOH, C.C., CLARKE, K.M., and NMEHIELLE, V.O., *The African Court of Justice and Human and Peoples' Rights in Context: Development and Challenges* (CUP 2019).

KUFUOR, K.O., *The African Human Rights System: Origin and Evolution* (Palgrave 2010).

MURRAY, R., *The African Charter on Human and Peoples' Rights: A Commentary* (OUP 2019).

OKAFOR, O.C., *The African Human Rights System, Activist, Forces, and International Institutions* (CUP 2007).

OUGUERGOUZ, F., *African Charter of Human and People's Rights: A Comprehensive Agenda for Human Dignity and Sustainable Democracy in Africa* (Nijhoff 2003).

VILJOEN, F., *International Human Rights Law in Africa* (2nd edn., OUP 2012).

WERLE, G., and VORMBAUM, M. (eds.), *The African Criminal Court: A Commentary on the Malabo Protocol* (Asser Press 2017).

---

[378] ACtHPR, Activity Report of the African Court on Human and Peoples' Rights (2021), EX.CL/1258(XXXVIII), pp. 11, 15; ACtHPR, Activity Report of the African Court on Human and Peoples' Rights (2020), EX.CL/1204(XXXVI), pp. 10, 16.

[379] M. du Plessis, 'Implications of the AU Decision to Give the African Court Jurisdiction over International Crimes', ISS Paper 235 (June 2012), 9–10; K.M. Clarke, C.C. Jalloh, and V. Nmehielle, 'Origins and Issues of the African Court of Justice and Human and Peoples' Rights in the Prosecution of Serious Crimes in Africa' in C.C. Jalloh, K.M. Clarke, and V.O. Nmehielle (eds.), *The African Court of Justice and Human and Peoples' Rights in Context: Development and Challenges* (CUP 2019) 1–53, 42–44; S. Ford, 'Between Hope and Doubt: The Malabo Protocol and the Resource Requirements of an African Criminal Court' in C.C. Jalloh, K.M. Clarke, and V.O. Nmehielle (eds.), *The African Court of Justice and Human and Peoples' Rights in Context: Development and Challenges* (CUP 2019) 1076–1100.

[380] S. Ford, 'Between Hope and Doubt: The Malabo Protocol and the Resource Requirements of an African Criminal Court' in C.C. Jalloh, K.M. Clarke, and V.O. Nmehielle (eds.), *The African Court of Justice and Human and Peoples' Rights in Context: Development and Challenges* (CUP 2019) 1076–1100, 1080; S. Adjolohoun, 'A crisis of design and judicial practice? Curbing state disengagement from the African Court on Human and Peoples' Rights' (2020) 20 *African Human Rights Law Journal* 1, 40.

PART IV

SUBSTANTIVE RIGHTS

The final part of this book extends across two chapters, both concerned with a range of specific rights. While it was not possible to include, in one book, the discussion of all possible human rights, it was particularly challenging to select key rights to engage with. Ultimately, deciding which rights to feature was based on consultations with different colleagues about the topics they cover in their respective courses.

Chapter 9 deals with more classical rights, which range from the right to life and the right to personal integrity—encompassing the prohibition of torture and cruel, inhuman, and degrading treatment—to the fundamental freedoms of opinion and expression, and of thought, conscience, and religion. We purposely decided not to differentiate rights across dated classifications concerning generations or categories; a discussion of the 'traditional' distinction of rights—and their respective obligations and means of implementation—between civil and political rights, and economic, social, and cultural rights was covered in the historical discussion about the development of the international law of human rights, provided in **Chapter 2**. We believe that traditional classifications of rights belong to the history of human rights, as a more comprehensive understanding of human rights discloses their interconnected individual, social, and collective dimensions and effects.

The substantive rights selected for **Chapter 10** place further emphasis on rights held by individuals as members of specific social collectives, to then focus on fundamental rights that belongs to a collective or people rather than to their members individually. The chapter starts with a discussion of the prohibition of discrimination, which is both a fundamental right and a general guarantee applicable to respecting and protecting all rights. Then, it delves into the discussion of rights held by individuals belonging to two social groups, covering the topics of women's rights and of children's rights. The chapter concludes by exploring the right to self-determination of peoples, a paradigmatic example of a right whose right-holder is a collective of individuals, and the topic of indigenous peoples' rights.

Along with the exploration of these rights, significant attempts have been made to provide an engagement with a plurality of monitoring bodies from across the world and their interpretation of the content and scope of the different rights. Moreover, the critiques presented in **Chapter 1** are brought back into the discussion of some rights to illustrate how these can be applied to provide a different interpretation that highlights existent shortcomings that are usually left unproblematized.

9

THE INTERNATIONAL PROTECTION OF SUBSTANTIVE RIGHTS (I)

9.1 THE RIGHT TO LIFE

9.1.1 NORMATIVE RECOGNITION

Undoubtedly, the right to life is an essential right; its effective protection acts as a prerequisite for the enjoyment of all other human rights.[1] Its fundamental character is recognized in all foundational instruments of the international law of human rights, even if the phrasing of this protection differs to some degree among the texts.[2] From these, the more comprehensive provisions are the ones provided by the International Covenant on Civil and Political Rights (ICCPR) and the European and American Conventions on Human Rights. These instruments recognize the importance of the right to life as an inalienable attribute of the individual,[3] from which no derogation is allowed, even in situations of armed conflict and public emergency.[4] Although, at the same time, these instruments all reveal a political compromise concerning the

---

[1] Special Rapporteur (Amos Vako), 'Summary or Arbitrary Executions', E/CN.4/1983/16 (1983) para. 22; IACtHR, *'Street Children' (Villagrán Morales et al.) v. Guatemala*. Merits. Judgment of November 19, 1999. Series C No. 63, para. 144; CCPR, General Comment No. 36 on the Right to Life, CCPR/C/GC/36 (2018), para. 2.

[2] Universal Declaration of Human Rights (adopted 10 December 1948) UNGA Res. 217.A(III), Art. 3; American Declaration of the Rights and Duties of Man (adopted 2 May 1948), Art. I; International Covenant on Civil and Political Rights (adopted 16 December 1966, entered into force 23 March 1976) 999 UNTS 171, Art. 6; European Convention on Human Rights (adopted 4 November 1950, entered into force 3 September 1953) 213 UNTS 221, Art. 2; American Convention on Human Rights (adopted 22 November 1969, entered into force 18 July 1978) 1144 UNTS 123, Art. 4; African Charter on Human and Peoples' Rights (adopted on 27 June 1981, entered into force 21 October 1986), OAU Doc. CAB/LEG/67/3 rev. 5, 21 I.L.M. 58 (1982), Art. 4; Arab Charter on Human Rights (adopted 22 May 2004, entered into force 15 March 2008), ST/HR/]CHR/NONE/2004/40/Rev. 1, Arts. 5–7; ASEAN Human Rights Declaration (adopted 18 November 2012), Art. 11.

[3] IACHR, Report 47/96, Case 11.436 (*Victims of the Tugboat '13 de marzo' v. Cuba*) (16 October 1996), Annual Report of the Inter-American Commission on Human Rights 1996 (14 March 1997), OEA/Ser.L/V/II.95 Doc. 7 rev., para. 79; ECtHR, *Streletz, Kessler and Krenz v. Germany* [GC], App. nos. 34044/96 and two others, § 94, ECHR 2001-II; CCPR, General Comment No. 36 on the Right to Life, CCPR/C/GC/36 (2018), para. 2.

[4] ICCPR, Art. 4; ECHR, Art. 15; ACHR, Art. 27.

scope of the right to life; its protection not expressed in the same absolute terms as the prohibition of torture—discussed in **Section 9.2**.[5]

The aforementioned treaties also present the most common features of the protection of the right to life under the international law of human rights. These are the prohibition of arbitrary deprivation of life, the existing restrictions on the use of the death penalty as a means of State punishment, and the obligation upon States to protect this right by domestic law. Each of these features will be discussed in turn, following a brief but important engagement with the debate surrounding the moment when the protection of the right to life begins.

9.1.1.1 The beginning of life

The precise moment at which the protection of the right to life begins has been the subject of extensive controversy, especially regarding the legal regulation of abortion.[6] During the drafting process of the Universal Declaration of Human Rights, it was discussed whether this instrument was to pinpoint when the protection of the right to life was to commence. Proposals to include the moment of conception as the beginning of life were rejected at different stages of the negotiation of the text,[7] with the Declaration's final phrasing stating: 'All human beings are *born* free and equal in dignity and rights'.[8] A similar discussion had ensued months earlier, during the adoption of the American Declaration of the Rights and Duties of Man, where proposals to indicate the precise moment at which the protection of life was to start were also rejected.[9]

Conversely, a somewhat unclear reference to the beginning of life managed to be included in the text of the American Convention on Human Rights, which states that the right to life shall be protected 'in general, from the moment of conception'.[10] Unsurprisingly, such an ambiguous expression has been the source of misinterpretations. Nevertheless, both the Inter-American Commission and Court have clarified that such a provision should not be interpreted as imposing upon States a duty to regulate restrictively the access to abortion within their jurisdictions, since it was actually a

---

[5] C.K. Boyle, 'The Concept of Arbitrary Deprivation of Life', in B.G. Ramcharan, *The Right to Life in International Law* (Nijhoff 1985) 221, 222–223; E. Wicks, *The Right to Life and Conflicting Interests* (OUP 2010) 42.

[6] IACHR, Resolution 23/81, Case 2141 (United States) (6 March 1981), Annual Report of the Inter-American Commission on Human Rights 1981–1982 (16 October 1981), OEA/Ser.L/V/II.54 Doc. 9 rev. 1; ECtHR, *W.P. v. UK* (dec.), App. no. 8416/78, 13 May 1980; ECtHR, *H. v. Norway* (dec.), App. no. 17004/90, 19 May 1992; ECtHR, *Boso v. Italy* (dec), App. no. 50490/99, 5 September 2002; CCPR, *Mellet v. Ireland*, CCPR/C/116/D/2324/2013 (17 November 2016), para. 7.7.

[7] R. Copelon et al., 'Human Rights Begin at Birth: International Law and the Claim of Fetal Rights' (2005) 13 *Reproductive Health Matters* 120, 121–122; C. Zampas and J. Gher, 'Abortion as a Human Right – International and Regional Standards' (2008) 8 *Human Rights Law Review* 249, 262–263. See: E/CN.4/AC.1/SR.12 (20 June 1947); E/CN.4/AC.1/SR.35 (17 May 1948); E/SR.215174 (25 August 1948).

[8] UDHR, Art. 1 (emphasis added).

[9] IACHR, Resolution 23/81, Case 2141 (United States) (6 March 1981), Annual Report of the Inter-American Commission on Human Rights 1981–1982 (16 October 1981), OEA/Ser.L/V/II.54 Doc. 9 rev. 1, para. 18; IACtHR, *Artavia Murillo et al. (In Vitro Fertilization) v. Costa Rica*. Preliminary Objections, Merits, Reparations and Costs. Judgment of November 28, 2012. Series C No. 257, paras. 195–198.

[10] ACHR, Art. 4.1.

reflection of the compromise reached by the drafters of the Convention in view of the diverging legislation existing among the American States in the 1960s when the text of the Convention was adopted.[11] An attempt to introduce a similar clause to the provision on the right to life under ICCPR—made by Belgium, Brazil, El Salvador, México, and Morocco, during the drafting process—was defeated by a vote within the General Assembly's Third Committee.[12]

The determination of the moment at which life begins was also a contentious issue during the drafting of the UN Convention on the Rights of the Child (UNCRC). A proposal, made by Ireland and the Holy See, aimed at clarifying, in the preambular part of the treaty, that the rights of the child were to commence before birth was rejected during the drafting process.[13] The adopted solution was to make no reference as to the beginning of life within the Convention, allowing States to determine this issue within their domestic legislation.[14] This open-ended approach prompted some States to include declarative interpretations, on their ratifying instruments to the Convention, stating their position on the matter. These included those which endorsed the moment of conception as the beginning of life—such as Argentina and Guatemala—, as well as those which clarified that nothing in the Convention could be interpreted as restricting their domestic laws and policies allowing for the interruption of pregnancies—such as France, Luxembourg, and Tunisia.[15]

In their interpretation of their respective treaties, the stance expressly adopted by both the European and American Courts of Human Rights is that it is not for an international court to determine a precise moment in which life begins and, therefore, when the protection of the right to life starts.[16] This has led the European Court to continue granting a rather wide discretion to States as to how abortion can be regulated under domestic laws, despite the existence of an overwhelming degree of consensus among European States on the matter.[17] Conversely, the approach adopted within the African human rights system has included the explicit normative recognition of women's reproductive rights in terms that clarify the right to have access to medical abortion in a range of situations, including that of sexual assault and where the continuation of a pregnancy endangers the mental and physical health of the woman.[18] Similarly, the

---

[11] IACHR, Resolution 23/81, Case 2141 (United States) (6 March 1981), Annual Report of the Inter-American Commission on Human Rights 1981–1982 (16 October 1981), OEA/Ser.L/V/II.54 Doc. 9 rev. 1, paras. 25–29; IACtHR, *Artavia Murillo et al. (In Vitro Fertilization) v. Costa Rica*. Preliminary Objections, Merits, Reparations and Costs. Judgment of November 28, 2012. Series C No. 257, paras. 204–211.

[12] Report of the Third Committee, A/3764 (5 December 1957), paras. 112, 119.

[13] G. Van Bueren, *The International Law on the Rights of the Child* (Nihoff 1995) 33–34.

[14] Only a passing reference to the safeguard and care needed by children, even before birth, appears in the preamble. See: UNCRC, preamble.

[15] See the status of ratification of UNCRC, available at: https://treaties.un.org/pages/ViewDetails.aspx?src=IND&mtdsg_no=IV-11&chapter=4 (accessed on 6 April 2023).

[16] ECtHR, *Vo v. France* [GC], App. no. 53924/00, § 82, ECHR 2004-VIII; ECtHR, *Evans v. the United Kingdom* [GC], App. no. 6339/05, § 54, ECHR 2007-I; IACtHR, *Artavia Murillo et al. (In Vitro Fertilization) v. Costa Rica*. Preliminary Objections, Merits, Reparations and Costs. Judgment of November 28, 2012. Series C No. 257, para. 185.

[17] ECtHR, *A, B and C v. Ireland* [GC], App. no. 25579/05, § 235–237, ECHR 2010.

[18] Protocol to the African Charter on Human and Peoples' Rights on the Rights of Women in Africa (adopted on 1 July 2003, entered into force 25 November 2005) ('Maputo Protocol').

Human Rights Committee has expressed its view that a restrictive access to voluntary termination of pregnancies can jeopardize the human rights of girls and women.[19]

9.1.2 THE PROHIBITION OF ARBITRARY DEPRIVATION OF LIFE

The first and foremost obligation imposed upon States concerning the protection of the right to life is the prohibition of arbitrarily depriving someone of their life. Obvious examples of the violation of such a prohibition are the cases of arbitrary, summary, or extrajudicial executions carried out by State agents.[20] However, the prohibition of *arbitrary* deprivation of life implies the existence of circumstances in which a deprivation of life attributable to the State might be considered legitimate, such as during armed conflict, in compliance with international humanitarian law, or when absolutely necessary to protect individuals from imminent threat of death or serious injury. In order to determine whether a deprivation of life entails the responsibility of the State, international monitoring bodies must examine, with the most careful scrutiny, the context in which the deprivation of life has occurred. The use of potentially lethal force for law enforcement is in itself an extreme measure that should only be resorted to when strictly necessary in order to protect life or prevent serious injury from an imminent threat.[21] When lethal force has been used by State agents, regard should be had both to the actions of the agents themselves and to the surrounding circumstances, including the planning and control of the actions under examination.[22] Given the gravity of the violation at stake, a deprivation of life attributable to the State would only be in conformity with the international law of human rights when the State can prove the absolute necessity of its agents' actions in order to fulfil a legitimate security operation.

9.1.2.1 Further reflections: forced disappearances[23]

Forced disappearance could be defined as the arrest, detention, abduction, or any other form of deprivation of liberty of a person, perpetrated by State agents, or by persons acting with the authorization, support, or acquiescence of the State, followed by an absence of information or a refusal to acknowledge that deprivation of liberty, or to give information on the whereabouts of that person, thereby placing such a person

---

[19] CCPR, General Comment No. 36 on the Right to Life, CCPR/C/GC/36 (2018), para. 8.

[20] CCPR, *Suarez de Guerrero v. Colombia*, Communication 11/45, CCPR/C/15/D/45/1979 (1982); CCPR, *Baboeram-Adhin et al. v. Suriname*, Communications 146/1983, CCPR/C/24/D/146/1983 (1985); IACtHR, *Aloeboetoe et al. v. Suriname*. Merits. Judgment of December 4, 1991. Series C No. 11; IACtHR, *El Amparo v. Venezuela*. Merits. Judgment of January 18, 1995. Series C No. 19.

[21] CCPR, General Comment No. 36 on the Right to Life, CCPR/C/GC/36 (2018), para. 12.

[22] ECtHR, *McCann and Others v. the United Kingdom*, 27 September 1995, § 150, Series A no. 324.

[23] Sometimes also referred to as 'enforced' or 'involuntary' disappearances.

outside the protection of the law.²⁴ This international crime entails the multiple and continuing violation of several human rights.²⁵ The arbitrary deprivation of liberty is a violation of the right to liberty and security of the person; the prolonged isolation and deprivation of communication are in themselves forms of cruel and inhuman treatment; the uncertainty that surrounds this crime, including the absence of due judicial scrutiny, is a breach of the rights to a fair trial and judicial guarantees, and of the right to an effective remedy; the situation of uncertainty in which the victim is placed, preventing them from exercising their rights in general, amounts to a breach of the right to recognition as a person before the law; and the refusal of the authorities to disclose the whereabouts of the victim allows inferring the violation of the right to life.²⁶

But it is not only the direct victim who suffers a violation of their human rights in cases of forced disappearance. This crime also entails the violation of the rights of the direct victim's next-of-kin, including their own right to personal integrity, given the suffering caused by the disappearance of a loved one, as well as their right to obtain justice for the crime against their family member.²⁷ Importantly, the multiple violations of rights caused by the crime of forced disappearance are of continuous duration until the time in which the fate of the victim is established by the State authorities.²⁸ A further legal development connected with the crime of forced disappearance has been the proclamation of a right to truth, which assists both the direct and indirect victims of this crime, as well as the society as a whole.²⁹ As affirmed by the Inter-American Commission of Human Rights: 'Every society has the inalienable right to know the

---

[24] Inter-American Convention on Forced Disappearance of Persons (adopted 9 June 1994, entered into force 28 March 1996), OAS Treaty Series 68, Art. II; International Convention for the Protection of All Persons from Enforced Disappearance (adopted 20 December 2006, entered into force 23 December 2010), 2716 UNTS 3, Art. 2.

[25] Report of the Working Group on Enforced or Involuntary Disappearances, 'Question of Human Rights of All Persons Subjected to any Form of Detention or Imprisonment, in Particular: Question of Missing and Disappeared Persons', E/CN.4/1435 (26 January 1981), paras. 184–187; IACtHR, *Velásquez Rodríguez v. Honduras*. Merits. Judgment of July 29, 1988. Series C No. 4, para. 155.

[26] UNGA, Declaration on the Protection of all Persons from Enforced Disappearance, Resolution 47/133 (18 December 1992), Art. 1.2; IACtHR, *Velásquez Rodríguez v. Honduras*. Merits. Judgment of July 29, 1988. Series C No. 4, paras. 155–158; IACtHR, *Anzualdo Castro v. Peru*. Preliminary Objection, Merits, Reparations and costs. Judgment of September 22, 2009. Series C No. 202, para. 103.

[27] CCPR, *Quinteros v. Uruguay*, Communication 107/1981 (1981), CCPR/C/19/D/107/1981, para. 14; IACtHR, *Bámaca Velásquez v. Guatemala*. Merits. Judgment of November 25, 2000. Series C No. 70, paras. 165–166, 195–196; IACtHR, *Anzualdo Castro v. Peru*. Preliminary Objection, Merits, Reparations and Costs. Judgment of September 22, 2009. Series C No. 202, paras. 118–119.

[28] IACtHR, *Velásquez Rodríguez v. Honduras*. Merits. Judgment of July 29, 1988. Series C No. 4, para. 155. See: UNGA, Declaration on the Protection of all Persons from Enforced Disappearance, Art. 17.1; Inter-American Convention on Forced Disappearance of Persons, Art. III; International Convention for the Protection of All Persons from Enforced Disappearance, Art. 8.1.(b).

[29] IACHR, Report No. 25/98 (Chile), OEA/Ser.L/V/II.98. Doc. 6 rev. (13 April 1998), para. 94; I/A Court H.R., *Bámaca Velásquez v. Guatemala*. Merits. Judgment of November 25, 2000. Series C No. 70, separate opinion of Judge A.A. Cançado Trindade para. 32; IACtHR, *Bámaca Velásquez v. Guatemala*. Reparations and Costs. Judgment of February 22, 2002. Series C No. 91, para. 76. See also: D. Gonzalez-Salzberg, 'El Derecho a la Verdad en Situaciones de Post-conflicto Bélico de Carácter No-internacional' (2008) 12 *International Law: Revista Colombiana de Derecho Internacional* 435.

truth about past events, as well as the motives and circumstances in which aberrant crimes came to be committed, in order to prevent repetition of such acts in the future.'[30]

The systematic practice of this State crime has been part of the repressive policy of multiple States throughout the twentieth century, from its use by the Nazi regime to its implementation during the Guatemalan conflict in the 1960s and their adoption by the dictatorships in the South Cone of the American continent in the 1970s.[31] The cruelty of such crime led to its examination by different international monitoring mechanisms. Within the United Nations, the Commission on Human Rights established the Working Group on Chile in 1975 — following the 1973 coup d'état—which placed special emphasis on the widespread use of torture by the Pinochet regime but also raised concerns about the practice of forced disappearance.[32] This paved the way for the creation of a Working Group 'to examine questions relevant to enforced or involuntary disappearances of persons', which continues to exist in our days.[33] The work of the Inter-American Commission on Human Rights in this area has also been remarkable, engaging with multiple governments that made use of forced disappearance as a systematic crime for decades.[34] In particular, it was the Commission's country report on Argentina, following its visit in 1979, that gained substantial notoriety due to its extensive engagement with the topic of forced disappearances under the military dictatorship.[35]

The prohibition of forced disappearance is solidly established under the international law of human rights, cemented by the adoption of a number of international instruments, including the 1992 UN Declaration on the Protection of All Persons from Enforced Disappearance, the 1994 Inter-American Convention on Forced Disappearance of Persons, and the 2006 International Convention for the Protection of All Persons from Enforced Disappearance. The prohibition of this international crime is of an absolute character, placing its prohibition within the realm of *jus cogens*.[36] It entails the aggravated responsibility of the State, encompassing more severe legal consequences, such as the

---

[30] IACHR, Annual Report of the Inter-American Commission on Human Rights 1985–1986, OEA/Ser.L/V/II.68. Doc. 8 rev. 1 (26 September 1986), Chapter V.

[31] Amnesty International, *Disappearances: A Workbook* (Amnesty International USA 1981) 1–3; R. Brody and F. González, 'Nunca Más: An Analysis of International Instruments on "Disappearances"' (1997) 19 *Human Rights Quarterly* 365, 366.

[32] Report of the Ad Hoc Working Group established under resolution 8 (XXXI) of the Commission on Human Rights to inquire into the situation of human rights in Chile, E/CN.4/1310 (1 February 1979).

[33] Commission on Human Rights, Resolution 20(XXXVI) Question of missing and disappeared persons (29 February 1980).

[34] R. Brody and F. González, 'Nunca Más: An Analysis of International Instruments on "Disappearances"' (1997) 19 *Human Rights Quarterly* 365, 367. See, for instance, IACHR, Report on the Status of Human Rights in Chile, OEA/Ser.L/V/II.34 Doc. 21 corr.1 (25 October 1974).

[35] IACHR, Report on the Situation of Human Rights in Argentina, OEA/Ser.L/V/II.49 Doc. 19 corr.1 (11 April 1980).

[36] When part of a systematic practice, this crime is considered a crime against humanity, located in the convergence of the international law of human rights and international criminal law. See: UNGA, Declaration on the Protection of all Persons from Enforced Disappearance, preamble; Inter-American Convention on Forced Disappearance of Persons, preamble; International Convention for the Protection of All Persons from Enforced Disappearance, preamble, and Art. 5; Statute of the International Criminal Court (adopted 17 July 1998, entered into force 1 July 2002), Art. 7.1.(i).

need to adopt wider measures of reparation, aimed at avoiding both impunity for the violation committed and recidivism. These remedies include not only the payment of compensation to the victim's next-of-kin but also the duty to undertake an investigation of the facts surrounding the crime, establishing both the truth about the victim's fate and the individual criminal responsibility of the perpetrators, as well as the adoption of measures that would preserve the collective memory of the facts and the victims. Moreover, States are banned from adopting any measures that would obstruct the investigation and prosecutions or even restrict or suppress the effect of the conviction, as discussed in **Section 9.1.4**.

9.1.3 THE DEATH PENALTY

The original protection of the right to life in the different international instruments did not include an absolute proscription on the death penalty but only contained a number of restrictions to its application. The European Convention established that the death penalty could only be applied to crimes for which it was provided by law and following a conviction and sentence imposed by a court of law.[37] To this, ICCPR added that the law could only contemplate such penalty for the most serious crimes and that such legislation needs to be contemporaneous to the commission of the crime—banning the possibility of retrospective laws.[38] In addition, ICCPR forbade the imposition of the death penalty for crimes committed by individuals younger than eighteen and prohibited its application to pregnant women.[39] The provision also states that anyone sentenced to death has the right to seek a pardon or the commutation of the sentence.[40] The American Convention went further in the regulation of the death penalty in an attempt to 'delimit strictly its application and scope, in order to reduce the application of the penalty to bring about its gradual disappearance'.[41] It set an absolute prohibition on re-establishing the death penalty in States that have abolished it and a complete ban on extending its applicability to crimes for which such a penalty was not provided for under domestic law at the time the State became Party to the Convention.[42] Following ICCPR, the American Convention also restricted the death penalty to the most serious crimes and clarified that it cannot be inflicted for political offences or related common crimes.[43] It also went further than ICCPR as to personal limitations, indicating that capital punishment cannot be imposed upon persons who, at the time the crime was committed, were under eighteen or over seventy years of age. Similarly, its application

---

[37] ECHR, Art. 2.1.   [38] ICCPR, Art. 6.2.
[39] The Arab Charter on Human Rights extends this 'moratorium' in the applicability of the death penalty to nursing mothers within two years from the date of delivery. See: Arab Charter, Art. 7.2.
[40] ICCPR, Arts. 6.4–6.5.
[41] IACtHR, *Restrictions to the Death Penalty (Arts. 4(2) and 4(4) American Convention on Human Rights)*. Advisory Opinion OC-3/83 of September 8, 1983. Series A no. 3, para. 57.
[42] ACHR, Art. 4.2–3; IACtHR, *Restrictions to the Death Penalty (Arts. 4(2) and 4(4) American Convention on Human Rights)*. Advisory Opinion OC-3/83 of September 8, 1983. Series A no. 3, op. para. 3.a.1.
[43] ACHR, Art. 4.4.

is banned not only banned to women but also to anyone who has applied for amnesty, pardon, or commutation of sentence while the petition is pending a decision by the competent authority.[44]

Following these initial restrictions, protocols aimed at the complete abolition of the death penalty have been adopted to complement the ICCPR and the European and American Conventions. Within the Council of Europe, a first protocol (Protocol 6) was adopted in 1983, establishing a complete prohibition of the death penalty, except with respect to acts committed in time of war—or of imminent threat of war. A subsequent protocol (Protocol 13) was adopted in 2002, which laid down an absolute ban on the death penalty in all circumstances.[45] Most States Parties to the Convention are Parties to the latter Protocol, with the exception of Armenia and Azerbaijan—or Russia, when still Party to the Convention.[46] Optional protocols on the abolition of the death penalty were also adopted to complement the restrictions imposed by ICCPR and the American Convention, respectively, in 1989 and 1990. Both these protocols established an absolute prohibition on the applicability of the death penalty in the territory under the jurisdiction of States Parties, only allowing the possibility of appending a reservation, at the time of ratification or accession, concerning the possibility of applying the death penalty in wartime for extremely serious crimes of a military nature.[47] Unfortunately, the level of ratification of these optional protocols is not as high as could be desired, with a much lower ratio of Parties than Protocol 13 to the European Convention.[48]

Nevertheless, the restrictions to the death penalty are of an evolving nature, including for States that have not become Parties to the mentioned additional protocols. For instance, the Human Rights Committee has found that under ICCPR the abolition of the death penalty is legally irrevocable—alike the regime existent under the American Convention—, States that have already abolished it cannot re-implement it, nor can they extend it to crimes that did not entail such punishment.[49] Similarly, the scope of the 'most serious crimes' for which the death penalty could be imposed has been gradually clarified,[50] and it is currently accepted that its application can only be considered for

---

[44] ACHR, Arts. 4.5, 4.6.

[45] Protocol No. 6 to the Convention for the Protection of Human Rights and Fundamental Freedoms concerning the Abolition of the Death Penalty (adopted 28 April 1983, entered into force 1 January 1985) ETS No. 114; Protocol No. 13 to the Convention for the Protection of Human Rights and Fundamental Freedoms, concerning the Abolition of the Death Penalty in All Circumstances (adopted 3 May 2002, entered into force 1 July 2003) ETS No. 187.

[46] See: https://www.coe.int/en/web/conventions/full-list?module=signatures-by-treaty&treatynum=187 (accessed on 1 May 2023).

[47] Second Optional Protocol to the International Covenant on Civil and Political Rights, aiming at the abolition of the death penalty (adopted by General Assembly Resolution 44/128 of 15 December 1989), Arts. 1, 2.1; Protocol to the American Convention on Human Rights to Abolish the Death Penalty (adopted 6 August 1990), OAS Treaty Series No. 73, Arts. 1, 2.1.

[48] See: https://indicators.ohchr.org/: http://www.oas.org/juridico/english/sigs/a-53.html.

[49] CCPR, General Comment No. 36 on the Right to Life, CCPR/C/GC/36 (2018), para. 34.

[50] CCPR, *Lubuto v. Zambia*, Communication 390/1990, CCPR/C/55/D/390/1990/Rev. 1 (1995), para. 72.2; IACtHR, *Raxcacó Reyes v. Guatemala*. Merits, Reparations and Costs. Judgment of September 15, 2005. Series C No. 133, paras. 71–72.

crimes involving intentional killing.[51] As to the personal restrictions to the death penalty, the Committee has affirmed that States must also refrain from imposing the death penalty on individuals who faced special barriers in defending themselves during trial, such as those with serious psychosocial or intellectual disabilities.[52]

Another clear restriction to the death penalty, acknowledged by the Human Rights Committee, the Inter-American Court of Human Rights, and the African Court on Human and Peoples' Rights, is that the legislation contemplating the death penalty cannot mandate its imposition for specific crimes, depriving the judicial organ of its ability to consider the defendant's personal circumstances or the circumstances of the particular offence.[53] In other words, criminal legislation that establishes the automatic application of the death penalty for a specific crime amounts to a violation of the prohibition against the arbitrary deprivation of life.[54]

On its part, the European Court of Human Rights has gone as far as to consider that, within the Council of Europe, there is enough State practice to indicate that 'the Convention has been amended so as to prohibit the death penalty in all circumstances'.[55] Consequently, even the States that have not yet become Parties to Protocol 13 would be under the obligation to refrain from applying the death penalty under their jurisdiction. It could be inferred that the Human Rights Committee is of a similar opinion with regard to ICCPR, as in its more recent General Comment on the right to life, it has stated that:

> The increasing number of States parties to the Second Optional Protocol to the Covenant, aiming at the abolition of the death penalty, other international instruments prohibiting the imposition or carrying out of the death penalty, and the growing number of non-abolitionist States that have nonetheless introduced a de facto moratorium on the exercise of the death penalty, suggest that considerable progress may have been made towards establishing an agreement among the States parties to consider the death penalty as a cruel, inhuman or degrading form of punishment.[56]

If this interpretation by the Committee is correct, then every State Party could be considered under the obligation to eliminate this type of penalty as a form of criminal punishment under general international law, given the peremptory character of the prohibition of cruel, inhuman, and degrading treatment.

---

[51] CCPR, Consideration of Reports, Algeria (9 October 1992), paras. 289, 297; CCPR, Consideration of Reports, Republic of Korea (9 October 1992), paras. 506, 517; CCPR, Concluding Observations on the Islamic Republic of Iran, CCPR/C/79/Add. 25 (1993), para. 8. See also: ACHPR, General Comment No. 3 on the African Charter on Human and Peoples' Rights: The Rights to Life (2015), para. 24.

[52] CCPR, General Comment No. 36 on the Right to Life, CCPR/C/GC/36 (2018), para. 49.

[53] CCPR, *Eversley Thompson v. St. Vincent and the Grenadines*, Communication 806/1998, CCPR/C/70/D/806/1998 (2000); IACtHR, *Hilaire, Constantine and Benjamin et al. v. Trinidad and Tobago*. Merits, Reparations and Costs. Judgment of June 21, 2002. Series C No. 94; ACtHPR, *Ally Rajabu and others v. Tanzania*, App. 7/2015, Judgment (28 Nov. 2019).

[54] IACtHR, *Hilaire, Constantine and Benjamin et al. v. Trinidad and Tobago*. Merits, Reparations and Costs. Judgment of June 21, 2002. Series C No. 94, paras. 103, 108.

[55] ECtHR, *Al-Saadoon and Mufdhi v. the United Kingdom*, App. no. 61498/08, § 120, ECHR 2010.

[56] CCPR, General Comment No. 36 on the Right to Life, CCPR/C/GC/36 (2018), para. 51.

Furthermore, it has been clearly established that the obligation to abolish the death penalty and abstain from its application also includes the duty not to extradite, deport, or otherwise transfer a person to a State in which they face criminal charges that carry the death penalty unless credible and effective assurances against the imposition of the death penalty have been obtained.[57] This obligation was initially developed under the European Convention, in the renowed *Soering v. United Kingdom* case, but has been later endorsed by other international monitoring bodies.[58]

> **ECtHR, *Soering v. the United Kingdom*, 7 July 1989, Series A no. 161**
>
> This well-known case concerned a German national who was detained in prison in the United Kingdom, pending extradition to the United States to face charges of murder in the Commonwealth of Virginia; a state that retained the death penalty as possible punishment for the crime. While the UK sought assurance that if the death penalty was imposed, it would not be applied, such assurance was not provided. The applicant applied to the European Commission, arguing that the likely imposition of the death penalty, if found guilty, and the 'death row phenomenon', including a wait of six to eight years between sentence and execution, amounted to inhuman and degrading treatment and punishment, in contravention of Convention Article 3. Although the Commission found that the extradition would not breach Article 3 of the Convention, it found that it would violate the right to an effective remedy (Article 13). The case was then referred to the Court by the Commission, the United Kingdom, and Germany.
>
> In its judgment, the Court took into consideration the lengthy period of time that individuals spent on death row in the USA, with the ever present and mounting anguish of awaiting execution, and the personal circumstances of the applicant, including his young age and his mental state at the time of the offence. It concluded that his extradition to the USA would expose him to a real risk of treatment against the prohibition of torture, inhuman, or degrading treatment or punishment. Therefore, the Court found that if the UK was to extradite the applicant, it would be in contravention of its obligations under Article 3 of the Convention.

9.1.4 POSITIVE OBLIGATIONS

Under the international law of human rights, the right to life cannot be sufficiently protected through States' abstentions. When becoming Parties to human rights treaties, States assume a range of positive obligations that need to be adopted to respect, protect, and guarantee the right to life to every person under their jurisdiction. These include the adoption of legislation to protect individuals' right to life, the implementation of measures to protect life from reasonably foreseeable threats, the procedural duty to investigate when a deprivation of life has taken place, and the obligation to adopt all reasonable actions to prosecute and convict the perpetrators of the crime.

---

[57] CCPR, General Comment No. 36 on the Right to Life, CCPR/C/GC/36 (2018), paras. 34, 36.

[58] CCPR, *Charles Chitat Ng v. Canada*, CCPR/C/49/D/469/1991 (7 January 1994), para. 16.4; IACtHR, *Wong Ho Wing v. Peru*. Preliminary Objection, Merits, Reparations and Costs. Judgment of June 30, 2015. Series C No. 297, para. 134.

The first positive duty of States is to set in place a legal framework that would protect the right to life under their jurisdiction. This encompasses legislation on a rather wide variety of issues, ranging from effective criminal prohibitions of all manifestations of violence that could result in the deprivation of lives and a clear regulatory framework for the use of force by State agents,[59] to measures that ensure that women are not forced to resort to unsafe abortions and special measures of protection towards persons in vulnerable situations.[60] The legal framework should also set in place appropriate procedures to guarantee that, if an arbitrary deprivation of life has taken place, the victim's next-of-kin can be awarded compensation for the pecuniary and non-pecuniary damages experienced as a consequence of losing a loved one.[61] In broader terms, the duty to protect life also requires States to 'take appropriate measures to address the general conditions in society that may give rise to direct threats to life or prevent individuals from enjoying their right to life with dignity', including high levels of criminality, serious environmental degradation, the prevalence of life-threatening diseases, widespread hunger and malnutrition, and extreme poverty and homelessness.[62]

Furthermore, States are under a more precise obligation to adopt preventive measures to protect the life of individuals when the authorities know—or can be expected to know—that there is a real and immediate risk to life.[63] This obligation can arise due to a risk posed intentionally by a public authority or a private person, as well as due to the undertaking of dangerous activities, or even due to natural disasters.[64] An essential element to determine the responsibility of States for failure to prevent a deprivation of life is whether the authorities knew, or ought to have known, about the existence of the risk and, if so, whether they adopted all measures that could have been reasonably expected, under the circumstances, to avoid the risk from materializing.[65]

A further positive obligation upon States, which has been extensively developed by international monitoring bodies, is the procedural duty to undertake an effective

---

[59] ECtHR, *Osman v. the United Kingdom* [GC], 28 October 1998, § 115, Reports of Judgments and Decisions 1998-VIII; ECtHR, *Makaratzis v. Greece* [GC], App. no. 50385/99, § 57, 59, ECHR 2004-XI; CCPR, General Comment No. 36 on the Right to Life, CCPR/C/GC/36 (2018), paras. 13, 20.

[60] CCPR, General Comment No. 36 on the Right to Life, CCPR/C/GC/36 (2018), paras. 8, 23–24.

[61] ECtHR, *Ringeisen v. Austria* (Art. 50), 22 June 1972, § 26, Series A no. 15; CCPR, *Suarez de Guerrero v. Colombia*, Communication 11/45 (1982), para. 15; IACtHR, *Velásquez Rodríguez v. Honduras*. Reparations and Costs (July 21, 1989). Series C No. 7, para. 26; ACtHPR, *Beneficiaries of Late Norbert Zongo Abdoulaye Nikiema, Ernest Zongo and Blise Ilboudo & the Burkinabe Movement on Human and Peoples' Rights v. Burkina Faso* (reparations), 1 AfCLR 258, para. 111.

[62] CCPR, General Comment No. 36 on the Right to Life, CCPR/C/GC/36 (2018), para. 26.

[63] ECtHR, *Osman v. the United Kingdom* [GC], 28 October 1998, § 115–116, Reports of Judgments and Decisions 1998-VIII; ECtHR, *Öneryıldız v. Turkey* [GC], App. no. 48939/99, § 71, 90, 101, ECHR 2004-XII; IACtHR, *Pueblo Bello Massacre v. Colombia*. Merits, Reparations and Costs. Judgment of January 31, 2006. Series C No. 140, para. 123.

[64] ECtHR, *Osman v. the United Kingdom* [GC], 28 October 1998, § 116, Reports of Judgments and Decisions 1998-VIII; ECtHR, *Öneryıldız v. Turkey* [GC], App. no. 48939/99, § 71, ECHR 2004-XII; ECtHR, *Budayeva and Others v. Russia*, App. nos. 15339/02 and four others, § 137, ECHR 2008.

[65] ECtHR, *L.C.B. v. the United Kingdom*, 9 June 1998, § 36, Reports of Judgments and Decisions 1998-III; ECtHR, *Osman v. the United Kingdom* [GC], 28 October 1998, § 116, Reports of Judgments and Decisions 1998-VIII; IACtHR, *Sawhoyamaxa Indigenous Community v. Paraguay*. Merits, Reparations and Costs. Judgment of March 29, 2006. Series C No. 146, para. 155.

official investigation when the death of an individual has occurred under suspicious circumstances, especially when the presumed perpetrator is a State agent.[66] Investigations into potential arbitrary deprivations of life must be independent, impartial, prompt, thorough, effective, credible, and transparent.[67] In particular, investigations should be capable of establishing the facts surrounding the deprivation of life and lead to the prosecution and conviction of the individuals responsible for it.[68] The adequacy of the investigations heavily relies on their independence, requiring the officials in charge to be sufficiently independent of the persons and institutions whose responsibility is potentially engaged.[69] Investigations need to be promptly initiated and conducted in a reasonably expedited manner, to avoid any appearance of tolerance of unlawful acts.[70] They should also entail a sufficient element of public scrutiny, which would vary depending on the circumstances, to secure accountability, and should allow the victim's next-of-kin to participate in the procedures, to safeguard their rights, and interests.[71]

The conviction of the individuals criminally responsible for an arbitrary deprivation of life, following their prosecution with due respect of judicial guarantees, is the expected outcome of the investigation.[72] When it concerns grave violations of human rights, including arbitrary or summary executions and forced disappearances, international monitoring bodies have developed an extensive jurisprudence concerning the obligation to bring wrongdoers to justice, impose appropriate sentences, and implement such convictions.[73] It follows that the duties to investigate, to prosecute, and to convict the perpetrators of these serious crimes inhibits States from the possibility of adopting amnesty laws, applying statutory limitation of criminal liability, or otherwise

---

[66] IACHR, Cases 1702, 1748 y 1755 (Guatemala), Case 1790 (Chile), Case 1798 (Bolivia), Case 1874 (Chile), Annual Report 1975, OEA/Ser.L/V/II.37, Doc. 20 corr. 1 (28 June 1976); CCPR, *Bleier v. Uruguay*, Communication 7/30 (1980), CCPR/C/15/D/30/1978, para. 15; IACtHR, *El Amparo v. Venezuela*. Reparations and Costs. Judgment of September 14, 1996. Series C No. 28, para. 61 and op. para. 4; ECtHR, *Paul and Audrey Edwards v. the United Kingdom*, App. no. 46477/99, § 69, ECHR 2002-II; ECtHR, *Menson v. the United Kingdom* (dec.), App. no. 47916/99, ECHR 2003-V, p. 12.

[67] CCPR, General Comment No. 36 on the Right to Life, CCPR/C/GC/36 (2018), para. 28.

[68] IACtHR, *El Amparo v. Venezuela*. Reparations and Costs. Judgment of September 14, 1996. Series C No. 28, para. 61; ECtHR, *Oğur v. Turkey* [GC], App. no. 21594/93, § 88, ECHR 1999-III.

[69] ECtHR, *Tahsin Acar v. Turkey* [GC], App. no. 26307/95, § 222, ECHR 2004-III; IACtHR, *Valencia Hinojosa et al. v. Ecuador*. Preliminary Objections, Merits, Reparations and Costs. Judgment of November 29, 2016. Series C No. 327, para. 138.

[70] ECtHR, *Hugh Jordan v. the United Kingdom*, App. no. 24746/94, § 108, 4 May 2001; IACtHR, *Bulacio v. Argentina*. Merits, Reparations and Costs. Judgment of September 18, 2003. Series C No. 100, para. 115.

[71] ECtHR, *Hugh Jordan v. the United Kingdom*, App. no. 24746/94, § 109, 4 May 2001.

[72] CCPR, *Bleier v. Uruguay*, Communication 7/30 (1980), CCPR/C/15/D/30/1978, para. 15; IACtHR, *El Amparo v. Venezuela*. Reparations and Costs. Judgment of September 14, 1996. Series C No. 28, para. 61; ECtHR, *Oğur v. Turkey* [GC], App. no. 21594/93, § 88, ECHR 1999-III.

[73] Concerns about problems underpinning this 'coercive' approach have been voiced in the literature. See: F. Basch, 'The Doctrine of the Inter-American Court of Human Rights Regarding States' Duty to Punish Human Rights Violations and Its Dangers' (2013) 23 *American University International Law Review* 195; N. Mavronicola, 'Coercive Overreach, Dilution and Diversion: Potential Dangers of Aligning Human Rights Protection with Criminal Law (Enforcement)' in L. Lavrysen and N. Mavronicola (eds.), *Coercive Human Rights: Positive Duties to Mobilise the Criminal Law under the ECHR* (Hart 2020) 183–202.

implementing any measure designed to eliminate the responsibility of those criminally responsible or to suppress the effect of the conviction.[74]

> **IACtHR, *Barrios Altos v. Peru*. Merits. Judgment March 14, 2001. Series C No. 75.**
>
> The case concerned the summary execution of 15 individuals and the injuring of four others in the Barrios Altos neighbourhood of Lima in 1991, which was carried out by six members of the Peruvian military forces in an operation of reprisal against alleged members of 'Sendero Luminoso'. The judicial authorities had only commenced a serious investigation of the attack in 1995, when the Peruvian Congress adopted an amnesty law that exonerated from criminal responsibility the members of the army, police force, and civilians who had violated human rights or taken part in such violations between 1980 and 1995. However, the judge in charge of the investigation of the 'Barrios Altos' massacre refused to apply the amnesty law to the case, finding it in breach of both constitutional and international norms. In response, the Peruvian Congress adopted a second amnesty law, which established that the initial amnesty could not be revised by the judiciary; thus, securing impunity for the perpetrators of the 1991 killings.
>
> The case was submitted to the Inter-American Court by the Commission, with a request to find that the 'Barrios Altos' massacre, and the subsequent adoption of the two amnesty laws, amounted to multiple violations of the American Convention, including the right to life (Article 4) and the right to access justice (Articles 8 and 25). The State acknowledged its international responsibility before the Court, which led it to rule that Perú had breached numerous Convention rights, including the right to life (Article 4), the right to personal integrity (Article 5), and the rights to judicial protection and fair trial (Articles 25 and 8). In a passage that would become part of its constant jurisprudence, the Court affirmed that: '... all amnesty provisions, provisions on prescription and the establishment of measures designed to eliminate responsibility are inadmissible, because they are intended to prevent the investigation and punishment of those responsible for serious human rights violations such as torture, extrajudicial, summary or arbitrary execution and forced disappearance, all of them prohibited because they violate non-derogable rights recognized by international human rights law' (para. 41).
>
> Finding the two amnesty laws to be incompatible with the American Convention and, therefore, to lack of legal effect, the Court ordered the State, among other measures of reparation, to undertake an investigation to determine the perpetrators of the summary executions, to prosecute and punish them, and to make the results of such investigation and trial accessible to the public.

---

[74] IACtHR, *Barrios Altos v. Peru*. Merits. Judgment March 14, 2001. Series C No. 75, para. 41; IACtHR, *Gómez Paquiyauri Brothers v. Peru*. Merits, Reparations and Costs. Judgment of July 8, 2004. Series C No. 110, para. 232; CCPR, General Comment No. 31, The nature of the general legal obligation imposed on States Parties to the Covenant (2004), CCPR/C/21/Rev.1/Add. 13, para. 18; ECtHR, *Ali and Ayşe Duran v. Turkey*, App. no. 42942/02, § 69, 8 April 2008.

9.1.5 THE RIGHT TO AN ADEQUATE STANDARD OF LIVING

The scope of the right to life is not exhausted by the elements previously discussed but necessarily incorporates aspects of the type of life individuals are entitled to live. As discussed in **Section 3.1.1.1**, human rights treaties are 'living instruments', meaning that their interpretation must adapt to the evolution of the times, leading to a broadening content and scope of protected rights. The right to an adequate standard of living can then be interpreted both as an indispensable extension of the socioeconomic dimensions of the right to life, building on the indivisibility and interdependence of rights, as well as an autonomous right in itself, which has been recognized in multiple international instruments, although mostly subjected to its progressive realization. Whichever the legal foundations we provide to the right to an adequate standard of living, it leads to acknowledging the existence of international obligations upon States with regards to its protection.

Article 25 of the Universal Declaration of Human Rights is among the international instruments that clearly recognizes the right at stake,[75] stating that: 'Everyone has the right to a standard of living adequate for the health and well-being of [themselves] and of [their] family, including food, clothing, housing and medical care and necessary social services, and the right to security in the event of unemployment, sickness, disability, widowhood, old age or other lack of livelihood in circumstances beyond his control.'[76] In seemingly more restrictive terms, ICESCR also provides recognition to this right, highlighting 'food, clothing and housing' as its main components, and establishing upon States Parties the obligation to take appropriate steps to ensure the realization of this right, while also acknowledging the importance of international cooperation to this effect.[77] Nonetheless, the Committee on Economic, Social and Cultural Rights (CESCR) has indicated that the enumeration of elements of the right to an adequate standard of living in Article 11.1 of the Covenant is not exhaustive and has, for example, identified the right to water[78] as another essential right that emanates from

---

[75] Others are the 1948 American Declaration of the Rights and Duties of Man (although focusing on the Right to Health and Well-being), the 1979 Convention on the Elimination of All Forms of Discrimination against Women (although only explicitly with regards to rural women), the 1989 Convention on the Rights of the Child, the 2003 Protocol to the African Charter on Human and Peoples' Rights on the Rights of Women in Africa (through the independent rights of food security and adequate housing) and the 2006 Convention on the Rights of Persons with Disabilities. See: ADRDM, Art. XI; CEDAW, Art. 14.2.(h); UNCRC, Art. 27; Maputo Protocol, Arts. XV, XVI; CRPD, Art. 28. Specifically on the Right to Food, see: San Salvador Protocol, Art. 12.

[76] UDHR, Art. 25.

[77] International Covenant on Economic, Social and Cultural Rights (ICESCR) (adopted on 16 December 1966, entered into force 3 January 1976) 993 UNTS 3, Art. 11.

[78] In addition to its conventional basis, the right to water can be claimed to exist as part of international customary law, with origins in the 1977 Mar del Plata Declaration. See: P. Thielbörger, 'Something Old, Something New, Something Borrowed and Something Blue: Lessons to Be Learned from the Oldest of the "New" Rights – the Human Right to Water' in A. von Arnauld, K. von der Decken, and M. Susi (eds.), *The Cambridge Handbook of New Human Rights* (CUP 2020) 70–78, 75–76.

it.[79] Following the work of this Committee, the present section will delve into three of the most fundamental components of this right; namely, the rights to food, water, and housing, all of which have been subject to analysis in pertinent general comments.[80]

Access to food and water is indispensable for an adequate standard of living. And yet, more than 840 million people throughout the world, most of them in developing countries, are chronically hungry, while over one billion people lack access to a basic water supply, and several billions do not have access to adequate sanitation.[81] The roots of this problem are not the scarcity of food or water, but the lack of access to these essential resources by large segments of the world's population due to structural poverty.[82] The rights to food and water entitle every individual—including those belonging to the most vulnerable or marginalized sections of the population—to have (physical and economic) access to sufficient, safe, and accessible food and water for their essential personal use at all times.[83] Food should be sufficient, in quantity and quality, to satisfy the dietary needs of individuals, free from adverse substances, and acceptable within a given culture,[84] and water must be safe and of acceptable colour, odour, and taste, and should be sufficient for personal use, including drinking, personal sanitation, washing of clothes, food preparation, and personal and household hygiene.[85]

The right to housing concerns the right to live somewhere in security, peace, and dignity.[86] Adequate housing must be habitable, in terms of providing the inhabitants with adequate space and protecting them from the inclemency of the weather, and should have access to safe drinking water, energy for cooking, heating, and lighting, sanitation and washing facilities, means of food storage, refuse disposal, and drainage. It should also provide a degree of security of tenure that guarantees legal protection against forced eviction.[87] Nevertheless, the sad reality is that significant problems of homelessness and inadequate housing exist worldwide, including in some of the most economically developed States.[88]

Former Special Rapporteur on the Right to Adequate Food as a Human Right, Asbjørn Eide, has explained that the enjoyment of the right to an adequate standard

---

[79] CESCR, General Comment No. 6, The Economic, Social and Cultural Rights of Older Persons (1995), E/1996/22, para. 32; CESCR, General Comment No. 15, The Right to Water (2002), E/C.12/2002/11, para. 3.

[80] CESCR, General Comment No. 4, The Right to Adequate Housing (1991), E/1992/23; CESCR, General Comment No. 7, The Right to Adequate Housing: Forced Evictions (1997), E/1998/22 Annex IV; CESCR, General Comment No. 12, The Right to Adequate Food (1999), E/C.12/1999/5; CESCR, General Comment No. 15, The Right to Water (2002), E/C.12/2002/11.

[81] CESCR, General Comment No. 12, The Right to Adequate Food (1999), E/C.12/1999/5, para. 5; CESCR, General Comment No. 15, The Right to Water (2002), E/C.12/2002/11, para. 1.

[82] CESCR, General Comment No. 12, The Right to Adequate Food (1999), E/C.12/1999/5, para. 5.

[83] CESCR, General Comment No. 12, The Right to Adequate Food (1999), E/C.12/1999/5, para. 6; CESCR, General Comment No. 15, The Right to Water (2002), E/C.12/2002/11, para. 2.

[84] CESCR, General Comment No. 12, The Right to Adequate Food (1999), E/C.12/1999/5, paras. 8, 14.

[85] CESCR, General Comment No. 15, The Right to Water (2002), E/C.12/2002/11, para. 12.

[86] CESCR, General Comment No. 4, The Right to Adequate Housing (1991), E/1992/23, para. 7.

[87] CESCR, General Comment No. 4, The Right to Adequate Housing (1991), E/1992/23, para. 8. See also: CESCR, General Comment No. 7, The Right to Adequate Housing: Forced Evictions (1997), E/1998/22 Annex IV.

[88] CESCR, General Comment No. 4, The Right to Adequate Housing (1991), E/1992/23, para. 4.

of living depends on a combination of individual efforts and States' duties. It is for the individual to take all measures within their capacity to secure an adequate standard of living for themselves and their families and for the State to supplement this personal effort when needed.[89] The right to an adequate standard of living and all of its essential components, imposes three types of State obligations; namely, to respect, to protect, and to fulfil (as discussed in **Section 3.2**). The obligation to respect requires States to abstain from any measures that result in preventing the access of individuals to water, food, or housing. The obligation to protect requires States to adopt measures to ensure that third parties do not deprive individuals of their access to adequate food, water, and housing, including by the adoption of legislation regulating the many activities through which goods and services concerning this right can be obtained, such as trade, labour, contractual relations in general, and the prohibition of discrimination.[90] In turn, the obligation to fulfil encompasses aspects of facilitation, promotion, and provision. The duty to fulfil (facilitate) means that States must proactively engage in activities intended to strengthen people's access to needed resources to ensure their livelihoods, such as food, water, and housing security. The obligation to fulfil (promote) requires States to ensure adequate education concerning the appropriate and fair use of resources, including their long-term sustainability. Moreover, whenever individuals or groups are unable, for reasons beyond their control, to secure access to food, water, or housing, States have the obligation to fulfil (provide) such access.[91]

Some of the measures required by the abovementioned obligations are of a more immediate nature, while others have a longer-term character to achieve progressively the full realization of the right to an adequate standard of living.[92] While economic constraints might make it impossible for less-developed States to provide access to food, water, and housing for everyone unable to secure such access by themselves, States are, nonetheless, obliged to make every effort to use all available resources to satisfy, as a matter of priority, a minimum level of protection of core aspects of the right to an adequate standard of living, while adopting policies that would lead to its progressive realization for everyone. This includes, at least, a strict restriction on the adoption of retrogressive measures on the protection of this right and a prohibition of discrimination in the fulfilment of obligations.[93] A minimum core level of the State's obligation to fulfil the right at stake involves securing that every individual is free from hunger and has access to essential amounts of water for personal and domestic uses,[94] as

---

[89] A. Eide, 'The Right to an Adequate Standard of Living Including the Right to Food' in A. Eide, C. Krause, and A. Rosas (eds.), *Economic, Social and Cultural Rights* (2nd edn., Nijhoff 2001) 133–148, 139–140.

[90] CESCR, General Comment No. 12, The Right to Adequate Food (1999), E/C.12/1999/5, para. 20; CESCR, General Comment No. 15, The Right to Water (2002), E/C.12/2002/11, paras. 23–24.

[91] CESCR, General Comment No. 12, The Right to Adequate Food (1999), E/C.12/1999/5, para. 15; CESCR, General Comment No. 15, The Right to Water (2002), E/C.12/2002/11, paras. 22–25.

[92] CESCR, General Comment No. 12, The Right to Adequate Food (1999), E/C.12/1999/5, para. 16; CESCR, General Comment No. 15, The Right to Water (2002), E/C.12/2002/11, para. 17.

[93] CESCR, General Comment No. 12, The Right to Adequate Food (1999), E/C.12/1999/5, para. 17; CESCR, General Comment No. 15, The Right to Water (2002), E/C.12/2002/11, paras. 17–19.

[94] CESCR, General Comment No. 12, The Right to Adequate Food (1999), E/C.12/1999/5, para. 17; CESCR, General Comment No. 15, The Right to Water (2002), E/C.12/2002/11, para. 37.

well as the adoption of a strategy and plan of action to ensure food, water, and housing security for all.[95]

States' failure to comply with the minimum level of obligations with respect to the right to an adequate standard of living can engage their international responsibility, as determined by international monitoring bodies. Unsurprisingly, CESCR has been one of the most active supervisory bodies to examine violations of this right. Since 2015, it has decided a number of important cases concerning the adequate housing component of the right to an adequate standard of living.[96] As discussed in **Section 2.3.2**, other bodies, including the African Commission on Human and Peoples' Rights and the Inter-American Court of Human Rights have also found violations of the right at stake through an expansive interpretation of the respective treaties.[97]

> CESCR, *Ben Djazia and Bellili v. Spain*, Communication 5/2015, E/C.12/61/D/5/2015 (2017).
>
> This was the second decision adopted by the Committee on a case regarding the right to an adequate standard of living under ICESCR, involving, in particular, the right to adequate housing. The authors were a married couple and their two minor children who had suffered an eviction from the private accommodation they rented, after failing to pay rent for a number of months. They complained that their court-ordered eviction, when lacking alternative accommodation, breached their rights under ICESCR.
>
> The Committee affirmed that even though the Covenant establishes, primarily, rights and obligations between the State and the individual, the scope of States' obligations also extend to the relations between individuals. States Parties not only have the obligation to respect Covenant rights, but also to protect them by adopting measures to prevent these rights being breached by private parties (para. 14.2). The Committee stated that States Parties have a duty to take reasonable measures to provide alternative housing to persons who are left homeless as a result of eviction, especially when evictions affect members of vulnerable groups, such as children (para. 15.2). When an eviction would render a person homeless, the State failing to provide alternative accommodation 'must demonstrate that it has considered the specific circumstances of the case and that, despite having taken all reasonable measures, to the

---

[95] CESCR, General Comment No. 4, The Right to Adequate Housing (1991), E/1992/23, paras. 11–12; CESCR, General Comment No. 12, The Right to Adequate Food (1999), E/C.12/1999/5, paras. 21, 29; CESCR, General Comment No. 15, The Right to Water (2002), E/C.12/2002/11, para. 37.

[96] All the earlier cases have been against Spain, which is one the twenty-six States that, by the end of 2020, have become Parties to the ICESCR Optional Protocol allowing for individual communications. See: CESCR, *I.D.G. v. Spain*, Communication 2/2014, E/C.12/55/D/2/2014 (2015); CESCR, *Ben Djazia and Bellili v. Spain*, Communication 5/2015, E/C.12/61/D/5/2015 (2017); CESCR, *López Albán v. Spain*, Communication 37/2018 (2019); *Gómez-Limón Pardo v. Spain*, Communication 85/2018, E/C.12/67/D/52/2018 (2020).

[97] ACHPR, *Free Legal Assistance Group and Others v. Zaire*, Communication No. 25/89, 47/90, 56/91, 100/93 (1995), para. 47; ACHPR, *Social and Economic Rights Action Center (SERAC) and Center for Economic and Social Rights (CESR) v. Nigeria ('Ogoni case')*, ACHPR/COMM/A044/1 (27 May 2002), para. 68; IACtHR, *Yakye Axa Indigenous Community v. Paraguay*. Merits, Reparations and Costs. Judgment of June 17, 2005. Series C No. 125; IACtHR, *Xákmok Kásek Indigenous Community v. Paraguay*. Merits, Reparations and Costs. Judgment of August 24, 2010. Series C No. 214.

maximum of its available resources, it has been unable to uphold the right to housing of the person concerned' (para. 15.5).

In the case, the Committee was not persuaded by the reasons given by the State for not providing alternative accommodation to the authors. It emphasized that the regional authorities involved had adopted retrogressive measures in respect of housing—selling part of its public housing—which was not duly justified by the State (paras. 17.5–17.6). The Committee concluded that it was not persuaded that Spain's failure to provide the authors with alternative accommodation took place despite having taken all necessary measures, to the maximum of available resources. Therefore, it found a violation of the right to an adequate standard of living (paras. 17.8–18).

Consequently, the Committee recommended that the State should provide the authors with adequate housing, if they still require it, and award them financial compensation. In addition, the Committee affirmed that the State had an obligation to prevent similar violations from occurring in the future and recommended Spain to implement, to the maximum of available resources, a comprehensive plan to guarantee the right to adequate housing for low-income persons (paras. 20–21).

9.2 THE RIGHT TO PERSONAL INTEGRITY

9.2.1 NORMATIVE RECOGNITION

The most evident illustration of the protection of the right to physical, mental, and moral integrity of the person that can be found under the international law of human rights is the prohibition of torture and other cruel, inhuman, and degrading treatment or punishment. The explicit prohibition of these types of ill-treatment can be found in all major human rights instruments,[98] as well as in norms pertaining to international humanitarian law and international criminal law.[99] The widespread prohibition of these unacceptable treatments is reflected in the adoption of multiple international instruments specifically concerned with them, which include: the 1955 Standard Minimum Rules for the Treatment of Prisoners (revised as the 2015 'Nelson Mandela Rules');[100] the 1975 Declaration on the Protection of All Persons from Being Subjected to Torture and Other Cruel, Inhuman or Degrading Treatment or Punishment;[101] the 1982 Principles of Medical Ethics relevant to the Role of Health Personnel, particularly

---

[98] UDHR, Art. 5; ECHR, Art. 3; ICCPR, Art. 7; ACHR, Art. 5; ACHPR, Art. 5; Arab Charter, Arts. 8–9; ASEAN Declaration, Art. 14; UNCAT.

[99] 1949 Geneva Convention (I), Arts. 3, 12, 50; 1949 Geneva Convention (II), Arts. 3, 12, 51; 1949 Geneva Convention (III), Arts. 3, 17, 87, 130; 1949 Geneva Convention (IV), Arts. 3, 32, 147; Statute of the International Criminal Court (adopted 17 July 1998, entered into force 1 July 2002), Arts. 7–8.

[100] First United Nations Congress on the Prevention of Crime and the Treatment of Offenders (Geneva, 1955), approved by ECOSOC's resolutions 663 C (XXIV) (31 July 1957); UNGA, Resolution 70/175, Annex (17 December 2015).

[101] UNGA, Resolution 3452 (XXX) (9 December 1975).

Physicians, in the Protection of Prisoners and Detainees against Torture and Other Cruel, Inhuman or Degrading Treatment or Punishment;[102] the 1984 Convention against Torture and Other Cruel, Inhuman or Degrading Treatment or Punishment (UNCAT);[103] the 1985 Inter-American Convention to Prevent and Punish Torture;[104] the 1987 European Convention for the Prevention of Torture and Inhuman or Degrading Treatment or Punishment;[105] and the 2000 Principles on the Effective Investigation and Documentation of Torture and Other Cruel, Inhuman or Degrading Treatment or Punishment ('Istanbul Principles').[106]

The prohibition of torture and other cruel, inhuman, and degrading treatment or punishment can be found among the non-derogable provisions in international human rights treaties, as these types of treatment are not allowed even in situations of armed conflict or public emergency.[107] The absolute character of the prohibition of torture and other ill-treatment is abundantly clear in all international instruments, with strict wording used to state this prohibition, which allows for no exceptions and applies to everyone.[108] As discussed in **Section 3.1.5**, the prohibition of torture is among the norms that have undoubtedly reached the status of *jus cogens*, as consistently recognized by the corresponding jurisprudence of multiple international courts.[109] This status of peremptory norm has also been achieved by the prohibition of other violations of the right to personal integrity that might not amount to torture, such as inhuman and degrading treatment.[110]

9.2.2 PROHIBITION OF TORTURE

Notwithstanding the widespread agreement on the absolute prohibition of torture, none of the general human rights treaties provide a definition of the prohibited conducts. Such a definition has appeared in specialist instruments that, however, do

---

[102] UNGA, Resolution 37/194 (18 December 1982).

[103] Convention Against Torture and Other Cruel, Inhuman or Degrading Treatment or Punishment (adopted 10 December 1984, entered into force 26 June 1987) 1465 UNTS 85 (CAT).

[104] Inter-American Convention to Prevent and Punish Torture (adopted 9 December 1985, entered into force 28 February 1987) OAS Treaty Series 67.

[105] European Convention for the Prevention of Torture and Inhuman or Degrading Treatment or Punishment (adopted 26 November 1987, entered into force 1 February 1989) ETS 126.

[106] OHCHR, HR/P/PT/8/Rev.1, Annex I.   [107] ECHR, Art. 15; ICCPR, Art. 4; ACHR, Art. 27.

[108] N. Mavronicola, *Torture, Inhumanity and Degradation under Article 3 of the ECHR: Absolute Rights and Absolute Wrongs* (Hart 2021) 16–17.

[109] ICTY (Trial Chamber), *Prosecutor v. Anto Furundzija*, Case No.: IT-95-17/1-T, 10 December 1998, paras. 137–139, 144, 154, 160; ECtHR, *Al-Adsani v. the United Kingdom* [GC], App. no. 35763/97, § 61, ECHR 2001-XI; ECtHR, *Selmouni v. France* [GC], App. no. 25803/94, § 95, ECHR 1999-V; IACtHR, *Maritza Urrutia v. Guatemala*. Merits, Reparations and Costs. Judgment of November 27, 2003. Series C No. 103, para. 92; ICJ, *Questions relating to the Obligation to Prosecute or Extradite (Belgium v. Senegal)*, Judgment, I.C.J. Reports 2012, p. 422, para. 99.

[110] ECtHR, *Selmouni v. France* [GC], App. no. 25803/94, § 95, ECHR 1999-V; IACtHR, *Caesar v. Trinidad and Tobago*. Merits, Reparations and Costs. Judgment of March 11, 2005. Series C No. 123, para. 100; IACtHR, *Fermín Ramírez v. Guatemala*. Merits, Reparations and Costs. Judgment of June 20, 2005. Series C No. 126, para. 117.

not fully circumscribe all the characteristics of the forbidden conducts. Arguably, the most accepted definition is the one provided by UNCAT—counting 173 States Parties by the end of 2022[111]—which drew heavily on the text of the 1975 UN Declaration,[112] and defines torture as:

> ... any act by which severe pain or suffering, whether physical or mental, is intentionally inflicted on a person for such purposes as obtaining from him or a third person information or a confession, punishing him for an act he or a third person has committed or is suspected of having committed, or intimidating or coercing him or a third person, or for any reason based on discrimination of any kind, when such pain or suffering is inflicted by or at the instigation of or with the consent or acquiescence of a public official or other person acting in an official capacity.[113]

It is possible to identify four main elements that such a definition establishes for the qualification of ill-treatment as torture: first, the high degree of pain or suffering (physical or psychological) the act inflicts; second, the intent to inflict this pain; third, the particular aim pursued by the infliction of pain, such as to obtain information, punish, intimidate, or for discriminatory reasons; and, last, the involvement of a public authority in the crime, either directly or indirectly.[114]

However, the existence of multiple instruments prohibiting torture means that the elements of this forbidden treatment differ under the different provisions. For instance, the definition adopted by the Statute of the International Criminal Court for the purpose of establishing the international responsibility of individuals, rather than States, describes torture as 'the intentional infliction of severe pain or suffering, whether physical or mental, upon a person in the custody or under the control of the accused'.[115] Compared to the aforementioned definition, that of the ICC Statute dispenses of the need of a particular purpose, as well as of the involvement of public authorities.[116]

Additionally, the interpretation of the multiple treaty provisions banning torture and ill-treatment, carried out by different monitoring bodies, can also lead to divergent understandings of what amounts to torture. Different international bodies have asserted that the purpose required for an act to be classified as torture is not limited to those expressly mentioned in UNCAT—to obtain information, as punishment, to

---

[111] N.S. Rodley, 'The Definition(s) of Torture in International Law' (2002) 55 *Current Legal Problems* 467, 474. See: https://indicators.ohchr.org/ (accessed on 29 March 2023).

[112] UNGA, Declaration on the Protection of All Persons from Being Subjected to Torture and Other Cruel, Inhuman or Degrading Treatment or Punishment, Resolution 3452 (XXX) (9 December 1975), Art. 1.

[113] CAT, Art. 1.

[114] M. Farrell, *The Prohibition of Torture in Exceptional Circumstances* (CUP 2013) 3; G. Zach, 'Convention Against Torture and Other Cruel, Inhuman or Degrading Treatment or Punishment, Part I Substantive Articles, Art.1 Definition of Torture' in M. Nowak, M. Birk, and G. Monina, *The United Nations Convention Against Torture and its Optional Protocol: A Commentary* (2nd edn., OUP 2019) 24.

[115] Rome Statute of the International Criminal Court (adopted 17 July 1998, entered into force 1 July 2022) 2187 UNTS 3.

[116] N.S. Rodley, 'The Definition(s) of Torture in International Law' (2002) 55 *Current Legal Problems* 467, 469.

intimidate, for discriminatory reasons[117]—leading to the interpretation that there exist an open-ended range of possible aims.[118] Similarly, the degree of engagement of a public authority that is required for an act to amount to torture is also varying. UNCAT states that for an act to be torture it should be 'inflicted by or at the instigation of or with the consent or acquiescence of a public official or other person acting in an official capacity'.[119] That is to say, the State's involvement, through at least its acquiescence, appears as required under the Convention.[120] Nonetheless, under general international law, States can be found responsible for a violation of the prohibition of torture for failing to adopt positive measures with regard to acts committed by private individuals, as will be discussed in **Section 9.2.4**.[121] Lastly, the level of severity of the pain or suffering experienced by the victim is not a clear-cut notion and whether such threshold has been met would also depend on the criterion followed by the supervisory organ undertaking the examination of the case, as will be further discussed in **Section 9.2.3**.

Although some elements of torture might vary depending on the criteria of the body assessing the violation, it is beyond dispute that torture is not limited to acts that cause physical pain and suffering but that psychological torture is comprehended by the absolute prohibition of this international crime. Psychological torture consists of the infliction of severe pain or suffering by creating a state of anguish and stress by means other than bodily assault.[122] This type of torture has been repeatedly recognized by extensive jurisprudence of international monitoring bodies and acknowledged in specialist international instruments, such as the 1975 UN Declaration, UNCAT, and the 1985 Inter-American Convention, all of which explicitly refer to the severe pain or suffering amounting to torture as either physical or mental.[123] Psychological torture

---

[117] M.E. Tardu, 'The United Nations Convention against Torture and Other Cruel, Inhuman or Degrading Treatment or Punishment' (1987) 56 *Nordic Journal of International Law* 303, 305–306.

[118] ECtHR, *Ireland v. the United Kingdom*, 18 January 1978, Series A App. no. 25, separate opinion of Judge Matscher para. 1; IACtHR, *González et al. ('Cotton Field') v. Mexico*. Preliminary Objection, Merits, Reparations and Costs. Judgment of November 16, 2009. Series C No. 205, concurring opinion of Judge Medina Quiroga, para. 3; Report by the Special Rapporteur on torture and other cruel, inhuman or degrading treatment or punishment, 'Extra-custodial use of force and the prohibition of torture and other cruel, inhuman or degrading treatment or punishment, A/72/178 (20 July 2017), para. 31.

[119] CAT, Art. 1.

[120] N. Mavronicola, *Torture, Inhumanity and Degradation under Article 3 of the ECHR: Absolute Rights and Absolute Wrongs* (Hart 2021) 84.

[121] CCPR, General Comment No. 20: Art. 7 (Prohibition of torture, or other cruel, inhuman or degrading treatment or punishment) (10 March 1992), paras. 2, 13; ECtHR, *H.L.R. v. France*, 29 April 1997, § 40, Reports of Judgments and Decisions 1997-III; IACtHR, *Bueno Alves v. Argentina*. Merits, Reparations and Costs. Judgment of May 11, 2007. Series C No. 164, para. 79; Report of the Special Rapporteur on torture and other cruel, inhuman, and degrading treatment or punishment (Manfred Nowak), A/HRC/7/3 (15 January 2008), para. 31; Committee against Torture, General Comment No. 2: On Implementation of Art. 2 by States Parties, CAT/C/GC/2 (24 January 2008), para. 18.

[122] European Commission of Human Rights, *The Greek case* (1969), App. no. 3321/67 (*Denmark v. Greece*), App. no. 3322/67 (*Norway v. Greece*), App. no. 3323/67 (*Sweden v. Greece*), App. no. 3344/67 (*Netherlands v. Greece*), p. 461.

[123] UNGA, Declaration on the Protection of All Persons from Being Subjected to Torture and Other Cruel, Inhuman or Degrading Treatment or Punishment, Resolution 3452 (XXX) (9 December 1975), Art. 1; CAT, Art. 1; Inter-American Convention to Prevent and Punish Torture, Art. 2.

can adopt many forms, such as the believable threat of physical punishment, including simulated executions, the threat to kill or torture relatives, and the use of total isolation and sensory deprivation.[124]

9.2.2.1 Further reflections: a feminist approach to the prohibition of torture

The prohibition of torture is one of the most fundamental norms in the international law of human rights. It is crafted in absolute terms—torture is not admitted under any circumstances—and constitutes one of the handful of universally accepted provisions; it is the paradigmatic example of a *jus cogens* norm. And yet, such a significant norm can be the subject of important critiques when approached from a feminist perspective. As is the case with most universal prohibitions under international law, this norm suffers from a clear gender bias.[125] Torture, as originally conceived, in terms of a prohibited ill-treatment under international law that should be brought to an end, is a clear reflection of men's, rather than women's, fears.

To begin, support for the claim that torture is a reflection of men's fears can already be found in the problematic use of male pronouns in UNCAT to refer to the 'universal' potential victim of torture:[126]

> For the purposes of this Convention, the term "torture" means any act by which severe pain or suffering, whether physical or mental, is intentionally inflicted on a person for such purposes as obtaining from *him* or a third person information or a confession, punishing *him* for an act *he* or a third person has committed or is suspected of having committed, or intimidating or coercing *him* or a third person, or for any reason based on discrimination of any kind, when such pain or suffering is inflicted by or at the instigation of or with the consent or acquiescence of a public official or other person acting in an official capacity. It does not include pain or suffering arising only from, inherent in or incidental to lawful sanctions.[127]

But what makes the male character of the prohibition of torture even more evident is the fact that, statistically, women are much more likely to be victims of the infliction of severe pain and suffering at the hands of private actors,[128] away from the protection provided by a norm focused on a public form of ill-treatment—connected to the

---

[124] CCPR *Estrella v. Uruguay*, Communication 74/1980 (29 March 1983), paras. 8.3, 10; Report by the Special Rapporteur (Mr P. Kooijmans) on torture and other cruel, inhuman or degrading treatment or punishment, E/CN.4/1986/15 (19 February 1986), p. 30; IACtHR, *Maritza Urrutia v. Guatemala*. Merits, Reparations and Costs. Judgment of November 27, 2003. Series C No. 103, para. 94.

[125] H. Charlesworth and C. Chinkin, 'The Gender of *Jus Cogens*' (1993) 15 *Human Rights Quarterly* 63, 75.

[126] The problematic reference to men as encapsulating the universal human had already been the subject of debate during the drafting of the Universal Declaration of Human Rights. See: A. S. Fraser, 'Becoming Human: The Origins and Developments of Women's Human Rights' 21 (1999) *Human Rights Quarterly* 853, 888.

[127] UNCAT, Art. 1.1 (emphasis added).

[128] Recent data from the World Health Organization (WHO) shows that approximately one-third of all women have been subject to physical or sexual violence by an intimate partner or sexual violence from a non-partner. See: WHO, 'Violence against women prevalence estimates, 2018: global, regional and national prevalence estimates for intimate partner violence against women and global and regional prevalence estimates for non-partner sexual violence against women' (2021), p. xvi.

operation of the State through its public officials.[129] This provides strong support to the feminist concern of the protection against torture being adopted to address a predominantly male concern, even if crafted in universal terms.[130] Far from truly surprising, this can be seen as an expected outcome of a process of norm creation under international law that had been traditionally dominated by men.[131]

Furthermore, the disparity in the protection against the infliction of severe pain and suffering is not simply a matter of granting universal and absolute character to the public risk of experiencing such harm, but not to the same danger when private. Almost a decade after the UN General Assembly had adopted UNCAT, prohibiting torture in absolute terms and imposing the duty to prosecute the culprits, the commitment of the international community of States to protecting women from domestic ill-treatment was still concerningly weak. For instance, in 1993, a lesser body of the United Nations—the Centre for Social Development and Humanitarian Affairs—adopted a 'manual' on 'strategies for confronting domestic violence', which included a section discussing 'Arguments for and against the criminalization of domestic violence'.[132] Similarly, that same year, the General Assembly proclaimed the Declaration on the Elimination of Violence against Women, which, while stipulatinged the obligation of States to prevent, investigate, and sanction acts of gender-based violence committed by private individuals,[133] was an instrument of soft law, lacking the binding character of a treaty.

As further discussed in **Section 10.2.3.1**, gender-based violence is a global crisis that affects over a third of women in their lifetime.[134] However, despite its magnitude, this pressing issue faced an uphill battle to become the subject of international protection, given that the structure of the international law of human rights itself has been mostly concerned with acts and omissions of State agents, rather than with the actions of private individuals—as discussed in **Section 3.2.2**.[135] It has taken a rather lengthy time for international actors to accept that the international responsibility of States can also follow from the actions of private actors, for their failure to act in accordance with positive obligations.[136] And yet, while the prohibition of torture amounts to one of the most fundamental norms of the international law of human rights, consistently recognized as a norm belonging to the realm of *jus cogens*, the same universal and

---

[129] H. Charlesworth and C. Chinkin, 'The Gender of *Jus Cogens*' (1993) 15 *Human Rights Quarterly* 63, 70.

[130] Report of the Special Rapporteur on torture and other cruel, inhuman or degrading treatment or punishment, Juan E. Méndez, A/HRC/31/57 (5 January 2016), para. 5.

[131] H. Charlesworth and C. Chinkin, 'The Gender of *Jus Cogens*' (1993) 15 *Human Rights Quarterly* 63, 68–69; H. Charlesworth and C. Chinkin, *The Boundaries of International Law: A Feminist Analysis* (2nd edn., Manchester University Press 2022) 120.

[132] UN, 'Strategies for Confronting Domestic Violence: A Resource Manual', ST/CSDHA/20 (1993) 13–15.

[133] Declaration on the Elimination of Violence against Women, General Assembly resolution 48/104 (20 December 1993), Art. 4.

[134] See: Declaration on the Elimination of Violence against Women, General Assembly resolution 48/104 (20 December 1993), preamble. See also: CEDAW Committee, General Recommendation No. 35: on gender-based violence against women, updating General Recommendation No. 19, CEDAW/C/GC/35 (26 July 2017).

[135] H. Charlesworth and C. Chinkin, 'The Gender of *Jus Cogens*' (1993) 15 *Human Rights Quarterly* 63, 69.

[136] H. Charlesworth and C. Chinkin, 'The Gender of *Jus Cogens*' (1993) 15 *Human Rights Quarterly* 73.

absolute character has not been recognized to the prohibition of gender-based violence.[137]

This feminist critique of the international prohibition of torture is not intended to question the value and pertinence of this norm nor its duly recognized *jus cogens* status. It is simply aimed at revealing the gender bias underpinning the adoption of such an important norm, which serves to construct male fears as universal interests while rendering similar concerns, affecting roughly half of the world population, with diminished legal protection.

9.2.3 PROHIBITION OF CRUEL, INHUMAN, OR DEGRADING TREATMENT OR PUNISHMENT

The provisions protecting the right to personal integrity not only prohibit torture in absolute terms but also cruel, inhuman, and degrading treatment or punishment. However, the definitional threshold between torture and other forms of ill-treatment is often unclear.[138] This is partly because 'torture' itself is not a specific type of act but the legal qualification given to certain acts, which attaches a special stigma to ill-treatment deliberately inflicted to cause very serious and cruel suffering to the victim.[139] Moreover, the evolving protection of the human person under the international law of human rights means that acts that might have been considered inhuman or degrading in the past could be classified as torture in the future, as affirmed by the European Court of Human Rights when deciding the *Selmouni* case.[140]

ECtHR, *Selmouni v. France* [GC], App. no. 25803/94, ECHR 1999-V.

This case was decided by the Court, sitting as a Grand Chamber, and concerned the alleged violations of the prohibition of torture and inhuman or degrading treatment (Article 3) and of the fair trial guaranteed by Convention Article 6. The applicant, a Dutch-Moroccan citizen, was detained by the French police and interrogated during three days on drug related charges, which led to a fifteen-year conviction. He complained of having been a victim of ill-treatment banned under Article 3 during police interrogation; an allegation supported by medical reports that showed that he had suffered extensive injuries while in police custody. He also claimed the violation of the right to a fair trial due to the length of the proceedings against the alleged perpetrators of the ill-treatment.

---

[137] ILC, Fifth report on peremptory norms of general international law (*jus cogens*) by Dire Tladi, Special Rapporteur, A/CN.4/747 (24 January 2022); ILC, Draft conclusions on identification and legal consequences of peremptory norms of general international law (jus cogens), A/77/10 (2022).

[138] Committee against Torture, General Comment No. 2: On Implementation of Article 2 by States Parties, CAT/C/GC/2 (24 January 2008), para. 3.

[139] ECtHR, *Ireland v. the United Kingdom*, 18 January 1978, § 167, Series A no. 25.

[140] ECtHR, *Selmouni v. France* [GC], App. no. 25803/94, § 101, ECHR 1999-V.

> The Court found a violation of Article 3, affirming that Mr Selmouni had endured repeated and sustained assaults inflicted by the police in the performance of their duties and that the physical and mental violence experienced had caused severe pain and suffering and had been particularly serious and cruel. It added that the pain was inflicted intentionally for the purpose of making him confess to the offence which he was suspected of having committed (para. 98). To determine whether such treatment should be classed as torture, the Court famously affirmed: '... having regard to the fact that the Convention is a "living instrument which must be interpreted in the light of present-day conditions" ... the Court considers that certain acts which were classified in the past as "inhuman and degrading treatment" as opposed to "torture" could be classified differently in future.' (para. 101). It, therefore, concluded that 'the physical and mental violence, considered as a whole, committed against the applicant's person caused "severe" pain and suffering and was particularly serious and cruel. Such conduct must be regarded as acts of torture' (para. 105). With regard to the claim under Article 6, the Court also found a violation, stating that the investigation and criminal proceedings against the perpetrators were still ongoing, more than six years after the initial formal complaint, which exceeded the requirement of 'reasonable time' prescribed by the Convention (para. 118).

There are different possible interpretations as to what allows attributing the label of 'torture' to certain acts of ill-treatment, distinguishing them from other forms of unacceptable treatment. One of the earliest approximations to the distinction among ill-treatments was made by the European Commission of Human Rights when deciding the *Greek case* (discussed in **Section 7.1.3**). The Commission interpreted the European Convention's provision banning torture, inhuman, and degrading treatment as providing three manifestations of ill-treatment that differ from each other in terms of degree.[141] It affirmed that all torture is inhuman treatment and that the latter is always degrading.[142] The Commission understood torture as an aggravated form of inhuman treatment, while it defined degrading treatment or punishment as that which grossly humiliates the victim before others or drives the victim to act against their will or conscience.[143] Nevertheless, a distinction of degree in between the forms of ill-treatment,[144] ranging

---

[141] It has, nonetheless, been proposed that the distinction between inhuman and degrading treatment is more of a qualitative distinction. See: N. Mavronicola, *Torture, Inhumanity and Degradation under Article 3 of the ECHR: Absolute Rights and Absolute Wrongs* (Hart 2021) 90.

[142] European Commission of Human Rights, *The Greek case* (1969), App. no. 3321/67 (*Denmark v. Greece*), App. no. 3322/67 (*Norway v. Greece*), App. no. 3323/67 (*Sweden v. Greece*), App. no. 3344/67 (*Netherlands v. Greece*), p. 186.

[143] The Commission's interpretation seems to have inspired the drafters of the 1975 Declaration, which reads: '[t]orture constitutes an aggravated and deliberate form of cruel, inhuman or degrading treatment or punishment.' See: N.S. Rodley, 'The Definition(s) of Torture in International Law' (2002) 55 *Current Legal Problems* 467, 471. See also: UNGA, Declaration on the Protection of All Persons from Being Subjected to Torture and Other Cruel, Inhuman or Degrading Treatment or Punishment, Resolution 3452 (XXX) (9 December 1975), Art. 1.2.

[144] IACtHR, *Loayza Tamayo v. Peru*. Merits. Judgment of September 17, 1997. Series C No. 33, para. 57.

from degrading treatment to torture, does not clarify whether the measured gravity is that of the severity of the act itself,[145] or that of the pain and suffering inflicted.[146]

Another possible interpretation is that the distinctive factor among types of ill-treatment is not a matter of degree but of the intention of the perpetrator. This understanding is supported by the fact that intention to cause severe pain and suffering is required for an act to be classed as torture, but not needed for other forms of ill-treatment.[147] A further possible reading is that it is the purpose of the act itself what allows distinguishing among divergent types of ill-treatment. In fact, in the aforementioned case, the European Commission also stated that for an act to be considered as torture, it needs to be inflicted for a specific purpose, such as obtaining information or as a form of punishment.[148] Similarly, specialist provisions concerning torture expressly indicate (non-exhaustive) purposes of torturous acts, while no indication in this respect is given when referring to other forms of unacceptable treatment.[149] This discussion is ongoing, as the multiple international monitoring bodies with jurisdiction over torture and ill-treatment have resorted to different criteria, which has even changed throughout the years.[150] Moreover, as aforementioned, the evolving protection of the human person means that prohibited conducts that might not be considered to amount to torture under present-day criteria might, nonetheless, be assigned the stigma of torture in the future.

As an illustration, it is possible to mention different findings of international bodies of breaches to the prohibition of cruel, inhuman, or degrading treatment that failed to reach the threshold of torture. For instance, the Inter-American Court of Human Rights found that forcing female inmates to remain nude in a hospital, watched over by armed men, constituted sexual violence that amounted to cruel and inhuman treatment.[151] The

---

[145] N. Mavronicola, *Torture, Inhumanity and Degradation under Article 3 of the ECHR: Absolute Rights and Absolute Wrongs* (Hart 2021) 87.

[146] ECtHR, *Ireland v. the United Kingdom*, 18 January 1978, § 162, Series A no. 25 ECtHR, *Ireland v. the United Kingdom*, 18 January 1978, § 167, Series A no. 25; ECtHR, *Selmouni v. France* [GC], App. no. 25803/94, § 105, ECHR 1999-V.

[147] ECtHR, *Ireland v. the United Kingdom*, 18 January 1978, § 162, Series A no. 25 ECtHR, *Ireland v. the United Kingdom*, 18 January 1978, § 167, Series A no. 25.

[148] European Commission of Human Rights, *The Greek case* (1969), App. no. 3321/67 (*Denmark v. Greece*), App. no. 3322/67 (*Norway v. Greece*), App. no. 3323/67 (*Sweden v. Greece*), App. no. 3344/67 (*Netherlands v. Greece*), p. 186.

[149] Report of the Special Rapporteur on torture and other cruel, inhuman and degrading treatment or punishment (Nigel S. Rodley), E/CN.4/1995/34/Add. 1 (16 November 1994), para. 71; N.S. Rodley, 'The Definition(s) of Torture in International Law' (2002) 55 *Current Legal Problems* 467, 489–490; M. Nowak, 'What Practices Constitute Torture? US and UN Standards' (2006) 28 *Human Rights Quarterly* 809, 830; CCPR, *Giri et al. v. Nepal*, Communication 1761/2008, CCPR/C/101/D/1761/2008 (24 March 2011), para. 7.5.

[150] CCPR, General Comment No. 20: Art. 7 (Prohibition of torture, or other cruel, inhuman or degrading treatment or punishment) (10 March 1992), para. 4; ECtHR, *Aydın v. Turkey*, 25 September 1997, § 82, *Reports of Judgments and Decisions* 1997-VI; IACHR, *Luis Lizardo Cabrera v. Dominican Republic*, Case 10.832, Report Nº 35/96, OEA/Ser.L/V/II.95 Doc. 7 rev. at 821 (1997), para. 83; IACtHR, *Cantoral Benavides v. Peru*. Merits. Judgment of August 18, 2000. Series C No. 69, para. 104; Report of the Special Rapporteur on torture and other cruel, inhuman or degrading treatment or punishment (Manfred Nowak), A/HRC/13/39 (9 February 2010), para. 60.

[151] IACtHR, *Miguel Castro-Castro Prison v. Peru*. Merits, Reparations and Costs. Judgment of November 25, 2006. Series C No. 160, para. 308.

European Court of Human Rights ruled that overnight detention in a police station's cell without food, water, and access to toilet facilities constituted inhuman treatment.[152] Both Courts agreed that the next-of-kin of victims of forced disappearance or arbitrary executions could themselves be considered victims of a violation of their personal integrity, which can amount to either inhuman or degrading treatment.[153]

Furthermore, while there is a general agreement that a certain level of severity is required for ill-treatment to reach the minimum threshold of the overall prohibition against torture or cruel, inhuman, or degrading treatment (*de minimis* rule),[154] multiple factors contribute to determining whether such a minimum level has been reached in a given case.[155] These factors are closely related to those use to distinguish among the different classification of ill-treatment, having encompassed the intention of the perpetrator, the purpose of the conduct, the gravity of the act, the duration of the treatment, and its effects, as well as the context in which the act was perpetrated and the personal characteristics of the victim, such as their age, gender, and health.[156] The European Court's ruling in the *Bouyid v. Belgium* case illustrated this point when considering whether a slap in the face could amount to degrading treatment. Moreover, it is worth re-emphasizing that all forms of ill-treatment that reach the threshold of cruel, inhuman, or degrading treatment are prohibited in absolute terms under the international law of human rights, not being susceptible to exceptions—even in times of public emergency or armed conflict.[157]

> **ECtHR, *Bouyid v. Belgium* [GC], App. no. 23380/09, ECHR 2015.**
>
> This case was decided by the Grand Chamber, following the applicants' request for a referral after the Chamber's ruling. It concerned the complaint of two young siblings—one of them a minor at the time of the events—alleging they both had been slapped in the face by police officers while in custody at the police station and claiming this had amounted to degrading treatment, prohibited under Article 3 of the Convention.
>
> Despite the high threshold the Court set to the standard of proof for cases concerning Article 3, it considered it was satisfied in the case. It then had to decide whether the wrongful

---

[152] ECtHR, *Fedotov v. Russia*, App. no. 5140/02, § 68, 25 October 2005.

[153] IACtHR, '*Street Children*' (*Villagrán Morales et al.*) *v. Guatemala*. Merits. Judgment of November 19, 1999. Series C No. 63, para. 174; ECtHR, *Gongadze v. Ukraine*, App. no. 34056/02, § 186, ECHR 2005-XI.

[154] N. Mavronicola, *Torture, Inhumanity and Degradation under Article 3 of the ECHR: Absolute Rights and Absolute Wrongs* (Hart 2021) 91.

[155] ECtHR, *Ireland v. the United Kingdom*, 18 January 1978, § 162, Series A App. no. 25; ECtHR, *Selmouni v. France* [GC], App. no. 25803/94, § 100, ECHR 1999-V; ACHPR, *Huri-Laws v. Nigeria*, Communication No. 225/98 (6 November 2000), para. 41.

[156] ECtHR, *Ireland v. the United Kingdom*, 18 January 1978, § 162, Series A App. no. 25; ECtHR, ECtHR, *Bouyid v. Belgium* [GC], App. no. 23380/09, § 86, ECHR 2015.

[157] CCPR, General Comment No. 20: Art. 7 (Prohibition of torture, or other cruel, inhuman or degrading treatment or punishment) (10 March 1992), para. 3; ECtHR, *Selmouni v. France* [GC], App. no. 25803/94, § 95, ECHR 1999-V; IACtHR, *Miguel Castro-Castro Prison v. Peru*. Merits, Reparations and Costs. Judgment of November 25, 2006. Series C No. 160, para. 271.

> act in question reached the minimum severity level to be considered degrading treatment. The Grand Chamber affirmed that ill-treatment that attains such a minimum threshold usually involves actual injury or intense suffering, but it clarified that this was not a necessary condition, as humiliating treatment that disrespects the victim or arouses feelings of fear, anguish, or inferiority might suffice. It further clarified that it might well be enough for the victim to be humiliated in their own eyes for the act to reach the level of degrading treatment (para. 87).
>
> The Court asserted that, in confrontation with law-enforcement officers, any recourse to force that is not strictly necessary might be sufficient to infringe the protection provided by Article 3 (paras. 88 and 100). It then surmised that a slap in the face inflicted by a policeman to a person entirely under their control amounts to a serious attack on the individual's dignity that could be classed as degrading treatment under the Convention. Therefore, it found the violation of Article 3 (paras. 102–103 and 111–112).

9.2.4 POSITIVE OBLIGATIONS

Similar to the discussion in **Section 9.1** concerning the right to life, the prohibition of torture and cruel, inhuman and degrading treatment or punishment entails both negative and positive obligations for States. Where the paradigmatic negative obligation is for the State to refrain from carrying out actions that would amount to ill-treatment—including to refrain from forcibly returning a person to a State where they might be subject to such treatment[158]—the bundle of positive obligations can be split into three: the duty to adopt adequate legislation in their domestic legal order; the duty to prevent individuals under their jurisdiction to be subject to prohibited ill-treatment, even from private actors; and the procedural obligations to investigate acts of ill-treatment inflicted under their jurisdiction, to prosecute the perpetrators, and to provide redress for the victims.[159]

As to the obligation to adapt the national legal system to make it conform to the obligations assumed under the international law of human rights, States must have criminal provisions that make the offence of torture punishable, in specific and distinct terms from those of common assault or other crimes, since naming, defining, and setting an appropriate level of punishment for the crime of torture contributes to raising

---

[158] Committee against Torture, *G.R.B. v. Sweden*, CAT/C/20/D/83/1997 (15 May 1998), para. 6.5.

[159] CCPR, General Comment No. 20: Art. 7 (Prohibition of torture, or other cruel, inhuman or degrading treatment or punishment) (10 March 1992), paras. 8, 13, 15; ECtHR, *H.L.R. v. France*, 29 April 1997, § 40, Reports of Judgments and Decisions 1997-III; ECtHR, *Assenov and Others v. Bulgaria*, 28 October 1998, § 102, Reports of Judgments and Decisions 1998-VIII; IACtHR, *Maritza Urrutia v. Guatemala*. Merits, Reparations and Costs. Judgment of November 27, 2003. Series C No. 103, para. 96; Committee against Torture, General Comment No. 2: On Implementation of Art. 2 by States Parties, CAT/C/GC/2 (24 January 2008).

awareness to its special gravity.[160] This positive obligation is inextricably linked to the States' duty to prevent, as the adoption of a legal framework that provides adequate protection to individuals could be subsumed into the States' preventive duty.[161] Among other requirements, such a legal framework needs to avoid imposing undue restrictions on the prosecution of unacceptable ill-treatment carried out by both public authorities and private actors.[162] Moreover, the preventive duty of States also extends to the adoption of reasonable measures to avoid a real and immediate risk of ill-treatment in the hands of private actors, when States' authorities know—or ought to know—about the existence of such a risk; an obligation that is heightened when the victims are in a situation of special vulnerability.[163]

An additional aspect of the positive obligations of States with respect to the prohibition of torture and cruel, inhuman, or degrading treatment is the States' duty to investigate allegations of forbidden treatment or punishment and to prosecute and convict the perpetrators of these crimes.[164] With regard to the investigation of credible allegations of ill-treatment, these must be carried out with speed, diligence, and transparency, with a view to establishing what had occurred and who was responsible, allowing the participation of the victim within the investigation to safeguard their legitimate interests.[165] Furthermore, when it concerns torture, States are under the obligation to refrain from adopting amnesty provisions, applying statutory limitations, or implementing any type of measure designed to suppress the responsibility of the perpetrators of this crime or to limit the effect of their conviction.[166] The only legal venue for a State to avoid its obligation to investigate alleged acts of torture and, if pertinent, to submit the case to the competent authorities for the purpose of prosecution, is to extradite the person to a State that can exercise jurisdiction over the crime, if a request

---

[160] Committee against Torture, General Comment No. 2: On Implementation of Art. 2 by States Parties, CAT/C/GC/2 (24 January 2008), paras. 8–11. Conversely, there does not seem to be an obligation upon States to have a specific crime of inhuman or degrading treatment, which could be prosecuted under other domestic offences. See: Committee against Torture, General Comment No. 2: On Implementation of Art. 2 by States Parties, CAT/C/GC/2 (24 January 2008), para. 10; IACtHR, *Quispialaya Vilcapoma v. Peru*. Preliminary Objections, Merits, Reparations and Costs. Judgment of November 23, 2015. Series C No. 308, paras. 223–229.

[161] ECtHR, *Mahmut Kaya v. Turkey*, App. no. 22535/93, § 115, ECHR 2000-III.

[162] ECtHR, *A. v. the United Kingdom*, 23 September 1998, § 22–24, Reports of Judgments and Decisions 1998-VI; CCPR, General Comment No. 31: The Nature of the General Legal Obligation Imposed on States Parties to the Covenant, CCPR/C/21/Rev.1/Add. 13 (26 May 2004), para. 18.

[163] ECtHR, *Mahmut Kaya v. Turkey*, App. no. 22535/93, § 115, ECHR 2000-III; ECtHR, *Z and Others v. the United Kingdom* [GC], App. no. 29392/95, § 73, ECHR 2001-V.

[164] ECtHR, *Assenov and Others v. Bulgaria*, 28 October 1998, § 102, Reports of Judgments and Decisions 1998-VIII; IACtHR, *Maritza Urrutia v. Guatemala*. Merits, Reparations and Costs. Judgment of November 27, 2003. Series C No. 103, para. 96; Committee against Torture, General Comment No. 2: On Implementation of Art. 2 by States Parties, CAT/C/GC/2 (24 January 2008), para. 18.

[165] N. Mavronicola, *Torture, Inhumanity and Degradation under Article 3 of the ECHR: Absolute Rights and Absolute Wrongs* (Hart 2021) 143–144.

[166] CCPR, General Comment No. 20: Art. 7 (Prohibition of torture, or other cruel, inhuman or degrading treatment or punishment) (10 March 1992), para. 15; IACtHR, *Barrios Altos v. Peru*. Merits. Judgment March 14, 2001. Series C No. 75, para. 41; ECtHR, *Ali and Ayşe Duran v. Turkey*, App. no. 42942/02, § 69, 8 April 2008. Committee against Torture, *Kepa Urra Guridi v. Spain*, CAT/C/34/D/212/2002 (17 May 2005), para. 67.

for extradition exists.[167] States Parties to UNCAT have assumed an express obligation of international cooperation against impunity for the crime of torture, which translate into the duty to either prosecute or extradite (*aut dedere aut judicare*) those individuals suspected of having incurred in criminal responsibility for torture.[168] Nevertheless, the nature of both obligations—to prosecute and to extradite—is not the same. Where prosecution is an international obligation, the violation of which amounts to a wrongful act, extradition is an option offered by the Convention to avoid engaging in international responsibility.[169]

Lastly, the obligation to investigate, prosecute, and punish is also indissolubly connected to the States' duty to provide redress to the victim of the crime, as this encompasses both access to an effective remedy as well as measures of reparation. Among the former, redress covers the right of the victim to know the truth about the crime, which requires the State to have investigated and prosecuted the perpetrators.[170] As to the latter, the redress provided by States should entail sufficient compensation for any economic loss suffered, as well as for the non-financial physical and mental harm experienced. Moreover, reparation should include due medical and psychological care, either through the reimbursement of expenses incurred or through the direct provision of these services by the State.[171]

9.2.5 FURTHER REFLECTIONS: THE 'FRUIT OF THE POISONOUS TREE' DOCTRINE

The 'fruit of the poisonous tree' is a *praetorian* doctrine elaborated by the Supreme Court of the USA to determine the inadmissibility in trial of illegally obtained evidence.[172] More precisely, it refers to the extension of the exclusionary rule to cover the inadmissibility of evidence indirectly discovered due to direct evidence that was illegally obtained.[173] The metaphor of the 'poisonous tree' serves to indicate that the secondary evidence obtained will be tainted by the illegal act that led to obtaining the primary evidence. A paradigmatic example is the discovery of real or physical evidence following a confession illegally obtained through torture.

---

[167] ICJ, *Questions relating to the Obligation to Prosecute or Extradite (Belgium v. Senegal)*, Judgment, I.C.J. Reports 2012, p. 422, paras. 94–95.

[168] CAT, Art. 7.1.

[169] ICJ, *Questions relating to the Obligation to Prosecute or Extradite (Belgium v. Senegal)*, Judgment, I.C.J. Reports 2012, p. 422, para. 95.

[170] Committee against Torture, General Comment 3: On Implementation of Article 14 by States Parties, CAT/C/GC/3 (13 December 2012), para. 16.

[171] Committee against Torture, General Comment 3: On Implementation of Article 14 by States Parties, CAT/C/GC/3 (13 December 2012), paras. 10–11.

[172] USSC, *Silverthorne Lumber Co. v. United States*, 251 U.S. 385 (1920); USSC, *Nardone v. United States*, 308 U.S. 338 (1939).

[173] M. Spurrier, 'Gafgen v. Germany: fruit of the poisonous tree' (2010) *European Human Rights Law Review* 513, 517.

The exclusion as evidence of any statement made as a result of torture is expressly recognized in UNCAT.[174] However, whether the exclusionary rule applies to information obtained under other forms of ill-treatment and whether it extends to secondary evidence is not explicit. Different international monitoring bodies have provided an affirmative answer to the first question, asserting that the domestic law of States must prohibit the admissibility in court of statements or confessions obtained not only through the use of torture but also through other forms of prohibited treatment.[175] Furthermore, the use of prohibited ill-treatment, even below the threshold of torture, would render inadmissible not only a statement or confession so forced, but also real evidence obtained directly through the use of inhuman or degrading treatment.[176] The question that remains unanswered is whether secondary evidence that was obtained indirectly, but as a result of a statement or confession illegally obtained, is also tainted by illegality, thus rendered inadmissible, under the international law of human rights.

In its rather controversial judgment in the *Gäfgen* case,[177] the European Court of Human Rights, sitting as a Grand Chamber, refused to apply the 'fruit of the poisonous tree' doctrine while explicitly acknowledging the use of this legal doctrine in certain jurisdictions. In its ruling, the Court recognized that evidence had been obtained as a direct result of police interrogation, in breach of the prohibition of ill-treatment under the Convention.[178] Nonetheless, the Court convinced itself that such evidence had not been determinant for the conviction of the applicant. Therefore, the Court ruled against finding a breach to the right to a fair trial.[179] With this ruling, although the Court did not explicitly accept the validity of the use of (poisoned) real evidence secured following a coerced confession, it certainly did not affirm the illegality of its use.[180]

A different stance has been adopted by the Inter-American Court of Human Rights. In its judgment in the case of *Cabrera García and Montiel Flores v. Mexico*, the Court affirmed that the rule of evidentiary exclusion does not only apply to torture but

---

[174] UNCAT, Art. 15.
[175] CCPR, General Comment No. 20: Article 7 (Prohibition of torture, or other cruel, inhuman or degrading treatment or punishment) (10 March 1992), para. 12; Committee against Torture, General Comment No. 2: On Implementation of Article 2 by States Parties, CAT/C/GC/2 (24 January 2008), para. 6; IACtHR, *Cabrera García and Montiel Flores v. Mexico*. Preliminary Objection, Merits, Reparations, and Costs. Judgment of November 26, 2010 Series C No. 220, para. 165. However, the Committee against Torture has later casted doubts as to its interpretation of this matter. See: Committee against Torture, *Kirsanov v. Russia*, Communication 478/2011, CAT/C/52/D/478/2011 (14 May 2014), para. 11.4.
[176] ECtHR, *Jalloh v. Germany* [GC], App. no. 54810/00, § 118–123, ECHR 2006-IX.
[177] ECtHR, *Gäfgen v. Germany* [GC], App. no. 22978/05, ECHR 2010. See: M. Spurrier, 'Gafgen v. Germany: fruit of the poisonous tree' (2010) *European Human Rights Law Review* 513; N. Mavronicola, 'Is the Prohibition Against Torture and Cruel, Inhuman and Degrading Treatment Absolute in International Human Rights Law? A Reply to Steven Greer' (2017) 17 *Human Rights Law Review* 479.
[178] ECtHR, *Gäfgen v. Germany* [GC], App. no. 22978/05, § 171, ECHR 2010.
[179] ECtHR, *Gäfgen v. Germany* [GC], App. no. 22978/05, § 188, ECHR 2010.
[180] The ECtHR has, nonetheless, referred to the 'fruit of the poisonous tree' doctrine when ruling on the second *Yaremenko v. Ukraine* case. See: ECtHR, *Yaremenko v. Ukraine (No. 2)*, App. no. 66338/09, § 66, 30 April 2015.

also extends to any form of duress that interferes with the spontaneous expression of a person's will under interrogation. The Court asserted that the exclusion of such evidence was necessary as means to discourage the use of any form of coercion as part of criminal investigations.[181] The Court stated that the exclusionary rule can only be duly guaranteed by excluding, as well, real evidence derived from information obtained by coercion; thus embracing the 'fruit of the poisonous tree' doctrine.[182] In agreement with the Inter-American Court, it should be emphasized that disallowing the 'fruit of the poisonous tree' doctrine weakens the absolute prohibition of torture and other forms of ill-treatment, as it could act as an incentive for the use of such means of interrogation.[183]

> **ECtHR, *Gäfgen v. Germany* [GC], App. no. 22978/05, ECHR 2010.**
>
> The case concerned the kidnap and murder of an eleven-year-old by the applicant who, following the murder, sought a ransom from the child's family and was arrested soon after, when collecting the payment. He was questioned by police and threatened with physical pain if he failed to reveal the boy's whereabouts. Following the threats, the applicant revealed the location of the body and was escorted by the police to the location where the body was found as well as further evidence against him. The criminal trial against the applicant excluded his confession as evidence, but not the real evidence secured as a consequence of the confession. The trial ended with the conviction of the applicant to a life sentence.
>
> Before the Court, the applicant claimed to have been a victim of ill-treatment in violation of Article 3, as well as of a breach of his right to a fair trial under Article 6, as the physical evidence obtained pursuant to an illegally obtained confession was allowed. After an adverse ruling by the Chamber, which rejected all his claims, the applicant requested a referral to the Grand Chamber, which was accepted. The Grand Chamber found that the applicant had been a victim of inhuman treatment in breach of Article 3, based on the threat of torture during police interrogation (para. 131). However, it rejected finding a violation of his rights under Article 6. The Grand Chamber considered that the applicant's conviction by the domestic court had been based on his confession in court and that the real evidence gathered following the illegally obtained confession at the police station had no bearing on the conviction, but was merely used to 'test the veracity of his confession' (paras. 179–180). It concluded that 'the failure to exclude the impugned real evidence, secured following a statement extracted by means of inhuman treatment, did not have a bearing on the applicant's conviction and sentence' (para. 187).

---

[181] IACtHR, *Cabrera García and Montiel Flores v. Mexico*. Preliminary Objection, Merits, Reparations, and Costs. Judgment of November 26, 2010 Series C No. 220, para. 166.

[182] IACtHR, *Cabrera García and Montiel Flores v. Mexico*. Preliminary Objection, Merits, Reparations, and Costs. Judgment of November 26, 2010 Series C No. 220, para. 167.

[183] K. Ambos, 'The Transnational Use of Torture Evidence' (2009) 42 *Israel Law Review* 362, 380; G. Monina, 'Convention Against Torture and Other Cruel, Inhuman or Degrading Treatment or Punishment, Part I Substantive Articles, Art. 15 Non-Admissibility of Evidence Obtained by Torture' in M. Nowak, M. Birk, and G. Monina, *The United Nations Convention Against Torture and its Optional Protocol: A Commentary* (2nd edn., OUP 2019) 417, 421–422.

> IACtHR, *Cabrera García and Montiel Flores v. Mexico*. Preliminary Objection, Merits, Reparations, and Costs. Judgment of November 26, 2010 Series C No. 220.
>
> The case revolved around the alleged violation of a series of Convention rights suffered by the two applicants. These included the ill-treatment experienced while detained in the custody of members of the Mexican army; the irregular criminal proceedings followed against them, such as the failure to bring them, without delay, before a judicial authority to oversee the legality of their detention; and the lack of an appropriate investigation into the alleged ill-treatment. The Court found multiple violations of the Convention to the detriment of the applicants. Among these, it considered that their detention by the army without judicial review for five days was a breach of their right to personal liberty (Article 7) (para. 102). It also ruled that the State had failed to promptly and seriously investigate the allegations of torture made by the applicants, which entailed the violation of the right to personal integrity (Article 5), as well as of the obligations México had assumed under the Inter-American Convention to Prevent and Punish Torture (para. 137). Furthermore, the Court considered that the statements made under alleged cruel and inhuman treatment, and any evidence obtained as a consequence of such treatment, should have been disqualified by the domestic courts and that their use for reaching the conviction of the applicants amounted to a violation of their right to a fair trial (Article 8.3) (para. 177).

9.3 FREEDOM OF THOUGHT, CONSCIENCE, AND RELIGION

9.3.1 NORMATIVE RECOGNITION

Freedom of thought, conscience, and religion is a fundamental right recognized in all main international human rights instruments.[184] The different instruments vary slightly as to the phrasing of the protection of this right, but they mostly protect two distinctive aspects. On the one hand, an internal aspect of the right that encompasses the right of every person to freedom of thought, conscience, and religion, including the right to have a freely chosen religion and the right to change such a religion, as well as to have no religion at all. This internal dimension of freedom of thought, conscience, and religion (usually referred to as *forum internum*) could be said to be absolute, as it admits no limitations whatsoever.[185] On the other hand, there is an external aspect of this right, which refers to the freedom, either individually or in community with others, and in public or private, to manifest the chosen religion or belief in worship,

---

[184] UDHR, Art. 18; ADRDM, Art. III; ECHR, Art. 9; ICCPR, Art. 18; ACHR, Art. 12; ACHPR, Art. 8; Arab Charter, Arts. 25, 30; ASEAN Declaration, Art. 22.
[185] CCPR, General Comment No. 22 (Art. 18), CCPR/C/21/Rev.1/Add. 4 (27 September 1993), para. 3; ECtHR, *Ivanova v. Bulgaria*, App. no. 52435/99, § 79, 12 April 2007.

observance, practice, and teaching. This external dimension of the right (*forum externum*) encompasses a wide range of actions. In a non-exhaustive explanation, the Human Rights Committee has affirmed:

> The concept of worship extends to ritual and ceremonial acts giving direct expression to belief, as well as various practices integral to such acts, including the building of places of worship, the use of ritual formulae and objects, the display of symbols, and the observance of holidays and days of rest. The observance and practice of religion or belief may include not only ceremonial acts but also such customs as the observance of dietary regulations, the wearing of distinctive clothing or headcoverings, participation in rituals associated with certain stages of life, and the use of a particular language customarily spoken by a group. In addition, the practice and teaching of religion or belief includes acts integral to the conduct by religious groups of their basic affairs, such as, inter alia, the freedom to choose their religious leaders, priests and teachers, the freedom to establish seminaries or religious schools and the freedom to prepare and distribute religious texts or publications.[186]

Unlike the *forum internum*, the external aspect of the freedom of thought, conscience, and religion is subject to limitations by States since not every behaviour governed by one's religion or belief would be deemed worthy of protection.[187] However, such restrictions need to be prescribed by law and necessary to protect essential public interests, such as public safety, public order, public health, public morals, or the fundamental rights and freedoms of others.[188] Moreover, neither aspect of the right should be subject to further limitations to those already mentioned, even in times of public emergency.[189]

9.3.2 SCOPE OF FREEDOM OF THOUGHT, CONSCIENCE, AND RELIGION

The right to freedom of thought, conscience, and religion is important both for the individual and for society as a whole. For the individual, this right can be considered 'one of the most vital elements that go to make up the identity of believers and their conception of life'.[190] Concerning society, this right acts as one of the foundational pillars of a democratic society, as the pluralism indissolubly linked to such a society depends on it.[191] Nonetheless, this right is not only fundamental in its religious dimension, but the

---

[186] CCPR, General Comment No. 22 (Art. 18), CCPR/C/21/Rev.1/Add. 4 (27 September 1993), para. 4. See also: UNGA, Declaration on the Elimination of All Forms of Intolerance and of Discrimination Based on Religion or Belief, Resolution 36/55 (25 November 1981), Art. 6.

[187] ECtHR, *Kalaç v. Turkey*, 1 July 1997, § 27, *Reports of Judgments and Decisions* 1997-IV; ACHPR, *Garreth Anver Prince v. South Africa*, Communication 255/02 (7 December 2004), para. 41.

[188] ECHR, Art. 9.2; ICCPR, Art. 18.3; ACHR, Art. 12.3.

[189] Although the European Convention does not recognize this right as non-derogable, the prohibition of the suspension of the enjoyment of this right is explicit both in ICCPR (Art. 4) and the American Convention (Art. 27).

[190] ECtHR, *Kokkinakis v. Greece*, 25 May 1993, § 31, Series A no. 260-A.

[191] ECtHR, *Kokkinakis v. Greece*, 25 May 1993, § 31, Series A no. 260-A.

beliefs it protects extend beyond religious convictions, encompassing theistic, atheistic, and non-theistic beliefs. These protected beliefs are to be broadly construed, not limited to 'traditional religions or to religions and beliefs with institutional characteristics or practices analogous to those of traditional religions'.[192] Nevertheless, for beliefs to be protected under the right to freedom of thought, conscience, and religion they need to be 'views that attain a certain level of cogency, seriousness, cohesion and importance'.[193] As an illustration, religious beliefs such as those held by Mormons or Jehovah's Witnesses, as well as non-religious convictions, such as pacifism or veganism, have all been considered to be protected under the freedom of thought, conscience, and religion.[194]

The existence of a State religion has been found to be compatible with freedom of thought, conscience, and religion by different international monitoring bodies, so long as the State's embrace of a particular faith does not result in the impairment of rights of those who do not profess such a religion.[195] For instance, access to public employment or public office cannot require individuals to belong to a specific religion, nor be subject to the swearing of an oath with religious connotations.[196] Imposing upon individuals religious imperatives from a faith they do not profess would infringe the State's duty of religious neutrality and impartiality.[197] States' duty of neutrality extends, in particular, to the ambit of public education, as States need to ensure the neutrality of the teaching curricula in public schools.[198] In fact, different international instruments include an additional regulation regarding freedom of thought, conscience, and religion in respect of the education of children, prescribing that States should respect the right of parents and legal guardians to ensure the education of their children in conformity with their own religious or philosophical convictions.[199] While States can provide education about religion, such instruction cannot amount to indoctrination. This means that States must ensure that religious information is conveyed in an 'objective, critical and

---

[192] CCPR, General Comment No. 22 (Art. 18), CCPR/C/21/Rev. 1/Add. 4 (27 September 1993), para. 2.

[193] ECtHR, *Campbell and Cosans v. the United Kingdom*, 25 February 1982, § 36, Series A no. 48.

[194] European Commission of Human Rights, *Arrowsmith v. United Kingdom*, App. no. 7050/75, 12 October 1978; European Commission of Human Rights, *W. v. United Kingdom* (dec.), App. no. 18187/91, 10 February 1993; ECtHR, *Religionsgemeinschaft der Zeugen Jehovas and Others v. Austria*, App. no. 40825/98, 31 July 2008; ECtHR, *The Church of Jesus Christ of Latter-Day Saints v. the United Kingdom*, App. no. 7552/09, 4 March 2014.

[195] European Commission of Human Rights, *Darby v. Sweden*, App. no. 11581/85, 9 May 1989, para. 45; CCPR, General Comment No. 22 (Art. 18), CCPR/C/21/Rev.1/Add. 4 (27 September 1993), para. 9; ECtHR, *Ásatrúarfélagid v. Iceland* (dec.), App. no. 22897/08, 18 September 2012, para. 27.

[196] ECtHR, *Buscarini and Others v. San Marino* [GC], App. no. 24645/94, § 39, ECHR 1999-I; Interim report of the Special Rapporteur on freedom of religion or belief (Ms. Asma Jahangir), A/63/161 (22 July 2008), para. 38.

[197] ECtHR, *Metropolitan Church of Bessarabia and Others v. Moldova*, App. no. 45701/99, § 123, ECHR 2001-XII. Similarly, States that apply Shari'a law cannot subject non-Muslim people to it but must provide secular tribunals for trials involving non-Muslims. See: ACHPR, *Amnesty International and Others v. Sudan*, Communications 48/90, 50/91, 52/91, 89/93 (1999), para. 73.

[198] CCPR, General Comment No. 22 (Art. 18), CCPR/C/21/Rev.1/Add. 4 (27 September 1993), para. 6; ECtHR, *Kurtulmuş v. Turkey* (dec.), App. no. 65500/01, 24 January 2006, p. 6.

[199] ECHR Protocol 2, Art. 2; ICCPR, Art. 18.4; ACHR, Art. 12.4.

pluralistic manner',[200] or that an exemption from these classes is available for students whose parents object to such teaching.[201] Moreover, determining what might encroach on parent's rights to have their children's education conforming with their beliefs is a rather complex task. The European Court of Human Rights has been called to engage with a variety of parents' complaints as to schools' teaching and activities allegedly breaching their rights, including, among others, the imparting of sex education, the need to participate in national holiday celebration parades, and the requirement of children to attend (mixed-sex) swimming lessons—neither of which was found to amount to a breach of rights.[202]

Perhaps surprisingly, this has been the topic of one of the most controversial and politically charged cases the European Court of Human Rights has ever decided,[203] that of *Lautsi and Others v. Italy*.[204] Parental concerns as to the presence of sizeable crucifixes in public schools' classrooms led to a Chamber's ruling that caused unprecedented political backlashes.[205] The case was referred to the Grand Chamber, at Italy's request, and ten States Parties to the Convention decided to intervene in its re-hearing, in support of the respondent State. This certainly added political pressure on the Grand Chamber to carefully (re-)think the Court's stance on the issue. In the end, the Grand Chamber characterized the crucifix affixed to the classrooms' wall as an 'essentially passive symbol',[206] in an attempt to distinguish it from the (controversial) characterization its past case law had made of headscarves in the context of schools (see **Section 9.3.3.1**). It, therefore, concluded that the presence of certain religious symbols in schools' classrooms was compatible with the protection of the freedom of thought, conscience, and religion of children who attended the school and with their parents' right to ensure education in conformity with their own religious or philosophical beliefs.[207]

---

[200] ECtHR, *Folgerø and Others v. Norway* [GC], App. no. 15472/02, § 84, ECHR 2007-III.

[201] CCPR, *Leirvåg v. Norway*, Communication 1155/2003 (3 November 2004), paras. 14.3, 14.6-7; ECtHR, *Folgerø and Others v. Norway* [GC], App. no. 15472/02, § 102, ECHR 2007-III.

[202] ECtHR, *Kjeldsen, Busk Madsen and Pedersen v. Denmark*, 7 December 1976, Series A App. no. 23; ECtHR, *Valsamis v. Greece*, 18 December 1996, *Reports of Judgments and Decisions* 1996-VI; ECtHR, *Osmanoğlu and Kocabaş v. Switzerland*, App. no. 29086/12, 10 January 2017.

[203] D. Tsarapatsanis, 'A political approach to *Lautsi and Others v. Italy*' in D. Gonzalez-Salzberg and L. Hodson (eds.), *Research Methods for International Human Rights Law: Beyond the Traditional Paradigm* (Routledge 2019) 201-226.

[204] ECtHR, *Lautsi and Others v. Italy* [GC], App. no. 30814/06, ECHR 2011.

[205] D. McGoldrick, 'Religion in the European Public Square and in European Public Life: crucifixes in the classroom?' (2011) 11 *Human Rights Law Review* 451, 470-472; K. Lemmens, 'Criticising the European Court of Human Rights or Misunderstanding the Dynamics of Human Rights Protection?' in P. Popelier, S. Lambrecht, and K. Lemmens (eds.), *Criticism of the European Court of Human Rights: Shifting the Convention System: Counter-dynamics at the National and EU Level* (Intersentia 2016) 23-40, 36; G. Marinico, 'Italy: Between constitutional openness and resistance' in P. Popelier, S. Lambrecht, and K. Lemmens (eds.), *Criticism of the European Court of Human Rights: Shifting the Convention System: Counter-dynamics at the National and EU Level* (Intersentia 2016) 177-197, 178.

[206] ECtHR, *Lautsi and Others v. Italy* [GC], App no. 30814/06, § 72, ECHR 2011.

[207] ECtHR, *Lautsi and Others v. Italy* [GC], App no. 30814/06, § 77-78, ECHR 2011.

> ECtHR, *Lautsi and Others v. Italy* [GC], App no. 30814/06, ECHR 2011.
>
> In this case, the Court was called to examine whether the presence of sizeable crucifixes in public schools' classrooms amounted to indoctrination, in violation of children's right to freedom of thought and conscience and of their parents' right to have their children educated in conformity with their own philosophical convictions. Following an adverse decision from the Chamber, the State requested a referral to the Grand Chamber, which was accepted.
>
> The Grand Chamber acknowledged that the existence of crucifixes—undoubtedly Christian symbols—in classrooms, provided a preponderant visibility to the State's majoritarian religion. Nonetheless, it found that this was not in itself sufficient to amount to indoctrination (para. 71). Characterizing the affixed crucifixes as 'essentially passive symbol[s]' (para. 72), the Grand Chamber concluded that the decision to place them in school classrooms was within the State's margin of appreciation (para. 76). Therefore, this controversial issue had not encroached on the protection of the freedom of thought, conscience and religion of children who attended the school or on their parents' right to ensure education in conformity with their own religious or philosophical beliefs.

9.3.2.1 Critical debates: conscientious objectors

In general terms, 'conscientious objection' refers to the refusal of an individual to perform a duty due to their conviction that doing so would be against their own religious, moral, or philosophical beliefs. The term has been mostly used to refer to the opposition to perform the State's military service, with the State's ability to force its citizens to undertake military service being recognized in most international human rights instruments as an accepted exception to the prohibition of forced labour.[208] However, the case law of international monitoring bodies has (gradually)[209] led to the recognition of the right to object to performing military service as falling within the scope of the right to freedom of thought, conscience and religion.[210] Therefore, States that continue imposing mandatory military service for citizens are under the obligation to provide an alternative civic service for those who oppose undertaking military training, which should not be a more burdensome duty.[211]

---

[208] ECHR, Art. 4.3.(b); ICCPR, Art. 8.3.(c).(ii); ACHR, Art. 6.3.b.

[209] The initial stance adopted by the Human Rights Committee and the European Court of Human Rights was against recognizing such a right; a position that was reversed with time. See: CCPR, *L.T.K. v. Finland*, Communication 185/1984, UN Doc. CCPR/C/25/D/185/1984 (9 July 1985), para. 5.2; ECtHR, *Thlimmenos v. Greece* [GC], App. no. 34369/97, § 43, ECHR 2000-IV.

[210] UN Commission on Human Rights, 'Conscientious objection to military service', Resolution 1989/59 (8 March 1989), para. 1; CCPR, General Comment No. 22 (Art. 18), CCPR/C/21/Rev.1/Add. 4 (27 September 1993), para. 11; IACHR, Annual Report of the Inter-American Commission on Human Rights (1997), OEA/Ser.L/V/II.98 Doc. 6 rev. (13 April 1998), Chapter VII; ECtHR, *Bayatyan v. Armenia* [GC], App. no. 23459/03, § 124, ECHR 2011.

[211] CCPR, *Maille v. France*, Communication 689/1996, UN Doc. CCPR/C/69/D/689/1996 (10 July 2000), para. 10.4; OHCHR, Civil and Political Rights, including the Question of Conscientious Objection to Military Service, E/CN.4/2004/55 (16 February 2004), para. 38.(g); OHCHR, Conscientious Objection to Military Service, A/HRC/35/4 (1 May 2017), paras. 54–55, 64.

Over the years, the topic of conscientious objections has extended beyond the ambit of military service, leading to rather complex scenarios where the right of those who object to perform a legal duty conflicted with the enjoyment of human rights by others, such as the case of health personnel opposing to take part in interventions that would lead to the interruption of pregnancies, or public officials refusing to celebrate same-sex marriages and civil partnerships. In recent years, the European Court of Human Rights has been called to deal with such cases. Concerning the former, the Court has considered that legislation requiring health practitioners to intervene in the voluntary interruption of pregnancies was a valid interference with the right to freedom of religion, as it pursued the legitimate aim of protecting the health of women seeking an abortion.[212] It affirmed that when a State has decided to provide abortion services, it has a 'positive obligation to organise its health system in a way as to ensure that the effective exercise of freedom of conscience of health professionals in the professional context does not prevent the provision of such services'.[213] As to the refusal of public officials to celebrate same-sex unions, it was raised within one of the four applications the Court decided in *Eweida and others v. the United Kingdom*.[214] The Court considered that freedom of religion does not grant public officials an exemption from performing same-sex civil partnerships and, consequently, they can be subject to disciplinary measures for their refusal to do so.[215]

> **ECtHR, *Eweida and Others v. the United Kingdom*, App. nos. 48420/10 and three others, ECHR 2013.**
>
> The case originated in four different applications against the United Kingdom; those of Ms Eweida, Ms Chaplin, Ms Ladele, and Mr McFarlane. All applicants alleged that the domestic law failed to protect their right to manifest their religion. The first two applicants (Ms Eweida and Ms Chaplin) complained about restrictions placed by their employers on their wearing of a cross around their necks. The other two applicants (Ms Ladele and Mr McFarlane) complained about sanctions adopted against them by their employers as a result of their objection to perform services which they considered to condone same-sex unions. Only Ms Eweida was successful in her claim.
>
> Ms Eweida worked for British Airways and complained about her inability to openly wear a cross while performing a client-facing role. Her refusal to conceal the cross or to take on a role without customer contact led her being placed on unpaid leave. Although the company eventually changed its dress code and allowed the open use of the cross, she was unsuccessful in her attempts to obtain damages for the time she was not paid. In Strasbourg, she complained that the domestic courts had failed to protect her right to manifest her religion by openly wearing

---

[212] ECtHR, *Grimmark v. Sweden* (dec.), App. no. 43726/16, 11 February 2020, para. 25; ECtHR, *Steen v. Sweden* (dec.), App. no. 62309/17, 11 February 2020, para. 20.
[213] ECtHR, *Grimmark v. Sweden* (dec.), App. no. 43726/16, 11 February 2020, para. 26; ECtHR, *Steen v. Sweden* (dec.), App. no. 62309/17, 11 February 2020, para. 21.
[214] ECtHR, *Eweida and Others v. the United Kingdom*, App. nos. 48420/10 and three others, ECHR 2013.
[215] ECtHR, *Eweida and Others v. the United Kingdom*, App. nos. 48420/10 and three others, § 106, ECHR 2013.

a cross. The Court found a violation of Article 9 in her case. It considered that a fair balance between the interests at stake had not been struck; namely, between the applicant's desire to manifest her religious belief and the company's wish to project a certain corporate image. The Court ruled that the domestic authorities accorded too much weight to the interests of the company, which was eventually willing to amend its dress code and allow for the visible wearing of religious jewellery, demonstrating that the earlier prohibition was not of crucial importance.

Ms Chaplin also complained of her inability to wear a cross in a necklace at work; she was a nurse working at a public hospital. The prohibition was grounded on health and safety guidelines, as it was considered that a chain and cross could cause harm to a patient who pulled on it. She claimed to be a victim of religious discrimination before domestic courts, but her claim was unsuccessful. The Court also ruled against her claim. It considered that the reason for the prohibition of wearing the religious symbol was the protection of health and safety on a hospital ward, which amounted to a justified restriction, considering the margin of appreciation allowed to the domestic authorities, which were better positioned to make decisions about clinical safety than an international court.

The third applicant was Ms Ladele, who was a registrar for a London local authority, in charge of marriages and civil partnerships. She identified as an Orthodox Christian and considered that marriage could only be the union of one man and one woman for life, believing that same-sex civil partnerships were contrary to God's law. Following her beliefs, she refused to comply with her duties as a registrar with regards to (same-sex) civil partnerships. Her refusal to perform her job led to the adoption of disciplinary measures that culminated with her losing the job; a decision that was upheld by the domestic courts. The Strasbourg Court considered that the balancing act between the protection of the applicant's religious views and the rights of others to have their union legally recognized had been fairly achieved by the State; hence, it did not find a violation of her rights.

The final applicant was Mr McFarlane, who worked as a sex therapist counsellor for a private company. He professed to hold a deep belief that the Bible viewed homosexual activity as sinful and, therefore, he should do nothing to endorse such activities. He was dismissed, as the company considered that it was uncertain whether the applicant would be willing to provide counselling without reservation on issues concerning same-sex sexuality. Before the domestic courts, Mr McFarlane claimed to have been unfairly dismissed on grounds of religious discrimination, but his claim was unsuccessful. The European Court also ruled against his claim. It found that State authorities had remained within their margin of discretion when deciding how to strike a fair balance between the applicant's right to manifest his religious belief and his employer's interest in securing the rights of others.

9.3.3 LIMITATIONS TO THE RIGHT TO FREEDOM OF THOUGHT, CONSCIENCE, AND RELIGION

As mentioned in **Section 9.3.1**, while the internal dimension of the right to freedom of thought, conscience, and religion is absolute, as it must be free from any inherence from States, the external aspect of the right, concerning the freedom to manifest the chosen religion or belief, can be subject to limitations. Nonetheless, for these restrictions to be valid under the international law of human rights, they need to fulfil a number of requirements, namely: to be prescribed by law, to be aimed at protecting an essential public interest—public safety, public order, public health, public morals, or the fundamental rights and freedoms of others—and to be necessary for achieving such a legitimate aim.

When there is a claim of a violation of the enjoyment of the right to freedom of thought, conscience, and religion the first issue to be determined is whether the person alleging such a breach has suffered an interference with their right; meaning that the State had adopted a measure that affected its free exercise. If such interference exists, the initial requisite it must fulfil to be valid is to be 'prescribed by law'. The European Court of Human Rights, the Human Rights Committee, and the African Court on Human and People's Rights all seem to be in agreement that the fundamental meaning of this requirement concerns the issue of foreseeability of the limitation. This means that the conditions and circumstances under which the restriction of the right are imposed must have been clearly stipulated in a legal provision that is accessible to all individuals, so that everyone is able to regulate their conduct in accordance with such a norm.[216] As to the legal provision itself, it is not required for it to emanate from the legislature, but could be based on well-established common law or on norms below the rank of statutes.[217] Conversely, the Inter-American Court has established that limitations of rights under the American Convention on Human Rights are only permissible by law in the formal sense; understood as general legal norms adopted by the democratically elected legislative bodies and, only exceptionally, and when allowed by constitutional provisions, by a delegated authority acting within its constitutionally established framework.[218]

The second main requirement that a legitimate limitation to freedom of thought, conscience, and religion has to fulfil is that it should pursue a legitimate aim. As aforementioned, the legitimate grounds provided by international treaties that could justify an interference with this right are the protection of public safety, public order, public health, public morals, or of the rights and freedoms of others. Importantly, the protection of 'national security', an accepted aim for the restriction of other rights, is not conceived as a valid justification for imposing restrictions on an individual's freedom of thought, conscience, and religion;[219] a reflection of the particular importance of this right.[220] The enumeration of legitimate aims should be construed as strictly exhaustive;[221] meaning

---

[216] ECtHR, *The Sunday Times v. the United Kingdom (no. 1)*, 26 April 1979, § 49, Series A no. 30; CCPR, General comment No. 34: Art. 19: Freedoms of opinion and expression, CCPR/C/GC/34 (12 September 2011), para. 25; ACtHPR, *Lohe Issa Konate v. Burkina Faso* (merits) (2014) 1 AfCLR 314, para. 128.

[217] ECtHR, *The Sunday Times v. the United Kingdom (no. 1)*, 26 April 1979, § 47, Series A no. 30; ECtHR, *Dogru v. France*, App. no. 27058/05, § 52, 4 December 2008.

[218] IACtHR, The Word 'Laws' in Art. 30 of the American Convention on Human Rights. Advisory Opinion OC-6/86 of May 9, 1986. Series A no. 6, paras. 35–38.

[219] ECHR, Art. 9.2; ICCPR, Art. 18.3; ACHR, Art. 12.3.

[220] ECtHR, *Nolan and K. v. Russia*, App. no. 2512/04, § 73, 12 February 2009.

[221] CCPR, General Comment No. 22 (Art. 18), CCPR/C/21/Rev.1/Add. 4 (27 September 1993), para. 8; ECtHR, *Svyato-Mykhaylivska Parafiya v. Ukraine*, App. no. 77703/01, § 132, 14 June 2007; ACHPR, *Centre for Minority Rights Development (Kenya) and Minority Rights Group (on behalf of Endorois Welfare Council) v. Kenya*, no. 276/03 (2009), para. 172.

that no public interest beyond those mentioned could be seen as legitimate to justify a restriction of the external dimension of the right to freedom of thought, conscience, and religion. Although, in the past, international monitoring bodies have accepted States' arguments concerning legitimate aims pursued, without performing an in-depth analysis of this requirement.[222]

The final requirement for the validity of a restriction to the right to freedom of thought, conscience, and religion is that such a limitation should be necessary to achieve the legitimate aim pursued. To determine whether a limitation could be considered necessary—a burden that lies on the State attempting to justify it—is essential to distinguish this notion from that of useful or desirable.[223] Necessity refers to the absence of other means of achieving the same aim that would interfere less seriously with the right at stake.[224] Whether a specific restriction of the external aspect of freedom of thought, conscience, and religion is to be considered 'necessary' and, therefore, valid under the international law of human rights would be for the pertinent international monitoring body to decide on a case-by-case basis. On the one hand, the European Court of Human Rights has developed the doctrine of the margin of appreciation (discussed in **Section 7.7**) as a tool for performing the analysis;[225] an approach that seems to be followed by the African Court on Human and People's Rights.[226] This means that when assessing whether an interference with the freedom of thought, conscience, and religion is necessary, the European Court would grant the State a certain margin of discretion for determining the necessity for such interference, considering that the domestic authorities are, in principle, better placed than an international supervisory body to evaluate local needs.[227] However, the scope of such margin of discretion granted by the Court varies depending on the importance of the interests at stake and also taking into account the existence of consensus among States as to how the particular issue should be regulated. The European Court of Human Rights would only find a violation of the right to freedom of thought, conscience, and religion when it considers that the State's interference with such a right has exceeded its margin of appreciation.[228] On the other hand, the Human Rights Committee and the Inter-American Court of Human Rights have not adopted the doctrine of the margin of appreciation as a method for deciding cases.[229] These bodies would decide on the necessity of any restrictions to a right in a principled manner on a case-by-case basis.

---

[222] P.M. Taylor, *Freedom of Religion: UN and European Human Rights Law and Practice* (CUP 2005) 302, 305.
[223] ECtHR, *Young, James and Webster v. the United Kingdom*, 13 August 1981, § 63, Series A no. 44 ECtHR, *Svyato-Mykhaylivska Parafiya v. Ukraine*, App. no. 77703/01, § 116, 14 June 2007.
[224] ECtHR, *Biblical Centre of the Chuvash Republic v. Russia*, App. no. 33203/08, § 58, 12 June 2014.
[225] ECtHR, *Kokkinakis v. Greece*, 25 May 1993, § 46, Series A no. 260-A.
[226] ACHPR, *Umuhoza v. Rwanda* (merits) (2017) 2 AfCLR 165, para. 137.
[227] ECtHR, *Leyla Şahin v. Turkey* [GC], App. no. 44774/98, §121, ECHR 2005-XI.
[228] ECtHR, *Bayatyan v. Armenia* [GC], App. no. 23459/03, § 123–124, ECHR 2011.
[229] CCPR, *Ilmari Länsman et al. v. Finland*, Communication No. 511/1992, UN Doc. CCPR/C/52/D/511/1992 (26 October 1994), para. 9.4; CCPR, General comment No. 34: Art. 19: Freedoms of opinion and expression, CCPR/C/GC/34 (12 September 2011), para. 36. With respect to the Inter-American Court of Human Rights, see discussion in **Section 6.7**.

9.3.3.1 Critical debates: the use of religious symbols and clothing

The wearing of religious clothing and symbols is a manifestation of the observance and practice of religion, encompassed by the external dimension of the right to freedom of thought, conscience, and religion and, as such, subject to State limitations that fulfil all aforementioned requirements. This topic has been the subject of extended examination by different international bodies, including the assessment of restrictions that affected the wearing of turbans, crosses, headscarves, and face veils.[230] Nevertheless, it has been the restrictions imposed on women's use of clothing associated with Islam, in particular in Europe, which has led to the largest number of cases brought to international supervisory mechanisms, leading to a significant level of controversy.

Although not the first case to be decided,[231] the one of *Leyla Şahin v. Turkey* is undoubtedly among the most significant cases on this topic, given that it was subject to a decision on the merits by the European Court of Human Rights sitting as a Grand Chamber. The Court assessed the compatibility of a circular issued by Istanbul University banning the use of the Islamic headscarf—as well as beards—and prohibiting those in breach to attend classes and examinations. The applicant in the case, Leyla Şahin, was a medical student who claimed that the imposed restriction amounted to a breach of her right to manifest her religion. However, the Court ruled against the claimant. While it acknowledged that the challenged regulation constituted an interference with the applicant's right to manifest her religion, it considered such a restriction to be justified. First, the Court found the legislation in place to be 'prescribed by law', as the forbidden conduct was sufficiently clear and was grounded in Turkish legislation as interpreted by the courts.[232] It further affirmed that the impugned interference pursued the legitimate aims of protecting the rights and freedoms of others and public order,[233] proceeding to then assess whether it could be considered necessary for achieving such goals. In doing so, the Court decided to grant the State a rather wide margin of appreciation for deciding how the conflicting interests at stake should be balanced. It reached such a decision, making reference to a lack of consensus among States as to how this type of situation should be regulated.[234]

The ruling was, however, permeated by rather strong assumptions about the Islamic headscarf. The Court recalled its past decision in *Dahlab v. Switzerland*, where it characterized the Islamic headscarf as a 'powerful external symbol', susceptible of having

---

[230] Among many others: CCPR, *Karnel Singh Bhinder v. Canada*, Communication 208/1986, UN Doc. CCPR/C/37/D/208/1986 (9 November 1989); European Commission of Human Rights, *Karaduman v. Turkey*, App. no. 7050/75, 3 May 1993; ECtHR, *Dahlab v. Switzerland* (dec.), App. no. 42393/98, 15 February 2001; CCPR, *Hudoyberganova v. Uzbekistan*, Communication 931/2000, CCPR/C/82/D/931/2000 (5 November 2004); ECtHR, *Ahmet Arslan and Others v. Turkey*, App. no. 41135/98, 23 February 2010; ECtHR, *Eweida and Others v. the United Kingdom*, App. nos. 48420/10 and three others, ECHR 2013; ECtHR, *S.A.S. v. France* [GC], App. no. 43835/11, ECHR 2014.

[231] European Commission of Human Rights, *Karaduman v. Turkey*, App. no. 7050/75, 3 May 1993; European Commission of Human Rights, *Bulut v. Turkey*, App. no. 18783/91, 3 May 1993; ECtHR, *Dahlab v. Switzerland* (dec.), App. no. 42393/98, 15 February 2001.

[232] ECtHR, *Leyla Şahin v. Turkey* [GC], App. no. 44774/98, § 78, 98, ECHR 2005-XI.

[233] ECtHR, *Leyla Şahin v. Turkey* [GC], App. no. 44774/98, § 99.

[234] ECtHR, *Leyla Şahin v. Turkey* [GC], App. no. 44774/98, § 109.

a proselytizing effect, and which 'appeared to be imposed on women by a religious precept that was hard to reconcile with the principle of gender equality'.[235] The Court then affirmed that it was the fundamental principle of secularism that provided support to the ban on the wearing of religious symbols in universities, a context in which 'the values of pluralism, respect for the rights of others and, in particular, equality before the law of men and women are being taught and applied in practice'.[236] It asserted that upholding secularism was consistent with the values underpinning the Convention and that conducts that deviated from that principle might be deprived of protection under the Convention. In conclusion, and having consideration to the discretion enjoyed by the State, the Court ruled against the applicant's claim.

The Court's judgment has been the subject of extensive academic criticism.[237] In particular, the paternalistic presumption that the headscarf is an undesired imposition on Muslim women and the suggestion that it could conflict with the prohibition of gender discrimination seem to be hard to support.[238] Moreover, the characterization of the Islamic headscarf as a 'powerful external symbol', while a sizeable crucifix could be seen as an 'essentially passive symbol' (see **Section 9.3.2**), has led to the suspicion that certain rulings might be underpinned by strongly Westernized views. Nonetheless, it is also possible to perform a harmonious reading of the case law if deference to the State's discretion is understood as the Court's paramount hermeneutic criterion governing the topic.

ECtHR, *Dahlab v. Switzerland* (dec.), App. no. 42393/98, 15 February 2001.

In this case, the applicant was a primary-school teacher in Switzerland, who converted to Islam and started wearing an Islamic headscarf while teaching. After more than three years of her wearing the headscarf, she was requested by the school authorities not to do so while performing her professional duties. Ms Dahlab claimed that the imposed restriction infringed on her freedom to manifest her religion, but the domestic authorities did not uphold her claim.

To reach its decision, the European Court took into account that the applicant's pupils were very young (aged between four and eight). It characterized the headscarf as a 'powerful external symbol' and cast doubts as to its potential impact on the children's own freedom of conscience and religion. The Court affirmed that, in the circumstances of the case, it was not possible to deny that the wearing of a headscarf might have some kind of proselytizing effect. It further stated its agreement with the Swiss domestic courts in that the headscarf seemed to be imposed on women by the Koran, making it hard to reconcile with the principle of

---

[235] ECtHR, *Leyla Şahin v. Turkey* [GC], App. no. 44774/98, § 111.
[236] ECtHR, *Leyla Şahin v. Turkey* [GC], App. no. 44774/98, § 116.
[237] Among many others: J. Marshall, 'Freedom of religious expression and gender equality' (2006) 69 *Modern Law Review* 452; C. Skach, '*Şahin v. Turkey*: case comment' (2006) 100 *American Journal of International Law* 186; N. Nathwani, 'Islamic headscarves and human rights: a critical analysis of the relevant case law of the European Court of Human Rights' (2007) 25 *Netherlands Quarterly of Human Rights* 221; I. Rorive, 'Religious symbols in the public space: in search for a European Answer' (2009) 30 *Cardozo Law Review* 2669.
[238] ECtHR, *Leyla Şahin v. Turkey* [GC], App. no. 44774/98, ECHR 2005-XI, dissenting opinion of Judge Tulkens.

> gender equality. The Court stated that it found difficult to square the wearing of the Islamic headscarf with the message of tolerance, respect for others and, above all, equality and non-discrimination that all teachers in a democratic society must convey to their pupils. After weighting the rights it understood to be in conflict in the case—the right of a teacher to manifest her religion, against the need to protect her pupils by preserving religious harmony—the Court ruled that the ban imposed on wearing a headscarf was within the State's margin of appreciation; hence, it was justified as necessary in a democratic society.

On its part, the Human Rights Committee has certainly distanced itself from the stance adopted by the European Court in this area. In a series of decisions, the Committee found regulations restricting women's use of headscarves in employment and education, as well as those that prohibit the use of a face veil in public, to be incompatible with the right to freedom of thought, conscience, and religion.[239] In particular, the Committee has rejected the argument of the headscarf being a powerful external symbol, in contrast to other religious clothes or instruments which would be mere passive symbols.[240] Similarly, the Committee has refuted the understanding that the wearing of gender specific religious clothing should be viewed as an imposition on women amounting to gender discrimination. While acknowledging that, in certain contexts, some women may be subject to family or social pressures to wear particular clothes, the Committee has stated that this may also be done out of free will.[241] Therefore, in the cases it examined, the Committee has found that the States' prohibition to wear headscarves or face veils amounted to intersectional discrimination based on religion and gender.[242]

> **CCPR, *F.A. v. France*, Communication 2662/2015, CCPR/C/123/D/2662/2015 (16 July 2018).**
>
> The author of the communication worked as an educator in a private childcare centre in France for about seventeen years. She had worn a headscarf while performing her job during most of these years, until she was told that the internal regulations did not allow this anymore. Her refusal to remove the headscarf led to her dismissal for insubordination, which prompted legal actions for discrimination against her employer. After the domestic courts ruled against her, she brought a communication to the Human Rights Committee, alleging that her dismissal had violated her right to manifest her religion.

---

[239] CCPR, *Hudoyberganova v. Uzbekistan*, Communication 931/2000, CCPR/C/82/D/931/2000 (5 November 2004); CCPR, *F.A. v. France*, Communication 2662/2015, CCPR/C/123/D/2662/2015 (16 July 2018); CCPR, *Sonia Yaker*, Communication 2747/2016, CCPR/C/123/D/2747/2016 (17 July 2018); CCPR, *Seyma Türkan v. Turkey*, Communication 2274/2013, CCPR/C/123/D/2274/2013/Rev.1 (17 July 2018); CCPR, *Miriana Hebbadj v. France*, Communication 2807, CCPR/C/123/D/2807/2016 (17 July 2018).
[240] CCPR, *F.A. v. France*, Communication 2662/2015, CCPR/C/123/D/2662/2015 (16 July 2018), para. 8.12.
[241] CCPR, *Sonia Yaker*, Communication 2747/2016, CCPR/C/123/D/2747/2016 (17 July 2018), para. 8.14.
[242] CCPR, *F.A. v. France*, Communication 2662/2015, CCPR/C/123/D/2662/2015 (16 July 2018), para. 8.13; CCPR, *Sonia Yaker*, Communication 2747/2016, CCPR/C/123/D/2747/2016 (17 July 2018), para. 8.17.

France argued that the restriction to which the author was subjected pursued the legitimate objective of protecting the rights and freedoms of the children that attended the centre and of their parents, who should not be exposed to a conspicuous display of religious affiliation, such as the wearing of a hijab, which had been characterized by the European Court of Human Rights as a 'powerful external symbol'. However, the Committee considered that the State's argument was not persuasive enough, failing to establish how the wearing of a headscarf by an educator in the childcare centre would amount to a violation of the fundamental rights and freedoms of the children and parents attending the centre. Consequently, the Committee found the restriction imposed not to be proportionate to the intended objective and, consequently, to amount to a violation of the author's freedom of religion under ICCPR.

CCPR, *Sonia Yaker*, Communication 2747/2016, CCPR/C/123/D/2747/2016 (17 July 2018).

The author of the communication was a Muslim woman who wore a full-face veil (niqab) when out in public. Based on the legislation adopted in France, she was stopped for an identity check while wearing her niqab on the street, which led to her conviction for the minor offence of wearing a garment to conceal her face in public, being ordered to pay a fine of 150 euros. Before the Committee, she claimed that the ban against concealing the face in public areas amounted to a violation of her right to manifest her religion and of the prohibition of discrimination.

To justify the questioned legal interference, France indicated two purposes the law was pursuing: the protection of public order and safety, and the protection of the rights and freedoms of others. The Committee rejected the validity of the first objective claimed, stating that, on the one hand, the State had failed to explain why the use of a niqab was banned, while face covering for numerous other purposes (such as sporting, artistic, and other traditional and religious purposes) was allowed. On the other hand, the Committee considered that even if the State could justify the existence of a specific and significant threat to public safety, it had still failed to demonstrate that a blanket ban was the least restrictive measure to ensure, at the same time, the protection of freedom of religion or belief.

As to the second public objective claimed, the Committee considered that France had not identified any specific fundamental rights or freedoms of others that were affected by the fact that some people in the street might decide to cover their faces. It stated that: 'The right to interact with any individual in public and the right not to be disturbed by other people wearing the full-face veil are not protected by the Covenant and therefore cannot provide the basis for permissible restrictions' (para. 8.10). Consequently, the Committee found that the legislation in place, which prohibited Muslim women to wear a full-face veil, amounted to a violation of the right to manifest their religion, as well as of the prohibition of discrimination based on gender and religion, given that it particularly affected Muslim women.

It is, nonetheless, possible to wonder whether the European Court of Human Rights would revisit its stance on the topic. There are indications that the Court has somehow started to modify, even if only slightly, its position on the validity of the restrictions concerning the wearing of religious clothing and symbols. On the one hand, there have been judgments in which the restrictions were not accepted,[243] including on the wearing of the hijab, although under very specific circumstances.[244] On the other hand, the reasoning of the Court, even when still validating the restrictions at stake, has drastically changed. This is particularly illustrated by the judgment adopted by the Grand Chamber in *S.A.S. v. France*.

In this case, the Court examined the 2010 French legislation that prohibited the wearing of clothing designed to conceal the face in public places, including the prohibition of the use of a full-face veil (niqab). While the Court ruled that such a restriction did not amount to a violation of the right to freedom of thought, conscience, and religion, it did perform a stricter scrutiny of the legislation, compared to prior rulings.[245] For instance, the Court decided to undertake a deeper examination of the legitimate aims claimed by the State, acknowledging its past deficiencies concerning this analysis. The State claimed that the legitimate purpose of its legislation was both the protection of public safety and the 'respect for the minimum set of values of an open and democratic society'.[246] Although the latter does not appear as a legitimate aim under the Convention—which could have given the Court enough reasons to reject it—the State argued that this objective could be linked to the accepted aim of the protection of the rights and freedoms of others, enumerating three underpinning values: the respect for equality between men and women, the respect for human dignity, and the respect for the minimum requirements of life in society. The Court accepted the protection of the third of the mentioned values but rejected the other two.

As to the argument based on gender equality, the Court even abandoned its past suspicions of gender discrimination with regard to women's use of Islamic clothing, affirming that:

> . . . a State Party cannot invoke gender equality in order to ban a practice that is defended by women – such as the applicant – in the context of the exercise of the rights enshrined in those provisions, unless it were to be understood that individuals could be protected on that basis from the exercise of their own fundamental rights and freedoms.[247]

Concerning the protection of dignity, the Court found this argument plainly unfounded to support the legislation. Conversely, the Court did accept the 'living together' argument as a potential legitimate aim, stating that 'the face plays an important role in social

---

[243] ECtHR, *Ahmet Arslan and Others v. Turkey*, App. no. 41135/98, 23 February 2010; ECtHR, *Eweida and Others v. the United Kingdom*, App. nos. 48420/10 and three others, § 106, ECHR 2013; ECtHR, *Hamidović v. Bosnia and Herzegovina*, App. no. 57792/15, 5 December 2017.

[244] In the case of *Lachiri v. Belgium*, the applicant was banned from entering a court, where she was to stand as party in the case against her brother's killer, due to her refusal to remove her hijab. The European Court ruled that such a restriction had been unjustified, in breach of Mrs. Lachiri's right to manifest her religion. See: ECtHR, *Lachiri v. Belgium*, App. no. 3413/09, 18 September 2018.

[245] R. Costello and S. Ahmed, 'Citizenship, Identity, and Veiling: Interrogating the Limits of Article 8 of the European Convention on Human Rights in Cases Involving the Religious Dress of Muslim Women.' (2023) 38 *Journal of Law and Religion* 81, 87–88.

[246] ECtHR, *S.A.S. v. France* [GC], App. no. 43835/11, § 114, ECHR 2014.

[247] ECtHR, *S.A.S. v. France* [GC], App. no. 43835/11, § 119, ECHR 2014.

interaction ... individuals who are present in places open to all may not wish to see practices or attitudes ... which would fundamentally call into question the possibility of open interpersonal relationships'.[248] Thus, the Court accepted that the full-face veil could be perceived as a barrier raised against others, which could conflict with the right of others to live in a space of socialization.

The Court then went on to assess whether the questioned norm could be considered necessary for achieving any of the two aims accepted as legitimate. As to the first one—public safety—the Court affirmed that a State might need to be able to identify individuals to prevent certain threats and to combat identity fraud, so an obligation to remove a face covering, if a risk has been established or if there are founded suspicions of identity fraud, could be an acceptable requirement for the protection of public safety. However, a blanket ban on the wearing of clothing designed to conceal the face in public places did not appear to be proportionate to the aim pursued.[249] As to the second accepted aim—the requirements of life in society—the Court asserted that in matters of general policy the State's margin of appreciation tends to be wider, which was reinforced by its understanding that there was no European consensus on the matter—although the Court did acknowledge that France was one of only two States that have adopted such a ban.[250] Based on this wide discretion the Court granted the State, it reached the decision that the prohibition under scrutiny did not exceed the margin of appreciation and was, therefore, acceptable under the Convention.[251]

In sum, the Court can still be seen as willing to accept the validity of States' restrictions on the wearing of religious clothing, even when confronted with problematic arguments and in the face of an opposing view supported by the Human Rights Committee. Nonetheless, the Court's examination of the topic has become more careful, placing an added level of rigour to the evaluation of the arguments presented by the State. It might, therefore, not be unconceivable for the Court to change its jurisprudence in the future.

9.4 FREEDOM OF OPINION AND EXPRESSION

9.4.1 NORMATIVE RECOGNITION

Freedom of opinion and expression is a fundamental right recognized by all main international human rights instruments,[252] even if its protection is provided for in these instruments with some relevant variations. Similar to freedom of thought, conscience, and religion (**Section 9.3**), the right to freedom of opinion and expression also has two

---

[248] ECtHR, *S.A.S. v. France* [GC], App. no. 43835/11, § 122, ECHR 2014.
[249] ECtHR, *S.A.S. v. France* [GC], App. no. 43835/11, § 139, ECHR 2014.
[250] ECtHR, *S.A.S. v. France* [GC], App. no. 43835/11, § 156, ECHR 2014.
[251] ECtHR, *S.A.S. v. France* [GC], App. no. 43835/11, § 157–159, ECHR 2014.
[252] UDHR, Art. 19; ADRDM, Art. IV; ECHR, Art. 10; ICCPR, Arts. 19, 20; ACHR, Arts. 13, 14; ACHPR, Art. 9; Arab Charter, Art. 32; ASEAN Declaration, Art. 23.

distinctive dimensions. On the one hand, freedom of opinion is in itself a right that guarantees its bearers the entitlement to hold and change opinions free from States' restrictions or coercion, encompassing all forms of opinion, such as those of 'a political, scientific, historic, moral or religious nature'.[253] Given its internal character, freedom of opinion is a right that admits no limitation at all.[254] Although the prohibition of suspending the exercise of this right in situations of emergency has not been explicitly provided for in international treaties,[255] its character as a non-derogable right can yet be affirmed.[256]

On the other hand, the right to freedom of expression includes the freedom to seek, receive, and impart information and ideas of all kinds, by any media, and regardless of frontiers.[257] The special place this right occupies within the realm of human rights cannot be overstated,[258] as will be further discussed in **Section 9.4.2**. However, this dimension of freedom of expression is subject to State restrictions, which must be prescribed by law and necessary for the protection of certain essential public interests, as discussed in **Section 9.4.3**. Moreover, the enjoyment of the right to freedom of opinion and expression is subject to explicit nuances established by further provisions in international human rights treaties. For instance, both ICCPR and the American Convention on Human Rights impose upon States Parties the obligation to prohibit by law any propaganda for war, as well as any advocacy of national, racial, or religious hatred that constitutes incitement to discrimination, hostility or violence.[259] In addition, the American Convention provides two further provisions that delineate a regulation of freedom of expression that differs from that of other instruments.[260] On the one hand, it establishes a prohibition on prior censorship, with the sole exception of access

---

[253] CCPR, General Comment No. 34 (Art. 19: Freedoms of opinion and expression), CCPR/C/GC/34 (12 September 2011), para. 9.

[254] M. Nowak, *UN Covenant on Civil and Political Rights: CCPR Commentary* (2nd edn., Engel 2005) 441.

[255] ECHR, Art. 15; ICCPR, Art. 4; ACHR, Art. 27.

[256] CCPR, General Comment No. 34 (Art. 19: Freedoms of opinion and expression), CCPR/C/GC/34 (12 September 2011), paras. 5, 9.

[257] UDHR, Art. 19; ADRDM, Art. IV; ECHR, Art. 10.1; ICCPR, Art. 19.2; ACHR, Art. 13.1; Arab Charter, Art. 32.1; ASEAN Declaration, Art. 23.

[258] Special Rapporteurships on this right have been created under the auspices of the UN Commission on Human Rights in 1993 (and then continued by the Human Rights Council), the Inter-American Commission on Human Rights in 1997, and the African Commission on Human and Peoples' Rights in 2004. Before them all, in 1952, the ECOSOC had also created a brief mandate on freedom of information held by Salvador López. See: UN Commission on Human Rights, Resolution 1993/45 (5 March 1993); IACHR, Annual Report 1997, OEA/Ser.L/V/II.98 Doc. 6 rev. (13 April 1998), Chapter II; African Commission on Human and Peoples' Rights, 'Resolution on the Mandate and Appointment of a Special Rapporteur on Freedom of Expression in Africa, Res. 71(XXXVI)04 (2004); ECOSOC, Resolution 442 C (XIV).

[259] A similar provision is also provided for by ICERD. See: ICERD, Art. 4.a; ICCPR, Art. 20; ACHR, Art. 13.5.

[260] IACtHR, Compulsory Membership in an Association Prescribed by Law for the Practice of Journalism (Arts. 13, 29 American Convention on Human Rights). Advisory Opinion OC-5/85 of November 13, 1985. Series A no. 5, para. 50.

by minors to public entertainments.[261] On the other hand, it also explicitly recognizes a right of reply, which can be exercised by anyone injured by inaccurate or offensive statements or ideas disseminated by communications outlets, allowing for a reply or correction to such information.[262]

9.4.2 SCOPE OF FREEDOM OF OPINION AND EXPRESSION

Freedom of opinion and expression is a fundamental human right. It constitutes the foundation stone of every free and democratic society. This right not only acts as a necessary condition for the realization of the principles of transparency and accountability, pillars of a democratic government, but also provides the essential grounds for the full enjoyment of a wide range of other human rights, from political rights and freedom of assembly and association, to the minimum conditions for the exercise of individuals' autonomy and self-development.[263] The right to freedom of expression encompasses both an individual and a collective dimension, which must be simultaneously guaranteed. In its individual dimension, freedom of expression includes the rights of individuals to impart and disseminate information and ideas through any media and regardless of frontiers.[264] In its social dimension, this right is 'a means for the interchange of ideas and information among human beings and for mass communication. It includes the right of each person to seek to communicate [their] own views to others, as well as the right to receive opinions and news from others'.[265]

The protection of this right encompasses the forms and means for the dissemination of information, as well as its content. As to the forms, these include 'spoken, written and sign language and such non-verbal expression as images and objects of art',[266] while the means comprehend 'books, newspapers, pamphlets, posters, banners, dress ... all forms of audio-visual as well as electronic and internet-based modes

---

[261] ACHR, Art. 13.2, 13.4. See: IACtHR, *'The Last Temptation of Christ' (Olmedo Bustos et al.) v. Chile*. Merits, Reparations and Costs. Judgment of February 5, 2001. Series C No. 73, para. 70.

[262] ACHR, Art. 14. See: IACtHR, Enforceability of the Right to Reply or Correction (Arts. 14(1), 1(1), 2 American Convention on Human Rights). Advisory Opinion OC-7/85 of August 29, 1986. Series A no. 7.

[263] ECtHR, *Handyside v. the United Kingdom*, 7 December 1976, § 49, Series A App. no. 24; ACHPR, *Media Rights Agenda and Constitutional Rights Project v. Nigeria*, Communication Nos. 105/93, 128/94, 130/94, 152/96 (31 October 1998), para. 54; CCPR, General Comment No. 34 (Art. 19: Freedoms of opinion and expression), CCPR/C/GC/34 (12 September 2011), paras. 2–4.

[264] IACtHR, Compulsory Membership in an Association Prescribed by Law for the Practice of Journalism (Arts. 13, 29 American Convention on Human Rights). Advisory Opinion OC-5/85 of November 13, 1985. Series A No. 5, paras. 31–33.

[265] IACtHR, Compulsory Membership in an Association Prescribed by Law for the Practice of Journalism (Arts. 13, 29 American Convention on Human Rights). Advisory Opinion OC-5/85 of November 13, 1985. Series A No. 5, para. 33.

[266] CCPR, General Comment No. 34 (Art. 19: Freedoms of opinion and expression), CCPR/C/GC/34 (12 September 2011), para. 12.

of expression'.[267] Concerning the content, a wide range of expressions are protected under the right at stake, such as political speech, views on affairs of public interest, cultural and artistic expressions, teaching and academic opinions, religious discourse, and commercial advertisement.[268] Importantly, the protection of expressions is not limited to information or ideas 'that are favourably received or regarded as inoffensive', but also includes 'those that offend, shock or disturb the State or any sector of the population'.[269]

However, the wide range of expressions covered under this right does not mean that all categories of speech are to be awarded the same level of protection.[270] The extensive case law of the European Court of Human Rights has highlighted the particular importance of protecting political speech,[271] while certainly being less emphatic when it concerned the protection of artistic expressions—yet undoubtedly protected—,[272] and even less so when it referred to commercial advertisement.[273] An important contribution of the organs of the Inter-American system to this classification of protected speech has been to emphasize that, in addition to political speech and that of matters of public interest, a specially protected form of expression is that which concerns the expression of essential elements of personal identity, such as through the use of a minority language, or through the expression of one's religious, sexual, or gender identity.[274]

Within democratic societies the press and mass media perform a particularly fundamental role, being tasked with imparting and disseminating information and ideas on matters of general interest, which deserves special protection under the right to freedom of opinion and expression.[275] Of special importance is the press' role as the government 'watchdog', securing that public authorities are held accountable to the public for their conduct, which has been confirmed numerous

---

[267] CCPR, General Comment No. 34 (Art. 19: Freedoms of opinion and expression), CCPR/C/GC/34 (12 September 2011), para. 12.

[268] CCPR, General Comment No. 34 (Art. 19: Freedoms of opinion and expression), CCPR/C/GC/34 (12 September 2011), para. 11.

[269] ECtHR, *Handyside v. the United Kingdom*, 7 December 1976, § 49, Series A App. no. 24.

[270] ECtHR, *Mouvement raëlien suisse v. Switzerland* [GC], App. no. 16354/06, § 61, ECHR 2012. See: D. Harris, M. O'Boyle, E. Bates, and C. Buckley, *Harris, O'Boyle and Warbrick: Law of the European Convention on Human Rights* (4th edn., OUP 2018) 608–618.

[271] ECtHR, *Wingrove v. the United Kingdom*, 25 November 1996, § 58, *Reports of Judgments and Decisions* 1996-V.

[272] ECtHR, *Müller and Others v. Switzerland*, 24 May 1988, § 27, Series A no. 133.

[273] ECtHR, *markt intern Verlag GmbH and Klaus Beermann v. Germany*, 20 November 1989, § 26, Series A no. 165.

[274] IACtHR, *López Álvarez v. Honduras*. Merits, Reparations and Costs. Judgment of February 1, 2006. Series C No. 141, para. 169; IACHR, Inter-American Legal Framework regarding the Right to Freedom of Expression, OEA/Ser.L/V/II, CIDH/RELE/INF. 2/09 (30 December 2009), para. 56.

[275] ECtHR, *Observer and Guardian v. the United Kingdom*, 26 November 1991, § 59, Series A no. 216; IACtHR, *Ivcher Bronstein v. Peru*. Merits, Reparations and Costs. Judgment of February 6, 2001. Series C No. 74, paras. 149–150; CCPR, General Comment No. 34 (Art. 19: Freedoms of opinion and expression), CCPR/C/GC/34 (12 September 2011), para. 13.

times in the international case law.²⁷⁶ The European Court of Human Rights has affirmed that '[i]n a democratic system the actions or omissions of the Government must be subject to the close scrutiny not only of the legislative and judicial authorities but also of the press and public opinion'.²⁷⁷ It is, therefore, incumbent on the press to impart information concerning matters of public interest, as it is the right of the public to receive such information.²⁷⁸ On its part, the Human Rights Committee has emphasized the important function of mass media in the dissemination of public information and the consequential need for States to adopt effective measures to secure the existence of a plurality of voices, avoiding both public and private monopolistic controls over the media, which would harm the desired diversity of sources and views.²⁷⁹ Further positive actions to be taken by States to secure a free press concern the protection of journalists against threats, intimidation, and attacks aimed at silencing their voices, which are sadly a frequent reality. States are under the obligation to promptly investigate such illegal acts and to prosecute the perpetrators.²⁸⁰

Furthermore, in our days, the large-scale dissemination of information and ideas is no longer limited to professional reporters and the traditional mass media.²⁸¹ The development of new technologies has radically changed communications worldwide. The wide accessibility to the internet and mobile devices has created a global network for the exchange of ideas and opinions that does not necessarily rely on traditional media.²⁸² These developments have led to the emergence of new duties upon States, such as fostering the access of individuals to this new means of communication,²⁸³ as well as obligations of protection towards those who could be harmed in their rights

---

²⁷⁶ ECtHR, *Pentikäinen v. Finland* [GC], App. no. 11882/10, § 89, ECHR 2015.

²⁷⁷ ECtHR, *Castells v. Spain*, 23 April 1992, § 46, Series A no. 236.

²⁷⁸ ECtHR, *Bladet Tromsø and Stensaas v. Norway* [GC], App. no. 21980/93, § 62, ECHR 1999-III.

²⁷⁹ CCPR, General Comment No. 34 (Art. 19: Freedoms of opinion and expression), CCPR/C/GC/34 (12 September 2011), para. 40. See also: IACtHR, *Compulsory Membership in an Association Prescribed by Law for the Practice of Journalism* (Arts. 13, 29 American Convention on Human Rights). Advisory Opinion OC-5/85 of November 13, 1985. Series A no. 5, paras. 33–34, 56; IACHR, 'Declaration on Freedom of Expression' (2000), Principle 12.

²⁸⁰ CCPR, General Comment No. 34 (Art. 19: Freedoms of opinion and expression), CCPR/C/GC/34 (12 September 2011), para. 23; Report of the Special Rapporteur on the promotion and protection of the right to freedom of opinion and expression, Frank La Rue, A/HRC/20 (4 June 2012), paras. 51, 65; IACtHR, *Vélez Restrepo and family v. Colombia*. Preliminary Objection, Merits, Reparations, and Costs. Judgment of September 3, 2012. Series C No. 248, para. 209.

²⁸¹ T. McGonagle, 'The development of freedom of expression and information within the UN: leaps and bounds or fits and starts?' in T. McGonagle and Y. Donders (eds.), *The United Nations and Freedom of Expression and Information: Critical Perspectives* (CUP 2015) 1–51, 5.

²⁸² CCPR, General Comment No. 34 (Art. 19: Freedoms of opinion and expression), CCPR/C/GC/34 (12 September 2011), para. 15.

²⁸³ Report of the Special Rapporteur on the promotion and protection of the right to freedom of opinion and expression, Frank La Rue, A/HRC/17/27 (16 May 2011), paras. 85–88; CCPR, General Comment No. 34 (Art. 19: Freedoms of opinion and expression), CCPR/C/GC/34 (12 September 2011), para. 15. See also: M. Best, 'Can the Internet Be a Human Right?' (2004) 4 *Human Rights & Human Welfare* 23.

and reputation by third parties.[284] As highlighted by the European Court of Human Rights:

> ... user-generated expressive activity on the Internet provides an unprecedented platform for the exercise of freedom of expression ... However, alongside these benefits, certain dangers may also arise. Defamatory and other types of clearly unlawful speech, including hate speech and speech inciting violence, can be disseminated like never before, worldwide, in a matter of seconds, and sometimes remain persistently available online.[285]

Moreover, the need for accountability of government policies and actions in a democratic society exposes another relevant facet of the right to freedom of expression, which concerns the right of access to information held by public authorities. As affirmed by the Inter-American Court of Human Rights: 'for the individual to be able to exercise democratic control, the State must guarantee access to the information of public interest that it holds.'[286] Therefore, two basic State duties follow the right of individuals to have access to information: on the one hand, States must 'proactively put in the public domain Government information of public interest' and, on the other hand, they should also enact procedures whereby individuals can gain access to information held by public bodies.[287]

9.4.2.1 Critical debates: Genocide denial

Freedom of expression not only provides protection to the dissemination of favourable or inoffensive opinions but also to views susceptible to offend, shock, or disturb others. A clear limit to protected speech can be found in the aforementioned provisions from different international treaties—such as ICERD, ICCPR, and the American Convention—,[288] which impose upon States a duty to ban certain categories of expression, commonly known as 'hate speech',[289] which advocate hatred

---

[284] CCPR, General Comment No. 34 (Art. 19: Freedoms of opinion and expression), CCPR/C/GC/34 (12 September 2011), para. 7.

[285] ECtHR, *Delfi AS v. Estonia* (GC), App. no. 64569/09, § 110, ECHR 2015.

[286] IACtHR, *Claude Reyes et al. v. Chile*. Merits, Reparations and Costs. Judgment of September 19, 2006. Series C No. 151, para. 87.

[287] IACtHR, *Claude Reyes et al. v. Chile*. Merits, Reparations and Costs. Judgment of September 19, 2006. Series C No. 151, para. 77; CCPR, General Comment No. 34 (Art. 19: Freedoms of opinion and expression), CCPR/C/GC/34 (12 September 2011), para. 19.

[288] ICERD, Art. 4; ICCPR, Art. 20.2; ACHR, Art. 13.5. See also: Additional Protocol to the Convention on Cybercrime, concerning the criminalization of acts of a racist and xenophobic nature committed through computer systems (adopted 28 January 2003, entered into force 1 March 2006), ETS No. 189.

[289] Hate speech has been defined as 'any kind of communication in speech, writing or behaviour, that attacks or uses pejorative or discriminatory language with reference to a person or a group on the basis of who they are, in other words, based on their religion, ethnicity, nationality, race, colour, descent, gender or other identity factor'. See: United Nations Strategy and Plan of Action on Hate Speech (18 June 2019). Available at: https://www.un.org/en/hate-speech/un-strategy-and-plan-of-action-on-hate-speech (accessed on 1 April 2023).

and are capable of inciting discrimination, hostility, or violence.[290] Nonetheless, the international duty to prohibit certain forms of speech has a rather high threshold for its application, as the limitation of free speech should remain exceptional.[291] In particular, the resort to criminal law for regulating speech—a rather contentious topic in itself[292]—is only allowed under the international law of human rights when it refers to the most severe forms of hatred and, in particular, those which call for violence or other criminal acts.[293] It is also paramount for the application of norms restricting freedom of expression to be carefully assessed by the courts, taking into consideration specific factual elements, such as the social and political context prevalent at the time the expression was conveyed and disseminated; the position and standing of the speaker; the intent behind the expression; the content, form, and style of the speech; the reach the expression is likely to have; and both the likelihood of the incitement to succeed and the possible imminence of the outcome.[294]

Whether the expression of views that deny heinous historical facts, such as genocide, should also fall into the category of speech that can (or even should) be criminalized under the international law on human rights has been the subject of debate. As a general principle, laws that criminalize the expression of erroneous opinions about, or incorrect interpretations of, historical facts are incompatible with the right to freedom of opinion and expression.[295] Nevertheless, numerous States have adopted so-called 'memory laws'; criminal legislation that prohibits expressions that deny, minimize, or

---

[290] V. Abramovich, 'Legal dilemmas related to the restriction of hate speech' (2022) 32 *Sur—International Journal on Human Rights*. Available at: https://sur.conectas.org/en/legal-dilemmas-related-to-the-restriction-of-hate-speech/ (accessed on 6 April 2023).

[291] OHCHR, Rabat Plan of Action on the prohibition of advocacy of national, racial or religious hatred that constitutes incitement to discrimination, hostility or violence, A/HRC/22/17/Add. 4 (5 October 2012), para. 18. See also: IACtHR, *Tristán Donoso v. Panama*. Preliminary Objection, Merits, Reparations and Costs. Judgment of January 27, 2009. Series C No. 193, para. 110.

[292] Final Report by Mr. Danilo Turk and Mr. Louis Joiner, Special Rapporteurs, 'The Right to Freedom of Opinion and Expression', E/CN.4/Sub.2/1992/9 (14 July 1992); IACHR, Annual Report 1994, OEA/Ser.L/V.88 Doc. 9 rev. 1 (17 February 1995), Chapter V; ECtHR, *Öztürk v. Turkey* [GC], App. no. 22479/93, § 66, ECHR 1999-VI; IACtHR, *Kimel v. Argentina. Merits*, Reparations and Costs. Judgment of May 2, 2008 Series C No. 177, para. 78; CCPR, General Comment No. 34 (Art. 19: Freedoms of opinion and expression), CCPR/C/GC/34 (12 September 2011), para. 47; CERD, General Recommendation No. 35: Combating racist hate speech, CERD/C/GC/35 (26 September 2013), para. 12.

[293] Report of the Special Rapporteur on freedom of religion or belief, Asma Jahangir, and the Special Rapporteur on contemporary forms of racism, racial discrimination, xenophobia and related intolerance, Doudou Diène, A/HRC/2/3 (20 September 2006), para. 47; ECtHR, *Mariya Alekhina and Others v. Russia*, App. no. 38004/12, § 223, 17 July 2018.

[294] OHCHR, Rabat Plan of Action on the prohibition of advocacy of national, racial or religious hatred that constitutes incitement to discrimination, hostility or violence, A/HRC/22/17/Add.4 (5 October 2012), para. 29. Note, however, that Art. 4 of CERD does not seem to require the presence of the last-mentioned element for the criminalization of the dissemination of racial hatred. See: CERD, General Recommendation No. 35: Combating racist hate speech, CERD/C/GC/35 (26 September 2013), para. 15.

[295] CCPR, General Comment No. 34 (Art. 19: Freedoms of opinion and expression), CCPR/C/GC/34 (12 September 2011), para. 49.

attempt at justifying specific historical facts, such as acts of genocide and other crimes against humanity.[296]

International monitoring bodies called to examine the application of 'memory laws' have found no general or absolute incompatibility between this type of legislation and the right to freedom of opinion and expression. Decisions as to whether criminal sanctions for acts of 'negationism' amount to a breach of freedom of expression have been made on the basis of the specific facts of the cases under examination.[297] The European Court of Human Rights is the body that has developed the widest jurisprudence on the topic, laying down important principles to determine why it considers the criminalization of the public denial of such heinous crimes to be consistent with the protection of freedom of expression.[298] The Court has explained that the justification for making the denial of the genocide perpetrated by Nazi Germany a criminal offence does not truly lie on the negation of an undoubtedly established historical fact but in that, in view of the historical and spatial context of the States concerned—Western European States—its denial connotes an antidemocratic and anti-Semitic ideology. It has further affirmed: 'Holocaust denial is thus doubly dangerous, especially in States which have experienced the Nazi horrors, and which may be regarded as having a special moral responsibility to distance themselves from the mass atrocities that they have perpetrated or abetted by, among other things, outlawing their denial.'[299] The European Court has considered that denying the reality of a mass atrocity such as the Holocaust can be considered an attempt at rehabilitating the Nazi regime and even of accusing the victims themselves of falsifying history. The Court has rendered such expressions of negationism a serious form of anti-Semitic defamation and of incitement to hatred, amounting to an abuse of rights, contrary to the fundamental values underpinning the European Convention on Human Rights and, therefore, unable to find protection under the Convention itself.[300]

---

[296] Due to obvious historical circumstances, these laws have been mostly adopted in European States, including Austria, Belgium, Czechia, France, Germany, Hungary, Liechtenstein, Lithuania, Luxembourg, Montenegro, Poland, Portugal, Romania, Slovakia, Switzerland, and Ukraine, as well as in Israel. See: J. Temperman, *Religious Hatred and International Law: The Prohibition of Incitement to Violence or Discrimination* (CUP 2016) 281–284.

[297] See, among others: CCPR, *Robert Faurisson v. France*, Communication No. 550/1993, UN Doc. CCPR/C/58/D/550/1993(1996); ECtHR, *Hans Jorg Schimanek v. Austria* (dec.), App. no. 32307/96, 1 February 2000; CCPR, *Malcolm Ross v. Canada*, Communication No. 736/1997 (18 October 2000); ECtHR, *Garaudy v. France* (dec.), App. no. 65831/01, 24 June 2003; ECtHR, *Witzsch v. Germany* (dec.), No. 7485/03, 13 December 2005; ECtHR, *Perinçek v. Switzerland* [GC], App. no. 27510/08, ECHR 2015; ACHPR, *Umuhoza v. Rwanda* (merits) (2017) 2 AfCLR 165.

[298] However, the Court's approach, rejecting some of these claims on admissibility grounds under Art. 17 (prohibition of abuse of rights), rather than following their examination as to the merits under Art. 10 (freedom of expression), has been subject to criticism. See: J. Temperman, *Religious Hatred and International Law: The Prohibition of Incitement to Violence or Discrimination* (CUP 2016) 151–152; J. Mchangama and N. Alkiviadou, 'Hate Speech and the European Court of Human Rights: Whatever Happened to the Right to Offend, Shock or Disturb?' (2021) 21 *Human Rights Law Review* 1008, 1021–1022.

[299] ECtHR, *Perinçek v. Switzerland* [GC], App. no. 27510/08, § 243, ECHR 2015.

[300] ECtHR, *Garaudy v. France* (dec.), App. no. 65831/01, 24 June 2003, pp. 22–23.

> **CCPR, *Robert Faurisson v. France*, Communication 550/1993, CCPR/C/58/D/550/1993 (8 November 1996).**[301]
>
> The author of the communication, a university professor who had been removed from his Chair in 1991, was prosecuted, convicted, and fined under the domestic legislation that criminalized contesting the existence of crimes against humanity for which Nazi leaders had been convicted by the International Military Tribunal at Nuremberg. The author had expressed in a magazine interview that he believed that the gas chambers used to exterminate Jewish people in Nazi death camps during the Second World War were a myth. Before the Committee, the author claimed that his conviction amounted to a breach of his right to freedom of expression.
>
> However, the Committee rejected the author's claim. It considered that the restriction had been adopted pursuant to existing domestic legislation, which pursued the legitimate aim of protecting the rights and reputation of others. It assessed such a restriction to be necessary in a democratic society, affirming that: 'the statements made by the author, read in their full context, were of a nature as to raise or strengthen anti-semitic feelings' (para. 9.6.). The Committee stated that the restriction served the 'respect of the Jewish community to live free from fear of an atmosphere of anti-semitism' (para. 9.6); hence, it found it compatible with the protection of freedom of expression under ICCPR.

> **ECtHR, *Garaudy v. France (dec.)*, App. no. 65831/01, 24 June 2003.**
>
> The applicant was the author of a book entitled 'The Founding Myths of Israeli Politics'; published and distributed in 1995 and 1996. The book contained a number of passages in which historically established characteristics of the Holocaust were questioned, including the number of victims, the cause of their deaths, and the use of gas chambers to kill them. He was prosecuted and convicted of the offences of disputing the existence of crimes against humanity, defamation in public of a group of persons—namely, the Jewish community—and incitement to racial hatred. He was sentenced to a suspended term of imprisonment and ordered to pay a fine, as well as limited compensation to the civil parties in the procedures. Before the European Court of Human Rights, he claimed that his conviction amounted to a breach of his right to freedom of expression.
>
> The Court declared his application inadmissible. To reach this conclusion, the Court considered that expressions contained in the book in question had amounted to Holocaust denial, which entailed one of the most serious forms of racial defamation against Jewish people and of incitement to hatred of them. It affirmed that there was 'no doubt that denying the reality of clearly established historical facts, such as the Holocaust, as the applicant does in his book, does not constitute historical research akin to a quest for the truth. The ... real purpose being to rehabilitate the National-Socialist regime and, as a consequence, accuse

---

[301] According to Michael O'Flaherty, member of the Human Rights Committee and Committee's Rapporteur for the drafting of General Comment No. 34 (2011), the stance the Committee adopted in that general comment with regards to the incompatibility of 'memory laws' with ICCPR entailed overruling the opinion rendered in *Faurisson v. France*. See: M. O'Flaherty, 'Freedom of Expression: Article 19 of the International Covenant on Civil and Political Rights and the Human Rights Committee's General Comment No 34' (2012) 12 *Human Rights Law Review* 627, 645, 652–653.

the victims themselves of falsifying history.' (p. 22). According to the Court, such acts were manifestly incompatible with the fundamental values underpinning the Convention, which subtracted them from the protection under Article 10 (freedom of expression). Consequently, in application of Article 17 (prohibition of abuse of rights), the Court rejected the application.

ACHPR, *Umuhoza v. Rwanda* (merits) (2017) 2 AfCLR 165.

The case concerned a Hutu Rwandan politician who, after living abroad for nearly seventeen years, returned to Rwanda to register an opposition political party to participate in upcoming elections. Upon her return, she gave public speeches and interviews in which she spoke about problems with reconciliation and ethnic violence. The authorities considered that her expressions amounted to the crime of minimizing genocide, propagating the ideology of genocide, and threatening State security. She was prosecuted and convicted on charges of spreading the ideology of genocide, as well as on an array of charges against national security, including terrorist related offences. She was initially convicted to eight years of imprisonment, increased to fifteen years on appeal.

The applicant resorted directly to the African Court on Human and People's Rights, as Rwanda had accepted the direct access of individuals—in fact, it was this case that prompted Rwanda's withdrawal of the declaration, as discussed in **Section 8.3**. Before the Court, she claimed that her prosecution, trial, and conviction amounted to the violation of the rights to a fair trial and of freedom and expression, protected under the African Charter. The Court found the State responsible for the violation of both rights. With respect to the latter, the Court affirmed ' . . . that it is fully aware and cognisant of the fact that Rwanda suffered from the most atrocious genocide in the recent history of mankind . . . This grim fact of its past evidently warrants that the government should adopt all measures to promote social cohesion and concordance among the people and prevent similar incidents from happening in the future' (para. 146). It, therefore, confirmed that it was entirely legitimate for the State to have introduced criminal laws that imposed restrictions on expressions that negate or minimize genocide. Nonetheless, the Court considered that the imposed restrictions could not be considered necessary in a democratic society; on the one hand, the applicant's expression did not seem to amount to a negation or minimization of genocide and, on the other hand, the sanctions imposed failed to meet a test of proportionality, as the aims pursued could have been achieved through less restrictive measures (para. 161).

9.4.3 RESTRICTIONS TO FREEDOM OF EXPRESSION

Despite its fundamental importance, freedom of expression is certainly susceptible to restrictions by States. Such limitations need to be prescribed by law and deemed necessary to protect essential public interests. The bundle of legitimate interests that can justify the restriction of freedom of expression by the State is similar to those discussed with regard to freedom of thought, conscience, and religion (**Section 9.3.3**) and includes the protection of the rights or reputations of others, as well as the protection of national security, public order, public health, and public morals.[302] When a claim of a violation of the right of freedom of expression arises, the first issue to be determined is whether the person alleging such a breach has suffered interference with the enjoyment of their right; meaning that the State had adopted a measure affecting its free exercise. If such interference exists, the initial requirement it must fulfil to be justified is to have been 'prescribed by law'. As discussed in **Section 9.3.3**, the European Court of Human Rights, the Human Rights Committee, and the African Court on Human and People's Rights are all in agreement that the meaning of this requirement concerns the issue of foreseeability of the limitation. This means that the conditions and circumstances in which the restriction to the right would be imposed are clearly stipulated in a legal provision that is accessible to all individuals so that everyone would be able to regulate their conduct in accordance with such norm.[303] As to the provision itself, it does not need to have been enacted by the legislative power, but could be based on well-established common law or on norms below the rank of statutes.[304]

The second main requirement a limitation must fulfil is its legitimate purpose. The aims enumerated in the pertinent provisions of international human rights treaties are exhaustive,[305] meaning that no public interest beyond those mentioned could act as legitimate justification for a restriction of freedom of expression. The legally grounded interference should not only serve to advance the purported legitimate aim[306] but must also be necessary to achieve the valid aim pursued, which is the third condition it must fulfil. To assess the necessity of the limitation and determine whether the State has discharged its burden of justifying the restriction at stake, it is essential to distinguish the concept of 'necessity' from those of usefulness or desirability, as the former implies the existence of a 'pressing social need'.[307] In particular, for an interference to be considered

---

[302] While this is the case under ICCPR and the ACHR, the ECHR has a more extensive enumeration of legitimate aims that can lead to the limitations of freedom of expression, expressly mentioning national security, territorial integrity, public safety, the prevention of disorder or crime, the protection of health and morals, the protection of the reputation or rights of others, preventing the disclosure of information received in confidence, and maintaining the authority and impartiality of the judiciary.

[303] ECtHR, *The Sunday Times v. the United Kingdom* (no. 1), 26 April 1979, § 49, Series A no. 30; CCPR, General Comment No. 34: Art. 19: Freedoms of opinion and expression, CCPR/C/GC/34 (12 September 2011), para. 25; ACtHPR, *Lohe Issa Konate v. Burkina Faso* (merits) (2014) 1 AfCLR 314, para. 128.

[304] ECtHR, *The Sunday Times v. the United Kingdom* (no. 1), 26 April 1979, § 47, Series A no. 30; ECtHR, *Dogru v. France*, App. no. 27058/05, § 52, 4 December 2008. As discussed in **Section 9.3.3**, this stance is not shared by the Inter-American Court.

[305] CCPR, General Comment No. 34 (Art. 19: Freedoms of opinion and expression), CCPR/C/GC/34 (12 September 2011), para. 22; IACtHR, Compulsory Membership in an Association Prescribed by Law for the Practice of Journalism (Arts. 13, 29 American Convention on Human Rights). Advisory Opinion OC-5/85 of November 13, 1985. Series A no. 5, para. 65.

[306] CCPR, General Comment No. 34 (Art. 19: Freedoms of opinion and expression), CCPR/C/GC/34 (12 September 2011), para. 22; ECtHR, *Bayev and Others v. Russia*, App. nos. 67667/09 and two others, § 83, 20 June 2017.

[307] ECtHR, *Handyside v. the United Kingdom*, 7 December 1976, § 48, Series A no. 24.

necessary the legitimate aim pursued should not be achievable through measures that are less restrictive than those in place.[308]

Whether a specific restriction is to be considered necessary would be for the pertinent international monitoring body to decide on a case-by-case basis. On the one hand, the European Court of Human Rights has developed the doctrine of the margin of appreciation (discussed in **Section 7.7**) as a tool for performing its analysis, an approach that seems to also be followed by the African Court on Human and People's Rights.[309] This means that when assessing whether an interference with freedom of expression is compatible with the European Convention, the Court grants the respondent State a certain margin of discretion for determining the need for the interference, considering that the domestic authorities are, in principle, better situated to assess local needs than an international supervisory body.[310] However, the scope of the margin of discretion granted to the State would vary depending on different factors, including the importance of the interests at stake and the existence of a consensus among European States as to how the particular issue should be regulated. The European Court of Human Rights would only find a violation of the right to freedom of expression if it considers that the State's interference with the right has exceeded its margin of discretion in the given case.[311] On the other hand, the Human Rights Committee and the Inter-American Court of Human Rights have not adopted the European Court's approach, rejecting the margin of appreciation as a method for deciding cases.[312] These bodies would rule on the necessity of any restriction to a right in a principled manner on a case-by-case basis.

9.4.3.1 Conflict of rights: freedom of expression and the protection of the rights and reputation of others

According to the Registry of the European Court of Human Rights, the protection of the rights and reputation of individuals is, by far, the legitimate aim most frequently relied on by States with regard to imposing restrictions on freedom of expression.[313] This is not surprising, as the recognition of this right in international treaties acknowledges that its exercise attracts special duties and responsibilities, as it can potentially clash with the enjoyment of other human rights that States are also under the obligation to protect. The topic of 'defamation', broadly understood as a statement that causes injury to someone's reputation, concerns one of such circumstances in which the right

---

[308] IACtHR, *Compulsory Membership in an Association Prescribed by Law for the Practice of Journalism* (Arts. 13, 29 American Convention on Human Rights). Advisory Opinion OC-5/85 of November 13, 1985. Series A no. 5, para. 79; ECtHR, *Glor v. Switzerland*, App. no. 13444/04, § 94, ECHR 2009; CCPR, General Comment No. 34 (Art. 19: Freedoms of opinion and expression), CCPR/C/GC/34 (12 September 2011), paras. 33–34.

[309] ACHPR, *Umuhoza v. Rwanda* (merits) (2017) 2 AfCLR 165, para. 137.

[310] ECtHR, *Handyside v. the United Kingdom*, 7 December 1976, § 48–50, Series A no. 24.

[311] ECtHR, *Zana v. Turkey*, 25 November 1997, § 62, Reports of Judgments and Decisions 1997-VII.

[312] CCPR, General Comment No. 34: Art. 19: Freedoms of opinion and expression, CCPR/C/GC/34 (12 September 2011), para. 36. With respect to the IACtHR, see discussion in **Section 6.8**.

[313] Registry of the ECtHR, 'Guide on Article 10 of the European Convention on Human Rights: Freedom of Expression' (31 December 2020), para. 109.

to freedom of expression conflicts with individuals' rights not to be attacked in their honour.[314] Nevertheless, restrictions imposed upon freedom of expression for the protection of the reputation of others need to be carefully drafted and applied, and take into consideration a number of conditions in order to achieve a fair balance between the enjoyment of both rights at stake.[315]

An initial element that the legal regulation of defamation must carefully establish is the minimum level of severity threshold that needs to exist for an expression to be susceptible of causing actual harm to a person's reputation,[316] bearing in mind that even ideas and opinions that offend, shock, or disturb, are still entitled to protection under the right to freedom of expression. Moreover, the degree of protection deserved by the dissemination of controversial information or opinions should be higher when it relates to the debate of matters of public interest.[317] As mentioned in **Section 9.4.2**, in a democratic society, political speech and that related to issues of public interest should benefit from enhanced protection. Of course, whether a matter can indeed be considered of public interest is in itself debatable. In an attempt to provide guidance on the issue, the European Court of Human Rights has asserted:

> Public interest ordinarily relates to matters which affect the public to such an extent that it may legitimately take an interest in them, which attract its attention or which concern it to a significant degree, especially in that they affect the well-being of citizens or the life of the community. This is also the case with regard to matters which are capable of giving rise to considerable controversy, which concern an important social issue, or which involve a problem that the public would have an interest in being informed about. The public interest cannot be reduced to the public's thirst for information about the private life of others, or to an audience's wish for sensationalism or even voyeurism.[318]

Whether the opinion or information concerns a private person or a public figure is another important aspect since the limits of acceptable criticism are wider when it comes to public personalities. Public personalities, in general, have laid themselves open to scrutiny by the press and the public at large and, therefore, should display a greater degree of tolerance to being criticized.[319] This is particularly true with regard to

---

[314] UDHR, Art. 12; ECHR, Art. 10.2; ACHR, Arts. 11, 13.2; ICCPR, Arts. 17, 19.3; Arab Charter, Art. 32.2.

[315] CCPR, General Comment No. 34: Art. 19: Freedoms of opinion and expression, CCPR/C/GC/34 (12 September 2011), para. 47; IACtHR, *Fontevecchia and D`Amico v. Argentina*. Merits, Reparations and Costs. Judgment of November 29, 2011. Series C No. 238, para. 50.

[316] Report of the Special Rapporteur on the promotion and protection of the right to freedom of opinion and expression (Ambeyi Ligabo), A/HRC/4/27 (2 January 2007), para. 47; ECtHR, *Axel Springer AG v. Germany* [GC], App. no. 39954/08, § 83, 7 February 2012.

[317] ECtHR, *Tammer v. Estonia*, App. no. 41205/98, § 68, ECHR 2001-I; IACtHR, *Herrera Ulloa v. Costa Rica*. Preliminary Objections, Merits, Reparations and Costs. Judgment of July 2, 2004. Series C No. 107, para. 128.

[318] ECtHR, *Satakunnan Markkinapörssi Oy and Satamedia Oy v. Finland* [GC], App. no. 931/13, § 171, 27 June 2017.

[319] ECtHR, *Lingens v. Austria*, 8 July 1986, § 42, Series A no. 103; IACtHR, *Herrera Ulloa v. Costa Rica*. Preliminary Objections, Merits, Reparations and Costs. Judgment of July 2, 2004. Series C No. 107, para. 129; ACHPR, *Umuhoza v. Rwanda* (merits) (2017) 2 AfCLR 165, para. 160.

politicians and State officials. In fact, States are bound to repeal any existing domestic legislation that prohibits criticism of those exercising political office, including heads of State and government.[320] Nonetheless, a further distinction should be made between information or opinions relating to the public functions of the person at stake and those concerning their private life. While in the former case, the dissemination of expression is connected to the needed transparency and accountability that underpins the operation of a democratic system, the circumstances in which the public's right to be informed can extend into aspects of the private life of public figures are much more restricted.[321]

Whether the expressions considered harmful are statements of facts—such as the attribution of the commission of an illegal act—or value judgments is also relevant. Domestic legislation might require proof of the truth of the former—and providing such proof should act as a valid defence—,[322] but this cannot be requested from the latter without amounting to a violation of freedom of expression.[323] When it is not possible to clearly distinguish between the factual and the evaluative elements of a statement, then, the expression as a whole should be considered an opinion.[324] However, even if proof of truth cannot be requested for critical opinions, the existence of a 'sufficient factual basis' could be, as value judgments without any factual basis at all to support them could be considered excessive.[325]

The type and severity of potential sanctions stipulated by domestic legislation in case of expressions that harm another person's reputation is another relevant aspect to consider. Stringent penalties, especially through the use of criminal law, could have a 'chilling effect' that amounts to censorship, as they could discourage the expression of criticism.[326] In turn, this could disrupt the role of the press as government watchdog with ghastly consequences for the healthy working of a democratic society.[327] Under the

---

[320] IACHR, Annual Report 1994, OEA/Ser.L/V.88 Doc. 9 rev. 1 (17 February 1995), Chapter V; CCPR, General Comment No. 34: Art. 19: Freedoms of opinion and expression, CCPR/C/GC/34 (12 September 2011), para. 38.

[321] ECtHR, *Standard Verlags GmbH v. Austria* (no. 2), App. no. 21277/05 § 53, 4 June 2009.

[322] ECtHR, *Castells v. Spain*, 23 April 1992, § 48, Series A App. no. 236; CCPR, General Comment No. 34: Art. 19: Freedoms of opinion and expression, CCPR/C/GC/34 (12 September 2011), para. 47; African Commission on Human and Peoples' Rights, 'Declaration of Principles on Freedom of Expression and Access to Information in Africa' (2019), Principle 21. The Inter-American Commission on Human Rights has gone even further, proposing the adoption of the 'actual malice' doctrine with regard to public officials and public figures, which proposes that in case of harm caused by the dissemination of false information, sanctions should only be applied when there was actual intent to cause harm, with full knowledge that the information was false or with manifest negligence in the determination of the truth. See: IACHR, 'Declaration on Freedom of Expression' (2000), Principle 10.

[323] ECtHR, *Lingens v. Austria*, 8 July 1986, § 46, Series A no. 103; IACtHR, *Kimel v. Argentina. Merits*, Reparations and Costs. Judgment of May 2, 2008 Series C No. 177, para. 93.

[324] N. Jayawickrama, *The Judicial Application of Human Rights Law: National, Regional and International Jurisprudence* (2nd edn., CUP 2017) 751–752.

[325] ECtHR, *Jerusalem v. Austria*, App. no. 26958/95, § 43, ECHR 2001-II; ECtHR, *Pedersen and Baadsgaard v. Denmark* [GC], App. no. 49017/99, § 76, ECHR 2004-XI.

[326] ECtHR, *Karsai v. Hungary*, App. no. 5380/07, § 36, 1 December 2009; IACtHR, *Fontevecchia and D´Amico v. Argentina*. Merits, Reparations and Costs. Judgment of November 29, 2011. Series C No. 238, para. 74.

[327] ECtHR, *Stoll v. Switzerland* [GC], App. no. 69698/01, § 154, ECHR 2007-V.

international law of human rights, States are strongly discouraged, if not yet obliged, to refrain from the use of criminal sanctions when it concerns the offence of defamation, and forbidden to resort to actual custodial sentences.[328]

9.4.3.2 Critical debates: blasphemy

According to a 2017 Report of the Special Rapporteur on Freedom of Religion, Ahmed Shaheed, more than seventy States have anti-blasphemy laws on the books.[329] This legislation criminalizes blasphemous acts or expression, which could be broadly defined as offences that consist of insulting or showing contempt or lack of reverence to deities, religious beliefs, or anything considered sacred.[330] While this type of legislation has been defended by some, as means to protect individuals' unhindered exercise of freedom of thought, conscience, and religion,[331] their European inception was aimed at preventing challenges to State-endorsed (Christian) faith, punishing error and heresy.[332] Anti-blasphemy laws tend to afford different levels of protection to different religions, privileging that which is State-endorsed or, at least, followed by the majority of the population. Therefore, these laws can become instruments of persecution, hostility, and violence against religious minorities, agnostics, atheists, and non-theists.[333]

As discussed in **Section 9.3**, freedom of religion is a fundamental human right, but it does not encompass the right to be free from criticism (or even from ridicule) of one's religion or belief.[334] Believers must tolerate the denial by others of their

---

[328] IACtHR, *Kimel v. Argentina. Merits*, Reparations and Costs. Judgment of May 2, 2008 Series C No. 177, para. 78; CCPR, General Comment No. 34: Art. 19: Freedoms of opinion and expression, CCPR/C/GC/34 (12 September 2011), para. 47; African Commission on Human and Peoples' Rights, 'Declaration of Principles on Freedom of Expression and Access to Information in Africa (2019), Principle 22. See also: Joint Declaration by the UN Special Rapporteur on Freedom of Opinion and Expression, the OSCE Representative on Freedom of the Media and the OAS Special Rapporteur on Freedom of Expression (2002).

[329] Interim report of the Special Rapporteur on freedom of religion or belief (Ahmed Shaheed), A/72/365 (28 August 2017), para. 26.

[330] Venice Commission, Report on the Relationship between Freedom of Expression and Freedom of Religion: The Issue of Regulation and Prosecution of Blasphemy, Religious Insult and Incitement to Religious Hatred, CDL-AD(2008)026 (23 October 2008), para. 24.

[331] UNGA, 'Combating defamation of religions', A/RES/62/154 (6 March 2008); HRC, 'Combating defamation of religions', Resolution 7/19 (27 March 2008). But, see also: HRC, 'Combating intolerance, negative stereotyping and stigmatization of, and discrimination, incitement to violence and violence against, persons based on religion or belief', A/HRC/RES/16/18 (12 April 2011); UNGA, 'Combating intolerance, negative stereotyping, stigmatization, discrimination, incitement to violence and violence against persons, based on religion or belief', A/RES/66/167 (27 March 2012).

[332] K. Boyle, 'The Danish Cartoons' (2006) 24 *Netherlands Quarterly of Human Rights* 185, 189; D. Grimm, 'Freedom of Speech in a Globalized World' in I. Hare and J. Weinstein (eds.), *Extreme Speech and Democracy* (OUP 2009) 11–22, 17.

[333] OHCHR, Rabat Plan of Action on the prohibition of advocacy of national, racial or religious hatred that constitutes incitement to discrimination, hostility or violence, A/HRC/22/17/Add. 4 (5 October 2012), para. 19; Interim report of the Special Rapporteur on freedom of religion or belief (Ahmed Shaheed), A/72/365 (28 August 2017), para. 27.

[334] ECtHR, *Otto-Preminger-Institut v. Austria*, 20 September 1994, § 47, Series A no. 295-A; OHCHR, Rabat Plan of Action on the prohibition of advocacy of national, racial or religious hatred that constitutes incitement to discrimination, hostility or violence, A/HRC/22/17/Add. 4 (5 October 2012), para. 19.

religious beliefs, as well as the expression of opinions hostile to their faith.[335] A limit to this admissible criticism is to be found in expressions that amount to 'hate speech' (see **Section 9.4.2.1**). While expressions of prejudice and hatred that incite violence or discrimination against the members of a religious group are placed beyond the scope of protected speech, the criticism of religious doctrine, tenets of faith, and even religious leaders should not be.[336] Nonetheless, the particular difficulty of drafting legislation that provides precise criteria to allow distinguishing between criticisms of religious beliefs, deities, and institutions from expressions that can be construed as prejudicial against individuals who embrace them should be acknowledged.[337]

The compatibility of anti-blasphemy laws with freedom of expression remains a contentious topic in our days, even if there is an increasing international trend that calls for their repeal.[338] Faced with challenges to domestic restrictions imposed on the dissemination of expressions, in particular through books, articles, and the screening of films, the European Court of Human Rights developed a long-standing case law in which anti-blasphemy legislation had been found to be compatible with freedom of expression.[339] It might seem that such jurisprudence has started to change, with the Court ruling on the violation of freedom of expression due to the imposition of domestic sanctions for the criticism of religious ideas, dogmas, and members of the clergy.[340] However, it is not (yet) possible to affirm that the Court's case law has decried

---

[335] ECtHR, *Otto-Preminger-Institut v. Austria*, 20 September 1994, § 47, Series A no. 295-A.

[336] CCPR, General Comment No. 34: Art. 19: Freedoms of opinion and expression, CCPR/C/GC/34 (12 September 2011), para. 48; CERD, General Recommendation No. 35: Combating racist hate speech, CERD/C/GC/35 (26 September 2013), para. 6.

[337] P. Cumpler, 'Blasphemy, Freedom of Expression and the Protection of Religious Sensibilities in Twenty-First-Century Europe' in J. Temperman and A. Koltay (eds.), *Blasphemy and Freedom of Expression: Comparative, Theoretical and Historical Reflections after the Charlie Hebdo Massacre* (CUP 2017) 137–166, 156–157; E. Howard, *Freedom of Expression and Religious Hate Speech in Europe* (Routledge 2018) 67.

[338] Parliamentary Assembly of the Council of Europe, Recommendation 1805 (2007), para. 15; Venice Commission, Report on the Relationship between Freedom of Expression and Freedom of Religion: The Issue of Regulation and Prosecution of Blasphemy, Religious Insult and Incitement to Religious Hatred, CDL-AD(2008)026 (23 October 2008), para. 89; CCPR, General Comment No. 34: Art. 19: Freedoms of opinion and expression, CCPR/C/GC/34 (12 September 2011), para. 48; OHCHR, Rabat Plan of Action on the prohibition of advocacy of national, racial or religious hatred that constitutes incitement to discrimination, hostility or violence, A/HRC/22/17/Add.4 (5 October 2012), para. 25; Interim report of the Special Rapporteur on freedom of religion or belief (Ahmed Shaheed), A/72/365 (28 August 2017), para. 76; Report of the Special Rapporteur on freedom of religion or belief (Ahmed Shaheed), A/HRC/40/58 (5 March 2019), paras. 23–24.

[339] ECtHR, *Otto-Preminger-Institut v. Austria*, 20 September 1994, Series A App. no. 295-A; ECtHR, *Wingrove v. the United Kingdom*, 25 November 1996, Reports of Judgments and Decisions 1996-V; ECtHR, *İ.A. v. Turkey*, App. no. 42571/98, ECHR 2005-VIII.

[340] ECtHR, *Giniewski v. France*, App. no. 64016/00, ECHR 2006-I; ECtHR, *Aydın Tatlav v. Turkey*, App. no. 50692/99, 2 May 2006; ECtHR, *Klein v. Slovakia*, App. no. 72208/01, 31 October 2006; ECtHR, *Tagiyev and Huseynov v. Azerbaijan*, App. no. 13274/08, 5 December 2019; ECtHR, *Rabczewska v. Poland*, App. no. 8257/13, 15 September 2022; ECtHR, *Bouton v. France* (dec.), App. no. 22636/19, 13 October 2022.

the validity of anti-blasphemy restrictions.[341] Conversely, when the Inter-American Court has had the opportunity to examine the restriction of the screening of a film that had been considered offensive to the honour and reputation of Jesus Christ,[342] it relied on the prohibition of prior censorship established in the American Convention to find a clear violation of freedom of expression.[343]

ECtHR, *Otto-Preminger-Institut v. Austria*, 20 September 1994, Series A no. 295-A.

The applicant was an association that sought to organize six showings of the film 'Council in Heaven' in Innsbruck; a film based on a nineteenth-century play that portrayed the Christian God, Jesus, and Mary in a satirical manner. At the request of the Catholic Church, the public prosecutor brought criminal proceedings against the association's manager, charging him with the act of 'disparaging religious doctrines' and, subsequently, requested the seizure and forfeiture of the film. The domestic courts granted the prosecutor's request; hence, the planned screening of the film did not take place.

The applicant resorted to the European Commission of Human Rights, claiming that the actions of the domestic authorities had amounted to a violation of freedom of expression. By a clear majority, the Commission agreed with the applicant and found a violation of the Convention. Following this decision, the case was referred to the European Court which, in a contentious (6-to-3) judgment, ruled that there had been no violation of Article 10 (freedom of expression).

The Court's reasoning included a paragraph that would be widely quoted in subsequent cases concerning the balancing of conflicting interests between freedom of expression and freedom of religion: 'Those who choose to exercise the freedom to manifest their religion, irrespective of whether they do so as members of a religious majority or a minority, cannot reasonably expect to be exempt from all criticism. They must tolerate and accept the denial by others of their religious beliefs and even the propagation by others of doctrines hostile to their faith' (para. 47). Nevertheless, this statement was followed by the understanding that the seizure and forfeiture of the film could be seen as necessary in the case. The Court ruled that the domestic authorities had not overstepped their margin of appreciation in determining how to balance what they considered to be a conflict of rights. It was, nonetheless, peculiar that the Court assessed the fact that the Roman Catholic religion was that of the overwhelming majority of the inhabitants of the region as a factor to be weighted in favour of the restrictive measure, rather than against it (para. 56).[344]

---

[341] ECtHR, *E.S. v. Austria*, App. no. 38450/12, 25 October 2018. See: T. Lewis, 'At the Deep End of the Pool Religious Offence, Debate Speech and the Margin of Appreciation before the European Court of Human Rights' in J. Temperman and A. Koltay (eds.), *Blasphemy and Freedom of Expression: Comparative, Theoretical and Historical Reflections after the Charlie Hebdo Massacre* (CUP 2017) 259–293, 260; J. Temperman, 'Blasphemy and the European Court of Human Rights: A Small Step Forward, a Giant Leap Back' in P. Czech et al. (ed.), *European Yearbook on Human Rights 2019* (Intersentia 2019) 221–236, 231–235.

[342] IACtHR, '*The Last Temptation of Christ*' *(Olmedo Bustos et al.) v. Chile*. Merits, Reparations and Costs. Judgment of February 5, 2001. Series C No. 73, para. 61.h.

[343] IACtHR, '*The Last Temptation of Christ*' *(Olmedo Bustos et al.) v. Chile*. Merits, Reparations and Costs. Judgment of February 5, 2001. Series C No. 73, op. para. 1.

[344] J. Temperman, 'Blasphemy and the European Court of Human Rights: A Small Step Forward, a Giant Leap Back' in P. Czech et al. (ed.), *European Yearbook on Human Rights 2019* (Intersentia 2019) 221–236, 226.

> IACtHR, *'The Last Temptation of Christ' (Olmedo Bustos et al.) v. Chile*. Merits, Reparations and Costs. Judgment of February 5, 2001. Series C No. 73.
>
> The case concerned the decision of the domestic authorities of Chile to forbid the screening of the film 'The Last Temptation of Christ' in movie theatres in the country. Although the film had obtained authorization for its exhibition for an adult audience, a petition filed in the domestic courts by a group of individuals in their own name and in representation of Jesus Christ led to the prohibition of the exhibition of the film.
>
> Following the decision of the judicial authorities, a group of individuals filed a petition before the Inter-American Commission of Human Rights claiming the violation of their right to receive information, due to the censoring of the film in question. The Commission decided in favour of the applicants and, following the State's lack of compliance with its recommendations, decided to submit the case to the Court.
>
> The Inter-American Court found that the censoring of the film amounted to a violation of the right to freedom of expression. It stated that prior censorship was not allowed under the American Convention—with the sole exception of the regulation of access of minors to public entertainment—and, therefore, the acts of the domestic authorities amounted to its violation. Furthermore, the Court affirmed that the domestic legislation that allowed for the adoption of acts of prior censorship (including Chile's Constitution) was in itself in conflict with the State's obligations under the Convention and ordered the State to amend such legislation within a reasonable period of time.

9.4.4 FURTHER REFLECTIONS: A POST-MODERN CRITIQUE OF FREEDOM OF EXPRESSION

As discussed in **Section 1.3.3**, a post-modern critique of human rights reveals concern over the regulatory power of rights, with rights conceived of, concomitantly, as protective tools against States' interferences and as manifestations of bio-power—a life-administrating power, involved in the regulation, control, and administration of the lives of individuals.[345] The right to freedom of expression is a particularly interesting subject for a post-modern critique, given its fundamental role as a pillar of the Western democratic State.[346] The following post-modern analysis of freedom of expression is grounded on three important and interrelated concepts from Foucault's writings: bio-power, knowledge, and discourse.

An important starting point is to appreciate that a given discourse is not just a means to describe reality but a site in which meanings and truth(s) are constructed; discourses can be understood as systems of ideas that have a claim to the truth on a given topic. Discourses require, produce, and reproduce knowledge, and both—discourses and knowledge—act as manifestations of bio-power. To illustrate this

---

[345] M. Foucault, *The History of Sexuality: An Introduction* (Penguin 1978) 136.
[346] N. Jayawickrama, *The Judicial Application of Human Rights Law: National, Regional and International Jurisprudence* (2nd edn., CUP 2017) 755.

point, Foucault explained that it was not coincidental that the emergence of an era of institutional repression of non-heteronormative sexualities in Europe, which started in the seventeenth century, was accompanied by an institutional incitement to speak about sex.[347] The religious practice of 'confession' was one of the most evident examples of the incitement to discourse, presenting an opportunity to unburden one's conscience, while obtaining forgiveness for one's soul.[348] This right and duty to 'confess' was one of the main sources of the production of knowledge about sex.[349]

In our days, the ritual of confession continues to be important for producing and re-producing knowledge, even if not assuming the shape of the Christian rite. In our digital era, secular confessions, such as through social media, are an (almost) social imperative. There is an incitement to discourse about all aspects of life. This sharing of abundant information with a plurality of (unknown) recipients is protected and fostered by 'freedom of expression'. However, these secular confessions are not merely a free exercise of expression but are also shaped in certain formats, as individuals self-regulate their discourse to fit expected patterns.[350]

Discourses circulated through the dissemination of information and ideas have an important regulatory power over how we conceive the world and ourselves within it. Bio-power does not only require knowledge; it also produces and reproduces it. The wide circulation of ideas, especially through mass and social media, plays an important role in the production of knowledge, the shaping of ideas and behaviours, and the construction of meaning and identities.[351] Discipline is learned through knowledge about how individuals, by themselves and as a collective, are expected to behave. In the words of Foucault: 'power produces; it produces reality; it produces domains of objects and rituals of truth'.[352] Power also produces the (disciplined) individuals that it seeks to regulate.

Therefore, the legal regulation of freedom of expression is quite telling from a post-modern perspective. As discussed in this chapter, the regulation in place rightfully finds fault with undue restrictions to the circulation of ideas, as well as with 'hate speech'—which spreads hatred and incites violence and discrimination. Nevertheless, as warned by Foucault, regulatory power operates by fostering the dissemination of discourses through an incitement to speak rather than through repression, regulation, and censorship. Consequently, a post-modern approach would be wary of equating greater freedom of expression with greater freedom from power. Wider freedoms cannot be seen as a path to reach an ideal state of liberation because (regulatory) power is as implicated in liberation as it is in domination, with no possible existence beyond

---

[347] M. Foucault, *The History of Sexuality: Volume I* (trans. R. Hurley, Pantheon Books 1978).
[348] M. Foucault, *The History of Sexuality: Volume I* (trans. R. Hurley, Pantheon Books 1978) 12–13.
[349] M. Foucault, *The History of Sexuality: Volume I* (trans. R. Hurley, Pantheon Books 1978) 63.
[350] M. Foucault, *The History of Sexuality: Volume I* (trans. R. Hurley, Pantheon Books 1978) 140; M. Foucault, *Discipline and Punish: The Birth of the Prison* (trans. A. Sheridan, Vintage Books 1979) 199.
[351] D. Grimm, 'Freedom of Speech in a Globalized World' in I. Hare and J. Weinstein (eds.), *Extreme Speech and Democracy* (OUP 2009) 11–22, 15.
[352] M. Foucault, *Discipline and Punish: The Birth of the Prison* (trans. A. Sheridan, Vintage Books 1979) 194.

power.[353] To clarify, a post-modern critique of freedom of expression would lead neither to the rejection of the value of this fundamental right, nor to more stringent legal restrictions on its exercise. However, it should lead to the understanding that while freedom of expression is certainly a precious right, it also operates as a powerful regulatory tool.

FURTHER READING

FARRELL, M., *The Prohibition of Torture in Exceptional Circumstances* (CUP 2013).

HARRIS, D., O'BOYLE, M., BATES, E., and BUCKLEY, C., *Harris, O'Boyle and Warbrick: Law of the European Convention on Human Rights* (4th edn., OUP 2018).

HOWARD, E., *Freedom of Expression and Religious Hate Speech in Europe* (Routledge 2018).

JAYAWICKRAMA, N., *The Judicial Application of Human Rights Law: National, Regional and International Jurisprudence* (2nd edn., CUP 2017).

MAVRONICOLA, N., *Torture, Inhumanity and Degradation under Article 3 of the ECHR: Absolute Rights and Absolute Wrongs* (Hart 2021).

NOWAK, M., BIRK, K., and MONINA, G., *The United Nations Convention Against Torture and its Optional Protocol: A Commentary* (2nd edn., OUP 2019).

TAYLOR, P.M., *Freedom of Religion: UN and European Human Rights Law and Practice* (CUP 2005).

TEMPERMAN, J., *Religious Hatred and International Law: The Prohibition of Incitement to Violence or Discrimination* (CUP 2016).

WICKS, E., *The Right to Life and Conflicting Interests* (OUP 2010).

---

[353] M. Valverde, 'Derrida's Justice and Foucault's Freedom: Ethics, History, and Social Movements' (1999) 24 *Law & Social Inquiry* 655, 667.

10

THE INTERNATIONAL PROTECTION OF SUBSTANTIVE RIGHTS (II)

10.1 THE PROHIBITION OF DISCRIMINATION

The prohibition of discrimination and its positive manifestation as the principle of equality constitute fundamental pillars of the international law of human rights,[1] given that this legal system rests on the belief that all individuals are born equal in dignity and rights.[2] The principle of equality and non-discrimination is clearly established in the most important international human rights treaties, appearing, in the majority of them, both as a general guarantee, applicable to the respect and protection of all rights, and an autonomous right.[3] As discussed in **Section 3.2.1**, there is an inseparable connection between the principle of equality and non-discrimination and the general obligations upon States concerning human rights, as States are obliged to respect, protect, and fulfil all human rights without discrimination.[4] The fundamental character of the principle of equality and non-discrimination can also be appreciated by the fact that the prohibition of discrimination has become a strict limit to the possible derogation of rights in times of emergency, as expressly recognized by both the International Covenant on Civil and Political Rights (ICCPR) and the American Convention on Human Rights,[5] with the

---

[1] IACtHR, *Proposed Amendments of the Naturalization Provisions of the Constitution of Costa Rica*. Advisory Opinion OC-4/84 of January 19, 1984. Series A no. 4, separate opinion of Judge Rodolfo Piza E. para. 10; CCPR, General Comment No. 18: Non-discrimination (1989), paras. 1–2. See also: Y. Dinstein, 'Discrimination and International Human Rights' (1985) 15 *Israel Yearbook on Human Rights* 11.

[2] An idea, however, disputed by Hannah Arendt, who insisted that, despite rhetoric, rather than being born equal, individuals become equals 'on the strength of our decision to guarantee ourselves mutually equal rights'. See: UDHR, Art. 1; H. Arendt, *The Origins of Totalitarianism* (Harvest 1973) 301.

[3] ICERD, Art. 2; ICESCR, Arts. 2.2, 3; ICCPR, Arts. 2, 26; CEDAW, Arts. 2, 3, 5–16; UNCRC, Art. 2; ICRMW, Arts. 1, 7, 18.1, 25, 27, 28, 43, 45.1, 48, 55, 70; UNCRPD, Arts. 5, 12; ECHR, Art. 14; Protocol 12 to the ECHR, Art. 1; ACHR, Arts. 1, 24; African Charter, Arts. 2, 3, 19; Arab Charter, Art. 2.

[4] IACtHR, *Juridical Condition and Rights of the Undocumented Migrants*. Advisory Opinion OC-18/03 of September 17, 2003. Series A no. 18, para. 85.

[5] ICCPR, Art. 4.1; ACHR, Art. 27.1.

Inter-American Court even daring to assert that the principle of equality and non-discrimination belongs to the realm of *jus cogens*.[6]

Notwithstanding discrimination being forbidden under the international law of human rights, not every distinction in treatment amounts to prohibited discrimination. An accepted definition of discrimination is provided by the Human Rights Committee, following the interpretation of different human rights instruments. According to the Committee, the term 'discrimination' should be understood to imply any distinction, exclusion, restriction, or preference which is based on prohibited grounds—which include, but are not limited to, race, colour, sex, language, religion, political or other opinion, national or social origin, property, birth or other status—and which has the purpose or effect of nullifying or impairing the recognition, enjoyment or exercise by all persons, on an equal footing, of all rights and freedoms.[7]

The general and broad character of the prohibition of discrimination has allowed for its use to provide an evolving protection of human rights, both in terms of rights not explicitly acknowledged in the text of international treaties, as well as in favour of members of vulnerable groups whose characteristics might not be expressly mentioned in the treaties. Among the former, it is possible to mention the use of the prohibition of discrimination by different international monitoring bodies to provide protection for pension rights, unemployment benefits, tenancy agreements, parental leave, adoption rights, and residency permits.[8] As to the latter, the non-exhaustive lists of protected characteristics under the prohibition of discrimination has been explicitly extended to cover, among others, age, nationality, immigration status, disability, sexual orientation, and gender identity.[9]

10.1.1 THE IDEAL OF EQUALITY

Although the idea of equality can have different meanings,[10] the traditional conception of equality that underpins the international law of human rights is grounded on the Aristotelian notion of distributive justice, which imposes the duty to treat similar cases

---

[6] IACtHR, *Juridical Condition and Rights of the Undocumented Migrants*. Advisory Opinion OC-18/03 of September 17, 2003. Series A no. 18, paras. 100–101; IACtHR, *Yatama v. Nicaragua*. Preliminary Objections, Merits, Reparations and Costs. Judgment of June 23, 2005. Series C No. 127, paras. 184–185; IACtHR, *Girls Yean and Bosico v. Dominican Republic*. Preliminary Objections, Merits, Reparations and Costs. Judgment of September 8, 2005. Series C No. 130, para. 141.

[7] CCPR, General Comment No. 18: Non-discrimination (1989), para. 7.

[8] CCPR, *Young v. Australia*, CCPR/C/78/D/941/2000 (18 September 2003); CCPR, *Sprenger v. The Netherlands*, CCPR/C/44/D/395/1990 (31 March 1992); ECtHR, *Karner v. Austria*, App. no. 40016/98, ECHR 2003-IX; ECtHR, *Konstantin Markin v. Russia* [GC], App. no. 30078/06, ECHR 2012; ECtHR, *E.B. v. France* [GC], App. no. 43546/02, 22 January 2008; ECtHR, *Taddeucci and McCall v. Italy*, App. no. 51362/09, 30 June 2016.

[9] ECtHR, *Schwizgebel v. Switzerland*, App. no. 25762/07, ECHR 2010; CCPR, *Mümtaz Karakurt v. Austria*, CCPR/C/74/D/965/2000 (4 April 2002); ECtHR, *Bah v. the United Kingdom*, App. no. 56328/07, ECHR 2011; ECtHR, *Glor v. Switzerland*, App. no. 13444/04, ECHR 2009; ECtHR, *Identoba and Others v. Georgia*, App. no. 73235/12, 12 May 2015; IACtHR, *Atala Riffo and Daughters v. Chile*. Merits, Reparations and Costs. Judgment of February 24, 2012. Series C No. 239.

[10] J. Clifford, 'Equality' in D. Shelton (ed.), *The Oxford Handbook of International Human Rights Law* (OUP 2013) 420–445, 420.

alike and dissimilar cases differently.[11] This notion of equality has led to the adoption of the legal prohibition of direct discrimination, which bans the differential treatment of individuals unless an objective and reasonable justification can be provided for treating certain individuals better than others. As aforementioned, the international law of human rights provides an expanding and non-exhaustive list of individual characteristics that, as a matter of principle, would not be considered valid grounds for differential treatment. These include race, ethnicity, gender, gender identity, religion, political opinion, age, disability, and sexuality. When a differential treatment is based on any of these suspected grounds, the level of scrutiny as to its validity is heightened, and very compelling reasons would need to be provided to justify the distinction.[12]

However, the prohibition of discrimination is not exhausted by the prohibition of direct discrimination but also includes measures adopted by the State that, although seemingly neutral, might still entail (indirect) discrimination. Indirect discrimination takes place when a measure does not involve prohibited grounds for distinction and yet disproportionately affects individuals who share a specific protected characteristic.[13] An illustrative example of the type of measure that could entail indirect discrimination is the existing prohibitions on wearing a head covering within a specific environment. While such a ban does not explicitly affect individuals based on a protected characteristic, it has a pernicious effect on individuals who, for religious reasons, believe in the use of a hijab, kippah, or pagri. Therefore, a general (and seemingly neutral) prohibition on wearing a head covering could amount to indirect discrimination on religious grounds unless proven reasonable and objective.[14] Although the prohibition of indirect discrimination is only explicitly stated in recent treaties—such as the 2013 Inter-American Convention against All Forms of Discrimination and Intolerance[15]—it has, nonetheless, been extensively developed by the jurisprudence of international monitoring bodies.[16]

---

[11] Aristotle, *Nicomachean Ethics* (Roger Crisp ed. and trans., Cambridge University Press 2004) xxii and 86. See: CERD, General Recommendation No. 32: The meaning and scope of special measures in the Convention, CERD/C/GC/32 (24 September 2009), para. 8; ECtHR, *Fábián v. Hungary*, App. no. 78117/3, 5 September 2017, joint concurring opinion of Judges O'Leary and Koskelo, para. 10; ECtHR, *Khamtokhu and Aksenchik v. Russia* [GC], App. nos. 60367/08 and 961/11, ECHR 2017, dissenting opinion of Judge Pinto de Albuquerque, para. 19.

[12] ECtHR, *Abdulaziz, Cabales and Balkandali v. the United Kingdom*, 28 May 1985, § 78, Series A App. no. 94; ECtHR, *D.H. and Others v. the Czech Republic* [GC], App. no. 57325/00, § 196, ECHR 2007-IV; IACtHR, *Atala Riffo and Daughters v. Chile*. Merits, Reparations and Costs. Judgment of February 24, 2012. Series C No. 239, para. 124.

[13] ECtHR, *Shanaghan v. the United Kingdom*, App. no. 37715/97, § 129, 4 May 2001; CCPR, *Rupert Althammer et al. v. Austria*, CCPR/C/78/D/998/2001 (8 August 2003), para. 10.2; CESCR, General Comment 20: Non-discrimination in economic, social and cultural rights, E/C.12/GC/20 (2 July 2009), para. 10.

[14] CCPR, *Karnel Singh Bhinder v. Canada*, CCPR/C/37/D/208/1986 (9 November 1989), para. 6.2.

[15] Inter-American Convention against all Forms of Discrimination and Intolerance (adopted 5 June 2013, entered into force 20 February 2020), Art. 1.2.

[16] ECtHR, *Shanaghan v. the United Kingdom*, App. no. 37715/97, 4 May 2001; ECtHR, *D.H. and Others v. the Czech Republic* [GC], App. no. 57325/00, ECHR 2007-IV; CCPR, *Rupert Althammer et al. v. Austria*, CPR/C/78/D/998/2001 (8 August 2003); CESCR, General Comment No. 20: Non-discrimination in economic, social and cultural rights, E/C.12/GC/20 (2 July 2009); CEDAW Committee, General Recommendation No. 28: Core Obligations of States Parties under Art. 2 of the Convention, CEDAW/C/2010/47/GC.2 (19 October 2010), para. 16.

ECtHR, *D.H. and Others v. the Czech Republic* [GC], App. no. 57325/00, ECHR 2007-IV.

This has been one of the most significant cases decided by the European Court of Human Rights on indirect discrimination. The eighteen applicants were individuals of Roma origin who, as children, had been placed in schools for children with intellectual difficulties. The applicants complained that their placement in such schools amounted to indirect discrimination. At the time, the decision to place a child in a school for children with intellectual difficulties was made on the basis of tests aimed at measuring the child's intellectual capacity, carried out in an educational psychology centre, and subject to the consent of the child's legal guardian. The applicants claimed that the system in place resulted in segregation and discrimination, as Roma children were disproportionally assigned to special schools. They raised such a complaint in the domestic jurisdiction, but it was dismissed.

Before the European Court, the applicants claimed indirect discrimination, in breach of Article 14 (prohibition of discrimination) in conjunction with Article 2 of Protocol 1 (right to education). They presented statistical evidence for their school district showing that more than half of the pupils placed in the local special schools were Roma children, whereas Roma children merely accounted for just over 2 per cent of the city's primary school children. However, the Chamber found no violation of the applicants' rights, which led to a request for referral to the Grand Chamber, which was admitted.

Although the Grand Chamber cast a degree of doubt on the reliability of the statistical evidence presented, the data was partly confirmed by both the respondent State and independent supervisory bodies. Therefore, the Grand Chamber considered those numbers to reveal that Roma children were vastly over-represented in special schools. It asserted that, despite being seemingly neutral, the system to determine who should attend a special school had a disproportionate impact on Roma children, compared to non-Roma children. It considered that there was a clear possibility that the tests were biased, with the results not being analysed in the light of the particular characteristics of the Roma children who sat them. In those circumstances, the tests in question could not serve as justification for the impugned treatment. The Grand Chamber affirmed that the circumstances evidenced a strong presumption of indirect discrimination, which made the burden of proof rest upon the State to show that the differential impact of the system in place was the result of objective factors, unrelated to the ethnic origin of the children.

Ultimately, the Grand Chamber was not satisfied that the difference in treatment between Roma children and non-Roma children was objectively and reasonably justified and that there existed a reasonable relationship of proportionality between the means used and the aim pursued. As it had been established that the relevant legislation, as applied at the material time, had a disproportionately prejudicial effect on the Roma community, the Court found a violation of the right to education in conjunction with the prohibition of discrimination in detriment of the applicants, as members of that community.

Furthermore, the existence of structural inequalities in society means that the equal treatment of individuals by the State (formal equality) is not sufficient for securing substantive (or de facto) equality.[17] As with the protection of all human rights, States are under the obligation to adopt positive measures to secure the realization of the principle of equality. Among these, States must adopt measures to protect individuals from discriminatory treatment by other private individuals, such as adopting effective legislation in this respect, including the duty upon both public and private actors to adjust policies, practices, and premises that hinder the inclusion of individuals from disadvantaged groups—usually referred to as 'reasonable accommodation'.[18] Moreover, to achieve a fair redistribution of social goods to secure de facto equality, States are required to undertake measures to offset existent disadvantages.[19] States are under the obligation to adopt transformative general measures, aimed at tackling existent patterns of subordination that specifically affect the members of vulnerable groups. They should promote respect for the equal dignity and worth of every person and provide positive affirmation of marginalized identities, addressing stigma, stereotyping, humiliation, and violence associated with membership in these groups.[20] However, a transformative approach also requires the adoption of temporary measures to swiftly address systemic inequalities until substantive equality is achieved. The topic of affirmative action is discussed below.

10.1.1.1 Affirmative action

As discussed in **Section 10.1.1**, the existence of structural inequalities in society means that the equal treatment of individuals (formal equality), far from leading to substantive equality, contributes to entrenching patterns of subordination. 'Affirmative action' is the term used to refer to a series of measures of a temporary character aimed at improving the living conditions of individuals who belong to specific disadvantaged

---

[17] CEDAW, General Recommendation No. 25: Temporary special measures (2004), paras. 4, 9; CERD, General Recommendation No. 32: The meaning and scope of special measures in the Convention, CERD/C/GC/32 (24 September 2009), para. 6.

[18] J. Lord and R. Brown, 'The Role of Reasonable Accommodation in Securing Substantive Equality for Persons with Disabilities: The UN Convention on the Rights of Persons with Disabilities' in M. Rioux, L. Basser, and M. Jones (eds.), *Critical perspectives on human rights and disability law* (Brill 2011) 273–307, 279. See also: CRPD, CRPD, General Comment No. 6: on equality and non-discrimination, CRPD/C/GC/6 (26 April 2018), paras. 23–27.

[19] CCPR, General Comment No. 18: Non-discrimination (1989), para. 10; IACtHR, *Juridical Condition and Rights of the Undocumented Migrants*. Advisory Opinion OC-18/03 of September 17, 2003. Series A no. 18, para. 104; CEDAW Committee, General Recommendation No. 25: temporary special measures, HRI/GEN/1/Rev.7 at 282 (2004), para. 7; IACHR, Report No. 26/09. Case 12.440 (*Wallace de Almeida v. Brazil*) (20 March 2009), para. 147; CERD, General Recommendation No. 32: The meaning and scope of special measures in the Convention, CERD/C/GC/32 (24 September 2009).

[20] S. Fredman, 'Providing Equality: Substantive Equality and the Positive Duty to Provide' (2005) 21 *South African Journal on Human Rights* 163, 167.

groups to help them achieve substantive equality.[21] These actions can adopt different forms, including legislative and administrative measures, budgetary and regulatory instruments, policies and programmes, including preferential regimes in areas such as employment, housing, education, culture, and participation in public life for the members of disfavoured groups.[22] These measures can pursue the objective of achieving substantive equality through different approaches. They can be aimed at securing that people from disadvantaged groups enjoy equal opportunities to those from more privileged sectors of society to compete for a social good, or can go further, focusing on securing equal results in the actual enjoyment of the given social good for the members of disadvantaged groups.[23] The appraisals of the need for the adoption of special measures must be undertaken on the basis of accurate data and their design and implementation should involve prior consultation with, and active participation of, the affected communities.[24]

The obligation upon States to adopt measures to address situations of systemic or structural discrimination against individuals who share a personal characteristic has been expressly acknowledged in a number of international instruments,[25] but even in the absence of a textual recognition, multiple international monitoring bodies have supported their adoption. These bodies have affirmed the need for States to undertake affirmative action in order to bring about substantive equality and to maintain these measures in force until such ultimate objective is met.[26] Given that affirmative action, by its nature, requires the adoption of differential treatment that would benefit individuals based on personal characteristics, their implementation has been contentious at times.[27] However, strong justifications exist to support their adoption to address structural discrimination.

---

[21] Sub-Commission on Prevention of Discrimination and Protection of Minorities, 'The concept and practice of affirmative action', Final report submitted by Mr. Marc Bossuyt, Special Rapporteur, in accordance with Sub-Commission resolution 1998/5, E/CN.4/Sub.2/2002/21 (17 June 2002), para. 6.

[22] CEDAW Committee, General Recommendation No. 5: Temporary special measures, A/43/38 (1988); CEDAW Committee, General Recommendation No. 25: Temporary special measures (2004), para. 22; CERD, General Recommendation No. 32: The meaning and scope of special measures in the Convention, CERD/C/GC/32 (24 September 2009), para. 13.

[23] C. Courtis, 'Dimensiones conceptuales de la protección legal contra la discriminación' (2008) 48 *Revista IIDH* 157, 165.; J. Clifford, 'Equality' in D. Shelton (ed.), *The Oxford Handbook of International Human Rights Law* (OUP 2013) 420–445, 428–429.

[24] CERD, General Recommendation No. 32: The meaning and scope of special measures in the Convention, CERD/C/GC/32 (24 September 2009), paras. 17–18.

[25] These include: ICERD, CEDAW, the 2013 Inter-American Convention against Racism, Racial Discrimination, and Related Forms of Intolerance, and the 2013 Inter-American Convention against all Forms of Discrimination and Intolerance.

[26] CEDAW, General Recommendation No. 25: Temporary special measures (2004), paras. 4, 9; CERD, General Recommendation No. 32: The meaning and scope of special measures in the Convention, CERD/C/GC/32 (24 September 2009), para. 6.

[27] M. Rodríguez, 'Igualdad, Democracia y Acciones Positivas' in R. Gargarella (ed.), *Teoría y Crítica del Derecho Constitucional: Vol. II* (Abeledo Perrot 2008), 619–657, 619; S. Fredman, *Discrimination Law* (2nd edn., OUP 2011) 233.

Perhaps the fight against the affront of structural discrimination acts as the most usual argument to support affirmative action, focusing on the disadvantaged position that the members of specific groups hold in society, with the objective to redistribute social goods in a more just manner.[28] However, other (supplementary) justifications exist, which turn the focus on either 'historical injustice' and or 'social utility'. The first one refers to addressing past wrongs, such as the historical discrimination suffered by the members of particular groups; the history of legally endorsed racial or gender discrimination constituting paradigmatic examples.[29] Following this justification, affirmative action would help to redress the disadvantaged position that individuals sharing a specific characteristic continue to experience in the present, due to the discrimination historically suffered by the members of the group. As to social utility, this argument proposes that the existence of diversity within different social domains could be seen in itself as a desirable outcome that maximizes the common well-being.[30] All these three types of justifications, either independently or jointly, have provided solid grounds for supporting the adoption of affirmative action by States and have led to their endorsement by multiple international monitoring bodies.

Nevertheless, as aforementioned, affirmative action is conceived to be temporary in character, as these measures are expected to cease when the pursued objective of substantive equality is achieved.[31] That is why affirmative action cannot be undertaken in isolation from transformative measures to bring structural and systemic inequality to an end.[32] Transformative measures should be aimed at permanently breaking the cycle of disadvantage experienced by the members of subordinated groups, facilitating their full participation in all aspects of society.[33] The building of an equal and just society is the only meaningful way to fulfil the promise of the Universal Declaration of Human Rights (UDHR) of individuals becoming equal in dignity and rights.

---

[28] M. Rodríguez, 'Igualdad, Democracia y Acciones Positivas' in R. Gargarella (ed.), *Teoría y Crítica del Derecho Constitucional: Vol. II* (Abeledo Perrot 2008),619–657, 634–636; A. McHarg and D. Nicolson, 'Justifying Affirmative Action: Perception and Reality' (2006) 33 *Journal of Law and Society* 1, 11.

[29] M. Rodríguez, 'Igualdad, Democracia y Acciones Positivas' in R. Gargarella (ed.), *Teoría y Crítica del Derecho Constitucional: Vol. II* (Abeledo Perrot 2008), 619–657, 630–634; S. Fredman, *Discrimination Law* (2nd edn., OUP 2011) 260; A. McHarg and D. Nicolson, 'Justifying Affirmative Action: Perception and Reality' (2006) 33 *Journal of Law and Society* 1, 9.

[30] M. Rodríguez, 'Igualdad, Democracia y Acciones Positivas' in R. Gargarella (ed.), *Teoría y Crítica del Derecho Constitucional: Vol. II* (Abeledo Perrot 2008),619–657, 636–640; A. McHarg and D. Nicolson, 'Justifying Affirmative Action: Perception and Reality' (2006) 33 *Journal of Law and Society* 1, 15–16.

[31] CEDAW Committee, General Recommendation No. 25: Temporary special measures (2004), para. 15; CESCR, General Comment No. 20: Non-Discrimination in Economic, Social and Cultural Rights, para. 9; CERD, General Recommendation No. 32: The meaning and scope of special measures in the Convention, CERD/C/GC/32 (24 September 2009), para. 27.

[32] J. Lord and R. Brown, 'The Role of Reasonable Accommodation in Securing Substantive Equality for Persons with Disabilities: The UN Convention on the Rights of Persons with Disabilities' in M. Rioux, L. Basser, and M. Jones (eds.), *Critical perspectives on human rights and disability law* (Brill 2011) 273-307, 276–277; J. Clifford, 'Equality' in D. Shelton (ed.), *The Oxford Handbook of International Human Rights Law* (OUP 2013) 420–445, 430.

[33] S. Fredman, 'Providing Equality: Substantive Equality and the Positive Duty to Provide' (2005) 21 *South African Journal on Human Rights* 163, 167.

10.1.2 FURTHER REFLECTIONS: RACIAL DISCRIMINATION

As discussed in **Section 5.4**, the International Convention on the Elimination of All Forms of Racial Discrimination (ICERD) was unanimously adopted by the UN General Assembly in 1965, a year before the adoption of the two human rights Covenants. It is not surprising that, at a time when conflicting political ideologies were obstructing the adoption of general treaties on human rights, the vast majority of States managed to find consensus on the universal repudiation of racial discrimination. The truth is that the scourge of racial discrimination, broadly understood, was impossible to ignore due to both past and contemporary tragedies.

Racial discrimination is in itself a broad concept that encompasses discrimination based on a multiplicity of characteristics, including race, colour, descent, and national or ethnic origin.[34] The history of racial discrimination discloses innumerable examples of this tragic phenomenon, including pervasive social discrimination, legally sanctioned segregation, colonial exploitation, slavery, 'ethnic cleansing', and genocide.[35] Colonialism and the slave trade are among the most wide-reaching expressions of racial discrimination, in which a Western view of racial superiority was used to justify the subjugation of entire populations, who could even be owned and exchanged as instruments of production (and reproduction).[36] In fact, the condemnation of colonialism and all practices of segregation and discrimination associated therewith are mentioned in the preamble of ICERD. The Convention's preamble also highlights that, at the time of the adoption of the text, racial discrimination was still present as part of governmental policies based on racial superiority, such as apartheid and segregation. While the Convention's mentioning of apartheid was directed to single out South Africa, the reference to segregation policies was also addressing the situation in many other (unidentified) States.[37] Moreover, it is impossible to forget that it had been the horrors of the Second World War, in particular the Jewish genocide committed by Nazi Germany, that led to the emergence of the international law of human rights as a whole, as a humane response to the despicable consequences produced by abhorrent ideas of racial superiority. The Convention's preamble also makes express reference to the States' conviction that 'any doctrine of superiority based on racial differentiation is scientifically false, morally condemnable, socially unjust and dangerous, and that there is no justification for racial discrimination, in theory or in practice, anywhere'.[38]

When the Convention was adopted, racism was anything but extinct. While traditional slavery had been universally condemned, and the Nazi regime had been defeated, racist policies continued to be deployed by numerous States. To name but a

---

[34] ICERD, Art. 1.1.
[35] G. Fredrickson, *Racism: A Short History* (Princeton University Press 2002) 9.
[36] G. Fredrickson, *Racism: A Short History* (Princeton University Press 2002) 30; A. Loomba, *Colonialism/Postcolonialism* (Routledge 2005) 132–133; E. Tendayi Achiume, 'Putting Racial Equality onto the Global Human Rights Agenda' (2018) 15 *Sur—International Journal on Human Rights* 141, 144.
[37] CERD, General Recommendation XIX: On Art. 3 (1995), para. 1.
[38] ICERD, Preamble.

few evident illustrations: many of the peoples of the African continent remained under the colonial domination of some of the most powerful Western States, including the UK, France, Spain, and Portugal; the apartheid regime in South Africa and South West Africa continued to enforce a policy of racial segregation and subordination; and in the USA the 'Jim Crow' laws had only recently been formally repealed, which certainly did not mean that racial discrimination had come to an end there.

Nowadays, the prohibition of racial discrimination has become one of the norms of the international law of human rights with universal acceptance. It is beyond dispute that this prohibition belongs to the realm of *jus cogens*,[39] not admitting any kind of derogation from it. Consequently, the obligations emanating from this essential provision are of an *erga omnes* character, being assumed by States towards the international community as a whole.[40] And yet, racial discrimination remains a reality of our times, casting doubts on the limitations of the effective power of the international law of human rights.

10.1.3 INTERSECTIONALITY

It was Kimberlé Crenshaw's seminal work that emphasized the need to examine discrimination as an intersectional phenomenon.[41] In her 1989 ground-breaking article, Crenshaw argued that individuals from disadvantaged groups—in her example, a black woman—are often the victims of multiple and overlapping forms of oppression. Therefore, attempting to comprehend this situation as a disadvantaged treatment based on a single personal characteristic fails to duly understand the broader problem. In other words, an approach to discrimination that focuses on identifying the one personal characteristic on which a disadvantageous treatment is based risks ignoring the manifold and concurrent roots of subordination suffered by the members of multiple disadvantaged groups. Similarly, affirmative action could suffer from the same deficit, as measures adopted to improve the situation of members of disadvantaged groups tend to focus on providing specific measures based on what is believed to be the one shared cause of subordination, overlooking the multifaceted character of the problem. In fact, a possible critique of affirmative action is that, usually, the most privileged members of the unprivileged groups are the ones likely to benefit

---

[39] ILC, Draft Articles on the Responsibility of States for Wrongful Acts, with commentaries (2001) 2 *Yearbook of the International Law Commission* 31, 85, 112; ILC, Fifth report on peremptory norms of general international law (*jus cogens*) by Dire Tladi, Special Rapporteur, A/CN.4/747 (24 January 2022), conclusion 23.

[40] ICJ, *Barcelona Traction, Light and Power Company, Limited*, Judgment, I.C.J. Reports 1970, p. 3, paras. 33–34.

[41] K. Crenshaw, 'Demarginalizing the Intersection of Race and Sex: A Black Feminist Critique of Antidiscrimination Doctrine, Feminist Theory and Antiracist Politics' (1989) *University of Chicago Legal Forum* 140.

from the adopted measures, while the most vulnerable individuals of the same group end up being further marginalized.[42]

The international law of human rights has been progressively embracing the understanding of discrimination as a multifaceted phenomenon. The Convention on the Rights of Persons with Disabilities (UNCRPD) provides one of the most evident examples of the normative recognition of overlapping forms of discrimination. In its preamble, the Convention emphasizes that persons with disabilities are subject to multiple forms of discrimination, which compound disadvantages suffered due to disabilities with discrimination experienced because of other characteristics—such as race, sex, religion, social origin, age, or other status—while in Article 6, the Convention specifically refers to the aggravated discrimination suffered by women and girls with disabilities.[43] In its authoritative interpretation of the Convention, the Committee on the Rights of Persons with Disabilities has asserted that both multiple and intersectional discrimination are complex expressions of discrimination that combine different personal characteristics. On the one hand, 'multiple discrimination' refers to a situation where a person experiences discrimination concurrently on two or several grounds.[44] On the other hand, intersectional discrimination 'is the situation where several grounds operate and interact with each other at the same time in such a way that they are inseparable and thereby expose relevant individuals to unique types of disadvantage and discrimination'.[45] In other words, intersectional discrimination refers to a particular form of subordination that cannot be simply reduced to a detrimental treatment based on the accumulation of characteristics but should be comprehended as a distinctive form of disadvantage that occurs at the intersection of different sites and systems of marginalization and which is experienced by the complex lived identities thereby located.[46]

This Committee is certainly not the only international monitoring body to have embraced intersectionality as a tool to better understand the complexities of discrimination. Numerous international supervisory organs, including the Human Rights Committee, the CEDAW Committee, the Committee on the Rights of the Child, the Committee on the Elimination of Racial Discrimination, the African Commission on Human and Peoples' Rights, and the Inter-American Commission and Court of Human Rights have acknowledged discrimination as a multifaceted phenomenon

---

[42] S. Carter, *Reflections of an Affirmative Action Baby* (Basic Books 1991) 71; L. Padilla, 'Intersectionality and Positionality: Situating Women on Color in the Affirmative Action Dialogue' (1997) *Fordham Law Review* 843, 881; D. Carbado and K. Crenshaw, 'An Intersectional Critique of Tiers of Scrutiny: Beyond "Either/Or" Approaches to Equal Protection' (2019) *Yale Law Journal Forum* 108, 123–124.

[43] UNCRPD, preamble and Art. 6.

[44] CRPD, General Comment No. 3: Women and girls with disabilities, CRPD/C/GC/3 (25 November 2016), para. 4(c); CRPD, General Comment No. 6: Equality and non-discrimination, CRPD/C/GC/3 (26 April 2018), para. 19.

[45] CRPD, General Comment No. 6: Equality and non-discrimination, CRPD/C/GC/3 (26 April 2018), para. 19.

[46] V. May, *Pursuing Intersectionality: Unsettling Dominant Imaginaries* (Routledge 2015) 82. See also: P. Hill Collins and S. Bilge, *Intersectionality* (2nd edn., Polity Press 2020) 2.

that concurrently operates on the basis of interlinked personal characteristics.[47] This jurisprudence, from a multiplicity of supervisory organs, has helped to identify the unique forms of discrimination experienced by members of multiple disadvantaged groups and is contributing to the development of specific measures to tackle them.

10.1.4 THE EXAMINATION OF A DISCRIMINATION CLAIM

As discussed in **Section 10.1**, the prohibition of discrimination is not breached by every differential treatment that is carried out by a State, but only by distinctions lacking an objective and reasonable justification.[48] How international monitoring bodies examine and decide applications pertaining to a violation of the prohibition of discrimination depends in part on whether the claim is based on a violation of the prohibition of discrimination as a general guarantee in the exercise of other human rights,[49] or on the autonomous right to equality before the law.[50]

When an allegation of discrimination in the exercise of another right is made, the monitoring body must first determine whether the facts of the case fall within the ambit of a human right protected by the respective treaty; what the European Court of Human Rights has labelled the 'within the ambit' test.[51] It is not required for the alleged discriminatory measure to have breached another human right, but only for the matter under examination to be covered within the general scope of the right.[52] Moreover, there is a degree of flexibility in assessing whether an issue falls within the scope of another right, which can encompass spheres that the State has opted to engage with in an effort to enhance the protection of rights and freedoms, even if there was no explicit

---

[47] CCPR, General Comment No. 28: The Equality of Rights Between Men and Women, CCPR/C/21/Rev.1/Add. 10 (9 March 2000), para. 30; CERD, General Recommendation XXV: On gender-related dimensions of racial discrimination, U.N. Doc. A/55/18, annex V (2000), paras. 1–3; CRC, General Comment 11: Indigenous children and their rights under the Convention, CRC/C/GC/11 (12 February 2009), para. 29; CEDAW Committee, General Recommendation 28: on the core obligations of States parties under Art. 2 of the Convention, CEDAW/C/GC/28 (16 December 2010), para. 18; IACHR, Report No. 64/11, Case 12.573 (*Marino López et al v. Colombia*) (31 March 2011), para. 379; ECtHR, *B.S. v. Spain*, App. no. 47159/08, 24 July 2012; ACHPR, 'Principles and Guidelines on the Implementation of Economic, Social and Cultural Rights in the African Charter on Human and Peoples' Rights' (12 May 2014), para. 38; IACtHR, *Employees of the Fireworks Factory of Santo Antônio de Jesus and their families v. Brazil*. Preliminary Objections, Merits, Reparations and Costs. Judgment of July 15, 2020. Series C No. 407, paras. 191–203; CESCR, General Comment No. 22: The right to sexual and reproductive health (Art. 12 of the International Covenant on Economic, Social and Cultural Rights), E/C.12/GC/22 (2 May 2016).

[48] ECtHR, *Case relating to Certain Aspects of the Laws on the Use of Languages in Education in Belgium* (Merits), Series A no 6, 23 July 1968, para. 10; ECtHR, *National Union of Belgian Police v. Belgium*, 27 October 1975, Series A no. 19, para. 46.

[49] ICCPR, Art. 2; ECHR, Art 14; ACHR, Art. 1; African Charter, Art. 2.

[50] ICCPR, Art. 26; ECHR, Protocol No.12, Art. 1; ACHR, Art. 24; African Charter. 3.

[51] D. Gonzalez-Salzberg, *Sexuality and Transsexuality under the European Convention on Human Rights: A Queer Reading of Human Rights Law* (Hart 2019) 98–99.

[52] D. Harris, M. O'Boyle, E. Bates, and C. Buckley, *Law of the European Convention on Human Rights* (2nd edn., OUP 2009) 580–581.

obligation to do so under the treaty.[53] Examples of matters falling within the general scope of a right, although not expressly recognized as human rights by specific treaties, are the right to adopt, pension rights, the right to succeed to a tenancy agreement, or the right to obtain a residence permit.[54]

As discussed in **Section 10.1.1**, a specific treatment will be in breach of the equality principle when similar cases are not treated alike (direct discrimination), as well as when dissimilar cases are given the same type of treatment (indirect discrimination).[55] The determination of direct discrimination comprehends two main questions: first, whether the applicant has been treated less favourably than someone else, in a comparable situation; an analysis usually referred to as the 'analogous situation' test.[56] Secondly, it would be assessed whether such treatment was justified. This requires the examination of whether the differential treatment pursued a 'legitimate aim' and, if so, whether there was a reasonable relationship of proportionality between the means employed and the aim sought to be realized.[57]

To determine whether two individuals who are being treated differently should be considered to be in a relevantly similar situation, human rights treaties provide a non-exhaustive list of protected characteristics that would render any differentiation based on them 'suspicious'.[58] This means that a difference in treatment based on certain personal characteristics would, in principle, be difficult to accept; hence, requiring the State undertaking such treatment to provide especially weighty reasons to justify its compatibility with the principle of equality. These personal characteristics include race, colour, sex, language, religion, political or other opinion, national or social origin, property, birth, or other status, and international monitoring bodies have extended the

---

[53] A. Baker, 'The Enjoyment of Rights and Freedoms: A New Conception of the "Ambit" under Article 14 ECHR' (2006) 69 *The Modern Law Review* 714, 716, 734.

[54] CCPR, *Young v. Australia*, CCPR/C/78/D/941/2000 (18 September 2003); CCPR, *Sprenger v. The Netherlands*, CCPR/C/44/D/395/1990 (31 March 1992); ECtHR, *Karner v. Austria*, App. no. 40016/98, ECHR 2003-IX; ECtHR, *Konstantin Markin v. Russia* [GC], App. no. 30078/06, ECHR 2012; ECtHR, *E.B. v. France* [GC], App. no. 43546/02, 22 January 2008; ECtHR, *Taddeucci and McCall v. Italy*, App. no. 51362/09, 30 June 2016.

[55] ECtHR, *Thlimmenos v. Greece* [GC], App. no. 34369/97, ECHR 2000-IV, para. 44; ECtHR, *D.H. and Others v. the Czech Republic* [GC], App. no. 57325/00, ECHR 2007-IV, para. 175; ECtHR, *Carson and Others v. the United Kingdom*, App. no. 42184/05, 4 November 2008, para. 77.

[56] D. Gonzalez-Salzberg, *Sexuality and Transsexuality under the European Convention on Human Rights: A Queer Reading of Human Rights Law* (Hart 2019) 99.

[57] ECtHR, *Case relating to Certain Aspects of the Laws on the Use of Languages in Education in Belgium* (Merits), Series A no. 6, 23 July 1968, para. 10; ECtHR, *Marckx v. Belgium*, 13 June 1979, Series A no. 31, para. 33; IACtHR, *Proposed Amendments of the Naturalization Provisions of the Constitution of Costa Rica*. Advisory Opinion OC-4/84 of January 19, 1984. Series A no. 4, para. 57.

[58] S. Ganty, 'Poverty as Misrecognition: What Role for Antidiscrimination Law in Europe?' (2021) 21 *Human Rights Law Review* 962, 981; N. Petersen, 'The implicit taxonomy of the equality jurisprudence of the UN Human Rights Committee' (2021) 34 *Leiden Journal of International Law* 421, 430, 440.

list to encompass, among others, age, nationality, disability, immigration status, sexual orientation, and gender identity.[59]

The subsequent step of analysis focuses on whether the distinction in treatment was justified. There is a shift in the burden of proof from this step of the analysis onwards. Once an applicant has shown the existence of a difference in treatment, it is for the State to convince the supervisory organ that such a distinction was justified.[60] As aforementioned, a difference in treatment is only discriminatory if it has no objective and reasonable justification. This happens when differential treatment does not pursue a legitimate aim or when there is no reasonable relationship of proportionality between the means employed and the aim sought to be realized.[61] Therefore, States would first need to justify the objective pursued by the distinction in treatment and, then, that the measure under analysis can be considered to be a proportionate means for achieving such a legitimate aim.

The assessment of proportionality for the purpose of determining discrimination is similar to that discussed regarding other rights in **Section 9.3.3** and **Section 9.4.3**. Consequently, the European Court of Human Rights performs this analysis, making use of the doctrine of the 'margin of appreciation', while bodies such as the Human Rights Committee and the Inter-American Court undertake a principled review. Whether mediated by the margin of appreciation or not, these international monitoring bodies are in agreement that distinctions based on suspected categories would almost necessarily entail discrimination, given that, in these cases, the principle of proportionality does not merely require the measure chosen to be suited for realizing the legitimate aim sought, but the State must show that in order to achieve its legitimate aim, it was necessary to exclude people based on a protected characteristic from the scope of application of the measure.[62]

When the case at stake concerns indirect discrimination, the first of the two main questions to be answered by the monitoring body (see earlier) would be slightly different. The first question could be phrased in the following terms: Does the measure

---

[59] ECtHR, *Schwizgebel v. Switzerland*, App. no. 25762/07, ECHR 2010; CCPR, *Mümtaz Karakurt v. Austria*, CCPR/C/74/D/965/2000 (4 April 2002); ECtHR, *Bah v. the United Kingdom*, App. no. 56328/07, ECHR 2011; ECtHR, *Glor v. Switzerland*, App. no. 13444/04, ECHR 2009; ECtHR, *Identoba and Others v. Georgia*, App. no. 73235/12, 12 May 2015; IACtHR, *Atala Riffo and Daughters v. Chile*. Merits, Reparations and Costs. Judgment of February 24, 2012. Series C No. 239; IACHR, Report No. 64/12, Case 12.271 (*Benito Tide Méndez et al. v. Dominican Republic*) (29 March 2012).

[60] ECtHR, *D.H. and Others v. the Czech Republic* (n 23), para. 177; ECtHR, *Timishev v. Russia*, App. nos. 55762/00 and 55974/00, ECHR 2005-XII, para. 57; ECtHR, *Chassagnou and Others v. France* [GC], App. nos. 25088/94, 28331/95, 28443/95, ECHR 1999 III, para. 92; IACtHR, *Atala Riffo and Daughters v. Chile*. Merits, Reparations and Costs. Judgment of February 24, 2012. Series C No. 239, paras. 124–125.

[61] ECtHR, *Karner v. Austria*, App. no. 40016/98, ECHR 2003-IX, para. 37; ECtHR, *Fretté v. France*, App. no. 36515/97, ECHR 2002-I, para. 34; ECtHR, *E.B. v. France* [GC], App. no. 43546/02, 22 January 2008, para. 91; ACtHPR, *Kambole v. Tanzania* (judgment) (2020) 4 AfCLR 460, para. 82.

[62] ECtHR, *Karner v. Austria*, App. no. 40016/98, ECHR 2003-IX, para. 41; IACtHR, *Atala Riffo and Daughters v. Chile*. Merits, Reparations and Costs. Judgment of February 24, 2012. Series C No. 239, paras. 127, 131; IACHR, Report No. 64/12, Case 12.271 (*Benito Tide Méndez et al. v. Dominican Republic*) (29 March 2012), para. 227.

or treatment in place have a disproportionately prejudicial effect against the members of the particular social group? The second question remains the same and concerns whether the measure or treatment under scrutiny is justified, entailing the examination of the legitimacy of the aim pursued and of the existence of a reasonable relationship of proportionality between the means employed and the objective sought to be realized. Statistical data is an extremely helpful tool to prove the suspected effects of an apparently neutral measure,[63] which would then lead to the examination of whether the State can justify the measure in place by providing persuasive reasons as to the legitimacy of the objective it pursues and the proportionality of the means employed.

10.1.5 CRITICAL DEBATES: DISCRIMINATION BASED ON SEXUAL AND GENDER IDENTITIES

Neither sexual orientation nor gender identity appears expressly mentioned in provisions protecting against discrimination in the major international human rights treaties, which is certainly not surprising when considering the time of their adoption.[64] However, in our days, it is widely established by the constant jurisprudence of international courts and treaty bodies that discrimination on the grounds of individuals' sexual and gender identities is prohibited.[65] The protection of sexual orientation under the international law of human rights finds its oldest renowned victory in the early 1980s with the decision of the European Court of Human Rights in the *Dudgeon* case. In this case, the Court ruled that the criminalization of homosexuality under the legislation of Northern Ireland amounted to a violation of the right to respect for private life, attributable to the UK.[66] Nonetheless, it would only be in the 1990s when sexual orientation was recognized as a category protected from discrimination. In *Toonen v. Australia*, decided in 1994, the Human Rights Committee was called to assess a case similar to *Dudgeon* but concerning the domestic legislation of the Australian State of Tasmania. Following reasoning akin to that of the European Court, the Committee found the domestic legislation criminalizing homosexuality to be in breach of the right to privacy, but it also went on to confirm that, under ICCPR, the

---

[63] CEDAW Committee, General Recommendation 9: Statistical data concerning the situation of women (1989); CEDAW Committee, General Recommendation No. 25: Temporary special measures (2004), para. 35; ECtHR, *D.H. and Others v. the Czech Republic* [GC], App. no. 57325/00, § 192–195, ECHR 2007-IV.

[64] For an in-depth discussion of this topic under the European Convention, see: D. Gonzalez-Salzberg, *Sexuality and Transsexuality under the European Convention on Human Rights: A Queer Reading of Human Rights Law* (Hart 2019).

[65] CCPR, *Toonen v. Australia*, Communication No. 488/1992, CCPR/C/50/D/488/1992 (31 March 1994), para. 8.7; ECtHR, *Salgueiro da Silva Mouta v. Portugal*, App. no 33290/96, ECHR 1999-IX, para. 28; ECtHR, *Identoba and Others v. Georgia*, App. no. 73235/12, 12 May 2015, para. 96; CESCR, General Comment No. 20: Non-discrimination in economic, social, and cultural rights (art. 2, para. 2 of the International Covenant on Economic, Social and Cultural Rights), E/C.12/GC/20 (2 July 2009), para. 32; IACtHR, para. 84; IACtHR, *Gender identity, and equality and non-discrimination with regard to same-sex couples*. Advisory Opinion OC-24/17 of November 24, 2017. Series A no. 24, para. 84.

[66] ECtHR, *Dudgeon v. United Kingdom*, Series A no. 45, 22 October 1981.

prohibition of discrimination on the grounds of 'sex' was to be interpreted to include individuals' sexual orientation.[67] This latter finding would be used by the Committee when, in *Young v. Australia*, it was called to examine whether the denial of a survivor's pension, following the death of a same-sex life partner, amounted to unacceptable discrimination under ICCPR.[68]

> **CCPR, *Young v. Australia*, CCPR/C/78/D/941/2000 (18 September 2003).**
>
> In this case, the Human Rights Committee examined under the equal treatment provision of ICCPR (Article 26) the right to a survivor's pension following the death of a same-sex life partner. After the death of his same-sex partner of thirty-eight years, Mr Young had been denied a survivor's pension, because he did not qualify under the Australian legislation at the time as a 'member of a couple', since he had not been 'living with a member of the opposite sex' (para. 10.2).
>
> Applying its earlier jurisprudence, the Committee reaffirmed that the prohibition against discrimination under ICCPR comprises discrimination based on sexual orientation, even though sexual orientation does not appear expressly mentioned by the Covenant as prohibited grounds of discrimination (para. 10.4). Consequently, the Committee was of the view that denying a survivor's pension based on the sexual orientation of the partners was a case of discrimination, in violation of ICCPR (para. 11).

Nevertheless, it was actually the European Court that, in 1999, first ruled on a violation of the prohibition of discrimination due to a distinction based on the sexuality of an applicant. In *Salgueiro da Silva Mouta v. Portugal*, the Court confirmed that the prohibition of discrimination under the Convention refers to the protection from differential treatment based on an illustrative list of non-exhaustive characteristics under which sexual orientation should be considered encompassed.[69] The development of the Court's case law has actually led to considering that, under the international law of human rights, discrimination based on sexual orientation is deserving of a similar level of repudiation to that afforded to race discrimination,[70] casting doubts as to the existence of any circumstances that could justify a differential treatment based on this personal characteristic.[71] However, such strong finding appears contradicted by the fact that the European Court continues to consider the regulation of same-sex marriage and

---

[67] CCPR, *Toonen v. Australia*, Communication No. 488/1992, CCPR/C/50/D/488/1992 (31 March 1994), para. 8.7.
[68] CCPR, *Young v. Australia*, CCPR/C/78/D/941/2000 (18 September 2003).
[69] ECtHR, *Salgueiro da Silva Mouta v. Portugal*, App. no 33290/96, ECHR 1999-IX, para. 28.
[70] ECtHR, *Lustig-Prean and Beckett v. United Kingdom*, App. nos. 31417/96 and 32377/96, September 1999, para. 90; ECtHR, *Smith and Grady v. United Kingdom*, App. nos. 33985/96, 33986/96, ECHR 1999-VI, para. 97.
[71] ECtHR, *Kozak v. Poland*, App. no. 13102/02, 2 March 2010, para. 92; ECtHR, *Genderdoc-M v. Moldova*, App. no. 9106/06, 12 June 2012, para. 51; ECtHR, *X and Others v. Austria* (GC), App. no. 19010/07, 19 February 2013, para. 99. See also: IACtHR, *Atala Riffo and Daughters v. Chile*. Merits, Reparations and Costs. Judgment of February 24, 2012. Series C No. 239, para. 93; IACtHR, *Gender identity, and equality and non-discrimination with regard to same-sex couples*. Advisory Opinion OC-24/17 of November 24, 2017. Series A no. 24, para. 84.

adoption by same-sex couples to fall under the States' margin of appreciation.[72] Within the past three decades, the prohibition of discrimination based on sexual orientation was confirmed by multiple international monitoring bodies,[73] and was extended to include the prohibition of discrimination on the grounds of gender identity as well.

> ECtHR, *Salgueiro da Silva Mouta v. Portugal*, App. no. 33290/96, ECHR 1999-IX.
>
> The case concerned the decision of the Portuguese domestic courts concerning the award of parental responsibility of a child. The courts had decided to award custody of the child to the mother, after taking into account the sexual orientation of the father as a determining factor for the decision. It was the first opportunity in which the Court dealt with parental rights of a gay father and it was also the first time in which it stated that sexual orientation was a prohibited category of discrimination under the European Convention, despite it not being expressly stated in Article 14.
>
> While Article 14 reads: 'The enjoyment of the rights and freedoms set forth in this Convention shall be secured without discrimination on any ground such as sex, race, colour, language, religion, political or other opinion, national or social origin, association with a national minority, property, birth or other status', the Court affirmed that the use of the words 'such as' clearly indicates that the list of protected characteristics is merely illustrative and not exhaustive (para. 28). It continued, stating that sexual orientation is a personal characteristic that should, undoubtedly, be considered included under the provision (para. 28). Following its assessment of sexual orientation as a prohibited characteristic of discrimination, the Court ruled that the decision of the domestic courts to deny parental responsibility of a child due to the sexuality of the father amounted to discriminatory treatment, in breach of the Convention (para. 36).

The protection of the gender identity of individuals under the international law of human rights also finds earlier victories within the jurisprudence of the European Court of Human Rights. However, it took the Court almost two decades of complaints regarding the right of individuals to amend their assigned legal gender in official documents to finally acknowledge that such a right was protected under

---

[72] ECtHR, *Schalk and Kopf v. Austria*, App. no. 30141/04, ECHR 2010; ECtHR, *Alekseyev v. Russia*, nos. 4916/07 and two others, § 83, 21 October 2010; ECtHR, *X and Others v. Austria* [GC], App. no. 19010/07, ECHR 2013; ECtHR, *Fedotova and Others v. Russia* [GC], App. nos. 40792/10 and two others, 17 January 2023.

[73] CRC, General Comment No. 3: HIV/AIDS and the rights of the child, CRC/GC/2003/3 (17 March 2003), para. 8; CAT, General Comment No. 2: Application of Art. 2 by States Parties, CAT/C/GC/2 (24 January 2008), para. 21; CESCR, General Comment No. 20: Non-discrimination and economic, social and cultural rights, E/C.12/GC/20 (2 July 2009), para. 32; CEDAW Committee, General Recommendation No. 27: On women of age and the protection of their human rights, CEDAW/C/GC/27 (16 December 2010), para. 13; IACtHR, *Atala Riffo and Daughters v. Chile*. Merits, Reparations and Costs. Judgment of February 24, 2012. Series C No. 239, para. 93.

the European Convention.[74] Moreover, the actual recognition of gender identity as a protected characteristic against differential treatment was further protracted, but is now fully recognized not only by the European Court, but also by multiple international monitoring bodies.[75] The Inter-American Court has even clarified that the protection of gender identity not only includes a prohibition of discrimination based on this personal characteristic, but also a right to obtain the rectification of all identity documents and public records to make them conform with the self-perceived gender identity of individuals, based exclusively on free and informed consent,[76] dispensing with any requirements of medical or psychological certification and with any kind of hormonal or surgical treatments.[77]

> **IACtHR,** *Gender identity, and equality and non-discrimination with regard to same-sex couples.* **Advisory Opinion OC-24/17. Series A no. 24 (24 November 2017).**[78]
>
> On 18 May 2016, Costa Rica requested the Inter-American Court to render an advisory opinion concerning LGBTQI rights. While the Court had ruled on cases concerning same-sex sexuality in the past, this was the first opportunity on which it was called to examine issues regarding gender identity. The main questions the Court was called to answered can be summarized as follows. With respect to gender identity, whether States were obliged to allow individuals to amend their name in accordance with their gender identity and, if so, whether the procedure for such an amendment should be administrative, rather than judicial. Regarding sexuality, the questions concerned whether States were under the obligation to provide same-sex couples

---

[74] ECtHR, *Rees v. the United Kingdom*, 17 October 1986, Series A no. 106; ECtHR, *Cossey v. the United Kingdom*, 27 September 1990, Series A no. 184; ECtHR, *Sheffield and Horsham v. the United Kingdom*, 30 July 1998, Reports of Judgments and Decisions 1998-V; ECtHR, *Christine Goodwin v. the United Kingdom* [GC], App. no. 28957/95, ECHR 2002-VI.

[75] ECtHR, *P.V. v. Spain*, App. no. 35159/09, 30 November 2010, para. 30; ECtHR, *Identoba and Others v. Georgia*, App. no. 73235/12, 12 May 2015, para. 96; CESCR, General Comment No. 20: Non-discrimination in economic, social and cultural rights, E/C.12/GC/20 (2 July 2009), para. 32; General Comment No. 22: The right to sexual and reproductive health, E/C.12/GC/22 (2 May 2016), paras. 9, 30; CCPR, Concluding observations on the initial report of Turkey, CCPR/C/TUR/CO/1 (30 October 2012), para. 8; CCPR, Concluding observations on Belize in the absence of a report, CCPR/C/BLZ/CO/1 (26 April 2013), para. 13; IACtHR, *Gender identity, and equality and non-discrimination with regard to same-sex couples.* Advisory Opinion OC-24/17 of November 24, 2017. Series A no. 24, para. 84.

[76] IACtHR, *Gender identity, and equality and non-discrimination with regard to same-sex couples.* Advisory Opinion OC-24/17 of November 24, 2017. Series A no. 24, paras. 116, 160, 171.

[77] Conversely, while the European Court has dispensed with the need for surgical requirements, it still allows States to subordinate gender recognition to medical or psychological certification. See: ECtHR, *A.P., Garçon and Nicot v. France*, App. nos. 79885/12 and two others, 6 April 2017; ECtHR, *X and Y v. Romania*, App. nos. 2145/16, 20607/16, 19 January 2021. See also: D. Gonzalez-Salzberg, 'An Improved Protection for the (Mentally Ill) Trans Parent: A Queer Reading of *AP, Garçon and Nicot v. France*' (2018) 81 *Modern Law Review* 526.

[78] For a critical discussion of this advisory opinion, see: D. Gonzalez-Salzberg, 'A queer approach to the Advisory Opinion 24/2017 on LGBT rights' in D. Gonzalez-Salzberg and L. Hodson (eds.), *Research Methods for International Human Rights Law: Beyond the Traditional Paradigm* (Routledge 2019) 98–122.

with equal patrimonial rights to those enjoyed by different-sex couples and, if so, whether these rights had to be made available through a specific institutional form (para. 3).

As to gender identity, the Court went further than originally requested. It held that, under the appropriate reading of the American Convention, individuals have a right to obtain the rectification of identity documents and public records to conform to their self-perceived gender identity (para. 116). The Court even spelled out the requirements that the procedure allowing for the amendment of gender markers should follow, which include being prompt, confidential, cost-free, and (preferably) administrative in nature. It emphasized that the procedure should be based exclusively on free and informed consent—excluding the requirement of any medical or psychological certifications, or any kind of hormonal or surgical treatments (paras. 160 and 171).

Concerning discrimination based on sexuality, the Court ruled that same-sex couples should be entitled to the same patrimonial rights as those enjoyed by different-sex couples. It also affirmed that same-sex couples should have access to all forms of legal recognition available within a State's domestic law, including access to same-sex marriage (paras. 199, 224–225 and 228). The Court's stance on both sexuality and gender identity adopted in this advisory opinion placed it at the forefront of the international protection of LGBTQI rights, having gone much further than the jurisprudence of any of the other international monitoring bodies.

10.1.6 FURTHER REFLECTIONS: A MARXIST CRITIQUE OF SOCIOECONOMIC DISCRIMINATION

Under the most important international instruments, the prohibition of discrimination in the enjoyment of human rights includes among the 'suspect categories' of unacceptable distinction that of 'property', 'economic status', 'fortune', or 'wealth'.[79] In other words, States actions that entail a distinction in treatment based on these conditions—which could be referred to as discrimination due to 'socioeconomic disadvantage'[80]—require serious justification.[81] States also have a positive duty to stop private actors from such discriminatory treatment. And yet, a Marxist critique would highlight that in our neoliberal world of market fundamentalism, being deprived of access to goods, services, and facilities due to the inability to afford them is not construed as socioeconomic discrimination.[82]

---

[79] ICCPR, Arts. 2.1, 26; ICESCR, Art. 2.2; ECHR, Art. 14 and A1P12; ACHR, Art. 1.1.; African Charter, Art. 2; Arab Charter, Art. 3.1.

[80] Report of the Special Rapporteur on extreme poverty and human rights, Olivier De Schutter, 'Banning discrimination on grounds of socioeconomic disadvantage: an essential tool in the fight against poverty', A/77/157 (13 July 2022), para. 20.

[81] ECtHR, *Garib v. the Netherlands*, no. 43494/09, 23 February 2016, joint dissenting opinion of judges López Guerra and Keller paras. 14–15; ECtHR, *Garib v. the Netherlands* [GC], App. no. 43494/09, 6 November 2017, dissenting opinion of judges Pinto de Albuquerque and Vehabović paras. 13, 39; Report of the Special Rapporteur on extreme poverty and human rights, Olivier De Schutter, 'Banning discrimination on grounds of socioeconomic disadvantage: an essential tool in the fight against poverty', A/77/157 (13 July 2022), para. 16.

[82] G. MacNaughton, 'Equality Rights beyond Neoliberal Constraints' in G. MacNaughton and D. Fey, *Economic and Social Rights in a Neoliberal World* (CUP 2018) 103–123, 105–106.

The prohibition of socioeconomic discrimination remains largely underexplored in the jurisprudence of international monitoring bodies. The majority of cases in which supervisory bodies have been called to engage with this provision have concerned property rights rather than discrimination due to a disadvantaged socioeconomic situation.[83] This fact in itself can be taken as an indication of the broader problem, as it hides the significance of poverty as a human rights issue,[84] rendering those who suffer from a disadvantaged socioeconomic background further 'invisibilized'.[85]

However, the recognition of socioeconomic disadvantage as grounds for discrimination against those living in poverty is slowly emerging within the international sphere. Throughout the years, the Office of the High Commissioner for Human Rights and the Special Procedure on Extreme Poverty and Human Rights, created by the UN Commission on Human Rights (and then the Human Rights Council), have engaged with the interconnection between poverty and human rights,[86] highlighting the need to use human rights strategies to tackle extreme poverty.[87] International monitoring organs have also begun to recognize that obstacles to access social goods and services faced by individuals in poverty amounts to discrimination due to socioeconomic disadvantage. Nevertheless, this incipient recognition has mostly taken place with regards to people experiencing multifaceted or intersectional discrimination,[88] where more traditional grounds of discrimination may have overshadowed socioeconomic

---

[83] See: CCPR, *Adam v. The Czech Republic*, Communication No. 586/1994, U.N. Doc. CCPR/C/57/D/586/1994 (1996); ECtHR, *Chassagnou and Others v. France* [GC], App. nos. 25088/94 and two others, ECHR 1999-III; CCPR, *Brok v. The Czech Republic*, Communication No. 774/1997, CCPR/C/73/D/774/1997 (2001); CCPR, *Haraldsson and Sveinsson v. Iceland*, Communication No. 1306/2004, CCPR/C/91/D/1306/2004 (2007); ECtHR, *Chabauty v. France* [GC], App. no. 57412/08, 4 October 2012.

[84] CESCR has defined poverty as 'a human condition characterized by sustained or chronic deprivation of the resources, capabilities, choices, security and power necessary for the enjoyment of an adequate standard of living', including hunger, poor education, discrimination, vulnerability, and social exclusion. See: CESCR, 'Substantive Issues Arising in the Implementation of the International Covenant on Economic, Social and Cultural Rights: Poverty and the International Covenant on Economic, Social and Cultural Rights', E/C.12/2001/10 (10 May 2001), paras. 7–8. See also: OHCHR, 'Human Rights and Poverty Reduction: A Conceptual Framework', HR/PUB/04/1 (2004).

[85] S. Ganty, 'Poverty as Misrecognition: What Role for Antidiscrimination Law in Europe?' (2021) 21 *Human Rights Law Review* 962, 966, 1007. See also: M. Ignatieff, *The Rights Revolution* (House of Anansi 2000) 92.

[86] M. Pinto, 'Los derechos humanos desde la dimensión de la pobreza' (2008) 48 *Revista IIDH* 43, 54–56; G. MacNaughton, 'Emerging Human Rights Norms and Standards on Vertical Inequalities' in G. MacNaughton, D. Frey and C. Porter (eds.), *Human Rights and Economic Inequalities* (CUP 2018) 33–62, 44–50.

[87] See, among many: OHCHR, 'Human Rights and Poverty Reduction: A Conceptual Framework', HR/PUB/04/1 (2004); OHCHR, 'Principles and Guidelines for a Human Rights Approach to Poverty Reduction Strategies', HR/PUB/06/12 (2005); Final draft of the guiding principles on extreme poverty and human rights, submitted by the Special Rapporteur on extreme poverty and human rights, Magdalena Sepúlveda Carmona, A/HRC/21/39 (18 July 2012); Report of the Special Rapporteur on extreme poverty and human rights, Olivier De Schutter, 'Banning discrimination on grounds of socioeconomic disadvantage: an essential tool in the fight against poverty', A/77/157 (13 July 2022).

[88] ECtHR, *B.S. v. Spain*, App. no. 47159/08, 24 July 2012; IACtHR, *Gonzales Lluy et al. v. Ecuador*. Preliminary Objections, Merits, Reparations and Costs. Judgment of September 1, 2015. Series C No. 298; CCPR, *Mellet v. Ireland*, CCPR/C/116/D/2324/2013 (2016); CESCR, *Trujillo Calero v. Ecuador*, E/C.12/63/D/10/2015 (2018);

disadvantage; hence, raising the question of the importance this ground would be granted on its own.[89]

Moreover, even if progressively providing a degree of human rights protection, the prohibition of socioeconomic discrimination is not interpreted as imposing upon States a general duty to guarantee equal access to social goods and services to those who cannot afford them. This is certainly not a surprising turn of events. As affirmed by Moyn, human rights can be seen as a companion of extreme inequality;[90] theoretically unambitious and practically ineffective to combat material inequality.[91] While agreeing with such a statement, a Marxist critique would object to Moyn's appraisal of the reasons behind the problematic association between material inequality and human rights.

As discussed in **Section 1.3.1**, Marxism finds a strong connection between human rights and capitalism, to the extent of believing human rights to be engrained in the capitalistic system.[92] From a Marxist perspective, human rights would be unable to address material inequality in any substantive manner, as they are a device designed to avoid questioning the root causes of the reigning political-economic system that created them and outside of which they have no existence. The international law of human rights works within the logic of the individual victim and the wrongdoer State, unable to search for responsibility in the actions of the true beneficiaries of the system in place.[93] Even if socioeconomic discrimination were to blossom into an established legal ground for determining the responsibility of States, this would be perceived as yet another systemic tactic to draw attention away from the actual root causes of the worldwide reality of widespread structural material inequality.

10.2 WOMEN'S RIGHTS

The recognition that women are entitled to equal legal rights to men, which seems so evident in our days, was actually centuries in the making. The eighteenth-century declarations of rights discussed in **Section 1.2.2**,[94] fruit of the social, economic, cultural, and political changes in the West, excluded women, among other subjugated groups,

---

[89] S. Ganty, 'Poverty as Misrecognition: What Role for Antidiscrimination Law in Europe?' (2021) 21 *Human Rights Law Review* 962, 1004.

[90] See also: W. Brown, '"The Most We Can Hope For . . . ": Human Rights and the Politics of Fatalism' (2004) 103 *South Atlantic Quarterly* 451, 461; P. O'Connell, 'On Reconciling Irreconcilables: Neo-liberal Globalisation and Human Rights' (2007) 7 *Human Rights Law Review* 483, 507–508.

[91] S. Moyn, 'A Powerless Companion: Human Rights in the Age of Neoliberalism' (2014) 77 *Law and Contemporary Problems* 147, 149–150, 168–169; S. Moyn, *Not Enough: Human Rights in an Unequal World* (Harvard University Press 2018) 213, 216–217.

[92] J. Whyte, *The Morals of the Market: Human Rights and the Rise of Neoliberalism* (Verso 2019) 19.

[93] S. Marks, 'Human rights and the bottom billion' (2009) *European Human Rights Law Review* 37, 48–49; S. Marks, 'Human Rights and Root Causes' (2011) 74 *Modern Law Review* 57, 76; R. Knox, 'A Marxist approach to *R.M.T. v. United Kingdom*' in D. Gonzalez-Salzberg and L. Hodson (eds.), *Research Methods for International Human Rights Law: Beyond the Traditional Paradigm* (Routledge 2019) 13–41, 17.

[94] Such as the 1776 Declaration of Independence of the United States and the 1789 French Declaration on the Rights of Man and the Citizen.

from their application.[95] These proclamations of the inalienable rights of men were followed by the demands of numerous women (and some men), who understood the need to fight for the recognition of women's rights. Two of the best-known documents that rightfully denounced the exclusion of women from the recognition of the inherent rights of all individuals are Olympe de Gouges' 1790 Declaration of the Rights of Woman and Mary Wollstonecraft's 1792 Vindication of the Rights of Women.[96] De Gouges' Declaration was addressed to the Queen, Marie-Antoinette, with a request for the French National Assembly to adopt an identical Declaration to that proclaimed in 1789, but this time in favour of women and the female citizen, recognizing women as subjects of rights in equal terms to men.[97] Sadly, de Gouges was persecuted due to her political activism and sentenced to the guillotine in November 1793.[98] On its part, Wollstonecraft's second treatise on rights—which followed her 1790 Vindication of the Rights of Man[99]—was an elaborated reflection of the similar nature of women and men, including a solidly grounded challenge to the recognition of rights to men that were denied to women. She strongly asserted the need to foster women's autonomy and the essential role that education should play in achieving such an aim.[100]

10.2.1 FURTHER REFLECTIONS: THE SUFFRAGIST MOVEMENT

While the claim for women's rights had been voiced by multiple actors, their legal recognition only started to progressively materialize when women organized themselves to campaign for their rights. The movement for the right to vote is perhaps one of the most paradigmatic illustrations of organized action for women's rights. The historic meeting known as the 'Seneca Falls Convention', which took place in July of 1848 in the USA, is credited as one of the founding moments of the organized movement for women's right to vote.[101] The meeting itself was a concerted call for women to organize and petition for the unalienable rights they were being denied. The Convention approved twelve resolutions designed to voice the need to fight for women's rights both in their public and private lives. However, it was the most contested resolution, the

---

[95] M. Ishay, *The History of Human Rights: from Ancient Times to the Globalization Era* (University of California Press 2004) 8; L. Hunt, *Inventing Human Rights: A History* (Norton and Company Press 2007) 18; C. Douzinas, *Human Rights and Empire: the political philosophy of cosmopolitanism* (Routledge 2007) 455.

[96] Certainly, these were not the first documents in which authors have decried the subjugation of women under the Law. For a more comprehensive discussion of the history of women's rights, see: A.S. Fraser, 'Becoming Human: The Origins and Developments of Women's Human Rights' (1999) 21 *Human Rights Quarterly* 853.

[97] O. de Gouges, 'The Declaration of the Rights of Woman' in D. Levy, H. Applewhite, and M. Johnson (eds), *Women in Revolutionary Paris 1789–1795* (University of Illinois Press 1979) 87–92.

[98] M.B. Dembour, *Who Believes in Human Rights? Reflections on the European Convention* (CUP 2006) 188.

[99] M. Wollstonecraft, *A Vindication of the Rights of Men* (Johnson 1790).

[100] M. Wollstonecraft, *A Vindication of the Rights of Woman: With Strictures on Political and Moral Subjects* (Johnson 1792).

[101] A.S. Fraser, 'Becoming Human: The Origins and Developments of Women's Human Rights' (1999) 21 *Human Rights Quarterly* 853, 874; S.D. O'Connor, 'The History of the Women's Suffrage Movement" (1996) 49 *Vanderbilt Law Review* 657, 659–660.

only one not unanimously passed, which is also the best remembered: the resolution claiming the need for women to secure political rights.[102]

National and international organizations of women were formed during the second part of the nineteenth and the beginning of the twentieth century, such as the International Council of Women, founded in 1888, and the International Woman Suffrage Alliance, constituted in 1904.[103] Although not restricted to campaigning for political rights, the right to vote was central to the claims put forward by these organizations. The denial of women's political rights was a worldwide affront that only began to be gradually addressed by different nations towards the end of the nineteenth and throughout the twentieth century. New Zealand, the Cook Islands, and parts of Australia and the USA can be counted among the first places where women's entitlement to political participation was acknowledged.[104] However, the recognition of women's political rights has been a lengthy process, with certain States only providing this basic degree of equality between genders in the late twentieth or even the twenty-first century.[105]

10.2.2 WOMEN'S RIGHTS UNDER INTERNATIONAL LAW

International law's engagement with women's rights evolved throughout the twentieth century. Some of the earlier international instruments concerning women's rights can be seen to adopt a rather paternalistic approach towards women, conceiving women as an object of protection rather than as a subject of rights.[106] Clear illustrations of this approach are the International Labour Organization (ILO) Conventions adopted to prohibit women from undertaking industrial night work and underground mine work, or the earlier conventions aimed at the suppression of women trafficking.[107] With the creation of the United Nations, this protective approach evolved into the recognition of women as full subjects of rights under international law.[108] From the onset, the UN Charter itself established the prohibition of discrimination based on sex in respect of

---

[102] International Council of Women, *Women in a Changing World: The Dynamic Story of the International Council of Women since 1888* (Routledge 1966) 7–8; R. Boggs Roberts, *Suffragists in Washington D.C.: The 1913 Parade and the Fights for the Vote* (History Press 2017) 25.

[103] International Council of Women, *Women in a Changing World: The Dynamic Story of the International Council of Women since 1888* (Routledge 1966) 3, 35; D.S. Helmer, Women Suffragists (Facts on File 1998) 121.

[104] C. Daley, *Suffrage and Beyond: International Feminist Perspectives* (Auckland University Press 1994), appendix.

[105] M. Nussbaum, 'Women's Progress and Women's Human Rights' (2016) 38 *Human Rights Quarterly* 589, 590.

[106] N. Hevener, 'International Law and the Status of Women: An Analysis of International Legal Instruments Related to the Treatment of Women' (1978) 1 *Harvard Women's Law Journal* 131, 135.

[107] ILO, Night Work (Women) Convention, 1919 (C004) (abrogated in 2017); ILO, Underground Work (Women) Convention (C045) (adopted 21 June 1935, entered into force 30 May 1937); ILO, Convention for the Suppression of the Traffic in Women and Children (adopted 30 September 1921, entered into force 15 June 1922); ILO, International Convention for the Suppression of the Traffic in Women of Full Age (adopted 11 October 1933, entered into force 24 August 1934); ILO, Indigenous and Tribal Populations Convention (C107) (adopted on 26 June 1957, entered into force 2 June 1959).

[108] N. Hevener, 'International Law and the Status of Women: An Analysis of International Legal Instruments Related to the Treatment of Women' (1978) 1 *Harvard Women's Law Journal* 131, 141–147.

human rights and fundamental freedoms.[109] Similarly, during the drafting process of the Universal Declaration of Human Rights (UDHR) there was an important debate on the avoidance of the use of 'man' as a universal term to refer to every person. Instead, either un-gendered terms, such as 'human being' or 'individual', or the expression 'men and women' were then used throughout the Declaration, in efforts to emphasize that human rights belong to all, regardless of gender.[110] Despite those laudable efforts, reference to 'man' as inclusive of all human beings remained present in the Declaration's preamble and male pronouns were used in multiple articles, 'himself' appearing in Articles 23 and 25 and 'his' in twelve different provisions.[111]

In 1946, the ECOSOC established a Commission on the Status of Women with a mandate that included the elaboration of reports and recommendations on the promotion of women's rights in political, economic, civil, social, and educational fields.[112] Over the years, the work of this Commission led to the adoption of different international instruments, such as the Convention on the Political Rights of Women, the Convention on the Nationality of Married Women, and the Convention on the Consent to Marriage, Minimum Age for Marriage, and Registration of Marriages.[113] In 1963, the UN General Assembly tasked the Commission with the elaboration of a draft declaration on the elimination of discrimination against women, which was to combine, in a single instrument, the international standards that articulated the equal rights of men and women.[114] This led to the adoption of the 1967 Declaration on the Elimination of Discrimination against Women. Although not a binding instrument *per se*, the adoption of the 1967 Declaration paved the way for the elaboration of a treaty that would provide binding force to the principles laid down.[115] In 1972, the Commission requested the UN Secretary-General to call upon UN Member States to transmit their views on the possible adoption of a convention and, the following year, a working group was appointed to consider the elaboration of such a binding instrument.[116]

---

[109] UN Charter (adopted 26 June 1945, entered into force 24 October 1945) 1 UNTS XVI, Art. 1.3.

[110] Hansa Mehta, the Indian delegate, has been credited with promoting this change in vocabulary within the drafting Committee. See: A.S. Fraser, 'Becoming Human: The Origins and Developments of Women's Human Rights' (1999) 21 *Human Rights Quarterly* 853, 888.

[111] UDHR, preamble and Arts. 10, 11, 12, 13, 15, 17, 18, 21, 22, 23, 25, 29.

[112] Initially created as a Sub-Commission, it was quickly granted status as a Commission. See: ECOSOC, Resolution 2/11 (21 June 1946).

[113] Convention on the Political Rights of Women (adopted 31 March 1953, entered into force 7 July 1954), 193 UNTS 135; Convention on the Nationality of Married Women (adopted 20 February 1957, entered into force 11 August 1958), 309 UNTS 65; Convention on the Consent to Marriage, Minimum Age for Marriage, and Registration of Marriages (adopted 10 December 1962, entered into force 9 December 1964), 521 UNTS 231. See: L. Reanda, 'Human Rights and Women's Rights: The United Nations Approach' (1981) 3 *Human Rights Quarterly* 11, 19; F. Gaer, 'Women, international law and international institutions: The case of the United Nations' (2009) 32 *Women's Studies International Forum* 60, 62.

[114] UNGA, Resolution 1921(XVIII) 'Draft declaration on the elimination of discrimination against women' (5 December 1963).

[115] A.S. Fraser, 'Becoming Human: The Origins and Developments of Women's Human Rights' (1999) 21 *Human Rights Quarterly* 853, 893–894.

[116] M. Campbell, *Women, Poverty, Equality: The Role of CEDAW* (Hart 2018) 36.

As discussed in **Section 5.7**, this process led to the adoption of the 1979 Convention on the Elimination of Discrimination against Women (CEDAW), which marked a turning point in the history of the protection of women's rights under international law.[117]

The United Nations also organized four world conferences on women's rights, which took place in México City in 1975, Copenhagen in 1980, Nairobi in 1985, and Beijing in 1995. The first of these conferences was the fruit of a recommendation from the Commission on the Status of Women[118] and set an ambitious plan of action with a comprehensive list of goals dealing with different aspects of women's rights that were to be achieved within five years.[119] At the end of that five year period, the Second World Conference was hosted in Copenhagen. It was then that the recently adopted CEDAW was opened for signature.[120] The conference undertook a review of the progress achieved over the previous five years and adopted another ambitious plan of action to improve the situation of women worldwide.[121] The third conference, held in Nairobi, also took to review past progress and succeeded in bringing international attention to the scourge of violence against women, particularly domestic violence, as an issue pertaining to the international law of human rights;[122] a topic further discussed in **Section 10.2.3.1**.

Before the Fourth World Conference on Women, two other important world conferences took place in 1993 and 1994. First, the 1993 World Conference on Human Rights took place in Vienna. This conference was extremely relevant for women's rights, with the Vienna Declaration and Programme of Action containing a specific section on the equal status and human rights of women. The Vienna Declaration expressly acknowledged that:

> The human rights of women and of the girl-child are an inalienable, integral and indivisible part of universal human rights. The full and equal participation of women in political, civil, economic, social and cultural life, at the national, regional and international levels, and the eradication of all forms of discrimination on grounds of sex are priority objectives of the international community. Gender-based violence and all forms of sexual harassment and exploitation, including those resulting from cultural prejudice and international trafficking, are incompatible with the dignity and worth of the human person, and must be eliminated.[123]

---

[117] L. Reanda, 'Human Rights and Women's Rights: The United Nations Approach' (1981) 3 *Human Rights Quarterly* 11, 12; H. Charlesworth and C. Chinkin, *The Boundaries of International Law: A Feminist Analysis* (2nd edn., Manchester University Press 2022) 216–217.

[118] Report of the World Conference of the International Women's Year, E/CONF.66/34 (1975), p. 116

[119] A.S. Fraser, 'Becoming Human: The Origins and Developments of Women's Human Rights' (1999) 21 *Human Rights Quarterly* 853, 896. See: Report of the World Conference of the International Women's Year, E/CONF.66/34 (1975), pp. 8–41.

[120] A.S. Fraser, 'Becoming Human: The Origins and Developments of Women's Human Rights' (1999) 21 *Human Rights Quarterly* 853, 900.

[121] Report of the World Conference of the United Nations Decade for Women: Equality, Development and Peace, A/CONF.94/35 (1980).

[122] F. Gaer, 'Women, international law and international institutions: The case of the United Nations' (2009) 32 *Women's Studies International Forum* 60, 63.

[123] Vienna Declaration (25 June 1993), para. 18.

For its part, the 1994 International Conference on Population and Development, held in Cairo, was also key in the advancement of women's rights. The adoption of the conference's programme of action entailed the recognition of sexual and reproductive health as a fundamental human right and emphasized the existence of States' obligations concerning the advancement of gender equality and the empowerment of women and girls, ensuring their ability to control their own reproductive capacities.[124]

The Fourth World Conference on Women took place in Beijing in 1995. The Beijing Declaration and Platform for Action was adopted at that conference, amounting to one of the strongest expressions of States' commitment towards women's rights and the empowering of women at the international level up to that point in time. It covered twelve critical areas where actions were in desperate need, identifying strategic objectives; among others, these areas included poverty, education, health, violence, economy, human rights, the media, the environment, and the girl child. Unfortunately, more than a quarter of a century has elapsed since the Beijing conference without its objectives being achieved, as confirmed by the progress assessment undertaken every five years to identify challenges and shortcomings and to provide recommendations.[125]

More recent efforts within the United Nations towards achieving equal rights for women included the creation, in 2010, of the UN Entity for Gender Equality and the Empowerment of Women (UN Women).[126] This is a specialized agency that centralizes the work of the organization concerning women's rights. It is aimed at working towards the elimination of discrimination against women, the empowerment of women, and the achievement of equality between women and men as partners and beneficiaries of development, human rights, humanitarian action, and peace and security. UN Women is tasked with supporting Member States to set and implement legislation, policies, and programmes for achieving gender equality within their respective jurisdictions and worldwide.[127] This UN agency is expected to make an important contribution to the organization's efforts towards the realization of Goal 5 of the United Nations Sustainable Development Goals: to achieve gender equality and empower all women and girls by the year 2030.[128]

---

[124] ICPD Programme of Action, A/CONF.171/13 (1994), esp. principle 4 and paras. 4.4, 4.17.
[125] UNGA, 'Further actions and initiatives to implement the Beijing Declaration and Platform for Action', A/RES/S-23/3 (16 November 2000); CSW, Report on the forty-ninth session, E/2005/27-E/CN.6/2005/11 (28 February–11 and 22 March 2005); CSW, Report on the fifty-fourth session, E/2010/27-E/CN.6/2010/11 (13 March and 14 October 2009 and 1–12 March 2010); CSW, Report on the fifty-ninth session, E/2015/27-E/CN.6/2015/10 (21 March 2014 and 9–20 March 2015); CSW, 'Political declaration on the occasion of the twenty-fifth anniversary of the Fourth World Conference on Women', E/CN.6/2020/L.1 (2 March 2020).
[126] UNGA, 'System-wide coherence', A/64/L.56 (30 June 2010).
[127] UN Secretary-General, 'Comprehensive proposal for the composite entity for gender equality and the empowerment of women', A/64/588 (6 January 2010), para. 5.
[128] UNGA, 'Transforming our world: the 2030 Agenda for Sustainable Development', A/RES/70/1 (21 October 2015).

10.2.2.1 Regional developments

Although the adoption of CEDAW is, arguably, the most significant step yet taken for the protection of women's rights under the international law of human rights,[129] the regional treaties celebrated within the Americas, Africa, and Europe cannot be overlooked. The treaty adopted within the African human rights system, the 2003 Protocol on the Rights of Women in Africa ('Maputo Protocol'), is wide in its scope and aims to ensure that the rights of women are promoted, realized, and protected so as to enable women to fully enjoy all human rights.[130] As discussed in **Section 8.1.2**, this Protocol established a legal framework for the protection of women in Africa, including a two-folded system of supervision of States Parties' obligations. First, the Protocol imposes upon States Parties the duty to inform the African Commission of the measures adopted to achieve the full realization of the protected rights through the periodic report mechanism contemplated in the African Charter. Secondly, the Protocol allows for resort to the African Court with regard to its interpretation arising from its application or implementation by States Parties and, according to a contextual reading of the Protocol, the Commission can also be seized in matters concerning its interpretation and application.[131]

On their part, the treaties adopted under the Organization of American States and the Council of Europe are focused on the affliction of violence against women, which is the topic of **Section 10.2.3.1**. In 1994, the OAS adopted the Inter-American Convention on the Prevention, Punishment and Eradication of Violence against Women ('Convention of Belém do Pará'), aimed at addressing the pandemic of violence against women in the region.[132] As discussed in **Section 6.1.5**, this treaty emphasized its applicability in both the public and private spheres, imposing upon States the obligation to take measures without delay to prevent, punish, and eradicate all forms of violence against women. The Convention established a double system of international supervision: first, through State reports to the Inter-American Commission of Women on measures adopted both to prevent and prohibit violence against women, as well as to assist the victims; and secondly, through individual complaints to the Inter-American Commission and Court for breaches of the main obligations of States concerning prevention and eradication of violence and the punishment of perpetrators.[133]

---

[129] L. Reanda, 'Human Rights and Women's Rights: The United Nations Approach' (1981) 3 *Human Rights Quarterly* 11, 12; H. Charlesworth and C. Chinkin, *The Boundaries of International Law: A Feminist Analysis* (2nd edn., Manchester University Press 2022) 216–217.

[130] At the end of 2022, forty-two of the fifty-five Member States of the African Union were Parties to the Protocol. See: https://au.int/treaties/protocol-african-charter-human-and-peoples-rights-rights-women-africa.

[131] Maputo Protocol, Art. XXVII. See: ACtHPR, *Association pour le Progrès et la Défense des Droits des Femmes Maliennes and the Institute for Human Rights and Development in Africa v. Mali* (merits) (2018) 2 AfCLR 380.

[132] At the end of 2022, all OAS Member States, with the exception of Canada and the USA, are Parties to the Convention. See: http://www.cidh.org/basicos/english/Basic14.Conv%20of%20Belem%20Do%20Para%20Ratif.htm.

[133] Inter-American Convention on the Prevention, Punishment and Eradication of Violence against Women (adopted 9 June 1994, entered into force 5 March 1995).

Within the Council of Europe, it was in 2011 that the Convention on Preventing and Combating Violence against Women and Domestic Violence ('Istanbul Convention') was adopted. The Convention established a comprehensive set of obligations upon States to address gender-based violence, including the need to adopt measures of prevention, protection, and support of the victims, as well as measures towards investigating and prosecuting harmful acts. The treaty set up a Group of Experts, to be elected by the Parties to the Convention, as its monitoring body to which States Parties should submit periodic reports.[134] Unlike the Inter-American and African treaties, the European one does not allow for individuals to access the regional Court when a violation of the treaty has taken place.[135]

10.2.3 CONTEMPORARY STATUS OF WOMEN'S RIGHTS

It is beyond dispute that women should enjoy equal rights to those of men. Nowadays, the prohibition of gender discrimination can be affirmed to belong to the realm of *jus cogens*,[136] despite opinions to the contrary.[137] However, women's unequal enjoyment of rights remains a reality worldwide, which is deeply embedded in tradition, history, and culture.[138] One of the long-standing causes of women's inequality can be found in the traditional separation between the public and private spheres of human activity, in which public life appears as the privileged ambit, and has been mostly populated by men, while women have been mainly relegated to the private or domestic sphere, which is treated as inferior and is associated with reproduction and the raising of children.[139] As accurately asserted by the CEDAW Committee: 'Men historically have both dominated public life and exercised the power to confine and subordinate women within the private sphere.'[140]

In order to modify the existent situation of unequal enjoyment of rights, grounded in the aforementioned historical reasons, the international law of human rights imposes upon States the obligation to adopt a range of measures. One of the most urgent

---

[134] Convention on preventing and combating violence against women and domestic violence ('Istanbul Convention') (adopted 11 May 2011, entered into force 1 August 2014), CETS No. 210.

[135] At the end of 2022, there were ten Member States of the Council of Europe not Parties to the Convention, including Turkey, which denounced it in 2021. See: https://www.coe.int/en/web/conventions/full-list?module=signatures-by-treaty&treatynum=210 (accessed on 13 April 2023).

[136] A. Edwards, *Violence against Women under International Human Rights Law* (CUP 2010) 310; A.W. Shavers, 'Using Customary International Law to Improve Women's Lives' in B. Lepard, *Reexamining Customary International Law* (CUP 2017) 266–306, 304.

[137] ILC, Fourth report on peremptory norms of general international law (jus cogens) by Dire Tladi, Special Rapporteur, A/CN.4/727 (31 January 2019), para. 135; ILC, Fifth report on peremptory norms of general international law (*jus cogens*) by Dire Tladi, Special Rapporteur, A/CN.4/747 (24 January 2022), conclusion 23.

[138] CCPR, General Comment No. 28: The equality of rights between men and women, HRI/GEN/1/Rev. 9 (Vol. I) (29 March 2000), para. 5

[139] CEDAW Committee, General Recommendation No. 21: Equality in marriage and family relations, A/49/38 (1994), para. 11; CEDAW Committee, General Recommendation No. 23: Political and public life, A/52/38 (1997), para. 8.

[140] CEDAW Committee, General Recommendation No. 23: Political and public life, A/52/38 (1997), para. 8.

obligations of States is to ensure that their legislation does not entail *de jure* gender discrimination and that women are legally entitled to enjoy all human rights on equal footing to men in both the public and the private sphere,[141] including ensuring that both single and married women have equal rights in regard to the ownership and administration of property.[142] Furthermore, States must adopt effective measures to secure the protection of human rights that specifically concern women, including access to the necessary means to avoid unwanted pregnancies, through guaranteed access to sex education, contraceptive methods, and family planning services.[143]

States must also adopt transformative measures—as discussed in **Section 10.1.1** — to bring systemic and structural gender inequalities to an end and help women achieve de facto equality. Transformative action should be aimed at achieving cultural changes in society, to modify dated ideas concerning gender roles, stereotypes, patterns, and behaviours.[144] In all societies worldwide, one of the most significant factors inhibiting women's ability to fully enjoy all rights has been the cultural framework of values and beliefs that reinforce the idea of the man breadwinner and the woman homemaker, which serve to confine women to the private sphere of activities, excluding them from active participation in public life.[145] Until such a transformation is achieved, States are under the obligation to adopt affirmative action—as discussed in **Section 10.1.1.1**— which can take the form of temporary supporting programmes, targeted recruitment, and quota systems.[146]

10.2.3.1 Gender-based violence

Gender-based violence is a global pandemic that affects over a third of women in their lifetime[147] and is rooted in long-standing gender inequality, unequal power relations, and existent harmful cultural norms.[148] And yet, reaching the understanding that

---

[141] ICCPR, Art. 3; ICESCR, Art. 3; CEDAW; Protocol to the African Charter on Human and Peoples' Rights on the Rights of Women in Africa ('Maputo Protocol') (adopted 1 July 2003, entered into force 25 November 2005), Art. II.

[142] CEDAW Committee, General Recommendation No. 21: Equality in marriage and family relations, A/49/38 (1994), para. 10; Report of the Special Rapporteur on violence against women, its causes and consequences, Ms. Radhika Coomaraswamy, E/CN.4/1996/53 (5 February 1996), para. 142; CCPR, General Comment No. 28: The equality of rights between men and women, HRI/GEN/1/Rev. 9 (Vol. I) (29 March 2000), para. 25; CEDAW Committee, General Recommendation: Economic consequences of marriage, family relations and their dissolution, CEDAW/C/GC/29 (30 October 2013), paras. 36–38.

[143] CEDAW Committee, General Recommendation No. 21: Equality in marriage and family relations, A/49/38 (1994), para. 22; CEDAW Committee, General Recommendation No. 24: Women and health, A/54/38/Rev. 1, chap. I. (1999), para. 31.

[144] CEDAW, Art. 5.a; Maputo Protocol, Art. II.2.

[145] CEDAW Committee, General Recommendation No. 23: Political and public life, A/52/38 (1997), para. 10.

[146] CEDAW Committee, General Recommendation No. 25: Temporary special measures (2004), para. 22.

[147] WHO, 'Violence against women prevalence estimates, 2018: global, regional and national prevalence estimates for intimate partner violence against women and global and regional prevalence estimates for non-partner sexual violence against women' (2021), p. xvi.

[148] Declaration on the Elimination of Violence against Women, General Assembly resolution 48/104 (20 December 1993), preamble. See also: CEDAW Committee, General Recommendation No. 35: on gender-based violence against women (updating General Recommendation No. 19), CEDAW/C/GC/35 (26 July 2017).

gender-based violence is a human rights issue was not a simple task.[149] An important obstacle could be found in the structure of the international law of human rights itself, given that this legal system is mostly concerned with acts and omissions of State agents (as discussed in **Section 3.2.2**), while gender-based violence is a torment most often occurring within the private sphere, committed by private persons.[150] As asserted by the CEDAW Committee: 'Family violence is one of the most insidious forms of violence against women. It is prevalent in all societies. Within family relationships, women of all ages are subjected to violence of all kinds, including battering, rape, other forms of sexual assault, mental and other forms of violence, which are perpetuated by traditional attitudes.'[151]

Nevertheless, progress within the international law of human rights has led to the recognition that States are not only internationally liable for the actions of their agents, but their responsibility is also engaged due to private acts when there is a failure to act in accordance with international obligations.[152] With regard to gender-based violence, a number of these obligations have indeed been imposed upon States, including, among others: the duties to set in place adequate legislation to address domestic violence, to act with due diligence to prevent violations of the rights of women by private actors, and to investigate, prosecute, and punish acts of gender-based violence.[153]

As mentioned in **Section 10.2.2.1**, within the Inter-American and European human rights systems specific treaties have been adopted concerning gender-based violence, while the more ambitious African treaty on women's rights (the Maputo Protocol) also covers States' obligations with regards to this crime.[154] Within the United Nations, the CEDAW Committee has been emphatic in that gender-based violence is a manifestation of gender discrimination as prohibited by the Convention.[155] Moreover, in 1993, the UN General Assembly proclaimed the Declaration on the Elimination of Violence against Women,[156] which defined gender-based violence as any act likely to result in physical, sexual, or psychological harm or suffering to women, including threats of such acts, regardless of whether these take place in the public or the private sphere.[157] The Declaration is clear as to the obligation upon States to adopt the necessary measures to

---

[149] A. Edwards, *Violence against Women under International Human Rights Law* (CUP 2010) 7.
[150] H. Charlesworth and C. Chinkin, 'The Gender of *Jus Cogens*' (1993) 15 *Human Rights Quarterly* 63, 69.
[151] CEDAW Committee, General Recommendation No. 19: Violence against Women, A/47/38, para. 23.
[152] H. Charlesworth and C. Chinkin, 'The Gender of *Jus Cogens*' (1993) 15 *Human Rights Quarterly* 63, 73.
[153] CEDAW Committee, General Recommendation No. 19: Violence against Women, A/47/38, paras. 9, 24; CEDAW Committee, General Recommendation No. 35: On gender-based violence against women (updating General Recommendation No. 19), CEDAW/C/GC/35 (26 July 2017), para. 24.
[154] Maputo Protocol, Arts. III–V.
[155] CEDAW Committee, General Recommendation No. 19: Violence against Women, A/47/38, paras. 1, 6, 7; CEDAW Committee, General Recommendation No. 35: On gender-based violence against women (updating General Recommendation No. 19), CEDAW/C/GC/35 (26 July 2017), paras. 1, 21.
[156] On the shortcomings of the Declaration, see: A. Edwards, *Violence against Women under International Human Rights Law* (CUP 2010) 21–25.
[157] Declaration on the Elimination of Violence against Women, General Assembly resolution 48/104 (20 December 1993), Art. 1.

prevent, investigate, and sanction acts of gender-based violence committed by private individuals.[158] While the Declaration could have been thought by some as soft law in the early 1990s, the obligations emanating from it are grounded in international customary law, as confirmed by the practice of the Special Rapporteurship created.

In 1994, the UN Commission on Human Rights decided to create the mandate of a Special Rapporteur on 'violence against women, its causes and consequences'; the first ever gender-specific mandate of a Special Rapporteur.[159] The mandate is ongoing, having been renewed by the Human Rights Council. The mandate holder is tasked with seeking and receiving information concerning gender-based violence from multiple sources and with issuing recommendations conducive to the elimination of all forms of violence against women, its causes, and consequences at the local, national, regional, and international levels.[160] Over the years, the mandate has made many important contributions to the understanding of gender-based violence as a grave violation of human rights and to the scope of States' obligations with regards to this type of violation. Among the established international obligations identified by the Special Rapporteur, it is possible to highlight the following: States should ensure that abusive practices are criminalized under their legislation, including marital rape and female genital mutilation; States should provide effective mechanisms by which victim-survivors can invoke States' protection, including the creation of special units or procedures within hospitals to help identify victims of gender-based violence; States should support victim-survivors, through the provision of shelter, counselling, and protection from contact from the aggressor; and States should carry out literacy campaigns concerning domestic violence and the legal rights of women.[161] However, as the fifteen-year review of the mandate revealed: 'The unfortunate fact remains that, for the most part, [violence against women] continues to be perpetrated with impunity, access to justice is ridden with obstacles, and accountability remains elusive within the domestic realm.'[162]

Gender-based violence is certainly an urgent and significant problem against which the international law of human rights will continue to face a rather tragic uphill battle. The gender-based violence pandemic will not be eliminated until States succeed in modifying social and cultural patterns of conduct of all individuals, leading to the

---

[158] Declaration on the Elimination of Violence against Women, General Assembly resolution 48/104 (20 December 1993), Art. 4.

[159] H. Charlesworth and C. Chinkin, *The Boundaries of International Law: A Feminist Analysis* (2nd edn., Manchester University Press 2022) 219.

[160] CHR, 'Question of integrating the rights of women into the human rights mechanisms of the United Nations and the elimination of violence against women' E/CN.4/RES/1994/45 (4 March 1994).

[161] Report of the Special Rapporteur on violence against women, its causes and consequences, Ms. Radhika Coomaraswamy, E/CN.4/1996/53 (5 February 1996), para. 142; Report of the Special Rapporteur on violence against women, its causes and consequences, Ms. Radhika Coomaraswamy, 'A framework for model legislation on domestic violence', E/CN.4/1996/53 (5 February 1996). See also: CEDAW Committee, General Recommendation No. 35: On gender-based violence against women (updating General Recommendation No. 19), CEDAW/C/GC/35 (26 July 2017).

[162] Y. Ertürk, '15 Years of the United Nations Special Rapporteur on Violence against Women (1994–2009): A Critical Review' (2009) 54.

elimination of prejudices and customary practices based on the idea of the inferiority or superiority of a given gender and stereotyped roles, abilities, and behaviours pertaining to men and/or women. The adoption of measures to achieve such a significant cultural change is indeed an international obligation assumed by States under the international law of human rights.[163]

> CEDAW, *A.T. v. Hungary*, Communication No. 2/2003 (26 January 2005).
>
> This was an extremely serious case concerning gender-based violence, in which the author (A. T.) had been victim of physical violence and threats for over four years at the hands of her former common-law husband, father of her two children. The author had been unsuccessful in obtaining a permanent order of protection forbidding her former partner to return to their apartment, while she had also been unable to leave the apartment herself, as the available shelters were unequipped to accept her together with her children, one of whom was disabled.
>
> The Committee found that the State had failed in its duty to provide A. T. with protection from the serious risk to her physical integrity, physical and mental health, as well as her life, posed by her former common-law husband. This amounted to a continuous breach of Article 2 (a), (b) and (e) of CEDAW, which, by establishing the obligation to adopt all necessary measures to prohibit and eliminate discrimination against women, must be interpreted to include the States' duty to prevent violence against women and to protect women from violence (para. 9.3). The Committee also found the situation to amount to the violation of Articles 16 and 5 (a) read jointly, which, respectively, impose upon States Parties the obligation to adopt all appropriate measures to eliminate discrimination against women in all matters relating to marriage and family relations, and to take measures to modify the social and cultural patterns of conduct of men and women, with a view to achieving the elimination of prejudicial and stereotypical gender roles (para. 9.4).
>
> The Committee recommended the State take immediate and effective actions to guarantee the physical and mental integrity of A. T. and her family and to ensure that she was given a safe home in which to live with her children, in addition to due reparation for the harm suffered (para. 9.6).

> ECtHR, *Opuz v. Turkey*, App. no. 33401/02, ECHR 2009.
>
> The case concerned a situation of gender-based violence in which the perpetrator had subjected both the applicant (his wife) and her mother to a series of very serious violent assaults, including some certified as life-threatening by medical doctors. Ultimately, the applicant's mother was shot and killed by the applicant's husband in 2002, when she was helping her daughter flee the matrimonial home. The repeated assaults had been reported to the authorities and criminal proceedings had been brought against the perpetrator, although some had been discontinued. The perpetrator had been convicted for two of those offences,

---

[163] CEDAW, Art. 5.a.; Convention of Belém do Pará, Arts. 6, 8; Istanbul Convention, Art. 12.

which included having stabbed his wife seven times and having run over his mother-in-law with the car, but for these offences he merely received a fine payable in instalments and a three-month sentence that was later commuted to a fine. In 2008, the perpetrator was finally convicted of murder, for the killing of the applicant's mother, and sentenced to life imprisonment, but he was released, pending appeal, and renewed his threats against the applicant.

The European Court found three separate violations of the Convention, given the way in which the domestic authorities mishandled the prolonged situation of gender-based violence. Concerning the killing of the applicant's mother, the Court ruled that the State's inaction was in breach of its positive obligations to prevent a violation of the right to life under Article 2, as the authorities knew of the existence of a real and immediate risk to the life of the victim and failed to take effective measures to avoid the risk from materializing (paras. 134–136 and 148–149). The Court also found a violation of the prohibition of ill-treatment under the Convention (Article 3), given the authorities' failure to protect the applicant against domestic violence perpetrated by her former husband (para. 176). Lastly, the Court also ruled on the violation of the prohibition of discrimination (Article 14) in conjunction with both the right to life and the prohibition of ill-treatment. It considered that the judicial passivity in Turkey mainly affected women, which amounted to gender-based violence itself; a manifestation of gender discrimination (paras. 200–202).

IACtHR, *González et al. ('Cotton Field') v. Mexico*. Preliminary Objection, Merits, Reparations and Costs. Judgment of November 16, 2009. Series C No. 205.

The case revolved around the disappearance and death of two girls and a woman, whose bodies were found in a cotton field in Ciudad Juárez in November 2001, and the State's passivity in adopting measures to protect the victims, prevent the crimes, or seriously investigate the murders. The three murders were part of a broader pattern of gender-based violence that characterized Ciudad Juárez from the early 1990s, with an unknown (but alarming) number of girls and women being killed that can be counted in the hundreds. The case was brought before the Court by the Commission, after considering that México had failed to adopt its recommendations.

Before the Court, the State made a partial acknowledgement of its international responsibility. The Court found the State in breach of different provisions of the American Convention, including the right to life (Article 4), the right to personal integrity (Article 5), and the right to personal liberty and security (Article 7), as well as of Article 7 of the Inter-American Convention on the Prevention, Punishment and Eradication of Violence against Women. The Court did not find the State directly responsible for the murder of the victims, as it was not proved that the crimes had been carried out by State agents, nor did the Court find a breach of the mentioned Conventions due to the State's failure to prevent the disappearance of the victims, despite it being aware of the general situation of risk for women in Ciudad Juárez.

Nevertheless, the Court did find the State to have breached its international obligations from the moment that its agents became aware of the disappearance of the victims, due to

> the lack of effective measures to find them (para. 279). The Court considered that the State had failed to act with the required due diligence to prevent the death and abuse suffered by the victims, given that the general circumstances surrounding the disappearance of the three victims meant that the State should have been aware of the real and imminent risk faced by them (paras. 283–284). Furthermore, the Court ruled that the State was also liable for the lack of an effective investigation into the crimes, capable of identifying and convicting the perpetrators. On the contrary, the investigations had been plagued with irregularities, attributable to the State agents involved, including the harassment of the victims' next of kin during their search for justice. This led to the Court's finding of the violation of the rights of access to justice and to judicial protection (Articles 8 and 25), as well as to the right to personal integrity of the victims' relatives—themselves indirect victims in the case (para. 402).
>
> The Court ordered a wide range of measures of reparation, which included the payment of compensation, as well as the obligation to seriously undertake criminal proceedings to identify, prosecute, and, if appropriate, punish the perpetrators and masterminds of the disappearance, ill-treatment, and deprivation of life of the victims (paras. 460 and 462). It also ordered the State to adopt a range of measures aimed at overcoming the general and systemic crime of gender-based violence in the region. These measures included: the erection of a monument in memory of the victims of gender-based murders in Ciudad Juárez; the amendment of the State's procedures for the investigation of gender-based crimes, to make them compliant with human rights standards; the creation of a database with the information available on the girls and women that had disappeared; and the implementation of education programmes on gender discrimination and gender-based violence for both public officials and the general population (paras. 471–472, 502, 512, and 541–543).

10.2.3.1.1 Critical debates: female genital mutilation

Female genital mutilation (FGM) refers to all procedures involving partial or total removal of the female external genitalia or other injury to the female genital organs for non-medical reasons.[164] Although most frequently performed within African societies, FGM is carried out in every region of the world and, within some cultures, is a requirement for marriage and believed to be an effective method of controlling the sexuality of women and girls. It has been estimated that between 100 and 140 million girls and women worldwide have been subjected to FGM.[165] FGM is a manifestation of gender inequality and gender oppression that is deeply entrenched in social, economic, and political structures and which has the effect of perpetuating normative and harmful gender roles.[166] FGM has been conclusively acknowledged as a multifaceted violation of human rights, including of the right to personal integrity, the right to health, and

---

[164] CEDAW Committee and CRC, Joint general recommendation (No. 31 CEDAW/No. 18 CERD) on harmful practices, CEDAW/C/GC/31-CRC/C/GC/18 (14 November 2014), para. 19.

[165] CEDAW Committee and CRC, Joint general recommendation (No. 31 CEDAW/No. 18 CERD) on harmful practices, CEDAW/C/GC/31-CRC/C/GC/18 (14 November 2014), para. 19.

[166] OHCHR, UNAIDS, UNDP, UNECA, UNESCO, UNFPA, UNHCR, UNICEF, UNIFEM, WHO, Eliminating Female genital mutilation: An interagency statement (2008), p. 5.

the prohibition of discrimination.[167] In fact, this harmful practice amounts to an intersectional form of oppression, which mainly affects girls due to their gender, age, and cultural background.

Within the societies in which FGM is practised, it tends to be upheld by local structures of power and authority, such as traditional and religious leaders, elders, and even some medical personnel.[168] While FGM can be forced in many cases, it can also be naturalized by the victims themselves as an important part of their cultural identity; understood as a rite of passage that prepares girls for adulthood and married life and provides a feeling of community membership.[169] However, under the international law of human rights, FGM is seen as a grave violation of women's rights and States are under the obligation to adopt measures to put an end to this practice. These measures include the duty to protect girls from this ritual practice, to enact effective legislation that prohibits FGM, to carry out literacy campaigns to raise awareness about the harmful consequences of this practice, and to provide support to local and national organizations working towards the elimination of FGM.[170]

10.3 CHILDREN'S RIGHTS

As discussed in **Section 5.9**, the United Nations Convention on the Rights of the Child (UNCRC) is the international human rights treaty with the largest number of State Parties, including all UN Member States, with the sole exception of the USA. This high level of ratification demonstrates the overwhelming consensus among States on the importance of providing due protection and legal recognition to children everywhere. This protected collective—children—is, however, a rather heterogeneous group, including persons with varying degrees of development in their personal capacities, given the wide range of ages it encompasses. The UN Convention establishes eighteen

---

[167] CEDAW Committee, General Recommendation No. 14: Female circumcision, A/45/38 (1990); CEDAW Committee, General Recommendation No. 19: Violence against women, A/47/38 (1992), paras. 19–20; CEDAW Committee, General Recommendation No. 24: Women and health, A/54/38/Rev.1, (1999), para. 15; CCPR, General Comment No. 28: Equality of rights between men and women, CCPR/C/21/rev. 1/Add. 10 (29 March 2000), para. 11; CESCR, General Comment No. 14: The right to the highest attainable standard of health, UN Doc. E/C.12/2000/4 (11 August 2000), paras. 22, 35; CRC, General Comment No. 4: Adolescent health and development in the context of the Convention, CRC/GC/2003/4 (1 July 2003), para. 24.

[168] OHCHR, UNAIDS, UNDP, UNECA, UNESCO, UNFPA, UNHCR, UNICEF, UNIFEM, WHO, Eliminating Female genital mutilation: An interagency statement (2008), p. 6.

[169] I. Gunning, 'Arrogant Perception, World-Travelling and Multicultural Feminism: The Case of Female Genital Surgeries' (1992) 23 *Columbia Human Rights Law Review* 189, 218; F. Ahmadu, 'Rites and wrongs: an insider/outsider reflects on power and excision' in B. Shell-Duncan and Y. Hernlund (eds.) *Female 'circumcision' in Africa: culture, controversy and change* (Lynne Rienner 2000), 283–313, 301–302; OHCHR, UNAIDS, UNDP, UNECA, UNESCO, UNFPA, UNHCR, UNICEF, UNIFEM, WHO, Eliminating Female genital mutilation: An interagency statement (2008), p. 6.

[170] CEDAW Committee, General Recommendation No. 14: Female circumcision, A/45/38 (1990); CEDAW Committee, General Recommendation No. 24: Women and health, A/54/38/Rev. 1, (1999), para. 15; CRC, General Comment No. 4: Adolescent health and development in the context of the Convention, CRC/GC/2003/4 (1 July 2003), para. 24.

years of age as the threshold between childhood and adulthood, although it allows States to set a lower age for attaining majority.[171] Other treaties have established the same age for reaching adulthood, some of them depriving States of the discretion to set a lower age for reaching adulthood.[172]

Undoubtedly, the adoption of UNCRC in 1989 was a milestone in the development of the legal recognition and protection of children under the international law of human rights. However, international law's concern for the protection of children did not start with the adoption of this Convention, nor was it finished therewith. As recognized by UNCRC's preamble, the need to provide particular care to children had been stated in the 1924 Geneva Declaration of the Rights of the Child, adopted under the auspices of the League of Nations;[173] a document that has been considered by some as the first human rights instrument ever proclaimed,[174] preceding those adopted in 1948 both in the Americas and within the UN by almost a quarter of a century. This short document affirmed, in its five articles, that mankind owed children everywhere a minimum level of protection against hunger, sickness, destitution, and distress to help their development. This concern about children's welfare was echoed by the United Nations, as illustrated by the creation of the International Children's Emergency Fund (UNICEF) in 1946; the inclusion of a particular provision acknowledging the special care and assistance required by children in the 1948 Universal Declaration of Human Rights (Article 25.2); and the adoption of the more comprehensive Declaration of the Rights of the Child, in 1959. In particular, the 1959 Declaration recognized, across ten principles, that children, by reason of their immaturity, should be provided with special safeguard and care, should be protected against all forms of neglect, cruelty, and exploitation, and should be entitled to enjoy, among other rights, the right to be free from discrimination, the right to a name and nationality, the right to education, the right to benefit from social security, and the right to play and recreation.[175]

Conventional protection of children regarding the specific area of labour was provided by the International Labour Organization (ILO). From its inception, through the 1919 Peace Treaty of Versailles, the ILO manifested a commitment towards the protection of children within the context of employment and the need to bring child labour to an end.[176] However, it was not until 1973 that the ILO adopted the 'Minimum Age Convention' (Convention No. 138), which imposed upon States Parties the obligation to pursue a domestic policy aimed at the effective abolition of child labour, as

---

[171] Convention on the Rights of the Child (adopted on 20 November 1989, entered into force 2 September 1990), Art. 1.

[172] African Charter on the Rights and Welfare of the Child (adopted 11 July 1990, entered into force 29 November 1999), OAU Doc.CAB/LEG/24.9/49 (1990), Art. 2 [hereinafter 'African Children's Charter']; European Convention on the Exercise of Children's Rights (ETS No. 160) (adopted 25 January 1996, entered into force 1 July 2000), Art. 1.1; Worst Forms of Child Labour Convention (No. 182) (adopted 17 June 1999, entered into force 19 November 2000), Art. 2.

[173] Geneva Declaration of the Rights of the Child (adopted 26 September 1924).

[174] G. Van Bueren, *The International Law on the Rights of the Child* (Nihoff 1995) 6.

[175] UNGA, Declaration of the Rights of the Child, Resolution 1386 (XIV), A/4354 (20 November 1959).

[176] Treaty of Peace of Versailles (adopted 28 June 1919, entered into force 10 January 2020), Part XIII.

well as the duty to progressively raise the minimum age for admission to employment.[177] In 1999, the ILO adopted the Convention on the 'Worst Forms of Child Labour'; the first ILO Convention to achieve universal ratification. It placed States Parties under the obligation to adopt, as a matter of urgency, immediate and effective measures to secure the prohibition and elimination of certain forms of child labour. These prohibited forms of labour included all activities that are either illegal or likely to harm the health and safety of children, such as all forms of slavery and similar practices, including the compulsory recruitment of children for use in armed conflict, child prostitution, and pornography, and activities linked to the production and trafficking of drugs.[178]

As discussed in **Section 5.9**, the adoption of UNCRC in 1989 came to confirm the recognition of children as subjects of rights rather than as mere objects of protection. This treaty imposed upon States Parties clear obligations in terms of the respect and protection of children's rights, encompassing civil, political, social, economic, and cultural rights.[179] Over the years, the substantive content of the Convention has been enriched by the work of the Committee of the Rights of the Child, as well as by the adoption of three Protocols. The first two Protocols, adopted in 2000, concerned, respectively, the prohibition of child prostitution and child pornography, and the regulation of children's participation in armed conflicts. A further Protocol was adopted in 2011, strengthening the operational capacities of the Committee by allowing for individual communications.[180]

10.3.1 REGIONAL DEVELOPMENTS

The progress made towards the protection of children and their recognition as subjects of rights under UNCRC has been complemented by efforts made under regional human rights regimes. As discussed in **Section 8.1.2.1**, the adoption of the African Charter on the Rights and Welfare of the Child followed only by months the UN Convention, making the African human rights system the first regional regime to adopt a treaty specifically focused on the protection of children.[181] The Charter provides a catalogue of children's rights to be protected by State Parties and established a 'Committee of Experts on the Rights and Welfare of the Child' tasked with the promotion and protection of children's rights and with monitoring the implementation of the treaty.[182] The Committee has created specific mandates to set standards and develop strategies to

---

[177] Minimum Age Convention (No. 138) (adopted 26 June 1973, entered into force 18 June 1976).
[178] Worst Forms of Child Labour Convention (No. 182) (adopted 17 June 1999, entered into force 19 November 2000).
[179] W. Vandenhole, G. Türkelli, and S. Lembrechts, Children's Rights: A Commentary on the Convention on the Rights of the Child and its Protocols (Elgar 2019) 6.
[180] Optional Protocol to the Convention on the Rights of the Child on the sale of children, child prostitution, and child pornography (adopted 25 May 2000, entered into force 18 January 2002); Optional Protocol to the Convention on the Rights of the Child on the involvement of children in armed conflict (adopted 25 May 2000, entered into force 12 February 2002); Optional Protocol to the Convention on the Rights of the Child on a communications procedure (adopted 19 December 2011, entered into force 14 April 2014).
[181] African Children's Charter.   [182] ACRWC, Arts. 32, 42.

improve the promotion and protection of children's rights, which have included special rapporteurs on violence against children, on health, welfare and development, on child marriage, on the right to education, on children and armed conflict, as well as working groups on children's rights and business and on children's rights and climate change. It has also started developing a rich jurisprudence that clarifies the scope of children's rights within the regional system (see **Section 10.3.3**).

Within the Council of Europe, the specific legal framework concerning children's rights is perhaps less developed than in other regions. While in 1979, the Parliamentary Assembly recommended the Committee of Ministers to undertake the elaboration of a 'European Charter on the Rights of the Child',[183] such a treaty never came to be adopted. In its place, we can find a number of regional treaties aimed at the protection of children,[184] such as the 1996 European Convention on the Exercise of Children's Rights, which expressly grants procedural rights to children in judiciary proceedings affecting them.[185] Additionally, the European Social Charter contains two provisions specifically aimed at children; Article 7 sets out the obligation to protect children from economic exploitation within the area of employment, while (revised) Article 17 mandates States to take the necessary measures to ensure that children are protected from negligence, violence, and exploitation, and that they receive the care, assistance, and education needed for their development.[186] Moreover, despite the absence of specific provisions addressing the rights of children under the European Convention on Human Rights, the Court has developed an evolving case law that recognizes that, in cases involving children, their best interests are of paramount importance and should be placed at the centre of all decisions susceptible to affect their rights and development.[187]

On its part, the American Convention on Human Rights has a specific provision titled 'Rights of the Child', which provides that children have the right to the measures of protection required by their condition as minors on the part of their family, the society, and the State.[188] Both the Inter-American Commission and Court have developed important guidelines as to children's rights under the Convention.

---

[183] PACE, Recommendation 874 (4 October 1979)

[184] Among them: European Convention on the Adoption of Children (ETS No. 058) (adopted 24 April 1967, entered into force 26 April 1968); the (revised) European Convention on the Adoption of Children (ETS No. 202) (adopted 27 November 2008, entered into force 1 September 2011); European Convention on the Legal Status of Children born out of Wedlock (ETS No. 085) (adopted 15 October 1975, entered into force 11 August 1978); Convention on Recognition and Enforcement of Decisions concerning Custody of Children and on Restoration of Custody of Children (ETS No. 105) (adopted 20 May 1980, entered into force 1 September 1983); Convention on Contact concerning Children (ETS No. 192) (adopted 15 May 2003, entered into force 1 September 2005); Convention on the Protection of Children against Sexual Exploitation and Sexual Abuse (CETS No. 201) (adopted 25 October 2007, entered into force 1 July 2010).

[185] European Convention on the Exercise of Children's Rights (ETS No. 160) (adopted 25 January 1996, entered into force 1 July 2000).

[186] European Social Charter (revised) (adopted 3 May 1996, entered into force 1 July 1999) (ETS No. 163)

[187] See, for instance: ECtHR, *Neulinger and Shuruk v. Switzerland* [GC], App. no. 41615/07, § 134–135, ECHR 2010; ECtHR, *Vavřička and Others v. the Czech Republic* [GC], App. nos. 47621/13 and five others, § 286–289, 8 April 2021.

[188] ACHR, Art. 19.

The Commission established a Rapporteurship on the Rights of the Child in 1998, aimed at the promotion of children's rights within the jurisdiction of the thirty-five OAS Member States. Fruits of the work of the Rapporteurship are numerous thematic reports that have contributed to solidifying standards of protection within the system.[189] Similarly, the Inter-American Court has produced an important jurisprudence on the topic, including two advisory opinions,[190] which confirmed that children are indeed subjects of rights, and not only objects of protection and that the best interests of the child, as a guiding principle, means that children's development and the full enjoyment of their rights must be considered when applying norms pertaining to any aspect of children's lives.[191] The Court even provided a wise and sobering warning concerning children, affirming that: 'a world which does not take care of its children, which destroys the enchantment of their infancy within them, which puts a premature end to their childhood, and which subjects them to all sorts of deprivations and humiliations, effectively has no future'.[192]

10.3.2 THE FOUR PRINCIPLES

In its fifth general comment, adopted in 2003, the Committee on the Rights of the Children highlighted four principles, which it considered underlying the whole system of UNCRC. While these principles do not appear as such in the text of the Convention, the Committee identified these principles from its early days of work, proposing them in the guidelines for States to prepare their initial reports to the Committee.[193] These four principles, which can now be said to underpin the protection of children's rights under the international law of human rights more broadly are the prohibition of discrimination, the best interests of the child, the right to development, and the right of children to freely express their own views.

---

[189] See, among others: IACHR, 'The Rights of the Child in the Inter-American Human Rights System', OEA/Ser.L/V/II.133, doc. 34 (29 October 2008); IACHR, 'Report on Corporal Punishment and Human Rights of Children and Adolescents', OEA/Ser.L/V/II.135, doc. 14 (5 August 2009); IACHR, 'Juvenile Justice and Human Rights in the Americas', OEA/Ser.L/V/II, doc. 78 (13 July 2011); IACHR, 'The Right of Girls and Boys to a Family. Alternative Care. Ending Institutionalization in the Americas', OEA/Ser.L/V/II, doc. 54/13 (17 October 2013); IACHR, 'Violence, Children and Organized Crime', OEA/Ser.L/V/II, doc. 40/15 (11 November 2015); IACHR, 'Towards the Effective Fulfillment of Children's Rights: National Protection Systems', OEA/Ser.L/V/II.166, doc. 206/17 (30 November 2017); IACHR, 'The Situation of Children in the Adult Criminal Justice System in the United States', OAS/Ser.L/V/II. 167, doc. 34 (1 March 2018).

[190] IACtHR, *Juridical Condition and Human Rights of the Child*. Advisory Opinion OC-17/02 of August 28, 2002. Series A no. 17; IACtHR, *Rights and guarantees of children in the context of migration and/or in need of international protection*. Advisory Opinion OC-21/14 of August 19, 2014. Series A no. 21.

[191] IACtHR, *Juridical Condition and Human Rights of the Child*. Advisory Opinion OC-17/02 of August 28, 2002. Series A no. 17, op. paras. 1–2.

[192] IACtHR, *Juridical Condition and Human Rights of the Child*. Advisory Opinion OC-17/02 of August 28, 2002. Series A no. 17, op. paras. 1–2, concurring opinion of Judge A.A. Cançado Trindade para. 3.

[193] R. Shackel, 'The United Nations Convention on the Rights of the Child: A Review of Its Successes and Future Directions' (2003) *Australian International Law Journal* 21, 27; K. Hanson and L. Lundy, 'Does Exactly What It Says on the Tin: A Critical Analysis and Alternative Conceptualisation of the So-Called General Principles of the Convention on the Rights of the Child' (2017) 25 *International Journal of Children's Rights* 285, 287, 291.

The first of the mentioned principles is the prohibition of discrimination; all children are entitled to the respect and protection of all human rights without discrimination of any kind.[194] Recalling the discussion of the principle of equality and non-discrimination from **Section 10.1**, it is important to emphasize that the prohibition of discrimination, especially when applied to children, does not equate to equal treatment for all, but requires the adoption of special measures in order to eliminate structural or systemic conditions of inequality that result in discrimination.[195] The discussion of intersectionality is particularly suitable for understanding discrimination against children, as children that belong to other vulnerable groups experience discrimination from overlapping and interrelated discriminatory social structures.[196] Therefore, the special measures of protection that need to be designed by States to empower children throughout their development should be adapted to the distinct needs of children belonging to different social groups. The Committee on the Rights of the Child, through its general comments has had the opportunity to highlight States' international obligation to adopt special measures of protection, which should be tailored to target the multifaceted and intersectional discrimination experienced by, for instance, indigenous children, disabled children, LGBTQI children,[197] or migrant children—and, in particular, girls —as their intersecting characteristics make them especially vulnerable.[198]

The second principle underlying children's rights is that of the best interests of the child as a primary consideration in all measures concerning children.[199] This principle, originally developed as a legal construction for the judicial determination of child custody, has now become a general principle for all issues affecting children's rights.[200]

---

[194] CRC, General Comment No. 5: General measures of implementation of the Convention, CRC/GC/2003/5 (27 November 2003), para. 12.

[195] CRC, General Comment No. 5: General measures of implementation of the Convention, CRC/GC/2003/5 (27 November 2003), para. 12.

[196] C. Ravnbøl, 'Intersectional Discrimination against Children Discrimination against Romani Children and Anti-Discrimination Measures to Address Child Trafficking', *Innocenti Working Papers* (United Nations), 30 Jun 2009, No. 2009/11, p. 14.

[197] Children who identify within the LGBTQI range of identities have been, unsurprisingly, absent in the text of the treaty, but are starting to find a certain degree of protection in the developing jurisprudence of the Committee. See: K. Sandberg, 'The Rights of LGBTI Children under the Convention on the Rights of the Child' (2015) 33 *Nordic Journal of Human Rights* 337; R. Linde, 'The Rights of Queer Children: The Denial of Children's Sexual Agency in the Convention on the Rights of the Child' (2019) 27 *International Journal of Children's Rights* 719; P. Gerber and A. Timoshanko, 'Is the UN Committee on the Rights of the Child Doing Enough to Protect the Rights of LGBT Children and Children with Same-Sex Parents?' (2021) 21 *Human Rights Law Review* 786.

[198] CRC, General Comment No. 9: The rights of children with disabilities, CRC/C/GC/9 (27 February 2007), paras. 8, 10, 79; CRC, General Comment No. 11: Indigenous children and their rights under the Convention, CRC/C/GC/11 (12 February 2009), paras. 5, 29; CRC and CMW, Joint General Comment (No. 3 CMW/No. 22 CRC) on the general principles regarding the human rights of children in the context of international migration, CMW/C/GC/3-CRC/C/GC/22 (16 November 2017), paras. 16, 18, 23.

[199] CRC, General Comment No. 5: General measures of implementation of the Convention, CRC/GC/2003/5 (27 November 2003), para. 12.

[200] P. Alston, 'The Best Interests Principle: Towards a Reconciliation of Culture and Human Rights' (1994) 8 *International Journal of Law and the Family* 1, 1; D. Gonzalez-Salzberg, *Sexuality and Transsexuality under the European Convention on Human Rights: A Queer Reading of Human Rights Law* (Hart 2019) 143.

Notwithstanding its almost universal acceptance, there is neither a general definition of this concept, nor clear criteria as to how the best interests of children should be established in every situation, leaving the content of this important principle vague and indeterminate to some extent.[201] According to the Committee on the Rights of the Child, the child's best interests is a threefold concept. First, it is a substantive right that entitles children to have their best interests assessed and taken as a primary consideration when making any decisions that concern them. Second, it is a fundamental interpretative legal principle, which mandates that when a legal provision is susceptible to multiple interpretations, the one that better serves the child's best interests should be chosen. Lastly, it is also a procedural rule, which should guide the decision-making process of any determination that will affect children, securing that the different possible impacts of the decision are examined and that the child's best interests are weighed against other policy considerations.[202]

The third principle concerns children's right to development.[203] Within this context, development should be interpreted in the broadest possible sense, as a holistic concept, embracing children's physical, mental, spiritual, moral, psychological, and social development.[204] Children's development is heavily determined by the environment in which they live; hence, the creation of a safe and supportive environment entails the duty of addressing both children's immediate environment (for example, family, schools, public services), as well as the wider community, which requires States to formulate policies and adopt legislation and programmes to foster the holistic development of children.[205] While the main obligation upon States is to create an environment that promotes and ensures the holistic development of every child under their jurisdiction, a duty to engage in international co-operation and assistance to contribute to the development of children worldwide can also be found under the international law of human rights.[206]

The fourth and final principle refers to children's right to freely express their views on all matters affecting them, given due weight to these views according to the

---

[201] S. Parker, 'The Best Interests of the Child – Principles and Problems' (1994) 8 International Journal of Law and the Family 26, 26; M. Freeman, A Commentary on the United Nations Convention on the Rights of the Child, Art. 3: The Best Interests of the Child (Nijhoff 2007) 27; W. Vandenhole, G. Türkelli, and S. Lembrechts, Children's Rights: A Commentary on the Convention on the Rights of the Child and its Protocols (Elgar 2019) 63.

[202] CRC, General Comment No. 14: On the right of the child to have his or her best interests taken as a primary consideration, CRC/C/GC/14 (29 May 2013), para. 6.

[203] Concerns as to the lack of clarity of the precise meaning and content of the concept of children's right to development have also been raised. See: N. Peleg, 'Time to Grow Up: The UN Committee on the Rights of the Child's Jurisprudence of the Right to Development' in M. Freeman (ed.), Law and Childhood Studies: Current Legal Issues (OUP 2012) 371–391, 389–390.

[204] CRC, General Comment No. 5: General measures of implementation of the Convention, CRC/GC/2003/5 (27 November 2003), para. 12.

[205] CRC, General Comment No. 4: Adolescent health and development in the context of the Convention, CRC/GC/2003/4 (1 July 2003), para. 14. See also: CRC, General Comment No. 16: State obligations regarding the impact of the business sector on children's rights, CRC/C/GC/16 (17 April 2013), paras. 19, 20.

[206] M. Nowak, A Commentary on the United Nations Convention on the Rights of the Child, Article 6: the Right to Life, Survival and Development: The Right to Life, Survival and Development (Brill 2005) 49.

child's age and maturity.[207] This principle emphasizes the role of children as active participants in the promotion, protection, and monitoring of their own rights.[208] It is fundamental for States to comprehend that children's views may add relevant perspectives and experiences to the process of elaboration of laws and policies susceptible to affect children's rights,[209] as well as to the evaluation of the measures adopted.[210] States should promote children's 'participation', which encapsulates the continuous process of 'information-sharing and dialogue' between children and adults,[211] in which children can learn how their views are taken into account and influence the outcome of the decision-making process concerning policies and programmes affecting their rights, both as a group and as individuals.[212] Consequently, States should encourage children to form an autonomous view on matters susceptible to affect them, providing an environment in which children feel respected and secure when freely expressing their opinions.[213] Moreover, the understanding of what sort of matters might be considered to affect children is not to be restricted to youth-specific policies, but extends as well to areas not typically associated with children that, nevertheless, affect them, and covers subjects as diverse as healthcare, the environment, or the media.[214] It is, ultimately, up to the children themselves to determine whether a particular matter is of relevance to them.

10.3.2.1 The evolving capacity and maturity of children

As holders of rights, even the youngest of children are entitled to express their feelings, views, and wishes concerning matters that affect them, and these should be given due weight in accordance with their respective age and maturity.[215] Participation in the decision-making process of measures affecting children does not require them to have comprehensive knowledge of all aspects of the issue at stake, but a level of understanding that is appropriate for forming an opinion on the matter should suffice.[216] The weight

---

[207] CRC, General Comment No. 12: The right of the child to be heard, CRC/C/GC/12 (20 July 2009), para. 15.
[208] CRC, General Comment No. 5: General measures of implementation of the Convention, CRC/GC/2003/5 (27 November 2003), para. 12.
[209] In fact, children had the opportunity to participate in the process of the drafting of the UN Convention on the Rights of the Child itself. See: G. Van Bueren, 'The UN Convention on the Rights of the Child' (1991) 3 *Journal of Child Law* 63, 63.
[210] CRC, General Comment No. 12: The right of the child to be heard, CRC/C/GC/12 (20 July 2009), para. 12.
[211] K. Sandberg, 'The Convention on the Rights of the Child and the Vulnerability of Children' (2015) 84 *Nordic Journal of International Law* 221, 246.
[212] CRC, General Comment No. 12: The right of the child to be heard, CRC/C/GC/12 (20 July 2009), paras. 3, 13.
[213] CRC, General Comment No. 12: The right of the child to be heard, CRC/C/GC/12 (20 July 2009), paras. 11, 23, 49.
[214] W. Vandenhole, G. Türkelli, and S. Lembrechts, Children's Rights: A Commentary on the Convention on the Rights of the Child and its Protocols (Elgar 2019) 149.
[215] CRC, General Comment No. 7: Implementing child rights in early childhood, CRC/C/GC/7/Rev.1 (20 September 2006) para. 14. On this topic, see: L. Krappmann, 'The Weight of the Child's View (Article 12 of the Convention on the Rights of the Child)' (2010) 18 *International Journal of Children's Rights* 501.
[216] CRC, General Comment No. 12: The right of the child to be heard, CRC/C/GC/12 (20 July 2009), para. 21.

that is given to children's views should then reflect their level of understanding of the issue.[217] No strict age limit should be set on the right of children to express their views, as age alone cannot uniformly determined capacity for understanding, nor maturity; these can only be assessed on a case-by-case basis.[218]

As mentioned in **Section 10.3**, children are a rather heterogeneous collective, encompassing individuals with varying degrees of capacities, which evolve through the process of maturation and learning, allowing them to progressively acquire competencies, understanding, and increasing levels of agency to assume responsibility and exercise their rights.[219] Bearing in mind the important differences among children during different stages of their development, the Committee on the Rights of the Child has issued two specific general comments, one focusing on early childhood (below the age of eight years), and one focusing on adolescence (covering the period between ten and eighteen years of age). In these, the Committee engaged with specificities as to the different range of measures States must adopt to provide due protection to children's rights in their different stages of development.[220] A central common theme throughout the Committee's views is the recognition that all children, no matter how young, are social actors,[221] with particular interests, capacities, and vulnerabilities.[222] All children are entitled to measures of special protection and, according to their evolving capacities, require guidance and support for the progressive exercise of their rights.[223]

CRC, *Y.B. and N.S. v. Belgium*, CRC/C/79/D/12/2017 (5 November 2018)

The case concerned a Moroccan child who had been taken in by a couple residing in Belgium under a *kafalah* arrangement, which consists of the fostering of an abandoned child. While a kafalah arrangement does not technically create a parent–child relationship, it does entail a commitment to take responsibility for the protection, education, and maintenance of the child, as a parent would for their children. As the kafalah agreement did not allow for a visa application on the grounds of family reunification under Belgian law, the couple applied for a long-term visa on humanitarian grounds to allow them to live in Belgium together with

---

[217] W. Vandenhole, G. Türkelli, and S. Lembrechts, Children's Rights: A Commentary on the Convention on the Rights of the Child and its Protocols (Elgar 2019) 152.

[218] CRC, General Comment No. 12: The right of the child to be heard, CRC/C/GC/12 (20 July 2009), paras. 21, 29

[219] CRC, General Comment No. 20: On the implementation of the rights of the child during adolescence, CRC/C/GC/20 (6 December 2016), para. 18.

[220] CRC, General Comment No. 7: Implementing child rights in early childhood, CRC/C/GC/7/Rev.1 (20 September 2006); CRC, General Comment No. 20: On the implementation of the rights of the child during adolescence, CRC/C/GC/20 (6 December 2016).

[221] M. Woodhead, 'Early Childhood Development: A Question of Rights' (2005) 37 *International Journal of Early Childhood* 79, 95.

[222] CRC, General Comment No. 7: Implementing child rights in early childhood, CRC/C/GC/7/Rev.1 (20 September 2006), para. 2.c.

[223] CRC, General Comment No. 7: Implementing child rights in early childhood, CRC/C/GC/7/Rev.1 (20 September 2006), para. 3.

their child. However, their request was denied by the Immigration Office and, while an appeal against the refusal was successful, the administrative authorities refused to issue the requested visa or even a shorter one that would have allowed the child to join them in Belgium.

The Committee found that the refusal to grant the child a visa to join their foster parents in Belgium amounted to multiple violations of the Convention on the Rights of the Child. It highlighted that in all actions concerning children, the best interests of the child must be a primary consideration and that the child's best interests must be assessed and determined in the light of the specific circumstances of the particular child (para. 8.3). It considered that when the second decision on the application for a humanitarian visa was made, the child was already five years old and would have been capable of forming her own views regarding the possibility of living permanently with her foster parents in Belgium (para. 8.8). Therefore, not allowing her to exercise her right to be heard during the proceedings amounted to a violation of such a right (Article 12), as well as of the best interests of the child (Article 3) under the Convention.

The Committee also found that when determining the best interests of the child, for the purpose of deciding whether to grant a residence permit to the child, the State should have taken into consideration the de facto ties forged with her foster parents, as the term 'family' must be interpreted in the broadest possible sense, including biological, adoptive, and foster parents, as well as members of the extended family or community as provided for by local custom. However, no consideration was given to the de facto family ties that existed in the case. On the contrary, the State failed to assess the visa application in a positive, humane, and expeditious manner, in breach of the child's right to family reunification under Article 10 of the Convention (paras. 8.11 and 8.12).

The Committee ruled that the State party was under the obligation to urgently reconsider the application for a visa in a positive spirit, ensuring the best interests of the child as a primary consideration, taking into account the family ties that have been forged, and securing that the child's views were heard (para. 9).

Undoubtedly, the approach to ensure the realization of the rights of adolescents differs significantly from those adopted for younger children.[224] Adolescents, in particular, should be appreciated as 'agents of change' and key social assets with the potential to contribute positively to society.[225] Therefore, States are under the obligation to foster an environment that acknowledges the intrinsic value of adolescence, adopting legislation and policies to help them thrive, explore their emerging identities, beliefs, sexualities, and opportunities, and build their capacity for making free, informed, and positive decisions and life choices.[226] At the same time, an important warning issued to States by the Committee is that, especially during adolescence, gender inequalities become

---

[224] CRC, General Comment No. 20: On the implementation of the rights of the child during adolescence, CRC/C/GC/20 (6 December 2016), para. 1.

[225] CRC, General Comment No. 20: On the implementation of the rights of the child during adolescence, CRC/C/GC/20 (6 December 2016), para. 2.

[226] CRC, General Comment No. 20: On the implementation of the rights of the child during adolescence, CRC/C/GC/20 (6 December 2016), para. 26.

more significant, with manifestations of discrimination against girls often intensifying, which can lead to more serious violations of their rights, such as forced marriage, early pregnancy, genital mutilation, gender-based violence, and sex trafficking.[227] Consequently, States are required to adopt proactive measures to challenge patriarchal gender norms, modify cultural standards that ascribe lower status to girls, and promote the empowerment of girls.[228]

> ECtHR, *M.K. v. Greece*, App. no. 51312/16, 1 February 2018.
>
> The case was about a child custody dispute. The applicant, a mother of two children, had been awarded custody of them following her divorce. She subsequently relocated from Greece to France, leaving her children in the temporary care of their grandmother but, after visitation, their father refused to return them to the grandmother's home. Following litigation, the domestic courts ordered that the youngest child was to move to France with the applicant, while the other child was allowed to remain in Greece with their father. However, after visiting his father and brother in Greece, the youngest child did not return to France, where he was living with his mother.
>
> The applicant initiated judicial proceedings to have the judgment awarding her custody enforced. The child, aged thirteen at the time, was heard repeatedly during the proceedings and unequivocally expressed his desire to remain in Greece with his brother and father. Despite the existence of a firm judgement, he remained in Greece. The applicant claimed before the European Court that the Greek authorities' failure to enforce the judicial decision granting her custody of her youngest son amounted to a breach of her right to respect for her family life (Article 8).
>
> However, the Court did not find a violation of the Convention. In so deciding, the Court placed special emphasis on the child's right to be heard and to participate in the decision-making process of any family proceedings affecting him. It ruled that the wishes expressed by the child, who was considered to have sufficient understanding of the situation and capacity to freely express his desired living arrangements, should have been paramount in the proceedings determining custody, and that the State had acted within its margin of appreciation by not enforcing a decision made against the child's wishes (paras. 91 and 93).

10.3.3 CRITICAL DEBATES: CHILDREN IN STREET SITUATIONS

The affliction of children in street situations is a long-standing reality worldwide. Children in street situations are a heterogeneous group that includes children who actually depend on the streets to live or work, as well as a wider population of children who have a strong connection with public spaces and for whom the street plays a vital role in their everyday

---

[227] CRC, General Comment No. 20: On the implementation of the rights of the child during adolescence, CRC/C/GC/20 (6 December 2016), para. 27.

[228] CRC, General Comment No. 20: On the implementation of the rights of the child during adolescence, CRC/C/GC/20 (6 December 2016), paras. 27–28.

lives.[229] The heterogeneity of the group is also marked by other personal characteristics, such as their age, gender, ethnicity, and sexual orientation, among others, which determine that their experiences, risks, and needs are different from one another.[230] Regardless of the level of socioeconomic development, under the international law of human rights, all States are under the obligation to adopt holistic and long-term strategies, and to make the necessary budget allocations, to address the needs of children in street situations.[231] Among the most essential obligations upon States, is the need to adapt their domestic legislation to suppress legal provisions that discriminate against children and their families on the basis of their street situation, including the abolition of any provision allowing for the arbitrary removal of children and their families from the streets or public spaces, as well as the suppression of any criminal norm that disproportionately affects children in street situations, such as those targeting begging, breach of curfews, loitering, vagrancy, and running away from home.[232]

Moreover, States should have legislation and policies in place that holistically address children in street situations. These strategic measures should be developed and implemented in close collaboration with key stakeholders, including children in street situations, who are themselves experts in their own lives.[233] These measures must tackle the multiple causes that lead children into street situations, ranging from structural inequalities to family violence.[234] The adopted programmes should account for the primordial role of the State, as main duty bearer with regards to children's rights, but also acknowledge the role of non-State actors, from parents and caregivers to the wider civil society and the business sector, as complementary actors in the protection of children's rights.[235] States should ensure that their child protection systems provide effective services on the street, including trained social workers, which can help children reconnect with family, local community services, and the wider society. Ultimately, States bear responsibility for ensuring that children in street situations can exercise their rights and gain access to basic services, such as health, education, justice, culture, and recreation.[236]

> ACERWC, *The Centre for human Rights (University of Pretoria) and La Rencontre Afaricaine pour la Defense des Droits de l'Homme (Senegal) v. Senegal.* **Decision 003/Com/001/2012 (15 April 2014).**
>
> The case concerned as many as 100,000 children between the ages of four and twelve—known as 'talibés'—who had been sent by their parents to Qur'anic schools ('daaras') in urban centres of Senegal to receive religious education, but were actually forced into begging on the streets

---

[229] CRC, General Comment No. 21: On children in street situations, CRC/C/GC/21 (21 June 2017), para. 4.
[230] CRC, General Comment No. 21: On children in street situations, CRC/C/GC/21 (21 June 2017), para. 6.
[231] CRC, General Comment No. 21: On children in street situations, CRC/C/GC/21 (21 June 2017), para. 13.
[232] CRC, General Comment No. 21: On children in street situations, CRC/C/GC/21 (21 June 2017), para. 14.
[233] CRC, General Comment No. 21: On children in street situations, CRC/C/GC/21 (21 June 2017), paras. 13–14.
[234] CRC, General Comment No. 21: On children in street situations, CRC/C/GC/21 (21 June 2017), para. 16.
[235] CRC, General Comment No. 21: On children in street situations, CRC/C/GC/21 (21 June 2017), para. 15.
[236] CRC, General Comment No. 21: On children in street situations, CRC/C/GC/21 (21 June 2017), para. 19.

by their instructors (paras. 2–3). To make matters even worse, these children were living under conditions of extreme deprivation and were forced to gain a certain level of daily collections or face further punishment (paras. 8–9). Despite the existence of legislation that criminalized forcing children into begging, it was claimed by the applicants that little effort was made by the State to put an end to the situation (paras. 3–4).

Assessing the situation, the African Committee of Experts on the Rights and Welfare of the Child found the State responsible for multiple ongoing violations of the African Children's Charter. It highlighted that the State was in violation of the Charter not only for its direct actions, but also for its omissions, for failing to protect children from the actions of third parties. Among the breaches found, the Committee highlighted the Charter's explicit prohibition on the use of children for begging (Article 29.b) and considered that, although the State had adopted legislation to comply with this provision, its failure to seriously enforce it disclosed a breach of the best interests of the child, of the prohibition of child labour, and of the obligation to eliminate harmful practices against children (Articles 4, 16, and 21) (paras. 37–39 and 73). It also ruled on the violation of the rights to survival and development, health, and of the prohibition against child abuse (Articles 5, 14, and 16), given the poor living conditions the children experienced in the daaras, since they were suffering from malnutrition, were not provided with clothes or shoes, and had no access to healthcare, education, clean water, a safe and clean environment in which to live, or protection from abuse and neglect (paras. 42–43, 55–56, and 68).

As to the right to education (Article 11), the Committee acknowledged that the existence of the daara system was partly due to the State's own failure in its obligation to provide children within its jurisdiction of an education that was available, accessible, and acceptable. Additionally, the State was then failing to monitor the education provided by third parties, securing its compliance with the respect of children's rights (paras. 48–50). Lastly, the Committee also found a breach of the prohibition of child trafficking (Article 29), given that many of the children in Senegal's daaras were trafficked from other States, including Guiné-Bissau and Mali (paras. 79–81).

The Committee issued an extensive list of recommendation for the State to undertake to redress the violations committed. These included, to ensure that all talibés were immediately taken back from the streets to their families; to provide them with appropriate psychological, medical, and social assistance; and to make sure that all perpetrators were brought to justice and that the applied penalties were commensurate to their crimes. It also ordered general measures of reparation, such as to review the national education policy and ensure that basic and compulsory education was made available for free, as well as to integrate the daaras into the formal education system and undertake regular inspections of them to ensure their compliance with the rights enshrined in the Charter, including minimum standards of health, safety, hygiene, and education content (para. 82).

CRC, *S.E.M.A v. France*, CRC/C/92/D/130/2020 (25 January 2023).

The case concerned S.E.M.A., an unaccompanied migrant child from Pakistan, who arrived in France and had to live in a street situation for almost a year and a half, as the authorities refused to recognize him as a minor and failed to provide him with emergency shelter and access to social services and education. The child underwent a flawed age determination procedure, in which the copies of his identity documents were neither trusted, nor validated with the pertinent Pakistani authorities, and where a short interview was conducted without an interpreter that spoke his birth language. The outcome of this initial assessment left him in a street situation, deprived of access to the child welfare system of the State. The decision's appeal to the judiciary was also unsuccessful. Even though original identity documents were provided to the court, these were disregarded, once again without seeking validation from the pertinent authorities. Recourse to the court of appeal took a year, during which S.E.M.A. remained unable to access child services, despite his request. Therefore, he was left without any support or means of subsistence, during the Covid-19 pandemic. By the time the court of appeal held its hearing, S.E.M.A. had reached the age of majority.

Before the Committee, the author complained of the breach of multiple rights by the situation he was forced to endured. The Committee agreed with his complaint. It found violations of the best interests of the child principle (Article 3), his right to be heard (Article 12), and the right to preserve his identity as a minor (Article 8). In particular, the Committee recalled its prior opinion on the fundamental characteristic that age assessment procedures should have, including being 'carried out in a prompt, child-friendly, gender-sensitive and culturally appropriate manner, including interviews of children ... in a language the child understands' (para. 8.6). And it reaffirmed that in the event of any doubts, the individual under assessment should be given the benefit of the doubt.

Moreover, the Committee ruled that France's failure to provide S.E.M.A. with measures of protection, despite his situation of abandonment and extreme vulnerability in the context of a health pandemic not only entailed a breach of the obligation to provide special assistance to children deprived of their family environment (Article 20), but also amounted to a violation of the prohibition of inhuman and degrading treatment (Article 37) (para. 8.11).

Consequently, the Committee recommended France to adopt a range of measures of reparation. These included: providing S.E.M.A. with the opportunity to regularize his administrative status in France, as well as amending the procedures for determining the age of young persons claiming to be minors, so situations like the one in this case did not happen again. The Committee clarified that, to be compliant with UNCRC, such procedure should be swift; appropriate to the capacity and maturity of the person assessed; include a qualified representative free of charge; and provide remedies to dispute its outcome, which should be prompt, effective, and accessible (para. 10).

10.4 GROUP RIGHTS

The discussion in **Chapter 9** and **Chapter 10** so far has focused on the rights of individuals, even if these were exercised collectively or were held as members of specific groups. The discussion in this section now turns to 'group rights' in the sense of fundamental rights that belong to a particular collective or people rather than to their members individually.[237] There are different examples of this type of rights, such as the right to peace, the right to development, or environmental rights,[238] but the most paradigmatic illustration of a collective right is the right to self-determination.[239]

10.4.1 THE RIGHT TO SELF-DETERMINATION

The principle of self-determination of peoples finds its genesis as a legal concept under international law in the aftermath of the First World War.[240] At the international level, both Lenin and US President Wilson have been identified as two of the main supporters of self-determination, although with a rather different understanding of this idea. Lenin proposed self-determination as a tool that could promote peoples' right to be free from external domination, which would apply both to the liberation of people under colonial subjugation as well as to ethnic or national groups living as minorities within a State.[241] Wilson initially understood this principle to encompass the right of people within a State to freely select the form of government, but his interpretation later extended to consider it a suitable guide for re-drawing the political borders of Europe, in particular with regard to the division of the Ottoman and Austro-Hungarian empires,[242] although allowing for important exceptions when it came to the population of the defeated States.[243] Nevertheless, at the end of the war, strong opposition from the victorious warring States, especially from those with colonial interests, led to any references to self-determination being excluded from both the Peace Treaties and the Covenant of the League of Nations.[244]

The principle of self-determination again became prominent during the Second World War, featuring in the 'Atlantic Charter' (discussed in **Section 1.2.6**). In that

---

[237] CCPR, General Comment No. 31: The Nature of the General Legal Obligation Imposed on States Parties to the Covenant, CCPR/C/21/Rev.1/Add. 13 (26 May 2004), para. 9. See also: Y. Dinstein, 'Human Rights of Peoples and Minorities' (1976) 25 *International and Comparative Law Quarterly* 102, 102–103; R. Kiwanuka, 'The Meaning of "People" in the African Charter on Human and Peoples' Rights' (1988) 82 *American Journal of International Law* 80, 85.

[238] African Charter, Arts. 20–24; UNGA, Resolution 41/128, 'Declaration on the Right to Development' (4 December 1986); UNGA, 'Declaration on the Right to Peace', A/RES/71/189 (2 February 2017); HRC, Resolution 48/13, 'The human right to a clean, healthy and sustainable environment', A/HRC/48/L.23/Rev. 1 (5 October 2021).

[239] ICESCR, Art. 1; ICCPR, Art. 1.

[240] Although the origin of the principle itself can be traced further back to the late eighteenth century with the independence of the British colonies of the Americas and the French Revolution. See: A. Cassese, *Self-determination of peoples: A legal reappraisal* (CUP 1995) 11; J. Castellino, 'Territorial Integrity and the "Right" to Self-Determination: An Examination of the Conceptual Tools' (2008) 33 *Brooklyn Journal of International Law* 503, 513.

[241] A. Cassese, *Self-determination of peoples: A legal reappraisal* (CUP 1995) 14–17; K. Senaratne, *Internal Self-determination in International Law: History, Theory, and Practice* (CUP 2021) 23–25.

[242] A. Cassese, *Self-determination of peoples: A legal reappraisal* (CUP 1995) 19–20; K. Senaratne, *Internal Self-determination in International Law: History, Theory, and Practice* (CUP 2021) 25–27.

[243] M. Shahabuddin, *Ethnicity and International law: Histories, Politics and Practices* (CUP 2016) 101–102.

[244] A. Cassese, *Self-determination of peoples: A legal reappraisal* (CUP 1995) 23; M. Shahabuddin, *Ethnicity and International law: Histories, Politics and Practices* (CUP 2016) 100–101.

joint declaration, made by US President Roosevelt and UK Prime Minister Churchill, self-determination appeared twice among the common principles on which a better post-war future could be built. The declaration stated that any territorial changes should be based on the wishes of the peoples concerned and that the form of government adopted should also be a choice of those peoples.[245] Certainly, Roosevelt's and Churchill's understanding of these statements regarding self-determination were not identical. As Churchill expressed to Parliament later that year, the proclaimed principle of self-determination should be understood to apply to the territories invaded by Nazi Germany but not to those under colonial territories under British domination.[246]

The inclusion of the principle of self-determination as a legal norm within the UN Charter was also contentious. The draft Charter agreed by the 'Four Powers'—the USA, the UK, the Soviet Union, and China—for discussion in the 1945 San Francisco Conference only included a reference to self-determination due to the pressure of the Soviet Union.[247] In San Francisco, anxieties as to the exact meaning and scope of this principle led to different objections from multiple States, including fears of secessionism or even of military annexations.[248] At the end, the principle of self-determination of peoples appeared recognized twice within the Charter, including within its first article, which affirms the development of friendly relations among nations, as a purpose of the organization itself, which must be based on the principles of equal rights and self-determination.[249] However, the meaning and scope ascribed to this legal principle remained uncertain;[250] thus, it became the task of States and UN organs—especially, the General Assembly—to develop its content through their practice.[251]

10.4.1.1 Self-determination as a 'human' right

Within the United Nations, the Soviets' understanding of self-determination, meaning the right of peoples to be free from external domination, gained support from the States from the Global South. Self-determination became an important rhetorical

---

[245] F.D. Roosevelt, State of the Union Address (6 January 1941). Available: https://millercenter.org/the-presidency/presidential-speeches/january-6-1941-state-union-four-freedoms (accessed on 13 April 2023).

[246] A. Cassese, *Self-determination of peoples: A legal reappraisal* (CUP 1995) 37; B. Ibhawoh, *Human Rights in Africa* (CUP 2018) 130–131.

[247] A. Cassese, *Self-determination of peoples: A legal reappraisal* (CUP 1995) 37; B. Ibhawoh, *Human Rights in Africa* (CUP 2018), 38. See: A. Cristescu, 'The Right to Self-determination, Historical and Current Developments on the Basis of United Nations Instruments', UN Doc. E/CN.4/Sub.2/404/Rev.1 (1981), para. 16.

[248] A. Cassese, *Self-determination of peoples: A legal reappraisal* (CUP 1995) 39–40.

[249] Besides being expressly mentioned in Arts. 1.2, and 55, the idea of self-determination appears implicitly in Chapters XI and XII of the Charter with regards to 'non-self-governing territories' and the trusteeship system. See: A. Cristescu, 'The Right to Self-determination, Historical and Current Developments on the Basis of United Nations Instruments', UN Doc. E/CN.4/Sub.2/404/Rev.1 (1981), para. 23.

[250] Different authors have proposed quite a pessimistic view as to the scope of the principle at the time of its adoption. See: R. Higgins, *Problems & Process: International Law and How We Use It* (OUP 1994) 111–113; A. Cassese, *Self-determination of peoples: A legal reappraisal* (CUP 1995) 41–43.

[251] R. Higgins, *Problems & Process: International Law and How We Use It* (OUP 1994) 113.

devise used in the fight against colonialism and racism, neo-colonialism and the foreign exploitation of natural resources, and the illegal occupation of the territory by another State.[252] Already in the early years, the UN General Assembly, placed special emphasis on the importance of self-determination,[253] even acknowledging it as a right of peoples that acted as a prerequisite for the enjoyment of all fundamental human rights.[254] Concordantly, and despite the opposition of Western States—especially, those which controlled colonial territories[255]—the Assembly decided that self-determination, as a collective right, was to be included in the text of the international Covenants on human rights that were being drafted at the time.[256] Moreover, as acknowledged by the International Court of Justice in its Advisory Opinion on the *Chagos Archipelago*, it was a resolution of the General Assembly that cemented the binding character of the right to self-determination of peoples, as a customary norm, even before its recognition by the mentioned treaties.[257] Resolution 1514 (XV) of 1960, on the Granting of Independence to Colonial Countries and Peoples, affirmed in normative terms that: 'All peoples have the right to self-determination; [and] by virtue of that right they freely determine their political status and freely pursue their economic, social and cultural development.'[258]

The binding nature of the right to self-determination was confirmed by shared Article 1 of ICCPR and ICESCR, which established that 'All peoples have the right of self-determination,'[259] pursuant to which they have a collective right to freely determine their political status, pursue their economic, social, and cultural development, and dispose of their natural wealth and resources.[260] On the interpretation of this common provision, the Human Rights Committee has affirmed that the right to self-determination is an inalienable right of particular importance, given that its realization acts as an essential condition for the effective guarantee and observance of individual human rights, which justifies its placement within the Covenants before all other human rights.[261]

Further insights into the importance of the right to self-determination were provided by the International Court of Justice. The Court has referred to this right as one of the essential principles of contemporary international law and clarified that it is a right

---

[252] A. Cassese, *Self-determination of peoples: A legal reappraisal* (CUP 1995) 45–46; K. Senaratne, *Internal Self-determination in International Law: History, Theory, and Practice* (CUP 2021) 134–135.

[253] For a detailed discussion of the development of the right to self-determination under the UN, see: ICJ, *Legal Consequences of the Separation of The Chagos Archipelago from Mauritius in 1965*, Advisory Opinion, I.C.J. Reports 2019, p. 95, separate opinion of Judge Cançado Trindade.

[254] UNGA, Resolution 637 (VII) of 16 December 1952.

[255] A. Cassese, *Self-determination of peoples: A legal reappraisal* (CUP 1995) 49–50.

[256] UNGA, Resolution 421 (V) of 4 December 1950; UNGA, Resolution 545 (VI) of 5 February 1952.

[257] ICJ, *Legal Consequences of the Separation of The Chagos Archipelago from Mauritius in 1965*, Advisory Opinion, I.C.J. Reports 2019, p. 95, para. 152.

[258] UNGA, Resolution 1514 (XV) of 14 December 1960. However, self-determination does not always equate with independence, as the UN recognized that free association with another State or even integration with a State can also be valid exercises of self-determination, so long that is the expression of the free and genuine will of the people. See: UNGA, Resolution 1541(XV) (15 December 1960).

[259] ICCPR, Art. 1.1; ICESCR, Art. 1.1.   [260] ICCPR, Arts. 1.1, 1.2; ICESCR Arts. 1.1, 1.2.

[261] CCPR, General Comment No. 12: Right to self-determination (13 March 1984), paras. 1–2.

that entails *erga omnes* obligations, meaning that every State has the duty to promote, through individual and joint actions, the realization of the right to self-determination of all peoples.[262] In our days, the right to self-determination has even entered the realm of *jus cogens*, with no derogations admitted from it,[263] as recently affirmed by the African Court of Human and Peoples' Rights.[264]

> **International Court of Justice,** *Legal Consequences of the Separation of the Chagos Archipelago from Mauritius in 1965***, Advisory Opinion, I.C.J. Reports 2019, p. 95.**
>
> In this advisory opinion requested by the UN General Assembly, the International Court of Justice clarified the situation of the Chagos Archipelago under international law. This archipelago, consisting of sixty-five islands, had been under the colonial domination of the United Kingdom since 1814, when its control was transferred from France, and governed as dependencies of (the colony of) Mauritius until 1965.[265] In 1965, the UK proceeded to the detachment of the islands from Mauritius and the constitution of a new colonial territory. The following year, the UK concluded an agreement with the United States, by which it leased the islands to the USA for fifty years for the establishment of a US military base in the Chagos Archipelago, including a commitment to de-populate the islands. In compliance with the agreement, the Chagossians were expelled from the islands and the military based, which subsists to our days, was established.
>
> In its advisory opinion, the ICJ affirmed that the right to self-determination of peoples was already part of customary international law by the end of 1960 and that the exercise of such a right required respect for the territorial integrity of non-self-governing territories. Applied to the situation of Mauritius and the Chagos Islands, the Court affirmed that the detachment of the Chagos Archipelago in 1965 did not allow for the lawful completion of the process of decolonization of Mauritius when reaching its independence in 1968, because part of its territory remained under colonial administration. In turn, this led the Court to consider the United Kingdom's continued administration of the Chagos Archipelago to amount to an internationally wrongful act of a continuing character. The Court also opined that it was for the UN General Assembly to establish the modalities needed for ensuring the completion of the decolonization of Mauritius.

---

[262] ICJ, *Case concerning East Timor (Portugal v. Australia)*, Judgment, I.C.J. Reports 1995, p. 90, para. 29; ICJ, *Legal Consequences of the Construction of a Wall in the Occupied Palestinian Territory*, Advisory Opinion, I.C.J. Reports 2004, p. 136, para. 155; ICJ, *Legal Consequences of the Separation of The Chagos Archipelago from Mauritius in 1965*, Advisory Opinion, I.C.J. Reports 2019, p. 95, para. 180.

[263] ICJ, *Legal Consequences of the Separation of The Chagos Archipelago from Mauritius in 1965*, Advisory Opinion, I.C.J. Reports 2019, p. 95, separate opinion of Judge Cançado Trindade, para. 118; ILC, Fifth report on peremptory norms of general international law (jus cogens) by Dire Tladi, Special Rapporteur, A/CN.4/747 (24 January 2022), conclusion 23.

[264] ACtHPR, *Bernard Anbataayela Mornah v. Benin, Burkina Faso, Côte d'Ivoire, Ghana, Mali, Malawi, Tanzania, and Tunisia*. Judgment, App. no. 028/2018 (22 September 2022), para. 298.

[265] For a discussion of the complex historical, legal, and political context of the case, see: D. Gonzalez-Salzberg and L. Hodson, 'A policy of "quiet disregard": the Chagos Islands, Islanders and international law' (2019) 19 *Revista do Instituto Brasileiro de Direitos Humanos* 107.

ACtHPR, *Bernard Anbataayela Mornah v. Benin, Burkina Faso, Côte d'Ivoire, Ghana, Mali, Malawi, Tanzania, and Tunisia.* Judgment, App. no. 028/2018 (22 September 2022).

The case was brought to the Court by the Chairman of the Convention People's Party of Ghana, on behalf of the Sahrawi people, claiming the failure of the eight respondent States to safeguard the independence of the Sahrawi Arab Democratic Republic (SADR), due to the continued occupation of its territory—known as 'Western Sahara'—by Morocco.

As context, the applicant explained that it was the admission of the Sahrawi Arab Democratic Republic to the Organization of African Unity that led to the withdrawal of Morocco from the OAU in 1984. His claim was that the admission of Morocco to the African Union in 2017 was inconsistent with the objectives and principles of the AU, enshrined in its Constitutive Act, the African Charter on Democracy, Elections and Governance, and the African Charter of Human and Peoples' Rights. He alleged that the respondent States were individually and collectively responsible for not opposing Morocco's admission and, in general, for failing to take action to protect the sovereignty, independence, and territorial integrity of the SADR and, among others, the right of its people to self-determination and to dispose of their wealth and natural resources (paras. 16, 86, and 122).

The Court considered that the main issue at stake was that of the right to delf-determination of the people of the SADR and whether the omissions of the respondent States entailed their international responsibility on the matter (paras. 285–287). The Court acknowledged that the occupation of the SADR by Morocco is unlawful under international law, in contravention with the right to self-determination of the people of SADR (paras. 301–303). It further affirmed that both negative and positive obligations stem from the right to self-determination and that States are required to adopt both individual and joint action to facilitate the realization of this right, including by providing assistance to people struggling for independence and freedom from domination, obligations that are *erga omnes* in character (paras. 297, 299, and 307).

However, the Court stopped short of finding the respondent States responsible for breaching their obligations with regards to the right to self-determination. It considered that although these States were under an obligation to adopt measures to facilitate the exercise of the right to self-determination of the Sahrawi people, there was no set list of actions that must be taken. The Court considered that stopping Morocco's admission to the AU was not among the mandatory measures to be adopted, as ultimately, the decision to admit the State was made by the AU itself, a separate entity to that of its Member States (paras. 314 and 318–319).

Consequently, the Court ruled that the respondent States had not failed to comply with their obligations with respect of the right to self-determination of the Sahrawi people, but it reminded them of their collective responsibility to find a permanent solution to the ongoing occupation and of their individual duty to avoid adopting any measures that would give recognition to such occupation as lawful (paras. 322–323).

Concerning the scope of the right to self-determination, this right has at least two dimensions, an internal and an external one. The first one is the Wilsonian conception of self-determination, which refers to the right of peoples to determine their form of government, granting a right to be free from anti-democratic or oppressive actions of their own State, while the latter—Lenin's understanding—concerns the right to be free from external domination, which applies to cases of colonial and neo-colonial subjugation and of foreign occupation.[266] Moreover, the right of peoples to self-determination is not limited to the political sphere, but includes economic, social, and cultural aspects, as expressly recognized by common Article 1 of ICCPR and ICESCR,[267] which has been referred to as socioeconomic self-determination.[268] For its part, the African Charter on Human and Peoples' Rights has provided an ever more developed recognition of the right to self-determination. The Charter weaved self-determination into the right of peoples to existence and explicitly embodied 'the right of colonized or oppressed peoples to free themselves from the bonds of domination and the right to the get assistance of the State Parties in their struggle for freedom'.[269] This provision is further strengthened by the subsequent Charter article, which recognizes the right of all peoples to benefit from the natural wealth and resources that traditionally belonged to them.[270]

Notwithstanding the importance of the right to self-determination, many uncertainties surrounding its scope and exercise remain.[271] While it might be clear that entire populations of recognized States or colonial territories enjoy the right to self-determination, it is uncertain whether sub-groups within such populations could also enjoy all or certain aspects of this right.[272] In other words, as discussed in **Section 3.3.2**, it could be difficult to determine which collectives actually qualify as 'peoples' to exercise the different aspects of the right to self-determination.[273] Closely related

---

[266] Special Rapporteur of the Sub-Commission on Prevention of Discrimination and Protection of Minorities (H. Gros Espiell), The Right to Self-Determination: Implementation of United Nations Resolutions E/CN.4/Sub.2/405/Rev. 1 (1980), para. 47; M. Nowak, *UN Covenant on Civil and Political Rights: CCPR Commentary* (2nd edn., Engel 2005) 22.

[267] ICJ, *Legal Consequences of the Separation of The Chagos Archipelago from Mauritius in 1965*, Advisory Opinion, I.C.J. Reports 2019, p. 95, separate opinion of Judge Cançado Trindade, para. 58.

[268] A.A. Yusuf, 'The Role that Equal Rights and Self-determination of Peoples can Play in the Current World Community' in A. Cassese (ed.), Realizing Utopia: The Future of International Law (OUP 2012) 375–391, 377.

[269] ACtHPR, *Bernard Anbataayela Mornah v. Benin, Burkina Faso, Côte d'Ivoire, Ghana, Mali, Malawi, Tanzania, and Tunisia*. Judgment, App. no. 028/2018 (22 September 2022), para. 295.

[270] F. Ouguergouz, *African Charter of Human and People's Rights: A Comprehensive Agenda for Human Dignity and Sustainable Democracy in Africa* (Nijhoff 2003) 272, 258.

[271] F. Tesón, 'Introduction: The Conundrum of Self-Determination' in F. Tesón (ed.), *The Theory of Self-Determination* (CUP 2016) 1–12, 1.

[272] R. Kiwanuka, 'The Meaning of "People" in the African Charter on Human and Peoples' Rights' (1988) 82 *American Journal of International Law* 80, 82, 88–89; F. Ouguergouz, *African Charter of Human and People's Rights: A Comprehensive Agenda for Human Dignity and Sustainable Democracy in Africa* (Nijhoff 2003) 210–211.

[273] ICJ, *Accordance with International Law of the Unilateral Declaration of Independence in Respect of Kosovo*, Advisory Opinion, I.C.J. Reports 2010, p. 403, separate opinion of Judge Cançado Trindade, para. 170.

to that discussion, is that of the circumstances of the applicability of the right itself. While colonialism appears as the most evident scenario in which the right to self-determination can be exercised, this right is also of extreme importance in a wider range of circumstances of alien subjugation, domination, and exploitation,[274] including comparable contemporaneous forms of neo-colonialism, imperialism, and tyranny.[275] However, determining what actions of a government or of a foreign State reach the threshold of severity to encroach on the right to self-determination is also contentious.

It seems to be accepted that, as a matter of principle, subsections of the entire population of a State, such as ethnic or national minorities, do not qualify as 'peoples' for the full enjoyment of the right to self-determination, as the principle of territorial integrity of States[276] imposes a restriction on a potential right of secession.[277] Nonetheless, such a minority group may be entitled to exercise the right to external self-determination under extreme circumstances,[278] such as when the State denies the group of the right of internal self-determination and subjects it to egregious violations of human rights or humanitarian law.[279] Moreover, minority groups can be considered entitled to the enjoyment of the internal dimensions of self-determination.[280] However, what this really entails for a specific minority is also unclear and seems to depend on the particular case.[281] At a minimum, internal

---

[274] UNGA, Resolution 1514 (XV), 'Declaration on the Granting of Independence to Colonial Countries and Peoples' (14 December 1960); UNGA, 'Declaration on Principles of International Law concerning Friendly Relations and Co-operation among States in accordance with the Charter of the United Nations', A/RES/2625 (XXV) (24 October 1970).

[275] Special Rapporteur of the Sub-Commission on Prevention of Discrimination and Protection of Minorities (H. Gros Espiell), The Right to Self-Determination: Implementation of United Nations Resolutions E/CN.4/Sub.2/405/Rev. 1 (1980), para. 47; ICJ, *Accordance with International Law of the Unilateral Declaration of Independence in Respect of Kosovo*, Advisory Opinion, I.C.J. Reports 2010, p. 403, separate opinion of Judge Cançado Trindade, paras. 175, 184.

[276] UNGA, Resolution 1514 (XV), 'Declaration on the Granting of Independence to Colonial Countries and Peoples' (14 December 1960); UNGA, 'Declaration on Principles of International Law concerning Friendly Relations and Co-operation among States in accordance with the Charter of the United Nations', A/RES/2625 (XXV) (24 October 1970).

[277] ICJ, *Accordance with International Law of the Unilateral Declaration of Independence in Respect of Kosovo*, Advisory Opinion, I.C.J. Reports 2010, p. 403, para. 82. See also: ACHPR, *Katangese Peoples' Congress v. Zaire*, Comm. No. 75/92 (1995); CERD, General Recommendation XXI: on the right to self-determination (1996), para. 6; IACHR, Report 'Right to Self-Determination of Indigenous and Tribal Peoples', OEA/Ser.L/V/II, doc. 413 (28 December 2021), para. 78.

[278] As well as in cases of agreement between the minority concerned and the government of the State. See: A.A. Yusuf, 'The Role that Equal Rights and Self-determination of Peoples can Play in the Current World Community' in A. Cassese (ed.), *Realizing Utopia: The Future of International Law* (OUP 2012) 375–391, 383; C. Anyangwe, 'The normative power of the right to self-determination under the African Charter and the principle of territorial integrity: competing values of human dignity and system stability' (2018) 2 *African Human Rights Yearbook* 47, 52.

[279] A.A. Yusuf, 'The Role that Equal Rights and Self-determination of Peoples can Play in the Current World Community' in A. Cassese (ed.), *Realizing Utopia: The Future of International Law* (OUP 2012) 375–391, 381.

[280] R. Kiwanuka, 'The Meaning of "People" in the African Charter on Human and Peoples' Rights' (1988) 82 *American Journal of International Law* 80, 92–94.

[281] K. Senaratne, *Internal Self-determination in International Law: History, Theory, and Practice* (CUP 2021) 116.

self-determination entails a right 'to participate in the political life of the state, to be represented in its government, and not to be discriminated against'.[282] In some cases, especially for geographically concentrated minority groups, it might extend to certain forms of autonomy and self-government within the State.[283]

Section 10.4.2 will focus, in particular, on the role played by the international law of human rights in the progressive recognition of the right to self-determination of indigenous peoples, collectives which were not the ones originally thought of when the right to self-determination was conceived.[284] Indeed, it has been a rather lengthy process for indigenous peoples to obtain the recognition of their right to self-determination, which has stopped short from acknowledging a right to secession and political independence from the State in which they are,[285] but encompasses a broad degree of autonomy for self-governance within the State and the right to concrete access to participate in the State's political decision-making process.[286]

10.4.2 INDIGENOUS PEOPLES

The notion that whole collectives can be entitled to group rights themselves has already been discussed. The development of the protection of indigenous peoples, in particular, is worth highlighting, as it has managed to find acceptance within various international regimes. A timid (and problematic) recognition of the need to protect indigenous communities under international law can already be found in the 1948 Inter-American Charter of Social Guarantees,[287] adopted by the OAS at the same conference that

---

[282] A.A. Yusuf, 'The Role that Equal Rights and Self-determination of Peoples can Play in the Current World Community' in A. Cassese (ed.), *Realizing Utopia: The Future of International Law* (OUP 2012) 375–391, 384.

[283] K. Senaratne, *Internal Self-determination in International Law: History, Theory, and Practice* (CUP 2021) 88–89.

[284] B.S. Santos, 'Human Rights: A Fragile Hegemony' in F. Crépeau and C. Sheppard (eds.), *Human Rights and Diverse Societies: Challenges and Possibilities* (Cambridge Scholars Publishing 2013) 17–25, 21–22.

[285] M. Scheinin, 'What are Indigenous Peoples?' in N. Ghanea and A. Xanthaki (eds.), *Minorities, Peoples and Self-Determination: Essays in Honour of Patrick Thornberry* (Nijhoff 2005) 6; U. Baxi, *The Future of Human Rights* (2nd edn., OUP 2008) 51–52; A. Anghie, 'International Human Rights Law and a Developing World Perspective' in S. Sheeran and N. Rodley (eds.), *Routledge Handbook of International Human Rights Law* (Routledge 2013) 109–125, 117.

[286] F. Ouguergouz, *African Charter of Human and People's Rights: A Comprehensive Agenda for Human Dignity and Sustainable Democracy in Africa* (Nijhoff 2003) 237, 258; M. Nowak, *UN Covenant on Civil and Political Rights: CCPR Commentary* (2nd edn., Engel 2005) 23–24; A. Carmen, 'International Indian Treaty Council Report from the Battle Field – The Struggle for the Declaration' in C. Charters and R. Stavenhagen (eds.), *Making the Declaration Work* (IWGIA 2009) 86–95, 93–94.

[287] The engagement with the original peoples of the Americas had been a topic of international political discussion for the States of the continent from as early as 1922, usually characterized by them as a 'problem'. See: D. Shelton, 'The Rights of Indigenous Peoples: Everything Old Is New Again' in A. von Arnauld, K. von der Decken, and M. Susi (eds), *The Cambridge Handbook of New Human Rights* (CUP 2020) 217–232, 219.

resulted in the proclamation of the American Declaration of the Rights and Duties of Man.[288] The mentioned Charter textually stated:

> In countries where the *problem* of an indigenous population exists, the necessary measures shall be adopted to give protection and assistance to the *Indians*, safeguarding their life, liberty and property, preventing their extermination, shielding them from oppression and exploitation, protecting them from want and furnishing them an adequate education.[289]

More extensive protection of the rights of indigenous peoples came with the adoption of two Conventions by the International Labour Organization (ILO). The first of these, Convention 107, adopted in 1957, was specifically aimed at 'the protection and *integration* of indigenous and other tribal and semi-tribal populations'.[290] For the purpose of the treaty, indigenous communities are defined:

> ...on account of their descent from the populations which inhabited the country, or a geographical region to which the country belongs, at the time of conquest or colonization and which, irrespective of their legal status, live more in conformity with the social, economic and cultural institutions of that time than with the institutions of the nation to which they belong.[291]

While the Convention had a rather emphatic integrationist approach,[292] it did attempt to provide communities with a certain degree of international protection of their rights, which includes 'enabling the said populations to benefit on an equal footing from the rights and opportunities which national laws or regulations grant to the other elements of the population',[293] and 'promoting the social, economic and cultural development of these populations and raising their standard of living'.[294] Moreover, the treaty mandated States to recognize '[t]he right of ownership, collective or individual, of the members of the populations concerned over the lands which these populations traditionally occupy'.[295]

In 1989, the ILO adopted a subsequent treaty on the same subject matter. ILO Convention 169 took a different approach to the protection of indigenous communities, leaving aside underpinning assumptions of a desired integration and making an important change in terminology from indigenous 'populations' to indigenous 'peoples'; the latter

---

[288] OAS, Final Act, Ninth Conference (1948), Resolution XXIX.
[289] OAS, Final Act, Ninth Conference (1948), Resolution XXIX, Art. 39 (emphasis added).
[290] International Labour Organization, Indigenous and Tribal Populations Convention (C107) (adopted on 26 June 1957, entered into force 2 June 1959), preamble (hereinafter 'ILO Convention C107') (emphasis added).
[291] ILO Convention C107, Art. 1.1.b.
[292] A. Eide, 'The Indigenous Peoples, the Working Group on Indigenous Populations and the Adoption of the UN Declaration on the Rights of Indigenous Peoples' in C. Charters and R. Stavenhagen (eds.), *Making the Declaration Work* (IWGIA 2009) 32–46, 37.
[293] ILO Convention C107, Art. 2.2.a.   [294] ILO Convention C107, Art. 2.2.b.
[295] ILO Convention C107, Art. 11.

being a term with strong connotations with regards to self-determination under international law, as discussed in **Section 10.4.1**. This modified approach placed emphasis on the protection of the human rights of indigenous peoples. It highlighted that special measures should be taken by States to protect 'the persons, institutions, property, labour, cultures and environment'[296] of indigenous peoples and clarified that when measures are adopted 'the social, cultural, religious and spiritual values and practices of these peoples shall be recognised and protected'.[297] The protection of the community's lands is made even stronger by stating the obligation of governments to 'take steps as necessary to identify the lands which the peoples concerned traditionally occupy, and to guarantee effective protection of their rights of ownership and possession',[298] as well as by stipulating that '[t]he rights of the peoples concerned to the natural resources pertaining to their lands shall be specially safeguarded'.[299]

10.4.2.1 The UN Declaration on the Rights of Indigenous Peoples

It was only in 1970 that the human rights of indigenous peoples became a significant topic of concern within the United Nations.[300] That year, the Sub-Commission on Prevention of Discrimination and Protection of Minorities recommended to ECOSOC that a complete and comprehensive study of the problem of discrimination against indigenous populations be undertaken.[301] Following authorization from ECOSOC, the Sub-Commission appointed a Special Rapporteur to carry out a study on the topic. The final output was a report concluded in 1984 by Special Rapporteur Martínez Cobo. The report proposed a 'working definition' of indigenous communities and peoples, suggesting that it should be a starting point for further reflection.[302] According to such a definition:

> Indigenous communities, peoples and nations are those which, having a historical continuity with pre-invasion and pre-colonial societies that developed on their territories, consider themselves distinct from other sectors of the societies now prevailing in those territories, or parts of them. They form at present non-dominant sectors of society and are determined to preserve, develop and transmit to future generations their ancestral

---

[296] ILO, Indigenous and Tribal Peoples Convention (C169) (adopted 27 June 1989, entered into force 5 September 1991), Art. 3.1 (hereinafter 'ILO Convention C169').
[297] ILO Convention C169, Art. 4.1.   [298] ILO Convention C169, Art. 14.2.
[299] ILO Convention C169, Art. 15.1.
[300] In 1948, Bolivia proposed the creation of a sub-commission to deal with the problems of the indigenous peoples of the Americas, but it was not successful. See: A. Willemsen-Diaz, 'How Indigenous Peoples' Rights Reached the UN' in C. Charters and R. Stavenhagen (eds.), *Making the Declaration Work* (IWGIA 2009) 16–31, 18.
[301] Sub-Commission on Prevention of Discrimination and Protection of Minorities, Resolution 4B(XXIII) (26 August 1970).
[302] Special Rapporteur of the Sub-Commission on Prevention of Discrimination and Protection of Minorities (J.R. Martínez Cobo), Study of the Problem of Discrimination against Indigenous Populations, Vol. V, Conclusions, Proposals and Recommendation, E/CN.4/Sub.2/1986/7/Add.4/Rev. 1 (1987), paras. 364–367.

territories, and their ethnic identity, as the basis of their continued existence as peoples, in accordance with their own cultural patterns, social institutions and legal systems.[303]

The report also highlighted specific areas of action where special measures needed to be taken by States in order to further protect the rights of indigenous peoples. These areas included health, housing, education, language, culture, employment, land, political and religious rights, and access to justice.

In the meantime, ECOSOC also authorized the Sub-Commission on Prevention of Discrimination and Protection of Minorities to establish a working group on indigenous populations, which was to meet annually to review developments pertaining to the promotion and protection of the human rights and fundamental freedoms of indigenous populations.[304] It was this working group that produced the initial draft of what would in time become the well-known UN Declaration on the Rights of Indigenous Peoples, adopted by the General Assembly in 2007.[305] The mentioned working group was later replaced, in 2007, by an Expert Mechanism on the Rights of Indigenous Peoples subsidiary to the Human Rights Council.[306] Under its 2016 revised mandate, the Expert Mechanism is in charge of providing the Human Rights Council with expertise and advice on the rights of indigenous peoples, and tasked with assisting Member States, upon request, to achieve the goals of the 2007 Declaration.[307] In addition to this mechanism, the former Commission on Human Rights and, subsequently, the Human Rights Council have established and renewed the mandate of a Special Rapporteur on the Rights of Indigenous Peoples,[308] which is empowered to formulate

---

[303] Special Rapporteur of the Sub-Commission on Prevention of Discrimination and Protection of Minorities (J.R. Martínez Cobo), Study of the Problem of Discrimination against Indigenous Populations, Vol. V, Conclusions, Proposals and Recommendation, E/CN.4/Sub.2/1986/7/Add.4/Rev. 1 (1987), para. 369. In 2005 the Working Groups of Experts on Indigenous Populations/Communities of the African Commission confirmed that it was neither necessary nor desirable to adopt a strict definition of 'indigenous peoples', but that outlining the major characteristics to identify who are the indigenous peoples in Africa could be helpful to provide the required protection for the particular groups whose cultures and ways of life are subject to discrimination and contempt and whose very existence is under threat of extinction (p. 87). It emphasized that the focus should be less on aboriginality (as all Africans are indigenous to Africa) and more 'on *self-identification* as indigenous and distinctly different from other groups within a state; on a *special attachment to and use of their traditional land* whereby their ancestral land and territory has a fundamental importance for their collective physical and cultural survival as peoples; on an experience of *subjugation, marginalization, dispossession, exclusion or discrimination* because these peoples have different cultures, ways of life or modes of production than the national hegemonic and dominant model' (pp. 92–93). See: Report of the African Commission's Working Group of Experts on Indigenous Populations/Communities Submitted in accordance with the 'Resolution on the Rights of Indigenous Populations/Communities in Africa' Adopted by The African Commission on Human and Peoples' Rights at its 28th ordinary session (2005).

[304] ECOSOC, Resolution 1982/34 (7 May 1982). See also: E-I. Daes, 'The Contribution of the Working Group on Indigenous Populations to the Genesis and Evolution of the UN Declaration on the Rights of Indigenous Peoples' in C. Charters and R. Stavenhagen (eds.), *Making the Declaration Work* (IWGIA 2009) 48–76.

[305] M. Davis, 'Indigenous Struggles in Standard-Setting: The United Nations Declaration on the Rights of Indigenous Peoples' (2008) 9 *Melbourne Journal of International Law* 439, 444–446.

[306] HRC, Resolution 6/36 (14 December 2007).

[307] HRC Resolution 33/25 (30 September 2016), para. 1.

[308] CHR, Resolution 2001/57 (24 April 2001); HRC, Resolution 6/12 (28 September 2007).

recommendations on measures and activities to prevent and remedy violations of the human rights of indigenous people,[309] as well as to examine ways to overcome obstacles to the full and effective protection of the rights of indigenous peoples.[310]

The Declaration on the Rights of Indigenous Peoples was the outcome of over two decades of work within the United Nations.[311] This work began in the 1980s, in the working group on indigenous populations, which produced a draft Declaration for consideration by the Commission on Human Rights.[312] The Commission established its own working group to consider the draft Declaration and it took over a decade of negotiations for an agreed-upon text to be adopted in 2006 by the Commissions' successor, the Human Rights Council.[313] However, it would take another year for the General Assembly to adopt the Declaration, as the African Group, led by Namibia, requested the deferment of its consideration by the General Assembly with a view to opening negotiations for making amendments that would consider 'the fundamental preoccupations of the African countries'.[314] These included their common concern that the right to self-determination of indigenous people,[315] recognized by Article 3 of the Declaration—and which had already been tempered by the addition of Article 4[316]—would be exercised 'within the context of a strict respect for the inviolability of borders and of the obligation to preserve the territorial integrity of States Parties'.[317]

The Declaration on the Rights of Indigenous Peoples was presented as a triumph for indigenous peoples worldwide,[318] given that it put in place a set of clear and

[309] CHR, Resolution 2001/57 (24 April 2001), para. 1.b; HRC, Resolution 6/12 (28 September 2007), para. 1.c.
[310] HRC, Resolution 6/12 (28 September 2007), para. 1.a.
[311] UNGA, Declaration on the Rights of Indigenous Peoples, A/RES/61/295 (2 October 2007).
[312] S.J. Anaya, *International Human Rights and Indigenous Peoples* (Aspen 2009) 55.
[313] S.J. Anaya, *International Human Rights and Indigenous Peoples* (Aspen 2009) 56; L.E. Chávez, 'The Declaration on the Rights of Indigenous Peoples - Breaking the *Impasse*: The Middle Ground' in C. Charters and R. Stavenhagen (eds.), *Making the Declaration Work* (IWGIA 2009) 96–106.
[314] M. Davis, 'Indigenous Struggles in Standard-Setting: The United Nations Declaration on the Rights of Indigenous Peoples' (2008) 9 *Melbourne Journal of International Law* 439, 441, 456–457; L.A. de Alba, 'The Human Rights Council's Adoption of the United Nations Declaration on the Rights of Indigenous Peoples' in C. Charters and R. Stavenhagen (eds.), *Making the Declaration Work* (IWGIA 2009) 108–137, 126–132; N. Kipuri, 'The UN Declaration on the Rights of Indigenous Peoples in the African Context' in C. Charters and R. Stavenhagen (eds.), *Making the Declaration Work* (IWGIA 2009) 252–262.
[315] A concern also shared by four Western States—Australia, Canada, New Zealand, and the USA—which had been lobbying against the adoption of the Declaration and were the only States to vote against it when adopted by the General Assembly. See: A. Eide, 'The Indigenous Peoples, the Working Group on Indigenous Populations and the Adoption of the UN Declaration on the Rights of Indigenous Peoples' in C. Charters and R. Stavenhagen (eds.), *Making the Declaration Work* (IWGIA 2009) 32–46, 39–40, 42.
[316] M. Davis, 'Indigenous Struggles in Standard-Setting: The United Nations Declaration on the Rights of Indigenous Peoples' (2008) 9 *Melbourne Journal of International Law* 439, 460.
[317] ACHPR, *Advisory Opinion of The African Commission on Human and Peoples' Rights on The United Nations Declaration on the Rights of Indigenous Peoples* (May 2007), para. 6; UNGA, Declaration on the Rights of Indigenous Peoples, A/RES/61/295 (2 October 2007), Art. 46.
[318] UN Secretary-General, 'Statement attributable to the Spokesperson for the Secretary-General on the adoption of the Declaration on the Rights of Indigenous Peoples' (13 September 2007). Available at: https://www.un.org/esa/socdev/unpfii/documents/2016-Docs-updates/Statement-SG-IDWIP-2007.pdf (accessed on 13 April 2023); OHCHR, 'High Commissioner for Human Rights Hails Adoption of Declaration on Indigenous Rights' (13 September 2007). Available at: https://www.ohchr.org/en/statements/2009/10/high-commissioner-human-rights-hails-adoption-declaration-indigenous-rightshttps://newsarchive.ohchr.org/CH/NewsEvents/Pages/DisplayNews.aspx?NewsID=6097&LangID=E (accessed on 14 September 2023).

comprehensive minimum standards on the protection deserved by indigenous peoples everywhere. Since its adoption by the General Assembly, it has become the source of confirmation of, and new impetus to, the recognition of both the individual members of indigenous communities and the communities themselves as subjects of rights under international law.[319] Nonetheless, by 2007, indigenous peoples had already gained legal standing to bring claims on their own behalf before international human rights bodies. This is clearly illustrated by the victories indigenous communities have achieved within the Inter-American and African human rights systems.[320]

10.4.2.2 The protection of indigenous peoples' lands and natural resources

As discussed in **Section 2.3.2.2**, the Inter-American Court of Human Rights has acknowledged that indigenous communities themselves enjoy a right to property, understanding that the recognition of this right under the American Convention needs not to be limited to a right to individual private property, but also includes the right to benefit from communal property.[321] From 2001 onwards, the Court started developing a consistent jurisprudence that recognizes indigenous (and tribal) communities communal ownership of their ancestral (or traditional) lands and natural resources.[322] In particular, the Inter-American Court has recognized the special close relationship that indigenous peoples have with their ancestral land, as that specific land plays an essential role in their cultural identity and worldview.[323] This jurisprudence has had

---

[319] See, among many: CCPR, *Chief Bernard Ominayak and the Lubicon Lake Band v. Canada*, Communication 167/1984, U.N. Doc. Supp. No. 40 (A/45/40) (26 March 1990); CERD, General Recommendation XXIII: The Rights of Indigenous Peoples, A/52/18, annex V (1997); IACHR, *Report on the Situation of Human Rights in Ecuador*, OEA/Ser.L/V/II.96, doc. 10 rev. 1 (24 April 1997); IACtHR, *Mayagna (Sumo) Awas Tingni Community v. Nicaragua*. Merits, Reparations and Costs. Judgment of August 31, 2001. ACHPR, *Social and Economic Rights Action Center (SERAC) and Center for Economic and Social Rights (CESR) v. Nigeria*, Communication 155/96 (October 2001); CESCR, General Comment No. 17: The right of everyone to benefit from the protection of the moral and material interests resulting from any scientific, literary or artistic production, E/C.12/GC/17 (12 January 2006), paras. 8, 9, 18, 32; CRC, General Comment No. 11: Indigenous children and their rights under the Convention, CRC/C/GC/11 (12 February 2009).

[320] See, among others: ACHPR, *Social and Economic Rights Action Center (SERAC) and Center for Economic and Social Rights (CESR) v. Nigeria*, Communication 155/96 (October 2001); IACtHR, *Mayagna (Sumo) Awas Tingni Community v. Nicaragua*. Merits, Reparations and Costs. Judgment of August 31, 2001. Series C No. 79; IACtHR, *Xákmok Kásek Indigenous Community. v. Paraguay*. Merits, Reparations and Costs. Judgment of August 24, 2010. Series C No. 214.

[321] IACtHR, *Mayagna (Sumo) Awas Tingni Community v. Nicaragua*. Merits, Reparations and Costs. Judgment of August 31, 2001. Series C No. 79, para. 148.

[322] IACtHR, *Mayagna (Sumo) Awas Tingni Community v. Nicaragua*. Merits, Reparations and Costs. Judgment of August 31, 2001. Series C No. 79; IACtHR, *Yakye Axa Indigenous Community v. Paraguay*. Merits, Reparations and Costs. Judgment of June 17, 2005. Series C No. 125; IACtHR, *Sawhoyamaxa Indigenous Community v. Paraguay*. Merits, Reparations and Costs. Judgment of March 29, 2006. Series C No. 146.

[323] IACtHR, *Mayagna (Sumo) Awas Tingni Community v. Nicaragua*. Merits, Reparations and Costs. Judgment of August 31, 2001. Series C No. 79, joint separate opinion of Judges A.A. Cançado Trindade, M. Pacheco Gómez, and A. Abreu Burelli; IACtHR, *Yakye Axa Indigenous Community v. Paraguay*. Merits, Reparations and Costs. Judgment of June 17, 2005. Series C No. 125, para. 154; IACtHR, *Sawhoyamaxa Indigenous Community v. Paraguay*. Merits, Reparations and Costs. Judgment of March 29, 2006. Series C No. 146, para. 118; IACtHR, *Kichwa Indigenous People of Sarayaku v. Ecuador*. Merits and Reparations. Judgment of June 27, 2012. Series C No. 245, para. 159. See also: ILO Convention C169, Art. 13.

far-reaching effects, having informed the reasoning on the topic of both the African Commission and Court on Human and People's Rights. Both these bodies have also recognized the rights of indigenous peoples as collectives and the protection offered to their rights by the African Charter.[324] Similarly, the Human Rights Committee has also affirmed, on numerous occasions in the concluding observations on State reports, that indigenous peoples 'must be able to freely dispose of their natural wealth and resources and that they may not be deprived of their own means of subsistence'.[325]

The recognition of indigenous communities' joint ownership of their ancestral lands, and of the natural resources of such lands,[326] brings attached a right to the conservation and protection of the environment and the productive capacity of their lands.[327] A further necessary corollary of such rights is the existence of an effective right of consultation, in relation to any project or activity likely to affect their lands and resources.[328] Neither can States carry out activities of exploration and extraction of natural resources on communal lands, nor can they authorize third parties to undertake them, without due prior consultation with the communities themselves.[329] States must guarantee the communities' rights to consultation and participation at all stages of the planning and adoption of any project or activity likely to affect their lands and resources.[330] The consultation process must follow culturally appropriate procedures, in accordance with the communities' traditions, and be undertaken in good faith.[331] The process should include appropriate risk assessments of the project at stake for the communities to be able to fully assess the social, spiritual, cultural, and environmental impact of the proposed activities.[332]

---

[324] ACHPR, *Centre for Minority Rights Development (Kenya) and Minority Rights Group (on behalf of Endorois Welfare Council) v. Kenya* (276/03) 25 November 2009; ACtHPR, *African Commission on Human and Peoples' Rights v. Republic of Kenya*, App. no. 6/2012, Judgment, 26 May 2017.

[325] CCPR, Concluding Observations on Canada, CCPR/C/79/Add.105 (1999), para. 8. See also: CCPR, Concluding Observations on Mexico, CCPR/C/79/Add.109 (1999); CCPR, Concluding Observations on Norway, CCPR/C/79/Add.112 (1999); CCPR, Concluding Observations on Australia, CCPR/CO/69/AUS (2000); CCPR, Concluding Observations on Denmark, CCPR/CO/70/DNK (2000); CCPR, Concluding Observations on Sweden, CCPR/CO/74/SWE (2002).

[326] ILO Convention C169, Art. 6; IACtHR, *Yakye Axa Indigenous Community v. Paraguay*. Merits, Reparations and Costs. Judgment of June 17, 2005. Series C No. 125, para. 137; IACtHR, *Sawhoyamaxa Indigenous Community v. Paraguay*. Merits, Reparations and Costs. Judgment of March 29, 2006. Series C No. 146, para. 118.

[327] UNGA, Declaration on the Rights of Indigenous Peoples, A/RES/61/295 (2 October 2007), Art. 29.1.

[328] ILO Convention C169, Arts. 14–15.

[329] IACtHR, *Saramaka People v. Suriname*. Preliminary Objections, Merits, Reparations, and Costs. Judgment of November 28, 2007 Series C No. 172, para. 158; ACHPR, *Centre for Minority Rights Development (Kenya) and Minority Rights Group (on behalf of Endorois Welfare Council) v. Kenya* (276/03) 25 November 2009, paras. 281–282, 291.

[330] IACtHR, *Kichwa Indigenous People of Sarayaku v. Ecuador*. Merits and Reparations. Judgment of June 27, 2012. Series C No. 245, para. 167.

[331] Case 245 para. 177. ACHPR, *Centre for Minority Rights Development (Kenya) and Minority Rights Group (on behalf of Endorois Welfare Council) v. Kenya* (276/03) 25 November 2009, para. 291.

[332] ILO, Indigenous and Tribal Peoples Convention, 1989 (No. 169), Art. 6; IACtHR, *Kichwa Indigenous People of Sarayaku v. Ecuador*. Merits and Reparations. Judgment of June 27, 2012. Series C No. 245, para. 204.

ACHPR, *Centre for Minority Rights Development (Kenya) and Minority Rights Group International on behalf of Endorois Welfare Council v. Kenya*, Communication 276/2003 (25 November 2009).

The case concerned the displacement of the Endorois community—an indigenous community of approximately 60,000 people—from their ancestral lands. The African Commission recognized the Endorois community as a distinct people, sharing a common history, culture, and religion, which entitled them to benefit from the collective rights provided for by the African Charter. In particular, the Commission acknowledged the intimately intertwined relationship of the culture, religion, and traditional way of life of the Endorois and their ancestral lands, which included Lake Bogoria and the surrounding areas. Consequently, it considered that the situation had led to the violation of multiple rights protected under the African Charter to the detriment of the Endorois people.

The Commission affirmed that the Endorois' forced eviction from their ancestral lands amounted to a violation of their right to property (Article 14). Moreover, this situation rendered it virtually impossible for the community to maintain their religious rituals, as these were linked to the access to the lands, entailing a violation of their freedom to practice their religion (Article 8). Similarly, the Commission affirmed that '[b]y forcing the community to live on semi-arid lands without access to medicinal salt licks and other vital resources for the health of their livestock, the respondent State have created a major threat to the Endorois pastoralist way of life ... the very essence of the Endorois' right to culture has been denied, rendering the right, to all intents and purposes, illusory' (para. 251). Furthermore, the situation amounted to the violation of the community's right to benefit from their own wealth and natural resources and to their right to economic, social and cultural development (Articles 21 and 22), given that they had received none of the economic benefits obtained from the exploitation of the natural resources of their lands.

Having found that the displacement of the Endorois community entailed the violation of multiple rights under the Charter, the Commission recommended Kenya to restitute the ancestral lands to the community and to recognize their ownership, including ensuring their unrestricted access to Lake Bogoria and its surrounding areas for their religious and cultural rituals. It also ordered the payment of royalties to the community from any existing economic activities taking place within their lands.

IACtHR, *Case of Kichwa Indigenous People of Sarayaku v. Ecuador*. Merits and Reparations. Judgment of June 27, 2012. Series C No. 245.

The case concerned Ecuador's granting of a contract for oil exploration and exploitation in the territory of the Kichwa Indigenous People of Sarayaku to a private oil company, without prior consultation with the community or obtaining their consent. The process of consultation and consent was the central element of analysis in the case. The Court considered that 'the close relationship between the indigenous communities and their land has an essential component, which is their cultural identity based on their specific worldviews, which, as distinct social and political actors in multicultural societies, must receive particular recognition and respect in a democratic society. Respect for the right to consultation of indigenous and tribal communities and peoples is precisely recognition of their rights to their own culture or cultural identity' (para. 159). The Court affirmed that this obligation to consult was not only treaty-based but also a general principle of international law, therefore, placing States under the obligation to carry out special consultation processes—which must respect the particular consultation system of each community—when the lands and resources of indigenous peoples are at stake.

In this case, the State had failed to undertake any type of consultation with the Sarayaku people and, while an environmental impact plan existed, it was prepared without the participation of the Sarayaku people, was implemented by a private entity subcontracted by the oil company, and did not take into account the social, spiritual, and cultural impact that the planned development activities might have on the community. Consequently, the Court found that Ecuador was responsible for the violation of the rights to consultation, to indigenous communal property, and to cultural identity, under Article 21 of the American Convention, to the detriment of the community. In addition, it found violations of the rights to judicial guarantees and to judicial protection (Articles 8 and 25), as the State had failed to provide an effective remedy in its domestic system to put an end to the claimed violations. The Court also found the State responsible for its acquiescence to the oil company's planting nearly 1,400 kilograms of pentolite explosives within the Sarayaku territory to carry out its activities. It considered this to be in violation of the Convention for 'severely jeopardizing the rights to life and to personal integrity' of the members of the community.

Among the measures of reparation ordered, and in addition to the payment of compensation, the Court indicated that the State must 'consult the Sarayaku People in a prior, adequate and effective manner ... in the event that it seeks to carry out any activity or project for the extraction of natural resources on its territory, or any investment or development plan of any other type that could involve a potential impact on their territory' (op. para. 3) and, more broadly, it should adopt the necessary measures in its domestic order to give full effect to the right to prior consultation of indigenous and tribal peoples with regard to any project that might affect them. Lastly, the Court also ordered the State to neutralize, deactivate, and remove all pentolite left in the territory of the Sarayaku People.

10.4.2.3 Further reflections: a postcolonial approach to indigenous peoples' right to self-determination

Starting with the invasion of the Americas from 1492, the history of the indigenous peoples' engagement with the European invaders reveals a saga of decimation of populations—both through violence and foreign diseases[333]—the pillage of vast extensions of lands and their natural resources, and the destruction of indigenous culture and ways of living.[334] As an outcome of this process of colonization, the few thousands

---

[333] D. Stannard, *American Holocaust: Columbus and the Conquest of the New World* (OUP 1992) ix–x; P. Sherman, 'Disease versus Genocide: The Debate over Population' in A. de Oliveira (ed.), Decolonising Indigenous Rights (Routledge 2009) 173–189.

[334] D. Stannard, *American Holocaust: Columbus and the Conquest of the New World* (OUP 1992) esp. 74, 84, 125–126; S.J. Anaya, *International Human Rights and Indigenous Peoples* (Aspen 2009) 61.

of indigenous communities that survived ended up dispossessed, dislocated, and living in conditions of extreme poverty, under the oppression of the Western populations brought to the indigenous lands,[335] when not being again the target of genocidal policies of extermination.[336] While certainly unable to redress the tragic history of injustice and domination that indigenous peoples continue to experience in our days, the international law of human rights has progressively provided for the recognition of the collective rights of indigenous peoples, but stopping short from acknowledging that their right to self-determination includes a right to secession and political independence.

However, why indigenous populations have been considered excluded from benefiting fully from the right to self-determination bears further consideration, especially from a postcolonial perspective.[337] As discussed in **Section 10.4.2.1**, it was a rather lengthy and contentious political process that led to the adoption of the 2007 United Nations Declaration on the Rights of Indigenous Peoples by the General Assembly. The proclamation of the right to self-determination of indigenous peoples (Article 3) was the most contentious issue within the process, as many States were concerned that such acknowledgement would pose a risk to their territorial integrity.[338] It has been argued that enjoying the possibility of external self-determination, with the potential of some indigenous peoples becoming politically independent from the State into which they were colonized,[339] was not the overwhelming desire of the indigenous peoples negotiating the Declaration.[340] And yet, this seems to have been desired by, at least, some indigenous peoples.[341]

---

[335] S.J. Anaya, *International Human Rights and Indigenous Peoples* (Aspen 2009) 1–2; C. Roy, 'Indigenous Peoples in Asia: Rights and Development Challenges' in C. Charters and R. Stavenhagen (eds.), *Making the Declaration Work* (IWGIA 2009) 216–231, 219; I. Watson, 'Aboriginal Laws and Colonial Foundation' (2017) 26 *Griffith Law Review* 469, 473.

[336] W. Churchill, 'A Travesty of a Mockery of a Sham: Colonialism as "Self-Determination" in the UN Declaration on the Rights of Indigenous Peoples' (2011) 20 *Griffith Law Review* 526, 529–530.

[337] J. Castellino, 'International Law and Self-Determination: Peoples, Indigenous Peoples, and Minorities' in C. Walter, A. von Ungern-Sternberg, and K. Abushov (eds.), *Self-Determination and Secession in International Law* (OUP 2014) 27–44, 43; J. Castellino, 'Territorial Integrity and the "Right" to Self-Determination: An Examination of the Conceptual Tools' (2008) 33 *Brooklyn Journal of International Law* 503, 567.

[338] J. Henriksen, 'The UN Declaration on the Rights of Indigenous Peoples: Some Key Issues and Events in the Process' in C. Charters and R. Stavenhagen (eds.), *Making the Declaration Work* (IWGIA 2009) 78–84, 80–81; L.E. Chávez, 'The Declaration on the Rights of Indigenous Peoples – Breaking the *Impasse*: The Middle Ground' in C. Charters and R. Stavenhagen (eds.), *Making the Declaration Work* (IWGIA 2009) 96–106, 102; A. Regino Montes and G. Torres Cisneros, 'The United Nations Declaration on the Rights of Indigenous Peoples: The Foundation of a New Relationship between Indigenous Peoples, States and Societies' in C. Charters and R. Stavenhagen (eds.), *Making the Declaration Work* (IWGIA 2009) 138–168, 146, 154.

[339] Independence is not the only possible outcome of external self-determination, as the free association with another State or even the integration with a State can be a valid exercise of self-determination, so long that is the expression of the free and genuine will of the people. See: UNGA, Resolution 1541(XV) (15 December 1960).

[340] S.J. Anaya, *International Human Rights and Indigenous Peoples* (Aspen 2009) 60; A. Eide, 'The Indigenous Peoples, the Working Group on Indigenous Populations and the Adoption of the UN Declaration on the Rights of Indigenous Peoples' in C. Charters and R. Stavenhagen (eds.), *Making the Declaration Work* (IWGIA 2009) 32–46, 41.

[341] A. Regino Montes and G. Torres Cisneros, 'The United Nations Declaration on the Rights of Indigenous Peoples: The Foundation of a New Relationship between Indigenous Peoples, States and Societies' in C. Charters and R. Stavenhagen (eds.), *Making the Declaration Work* (IWGIA 2009) 138–168, 146, 157; I. Watson, 'Aboriginal(ising) International Law and Other Centres of Power' (2011) 20 *Griffith Law Review* 619, 632. See also: Baguio Declaration (22 April 1999).

Worryingly, the truncated form that self-determination took in the 2007 Declaration can be interpreted as transforming self-determination into its very opposite, the denial of indigenous peoples' right to free themselves from the structures of internal colonial domination that have oppressed them.[342] The Declaration came to re-affirm the colonizer's sovereignty over indigenous peoples' ancestral lands.[343] It confirmed the validity of the political borders established by the Imperial powers, who appropriated lands by the authority granted by the Christian god under the (recently disavowed) doctrine of 'discovery'.[344] A doctrine which had provided the grounds for the appropriation of indigenous lands by Western powers since such territories were considered to be *terra nullius*—a territory belonging to no one,[345] as discussed in **Section 1.3.4**. The operation of another controversial Latin principle, that of *uti possidetis*, allowed States that gained independence from the Imperial powers—such as those in the Americas and Oceania—to enjoy the continuation of the existent colonial boundaries,[346] thus, re-colonizing the indigenous peoples within the same borders. In 2007, a Declaration that avowed to recognize indigenous peoples' rights came to validate this contentious state of affairs, disavowing the right to external self-determination of indigenous peoples on the grounds that it would affect the territorial integrity of existing States.

While the Declaration confirms the colonizer's sovereignty over indigenous lands, it does provide for the recognition of the indigenous communities' ownership of such lands. Yet another problematic idea. The understanding of indigenous lands as susceptible of ownership entails in itself the colonization of indigenous epistemologies surrounding the relationship between peoples and lands.[347] Indigenous lands are not a commodity, owned by indigenous peoples either individually or jointly.[348] These lands and their people exist as one, interdependently, and are not susceptible to Western ways

---

[342] W. Churchill, 'A Travesty of a Mockery of a Sham: Colonialism as "Self-Determination" in the UN Declaration on the Rights of Indigenous Peoples' (2011) 20 *Griffith Law Review* 526, 527.

[343] I. Watson, 'Aboriginal(ising) International Law and Other Centres of Power' (2011) 20 *Griffith Law Review* 619, 630–631, 638; C. Samson, *The Colonialism of Human Rights: Ongoing Hypocrisies of Western Liberalism* (Polity Press 2020) 181–184.

[344] R.J. Miller, 'The Doctrine of Discovery' in R.J. Miller, J. Ruru, L. Behrendt, and T. Lindberg, *Discovering Indigenous Lands: The Doctrine of Discovery in the English Colonies* (OUP 2010) 1–25, 5–6, 9–15. See also: Permanent Forum on Indigenous Issues, 'Preliminary study of the impact on indigenous peoples of the international legal construct known as the Doctrine of Discovery', E/C.19/2010/13 (4 February 2010).

[345] J. Castellino, 'Territorial Integrity and the "Right" to Self-Determination: An Examination of the Conceptual Tools' (2008) 33 *Brooklyn Journal of International Law* 503, 526; S. Huh, 'Title to Territory in the Post-Colonial Era: Original Title and *Terra Nullius* in the ICJ Judgments on Cases Concerning *Ligitan/Sipadan* (2002) and *Pedra Branca* (2008)' (2015) *European Journal of International Law* 709, 715–716.

[346] M. Shahabuddin, *Minorities and the Making of Postcolonial States in International Law* (CUP 2021) 89–90, 97–100, 281–282.

[347] B. Izquierdo and L. Viaene, 'Decolonizing transitional justice from indigenous territories' (2018) 34 *Peace in Progress* 16, 17–18; I. Watson, 'Aboriginal Relationships to the Natural World: Colonial Protection of Human Rights and the Environment' (2018) 9 *Journal of Human Rights and the Environment* 119, 119–121, 124.

[348] I. Watson, 'Aboriginal(ising) International Law and Other Centres of Power' (2011) 20 *Griffith Law Review* 619, 638; I. Watson, 'Aboriginal Relationships to the Natural World: Colonial Protection of Human Rights and the Environment' (2018) 9 *Journal of Human Rights and the Environment* 119, 119–121.

of ownership. These lands are sacred and cannot be subject to consent for exploitation for capitalist gains, even by their people.[349] Therefore, from a postcolonial perspective, it is possible to raise doubts as to whether the 2007 Declaration can be labelled a 'triumph' (see **Section 10.4.2.1**) and, if so, allows questioning who are the ones who triumphed with its adoption.

FURTHER READING

ANAYA, S.J., *International Human Rights and Indigenous Peoples* (Aspen 2009).

CHARTERS, C. and STAVENHAGEN, R. (eds.), *Making the Declaration Work: The United Nations Declaration on the Rights of Indigenous Peoples* (IWGIA 2009).

CASSESE, A., *Self-Determination of Peoples: A Legal Reappraisal* (CUP 1995).

CHARLESWORTH, H., and CHINKIN, C., *The Boundaries of International Law: A Feminist Analysis* (2nd edn., Manchester University Press 2022).

EDWARDS, A., *Violence against Women under International Human Rights Law* (CUP 2010).

FREDMAN, S., *Discrimination Law* (2nd edn., OUP 2011).

GONZALEZ-SALZBERG, D., *Sexuality and Transsexuality under the European Convention on Human Rights: A Queer Reading of Human Rights Law* (Hart 2019).

MAY, V., *Pursuing Intersectionality: Unsettling Dominant Imaginaries* (Routledge 2015).

VANDENHOLE, W., TÜRKELLI, G., and LEMBRECHTS, S., *Children's Rights: A Commentary on the Convention on the Rights of the Child and its Protocols* (Elgar 2019).

---

[349] I. Watson, 'Aboriginal Laws and Colonial Foundation' (2017) 26 *Griffith Law Review* 469, 469 and 475; B. Izquierdo and L. Viaene, 'Decolonizing transitional justice from indigenous territories' (2018) 34 *Peace in Progress* 16, 17–18; I. Watson, 'Aboriginal Relationships to the Natural World: Colonial Protection of Human Rights and the Environment' (2018) 9 *Journal of Human Rights and the Environment* 119, 121, 129.

INDEX

abortion 478–80
adequate standard of living, right to 490–4
  food and water 491
  housing 491, 493–4
  State's obligations 492–3
African Charter of Human and Peoples' Rights (1981) 423–30
  African Commission *see* African Commission on Human and Peoples' Rights
  African values and their implication 423–7
    duties of individuals 425–6
    socioeconomic and collective rights 424–5
  claw-back clauses 427
  collective rights 167
  denunciation 125, 423
  derogation provisions, absence of 427–9
  economic, social, and cultural rights 84–6
  indigenous peoples 603
  nature of obligations imposed 138
  normative framework 429–37
    Maputo Protocol (2003) 86, 429, 438, 443, 568, 571
    other AU human rights treaties 430
    Protocol on the Rights of Older Persons in Africa (2018) 87, 430, 438
  pro homine principle 119
  Protocol on the Rights of Older Persons in Africa (2018) 87, 430, 438
  Protocol on the Rights of Women in Africa 86
  reporting obligations 88–9
  right of individual petition 92–3, 166
  self-determination 595
  universalism/relativism debate, and 16, 17

African Charter on the Rights and Welfare of the Child (1990) 87, 430–7, 578–9
  background 430–1
  child soldiers 432
  children's responsibilities 432
  children's rights protected by States Parties 431, 578
  Committee of Experts 432–6, 578–9
  communications concerning violation 433–7
    admissibility requirements 434
    amicable settlement of cases 434
    enforcement of decisions 435–6
    provisional measures 434
    on-site visits 434, 436
    recommendations 434–5
African Commission on Human and Peoples' Rights (ACHPR) 85–6, 89, 437–40
  admissibility of communications 461–2
    admissibility criteria 463, 465
    timeframe for submission 464
  advisory opinions 466
  amicable settlements 460–1, 468
  composition 437
  'effective control' test 164
  freedom of opinion and expression 531
  functions 438
  general comments 466
  indigenous peoples
    collectives, rights of 603
    forced eviction 604
  individual communications 447–53
    admissibility 448
    binding nature of decisions 450
    decisions on merits 448

implementation of recommendations 450–3, 473
  procedure 447–8
  process 45
  referral to the Court 452
  reparations 449–50
  standing 448
inter-State communications 468–9
lack of adequate resources 438, 473
missions (promotional and protective) 440
on-site investigations 91, 440
pro homine principle 119
provisional measures 458
reporting mechanism 438–9
right of individual petition 166
sessions 437
special mechanisms 439–40
Special Rapporteurs 439–40
Working groups and committees 440
African Court on Human and Peoples' Rights (ACtHPR) 85–6, 441–7
access to 93
admissibility of cases 453, 461–6
  admissibility criteria 463
  material jurisdiction 462–3
  personal jurisdiction 462
  prior exhaustion of domestic remedies 464–5
  temporal jurisdiction 463
  timeframe for submission 464–5
advisory opinions 442, 466, 466–7
amicable settlements 460
background 441
cases before the Court 453–8
  admissibility 454, 461–5

African Court on Human and
     Peoples' Rights (Cont.)
  amicable settlements 461
  compliance with
     judgments 457-8, 473
  jurisdiction 454
  procedure 454
  process 456
  rectification, interpretation,
     and review of
     judgments 454
  reparations 455-7
  contentious and material
     jurisdiction 442-3
  criminal jurisdiction,
     future 153
  direct access to Court, lack of
     declarations for 473
  engagement with
     jurisprudence of multiple
     supervisory organs 120
  fair trial 457, 532
  indigenous peoples as
     collectives, rights of 603
  judges 447-8
  lack of adequate
     resources 473
  legal entities 169
  personal jurisdiction 445-6
  provisional measures
     458-9
  right of individual
     petition 166
  standing 444-6, 448, 452
African human rights
     system 84-7, 418-74
  abortion 479-80
  ACHPR see African
     Commission on Human
     and Peoples' Rights
     (ACHPR)
  ACtHPR see African Court
     on Human and Peoples'
     Rights (ACtHPR)
  African Charter see African
     Charter on Human and
     Peoples' Rights
  background 417-22
  economic, social, and cultural
     rights 84-7
  individual, and 447-53
  OAU see Organization of
     African Unity (OAU) 89
  towards a new African
     Court 469-72

African Union 298
  African human rights system
     see African human rights
     system
  successor to OAU 419, 430,
     469
aggression, crime of 197
  ICC, and 106, 136
American Anthropological
     Association 14, 15
American Convention on
     Human Rights 1969
     (ACHR) 81, 306-8
  amendments to 308-9
  background 306-7
  children 579
  death penalty 483, 484, 485
  denunciation 125, 308
  derogation provisions 427
  economic, social, and cultural
     rights 81-3, 90
  extra-territorial scope
     of human rights
     obligations 156-7
  federal clauses 155
  individual petitions 92, 309,
     323
  inter-State
     communications 351
  nature of obligations
     imposed 138-9
  pro homine principle 118
  Protocol of San Salvador
     81-2, 90, 309
  Protocol on abolition of death
     penalty 309-10
  Protocols, adoption of 308
  ratification, limited nature
     of 307-8, 358
  reporting obligations 90
  reservations 122
  right to life 477, 478, 479, 483,
     484, 485
  see also right to life
  States Parties to 307-8
American Declaration of the
     Rights and Duties of
     Man 81, 598
  extra-territorial scope of human
     rights obligations 156
  general principles of law,
     and 129
  Inter-American Commission
     on Human Rights, and 82
Andean Community 298

Aquinas, Thomas 21
Arab Charter on Human Rights
     (2004) 297
  denunciation 125
  reporting system 89, 297
Arab League 297
Aristotle 20, 544-5
ASEAN (2012) 297
Asian-African Legal Consultative
     Committee 131

Bentham, Jeremy 39, 40
biomedicine
  Convention on Human
     Rights and Biomedicine
     (1997) 363
blasphemy 537-40
Burke, Edmund 39, 40, 43-4

Cançado Trindade, Judge
     Cançado
  IACtHR, and 355-8
  ICJ, and 218, 221-2, 223-4,
     227, 247
Caribbean Community
     (CARICOM) 298
characteristics of human rights
     see meaning of human
     rights
children and children's
     rights 576-89
  ACHR 579
  African Children's Charter see
     African Charter on the
     Rights and Welfare of the
     Child
  African Network for the
     Prevention and Protection
     Against Child Abuse and
     Neglect 431
  African Youth Charter
     (2009) 430
  child soldiers 148, 232, 271, 431
  Council of Europe Convention
     on the Protection of
     Children against Sexual
     Exploitation and Sexual
     Abuse (2007) 365
  CRC see Committee on the
     Rights of the Child (CRC)
  Declaration of the Rights of
     the Child (1959) 577
  Declaration on the Rights and
     Welfare of the African
     Child (1979) 431

European Convention on the Exercise of Children's Rights (1996) 365, 579
evolving capacity and maturity of children 583–46
European Social Charter 579
four principles *see under* Committee on the Rights of the Child (CRC)
Geneva Declaration of the Rights of the Child 31, 577
ILO Conventions 577–8
International Children's Emergency Fund (UNICEF) 431, 577
migrant child, unaccompanied 588–9
Rapporteurship on the Rights of the Child 580
regional developments 578–8
street situations, children in 586–9
UDHR, and 577
UNCRC 148, 431, 576–7
 age of majority 576–7
 background 269–70
 children as subjects of rights 578
 core human rights treaty, as 231
 importance of 269–70
 Protocol for individual petitions 232
 Protocol on children in armed conflicts 148, 232, 271
 Protocol prohibiting child prostitution and child pornography 232, 270–1
Vienna Declaration 97
Cold War 69, 70, 95, 97, 104, 212
colonialism
 de-colonization *see* de-colonization
 exclusion of colonized people from rights of man 53
 history of 51–2
 indigenous peoples 605–6
 international law legitimising 52–3
 lasting effects of 52
 racial discrimination, as 550

self-determination, and 596
UDHR, and 54
universalization of rights, colonial project and 54–5
Committee against Torture (CAT) 265–9
 composition 265
 establishment 265
 general comments 266
 individual complaints 265–6, 269
 inquiries 266
 inter-State complaints 265, 266
 refoulement 103
 simplified procedure for State reporting 237
Subcommittee on Prevention of Torture (SPT) 90–1, 232, 267–8
 reports and recommendations 267–8
 SPT undertaking country visits 267
 States' obligation to set up National Preventive Mechanisms 268
Committee on Economic, Social and Cultural Rights (CESCR) 72, 76, 77–8, 87, 254–60
 adequate standard of living, right to 490–1
 composition 255
 created and members elected by ECOSOC 233, 255
 general comments 238, 255–6
 ICESCR, and 72, 76, 77–8, 87
 individual communications 241, 257–8, 258–60
 inquiries into grave or systematic violations 257
 inter-State communications 257–8
 statements 256
Committee on Enforced Disappearances (CED) 283–8
 composition 286
 establishment 286
 individual communications 286, 287–8
 initial concerns over 285–6

inquiries into grave or systematic violations 286–7
inter-State communications 286
referral procedure 287
sunset clause requiring evaluation of 286
urgent action procedure 287
Committee on the Elimination of All Forms of Racial Discrimination (CERD) 245–9
 composition 245
 compulsory mechanism for inter-State communications 247
 early warning and urgent action procedures 248–9
 general comments/ recommendations 238, 246
 individual communications 241, 247–8
 inter-State complaints 92, 240, 247
 legal entities 169
 proactively intervening to prevent violations 248
 review procedure 237
Committee on the Elimination of Discrimination against Women (CEDAW Committee) 238, 260–5
 causes of women's inequality 569
 family violence 571
 gender-based violence 571, 573
 general recommendation 263–4
 individual communications 262–3
 inquiries into grave or systematic violations 263, 264–5
 inter-State communications 240
 limited powers initially conferred 261–2
Committee on the Protection of the Rights of all Migrant Workers (CMW) 274–9
 composition 277

Committee on the Protection of the Rights of all Migrant Workers (*Cont.*)
  general comments 277, 278–9
  individual communications 277
  inter-State complaints 277
  monitoring function 277
Committee on the Rights of Persons with Disabilities (CRPD)
  composition 281
  general comments 281–2
  individual communications 282, 283
  inquiries into grave or systematic violations 282
  intersectionality 552
  inter-State communications 240
  monitoring function 281
Committee on the Rights of the Child (CRC) 269–74
  composition 270
  four principles 580–5
    best interests of the child 581–2, 583–4
    prohibition of discrimination 581
    right of children to freely express their own views 582–3, 584–5, 586
    right to development 582
  general comments 271, 584
  individual communications 241, 271–2
  inquiries into grave or systematic violations 271, 272–4
  inter-State communications 271
  limited monitoring powers 270
committees/treaty monitoring bodies 233–49, 293–4
  communication: inter-State and individual 240–4
    individual communications 241–4
    inter-State disputes 240–1
  composition 233–4
  election of committee members 233–4
  general comments/ recommendations 238–9
  legal nature 239
  improving treaty body system 288–9, 294
    committee members, improvements in selection of 294
    harmonized guidelines on State reporting for all committees 289
    problems with current system 288–9, 290
    proposal to consolidate committees into one standing body 290
    proposals to strengthen treaty body system 290–2
    uniform reporting calendar across committees, need for 294
    world human rights court, proposal for 292–3
  individual communications 241–4
    admissibility requirements 241, 242
    low level of compliance with committees' views 244
    procedure 242
    recommendations to respondent State 243
    submission requirements 241–2
    views/decision of committees 242–4
  inquiry procedures 244
  main functions of committees 234–44
  meetings 234–5
  State reporting system *see* State reporting system
  supervisory organs composed of human rights experts, as 233
Commonwealth of Independent States (CIS) 297
CIS Convention on Human Rights and Fundamental Freedoms (1995) 297
complaints systems 91–4
  HRC *see under* Human Rights Council (HRC)
  inter-State communications 91
  litis pendentia and *res judicata*, application of 94
  multiple international resources for protection of their rights 94
  prior exhaustion of domestic remedies 93–4
  right of individual petition 92–4
Convention against Torture and Other Cruel, Inhuman or Degrading Treatment 1984 (UNCAT) *see* torture and cruel, inhuman or degrading treatment
Convention on the Elimination of All Forms of Discrimination Against Women 1979 (CEDAW) *see* women and women's rights
Convention on the Rights of Persons with Disabilities 2006 (UNCRPD) *see* disabilities, persons with
Convention on the Rights of the Child 1989 (UNCRC) *see* children and children's rights
crimes against humanity
  general principles of law, and 106
  grave violations of human rights, as 130
  ICC, and 106
  jus cogens, as 135
criminal jurisdiction *see* international criminal jurisdiction
critiques of human rights 38–56
  feminist critiques 43–7
  intellectual opposition to inherent rights of man 39
  Marxist critiques 40–3
  nature of critiques 39–40
  postcolonial critiques 51–5
  postmodern critiques 47–50
cultural relativism
  cultural evolutionism, as reaction to 15
  definition of 15

incompatibility of rights
    with values of particular
    cultures 15–16
  margin of appreciation 17–19
  universality, and 14–17, 38–9
customary international law
  definition of international
    custom 126
  objective element (existence of
    State practice) 126, 127
  opinio juris communis,
    emergence of 127–8
  source of international law,
    as 126–8
  subjective element (*opinio
    juris*) 126, 127–8

de Gouges, Olympe 24, 43, 563
de Las Casas, Bartolomé 21
de Vitoria, Francisco 21
death penalty
  ACHR 309–10
  duty not to extradite or deport
    to State with death
    penalty 486
  ECHR 483, 484, 485, 486
  IACtHR 333–4
  ICCPR 232, 483, 484
  ICJ cases 220–2
  restrictions to 483–4, 484–5
  right to life, and 483–6
de-colonization 52, 70–1, 180
  membership of UN 71
  self-determination 71
denunciation *see under* treaties
disabilities, people with
  CRPD *see* Committee on the
    Rights of Persons with
    Disabilities (CRPD)
  disability, nature of 281
  Inter-American Convention
    on the Elimination of All
    Forms of Discrimination
    against
    Persons with
    Disabilities 312
  mental health issues 424
  UNCRPD 149
    background 279–81
    core human rights treaty,
      as 232
    overlapping forms of
      discrimination 552
    Protocol for individual
      petitions 232

regional integration
  organizations, open to
  281
States Parties having
  independent mechanisms
  on implementation 282
discrimination, prohibition
  of 543–62
  affirmative action 246, 547–9
  definition of
    discrimination 143, 544
  equality 544–9
  examination of a
    discrimination
    claim 553–6
  importance of 543–4
  indirect discrimination
    545–6, 555–6
  Inter-American Convention
    against all Forms of
    Discrimination and
    Intolerance (2013) 312,
    545
  intersectionality 551–3
  limit to possible derogation
    of rights in emergencies,
    as 543
  positive measures, adoption
    of 547
  prohibition of discrimination
    as general
    guarantee 142–3
  prohibition of discrimination
    as *jus cogens* 136, 142–3,
    544
  racial discrimination *see* racial
    discrimination
  sexual orientation and gender
    identity 132, 205–7,
    556–60
  socioeconomic discrimination,
    Marxist critique of
    560–2
  Sub-Commission on
    prevention of
    discrimination 184–5
  systemic or structural
    discrimination 548–9
  women, and *see* women and
    women's rights
domestic law 170–1
domestic violence *see under*
  women and women's
  rights
dualism 170

East African Community 298
Economic and Social Council
  (ECOSOC) 178–9
  creating UN Commission on
    Human Rights 60–1
  draft UDHR, and 64
Economic Community of
  West African States
  (ECOWAS) 298
Enlightenment 11, 22, 28, 47,
  49, 53, 67
equality *see* discrimination,
  prohibition of
erga omnes obligations 136–7,
  219, 245
European Commission of
  Human Rights 363
  Committee of Ministers,
    and 362–3
  establishment of 363
  individual petitions 363
  margin of appreciation
    18–19, 409
  torture and ill-treatment 501–2
European Convention
  on Human Rights
  (ECHR) 17, 79
  amendments to 308
  colonial clause 54, 154
  death penalty 483, 484, 485,
    486
  denunciation 125
  derogation provisions 427
  economic, social, and cultural
    rights, and 79
  general principles of law,
    and 129–30
  institutional framework 362–3
  jurisdiction 157
  legal entities 169
  margin of appreciation 398,
    408
  nature of obligations
    imposed 138
  Protocols 363–4
  reporting obligations 90
  retroactivity 129–30
  right of individual petition 92
  right to life 477, 479, 483, 484,
    485, 486
  see also right to life
  subsidiarity, principle of 398,
    408
  territorial scope of human
    rights obligations 154–5

European Court of Human
    Rights (ECtHR) 362,
    373–417
  abortion 479
  admissibility of
    applications 383–95
    abuse of right and
      'manifestly ill-founded'
      applications 387–8
    anonymous applications
      and duplicity of
      proceedings 385–7
    exhaustion of domestic
      resources and four-
      month rule 384–5, 408
    hardening of 396, 398
    jurisdiction 383–4
    nature of applicants 383
    significant
      disadvantage 388–9,
      396, 398
    subsidiarity, principle
      of 398, 408, 417
  advisory jurisdiction 404–8
    advisory opinions requested
      by domestic courts 398,
      406, 417
  backlashes 370
  caseload 395–8
    backlog 395–6, 397, 416
    changes to Court's
      formations 396–8
    Filtering Section 397–8
    pilot judgments 394–5
    reform through Protocols
      14–16 396–8, 416, 417
  colonial clause 154–5
  complementarity, principle
    of 383
  composition 373–5
  discrimination 546, 556,
    557–9
  economic, social, and cultural
    rights, and
    79–80
  establishment of 363
  extra-territorial scope
    of human rights
    obligations 157–63
    circumstances leading
      to 157–8
    exercise of 'control' 158–64
  fair trial 381, 382, 393, 500,
    507, 508
  freedom of opinion and
    expression 526, 528, 530,
      531–2, 534
    blasphemy 538, 539
    margin of appreciation 534,
      539
  freedom of thought,
    conscience, and
    religion 518–20, 521–3
    margin of appreciation 513,
      515, 517, 518, 520, 523
  gender-based violence 573–4
  general principles of law 130
  Grand Chamber 379–80
  horizontal effect of
    international human
    rights 144, 145, 147
  human rights treaties 115
  individual applications 363,
    375–89
    admissibility of
      applications 383–95
    contentious phase 377–8
    friendly settlement
      phase 376–7
    Grand Chamber 379–80
    priority policy 376, 398
    procedure 375–6
    process of 380
    striking out applications
      378–9
  interim measures (Rule
    39) 381–2
    binding nature of 381, 382
    procedure 382
    real risk of serious and
      irreversible harm 381
  international organisations,
    international
    responsibility of 149–50
  inter-State cases 399–401
  investigation of violations,
    duty of 142
  judges 373–5
  judgments, compliance
    with 401–4
    action plans 401
    binding nature of
      judgments 401
    enhanced supervision
      401–2
    infringement
      proceedings 402–4
    peer pressure and effective
      political leverage, reliance
      on 402
  legal entities 169
  'living instrument'
    doctrine 109, 117, 118
  margin of appreciation 351,
    398, 408–16
    adoption of 18–19, 409
    definition of 17–18, 409,
      410–11
    discretion not unlimited 18
    discrimination,
      determining 555
    ECHR 398
    freedom of opinion and
      expression 534, 539
    freedom of thought,
      conscience, and
      religion 513, 515, 517,
      518, 520, 523
    origins of 409–10, 411
    self-restraint on power of
      review, as 17, 352
    margin of appreciation, scope
      of 411–16
      criticisms of 415–16
      European consensus,
        existence or absence
        of 414–15
      importance of specific
        issue 413
      nature and purpose of
        State's interference with
        Convention right
        413–14
      nature of right at stake
        412–13
  non-State actors,
    responsibility of States
    for 144, 145, 147
  positive measures, need
    for 80
  principle of effective
    interpretation 116
  prohibition of torture as *jus
    cogens* 135
  rectification, revision,
    and interpretation of
    judgments 381
  refoulement 103
  relativist approach to
    protection of human
    rights 17–19
  reparations (just
    satisfaction) 389–95
    compensation 390–2
    general measures 392–5

INDEX

individual measures 392, 393
non-pecuniary damage 391–2
pilot judgments 394–5
reservations 122, 123
right of individual petition 92, 166
torture or ill-treatment, exclusion of evidence obtained by 507, 508
European human rights system 79–80, 360–417
Council of Europe membership 369–72
creation of 360–72
background 360–2
evolution of European human rights system 362–4
European Commission of Human Rights *see* European Commission of Human Rights
ECHR *see* European Convention on Human Rights (ECHR)
ECtHR *see* European Court of Human Rights (ECtHR)
normative framework 364–9
Commissioner for Human Rights 368–9
Committees of experts 365
European Social Charter 79, 90, 365–7, 579
multiple human rights treaties 365
European Union 149, 298
Court of Justice of the European Union 298
ECHR, and 149
UNCRPD, and 149

fair trial 109, 481
ACtHPR 457, 532
ECtHR 381, 382, 393, 500, 507, 508
IACtHR 333, 346, 353, 489, 509
jus cogens, and 136
provisional/interim measures 346, 381
female genital mutilation 575–6

feminist critiques of human rights 43–7, 52, 53
definition of 'feminist' 44
exclusion of women as subjects of inherent rights 43–4
'liberal' feminism 44–5
patriarchal order, human rights as product of 44, 45–6, 47
postmodern feminism 44, 46
radical feminism 45–6
'women's liberation' movement 45
food and water, right to 491
forced disappearance
CED *see* Committee on Enforced Disappearances (CED)
definition of 'enforced disappearance' 285
IACtHR 311
ICPPED 103, 482
background 283–5
core human rights treaty, as 232
denunciation 125, 250
individual communications 241
Inter-American Convention on the Forced Disappearance of Persons (1994) 284, 310, 344, 482
international crime of forced disappearance as *jus cogens* 135, 285, 482
prohibition of arbitrary deprivation of life, and 480–3
refugees' protection against 103
UN Declaration on the Protection of All Persons from Enforced Disappearance (1992) 284, 482
Working Group on Enforced or Involuntary Disappearances 285–6
Foucault, Michel 46
bio-power 48–9, 50
postmodernism 48–50, 540–1

France
Declaration of the Rights of Man and of the Citizen (1789) 23–5, 39, 40–1, 41–2, 53
slavery 25, 26
freedom of opinion and expression 523–42
blasphemy 537–40
fundamental human right, as 525
normative recognition 523–5
post-modern critique of freedom of expression 540–2
restrictions to 532–40
limitation must fulfil is its legitimate purpose 533–4
margin of appreciation 534
national security, public order, public health, and public morals 533
protection of rights or reputations of others 533, 534–7
scope of 525–32
access to information held by public authorities 528
forms and means for dissemination of information 525–6
genocide denial 528–32
hate speech 528–9
new technologies 527–8
political speech 526
press and mass media 526–7
freedom of thought, conscience, and religion 509–23
conscientious objection 513–15
Declaration of Principles on Freedom of Expression (2000) 313
limitations to the right 515–17
foreseeability of the limitation 516
legitimate aim, pursuit of 516–17
limitation necessary to achieve legitimate aim 517

freedom of thought, conscience, and religion (*Cont.*)
  normative recognition 509–10
  religious symbols and clothing, use of 514–15, 518–23
  scope of 510–15
    education in schools 511–13
    State religion 511, 513

gender-based violence *see under* women and women's rights
gender identity *see* sexual orientation and gender identity
general comments *see under* committees/treaty monitoring bodies
general principles of law 128–30
  formal source of international law, as 128
  fundamental nature of 129
  law 'recognized by civilized nations', problematic nature of 128–9
Geneva Conventions 29–30
  Additional Protocols (1977) 100
  armed groups 148
  basic fundamental rights, recognition of 100
  non-international armed conflicts 100
genocide
  effective control test 159–61
  erga omnes obligations 136
  general principles of law, and 106
  genocide cases in ICJ 222–4
  genocide denial 528–32
  grave violations of human rights, as 130
  ICC, and 106
  jus cogens, and 120–1, 134
  Nazi Germany 36, 550
Grotius, Hugo 21
Gulf Cooperation Council 298

High Commissioner for Human Rights 211–17, 229
  appointment of 212–13
  creation of post 211–12

functions of 213–14
Office of the High Commissioner for Human Rights 213, 214
  assessing implementation of human rights norms 215–17
  human rights indicators 215–17
histories of human rights 19–38
  declarations of 18th century 22–5
  international humanitarian law 28–31
  League of Nations 31–2
  natural law 20–2
  slavery, evolving prohibition of 25–8
Hobbes, Thomas 22
housing, right to 491, 493–4
Human Rights Committee (CCPR) 250–4
  composition 250–1
  denunciation 125–6, 250, 253–4
  discrimination
    definition of 143
    sexual orientation and gender identity 556–7
  establishment 250
  extra-territorial scope of human rights obligations 155–6
  'effective control' test 164
  freedom of expression 531
  general comments 252
  ICCPR, monitoring 72, 76
  main monitoring functions 251
  individual communications 252
  inter-State complaints 251–2
  investigation of violations, duty of 142
  legal entities 168–9
  non-derogable rights and *jus cogens* 136
  refoulement 103
  religious symbols and clothing, use of 520–1
  reservations 120, 122–3
Human Rights Council (HRC) 78, 88, 185–211, 227–8

Advisory Committee 210–11
complaints procedure 208–10
  actions and remedies 209–10
  complaints from individuals 93, 208
  procedure 208–9
  Working Group on Communications 208–9
  Working Group on Situations 209
creation of 185
fact-finding 90
functions 187
Israel, and 188–92, 228
  country-specific mandate on Occupied Palestinian Territory 190
  enhanced focus on Israel 189–90
  HRC bias, counter-productive nature of 191
  permanent agenda item, Israel as 189
  urgent fact-finding missions, deployment of 189–90
meetings 187
membership
  election of members 186
  suspension of 186
  tenure of members 186
  US, and 186–7
powers, restricted nature of 187–8
review of own work 188
right of individual petition 166
special procedures 199–207, 227, 229
  functions of mandate holders 204–5
  independent commissions of inquiry 203
  mandates for country-specific investigations 199–201, 202–3
  sexual orientation and gender identity, independent expert on 205–6
  system of human rights protection, 2 204–5
  thematic mandates 201–2, 203–4

succeeding UN Commission on Human Rights 166, 177, 182, 185
UDHR as customary law 128
Universal Periodic Review 128, 186–7, 192–9, 228–9
  concerns as to actual efficiency of 196
  cycles of 196
  nature of 192–3, 194–5
  objective of 192
  outcome report 195
  sources of information 194
  UK, and 196–9

inalienability of human rights 12–13
indigenous people
  American Declaration on the Rights of Indigenous Peoples (2016) 313
  collectives, rights of indigenous peoples as 603
  colonization, and 605–6
  ILO Conventions, and 598–9
  Inter-American Charter of Social Guarantees (1948) 597–8
  legal entities, as 169
  protection of indigenous peoples' lands and natural resources 602–5
    consultation 604–5
    eviction from ancestral lands 425, 604
  self-determination 597–608
    post-colonial approach to 605–8
  Special Rapporteur on the rights of indigenous peoples 600–1
  UN Declaration on the Rights of Indigenous Peoples (2007) 131–2, 599–602, 606–8
  Vienna Declaration 97
inherence of human rights 11–12, 13
  opposition to concept of 38–9
Inter-American Commission on Human Rights (IACHR) 82, 303, 313–16

abortion 478–9
American Declaration of the Rights and Duties of Man, and 303
autonomous entity of OAS, as 305
backlash against 349–51
children 579, 580
composition 313–14
convergent application of legal regimes 101–2
creation of 304–6
extra-territorial scope of human rights obligations 156–7
  'effective control' test 164
forced disappearance 481–2
functions and powers 314–15
individual communications 306, 323
  admissibility requirements 324
  friendly settlements 324
  process of petitions 327
  recommendations 325, 326
  referral to the Court 325, 326
  report on the merits 325–6
  standing 323
inter-State cases 351–2
mandate 305
  enlargement of 306
on-site investigations 91, 314, 315–16
precautionary measures 344–5, 347
recommendations 314
refugees 101–2
reporting system 315–16
  annual reports 316
  country reports 315–16
  thematic reports 316
right of individual petition 92, 166, 314–15
studies and reports 314
underfunding affecting the activities of 348
Inter-American Court of Human Rights (IACtHR) 317–23
  abortion 478–9
  admissibility of individual petitions and cases 337–44
    admissibility criteria of petitions 340–1

duplicity of proceedings and res judicata 342–3
exhaustion of domestic remedies and six-month rule 341–2
jurisdiction, operation of 339–41
material jurisdiction 339
objections based on Commission's proceedings 343–4
personal jurisdiction 338
temporal jurisdiction 338–9
advisory jurisdiction 319–23
  importance of 321
  legal effect 322–3
  scope of 320–1
American Declaration of the Rights and Duties of Man, and 304
backlash against 349–51
conventionality control 352–55
  meaning of 353, 354
economic, social, and cultural rights 82–4
fair trial 333, 346, 354, 489, 509
federal clauses 155
forced disappearance 311
freedom of opinion and expression 528, 540
functions 317
gender-based violence 574–5
gender identity 559–60
general principles of law 130
horizontal effect of international human rights 144–5, 145–6, 147
human rights treaties 115
IACHR referrals to 325, 326
indigenous communities' right to property 602–3
individual petitions 92, 166
  admissibility of 337–44
individuals, evolving role of 327–9
  Inter-American Defender 328
  legal assistance fund 328–9
  recognition of individual's legal standing 328, 329
interpretation, rectification, and revision of judgments 337–8

Inter-American Court of Human Rights (*Cont.*)
  investigation of violations, duty of 141–2, 147
  Judge Antônio Augusto Cançado Trindade, reflections 355–8
  judges 317
    ad hoc judges 318–19
    president 317–18
  legal entities 169
  'living instrument' doctrine 109
  margin of appreciation 352–3
  nature of Convention obligations 138–9
  prevention of violations, duty of 146, 147
  principle of effective interpretation 116–17
  procedure for cases 329–30
  prohibition of discrimination as *jus cogens* 136, 142–3
  prohibition of torture as *jus cogens* 135
  provisional measures 344, 345–7
  self-determination right as *jus cogens* 136
  refoulement 103
  reparations and compliance 330–7
    compensation 330–1, 333
    ending impunity and avoiding recidivism 331, 332
    measures of satisfaction 331–2
    monitoring compliance 334–7
    restitution 330, 331
    wide range of measures 332–3
  reservations 120, 122
  right of access to justice as *jus cogens* 136
  self-determination 594
  sessions 317
  slavery prohibition as peremptory norm 135
  torture or duress, exclusion of evidence obtained by 507–8, 509
  underfunding affecting the activities of 348

Inter-American human rights system 81–2, 299–359
  backlashes and lack of financial support 348–51
  creation and development of 259–313
    ACHR *see* American Convention on Human Rights (ACHR)
    additional regional human rights instruments 308–13
    American Declaration of the Rights and Duties of Man (1948) 81, 302–4, 306, 323
    history 299–301
    OAS membership 301–2
  economic, social, and cultural rights 81–3
  IACHR *see* Inter-American Commission on Human Rights (IACHR)
  IACtHR *see* Inter-American Court of Human Rights (IACtHR)
  individual, and 323–47
  Inter-American Democratic Charter (2001) 313
  reform proposals 359
  Social Charter of the Americas (2012) 313
Inter-American Juridical Committee 62, 131, 301, 304–5
International Committee of the Red Cross 29, 102
International Convention for the Protection of All Persons from Enforced Disappearance 2006 (ICPPED) *see* forced disappearance
International Convention on the Elimination of All Forms of Racial Discrimination 1965 (ICERD) *see* racial discrimination
International Convention on the Protection of the Rights of All Migrant Workers 1990 (ICRMW) *see* migrants and migrant workers
International Court of Justice (ICJ) 218–27

  advisory opinions 218
  conservative approach 218
  customary international law 126, 127
  death penalty cases 220–2
  effective control test 159–61
  erga omnes obligations 136–7, 219
  extra-territorial scope of human rights obligations 156
  function of 113
  general comments, increasing reliance on 239
  genocide cases 222–4
  international organisations, responsibility of 149
  Israel, and 191–2
  Judge Cançado Trindade, judgments 218, 221–2, 223–4, 227, 247
  judicial decisions as sources of international law 130–1
  jus cogens 134, 219
    genocide 120–1, 134
    torture 135
  'living instrument' doctrine 109, 110
  non-State actors 159–61
  nuclear weapons 224–7
  reservations 120–1
  self-determination as 592–3
  standing 218
  Statute of the International Court of Justice
  sources of international law of human rights 113
  UN Charter and UDHR 66, 219
  violation of a human rights treaty, first declaration of 219–20
International Covenant on Civil and Political Rights 1966 (ICCPR) 59, 65, 250
  adoption 72
  background 69–72, 74–5
  CCPR *see* Human Rights Committee (CCPR)
  collective rights 167
  'colonial clause', exclusion of 70–1
  core human rights treaty, as 231
  death penalty 232, 483, 484

denunciation 125–6, 250
derogation provisions 427
nature of obligations
 imposed 138
non-derogable rights 136
Protocol for individual
 petitions 232
Protocol on abolition of death
 penalty 232
retroactivity 129–30
right to life 477
see also right to life
self-determination 71, 592,
 595
States' obligations 75–6
territorial scope of human
 rights obligations 154
International Covenant on
 Economic, Social and
 Cultural Rights 1966
 (ICESCR) 59, 65
adequate standard of living,
 right to 490
adoption 72
background 69–72, 74–5
CESCR *see* Committee on
 Economic, Social and
 Cultural Rights (CESCR)
collective rights 167
colonial clause', exclusion
 of 70–1
core human rights treaty,
 as 231
denunciation 125, 250
health, right to 216
Limburg Principles (1986) 87,
 132
Optional Protocol 78, 232,
 256–7
self-determination 71, 592,
 595
States' obligations 75–6, 77–8
International Criminal Court
 (ICC)
core crimes 106
creation of 104–5
jurisdiction 105–6
members of organized armed
 groups 148
torture, definition of 496
international criminal
 jurisdiction
ad hoc international
 tribunals 105
creation of 104–6

ICC *see* International
 Criminal Court (ICC)
individuals, responsibility
 of 148
Nuremberg and Tokyo
 tribunals 104
retroactivity, and 129–30
State to individual
 responsibility, from
 104–6
TNCs 152–3
International Criminal Tribunal
 for Rwanda (ICTR) 105,
 131
International Criminal Tribunal
 for the Former Yugoslavia
 (ICTY) 30–1, 105, 131
effective control test 160–2
prohibition of torture as *jus
 cogens* 135
protection of human dignity
 of all individuals as aim
 of 30–1
purpose 30
international humanitarian
 law 28–31
armed groups 148
Geneva Conventions *see*
 Geneva Conventions
nature of 28–9
original aim of regulating
 conduct of armed
 conflicts 30
origins 29–30
protection of human dignity
 of all individuals as aim
 of 30
wounded and sick combatants,
 first treaty on 29
International Labour
 Organization (ILO)
children 577–8
creation of 32
indigenous peoples 598–9
migrant workers 275
 ICRMW, consultative role
 in 277–8
State reporting 244
treaties on standards of
 work and protection of
 workers 32
women workers, restrictions
 on 564
International Law
 Commission 98, 131

Articles on the Responsibility of
 States for Internationally
 Wrongful Acts 137
Draft Articles on Crimes
 against Humanity 153
Draft Articles on the
 Responsibility
 of International
 Organizations 149
international criminal
 responsibility 104–5
reservations 122, 123
international law of human
 rights 58–112
development and
 expansion 58–9
human person, protection
 of 99–107
evolving convergence of
 legal regimes 99–102
fundamental principles 102
hostilities, during 99–100
impunity, and *see*
 international criminal
 jurisdiction
migrants *see* migrants and
 migrant workers
*non-refoulement see non-
 refoulement*, principle of
refugees *see* refugees
implementation stage 87–99
complaints system 91–4
mechanisms of
 implementation 88–94
reporting systems 88–90
on-site investigations 90–1
second World Conference
 on Human Rights
 (1993) 59, 95–9
legislative stage 59–74
African system of human
 and peoples' rights 84–7
civil and political rights,
 and economic, social, and
 cultural rights 74–87
European human rights
 system 79–80
first three core human
 rights treaties, adoption
 of 69–72
first World Conference
 on Human Rights
 (1968) 59, 73–4
Inter-American human
 rights system 81–4

international law of human
    rights (*Cont.*)
  regional human rights
    systems 79–87
  UDHR *see* Universal
    Declaration of Human
    Rights 1948 (UDHR)
  nature of 58
  normative framework of
    human rights 113–72
  interaction of international
    and domestic law 170–1
  nature of obligation *see*
    nature and scope of
    human rights obligations
  protected subjects *see*
    protected subjects of
    human rights
  sources *see* sources of
    international law of
    human rights
  passage of time, and 107–11
    duty to continuously
      advance scope of
      protection of human
      rights 110–11
    'living instrument'
      doctrine 109–11
    potential victims, notion
      of 108–9
    urgent measures, adoption
      of 108–9
  sources *see* sources of
    international law of
    human rights
international organisations,
    international
    responsibility of 149–50
Israel
  HRC, and *see under* Human
    Rights Council (HRC)
  ICJ, and 191–2

judicial decisions and doctrinal
    work 130–1
jus cogens 131, 133–8
  consequences of violation
    of 137–8
  crimes against humanity 135
  definition of 133
  discrimination 136
  erga omnes obligations 136–7
  fair trial 136
  forced disappearances 135, 285
  genocide 120–1, 134
  ICJ, and *see* International

    Court of Justice (ICJ)
  non-derogable rights,
    and 135, 136
  non-refoulement, principle
    of 103
  objective illegality, regime
    of 136
  open category, as 133–4, 219
  racial discrimination
    245, 551
  right of access to justice 136
  slavery 135
  summary and extra-legal
    executions 135, 136
  torture 135, 136, 495
  VCLT, and 133
justice
  fair trial *see* fair trial
  right of access to justice as *jus
    cogens* 136

League of Nations 19, 31–7
  aims of 31
  Covenant 33
  demise of 36
  establishment of 31
  international instruments
    for protection of
    women, children, and
    refugees 31–2
  International Labour
    Organization as affiliated
    agency 32
  mandate system 32–3,
    165–6
  minorities, system for
    protection of 34–6,
    165–6
  Nazi Germany's withdrawal
    from 36
  slavery, abolition of 28
  UN, from League of Nations
    to 36–8
liberalism
  'liberal' feminism 44–5
  political liberalism 44–5
life, right to *see* right to life
Limburg Principles (1986) 87,
    132
'living instrument'
  doctrine 109–11
Locke, John 22

margin of appreciation
  ECtHR *see* European Court of
    Human Rights (ECtHR)

  IACtHR 351–2
  Inter-American system of
    human rights 350
Marxist critiques of human
    rights 40–3, 45, 50,
    52, 56
  class, human rights and 42–3
  criticism of French
    Declaration on Rights of
    Man 40–1, 41–2
  historical materialism 41–2
Marxist critique of socioeconomic
    discrimination 560–2
meaning of human rights 3–4
  definition of human rights 3,
    11
  legal rights, human rights
    as 4
  main characteristics of human
    rights 11–19
    inherent and
      inalienable 11–13
    universality 13–19
  moral conceptions of
    human rights *see* moral
    conceptions of human
    rights
  political conceptions of
    human rights *see* political
    conception of human
    rights
migrants and migrant workers
  CMW *see* Committee on the
    Protection of the Rights
    of all Migrant Workers
    (CMW)
  European Convention on the
    Legal Status of Migrant
    Workers (1977) 365
  ICRMW 93
    adoption of 276
    background 275
    core human rights treaty,
      as 231
    ICJ, access to 277
    ILO's consultative
      role 277–8
    inter-State
      communications 240
    low level of States
      Parties 274, 276–7
    right of petition 93, 166
  International Organization for
    Migration (IOM) 274
  migrant child,
    unaccompanied 588–9

trafficking 275
Vienna Declaration 97
see also refugees and internally displaced persons
minorities
  collective rights 34
  European Charter for Regional or Minority Languages (1992) 365
  Framework Convention for the Protection of National Minorities (1995) 365
  obligations as fundamental law 34–5
  procedural measures for breaches of obligations 35–6
  rights of minority members 34
  system for protection of 34–6
  Sub-Commission on protection of minorities 184–5
  termination of system 36
  UN Sub-commission on Prevention of Discrimination and Protection of Minorities 139, 284
monism 170
moral conceptions of human rights 4–5, 5–8
  consensus approach 6–8, 10
  grounding principles 6
  orthodox approach, as 5–6
  universality 13

National Human Rights Institutions 194, 210, 236, 237, 252, 290, 471
  Paris Principles 282
National Preventive Mechanisms 268
natural law (jusnaturalism) 20–2
  detachment of natural law from religious dictates 21
  development of theory of natural law 20–1
  natural rights 21–2
nature and scope of human rights obligations 138–64

abstentions and positive duties/measures 140–1
accessible and effective remedies, availability of 140–1
extra-territorial scope of human rights obligations 155–64
investigation of violations, duty of 141–2, 146, 147
nature of Convention obligations 138–9
obligations to respect, to protect, and to fulfil 139–40, 143
prevention of violations, duty of 141, 146, 147
prohibition of discrimination as a general guarantee 142–3
scope of international human rights obligations (personal dimension) 143–53
  horizontal effect of international human rights 144–5
  international organizations 149–50
  international responsibility of non-State actors 147–53
  States' responsibility for actions of non-State actors 144–7
scope of international human rights obligations (temporal/territorial) 153–64
  extra-territorial scope of human rights obligations 155–64
  federal clauses 155
  retroactivity 153
  territorial scope of human rights obligations 153–5
Nino, Carlos 6
non-refoulement, principle of 100, 102–3
  application of 102
  basic principle of international refugee law, as 102
  irreducible minimum of protection of rights of persons, as 103
  jus cogens, as 103
  normative content 102–3

non-State actors
  horizontal effect of international human rights 144–5
  international responsibility of non-State actors 147–53
    accountability 147–8
    armed groups, members of 148
    individuals, responsibility of 148
    international organizations 149–50
    transnational organizations 150–3
    meaning of 147
  States' responsibility for actions of non-State actors 144–7
nuclear weapons 224–7
Nuremberg and Tokyo tribunals 104

older persons 204
  Inter-American Convention on Protecting the Human Rights of Older Persons (2015) 312–13
  Protocol on the Rights of Older Persons in Africa (2018) 87, 429–30, 438
on-site investigations 90–1
  Israel, and 190–1
Organization of African Unity (OAU)
  African human rights system *see* African human rights system
  Banjul Charter 419, 421–2, 432
  objectives 418
  transformation into African Union 419, 430, 469
Organization of American States (OAS)
  aims of 299
  Charter 303–4
    denunciation 302–3
    Protocol of Buenos Aires (1967) 306
  composition 299
  contentious membership of 301–2
  establishment of 299
  Inter-American human rights system *see* Inter-American human rights system

Permanent Court of
    International Justice
  main judicial body of League
    of Nations, as 35
  Statute of the Permanent
    Court of International
    Justice 113, 128, 130
personal integrity, right
    to 494–509
  normative recognition 494–5
  multiple international
    instruments 494
  prohibition of torture *see* torture
    and cruel, inhuman or
    degrading treatment
political conception of human
    rights 6, 8–11
  complementarity of
    moral and political
    approaches 9–10
  human rights 'inflation',
    dangers of 10
  lists of human rights,
    differences in 9–10
  practical conception of human
    rights 9
  Rawl's theory 8–9
  universality 13
postcolonial critiques of human
    rights 51–5
  colonialism 51–3
  concept of postcolonialism 51
  emergence of 52
  rights of man as rights of only
    certain individuals 53
  UDHR, colonialism and 54
  universalization of rights,
    colonial project and 54–5
  Western international law,
    colonialism and 52–3
postmodern critiques of human
    rights 47–50, 52
  bio-power 48–9, 50
  concept of postmodernity 47
  Foucault 48–50
  postmodern feminism 46
  postmodern thinkers 48
poverty
  chronic poverty as deprivation
    of all human rights 83
  extreme poverty as violation
    of human dignity 98
  health, and 424
  human rights issue, as 561
  indigenous peoples 606
  States' duty to address extreme
    poverty 487
  structural poverty 491
  Vienna Declaration 98
  widespread 74
prisoners
  conditions of detention 333
    inhuman treatment, and 503
  forced disappearance 287–8
  National Preventive
    Mechanisms to examine
    treatment of 268
  Principles and Best Practices
    on the Protection of
    Persons Deprived of
    Liberty in the Americas
    (2008) 313
  Principles of Medical Ethics
    relevant to the Role of
    Health Personnel 494–5
  UN Standard Minimum Rules
    for the Treatment of
    Prisoners 132, 495
pro homine principle 116,
    118–20
  cross-fertilization 119–20
  limitations or restrictions,
    restrictive interpretation
    of 119
  meaning of 118
proportionality, principle
    of 351, 532, 546, 554,
    555–6
protected subjects of human
    rights 164–71
  individuals 164–7
    right of individual
      petition 71, 164–7
  legal entities 168–9
    exclusion of 168–9
    inclusion of 169
  indigenous people 169
  non-governmental
    organizations 169
  trade unions 169
  peoples 167–8
    characteristics describing
      'peoples' 168
    collective rights 167
    definition of 'peoples' 167–8

racial discrimination
  broad concept, as 550
  CERD *see* Committee on the
    Elimination of All Forms
    of Racial Discrimination
    (CERD)
  erga omnes obligations 136,
    219, 245
  ICERD 550–1
    adoption of 71, 72
    affirmative action 246
    background 69–72
    core human rights treaty,
      as 231
    definition of racial
      discrimination 246
    dispute settlement
      mechanism 240–1
    explicit ban on racial
      discrimination 245
    ICJ, access to 247
    individual petitions 71,
      92, 240
    inter-State
      communications 240
    legal entities 169
    reservations 124
    importance of 245
  Inter-American Convention
    against Racism, Racial
    Discrimination and
    Related Forms of
    Intolerance (2013) 312
  prohibition of racial
    discrimination as *jus
    cogens* 245, 551
  Vienna Declaration 97
Rawls, John 8–9
refugees and internally displaced
    persons
  convergence between
    regimes 100–2
  forced disappearance,
    protection against 103
  Inter-American Commission
    of Human Rights 101–2
  Kampala Convention
    (2009) 86–7, 430
  *non-refoulement see non-
    refoulement*, principle of
  OAU Convention Governing
    Specific Aspects of
    Refugee Problems in
    Africa (1969) 430
  Palestine occupied
    territories 101
  protection of 100–2
  UDHR 100
  UN High Commissioner for
    Refugees 101, 102
  UN Refugee Convention
    (1951) 31, 100

Vienna Declaration 97
  see also migrants/migrant
     workers
reporting systems 88–90
reservations see under treaties
right to life 477–94
  death penalty see death
     penalty
  inalienable attribute of the
     individual, as 477
  normative recognition 477–5
  beginning of life 478–80
  positive obligations 486–9
     duty to investigate 487–9
     establishing legal
        framework 487
     preventive measures,
        adoption of 487
  prohibition of arbitrary
     deprivation of life 480–3
  forced disappearances
     480–3
  right to an adequate standard
     of living 490–4
religious symbols and clothing,
  use of 514–15, 518–23
right to personal integrity see
  personal integrity, right
  to
Rousseau, J.J. 22

Second World War
  genocide by Nazi
     Germany 36, 550
  human rights violations 36, 60
  racist legislation in
     Germany 35–6
self-determination 590–7
  Atlantic Charter 36–7, 590
  historically 590–1
  human right, self-
     determination as 591–7
  indigenous people see under
     indigenous peoples
  right to self-determination as
     jus cogens 136
  UN Charter 591
  uncertainties on scope and
     exercise of right 595–7
sexual orientation and gender
  identity
  discrimination, and 132,
     205–7, 556–60
  independent expert on
     protection against
     violence and

discrimination 205–7
  conversion therapy 206–7
  Yogyakarta Principles
     (2007) 132
slavery
  erga omnes obligations 136,
     219
  evolving prohibition of 25–8
  general principles of law,
     and 106
  grave violations of human
     rights, as 130
  prohibition of slavery as
     peremptory norm 135
  slave trade as racial
     discrimination 550
  Slavery Convention 32
soft law 131–2
Southern African Development
  Community (SADC) 298
Southern Common Market
  (MERCOSUR) 298
sources of international law of
  human rights 113–38
  customary international
     law see customary
     international law
  formal sources 113
  general principles of
     law 128–30
  hierarchy of international
     norms 132–8
  jus cogens (peremptory
     norms) see jus cogens
  UN Charter 132–3
  other sources 130–2
State reporting system 235–7
  consideration of State
     reports 236–7
  emphasis on activities at
     domestic level 235
  objectives 235–6
  relatively low level of States'
     compliance 235, 237
  review procedure 237
  simplified procedure for State
     reporting 237
  transition towards enhanced
     coordination 236
subsidiarity, principle of 350,
  383, 398, 408, 417

torture and cruel, inhuman or
  degrading treatment
  CAT see Committee against
     Torture (CAT)

conditions of detention 333
Declaration on the Protection
  of All Persons from Being
  Subjected to Torture
  (1975) 494
European Convention
  for the Prevention of
  Torture and Inhuman or
  Degrading
  Treatment or Punishment
  (1987) 90, 365, 495
exclusion of evidence obtained
  by torture 507
'fruit of the poisonous
  tree' 506–9
Inter-American Convention
  to Prevent and Punish
  Torture (1985) 310, 495,
  509
Istanbul Principles 495
on-site investigations 90–1
positive obligation 504–5
  adoption of reasonable
     measures to avoid risk of
     ill-treatment 505
  duty to adopt adequate
     legislation 504–5
  duty to investigate 505
prisoners see prisoners
prohibition of cruel, inhuman,
  or degrading treatment
  or punishment 500–4
  certain level of
     severity required
     to reach minimum
     threshold 503–4
  definitional threshold 500–1
  distinction of degrees
     between forms of ill-
     treatment 501–3
  intention of
     perpetrator 502
  next-of-kin of victims,
     violation of personal
     integrity and 503
prohibition of torture 495–500
  definition of prohibited
     conduct 495–6, 497, 501
  engagement of a public
     authority 497
  feminist approach
     to 498–500
  intention of
     perpetrator 502
  jus cogens, as 135, 136,
     495–8

torture and cruel, inhuman or
    degrading treatment
    (*Cont.*)
  psychological torture 497
  purpose of torture,
    and 496–7, 502
  refugees, and 103
  UNCAT 90–1, 98, 103, 265,
    495, 499
    core human rights treaty,
      as 231
    definition of torture 495–6,
      497–8
    engagement of public
      authority 497
    exclusion of evidence
      obtained by torture 507
    ICJ, access to 266
    international cooperation
      against impunity for
      torture 506
trafficking
  child trafficking 588
  Council of Europe Convention
    on Action against
    Trafficking in Human
    Beings (2005) 365
  migrants 275
  women 31, 204, 564, 566, 586
transnational corporations
    (TNCs)
  ILO Tripartite Declaration of
    Principles concerning
    Multinational
    Enterprises 151
  international responsibility
    of 150–3
    'Guiding Principles on
      Business and Human
      Rights' 152
    increasing influence of 150
    international criminal
      responsibility of
      TNCs 152–3
    regulation of 150–2
  norms on the responsibilities
    of transnational
    corporations' 131
  OECD Guidelines for
    Multinational
    Enterprises 151
  UN Global Compact 151
treaties
  character of human rights
    treaties 115

core human rights
    treaties 231–2
degree of protection
    dependent on
    reservations 114
denunciation 124–6
  definition of 12
  VCLT, and 124–5
human rights treaties 115
humanization of the law of
    treaties 116, 124
interpretation of treaties
    116–20
  elements of interpretation
    under VCLT 116
  principle of autonomous
    meaning 116, 117
  principle of effective
    protection (*effet
    utile*) 116–17
  principle of evolutive/
    dynamic
    interpretation 116,
    117–18
  pro homine principle 116,
    118–20
nature of 114
reservations 114, 120–4
  definition of 120
  ICJ, and 120–1
  ILC, and 122, 123
  supervisory organs deciding
    on validity of 122–3
  system of reservations,
    improvements to
    123–4
  VCLT, and 120, 121, 122
source of international
    law 114–26
  principal source of
    obligations, treaties
    as 114
  strength of the protection
    based on level of
    ratification 114
treaty monitoring bodies
    see committees/treaty
    monitoring bodies
VCLT
  denunciation 124–5
  good faith
    interpretation 116
  governing treaties 114
  interpretation of
    treaties 116–17

jus cogens/peremptory
    norms 133
literal interpretation 116,
    117
principle of universal
    respect and observance of
    human rights 115
prohibition of invocation of
    reciprocity 115
reservations 120, 121, 122
retroactivity 153
systematic
    interpretation 116
teleological
    interpretation 116
treaty interpretation 116

United Kingdom
  colonialism 70
  ECtHR, and 371–2
  slavery, abolition of 26–7,
    27–8
  Universal Periodic Review,
    and 196–9
United Nations (UN)
  Charter *see* United Nations
    Charter
  complaints procedure 93
  creation of 19–20, 31
  Declaration by United
    Nations 37
  international trusteeship
    regime replacing
    mandate system 33
  League of Nations, from
    36–8
  membership 70
  reporting obligations of
    Members 88
  San Francisco Conference
    37–8, 60, 179, 591
United Nations Charter
  adoption of 37, 38, 60
  hierarchy of norms
    132–3
  human rights 38, 60, 65–6,
    133, 177–9
  prohibition of
    discrimination 60
  self-determination 591
  UDHR, and 65–6
  women, and 564–5
United Nations Commission on
    Human Rights 179–85,
    227

INDEX

first three core human rights
  treaties, adoption of
  69–72
creation of 60
discredited 182–4
  Human Rights Council
    succeeding 166, 177, 182
  membership issues 182–3
  over-politicization 183–4,
    188
forced disappearance 482
functions 179, 181
Israel, bias against 189
lack of power to respond to
  complaints 179
membership, changes
  in 180–1, 182–3
procedures to supervise
  compliance with human
  rights 181–2
Special Rapporteur in
  Palestine occupied
  territories 101
Sub-Commission on prevention
  of discrimination
  and protection of
  minorities 184–5
UDHR, and 60–3
United Nations Educational,
  Scientific and Cultural
  Organization (UNESCO)
international bill of human
  rights 61, 65, 69
UDHR, contribution 62–4
United Nations Global
  Compact 151
United States (US)
  Declaration of Independence
    (1776) 23
  HRC, and 186–7
  racial policies 70
  slavery 25–6, 28
Universal Declaration of Human
  Rights 1948 (UDHR) 4,
  59, 60–8, 75
adoption of 38, 59, 64–5
adequate standard of living,
  right to 490
bio-power, and 50
children 577
colonialism, and 54
conceived as first part of
  International Bill of
  Human Rights 61, 62, 65
customary norms, provisions

evolving into 128
developing consensus on
  human rights 7–8
drafting of 14, 129
fundamental principles
  of international law,
  enunciating 66, 219
general principles of law,
  and 129
human rights as intrinsic and
  inextricable 11–12, 38–9
individuals born equal in dignity
  and rights 142, 478
non-Western
  contributions 67–8
origins in Frech Declaration of
  the Rights of Man 24–5
refugees see refugees and
  internally displaced
  persons
right to life 478
self-determination, and 71
significance of 72
UN Charter, and 65–6
UN Commission on Human
  Rights, and 60–3
UNESCO's contribution 62–4
universal rights, critical debate
  on 66–8
universal human rights,
  emergence of 59
Western provenance of 67
universality of human
  rights 13–19
backlashes to concept of 38–4
margin of appreciation 17–19
meaning of universality 13
objections to 13–14
'synchronic' universality 14
universality and cultural
  relativism 14–17
universalization of rights,
  colonial project 54–5
urgent measures, adoption
  of 108–9

Vienna Convention on Consular
  Relations (1963) 109,
  111, 220, 221, 320
Vienna Convention on the Law
  of Treaties 1969 (VCLT)
  see under treaties
Vienna Declaration and
  Programme of Action
  (1993)

CEDAW 262
Declaration 96–9, 566
Programme,
  recommendations in 98
prohibition of
  discrimination 97
universal nature of human
  rights 97
women, and 97, 566
Virginia Declaration of Rights
  (1776) 22

war crimes 104
general principles of law,
  and 106
grave violations of human
  rights, as 130
ICC, and 106
Wollstonecraft, Mary 43–4, 563
women and women's
  rights 562–76
abortion 478–80
CEDAW
  background 260–1, 566
  core human rights treaty,
    as 231
  denunciation 125, 250
  gender equality in the field
    of education 216
  importance of 568
  Optional Protocol for
    individual petitions 232,
    262–3
  reservations 261
CEDAW Committee
  see Committee on
    the Elimination of
    Discrimination against
    Women (CEDAW
    Committee)
contemporary status of
  women's rights 569–76
causes of inequality 569
female genital
  mutilation 575–6
gender-based violence 80,
  197, 365, 499, 566, 568,
  569, 570–5
States' obligations to end
  gender inequalities 570
feminist critiques of human
  rights see feminist
  critiques of human rights
Inter-American Commission
  of Women 300, 311, 568

women and women's rights (*Cont.*)
  international law, women's rights under 24, 25, 564–9
    Commission on the Status of Women 260, 262, 565, 566
    Convention of Belém do Pará 310–11, 568
    Declaration on Elimination of Discrimination against Women (1967) 260, 565
    ILO Conventions 564
    International Conference on Population and Development (1994) 567
    Istanbul Convention 197, 365, 569
    Maputo Protocol (2003) 86, 429, 438, 443, 568, 571
    regional developments 568–9
    UDHR, and 565
    UN Charter, and 564–5
    UN Sustainable Development Goals 567
    UN Women 567
    world conferences on women's rights 566–7
  Suffragist movement 563–4
  trafficking in women 31, 204, 564, 566, 586
  Vienna Declaration 97, 566
  violence, and
    Convention of Belém do Pará 310–11, 568
    Declaration on the Elimination of Violence against Women (1993) 571–2
    gender-based/domestic violence 80, 197, 365, 499, 566, 568, 569, 570–5
    Istanbul Convention (2011) 197, 365, 569
    prohibition of torture, feminist approach to 498–500
    Special Rapporteur on violence against women 572
    States' obligations on gender-based violence 571
World Conference on Human Rights (Tehran, 1968) 59, 73–4
World Conference on Human Rights (Vienna, 1993) 59, 95–9, 262, 566
  convergence of legal regimes 102
  High Commissioner for Human Rights, proposal for 212
  preparatory meetings 95–6
  Vienna Declaration and Programme of Action 96–9
world human rights court, proposal for 292–3